MANAGEMENT INFORMATION SYSTEMS

SYSTEMS

THE MANAGER'S VIEW

F O U R T H   E D I T I O N

MANAGEMENT INFORMATION SYSTEMS
THE MANAGER'S VIEW

ROBERT SCHULTHEIS
MARY SUMNER

both of
Southern Illinois University at Edwardsville

Integrated Cases Prepared by Douglas Bock
Southern Illinois University at Edwardsville

Boston   Burr Ridge, IL   Dubuque, IA   Madison, WI   New York   San Francisco   St. Louis
Bangkok   Bogotá   Caracas   Lisbon   London   Madrid
Mexico City   Milan   New Delhi   Seoul   Singapore   Sydney   Taipei   Toronto

Irwin/McGraw-Hill

A Division of The **McGraw·Hill** *Companies*

MANAGEMENT INFORMATION SYSTEMS: THE MANAGER'S VIEW

This book is printed on acid-free paper.

1 2 3 4 5 6 7 8 9 0 VNH/VNH 9 0 9 8 7

ISBN 0-256-25195-9

Editorial director: *Michael W. Junior*
Senior sponsoring editor: *Rick Williamson*
Developmental editor: *Christine Wright*
Marketing manager: *James Rogers*
Project supervisor: *Paula M. Buschman*
Production supervisor: *Lori Koetters*
Designer: *Barb Gibson/Michael Warrell*
Prepress buyer: *Heather D. Burbridge*
Compositor: *Interactive Composition Corporation*
Typeface: *10/12 Garamond Book*
Printer: *Von Hoffmann Press, Inc.*

Library of Congress Cataloging-in-Publication Data
Schultheis, Robert A.
    Management information systems: the manager's view / Robert
Schultheis, Mary Sumner. — 4th ed.
      p. cm.
    Includes bibliographical references and index.
    ISBN 0-256-25195-9. — ISBN 0-07-115548-1
    1. Management information systems. I. Sumner, Mary. II. Title.
T58.6.S328 1998
658.4'038'011—dc21   97-25011

http://www.mhcollege.com

PREFACE

THE APPROACH

Management Information Systems: The Manager's View, fourth edition, represents a managerial approach to information systems concepts and applications. It is a cliché to say that computers have become pervasive in every aspect of our lives. Networks, including the Internet, have made computer facilities almost ubiquitous. As a result managers have a major responsibility for determining their information system needs and for designing and implementing information systems that support these needs. At the same time computer technologies have created opportunities for managers to improve customer service, reduce costs, improve productivity, increase market share, and increase profits.

Students who are majoring in general management, human resource management, accounting, marketing, production, finance, and management information systems (MIS) should understand how information systems technologies support key organization functions, what information resources are available to them, and how MIS and other professionals are involved in the systems development process.

This book serves the needs of graduate and undergraduate students enrolling in their first MIS course who may not yet have decided to become MIS majors. The book also provides MIS majors with the user-manager's viewpoint of information systems. The book also supports introductory information systems courses required by many other programs, such as political science, allied health, and educational administration.

WHY WE WROTE THIS BOOK

Many students who enroll in entry-level management information systems courses are not MIS majors. These students are drawn to an entry-level course for many reasons. Some are required to take the course as part of their major fields in the hope that they will then understand how information systems can be used in their disciplines. Most students majoring in a discipline within a school of business are required to take an introductory management information systems course. Others take the course because they wish to complete several MIS courses to make themselves more marketable. Some enroll because they are simply interested in computers and hope that they will find the study of information systems interesting.

For whatever reason, the field of management information systems is always popular with students who are not MIS majors. Most of these students begin their study of the field by enrolling in the introductory management information systems course at either the undergraduate or graduate level. Nearly all of these students are studying to become managers: business managers, managers of governmental agencies, managers in the music industry, managers in the health industry, managers in the agricultural industry—in fact, managers in a broad array of industries and disciplines.

This book was written to serve these types of students. Thus we designed the text to do the following:

1. Emphasize how managers can and should be involved with systems planning, development, and implementation.

2. Emphasize what information systems resources are available to managers for decision support.

3. Emphasize how these resources can be used at all levels of decision making and in the major functional management areas.

4. Show how information technology can be used to support organization strategy without overwhelming students with technical details.

WHAT'S NEW IN THIS EDITION

This edition incorporates a number of additions and modifications to the third edition.

Updates for New Technology and Practices

Management information systems is an extremely dynamic area of study. It should be no surprise to find, therefore, that in the three years since the third edition, numerous changes have taken place in computer hardware, software, and information systems theories, practices, and technologies. A thorough revision and updating of the third edition was necessary to incorporate these changes. For example, net PCs, WebTV, and convergent computers; digital video disks; intranets, extranets, the Internet, and the Web; data warehousing, data marts, and online analytical processing; and hypermedia, universal databases, push technology, and computer telephony are just a few of the new topics that have been added to the fourth edition.

In addition, many topics have received increased space in the text because they have received increased attention in the industry. For example, collaborative computing, desktop conferencing, e-mail, wireless computing, client/server computing, parallel processing, multiuser operating systems, multimedia systems, EDI and electronic commerce, and imaging systems are just a few of the topics that received more attention in this edition than in the last.

New concepts are also included in this revision. In Chapter 4, a new chapter on reengineering, you will learn how companies are reengineering business processes in order to cut bureaucracy and improve their ability to serve customer needs. An entire chapter (Chapter 3) is devoted to the strategic uses of information technology. This chapter includes a discussion of information partnering, the electronic marketplace, and capabilities-based competition. It also includes an analysis of the risks and impacts of strategic information systems. Decision support systems and expert systems have been combined into one chapter (Chapter 12) so that these concepts are integrated.

In Chapter 13, Information Systems Planning, three strategies managers can use to determine their information system needs are described, ana-lyzed, and compared. These are critical success factors, business systems planning, and ends/means analysis. In Chapter 14, "Systems Analysis and Design," there is a new case study that involves the analysis of business processes in a financial services company. In addition, Chapter 15 has been reorganized to focus on the analysis of alternative design options for systems development.

New Chapters

Five new chapters have been added to the text. These include a chapter on business process reengineering (Chapter 4); distributed systems, the Internet, and office communications (Chapter 9); applications of operational information systems to common business areas (Chapter 10); applications of tactical and strategic information systems to common business areas (Chapter 11); and alternative application development approaches (Chapter 15). Additionally, the chapter on the introduction to information systems has been substantially rewritten.

In past editions, we had dedicated four chapters to a discussion of how information systems affect the four functional business areas of accounting and finance, marketing, production, and human resources. Many instructors had difficulty in using all of these chapters in a semester course. In order to provide instruction in the application of information systems to the four functional areas in a more concise fashion, we reorganized the content of the four chapters into two: "Applications of Operational Information Systems to Business" (Chapter 10) and "Applications of Tactical and Strategic Information Systems to Business" (Chapter 11). This reorganization should permit instructors to provide an overview of how information systems affect common business functions within a semester time constraint.

More Problems and Cases

The number of questions at the end of each chapter has been increased when needed to reflect updated technology and issues. The number of cases found at the end of most chapters has also increased.

New Integrated Cases

A new series of comprehensive, integrated cases, all based on the same firm, has been added, with one case appearing at the end of each part of the text.

These cases allow students to integrate what they have learned from the chapters that precede the cases.

WHAT THIS BOOK IS ALL ABOUT

The most important activity in which managers engage is decision making, and many managers must make decisions in a very competitive environment. This text focuses on how information systems support managerial decision making. Specifically, the text is organized around the three major levels of managerial decision making: operational decisions, tactical decisions, and strategic planning decisions. This organizational theme is followed throughout the text to focus students on the types of decisions that managers must make. The book also emphasizes how information systems help managers provide their organizations with a competitive advantage. This approach recognizes that the design and use of information systems have become part of every manager's job and that information systems planning is no longer the sole province of information systems professionals.

Typical introductory texts in management information systems present the field from the specialist's view. Even many texts that assume a management perspective still present many information systems topics from the traditional, specialist viewpoint. This text overcomes these limitations by providing the following elements.

A user-manager perspective. Many texts cover the systems life cycle from the traditional systems analyst perspective instead of from a user-manager perspective. They provide detailed descriptions of the systems analyst's role in requirements definition, design, and implementation rather than explaining how the user-manager should be involved in these cycle activities. In short, many texts lead students through the various stages of the systems life cycle as if they were expected to become professional systems analysts. This book leads students through the cycle expecting them to become functional area managers.

A managerial emphasis. Many texts present technical hardware and software concepts in too detailed a manner for students who are not MIS majors. The underlying criterion for selecting the content for this text was, Does the manager need to know it? Thus even in the chapters that cover computer hardware, computer software, database management systems, and communications systems, the overriding concern is, What does the manager need to know about these topics? We believe that students will find these chapters interesting and easy to read. We also believe that students will appreciate that these chapters continuously refer to why managers need to know the technical concepts presented and provide many examples of how managers can use technical information in decision making.

Practical, management-oriented cases. Many texts do not provide enough problems and cases that place students in the role of user-managers and ask them to use information systems skills and concepts. This text provides many problems and cases in which students must assume the role of managers and make decisions about information systems problems. Some of these problems and cases are software supported; that is, they can be used in conjunction with templates or data files contained on the Instructor CD-ROM that is available from the publisher or from the text's Web site. In addition to the end-of-chapter cases, the text also includes five integrated, comprehensive cases involving experiences at one company following each part of the text.

Managerial coverage. Many introductory texts provide a survey of information systems topics. Thus the texts really are short systems courses. This text selects information system topics on the basis of their importance to the manager. Rather than providing a survey course for majors, this text helps managers understand information systems concepts and applications.

The integration of information theory and practice. Major information management theories important to the manager are covered. These include

1. Hammer's framework for categorizing the impact of information systems (IS)—efficiency, effectiveness, and transformation (Chapter 4).
2. Anthony's paradigm of decision making—operational, tactical, and strategic decisions (Chapter 1).

3. Nolan's stage assessment for the analysis of the evolution of information systems (Chapter 1).

4. Keen's theories of decision support systems design (Chapter 12).

5. Buchanan and Linowes's concept of distributed data processing (Chapter 16).

6. Porter's analysis of competitive strategy (Chapter 3).

7. Porter and Millar's value chain analysis of organizational activities (Chapter 3).

8. Rockart's critical success factors (Chapter 13).

9. Gremillion and Pyburn's framework for evaluating systems development alternatives (Chapter 15).

10. McFarlan's portfolio approach to evaluating the risks of systems development projects (Chapter 15).

11. Information partnering and electronic marketplaces (Chapter 3).

12. Group decision support systems and electronic meeting systems (Chapter 12).

13. Reengineering business processes (Chapter 4).

The book presents each theory or framework and then applies it to real information systems issues so students can develop an understanding of how to apply the theories to real-life situations.

New information technology. New information technology is presented throughout the text. Students will have opportunities to learn how new technology creates opportunities for an organization by providing a competitive advantage, by identifying new markets, by reducing costs, by improving customer service, or by improving productivity. To cite a few examples, students learn about data warehousing (Chapter 7), networks (Chapter 8), the Internet (Chapter 9), decision support tools (Chapter 12), executive information systems (Chapter 12), expert systems and artificial intelligence (Chapter 12), and computer-assisted software engineering tools (Chapter 14).

Microcomputer technology. The use of microcomputer systems to support management decision making has become commonplace. As a result information about the use of microcomputers and microcomputer software is integrated extensively throughout the text. The technology of microcomputers is first presented in Chapters 5 and 6. Microcomputer software used by managers is then presented in Chapters 6 and 7 as part of the database and communications systems chapters and again in the chapters pertaining to the functional business areas (Chapters 10 and 11).

The Internet. The Internet and all its features, including e-mail, newsgroups, file transfer, and the Web, are changing not only the information systems world but also the lives of nearly everyone. The impact of the Internet on organizations has been swift in coming and continues to grow. The effect of the Internet on organizations is included in almost every chapter and receives close attention in Chapter 9.

FEATURES

This text has numerous features of use to both teachers and students.

End-of-Chapter Questions

Each chapter ends with a series of short questions that are designed to measure student understanding of the facts and concepts presented in the chapter. Students will find that reading these questions before they read the chapter will help them focus on the important points developed in the chapter. They also will find that answering the questions after reading a chapter is an effective means of reviewing the content of the chapter. Teachers may use these questions as part of quizzes or examinations.

Following the review questions are a series of more complex questions that usually ask the students to compare or evaluate what they have learned. These questions are useful as discussion questions for a classroom session.

Problems

Like most instructors, we like to provide our students with many practical, hands-on activities. This text provides numerous practical problems and cases at the end of each chapter. A number of the problems are supported by software, in the form of data sets for data-based and spreadsheet templates for what-if problems. In many chapters students can choose among problems requiring use of spreadsheet software or database software.

Chapter Cases

Most chapters contain two to five cases for students to solve. These cases are primarily targeted to the content presented within the chapter. They require students to analyze organizational situations using the information from the chapter.

Integrated Cases

At the end of each part of the text is a comprehensive case that requires students to integrate what they have learned from the preceding chapters.

Examples and Manager's Memos

Most chapters contain many practical, management-oriented examples and cases. Most chapters also present current, real-life examples of information systems in Manager's Memos within the narrative.

Other Student Study Features

Student study skills are enhanced through an introduction to each chapter ("Manager's View"), a chapter summary ("Management Summary"), the highlighting of key terms ("Key Terms for Managers"), and the glossary of terms at the end of the text.

Text Style

The text is written in a clear, readable writing style with a "you" emphasis to help students relate to the concepts and ideas presented. Although many of the concepts presented are complex, the way in which they are presented is designed to be just the opposite.

How This Book Was Developed

This book was developed recognizing that the introductory information systems course often consists of large numbers of students, including majors and nonmajors. We have tested the content and sequence of the text and the problems and cases in our own classes. Our students provided important feedback that we used to revise the content, problems, and cases. However, the text was not based solely on our own perspective. Many faculty members throughout the country, both those who use the text and those who do not, reviewed the revision of the text continuously as it was developed.

Their pointed criticisms and suggestions improved the organization, content, and style of the text.

The Instructional Materials Package

The instructional package consists of several components.

Text

The text consists of 17 chapters organized into five parts:

> Part I—Information Systems
> Part II—Computer System Resources
> Part III—Common Business Application Areas
> Part IV—Planning and Development of Information Systems
> Part V—The Management of Information Systems

Each chapter begins with "Manager's View," which describes why current and future managers need to learn the topics in the chapter. Each chapter closes with a summary, key terms, review questions and discussion questions, practical problems, and cases. A comprehensive case appears at the end of each part.

Instructor CD-ROM

An instructor CD-ROM containing all the files for the following list of supplements will be available to adopters of the text. Instructors will be able to run the PowerPoint show directly from this CD–ROM or view, edit, and print out individual pages or copies of the following supplements.

Data files. Data files provide data sets and spreadsheet templates. The data sets are designed to be used by dBASE IV; however, they can be read by many other microcomputer database management systems. The spreadsheet templates can be read by Excel, Lotus 1-2-3, 1-2-3 clones, or by any spreadsheet program that can read Excel files.

Instructor's manual. A companion instructor's manual prepared by Douglas Bock provides the following elements for each chapter:

Teaching suggestions. These provide various ideas for presenting each chapter and the integrated cases, including suggestions for introducing topics, overcoming typical student learning problems, using the PowerPoint software and sequencing the topics.

Answers to chapter questions, problems, cases, and the integrated cases. Suggested answers to end-of-chapter exercises and integrated cases are provided on a chapter-by-chapter basis.

Assignment schedule. A suggested schedule for a semester course is included in the instructor's manual.

Suggestions for use of PowerPoint software. Suggestions for using the PowerPoint software for in-class lecture presentation are provided for each chapter.

Test bank. A third companion document prepared by Alan Carswell provides a series of true-false, multiple choice, and short answer questions for each chapter along with the suggested answers. A 50-question mid-term exam and a 100-question final exam are also provided.

Computest 4. A computerized testing package, Computest 4, allows you to select test questions, organize the questions in the order you want, and print them for exams.

PowerPoint classroom presentation software. PowerPoint slides prepared by Doug Bock that provide lecture notes for each chapter are available. You may want to adapt the slides to your needs and the needs and interests of your students. You may also wish to provide students with copies of the lectures by printing the outline view of the slide presentations.

Classroom video support. Thirteen videotapes are available from the Irwin Information Systems Video Library for use with this text. The videos cover the following topics: Introduction to Information Systems (Chapter 1), Business Process Reengineering (Chapter 4), Technology (Chapters 5–9), Multimedia Presentations (Chapters 5 and 6), Telecommunications (Chapter 8), Client/Server Computing (Chapter 9), Finance Systems (Chapters 10 and 11), Marketing Systems (Chapters 10 and 11), Manufacturing Systems (Chapters 10 and 11), Human Resource Management Systems (Chapters 10 and 11), Corporate Training Systems (Chapters 10 and 11),

and Information for the Retail Market (Chapters 10 and 11). The videotapes are all about 10 to 12 minutes in length and can be used to enrich and supplement regular classroom instruction.

Internet Support

Internet support for faculty and students is provided in several ways:

1. A Web page (http://www.mhhe.com/ business/mis/schultheis) contains *additional cases* and *problems* for your use. Those of you who have used the text before will appreciate the problems from the previous edition that are found on the Web page. The Web page also contains *data files* needed for problems, lecture slide-show files, and case slide-show files.

2. Web *references* are provided at the end of each chapter so that you and your students can explore the topics in the chapter further on the Internet.

3. An e-mail address and link are provided for the authors so that you can contact them if you have questions or suggestions.

ACKNOWLEDGMENTS

We would like to acknowledge the contributions made by a number of people who helped us in the development and refinement of this text. First, we would like to thank Rick Williamson and Christine Wright who reviewed our ideas and our work and managed the text development process.

Second, many faculty members in management information systems and computer information systems departments who used the text reviewed our work constantly as we developed and refined it. Additional faculty, who did not use the text, also reviewed our work. Their criticisms and suggestions were extremely valuable. The reviewers were

Jeff Butterfield, University of Idaho

Patricia Carlson, Suffolk University

Alan D. Carswell, University of Maryland— College Park

K. Dale Foster, Memorial University

Nancy J. Johnson, Metropolitan State University

Sharad K. Maheshwari, Hampton University

Larry Meile, Boston College

Vincent Yen, Wright State University

A special thanks goes to our colleague, Douglas Bock, who prepared the integrated cases that appear at the end of each part of the text and who created the instructor's manual and PowerPoint software.

We would also like to thank the students at Southern Illinois University at Edwardsville who tested the text materials and provided us with many ideas for improvement.

Robert A. Schultheis
Mary Sumner

Contents in Brief

PART I
INFORMATION SYSTEMS, **1**

CHAPTER 1
A MANAGER'S VIEW OF INFORMATION SYSTEMS, 2

CHAPTER 2
AN INTRODUCTION TO CONCEPTS OF SYSTEMS
AND ORGANIZATIONS, 30

CHAPTER 3
STRATEGIC USES OF INFORMATION TECHNOLOGY, 56

CHAPTER 4
BUSINESS PROCESS REENGINEERING
AND INFORMATION TECHNOLOGY, 86

PART II
COMPUTER SYSTEM RESOURCES, **117**

CHAPTER 5
COMPUTER HARDWARE, 118

CHAPTER 6
COMPUTER SOFTWARE, 168

CHAPTER 7
FILE AND DATABASE MANAGEMENT SYSTEMS, 210

CHAPTER 8
COMMUNICATIONS SYSTEMS BASICS, 252

CHAPTER 9
DISTRIBUTED SYSTEMS, THE INTERNET,
AND OFFICE COMMUNICATIONS, 300

PART III
APPLICATIONS OF INFORMATION SYSTEMS TO
FUNCTIONAL BUSINESS AREAS, **355**

CHAPTER 10
APPLICATIONS OF OPERATIONAL INFORMATION
SYSTEMS TO BUSINESS, 356

CHAPTER 11
APPLICATIONS OF TACTICAL AND STRATEGIC INFORMATION
SYSTEMS TO BUSINESS, 402

CHAPTER 12
DECISION SUPPORT SYSTEMS AND EXPERT SYSTEMS, 458

PART IV
PLANNING AND DEVELOPMENT
OF INFORMATION SYSTEMS, **515**

CHAPTER 13
INFORMATION SYSTEMS PLANNING, 516

CHAPTER 14
SYSTEMS ANALYSIS AND DESIGN, 542

CHAPTER 15
ALTERNATIVE APPLICATION DEVELOPMENT
APPROACHES, 582

PART V
THE MANAGEMENT OF INFORMATION SYSTEMS, **623**

CHAPTER 16
ORGANIZATION OF INFORMATION SYSTEMS
AND END-USER COMPUTING, 624

CHAPTER 17
SECURITY AND ETHICAL ISSUES
OF INFORMATION SYSTEMS, 650

GLOSSARY, 698

NAME INDEX, 723

SUBJECT INDEX, 725

CONTENTS

PART I
INFORMATION SYSTEMS, **1**

CHAPTER 1
A MANAGER'S VIEW OF INFORMATION SYSTEMS, 2

Manager's View, 3
The Functions of Management, 3
Managerial Roles, 4
The Levels of Management, 7
The Activities of the Organization, 8
A Framework for Information Systems, 9
   Operational Systems, 9
   Tactical Systems, 10
   Strategic Planning Systems, 12
Sequence of Development of Management
   Information Systems, 15
   General Life Insurance Company, 15
   Dellco Foods, Inc., 17
   Sea Lake County Welfare Department, 17
The Stage Evolution of Data Processing, 19
An Update to the Original Theory, 21
   Stages of New Information Technology
     Growth, 23
Management Summary, 25
Key Terms for Managers, 25
Review Questions, 25
Questions for Discussion, 26
Problems, 26
Cases, 27
Selected References and Readings, 28

CHAPTER 2
AN INTRODUCTION TO CONCEPTS OF SYSTEMS
AND ORGANIZATIONS, 30

Manager's View, 31
Systems Concepts, 31
   System Boundaries, 32
   Systems and Subsystems, 32
   Outputs and Inputs, 32
   Subsystem Interface and Interface
     Problems, 33

Systems and Their Environments, 34
   Open and Closed Systems, 34
   System Feedback, 35
   System Entropy, 36
   System Stress and Change, 37
How a System Works, 38
   Systems Concepts in Business, 38
   An Information System as a System, 39
   Subsystems, 40
   Output and Inputs, 41
   Hierarchy of Subsystems, 42
   System Feedback, 42
   Subsystem Interfaces, 42
   Internal Controls, 42
   Effect of the Systems Approach on Information
     Systems Design, 43
   The Structure of an Enterprise, 43
Using the Systems Approach in Problem Solving, 44
   Define the Problem, 44
   Gather Data Describing the Problem, 44
   Identify Alternative Solutions, 45
   Evaluate the Alternatives, 45
   Select and Implement the Best Alternative, 46
   Follow Up to Determine Whether the Solution
     Is Working, 46
Using Information Systems for Feedback, 46
   What Has Changed?, 46
   Guidelines for Designing and Implementing
     a "Manage by Wire" System, 48
Making the Transition to the Learning
   Organization, 49
   The Disciplines of the Learning
     Organization, 49
   Learning Disabilities of Current
     Organizations, 50
   Using the Systems Approach to Make the
     Transition to the Learning Organization, 50
   Feedback in the Learning Organization, 51
   Conclusion, 52
Management Summary, 52
Key Terms for Managers, 52
Review Questions, 53

Questions for Discussion, 53
Problems, 53
Cases, 55
Selected References and Readings, 55

CHAPTER 3
STRATEGIC USES OF INFORMATION TECHNOLOGY, 56

Manager's View, 57
How Information Technology Supports Business
    Activities, 57
Using Information Technology for Competitive
    Advantage, 61
    Industry-Level Effect, 62
    Firm-Level Effect, 63
    Defining Competitive Strategy, 68
    New Business Opportunities, 68
    *Using Information Technology to Improve
        Customer Service, 69*
Interorganizational Systems, 70
    Information Partnering, 70
    The Electronic Marketplace, 71
The Strategic Impact of the Internet and Electronic
    Commerce, 73
    About the Internet, 73
    An Overview of Internet Applications, 73
    Business Uses of the Internet, 74
    *Electronic Marketing and On-Line
        Communities on the World Wide Web, 75*
Strategic Information Systems: The Risks, 76
    Shifting the Balance of Competition, 77
    *Failure to Upgrade the Capabilities
        of a Strategic System, 77*
    Litigation, 77
Do Information Systems Provide a Competitive
Edge?, 77
    Shifting to Capabilities-Based Competition, 78
    An Update to SABRE, 79
Management Summary, 80
Key Terms for Managers, 81
Review Questions, 81
Questions for Discussion, 81
Problems, 82
Cases, 82
Selected Internet Reference Sites, 84
Selected References and Readings, 85

CHAPTER 4
BUSINESS PROCESS REENGINEERING
AND INFORMATION TECHNOLOGY, 86

Manager's View, 87

The Impact of Information Technology, 87
    Impact on the Individual, 88
    Impact on the Functional Unit, 89
    Impact on the Organization, 89
The Reengineering of Work, 90
    Background, 90
    What Has Changed, 90
    *How Organizations Are Reengineering
        Work, 91*
    The Process of Reengineering Work, 94
    Organizational Impacts of Reengineering, 96
    Who Will Reengineer the Corporation? 96
Information Technology and Business Process
    Redesign, 97
    Case Studies in Business Process Redesign, 99
    *Types of Business Processes and the Role
        of Information Technology, 100*
    *How Information Technology Applications
        Improve Business Processes, 101*
    *Management Challenges in Business Process
        Redesign, 103*
Information Technology and Organizational
    Structure, 104
Management Summary, 104
Key Terms for Managers, 104
Review Questions, 104
Questions for Discussion, 105
Problems, 105
Selected Internet Reference Sites, 106
Selected References and Readings, 107

INTEGRATED CASE I
SOLVING PROBLEMS AT SOFTWARE REENGINEERING
COMPANY (SRC), INC., 108

PART II
COMPUTER SYSTEM RESOURCES, 117

CHAPTER 5
COMPUTER HARDWARE, 118

Manager's View, 119
Computer Systems, 120
    Supercomputers, 120
    Mainframe Computers, 120
    Minicomputer Systems, 120
    Microcomputer Systems, 120
    Professional Workstations, 121
    Laptop, Notebook, and Palmtop Systems, 121
    Network Computers, 123
    Convergent Computers, 123

Computer Platforms and the Manager, 124
Central Processing Units, 125
Memory, 129
Computer Power, 131
Using More Than One Processor, 132
Types of Computer System Processing, 133
Secondary Storage Media and Devices, 134
  Disk Storage, 135
  Optical Storage, 140
  Tape Storage, 142
  Hierarchical Storage Systems, 143
Input and Output Devices, 143
  Input Devices, 144
  Output Devices, 149
Hardware Standards, 155
  Compatibility, 155
  Expandability, 156
  Reliability, 156
Other Acquisition Issues, 156
  Timing the Acquisition, 156
  Renting, Leasing, and Buying, 157
  Deciding on the Acquisition, 158
  Choosing a Hardware Vendor, 158
  Installation, Maintenance, and Training, 159
  Operating Costs and the Environment, 159
  The Ergonomics of the Computer Workstation, 160
Management Summary, 161
Key Terms for Managers, 161
Review Questions, 162
Questions for Discussion, 163
Problems, 163
Cases, 164
Selected Internet Reference Sites, 166
Selected References and Readings, 166

CHAPTER 6
COMPUTER SOFTWARE, 168

Manager's View, 169
Systems Software, 170
  Operating Systems, 171
  Multiprogramming, 172
  Time-Sharing, 172
  Multiprocessing, 173
  Parallel Processing, 173
  Virtual Storage, 173
Communications Software, 173
Other Systems Software, 174
Microcomputer Operating Systems, 174
  Single- and Multitasking Operating Systems, 174

  Task Switching, 175
  Kernel, 175
  Utilities, 176
  Third-Party Software Vendors, 176
  Hardware Dependence, 177
  Operating System Interfaces, 177
  Command-Line Interfaces, 177
  Graphical User Interfaces, 177
  Windowing, 178
  Dynamic Data Exchange, 178
Application Software, 179
  Custom versus Commercial Software, 179
  Shareware and Freeware, 179
  Application Program Library, 179
  Portability, 179
  Single-User/Multiuser Programs, 180
  Categorizing Application Software by Use, 180
  Desktop Suites, 180
Development Software, 187
  Programming Languages, 187
  CASE Tools, 193
  Object-Oriented Programming, 193
General Software Features and Trends, 194
  Graphical User Interface, 194
  Windowing, 194
  Object Linking and Embedding, 194
  Multiplatform Capability, 194
  Network Capabilities, 195
  Licensing, 195
  Portability, 195
  Group-Work Capabilities, 196
  Compatibility with Other Software, 196
  Compatibility with Peripherals, 196
  Ease of Use, 197
  Sophistication, 197
  Wizards and Agents, 197
  Ease of Installation, 198
  Hardware Demands, 198
  Memory Requirements, 199
  Cost, 199
  Applets, 199
Selecting Microcomputer Software, 199
  Step 1: Identifying Your Application Needs, 199
  Step 2: Seeking the Right Software, 199
  Step 3: Choosing the Software That Best Fits Your Business Needs, 201
  Step 4: Choosing the Hardware, 201
  Step 5: Choosing a Software Vendor, 201
Management Concerns, 202

Management Summary, 203
Key Terms for Managers, 204
Review Questions, 205
Questions for Discussion, 205
Problems, 206
Cases, 207
Selected Internet Reference Sites, 209
Selected References and Readings, 209

CHAPTER 7
FILE AND DATABASE MANAGEMENT SYSTEMS, 210

Manager's View, 211
File Concepts, 212
File Structures, 214
    Sequential File Structure, 214
    Direct File Structure, 215
    Indexed Sequential File Structure, 215
Accessing Records, 216
    Inverted Files, 217
    Linked Lists, 217
File Structures and Processing Methods, 217
    *File Structures in On-Line, Real-Time
        Processing, 217*
    File Structures in Batch Processing, 217
Database Concepts, 218
    Data Independence, 219
    Data Redundancy, 219
    Data Consistency, 219
Database Management Systems, 220
Components of a Database Management
    System, 221
    Data Dictionary/Directory, 221
    Data Languages, 222
    Teleprocessing Monitors, 222
    Application Development Tools, 222
    Security Software, 222
    Archiving, Backup, and Recovery Systems, 222
    Report Writers, 222
    Query Languages, 222
    Multiple-Platform Databases, 223
    Web Server Software, 224
The Database Administrator, 225
Views of the Data, 227
    The Schema, 227
    Subschema, 227
Database Models, 228
    *Hierarchical and Network Database
        Models, 228*
    Relational Database Model, 229

    Object-Oriented Databases, 231
Advantages of Database Management Systems, 233
    Data Sharing, 233
    Reduced Data Redundancy, 233
    Improved Data Consistency, 233
    Data Independence, 234
    *Increased Application Programmer and User
        Productivity, 234*
    *Improved Data Administration and
        Control, 234*
    *Increased Emphasis on Data as a Resource,
        234*
Problems of Database Management Systems, 234
    Concurrency Problems, 235
    Resource Problems, 236
    Security Problems, 236
Specialized Databases, 236
    Intranet and Hypermedia Databases, 236
    On-Line Databases, 237
    Data Warehousing, 239
    Data Marts, 240
    On-Line Analytical Processing, 241
    Image Databases, 242
    Document Databases, 242
Universal Database Systems, 243
Management Summary, 243
Key Terms for Managers, 244
Review Questions, 245
Questions for Discussion, 246
Problems, 246
Cases, 248
Selected Internet Reference Sites, 251
Selected References and Readings, 251

CHAPTER 8
COMMUNICATIONS SYSTEMS BASICS, 252

Manager's View, 253
Communications Systems Elements, 255
Communications Modes and Codes, 256
    Analog and Digital Transmission, 256
    Data Codes, 256
    Asynchronous Transmission, 257
    Synchronous Transmission, 257
    *Simplex, Half-Duplex, and Full-Duplex
        Transmission, 258*
    Circuit Switching, 258
    Message Switching, 258
Communications Media, 260
    Speed and Capacity, 260

Twisted Pair, 260
Coaxial Cable, 260
Fiber Optics, 260
Wireless, 260
Sources and Products, 262
Dial-Up Telephone Lines, 264
Leased Telephone Lines, 264
Wireless Networks, 265
Common Network Components, 268
Hosts and Servers, 268
Terminals or Workstations, 268
Protocol Converters, 269
Modems, 270
Terminal Connection Equipment, 270
Network Connection Equipment, 272
Network Topologies, 273
Point-to-Point or Star and Hierarchical
Topologies, 273
Multidrop or Bus and Ring Topologies, 273
Mesh, 274
Wireless Topology, 277
Network Types, 277
Local Area Networks, 277
Wide Area Networks, 278
Enterprise Networks, 278
International Networks, 279
Remote Access, 280
Transferring Data Files between
Microcomputers, 280
Connecting Your Remote PC to Your Office
Desktop, 281
Connecting to the Internet and On-Line
Databases, 281
Connecting to a Remote Local Area Network,
281
Connecting to a Minicomputer
or Mainframe, 282
Reasons Managers Implement Networks, 283
Sharing Peripherals, 283
Sharing Data Files, 283
Sharing Applications, 283
Reducing the Costs of Acquiring, Installing,
and Maintaining Software, 284
Connecting to Other Networks, 284
Capturing Data at Its Source, 284
Increasing Productivity, 284
Permitting Expansion, 284
Increasing Timely Communications, 285
Increasing Management Control, 285

Network Concerns for the Manager, 285
Network Reliability, 285
Network Response Time, 285
Network Costs, 286
Compatibility, 286
Network Access and Security, 287
Voice Systems, 287
PBXs, 287
Centrex, 287
Reasons for Implementing a PBX, 288
PBX Hardware and Software, 290
Voice Systems Concerns for the Manager, 292
Communication Standards and the Manager, 292
Management Summary, 293
Key Terms for Managers, 294
Review Questions, 294
Questions for Discussion, 295
Problems, 295
Cases, 297
Selected Internet Reference Sites, 298
Selected References and Readings, 298

CHAPTER 9
DISTRIBUTED SYSTEMS, THE INTERNET,
AND OFFICE COMMUNICATIONS, 300

Manager's View, 301
Distributed Processing, 303
Reasons for Implementing Distributed
Processing, 303
Distributed Processing Concerns for
Managers, 305
An Effective Distributed Processing System, 306
Distributed Databases, 307
Replicated Databases, 307
Partitioned Databases, 308
Advantages and Disadvantages of Distributed
Databases, 308
Client/Server Computing, 309
SQL Servers, 309
Downsizing, 311
Interorganizational Information Systems, 311
Electronic Data Interchange, 312
Electronic Market Systems, 313
Internet Communications, 313
Internet Features, 313
Browsing Documents, 314
Searching for Information, 316
Push versus Pull Internet, 318
Internet Connection Problems, 319

Sending E-Mail, 320
Electronic Discussion Groups, 320
Transferring Files, 320
Running Programs on Remote Computers, 321
Network PCs and the Internet, 321
*Internet Telephony and Desktop
    Conferencing, 321*
Internet Commerce, 322
Intranet Communications, 323
  Extranet Communications, 324
Office Communications, 325
  Electronic Mail Systems, 327
  Voice Processing Systems, 329
  Electronic Conferencing Systems, 331
  Fax Systems, 334
  The Virtual Office, 336
  Groupware Systems, 337
  Workflow Automation, 338
  The Paperless Office, 340
Management Summary, 342
Key Terms for Managers, 342
Review Questions, 343
Questions for Discussion, 344
Problems, 344
Cases, 345
Selected Internet Reference Sites, 347
Selected References and Readings, 348

INTEGRATED CASE II
UPGRADING COMPUTER INFORMATION SYSTEMS FOR THE
U.S. ARMY RESERVE PERSONNEL CENTER, 349

PART III
APPLICATIONS OF INFORMATION SYSTEMS TO
FUNCTIONAL BUSINESS AREAS **355**

CHAPTER 10
APPLICATIONS OF OPERATIONAL INFORMATION SYSTEMS
TO BUSINESS, 356

Manager's View, 357
  *The Nature of Operational Information
    Systems, 357*
  Management Advantages, 357
Operational Accounting and Financial Information
Systems, 359
  Financial Accounting Systems, 359
  Importance to Decision Making, 359
  General Ledger System, 360

Fixed Assets System, 360
Sales Order Processing System, 361
Accounts Receivable System, 361
Accounts Payable System, 363
Inventory Control System, 364
Purchase Order Processing System, 364
Payroll System, 364
Financial Accounting Software, 364
Operational Marketing Information Systems, 365
  Sales Force Automation Systems, 366
  *Micromarketing and Data Warehouse
    Systems, 368*
  Telemarketing Systems, 369
  Direct Mail Advertising Systems, 370
  Point-of-Sale Systems, 370
  Delivery Tracking and Routing Systems, 370
  Electronic Shopping and Advertising, 372
Operational Production Information Systems, 375
  Purchasing Systems, 375
  Receiving Systems, 376
  Quality Control Systems, 376
  Shipping Systems, 378
  Cost Accounting Systems, 378
  Inventory Control Systems, 378
  Automated Material Handling Systems, 380
  *Computer-Aided Design and Manufacturing
    Systems, 380*
  Image Management Systems, 382
  Material Selection Systems, 382
  Shop-Floor Scheduling Systems, 382
  *Mass Customization and Agile Manufacturing
    Systems, 382*
Operational Human Resource Information
  Systems, 383
  Position Control Systems, 384
  Employee Information Systems, 385
  Performance Management Systems, 385
  Government Reporting Systems, 387
  *Applicant Selection and Placement Systems,
    389*
  Training Systems, 389
Management Summary, 391
Key Terms for Managers, 391
Review Questions, 392
Questions for Discussion, 393
Problems, 393
Cases, 394
Selected Internet Reference Sites, 399
Selected References and Readings, 400

CHAPTER 11
APPLICATIONS OF TACTICAL AND STRATEGIC
INFORMATION, 402

Manager's View, 403
The Nature of Tactical and Strategic Information
    Systems, 403
Tactical Accounting and Financial Information
    Systems, 405
    Budgeting Systems, 405
    Cash Management Systems, 407
    Capital Budgeting Systems, 408
    Investment Managing Systems, 410
Strategic Accounting and Financial Information
    Systems, 412
    Financial Condition Analysis Systems, 412
    Long-Range Forecasting Systems, 413
Tactical Marketing Information Systems, 415
    Sales Management Systems, 416
    Advertising and Promotion Systems, 419
    Pricing Systems, 421
    Distribution Channel Systems, 423
    Competitive Tracking Systems, 423
Strategic Marketing Information Systems, 425
    Sales Forecasting Systems, 425
    Marketing Research Systems, 426
    *Product Planning and Development
        Systems, 427*
Tactical Production Information Systems, 428
    Materials Requirements Planning Systems, 430
    Just-in-Time Systems, 431
    Capacity Planning Systems, 431
    Production Scheduling Systems, 433
    Product Design and Development Systems, 434
    Manufacturing Resource Planning Systems, 435
    *Computer-Integrated Manufacturing
        Systems, 436*
Strategic Production Information
    Systems, 436
    Site Planning and Selection Systems, 437
    *Technology Planning and Assessment
        Systems, 437*
    Process Positioning Systems, 437
    Plant Design Systems, 438
Tactical Human Resource Information Systems, 438
    Job Analysis and Design Systems, 439
    Recruiting Systems, 440
    Compensation and Benefits Systems, 441
    Succession Planning Systems, 442
Strategic Human Resource Information Systems, 443

Workforce Planning Systems, 443
*Information Systems Supporting Labor
    Negotiations, 445*
*Other Strategic Uses of Human Resource
    Information Systems, 445*
HRIS Software, 446
Management Summary, 447
Key Terms for Managers, 447
Review Questions, 448
Questions for Discussion, 449
Problems, 450
Cases, 453
Selected Internet Reference Sites, 456
Selected References and Readings, 457

CHAPTER 12
DECISION SUPPORT SYSTEMS AND EXPORT SYSTEMS, 458

Manager's View, 459
Manager's Systems Needs, 459
Characteristics of the Decision-Making Process, 460
    Phases of Decision Making, 461
    Types of Decision Problems, 461
    Attributes of the Decision Maker, 461
    Strategies for Decision Making, 462
    *Implications of Decision Making for Decision
        Support Systems, 462*
Important Features of Decision Support Systems, 462
    Support of Semi-structured Decisions, 463
    Support for Database Access and Modeling, 463
    *Support for All Phases of the Decision-Making
        Process, 463*
    *Support for Communications among Decision
        Makers, 464*
    Availability of Memory Aids, 465
    *Availability of Control Aids for Decision
        Making, 465*
Components of a Decision Support System, 465
    *Data Components of a Decision Support
        System, 465*
    Building a Data Warehouse, 465
    Data Mining and Intelligent Agents, 466
    Model Component, 467
The Tools of Decision Support, 468
Cases in Managerial Decision Support Systems, 471
    A Production Planning System, 471
    A Financial Control System, 472
    An International Loan System, 472
The Development of Decision Support Systems, 474
    *The Decision Support Systems Development
        Life Cycle, 475*

The Benefits of Decision Support Systems, 477
The Risks of Decision Support Systems, 478
  Lack of Quality Assurance, 478
  Lack of Data Security, 478
  Failure to Specify Correct Requirements, 478
  Failure to Understand Design Alternatives, 479
Group Decision Support Systems, 479
Artificial Intelligence and Expert Systems, 481
Expert Systems and Decision Support Systems, 482
The Characteristics of Expert Systems, 483
  The Knowledge Base, 484
  The Inference Engine, 484
  *The Knowledge Acquisition and Explanation
    Subsystems, 485*
How an Expert System Works, 485
  Rule-Based Systems, 485
  Frame-Based Systems, 486
  *How an Expert System Differs from a
    Conventional Information System, 487*
  *The Kinds of Problems an Expert System Can
    Solve, 487*
Expert Systems Applications in Business, 489
  *The Kinds of Opportunities Expert Systems
    Address, 490*
  How Expert Systems Are Developed, 490
  The Stages of Building an Expert System, 491
  *The Roles of the Knowledge Engineer and the
    Expert, 491*
  *The Prototyping Approach in Expert Systems
    Development, 492*
  How Knowledge Is Acquired from Experts, 492
The Advantages of Expert Systems, 493
  The Limits of Expert Systems, 493
  Expert System Tools, 494
Management Summary, 495
Key Terms for Managers, 496
Review Questions, 496
Questions for Discussion, 497
Problems, 497
Cases, 499
Selected Internet Reference Sites, 505
Selected References and Readings, 505

INTEGRATED CASE III
ANALYZING THE COMPUTER PERSONNEL ALLOCATION
PROBLEM AT SOFTWARE REENGINEERING COMPANY (SRC),
INC., 507

PART IV
PLANNING AND DEVELOPMENT OF
INFORMATION SYSTEMS, **515**

CHAPTER 13
INFORMATION SYSTEMS PLANNING, 516

Manager's View, 517
Information Systems Planning Strategies, 517
Problems with Determining Information
    Requirements, 517
Managing by Wire in a Complex Business
    Environment, 519
Critical Success Factors, 520
  Defining Critical Success Factors, 521
  Defining Measures, 522
  Advantages and Limitations, 522
Business Systems Planning, 523
  BSP Study Activities, 523
  The Study Team, 524
  Method of Analysis, 524
  Assessment of Business Problems, 526
  Determining Priorities, 526
  Information Systems Management, 527
  The Action Plan, 527
  Implications of the BSP Method, 527
Ends/Means (E/M) Analysis, 528
  Comparison of the Three Methods, 529
  *Information Systems Planning at the
    Organizational Level, 530*
  *How Information Technology Supports
    Business Strategy, 530*
  The Information Planning Grid, 531
  Management Strategies, 532
Technology Planning in an Age of Uncertainty, 534
  Schein's Theory of Technology Assimilation, 534
  Planning in a Dynamic Environment, 535
Organizing the Information Systems Plan, 536
  Application Development, 536
  New Technology, 536
  *Organization and Management of
    Information Processing, 537*
  *The Changing Role of the Chief Information
    Officer, 538*
Management Summary, 539
Key Terms for Managers, 539
Review Questions, 539
Questions for Discussion, 540

Problems, 540
Selected References and Readings, 541

CHAPTER 14
SYSTEMS ANALYSIS AND DESIGN, 542

Manager's View, 543
The Systems Development Process, 543
  The Systems Development Life Cycle, 544
Systems Analysis, *547*
  Case Study: A Law School Admissions Office, 548
  The Systems Interview, 548
  Using Questionnaires in Systems Analysis, 549
Structured Systems Analysis and Design, 551
  *Developing a Logical Data-Flow Diagram
    of the Current System, 552*
  Case Study: The Reliable Finance Company, 554
  Developing Business and System Objectives, 559
  *Preparing the Proposed System Data-Flow
    Diagram, 560*
  *Specifying Process Logic Using Decision Trees
    and Tables, 562*
  *Describing Data Flows and Data Stores in the
    Logical Data Dictionary, 563*
Evaluating Alternative Design Options, 563
  Alternative Processing Modes, 563
  Computer Design Alternatives, 564
  Software Development Alternatives, 565
Analysis of Alternative Design Options, 567
The Organizationwide Data Dictionary, 573
Management Summary, 577
Key Terms for Managers, 578
Review Questions, 578
Questions for Discussion, 579
Problems, 579
Cases, 580
Selected References and Readings, 581

CHAPTER 15
ALTERNATIVE APPLICATION DEVELOPMENT APPROACHES, 582

Manager's View, 583
Strategies to Overcome the Systems Development
  Bottleneck, 583
  Software Packages, 584
  Prototyping, 584
  User Development of Information Systems, 585
  *Factors to Consider in Selecting a Development
    Approach, 586*

Project Management and Control, 587
A Portfolio Approach to Project Management, 590
  Risk Factors, 590
  Strategies for Minimizing Project Risk, 590
  *Using Appropriate Strategies to Manage
    Projects, 591*
Cost-Benefit Analysis, 592
  The Benefits of Information Systems, 592
  The Costs of Information Systems, 593
Detailed Design: Transforming Logical
  Specifications into Physical Specifications, 595
  Structured Design, 595
  Physical Design Specifications, 597
  Program Specifications, 598
  Documentation, 598
Implementation, 600
  Programming and Testing, 600
  Training, 601
  Conversion, 602
  Human Factors in Systems Implementation, 602
User Involvement in System Selection, 604
  Developing an RFP, 604
  Evaluating a Database Program, 604
  Hardware Evaluation, 606
Management Summary, 608
Key Terms for Managers, 608
Review Questions, 608
Questions for Discussion, 609
Problems, 609
Cases, 611
Selected Internet Reference Sites, 613
Selected References and Readings, 613

INTEGRATED CASE IV
SYSTEMS DEVELOPMENT BY SOFTWARE REENGINEERING
COMPANY (SRC), INC., 614

PART V
THE MANAGEMENT OF INFORMATION SYSTEMS, **623**

CHAPTER 16
ORGANIZATION OF INFORMATION
AND END-USER COMPUTING, 624

Manager's View, 625
The Organization of Data Processing, 625
  The Evolution of Computing, 625
  Centralized Data Processing, 626

Decentralized Data Processing, 628
Distributed Data Processing, 629
Allocation of Responsibilities in Distributed
    Data Processing, 632
Effective Organization of Information
    Processing Activities, 633
Roles and Responsibilities of Information
    Systems Professionals, 635
Career Paths and Management of Data
    Processing, 638
The Organization and Management of
    End-User Computing, 639
Users and User-Developed Applications, 640
Management and Control Issues, 641
Departmental Computing, 642
The Future of the Information Systems
    Organization, 643
Management Summary, 644
Key Terms for Managers, 644
Review Questions, 645
Questions for Discussion, 645
Problems, 645
Cases, 647
Selected Internet Reference Sites, 648
Selected References and Readings, 649

CHAPTER 17
SECURITY AND ETHICAL ISSUES OF INFORMATION
SYSTEMS, 650

Manager's View, 651
Viewing Information Systems Security, 653
Risks, 653
    Risks, Threats, and Vulnerabilities, 653
    Assessing Risks, 653
Common Controls, 655
    Physical Controls, 655
    Electronic Controls, 655

Software Controls, 655
Management Controls, 655
Common Threats, 656
    Natural Disasters, 656
    Employee Errors, 656
    Computer Crime, Fraud, and Abuse, 657
    Program Bugs, 665
Protecting Information Systems, 666
    Securing Information Systems Facilities, 666
    Securing Communication Systems, 668
    Securing Database Information Systems, 672
    Securing Information Systems Applications, 675
Ethical Issues and Information Systems, 679
    Ethical and Contractual Behavior, 679
    Privacy, Access, and Accuracy Issues, 679
    Property Issues, 683
    The Widespread Impact of Information
        Systems, 685
    Management Responsibility, 686
Management Summary, 686
Key Terms for Managers, 687
Review Questions, 687
Questions for Discussion, 688
Problems, 688
Cases, 689
Selected Internet Reference Sites, 691
Selected References and Readings, 691

INTEGRATED CASE V
CLIENT COMPUTER SYSTEMS
SUPPORT BY SOFTWARE REENGINEERING COMPANY
(SRC), INC., 693

GLOSSARY, 698

NAME INDEX, 723

SUBJECT INDEX, 725

INFORMATION SYSTEMS

AS A MANAGER, you will use computer-based information systems throughout your career. Information technology supports every business function, from the purchasing of goods and services to the servicing of products. To be useful, information technology should serve business needs. An on-line diagnostic hotline connected to an appliance-maintenance database can provide customers with timely help diagnosing small appliance problems. A frequent flight bonus program can create customer loyalty to an airline. A national rental car reservations information system can provide customers with access to rental information in remote sites.

To be a successful manager, you must be able to identify information systems needs that create a business advantage. That is, you must understand how information technology can provide better products, enhance existing services, and create new business opportunities. Then you will be able to plan and develop information systems that improve market share, counteract rivals, and facilitate linkages with customers and suppliers.

Chapter 1 will start you on the road to being a successful manager by describing the fundamental concepts of information systems in business. You will learn how information systems support three types of business objectives: efficiency, effectiveness, and transformation. You will also learn how information technology provides some organizations with a competitive advantage.

Chapter 2 explains the systems approach and how it can be useful in problem solving. You learn about various types of organizational structures and how information systems are used in each. This chapter provides fundamental knowledge that you can apply throughout the text, particularly in analyzing management case studies.

Chapter 3 describes how organizations are using information technology to gain a competitive advantage. You will learn about the *strategic* uses of information technology, the emerging electronic marketplace, and how information partnerships are being organized to address the needs of customers, buyers, and suppliers.

Chapter 4 covers the challenges of analyzing and redesigning business processes to improve performance and productivity. Information technology can facilitate business process redesign, by providing tools for integrating information in shared databases and providing network access to common information resources.

CHAPTER 1
A MANAGER'S VIEW
OF INFORMATION
SYSTEMS

CHAPTER 2
AN INTRODUCTION
TO CONCEPTS
OF SYSTEMS AND
ORGANIZATIONS

CHAPTER 3
STRATEGIC USES
OF INFORMATION
TECHNOLOGY

CHAPTER 4
BUSINESS PROCESS
REENGINEERING
AND INFORMATION
TECHNOLOGY

A MANAGER'S VIEW OF INFORMATION SYSTEMS

CHAPTER OUTLINE

Manager's View

The Functions of Management

Managerial Roles

Managerial Performance

The Levels of Management

The Activities of the Organization

A Framework for Information Systems

Sequence of Development of
Management Information Systems

The Stage Evolution of Data
Processing

An Update to the Original Theory

Management Summary

Key Terms for Managers

Review Questions

Questions for Discussion

Problems

Cases

Selected References and Readings

THE PROCESS OF MANAGEMENT involves planning, organizing, directing, and controlling people and activities. At each level of management, the responsibilities for handling these tasks differ. Top-level managers are responsible for establishing organizational objectives. Middle-level managers organize and control the organization's resources to achieve these objectives, whereas lower-level managers supervise day-to-day activities. Each of these three levels of management has distinct information systems needs. First-line supervisors require feedback about day-to-day activities. Middle-level managers need information that will enable them to reallocate resources to achieve objectives. Top-level managers use external information to identify new business opportunities and to establish goals for the firm.

This chapter helps you understand information systems that support management decision making at the operational, tactical, and strategic planning levels. Knowledge of the nature of operational, tactical, and strategic planning information systems is necessary to understand the application of these information systems to the problem of managing the marketing, finance, accounting, production, and human resource functions. The development of information systems within organizations has been characterized by a process of evolution involving more than technology alone. This process requires planning, a balanced mix of application development, and leadership on the part of both management information systems (MIS) professionals and user-managers. In this chapter you'll learn about the roles and responsibilities of user-managers in determining which types of data processing projects support business goals and in working with the MIS function to accomplish these projects.

THE FUNCTIONS OF MANAGEMENT

Management is the process of directing tasks and organizing resources to achieve organizational goals. The main functions of management are planning, organizing, leading, and controlling. **Planning** is deciding what to do. This function entails evaluating the organization's resources and environment and establishing a set of organizational goals. Once these goals are established, the manager must develop tactics to achieve these goals and create a decision-making process that will monitor the results.

Let's take the example of an office equipment dealership. During the mid- to late 1970s, the dealership's primary product was copier equipment. Growing competition, brought on by the introduction of Japanese products and an increase in the number of dealers in the market area, forced top management to realize that it would have to introduce new products or create more effective advertising and service programs. As a result, a company goal was established: to generate at least 50 percent of the company's revenues from microcomputer and related devices by 1990.

3

The second managerial function is **organizing.** Organizing is the art of deciding how to achieve goals. This decision requires developing the best organizational structure, acquiring and training personnel, and establishing communications networks. The manager of the office equipment dealership will have to organize resources to achieve the objective. A computer department may be organized and staffed with salespeople, technical support representatives, training personnel, and systems analysts to help support the marketing effort. Communications channels between managers, customers, manufacturers, salespeople, and technical specialists will all have to be established under this new plan.

Leading, the third managerial function, involves directing and motivating employees to achieve the organization's goals. The manager of the office dealership may need to develop incentive programs to motivate salespeople and to organize team-building efforts to maintain good morale. The fourth managerial function, **controlling,** enables the manager to determine if the organization's performance is on target. He or she may develop and use performance standards to assess employee performance. Information systems can also provide feedback on how effectively financial and physical resources are being used to achieve business goals. Reports that summarize sales statistics and compare planned versus actual expenses provide information that managers can use to control the use of the organization's resources. The basic managerial functions are summarized in Figure 1–1.

Besides handling the basic managerial functions of planning, organizing, leading, and controlling, managers are also responsible for adapting to changes in the internal and external environment. When a new competitor unexpectedly enters the marketplace or when a key manager suddenly quits, the manager of the office equipment dealership has to investigate possible alternatives and solutions. These decisions, too, may require access to information on an on-demand or ad hoc basis.

MANAGERIAL ROLES

Successful management also requires performing a variety of managerial roles. Mintzberg (1975) studied three managerial roles: *interpersonal, informational,* and *decisional.*

The manager's interpersonal roles include the figurehead role, the leader role, and the liaison role. In the figurehead role, the manager performs ceremonial duties such as greeting job candidates and dignitaries. Managers spend as much as 12 percent of their time in these roles. In the leadership role, the manager must hire, train, and motivate employees. Finally, in the liaison role, the manager makes contacts outside the vertical chain of command. Most studies of managers show that they spend as much time with their peers and with people outside their units as they do with their own

Figure 1–1
Managerial functions

Planning	• Establishing organizational goals • Developing strategies to achieve goals
Organizing	• Developing the structure of the organization • Acquiring human resources
Leading	• Motivating and managing employees • Forming task groups
Controlling	• Evaluating performance • Controlling the organization's resources

subordinates. For example, in a study of foremen, Robert Guest found that managers spent 44 percent of their time with peers, 46 percent of their time with people inside their units, and only 10 percent of their time with their superiors. Chief executives make contact with a wide range of people, including subordinates, clients, business associates, government officials, trade union officers, and suppliers.

The second type of role Mintzberg depicts is the informational role. Managers have formal access to information from virtually every internal staff member as well as extensive external information. In Mintzberg's research, 70 percent of incoming mail was informational. Communications is a large part of the manager's job. In fact, monitoring or scanning the environment for information is one of the most important tasks of managers.

The manager is also a disseminator of information. In this role, the manager may choose to pass certain information along to peers and to subordinates. In the spokesperson role, the manager provides information to the external community: to suppliers, to the press, to lobbying organizations, and to government officials.

The decisional roles of the manager are of primary importance. They include the entrepreneurial role, the disturbance handler role, the resource allocator role, and the negotiator role. In an entrepreneurial role, the manager is constantly looking for new ideas. An effective chief executive may initiate and keep track of as many as 50 different projects. Some of these may involve new products, others may relate to organizational changes, and still others may attempt to identify new markets. "Like jugglers, chief executives keep a number of projects in the air; periodically, one comes down, is given a new burst of energy, and sent back to orbit" (Mintzberg, 1975).

Sometimes the manager has to be a disturbance handler. When internal or external disputes affect the company's operations, a senior manager may have to respond to pressures. The manager must act when a strike occurs, when a major customer cancels an order, or when a supplier defaults on a contract.

Another decisional role is the resource allocator role. As a resource allocator, the manager determines who will get what. He or she may decide how much money to spend on recruiting and training new sales personnel and how much time to spend on developing an advertising program. In the role of resource allocator, executives face very complex choices. One common solution to selecting what projects to support is to pick the person, not the proposal. The manager tends to support the projects that people he or she trusts propose.

The final decisional role is negotiator. The manager is responsible for representing the organization in bargaining with others—with customers, with shipping companies, and with manufacturers. Negotiating with equipment manufacturers for exclusive marketing and service rights for certain lines of equipment is an example of this role.

The interpersonal, informational, and decisional roles of managers are summarized in Figure 1-2. Although the basic tasks of planning, organizing, leading, and controlling are significant activities, most managers are constantly responding to internal and external changes and are responsible for communicating information within the firm and to external groups.

MANAGERIAL PERFORMANCE

One of the keys to managerial performance is the ability to distinguish between efficiency and *effectiveness*. **Efficiency** is "doing things right," whereas **effectiveness** is "doing the right things right." In a business context, *efficiency* means being able to achieve high levels of output with a given base of inputs, or resources. An *efficient*

Henry Mintzberg discussed the role of the manager in his classic article, "The Manager's Job: Folklore and Fact," which appeared in the *Harvard Business Review.* In the classic view managers are responsible for planning, organizing, coordinating, and controlling. In reality, Mintzberg argues, these words tell us little about what managers actually do. The following four myths are not confirmed by the facts.

Folklore: Managers plan in a careful and systematic way.

Fact: Managers work at an unrelenting pace, focusing on hundreds of brief and varied activities.

Chief executives encounter a steady stream of callers and mail from morning until night. In one study Guest found that foremen averaged 583 activities per eight-hour shift, or one every 48 seconds. Rather than planned, 93 percent of the verbal contacts of executives are ad hoc. Managers are constantly interrupted; they try to balance the time they have available for ever-present obligations with the time they need to invest in getting things done. Rather than charting complex strategic plans, most senior executives have intentions that loom in their heads and guide their decisions.

Folklore: Effective managers spend most of their time planning and delegating and less time doing regular duties such as seeing customers and negotiating disputes.

Fact: Managers spend a great deal of their time doing regular tasks, participating in ritual activities, and processing "soft" information about the external environment.

Many senior executives spend a good deal of their time performing ceremonial duties, such as presiding at holiday dinners and giving out gold watches. They also may have access to soft external information (e.g., favorite golf course) about customers or competitors. Sometimes they are called upon to greet important incoming visitors, job candidates, and vendors. All these activities are fairly routine tasks, but they still need to be done.

Folklore: Senior managers use aggregated and summarized information that a management information system provides.

Fact: Managers prefer information from telephone calls, personal conversations, and meetings.

On the average, according to Mintzberg's data, managers spend about 80 percent of their time in verbal communications. In addition, managers are inundated by mail—even though not much of the mail provides interesting, current information on such things as competitor strategies and customer preferences. In one study five executives responded to 2 out of 40 routine reports and to 4 items out of 104 periodicals in five weeks. In contrast to the hard data they receive, managers love soft information, especially hearsay and speculation. Managers use information in two important ways: to identify problems and opportunities and to build mental models of such things as budget forecasts and customer buying patterns. In specific decision situations, managers use small tidbits of data to build models.

Richard Neustadt, who studied the information-collecting habits of Presidents Franklin Roosevelt, Truman, and Eisenhower, commented that "it is not information of a general sort that helps a president see personal stakes; not summaries, not surveys. Rather . . . it is the odds and ends of tangible detail that pieced together in his mind illuminate the underside of issues put to him. To help himself, he must reach out as widely as he can for every scrap of fact, opinion, or gossip bearing on his interests and relationships as president. He must become his own director of his own central intelligence."[1] Managers cherish hearsay because today's gossip may be tomorrow's fact. Managers rely on verbal information that is stored in people's brains, not in their files. Sometimes managers have difficulty delegating tasks because much of the critical detail they expect to be used in making decisions is stored in their memories, not in reports and office records.

Folklore: Management is a science and a profession.

Fact: Management is not a science; managers process information and make decisions using judgment and intuition, not preprogrammed logic.

If management were a science, managers could make decisions using systematic, predetermined programs and procedures. But this is not the case. Managers must make hundreds of judgment calls per day, given the hundreds of brief, fragmented issues and problems they must confront. They use verbal communications extensively to grasp critical facts. The nature of managerial work does not lend itself to scientific improvement.

As you can see from Mintzberg's article, managers have a variety of roles. Their performance depends largely on how well they respond to the pressures of their jobs. A large part of their time is spent assimilating and disseminating important information about the organization's people and problems through verbal communications. In general, the pressures of a manager's job encourage constant interruption, the need to respond to many different stimuli, the desire to get tangible details, and the importance of making small but crucial decisions.

[1] H. Mintzberg, "The Manager's Job: Folklore and Fact," *Harvard Business Review,* March–April 1990, pp. 163–76. Originally appeared in *Harvard Business Review* July–August 1975.

Figure 1–2
Managerial roles

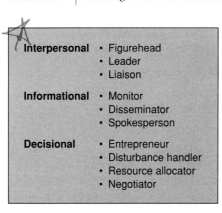

Interpersonal
- Figurehead
- Leader
- Liaison

Informational
- Monitor
- Disseminator
- Spokesperson

Decisional
- Entrepreneur
- Disturbance handler
- Resource allocator
- Negotiator

✱ discussed in class

secretary, for example, may be able to type 75 words per minute and to generate hundreds of letters per week. But she or he would be considered *effective* only if these efforts support the goals of the business.

Most managers are responsible for monitoring the performance of people, programs, and other resources that support organizational goals. Managers are responsible for maintaining existing performance as well as for organizing resources to improve performance. They must also develop criteria to measure successful performance. The information they use to make decisions should provide measures of performance that relate to the successful achievement of business goals. If performance is not suitable, information from reports should highlight the discrepancy between planned and actual performance so that the manager can study the situation and reallocate resources effectively.

The Levels of Management

The levels of management consist of top, middle, and first-line management. Members of top management are the organization's senior executives. Their most important role is establishing the goals of the organization. They are typically responsible for interacting with representatives of the external environment, such as financial institutions, political figures, and important suppliers and customers.

Middle-level managers are responsible for allocating resources so that the objectives of top management are accomplished. They do so by implementing plans and by supervising lower-level managers under their functional area of responsibility. A sales manager, for example, organizes resources—salespeople's time, training budgets, entertainment budgets—to achieve sales results that are consistent with the growth plans of top management. If these goals are not being met, then the sales manager needs to study the existing scope and level of sales force activity and reallocate resources accordingly. Other types of middle-level managers are research directors, plant managers, market research directors, and directors of information systems.

First-line supervisors are responsible for supervising day-to-day operations. They typically supervise functions such as order entry, credit checking, inventory control, and preventive maintenance. If problems such as errors in pricing or frequent breakdowns of equipment on the plant floor occur, first-line supervisors work to solve them. They use information such as quality control reports and inventory turnover reports to supervise the activities for which they are responsible and to make sure that performance is suitable.

THE ACTIVITIES OF THE ORGANIZATION

The activities of an organization are of three kinds: operational, tactical, and strategic planning, as shown in Figure 1–3. Operations are the day-to-day activities of the firm that involve acquiring and consuming resources. First-line supervisors must identify, collect, and register all transactions that result in acquiring or expending these resources. When sales are made or goods are shipped, a department manager needs to record these events. These day-to-day transactions produce data that are the basis for operational systems.

The tactical function of an organization is the responsibility of its middle-level managers. They review operational activities to make sure that the organization is meeting its goals and not wasting its resources. The time frame for tactical activities may be month to month, quarter to quarter, or year to year. For example, orders for raw materials might be monitored monthly, productivity might be assessed quarterly, and department budgets might be reviewed annually. Managers responsible for control have to decide how to allocate resources to achieve business objectives. Data that can be used to predict future trends help managers make these resource allocation decisions.

The top management of the organization carries out strategic planning. Though managers responsible for operational and tactical decision making are primarily involved in reviewing internal data, the managers responsible for planning are also interested in external information. They need to set the organization's long-range goals, for example, by deciding whether to introduce new products, build new physical plant facilities, or invest in technology. To make these decisions they need to know the activities of competing firms, interest rates, and trends in government regulation. Strategic planners address problems that involve long-range analysis and prediction and often require months and years to resolve.

Figure 1–3

The activities of an organization

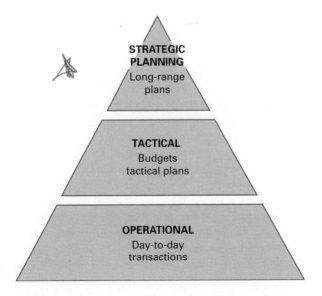

A Framework for Information Systems

Each level—operational, tactical, and strategic planning—requires specific information systems, as shown in Figure 1-4.

Operational Systems

At the **operational systems** level the primary concern is to collect, validate, and record transactional data describing the acquisition or disbursement of corporate resources. Financial data on accounts receivable, accounts payable, payroll, and cash receipts must be recorded as they occur. When a sale occurs, data on the items ordered are recorded, the inventory level for these items is adjusted, a shipping label and packing slip are prepared, and an invoice is generated. The original transaction—the sale of the item—creates numerous transactions in order processing, inventory, and billing.

Operational-level information systems often have the following characteristics.

 Repetitiveness. The information operational-level information systems produce is #9 usually generated repetitively at periodic intervals, such as daily, weekly, or monthly.

 Predictability. The information usually does not contain any surprises or unexpected results for the manager or other users of the system. That is, people are paid what they were expected to be paid, and customers are billed for what they purchased during the month.

Emphasis on the past. The information usually describes past activities of the organization. For example, the output of a payroll system describes employees' past work. The checks to vendors describe past purchases by the organization. Customer invoices describe past sales to them. Stock reports describe past changes in inventory.

Detailed nature. The information is very detailed. That is, paychecks provide detailed information on the workweek of each employee and the specifics of each employee's gross and net pay. Customer invoices specify details regarding purchases

Figure 1–4

A framework for information systems

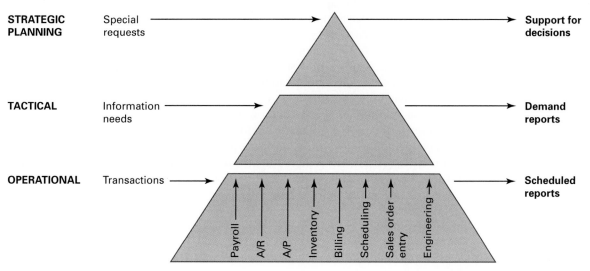

made during the period, the terms under which the purchases must be repaid, and the total amount, including taxes and other charges, due.

Internal origin.   The data for operational systems usually spring entirely from internal sources. That is, the data for paychecks come from internal documents such as time cards and employee master records. The data for customer invoices come from sales orders and shipping documents.

Structured form.   The form of the data used as input and the form of the information produced by operational-level systems are usually very structured. That is, the data on time cards are carefully formatted in identical fashion on each, or the data on each customer invoice are carefully formatted in identical fashion. In short, the form and format of the data input and the information output of the systems are highly structured.

Great accuracy.   The accuracy of the data used as input to such systems and of the output produced by such systems is usually very high. The data input and information output are carefully checked.

Tactical Systems   The second level in the framework consists of **tactical systems.** Tactical systems provide middle-level managers with the information they need to monitor and control operations and to allocate their resources effectively. In tactical systems, transactions data are summarized, aggregated, or analyzed. Tactical systems generate a variety of reports, including summary reports, exception reports, and ad hoc reports.

      Summary reports provide management with important totals, averages, key data, and abstracts on the activities of the organization. An example of a summary report might be a list of the total regular and overtime hours earned at each plant for the week by job classification. Another example is a list of total weekly sales, by salesperson, by product, and by sales region.

      Exception reports warn managers when results from a particular operation exceed or do not meet the expected standard for the organization. An example of an exception report is a list of all plants that have logged more overtime hours than expected for the week. Another example is a list of those sales personnel whose sales fall in the top and bottom 10 percent of the organization.

      Ad hoc reports are reports that managers need, usually quickly, that may never be needed again. Ad hoc reports present information that the manager needs to solve a unique problem. An example of this type of report might be a list of the total number of employees absent during the week arranged by plant and by job title along with the hours or days missed. Another example might be a report that presents the production record of each plant for the week. A manager might request these reports only when an exception report shows high overtime earnings at certain plants. The manager may ask for a number of ad hoc reports such as these to identify the nature of the overtime problem.

      Tactical information systems differ from operational information systems in their basic purpose: the purpose of tactical information systems is not to support the execution of operational tasks, but to help the manager control these operations. As a result, the types of data used as inputs and the information produced as outputs also differ from the types of data involved in operational information systems. Tactical information systems often have these characteristics.

Periodic nature.   The information from a tactical system is sometimes produced periodically. For example, a branch credit manager for an organization may receive a weekly report showing the total dollar amount of accounts that are more than 60 days overdue, 90 days overdue, and in the hands of a collection agency. The report might also compare these three dollar amounts with the same data from other branches of the organization and with the same data for last year at this date and last month at this date. Using the data from other branches and from previous periods as standards for comparison, the credit manager can decide whether the overdue account totals are within the normal range for the branch or whether the difference between the amounts warrants special managerial action or decisions. This information system provides the means by which the credit manager can quickly identify problems and bring them under control.

Tactical information systems may also produce information when it is needed, that is, on an ad hoc basis. For instance, once the credit manager has identified a problem with overdue accounts, he or she may wish to query the accounting system database to find out what customer data, if any, correlate with those who have credit problems. For example, is there a relationship between family income and credit difficulty? Is there a connection between location or address and credit difficulty? Is there a relationship between age and credit difficulty? Is there a link between the number of years that customers have resided in the same home or apartment and credit difficulty? Is there a connection between home ownership versus renting and credit difficulty?

The answers to these questions, and others that the credit manager pursues by querying the accounting system records, may assist in identifying the problem or proposing new credit limitations or requirements for credit status within the organization.

Unexpected findings. A tactical information system may produce unexpected information. For example, in querying the accounting system database, the credit manager may find that the major customer characteristic correlating with credit difficulty is the relationship between type of position and type of employer. Further investigation may reveal that organizations in a particular industry have cut their workforces and have laid off selected workers in certain positions. Such findings may lead to a review of all customers who work in similar positions in that industry to find ways to solve or ease their credit problems and to prevent them from becoming bad debts to the organization.

Comparative nature. The information is usually comparative in nature rather than merely descriptive. Tactical information systems should provide managers with information that alerts them to variances from accepted standards or to results that are outside the normal range so that they can take remedial action swiftly. This type of tactical information system is analogous to process control systems that monitor output constantly and provide feedback when output parameters are at variance with accepted standards.

An example of this type of feedback is a home heating system. As long as the temperature of the air in the house falls within the range specified on the thermostat, the heating system remains inactive. When the air temperature falls below the thermostat setting, however, the thermostat sends a signal to the furnace to turn on. When the air reaches the temperature on the thermostat, it sends a signal to the furnace to turn off.

With comparative overdue account information from other branches and other periods, the credit manager can determine whether the amount overdue is normal or beyond acceptable limits. In some cases, top management sets the standard. That is, top management may have set a credit goal of no more than 5 percent bad debts. Reports comparing the actual bad debts to this standard help the manager spot credit problems quickly.

Summary form.   The information is usually not detailed, but in summary form. The credit manager is not interested in a detailed listing of each customer account and its balance. In large organizations, that would be an enormous quantity of data and would not, therefore, be useful information to the manager. The manager needs only summary information relating to credit performance or balances of accounts that are overdue or in collection.

Both internal and external sources.   The data used for input to the system may extend beyond sources internal to the organization. In our example the credit manager compared the information pertaining to problem customers to other branches, to other periods from the same organization, or to a goal set by top management. The credit manager might also have compared the branch's credit information with the average overdue account experience reported for the whole industry of which the organization is a part. Such a comparison might show that though the branch is experiencing an increase in credit problems, so is the whole industry. Further investigation may reveal that a downturn in the economy is the likely culprit, not any unusual credit policies of the organization.

Thus tactical information systems differ from operational information systems not only in their intended purpose but also in the regularity with which information is produced, the predictability of the results, the comparative nature of the information, the amount of detail produced, and the rigidity of the structure of the information.

Strategic Planning Systems

The third level in the framework for information systems is **strategic planning.** Strategic planning information systems are designed to provide top managers with information that assists them in making long-range planning decisions for the organization. The distinction between strategic planning information systems and tactical information systems is not always clear because both types of information systems may use some of the same data. For example, when middle-level managers use budgeting information to allocate resources to best meet organizational goals, budgeting becomes a tactical decision activity. When top management uses budgeting information to plan the long-term activities of an organization, budgeting becomes a strategic planning activity. In either case, accurate budget information delivered in a timely fashion to managers is an important function of the financial information system of the organization. However, the key differences between the systems have to do with who uses the data and what they are using it for.

Top management ordinarily uses strategic planning information systems for setting long-term organizational goals. Middle managers typically use tactical information systems to control their areas of supervision and to allocate resources to meet organizational goals set by top management. Though the data used in tactical and strategic planning information systems sometimes overlap, usually differences exist in the data that the two information systems use. Strategic planning information systems often have these characteristics.

Ad hoc basis.   The information may be produced either regularly or periodically. For example, top management uses periodic accounting system reports such as the income statement, balance sheet, statement of sources and uses of funds, and capital statement in its planning function. However, strategic planning information is more often produced on an ad hoc basis. For example, organization planners may request marketing analysis information pertaining to a new product or to a new cluster of stores when they are considering the addition of several new stores in a new region.

Manager's Memo 1–2 | **HOW INFORMATION TECHNOLOGY SUPPORTS TACTICAL DECISIONS**

Information technology—which includes databases, telecommunications networks, personal computers, optical scanners, and a host of other technologies—has rapidly become an effective tool for monitoring and tracking critical data. These examples will show you how.

One food marketing company transmits data via a telecommunications network to inform manufacturing plants to beef up inventories in response to unanticipated sales trends. Timely data help management reduce the "react time" when actual sales are greater than forecasted sales.

Sometimes shifts in laws require quick alterations in business strategy. In 1986 Congress passed a tax law affecting insurance companies. One insurance firm immediately extracted policyholder data from its files in order to inform its clients of the changes, whereas other companies had to scramble to obtain lists of customers who would be affected by the change. The first company encouraged its customers to pay back loans against their whole life policies because loan interest was no longer deductible. The net effect of the program was that customers were convinced to repay millions of dollars in loans and to reinvest in single-premium life insurance programs, which were considered liquid and nontaxable under the new law.

Modern tactical systems can also detect deviations in equipment performance in a manufacturing environment. If problems are cited early, preventive maintenance procedures can minimize equipment downtime. Carefully tuned production machinery can also improve the quality of manufactured goods. For example, paper companies use sophisticated monitoring devices to double-check paper thickness and enable engineers to make modifications in production processes if flaws are detected.

Information systems can also help managers market new products and services. Trust officers at one commercial bank scanned through a database of trust accounts to find the names of beneficiaries. When the trust initiator died, these beneficiaries were good prospects for banking services. With the use of a tracking system to generate their names when they became the eligible age, the trust officer could establish a banking relationship with inheritors at an opportune time. Still other information systems enable manufacturers to control their inventories. An automobile manufacturer is linked electronically to the order-entry system of one of its major suppliers, a steel company. By ordering electronically, the manufacturer can rely on timely delivery and reduce its own in-house inventory investment. For decades

Japanese electronics manufacturers have been linked to their suppliers, in some cases ordering inventory at the beginning of each day for that day's manufacturing operations. This strategy, known as *just-in-time manufacturing,* has become a reality in many U.S. companies because of information systems linking buyers and suppliers.

Another example from the food industry shows how computer systems can aid just-in-time delivery. One national food company uses sales trends for various inventory items to stock the grocery stores it serves. Each store has a different inventory mix because of regional and ethnic differences in various neighborhoods. Truck drivers with inventory items did not always have timely information on the previous day's items sold to adjust their deliveries. That situation changed when the food company put microcomputers in its 1,000 delivery trucks. Each morning, each driver's microcomputer receives data on the recommended stock mix for each store on his or her route. At the end of the day, drivers key in information on deliveries made and stale stock removed from the store shelves. This system helps the drivers respond to local store sales trends and also enables the food company's customers, the grocery stores, to manage their inventories more effectively.

Finally, intelligent information systems can create incentives for customers to buy more. Traditionally, customer discounts are based on volume purchases. For example, opticians receive consignment inventory from a contact lens manufacturer, based on their ability to turn it over 13 times a year. In response to this benefit, the opticians attempt to push this manufacturer's line. On-line information about inventory turnover in each store helps the contact lens manufacturer adjust production in response to sales trends and boosts the firm's market share.

In general, tactical systems have become more flexible and more closely tied to a firm's competitive strategy. Information systems enable a manufacturer to cut inventories and to troubleshoot equipment downtime problems. They help marketers zero in on the most profitable market targets and help financial services companies identify their most profitable products and services. Throughout this text you will learn more about tactical systems and how they enable managers to allocate resources more effectively.

Unexpected information.   The system may produce unexpected information. For instance, economic forecast information may be requested for the economy as a whole and for the industry in particular. The results of the economic forecast may be a surprise to organization planners. Or the marketing survey described above may produce store locations that the planners had not predicted or expected.

Predictive nature.   The information is usually predictive of future events rather than descriptive of past events. Long-range planners try to set a course for an organization through an uncharted future. Their primary task is to choose a route that will improve the organization's level of success. The information that the strategic planning system provides should help these planners reduce the risks involved in their choice of routes.

Because organizational long-range planning groups make decisions that will affect the organization for some time in the future, much of the information used in the system is future oriented and predictive in nature. For example, forecasts of future economic conditions, projections of new product sales, and forecasts of the changing demographic characteristics of target customer groups are all forms of strategic planning information that help planners make decisions.

Summary form.   The information is usually not detailed, but in summary form. Long-range planners are not usually interested in detailed information; they are usually concerned with more global data. For instance, long-range planners are not ordinarily concerned about the details of customer invoices. They are more likely to be interested in the overall buying trends reflected in the summaries of sales by product group. In addition, long-range planners are not usually interested in the specific demographic characteristics of a particular customer. They are more likely to be concerned with the overall demographic characteristics of groups of customers.

External data.   A large part of the data used for input to the system may be acquired from sources external to the organization. For example, information pertaining to investment opportunities, rates of borrowed capital, demographic characteristics of a market group, and economic conditions must be obtained from data maintained outside the organization.

MIS personnel may help long-range planners select various on-line external databases to find the information they need quickly and in a form that can be manipulated further. Long-range planners may wish to access databases containing economic data from which they can make forecasts, for example. They may also wish to access databases that contain census data from which they can draw demographic trends and forecasts.

Unstructured format.   The data used for input to the system may contain data that are unstructured in format. For instance, forecasts of future market trends may use the opinions of store buyers, salespeople, or market analysts obtained in casual conversations.

Subjectivity.   The data used for input to the system may be highly subjective and their accuracy may be suspect. For example, forecasts of future stock market trends may be based partly on rumors reported by brokers. Forecasts of the expected market share of your organization within the industry might use the opinions of industry observers who are basing their information on rumors and on conversations held with industry personnel.

A summary of the characteristics of information systems at the operational, tactical, and strategic planning levels is shown in Figure 1–5. As you can see from this chart, first-line supervisors use operational information systems and middle-level managers use tactical information systems. The top executives of the organization use strategic planning systems.

Figure 1–5

A comparison of information systems in operational, tactical, and strategic planning systems

Summary Classification of Information Systems			
Characteristic	**Operational**	**Tactical**	**Strategic planning**
Frequency	Regular, repetitive	Mostly regular	Often ad hoc
Dependability of results	Expected results	Some surprises may occur	Results often contain surprises
Time period covered	The past	Comparative	Predictive of the future
Level of detail	Very detailed	Summaries of data	Summaries of data
Source of data	Internal	Internal and external	Mostly external
Nature of data	Highly structured	Some unstructured data	Highly unstructured
Accuracy	Highly accurate data	Some subjective data	Highly subjective data
Typical user	First-line supervisors	Middle managers	Top management
Level of decision	Task oriented	Oriented toward control and resource allocation	Goal oriented

SEQUENCE OF DEVELOPMENT OF MANAGEMENT INFORMATION SYSTEMS

The base of operational systems has to be in place before tactical systems can be built because the data input into operational systems become the source of data for tactical systems. For example, sales transactions must be captured at the operational level to summarize these data over a six-month or yearly time frame for use in summary reports. However, tactical systems do not necessarily have to be in place for strategic planning systems to be developed because the latter rely heavily on external data sources.

Data and information differ. *Data* are the individual elements of a transaction, such as item number, item quantity, and price on a sales order transaction. *Information,* on the other hand, is data with meaning for decision making. *An information system* is a set of procedures organized to generate information that enables managers to review operational, tactical, and strategic planning activities. *A management information system,* in particular, is designed to provide information for effective planning and tactical decision making. Data are often aggregated to provide the information needed for tactical information systems. Therefore, most management information systems need a foundation of operational-level data systems.

In the next sections, we'll examine information systems in an insurance company, a food marketing company, and a county welfare agency. These cases illustrate a range of applications that are designed to produce information for operational and tactical decision making, and each system supports important business objectives.

General Life Insurance Company

Massive amounts of paperwork involved in creating, maintaining, and generating bills for policies make computer systems essential at General Life Insurance Company. On-line systems supporting policy screening, creation, and issuance were designed in the 1970s. Using an on-line system, an operator keys in new application information at a computer terminal. New information arriving from physicians is used to update policy information on-line. When all information is compiled, a worksheet is created for an underwriter who evaluates the insurability of potential customers. Policy information is then entered into the system and a policy data sheet is created. On-line access to policy information makes it possible to handle inquiries from policyholders and from agents seeking information about policy status.

During the 1970s an on-line data communications network was set up to link the home office with insurance sales agencies. This system enables sales agents to inquire on-line about policies and to enter application information at remote sites. It also makes it possible to update policies in the home office.

Many of the newer systems at General Life provide the firm with a competitive advantage in product marketing and customer service. General Life has developed software available through its network that enables local sales agents to analyze alternative product and service options on a timely basis (for example, what if a customer changes to one option after 10 years instead of 5?). This software provides the information agents need to close many sales immediately.

One of the major projects at General Life today is developing software for producing new insurance products. With competitors introducing new products all the time, it is important to have new services and product options "on the shelf" for new marketing efforts. Market studies forecasting customer needs can provide senior management with valuable information for new product planning.

Figure 1–6 summarizes the operational, tactical, and strategic planning applications at General Life Insurance Company.

New systems projects are clearly directed at cutting costs, improving productivity, and providing managers with better information for decision making. Increasingly, sales managers are designing applications that will help them analyze product profitability, agent profitability, customer profitability, and the impact of marketing strategies on sales. Information on customer profitability, for example, helps the company concentrate its resources (such as salespeople's time or in-house presentations) on the most profitable customers. This supports the tactical objective of achieving maximum profitability.

Figure 1–6

Information systems in an insurance company

Dellco Foods, Inc.

At Dellco Foods, Inc., a company that manufactures, markets, and distributes food products, the information systems at the operational and tactical levels support marketing, physical distribution, production, and administration.

The information systems in physical distribution are operational. Orders are entered at six service centers, and order data are used to update accounts receivable and distribution files. Invoices can be printed out either at the originating location or at a service center nearest the customer's location. As a result, payments are received faster, and cash flow improves. An accounts receivable status report provides on-line credit checking so that orders submitted by delinquent accounts will not be filled without prepayment.

Once order data are keyed in, customer service personnel have immediate access to an open order file that can be used to respond to customer inquiries about deliveries and shipments. When cash payments from customers are received, they are applied almost automatically to customers' accounts.

A number of tactical information systems at Dellco Foods, Inc. support the marketing efforts of the company. The basis for much of the sales analysis is a customer product information file with 24 months of order history data on purchases. These data are used to generate reports on monthly sales by product line within each territory. Other reports supporting tactical decisions are an important account report, showing sales activities within major accounts, and a new product report, showing a reorder analysis of newly introduced products.

Other operational systems are in the production area. A bill-of-materials file containing the list of ingredients and fixed batch sizes for each product is computerized. Recipes, or sets of instructions on how to make products, are merged with the bills of material to produce the manufacturing orders for each batch of the product.

The product specifications file, another operational data file, serves as a database of raw materials information for reference and for printing text on purchase orders. After production, finished goods inventory must be transferred to branch warehouses. Forecasting reports guide inventory management personnel in allocating warehouse stock to various field locations, based on anticipated demand.

In finance and administration, an accounts receivable application is updated with customer billings and cash receipts. Aged trial balance reports are generated monthly, producing account collection letters at specified intervals.

Figure 1-7 summarizes the information systems at Dellco Foods, Inc. These operational systems enable Dellco Foods, Inc. to process orders on a timely basis, to manage inventories, and to organize production. These systems cut costs, increase revenues, and improve service to customers. For example, the order processing system that generates invoices and shipping orders automatically at remote distribution centers cuts down order processing time by days and allows the company to collect accounts on a timely basis. Tactical information systems enable managers to analyze sales, by product and by territory, so that they can allocate marketing efforts to serve demand. Strategic planning systems provide senior managers with competitive industry data so that they can identify emerging trends in the marketplace.

Sea Lake County Welfare Department

The Sea Lake County Welfare Department offers an example of information systems in the public sector. The department provides financial assistance to residents, including medical assistance, a food stamp program, social services (for instance, adoptions and foster home placements), and special services (day care, school services, family planning, housing, legal services, and so on). The major information systems are designed to process new applications and to pay welfare recipients.

Figure 1–7

Information systems at Dellco Foods

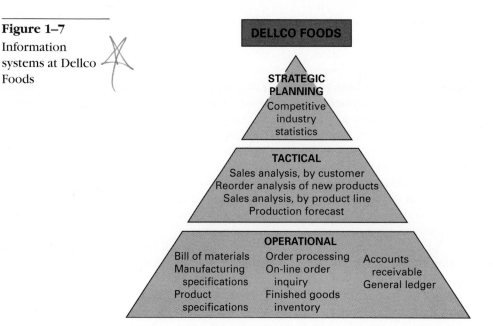

When a welfare applicant applies and becomes eligible, new on-line records are created for public assistance and for the food stamp program. The system automatically prints an identification card from the welfare payroll master file that entitles the client to services for which the welfare department is charged. On-line inquiry and on-line update of client records are also possible. The welfare payroll master file generates the welfare check and a listing on the payroll register. Public assistance also entitles the welfare recipient to participate in the food stamp program. Recipients apply for food stamp authorizations, which are mailed out periodically.

Although most of the welfare department data processing applications are operational in nature, several tactical information systems exist. For example, reasons for welfare denial are accumulated and reported for management analysis. Welfare participant data can also be accumulated and analyzed on a long-term basis to detect trends in client needs and to predict needed services. Information about changing government regulations provides senior managers with input into the planning process. A summary of welfare department applications at the operational, tactical, and strategic planning levels is shown in Figure 1–8.

These three case studies show that many of the original information systems within organizations are operational systems supporting transactions processing. These systems are a necessary foundation for the development of tactical information systems. In contrast, strategic planning systems often use external data about markets, competitors, and government regulations. The growth of data processing within organizations involves investments in technology and in application development. But the evolution of information processing involves more than the construction of application systems; it also entails the organization of a data processing function, user involvement in project selection, and the introduction of planning and control strategies. Nolan's stage theory describes the factors that contribute to the evolution of information processing.

Figure 1–8

Information systems in a welfare agency

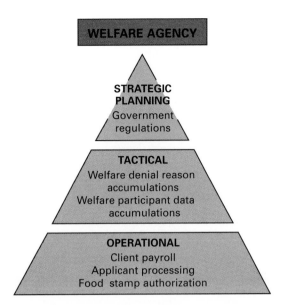

WELFARE AGENCY

STRATEGIC PLANNING
Government regulations

TACTICAL
Welfare denial reason accumulations
Welfare participant data accumulations

OPERATIONAL
Client payroll
Applicant processing
Food stamp authorization

THE STAGE EVOLUTION OF DATA PROCESSING

In his article "Managing the Crises in Data Processing," Nolan argues that the growth of data processing involves growth in technology and application development, changes in planning and control strategies, and changes in user involvement. His six-stage theory of data processing growth describes a learning curve that he argues cannot be overcome. Nolan believes that organizations need to experience the growth characteristics associated with each stage of evolution. A stage of growth cannot be skipped because of the learning process associated with it. Understanding this learning curve can help organizations manage this evolutionary process effectively. Figure 1–9 depicts the six stages of data processing growth that Nolan outlines.

The first stage of data processing growth is *initiation,* when cost-effective transaction-processing systems like accounts receivable and payroll are introduced. Technical specialists within functional areas such as accounting develop most of these systems. This stage has few controls over data processing expenditures, and users have a "hands off" attitude.

This initial success with data processing moves the organization into stage 2, which Nolan calls *contagion.* A proliferation of applications occurs during this stage, and data processing specialists are given the go-ahead to pursue many different kinds of automation opportunities. Because controls are virtually nonexistent, expenditures for computers and data processing personnel skyrocket and cause corporate management to become concerned about the business benefits of investments in information systems.

This concern brings about stage 3, *control.* Motivated by the need to control data processing expenditures, management organizes steering committees with representatives from user areas who become responsible for setting priorities for application development projects. The MIS function becomes a formal department and begins to control its internal activities, using project management plans and systems development

Figure 1–9

The six stages of data processing growth

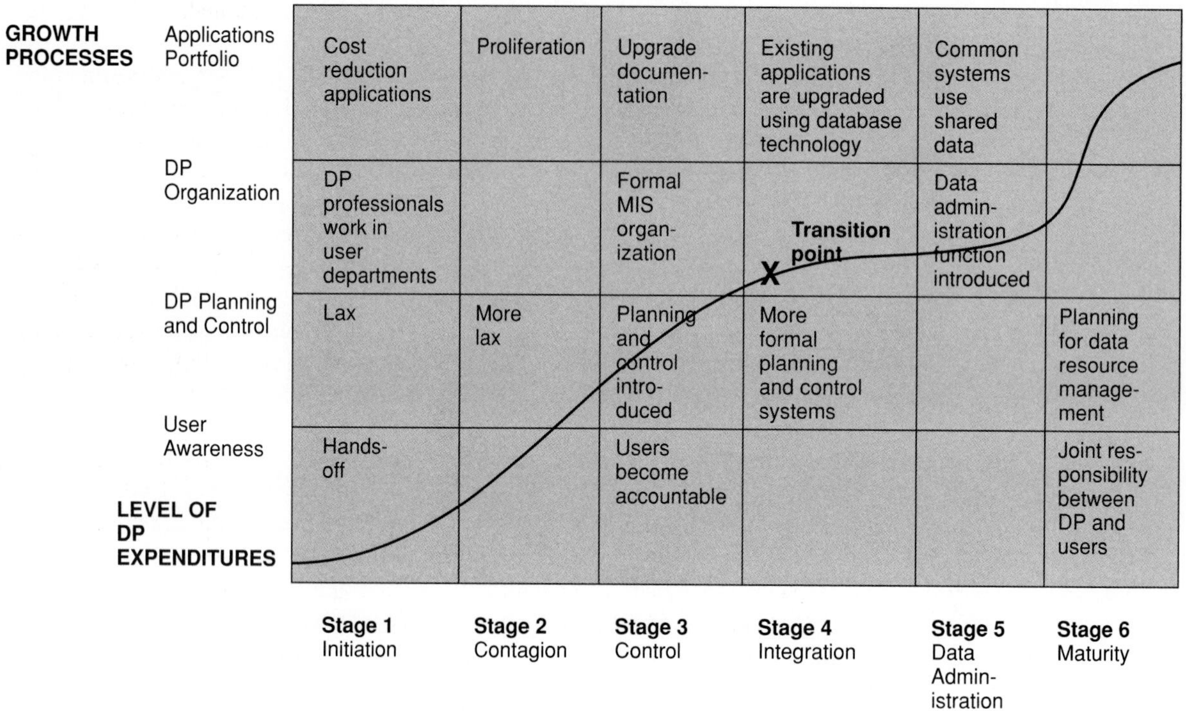

GROWTH PROCESSES	Stage 1 Initiation	Stage 2 Contagion	Stage 3 Control	Stage 4 Integration	Stage 5 Data Administration	Stage 6 Maturity
Applications Portfolio	Cost reduction applications	Proliferation	Upgrade documentation	Existing applications are upgraded using database technology	Common systems use shared data	
DP Organization	DP professionals work in user departments		Formal MIS organization	**Transition point** X	Data administration function introduced	
DP Planning and Control	Lax	More lax	Planning and control introduced	More formal planning and control systems		Planning for data resource management
User Awareness	Hands-off		Users become accountable			Joint responsibility between DP and users

LEVEL OF DP EXPENDITURES

methods. Existing applications that lack documentation are upgraded to provide a better foundation for the development of tactical information systems in later stages of growth.

Between stages 3 and 4, Nolan argues, an important transition occurs—from managing the computer to managing data as a resource. Systems developed during stages 1 to 3 were generally created as independent entities. Beginning in stage 4, *integration*, a major effort is made to integrate existing information systems by using database and telecommunications technologies. The introduction of database technology drives the shift from traditional files supporting single applications to the design of logical databases supporting multiple applications during stage 5, *data administration.*

As the organization moves from technology management to data resource management, in stage 6—which Nolan calls *maturity*—a number of changes occur. As upper-middle and senior management recognize that management information systems are a foundation on which the organization relies, formal planning and control systems for data resource planning are put into effect to make sure that MIS plans support business plans. Priority setting by data processing management is replaced by joint priority setting by top management and data processing management.

During this time frame, corporate data processing establishes the capability to manage computer power for the firm, including mainframe-based data systems, telecommunications networks, and links with distributed systems. Application development groups, responsible for the analysis, design, and implementation of information systems, are organized within operating companies. Transition beyond stage 3 is also accompanied by a greatly increased awareness on the part of noninformation systems professionals about the importance of information systems. In particular, users begin to build their own systems using personal computers and mainframe-based data query and reporting tools.

Nolan's framework enables companies to chart a course for managing information systems development and technology. He argues that the evolution of data processing depends on achieving a balance among technology, application development, user involvement, and organizational control. This organizational learning process can be managed. For example, deliberate slack or lack of controls at stage 2, he contends, can accelerate learning about technology and its uses. Without this period of experimentation, many of the most business-effective uses of information technology may not be discovered. Stage 2 is an "out of control" situation that forces management to recognize the need to establish effective controls and user accountability in stage 3. In stage 5, however, high control is necessary to move into data resource management.

In summary, Nolan's stage theory helps organizations evaluate their current stage of data processing evolution and identify strategies to move ahead to the next phase. These recommendations not only identify what application projects will support business needs; but also explain what kind of planning and control strategies, user involvement, and MIS management will be needed to achieve growth.

AN UPDATE TO THE ORIGINAL THEORY

In an update to his original theory, Nolan presents a new framework for understanding the evolution of information technology within organizations. This framework describes three eras: the data processing or DP era, the information technology (IT) era, and the network era (see Figure 1–10).

In the first era, the DP era, organizations were functional hierarchies. Some of these organizations evolved into a divisionalized form of organizational structure, with functional hierarchies within each division. Work methods and procedures were well-defined, and control systems were designed to monitor the outputs of functional units.

Figure 1–10

The three eras of information technology

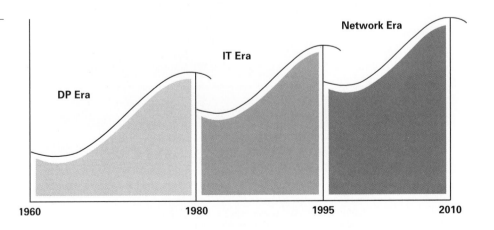

Data processing technology was originally introduced into these forms of organization to automate specific tasks. Transaction processing systems supported paperwork processing, such as generating sales orders and invoices. Tactical-level information systems were designed to provide information for better allocation and control of resources.

The IT era, beginning in the early 1980s, refocused the use of information technology on the knowledge worker. Financial analysts, stock brokers, and production planners used PC workstations, primarily for what-if types of analysis.

In the mid-80s, another major shift occurred. Instead of managing data processing alone, MIS management discovered new application portfolios, depicted in Figure 1–11. Besides the traditional data processing portfolio, application portfolios for office automation, microcomputing, computer-assisted design, and robotics emerged. All these portfolios were characterized by different stages of evolution, with DP at a fairly mature stage of evolution compared with other technologies.

In the network era, the move toward using information technology to leverage business results is becoming most pronounced. If major productivity improvements are to occur, Nolan argues, new technology must be introduced along with new forms of organizational structure. Information technology alone will not enable organizations to achieve the business results they seek, but information technology combined with new organizational forms will bring about dramatic productivity improvements.

Nolan predicts that information technology, combined with networked forms of organizing people and their work, will create 10-fold productivity increases. The networked form of organization will create opportunities for multidisciplinary teams to accomplish projects. Traditional departmental barriers will be blurred, and new methods of accomplishing tasks will emerge as work is reengineered.

Figure 1–11

New application portfolios

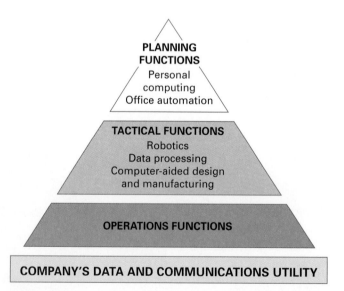

Stages of New Information Technology Growth

Many of the MIS issues you have learned about involve the organization assimilating advanced technologies. Edgar Schein has proposed a framework depicting the evolution of new information technology within organizations that provides a holistic view of the organizational change process. In some ways, his theory is similar to Nolan's stage theory. Schein's phases include (1) investment or project initiation, (2) technology learning and adaptation, (3) management control, and (4) widespread technology transfer. These phases are depicted in Figure 1–12.

In the investment phase, the organization decides to invest in a new information technology such as office automation. If this new technology seems to have merit, this initial phase leads to the second phase, technology learning and adaptation. However, if users are not involved in the initial system selection or if vendor-related problems occur, stagnation A may occur. Stagnation A, which may result from significant cost overruns, poor project management, and unanticipated technological problems, delays further evolution of new information technology indefinitely.

In successful projects, the introduction of new technology leads to the second phase—trying the technology—during which users learn how to use the technology for tasks beyond those initially planned. For example, microcomputers may be introduced for word processing during project initiation. Experimentation with word processing and database software may lead secretaries to set up mailing list files and office record-keeping systems. Experimentation causes new technology to

Figure 1–12

Phases of new information technology growth

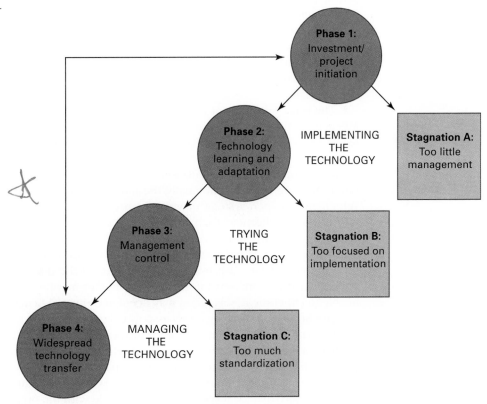

Source: Adapted from J. McKenney and F. W. McFarlan, "The Information Archipelago—Maps and Bridges," *Harvard Business Review,* September–October 1982, p. 115.

be used in ways different from those originally planned and brings about unforeseen benefits.

If users have an opportunity to develop a better understanding of new technology and its benefits during phase 2, the organization will move into phase 3. However, premature controls can cause failure to learn how to use new technology and lead to stagnation B. For example, stagnation B occurred in an organization that introduced word processing to automate mass mailings. This application cut the costs of clerical work, and the organization had no motivation to expand the scope of office automation to new tasks based on its experience with the mailing application. Because of the premature focus on cutting clerical costs, the organization was unable to reap the potential benefits of expanded uses of office automation.

Phase 3—management control—occurs when the organization recognizes the importance of the technology and introduces precise controls over systems development and implementation that help to ensure the cost-effectiveness and success of the applications that result. If this phase is successful, the organization then begins to transfer this application to other groups within the organization.

However, if excessive controls are introduced, stagnation C results. Stagnation C may inhibit further transfer of the technology into other organizational units. For example, in one organization a local area network was established within a research department. To justify the network, its users focused on paperwork reduction and operational efficiency. As a result, the enthusiasm for innovation was lost, and the new technology failed to be transferred to other offices throughout the organization. Stagnation C may also lead to surreptitious experimentation with altogether different technologies, causing evolution beginning with phase 1 again.

If technology is successfully implemented, phase 4—widespread technology transfer—should occur. During this phase, a technology such as local area networking is transferred to other parts of the organization. Technical expertise should be transferred by user analysts and technical support personnel along with the technology itself.

The stage evolution of new technology assimilation creates new challenges for MIS management because organizations may be in different phases of growth for different types of technologies. For example, success with the development of on-line transactions systems may put an organization in phase 4 with regard to data processing technology. Gradual assimilation of word processing may result in a phase 3 evolution in office automation. Finally, the introduction of software supporting the development of expert systems may put the organization in phase 1 in the development of artificial intelligence. Each phase requires different types of management techniques and control strategies. Improper management and premature controls may create the various forms of stagnation that retard further development.

The stage theory also points out that some of the disorderliness accompanying experimentation with new information technology may be necessary. If managers are unable to experiment, stagnation may occur and the real benefits of new technology may not be found or will be unnecessarily delayed.

Premature controls may also block further learning. Users who construct departmental systems may not be convinced of the importance of data security, documentation, and backup procedures until these applications develop business importance. Eventually, users may take responsibility for developing adequate standards and controls to be sure that local systems are compatible with the organization's information processing network and to ensure that these applications are correctly designed.

MANAGEMENT SUMMARY

In this chapter you have learned about the functions of managers and how information systems support these functions. The activities of an organization include day-to-day operations, effective allocation of resources, and strategic planning. Information systems are designed to support decisions at these three levels. Operational information systems process transactions describing the acquisition and disbursement of corporate resources. First-line supervisors use operational systems to monitor day-to-day activities. Accounts receivable, accounts payable, and payroll systems are examples of operational systems.

Tactical information systems provide middle managers with the information they require to allocate resources needed to achieve organizational goals. Often, these tactical systems summarize or aggregate data generated from operational systems. Strategic planning systems help senior managers identify organizational goals. Information for strategic planning often comes from external sources such as demographic data and competitive industry statistics.

Information systems have evolved within organizations over the past 20 to 25 years. This growth involves the construction of operational, tactical, and strategic planning information systems to support the managers of the business. However, the growth of data processing systems involves more than technology and applications. It requires user involvement in application development, the organization and management of an MIS function, and the development of effective planning and control strategies. In Nolan's stage theory, you learned about the characteristics of various stages of data processing growth and how to identify strategies to move from one stage to the next.

Many organizations today are building information systems to achieve a competitive edge. Information systems can be used to cut costs, to add value to products and services, and to expand competitive scope. The information systems opportunities that the management of a firm selects may depend on these competitive plans.

KEY TERMS FOR MANAGERS

ad hoc report, 10	exception report, 10	planning, 3
controlling, 4	leading, 4	strategic planning, 12
effectiveness, 5	operational systems, 9	summary report, 10
efficiency, 5	organizing, 4	tactical systems, 10

REVIEW QUESTIONS

1. What are the planning functions of the manager?

2. What are the organizing functions of the manager?

3. What are the leading functions of the manager?

4. What are the controlling functions of the manager?

5. What informational roles does the manager have?

6. What interpersonal roles does the manager perform?

7. Give an example of a manager's decisional role.

8. What is the difference between *efficiency* and *effectiveness?*

9. What is the difference between *data* and *information?*

10. What are the characteristics of an operational information system?

11. What types of reports are generated from a tactical information system?

12. What are the characteristics of a strategic planning system?

13. In what stage of Nolan's stage theory are steering committees formed to establish application development priorities?

14. In what stage does a proliferation of applications occur?

15. In what stage are common databases designed to support multiple applications?

16. Between what two stages is there a transition from the management of computer resources to the management of data resources?

Questions for Discussion

1. Why is tactical-level information so important to middle-level managers?

2. What kind of tactical information would be useful to a branch manager of a Coca-Cola or Pepsi distributorship?

3. What kind of strategic information would be useful to the president of a four-year liberal arts college?

4. In Nolan's stage theory, why are slack and the lack of effective planning and control systems useful during early phases of evolution?

5. How can the stage theory approach help MIS managers chart a course for future evolution?

6. Nolan's stage theory identifies the organizational and management factors influencing the evolution of data processing technology. Explain what types of organizational and management factors influence DP evolution.

7. Mintzberg cites a myth that the manager plans in a careful and systematic way. How does the manager really work, and why?

8. In Mintzberg's analysis, what type of information is most valuable to the manager? Why?

Problems

1. ABC Industries. At ABC Industries managers at various levels need to make the following types of decisions. Categorize each of the following decisions by the type of decision it represents. Choose from operational, tactical, and strategic planning.

a. Rejecting credit for a company with an overdue account.

b. Analyzing sales by product line within each geographic region, this year to date versus last year to date.

c. Using a simulation model to forecast profitability of a new product, using projected sales data, competitive industry statistics, and economic trends.

d. Comparing planned versus actual expenses for department staff.

e. Allocating salespeople's time to the highest potential market prospects.

2. Essex Industries, Inc. The president of Essex Industries, Inc., a $400,000,000 company in the electronics business, is annoyed with the information systems department in her company. She feels that the computer-based information systems are generating too many reports about day-to-day activities and that managers are not using much of this information for decision making. Even though the firm is spending over $15,000,000 per year on computers and data processing personnel, she can't see what they are getting for this kind of investment. Currently, data processing projects are requested by user-managers and selected by the information systems director. Since there is a two-year backlog of projects, the president is considering bringing in consultants or hiring a service bureau to get some of the work done. However, she isn't sure if all these projects are necessary. What steps should the president take to make sure that information systems are more responsive to the needs of the firm?

CASES

1. **Sherwood Stores, Inc.**   Sherwood Stores, Inc. is a retail grocery store chain with a central distribution center and 14 retail stores in a major metropolitan area. Managers at all levels at the headquarters office, at the distribution center, and in the retail stores use reports from various information systems.

    One of the important information systems is the inventory system that keeps track of physical inventory by product line. Sales information gathered at point-of-sale checkout terminals is used to update inventory levels. At the end of each day, the store manager receives a reorder report indicating which items in inventory have reached their reorder point and need to be reordered from the distribution center. The inventory system also includes a report of items on order by product line, prices, and expected delivery dates.

    Each department manager within each store develops a sales plan that indicates the expected sales volume for each item for the subsequent week. Actual sales for each item are compared with the planned sales activity on a weekly basis and a sales analysis summary report is generated that provides information on planned versus actual sales for each item. Department managers in each store use this report to develop a new weekly sales plan. The report is also useful in determining new safety stock levels for each inventory item and for estimating shelf-space allocations.

    All orders from the local stores are filled from the central distribution center. The central distribution center purchases inventory from suppliers and allocates it to the local stores based on a sales forecasting report. If a local store needs to replenish its stock because an item has fallen below a desired inventory level, the store manager can request additional stock from the central distribution center.

    At the central distribution center, a purchasing system is used to generate purchase orders for stock. One byproduct of this purchasing system is a purchase order

    due-in report that indicates when shipments are scheduled to arrive, the shipper, and the warehouse location for the shipped merchandise. Another report helps monitor the performance of various suppliers by providing information on planned versus actual shipment dates and on the quality of the shipped merchandise. For example, if six cases of eggs are damaged in shipment, the damage is indicated on the shipment report. In addition, an accounts payable system keeps track of payment amounts and due dates for Sherwood's suppliers.

    Sherwood Stores, Inc., has 24 trucks making deliveries to local stores daily. An information system provides drivers with a computerized schedule of store deliveries. Distribution managers develop standards for truck unloadings based on shipment quantity and weight. Actual delivery data are compared with delivery standards in reports to distribution managers.

    Finally, planners on the headquarters staff use external market data and demographic data to forecast sales trends in various regions. They build these data into reports that analyze the sales potential of alternative store sites. Store site selection is an important issue for top managers at Sherwood Stores, Inc. because they would like to expand the number of stores from 14 to 24 within the next three to five years. The information systems at Sherwood Stores, Inc. are essential to its ability to control inventories, manage the distribution process, and analyze sales trends affecting various product lines and store sites.

    a.   What information systems are described in the case?
    b.   What business objectives are supported by each system?
    c.   What level of decision making (operational, tactical, strategic planning) does each information system support?

2. **Clark Products, Inc.**   At Clark Products, Inc., office automation was introduced in the late 1970s when a word processing center was organized. The primary purpose of the word processing center was to efficiently

produce thousands of repetitive letters supporting a variety of applications.

While other companies were beginning to experiment with other applications of office automation, such as electronic mail, desktop publishing, and local area networks, Clark Products seemed to be in a rut. Requests for office automation systems within user departments were virtually nonexistent. Secretaries maintained records and filed pretty much as they had in the 1950s. Major production jobs, such as mass mailings of repetitive letters and heavily revised financial reports, were always sent to the word processing center, so secretaries had little or no exposure to office automation.

The president of Clark Products is skeptical about the firm's lack of progress in office automation. Other companies are busily experimenting with new information technology, but little interest in these emerging technologies seems to be surfacing at Clark Products.

As a result, Ralph Mattheus, the president, has called in Thomas Morris, a consultant specializing in office automation. Assume that you are Thomas Morris and answer the following questions:

a. Using Schein's theory of new information technology growth, at what stage would you place Clark Products in terms of the evolution of office automation?

b. What strategies would you recommend to change the direction of office automation at Clark Products?

SELECTED REFERENCES AND READINGS

Anthony, R. *Planning and Control Systems: A Framework for Analysis.* Boston: Harvard University, Division of Research, Graduate School of Business Administration, 1965.

Mintzberg, H. "The Manager's Job: Folklore and Fact." *Harvard Business Review* 53, no. 4, (July–August 1975), pp. 49–61.

Nolan, R. L. "Managing the Crises in Data Processing." *Harvard Business Review,* March–April 1979, pp. 115–26.

An Introduction to Concepts of Systems and Organizations

Chapter Outline

Manager's View

Systems Concepts

Systems and Their Environments

How a System Works

Using the Systems Approach in Problem Solving

Using Information Systems for Feedback

Making the Transition to the Learning Organization

Management Summary

Key Terms for Managers

Review Questions

Questions for Discussion

Problems

Cases

Selected References and Readings

WHEN YOU BEGIN THE STUDY OF **INFORMATION** SYSTEMS, you should become acquainted with a theoretical framework for understanding their use, development, and effect on organizations; that is, you need to have an understanding of systems concepts as a foundation for further study. The word *system* is often misunderstood—some people think you are referring to a computer system when you use the term, but you may hear people talk about financial systems, air-conditioning systems, school systems, and investment systems as well as about **information systems.** A system is a collection of people, machines, and methods organized to accomplish a set of specific tasks. Information systems—which are a major topic in this text—have the same components and characteristics as systems in general.

This chapter introduces the concepts of systems, their characteristics, and their interaction with the environment. As a manager, you'll constantly be dealing with systems, and you'll need feedback about their performance. Information is the feedback you need to determine if systems are achieving their objectives, operating with the necessary components, and meeting the necessary standards. Information systems are designed to give managers the information they require as feedback.

In this chapter you will learn about the systems approach to problem solving. As a manager, you will be dealing with many types of systems, and you will be responsible for improving their performance. For example, you'll determine if procedures, personnel, and equipment need to be changed to achieve objectives. Or you'll need to assess the effect of new equipment on current work methods, procedures, and organization. The systems approach to problem solving will help you deal with these kinds of tasks.

Finally, this chapter explains how organizations operate as systems, with unique characteristics, information flows, and decision processes. You will learn about the components of organizations and about different types of organizational structures. You will need to recognize the structures of organizations to understand the decision-making processes that occur within different types of organizations.

SYSTEMS CONCEPTS

A **system** is an integrated set of components, or entities, that interact to achieve a particular function or goal. Systems have characteristics such as boundaries, outputs and inputs, methods of converting inputs into outputs, and system **interfaces.** Systems are composed of interrelated and interdependent **subsystems.** Examples of systems are all around us—in fact, an excellent example is a college class. The components of the classroom situation, including an instructor, the students, textbooks, and facilities, all interact to make the accomplishment of learning goals possible. Figure 2-1 depicts a classroom system.

Figure 2–1

A classroom system

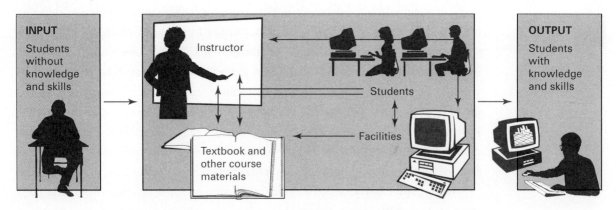

A business is also a system. A business uses resources such as people, capital, materials, and facilities to achieve the goal of making a profit. Business procedures, such as order handling, marketing research, financial planning, and manufacturing, are the interactions that need to be managed to achieve this objective.

System Boundaries

Every system has a **boundary** that defines its scope of activities. For example, the activities in a class include lectures, discussion, testing, grading, and preparation of assigned course work. These activities may represent the boundary of the system for which a teacher is responsible. Within the system of the classroom, the teacher is responsible for organizing class time, assigning homework to students, and evaluating student progress. The boundary, then, delineates an area of responsibility. When defining a system, you must establish a boundary.

System boundaries are also established within a business system. A sales manager may be responsible for managing, motivating, and evaluating the performance of a sales organization. The owner of the business, however, faces different boundaries and may develop a financial plan, a marketing strategy, and a long-range business plan.

Systems and Subsystems

Systems may consist of numerous subsystems, each of which has elements, interactions, and objectives. Subsystems perform specialized tasks related to the overall objectives of the total system. For example, an educational system may consist of individual courses that are subsystems. Each course provides specific knowledge that is a part of the overall educational system and contributes to its goals.

In a business system, various functions are subsystems. Marketing, finance, and manufacturing, for example, are subsystems. Within the marketing subsystem, the sales order-entry and credit-checking functions are subsystems. Each subsystem uses its resources to meet specific objectives. Successful achievement of these goals requires good management of internal resources. For instance, in managing the sales order-entry function, the supervisor needs to develop sales order procedures, maintain sales order records, and train sales order personnel.

Outputs and Inputs

The inner workings of a system or subsystem are organized to produce outputs from inputs. In this conversion process, some value or utility should be added to the inputs. For example, a training program should produce trained employees with certain skills, knowledge, or behavior from its inputs—untrained employees.

The outputs of one subsystem usually become inputs into the next. The outputs of a course in introductory data processing concepts, for instance, become inputs into the next course in COBOL programming. These two subsystems are depicted in Figure 2–2.

As you'd expect, the outputs of a subsystem have to adhere to certain standards to be acceptable to the next. If students coming out of the introductory data processing course don't understand basic concepts of file organization and file processing, they won't have the prerequisite skills needed for COBOL. If they're not permitted to enter COBOL until they meet certain standards, though, the problem would be alleviated. The more exactly standards are adhered to, the easier it will be to interface the two courses, or subsystems.

An *interface* is a connection at system or subsystem boundaries. An interface serves as a medium to convey the output from one system to the input of another system. An example will help clarify this concept. Two typical business systems that interface with each other are inventory control and purchasing. If inventory levels drop below a certain level, then additional stock of these items should be purchased. Purchasing will need to know what quantity of a particular item to obtain to replenish the stock and information on sales and inventory turnover to learn which items are in greatest demand so these items can be replenished on a timely basis. An inventory control system will provide information on stock to be reordered based on sales and inventory turnover trends.

However, if the inventory control subsystem triggers erroneous information about the amount of stock to be reordered, then inputs into purchasing will be wrong. This problem can be partially overcome by establishing an economic order quantity, or the quantity of an item that is most economical to buy, for each item in inventory. This quantity, derived from order history and inventory turnover rate, can serve as a standard and prevent reordering too much or too little stock.

Subsystem Interface and Interface Problems

In the previous section we mentioned that adhering to standards can alleviate some interface problems. However, you might encounter other types of interface problems. Sometimes the output of one subsystem is not sufficient to accommodate the needs of the next subsystem. For example, the production subsystem may not be able to produce enough stock to meet sales demands during certain peak periods. One way of handling this interface problem is through the use of slack resources. In this

---

Figure 2–2

Typical subsystems: An example

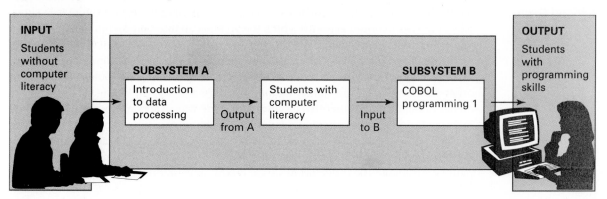

situation a business can build excess inventory during slack times to meet the demand for inventory at peak times.

Another system interface problem can occur between the authoring subsystem and the editorial subsystem in the development of a textbook. Authors who wait until the last minute to finish their writing may not be able to produce a manuscript fast enough to meet production schedules, which involve editing, artwork, layout and design, typesetting, and proofreading tasks. The publisher can avoid this problem in several ways. First, the publisher can ask the author to complete several chapters before production activities begin. This procedure is another example of using slack resources.

Second, the publisher can ask the author to adhere to certain standards for input into the production subsystem. For example, the author can create and store all text using a word processing package that can be transported to a computer-based typesetting system without rekeying.

Third, the author could hire a library researcher, photo researcher, and typist to provide a support subsystem to expedite the development of manuscript. This method creates a new subsystem to solve a system interface problem.

Another situation in which designing a new subsystem can solve a system interface problem occurs at a college when it accepts some students with deficiencies in their academic backgrounds. To bridge the gap between high school and college, the college can create a remedial subsystem to help students develop prerequisite skills for college work. For instance, the college may require students deficient in basic writing skills to take a remedial writing class to learn spelling, grammar, punctuation, and composition skills before they can enroll in literature classes.

SYSTEMS AND THEIR ENVIRONMENTS

The system's environment consists of people, organizations, and other systems that supply data to or that receive data from the system. Not surprisingly, different managers perceive the environment differently. A sales manager, for example, may envision the system environment to be the company's customers and vendors of the products and services being marketed. On the other hand, the owner of the business may perceive the environment to include the firm's competitors, financial institutions that provide resources for expansion, and government agencies with jurisdiction over company plans and products. Moreover, various kinds of systems may interact with the environment in different ways.

Open and Closed Systems

Open systems operate in an external environment and exchange information and material with that environment. The external environment consists of the activities external to the system boundary with which the system can interact. An open system needs to receive feedback to change and to continue to exist in its environment. For example, a marketing system, which is an open system, operates in an environment of competition. If a competitor introduces new technology by providing customers with on-line order-entry terminals, the marketing function must adapt to the change in the environment or remain at a competitive disadvantage. One way of accommodating the change in the environment is to offer a similar on-line order-entry service. The same type of adjustment is necessary when an airline offers a new service, such as a frequent flier bonus program. Though the new service may temporarily give the air carrier a competitive advantage, the other airlines soon follow suit and offer similar programs.

In contrast, a **closed system** is relatively self-contained; it doesn't exchange information with its environment. Closed systems don't get the feedback they need from the external environment and tend to deteriorate. For instance, if a training program administrator doesn't respond to the needs of the business environment for trained graduates, students may no longer be able to get jobs and may go elsewhere for training. Eventually, the training program may be discontinued.

You might wonder why closed systems exist at all. More often than not, participants in a system become closed to external feedback without fully being aware of it. For example, a university may offer graduate courses only during the daytime hours because it has always scheduled these courses in this way. Without recognizing the growing number of working adults wishing to enroll in evening graduate programs, the university may find registrations dwindling and may even have to discontinue certain courses. If university officials had been more responsive to student needs, however, the school might have enjoyed booming enrollments among the population of adult evening students.

System Feedback

A system needs feedback to do its job. **Feedback** is an indicator of current performance rates when compared to a set of standards. With effective feedback, continuing adjustments in the activities of a system can be made to assure that the system achieves its goals. Measuring performance against a standard is an effective control mechanism. Employees need feedback to learn how well they are achieving job goals. Students receive grades or other kinds of evaluations from instructors that show whether the students are meeting course objectives.

The good thing about feedback is that it usually increases effort. For example, tennis players often perform better when they are keeping score. When salespeople receive positive feedback, it increases their motivation to achieve a sales quota. Negative feedback may also serve a useful purpose. Negative feedback is designed to correct or guide activities that are not consistent with achieving the goals of the system. If salespeople are not achieving quotas, they may want to rethink current sales techniques or reorganize their time. Similarly, if students receive low grades, they may need to improve study habits, obtain tutoring, or enroll in courses that better match their abilities or backgrounds.

Product managers also need feedback on how well new products fare in certain markets. They conduct market research studies in test markets to compare new products with established products. They can use feedback from these market tests to redesign a new product or identify target markets for which the product is suitable before its introduction. Products such as shampoos, honey-roasted peanuts, and detergents are all market tested in this way. Sometimes a company receives enormous amounts of feedback after introducing a new product. When Coca-Cola introduced new Coke, negative feedback from customers forced the company to reintroduce its original formula as Classic Coke.

Trainers in companies also need feedback about how well their programs are equipping trainees for job tasks. Feedback from supervisors may provide suggestions on what skills trainees need to perform successfully on the job. For example, employees who take a training program to learn how to use Lotus 1-2-3, a popular microcomputer spreadsheet program, may not be taught how to copy formulas from one cell to a range of cells and may experience difficulty performing this procedure on the job. Trainers can use this feedback to build more exercises on the copy command into training classes. Figure 2-3 depicts a training system and its environment.

Figure 2–3

A training system
and its
environment

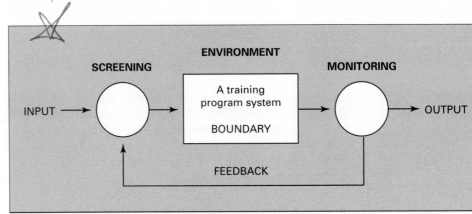

It also shows how feedback from the external environment can be used by managers to modify or improve the system's internal workings.

So far we've emphasized the constructive aspect of feedback. Sometimes, however, the wrong kind of feedback is provided. For example, if students are rewarded for the number of book reports they complete, rather than for the quality of the reports, they may skim books to get just enough information to complete and submit each report without developing comprehension and reading skills—the real objectives of the exercise. Or if employees get the wrong kind of feedback, they may increase their efforts in areas that aren't useful in achieving the objectives of the system. For example, if salespeople are rewarded for the number of sales calls they make, instead of the number of sales they close, they will try to fit in as many calls a day as they can, rather than spending the time with each customer to make a sale. As a result, the company may lose business and not achieve its objectives.

Such considerations make it clear that managers must design feedback mechanisms for effective control of business functions within an organization. In a business setting, an inventory manager needs to manage the inventory levels of hundreds of items to avoid shortages of items in demand and to prevent excess inventory levels of items that do not turn over frequently. The inventory manager needs feedback to control these inventory levels and determine when to order new stock of certain items. An inventory control system can automatically generate a purchase order for stock replenishment when an item in inventory falls below its reorder point. (The *reorder point* is the inventory level of an item that signals when that item needs to be ordered.) This reorder system is an effective control device because if inventory levels fall below a safe level, the company cannot fill incoming customer orders. This system also reduces excess inventory, which ties up cash unnecessarily.

In short, many information systems provide managers with information they need to allocate their resources to achieve business goals. By having information about current business activities, managers can control production, inventory, and marketing resources and invest these resources in the most profitable ways. For example, managers can use information on planned versus actual sales to detect slow-moving items and cut production appropriately. Fast-moving items should trigger production so the sales function can take advantage of market demand.

System Entropy   Systems can run down if they are not maintained. **Systems entropy** corresponds roughly to chaos or disorder—a state that occurs without maintenance. If employees do not have opportunities to learn new concepts and techniques, the skills they apply to performing job tasks will become out of date. The process of maintaining a system is a process of decreasing entropy or increasing orderliness. Sending automobile mechanics to training classes to learn new diagnostic techniques is an example of decreasing entropy. Orderliness can be achieved through preventive maintenance checks, such as a yearly physical examination for an employee or a routine tune-up for an automobile, and then taking action as a result of these regular checks. These checks provide valuable feedback to help detect faults or problems when none have been anticipated. Diagnostic tools for equipment and machinery help prevent downtime, which may cause delays in production and cost thousands of dollars in lost business.

System Stress and Change

Systems change over time. Some of these changes occur because of identified problems, new business opportunities, and new management directives. Systems may also change as a result of stresses. The achievement levels needed to meet existing goals may change. For example, because of reduced profit margins on sales, a division sales manager may insist on a sales increase of 10 percent instead of 7 percent to achieve the same profits. The tendency is to localize the stress so that only one subsystem, in this case the division sales force, feels most of the pressure for adjusting to new demands.

It is easier to deal with change within one subsystem than within the total system because stress may require rethinking existing work methods and organization. In this case the sales manager may have to develop more effective procedures to improve the profitability of sales. The sales manager may recommend cutting down calls to smaller customer accounts and substituting telemarketing to service their needs. Salespeople might need to reallocate their time so they can pay special attention to customers who purchase the most profitable product lines and encourage customers who purchase less profitable lines to look at high-margin products. All these procedures require a close analysis of the current system, changes in work procedures, and effective time management.

Another source of system stress occurs if inputs cannot be monitored but the system is expected to produce the same quality of output. Many colleges and universities screen applicants using standardized test scores, high school grades, and references. Some educational institutions, however, have open admissions policies that allow all high school graduates to apply and be admitted. Because admitting candidates without the necessary academic skills for college study places undue stress on the entire educational system, colleges with open admissions policies typically localize this stress by establishing remedial programs and hiring specially trained teachers for these students. Students are expected to pass remedial course work before entering regular college courses.

In a business situation, the same thing happens. New workers participate in training programs before they begin to work in the firm. During the training period, they learn specific job-related practices so they can become productive in the work environment as soon as possible. After training, they receive jobs and responsibilities consistent with their skill levels and backgrounds. This orientation and training process helps minimize the stress that might occur if the new employees were placed directly into positions within the firm.

Although one way to deal with stress is by changing the activities of a subsystem, it is also important to remember that the subsystem is a part of the whole system and interacts with other subsystems to achieve the organization's overall objectives. Therefore, managers may need to consider the entire system in responding to a problem and to modify activities in other subsystems as well.

HOW A SYSTEM WORKS

You can get a better idea of how a system works by considering the activities of a professional baseball team. A professional baseball team consists of components that are organized to achieve its objectives. One of the major objectives of a baseball club is to win games. To achieve this goal, the owner and manager may recruit players, organize training programs, and develop marketing campaigns. When the team needs a good catcher, the manager may acquire a new player by making a trade. All these components—players, management, training, and promotion—interact to enable the ball club to achieve its objectives.

A professional baseball team interacts with its environment, just as other systems do. It accepts feedback from the external environment in order to organize its resources more effectively. It receives feedback from many sources. Sportswriters provide feedback on trades, team strategy, and performance. Fans provide feedback by their support (or lack of it) for the team. The manager and coaches give players specific feedback about their performance. All this feedback provides the manager, coaches, and players with information they need to reallocate resources to meet objectives.

Systems differ in terms of their goals, components, and characteristics. The objective of one ball club may be to win games. To achieve this goal, it may recruit highly paid professionals throughout the season to fill gaps in the lineup. In contrast, the objective of another team may be to make money. Instead of recruiting highly paid athletes, this second team may enlist talented rookies, hoping to fill the ballpark with dedicated fans. Each of these two ball clubs has a different system with different objectives. The measures of success that each club uses to evaluate its performance vary. In the first case, game and player statistics help measure the ability to win games. In the second, box office receipts are a measure of success.

A professional baseball team can exhibit signs of entropy if it is not successfully managed and maintained. New players have to be brought in to fill critical positions and others need to be retrained. Owners and managers need constantly to formulate team strategy to address the competition. The purpose of all these efforts is to maintain the system and to prevent it from becoming noncompetitive in its environment.

Systems Concepts in Business

Now that you have a general picture of how a system works, it will be helpful to look more closely at business systems. The systems approach is a way of analyzing business problems. This approach views the business organization as a system of interrelated parts designed to accomplish goals. Each subsystem is both a self-contained unit and a part of a larger system. Managers must understand the goals of the total system and design the function of subsystems within the total system to accomplish these goals.

More specifically, *management* is the practice of organizing resources, including people, materials, procedures, and machines, to achieve objectives. In other words, it entails organizing subsystems to accomplish specific tasks. Using a systems approach, a manager organizes various activities of the business into separate organizational subsystems. The subsystems of the business are connected by resource flows throughout the firm.

To consider an example, the market research subsystem of the business may obtain information from customers about modifications that need to be made in the firm's products and services. The market research subsystem can transmit this information to the manufacturing subsystem that builds product design changes into its processes. Finally, the marketing subsystem sells the finished products to customers. If technical

Figure 2–4

The firm's subsystems

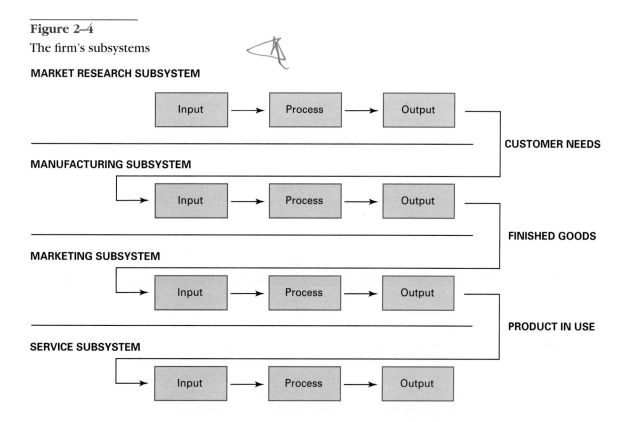

problems occur, the service subsystem may need to provide follow-up support. The interactions among these functional subsystems are depicted in Figure 2–4.

An Information System as a System

In many ways, information systems have the same characteristics as systems in general. The major purpose of an information system is to convert data into information—*information* is data with meaning. In a business context, an information system is a subsystem of the business system of an organization. Each business system has goals, such as increasing profits, expanding market share, and providing service to customers. An Chapter 1, you learned that the operational information systems of an organization provide information on the day-to-day activities of a business, such as processing sales orders or checking credit. Information systems that provide information that lets management allocate resources effectively to achieve business objectives are known as tactical systems. Finally, information systems that support the strategic plans of the business are known as **strategic planning systems.** To sum up our discussion so far, information provides managers with the feedback they need about a system and its operations—feedback they can use for decision making. Using this information, a manager can reallocate resources, redesign jobs, or reorganize procedures to accomplish objectives successfully.

An information system consists of components that interact to achieve the objective of providing information about day-to-day activities that managers can use to control business operations. Information systems can also provide information to enable managers to allocate resources and establish long-range business plans. An information system contains such elements as hardware, software, personnel, databases, and procedures to accomplish its objectives. The **hardware** consists of the computer devices that support data processing, communications processing, and other computer-related activities. **Software** consists of the instructions that the hardware uses to process information. Software includes both **application software** and **system software.** Application software consists of the programs written to support specific business functions, such as order entry, inventory control, and accounts receivable. System software enables the hardware to run application software. System software consists of the programs that handle such functions as sorting data, converting programs into the machine language the computer can understand, and retrieving data from storage areas.

Information-processing personnel, such as systems designers and programmers, design and write the application programs to support information processing activities. Operations personnel, such as data entry operators and equipment operators, handle day-to-day operations activities. Finally, all personnel have to follow specific procedures to organize and manage a company's information-processing activities. These procedures include designing and implementing programs, maintaining hardware and software, and managing the operations function. The interactions among these elements constitute the information-processing procedures that are used to generate information needed for decision making. (A general model of an information system is shown in Figure 2–5.)

Subsystems

Operational systems, which are designed to provide information about day-to-day activities, are composed of subsystems that accomplish specialized tasks. A mail-order business, for example, needs a system to process customer orders. The order-processing system actually consists of subsystems set up to handle incoming orders, update inventory levels, and bill customers. Other subsystems are created to purchase new stock, to handle accounts payable transactions, and to apply cash receipts from customers to outstanding accounts receivable balances. Each subsystem performs a specialized task that supports the business objectives of increasing sales and providing customer service. You can see how these subsystems are organized in Figure 2–6.

Figure 2–5

A model of an information system

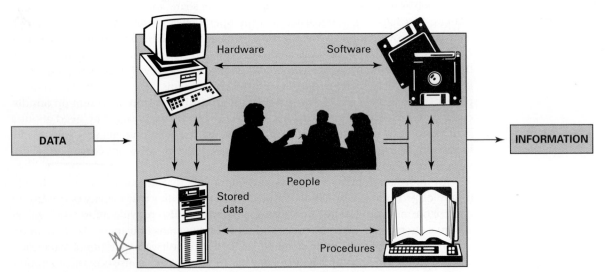

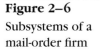
Figure 2–6
Subsystems of a
mail-order firm

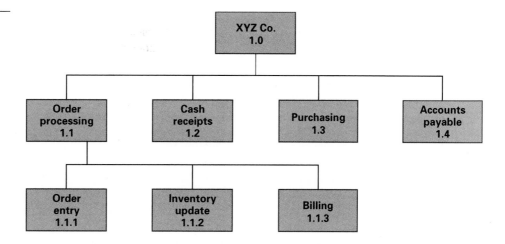

If one of these subsystems breaks down, the overall business will feel the effect. For example, if the mail-order company does not maintain sufficient inventories, customers may become frustrated with constant back orders and shift their business to other companies.

Outputs and Inputs

An information system, like any other system, receives inputs of data and instructions, processes the data according to these instructions, and produces outputs. This information-processing model can be used to depict any information system. An inventory update system is shown in Figure 2-7.

In an inventory update procedure, the inputs are sales order transactions and an old inventory master file. During the update procedure, the item quantities for each item on a sales order transaction are subtracted from the existing inventory level for that item in stock. The new inventory level is then written to the new inventory master file. The outputs of this system are an updated inventory master file, a reorder report, and a sales listing. A reorder report lists any items in inventory that have fallen

Figure 2–7
An inventory
update system

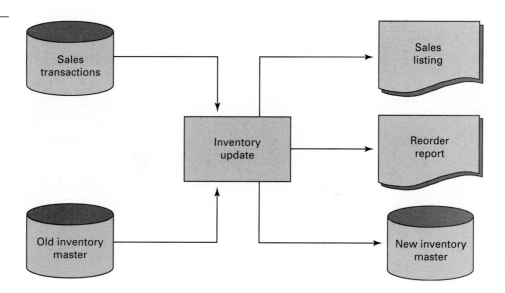

below their desired inventory level and provides a purchasing manager with feedback about items that need to be reordered.

Hierarchy of Subsystems

The subsystems within an information system can be organized into a hierarchy to represent their functions within the overall system. Each subsystem performs a specialized function. In the inventory update example, one subsystem may record sales transactions as input, another subsystem may check customer credit, and another may check inventory availability. Other subsystems may update inventory, generate a reorder report, produce information for billing, and so on.

System Feedback

An information system provides system feedback to a manager about day-to-day activities and about deviations from planned activity. The manager can use this information to supervise daily operations, such as credit checking and billing, and to reorganize resources to achieve objectives more effectively. In the inventory control example, one of the outputs was a reorder report indicating which inventory items need to be reordered. A purchasing manager could use this report to reorder additional stock on a day-to-day basis. An example of a reorder report is shown in Figure 2–8.

Middle managers might want feedback about which items in inventory are moving rapidly and which items are moving slowly so they can reallocate the investment in inventory to minimize waste and maximize profitability. The information systems providing feedback that can be used to allocate resources effectively, such as inventory and personnel, are called **tactical systems.**

Subsystem Interfaces

As with other systems, interfaces exist between the subsystems of an information system. Again, the outputs of one subsystem become the inputs into the next. For example, the outputs of a sales order entry system become the inputs into an invoicing system. If the outputs of one system are not correct, however, the next subsystem will be affected. If the price of an item is entered incorrectly during order entry, then the charges to the customer may be incorrectly calculated during billing.

Internal Controls

Good information systems also have internal standards to make sure that data are processed accurately. Input controls, for example, ensure that input data are valid before they are processed. Another type of control is a password security procedure designed to protect against unauthorized access and update of data. All in all, standards make sure the system works properly. Without controls, the data printed out on reports may be inaccurate, and managers may not be able to trust the information sys-

Figure 2–8

A reorder report

REORDER REPORT
American Office Supply

DATE: 01/01/98

Item No.	Item Description	Unit	Quantity On Hand	Quantity On Order	Quantity Back Order	Reorder Point	EOQ
5045	3-ring binder	EA	100	0	0	120	40
6565	Pencil sharpener	EA	34	10	0	50	10
7231	Manila folder	BX	0	50	20	50	50

tem to provide valid results. If unauthorized users update data files or if input data are not valid, managers may not even know that the output generated in reports is invalid, and thus they may make decisions using erroneous information.

Effect of the Systems Approach on Information Systems Design

Many of the ideas that are part of the systems approach have implications for the design of information systems. You can learn about the design of an information system by putting yourself in the shoes of an owner of a microcomputer dealership, for example. Systems have objectives, and in this case the owner's objective is to make a profit on the sales of microcomputers, software, and related peripheral equipment.

The Structure of an Enterprise

The entire enterprise has been organized into subsystems, including the marketing subsystem, the service subsystem, and the administrative subsystem. The marketing subsystem promotes and markets microcomputer products and services. When customers have problems with their microcomputers or need preventive maintenance, they use the service subsystem. Finally, the administrative subsystem takes care of billing customers, purchasing equipment and supplies from vendors, paying vendors, and handling accounting activities. The organizational structure of the dealership is depicted in Figure 2-9.

The marketing subsystem of the dealership is managed by a sales manager who recruits salespeople, including experienced veterans and new trainees, to demonstrate and sell the equipment. These salespeople are trained to follow certain procedures, such as giving equipment demonstrations and making follow-up calls. These procedures are an important part of the "system" of selling microcomputer hardware and software. When they are not followed, profitability suffers.

The sales manager needs an information system to provide feedback on how the system is working. On a day-to-day basis, he may receive information about salespeople who have successfully closed sales, about customers who are complaining, and about technical problems with equipment. This feedback makes it possible to review the procedures and activities of the current system. For example, if a particular

Figure 2–9

Organizational structure of the dealership

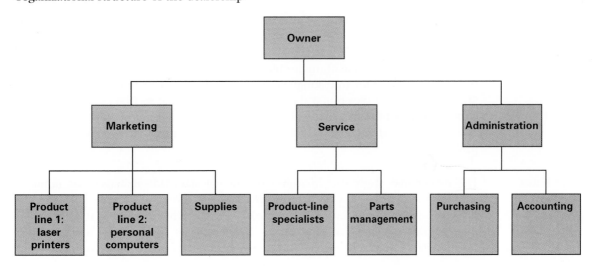

model of microcomputer is breaking down too often, the sales manager may encourage the salespeople to push alternative lines of equipment until manufacturer technical problems are resolved.

The sales manager also needs to organize personnel resources to achieve the desired objectives. If a certain salesperson is unable to make quota month after month, a more effective training program may be needed. If experienced salespeople seem to be selling more effectively to large accounts, the sales manager may assign them to these accounts.

You can now see that the information the sales manager uses to monitor and control the activities of the marketing system is critical to achieving the objectives of the business. Some of this information may be obtained by word of mouth, and other information may be generated from a computer. A product profitability report, for example, may give the sales manager feedback on the product lines that generate the greatest gross profit. The manager uses informal feedback, computer-generated reports, or both to organize people, procedures, and activities to accomplish objectives.

USING THE SYSTEMS APPROACH IN PROBLEM SOLVING

An owner of a business like the microcomputer dealership must constantly analyze problems and reorganize the resources of the system to deal with these problems effectively. The systems approach is a valuable method of problem solving that takes into account the goals, environment, and internal workings of the system. The systems approach to problem solving involves the following steps:

1. Define the problem.
2. Gather data describing the problem.
3. Identify alternative solutions.
4. Evaluate these alternatives.
5. Select and implement the best alternative.
6. Follow up to determine whether the solution is working.

We can understand how the systems approach works by applying it to a problem that the microcomputer dealer might experience.

Define the Problem

The first step in the systems approach to problem solving is to define the problem. Defining the problem is one of the most important parts of the system study, because if the wrong problem is identified, the entire effort to change the system will be off track. At the outset, some of the problems that are identified may be symptoms of the real problem. In order to distinguish between symptoms and problems, it is necessary to gather data describing the problem. Let's say that in this case the owner is concerned about the fact that many of the salespeople are not meeting their quotas. She decides to start a systems study by collecting more information about the problem.

Gather Data Describing the Problem

The owner may study the environment, current standards, management, input resources, and internal procedures to gain an understanding of the problem. The first place the owner might look is the *environment*. The environment of the microcomputer dealer includes its vendors, its customers, its competitors, and the local community. From this investigation, the owner might learn that local competitors are selling comparable microcomputers at prices 10 percent to 15 percent less than the firm can offer.

Next, she might look at the dealership's *standards* to determine if they are valid in the face of the competitive environment. It might turn out that a goal of increasing gross sales by 10 percent for the year is unrealistic when the competition is cutting prices. Another area the owner can analyze is *management*. The owner needs to learn if the sales manager is doing a good job. If the sales manager is not providing salespeople with effective training and feedback regarding their performance, they may feel frustrated.

Input resources are another area that should be analyzed. The owner needs to find out if new sales and technical representatives are being recruited and if these employees are trained to demonstrate computer equipment and software. If new recruits lack knowledge of the technical features of the equipment, for example, they will fail to win new business. If sales materials are not kept up-to-date, customers may not learn about new product features. *Work methods and procedures* also need to be studied. If salespeople are not trained to follow up on new prospects, the company could lose valuable business. If technical support personnel cannot diagnose and solve service problems on a timely basis, customers may hesitate to purchase more equipment.

One of the major problems identified in this case is that competitors are charging lower prices for comparable products. Many of the difficulties the dealer has identified are symptoms of this fundamental problem. To address it, the owner has to identify and evaluate some alternatives.

Identify Alternative Solutions

Given the fact that competitors have dropped their prices on comparable microcomputers, the owner needs to identify some alternatives responses. These alternatives might include the following:

> *Alternative 1:* Investigate alternative manufacturers of microcomputers to obtain products at a lower cost per unit.
>
> *Alternative 2:* Decrease the cost of sales by introducing mail-order sales supported by telemarketing. Use salespersons for large accounts only. Cutting the cost of sales efforts would make it possible to reduce machine prices to a more competitive level
>
> *Alternative 3:* Differentiate the dealership's products by offering on-line diagnostic support services for machine failure, service response time within 5 hours on a 24-hour basis, and annual service checks.

Each alternative supports a slightly different strategy. Finding lower-cost manufactured goods represents a cost-cutting strategy. The second alternative, using mail-order sales and telemarketing, also supports a low-cost strategy because the cost of mail-order sales would be less than the cost of a large sales staff. Finally, introducing on-line diagnostic support services provides a "value added" feature. Upgraded technical support would justify slightly higher equipment costs.

Evaluate the Alternatives

The owner evaluates the extent to which each alternative enables the organization to achieve its objectives. As we saw, the owner's objective was to increase the overall performance of sales personnel. Purchasing lower-cost products from suppliers would enable the owner to cut prices, as suggested in the first alternative, but would create difficulty at the service end if these microcomputer products were less reliable. This strategy might make it more difficult for salespeople to meet their objectives. Introducing a mail-order program would cut the cost of sales overhead. However, the mail-order program would require creating a database of customer prospects and developing specialized promotional materials. This strategy might free sales representatives to concentrate on direct sales to high-potential accounts while using a less costly strategy to maintain the business of smaller accounts.

The final alternative would offer customers additional levels of service and technical support that add value to the firm's products. Because service is one of the key criteria for microcomputer selection, this strategy might work. However, it is costly and might not satisfy the needs of economy-conscious small businesses that represent a large potential market share.

Select and Implement the Best Alternative

Let's say that the owner decides to develop and implement a mail-order program to reduce the cost of sales overhead to smaller accounts and to enable sales personnel to focus on high-potential accounts. This new strategy would require the owner to recruit new customer service representatives or train current employees for telemarketing. The owner would also have to develop and establish customer prospect databases, as well as a system for shipping merchandise, billing, and authorizing credit transactions.

Follow Up to Determine Whether the Solution Is Working

The last step in the systems approach to problem solving is follow-up. In the case of the mail-order sales alternative, the owner needs to determine if the system is meeting its goals. If not, she has to make changes in management, standards, resources, and procedures to achieve the objectives. If either one of the other two alternatives is selected, the owner also needs to follow up to determine if the approach is improving sales. As you can see from this example, the systems approach to problem solving is an important technique for the manager. Every manager needs feedback to determine if the goals of the system are being achieved. One of the most difficult tasks in a systems study is identifying information that managers can use to determine how the system is working. This problem is as true in an organization with a simple structure as it is in a more complex organization. The next section discusses the characteristics of organizations with various structures.

USING INFORMATION SYSTEMS FOR FEEDBACK

What Has Changed

Today's business environment is making it necessary to use information systems to provide feedback. Flexibility, responsiveness, competitiveness, and effectiveness all require the ability to sense and to respond to changes in customer needs. Success depends upon the ability to acquire, interpret, and act upon information.

In a recent article in the *Harvard Business Review,* Haeckel and Nolan refer to this responsiveness as "managing by wire." In some respects managing by wire in today's business environment is similar to what airplane pilots experience when they "fly by wire." In flying by wire, pilots use computer systems to acquire, assimilate, and react to changing environmental information, such as oncoming aircraft. The computer helps the pilot analyze alternative responses, and when the pilot makes a decision to take evasive action (e.g., veer away from another aircraft), the computer system accepts the pilot's command and translates it into thousands of detailed instructions that are executed in a real-time basis. In a modern jet, a fly-by-wire system may require more than 20,000,000 lines of code.

The Air Force characterizes the pilot's ability to respond by introducing the concept of a learning loop. The most effective fighter pilots are adept at assimilating and interpreting real-time information quickly and accurately.

The four processes in the learning loop are:

- Observation: sensing environmental signals.
- Orientation: interpreting these signals. *- alternatives*
- Decision: selecting from a set of available responses.
- Action: executing the response selected.

See Figure 2–10 for a depiction of the Air Force learning loop.

In today's business environment, the manager has to be able to respond to competitors and customers in a real-time basis. The most effective managers will be those who can sense, interpret, and make decisions, and act upon them in a quick and timely manner. The feedback they need will consist of changing information models that can react to changes in the external environment.

See Figure 2–11 for a depiction of the business learning loop.

Here are several examples of businesses that have created feedback mechanisms that simulate the capabilities of a fly-by-wire or autopilot system:

- In each Mrs. Fields Cookies store, local managers use a computing system to project sales for the day based on prior sales and inventory turnover. The software develops a production plan and generates information on how many batches of cookies to make, when to reorder materials (e.g., chips), and how to schedule workers to achieve the desired result. The Retail Operations Intelligence System includes modules for inventory control, activity scheduling, financial reporting, and other administrative functions.

- Wal-Mart transmits information about each day's sales to Wrangler. The information model developed by Wal-Mart provides information regarding specific quantities and specific sizes and colors of jeans needed in specific stores. The resulting "learning loop" provides feedback to Wrangler that enables Wal-Mart to cut inventory costs while minimizing stockouts and providing needed products to customers.

Figure 2–10

The Air Force learning loop

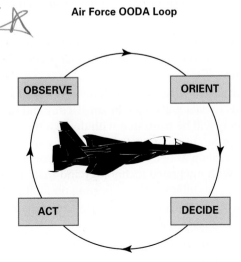

Air Force OODA Loop

Figure 2–11
The business
learning loop

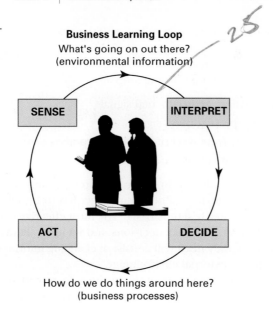

Business Learning Loop
What's going on out there?
(environmental information)

SENSE   INTERPRET

ACT   DECIDE

How do we do things around here?
(business processes)

- At a major global insurance company, a decision support system provides feedback on product development, underwriting, and sales strategies. Using a laptop computer with access to the firm's corporate network, an insurance agent can tailor an insurance policy to a client's specific situation, such as income, investment preferences, children's ages, and future goals. Decision-to-action times have been reduced by 400 percent to 700 percent on many business decisions, enabling the company to compete effectively with smaller companies that target their products to niche markets.

Guidelines for Designing and Implementing a "Manage by Wire" System

In designing a manage-by-wire capability, the modern corporation needs leadership that is willing to make tough decisions with respect to organizing information technology, data, and information-sharing capabilities. Some guidelines for organizing include:

- Does the current information technology link information sources, media, locations, and users? Islands of incompatible, independent networks will inhibit information sharing.
- Does the company have an institutional ability to share data using integrated technology? Islands of data will create inconsistency and duplication of effort. Customers ultimately will be frustrated with duplicative efforts. For example, in a company with a group of unintegrated technology and data, customers would receive multiple premium notices from the same insurance company for its different policies. With integrated technology and shared data, customers would receive an integrated premium notice reporting on multiple policies.
- Does the company provide managers with access to data that is classified, organized, related, and used in a meaningful way?
- Is information shared among business units where there are value-added implications to sharing data?

- Are the company's executives willing to commit to a managing-by-wire strategy and to steer the process of integrating data across multiple business units in a expedient way?

If employees resist the shared data approach, then corporate management might want to select an application area that represents a cost-effective opportunity to pilot the shared data approach. An example of this methodology might be to pilot a customer information system that integrates customer data from various business units. The pilot system should produce results that illustrate the benefits of an integrated approach to managing data in support of multiple business processes. Managers overseeing various functional units may then recognize the importance of a shared data approach and find additional applications where they can use this approach.

Making the Transition to the Learning Organization

As we move into the year 2000, the most successful corporations will be the learning organizations, and the ability to learn faster than the competition will be the key to maintaining a sustainable competitive advantage. In his text, *The Fifth Discipline: The Art and Practice of the Learning Organization,* Peter Senge defines learning organizations as "organizations where people continually expand their capacity to create the results they truly desire, where new and expansive patterns of thinking are nurtured, where collective aspiration is set free, and where people are continually learning how to learn together."

In this closing section, you will learn about the disciplines of the learning organization, the "learning disabilities" that most modern organizations experience, and about how corporations can use the systems approach to become learning organizations.

The Disciplines of the Learning Organization

The five disciplines of **the learning organization** are personal mastery, mental models, building shared vision, team learning, and systems thinking. A brief description of each discipline will help you understand how these disciplines have to work together to achieve a desired result.

- *Personal mastery* is the discipline of clarifying our personal vision, of focusing our energies, of developing patience, and of seeing reality objectively. It requires a commitment to lifelong learning, and it is a foundation for the learning organization.
- *Mental models* include biases, predispositions, and prejudices that get in the way of clear communications, open inquiry, advocacy, and "learningful" conversations.
- *Building shared vision* is essential because people need to bind together around a common identity and a sense of destiny; when there is vision, people bind together—not because they are told to, but because they want to.
- *Team learning* is essential because teams are the fundamental learning unit in most organizations. Unless teams can learn, the organization cannot learn.
- *Systems thinking* is the **fifth discipline.** Systems thinking is essential to achieving the vision of the organization. The vision of the future cannot be achieved without an understanding of the forces that must be mastered to achieve these goals, and the systems approach provides this understanding.

Combined with the other disciplines, systems thinking facilitates the shift in mindset that is essential for the learning organization. Personal mastery fosters personal motivation for learning. Mental models enable us to understand the shortcomings of our present way of visualizing the system. Team learning enables individuals to work together to achieve goals that lie beyond individual perspectives. The systems approach demands that we shift from seeing problems as caused by outside forces to taking responsibility for our own actions and recognizing that these actions sometimes create the problems we experience.

Learning Disabilities of Current Organizations

Most organizations are characterized by learning disabilities that interfere with systems thinking. Some of these disabilities follows.

- Individuals focus on their own position, don't see how their actions affect other people's positions, and don't recognize that they can be responsible for the results that occur when all the positions interact.

- When problems arise, individuals blame someone else or entities outside their control. For example, American companies blame Japanese competition, labor unions, government regulators, customers, and suppliers.

- Proactiveness may be reactiveness in disguise. Many strategies are ways of aggressively fighting the enemy and are essentially reactions.

- Individuals spend much time focusing on events, rather than on slow, gradual processes. As a result, many managers spend a good deal of their time fighting fires, rather than recognizing and understanding long-term trends that may have far greater impact than immediate, concrete issues.

- Functional hierarchies tend to organize into fiefdoms, making it difficult or impossible to analyze problems from a cross-functional perspective.

- Organizations tend to believe the myth of the management team, whereas most teams in business consist of individual members who are fighting for their own turf, seeking to squelch disagreement, and orchestrate compromises that everyone can live with.

In general, most organizations demonstrate "skilled incompetence" and consist of teams of people who become proficient at keeping themselves from learning. The various teams may become so involved with blaming the other players for their own problems that it is difficult for anyone to learn from someone else's experience. For example, manufacturing blames engineering, engineering blames marketing, and so forth. Without a systems approach, the learning disabilities prevail and contradict the processes of the learning organization.

Using the Systems Approach to Make the Transition to the Learning Organization

Systems thinking is a discipline of seeing wholes; it provides a framework for seeing interrelationships, rather than static events and snapshots. Systems thinking provides an antidote for a sense of helplessness that prevails in complex situations. Systems thinking builds in a feedback loop that does not imply causality and does not establish blame. In systems thinking everyone shares responsibility for the problems, and everyone shares responsibility for overcoming these problems.

Corporations can use the systems approach to analyze and understand some of the problems that occur in business systems.

- "Today's problems come from yesterday's solutions." Some solutions merely shift the problem from one part of the system to another. When police start to arrest drug dealers on 14th Street, they may just be shifting the problem to another jurisdiction. The reason that this situation can continue is that the team that attempts to solve the first problem is often not the team that inherits the new problem.

- "The harder you push, the harder the system pushes back." Stated another way the more effort you expend trying to improve matters, the more effort that seems to be required. A good example of this problem occurs frequently in product marketing. Let us say that one of a company's major products begins to lose market share. When marketing executives push for more aggressive marketing and spend new dollars on more effective advertising, they have to shift resources from other areas and may actually cut down on customer service, which may drive more customers away.

- "The easy way out usually leads back in." When you push harder and faster with the same solutions to problems, you may make matters worse.

- "Faster is slower." The American business ethic drives fast, faster, fastest. This mentality may go against the natural growth rates of an industry and become counterproductive, or even destructive. The rapid rise and fall of People's Express is a case in point. When its market share began to fall, People's cut costs, reduced service, and eventually could compete only on the basis of lower and lower airfares. Eventually, the company couldn't survive on such low profits.

- "Cause and effect are not closely related in time and space." If there is a problem in marketing, we look for a cause in marketing. If there is a problem getting sales, we create a new sales incentive plan. If there is inadequate housing, we build more. None of these steps use the systems approach to analyze problems from a cross-functional perspective.

- "Dividing an elephant in half does not produce two small elephants." If you study individual, isolated functional units (marketing, manufacturing, engineering), you will come up with a completely different set of problems than if you try to understand the interactions among these functions.

- "You can have your cake and eat it too—but not all at once." Automotive manufacturers constantly debate the trade-off between quality and low cost, assuming that quality costs more. But by investing in up-front quality manufacturing, today's automakers can achieve both goals, because quality ultimately cuts the cost of ongoing maintenance and technical support.

- "There is no blame." Avoid the tendency to blame outside entities—the press, the competitors, the marketplace—and internal factors—other functional units. In the systems approach, everyone is to blame, and no one is to blame. Everyone shares responsibility for the problems generated by a system, and everyone shares the responsibility for overcoming them.

Feedback in the Learning Organization

Without question, the issue of feedback is critical to understanding an organization from a systems perspective. Information systems become the feedback mechanism for the business systems. Some feedback is reinforcing. Effective sales of a new product provides positive feedback and generates new sales. Positive feedback influences successful performance, as in the Pygmalian effect, where a teacher's high expectations for a student can influence the successful performance of that student.

Balancing feedback is another type of feedback that the systems approach helps explain. Balance means stability, and systems try to achieve stability. In balancing a system, you make corrective adjustments to maintain some goal or to achieve some target. Filling a new position is a balancing process because a firm needs to maintain a skilled workforce. Steering a car is a balancing process because a car needs to go in the right direction.

Balancing processes are difficult to diagnose, because it looks like nothing is happening. The system is simply moving to achieve its goals, which is why change is so problematic. When a new leader seeks to orchestrate a major change, it is often in conflict with balancing processes which may be implicit. It may seem that resistance is coming from nowhere, when in fact the new strategies are coming in conflict with the status quo. Resistance to change is a response by the system that is attempting to maintain an implicit system goal. Unless this goal is understood, the change effort may be doomed. For change to be successful, the leader may need to establish new models and to enlist support for new goals.

Conclusion

In summary, systems thinking is critical to the learning organization. Systems thinking tries to uncover patterns and relationships; it tries to understand processes rather then isolated events. Feedback is a critical concept and must exist to maintain existing standards, to generate additional successes, and to diagnose problems with current work methods. Systems thinking is the key to bringing about a shared responsibility for change and for providing motivation for achieving a shared vision through teamwork and individual performance.

MANAGEMENT SUMMARY

This chapter introduces systems concepts that provide a foundation for understanding information systems in general and management information systems in particular. Managers have to understand systems, their objectives, their components, and their activities. Information about how a system is working provides them with the feedback they need to allocate resources to achieve their business objectives. Depending on the objectives of a system, its components, standards, and interactions may differ. We have seen that an information system provides feedback about the activities of the business. Information systems have the same characteristics as other systems, including inputs and outputs, processes that transform inputs into outputs, and methods of system control. In designing an information system, the outputs must be defined, the interactions must be established, and the standards of system control must be organized.

A management information system in particular must be designed to provide information for effective planning and control of business activities. Decision making requires converting data into information. Information is data that have meaning in the decision-making process. An information system must be designed to provide feedback for the business system. Managers use this feedback to reorganize, simplify, and improve activities in the business system so that the system can achieve goals more effectively. In the information-based organization, managers must define their information needs and use information as feedback.

KEY TERMS FOR MANAGERS

application software, 40
balancing feedback, 51
boundary, 32
closed system, 35
feedback, 35
fifth discipline, 49
hardware, 39

information, 31
information system, 31
interface, 31
open system, 34
operational systems, 40
software, 40
strategic planning systems, 39

subsystem, 31
system, 31
system software, 40
systems entropy, 36
tactical systems, 42
the learning organization, 49

REVIEW QUESTIONS

1. What is a system? Which of the following are systems? Give reasons for your answers.
   a. A house
   b. A football team
   c. A textbook
   d. A soccer game

2. For each of the following systems, identify the subsystems
   a. An educational system
   b. A professional baseball team
   c. A library

3. What forms of feedback can be used to control the following systems or subsystems?
   a. A student organization
   b. A retail department store
   c. An insurance agency

4. Discuss how interface problems can be solved using an interface subsystem, standards, or slack resources in each of the following examples:
   a. A limited supply of concert tickets with great consumer demand.

b. A two-year degree in office management that produces students with good technical skills but inadequate communications skills with a four-year program in business that requires effective speaking and writing skills.
   c. Components of a microcomputer system.

5. What is the difference between data and information?

6. What information can be used to provide feedback about each of the following?
   a. Employee morale
   b. New-product sales
   c. Salesperson performance

7. Classify the following systems as either open systems or closed systems. Give reasons for your answers.
   a. A real estate agency
   b. A country club
   c. A symphony orchestra
   d. A prison
   e. A dentist's practice

QUESTIONS FOR DISCUSSION

1. Why is feedback useful in controlling the internal workings of a system?

2. Why is a closed system likely to deteriorate?

3. What are some methods of decreasing entropy affecting a newly purchased automobile?

4. Why do many managers use the systems approach to problem solving?

5. How can a graduate program in music at a university use standards as a method of system control?

6. Why is "soft information," which is intangible and speculative, so valuable to managers?

7. What is the learning organization? What are the five disciplines of the learning organization? What is the fifth discipline, and why is it important?

8. Name four learning disabilities that interfere with systems thinking.

9. In systems thinking, "there is no blame." Explain.

10. What is the difference between balancing feedback and reinforcing feedback?

PROBLEMS

1. **New job skills.** Many of the newly hired programmer analysts at Epcon Industries have good technical skills, but they are falling down on the job because of poor communications skills—particularly writing ability. This situation is causing the personnel department to think seriously about requiring a prescreening test in basic writing skills, including grammar, punctuation, and spelling. The personnel department has also contacted several local universities to express its concern about the problem of communications skills. Diagnose this problem from a systems standpoint and suggest some possible solutions.

2. **Town and Country Tennis and Golf Club.**
Town and Country Tennis and Golf Club is a rapidly expanding club in suburban Baltimore County. It currently has about 1,200 members but may expand to as many as 3,000 members within the next five years. An 18-hole golf course and eight tennis courts are its major attractions. The club has two restaurants, one of which is casual and one of which is formal, and a bar. It also offers a golf shop and a tennis shop that sell sports equipment and clothes. Members can take golf and tennis lessons, enroll in weekly scheduled events, participate in tournaments, and invite guests for certain activities. A prospective member needs to obtain three letters of reference from current members of the club. Then the applicant and family are interviewed by a subcommittee of the board of directors. Once admitted, the member is responsible for paying an entry fee plus monthly dues. When the club does not meet revenue projections, members are assessed an additional fee to cover operating losses. A board of directors oversees club management, hires staff, and monitors the budget. Subcommittees are responsible for recruiting new members, organizing social events, managing golf and tennis programs, and ensuring that members adhere to club rules and regulations. With the objective of building membership, the club has recently renovated its facilities, improved several areas of the golf course, and added two tennis courts. Club management is aggressively marketing banquet facilities and special events. Identify the major systems and subsystems of the club. What are the boundaries of these systems? What are the objectives of each subsystem? What elements interact in these subsystems? What methods does the club have to screen input? What types of control mechanisms are in place? Is the club an open system or a closed system? What types of feedback from the environment does the club use?

3. **Amalgamated Paper, Inc.** The MIS department at Amalgamated Paper, Inc., built many data processing systems in the 1960s and 1970s. These systems were written in COBOL, a procedural language, and were maintained by programmer analysts with technical backgrounds. Many of these data processing systems handled the day-to-day paperwork of the company, including order entry, accounts receivable, and inventory control. In the mid- to late 1970s, many line managers became dissatisfied with the computer-generated information they were receiving. They wanted more information on such issues as customer profitability and product profitability. However, the MIS department continued to focus on upgrading hardware, converting old systems to new systems, and resolving technical problems. It was not able to respond to the users' requests for better information. As a result, many user-managers started solving their own problems by purchasing their own microcomputers and database programs. By the time the MIS department started to react to this situation, many of the users had developed considerable expertise in managing hardware, software, and data. Although the MIS department wanted to offer mainframe-based tools supporting database query, most of the users had made considerable investments in acquiring and learning how to use microcomputer-based tools and were not interested in MIS support for mainframe-based tools. Was the MIS department an open or a closed system? Diagnose the problem described in this situation by using the open versus closed system concept.

4. **A fast-food restaurant.** At a popular fast-food restaurant, an assembly line is in place to mass-produce hamburgers. The best-selling hamburger has pickles, cheese, ketchup, lettuce, tomato, and onions. Work is highly specialized, and specific workers are responsible for cooking, putting on relishes, wrapping, and distributing the finished hamburgers. When a customer requests a plain hamburger or a hamburger with ketchup only, the system breaks down. A special order has to be placed, and the customer may have to wait for 15 minutes or more to get the finished product. This wait really irritates some customers. How would you change the system to accommodate special orders?

CASES

1. **Tip Top Diner.** The Tip Top Diner, a busy restaurant in the downtown area of a major city, is having a problem providing adequate service to customers during the hectic lunch-hour period. Often, they have to wait 20 to 30 minutes to get served, and sometimes items on the menu are not available. The restaurant is a system. The objectives of the restaurant are to provide good service at low cost and to make a profit of 10 percent of total sales volume. (Much of this profit has been eroded by the hiring of additional part-time workers to handle the busy workload, however.) The components of the restaurant include waitresses, dining facilities, menu items, a kitchen staff, food supplies, kitchen facilities, and a manager. Interactions in the restaurant include ordering, cooking, serving, and collecting cash receipts. The manager has asked you to study the components, interactions, and other aspects of the restaurant to diagnose its problems and to identify a solution. Develop a plan for conducting your study and explain what activities you would accomplish during each step of your study.

2. **Maine Custom Jewelry, Inc.** Maine Custom Jewelry, Inc., is a large manufacturer and marketer of quality jewelry. Currently, the company employs about 50 jewelry craftsworkers and has been growing at the rate of 20 percent per year over the past three years. Management does not expect this growth rate to continue in the future, but it does predict a steady growth rate of 5 percent over the next decade. Its product line features a variety of costume jewelry in silver with semiprecious stones. Stock products make up only 50 percent of the output from the craftworkers. The remaining products are produced to special order. This service is possible because each jewelry craftsperson is responsible for the complete manufacturing of a given product. The company does not use production-line techniques. When a custom order is received, the specifications for the order are posted along with an expected shipping date. Each craftsworker is then eligible to bid on all or part of an order. Once the bids are evaluated, the company accepts the lowest bid for production. The custom part of the business has shown the greatest growth in recent years. During the last 12 months, an average of 500 orders have been in process at any one time.

   The firm has experienced many difficulties related to providing consistent, on-time delivery. The skilled craftsworkers often fail to meet deadlines. Moreover, management has never had a satisfactory means of ensuring that orders are worked on in a priority sequence. Other problems, such as craftsworkers overcommitting themselves in a given time period or simply losing an order, are also becoming more serious. Identify and discuss Maine Custom Jewelry's problems from a systems standpoint. Consider the environment, standards, management, input resources, and work methods and procedures. What recommendations would you make for improving the current system?

SELECTED REFERENCES AND READINGS

Boulding, K. "General Systems Theory—The Skeleton of Science." *Management Science,* April 1956.

Luchsinger, V. P. and V. T. Dock. "An Anatomy of Systems." In *MIS: A Managerial Perspective,* ed. V. T. Dock; V. P. Luchsinger; and W. R. Cornette. Chicago: SRA, 1977, pp. 3–12.

Mintzberg, H. *The Structuring of Organizations.* Englewood Cliffs, NJ: Prentice Hall, 1979.

Senge, P. *The Fifth Discipline: The Art and Practice of the Learning Organization.* New York: Doubleday, 1990.

Von Bertalanffy, *General Systems Theory: Foundations, Development, Applications.* New York: Braziller, 1968. Haeckel, S. H. and R. Nolan, "Managing by Wire," *Harvard Business Review,* September–October 1993.

3

STRATEGIC USES OF INFORMATION TECHNOLOGY

CHAPTER OUTLINE

Manager's View

How Information Technology Supports Business Activities

Using Information Technology for Competitive Advantage

Interorganizational Systems

The Strategic Impact of the Internet and Electronic Commerce

Strategic Information Systems: The Risks

Do Information Systems Provide a Competitive Edge?

Management Summary

Key Terms for Managers

Review Questions

Questions for Discussion

Problems

Cases

Selected Internet Reference Sites

Selected References and Readings

As a manager, you will be in a position to assess how information technology can be used to support business activities. Traditionally, data processing applications have supported "back office" operations, such as transaction processing. However, the introduction of information systems such as American Hospital Supply's ASAP system, which electronically linked purchasing personnel with American's order-entry system, proved that businesses could use information technology to gain a competitive advantage. American Hospital Supply's ASAP system made it easier for hospitals to order, created access to inventory and delivery information, and provided an electronic interface that eliminated a great deal of costly paperwork. The dramatic increase in American Hospital Supply's orders clearly demonstrated that an information system could become a powerful competitive force. This chapter shows how businesses can use information technology for competitive advantage and how interorganizational systems have transformed the competitive marketplace.

How Information Technology Supports Business Activities

One of the first challenges managers face is understanding how they can use information technology to support business activities. Porter and Millar's concept of the **value chain** helps explain which business activities can be analyzed and transformed through the use of information technology. The value chain divides a company's activities into **value activities,** the distinct activities it must perform to do business. In Figure 3–1, you can see these value activities.

Value activities consist of primary activities and support activities. Primary activities include inbound logistics, operations, outbound logistics, marketing, and service. For a manufacturing organization, activities that support inbound logistics

Figure 3–1

Value activities in the value chain

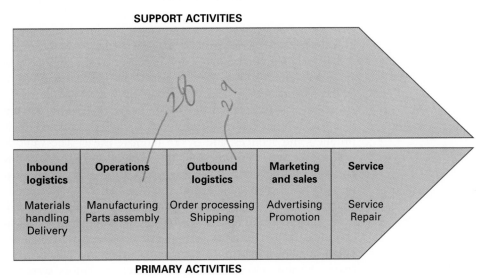

SUPPORT ACTIVITIES

Inbound logistics	Operations	Outbound logistics	Marketing and sales	Service
Materials handling Delivery	Manufacturing Parts assembly	Order processing Shipping	Advertising Promotion	Service Repair

PRIMARY ACTIVITIES

Source: Adapted from Porter & Millar, 1985.

Figure 3–2

Support activities in the value chain

SUPPORT ACTIVITIES

Organization				
Human resources				
Technology				
Purchasing				

Inbound logistics	Operations	Outbound logistics	Marketing and sales	Service
Materials handling Delivery	Manufacturing Parts assembly	Order processing Shipping	Advertising Promotion	Service Repair

PRIMARY ACTIVITIES

Source: Adapted from Porter & Millar, 1985.

include delivery and handling of incoming materials. Operations activities include manufacturing-related functions, such as parts assembly and quality assurance. Outbound logistics activities support order processing and shipping goods and services to customers. Marketing and sales activities include advertising, promotion, and sales force management. The company also organizes activities to support repair and maintenance of its goods and services.

Support activities include the resources that support the primary activities of the business. You can see some of these support activities in Figure 3–2. They provide the organization, human resources, and technologies to deliver primary activities. The firm's organization, which includes activities such as general management, legal work, and accounting, supports the entire value chain.

In Porter's view the value chain is a system of interdependent linkages. In other words, the way one activity is performed may affect the performance of others. As an example, investments in a more expensive product design and superior materials may reduce after-sale service costs.

To obtain a competitive edge, Porter argues, a firm must be able to perform its value activities at a lower cost than its rivals or in a way that provides its buyers with added value or service. The value chain of a particular industry works within a larger system of activities called the value system. The **value system** includes the value chains of suppliers, of the firm, of the channels through which the firm distributes its products and services, and of the ultimate buyer. The value system is depicted in Figure 3–3. According to Porter, the value chain of the firm interacts with the value chain of its suppliers because the suppliers provide the raw materials that are inputs into the firm's own value chain. The distribution activities that are part of the value chain of the firm's suppliers interact with the raw material–handling activities of the firm's value chain. If links between the value activities of the supplier and buyer are coordinated, then both firms can cut costs. For example, an automobile manufacturer obtains raw material from steel manufacturers as a part of its value chain. A link between the automaker's and the steelmaker's inventory systems can provide information on prices and delivery dates and facilitate ordering and delivery.

Figure 3–3

The value system

Supplier value chain(s) → Firm value chain(s) → Channel value chain(s) → Buyer value chain(s) →

Source: Adapted from Porter & Millar, 1985.

The company's products and services sometimes pass through channel value chains on their way to the ultimate buyer. A channel value chain occurs between a supplier and a buyer, for example, a dealer or distributor. In the case of the automobile industry, the dealership provides a channel value chain between the manufacturer and the automobile buyer. Information technology can provide a more effective interface between the buyer and the channel. For example, an automobile buyer may visit a Buick dealership in St. Louis, Missouri, but not be able to locate an automobile with the exact features she wants. Buick dealers use a system called EPIC to enable prospective car buyers to locate automobiles with the features they want in local and regional dealerships. The EPIC system gives the manufacturer a competitive edge by providing instant information about the availability of Buicks and preventing prospective buyers from searching for alternatives.

Information systems that link suppliers and buyers, manufacturers and distributors, and distributors and buyers are known as **interorganizational systems (IOSs).** These systems benefit both participants. For example, a large drug distributor places order-entry terminals in drugstores, allowing pharmacists to order directly. In this way, the manufacturer gets timely information about buying trends, and the pharmacists get timely delivery of their orders. Large retailers such as Sears and J. C. Penney enable customers to view merchandise using electronic catalogs and to place orders using terminals and personal computers. With technology, these retailers can give customers access to information about a wide range of products and services.

As you can see from these examples, information technology affects the value chain by transforming the way value activities are performed. Each activity in the value chain has a physical component and an information-processing component. The physical component encompasses the physical tasks needed to perform the activity, and the information-processing component includes the steps involved in capturing, manipulating, and channeling the data necessary to carry out the activity. Take Wal-Mart's inventory management activity as an example. The physical task is to stock sufficient inventory to meet customers' needs. The information-processing component must be designed to provide feedback on inventory requirements based on sales history data.

The information-processing component of each value activity is being increasingly supported by information technology, as you would expect. Examples of how technology supports primary activities appear in Figure 3–4.

In the Wal-Mart example, information technology supports inbound logistics. For example, Procter & Gamble supplies Wal-Mart stores with just-in-time inventory of Pampers, reducing both ordering and holding costs. Procter & Gamble has access to

Figure 3–4
How information
technology
supports value
activities

VALUE ACTIVITY	USE OF INFORMATION TECHNOLOGY
Inbound logistics	Just-in-time inventory
Operations	Process control systems
Outbound logistics	On-line links to the order-entry systems of suppliers
Marketing and sales	Laptops for direct sales
After-sale service	Electronic dispatch of technical support

sales history and inventory turnover information, and it uses this information to determine inventory requirements for its customer Wal-Mart. As a result, it fills Wal-Mart's orders automatically.

Information technology also supports operations. Process control systems monitor oil refinement, chemical production, and even assembly of ingredients in the manufacture of paints and cookies. These systems assure quality, timely production, and economy in using raw materials.

An insurance salesperson equipped with a laptop computer and a spreadsheet program can simulate the earnings of an insurance portfolio. This application is an effective use of technology in marketing insurance plans. In another example a food company has created a national database of product sales information. Marketing representatives can obtain access to this information via a worldwide network.

A good example of technology support for after-sale service is Otis Elevator's Otisline system. This system automatically dispatches elevator service calls to technicians with the proper training. Remote diagnostics of plant equipment is another way that technology can provide a competitive edge. At Xerox Corporation an on-line database matches service calls with the capabilities of service technicians. Using information about customer service histories, service managers are able to anticipate technical problems, assign qualified service technicians, and make sure that needed parts are available for service calls.

In addition to supporting primary value activities, information technology can also support the secondary activities of the value chain, as shown in Figure 3–5.

The use of information technology can also reinforce the support activities that are part of the value chain. A corporatewide electronic mail system can facilitate interaction among all levels of the management structure and create a more flexible, dynamic organization. Managers can use electronic mail to give their employees timely feedback about project-related activities. Workers can also supply feedback to help their managers diagnose problems and reallocate resources more effectively.

An on-line personnel information system with a skills database can support the management of human resources. A *database* is a repository of information that can be organized for inquiry and reporting purposes. A skills database is a valuable tool that enables management to identify employees with skills needed for particular assignments on a timely basis. For example, a sales manager can query an employee database for individuals who have college degrees in marketing, the ability to speak German, and a willingness to relocate.

Technology can be a critical part of the support infrastructure. For example, computer-aided design/computer-aided manufacturing (CAD/CAM) systems are essential in the aerospace industry. Procurement systems that provide on-line access to

Figure 3–5

How information technology supports secondary activities

SECONDARY ACTIVITY	USE OF INFORMATION TECHNOLOGY
Management communications	Electronic mail
Human resources	On-line access to personnel files with a skills database
Technology	Computer-aided design and manufacturing
Procurement	On-line access to suppliers' inventory files

suppliers' inventory databases can support purchasing. Using American Hospital Supply's on-line inventory databases, purchasing personnel can check inventory availability of specific items before placing orders using the system.

Examples of how information technology supports activities in the value chain are summarized in Figure 3–6.

Because information technology affects business at every level, more managers are using it to support and control their business activities. As a result, technology is being distributed "to the desktop," and managers at all levels of the organization are using desktop workstations to make decisions about day-to-day activities. Using these desktop workstations, managers can gain access to shared databases and communications networks.

USING INFORMATION TECHNOLOGY FOR COMPETITIVE ADVANTAGE

New developments in information technology, such as telecommunications, computer-aided design, and office automation, have created unprecedented opportunities. Managers in most organizations are looking for ways to use new information technology to support business strategy. Gregory Parsons, in his work on information

Figure 3–6

Information systems supporting value activities

SUPPORT ACTIVITIES

Organization: Office automation

Human resources: Skills databases

Technology: Computer-aided design and manufacturing

Purchasing: On-line links to suppliers

Inbound logistics	Operations	Outbound logistics	Marketing and sales	Service
Automated warehousing systems	Process control Manufacturing control systems	On-line order entry systems	Market analysis Product profitability	Remote machine diagnostics

PRIMARY ACTIVITIES

Source: Adapted from Porter & Millar, 1985.

technology and competitive strategy, introduces a three-level framework to help managers assess the current and potential effect of information technology. This framework is shown in Figure 3–7.

Industry-Level Effect

Information technology can change the nature of the industry in which the firm competes. The introduction of information technology can affect products and services, markets, and production economics.

Products and services.   Information technology can change the nature of products and services by altering the product development cycle or by increasing the speed of distribution. An example of speeding up the product development cycle comes from the publishing business. If a textbook publisher uses word processing and computer-based typesetting to generate publications, it may be able to reduce the product development life cycle by 30 to 40 percent and to cut the costs of document preparation, revision, and distribution by half. A publisher using word processing and typesetting could bring out a revision of a text in 12 months instead of the traditional 24-month product development life cycle, giving it an automatic competitive advantage in the textbook marketplace. Texts produced in this way are more timely and more responsive to market needs.

New information technologies also affect an industry's products and services. Technology like videoconferencing, for example, affects hotel conference centers. Large hotel chains, such as Holiday Inn and Sheraton, have set up videoconferencing centers in various metropolitan hotels so that companies can book on-site electronic conference rooms. This strategy is designed to address the potential threat of electronic meetings to their traditional hotel business as well as to establish technological leadership in the videoconferencing business.

Production economics.   The second industry-level effect of information technology has to do with production economics. A food marketer with a nationwide network of distribution centers can serve regional markets and also reallocate inventories to serve the national market. For example, if inventories of spaghetti sauce at a midwestern distribution center are too low to fill local orders, the food marketer can

Figure 3–7
The three-level effect of information technology

INDUSTRY LEVEL	Information technology changes an industry's
	• Products and services
	• Production economics
	• Markets
FIRM LEVEL	**Information technology affects key competitive forces**
	• Buyers
	• Suppliers
	• Substitute products
	• New entrants
	• Rivals
STRATEGY LEVEL	**Information technology supports a firm's strategy**
	• Low-cost leadership
	• Product differentiation
	• Market specialization

Figure 3–8
Industry-level
impacts

TYPE OF IMPACT	HOW INFORMATION TECHNOLOGY IS USED
Products and services	Computer-based word processing and typesetting
Production economics	Nationwide inventory tracking
Markets	ATMs Point-of-sale systems

automatically check inventories of spaghetti sauce in other centers and fill the orders from the next most convenient location. A food marketer without a nationwide distribution system like this would have great difficulty satisfying customer orders that could not be handled locally.

Markets.   Consumers have become increasingly computer literate. They are accustomed to banking with automatic teller machines (ATMs) and shopping where point-of-sale scanners are used. Organizations that are not able to offer electronic services to their customers may be at a competitive disadvantage. Figure 3–8 summarizes the industry-level impact of competitive systems.

**Firm-Level
Effect**

At the firm level, the competitive forces facing the firm determine the effect of information technology. Five competitive forces influence the profitability of an industry: buyers, suppliers, substitute products, new entrants, and rivals. These competitive forces, shown in Figure 3–9, are described in depth by Michael Porter in his book *Competitive Strategy*. Information technology can be used to address these competitive forces in the following ways.

Buyers.   The first competitive force is the power of buyers, a force that can reduce an industry's profits. Businesses can use information technology to reduce the power that buyers have by introducing switching costs. The American Hospital Supply case we discussed earlier is a good example. When American Hospital Supply gave purchasing agents in hospitals terminals tying them to its order entry system,

Figure 3–9
Five competitive
forces

Source: Adapted from Porter & Millar, 1985.

they introduced switching costs. Once the purchasing agents learned how to use the American Hospital Supply system to check order and delivery status, they could more easily order from American Hospital Supply than from its competitors.

Information technology can also provide market analysts with the tools they need to analyze buyer profitability. A financial services company, for example, used prior loan data to design an information system depicting the characteristics of potentially delinquent loan applicants. When the firm used these characteristics to screen out potential bad risks, it cut the costs of its delinquent loans dramatically. Decision-support tools can be developed to analyze the profitability of specific market groups and to deliver products and services to these groups, raising potential margins and revenues.

Suppliers.   The second competitive force is the power of suppliers. Firms can compete more effectively if they are able to control the power of suppliers. The automobile industry, for example, has had to rely on high-priced labor as a major supplier of services. Use of robots to handle assembly-line tasks has partially offset the accelerating costs of unionized labor. Information systems that are designed to track labor efficiency can be tied directly to wage incentive systems and can also provide management with an important advantage in rewarding productivity improvements.

Today, suppliers have to be more cautious because of the sophisticated quality control systems users have designed. Steel producers, for example, must be more quality conscious because the automobile industry has implemented sophisticated quality control systems. The automobile manufacturers use their quality control systems to check incoming shipments from steel manufacturers. In this way they exercise more control over their suppliers.

The average consumer can gain power over suppliers simply by having access to more information. In the past when consumers purchased automobiles, the dealer had all the information. Now that consumers have access to information about dealer invoice costs, they can negotiate more effectively. This information reduces the power of dealers, the suppliers.

Substitute products.   Another competitive strategy is to deter customers from finding substitutes for existing products and services, for example, using margarine for butter. Cost-effective substitutes for products and services can hurt a firm's profits. A firm can attempt to deter its customers from buying substitutes by lowering the cost of its products and services or by improving their perceived performance and value. The Merrill Lynch Cash Management Account (CMA) is an excellent example of this approach. The CMA bundles a brokerage account, a money market account, a Visa card, and a checking account—financial services previously available only as separate products—in one package. As a result, customers find it difficult to substitute for the CMA. With the CMA, Merrill Lynch was able to bring in 450,000 new brokerage accounts and $60,000,000 in annual fees for managing the liquid asset funds. For a number of years, no other brokerage firm was able to come out with a similar product, making a substitute difficult to find. Because it took Merrill Lynch's competitors years to catch up with the CMA-type account, Merrill Lynch was able to create switching costs among its customers and to attain a permanent competitive edge in the marketplace.

New entrants.   The threat of new entrants is a competitive force that established firms in an industry would like to deter or minimize. New entrants can draw profits from firms in an industry. Entry barriers that enable established firms to block the entry of newcomers include reputation, service levels, and distribution channels.

Information technology can create entry barriers by preventing new entrants from gaining market share or from entering the industry at all. Leading insurance companies such as Massachusetts Mutual Life Insurance Company have created effective entry barriers by constructing on-line telecommunications networks linking sales agents to home office databases with information about policies and claims. These networks allow local agents to update policies, to receive sales illustrations on new insurance programs, and to obtain local access to training and promotional materials. Without this kind of support for its sales agents, a new entrant would be at a competitive disadvantage. The million-dollar investment in these large-scale telecommunications networks creates a considerable entry barrier to potential new entrants into the insurance business.

The airline industry has created a similar entry barrier with on-line reservations systems. The reservations systems built by American, TWA, and United Airlines in the 1970s cost millions of dollars in development and equipment costs. To win the business of travel agents and business travelers, smaller airlines without reservation systems are forced to list their flights on the reservations systems of the major carriers. These smaller airlines are at an automatic disadvantage because the host carrier has access to information on their flights, their fares, and their bookings. In addition, the smaller airlines may be forced to pay the host airline a percentage of each flight booked on that airline's information system, creating a further disadvantage.

The history of the SABRE system, American Airlines' reservation system, shows how potent a competitive information system can be. SABRE began as a way of assigning seats on airplanes—it listed American flights as well as the flights of other airlines. In the mid-1970s SABRE was upgraded to generate flight plans, track spare parts, and schedule crews. All these applications supported internal operations. By the late 70s, however, SABRE was enhanced significantly with the addition of new services, including hotel and rental car reservations, to the database.

SABRE has been repeatedly upgraded since its origin in the early 70s. Today SABRE is a virtual electronic supermarket, a computerized middleman that links suppliers of travel services (e.g., Broadway shows, packaged tours, currency rates) with travel agents and that provides a computerized reservation system for American Airlines, Marriott, Hilton, and Budget Rent-A-Car companies. These enhancements to the original SABRE system provide an even greater barrier to entry.

Rivals.   The fifth competitive force that influences the profitability of an industry is rivals. All industries have rivalry among competitors. Competition is valuable because it establishes a market price and enables successful firms to earn profits. Information technology has made it possible for many firms within an industry to deal effectively with rivals. The airline reservations systems have been notorious for their impact on rivals. Frontier Airlines, in testimony before the Civil Aeronautics Board, argued that United's APOLLO reservation system employed an unfair competitive advantage by enabling United to check on prices of Frontier flights and then deliberately lower its prices to meet or to undercut them. In effect, Frontier argued that United had computerized access to confidential information about Frontier's flights, including prices, loading factors, and schedules in competitive markets. In addition, Frontier argued that United flights were preferentially listed on the APOLLO system and that Frontier flights were sometimes dropped without explanation. When Frontier introduced a special fare, such as a $99 one-way fare, United could use its system to send messages to travel agents notifying them that it would match these new fares. United reinforced its strong allegiance to its travel agents by rewarding exclusive APOLLO agents with add-on features such as automatic boarding-pass generation.

Firms within an industry can use information technology to compete with rivals in other industries. Firms in the railroad industry have joined to establish communications networks to track freight locations and schedules for their customers, making successful competition against their rivals in the trucking industry possible.

Sometimes the small players in an industry team up to compete with larger firms in the same industry. Some of the smaller airlines have combined resources to develop airline reservations systems to compete with the larger airlines' systems. In another instance, Philadelphia National Bank (PNB) and other smaller banks pooled their resources and formed an ATM network, the Money Access Center (MAC), as a generic ATM service available to all area banks. The MAC system directly counteracted the ATM network launched earlier by a formidable competitor, Girard, a large Philadelphia-based financial institution.

In considering ways to use information technology for competitive advantage, a firm has to assess the forces affecting its industry position and to develop a strategy that addresses buyers, suppliers, substitute products, new entrants, or rivals. Figure 3–10 summarizes the firm-level competitive impacts of information technology.

In *Competitive Strategy* Porter argues that three generic strategies can be used to achieve a competitive edge in an industry: *low-cost leadership, product differentiation,* and *market specialization.* The effective use of information technology can support each of these strategies, as illustrated by the examples given in this section.

Low-cost leadership. **Low-cost leadership** refers to the ability to reduce costs or to improve productivity without incurring additional costs. If a commercial bank can process thousands of demand deposit transactions per day at 2 cents per transaction, and one of its competitors processes a similar volume at 4 cents per transaction, the first bank will achieve a competitive advantage in cost leadership. A computer-based information system that cuts the cost of transaction processing will support this low-cost leadership strategy.

A magazine distributor has been able to achieve a position of low-cost leadership by using a computer-based information system to sort and distribute magazines and newspapers to newsstands. Many organizations have introduced office automation systems that mechanize office paperwork and cut administrative costs, supporting a low-cost leadership strategy. Law firms that have introduced word processing, for example, have cut the cost of creating, editing, and distributing documents by as much as one-third.

Figure 3–10
Firm-level impacts

COMPETITIVE FORCE AFFECTED	EXAMPLE OF AN INFORMATION SYSTEM AND ITS COMPETITIVE IMPACT
Buyers	American Hospital Supply system introduces switching costs to buyers
Suppliers	Use of robots to do assembly line tasks reduces the cost of the labor supply
Substitute products	Merrill Lynch's CMA provides a "bundled" set of financial services
New entrants	On-line telecommunications networks link insurance agents and home office systems Airline reservations systems

Inventory control systems that reduce the cost of excess inventories in plants and warehouses support a low-cost leadership strategy. Production control systems that minimize excess raw materials and control the costs of production also support this strategy.

Product differentiation. **Product differentiation** is achieved by adding value or unique features to a product to improve its image, quality, or service. A good example of product differentiation is giving customers electronic access to an on-line service network. Owners of Gateway computers have access to a bulletin board system that provides up-to-date information on technical issues and product features. Another form of product differentiation is providing value-added features to existing products or services. Frequent fliers on most airlines today receive frequent flier miles that translate into special discounts and bonuses. Sometimes "value added" features are embedded in the use of a product. For example, a tire manufacturer has introduced sensors that detect problems and display diagnostic messages about air pressure and tire maintenance that could cut costs and enhance safety.

Sometimes the ability to provide customers with better information is a source of product differentiation. An innovative travel agency, Rosenbluth Travel, has created a travel supermarket by offering information management services. Rosenbluth can search through its airline reservations system databases and select flights based upon ticket price. By shopping for the best price, Rosenbluth can offer its clients the best fares. Rosenbluth differentiates its services further by offering its clients access to a back-office expense tracking system that not only controls corporate travel expenses but also provides Rosenbluth with the clout to negotiate preferred rates with the major air carriers based on the amount of business some of its major clients represent.

A firm can differentiate its products by providing reliable service, quick responses to customer questions, and additional product features. For example, computer-aided design can create better-quality product designs for shoes, automobiles, and other consumer items. For years, Italian shoemakers and auto designers have designed products that "look better" than their counterparts made elsewhere. Computer-aided design has helped some American firms win back some of the business lost to Italian manufacturers.

Information technology can also support sales and service levels. A large computer manufacturer provides an 800 number for hotline access to a customer support center, allowing customers to troubleshoot technical problems with specialists. National hotel chains provide access to their reservations systems through 800 numbers. A large beer manufacturer provides its distributors with on-line access to pricing, promotion, and delivery information via an electronic mail network. All these services are examples of product differentiation.

Market specialization. The third competitive strategy Porter describes is **market specialization,** which is achieved by concentrating on a particular market or product niche. Information systems that support the market specialization strategy provide information about the profitability of specific market segments and enable manufacturers and distributors to design and market products and services addressing the needs of a particular market niche. An example of a service attracting a specific market segment is electronic library access, which would appeal to personal computer owners in academics and business. Figure 3–11 summarizes the strategy-level impacts of information technology.

Figure 3–11
Strategy-level
impacts

STRATEGY-LEVEL IMPACT	USE OF INFORMATION TECHNOLOGY
Low-cost leadership	Office automation Inventory control systems
Product differentiation	Computer-aided design Hotline to technical support
Market specialization	Electronic library access for PC owners Market profitability analysis

Defining Competitive Strategy

A firm needs to determine what its competitive strategy should be before deciding how to use information technology, which means understanding its competitive position, the competitive forces affecting it, and its overall business strategy. The applications a firm selects should support its competitive strategy and enable it to deal effectively with the competitive forces in its industry. Once the competitive uses of information technology are defined, these plans have to be translated into technology plans.

New Business Opportunities

New information technology is also fostering new business opportunities. Videoconferencing, a technology that makes it possible to hold electronic meetings, could hurt the airline and hotel businesses in the next 5 to 10 years. Holiday Inns has decided to counter this threat by offering videoconferencing facilities for business meetings and in this way has created an entirely new market.

As you might suspect, information technology has brought many organizations into the information services business itself. Union Pacific Railroad bought the smaller Missouri Pacific Railroad, the designer of an automated freight-car tracking system, because of its experience in developing a sophisticated telecommunications network and the software to support it. The information systems developed by Missouri Pacific have become one of the most valuable assets in its industry.

Once information technology is in place, companies can market new products and services via existing networks and databases. Sears uses its massive customer databases to market new consumer products. One database, for example, includes information about all customers who have purchased Sears Kenmore appliances, including name, address, date of purchase, model, and store of purchase. Telemarketing representatives use this database to contact new appliance owners to offer service maintenance contracts. Marketing personnel also search through the massive sales history databases for the phone numbers of appliance owners who made their purchases over seven years ago and contact these prospects with trade-in offers and equipment upgrades.

Supermarkets with point-of-sale bar-code scanners have become research laboratories for market research firms. One market research firm in Chicago uses two test markets to evaluate the effects of alternative marketing and sales promotional strategies on buyer behavior. Consumers in these test markets are exposed to various marketing programs via radio and television advertising, store coupons, and point-of-purchase specials. Their actual purchases are recorded via point-of-sale systems in regional supermarkets. With the help of these point-of-sale systems, the market research firm can measure the effect of advertising and promotion strategies on actual customer purchases. This innovative use of information technology enables the market research firm to differentiate its services by offering a unique method of assessing the impact of marketing strategies.

Finally, companies with excess computing capacity are able to market information services as a new business opportunity. Sears, for example, markets its know-how in processing credit card accounts to other companies. A. O. Smith, a manufacturer of automotive parts, has used its expertise in building telecommunications networks to win a contract to run a network of automatic teller machines for a bank consortium. A number of companies market internally developed software to external companies. For example, a copier distributor has marketed the prospect information system it developed to other distributors throughout the Midwest. This system has a prospect database enabling managers to make queries and generate reports about prospects for different types of products in various sales regions. All these examples illustrate how firms have been able to take advantage of their investment in information technology to create new business opportunities for themselves.

Using Information Technology to Improve Customer Service

One of the most important challenges today is to provide effective customer service. In dealing with large retail chains, customers don't have access to the personalized service of the mom-and-pop hardware store or the small grocery store of the 50s and 60s. Yet, good customer service today can provide a competitive edge. Information technology can enable even the smallest organization to augment its service to customers.

In their article "Can Information Technology Revitalize your Customer Service," Ives and Mason describe how technology can help businesses provide "personalized" service to customers. Imagine an airline database that keeps track of the types of seating customers prefer? Would you be impressed by a mail-order retail sporting goods chain that maintained a database of your preferences and contacted you when it offered specific promotions or special pricing on items for which you had indicated a preference? Both of these examples rely upon information databases that pull information together and support on-line query capability so that managers can gain access to customer preferences on a timely basis.

Another type of customer service that information technology can support is "augmented service." *Augmented service* means adding value to a product or service by providing the customer with additional support through the product life cycle, beginning with the acquisition of the product and going through to its retirement or resale. CompUSA, a retail computer chain, has developed an Internet site that enables prospective customers to check on the availability of new and refurbished desktop computers and laptops and to order items over the Web. On-line technical support is also available.

In general, the use of information technology can provide companies with a strategic advantage by giving them more information about their customers and enabling them to serve their customers better. By establishing customer profiles and by electronically storing information on client history and personal characteristics, businesses can respond to customer needs and once again offer the personalized and augmented service that defined the small retail hardware or grocery store of the 50s and 60s.

To summarize, the use of information technology has changed the nature of competition and has created new opportunities for using and marketing information services. As a manager, you will have a chance to determine how your organization can use information technology to support activities that are a part of the value chain (for example, buying and selling) of the business. Using information technology successfully to reduce the cost of value activities or to add value to existing products and services can provide a competitive edge. No matter what industry you find yourself in, you will be relying on information services to a larger extent than has ever been the case before.

INTERORGANIZATIONAL SYSTEMS

Many of the examples of the strategic uses of information technology you have learned about in this chapter involve links between buyers and suppliers. For example, an automobile manufacturer has established a computer-based communications system linking it with its primary suppliers in order to implement a just-in-time inventory system. Just-in-time inventory means that the automobile manufacturer can order parts and components to meet its manufacturing requirements on a day-to-day basis, rather than stockpiling large quantities of excess inventory. This section explains some of the forces behind **interorganizational systems (IOS)**, the participants in IOS, and information-partnering arrangements that have evolved because of IOS.

In general, interorganizational systems have evolved to facilitate the timely exchange of information in a highly competitive marketplace. For example, drugstores and pharmacies use McKesson's Economost system to place orders electronically. A store employee orders merchandise in the proper quantities to replenish stocks by using a wand to record inventory items in short supply. Ninety-nine percent of McKesson's orders arrive electronically.

The evolution of standards such as the universal product code (UPC), magnetic-ink character recognition (MICR), and automatic teller machines (ATMs) has reinforced IOS development. These standards create opportunities to develop information systems based on common data and interface standards.

Most of the organizations using IOS are suppliers, customers, manufacturers, vendors, and others who need to use IOS to exchange information to conduct a primary business process such as order entry, inventory management, electronic funds transfer, or purchasing. In the IOS environment, a new role has emerged, the IOS facilitator.

The **IOS facilitator** provides the information utility or the network that allows participants to exchange information. The CIRRUS network, which permits nationwide processing of ATM transactions 24 hours a day, is an IOS facilitator. With CIRRUS, customers have 24-hour, coast-to-coast access to their ATMs. CompuServe's electronic information services are another example. An individual can use CompuServe to gain access to electronic mail networks, electronic databases, and home-shopping services. Using the information superhighways offered by these IOS facilitators has become an essential element in doing business.

Information Partnering

Information partnering, or forming strategic alliances, is the driving force behind the emerging electronic marketplace. For example, at one time IBM and Sears teamed up to provide Prodigy, a package of several hundred electronic data services, including home banking, stock market quotations, and airline reservations. American Airlines has joined with Marriott and Budget Rent-A-Car in offering AMRIS, an electronic travel supermarket. Other examples are the Insurance Value-Added Network (IVANS), the Singapore TradeNet, and the Baxter Healthcare System.

IVANS links hundreds of insurance companies' home offices to thousands of independent insurance agents. IVANS makes it possible for independent insurance agents to gain access to information on policies offered by many of the smaller insurance companies. Consequently, agents can locate the most competitive prices and policies for their clients and maintain a competitive marketing environment that would not be possible without the multiple providers that have access to the network.

The Singapore TradeNet manages the operations activities of the world's largest shipping port by linking shipping companies, banks, and insurers with relevant government entities, including customs and immigration officials. The TradeNet, which cost the government over $50 million, enables vessels to clear the port in 10 minutes—a striking improvement from the two- to four-day interval required before.

The Baxter Healthcare System links a variety of medical supply manufacturers with buyers, including hospital purchasing agents. This system was developed and replaced from the original American Hospital Supply order entry system that enabled purchasing agents in hospitals to generate purchase orders electronically. As time went on, the Baxter System added on other hospital suppliers, thereby giving the purchasing agents access to order, inventory, and delivery information from multiple hospital supply organizations.

These information partnerships are representative of the new marketing environment. In most cases, an information facilitator provides the network through which the various participants can interact. An industry trade association initiated the insurance network IVANS because its members were concerned about the loss of market share to direct sales forces representing larger insurers such as Allstate and State Farm. The Singapore TradeNet was a government-sponsored project designed to make the port more competitive. The Baxter Healthcare System evolved from the American Hospital Supply system and grew to accommodate the needs of the medical supply industry.

At times, a company may acquire another company to form an information partnership that will help them both compete more effectively. Union Pacific Railroad acquired Missouri Pacific Railroad to utilize MoPac's sophisticated freight dispatching and tracking system. Strategic alliances such as these are critical to achieving market success.

Increasingly, companies find themselves organizing partnerships to compete with other alliances. Since American joined forces with Marriott and Budget Rent-A-Car, other airlines have also teamed up with hotel and rental car chains. The only downside of an information partnership is the possible transfer of authority to the partners. To participate in an information partnership, a firm must also create and manage a technical capability that supports the alliance. Because electronic communications is an essential element of information partnering, businesses must invest in telecommunications planning and design to participate in the electronic marketplace follow.

The Electronic Marketplace

The emergence of the electronic marketplace is an important trend in the 1990s. Electronic sales channels reduce the costs of locating suppliers, ordering merchandise, and reconciling errors. Customers can save money by ordering just-in-time inventory via electronic market channels. The players in the electronic marketplace include suppliers and buyers, retailers and customers, and manufacturers and dealers (see Figure 3-12). Some examples of players in the electronic marketplace follow.

Inventory Locator Service (www.go-ils.com), a subsidiary of Ryder System, offers an airline parts inventory database that enables the airlines to locate suppliers of the parts they need for repair and maintenance. Now planes that used to be grounded for days can fly within hours.

Some of the on-line shopping malls and catalogs on the Web include: Access Market Square (www.icw.com/ams.html), Barclay Square Shopping Mall (www.itl.net/barclay/square), the Branch Mall (branch.com), Cyberspace Malls International (cyspacemalls.com/), iMall (www.imall.com/homepage.html), Interactive Super Mall (supermall.com), Internet Shopping Network (www.internet.net/), Mall 2000 (www.mall2000.com), and marketplaceMCI (www.internetmci.com). The commercial on-line services, including America Online and CompuServe, also have Web-based shopping facilities.

Figure 3–12

One of the players
in the electronic
marketplace

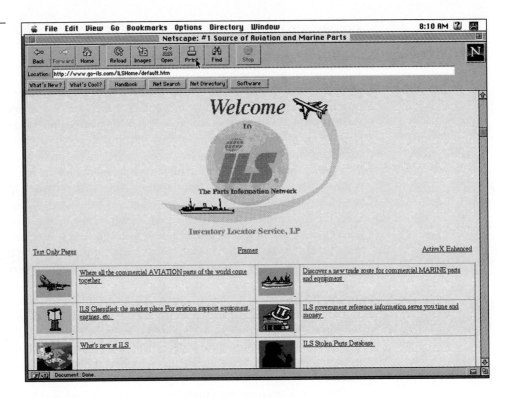

Telcot, an electronic market for cotton, enables 12,000 farmers to sell their products. Telcot was established by a cooperative association of cotton farmers in Oklahoma and Texas.

MEMA/Transnet, an electronic order system for automotive parts, serves more than 100 manufacturers and over 4,000 customers. MEMA/Transnet was invented by the Motor and Equipment Manufacturers Association, a trade association.

IVANS, the network that links insurance agents, insurance carriers, and other information sources for insurance agents, was created by an industry association of independent insurance agents. As you learned earlier, IVANS links many independent agents with smaller insurance carriers.

SABRE and APOLLO, the airline reservations systems of American and United, not only have added the flights of competitive carriers but also have become electronic travel supermarkets for related services, such as hotel and rental car reservations. These information systems link the airlines with travel agents and provide the travel agents with a wide range of travel information.

Med Facts, an electronic market for physicians, lists fees, educational backgrounds, and the specialties of over 1,400 physicians in the Miami area. This kind of information system will become more and more common in many cities in the United States.

As you can tell from these examples, the "competitive" systems designed by American Hospital Supply, United Airlines, and McKesson have evolved into electronic marketplaces that include many suppliers' goods. Although the APOLLO system originally offered only United flights, it was quickly changed to include the flights of competitive carriers. The American Hospital Supply order entry system is now being operated by Baxter Healthcare and includes a wide variety of medical supplies manufactured by multiple suppliers, including Baxter's competitors. In essence, then, electronic markets offer customers access to offerings from competing suppliers.

Electronic markets help the buyer because they enable both companies and consumers to search through the databases of competitive products and find the most cost-effective goods and services. In general, the electronic marketplace reduces the costs of locating vendors, comparing products and services, comparing costs, and handling paperwork.

The reduction in transactions costs associated with evaluating, ordering, and purchasing has a related effect. Because ordering via the electronic marketplace is so easy, many companies will inevitably choose to buy rather than to make the products and services they need. What may emerge in this environment is a group of specialized suppliers linked to major firms via the electronic marketplace. A number of components, such as computer parts, and a variety of specialized services, such as specialty printing, will be outsourced to the electronic marketplace because it will be more cost-effective to purchase these goods and services than to manufacture or to create them internally.

In summary, strategic alliances between suppliers and vendors, manufacturers and distributors, and retailers and buyers will become commonplace. Companies that want to remain competitive must build internal information systems and design telecommunications networks that enable them to participate in the electronic marketplace.

THE STRATEGIC IMPACT OF THE INTERNET AND ELECTRONIC COMMERCE

The Internet has become the major factor in *electronic commerce.* Managers in every organization—both large and small—are asking, What is the impact of the Internet on electronic commerce? How does the Internet affect how organizations do business? Companies are using global networking and technological innovation as powerful assets, and electronic marketing is rapidly providing many organizations with a competitive advantage. In this section of the chapter, you will learn about Internet applications, the business uses of the Internet, how the Internet is being used in electronic marketing, and the business potential of on-line communities.

About the Internet

The Internet is a network of networks. It is made up of over 25,000 networks that can transfer data via many routes. According to industry estimates, more than 100,000,000 people will use the Internet by 1998. Over 2,200,000 host computers are connected to the Internet, and its growth rate is close to 10 percent a month. To obtain access to the Internet, users can obtain accounts from an Internet service provider, a commercial on-line service, or a university-based computer system. Internet access provides electronic mail and file transfer capability and access to the *World Wide Web,* including a variety of search engines and tools.

An Overview of Internet Applications

In their text *Frontiers of Electronic Commerce,* Kalakota and Whinston describe some applications of the Internet that create opportunities for business. For example:

- Individual-to-group communications (group conferencing, telemeetings, electronic bulletin board systems, newsgroups) for research, collaboration, and distance education across institutional, state, and national boundaries.
- Information transfer and delivery services (electronic mail, newsgroups, bulletin boards, electronic data interchange (EDI), and multimedia electronic mail).

- Information databases, including access to full-text databases and virtual libraries containing both text and multimedia information. Information databases can be searched using Internet tools such as Gopher, World Wide Web browsers, and news gathering agents. **Gopher,** for example, is an information search and access method that lists different host computers and the subject areas of information they contain.   Examples of databases are Securities and Exchange Commission (SEC) databases with information on the health of companies, National Weather Service satellite photos, and the Library of Congress catalog.

- Information access using anonymous **FTP** (file transfer protocol), which allows the user to connect and download files from a remote computer.

- World Wide Web access to obtain information in a multimedia format with graphics, audio, and video.

- Information processing services—remote access to a variety of software programs for operations research, statistics, simulation, and visualization.

These Internet applications will be discussed in greater depth in upcoming chapters on telecommunications and networking systems. This chapter focuses on how the Internet can support business strategy and create competitive advantage.

Business Uses of the Internet

Today the Internet is becoming an electronic marketplace, and business uses of the Internet are growing more rapidly than any other application. An indicator of the growth of the business sector on the Internet is the growing number of electronic publications, such as *The Internet Business Journal, Internet World, The Internet Letter, The Internet Business Report,* and *Bits and Bytes Online.*

Many companies are using the Internet for electronic communications, data transfer, market research, and the creation of electronic storefronts (see Figure 3–13). For example, the Ford Motor Company uses the Electronic Car Showroom to promote its Lincoln line of cars and provides information about leasing, sales, and road test results through the Electronic Newsstand. Lufthansa Airlines uses a Gopher site to market special flights, prices, and travel packages.

Hundreds of businesses are using the Internet to market products and services. Some of the reasons for using the Internet to gain a presence in the electronic marketplace are globalization, competitive advantage, cost containment, sales and marketing, and electronic communications.

- Globalization. As companies move into the international marketplace, the Internet provides a global communications network that is vital to creating a global business presence. The Internet allows companies of any size to pursue customers on a worldwide basis.

- Competitive advantage. Using the Internet as a marketing tool, businesses can provide up-to-date information about products, technological developments, and research to millions of prospective customers and users.

- Information access. Using the Internet, businesses can access information, including government databases, industry statistics, and competitor practices.

- Cost containment. Doing business electronically is much less expensive than using paper communications, phone contact, and information distribution by paper and by mail.

- Sales and marketing. Using the Internet, customers can obtain information about products, services, advertisements, prices, schedules, contact persons, service capabilities, and business opportunities. Thousands of potential customers can

Figure 3–13

An example of an electronic storefront on the Web

access information in a labor-efficient and cost-effective way. Using the Internet, companies can create up-to-date postings of the latest customer information.

- Electronic communications. Using the Internet, businesses have access to an international electronic communications network that facilitiates communications and interactions among customers, vendors, and competitors in far-flung locations.

Electronic Marketing and On-Line Communities on the World Wide Web

The growth of commercial applications on the World Wide Web is spectacular. According to one source, the number of Web sites on the Internet has risen from four in 1970 to over 5,000,000 in 1996. In one classification scheme, corporate uses of the World Wide Web include (1) creating a marketplace awareness for a company's goods and services, (2) providing customer support, (3) selling products and services, (4) developing Web-based advertisements, and (5) providing electronic information services.

Another way of classifying the uses of the Web is in terms of the types of electronic communities it has created. The World Wide Web provides a powerful vehicle for letting customers interact with each other as participants in **on-line communities.** In an article entitled "The Real Value of On-Line Communities," Armstrong and Hagel describe various types of on-line communities.

- Communities of transaction facilitate the buying and selling of products and services and provide information related to those transactions. For example, a customer can select and order wines on-line from Virtual Vineyards, a Web-based wine site.

- Communities of interest allow participants to trade information with each other. For example, Motley Fool, a Web site for interactive feedback on stock investments, enables participants to exchange information on stock choices, insider trading, and other investment topics.

- Communities of relationship enable individuals to join on-line electronic discussion groups. Most of the commercial on-line services, such as America Online and CompuServe, have on-line chat rooms that enable participants to exchange information on various topics. The Cancer Forum, an on-line discussion group for cancer patients, gives people a forum for sharing experiences about treatments, medical research, and medication.

The potential value of these electronic communities is enormous. Participants in electronic communities develop a sense of loyalty and participation through their ongoing interactions. Web-based discussion groups may provide an effective vehicle for gaining unsolicited feedback about products and services from customers. The Web has the potential to revolutionize marketing research because of the potential value of unsolicited, unstructured feedback. Most of today's market research asks for responses to predefined questions; marketing research questions on the World Wide Web will be generated by current and prospective customers themselves and may lead to new insights that would not have been accessible using traditional methods.

As companies embark on efforts to place their businesses on the World Wide Web, they must answer a number of questions regarding the participation in and management of on-line communities. Some of these questions follow:

- How large is the economic potential of the electronic community?
- How intense is competition likely to be?
- Do we need to create an electronic community in order to defend an existing business niche, to create a new one, or both?
- How can we organize or segment the electronic community?
- Do we want to locate our electronic community directly on the Internet, or do we want to use an existing on-line service such as America Online or CompuServe?
- Do we want to form an electronic community on our own or in conjunction with an alliance of partners?

The Internet has become an exploding electronic marketplace. As electronic commerce applications are built more and more quickly, customers will interface with retailers, retailers will interface with manufacturers, and manufacturers will interface with suppliers over the Internet. The issues of cost, security, control, and expansion are all issues that will be played out in the years ahead and will ultimately determine the value and impact of the Internet on American business.

STRATEGIC INFORMATION SYSTEMS: THE RISKS

This chapter has given you insight into the competitive impacts of information technology and the benefits of interorganizational systems, but there are risks as well. These risks include shifting the balance of competition, failure to upgrade the capabilities of a strategic system, and litigation.

Shifting the Balance of Competition

Using information systems to link buyers with suppliers can shift the balance of competition. Let us say that a furniture retailer in St. Louis links up to the order-entry system of a furniture manufacturer in North Carolina. This link gives a competitive advantage to the supplier, the furniture manufacturer. Why? The electronic link to the supplier's order-entry system helps the furniture retailer to check prices, confirm delivery dates, and place orders with that particular supplier. Eventually, the furniture manufacturer creates switching costs that can cause the furniture retailer to do most of its business with that supplier. This environment creates an advantage for the supplier (the furniture manufacturer) over the buyer (the furniture retailer).

As time goes on, other furniture manufacturers may develop their own electronic order-entry systems. The furniture retailer in St. Louis can now hook up to the order-entry systems of multiple manufacturers, check the cost of goods being offered by various manufacturers, and place an order with the manufacturer that offers the best price. Now the competitive advantage has shifted to the buyer, the furniture retailer.

Although this example may seem like an isolated instance, this experience has been duplicated throughout many different industries. For example, the first airline to introduce frequent flight bonus points developed a competitive advantage, but soon all the major airlines followed suit and offered similar programs. Consequently, frequent flight programs raised the investment in information systems that airlines must build to compete in their industry without giving any one airline a competitive advantage. Although the first airline to offer such a program may gain an advantage, this advantage is only temporary.

Exceptions can occur when the innovator maintains its leadership by continually adding features to an already established competitive system. You learned about SABRE earlier in this chapter. SABRE was originally developed in the early 1970s to monitor airline seats. Since then, it has evolved into a computerized middleman linking suppliers of travel services (tours, rental cars, etc.) to travel agents. American also participated in the joint venture AMRIS, which includes Marriott, Hilton, and Budget Rent-A-Car companies. Information systems that start early and continue to add new services are extremely valuable.

Failure to Upgrade the Capabilities of a Strategic System

Another type of risk occurs if a company makes a one-time move by introducing a competitive information system and then fails to upgrade its capabilities. For example, American Hospital Supply's ASAP system was designed to enable hospitals to link with American's order-entry system. However, when ASAP was not enhanced for several years, American's competitors caught up and offered better systems. Eventually, ASAP evolved into the Baxter Healthcare system, which lists the offerings of multiple suppliers.

Litigation

Another risk involves possible litigation. Both United and American Airlines have been the subjects of lawsuits claiming that their reservations systems have created unfair trade practices, such as biased screen displays. Although both United and American have agreed to provide unbiased displays, the litigation on this issue has taken years to resolve.

DO INFORMATION SYSTEMS PROVIDE A COMPETITIVE EDGE?

As you have seen, information technology has created a competitive edge for many organizations. You have also seen that once a competitor introduces an information-based service, such as a frequent flight bonus program, other firms in the industry catch up, eliminating the innovator's original competitive advantage and raising the stakes of participating in an industry. Strategic information systems become a strategic necessity—a part of doing business.

Firms such as American Airlines, American Hospital Supply, and McKesson first designed competitive information systems to establish linkages between themselves and their customers. None of these firms was able to sustain a long-term competitive advantage because of their initial systems. Now that their systems provide linkages between customers and multiple suppliers, they are participants in the electronic marketplace.

In this scenario, what happens to smaller firms that cannot afford to design competitive information systems? In both the airline and pharmaceutical industries, smaller firms that could not afford to develop information systems themselves either were absorbed by larger firms or left the industry. In many industries, including insurance, retailing, and automobile manufacturing, the strategic use of information technology is necessary for survival. Information technology may not provide a long-term competitive advantage, but it is essential for participation in many industries. The focus today should be not to use information technology for its own sake, but rather to identify competitive uses of technology that reinforce the firm's basic capabilities.

Shifting to Capabilities-Based Competition

You have learned that the key building blocks of corporate strategy today are not products and markets, but business processes. In **capabilities-based competition,** competitive success depends on transforming key processes into capabilities that provide superior value to the customer. The following rules apply:

1) Set aggressive, customer-oriented goals.

2) Make sure that employees have the skills and resources they need to achieve the chosen capability.

3) Align measurements and rewards. For example, if the goal is to provide more effective customer service, then you should measure employees' performance in terms of their ability to provide effective customer support.

4) Have the CEO provide leadership for the transformation. Without top management support, the transition to a customer-focused, market-driven organization will not happen.

5) Drive down business decision making to those directly participating in the key business processes, the sales and service staffs.

Wal-Mart has been able to overcome Kmart by introducing new business processes such as cross-docking, the continuous dispatching of goods to stores, and managing of its own trucking fleet. Wal-Mart's 2,000 company-owned trucks replenish inventory to its stores within 48 hours, whereas its competitors rely on subcontractors for trucking. In both cross-docking and trucking-fleet management, Wal-Mart uses applications of information technology that support its key business processes. These business processes allow customers to find the goods they want when they shop at a Wal-Mart store.

To help store managers order stock on a timely basis, Wal-Mart provides them with information systems detailing consumer buying trends. Store managers even participate in videoconferences via Wal-Mart's satellite communications system to exchange information about customer trends. Both of these systems are designed to enable Wal-Mart's managers to focus on satisfying customer needs. In so doing, Wal-Mart's store managers have an opportunity to make decisions on stocking levels of inventory items.

Information systems describing buyer behavior and an inventory management system that virtually guarantees timely deliveries from distributors support the store managers. Other organizations have also applied the rules of capabilities-based competition. At Medequip, a medical equipment supplier, on-site service representatives work with selected customer accounts to offer personalized service. Honda provides its dealers with operating policies and procedures for more effective merchandising, selling, floor planning, and service management and reinforces its policies with dealer training. By making its dealers more effective, Honda has created a system that earns its dealers the highest ratings for customer satisfaction.

Another example of capabilities-based competition comes from the banking industry. Two banks, Wachovia and Banc One, are today among the nation's fastest growing regional banks. What are the keys to their success? In Wachovia's case, 600 personal bankers provide a total portfolio of banking services, using an integrated customer-information database. Banc One gives its 51 affiliate presidents autonomy over pricing, credit decisions, and management policy making. In both cases, the key to success is placing decision making with the people responsible for conducting the key business processes: the personal bankers at Wachovia and the affiliate presidents at Banc One. Technology plays a critical role in capabilities-based competition. The personal bankers at Wachovia, the store managers at Wal-Mart, and the on-site service representatives at Medequip all use information systems and customer databases to make decisions.

IBM Credit's deal structurers use information systems to authorize credit decisions, and accounts payable representatives use an integrated database to authorize payments to suppliers. The single most significant factor making it possible to decentralize decision making to the individuals responsible for key business processes is the use of information technology.

As we move through the 1990s and beyond, the strategic uses of information technology must focus upon reinforcing capabilities-based competition. That is, technology must support key business processes like customer service, order follow-up, and inventory control. Although many of these uses of technology may not be innovative, they are rapidly becoming an integral and essential part of doing business. Strategic information systems provide a competitive edge, but they are also becoming a strategic necessity.

An Update to SABRE

As you recall, SABRE, the American Airlines on-line reservation system, was one of the first examples of an information system that was used for competitive advantage. Max Hopper, the chief information officer at American Airlines, talked about SABRE 25 years later in an article in the *Harvard Business Review*. In this article Hopper discussed the changing technology environment, the current impact of SABRE, and its role in providing American Airlines with a competitive advantage.

American Airlines started working on the development of SABRE in the mid-50s, and it made its debut in 1963. At that time SABRE processed data related to 85,000 phone calls, 40,000 reservations, and 20,000 tickets per day. The database now holds 45,000,000 fares, and 40,000,000 changes are entered each month. During peak use, SABRE handles 2,000 messages per second and creates more than 300,000 passenger records per day.

When it was originally envisioned, SABRE was an inventory control system, capable of keeping track of available seats and attaching passenger names to each seat. By the mid-70s SABRE generated flight plans, tracked spare parts, scheduled crews, and developed a range of decision support systems for management. In 1976 the first

SABRE terminal was placed in a travel agency; today SABRE has over 14,300 travel-agency subscriber locations in 45 countries.

In the late 70s and 80s, SABRE grew to include hotel and rental car reservations systems. Today SABRE is an electronic travel supermarket linking many suppliers of travel services (Broadway shows, rental cars, packaged tours, hotel reservations) with the travel agent or customer. A joint venture among American Airlines, Marriott, Hilton, and Budget has developed computerized reservations systems and services encompassing the airline, hotel, and rental car businesses, respectively.

One of the most interesting questions relating to SABRE is whether it has provided American Airlines with an ongoing competitive edge. One of the subsystems with the greatest competitive impact, SABRE's yield-management system, is a good case in point. The yield-management subsystem is the system that establishes different prices for seats on flights in order to maximize revenues. After guarding this software for years, American Airlines is now selling the yield-management software to other companies because it believes that this software is the best in the world and because it can gain excellent profits by selling information services and software.

In line with this thinking, Hopper draws several conclusions that summarize some of the major points and identify some of the major trends affecting the information technology and information services businesses.

- Information systems may no longer provide an enduring business advantage because most companies have built these systems as a necessity; businesses must have these systems to compete, but they no longer guarantee competitive success.

- The age of building proprietary software for competitive advantage is over. Buying hardware and software solutions from third-party vendors is far more cost-effective. Of course, if American purchases critical software solutions from vendors, so can its competitors. This situation reinforces the argument that competitive systems are a strategic necessity; the advantage comes in how these systems are used.

- The information utility is becoming more and more important. A standardized networking and communications infrastructure must support powerful workstations. The technology platform is a central nervous system that provides access to shared databases and organizes the convergence of a number of critical systems and technologies, including desktop computing, administrative data processing, and office automation.

MANAGEMENT SUMMARY

As you can see from this chapter, information technology can provide organizations with a competitive edge. You have learned how American Hospital Supply electronically linked its customers to its order entry system, how Merrill Lynch created the CMA, and how American Airlines created an electronic travel supermarket by enhancing its SABRE on-line reservation system.

While many of these information systems have created a competitive edge, they have transformed the basis of competition within many industries. For example, it is virtually impossible to compete in the airline business today without a computer-based reservation system. Today most businesses find themselves in an electronic marketplace. To compete effectively in this environment, organizations like American Airlines and Sears have established information partnerships. Some of the original strategic information systems such as American Hospital Supply's order-entry system have been opened up to other suppliers. It is increasingly important for all companies to use technology-based capabilities as an integral part of doing business.

KEY TERMS FOR MANAGERS

capabilities-based competition, 78
FTP, 74
Gopher, 74
interorganizational systems (IOS), 61
IOS facilitator, 70

low-cost leadership, 66
market specialization, 67
on-line communities, 75
product differentiation, 67
value activities, 57

value chain, 57
value system, 58

REVIEW QUESTIONS

1. How can publishers use information technology to produce and distribute textbooks?

2. What are the five competitive forces that information technology can address at the firm level?

3. How can automobile manufacturers use information technology to add value or features to an automobile to prevent consumers from substituting alternative products?

4. How can insurance companies use information technology to block new entrants from entering the insurance industry?

5. How can a computer manufacturer use information technology to achieve low-cost leadership?

6. How can a manufacturer of designer shoes use information technology to differentiate its products?

7. Describe the competitive impact of each of these information systems:
   a. SABRE
   b. IVANS
   c. Singapore TradeNet
   d. Baxter Healthcare System

8. Explain the role of the interorganizational systems (IOS) facilitator.

9. What changes have occurred with these competitive systems, and what are their current roles in the electronic marketplace?
   a. SABRE
   b. McKesson's Economost system
   c. American Hospital Supply's ASAP system

10. How has Wal-Mart used information technology to reinforce capabilities-based competition?

11. What Internet applications can provide effective business tools?

12. Describe several types of on-line communities on the Internet.

QUESTIONS FOR DISCUSSION

1. How could a financial services company specializing in mortgage loans use information about its customers to gain power over its customers (buyers)?

2. If a furniture dealer gains access to the order-entry systems of four different furniture manufacturers and can check prices and delivery dates on each of these systems, how will the balance of power be affected? Will the dealer (buyer) have power over the manufacturer (supplier), or vice versa?

3. How could a national magazine distributor gain a competitive edge by using information technology to pursue a low-cost leadership strategy?

4. How can a computer manufacturer use information technology to pursue a product-differentiation strategy?

5. What applications of information technology can have a significant impact on improving customer service?

6. Give three examples of Internet applications that have business uses.

7. How can establishing on-line electronic communities contribute to the successful marketing and development of products and services?

8. What major changes and modifications have been made to SABRE, the American Airlines reservation system, over the years?

PROBLEMS

1. **Information systems for competitive advantage.** The following examples illustrate how companies are using information systems for competitive advantage:

   a. Airline companies have developed information systems so that they can offer frequent flight bonus programs to their customers.

   b. Digital Equipment Corporation (DEC) has developed an expert system to design appropriate computer configurations for its customers.

   c. Walgreen's pharmacies have a prescription information database that enables customers to fill their prescriptions at any Walgreen's pharmacy in the nation.

   d. Xerox Corporation has a field-service support system that matches information about service calls to the workloads and capabilities of its technical support representatives.

   e. Mrs. Fields Cookies has an electronic mail system that links each store manager to the boss, Mrs. Fields.

   Discuss the major impact of each of these information systems, identifying the level of impact and the type of impact. The impact can be at the industry level (products and services, markets, production economics), at the firm level (buyers, suppliers, substitute products, new entrants, and rivals), and at the strategy level (low-cost leadership, product differentiation, market specialization).

2. **An update on SABRE.** Throughout this chapter, you have learned about SABRE, the American Airlines reservation system. In an article entitled "Rattling SABRE—New Ways to Compete on Information," Max Hopper mentions that SABRE has the most sophisticated yield-management system ever designed. Its yield-management system reviews historical booking patterns to forecast the demand for flights up to a year in advance of their departure. The system monitors bookings at regular intervals, compares American's fares with competitors' fares, and determines the best price to charge for an airline seat to maximize revenue at any given point in time.

   American spent years and millions of dollars developing its yield-management information system. Today it markets this software to its competitors. Why do you think American decided to market its yield-management system to its competitors?

3. **Competitive advantage versus strategic necessity.** In his article "Corporate Strategies for Information Technology: A Resource-Based Approach," Eric Clemons argues that strategic information systems no longer provide a competitive advantage; they have become a "strategic necessity."

   What do you think Clemons means? Can you identify any firms that have been innovators in using information technology for competitive advantage, only to find that they lose their edge after their competitors develop the same capabilities?

CASES

1. **State Mutual Life Insurance Company.** State Mutual Life Insurance Company is a well-established company dedicated to providing quality and service to its upper-middle-class insurance customers. It has achieved its position in the insurance

industry by offering popular term life and whole life programs. More than 800 insurance agents around the country market State Mutual policies and handle claims.

In the early 1970s, the company developed information systems to automate the paperwork associated with policy creation and maintenance and claims administration. In the late 1970s, State Mutual upgraded most of these early batch systems to on-line systems, enabling local sales agents to create and maintain policyholder records from local agency locations. The new system meant that policy information could be updated in hours, rather than in days. By 1980 more than 800 sales agents were linked into State Mutual Life's on-line network.

In the early 1980s, State Mutual used its telecommunications network to provide new services to its agents. Agents were able to receive training and promotional materials about new product and service offerings at their local sites. In addition, they could use programs to analyze alternative policy options for their clients. By 1985 State Mutual had designed policy analysis systems for personal computers so that agents could use spreadsheet programs to determine the results of what-if questions. State Mutual also began developing PC-based software enabling local agents to create prospect databases and use them to make queries and generate mailing labels for promotional mailings.

By 1980 the insurance industry had changed dramatically. Competitors were designing new financial services, and new insurance products were being introduced daily. The two- to five-year product development cycle for insurance products was reduced to less than a year. To speed up the product development life cycle, State Mutual Life purchased a fourth-generation language and began to use the prototyping approach in systems development. It was able to reduce the lead time for introducing a new product offering by over a year using this approach. Programmers were also charged with developing information systems for new products so that State Mutual could have insurance products "on the shelf" for introduction at convenient times.

During the early 1980s, office automation systems were introduced at corporate headquarters to improve white-collar productivity. A number of personal computer–based systems were also developed to provide better information about the profitability of certain buyer groups and the profitability of various policies. Using this information, State Mutual executives planned to develop a target marketing strategy. According to this approach, specific insurance products would be designed and offered to highly profitable customer groups.

Given the information about State Mutual Life Insurance Company's information systems, identify which systems are providing the firm with an advantage in its industry by supporting a particular competitive strategy. Use the framework in this chapter that describes how information systems can be used to support various competitive strategies at the industry, firm, and strategy levels to explain which competitive strategies the various information systems projects at State Mutual support.

2. **People's Airlines.** The airline industry has been very aggressive in using information technology for a competitive edge. Airlines with computer-based information systems have consistently been in the forefront. In this environment it is difficult to understand how a small airline such as People's Airlines could succeed. People's Airlines is a small carrier with a fleet of 737s that provides shuttle service between major Texas cities, such as Dallas/Fort Worth, Houston, San Antonio, and El Paso. It is basically a commuter airline specializing in business travelers' needs. Unlike many of the major airlines, People's advertises itself as a "no nonsense" airline. It does not have meal service, reserved seating, frequent flight bonus miles, or other traditional add-ons. It offers an economical price and good service to its customers.

In the era of strategic alliances, People's is in a predicament. While other airlines are teaming up with rental car companies, hotel/motel chains, and even ticket agencies, People's is still just an airline specializing in a certain market niche. Can People's survive in its industry by remaining a no nonsense airline or will it need to consider creating the same kinds of strategic alliances its competitors have to stay in business over the long term?

Use your best judgment to make recommendations to executives at People's Airlines about its future in the electronic marketplace.

SELECTED INTERNET REFERENCE SITES

Airlines

Aeroflot   www.seanet.com/Bazar/Aeroflot/Aeroflot.html

American Airlines
www.amrcorp.com/aa_home/aa_home.html

Canadian Airlines   www.cdnair.ca/

Cathay Pacific Airlines   www.cathay-usa.com/

KLM—Royal Dutch Airlines
www.ib.com.8080/business/klm/klm.html

Lufthansa   www.tkz.fh-rpl.de/tii/lh/lhflug-e.html

Mexicana Airlines
www.catalog.com/cgibin/var/mx/index.html

Qantas Airways   www.anzac.com/qantas/qantas.html

Southwest Airlines Home Gate   www.iflyswa.com/

Swissair   www.swissair.ch/

United Airlines Flight Center   www.ualfltctr.com/

Careers

Academe This Week
chronicle.merit.edu/.ads/.links.html

America's Job Bank   www.ajb.dni.us/

Career Magazine   www.careermag.com/careermag/

CareerMosaic   www.careermosaic.com.cm/cm12.html

Career Web   www.cweb.com/

E-Span Employment Database
www.espan.com.egi-bin/ewais

Heart Career Connections   www.career.com/

HiTechCareers   www.hitechcareer.com/hitech

JobCenter   www.cocenter.com

Jobs in Consulting
www.cob.ohio-state.edu/dept.in/consult.htm

Jobs Online   www.ceweekly.wa.com

Kansas Mentor Project   www.ksu.edu/~dangle

Monster Board Career Site   www.monster.com/

Online Career Center   www.occ.com/

TalkPower Training Programs
com.primenet.com/seminars/

Training and Development Job Mart
www.tcm.com/trdev/jobs/

Finance

Barclaycard   www.barclaycard.co.uk

Charles Schwab Online   www.schwab.com/

Chicago Mercantile Exchange   www.cme.com

Daily Stock Market Data
www.ai.mit.edu/stocks/prices.html

Fidelity Investments   www.fid-inv.com

FinanceNet   www.financenet.gov

MasterCard   www.mastercard.com

NetWorth
networth.gait.com/www/home.networth.html

SEC EDGAR Database   town.halt.orgedgar/edgar.html

Wells Fargo   www.wellsfargo.com

Insurance

Aetna Life and Casualty
marketplace.internetMCI.COM/marketplace/aetna

Allstate Motor Club
www.shopping2000.com/shopping2000/allstate/

Armed Forces Insurance   www.afi.org/

Great-West Life and Annuity Insurance   www.gwla.com/

ITT Hartford Insurance   www.itt/hartford.com/

Kansas City Life Insurance
www.omg.com KCLife/kclife.htm

Nationwide Insurance   www.nationwide.com/

Old Line Life Insurance   www.oldline.com

Progressive Insurance   www.auto-insurance.com/

Reference

Barlett's Familiar Quotations
www.cc.columbia.edu/acis/bartlett/

Britannica Online   www.eb/.com/

CEDAR National Address Server
www.cedar.buffalo.edu/adserv.html

Cool Jargon of the Day   www.bitecn.com/jargon/cool

Hypertext Webster Interface
c.gp.cs.cmu.edu.5103/prog/webster

U.S. Postal Rates
www.pitneybowes.com/rates/rates.htm

Virtual Library: Law Schools & Libraries
www.law.indiana.edu/law/lawschools.html

Resources

AT & T   www.att.com

AT & T 800 Directory   att_net/dir800

Better Business Bureau   www.bbb.org/bbb/

BizWeb   www.bizweb.com

Federal Express   www.fedex.com

MCI Small Business Center   www.mci.com

National Business Association
www.natlbiz.com/~douglas/INDEX.HTML

United Parcel Service   www.ups.com

ZDNet   www.zdnet.com/

Clothing

2(x)ist Men's Underwear   www.digex.net/2xist.html

Burlington Coat Factory   www.coat.com

Graphiti T-Shirt Design
philadelphia.libertynet.org/~graphiti/link20.html

Jungle Jim's Jungle Wear
www.webcom.com/-jungle/warning.html

Matanuska Outfitters
ww.nauticom.net/users/mata/mata.html

Namark Cap & Emblem   www.accessnv.com/namark/

Neo Video Interactive Wear
adware.com/mall/neovideo/welcome.html

Netgear E-mail Address Polo Shirts
www.netgear.com/NetGear/

The Official Bubba Collection   www.com/bubba/

Shopping In   www.onramp.net/shopping_in/

Gifts

1-800-FLOWERS   www.800flowers.com

Apple Basket Antiques and Gifts
wmi.cais.com/abasket/index.html

Bridal: China, Silver, and Crystal

blackwidow.questar.com/bri/dalnet/tabletop.htm

Cookie Express   www.winc.com/commerce/cookiex/

Cybercalifragilistic   www.webcom.com/~getagift/

Dial-a-Gift   www.Icw.com/dialgift/homepage.html

Flags of the World   www.mallmart.com:80/flags/

Goodies from Goodman
branch.com/goodies/goodies.html

Innovations Online   www.innovations.co.uk/giftpoint/

Order a Personalized Birthday Home Page
ww.webcom.com/~getagift/Order_A_Birthday_Home_
   Page./html

Superflora
shopping2000.com/shopping2000/superflora/
   superflora/superflora.html

Online Malls & Catalogs

Access Market Square   www.icw.com/ams.html

Barclay Square Shopping Mall
www.itl.net/barclaysquare/

Branch Mall   branch.com

Cyberspace Malls International   cyspacemalls.com/

iMall   www.imall.com/homepage.html

Interactive Super Mall   supermall.com

Internet Shopping Network   www.internet.net/

Mall 2000   www.mall2000.com/

marketplace/MCI   www.internetmci.com

Redwood Country Unlimited
www.northcoast.com/unlimited/product_directory/
   product_directory.html

Selected References and Readings

Armstrong, A. and J. Hagel III "The Real Value of On-Line Communities," *Harvard Business Review*, May–June 1996.

Blake Ives and R. Mason "Can Information Technology Revitalize Your Customer Service?" *Academy of Management Executives* 4, no. 4, 1990.

Cash, J. and B. Konsynski. "IS Redraws Competitive Boundaries." *Harvard Business Review*, March–April 1985, pp. 134–42.

Clemons, E. "Corporate Strategies for Information Technology: A Resource-Based Approach." *IEEE Computer*, November 1991, pp. 23–35.

Hopper, M. "Rattling SABRE—New Ways to Compete on Information." *Harvard Business Review*, May–June 1990, pp. 118–25.

Kalakota, R. and A. Whinston *Frontiers of Electronic Commerce,* Reading, MA: Addison Wesley Publishing Co., 1996.

Malone, T.; J. Yates; and R. Benjamin. "The Logic of Electronic Markets." *Harvard Business Review,* May–June 1989, pp. 166–70.

Parsons, G. L. "Information Technology: A New Competitive Weapon." *Sloan Management Review*, Fall 1983, pp. 3–13.

Porter, M. *Competitive Strategy: Techniques for Analyzing Industries and Competitors.* New York: Free Press, 1980.

Porter, M. "How Competitive Forces Shape Strategy." *Harvard Business Review*, March–April 1979, pp. 137–45.

Stalk, G.; P. Evans; and L. Schulman. "Competing on Capabilities: The New Rules of Corporate Strategy." *Harvard Business Review,* March–April 1992, pp. 57–69.

BUSINESS PROCESS REENGINEERING AND INFORMATION TECHNOLOGY

CHAPTER OUTLINE

Manager's View

The Impact of Information Technology

The Reengineering of Work

Information Technology and Business Process Redesign

Information Technology and Organizational Structure

Management Summary

Key Terms for Managers

Review Questions

Questions for Discussion

Problems

Cases

Selected Internet Reference Sites

Selected References and Readings

A NUMBER OF TRENDS affect today's business environment. One of them is the transition from an industrial economy to an information services economy. Beginning with the Industrial Revolution, productivity gains in the U.S. economy were tied to industrial production and manufacturing of goods and services. Since the 1960s, 50 percent of all productivity gains have been attributable to the use of information technology. The ability to capture, store, process, and distribute information is critical to most organizations.

Today the traditional organization is being transformed into the information-based organization, which uses information and information technology to produce significant changes in work patterns. The organization of the past was highly structured and composed of many different functions. In this type of organization, each unit maintained its own information. The organization today has a more flexible, changeable structure. Teams consisting of specialists from various functional areas work together on projects that address new market opportunities. Shared information databases link individuals together.

Managers in the information-based organization are becoming responsible for using and managing technology. They use information technology (IT) as a tool to provide effective customer service, analyze marketing opportunities, and manage production and manufacturing operations. IT has become an integral part of business. To understand the information-based company of today and of the future, let's first learn about the impacts of information technology.

THE IMPACT OF INFORMATION TECHNOLOGY

This section provides a framework for determining the applications of information technology that have an impact upon the individual, the functional unit, and the organization as a whole. These applications can be placed into three categories: those designed to improve *efficiency,* those designed to improve *effectiveness,* and those designed to facilitate *transformation.*

Efficiency can be defined as doing things right. An efficient office worker, for example, can update hundreds of documents per hour. An efficient information system can update thousands of employee or student records per minute. Historically, computer-based information processing systems have supported efficiency by automating routine paperwork processing tasks.

Effectiveness can be defined as doing the right things or as doing the things that need to be done to achieve important business results. An effective sales manager, for example, focuses on tasks that pay off in increased sales volumes. Information systems can help managers be more effective. For example, a prospect database housed on a PC may enable a sales manager to identify sales prospects with high potential and direct his staff's attention to contacting those prospects.

Figure 4–1

A framework for
applications of
information
technology

	INDIVIDUAL	FUNCTIONAL UNIT	ORGANIZATION
Efficiency	Task mechanization	Process automation	Boundary extension
Effectiveness	Work improvement	Functional enhancement	Service enhancement
Transformation	Role expansion	Functional redefinition	Product innovation

Figure 4–1

A framework for
applications of
information
technology

The third objective of applying information technology is **transformation—** using information technology to change the way you do business. Meeting this objective may mean changing the nature of the product or service you deliver or entirely transforming the way a functional unit or an entire organization does business. For example, for years Sears has maintained extensive databases on customer sales histories and buying preferences that allow the company to target its marketing and promotion strategy to high-potential prospects. Now, Sears is selling access to its customer databases, thus offering a service that is totally different from its traditional line of business, retailing. An information-based service has in some ways transformed Sears' original business.

Next we'll consider how applications that achieve the objectives of efficiency, effectiveness, and transformation affect the individual, the functional unit, and the organization as a whole. Figure 4-1 summarizes these objectives.

Impact on the Individual

At the individual level, applications of information technology impact efficiency, effectiveness, and transformation. An individual can use a word processing program, for example, to automate retyping letters. A manager can use a spreadsheet to automate routine budget calculations. These applications improve efficiency by providing automated tools to support specific tasks.

Other applications improve the effectiveness of the secretary or manager. If a secretary uses a prospect database to merge prospect data with follow-up letters on sales calls, the combination word processing–database application improves effectiveness because these letters can improve sales—a fundamental objective of the business.

In some ways transformation is the most challenging outcome of information technology. By using a portable personal computer, a manager can perform "what-if" analyses for investment prospects during sales calls. A prospective customer, for example, may be weighing the advantages and disadvantages of alternative investment options—say, in stocks, bonds, and mutual funds. Sitting in the customer's living room with a PC in hand, the salesperson can compare the anticipated yields on different investment alternatives and give the customer a much better idea of the potential returns on different programs. This capability is an example of transformation; it changes the way the salesperson sells investments. Figure 4-2 summarizes applications of information technology that impact the individual.

Figure 4–2

Applications
impacting the
individual

Efficiency	Task mechanization	Word processing Using a spreadsheet to do a budget plan
Effectiveness	Work improvement	Using a prospect database to generate sales letters
Transformation	Role expansion	Using a portable PC to do "what-if" analyses for investment clients

Figure 4–3
Applications that impact the functional unit

Efficiency	Process automation	Order-entry; credit checking
Effectiveness	Functional enhancement	Computer-aided design Computer-aided manufacturing
Transformation	Functional redefinition	CD-ROM disks for business research

Impact on the Functional Unit

Applications that automate specific business processes, such as order-entry or credit checking, are examples of information technology's impact on the efficiency of the business function. Automated order processing and inventory control systems are other examples of these applications.

An example of an application that improves the effectiveness of the functional unit is using computer-aided design to improve the quality of the design of shoes, automobiles, or airplanes. Improved designs may lead to better sales.

Finally, information technology can transform the nature of the product or service the functional unit offers. A publishing company may sell business research information on CD-ROM disks. These disks provide access to enormous volumes of business information via PC. Hence, this new technology has produced an altogether new product line. Figure 4–3 summarizes applications of information technology that impact the functional unit.

Impact on the Organization

The last group of applications of information technology has an impact on the organization as a whole. Linking customers to the order-entry system of a supplier can improve efficiency. For example, furniture retailers can use terminals linked to the order-entry system of a furniture manufacturer to place orders, check on prices and delivery dates, and manage their own inventories. This system improves the efficiency of placing orders by cutting down on paperwork and enabling retailers to check on available stock before placing orders. The system also gives the furniture manufacturer a competitive advantage because it links customers electronically to the order-entry system, making it easier to place orders with this manufacturer than with other suppliers.

The second objective of information technology is effectiveness. The organization can be more effective by providing better service to its customers. General Electric's diagnostic hotline enables customers to call an 800 number to link into a diagnostic database for small electric appliances. Otis Elevator Company has in-car phones so people trapped in an elevator can call emergency service technicians who are dispatched to the problem area immediately.

Information technology can transform the way an organization does business by enabling the organization to introduce new products and services made possible by technology. Holiday Inns introduced videoconferencing facilities so its business clients could arrange electronic meetings with counterparts in other cities. In this way the hotel chain was able to use a new technology to open up a new business opportunity.

Numerous organizations are using technology to open up new business opportunities. An aggressive market-research firm used point-of-sale systems in local grocery chains to record data on customer buying behavior in response to various advertising and promotional strategies. Its advertising impact studies were superior to those of its competitors because it could tie the impact of advertising to an organization's strategy. Figure 4–4 summarizes applications that affect strategy.

As you can see, most applications of information technology are directly linked with improving business performance. In many cases they impact the products and

Figure 4–4

Applications that impact the organization

Efficiency	Boundary extension	On-line order entry linking customers and suppliers
Effectiveness	Service enhancement	On-line diagnostic databases for electrical appliances
Transformation	Product innovation	Holiday Inn's videoconferencing

services the business unit provides. This text will show how organizations can use information technology to cut operating costs, add value to products and services, and open up new business opportunities.

THE REENGINEERING OF WORK

Every exit is an entry somewhere else.

—Tom Stoppard, American dramatist

Background

Historically, organizations have become hierarchies of complex functions over time. One of the fundamental principles influencing the evolution of industrial organizations was specialization of labor. The division of labor led to the fragmentation of work, with workers in many different areas—marketing, manufacturing, accounting, and so on—performing specialized tasks.

A second factor in the development of modern organizations is the command-and-control structure, which can be traced to early railroad companies, and required predictable, safe control systems. Today's business bureaucracy, with its formalized operating procedures and formal lines of authority, evolved from these early railroad organizations. The standard pyramid, with work broken down by departments—each with its own budget and control system—is still a common organizational form.

The third factor influencing the performance of modern organizations was the nature of the post–World War II market: it was a seller's market. Given the unrelenting demand for goods and services, customers were willing to buy anything that was available. Customer service was not necessarily a critical success factor.

What Has Changed

In the 1990s the nature of the market changed. Customers have power over suppliers that they didn't have before. Part of this customer power comes from access to information. When prospective car buyers can look up dealer-invoice cost of a new auto in *Consumer Reports*, they gain new leverage over the dealer.

Second, competition has changed. Look at the success of Wal-Mart. As you learned in Chapter 3, Wal-Mart changed the retailing equation by developing new strategies that focused on customers' needs. By continuously dispatching goods from distribution centers to its stores, a process called *cross-docking,* Wal-Mart made sure that popular retail items were always in stock. Using its own fleet of 2,000 company owned trucks, Wal-Mart replenishes store inventories continuously. Such increased responsiveness to customer needs is a key factor in competitive success in the 1990s.

The third factor influencing business in the 1990s is technology. Information technology is a factor in Wal-Mart's success. Wal-Mart uses a private satellite communications system to send point-of-sale data directly to its 4,000 vendors so they can meet Wal-Mart's purchasing needs on a more timely basis. Technology also makes it possible for Wal-Mart store managers to exchange information with each other and with management via regular videoconferences.

Information technology provides a means to focus on the customer. By carefully tracking and analyzing customer buying behavior, companies like Wal-Mart can allocate inventory to meet customer needs. They can also use information technology to provide better customer service. Whirlpool has a customer service network that routes customer calls to the same service representative again and again, thus creating a sense of personal service. Otis Elevator uses a service management network to provide on-line technical service for almost 100,000 elevators. When a support call is dispatched to service technicians, the system automatically provides data on the maintenance history of a particular elevator. Many microcomputer vendors give their customers access to bulletin board systems that provide up-to-date technical information on product features.

Finally, information technology is transforming the scope of doing business. Worldwide communications networks enable businesses to operate in global markets and to reach new customers. Information technology also makes it possible to do business 24 hours a day. Individuals on project teams may work in distant locations and interact using electronic communications networks and videoconferencing facilities. For example, programmers in India can work with project leaders in Cincinnati on large software development projects, coordinating their efforts through electronic mail. This chapter and subsequent chapters explain more about how information technology is extending organizational boundaries.

How Organizations Are Reengineering Work

In the 1990s and beyond, there will be winning companies and losing companies—the difference is likely to be the ability to serve customers better with the products and services they want. The ability to serve customers will mean a fundamental shift in the way many companies do business that will involve redesigning basic business processes.

The reason many companies are inefficient today is that no one is in charge of fundamental business processes such as order fulfillment or accounts payable. Companies consist of dozens of fragmented units, and processes are broken down into many different pieces. Information is also fragmented because it is "owned" by each unit involved in the process. The result is that simple processes get bogged down in the fragmentation of work, backlogs occur, and ultimately the customer suffers. For example, a customer who requests a home improvement loan may wait days while the application is moved from desk to desk. At each step workers may check different files and update different databases. Figure 4–5 shows the isolated "buckets" of data that can develop to support specific business functions.

We can cite several examples of businesses that improved their performance by **reengineering** the traditional ways business processes are organized. Hammer and Champy describe a number of reengineering examples in their book *Re-engineering the Corporation*. In almost every case, information technology is a critical factor in changing business processes.

Ford Motor Company's accounts payable system. Ford's widely known revamping of its accounts payable system was motivated by a striking comparison: Ford had 500 people in accounts payable, whereas Mazda had only five. The factor that accounted for the difference was that Ford's accounts payable procedure involved

Figure 4–5

Data maintained by many organizational units

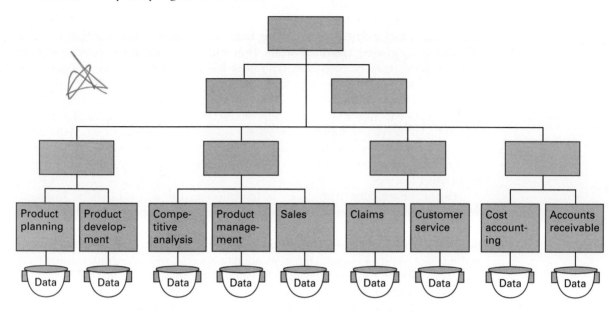

multiple departments: purchasing, receiving, and accounts payable. In the old process, purchasing sent a purchase order to the vendor and a copy to accounts payable. When the vendor shipped the goods, a clerk in receiving completed a receiving document and sent it to accounts payable. When accounts payable received the invoice from the vendor, it matched the invoice with the purchase order and the receiving document. If these three documents didn't match, then more people became involved. Time and paperwork complicated the process.

The new process (see Figure 4–6) applies this business rule:"We pay when we receive the goods," instead of "We pay when we receive the invoice." In the new process, the purchase order amount is entered into a database when a purchase order is generated. When the goods arrive, a clerk in receiving checks the terminal to determine if the shipment contents correspond to the outstanding purchase order amount in the database. If the shipment is correct, a check is sent to the vendor. This new process circumvents the possibility that the invoice won't match the purchase order or the receiving document, and it focuses upon the critical issue: paying for goods that are received.

Technology is an important part of the new process. The shared purchasing/ receiving/accounts payable database makes it possible to integrate the three functions to accomplish the overall business process, order procurement, successfully.

IBM Credit. A second example of reengineering comes from IBM Credit, a subsidiary of IBM responsible for financing the computers, software, and services that IBM Corporation sells. A customer request for financing in the original system began a multistep credit authorization process involving multiple departments. This process could drag on for as long as two weeks, even though the actual work took only 90 minutes. Too many people—a pricer, a checker, and so on—were involved.

In the old system, an IBM sales representative called in a credit request. Then a credit specialist entered the information into a computer system and checked the borrower's creditworthiness. Next the credit specialist dispatched the results to the business practices department, which modified the loan contract in response to the

Figure 4–6

The reengineered accounts payable process at Ford

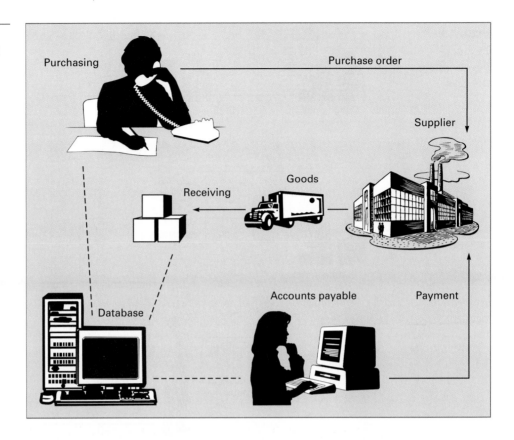

customer request and updated a computer file. Then the credit information was transmitted to a pricer who keyed it into another computer file and determined the interest rate. Finally, information on the credit decision was relayed to a clerical group, which generated a quote letter for the salesperson to give to the customer. This process took from six days to two weeks and sometimes caused customers to seek alternative financing sources.

The redesigned credit issuance process included a newly created position, the "deal structurer," who is equipped with a desktop workstation with various databases needed to make the credit authorization decision from beginning to end. As you can see, information technology was critical to reengineering this process.

Xerox's product development process. The product development process at Xerox was a good candidate for reengineering. Xerox's original product development process was predominantly sequential, which meant that workers on parts of the process had to wait until previous steps were completed. This procedure created numerous bottlenecks and delays.

In the new process, called *concurrent engineering*, (see Figure 4–7), information technology plays a critical role. Using a computer-aided design and manufacturing (CAD/CAM) system and an integrated database, engineers can develop design specifications for products in half the time.

Wal-Mart's inventory management process. As you learned earlier, Wal-Mart reengineered the management of its Pampers inventory by letting the vendor, Procter & Gamble, take control. Wal-Mart lets Procter & Gamble know how much stock it moves from its distribution centers into its stores, and Procter & Gamble in turn lets

Figure 4–7
Product
development
process

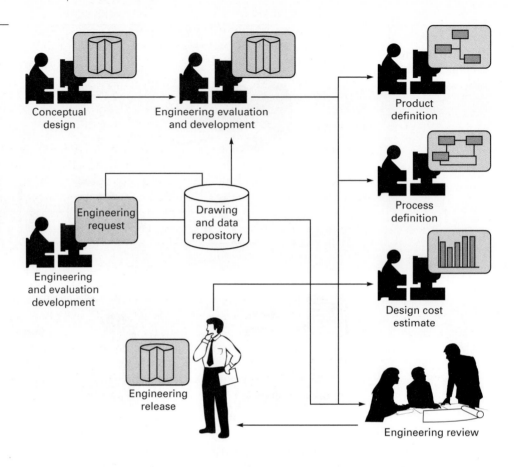

Wal-Mart know how much it needs to reorder. With this reorder information, Procter & Gamble can anticipate Wal-Mart's demand and schedule its production to replenish the Wal-Mart stores continuously. Wal-Mart benefits from this program because it can offload its inventory management function to a vendor and receive inventory into its stores even before it pays Procter & Gamble.

Hewlett-Packard's purchasing process.   A final example shows how technology enabled Hewlett-Packard to integrate a centralized purchasing process with decentralized operations. To improve local operations, Hewlett-Packard gave its divisions autonomy over purchasing. Although decentralized purchasing could have resulted in the loss of corporatewide quantity discounts, Hewlett-Packard overcame the problem by creating a standard purchasing database. When a division wanted to order copiers, for example, it could look up the corporate volume discounts and use these prices for its orders. The use of a shared database provided decentralized autonomy along with centralized control.

**The Process of
Reengineering
Work**

Confusion is a word we have invented for an order which is not yet understood.
—Henry Miller, American novelist

As you can see, reengineering work requires the ability to rethink traditional work methods and procedures. Why is this done in this way? is a critical question. Why does the division manager need to sign all travel requisitions? is another. If the answers indicate that some existing procedures can be eliminated, they should be. The process of reengineering work has several principles that you should take into account.

1. Organize around outcomes, not around tasks. This principle means assigning one person or a team to accomplishing a task, rather than using the traditional assembly-line approach with many people conducting many different steps. The case manager at Mutual Benefit Life, for example, was responsible for accomplishing an outcome: processing an insurance application. In an electronics company, a customer service representative is responsible for all order-filling, assembly, delivery, and installation tasks.

2. Have those who use the output of a process actually perform the process. If a marketing manager wants to purchase something in most organizations, he has to submit a purchase requisition to the purchasing department. Why does the marketing manager have to be a customer of the purchasing department? In a reengineered system, department managers can make their own purchases using a shared database of approved vendors. This system eliminates the costly paperwork of traditional purchasing procedures, yet safeguards the role of purchasing in negotiating the best vendor terms.

3. Treat geographically dispersed units as if they were centralized. Some of the greatest inefficiencies occur because decentralized divisions all maintain their own information systems. For example, each of Hewlett-Packard's 50 manufacturing units had its own purchasing department. This redundancy was costly and prevented HP from negotiating favorable prices. In redesigning the system, HP provided each manufacturing unit with access to a shared vendor database. Central purchasing officials maintained the database and used purchasing histories to negotiate contracts for the entire corporation.

4. Link parallel activities during the process, rather than at the end of the process. In complex manufacturing design and engineering projects, for example, multiple activities can be accomplished by different teams working concurrently with the use of shared databases that make it possible to integrate the final result. Electronic communications systems are also useful in coordinating work groups. One major defense contractor implemented a computer-based videoteleconferencing network to enable work groups in dispersed locations to communicate the progress of various work activities.

5. Capture information once at the source. One of the problems with traditional information systems is that the same information may be created, maintained, and used in many different places. In the insurance application screening process at Mutual Benefit Life, for example, the same information was individually entered into as many as five different databases. When the process was reengineered, integrated databases were designed. Integrated databases not only eliminated the repetitive data entry but also assured better data integrity.

The process of reengineering is difficult to accomplish because it challenges traditional work methods, job designs, and departmental functions. However, for drastic changes to occur, executive leadership needs to challenge traditional assumptions. Information technology can provide communications networks, access to shared databases, and access to on-line videoconferencing facilities that can completely change the way in which traditional functions are performed. This is what Michael Hammer meant by *transformation,* described earlier in this chapter. When transformation occurs, drastic changes result. Dramatic productivity improvement increases, such as the ability to cut overhead by 75 percent or the ability to eliminate errors by 80 percent, are the result. In the 1990s information technology is the means to accomplishing transformation through reengineering business processes.

Figure 4–8
Transition to the information-based organization

ELEMENT	TRADITIONAL	INFORMATION-BASED
Job design	Narrow	Broad
Structure	Layered	Flat
Career path	Vertical	Horizontal
Work standards	Procedures	Judgment
Management style	Supervision	Leadership
People needed	Structured	Adaptive
Training	Hard skills	Education

Organizational Impacts of Reengineering

The transformation that occurs as a result of reengineering has an impact on jobs, organizational structure, management practices, and training. See Figure 4–8 for a brief summary of these impacts.

As you can see, the nature of work in the information-based organization emphasizes adaptability, teamwork, and judgment. Rather than moving step-by-step up the ranks, individuals will become members of cross-functional teams and will make career shifts across departmental boundaries. Teams will assemble and disassemble as needed to accomplish projects. Instead of relying upon a layer of middle managers to specify work procedures, individuals will have considerably more job autonomy and decision-making capability. They will be free to respond to customer needs in a timely way.

Who Will Reengineer the Corporation?

Some of the roles in business reengineering include the sponsor, the steering committee, design teams, the champion and the implementation team. You will find some attributes of each of these participants in Figure 4–9.

As you can see from Figure 4–9, a number of participants play a role in reengineering. The sponsor articulates the overall goals—cutting headcount by one-third, cutting the time it takes to approve credit from 20 days to 2 days—and directs resources to the project. The sponsor recognizes the role that information technology plays in orchestrating these outcomes by providing electronic communications among geographically dispersed workers and by providing operational-level workers with the information they need to make decisions. A steering committee oversees the reengineering project, reviews its status, and identifies concerns along the way. Although managers on the committee represent various functional areas, they need to see beyond their own functional areas in order to make decisions that will benefit the larger organization. Their participation is needed to make the changes work.

The members of the design teams translate the sponsor's goals into new processes. Members must be collaborative, creative, and analytical. The design teams must be able to identify the processes to be redesigned, understand the existing processes, understand how information technology can help, and build working models or prototypes of the new processes. Finally, a champion is needed to coordinate the activities of the various design teams and to keep the sponsor informed. In effect, the champion keeps the ball rolling and promotes the projects to others throughout the organization. The members of the implementation team implement the work of the design teams and play a critical role in motivating others to cooperate with the changes. Sometimes a pilot test must be conducted to assess the impact of the changes. For example, Wal-Mart and Procter & Gamble tested their interorganizational system for inventory management with one product line within three stores before disseminating the changes on a widespread basis.

Figure 4–9

Participants in reengineering

Sponsor	Sees the big picture
	Provides the resources—people and money
Steering committee	Represents the affected units
	Provides guidance, insight
Design teams	Knowledgeable operating managers
	Represent various functional units
	Collaborative, creative
Champion	Middle manager with leadership role
	Direct line to sponsor
	Coordinates multiple design teams
Implementation team	Focuses on implementation
	Open to change
	Able to motivate others to change

Source: Adapted from J. I. Cash, R. G. Eccles, N. Nohria, and R. L. Nolan, *Building the Information-Age Organization: Structure, Control, and Information Technologies* (Burr Ridge, IL: Irwin, 1994), p. 410.

INFORMATION TECHNOLOGY AND BUSINESS PROCESS REDESIGN

Entrepreneurs see change as the norm and as healthy. Usually they do not bring about the change themselves. But—and this defines entrepreneur and entrepreneurship—the entrepreneur always searches for change, responds to it, and exploits it as an opportunity.

—Peter Drucker

The purpose of this section is to describe how information technology can be applied to redesign business processes that cross functional boundaries. **Business process redesign** can be defined as the analysis and design of work flows and processes within and between organizations. Information technology—the capabilities offered by computers, software, and telecommunications—is a key factor in making business process redesign possible.

First of all, it is important to define the term business process. A **business process** consists of a set of logically related tasks performed to achieve a defined business outcome. Business processes have two important characteristics: (1) they have customers; and (2) they cross functional boundaries. Business processes include such things as developing a new product, ordering goods from a supplier, processing an insurance claim, and creating a marketing plan. Analyzing business processes sometimes shows that certain processes can be quite lengthy and unwieldy. For example, analysis of a customer ordering process may show that the elapsed time from a customer's order to delivery is much greater than what the competition can offer. Analysis of the existing process may reveal bottlenecks that occur when each department organizes to maximize its own performance but fails to coordinate its piece of the process with other entities in order to maximize the desired outcome: timely delivery of an order to the customer.

Information technology (IT) can have a critical and important impact on the redesign of business processes. To determine how the use of technology can support new processes, it is useful to apply a framework for understanding the impact of IT. Possible impacts of technology include routinizing transactions, bridging geographical boundaries, automating human tasks, and facilitating simultaneous completion of tasks. Figure 4–10 describes the organizational impacts of information technology.

Steps in business process redesign.   Two important questions are, How can IT support business processes? and How can business processes be transformed using IT? These questions can be answered by understanding the five steps to redesigning business processes with IT.

Figure 4–10

IT capabilities and their organizational impacts

IT CAPABILITY	ORGANIZATIONAL IMPACT
Transactional	IT can transform unstructured processes into routinized transactions.
	Example: IT can support an admissions decision process by building predefined minimum admissions criteria into an admissions application-screening process with the use of an automated system.
Geographical	IT can transfer information with rapidity and ease across large distances, making processes independent of geography.
	Example: Application-development teams in India can use COBOL and other procedural languages to create business information systems that are implemented, tested, and ultimately used by many American firms.
Analytical	IT can bring complex analytical methods to bear in a process.
	Example: American Express has designed an expert system for credit authorization that capitalizes on the knowledge and experience of expert credit authorizers and applies expert analytical methods to the credit decision-making process.
Informational	IT can bring vast amounts of detailed information into a process.
	Example: In the process of making budgetary decisions, managers need access to details of past activity. A budget database can provide access to detailed historical information and can effectively support the budgetary analysis process.
Sequential	IT can enable changes in the sequence of tasks in a process, often allowing multiple tasks to be worked on simultaneously.
	Example: The redesign of the new product design and manufacturing process at Xerox was made possible through the design of a centralized database of product-design specifications, which could be updated and referred to during various stages of the product-development process.
Knowledge Management	IT allows the capture and dissemination of knowledge and expertise to improve a process.
	Example: The use of group support systems, including electronic mail, computer-based meeting systems, and electronic conferencing, provides opportunities for the sharing of meeting minutes, agenda, and historical information on business plans and activities.
Tracking	IT allows the tracking of task status, inputs, and outputs.
	Example: The use of a project-management reporting system can provide information on project status, activities, and deliverables to team members and to management on an ongoing basis and as these activities and accomplishments are updated.
Disintermediation	IT can connect two parties within a process who would otherwise communicate through an intermediary.
	Example: Many applications in electronic commerce are eliminating the middleman. Using Internet-based facilities, customer can order computers, T-shirts, office supplies, and a vast array of other products and services over the World Wide Web.

1. Develop business vision and process objectives. Business objectives are time and cost reductions as well as quality improvement. These objectives should be quantified (e.g., we will increase productivity by 40 percent) and prioritized.

2. Identify processes to be redesigned. It is important to identify critical or bottleneck processes. Two approaches for doing so are the exhaustive approach and the high-impact approach. In the exhaustive approach, management identifies all the business processes and prioritizes them. In the high-impact approach, management selects candidate processes by asking, What is broken? The exhaustive approach can be quite time-consuming, while the high-impact approach focuses on the most critical items.

3. Understand and measure existing processes. It is important to understand the problems of the current system. Since a baseline is needed in order to measure the outcomes of the redesigned process, the time, cost, and outcomes of the current process must be defined before the reengineering effort begins.

4. Identify IT levers. The range of opportunities and ideas for using information technology to support business processes can be investigated and expanded through brainstorming. Participants in this process should be functional-area specialists, information systems professionals, and managers representing various units that could be potentially affected by the process.

5. Design and build a prototype of the process. A prototype of the reengineering process should be implemented. The prototype should be designed to satisfy the original process-design objectives. As you will see, experience gained from implementing the prototype will offer some new ideas and will contribute to an iterative approach to developing a new technology-supported process.

Case Studies in Business Process Redesign

The following case studies, apply IT to the five steps in business process redesign.

Case: Mutual Benefit Life

1. Develop business vision and process objectives.

Mutual Benefit Life wanted to reduce the time and cost of underwriting an insurance policy in order to provide competitive, timely service to its customers.

2. Identify processes to be redesigned.

The process to be redesigned is underwriting an insurance policy. The current process involves 40 steps, more than 100 people, 12 functional areas, and 80 separate jobs.

3. Understand and measure existing processes.

After identifying the current problems and setting the baseline, management established a goal of improving productivity by 40 percent.

4. Identify IT levers.

In reengineering the underwriting process, Mutual Benefit Life created a new role (the case manager) to perform and coordinate all underwriting tasks centrally. This decision-making process was made possible by providing each case manager with a workstation-based computer system capable of pulling data from all over the company to support underwriting decisions.

5. Design and build a prototype of the process.

In the prototyping process, Mutual Benefit Life made some organizational changes. After a brief startup period, the firm learned that some underwriting cases needed two additional roles: specialists, such as lawyers or medical directors in knowledge-intensive fields, and clerical assistance. With the new roles and the redesigned process, senior managers at Mutual Benefit Life believed the company would reach the 40 percent productivity improvement goal.

Case: Use of an Executive Information System at Xerox

1. Develop business vision and process objectives.

In this case technology was used to improve the review of division-based strategic plans at Xerox. The primary objectives were to cut the time and cost of management decision making and to improve the quality and effectiveness of decision making as well.

2. Identify processes to be redesigned.

The process to be redesigned was the corporate-planning process. It involved the reporting, analysis, and compilation of division-based strategic plans and their integration into an overall corporate plan.

3. Understand and measure existing processes.

Prior to the redesign of the planning process, the current process was somewhat haphazard, with each division preparing planning documents in different formats and supplying different types of information to the corporate headquarters. The problems were lack of communication, poor coordination, and delayed decision making.

4. Identify IT levers.

With the design of an executive information system, division plans were sent over the Xerox network to all corporate management committee members so that the members could read and discuss the plans beforehand and could move forward to making decisions at the review meetings. The benefits were access to timely information and better communication. As one manager put it, "The system enables us to communicate at higher speed and in greater depth."

5. Design and build a prototype of the process.

As Xerox executives gained experience with the executive information system, they were able to develop additional uses for it.

Types of Business Processes and the Role of Information Technology

In determining how information technology can support the redesign of business processes, it is useful to use two additional frameworks.

The first framework describes how information technology can affect *entities,* including interorganizational, interfunctional, and interpersonal entities.

Interorganizational processes take place between two or more business organizations. An example of a process affecting interorganizational entities is the process of ordering from a supplier. Information technology can impact this process by lowering transactions costs. For example, when Dillards finds that a style of pants falls below a specific inventory level, it electronically notifies Haggar, the supplier. If Haggar doesn't have the cloth to manufacture the pants, it electronically notifies Burlington Industries, the manufacturer. These electronic linkages between the retailer and supplier and between the supplier and manufacturer enable all parties to cut costs, maintain sufficient inventories, and meet customers' needs.

Interfunctional processes cross several functional or divisional boundaries. For example, information technology can facilitate new-product development by creating opportunities to work across geographical boundaries and by affording greater simultaneity. The May Company network, which includes such retail chains as Lord and Taylor, Filene's, Hecht's, Kaufmann's, Strowbridge and Clothier, and Famous Barr, illustrates this process. At May's corporate headquarters in St. Louis, product designers prepare manufacturing specifications for new garments, such as jackets and shirts. These specifications are communicated to manufacturing plants in Seoul, Kuala Lumpur, Hong Kong, and other Far Eastern cities over a satellite-based high-bandwidth areawide network, making it possible for May Company managers to receive competitive bids from these manufacturers and to place orders for finished goods on a timely basis. The network allows the May Company to provide timely merchandise to a nationwide network of over 350 retail stores in a cost-effective and timely manner.

Interpersonal processes involve tasks within and across small work groups, typically within a function or department. An example of an interpersonal process is approving a bank loan. Information technology can impact this type of process by creating opportunities for role and task integration through access to network-based applications and shared databases. Using both internal and external databases available via a network, a bank loan officer can handle decision making from the desktop, thereby avoiding delays and fragmentation. Network-based applications that support decision making include electronic mail, computer conferencing, and electronic meetings. The case managers at Mutual Benefit Life Insurance also used computer-based databases to integrate information and decentralize decision making to the desktop so that they could make underwriting decisions on a timely basis.

Another framework that is useful in describing how information technology supports business activities describes both operational and managerial activities.

Operational activities involve the day-to-day carrying out of the organization's basic business purpose, such as filling a customer order. Information technology can support operational activities by reducing time and cost and by increasing the quality of output.

Managerial activities enable managers to control, plan, or provide resources for operational processes. An example is developing a budget. Information technology can support this type of process by improving analysis or by increasing participation in decision making. Automated tools supporting managerial productivity, including spreadsheet software, electronic mail, computer conferencing, and access to shared databases, are influential in providing technology support for managerial activities. In this chapter, you have already learned about Xerox's Executive Information System that provides automated support for corporate planning.

How Information Technology Applications Improve Business Processes

There are many examples of how information technology can become an enabler of process innovation. To get a better understanding of this topic, you should become familiar with generic applications for three important types of business processes: product development, order fulfillment, and logistics.

Applications supporting product development processes.   Five key applications of information technology deal with product development. Information technology can support *automated design* processes that improve the speed of design and prototyping. At Xerox, for example, an automated design tool optimizes paper path designs for new copiers. *Simulation* technology enables process designers to test the workings of a proposed systems design before building it. *Tracking systems* enable managers to continuously track the status of products or processes throughout the systems development life cycle. The fourth product development application, *decision analysis systems,* provides information on when to send a product to market, or when to delay its entry. Finally, *interorganizational communications systems* help coordinate the product development process by providing repositories of common information on product designs, components, and specifications via electronic messaging, electronic conferencing, and bulletin board systems.

Applications supporting order fulfillment processes.   In terms of order fulfillment, information technology can improve processes that begin when a customer makes a request and end when revenue is collected. These order fulfillment processes range from product choice and electronic messaging to electronic data interchange (EDI). *Product choice systems* are designed to match customers' needs with product solutions like, Digital's XCON, an expert system designed to configure computer systems to meet customers' needs. Another set of applications deals with *forecasting,* or predicting customer demand. For example, the airlines use complex yield-management software to manipulate seat prices to maximize revenue. Another simple, yet effective, use of technology is *voice communications.* Voice messaging systems can facilitate effective communications between customers and sales representatives and even be used to transfer calls to the appropriate destination. *Electronic marketing applications* enable customers to order many products and services over the Internet. Finally, EDI networks enable corporate customers to send and receive orders, to check the shipment status on orders, and to exchange forms of various types.

Applications supporting logistical processes.   Logistical processes deal with the transmission of goods between an organization and its suppliers and customers. Information technology can support logistical processes in a number of ways, using locational, recognition, asset management, and logistical planning systems. *Locational systems* provide information on the location of people and goods. As an example, the Shipment Management System developed by Union Pacific Technologies enables customers such as Dow Chemical and Ford Motor Company to track freight shipments on-line and receive timely reports regarding shipment and delivery status. A second type of system that supports logistical processes is a *recognition system.* One of the most common recognition systems is the bar-coding system used in most retail stores.

Another type of logistics system is the *asset management system.* This type of system tracks the availability of assets, including physical inventory, human resources, and even financial assets. "Smart warehouses," which track incoming and outgoing inventory, are examples of asset management systems.   Finally, *logistical planning systems* are designed to solve complex problems in routing, scheduling, and assigning resources. These systems move men and materiel around the world in military operations, such as the Gulf War, and also allocate inventory from production plants to regional distribution centers in the retail and food manufacturing businesses.

These examples of applications that support product development, order fulfillment, and logistical processes demonstrate how information technology can improve processes by streamlining business procedures and by augmenting productivity and service. In redesigning business processes, the use of automated technology is a critical factor in achieving these ends.

Management Challenges in Business Process Redesign

Business process redesign includes all the challenges of any organizational change. Some of the strategies that apply to orchestrating organizational change also apply to business process redesign. In his book *Managing Transitions,* William Bridges discusses strategies for managing the transition to strategic change.

- Figure out how people will have to modify their behavior and attitudes to make the change work. People need to understand what they must stop doing and what they are going to have to start doing.
- Deal with potential resistance to change by attempting to understand who stands the most to lose under the new system. People resist the process of letting go of the old order, not the change in and of itself.
- Allow managers to experience the problem first hand. For example, create opportunities for managers to field complaints or to deal directly with service problems. It is important to give managers a chance to diagnose the problem and to develop solutions. Then you won't have to sell the solutions because they will belong to the managers.
- Solicit as much feedback from individuals as possible. Managers may not realize that a problem exists. They may resist direct criticism by becoming defensive. If they are asked about the problems they are having, they will be in a better position to recognize and understand the need for changes.
- Stress effective communications. People can deal with transition more effectively if they understand what is going on and how it may affect them.

Managing the transition resulting from business process redesign requires an understanding of organizational changes that occur. In general, the organizational impacts include less reliance on hierarchy, more cross-functional communication and cooperation, and more decision making by middle and lower-level management.

Some specific guidelines for orchestrating organizational change through business process redesign include the following:

- Create task forces with representatives from key line groups, across functional lines.
- Have redesign teams work closely with managers and staff in the units to be affected.
- Encourage the information systems group to take on an advocacy role by convincing management of the power offered by technology to support process redesign.
- Build a new team of industrial engineers. The members should have strong interpersonal skills; an understanding of multiple functional areas; and an understanding of process measurement, systems analysis, and business process redesign.
- Build IT technology platforms that support cross-functional applications— which implies a standardized architecture with extensive communications capability between computing nodes and access to shared databases.

Information Technology and Organizational Structure

In conclusion, you should understand how information technology will impact the structuring of organizations. Today, most organizations are striving to use communications systems to flatten the organizational structure and to provide top management with timely access to information about activities at the operating core.

The flattening of organizational structure has another benefit. In dynamic environments, where responsiveness to customer needs is critical, decision making should be pushed down to first-line managers. The use of powerful desktop workstations that provide access to internal data resources and communications networks support decentralized decision making. The empowerment of the decision maker at the operating level is a fundamental concept of business process reengineering.

Management Summary

The evolution of computers shows that Leavitt and Whisler's prediction over 30 years ago that computers would change organizational structure and the nature of managerial work is coming true. Early attempts to manage paperwork used computers to mechanize tasks such as information retrieval. In the 1980s and 1990s, organizations learned that information technology could provide a competitive edge by adding value to products and services. Telephone links to diagnostic databases, vendor hotlines, and dealer networks supported by telecommunications links all provide better service to customers. Computer systems can link buyers and sellers, manufacturers and dealers, and home offices and branch offices.

Today, as most organizations make the transition to becoming information-based organizations, managers must understand emerging technologies and their applications. These applications should be focused upon efficiency, effectiveness, and transformation. The key to the 1990s will be using information technology to do things that were altogether impossible before.

As a future manager, you will want to become thoroughly acquainted with the challenges that information technology provides. This text will give you an opportunity to learn about information systems, to use information systems tools, and to become familiar with the systems development process—all from the manager's viewpoint.

Key Terms for Managers

business process, 97
business process redesign, 97
effectiveness, 87
efficiency, 87

interfunctional processes, 101
interorganizational processes, 100
interpersonal processes, 101
managerial activities, 101

operational activities, 101
reengineering, 91
transformation, 88

Review Questions

1. What problems occur when data are maintained by different organizational units?

2. What did Ford do to reengineer its accounts payable process?

3. How did a central database help Hewlett-Packard reengineer its purchasing process?

4. Describe an application of information technology that supports the efficiency of the individual manager.

5. Describe an application of information technology that improves the effectiveness of a functional unit of the business.

6. What is *transformation?*

7. Describe an application of information technology that supports transformation of the work of the individual.

8. Describe an application of information technology that supports transformation of the work of a functional unit of the business.

QUESTIONS FOR DISCUSSION

1. Identify two factors that are forcing organizations to rethink existing work methods and procedures?

2. Why is reengineering critical to the process of transformation?

3. Why is it important to focus on reengineering work processes to achieve true productivity gains?

4. Give an example of how work can be reengineered to achieve the following rule: Have those who use the output of a process actually perform the process.

5. Why is the process of reengineering work so difficult to accomplish?

6. What is the role of the champion in business reengineering?

7. What are the five steps in redesigning business processes?

8. What is the difference between the exhaustive approach and the high-impact approach to identifying business processes to be redesigned?

9. How can information technology capabilities be used to leverage the redesign of business processes? Give several examples.

10. What is meant by the geographical capability of information technology as it impacts organizations?

11. How can information technology support the effectiveness of interorganizational entities?

12. How can information technology support managerial activities?

13. Why is information technology a critical factor in making the transition to a "networked" organizational structure?

14. Why do some organizational theoreticians argue that many organizations no longer need a layer of middle management?

PROBLEMS

1. **Impact of technology.** Using the framework for describing applications of information technology shown below, identify the type of impact of each application (e.g., efficiency) and the scope of its impact (e.g., individual).

   a. With the introduction of point-of-sale inventory systems, store managers have timely reports on inventory turnover. When scanners replaced older inventory systems, store managers could use the reports they generated to reduce stock of slow-moving items and to adjust inventory levels to serve customers' needs.

   b. At Windsor University students register for classes using a touch-tone telephone system from home or work, making it much more convenient for them to enroll in classes and giving the university a competitive edge in obtaining students. With the system, students can key in desired course information, check prerequisites, and enter a Visa or MasterCard number for payment.

c. A consumer loan company has experienced difficulty reducing the percentage of bad-debt expense incurred when customers default on loans. In response to this problem, the firm developed a database of loan-applicant information and began to identify the characteristics of customers who were most likely to default on their loans. This system enables the company to screen out high-potential delinquents during the application review process, which has greatly reduced the bad-debt problem.

d. A textbook publisher has developed an inventory control system linking its branches. If one branch has insufficient stock of a text, the distribution manager can query databases of other branches to determine where sufficient stock exists. In this way the publisher can rely on a nationwide inventory of texts to fill orders.

e. Information technology can help sales managers align their sales incentive strategies with market trends. One retail bank developed a system to allocate its salespersons' time to pushing new financial services with the highest number of potential clients. With data on customers' financial holdings, the salespersons could direct their attention to the most profitable prospects.

2. **Reengineering case studies.**   In this chapter you learned how the following organizations used reengineering. Explain how information technology was a major factor in facilitating the reengineering of each process.

a. Ford's accounts payable process.
b. Mutual Benefit Life's application-screening process.
c. Hewlett-Packard's purchasing process.

3. **IT and reengineering.**   In this chapter you also learned how information technology is critical to the reengineering of business processes and the ultimate transformation of organizations. How can managers participate in the reengineering effort? How can MIS professionals contribute to business reengineering and business process redesign?

4. **Interview.**   Arrange an interview with an MIS manager in a local business or company. Ask the following questions about a business process that has been redesigned and supported with the use of information technology:

a. What were the overall business objectives to be achieved by using technology to support a business process?
b. What specific business process(es) are being redesigned?
c. What problems with the existing business process(es) led to the redesign effort?
d. How was information technology used to support the redesign of the business process(es)?
e. What was the role of management in the business process redesign effort? What was the role of the information systems group?
f. What has been the overall impact of the project?
g. What are the current issues confronting MIS in your firm?

SELECTED INTERNET REFERENCE SITES

Reengineering

Reengineering the Reengineering Process
www.flex.net/users/mcgovern/index.shtml

Software Reengineering Web Home Page
www.erg.abdn.ac.uk/users/brant/sre/index.html

Reengineering Forum   www.reengineer.org/

Reengineering—Business Process Reengineering
www.prosci.com/xbpr_ah1.htm

Reengineering…Japanese Style
techweb.cmp.com/iw/509/04mtsr.htm

SEI Reengineering Center: Perspectives on Legacy
     System Reengineering
www.sei.cmu.edu/~reengineering/guide/lsysree.html

The Change Management Toolkit for Reengineering
www.utsi.com/wbp/reengineering/index.html

BAI Software Reengineering
www.baiengineering.com/reeng.html

Re-engineering of Internal Services
www.nrcan.gc.ca/reengin/reengin_.htm

The Hocus-Pocus of Reengineering
www.strassmann.com/pubs/hocus-pocus.html

Reengineering Resource Repository: Research Groups
www.ee.gatech.edu/users/linda/revengr/revgps.html

Reengineering Survey
www.flex.net/users/mcgovern/reengineering.html

Enabling Reengineering with Client-Server Computing
www.csc.com/about/cli_serv.html

SELECTED REFERENCES AND READINGS

Benjamin, R.; C. Dickinson; and J. Rockart. "Changing Role of the Corporate Information Systems Officer." *MIS Quarterly* 9, no. 3 (1985), pp. 177–88.

Cash, J. I.; R. G. Eccles; N. Nohria; and R. L. Nolan. *Building the Information-Age Organization: Structure, Control, and Information Technologies.* Burr Ridge, Il.: Richard D. Irwin, 1994.

Davenport, T. *Process Innovation: Reengineering Work Through Information Technology.* Boston: Harvard Business School Press, 1993.

Hammer, M. "Reengineering Work: Don't Automate, Obliterate." *Harvard Business Review* 68, no. 4 (July–August 1990), pp. 104–12.

Lucas, H. C. Jr. "Utilizing Information Technology: Guidelines for Managers." *Sloan Management Review,* Fall 1986, pp. 39–47.

SOLVING PROBLEMS AT SOFTWARE REENGINEERING COMPANY (SRC), INC.

BACKGROUND

In early 1969 Stanley Pyszynski retired from a division of a very large computer company that provided computer services to the United States Department of Defense (DOD). He had worked for the last 10 years in the burgeoning computer industry and had quite a reputation as a senior systems analyst and computer programmer. Shortly after his retirement, his old firm asked Stanley if he would like to continue to work in a consulting capacity. Stanley agreed and formed the Software Support Company (SSC). SSC was located in St. Louis, which was home to many large DOD civilian and military agencies.

SSC started out as a very small firm. In fact, Stanley was the sole proprietor and sole employee, but business grew rapidly. Stanley hired new employees to handle the additional computer programming contracts SSC landed in the early 1970s. SSC's line of business was somewhat unusual because most large companies in the 1970s had their own data processing department. These companies could afford the cost of expensive mainframe technology in use in the 1970s and did not need to contract for outside computer programming assistance. For this reason SSC focused on winning government contracts.

In 1975 Stanley took the firm public with an initial stock offering. By now the firm employed more than 200 full-time workers. SSC continued to prosper, and in 1979 Stanley retired for good; his son Joseph took over leadership of the firm. Joe had a bachelor's degree in computer science and a master's of business administration degree with a specialization in management information systems. He had worked for his father for a number of years and understood the software contracting business.

One of Joe's first moves was to change the firm's strategic direction. Joe wanted to continue the firm's "bread and butter" business in DOD contract software development, but he also recognized the growing demand for contract software development within private industry. For years, data processing departments in many large firms had been unable to meet the increased demand for information systems within their firms. Joe believed that many of these firms might be willing to hire other companies to develop information systems on a contract basis.

Joe changed the name of the firm to Software Reengineering Company (SRC), Inc. He was well ahead of his time in using the term *reengineering,* or the redesign of existing computer-based information systems to add new functionality. New functionality typically improves existing business processes, that is, the ways in which businesses do business. Joe recognized that many computer information systems need to be upgraded to take advantage of new computer technologies, such as database management systems. SRC enjoyed a considerable advantage in the contract software development industry because very few firms were providing this type of service. Joe also moved the corporate headquarters to Alexandra, Virginia, in order to be close to the headquarters of major DOD agencies because DOD software development was still the firm's main business.

Today SRC is a nationwide firm with offices in a number of U.S. cities. A large regional office is still maintained in St. Louis. Other regional centers are located in Chicago (Illinois), Tuscaloosa (Alabama), and San Jose (California). Current new site proposals include Seattle and New York. SRC organizes its regional offices along divisional lines. Each office has three divisions: defense contract software division; corporate contract software division; and contract training/support division. The defense contract software division is responsible for developing information systems on a contract basis for various agencies of the U.S. Government's Department of Defense. The corporate contract software division performs similar services for client firms in private industry. The contract training support division provides training and support on an outsourcing basis for both DOD and private industry clients.

CURRENT SITUATION

On Friday afternoon, Malivai Washington, executive vice president in charge of the St. Louis regional office, was reviewing a progress report he had received from Susan Liu, regional vice president of marketing. Ms. Liu had been hired two years ago, and Malivai had confidence in her skill and knowledge of contract computer software sales.

In his seven years with the firm, Malivai had never read such a negative report. In it Ms. Liu provided detailed information that clearly showed that SRC was losing market share in its main market, DOD contract software development (see Figure C1-1). The private industry contract software development area wasn't growing, but at least it wasn't losing market share. Most alarming was the fact that Ms. Liu expected this trend to continue at least for the near future. The only market area where growth was evident was in SRC's software training/support business, and market share in this area was growing very slowly.

The report pinned blame for DOD market share losses on the firm's inability to deliver contract software products to customers on time and within estimated contract costs. Even when projects were completed on time, the actual software development time required to complete a project was generally excessive compared to the development time that Malivai knew competitors were achieving. Although Ms. Liu did not directly accuse any specific manager of incompetence, the report indirectly cast doubt on the performance of Marvin Albert, regional chief of the defense contract software division.

Malivai had been developing doubts about Mr. Albert's abilities for the past year or so, even though Marvin had 9 years of experience with SRC on the job and 12 years of previous experience as a senior systems analyst/programmer and MIS project manager. How, Susan asked in her report, could her sales contracting people be expected to meet the firm's revenue and cost targets if Marvin's side of the firm continually took more time than was contracted for to complete projects? Malivai decided to meet with Marvin early next week to discuss the situation.

Figure C1–1

Market share projections

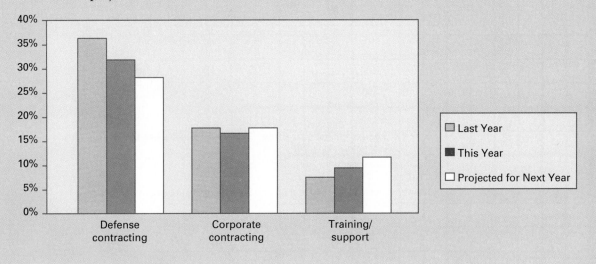

SRC's Three Business Areas

The St. Louis office is typical of other SRC satellites. Located on the west side of St. Louis at the Del Monte Plaza in the Platinum Building, it is divided into the three divisions already noted. Each division has a division chief and several permanently assigned project team leaders. In addition, a pool of skilled computer professionals is assigned to each division, although these personnel may be cross-assigned to another division to meet contract requirements. (See Figure C1–2 for the typical contract software division organization.)

SRC provides software development and training to DOD agencies and private firms in a variety of ways. When a company contracts for outside computer support, this is commonly termed *outsourcing.* Here's how outsourcing works. Most large firms have an internal information systems department (formerly termed *data processing,* but now referred to by the acronym *MIS*-management information systems). An in-house MIS department is an expensive, though necessary, department in industries that are information-intensive, such as the insurance industry, the banking industry, or the U.S. Army personnel management business. Most of the expense of operating an MIS department arises from the salaries that information systems professionals command. A senior MIS analyst/programmer may be paid anywhere from $45,000 to $75,000 per year. A skilled database administrator may command a salary in excess of $70,000 per year.

An additional factor that affects the cost of information systems development in companies is the tremendous demand for MIS support. Computer technology has been integrated into almost every area of business from personnel management to marketing research to financial management to job scheduling. Typical company offices are highly dependent on computer support for their daily activities. In many firms the demand for information systems support outstrips the capabilities of the internal MIS department to meet demand. These companies often search for an outside agency or firm to help provide the MIS support they need. This situation occurs in both public and private industry; thus SRC is positioned perfectly from a market standpoint to meet the needs of these client firms.

When a firm signs an outsourcing contract with SRC, the contract usually stipulates in detail the nature of the information systems product that SRC will deliver. Typically, SRC is asked to reengineer an existing information system in order to enable the client firm to upgrade to new computer technology. For example, SRC contracted with one large, regional retail firm to reengineer its sales-

Figure C1–2

Typical contract software division organization at SRC

Division chief (1)	
Team 1—Project team leader	**Team 2—Project team leader**

Pool of trained MIS professionals available to be assigned to a team
- Project team leaders (2 to 3)
- Senior analysts (4 to 6)
- Analyst/programmers (12 to 14)
- Scientific programmers (2)
- Fourth-generation-language experts (2 to 4)
- Systems programmers/administrators (2 to 3 who usually serve both teams and report to the division chief)
- Database administrator (1 who serves both teams and reports to the division chief)
- Data communications engineer (1 who serves both teams and reports to the division chief)
- Client/server systems administrator (2 who usually serve both teams and report to the division chief)

order-entry system to incorporate database management systems technology and client/server computer technology to replace an aging mainframe computer system. (See Figure C1–3 for a GANTT chart showing the typical phases and tasks involved in completing a contract software programming project. Note the overlap in task phases).

SRC's approach to large software development contracts is to organize a project team with a team leader and the appropriate mix of skilled MIS professionals (systems analysts, computer programmers, systems engineers, data communications specialists, etc.) to accomplish the job. This same approach is used within both the defense contract software and corporate contract software divisions.

SRC's contract training/support division also provides computer information systems training and support on an outsourcing basis. SRC provides this service in a number of ways. One approach is for SRC to send training instructors to the location of the contracting firm. SRC trainers provide instruction on the use of computer technology and information systems for periods that range from as little as one day to as long as two weeks. For example, SRC recently completed a very successful training session for personnel managers at the U.S. Army's Reserve Personnel Administration Center in St. Louis. The managers learned how to use a new computer system for tracking the assignment of Army reservists around the world.

SRC also uses training rooms at its St. Louis regional center and at other regional centers to provide scheduled training that is advertised to all of SRC's client firms. Client firms typically send their workers to the SRC training site for schooling in new computer technologies such as client/server development software.

The contract training/support division also provides on-site support on an outsourcing basis. Client firms contract with SRC to provide skilled MIS professionals who have special skills, such as data communications, to be on-site for extended time periods, often for as long as one year. Client firms pay more to SRC to provide such professionals than they would if they hired a full-time worker, but when the job is finished, the SRC worker is released back to the firm and the outsourcing arrangement is terminated. This approach is more satisfactory than one that involves hiring a full-time worker based on temporary job demands.

Figure C1–3

Typical tasks in a contract software project

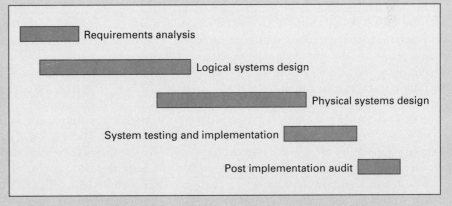

Time duration for each phase (task) in a software project

Note: Logical systems design includes (1) screen layout designs, (2) report designs, (3) database modeling/design, and (4) programming specification writing, (5) process flow modeling, (6) menu/window design, and (7) other design tasks.

Physical systems design includes (1) program coding and testing, (2) development of the test/implementation plan, (3) building system components using Computer-Aided Software Engineering tools, (4) database implementation, and (5) other design tasks.

THE MEETING

"Marv, I'm extremely concerned about our ability to meet our customer's needs," Malivai said in getting directly to the point of the meeting. "Take a look at this chart showing our market share over the last two years and projecting next year's performance." Malivai showed Marvin the data from Figure C1–1.

"Yes, sir. I received a copy of Ms. Liu's report last week. I went over it again this morning," replied Marvin. "I've been investigating the situation in order to develop a plan to respond to this report. Actually, I believe we are in pretty good shape."

"Really?" queried Malivai with a look of disbelief. "Maybe you can give me some advance idea as to your findings." So, Marvin proceeded to explain the problem from his perspective. SRC supports many projects each day. In fact, a given project team may be organized with personnel to support many projects on a concurrent basis. The contract provides guidelines on how long SRC expects each task in a project to take for completion. Of course, these guidelines are for the average MIS professional worker. Total project time does not reflect the time that these workers must spend in activities other than those associated with a project, such as attending mandatory meetings and studying new computer technologies.

Marvin explains that most project task estimates are based on the firm's past performance with similar activities. Actual task times may vary depending on an MIS professional's experience and skill level. For example, the task of using a computer-aided software engineering (CASE) tool to design the layout for a computer window screen that is part of a computer software product may take a new analyst/programmer twice as long as it would take a senior analyst/programmer. On the other hand, a new analyst/programmer might accomplish a task quicker than the senior worker if the new employee has recent experience with a new CASE tool that is in use on a particular project. "Quite simply, employees are not equally interchangeable," explains Marvin.

Further, each software team also support computer information system products that have been recently delivered to client firms. New software, especially the programs that make up the software, often have software 'bugs' that are actually errors in program coding. Sometimes an MIS worker must be pulled off a new project to respond to an emergency request to repair a 'bug' in a recently delivered system. When the MIS worker returns to the new development task, he or she may have forgotten what approach he or she was using to write a computer program or complete a design task. The worker may have to start the task all over again, resulting in some lost time.

"But you can be certain that we get the job done as quickly as anyone could, given the circumstances," beamed Marvin. "Our MIS professionals often work late into the night to get the job done. I've also been able to improve our internal communications by having all employees carry a beeper and a cellular telephone so that they can be reached at any time, day or night. Of course, we have also had to deal with employee turnover. As you know Malivai, there's tremendous demand for MIS professionals these days. Almost every week a headhunter lures one of our employees into taking a job elsewhere. Then we have to hire and train replacements."

"What effect does this have on getting projects completed?" queried Malivai. "Well, I'm not certain that it has any significant impact on our delivery of projects," replied Marvin, although he didn't look very convincing. "For example, recently one of my best senior programmers was assigned a really tough programming task. Of course, with her skills, I also use her to put out the fires so to speak whenever a bug surfaces in one of our new information systems. Why just last week, I had to pull her off of a tough programming task several times to help with problems elsewhere. But each time she returned and worked that much harder. She had to stay until 3.00 AM last night, er, I mean this morning, but she finished the project. I told her how proud I was of her," said Marvin in a beaming fashion as he continued to discuss details of the project.

"Well, that's very good Marvin," interrupted Malivai with a little edge of irritability in his voice. "But we need to focus on this report. As you can see, about 20 percent of the contract projects your division completed within the last six months were delivered anywhere from two weeks to two months after the estimated project completion date. Almost 60 percent were over cost in terms of the number of worker hours actually used to complete the projects. We have to absorb the cost of paying our workers for their overtime because we can't bill a DOD agency more than the dollar amount for which we contracted. Susan's latest report also shows that our recent projects have more programming errors after project completion than we historically experienced. What can we do about these problems?"

"Maybe we need more training," answered Marvin with a shrug of his shoulders.

PROBLEM SOLVING

Problem-Solving Processes

One of the most important responsibilities you will someday have as a manager is problem solving. Fortunately for us, as the chapters in this section of the textbook indicate, the ability to resolve problems can be learned and improved on by studying various techniques that aid the problem-solving process.

Figure C1–4 provides a conceptual diagram of the problem-solving process. Quite simply, solving a problem requires taking action that moves you from the *present state* to the *desired state*. The state of existence is evaluated by using one or more performance measures to determine the achievement of an established standard(s) or ob-

jective(s). When a problem does *not* exist, the evaluation will reveal the present and desired state to be one and the same; that is, the standard is being met or exceeded.

The problem-solving process has several elements. You must be skilled at defining the problem. Conceptually, this is quite simple. The *problem* is defined as the failure to be in the desired state. This failing is best recognized when the system under evaluation has a clearly specified *performance standard* or *objective*. For example, production output at a factory work site may be low. Low output is the present state. The desired state is one that includes high production output. The low output is easier to recognize if a standard for production exists.

In actual practice defining a particular problem can be difficult. Many people tend to confuse the problem with symptoms of the problem. *Symptoms* are conditions produced by a problem. Low factory production may be a symptom of poor employee motivation. In turn, poor employee motivation can result from an inadequate benefit package, faulty supervision, inferior work conditions, or a number of other factors. To identify the problem properly, you must gather evidence by working through the cause–effect chain of events. If a firm appears to have a multitude of problems, you should ensure that you are not confusing symptoms with problems. In fact, one or just a few problems can make it appear that a firm is overwhelmed with difficulties.

Figure C1–4

The problem-solving process

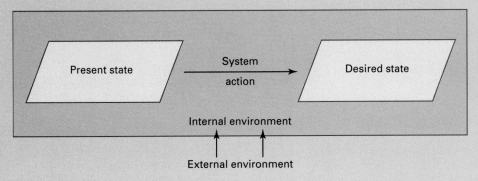

Once a problem is identified, some managers are quick to implement a plan of action to resolve the situation. When time is of the essence, this approach may be the only one that is satisfactory. However, when time allows, managers should identify *alternative* courses of action. The tendency to skip this step in problem-solving must be avoided whenever possible.

Occasionally, managers may find that some alternatives, regardless of how attractive they appear, result in failure because constraints upon the situation are not factored into the decision-making process. *Constraints* represent internal or external limits on courses of action. Constraints affecting employee morale can include the lack of a union labor relations contract, nonavailability of replacement personnel, or limits on funds allocated for worker benefits.

Problem-Solving Approaches

Various approaches to problem solving are available. One technique is to conduct the analysis based on a theory or hypothesis that is relevant to the situation. Another approach involves the use of intuition. When using intuition in problem solving, we primarily rely on past experience. As with other approaches, intuition may require you to make assumptions about the problem situation. By combining past experience, assumptions, and knowledge of the current situation, you select the best course of action.

One of the more favored techniques for analyzing and solving problems is the *systems approach*. This technique is a multiple-step method that is based on systems theory as described in Part I of the textbook.

The Systems Approach

We recommend the systems approach as both a method for analyzing this and other cases in the text and for diagnosing problems you may later encounter in operational settings. An advantage of the systems approach is that it enables you to incorporate other techniques. Additionally, the systems approach provides sufficient structure to the problem-solving process to reduce the probability of skipping a critical stage of the analysis procedure. In solving the cases in this text, you should combine the systems approach with the application of appropriate theory.

The steps in the systems approach outlined in this section of the textbook can be summarized as follows:

1. Define the problem based on the performance criteria.
2. Accumulate evidence about the problem.
3. Identify alternative courses of action.
4. Evaluate the alternatives.
5. Select the best alternative.
6. Evaluate the result based on the performance criteria.

Additionally, understanding the system within which the problem seems to lie will help you define the problem. This process requires you to identify the system in terms of the boundaries, inputs, and outputs. You should also determine if management is adequately monitoring output quality and screening input quality. Another important question to answer is whether or not management has in place the necessary information technology to aid in monitoring the overall system's functioning components.

Any assumptions you make during an evaluation—that is, information not available in a case or operational setting—need to be clearly stated. You should provide your rationale for making assumptions to show that they are reasonable, logical extensions of material evidence uncovered during your investigation.

Case Questions and Exercises

1. Do any of the officers within SRC's St. Louis regional center have clearly specified performance objectives for the operations within the center? Are these objectives measurable? Is there a standard of performance for contract computer software projects? If so, how is it being measured?

2. Analyze the case from a systems perspective. Identify the business system that would be labeled "contract computer

software development" and the various system components. Suggest which component or components are faulty.

3. Using a systems approach to problem solving, analyze SRC's problem in meeting contract project completion dates. Analyze Marvin's use of MIS professionals to fix problems that arise with contract information systems that have already been delivered.

4. Based on your analysis in questions 1, 2, and 3, write a detailed report analyzing SRC's

situation. If any procedures or resources are required to achieve objectives, determine the impact of the new procedures or resources on the St. Louis regional center's operations. Clearly specify any assumptions you make. Ensure that you clearly specify what you believe to be the problem or problems in this situation and then list the symptoms that led you to the identification of the problems.

COMPUTER SYSTEM RESOURCES

PART TWO IS A CONCISE SURVEY of the basic computer resources available to the manager. These resources include computer systems, hardware and software, file management and database systems, and communications systems hardware and software, including distributed systems, the Internet, and office communications systems.

    Whether you are reviewing the material or reading about it for the first time, it is essential that you have a basic knowledge of these computer resources so that you may learn how to use them to help you manage successfully.

CHAPTER 5
COMPUTER
HARDWARE

CHAPTER 6
COMPUTER
SOFTWARE

CHAPTER 7
FILE AND DATABASE
MANAGEMENT
SYSTEMS

CHAPTER 8
COMMUNICATIONS
SYSTEMS BASICS

CHAPTER 9
DISTRIBUTED
SYSTEMS, THE
INTERNET, AND
OFFICE
COMMUNICATIONS

5

COMPUTER HARDWARE

CHAPTER OUTLINE

Manager's View

Computer Systems

Computer Platforms and the Manager

Central Processing Units

Memory

Computer Power

Using More Than One Processor

Types of Computer System
Processing

Secondary Storage Media and Devices

Input and Output Devices

Hardware Standards

Other Acquisition Issues

Management Summary

Key Terms for Managers

Review Questions

Questions for Discussion

Problems

Cases

Selected Internet Reference Sites

Selected References and Readings

- A sales manager wants to know what type of computer system she should buy for her salespeople, given that the salespeople work almost entirely on the road and need to take the computer to the customer's site.

- A production manager wants to know whether he should buy or lease some computer systems that he wants his product engineers to use to improve their design of new products. The production manager estimates that the computer systems should not become obsolete for at least three years.

- A receiving department manager wants to know what kinds of computer systems her forklift truck operators can use to enter data about palettes of parts they remove from freight cars and place in inventory. To speed the unloading process, she doesn't want the operators to dismount from the trucks to enter data.

- A human resource director wants to identify computer systems that would be the least stressful to the physical health of his organization's work force . He wants to know how to avoid the common complaints from workers who must use computers repetitively and constantly throughout the day.

- The top management of a corporation is faced with replacing its large computer system and wants to know what its options are. It wants to know whether it should replace its large computer system with smaller computer systems and the downside to using smaller computer systems.

- The proprietor of an accounting firm wants to know whether she should replace her outdated computer systems now or wait a few months when prices for these computer systems will probably be lower.

Computers have become a common tool on managers' desks. It is almost certain that as a manager you will use a computer system. Many managers rely on computer-generated information to help them make decisions. Furthermore, decisions regarding the acquisition and use of computer systems, especially small computer systems, are increasingly being made at the department level of organizations. As a result, management concerns regarding the acquisition of computer systems have grown and include not only what systems should be acquired but also when, how, and from whom they should be acquired. Because rapid change in computer technology is ongoing, acquisition decisions are always made in a very dynamic environment. To help departmental managers make rational decisions about computer systems in such a complex and dynamic environment, they need a basic understanding of computer systems.

The computer industry is undergoing constant change. The major vendors of yesterday may not be the major vendors of tomorrow. Many types of computers produced today are regarded as commodities, and the names of their manufacturers do not carry the weight they did in the past with buyers. Earlier, many computer systems were purchased directly from the manufacturer, who delivered and installed them on the buyer's site. Today, many computers are purchased through the mail or from discount stores and the buyer is expected to assemble the hardware and install some or all of the programs. Managers in this environment must become knowledgeable about computer systems so that they can set specifications for the systems they buy and deploy the systems they purchase.

To be an effective computer user, you must not view computer systems as mysterious devices, but rather as everyday working tools. Fortunately, computer systems have become much more user-friendly. That is, they have become easier to use for people who are not computer experts. In fact, managers have become directly involved in developing computer information systems that serve their needs. Development of computer information systems by users, or end-user computing, has become an important part of management information systems.

COMPUTER SYSTEMS

Computer systems consist of numerous components, as you will learn in this and the following chapter. One of those components is computer hardware. The term **hardware** refers to computer equipment, the actual machinery used in a computer system. Today, computer system hardware comes in nearly every conceivable shape and size to serve the varying needs of organizations.

Super-computers

Supercomputers are very powerful and specialized computer systems. A supercomputer system is comprised of multiple processors that work together. Supercomputer systems are usually designed to handle scientific and engineering calculations very quickly. Defense agencies and scientific organizations often use these computer systems to process enormous amounts of data rapidly. Because much less powerful and much less expensive systems are able to handle common business applications, supercomputers are not likely to be used for these tasks. A supercomputer system with its attachments may fill a large room and cost many millions of dollars.

Mainframe Computers

Mainframe computer systems are large computers frequently used in large organizations. Some very large organizations use several mainframe computer systems to handle their activities. Mainframe computer systems and their attached devices usually take up an entire room, and they cost from hundreds of thousands to millions of dollars (see Figure 5–1).

Minicomputer Systems

Another type of computer system is the **minicomputer system,** which small organizations or departments in a large organization may use for all their computing needs. Minicomputer systems, costing between $10,000 and $500,000, can fit on a desktop or under a desk. High-powered minicomputers can challenge the power of mainframe systems.

Microcomputer Systems

Microcomputer systems are used by small organizations, executives in large organizations, and even by professionals working out of their homes. In the past IBM set the standards for microcomputer hardware. Many other firms developed microcomputer systems that worked like, or emulated, the IBM-PC, or personal computer. These

Figure 5–1

A mainframe computer system with computer console and disk drives

Courtesy of the International Business Machines Corporation

work-alikes, referred to as IBM-PC *compatibles* or IBM clones, make up one of the two major types of microcomputers sold today in the United States, the other being Apple and Macintosh computer systems. The price of microcomputers varies substantially, ranging from a few hundred to several thousand dollars.

High-powered microcomputers often control and provide resources to other computers in a network. The ability of these systems to handle the volume and complexity of an organization's information-processing tasks challenges minicomputer systems.

Professional Workstations

Some technical and professional persons need high-powered microcomputer systems with high-quality display screens, often called **workstations,** to perform their work (see Figure 5–2). For example, draftsmen may need workstations to create and edit detailed drawings. Computer programmers may need workstations to create and edit complex charts that illustrate the logic of the computer programs they write.

Laptop, Notebook, and Palmtop Systems

The trend for computer systems has been to smaller and smaller sizes (see Figure 5–3). **Desktop** microcomputers were followed by portable computers in the early 80s, which were followed by **laptop** computers in the late 80s, and then by **notebook** and **palmtop** computers in the early 90s.

Personal digital assistants, or PDAs, are small, handheld computer systems that you can use to take notes, keep track of appointments, receive faxes and pages, and complete forms (see Figure 5–4). They include pen-based computers, electronic clipboards, pocket organizers, and other special-function devices. The Apple MessagePad, which weighs about 1 pound, is an example.

Pen-based computers allow you to write or mark on a tabletlike screen with an attached or cordless device that looks like a pen. The handwriting-recognition software converts written or marked data into printed text or other output. The pen can also be used as a pointing device, similar to a mouse. In some applications the tablet screen may display a form to be filled in.

Pen-based computer systems are useful devices for field personnel, such as meter readers, delivery personnel, salespeople, inventory workers, pipeline workers, and even judges at sporting events. A common application for these devices is to display

Figure 5–2

A professional
workstation

Courtesy of Sun Microsystems, Inc.

a form in which you can record data with ease. For example, sales reps can use the devices to take inventory at customer stores and record competitor prices. Also, customer data can be stored in the devices so that the sales rep will not forget a customer's birthday, address, telephone number, or opening or closing times. Some physicians are using pen-based computers to store medical reference material and patient data.

Figure 5–3

The shrinking size
of computer
systems

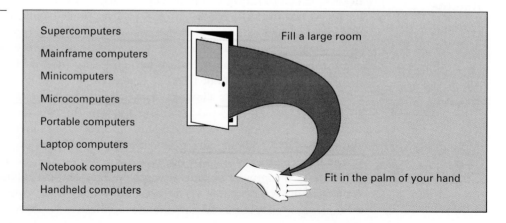

Supercomputers

Mainframe computers

Minicomputers

Microcomputers

Portable computers

Laptop computers

Notebook computers

Handheld computers

Fill a large room

Fit in the palm of your hand

Figure 5–4

A personal digital assistant

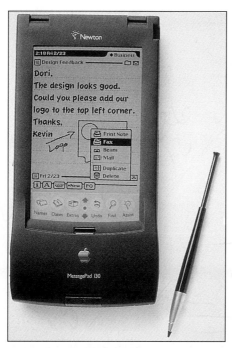

Courtesy of Apple Computers, Inc.

Pocket organizers are palmtop devices that provide a small screen and keyboard or an attached pen. The pocket organizer usually includes a calendar, calculator, address book, notepad, and other handy desktop tools.

Network Computers

Network computers are low-cost computer systems that use the computing power, software, and intelligence of other computer systems to which they connect. Their primary features are their ability to connect quickly and easily to networks, including the Internet. They permit users to view data stored on other computers and to run programs on other computers. Because they use computing resources on other systems, network computers may cost less than other systems.

Classifying a computer system as a microcomputer, minicomputer, mainframe computer, or supercomputer system usually depends on such factors as the amount of memory the system possesses (see the section on memory later in this chapter), the amount of data it can handle at one time (see the discussion of word size later in this chapter), and how many tasks and users it can handle concurrently (see the section on operating systems in the next chapter). Because of advances in technology, the classification system has become fuzzy. That is, many microcomputers are now as powerful as older minicomputers, and newer minicomputers have power that was formerly associated with mainframe computers. Nonetheless, these terms provide a convenient way to classify computers, and they remain in common use. As a manager, however, you should be less concerned with how people classify your computer systems and more concerned with whether those systems fit your needs.

Convergent Computers

Convergent computer systems bring together multiple technologies, such as a multimedia computer system with radio, television, speakerphone, fax/modem, voice-mail machine, compact disk player, and videoconferencing support. Aimed primarily at the home market, the devices appeal to people who wish to combine Internet

Figure 5–5

Sony web TV set—top box and remote control

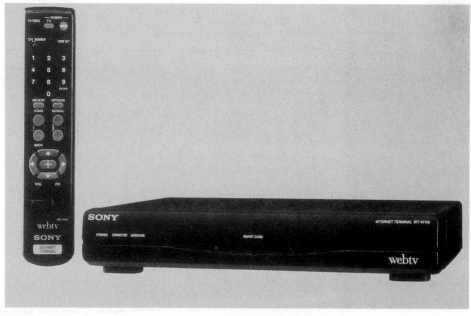

Courtesy of Sony, Inc.

access, computer games, and serious work with a host of other features. Future versions of these devices may include hardware and software to control home systems, such as burglar alarms, interior and exterior lights, and even your coffeepot.

One type of convergent computer system that has reached the market is *web TV* (see Figure 5-5). A web TV device is a television set that also allows users to access the Internet without a full-blown computer system. A box attached to the TV provides for the computing and communications services. The TV screen provides the display unit. Users can switch back and forth from traditional TV fare to Internet access quickly and easily using a remote control device.

Some feel that the recent Federal Communications Commission ruling setting the standard for high definition TV (HDTV) is likely to increase the convergence of TV and computing resulting in a variety of new products. Others feel that browsing the Internet is a personal, not a group, activity. Thus, the success of devices that converge Internet and TV usage is being debated at this writing.

COMPUTER PLATFORMS AND THE MANAGER

The type of computer system you are using for your organization's tasks is often referred to as a **computer platform.** That is, a firm that is using a mainframe computer system to process its sales orders is said to be running its order-entry system on a mainframe platform. All this talk about computer types and platforms may seem academic, but it is really very important to the manager. Because the computing power of minicomputer and microcomputer platforms has increased so greatly, many firms using mainframe computer systems have opted to **downsize** to minicomputer or microcomputer systems (see Manager's Memo 5-1). The major reason for downsizing is to reduce costs. Mainframe computer systems usually cost much more to acquire and less to operate than minicomputer or microcomputer systems do. Smaller computer systems are also usually less expensive to scale up or down to fit an in-

---

Manager's Memo 5–1	DOWNSIZING MAINFRAMES

◤ Many companies are choosing to use high-end microcomputers instead of minicomputers and mainframe computer systems. *The Wall Street Journal* reports that a national food chain dumped its $250,000 mini for a $25,000 multiprocessor microcomputer system. Analysts expect that multiprocessor microcomputers will be able to provide enough computing power to support most organizational tasks. The Jour-

nal quotes Compaq Computer's marketing director as saying:"By the end of the decade, there will be no computing task that you can't perform on a PC-based server."

Source: *The Wall Street Journal*, section B3, January 17, 1995 as described by J. Gehl and S. Douglas in *Innovations*, an on-line electronic magazine, January 22, 1995.

---

creased workload. That is, if a mainframe computer system has reached its maximum capacity, handling even a small additional workload would require the acquisition of another whole mainframe. When a minicomputer or microcomputer is at its maximum, responding to increased workloads requires the acquisition of smaller computing units, with an attendant reduction in cost. On the other hand, managing many small computer systems that have been connected together to do the job of one mainframe may prove to be more complex and more difficult than managing one, large computer system. Thus decisions about computer platforms are important for an organization.

The future of mainframe computer systems remains somewhat clouded. Although mainframe computer system sales dropped in the past as organizations sought to downsize their computer operations, recently mainframe sales have increased. A survey by *Datamation*[1] showed that:

> [A mainframe's use as . . . a server] seems to be relegating [it] to a more specialized role, however. When it comes to implementing new applications, respondents continue to express the trend of past years. New applications will be increasingly put on PCs and workstations. Whereas last year respondents estimated on average that 28% of new applications were scheduled to be installed on PCs, this year they put the figure at 34%. Conversely, new applications for mainframes fell from 53% last year to 42% of new applications this year. And this trend should accelerate in coming years. When asked about the long term, mainframes accounted for only 29% of planned new applications, with PCs and workstations accounting for 44%.

Other reasons for managers to opt for downsizing to computer platforms smaller than mainframes are presented in Chapters 9 and 16.

Regardless of their size and shape or how they are classified, however, all computer systems contain similar basic components. For example, all computer systems contain a **central processing unit (CPU)** and one or more devices to get data into and out of the CPU. Let's look first at the CPU.

CENTRAL PROCESSING UNITS

The CPU is often referred to as the "brain" of the computer system because it contains the *control unit* and *arithmetic/logic unit* (see Figure 5-6). The control unit obtains instructions from the computer system's memory, interprets them, and notifies the

---

[1] F. Guterl, "Mainframes Are Breaking Out of the Glass House," *Datamation* (June 15, 1995) (http://www.datamation.com/PlugIn/issues/June15/DATAM.htm).

other components in the system to carry them out (see Manager's Memo 5–2). The arithmetic/logic unit processes data obtained from memory under the direction of the control unit. The arithmetic/logic unit basically is able to process data in only two ways: (1) arithmetically, such as by adding, subtracting, multiplying, or dividing data; and (2) logically, such as by comparing one group of data with another. Logical processes include comparing one group of data with another to determine whether one group is

- Equal to the other (A = B).
- Not equal to the other (A ≠ B).

Manager's Memo 5–2 | **INSTRUCTION SETS**

One of the differences among CPUs is the *instruction set* they use, or the group of program commands that they understand and can execute. One group of CPUs is *CISC*, or complex instruction set computing systems. The other group is based on *RISC*, or reduced instruction set computing architecture. RISC systems use a small set of frequently used instructions; CISC systems use a larger set of instructions than RISC systems use. For processing that requires only these instructions, RISC systems are very fast. For processing that requires instructions that are not part of the RISC set, RISC systems can be relatively slow.

IBM introduced RISC technology in 1974. Since that time, RISC technology has been used in professional workstations and in other computer systems designed for special uses. IBM introduced a whole line of RISC workstations in the early 1990s based on its RS/6000 processing chip set. This set comprised seven to nine separate chips but was still a 32-bit system. Soon thereafter, a consortium (IBM, Apple, and Motorola) began development of a microcomputer processing chip that would combine the RS/6000 chip set into a single chip called the PowerPC chip. Although the consortium broke up, the PowerPC chip survived.

Microcomputer systems based on Intel's *Pentium* microprocessor debuted in 1993. The Pentium chip, like its Intel predecessors, the 80286, 80386, and 80486, is a CISC chip. Apple Macintosh computer systems use Motorola's 68040 chip, which, like the Pentium, is a CISC processor.

The latest version of Intel's Pentium chip is the MMX (which stands for multimedia extensions) chip. Some people say the MMX represents the greatest change in the architecture of the Intel-based PC in a decade. The chip provides a larger instruction set (57 more instructions) than the standard Pentium chip. These additional instructions allow a computer system to handle video, digital sound, and animation faster than the standard Pentium chip. The chip boosts the performance of multimedia computer systems and is expected to become the standard Intel chip in the near future.

Figure 5–6

A simple model of a CPU and main memory showing the relationship of the control unit, arithmetic/logic unit, and main memory

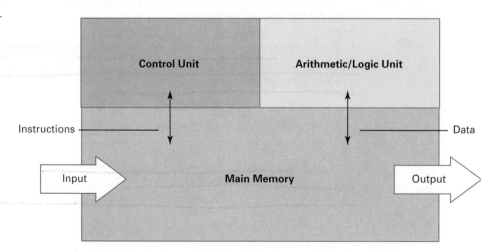

Figure 5–7
The Intel
PentiumPro chip

Courtesy of Intel Corporation.

- Less than the other (A < B).
- More than the other (A > B).
- Equal to or less than the other (A ≤ B).
- Equal to or more than the other (A ≥ B).

Considering the limited functionality of its arithmetic/logic unit, a CPU can perform an astonishing number of varied and complex tasks. The fundamental arithmetic processes and six logical comparisons allow the device to process complex mathematical relationships, control space vehicles, draw detailed pictures on a screen, create musical compositions, emulate some human thought processes, or simply produce paychecks at the end of the week.

On some computers the circuitry for the control unit and the arithmetic/logic unit is contained in a single *silicon chip* (see Figure 5-7) called a **microprocessor.** On a microcomputer the microprocessor chip for the control unit and the arithmetic/logic unit is placed on a board, often called the *motherboard* (see Manager's Memo 5-3), that comprises the heart of the central processing unit.

Computer systems of the future will likely be on a single chip. That is, while the control unit and arithmetic/logic unit are now placed on a microprocessor, future chip technology will allow manufacturers to place all the circuitry for an entire computer system, a phone, or even a digital camera on a single chip. This miniaturization will likely lead to advances in portable computer systems and in the integration of computers with other technologies, such as networking technologies.

Figure 5–8

A simple program for printing address labels

```
1000   OPEN "A", #1, "B : ADLABELS"
1010   WHILE NOT EOF
1020   INPUT #1, LNAME$, FNAME$, MNAME$, ADDRESS$, CITY$, STATE$, ZIP$
1030   LPRINT
1040   LPRINT FNAME$; MNAME$; LNAME$
1050   LPRINT ADDRESS$
1060   LPRINT CITY$; STATE$; ZIP$
1070   LPRINT
1080   LPRINT
1090   WEND
1100   END
```

Manager's Memo 5–3 | **INSIDE A PERSONAL COMPUTER**

◤ Here are some basic components that you will find inside your computer system:

Expansion slots—These slots let you add expansion boards to your computer system. They might include boards that provide parallel and serial ports, mouse ports, faxes, modems, sound, and video adapters.

Single in-line memory modules (SIMMS)—These modules provide the RAM for the system. RAM is where the computer system holds part or all of the programs you use and the data on which you are working.

Motherboard—This board is the heart of the computer system. It provides the electrical connections between the computer system's components, such as the CPU, ROM, and RAM.

Disk controller board—This board connects the disk drives to the CPU and allows the computer system to save and retrieve data from the drives. Many systems provide the connection to the disk drives directly on the motherboard and do not use a special controller board.

Video board—This board allows you to display text, data, and images on your monitor. Your monitor cable connects to this board through the monitor port on the back of your computer system.

Power supply—This component regulates the supply of electricity to the other components of the computer system.

Read-only memory (ROM)—These chips contain the commands your computer needs to get itself going when the power is turned on.

CPU—The brain of the computer system.

Hard drives—These devices allow you to store large amounts of data.

Floppy drives—These devices allow you to store data to and retrieve data from floppy disks.

Source: *PC Today,* April 1990, pp 96-7.

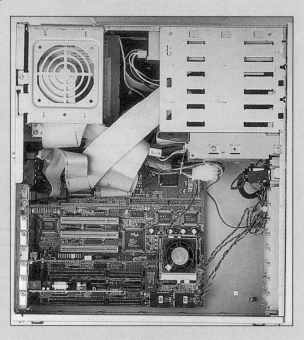

MEMORY

The data you wish the computer system to process is stored in internal memory or **main memory** along with a set of instructions for processing the data called a **computer program** (see Figure 5–8). Chapter 6 discusses computer programs in detail. Main memory usually must contain (1) part or all of the data you want to work on and (2) part or all of the instructions necessary to process the data.

Main memory has three important characteristics: It is usually volatile, it can be accessed randomly, and it is fast. It is usually volatile because the type of memory commonly used for main memory retains data and programs only as long as the system is on. When the system is turned off, all data and programs stored in main memory are lost. Main memory is also called **random access memory (RAM)** because it consists of storage locations in which data can be stored and retrieved directly (see single in-line memory modules, Manager's Memo 5–3). That is, the computer system is able to place or find data at any storage location without having to start at the beginning of main memory and work sequentially through all the locations. To permit the direct access of these memory locations, each location has its own *address*. Main memory is also called *primary storage*.

Main memory, or RAM, is usually more expensive than other types of memory on the basis of the cost per character of data stored. It is also usually faster than other types of memory. When large amounts of data must be stored, other, less expensive and usually slower forms of memory are used. As a result, most computer systems will have *auxiliary memory,* or **secondary storage,** in addition to main memory, or primary storage. Secondary storage usually takes the form of magnetic disks and tapes. Secondary storage devices permit you to store more data and programs than main memory would allow. Thus main memory only has to be big enough to store the current instructions and current data on which you are working. You can store your other instructions and other data externally on magnetic disks or tapes. Both disk and tape systems are explained later in this chapter. For now, you can get the idea of a magnetic disk by visualizing an old phonograph record. You can get the idea of a magnetic tape by visualizing a reel of audiotape.

Data and instructions, or the computer program, are stored in both main memory and secondary storage as *bits,* or *binary digits*. The binary number system uses only two numbers: one and zero. Thus a binary digit has only two states: on and off. "On" and "off" bits form characters such as letters of the alphabet, numerals, and special characters using a code. Samuel Morse used a similar scheme, combining short and long signals (dots and dashes) to represent letters, numerals, and special characters for the Morse code. To complicate matters, several computer codes are in use. Two of the most commonly used codes are *ASCII,* or American Standard Code for Information Interchange, and *EBCDIC,* or Extended Binary Coded Decimal Interchange Code. Figure 5–9 shows how these two codes represent characters.

The EBCDIC code uses eight bits to make up a character. The eight-bit set that represents a letter, numeral, or special character is called a *byte*. The computer system may add another bit to each byte, called a *parity bit,* which the computer uses for checking purposes. ASCII code is often used by personal computer systems. It uses seven bits to construct a character, or a total of eight bits with the parity bit added. IBM mainframe computer systems typically use EBCDIC code. The Digital Equipment Corporation's VAX 9000 mainframe computer system and most microcomputers use ASCII code.

Figure 5–9

ASCII and EBCDIC codes for numerals and letters

Character	EBCDIC	ASCII	Character	EBCDIC	ASCII
0	1111 0000	011 0000	I	1100 1001	100 1001
1	1111 0001	011 0001	J	1101 0001	100 1010
2	1111 0010	011 0010	K	1101 0010	100 1011
3	1111 0011	011 0011	L	1101 0011	100 1100
4	1111 0100	011 0100	M	1101 0100	100 1101
5	1111 0101	011 0101	N	1101 0101	100 1110
6	1111 0110	011 0110	O	1101 0110	100 1111
7	1111 0111	011 0111	P	1101 0111	101 0000
8	1111 1000	011 1000	Q	1101 1000	101 0001
9	1111 1001	011 1001	R	1101 1001	101 0010
A	1100 0001	100 0001	S	1110 0010	101 0011
B	1100 0010	100 0010	T	1110 0011	101 0100
C	1100 0011	100 0011	U	1110 0100	101 0101
D	1100 0100	100 0100	V	1110 0101	101 0110
E	1100 0101	100 0101	W	1110 0110	101 0111
F	1100 0110	100 0110	X	1110 0111	101 1000
G	1100 0111	100 0111	Y	1110 1000	101 1001
H	1100 1000	100 1000	Z	1110 1001	101 1010

The memory capacity of a computer system component is usually measured in terms of the number of bytes, or characters, that it can hold. Usually the measuring unit is 1,024 bytes, or 2^{10} bytes. Because this number is somewhat inconvenient to multiply easily, we usually round off 1,024 bytes to 1,000. Furthermore, we also refer to groups of 1,000 bytes of memory as **kilobytes** (kilo = 1,000) or **KB.** For example, many computers in the past were sold with an advertised main memory of 640KB, which means that they really held 640 × 1,024— or 655,360— bytes of data in main memory. Capacity in bytes is often shortened still further so that 640KB becomes 640K in everyday conversation.

As the amount of memory used in computer systems has grown, the terms **megabytes** (mega = 1,000,000) or **MB** and **gigabytes** (giga = 1,000,000,000) or **GB** of memory have become more common. For example, microcomputer systems with main memory capacities of 32MB can store 32,000,000 bytes of data in main memory. A secondary storage device may store 4GB, or 4,000,000,000 bytes of data.

Software designed for microcomputers often requires megabytes of RAM storage space, and the RAM required for microcomputer applications probably will continue to increase. One way to increase RAM in a microcomputer (and other types of computers, for that matter) is to add *memory boards* to the special memory-board

Figure 5–10

A SIMM board

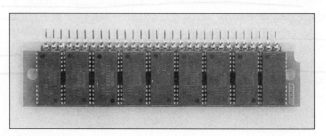

Courtesy of Jameco Electronics Components

slots on the motherboard. These memory slots accept *SIMM boards,* or single in-line memory modules (see Figure 5–10). A SIMM memory board is small and may contain 1MB, 4MB, 8MB, 16MB, or more of RAM. The amount of memory packed on these boards is constantly growing. One vendor has developed a prototype of a 1GB RAM chip.

Many microcomputer systems provide four SIMM memory board slots. If 8MB SIMM boards are used, the internal memory capacity of those microcomputers becomes 32MB of RAM.

The internal memory of your computer system also contains **read-only memory,** or **ROM** (see Manager's Memo 5–3). ROM usually contains programs that help the computer system start up and operate. However, ROM can only be read; it cannot be written to or altered by the user. Also, ROM is not lost when the power is shut off, which is the reason ROM is used for these special programs. You cannot alter the programs in ROM, and the programs are not lost when you turn off the power. ROM programs are represented by electronic circuitry in the form of ROM chips and are sometimes called *firmware.* If the ROM programs currently in your computer system need to be changed, the old ROM chips must be removed and new ROM chips containing the new programs inserted in their place.

Several types of ROM are available. For example, *programmable read-only memory* (PROM) is a form of ROM that allows you or the manufacturer to read a program into it. *Erasable programmable read-only memory* (EPROM) allows programs in ROM to be altered with special equipment.

COMPUTER POWER

One measure of the power of a computer is its *word size,* or how many bits of data it can transfer between the CPU and main memory at one time. A machine with a 32-bit word size can pass data through a 32-bit data path. This data path is a set of

---

| **Manager's Memo 5–4** | **BREAKING THE BUS BOTTLENECK** |

The bus used in many computers is called the AT bus because it is like the bus used on the venerable IBM PC/AT, an early PC that was very popular. Data runs on that bus at a speed of 8 MHz. Many microprocessor chips, however, run at speeds in the hundreds of megahertz. It doesn't make much sense to have a chip that can process data at 200 MHz if the chip has to slow down when it gets data from main memory, puts data into main memory, or exchanges data with other circuit boards. To allow computer systems to utilize fully the faster, more powerful microprocessor chips, a consortium of computer makers developed a faster bus standard that will also accept the old, AT bus expansion cards. This bus structure is called the Extended Industry Standard Architecture (EISA) bus. EISA bus machines, at this writing, are primarily used for computers that act as hosts on networks.

The Video Electronics Standards Association then developed the VL bus architecture that allowed some circuit boards, such as the boards that control the video screen and hard disks, to run at the same speed as the microprocessor chip. This bus architecture was usually called *local bus* architecture and was adopted by many large electronics firms and major manufacturers of video circuit boards. The local bus architecture is fading from the scene in favor of a bus architecture developed by Intel Corporation, a major manufacturer of computer chips. Intel developed a different local bus architecture called the Peripheral Component Interconnect (PCI) bus standard, which has been adopted by most major microcomputer manufacturers.

A major purpose of the PCI bus architecture is to provide fast processing of video signals because popular programs for microcomputers, with their flashy screens, require it. The old AT bus simply does not handle these programs fast enough.

| Manager's Memo 5–5 | INTEL'S MERCED CHIP |

At this writing, Intel Corporation is working on its next generation of computer chips, code named Merced, or the P7, for Pentium 7. The chip is a 64-bit design and is expected to reach clock speeds of 1 gigahertz (GHz). That kind of speed will blow away current microprocessors used in PCs, the fastest of which right now are from Digital Equipment Corporation and run at 500 MHz.

Besides running at a faster pace, the chip will also process many instructions simultaneously. Thus, the performance of the chip is likely to be a substantial improvement over current models.

Industry experts expect the chip to reach production in 1999.

wires through which data passes between the CPU and its components. The data path is also called the *bus* (see Manager's Memo 5–4). In other words, the data path, or word size, is four characters wide (32 bits). Many older personal computers and some minicomputers use a 16-bit data path or word size. Mainframe computers, many minicomputers, and many of the new microcomputers have 32-bit and 64-bit data paths. Think of a 16-bit machine as a highway with two lanes. Only two cars can use the highway at one time. A 32-bit machine is a four-lane highway, allowing four cars to pass concurrently, and a 64-bit machine is an eight-lane highway, on which eight cars can pass at once.

Another way to measure the power of a computer is the speed at which the central processing unit completes its internal processing tasks. The speed is referred to as a computer system's *clock speed,* and it is measured in millions of clock ticks per second, or *megahertz* (MHz). A computer system operating at a clock speed of 200 MHz completes its internal processing tasks faster than a computer system operating at a clock speed of 166 MHz. (See Manager's Memo 5–5.)

Still another measure of computing power is the number of instructions that the CPU can process in a given time period. The unit of measure used here is *millions of instructions per second* (MIPS). One microcomputer CPU, for example, may process between 20 and 80 MIPS; a more powerful microcomputer may handle 400 MIPS or more.

Although the power of a computer can be and often is expressed in word size, megahertz, and MIPS, these measures are really only rough guidelines. Many other factors contribute to a computer's speed and processing ability. The real power of a computer is *throughput,* or the time it takes to get the job done.

USING MORE THAN ONE PROCESSOR

Most computer systems use more than the central processing unit to do their work. Many computer systems use *coprocessors* to assist the central processor with its work. For example, a coprocessor may be used for math calculations, control of secondary storage devices, and video display units. Large computer systems may use special processors to control the input or output of data to secondary storage and printers. The latter processors are called *I/O channels.* By offloading special tasks to special processors, the central processor can concentrate on the work it has at hand and become more efficient.

Some computer systems use more than one central processing unit to run several programs simultaneously on a system. A computer system that has more than one processor and uses them to process more than one program simultaneously has *multiprocessing* capability.

Still other computer systems use more than one central processing unit to complete several processing tasks necessary for a single program simultaneously. These computer systems operate their processors in parallel to complete many steps in a program at once, which is called *parallel processing.*

TYPES OF COMPUTER SYSTEM PROCESSING

Events that occur in an organization's day are called transactions. For example, a sale at a store is a transaction. When you enter a sale into a computer terminal connected directly to the store's computer system and the system processes that sale immediately, the computer system processes that transaction using **on-line transaction processing (OLTP).** With OLTP you enter data into a device that is directly connected, or on-line, to the computer system, and the computer system handles each transaction as it is entered (see Figure 5–11). Because the transactions are processed immediately, these systems may also be called on-line, *real-time,* transaction processing systems.

When transactions are accumulated into a batch for processing at a later time, the computer system is performing **batch processing.** You may or may not be on-line, or directly connected to the computer system, at the time you enter the data to be processed. The important feature is that the batch of data you enter will be processed later as a group. For example, you may enter many sales transactions during the day into some type of storage device. Later, the entire group of sales transactions is processed in a batch (see Figure 5–12).

OLTP has many advantages. In the example described, transaction processing keeps the customer files and sales files current. It also allows you to provide information to the customer immediately if the sales transaction demands it—as would be the case when a customer tries to purchase an airline ticket. In contrast, many types of transactions can be handled quite nicely through batch processing methods. For

Figure 5–11

A systems flow-chart of an on-line sales order system

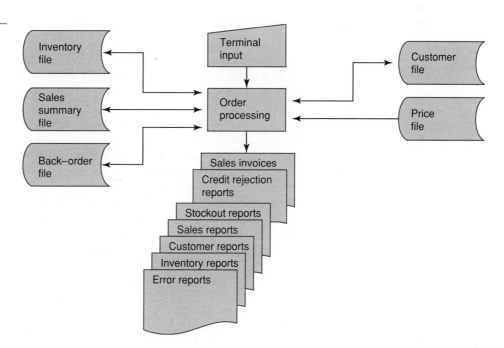

Figure 5–12

A systems flow-chart of batch processing of sales invoices

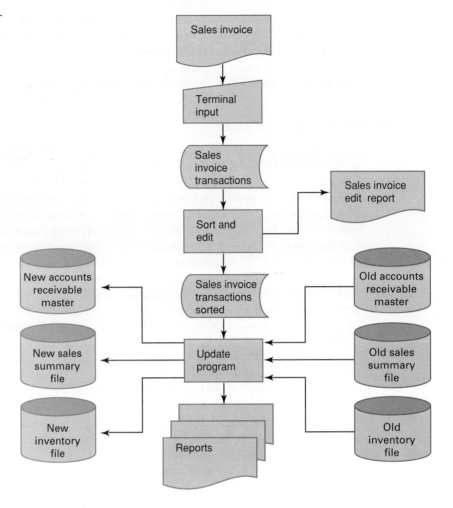

example, the daily hours worked by every employee are usually accumulated each day for processing in a batch at the end of the week. Constant processing of the hours worked for each employee is unnecessary because paychecks are prepared only once each pay period. Constant processing would be an inefficient use of employee time and computer resources. Batch processing allows you to delay the processing of some tasks that do not require immediate processing to times when your computer system resources are more available. Batch processing is especially appropriate if the delayed tasks require intensive processing and make heavy demands on the computer system.

SECONDARY STORAGE MEDIA AND DEVICES

Bytes, or characters of data, are composed of bits. Records, such as customer accounts, are made up of bytes. Files, such as customer files, consist of records. Because the number of records within a file can become large and because the number of files you want to work with can also be large, the amount of main memory you have in your computer system may not be large enough to hold all the necessary data.

Secondary storage allows you to store many more bytes of both data and programs than main memory does. Two of the most common devices used for secondary storage are **disk drives** and **tape drives.**

Disk drive storage devices are called *direct access storage devices* (DASD) because they permit data to be stored and retrieved directly; it is not necessary to scan all the other data on the medium sequentially. Like main memory, direct access storage devices achieve direct access by dividing the available storage space into discrete locations and giving each location a unique address.

Tape drive storage devices are called *sequential access storage devices* (SASD) because they permit data to be stored and retrieved only sequentially. For you to read record 1,056 in a file of 3,000 records, the system has to scan the file starting with record 1 until it reaches the record you want.

The ability to access a record directly rather than sequentially is very important. Suppose you need to view a record of a customer's account rapidly because the customer is in your office waiting for information. Direct access storage devices permit you to retrieve and view the customer's record directly. If you were using sequential access storage devices, however, you would have to scan every record from the beginning of the file to the customer's record. If the customer file was a large one, you— and the customer—might have to wait minutes or hours before the record was found, instead of seconds. However, direct access storage systems typically cost more than sequential access storage systems.

To perform on-line transaction processing, you must be on-line to the computer system and have your data stored on direct access storage devices. To perform batch processing, you may or may not need to be on-line to the computer system and may or may not have your data stored on sequential access storage devices.

Both disk drives and tape drives use *magnetic storage media.* On magnetic media, bits of data are stored on the media surfaces in the form of magnetic spots. As you might expect, data on these surfaces are easily altered or destroyed through careless handling, heat, static electricity, dust, and a host of other causes. Because of this vulnerability, managers must be sure that secondary storage media are handled carefully and that **backup,** or **archive, copies** of the data are created. It would not do to have all your accounts receivable data destroyed because a careless user accidentally erased the media on which they were stored.

Disk Storage

Disk drives are of two general types: floppy drives and hard drives. **Floppy drives** use flexible diskettes, or **floppy diskettes,** as storage media (see Figure 5-13). **Hard drives** use polished metal platters as storage media (see Figure 5-14).

Floppy diskettes.   Floppy diskettes are made of plastic and store data in magnetic form in concentric circles or tracks. The tracks are divided into pie-shaped sectors, which hold the amount of data that can be transferred from the disk to main memory or back again in one operation. These invisible tracks and sectors represent magnetic storage patterns on the recording surface. Floppy diskettes come in several sizes. Microcomputers, the systems with which you are most likely to work, commonly use 3 1/2-inch diskettes, although older machines may use 5 1/4-inch diskettes. Microcomputer floppy diskettes may store data in different densities. For example, a double-density floppy may store 720KB of data; a high-density diskette may store 1.44MB of data. Density refers to how compactly the data is stored on the diskette. Common storage capacities for Macintosh computer systems are 800KB and 1.6MB. Floppy disk drives (see Figure 5-13b) allow computer systems to read data from and write data to the floppy diskette.

Figure 5–13

(a) A diskette showing component parts; (b) A diskette being inserted into a disk drive

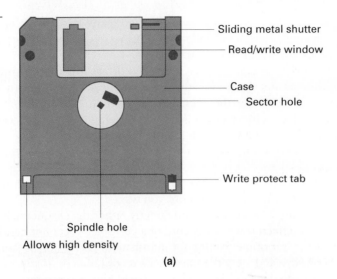

Sliding metal shutter

Read/write window

Case

Sector hole

Write protect tab

Spindle hole

Allows high density

(a)

(b)

Hard disks.   Hard disk drives allow you to access data faster and usually hold much more data than floppy disk drives hold. But as you might expect, they cost more. One model disk drive stores about 2.6GB of data, and the average time it takes to get data from this unit's hard disks to main memory is 8 milliseconds (a millisecond is a thousandth of a second). By comparison, the average time for data to get from one model of a floppy diskette to main memory is 350 milliseconds. However, the speed with which a CPU can move data around within main memory is usually measured in nanoseconds (billionths of a second). Thousandths, millionths, and billionths of a second are incredibly small units of time—probably too small for us to imagine. You may think that you will not notice the differences when processing data at these speeds, but if you must process large files of data, you will become a believer.

Hard disk units may use one or more disks, or platters, for storage. Hard disk drives may also use removable *disk packs,* or disk cartridges that contain one or more platters mounted together in a stack. As with floppy diskettes, each platter has two sides, and the writing surfaces are divided into tracks and sectors (see Figure 5-14a).

Figure 5–14

(a) Hard disk platters showing tracks, sectors, and cylinders in a disk pack; (b) A hard disk pack with exposed platter and actuator arm

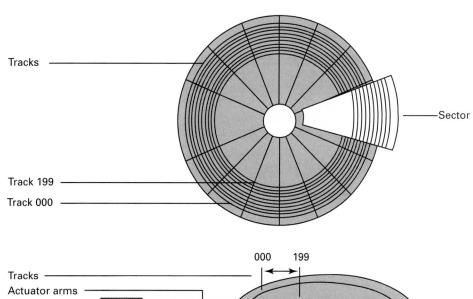

Tracks

Sector

Track 199

Track 000

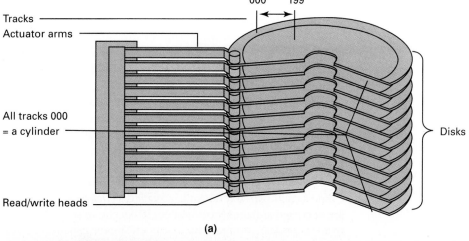

000   199

Tracks

Actuator arms

All tracks 000
= a cylinder

Disks

Read/write heads

(a)

Courtesy of Seagate Technology   **(b)**

137

Accessing data.   To access data from either a hard disk or a floppy diskette, the disk drive unit goes through four operations. The first operation is to move the read/write heads (see Figure 5-14a) to the track on which the data are stored. The time this operation takes is called *seek time.* The next operation is to select which read/write head to use. This operation is called *head switching.* The next operation is to allow the data on the track to rotate under the selected read/write head. The time this operation takes is called *rotational delay.* Finally, the selected read/write head reads the data and transmits it to main memory. The time it takes for this transmission is called *transfer time.* As you might expect, seek time is by far the longest of these time periods. Because the read/write heads used to read a disk pack move in unison, arrangement of data provides an opportunity for the computer system to minimize seek time. If the computer system stores data from one file on the same track on each side of each platter, moving the read/write head to that track allows the system to obtain all records in that file with a single movement of the read/write heads. The collection of tracks that can be accessed by a single movement of all the read/write heads is called a *cylinder,* and the method of storing data on the tracks of a cylinder is called the *cylinder method of storage.* On systems that use a single platter or a floppy diskette, the method used to reduce seek time is to store data from one file on contiguous tracks. Though this method reduces read/write head movement, it does not eliminate it.

Another method used to reduce access time is **cache memory.** Cache memory is a small part of a computer system's high-speed memory that is reserved for data that has been recently accessed. Cache memory is based on the idea that a system is likely to use the data it has just accessed more than once. Thus the data are stored in cache memory when they are first accessed from secondary storage. When the CPU needs more data, it first checks in cache memory. If the CPU finds the data it needs there, it is called a *cache hit.* If it doesn't, it's called a *cache miss.* If the data are in cache, the data are accessed at nanosecond speed. If a cache miss occurs, the CPU has to get the data from secondary storage, which is much slower, usually operating at millisecond speed.

RAID systems.   Still another method for improving access time is to use multiple hard drives so that more than one drive may be accessed at the same time. One method of using multiple hard drives is called the **redundant array of inexpensive disks (RAID).** Basically, RAID systems work by spreading chunks, or blocks of data, across many hard disks. When a user tries to access data that is spread across many disks, RAID systems are able access the blocks of data on each drive simultaneously.

Winchester drives.   On some computers, hard disks are not removable and are called *fixed disks.* Because smaller computers with fixed disks might be placed on factory floors or in rigorous environments, the hard disks they use may be sealed in a container with the read/write heads to prevent dust, dirt, or water from damaging the data on the disks. Sealed hard disks like those just described are usually called *Winchester drives.*

PC cards.   As computers have shrunk in size, manufacturers have sought ways to add features to these miniature boxes of technology. Enter PCMCIA technology. PCMCIA is a peripheral standard for small computer systems that was developed by the Personal Computer Memory Card International Association. The standard was developed for credit-card sized add-in boards for very small computer systems.

Currently, PCMCIA slots are being added to handheld computers, such as personal digital assistants, and notebook computers to allow users of these Lilliputian devices to add memory, fax capability, modems, hard disks, and other peripherals. The cards

Figure 5–15

PCMCIA card
(PC card)

Courtesy of US Robotics.

developed for the slots are thin, lightweight, and rugged and use little power (see Figure 5-15). Three types of PCMCIA cards, or **PC cards,** are available. All three are 2.1 inches wide by 3.4 inches long, although some cards are longer and stick out of the socket. Type I cards are 3.3 mm thick, Type II cards are 5.0 mm thick, and Type III cards are 10.5 mm thick. Type I cards are usually used for flash memory (see the following section), Type II cards are often used for modems and faxes (see Chapter 8), and Type III cards are thick enough to accommodate small hard disks.

Flash memory. **Flash memory** chips are memory chips that, unlike RAM, do not require power to retain their data. Manufacturers offer flash memory chips on cards that can substitute for a small hard drive. The advantage of the flash memory on a card is that it operates at or close to the speed of RAM while simulating a small hard disk. Remember, RAM runs at nanosecond speed, whereas most hard disks run at millisecond speed. However, flash memory cannot be written to at the same speed that it can be read from. Thus, you can store data or programs on the card as if it were a hard disk but read and write to the card at or close to RAM speeds.

Flash memory is usually lighter and cheaper, uses less power, and is more rugged than conventional RAM. However, data stored on flash chips must be written or erased in blocks, not bytes, and the chips wear out after extended use. The primary uses of flash memory have been to provide memory cards for small computer systems and ROM chips for all types of computer systems (see Figure 5-15). Some experts envision using flash memory for data-logging purposes, basically replacing a tape recorder or similar device. For example, flash memory could be used in seismographs or weather stations that are dropped into a site from a plane. They could also be used as black boxes for cars to record engine performance.[2]

---

[2] J. Lyle, Troubador Technologies Web site (http://www.troubadortech.com/flash/), last modified, July 3, 1996.

Figure 5–16
CD-ROM disk and
disk drive

Courtesy of Toshiba America, Inc.

Optical Storage

Optical storage systems use **optical disks** that are read by beams of laser light rather than by magnetic means. Several types of optical storage systems are commonly available.

CD-ROM drives.   One optical storage system is called **CD-ROM,** or compact disk–read only memory (see Figure 5-16). CD-ROM only lets you read from the optical disk, not write to it. A single CD-ROM disk used on microcomputer systems typically holds 650MB of data and has an average access time of 120 milliseconds. Mainframe CD-ROM systems may use larger disks than PC systems.

CD-ROM storage systems are often used to store static information, such as reference materials. Reference materials may include encyclopedias, directories, the complete annual issues of journals and magazines, census data, and statistical reports. For example, Computer Select offers 12 CD-ROM disks to subscribers annually that contain articles and abstracts drawn from over 120 computer, technical, and business periodicals on each monthly disk. The disks also contain hardware and software product specifications, computer company profiles, and a glossary of computer terms.

DVD-ROM drives.   **Digital video disk (DVD),** or high-density compact disk, technology provides much greater storage capacity than CD-ROM technology. While the look, feel, and dimensions of both media are the same, one side of a DVD-ROM will store up to 4.67GB of data, enough to hold 133 minutes of a running movie, including video, multiple sound tracks, and even subtitles. That's about seven times the capacity of a CD-ROM disk. Compared to current CD-ROM technology, DVD allows much more varied content for multimedia computer systems (see Manager's Memo 5–6). Furthermore, DVD-ROM drives can read both DVD-ROM and the older CD-ROM disks. Future plans of vendors include using a double-layered DVD disk capable of holding up to 8.5GB and developing WORM and rewritable systems.

WORM systems.   Another type of optical storage system allows you to write to a disk, but only once, although the disk can be read many times. The latter optical systems are called *WORM,* for write once, read many times. The media used for these systems will hold gigabytes, or billions of bytes, of data.

| **Manager's Memo 5–6** | **MULTIMEDIA HARDWARE** |

Many vendors offer multimedia computer systems. Multimedia technology typically allows you to link data, text, sound, images, video, and audio into a presentation or sequence of screens that might be used to introduce a product, show how a product can be used, or show how it can be fixed. Multimedia systems combine one or more of these technologies:

- Digitized audio for music, voice, or sound effects.
- MIDI Musical Instrument Digital Interface (MIDI) music and sound effects generated by synthesizers.
- Drawings and other graphics.
- Digitized photographs.
- Animation.
- Full-motion video with synchronized sound.

To create or show multimedia presentations, your computer system commonly needs several hardware components, including these:

- Lots of RAM.
- Fast CPU (preferably a CPU designed specifically for multimedia).
- High-resolution color display screen.
- Fast video display board.
- Large hard drive.
- A pointing device, such as a mouse or trackball.
- Speakers.
- Headphones.
- Sound board.
- CD-ROM drive.
- Color scanner.
- Video capture/display board for VCR and TV images.

Rewritable optical disk systems.   *Rewritable optical disk systems* permit data to be written to disk many times. Like WORM systems, the media for erasable optical disk systems hold gigabytes of data. For example, one vendor's rewritable optical disk drive model holds 1.5GB of data and has an average seek time of 45 milliseconds. Higher-end models are available that hold 2.6GB and 4.6GB drives and have access times around 25 milliseconds.

Optical disk systems include *jukebox storage systems* that allow you to access multiple CD-ROM, WORM, and rewritable optical disks. These systems select and switch optical disks from their stacks in a few seconds, providing you with access to many gigabytes of data. One current high-end system lets you switch between 300 optical disks putting 1.27 **terabytes (TB)** (a thousand gigabytes, or a trillion bytes) on-line for your use.

Tower CD-ROM systems place multiple CD-ROM drives in a single cabinet, allowing the user to access data from each of the CD-ROM disks in each drive. One tower system provides seven CD-ROM drives, placing 4.55GB of data on-line at one time.

Floptical drives.   The standard 3 1/2-inch high-density diskette, holding 1.44MB of data, is becoming a headache for many microcomputer users today. Many files that they wish to store are larger than the capacity of the diskette. For example, a salesperson can easily develop a slide presentation that exceeds 1.5MB in size. A need has developed for a very high capacity, removable media that is inexpensive and easy to use. Enter floptical drives (see Figure 5–17).

Floptical drives store data magnetically, but use optical technology for precision. The degree of precision allows much more data to be stored on a 3 1/2-inch diskette. Current models allow 100MB or more of data to be stored on a 3 1/2-inch diskette.

Figure 5–17

Samsung's floptical drive

Courtesy of Samsung International.

The drive gives the user a removable, rugged, high-capacity storage medium. Access speeds vary from 29 milliseconds to more than 100 milliseconds.

Because of their vast storage capabilities and because optical disk drive systems can be placed on-line to computer systems, optical memory systems have become an important mass storage technology when large amounts of data must be stored but also kept on-line. These systems also allow data to be accessed randomly, rather than sequentially.

Tape Storage

A second major type of secondary storage media is **magnetic tape.** Magnetic tape is a strip of plastic kept on a reel or in a cassette. Minicomputers and microcomputers, for example, can store backup copies of data and programs on magnetic tape cassettes. Mainframe computers have used magnetic tape reels for secondary storage for many years. Today, however, mainframe systems use tape reels primarily to back up data stored on hard disks.

Magnetic tape reels used in mainframe systems vary in length and in density, or the amount of data they can hold. Common densities found in existing computer systems are 1,650 and 6,250 bytes of data per inch of tape (bpi). A popular tape reel contains 2,400 feet of 1/2 -inch-wide tape that can hold between 100MB and 200MB of data. To read data from or record data to the tape, the reel is placed on a *magnetic tape drive* (see Figure 5-18).

This drive may read the tape at rates in excess of 100 inches per second. When this speed is combined with a high data density, it provides a fast transfer rate—in excess of 1 megabyte per second. Furthermore, a tape reel is very inexpensive, typically costing around $20 to $40. Thus, magnetic tape systems store a great deal of data, are relatively fast, and are relatively inexpensive. It should come as no surprise, therefore, that many large organizations have chosen magnetic tape for backing up or archiving the data they have on their hard disks.

The tape storage devices used in minicomputer and microcomputer systems often use tape cassettes and cartridges, and tape cartridge systems are available for mainframes. The tape drive may be installed internally in the computer system, or it may be external. Typical minicartridge systems store from 40MB to 250MB of data. Frequently, *QIC* systems, or quarter-inch cartridge systems, store up to 2GB of data, and *DAT* systems, or digital audiotape cartridges, store up to 8GB of data. The tapes may also be stored in jukebox storage systems that hold many tapes. One company of-

Figure 5–18

Mounting a tape reel on a tape drive

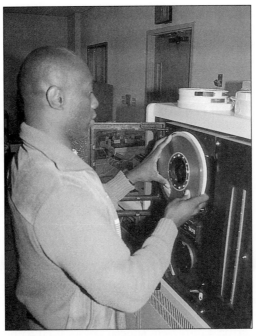

Courtesy of Hewlett-Packard Company

fers a jukebox system with 12 tapes that hold 8GB of data each, providing 96GB of overall storage. The average access time for this system is between 20 and 30 seconds.

Many organizations will probably switch to optical systems for archival storage for several reasons. The capacity of optical system media is much greater than tape. The cost of the media continues to drop and, on a cost per byte basis, the media is less expensive than tape. Optical systems and their media occupy a fraction of the space that tape systems require. Finally, the archival data stored on optical media are accessible on a random rather than sequential basis.

Hierarchical Storage Systems

Hierarchical storage systems combine hard drives, optical drives, and tape drives into a multilayered system for storing large amounts of data. These systems automatically move unused or little-used data from speedy but expensive hard drives to slower but less expensive media based on rules you have formulated. For example, you may decide that you want the system to move data that has not been used for three months from a hard drive to an optical drive. If the data has still not been used after another three months, you may want the system to move it to magnetic tape. After instructing the hierarchical storage system in these rules, the system carries them out automatically.

INPUT AND OUTPUT DEVICES

Each computer system must have a means of **input,** or putting data into the system, and **output,** or getting data out of the system. Input and output devices include keyboards, display screens, printers, disk drives, tape drives, and other devices that are located next to or outside of the CPU. These devices are often called **peripherals.**

Input Devices

One of the most common input devices is a **computer terminal.** The typical terminal has a keyboard so that data can be typed into the computer and a screen to display what is being typed.

Terminals can be classified according to their intelligence. Some terminals are given little logic or storage capability and are called **dumb terminals.** Dumb terminals rely on the intelligence of the computer to which they are attached to function. They are capable of transmitting data to the computer, but they are not capable of storing and processing the data. "Intelligent" or **smart terminals,** on the other hand, have a "brain," or CPU, of their own. They can use their own CPU to process data, or they can rely on the intelligence of another computer to which they are attached. Often, intelligent terminals are used to edit data before the data are sent to the main CPU, thus increasing the accuracy of the transmitted data. Microcomputers are increasingly being connected to computer networks and used as intelligent terminals.

Scanner technologies.   The quality of the data depends, in part, on the accuracy with which it is keyed in to the computer system by the computer terminal operator. The terminal, with its keyboard and screen, represent a point at which errors can be introduced into an information system. Thus careful selection of the computer terminals used for input is important to the quality of the manager's data. A badly designed keyboard, a screen highly susceptible to glare, or a fuzzy, difficult-to-read screen can increase operator error. Conversely, special colors used to highlight directions and data on a terminal screen reduce operator error.

Entering data using a keyboard also costs money. Operators must be trained and paid to do their work. Furthermore, operators make errors entering data using a keyboard. A number of input devices are available that are specifically designed to reduce the keystrokes used to input data into a computer system. These include *point-of-sale terminals,* which capture transactions at their point of origin or source. For example, a point-of-sale terminal in a store captures sales data when the customer buys, thus avoiding rekeying of data and potential rekeying errors.

There are many other ways to reduce or avoid keystrokes. For example, fast-food stores often use point-of-sale terminals with special keys to represent each item of food purchased. Another means is through the use of *bar-code readers,* which you have probably seen at the checkout counters of supermarkets. These bar-code readers read special bar codes printed on grocery items when they are manufactured. The special bar codes follow the *Universal Product Code* adopted by the grocery industry (see Figure 5–19d). Bar-code readers are also used in stock or inventory applications outside the grocery industry. Special bar codes are placed on inventory items or on the shelves that contain the items in warehouses or stores. Then bar-code readers are used to track inventory levels. These bar-code readers may be located in a hand-held wand or recessed in the sales counter. In automated factories bar codes are placed on items as they move through the production line. Computers use bar-code readers to determine the status of items as they are being produced. By reducing keyed input, monitoring stock is faster and more accurate.

Other input devices that reduce keystrokes are *optical character readers* (OCR), which read optical characters (see Figure 5–19a); *mark-sense readers,* which read optical marks (see Figure 5–19c); and *magnetic-ink character recognition* (MICR) readers, which read special characters written in magnetic ink (see Figure 5–19b). OCR, mark-sense, and MICR input devices enable workers to input data into a computer system with a minimum of keystrokes. Fewer keystrokes mean less cost and less chance for incorrect input. OCR equipment is often used in offices to convert hard copies of

Figure 5–19

Four types of data that can be read by optical-scanning equipment

VISA, the band design and the dove design are registered trademarks of VISA International and are reproduced here with permission

(a)

Courtesy of James M. Mejuto Photography.

(b)

Courtesy of the International Business Machines Corporation

(c)

(d)

Figure 5–20

Optical scanner

Courtesy of Hewlett-Packard Company.

documents to magnetic media so they can be edited on word processors. It is also commonly used to convert hard-copy records into records computer systems can use and to convert the records from one computer system to another. In the latter case, the records from one computer system are printed out, scanned by the OCR equipment, and then converted into the format of the new computer system. OCR and mark-sense devices are frequently used in meter reading for power companies and in scoring examinations, and banks have used MICR devices to process checks for many years. Bar-code devices, optical character and mark devices, and magnetic-ink character devices are examples of optical-scanning equipment.

Devices that read bar codes, MICR, text, and images are called **scanners** (see Figure 5–20). Many general-purpose scanners are available that, when accompanied by the appropriate programs, allow you to scan text and images and store them on disk where they can be read, edited, and otherwise manipulated. Scanners are available in several sizes from hand scanners that scan about 4 inches of a page to full-page scanners.

Pointing devices.   Other devices provide input for special situations. For example, a number of **pointing devices** allow you to enter data or make selections from a computer screen. One pointing device, a **mouse** (see Figure 5–21a & b), is a handheld device connected to the computer terminal with a cable that allows you to make entries without using the keyboard. There are also wireless or remote mice. The movement of a roller at the base of the mouse sends signals to the terminal that are converted into computer commands. Variants of the mouse, the **trackball** and **pointing stick** (see Figure 5–21c), are often used with notebook computers.

Figure 5–21

(a and b) A mouse on a desktop computer, (c) a pointing stick on a notebook computer

Courtesy of International Business Machines Corporation.

(a)

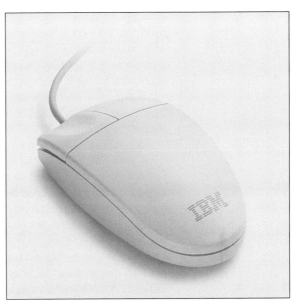

Courtesy of International Business Machines Corporation.

(b)

Courtesy of International Business Machines Corporation.

(c)

Other input devices.   Still another input medium that is gaining acceptance is voice input. **Voice-recognition technology** consists of a sound board and software that convert the analog waves of sound into digital data that can be stored on disk. In addition to the board, there is usually a microphone to allow input. Voice-recognition technology can be especially helpful when manual input is inconvenient or impossible. For example, forklift operators or factory workers can input data about the quantity of the products they have delivered or worked on without stopping work. IBM has developed voice-recognition technology that it feels is sufficiently versatile to allow users to dictate directly into a word processor. The company provides industry-specific vocabulary files, for such fields as radiology, emergency medicine, journalism, and law.

Card and badge readers, which read magnetic data contained on a card or badge, are frequently used to record automatically the in and out times of employees for payroll purposes.

A reemerging input technology that has been applied to very small computer systems is the *light pen.* The light-sensitive pen, or stylus, is connected to a screen or tablet by wire and is used to draw, write, mark, or make selections from a menu. *Touch screens* are another way to input data. The operator touches menu items or other objects displayed on the screen to enter data or make choices.

Systems that permit you to capture video images from live TV or a VCR tape have become popular. These systems capture video as individual frames, convert them to a format that can be stored on a hard disk or optical disk, and then use graphics software to manipulate the images or sequences of images (see Figure 5–22). **Desktop video technology** allows you to grab frames from a training tape and insert them in an accompanying training document. It also allows you to insert full-motion video, for example, a sequence that shows how to install an adapter board in a slot on a microcomputer motherboard, into a multimedia presentation.

Digital cameras have also grown in demand and use. Digital cameras look much like ordinary cameras but they capture the images they take in a format that can be stored on disk. The images can then be manipulated with graphics software. The technology allows you to insert the pictures you take into data files, documents, or presentations. For example, you can insert pictures of employees into employee files, pictures of products into advertising brochures, and pictures of a factory into a graphics presentation.

Figure 5–22

Desktop video technology

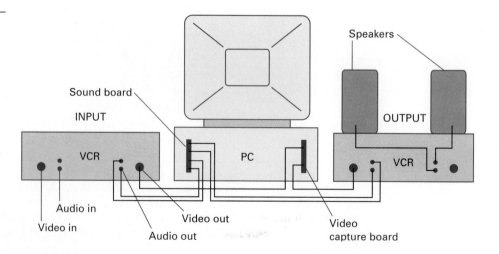

Output Devices   You have learned that the most common input device is a computer terminal. However, the computer terminal is also the most common output device. The screen of a computer terminal displays data; thus it is an output device. In fact, many input devices also serve as output devices.

Display Screens.   The screen of a computer terminal is called many names: *CRT* (for cathode ray tube), *VDT* (for video display terminal), *monitor,* **display screen,** or just plain *screen*. Display screens usually look like TV screens. The displays may be in color or monochrome. Monochrome screens usually are black and white, amber, or green. Displays vary in resolution and size. Screen **resolution** refers to the number of pixels (picture elements) per inch. Size refers to how many columns wide and how many lines long the screen is.

Color terminals have become standard on desktop microcomputers and for mainframe and minicomputer systems. The screens on color terminals vary in the number of hues they can display. Some screens can represent many colors and many different shades of each color. Color screen resolution is often measured in dot pitch, or the distance between dots of the same color. The lower the dot pitch, the sharper the image.

Special-purpose screens are also available. For example, you can buy a full-page screen (80 columns by 66 lines), a wide screen (120 or 132 columns wide), and even a two-page screen (pages appear side by side). Screens are also commonly available for desktop computers in 14-, 15-, and 17-inch sizes.

Liquid crystal display (LCD) screens are often used on notebook and laptop computers because they are flat and lightweight. However, the principal problem with notebook and laptop computers has been the poor quality of the screen images. The LCD technology requires that the screen image be exposed to a lot of light to achieve satisfactory resolution. Recent advances in LCD screen displays have improved the quality of these screens considerably. Furthermore, LCD screens are much more expensive than CRT screens. However, manufacturers of LCD screens are developing less-expensive flat panel screens and hope these screens will replace the bulky CRT screens on desktop machines in the near future.

Some computer terminals are also *printing terminals.* These terminals have keyboards built into printers and usually do not have screens. The keyboards can be used for data input, and output from the computer systems is printed on paper.

Still another output device is the ordinary television screen. Using desktop video technology and sound technology, the digital output of a computer system can be converted into the sound and visual signals that are the standard in the television industry. The result is that you can display output with sound using an ordinary TV. This technology allows you to use a large TV, for example, as a display device for a business presentation.

Some vendors have begun to combine computer systems with entertainment-center components such as big screen TV and high-quality stereophonic sound. The systems, equipped with fax/modems, CD-ROMs, and wireless pointing devices, are an attempt to move the computer into the family room. Families can watch TV, browse the Internet, play interactive games, or even capture movie screen images to disk.

Printers.   Many types of printers are available for computer systems. These printers can usually be grouped into two major categories: **impact printers** and **nonimpact printers.** Impact printers bring the paper or other medium into contact with the print element. Nonimpact printers place the print on the medium in other ways.

Impact printers are used to print multipart forms. Nonimpact printers are typically used when there is a need for high-quality documents or when the surface of the printed material is not even, such as wrapped boxes.

Two common types of impact printers are line printers and dot-matrix printers. *Line printers* print whole lines of text or numbers at one time. They may be used when large numbers of documents must be printed rapidly, such as invoices, paychecks, statements of account, or multipart forms. Because of the quality of print, line printers are not ordinarily used for text documents, such as reports or letters. Speeds of line printers range from hundreds to thousands of lines per minute. For example, IBM makes a line printer that prints 2,200 lines per minute and can print documents requiring up to 132 characters on a line (see Figure 5–23). Because nonimpact printers are faster, quieter, and offer better print quality, line printers are not as popular today as they have been in the past.

Another type of impact printer is the **dot-matrix printer.** Dot-matrix printers form characters by using thin rods, or pins, to produce dots on a page. The quality of the end product depends on the number of pins used to form each character. Inexpensive dot-matrix printers may use nine pins to form characters in a rectangle. More expensive dot-matrix printers use 24 pins to create very tightly formed characters.

Dot-matrix printers are often used to produce rough drafts of documents and informal, internal documents, such as memos. Typical speeds of inexpensive dot-matrix printers are 120 to 200 characters per second. Fast dot-matrix printers may reach speeds over 500 characters per second, and even faster ones measure their speeds in lines per minute. Some dot-matrix printers achieve what is called "near letter quality" output by having the print head make more than one pass on each line of print or for each character. Each time the print head makes a pass, it moves a small increment to the right or left of the first pass. By making several such passes,

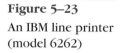

Figure 5–23

An IBM line printer (model 6262)

Courtesy of International Business Machines Corporation.

the dots fill in the spaces of each letter and give the appearance of a letter-quality character.

The advantage of near-letter-quality dot-matrix printers is that they can quickly print rough drafts and in-house documents, print letter-quality documents at a slower pace, and also print graphic images. Thus a single printer can produce all three types of output. Dot-matrix printers also are relatively inexpensive.

Two common types of nonimpact printers are laser printers and ink-jet printers. **Laser printers** print a whole page at once and are also called *page printers*. Laser printers are often used when drawings, photographs, and graphic images must be reproduced with high quality or in color, or when a large number of pages must be printed and both quality and speed are important. Laser printers offer a large number of type styles and allow you to merge multiple print styles, graphics, and other images on a single page (see Figure 5–24).

Laser printers are usually fast. A typical speed for an inexpensive laser printer is eight pages per minute (ppm). High-output laser printers produce hundreds of pages per minute. Laser printers are also much quieter than impact printers. However, when you switch to color printing, the speed of the printers slows dramatically. A laser printer that prints 10 ppm in monochrome mode may slow down to 2 to 3 ppm in color mode.

Another type of nonimpact printer is the **ink-jet printer.** These printers form characters by spraying ink on the paper. As a result, special types of ink-jet printers can print on surfaces that are not entirely flat, such as packages. Of course, neither

Figure 5–24

A laser printer with printer output

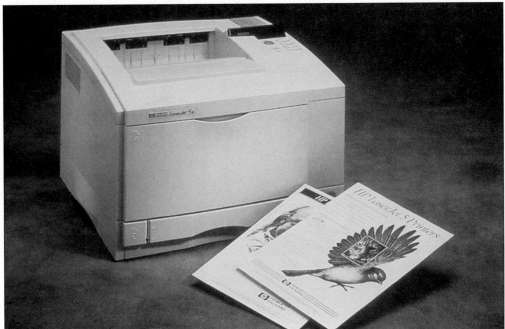

Courtesy of Hewlett-Packard Company.

ink-jet printers nor laser printers can be used where carbon copy forms must be printed, since they are not impact printers; that is, they do not have a print element that strikes the paper. Speeds of ink-jet printers range from slower models with print speeds measured in characters per second (CPS) to faster models that print pages per minute. Like laser printers, ink-jet printers that have a speed of eight ppm in monochrome mode may slow down to one ppm to print in full-color mode. Because ink-jet printers offer higher resolution printing than dot-matrix printers do and because there is only a small difference in their prices, ink-jet printers have replaced dot-matrix printers in many organizations as inexpensive, desktop printers.

Many vendors now offer printers that are bundled with other technologies. For example, you can buy a printer that is also a fax machine, or a machine that is a fax, printer, copier, and scanner all in one. Combination devices can be cost-effective for

Figure 5–25

A plotter

Courtesy of Hewlett-Packard Company.

small firms where the volume of work is low but the need to perform all these functions on a small scale occurs often. (Fax technology is discussed in Chapter 9.)

Other output devices. For special purposes, manufacturers have produced special output devices. For example, you can use _plotters_ to print maps, charts, and graphs (see Figure 5–25). One model of plotter prints high-quality color images as large as 3 feet by 9 feet.

Another special-purpose output device is a voice synthesizer. Its output is in voice form and is used in a variety of situations such as subway station alerts, telephone-marketing systems, and voice-mail systems. (Voice mail is discussed in more detail in Chapter 9.) Voice output usually consists of computer-controlled playback of stored speech segments, such as numbers and words.

Other devices can transfer computer output to microfilm. These devices, called _computer output microfilm_ (COM) recorders, can archive large amounts of records in a form that can be stored relatively inexpensively in reduced size (see Figure 5–26).

As you can see, there are many specialized input and output devices for computer systems—too many to describe in one chapter. However, for your information, Figure 5–27 provides a partial list of these devices.

The capacity of the storage media and the speed with which a computer system can access data from these media and other input devices are important considerations when you choose a computer system. Storage media and input devices that cannot keep up with the computer system will cause your system to be _input_

Figure 5–26

A computer output microfilm system

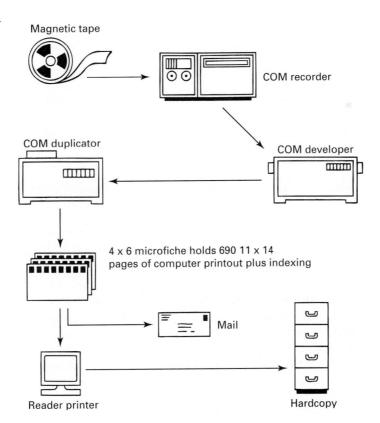

Magnetic tape

COM recorder

COM duplicator

COM developer

4 x 6 microfiche holds 690 11 x 14 pages of computer printout plus indexing

Mail

Reader printer

Hardcopy

Figure 5–27

Some examples of
input and output
devices

Input Devices	
Badge reader	Magnetic-ink character reader
Bar-code reader	Microphone
Cartridge drive	Mouse
Cassette drive	Optical character reader
CD-ROM drive	Optical mark reader
Digital camera	Pointing stick
Digitizing tablet	Punch card reader
Disk drive	Scanner
Erasable optical drive	Tape drive
Exoskeleton gloves	Touch screen
Eye and head movement tracker	Touch tablet
Floptical drive	Trackball
Foot controller	Video display terminal
Full-page scanner	Voice-recognition device
Joy stick	WORM drive
Keyboard	
Light pen	

Output devices	
Cartridge drive	Line printer
Cassette drive	Magnetic-ink character coder
CD-ROM drive	Plotter
Computer output microfilm	Robot
Daisy-wheel printer	Speech synthesizer
Disk drive	Tape drive
Dot-matrix printer	Television screen
Erasable optical drive	Thermal printer
Ink-jet printer	Video display terminal
Laser printer	WORM drive

bound. For example, your CPU may be idle because it has to wait for data to be transmitted from a slow storage device. One means of reducing the time that CPUs wait is to use cache memory to store data taken from a slower disk drive or other storage medium.

In the same way, the speed of output devices is important to the overall performance of a computer system. Output devices that cannot keep up with the CPU will cause the system to become *output bound* unless there is a place for the CPU to store the data that it has already processed. For output devices, that place is usually called a *buffer,* or small amount of memory. The buffer storage may be part of main memory allocated for that task, it may be located in a device positioned between the output device and the CPU, or it may be located in the output device itself. Many printers have buffer storage, for example. A computer system that is input/output bound, or *I/O bound,* is inefficient and wastes valuable resources.

As a manager, you must be certain your equipment has sufficient main memory to handle both your programs and data. You also should be sure that the secondary storage devices you use provide sufficient memory to store the programs and data the

Manager's Memo 5-7	TALK ABOUT THE FUTURE

As you have learned from reading the text, there are many, many types of input and output devices for computer systems. Some of these devices can get pretty exotic. For example:

Mind over Matter. Cyberlink Mind Systems, Inc., has developed the Cyberlink Interface. The device is a headband with three sensors and an amplifier in it. The sensors detect electrical signals from activity of the brain and muscles. The amplifier then increases the power of the signals by 20,000. The device is being developed to allow pilots to control their aircraft by thinking what has to be done instead of physically maneuvering aircraft. Currently, disabled people are using the Cyberlink Interface to operate computer systems. A wheelchair, capable of being steered by Cyberlink, is also being marketed in 1997. In addition, the company is exploring ways to help people with spinal injuries. They want people to be able to skip the spine and send signals directly to muscle stimulators in their legs. The company also produces a general-purpose device for playing games and interacting with the Internet that retails for about $650.[1]

An Eye on the Future. One of the largest components of computer systems remains the monitor or display screen. While the processor can fit in the palm of your hand, a 26-line screen still takes up as much space as a keyboard. Now, however, a company called Micro Vision has developed a system called a virtual retinal display. The system is made up of a small computer that fits to your waist, a fiber optic cable, and pair of special eyeglasses with movable mirrors. The computer system generates an image that is passed to the mirrors, which beam the image directly to the retina. In effect, the retina becomes a display screen.

Todd MacIntyre, one of the company's VPs, says, "You already have this high-performance, dynamic screen built into your head—it's called the eye. We're just leveraging the eye's response to light, only instead of reflected light we're using directed light." The company expects to develop its first systems for medical and military uses.[2]

[1] C. Liu, "Brain Signals Help Disabled Run Machines," *St. Louis Post-Dispatch*, December 7, 1996, p. 7.

[2] E. Weise, "Computer Uses Eye as Screen," *St. Louis Post-Dispatch*, November 27, 1996, p. 5C.

computer is not using at the moment. Finally, you should select input and output equipment that fits the jobs your computer system performs (see Manager's Memo 5-7).

HARDWARE STANDARDS

The computer hardware you acquire as a manager must fit in with the acquisition scheme of the entire organization. Casual or opportunistic purchasing of equipment can easily lead to many different computer system models, display screen types, bus structures, boards, printers, and other peripherals. Having an array of different hardware types may lead to many problems, including lack of compatibility, expandability, and reliability. To avoid these problems, many organizations attempt to set standards for the computer hardware they acquire.

Compatibility

If an organization does not set standards for computer hardware, each department or each employee may decide to acquire different, incompatible hardware. An expansion board that works in a computer with one bus structure, for example, may not work in a computer system with another bus structure. The output of one computer system may not be useable as input to another computer system without either additional hardware or software to convert the data from one type to another. Connecting one type of terminal to a mainframe that requires another type of terminal requires additional hardware and software. A computer program developed for one type of hardware may not run on other computer systems, so an organization may need to develop or purchase programs for each type of computer system acquired. The cost of making one system work with another may be higher than the benefit derived from doing so.

Standards for computer hardware affect costs in other ways. For example, maintaining computer system hardware requires expertise with the hardware. If an organization has many hardware types, it will need people who have expertise with many systems. That may translate into the need for more people, more training, or both. Maintenance may require an inventory of spare parts, but keeping spare parts for many different hardware types may require storing a large number of parts. Purchasing one type of hardware in large quantities offers opportunities for quantity discounts or a lower negotiated price.

Expandability

As an organization's computer needs grow, it may outgrow the capacity of its present computer systems. However, some computer systems can be upgraded to allow increased capacity. Computer systems are also continually changing—the computer industry announces new models with new features daily. The ability of a computer system to grow, add capacity, or add new features means that the computer system's life can be extended, and the organization's costs for developing a new system, including system acquisition, start-up costs, and training costs, can be forestalled or reduced. The expandability of hardware is an important consideration when setting standards for an organization to allow future growth and improvement in hardware with minimal cost and disruption to the organization.

Reliability

Purchasing hardware on the cutting edge of technology is appealing to many buyers. The allure of getting the latest technological developments with all the bells and whistles shown in the advertising brochures is tantalizing. However, managers should recognize that cutting-edge technology often has problems that are not described in the advertising brochures. After new products are announced, the trade and computer magazines usually are filled with articles about the various problems users have found that designers overlooked. Buying computer hardware that has not been thoroughly tested in the marketplace is similar to buying the first car of a new model. You can usually expect problems to occur in the early cars because testing rarely can duplicate fully the driving conditions created by real drivers on real roads.

Purchasing hardware fresh from the designer's drawing board is usually unwise. Instead of the cutting edge, you may find yourself on the "bleeding edge" of technology. Organizations should develop standards for hardware acquisition to ensure that the hardware acquired is compatible, expandable, and reliable. Managers of departments should use those standards to help them in the acquisition process.

OTHER ACQUISITION ISSUES

In addition to establishing and maintaining hardware standards, managers face a number of other issues when acquiring hardware.

Timing the Acquisition

Since computer systems became popular in the 1960s, their power has continually increased and the costs of acquiring them have continually decreased. These two trends have not abated. A manager can usually depend on the new models of computer hardware to be more powerful than the old models and the relative costs of those models to be lower. Thus buyers have a tendency to defer purchasing new or additional computer systems. When buyers finally acquire hardware, they are often upset when subsequent models provide more power at a lower cost.

However, you must realize that future hardware will continue to provide increased power at lower cost. Your acquisition decision should be based on careful estimates of the costs of the system to you and the benefits it will offer you. If you find that the benefits of acquiring a system outweigh its costs, then it matters little how much better and less expensive future models are. If you choose to defer acquisition because future models are likely to be improved or less expensive, you will wait forever—computer systems will always be less expensive and better in the future. In the meantime, you will lose the difference between the costs and benefits that the current system could offer you.

Renting, Leasing, and Buying

The costs of many minicomputer and microcomputer systems have dropped to the point that many organizations do not consider whether they will lease or buy these systems—they simply buy them (see Manager's Memo 5–8). Mainframe computer systems and some high-end minicomputers, and even some microcomputers, however, still represent substantial investments, even for large organizations. You should determine the costs both of buying and of leasing the computer systems you wish to acquire. If you will need the equipment for less than 12 months, you should also price renting it. If the applications you must use computers to perform have been very stable over the years, you might even consider buying used equipment.

The advantages and disadvantages of purchasing or leasing computer equipment are basically the same as those for acquiring any durable good. Rental arrangements usually cost the most on a monthly basis but offer the least risk of obsolescence. Leasing costs, on a monthly basis, are usually lower than rental costs but higher than outright purchase costs. Purchasing provides the buyer with ownership and a residual value but tends to lock in the equipment decision because changing equipment will involve trading it in or selling it.

Manager's Memo 5–8	RENTING, LEASING, OR BUYING

 ADVANTAGES

DISADVANTAGES

Renting
Short-term commitment
Least risk of obsolescence
Requires no up-front capital investment

Renting
More expensive than leasing
Equipment may be used
Some equipment vendors do not rent

Leasing
Lower risk of obsolescence
No immediate capital investment
May provide purchase option
Payments may include service
Less expensive than renting

Leasing
May be more expensive than purchase
No residual value to owner

Buying
Residual value to owner
Usually less expensive than leasing over
  the long term

Buying
Requires capital investment or borrowing of funds
Locks buyer into decision
Owner must obtain or provide maintenance services

Deciding on the Acquisition

Responsibility for acquiring computer systems may rest in several places in an organization. The decision may be centralized in a data processing or management information systems department. Alternatively, the decision may be centralized in a computer committee in the organization. In such cases this department or committee must approve system purchases. On the other hand, the decision may be decentralized to the department level. In this case approval from the department is necessary before acquisition can be completed. In some organizations, individuals may be able to make their own decisions.

In any case the decision to acquire computer systems for an individual or department usually begins with the manager. That decision may then be forwarded for approval to a department committee, the MIS department, or a computer committee that represents the entire organization. In many large firms, the MIS department provides special services for departments or individuals who wish to acquire computer equipment. The special services are usually provided through an office devoted to the users of computing equipment, such as managers, supervisors, clerical personnel, and other noncomputing specialists. The office helps these buyers plan their acquisitions, select, acquire, and install the systems, and train users.

The issues surrounding the organization of computing resources are discussed in greater detail in later chapters.

Choosing a Hardware Vendor

The selection of a vendor for your hardware may not be an option open to you as a manager. Your organization may already have a relationship with one or more hardware vendors. The special relationship may provide your firm with volume discounts, faster service, special training, custom installation, or other services.

If you are able to select the vendor to supply the hardware you want, the vendor you choose depends to some extent on your knowledge of the systems you are acquiring and the help you will need to purchase, install, and use them. You can buy hardware from many types of vendors, including hardware manufacturers, computer sales and service dealers, and mail-order firms.

Many businesses buy their hardware directly from the manufacturer. Some manufacturers provide a great deal of support to the buyer, including selection advice, on-site installation, and user training. Others provide little or no support and merely ship you boxes of hardware with written installation directions. To help you make your decision, you may ask manufacturers' sales representatives to provide on-site demonstrations of their products or visit a dealer to inspect and use the hardware.

Some vendors provide hot-line technical support to customers, sometimes through an 800 phone service that allows customers to talk directly to technicians if they have problems installing or using the systems. Other vendors answer inquiries through the regular mail or through electronic mail systems. Still others provide no technical support at all to the buyer. Clearly, *before* you buy the systems you should find out what level and types of help the vendor will provide *after* you buy the systems.

If you are very knowledgeable about the hardware you want to buy, you may choose to buy from mail-order companies. Ordinarily, their prices are lower than other sources. However, you may find that the hardware or software you have purchased is not what you wanted. Some mail-order companies allow you to return your purchases. Some allow returns with penalties, and others allow you to return your purchases with a full refund, under certain conditions. Of course, you should find out the purchase terms before you commit yourself.

Buying from mail-order firms has become popular today because many of them have made the purchase of computer systems easy. Mail-order firms now typically pre-install much of the hardware and any programs that come with the computer systems you are buying. When the boxes are shipped, you will probably find all the software that was bundled with the hardware, the expansion cards, and the memory boards already installed. You still have to connect the major parts, such as the CPU, the screen, and the keyboard. However, once that job is done, you may be able to turn the computer on and be ready to start using the programs. When you are buying hundreds of machines, preinstallation of the various hardware components and software saves you an enormous amount of time.

It is important, especially for large purchases, that you carefully evaluate every vendor you are considering. For example, how many technical support people do they employ? Where are their nearest service centers? Do the service centers have a complete stock of spare parts? How long have the vendors been in business? What other organizations are customers of the vendors? How sound financially are they? Where are their nearest training centers? How often do they run classes? What level of training do they offer? How comprehensive are their course offerings?

Ordinarily, if you are not knowledgeable about what you need to buy, you should select vendors that provide you with considerable support. For the inexperienced buyer, obtaining hardware from competent, reliable vendors who are helpful both before and after the purchase makes the acquisition and implementation of computer systems much easier. You must realize, however, that providing such support costs money. Support costs may be charged directly to you as line items on an invoice, or they may be reflected in comparatively higher prices for the systems than those offered by vendors providing little or no support.

If your operations are worldwide, you should find a vendor that can provide international on-site support, can deliver worldwide, and can diagnose and repair your equipment worldwide. Communications technology and overnight shipping allow manufacturers to support computer systems in remote and exotic locations. However, you should always understand the nature and extent of the support a vendor provides before you buy.

Installation, Maintenance, and Training

Acquiring computer systems is only one step in deploying them in your organization. Once delivered, computer systems must be installed and maintained. Installation may require substantial modification of your facility. You may need to add additional air-conditioning, special wiring, cabling, electrical systems, and/or special security systems. Furthermore, employees are likely to need training in the use of the computer systems. The ease with which computer systems can be installed, the costs and difficulties of maintaining them, and the ease with which they can be used are important management concerns; the original acquisition costs are only one part of the total costs.

Operating Costs and the Environment

The Environmental Protection Agency estimates that PCs gobble up 74 percent of office equipment power usage. However, microcomputer vendors offer systems that are much less taxing on the environment and on your energy budget. The systems are advertised as "green" or "Energy Star" computer systems because they conform to the EPA's Energy Star guidelines for low energy consumption. Energy Star systems are much more energy efficient than the standard microcomputer systems on the market today. For example, one vendor's green machine uses only three-fourths of the power required by conventional systems. Conventional PCs may use from 60 to 150 watts when running. To meet the EPA's Energy Star requirements, however, a PC must use less than 30 watts when it is "idling" —when it is running but not otherwise being used. The EPA estimates that the use of green machines can cut energy costs by $1 billion, reduce CO emissions by the amount of CO produced by 2,500,000 cars, and save more than $100 per system per year.[3]

A common way for the green systems to reduce power usage is to power down the CPU and the screen automatically during periods of nonusage. While the green machines save energy for our globe and reduce a company's energy bill, they also lengthen the uptime for battery-driven laptops and other nondesktop computer systems. The longer the uptime for such systems, the more acceptable they become to users. Everybody seems to win.

Brian Nadel[4] offers some other ways that PC users can reduce their load on the environment:

1. Turn off your PC when you will not be using it for some time. Don't leave it running continuously.
2. Set your screen saver to blank instead of using some snappy, high-color, dynamic screen display.
3. View your documents electronically instead of printing them.
4. Use electronic mail instead of interoffice mail.
5. Recycle your printer and copier toner cartridges.
6. Recycle your laptop, notebook, or other computer batteries.
7. Recycle your printouts.

The Ergonomics of the Computer Workstation

Ergonomics in the workplace is the science of adapting employee workstations, including computer workstations, to fit the worker. The purposes of applying ergonomics are manifold and include: removing work conditions pertaining to the workstation that can harm employees, improving employee productivity, reducing employer liability for work-related injuries, and improving employee morale. For example, providing workers with tables and chairs that are adjustable can reduce or eliminate back, wrist, and neck strain. Attention to how chairs and tables fit the workers who use them also can improve productivity and make work more pleasant.

A persistent work-related problem in the computer field is carpal tunnel syndrome that can cause severe pain to people who perform repetitive tasks with their wrists and hands, for example, data entry personnel. The pain can become so severe that the worker can no longer function on the job. Placing the keyboard at the right height, using a well-designed keyboard, and providing a wrist rest can reduce the incidence of this syndrome.

Another persistent complaint from employees who spend a great deal of time in front of a computer screen is eye strain. Providing high-resolution computer screens that are glare free and large enough to make text easy to read can reduce eye strain, improve employee morale, and improve employee productivity. After all, it is hard to spot errors in text that is small and fuzzy.

---

[3] T. Quinlan, "Intel 486 Line Gains SL Power-Saving Features," *InfoWorld* 15, no. 25 (June 21, 1993) p.27.
[4] B. Nadel, "The Green Machine," *PC Magazine* 12, no. 10 (May 25, 1993), p.112.

Reducing employer liability for work-related injuries is an important aspect of ergonomics. In fact, the Occupational Safety and Health Administration (OSHA) of the U.S. Department of Labor has training courses in the application of the principles of ergonomics to work environments.

Evaluating the ergonomic features of computer equipment is an important step in acquiring it and should be part of any computer system acquisition plan.

Management Summary

Computers are often classified as supercomputers, mainframe computers, minicomputers, and microcomputers. These classifications have become fuzzy over time because the power of computers in a lower category may exceed the power of computers in a high category. However, they are still commonly used.

All computer systems have a CPU, which consists of a control unit and arithmetic/logic unit. Computer systems also have two types of memory: main, or internal memory, and secondary storage, or external memory. Main memory is composed of RAM, or random access memory. RAM is volatile, and data stored in RAM can be accessed directly. Computer systems also store programs in ROM, or read-only memory. Common forms of secondary storage include disk drive and tape drive systems.

Computer systems operate under the direction of a program, and they must have parts or all of both the program and the data to be processed in main memory to operate. Computers store programs and data in bytes of code. Each byte is formed by a number of bits, which varies with the code used. The number of bits a computer can transfer between main memory and the control unit and arithmetic/logic unit at one time is called a word. The number of instructions a CPU can process in a second is measured in millions of instructions per second (MIPS). Word size, megahertz, and MIPS are measures of computer power. Memory in secondary storage consists of bytes stored on hard disks, diskettes, tapes, or other devices. Input and output devices attached to the computer allow data to enter or exit from the system. Common input and output devices are computer terminals with keyboards, display screens, disk drives, and printers. Many other input and output devices are available for special purposes. The CPU, main memory, and input and output devices are called computer hardware.

The acquisition of computer systems generates many organizational issues and provides many concerns for the manager. These issues and concerns include when computer systems should be acquired; whether they should be rented, leased, or purchased; who should decide what systems will be acquired; how the systems should be installed and maintained; and what training for employees should be required.

Managers must also be concerned with developing or following hardware standards to ensure hardware compatibility, expansion, upgradability, and reliability. However, computer hardware is only part of a computer system. To make the hardware run—to make it do what you want it to do—the hardware must be told precisely when and how to act. This is the job of computer programs, or software, and computer software is the subject of the next chapter.

Key Terms for Managers

archive copy, 135	computer platform, 124	digital cameras, 148
backup copy, 135	computer program, 129	digital video disk (DVD), 140
batch processing, 133	computer terminal, 144	disk drives, 135
cache memory, 138	convergent computer systems, 123	display screen, 149
CD-ROM, 140	desktop microcomputers, 121	dot-matrix printer, 150
central processing unit (CPU), 125	desktop video technology, 148	downsize, 124

dumb terminals, 144

flash memory, 139

floppy diskettes, 135

floppy drives, 135

gigabytes (GB), 130

hard drives, 135

hardware, 120

impact printers, 149

ink-jet printer, 151

input, 143

kilobytes (KB), 130

laptop computers, 121

laser printers, 151

magnetic tape, 142

main memory, 129

mainframe computer systems, 120

megabytes (MB), 130

microcomputer systems, 120

microprocessor, 127

minicomputer system, 120

mouse, 146

network computers, 123

nonimpact printers, 149

notebook computers, 121

on-line transaction processing (OLTP), 133

optical disks, 140

output, 143

palmtop computers, 121

PC cards, 139

peripherals, 143

personal digital assistants (PDAs), 121

pointing devices, 146

pointing stick, 146

random access memory (RAM), 129

read-only memory (ROM), 131

Redundant array of inexpensive disks (RAID), 138

resolution, 149

scanners, 146

secondary storage, 129

smart terminals, 144

supercomputers, 120

tape drives, 135

terabytes (TB), 141

trackball, 146

voice-recognition technology, 148

workstations, 121

Review Questions

1. Describe the main parts of a CPU. Explain what each part does.

2. Explain the differences between RAM and ROM.

3. What is a bit? What is a byte? What do 2MB, 2GB, and 2TB mean?

4. Explain what 640KB of RAM means. How many characters of data can be stored in this much RAM?

5. Explain why word size is important to the processing speed of a computer.

6. Explain why megahertz is important to the processing speed of a computer.

7. Describe two major classifications of printers. Identify and describe one example from each printer classification.

8. What are MIPS and how do MIPS affect the performance of computer systems?

9. What is the difference between on-line, real-time transaction processing, and batch processing?

10. What is the difference between primary storage and secondary storage? Which is usually faster to access?

11. What is a hard disk? How does a hard disk differ from a floppy diskette in terms of storage capacity? in terms of access speed?

12. Describe the four operations that are necessary to transfer data from a direct access storage device to main memory.

13. Explain what a disk pack is and what a cylinder on a disk pack is. How does the cylinder method of storing data speed up access time?

14. Explain how magnetic tape systems are frequently used in mainframe computer systems.

15. What is flash memory? How does it differ from RAM?

16. Identify major concerns managers should have when they consider acquiring computer systems.

17. What is a RISC system? How does it compare to a CISC system?

18. What is cache memory? How does it increase the speed of data access?

19. What is a professional workstation? What is an example of how a professional workstation might be used?

20. What does RAID mean? How can it improve the performance of a computer system?

QUESTIONS FOR DISCUSSION

1. What features should managers look for in computer terminals that are used for data entry by data entry clerks? Explain how each feature will aid management.

2. The business world often uses the terms *supercomputer, mainframe computer, minicomputer,* and *microcomputer.* What do these computer systems have in common? How might these computer systems differ?

3. Describe some options for data input that do not require a keyboard. What are the advantages of these options?

4. Why are hardware standards important to a manager?

5. Describe why it is important to make backup copies of data files stored on magnetic media.

6. Describe the power of a central processing unit. What additional characteristics of a complete computer system should be examined when comparing the power of one system to another?

7. What does it mean when a computer system is I/O bound? How might a computer system become I/O bound?

8. What is a multimedia PC? What hardware features are common to multimedia PCs?

9. What is PCMCIA? How is PCMCIA technology useful to managers?

10. What is a hierarchical storage system? What advantages does it provide?

11. What does downsizing mean in terms of computer hardware?

PROBLEMS

1. **The Jolincraft Corporation.** Jolincraft is a small company that produces cedar furniture for outdoor patios. The company has been in business only one year, but the sales of its products have been growing rapidly because the furniture is relatively inexpensive, strong, and free of maintenance. The company is considering the acquisition of a minicomputer system to improve the efficiency of its accounting system. It realizes that it will need to purchase one or more printers for the computer system to produce printed, multipart customer invoices, purchase orders, customer statements, and employee W-2 forms, periodic financial statements for the firm, paychecks, and other accounting forms and reports.

   a. What factors should the company consider when selecting its printer(s)?

   b. What types of printers might the company consider to accomplish its work?

   c. What type of printer(s) do you recommend for it and why?

2. **Secondary storage systems.** Prepare a paper analyzing one of the following secondary storage systems:

   a. Optical disk systems

   b. Winchester disk systems

   c. Flash memory cards

   d. Floptical disk systems

   Include in your paper data pertaining to system components, costs, storage capacities, and access times or transfer rates. Use as your sources of information any of the following: (1) on-line computer magazines (ezines), (2) Internet search tools, (3) the *Computer Literature Index,* published by Applied Computer Research, Inc., Phoenix, Arizona, (4) Internet Web sites of vendors, and (5) the CD-ROM database Computer Select.

3. **CISC versus RISC.** Complete a paper that compares one CISC to one RISC system in terms of power (MHz, MIPS, word size, cost, and compatibility). Use as your sources of information any of the following: (1) on-line computer magazines (ezines), (2) Internet search tools, (3) the *Computer Literature*

Index, published by Applied Computer Research, Inc., Phoenix, Arizona, (4) Internet Web sites of vendors, and (5) the CD-ROM database Computer Select.

4. **System specifications.** Browse to the Internet site of a major computer manufacturer and examine the vendor's newest desktop microcomputer system and newest notebook computer system. Gather the specifications for both systems. Then use Internet search tools to obtain additional information about the models, such as articles or product reviews. Alternatively, use the *Computer Literature Index* or the *Guide to Business Periodicals* to find articles that review the computer systems. Prepare a written review comparing the features of each system. Web addresses for several major personal computer vendors are listed at the end of this chapter under "Selected Internet Reference Sites."

CASES

1. **Toronto Office Supply Company.**
Gerald Clark is president of Toronto Office Supply Company in Toronto, Canada. The company began with one store two years ago and has quickly added six branch stores in the Toronto metropolitan area. However, it has not computerized its operations. As a result, costs for record keeping have been escalating. Clark responds to criticism about the lack of computerization by remarking that he has been too involved with the growth of the company to pay attention to this part of the operations. However, rising clerical costs, mainly the personnel costs needed to maintain records, and sluggish office operations, have compelled Clark to face this issue. As a result, he hired Maple Leaf Associates, a computer consulting firm, to advise him on the computerization of all seven of his retail outlets. After visiting the company and talking with Clark and various managers, sales personnel, and office clerks, a consultant from Maple Leaf Associates recommended that Clark purchase and install a number of computer systems, all based on a major vendor's just-introduced chip. She also made recommendations about purchasing computer programs and providing installation, training, and maintenance.

When Clark discussed the Maple Leaf recommendations with his senior staff, however, there was some dissent. Charles Robertson, the company's financial officer, felt that the cost of the computers themselves was too high. He recommended that the company wait a few months for the price of these computer systems to settle down. He pointed out that computer prices have been falling a great deal lately. He didn't see any reason why the company could not wait a few months more to get much better prices for the equipment. Sarah Blake, the company's marketing officer, was concerned that the company was purchasing computer systems that were already obsolete. She pointed out that the computer systems Maple Leaf Associates recommended were based on a chip that is likely to be pushed aside soon, since the chip maker was already at work on its next chip model.

  a. What is your analysis of Robertson's objection?
  b. What is your analysis of Blake's objection?
  c. What is your analysis of the consultant's recommendation?

2. **Deluxe Deliveries.** Donna Carlino started a packaging and delivery service about three years ago in a small town near a major metropolitan area. Her business offers wrapping, boxing, insurance, delivery, and other services associated with mailing or delivering packages for individuals and small businesses. She operates the store herself for much of the day, relying on part-time help during seasonal peaks and weekends. She also has employees who drive company

trucks to pick up and deliver packages for customers.

Carlino believes now is the time for her to automate some of her operations, specifically, accounting and delivery. Output of the system would be primarily accounting reports, delivery schedules, and customer invoices. Marcus Sykwuz, who runs the only computer store in town, suggested that she purchase a high-end microcomputer system. The system comes with a very high resolution color screen; the maximum amount of RAM; the largest hard drive possible for that model; and a microphone, speakers, and sound board. He suggested also that she purchase a laser printer for her documents, including the multipart sales invoices. If you were asked to advise Carlino, would you agree with Sykwuz's recommendations? If not, what would you suggest that Carlino consider in the way of a computer system and peripherals?

3. **Roscoe Manufacturing Company.** The staff of Roscoe Manufacturing Company has been using IBM compatible computer systems from a major manufacturer for several years to write letters, memos, reports, and other documents and to prepare budgets and other financial reports. The computer systems were purchased from a local computer dealer who delivered, installed, and trained the staff in the use of the systems. The same dealer has maintained the equipment since its purchase.

Because the company has grown and its staff increased, the company needs to buy additional computer systems. Dale Vincent, who is in accounting, would like to purchase these computer systems as cheaply as possible. He feels that the company ought to purchase a number of computer systems from a mail-order vendor in order to get the lowest price. He claims that these machines can be purchased for quite a bit less than machines bought from a local computer dealer. Rose Delaney, who is in marketing, wants the company to consider buying Macintosh computer systems because she has heard that Macintosh computers offer

the best graphic capabilities, permitting her to produce attractive product announcements, customer newsletters, and other marketing materials. Shiela Ruggins, who is in engineering, wants the company to consider purchasing a Digital Equipment Corporation VAX minicomputer system so that the staff of the engineering department can be attached to the same minicomputer. She believes that this system would facilitate communications and reduce paper handling. Chuck Demond, who is in production, wants the company to consider buying the new Breeze computer system offered by WhirlWind Computer Systems. WhirlWind Computer Systems will offer the Breeze computer system commercially in just two months, and Chuck wants to wait for the new system to avoid buying existing equipment that will quickly become obsolete. Felix Mannix, who is in personnel, thinks that each department should be allowed to buy the system that best fits its needs. You are in charge of acquiring the additional computer resources. What concerns should you have about the recommendations of Dale Vincent, Rose Delaney, Sheila Ruggins, Chuck Demond, or Felix Mannix?

4. **Findley Automotive Parts Company.** Findley Automotive Parts Company is a wholesale automotive parts distributor that sells auto parts in a large metropolitan area. The company has one warehouse for its parts, located in the same building as its office, and employs 14 salespeople who spend most of their time in the field calling on retail stores and auto parts shops in a metropolitan area that contains many cities and towns. When salespeople call on customers, the salespeople complete sales order forms for the merchandise the customer wants to buy. The salespeople drop off those sales orders at the office at the end of each day. At the office, four order-entry clerks use key-to-tape machines to key in the sales order data dropped off by the salespeople the previous day. On some large orders from important customers and on

rush orders, the salespeople will call in the orders directly to the order-entry clerks. The tapes produced by the order entry clerks are mounted on tape drives and read into the computer system on the day following their entry. At the same time, the original orders are sent to the shipping department to be filled. This system, however, is not working well at Findley. For example, salespeople complain that they have to spend too much time traveling to the office to deliver sales orders. Generally, salespeople end their sales day early to drop off the orders, or they drop them off in the morning of the second day. They would rather spend their time selling. The order-entry clerks complain that they often have trouble reading the handwritten sales orders. Conversely, salespeople complain that there are too many errors in filled orders. That is, too many orders are filled with the wrong amount or type of merchandise. Also, salespeople report that customers are waiting too long for their orders to be delivered and that too often the goods they ordered are out of stock.

a. Which features of the current system might be responsible for slow deliveries and stockouts?

b. Which features of the current system might be responsible for order errors?

c. What changes in procedures and hardware might improve the order-entry process at Findley? Specifically, which technologies could Findley use to reduce errors in sales order entry, increase the efficiency of salespeople, and shorten delivery time?

Selected Internet Reference Sites

Apple Computer, Inc. (http://product.info.apple.com).

Digital Equipment Corporation (http://www.dec.com).

Florida Academy of Family Physicians (http://www.med.ufl.edu/medinfo/ffp/pda.html), last revised December 10, 1995.

Free On-line Dictionary of Computing (http://wombat.doc.ic.ac.uk).

IBM Corporation (http://www.ibm.com).

Intel Corporation (http://www.intel.com).

Physix (http://www.physix.com/), last revised September 16, 1996.

RAID storage systems (http://www.tritec.de/sunworldonline/swol-09-1995/swol-09-raid5.html), last updated September 1, 1995.

Sun Microsystems, Inc. (http://www.sun.com).

Selected References and Readings

Alsop, S. "These Guys Want to Take Away Our PCs." *Fortune,* October 14, 1996, p. 228.

Applied Computer Research. *Computer Literature Index.* A monthly index of computer publications, including those covering mainframe, minicomputer, and microcomputer systems.

Brown, B. "An Ink Jet in Every Pot." *PC Magazine,* May 28, 1996, p. 301.

Cahlin, M. "10 Tips for Buying a Notebook." *PC Today,* April 1996, p. 96.

Cope, J. "I/O Technologies: How Do They Compare?" *PC Today,* February 1996, p. 84.

Copy, J. "Zip vs. EZ: Removable Drives Aim to Fill Low-Cost Void." *PC Today,* October 1995, p. 58.

Datapro Corporation. *Datapro Reports.* A series of reports pertaining to topics in computer systems, including mainframe, minicomputer, and microcomputer systems.

Doolittle, S. "The Art of Acquisition." *PC Today,* September 1996, p. 78.

Germain, J. M. "The Changing Face of CD-ROM Technology." *PC Today,* January 1996, p. 82.

Grotta, D. and S. W. Grotta. "The Death of Film." *PC Magazine,* February 6, 1996, p. 145.

Huttig, J. W. "Power (PC) Struggle." *PC Today,* January 1995, p. 19.

Jacobs, D. S. "How to Build a Creation [multimedia] Workstation." *Multimedia World,* May 1996, p. 74.

Martin, M. "When Info Worlds Collide." *Fortune,* October 28, 1996, p. 130.

Ozer, J. "Digital Video: Shot by Shot." *PC Magazine,* April 11, 1995, p. 104.

Thomas, S. G. "The Ultimate Home PC." *U.S. News & World Report,* November 25, 1996.

Whiting, R. "Spoilt for Choice." *Client/Server Computing,* October 1996, p. 40.

Microcomputer magazines: *Computer Shopper* is a monthly magazine that contains advertisements and articles for all kinds of computer hardware and programs; *VAX Professional* and *Digital Review* emphasize Digital Equipment Corporation computers; *Macworld* emphasizes Macintosh computer systems; *PC Week, PC World,* and *PC Magazine* report on IBM and IBM clones; *Byte* and *InfoWorld* report on microcomputer systems in general; *PC Today* offers information about microcomputer systems and peripherals and lists low-priced microcomputer hardware and software.

6 CHAPTER

COMPUTER SOFTWARE

CHAPTER OUTLINE

Manager's View

Systems Software

Communications Software

Other Systems Software

Microcomputer Operating Systems

Application Software

Development Software

General Software Features and Trends

Selecting Microcomputer Software

Management Concerns

Management Summary

Key Terms for Managers

Review Questions

Questions for Discussion

Problems

Cases

Selected Internet Reference Sites

Selected References and Readings

- An investment manager of a trust department wants to upgrade the computer systems in his department so that his staff can improve their financial analyses, especially the analyses of alternate investments of his client's funds. Friends have told the manager that one hardware vendor's equipment is usually more reliable and less expensive than the computer systems of other manufacturers. But he does not know whether that vendor's equipment will run software that will improve his staff's investment analyses.

- A marketing vice president wants to be able to access company data and get answers to her questions about problems that occur in sales and advertising at irregular intervals. Many of her questions are one-time questions; that is, she wants answers to questions she is not likely to ask again.

- An affirmative action manager of a large organization must decide whether to purchase commercial software to assist his department in completing government reports or have the company's information systems department create software specifically designed for his department's needs.

- A purchasing manager has just received purchase requests from two departments in the firm. Each department wants to order different brands of word processors, and neither of these word processors is the same as the one currently used by most departments.

So far, you have learned about computer system hardware, or the electronic and electromechanical devices that are part of a computer system. The features, or the bells and whistles, of computer hardware are very exciting. In fact, the advances that have taken place in computer hardware are breathtaking. However, the key issue for the manager is to get the computer system, with all its bells and whistles, working on problems that must be solved. Knowing that some computer terminals offer high-resolution screens or have lots of memory is not the same as knowing how to retrieve the right data from a computer system when you need to make a decision. In other words, the computer system is most useful when it can do the work you need done. It is the applications of the computer system that should most interest the manager.

For all its bells and whistles, computer hardware is pretty stupid. It is not able to operate without detailed instructions, or programs, called computer **software.** It is the software that makes computer hardware apply itself to your problems and makes the system useful to you. Thus you must have a clear notion of what software is really all about, what software is available to you, and how you can use this software in your work.

Computer system software may be classified into three broad categories:

- Systems software
- Application software
- Development software

Systems software manages the computer system hardware. **Application software** processes your data in the way you want it processed. Both types of software are essential to a computer system. **Development software** is used to create software of all types.

This chapter explains the basics of systems, application, and development software. Chapters in Part III of the book are devoted to specific types of application software and their use in management decision making.

SYSTEMS SOFTWARE

A computer system represents a number of resources that must be managed. These resources include the hardware components of the system: the central processing unit, memory, and peripherals such as secondary storage devices and printers. In many organizations, these resources cost a great deal of money, and their use should be carefully managed. To manage a computer system's hardware components, to coordinate them so that they work together efficiently, and to schedule them to make the best use of the computer's time, it is necessary to add a set of instructions that monitors and manages the system. This set of instructions is commonly referred to as *systems software.* By managing a computer system's hardware and available time, systems software acts as the linkage, or *interface,* between the computer system and the application programs the user wants to run (see Figure 6–1).

People who write or maintain systems software are called *systems programmers.* Systems programmers are also responsible for optimizing the performance of the organization's computer systems. Organizations with large computer systems usually include systems programmers on their staffs to tailor the systems software they use to the special needs of their organizations.

Systems software includes many different types of programs, such as operating systems software, communications software, and systems utility software.

Figure 6–1

The systems software interface

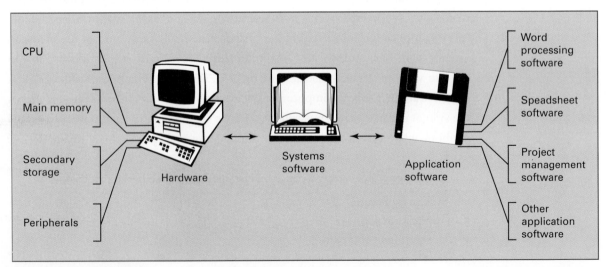

CPU		Word processing software
Main memory		Speadsheet software
Secondary storage	Hardware ↔ Systems software ↔ Application software	Project management software
Peripherals		Other application software

Operating Systems

An **operating system** is a set of programs that manages and controls computer resources, including the CPU, peripherals, main memory, and secondary storage. On large computers, operating systems often comprise many programs. On small computers, operating systems may consist of only a few programs. In either case, part or all of the operating system must be loaded into main memory for the computer system to function completely.

Operating system programs coordinate hardware through such activities as scheduling jobs to be run, queuing jobs, allocating memory to various job tasks, and communicating to the computer operator the status of the jobs and the computer system. Before operating system programs were developed, computer operators manually had to accomplish these activities. Computer operators scheduled jobs to run on the computer, loaded the programs and the data for each job, prepared printers or other devices to receive the output, and otherwise managed the tasks to be accomplished. The problem with this system was that computers operate at billionths of a second and computer operators perform at human rates of speed. While the human operators were setting up the next program and data to be run, the computer sat idle. In fact, studies of the use of computer systems in those days showed that they were idle most of the time. Thus much computer time was wasted. Operating systems software was designed to eliminate these inefficiencies and to manage computer time more effectively. Basically, it accomplishes these objectives by automatically performing the work formerly done by computer operators, or "operating" the computer system much as computer operators once did.

Operating systems typically include supervisory programs, job management programs, and input/output (I/O) management programs (see Figure 6-2). *Supervisory programs* are the heart of the operating system and are primarily responsible for managing computer resources. Frequently used supervisory programs usually are kept loaded, or *resident,* in main memory. These programs are called *resident programs.* The other supervisory programs and other components of the operating system typically are kept on a direct access storage device, such as a hard disk, so that they may be transferred to main memory quickly when needed. These programs are called *transient programs* (see Figure 6-3).

Figure 6–2

Components of an operating system

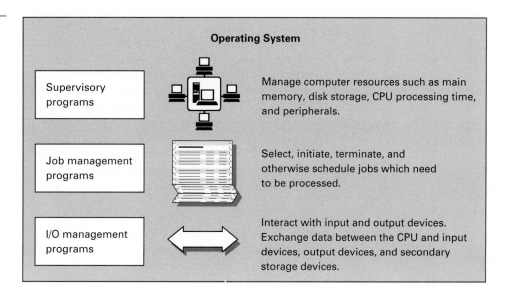

Operating System

Supervisory programs — Manage computer resources such as main memory, disk storage, CPU processing time, and peripherals.

Job management programs — Select, initiate, terminate, and otherwise schedule jobs which need to be processed.

I/O management programs — Interact with input and output devices. Exchange data between the CPU and input devices, output devices, and secondary storage devices.

Figure 6–3

A model showing the allocation of main memory when an operating system, more than one application program, and more than one data file are resident

Main Memory

Resident supervisory programs
Transient operating systems programs
Application program 1
Data for application program 1
Application program 2
Data for application program 2

Job management programs select, initiate, terminate, and otherwise schedule jobs that need to be processed. These programs maximize the efficiency with which the computer resources are used and the processing is performed. Computer resources include the time a program will take to run, the input and output devices the program will need, and the amount of memory the program will need.

I/O management programs assign input and output resources to programs and manage the transfer of data between main memory and these resources, including disk drives, tape drives, and printers. When data is needed from a disk or data needs to be sent to the printer, the supervisory program turns these duties over to the I/O management programs.

Multi-programming

One of the important ways operating systems manage computer resources efficiently is to allow multiple programs to run seemingly at the same time through **multiprogramming.** Operating systems achieve multiprogramming by allowing more than one program and its associated data to reside in main memory at the same time. Operating systems divide main memory into partitions, and place each program and its data in separate partitions (see Figure 6–3).

Operating systems that are capable of multiprogramming take advantage of the differences in the speeds of I/O and CPU processing. While the CPU is waiting for data from a hard disk drive to complete one application program, it can complete calculations or other processing for another application program. In fact, because the time it takes to access the data from hard disk is likely to be measured in milliseconds (thousandths of a second) and the processing by the CPU is likely to be measured in nanoseconds (billionths of a second), the CPU has plenty of time to complete processing for several application programs while it waits for data for another application program. By carefully scheduling what the computer system does, control programs can coordinate the running of many application programs so that idle time of the CPU and peripherals is kept to a minimum.

Time-Sharing

Another way to allow many programs to run seemingly at the same time is to offer each program a brief amount, or slice, of computer time to process its data. This procedure is called **time-sharing** or *time slicing.* Using time-sharing, the system rapidly moves from program to program, performing work. The system moves so quickly that to any one user it appears to be devoted exclusively to his or her program. The difference between multiprogramming and time-sharing is that in time-sharing the operating system allots a fixed amount of time to each program. In multiprogramming, the operating system moves from program to program when it encounters a logical stopping point, such as having to wait for data to be read into main memory from secondary storage.

It should be emphasized that although multiprogramming and time-sharing operating systems interweave the processing of several programs, they don't actually permit a single CPU to process data from several programs simultaneously; it just seems that way to the user.

Multiprocessing

Multiprocessing operating systems permit the simultaneous processing of several application programs by controlling more than one CPU at a time. The operating systems allow two or more CPUs to work together, sharing memory and peripheral devices. Thus each program that is being processed may be processed by separate CPUs dedicated to one program. This type of multiprocessing is called *asymmetric multiprocessing.* Another form of multiprocessing also uses multiple CPUs. One CPU acts as the controller of the others and assigns any CPU any application task. The main CPU also controls I/O tasks. This type of multiprocessing is called *symmetric multiprocessing.*

Parallel Processing

Some operating systems use more than one CPU to permit many tasks from *one* program to be completed simultaneously through **parallel processing.** That is, several steps in a program are processed in parallel using multiple CPUs.

Virtual Storage

Operating systems may offer **virtual storage,** or virtual memory, to overcome the size limitations of a computer system's main memory. For example, suppose that the program you wished to use required more main memory than you have in your computer system, or even more main memory than you could possibly have in your computer system. To solve the problem, the computer keeps parts of the program that are not needed immediately in secondary storage until they are required. When these parts are needed, they are read into main memory. The secondary storage device typically used is a hard disk because of its speed in retrieving the parts of the program directly. As a result, you have *virtually* as much main memory capacity as you have in main memory plus the memory capacity that has been allocated on the hard disk. Virtual memory creates the illusion of larger main memory by letting programs and data alternate their usage of main memory.

COMMUNICATIONS SOFTWARE

Communications software is really an extension to the operating system of a computer—it provides the additional logic for the computer system to control a variety of communications equipment so that it can communicate with peripherals, such as display terminals located far from the CPU. Communications software supervises such functions as communicating with remote terminals, monitoring communications equipment and lines, managing traffic on communications lines, logging and analyzing communications traffic, and diagnosing communications problems. Many personal computer operating systems now include communications programs as part of their standard package.

On mainframe computers communications software is a collection of programs costing many thousands of dollars and involving a host of peripheral equipment. On microcomputers communications software permits a microcomputer to connect to local or remote networks. Connecting to these networks may then allow the PC to "talk" to a mainframe, a minicomputer, or another microcomputer from a remote location or to connect to a group of microcomputers in a room, floor, or building.

Of special interest to many managers is software that allows their home or notebook microcomputers to connect to their organization's networks so that they can use these microcomputers as remote workstations. Communications hardware and software will be presented in depth in Chapters 8 and 9.

OTHER SYSTEMS SOFTWARE

There are many other types of systems software, only one of which is mentioned here: system utility software. *System utility programs* are just that—programs that operating system users find useful. Most system utility programs are designed to handle repetitive functions such as sorting records in files, finding data and programs on a hard disk, listing the data files and programs stored on hard disks, merging one group of data with another, copying data and programs from one secondary storage device to another, making copies of data and programs, diagnosing system performance, formatting magnetic media so that the media can be used, compressing files, and providing system security.

MICROCOMPUTER OPERATING SYSTEMS

As a manager, you may use a computer terminal attached to a mainframe or minicomputer system. In these situations you may not have much direct contact with the operating system your computer system uses. If you use a microcomputer, however, you almost certainly will make direct, hands-on use of its operating system. Because there is a high probability that you will use a microcomputer in your work, you should know something about typical microcomputer operating systems (see Manager's Memo 6–1).

Single- and Multitasking Operating Systems

Many microcomputer operating systems, such as MS-DOS, are *single-user,* **single-tasking operating systems.** They allow only one person to run *one* program at a time. In the past the term **multitasking operating systems** referred to microcomputer operating systems with multiprogramming capabilities that were limited to a single user, such as the System 7 operating system for Macintosh computers. The term *multitasking* has evolved, however. Microcomputer versions of the UNIX operating system, for example, are characterized as being multitasking and *multiuser* because they permit more than one program to run and more than one person to use the system at one time.

Multitasking microcomputer operating systems may allow you to receive a fax message at the same time you are editing another document or to search a large data file for a specific record while you are entering data into a new record. In multitasking systems the task that the operating system is working on (searching for a record) while you complete another is called a *background task.* The task that you are working on (entering data into a new record) is called a *foreground task.* When the CPU

Today's powerful microcomputers (see Chapter 5) are being driven by ever more powerful operating systems. Some new and some old operating systems for these new microcomputers include:

- *Windows NT*   Developed and sold by Microsoft, Windows NT is expected to become as dominant in its arena as MS-DOS and Windows became in theirs. Windows NT is a 32-bit graphical-user interface (GUI) operating system offering multiuser, multitasking, multiprocessing, and built-in networking capabilities. It is capable of running on computer systems designed using either CISC or RISC architectures, including computer systems using Digital Equipment Corporation's Alpha chip (see Chapter 5).

- *Windows 95*   This 32-bit, multitasking operating system replaces Windows 3.1 and provides integrated networking support. Windows 95 also includes "plug and play" capability, automatically configuring expansion boards without requiring users to set switches and jumpers. It will be upgraded to Windows 97 in 1997.

- *DOS*   This is a single-user, single-tasking operating system for 16- to 32-bit machines with versions offered by Digital Research Corporation, Microsoft, and IBM.

- *OS/2*   Sold by IBM, OS/2's latest version offers 32-bit processing and multitasking along with a GUI environment. It also supports voice recognition (in six languages) and comes with a built-in vocabulary of 22,000 words.

- *UNIX*   Several companies offer various versions of the UNIX operating system, such as AIX, Xenix, and Ultrix. These versions offer a 32-bit multiuser, multitasking operating system with built-in networking capabilities. The version developed by SunSoft adds multiprocessing capabilities, a GUI environment, and the ability to run on computer systems based on either CISC or RISC architectures.

- *Macintosh Operating System*   The versions of System 8 are single-user, multitasking operating systems for 32-bit Macintosh computers. Apple plans to merge System 8 and the next operating system into a new product call Rhapsody.

has no actions to take on foreground tasks, it operates on the background tasks. Given that even the fastest keyboarders type at speeds measured in words per minute, the CPU, which measures its work in nanoseconds, is yawning from lack of work between each key we strike. Therefore, the CPU works on the search task in what appear to it as enormous gulfs of time between the keystrokes of our fast-flying fingers.

Task Switching   Some microcomputer operating system software may let you load more than one program at a time and switch between these programs. You can have one program running in the foreground and several others suspended in the background. It is important to notice that the programs in the background do not continue to run—their operation is suspended. This process is called **task switching.** These operating systems typically let you task switch from one program to another by striking only one or two hot keys. *Hot keys* are simple combinations of one or two keys that allow you to suspend the operation of one program and move to another. For example, the hot keys might be the Alt key and the Tab key.

Kernel   On microcomputers, the frequently used portion of the operating system is called the *kernel,* and the kernel is what is loaded into the microcomputer's main memory. The remainder of the operating system and most of the utility programs usually remain stored on a hard disk to be used when needed. Ordinarily the operating system kernel must be on a diskette in the main diskette drive or on the hard drive of the microcomputer when the computer is first turned on. When the microcomputer is turned on, the kernel is *booted,* or loaded, into main memory automatically.

Utilities

Some of the most commonly used utilities of a microcomputer operating system include those that allow you to

- Copy the contents of one diskette to another diskette allowing you to make a *backup* or *archive copy* of a data diskette or an application program.
- Copy just one file or a group of files rather than the entire contents of the diskette.
- Prepare, or *format,* a new, blank diskette to receive data from the computer system. You can't store data on a diskette until it is formatted, or initialized. The formatting process writes the sectors on the diskette so that the operating system is able to place data in these locations.
- Delete files stored on a diskette.
- View the contents of files.
- List the file names and file details contained on a diskette, including the size of files, the time and day they were last revised, and how much unused memory is left on the diskette.
- Compress the data on a drive in order to store more data on that drive (Manager's Memo 6–2).
- Provide security by such means as blanking screens, locking keyboards, preventing files from being deleted, or demanding passwords for access.

Third-Party Software Vendors

Many users are not satisfied with the number, features, or quality of the system utilities their operating system offers. When this happens, they may purchase system utilities from a software firm other than the one that developed the operating system they use. In other words, they buy these utilities from a *third-party software vendor*. For example, many microcomputer users purchase a compression utility program (for example, PKZIP), or they purchase a suite of utility programs, including a backup program, bundled into one package (for example, Norton Utilities).

Manager's Memo 6–2	**DATA COMPRESSION**

◤ Many computer users fill their hard disks and other secondary storage media very quickly, much like they probably fill their attics. Whether they fill their media with old junk or important files, data compression systems can help them store more.

Data compression reduces the space that data occupy by various means, such as eliminating space wasted on inefficient data coding, repetitions of identical patterns of data, and data formatting. For example, compression systems usually look for multibyte repetitions of data, such as a string of zeros in a number, and then use a one- or two-byte "token" to substitute for that data sequence wherever it occurs. The longer these data sequences are and the more frequently they occur, the greater the compression that can be achieved.

The type of data that you have on disk or tape also alters the amount of space you save. Usually you can compress program files very little. You can compress

text or document files much more, usually somewhat less than 2 to 1. However, you can compress graphics files a great deal, usually more than 2 to 1. Many experts suggest that you can expect almost to double your hard disk capacity with compression. For example, your 1GB hard disk can be expanded to hold almost 2GB of data.

The population of attic fillers must be very large because the demand for disk compression has been very great. For PCs, disk compression is available by buying disk compression hardware, software, or both or by buying an operating system that provides disk compression.

Another major use of compression is to make files smaller for transmitting over communications lines. By compressing files into smaller sizes, the time needed to transmit them is reduced, along with transmission costs.

Hardware Dependence

An operating system may be limited to running on specific hardware or may have versions that allow it to run on many different types of computer systems. For example, Windows 95 runs on computer systems using Intel's complex instruction set (CISC) CPU chips. System 7 is an operating system that works on Macintosh computers using Motorola CPU chips. Windows operating systems will not work on Macintosh machines unless they are specially fitted with additional hardware or software; likewise, System 7 will not work on IBM PC clones. Versions of Windows NT, however, will run on both reduced instruction set (RISC) and CISC computer systems.

Operating System Interfaces

The ease with which you can use an operating system is important to the manager. Clearly, easy-to-use operating systems allow managers and other users to save learning and operating time. The operating system features by which the user interacts, or interfaces, with the operating system is called the **user interface.** For example, users interact with the MS-DOS and UNIX operating systems by typing keyboard *commands* (the keystroke combinations that make the program do what you want it to) at a *system prompt*. A systems prompt is a character, symbol, or combination of the two that tells you that the system is waiting for you to give it a command.

Command-Line User Interfaces

If you were using the MS-DOS operating system and wanted to find the names of files stored on a diskette, you would place the diskette into drive A and type the command below (DIR) at the systems prompt (A:>):

A:>DIR

The screen would then display a listing or directory of the files that are on your diskette. For example, the following files might be displayed on your screen:

CONTRACT DOC	1320	10-09-97	4:56p
FOLLOWUP TXT	4590	10-12-97	3:22p
MARSHAL DOC	5198	10-12-97	3:56p

In response to the command DIR, the operating system has listed the names of each file on the diskette, the size of the files in bytes, and the date and time that the files were created or last changed.

MS-DOS and UNIX are said to provide *command-line user interfaces* because you must type commands on a line. You use the keyboard to interface with the operating system.

Graphical User Interfaces

Learning, remembering, and using many different keyboard commands can be intimidating. To provide an easier method to talk to the operating system, most software companies offer a **graphical user interface (GUI)**—pronounced "gooey." A GUI uses dialog boxes, drop-down and pop-up menus, buttons, icons, scroll bars, pointers, and other devices instead of requiring commands (see Figure 6–4). You may move a pointer around the screen with a mouse to activate programs, data files, or features. Instead of keying in commands, you "point and click"—that is, move a pointer to an icon and click a mouse button. You may also point to icons using a light pen on some systems or use your fingers with a touch-screen system. Some systems even use voice synthesizing to let you activate GUI icons by speaking. Instead of pointing to a screen feature, like an icon, and clicking the mouse, you simply say the word that represents the icon. Pointing at an icon and clicking a mouse button or speaking a word to run a program is a lot simpler than learning a series of commands.

Figure 6–4

Windows 95, an operating system that uses a GUI

Icons   Buttons   Windows   Scroll Bars

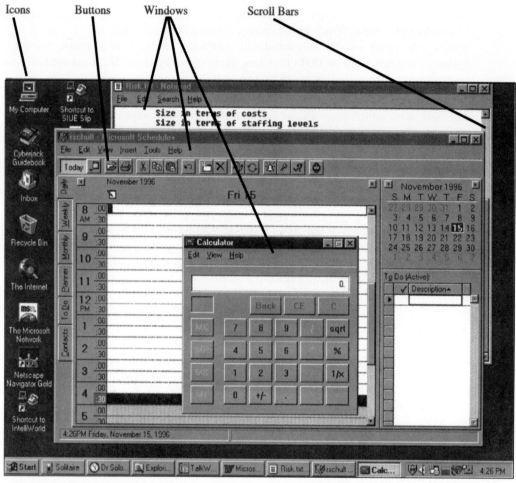

Courtesy of Microsoft Corporation.

Windowing

Operating system software may also allow you to run several programs simultaneously, view multiple data files at the same time, or both by splitting your display screen into parts called *windows*. Your display may show a document you are editing using one program in one window, a schedule you are creating using another program in another window, and a calculator you are using in still another window (see Figure 6-4).

Dynamic Data Exchange

Often users prepare a report on a project using a word processor and a budget for the same project using a spreadsheet. If the user changes an amount in the budget, the information in the document also has to be changed. Making such changes in some operating systems can be awkward. The user may have to close the budget file, exit the spreadsheet program, load the word processing program, load the report document, and then enter the changes to make the document conform to the revised budget.

Microsoft windows operating systems, however, have a feature called *dynamic data exchange* (DDE) that automatically links data in one document with another so manual updating is not necessary. In our example, DDE will automatically update the report to conform to the changes made in the budget. The operating system provides this linking process in real time; that is, as you make the changes in the spreadsheet, the changes are also made in the document, provided both the spreadsheet and word processor are loaded in memory.

APPLICATION SOFTWARE

Application programs perform specific data or text processing functions. For example, word processing and payroll programs are application programs. Programmers who develop application programs are called *application programmers*. To develop programs, application programmers use a programming language or other development software.

Custom versus Commercial Software

Many of the application programs used by organizations that have mainframe or minicomputer systems were written and developed by the application programmers employed in the data processing departments of those organizations. That is, the programs were "built" *in-house*. In other cases, the software was custom written by outside consultants or programmers. *Custom-written* software is often very expensive, but like software developed in-house, it may be the only way the organization can secure the kind of software it needs.

Increasingly, the application programs used on mainframes and especially the programs used on minicomputers and microcomputers are produced by professional software development companies. These commercially developed software application programs are bought "off the shelf" by computer users to satisfy their specific application needs. Commercially developed application software programs are called *canned programs* or *commercial software*.

Shareware and Freeware

Two inexpensive sources of off-the-shelf application and systems utility programs for microcomputers are *shareware* and *freeware*. Shareware is relatively inexpensive software that often is produced by individuals or "mom and pop" vendors and frequently distributed on the honor system through electronic bulletin boards or the Internet (see Chapter 9); that is, you can download the software from a bulletin board or the Internet without a charge. However, if you try the software, like it, and use it, you should pay the small fee to the developers. Prices for shareware software packages frequently range from $15 to $50. There are thousands of shareware programs that can be of great benefit to small businesses and even major corporations. Freeware, or *public domain software*, is similar to shareware except that freeware programs are entirely free.

Application Program Library

Regardless of the source of development, application programs are always written to run under a specific operating system. An important feature of any operating system, then, is the quantity and diversity of application programs that have been written for it, often referred to as its *library* of application programs.

Portability

At the same time, many software companies develop software that is *portable*. Software is considered portable when it (1) has different versions for many operating systems, (2) is able to switch between two or more operating systems, or (3) can be converted easily from one operating system to another. Portable software allows you to use what is or appears to be the same application program regardless of your computer system. You may use a mainframe computer at times and a minicomputer or microcomputer at other times, or you may switch between different types of microcomputers at your home and office. With portable software you may not have to learn how to operate several word processors simply because you must switch computer systems from time to time. An organization that adopts software that has versions for most or all of its computer systems saves training time and allows personnel to move easily from one job assignment and location to another.

Single-User/ Multiuser Programs

Like operating systems, application programs may be *single-user* or *multiuser* programs. For example, a word processing program may allow only one user to work on a specific document at one time, or it may allow many users to work on one document concurrently.

Categorizing Application Software by Use

Application software can also be categorized into general purpose software, function-specific software, and industry-specific software. *General purpose software* can be used by people in many different industries, at many different levels of organizations, and with many different job titles. For example, anyone who must create and edit documents can use word processing software. *Function-specific software* is designed to address the needs and problems of major business functions, such as accounting software, financial analysis software, marketing software, personnel management software, and manufacturing software. *Industry-specific software* includes programs that are tailored to the problems and needs of a particular industry. For example, job estimating programs are available for the construction industry and accounting programs are available specifically for the health industry. Industry-specific software programs are often developed by companies within the industry that spend the time and energy to create a program for their own needs. Once developed, the companies try to spread the program development costs by selling copies to other organizations.

Desktop Suites

Commercial software may be sold as *stand-alone packages* or as *suites* of integrated and compatible packages that are designed to work together. For example, a mainframe COBOL-language processor may be designed for a specific mainframe operating system and sold by itself. A microcomputer spreadsheet may be designed for a specific operating system and also sold by itself.

Stand-alone packages may pose problems for the manager. For instance, the manager may have a sales proposal prepared for a customer using a word processor and then prepare a budget using a spreadsheet. If the two products are stand-alone packages from different software companies, they may not be compatible. That is, the word processor may not be able to read the budget file prepared by the spreadsheet package. As a result, the budget may have to be printed out on paper using the spreadsheet package and then rekeyed into the word processing file to complete the proposal document. Software incompatibility causes a good deal of frustration and also costs time and money.

Suites of software that are compatible and integrated offer real advantages. First, these packages are compatible in that the **menus** (lists of program choices you are shown on a screen), **prompts** (usually helpful hints on the screen about what to do next), and commands are either the same or very similar throughout the applications. Second, the output of one application is readable by the others. Thus, using a suite of compatible software packages rather than incompatible stand-alone packages offers great benefits. Not only can each program you use read files prepared by the other applications, but also you do not have to learn multiple sets of commands. The former reduces the costs and errors that occur because data must be reentered; the latter reduces employee training costs.

However, software suites have some drawbacks. For example, the spreadsheet package of a suite might meet your needs, but the word processor might not have the features you require.

Personal computer systems purchased today are often sold "bundled" with a suite of commonly used application software packages. These **software suites** may include a word processor, a spreadsheet program, database software, and a presentation graphics program. For example, Microsoft bundles together Word (a word processor), Excel (a spreadsheet program), PowerPoint (a presentation graphics program), and Access (a database management program) into a suite of programs called Microsoft Office. Corel Corporation offers a similar suite called Office Professional.

Word processing software. **Word processing software** is a collection of application programs that permit the user to create, edit, and print documents primarily composed of text, although these documents may also contain data, images, tables, charts, and even sound (see Figure 6–5).

Word processing software may come with a variety of integrated proofing tools, such as an on-line spell checker, grammar checker, and thesaurus, as well as programs that create drawings, outlines, indexes, footnotes, and tables of contents (see the drop-down menu of tools in Figure 6–5): merge documents with addresses in a database file for mass mailings; and fax documents through your computer's modem. They also have programs that let you convert documents produced by other word processors.

Figure 6–5

A drop-down menu from WordPerfect for Windows showing many integrated support programs such as an on-line spell checker, grammar checker, and thesaurus

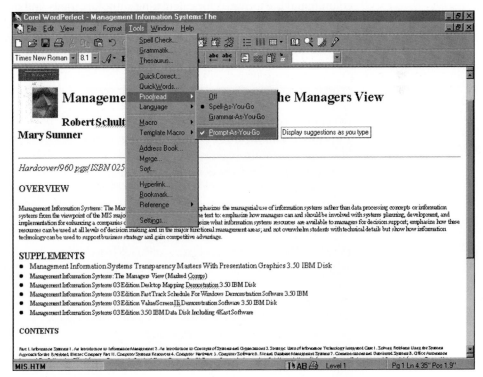

Courtesy of Corel Corporation.

The economic value of word processing software is often measured by the increased productivity of the clerical and secretarial employees who use that software. Though preparing documents the first time is easier and faster with a word processor, the real gains in productivity occur when revisions to the original document must be made. The ability to make revisions quickly, without having to retype the entire document, reduces document preparation costs substantially. Also, the ability to merge customer names and addresses with a form sales letter and print out the finished product on letterhead paper automatically reduces clerical costs enormously.

At the same time, because the use of microcomputers by managers has become widespread, many managers now prepare or edit their own documents—something a secretary would have done in the past. Substituting higher-cost managerial time for lower-cost clerical time to produce or edit documents increases document costs substantially.

Spreadsheet software.   **Spreadsheet software** allows managers to prepare budgets, tax analyses, investment portfolio analyses, sales and profit projections, and many other financial documents with ease. Sometimes referred to as an electronic scratch pad, spreadsheets are frequently used to solve financial problems presented in columnar fashion. Often, these problems were completed laboriously with a calculator in the past.

Spreadsheet software allows the manager to design partially completed tables or forms called **templates** (see Figure 6-6), which contain the headings and names of the items in the spreadsheet. The templates also contain the formulas used to calculate column or row totals, column or row averages, and other statistical quantities on the values entered into the template. For example, a budget template might include the table heading; the column headings; the names of the budget line items in the first column; and the formulas for calculating subtotals, totals, and percent changes. A manager can use a well-designed template (see Manager's Memo 6-3) time after time simply by entering the specific amounts for each line item and correcting the dates.

Figure 6–6

Part of a template for a budget spreadsheet

	A	B	C	D
1	Receiving Department			
2	Budget Estimate			
3	1/1/-- - 12/31/--			
4				
5		Actual	Estimated	
6		Payments	Payments	Percent
7	Budget Items	19--	19--	Change
8				
9	Salaries	0	0	0.00%
10	Wages	0	0	0.00%
11	Telephone	0	0	0.00%
12	Equipment	0	0	0.00%
13	Services	0	0	0.00%
14	Supplies	0	0	0.00%
15	Travel	0	0	0.00%
16	Postage	0	0	0.00%
17	Other	0	0	0.00%
18				
19	Totals	0	0	
20	Goal		0	
21	Difference		0	
22				

The most powerful use of spreadsheet software involves the ability to enter formulas as well as data so that the user may simulate various solutions to problems, using a what-if approach. That is, the user may enter a number of different values, such as production costs, and see the effect on the results, such as product profit margins. The formulas entered may vary from a simple column total or percentage to the more complicated return on investment or net present value calculation. Because it allows managers to answer "what-if" questions pertaining to financial problems, spreadsheet software provides an important managerial decision support tool.

Looking at the simple budget shown in Figure 6–7—the budget template in Figure 6–6 with the data filled in—the manager can quickly see the effects of increases and decreases in the amounts estimated for salaries, services, or other budget items by entering different percentages in one or more of the lines in the Percent Change column of the spreadsheet. For example, the manager can easily see the effect on the total budget if the estimated percent change for telephone expenses is 5 percent instead of 2 percent. Of course, the example shown is a simple one; real budget spreadsheets are usually much more complex. However, if the spreadsheet is designed properly, simulating the effects of different values is no more difficult than in our budget example.

The budget shown in the illustration is a simple financial model of a department. Spreadsheets allow the manager to develop quantitative models to help solve many organization problems. One model that can be developed using a spreadsheet allows managers to compare the differing costs related to buying, leasing, or renting an asset. Such a model usually compares the net present value of the cash flows resulting from the acquisition of an asset through purchase, lease, rental, and lease/purchase plans. The ability of the spreadsheet to display the data in both tabular and chart forms makes reading or presenting the budget easier.

Manager's Memo 6–3 | **EVALUATING YOUR SPREADSHEET DESIGN**

 1. Did you include the name of the developer or reviser in the spreadsheet?

2. Did you include the date of construction or revision in the spreadsheet?

3. Did you briefly describe the purpose of the spreadsheet in the spreadsheet?

4. Did you identify the sources of data for the spreadsheet?

5. Did you include a legend that defines any special symbols, abbreviations, or terms used?

6. Did you name cells used in formulas where appropriate? For example, in a budget spreadsheet, naming the sum of an actual payments column *actpay* and the sum of budget allocations *budalloc* lets you create a variance column total with this formula: actpay − budalloc.

7. Did you use cell references in spreadsheet formulas instead of absolute numbers? For example, you might set up a row that defines the

FICA tax rate at 7.51 percent and refer to that cell whenever the FICA rate is needed in a formula. Then, when the FICA rate changes, you need to change the actual numerical rate only in one place.

8. Did you format the worksheet so that it is easy to read and navigate? For example, did you:
   a. Round numbers to remove unnecessary detail when appropriate?
   b. Center labels, column titles, or data when useful?
   c. Indent and double space when useful?
   d. Place related columns and rows together?
   e. Divide a long spreadsheet into separate screens so that it can be easily navigated using the page up and page down keys?

9. Did you use techniques to avoid errors in data entry, such as using column widths to control maximum character length or using the protect feature to lock all cells except the input cells?

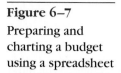

Figure 6–7
Preparing and charting a budget using a spreadsheet

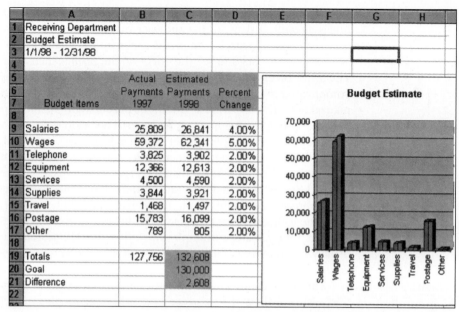

It is important to identify the types of analyses you wish to perform and to make certain that the spreadsheet software you acquire can perform these types of analyses quickly and easily. For example, many spreadsheet software products provide a built-in function for calculating the future value of investments. All you have to do is enter the name of the function, the current interest rate, and the location in the spreadsheet of amounts for which you wish to calculate the future value. Other popular spreadsheet functions are statistical functions, mathematical functions, and financial functions.

If the budget you prepare or work with results from the consolidation of many other budgets, choose a spreadsheet that can consolidate separately prepared budgets into a single budget. The ability to consolidate department budgets into one divisional budget is a very helpful feature of some spreadsheets.

If your templates require a great deal of input from data already in the organization files, you should select spreadsheet software that can *import* data from your organization's files located on other computer systems. This feature also makes it convenient to update data in your spreadsheet to correspond with current information. For example, if you are using a spreadsheet to help you manage cash, you might need to update information about your organization's cash balances regularly from information located on a mainframe to provide effective management of idle cash flows.

If you must create complicated models, many spreadsheet programs allow you to link data from one spreadsheet to another. If the model is a budget, this feature allows you to create separate, detailed spreadsheets for individual budget lines and link each spreadsheet total to a master budget spreadsheet.

Instead of creating your own spreadsheet templates, you may buy commercially prepared templates. Many software companies sell templates, and their products serve nearly every conceivable type of financial analysis (see Manager's Memo 6–4).

Database management software. **Database management software** allows users to prepare reports based on data found in many different types of records. For example, managers may wish to prepare reports that relate data about employees in

Manager's Memo 6–4	TEMPLATES FOR SPREADSHEETS

 The selected products below illustrate the variety of spreadsheet templates available.

Product	Vendor	Description
PowerSheets	Scope International, Inc.	200 templates for both personal and business uses
Spreadsheets on topics of interest to farm managers	Extension Software Services, Iowa State University	Many and varied spreadsheets covering beef, sheep, farm machinery, crop-yield analysis and management, financing alternatives, cash flow for land purchases
Computer-Aided Profit Plan spreadsheets	S3PS, Inc.	Spreadsheets for labor budget, profit plan, financial performance, project budgeting, revenue projections, manpower requirements, and more
Mutual Fund Portfolio Tracker and Mutual Fund Performance Tracker	Mutual Fund Tracker Enterprises	Fund and performance tracking spreadsheet
Fast Answer series	Village Software	Forecasting, ratio analysis, portfolio management, lease vs. buy analysis, business troubleshooter, retirement planner, sales planner, staff scheduler, and more
SmartForecasts	Smart Software Inc.	Supports statistical tools for forecasting
101 Quick Forms and You're in Business	TitleWave Press	101 spreadsheet templates for common business forms and 28 for financial analyses
Income Tax Spreadsheets	Tax Cruncher Software, Inc.	Income tax spreadsheets for Canada
Financial Forecast, Portfolio Manager, Mortgage Analysis Tool, others	Microsoft Corporation	Free financial templates for Excel
Value Expert	Innovative Professional Software, Inc.	A template for valuing a business in many different ways

personnel records to data about employees in payroll records. Financial managers may wish to analyze the relationship between data about customers found in customer invoice records and data about products found in inventory records.

As you will soon learn, database management software is an important managerial decision support tool for managers at all levels of an organization. Database management software is presented in more depth in Chapter 7.

Presentation graphics software. **Presentation graphics software** lets managers prepare slides containing charts, text, images, and sound to tell a story (see Figure 6–8). Managers then use the *slide-show feature* of the software that permits the timed and sequenced display of each slide on a display screen. Presentation graphics software usually provides libraries of clip art images that you can "cut and paste" into a slide to make the slide more attractive and informative. For example, a presentation graphics package might provide libraries of images for business, education, the military, science, and health. The library of business images might contain images of

Figure 6–8

Using presentation graphics software to create a slide show

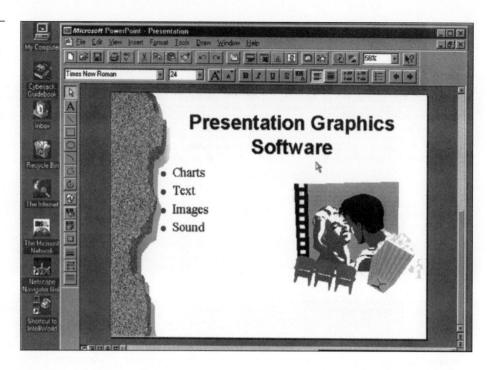

people in business attire, filing cabinets, computers, telephones, offices, and other pictures or scenes commonly found in business environments.

Many presentation graphics packages also include drawing and image manipulation features. Most presentation graphics packages allow you to create slides of text by simply preparing an outline, which is then automatically converted into bullet slides. You can dress up the bullet slides by adding color, special fonts, clip art, and other features. Most presentation graphics software provides a variety of "transition effects" to add interest when you move from slide to slide in your presentation. For example, you can use "fading" to end one slide and start another—the first slide will gradually fade out on the screen and be replaced by the other.

A presentation graphics software program may require a special display terminal and a special printer to produce the high resolution and colors the program can deliver (see Manager's Memo 6-5).

Add-on software. Many commercial software programs seem to leave out features that users want, at least when they are first developed. To fill these gaps, third-party software companies develop *add-on* software. For example, many add-on programs were developed to improve the graphics and document features available on commercially developed spreadsheet software. As time goes by, commercial software companies either develop or buy and incorporate these add-on programs into their products. By doing so, they add features to their product and hopefully differentiate their products from the competition.

Other application software types. Many types of general purpose application software are available. Manager's Memo 6-6 provides a brief description of the most common software categories.

Manager's Memo 6–5	MULTIMEDIA SYSTEMS

Multimedia systems consist of a set of hardware (see Chapter 5) and software tools that allow you to present information in many forms, such as data, text, images, live or taped video, and live or taped audio. Multimedia systems permit you to merge these presentation types into a collection or a file of screens that users can access in any order they choose.

The most obvious applications of multimedia are in marketing, entertainment, and education. Some companies use multimedia systems to train their sales representatives about their products and services or to make product presentations to customers. Other companies create multimedia software products. For example, if you buy a copy of the *New Grolier Multimedia Encyclopedia,* you will get all 21 volumes of the encyclopedia on a single CD-ROM disk. Besides the usual text and pictorial entries, the encyclopedia provides animations of the solar system, weather, and the human body. You will be able to listen to famous speeches, music, animal sounds, and bird songs. Museums and even tourist bureaus use multimedia systems. One city uses multimedia kiosks to give tourists and residents an overview of the city, information about job opportunities, and local news. This information is all kept up-to-date via modem.

Multimedia is often used to provide *computer-based training* (CBT) for employee training or education. Multimedia CBT programs usually are interactive; that is, they require or allow users to respond to questions, menus, or other stimuli and then present information to the user based on those responses. Consequently, how a user is routed through a sequence of screens depends on how he or she responds to these stimuli. CBT software can be used to develop skills and knowledge in any field. Training software is available for nearly every conceivable topic, including foreign languages, mathematics, chemistry, keyboarding, and human relations.

The software used to develop multimedia applications is a set of tools referred to as *authoring software.* One type of authoring software, called *hypertext,* stores text, images, sound, and other materials on pages. Users can navigate through the materials by "turning" the pages in sequence, by following a sequencing script developed by others, or by clicking on links to other pages embedded in the pages. Links may be words, icons, images, or buttons that move users to other pages. For example, imagine a user reading a page about politicians. Imagine further that the reader clicks on a link about Lincoln. On that page the reader finds the words *Gettysburg address,* in color and underlined to show that they are a link to other pages. Clicking on that link might move the reader to a series of pages describing the situation at Gettysburg when the address was made and a page containing a digitized photo of Lincoln. When the reader clicks on an icon of a stereo speaker in one corner of the photo, he or she might hear an actor giving the address.

Hypertext is also frequently used for the on-line help feature of application software and for *tutorial software* (see Figure 6-11). Tutorial software teaches computer users how to do a task, such as how to use a particular computer system or software program. Many software programs sold today include hypertext tutorial software to help the beginning user learn the commands and features of the programs.

DEVELOPMENT SOFTWARE

Development software allows programmers and other information system development personnel to create software for whatever jobs must be accomplished. Development software includes software that is used only by highly trained MIS professionals and software that may be used by people with little background or training in computer systems.

Programming Languages

Systems programmers, who develop and maintain systems programs, and application programmers, who develop application programs, use **programming languages** to create and maintain their programs. These languages consist of programming commands and other words that are put together into programming statements that tell computer systems what to do and when to do it. Programming statements are often

Manager's Memo 6–6 | **APPLICATION SOFTWARE FOR PERSONAL COMPUTERS**

Application software is diverse. Some common types of commercially available application software, in addition to the desktop suites discussed in the chapter, are described below. Many other types of application software are described in the chapters that follow.

Desktop publishing software. When combined with high-resolution printers, computer screens, and optical scanners, desktop publishing software forms document processing systems that can produce hard copy that challenges traditional photocomposition systems frequently found in printing houses.

Statistical software. Statistical software offers an easy way to treat data statistically and to display the data in graphic modes, such as pie, bar, and line charts.

Personal information management (PIM) software. PIMs provide a diverse set of desktop organizing features such as a calendar, schedule, phone book, phone log, task list, agenda, expense log, and index cards. Many salespeople use PIMs to manage their sales contacts.

Graphics software. Graphics software provides one or more of the following components: drawing programs, image manipulation programs, scanner programs, and screen capture programs. Drawing programs allow you to draw your own images to be printed or *exported* to other documents, such as a report or a slide-show presentation. Drawing programs provide drawing tools to edit or draw and size boxes, circles, lines, and arcs and that help you add shading, color, and text to improve the finished product. *Screen capture* programs take a "picture" of a computer screen and store it in a computer file. The graphics software provides features to crop (cut off), rotate, resize, and otherwise manipulate the captured image.

Project management software. Project management software provides tools, such as Gantt charts and PERT (program evaluation and reporting technique) charts to help manage projects. It also allows managers to ask what-if questions with the sequence of project events and the use of project resources to optimize resources, including time, for the completion of projects.

Desktop organizer software. Desktop organizer software offers a variety of useful features designed to clear your desktop of calculators, memo pads, telephone directories, calendars, and the like.

Expert systems software. Expert systems codify the experience and judgment of experts into (1) a knowledge base and (2) a set of procedures that software can then execute when faced with appropriate problems. For example, a college might codify the experience and judgment of its best academic advisors using expert systems software. The resulting expert system can then be used to help new or less-experienced advisors or students directly. The result is that many more students can be served by expert advisors than would be possible without the expert system program and at a lot less cost. You will learn more about expert systems in Chapter 12.

Security software. Security software protects computer systems from a variety of threats, such as unauthorized access to your firm's data; computer viruses (programs that can corrupt your data, destroy your data, or simply annoy you); and violations of site licenses. Computer viruses and security software are presented in detail in Chapter 17.

Groupware. Groupware is software that helps people work together. Groupware enable people who work together to track their work, share voice and written messages, share calendars and meeting schedules, share to-do lists, and share other information related to the work group.

Communications software. Communications software connects people and computer systems and includes software for e-mail, voice mail, faxing documents, connecting to the Internet, using a modem, and connecting to other computer systems. This software is described in detail in Chapters 8 and 9.

Utility software. This broad category of software includes programs that find, copy, delete, and move files and directories; format and copy diskettes; view files; find duplicate files; convert files in one format to another; compress and decompress files and drives; provide images for screen backgrounds; and perform other useful tasks that supplement or improve your operating system software.

Training and tutorial software. Many organizations use software to train employees in a variety of tasks. Multimedia software and presentation graphics software may be used to develop the training application. See Manager's Memo 6–5 for a more detailed description of training and tutorial software.

called *program code,* and the process of writing programming statements is referred to as *coding.*

There are many programming languages. These programming languages can be sorted into levels that indicate their degree of user-friendliness, or how easily humans can understand them.

Machine languages. At the first level is *machine language,* which is a language that the computer system actually can read and understand. As you might expect, the statements in this language are not readily recognizable to a person because they are written in binary representation. For example, a program statement in machine code might look like this:

01011000 01000000 00100011

which means: *load register 1 with 0.*

The statements found in all other programming languages must be translated into machine language so the computer system can execute them.

Programming in machine language is difficult and tedious because the programmer must use almost unintelligible commands to tell the computer system every step it must take in detail, including how to allocate the specific storage locations to be used for data and instructions. Machine language is the lowest level of all programming languages and requires that the programmer know a great deal about the physical organization of the computer system for which the programming code is being written. Machine language is almost never used by programmers today because they can achieve the same level of control over a computer, without the problems, by using assembly language.

Assembly languages. To relieve the programmer of some of the detail required by machine language and to provide a set of commands that are more readily understandable, higher levels of programming languages were developed. The first of these were *assembly languages* which use mnemonics as symbols for machine operations. For example, L may be used as the command for load, ST for store, and A for add. A program statement in assembly language might look like this:

AR 1,2

which means: Add register 1 to register 2

Symbolic programming commands and statements were much easier to work with than machine language and improved the productivity of programmers.

To be executed by a computer system, an assembly-language translator program, or *assembler,* translates the assembly-language instructions into machine language. The assembly-language program code is called *source code,* and the machine-language code that results from the assembler translation of the source code is called *object code.*

Unfortunately, assembly languages are machine specific; that is, they are limited to use on the machine for which they were developed. Therefore, a programmer who works with several machines must know the assembly language written for each.

Third-generation languages. Although working with assembly languages is easier than working with machine languages, neither language is very efficient in terms of programmer time. As a result, *third-generation languages* were developed. They used commands and programming statements that were even more like English and required less knowledge of the specific computer system for which the program was

---

| Manager's Memo 6–7 | THE YEAR 2000 PROBLEM |

For years programmers shortened the year field in records to two digits (97) instead of four (1997). For example, it is common for data input screens to display a field similar to the following in a data entry form:

Year: 19_ _

The data entry operator is expected to enter the last two digits of the year, such as 96, 97, 98, or 99. This programming shortcut saved space and simplified data entry for users—until the millenium. Now, unless changed by the year 2000, this connection is likely to wreak havoc with many programs. The year field is often used for calculations in programs, and without change, programmed calculations will return incorrect values. So much programming code will have to be changed that the change process is estimated to cost billions of dollars. For example, Union Pacific estimates that more than 80 percent of its programs will be affected. The company has almost 7,000 COBOL programs, and managers estimate that it will take 200,000 man hours to fix the problem.[1]

Because of the immensity of the problem, there has been a big increase in demand for third-generation programmers, the generation of code in which most of the "problem" programs are written. To ease resolution of the problem, a number of companies have begun to offer software to help organizations find and change the two-digit year fields in programs.

[1]D. Baum, "Union Pacific Stays on Track for 2000" *Datamation* (on-line magazine), January 1, 1996, (http://datamation.com/PlugIn / issues/1996/jan1/UnionPacificStays.html).

---

being written. Examples of third-generation programming languages include COBOL (COmmon Business-Oriented Language), Fortran (FORmula TRANslator), BASIC (Beginner's All-Purpose Symbolic Instruction Code), C, and Pascal.

An example of a coded program statement written in COBOL follows.
MULTIPLY EMP-HOURS BY EMP-RATE GIVING GROSS-PAY ROUNDED

As you can see, the program statement tells the computer system to multiply the employee's hours by the employee's rate of pay and to store the result in a location called gross pay and, by the way, to round the result to the nearest cent.

Like instructions written in any program language, program code written in a third-generation programming language is called source code. The source code must be converted into machine language, or object code, before the program can be run. See Manager's Memo 6–7 for more on third-generation programmers.

Fourth-generation languages.   Computer programming languages have evolved through a number of generations. These generations parallel the levels of user-friendliness of programming languages already discussed (see Figure 6–9). **Fourth-generation languages (4GLs),** such as FOCUS or dBASE IV, are written at a very high level of user-friendliness and require little knowledge of machine specifics. These languages allow relatively naive computer users to retrieve, manipulate, and analyze data from computer storage.

Third-generation languages required the programmer to spell out in detail each step and the exact order of steps the computer system must take to accomplish a task. Because detailed procedures must be described, these languages are called *procedural languages.* Fourth-generation languages may not require programmers to spell out the steps and sequence a computer system must follow to perform a task. When they don't, they are called *nonprocedural languages.* To understand a non-

Figure 6–9

Evolution of
programming
languages

			Degree of	
Generation	Language	Characteristics	User Orientation	Machine Orientation
First	Machine languages	Commands written in binary representation. Each language can be used only on a specific processor.		↑
Second	Assembly languages	Commands written using simple mnemonics. Each language can be used only on a specific processor.		
Third	High-level languages: COBOL, FORTRAN, BASIC, Pascal, C	Commands can be used on many machines with little change. Requires less knowledge of machine specifics.		
Fourth	FOCUS, dBASE IV	Commands closer to natural English. Requires little or no knowledge of machine specifics.	↓	

procedural language, consider the instructions a manager might give to a good administrative assistant when the manager wants to organize a meeting of branch managers. The manager might simply tell the assistant to set up a meeting with branch managers for next week sometime. The assistant would, without further instructions, contact each manager to find matching free times, schedule the use of a room, send reminder memos to each manager, arrange for a person to record the minutes of the session, order coffee or other refreshments if that is the accepted practice, and even prepare a proposed agenda for the manager to review. In short, the manager simply told the assistant what needed to be done. The manager did not tell the assistant how to do it—the steps to take and the sequence of steps to follow to get the job done. Nonprocedural fourth-generation languages allow you to describe what you want the computer system to do for you without requiring you to provide detailed instructions on how to get it done. Nonprocedural fourth-generation languages accept your request and develop the programming code to get the job done.

Although fourth-generation languages are easy to use, they do have some disadvantages. They often produce computer code that is less efficient than code written in lower-level languages. This may mean that the programs written in fourth-generation languages take longer to process your data than if the same programs were written in lower-level languages.

When used by an application programmer, fourth-generation languages improve productivity considerably over third-generation languages such as COBOL. Some people have claimed that programmers using a fourth-generation language have been able to write as much as 5 or 10 times as many lines of code in a day as they would have been able to had they used a third-generation language.

Fourth-generation languages are not defined very well by the information systems profession. Some professionals define fourth-generation languages as easy-to-use languages used primarily to develop applications related to a database. Others define fourth-generation languages broadly to include such software as query languages, report generators, application generators, object-oriented programming languages, computer-aided software engineering tools, decision support tools (such as spreadsheets), and natural languages. Some of these terms are used interchangeably, and certainly some of their definitions overlap.

Query languages.   Many database management systems provide end users with a relatively easy-to-learn *query language*. A query language is a set of commands through which end users can ask questions and retrieve data from computer files. For example, using a query language, you might retrieve the names of all customers who live in Chicago, Illinois, with these statements:

SELECT CUSTNAME FROM CUSTFILE WHERE CITY = CHICAGO

This statement opens a customer file with the name CUSTFILE and displays on the screen the names of all customers whose addresses include the city of Chicago. Query languages are described further in Chapter 7.

Report generators.   User-friendly fourth-generation languages also provide easy-to-use *report generators,* or tools that allow end users to generate reports quickly and easily without knowing any programming simply by making selections from drop-down menus.

Natural languages.   **Natural languages** are languages that are very close to ordinary English. That is, the user enters requests for information in normal, conversational English. The language program then translates that language into commands that the computer system understands and returns the information to the user on a screen or in a printed report (see Figure 6–10).

Application generators.   *Application generators* are fourth-generation language packages that can produce a set of programs for a complete application, such as billing or payroll, largely or wholly without requiring you to write programming code. Developing a complete application means that the generator must be able to create input screens so data can be input to the application. It must be able to create the

---

Figure 6–10

A conversation with a natural language program

A conversation between a manager at Trend Technology, Inc. (in regular type style) and a computer (in italics) that uses a natural language program might look like this:

How many people do we have working at branch offices in the city?

What do you mean by we?

Trend Technology, Inc.

What do you mean by city?

St. Louis.

Trend Technology, Inc., has 215 people working at branch offices in St. Louis.

records and files needed for the application. It must be able to create output reports so reports or other outputs, such as billing invoices and payroll checks, can be produced. It also must be able to create the processing steps to be taken to compute the payroll or to create customer bills. It must create the screens that can be used to delete or update records. Finally, it must be able to coordinate each of these elements into a complete system.

CASE Tools

CASE stands for **computer-aided software engineering.** CASE software products usually comprise a bundle of tools to help application developers complete their software development faster and better than when they use standard application development methods. CASE tools might include a fourth-generation language, a program code generator, a library routine developer, a data descriptor, and a data flow diagramming feature. CASE tools also assist developers in application planning, analysis, design, and testing.

Object-Oriented Programming

In a procedural language, the data to be processed and the operations to be used on the data are usually kept separate. In **object-oriented programming (OOP)** languages, the program operations, called *methods,* are joined with the data to form an *object.* A programmer might join a record with the operation *print.* Merely pointing and clicking on the record then will print it out.

The advantage of object-oriented programming is that the objects can be used over and over again in different applications. Programs can be built from libraries of objects that are already available and have been used and tested, instead of developing them from scratch. Application programmers who have a great deal of experience working with procedural languages often find it difficult to switch to object-oriented programming languages. For many the switch represents a major change in the way they approach their work. The payoff, however, can be great. As companies create large libraries of objects, they hope to find that the time needed to develop new programs will diminish substantially. The library of objects, containing developed and tested code, should help companies reduce their backlog of information systems application requests.

To support object-oriented programming, **visual programming** languages have been created. Visual programming allows the programer to use graphical tools to help construct information systems. Visual programming languages may be used to create a user interface by dragging and dropping scroll bars, buttons, and menus to a screen form; to create visual models of a system that can simulate the operation of the system, and to create actual programs. While visual programming helps programmers build systems graphically, some code writing is required.

OOP languages have been around since the late 1960s. However, they did not become very popular until GUI applications became popular. OOP languages seem to be especially effective for developing GUI applications. For example, the OOP language Actor can be used to develop Microsoft Windows applications. Hypertalk is an OOP language that is used in HyperCard, a program that is included in every Macintosh computer system. Some OOP languages come bundled with a library of previously constructed objects, such as file drawers, file folders, records, and file indexes, which are combined with actions, such as display, report, and compute. (Object-oriented databases are described in Chapter 7.)

GENERAL SOFTWARE FEATURES AND TRENDS

In general, software is becoming easier to use, more graphical, and loaded with more and more features. Software also requires increasingly more powerful hardware, especially greater amounts of main memory, secondary storage, and fast screens.

Graphical User Interface

The graphical user interface has become popular in all types of software, not just operating system software. Every type of software now has commercial applications that use a GUI, including word processing, spreadsheet, project management, and even utility software packages.

Windowing

Many software programs provide some **windowing** capabilities in addition to those provided by a windowing operating system. Many word processors, for example, permit you to open, view, and edit more than one document at a time. Many spreadsheets allow you to open, view, and edit several spreadsheet files at one time. Programs that offer windows also usually allow you to copy or move information from one document or file to another easily.

Object Linking and Embedding

Compound documents are documents that contain several objects. An object can be any piece of data or file created by a program. A letter created by a word processing document, a chart created by a spreadsheet program, a drawing created by a drawing program, a sound or voice annotation created by dictating into a mike, even full-motion video can all be objects. The chapter you are reading is considered a compound document because it contains text, photographs, and illustrations. Compound word processing documents may be created with word processors, spreadsheet software, database software, and other common software with compound document capability.

Linking data between these objects has become an important feature of many desktop suites. For example, you may link a chart produced in a spreadsheet program to a word processing document. Rather than actually containing the spreadsheet chart, the word processing document contains a pointer to the chart. Any changes made to the chart while it is in the spreadsheet program are automatically reflected in the word processing document. Consequently, if you create a budget with a spreadsheet for a report on a project produced by a word processor and you link the budget to the project report, any changes or updates you make to the budget automatically appear in the project report.

Embedding places the object directly into the document. For example, if you embed the spreadsheet budget into the project report, you will have only one file: a compound document made up of a word processing document and a spreadsheet document.

Both object linking and embedding provide in-place editing. That is, if you are in the project report described above and click on the budget, the spreadsheet program will be loaded and the menus will change to allow you to alter the spreadsheet object.

Multiplatform Capability

Software vendors are increasingly providing products that are capable of running on more than one hardware platform. For example, Microsoft Corporation provides versions of Excel, a spreadsheet program, that run on computers constructed around Intel's 80X86 chip family and Motorola's 64000 chip family. The operating systems Windows NT and UNIX have versions that run on Intel chip computers and RISC computers (see Chapter 5).

Network Capabilities

Connec'ing computers to each other has become very important in developing information systems to serve organizations. It is very likely that some of your applications will require a computer network. Thus the ability of software to run on a network of connected computers, and in fact, to take advantage of the network, is usually an important consideration.

Licensing

If you plan to use the microcomputer software in more than one machine, you should check on the software company's copyright agreements. Many software companies require that you purchase one copy of the software package for each workstation. Other companies allow you to pay a flat rate for the use of the software on all or a specified number of stations within your organization or at your location. That is, you will sign a *site licensing agreement* allowing you to pay a flat fee for the software and then use the software on many workstations. Still other software can be purchased on a *concurrent-use license* basis. Concurrent-use licensing allows you to make the software available to everyone on a network but pay only for those machines that are actually running the software. Thus a firm may place a program on its network but sign a license allowing the use of the software by only 50 computers concurrently. Thus, when the 51st computer tries to use the software, it might receive a "busy" message.

Concurrent licensing can save firms a great deal of money because while nearly all people may need to use a program from time to time, only a few may need to use it at the same time.

Portability

If you have more than one type of computer system or platform in your firm, your software should be available in versions that will run on all or most of them. As already discussed, software that is portable to many computer platforms reduces learning time and training costs for an organization.

Portable documents. One of the most frustrating tasks is trying to share documents created by different word processors or spreadsheets. Although most word processors and spreadsheets today provide conversion programs for documents created by other word processing and spreadsheet software, the converted document is almost never free from errors or formatting anomalies. (Table formats, paragraphing, and font changes are especially vulnerable to conversion problems.) Problems that occur in the conversion process usually require the operator to spend tedious time reformatting the document. When you try to view documents from another word processor using a different word processor, you often see strange characters and formatting that make the documents difficult to read or use. To address this problem, several new software packages have been created. These software packages, including Adobe's Acrobat, create **portable documents,** or documents that can be read and printed by another user *exactly* like the original regardless of the software the other person is using. The documents do not lose any of their original styles, fonts, formats, or graphics. For example, Acrobat is a portable document software package that allows one user to create a document that can be read by an Acrobat viewer regardless of the computer platform used by another person. If the other person does not have an Acrobat viewer, the software will either send or store the document and the viewer together. The viewer can be distributed to others freely, and its distribution does not violate any license provision.

Standard Generalized Markup Language (SGML). A more powerful way to exchange documents between different word processors, however, has been available for almost two decades but has not been implemented widely. This technology is **Standard Generalized Markup Language (SGML).** SGML provides standard rules and procedures for describing document formatting features. In other words, it codes documents by structure. For example, it adds a specific tag to indicate the beginning of a paragraph, another tag to indicate a first-level heading, and more tags to describe features such as font styles, type sizes, paragraph indents, and line spacing. Document software that is SGML-compliant places appropriate tags to identify each formatting feature of a document as it is being created and can read the SGML tags in documents created by other software.

SGML is platform independent; that is, as long as documents are defined with SGML codes the documents can be read, viewed, or otherwise moved from one computer system to another with relative ease. Furthermore, SGML is used not only on text documents but also on graphical documents and on documents containing images and charts.

Hypertext Markup Language (HTML).   More recently, a subset of SGML, HTML, has been developed for creating and viewing documents placed on the Internet or an organization's intranet (see Chapters 7, 8, and 9). Software that converts existing documents to HTML is also available.

Group Work Capabilities

In the last few years, integrated software products aimed specifically at improving the productivity of people who are collaborating to achieve common goals have evolved. These packages, called **groupware,** offer integrated support for many of the typical activities needed by work groups. Groupware will be presented in greater detail in Chapter 9. However, many newer software packages have features that facilitate group work. For example, some word processors have multiuser document annotation to permit many users to add comments to and revise documents prepared by other users. The feature usually allows users to track and catalog revisions made by others. Direct faxing of documents or direct distribution of documents via electronic mail to others also facilitates group work, as does automatic conversion of documents to formats used by other programs.

If your work must be shared and used by others in a group setting, you should review the collaborative features of any software you wish to acquire.

Compatibility with Other Software

The importance of compatibility of software has already been described in the discussion of suite software. However, compatibility is also important when you are updating the software you currently use with a new version. That is, the new version of the software should be able to read and use the data files you created with your old version of the software. This feature of software is called *backward compatibility*. At the very least, the new version should be able to convert the old files to the format of the new version easily.

File-conversion features have become increasingly common on word processors, spreadsheets, databases, and other popular software packages. These conversion features enable users to read, copy, and use files prepared by other programs.

Compatibility with Peripherals

It is easier to use a software package if it is already set up to use your printer or other peripherals. Many packages have procedures for installing the software on your computer system. The installation procedures may ask you to identify the type and amount of main memory, the type of monitor, the type and number of disk drives, and the type of printer you are using. An easy-to-install package will lead you through the installation process with lots of menus and prompts. For example, the installation procedu.es may include a screen showing you a menu of the printers the package supports. Installing the software for your printer is merely a matter of selecting a menu item. Some software packages, especially those of more recent vintage, almost install themselves, automatically identifying most elements of the computer system you are using.

At the very least, you should find out if the software package you want to buy will run your printer and other peripherals. For example, some software requires certain types of display screens and certain amounts of main memory. If you can, read the installation section of the software manual before you buy the software to make sure that the software will fit your system.

Ease of Use

A number of factors make software *user-friendly,* including

1. The readability and clarity of the documentation, or manual, for the software package.
2. The clarity of the menus and prompts displayed on the screen.
3. *On-line help* that explains the prompts and commands.
4. Tutorials that teach you how to use software. Many programs now offer on-line tutorials. Also, a number of companies develop on-line tutorials for popular software. The tutorials may be on disk or use a variety of audio and visual media, such as videotapes.
5. A graphical user interface. A GUI, with its point-and-click environment, makes many complex software packages seem easy to operate. Complex programs require a very large number of keyboard commands to make the programs do all that they are able to do. Learning to use all those commands and becoming proficient in them may take employees many months. It is much simpler for an employee to point an arrow at an icon representing a task and click a mouse.

Sophistication

Software packages range from the very simple to the very complex. Simple programs provide few of the sophisticated features of the more complex and expensive programs. But simple programs are usually easy to learn, cost less, and are appropriate for those who use the software infrequently. Sophisticated programs are more difficult to learn, provide many features, cost more, and are appropriate for those who use the software as a major part of their work.

Competition among software vendors has resulted in software packages that acquire more features each year. For example, most word processing packages today contain features that were available in the past only by purchasing separate, add-on software. Word processors now typically offer such features as font scaling, footnoting, outlining, drawing, graphics, on-line thesaurus, on-line grammar and spelling checkers, mail merge, direct faxing, and conversion of documents from other word processors. High-end word processors are becoming almost indistinguishable from desktop publishing software.

Wizards and Agents

Many software packages today employ "wizards" and "agents" to help users complete complex tasks (see Figure 6–11). Basically, a *wizard* is a series of menus presented to users to lead them through a difficult or lengthy activity. Users interact with screens that ask them to make decisions about how they want to accomplish the task. For example, wizards can help users install software; identify problems if software is

Figure 6–11
A wizard that helps
you develop an
employee database

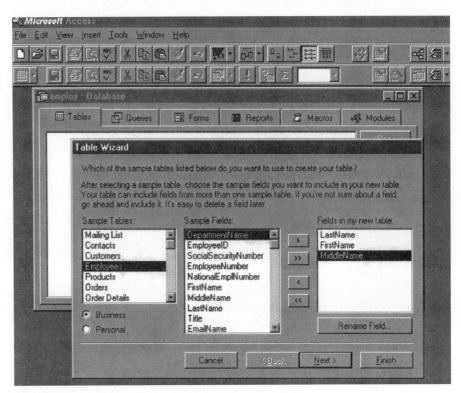

Courtesy of Microsoft Corporation.

not working properly; or design and format a slide presentation, a spreadsheet chart, a database report, or a word processing document.

An *agent,* or intelligent agent as it is sometimes called, is an automatic process that communicates with other agents to perform a task for a user. For example, that task may be to prepare data on one computer system so that it can be used by another computer system, it may be to transfer data from one computer to another, it may be to run a program on another computer, or it may be to accomplish all of those tasks for the user—automatically and without the user needing to know the details.

Wizards and agents remove the complexity of computer operations from users, making their work easier and faster. They also reduce training time and costs and permit users to get up and running with new software swiftly. Wizards often make upgrading to a new version of software or to a new software package relatively painless for users.

**Ease of
Installation**

Software has also become easier to install. Ordinarily, when you load a software package on your system for the first time, you must install it, or tell the software what type of screen, printer, and other peripherals your system possesses. Many programs today, however, can sense many of your system's features and install themselves with little intervention from you.

**Hardware
Demands**

Software that is smarter and uses a graphical-user interface requires more lines of program code than single software. That also means that this software requires more main memory and more secondary storage than single software. The complete code for a suite of these same programs may require more than 100MB of hard disk storage space.

Sof'ware that uses graphics may require special graphic boards and display screens. The boards and screens may deliver very high density images, but they also cost much more than ordinary screen display systems.

Complex software may require high-speed processors with large word sizes to work well. Many programs may be written only for high-speed and large word-size processors.

Memory Requirements

Software packages vary in the amount of main memory (RAM) they require. Because memory costs money, you should know if the program you want will fit within the typical memory sizes provided by microcomputer manufacturers. If the program requires more memory, find out what type of memory is needed and how much more that memory will cost.

Cost

The cost of the software is always an important consideration. However, you should recognize that often the cost difference between low-end and high-end software is only a few hundred dollars. You should not let a few hundred dollars dissuade you from purchasing a package better suited to your needs, given that you will use the package for several years.

Applets

Some people are predicting that a large market will grow for software that is simpler and runs on network computers (see Chapter 5). Simple word processing software, for example, could be loaded on a network computer, and if the user needs features that the simple package lacks, those features, in the form of small applications, or applets, would be downloaded from another computer to which the network computer is attached. Some experts are predicting that the need for expensive, powerful computer systems and complex office software suites would not be required for every worker in an organization. Instead, many workers could perform their work quite well using network computers that borrow applets from an organization's host computer system when needed.

SELECTING MICROCOMPUTER SOFTWARE

Unfortunately, many managers select the computer system as their first step to meet their information needs. This approach often proves disastrous because they may not be able to find appropriate application software that runs on the computer system they bought. Here are the steps you should take to select the software you need.

Step 1: Identifying Your Application Needs

Selecting a computer system should not begin with the computer hardware. The starting point should be a clear identification of your application needs. For example, you might identify sales forecasting as the major application you need to computerize. You should then spell out in some detail the features of a forecasting system you need: the ability to display color graphics, the ability to print displays to transparency acetate, the ability to perform specific statistical functions, the ability to access mainframe data for analysis, and so forth.

Step 2: Seeking the Right Software

Once you have listed your application requirements, you should then identify software that may meet your requirements. Here are some sources that can help you find the software you need.

Trade associations.   Identify the state, regional, national, and international trade and marketing associations that are appropriate to your tasks. Then obtain copies of their publications for the last six months. Usually copies of association publications are readily available in a university or company library. If a software developer creates a software package for a specific function or a specific industry, the most likely place for that developer to advertise the software will be in these association journals. You might also want to contact authors whose articles appear in these publications and ask them for further information about the software they described.

Software companies.   Call or write the companies that advertise appropriate software or whose software was described in the journal articles to ask for further information. Many software companies will send you free or very inexpensive demonstration diskettes of their software so that you can get some idea of its features. Other companies will provide examination copies of the software so that you can try it out on your hardware before buying it. Still others provide all their software packages on a CD-ROM disk. If you like any of the products, you can call the vendor to arrange for payment. The vendor then gives you a code to unlock the software from the CD-ROM disk so you can copy it to your hard disk.

Software databases.   Search software databases for programs that meet your needs. For example, if you were to search the Computer Select CD-ROM database, you would start in the "Software Product Specifications" section. You might then enter the search words, "sales forecasting" and browse the products that meet the search criteria. Each product description contains information about the company and the product. You could then contact the companies for details, demonstration diskettes, or examination copies of the actual programs.

The Internet.   Using search tools on the Internet (see Chapter 9), you can usually find articles, reviews, and other information about many types of software, including Internet sites that allow you to download demonstration or examination copies of the software. Such searches will often identify the Internet sites of vendors who offer commercial software as well as shareware and freeware packages.

Computer magazines.   Examine computer magazines. These magazines are a useful source of information about software. Many dedicate one issue annually to the review of a major software type. Look for an issue that features the type of software you are interested in. Many magazines also carry the advertisements of wholesale computer distributors who will sell the software you need at substantial discounts from list price.

Some computer magazines are especially well suited for searches. For example, *Computer Shopper* is a monthly magazine that fills its 900-plus pages with articles and advertisements on computer software as well as hardware.

Consultants.   Contact consultants who are knowledgeable about computer systems and computer software. Seeking advice from experienced consultants can save you many hours of search time. On the other hand, be aware that the experiences of some consultants can be quite narrow and limited to a few systems. Consultants with limited experience in software may restrict their recommendations to the software they know, limiting the options you consider.

Step 3: Choosing the Software That Best Fits Your Business Needs

After identifying potential software packages that may serve your application needs, you should compare the features of each package to the specific features your application requires, which you identified in step 1. For example, you may need human resource management software that can list employees by physical handicap or as members of more than one department.[2] You may need a word processor that can import a specific type of image file and merge letters with names and addresses that are part of a specific database.

Once you evaluate software in terms of the specific features you require, you should evaluate the packages in terms of their general features (see the previous section "General Software Features and Trends").

A good way to compare software packages in terms of their features is to use some form of the weighted-average method. That is, you list the features that you want in the application and then weight them. Then you rate the quality of those features in each package that you review. Finally, you multiply the weight times the quality for each package, find the average of the results, and choose the package with the highest average.

Reading the evaluations of software packages in computer magazines is very helpful, particularly in identifying features that may be important to your application. However, the overall rating of the software in the article may be misleading in terms of the choice you should make. The writer of an article will often weight very highly features that are unimportant or of little importance to you, or the reverse. If you rely on such reviews as your only method of selection, you may choose the wrong software.

Many software packages are under constant revision. Make sure you are buying the latest version of the software you want. Also, some software vendors offer updated versions of their software to existing users at a substantially reduced charge. Find out about the software company's update policy before you buy the software.

Step 4: Choosing the Hardware

Once you have found the software that meets your specific requirements, you should select the computer hardware that uses an operating system that will run that software. You should also consider the other hardware-selection issues described in this text (see Chapter 5). In other words, you should select the hardware after you select the software.

Step 5: Choosing a Software Vendor

How you choose a vendor to supply the software you have selected depends to some extent on the knowledge you have of the software you are acquiring and the help you will need to purchase, install, and use it. Like hardware, you can buy software from many types of vendors, including software companies, computer sales and service dealers, and mail-order firms.

Some vendors provide *hot-line* technical support to customers. Others provide bulletin board, Internet, or e-mail service through which you can leave messages for technical experts and view their responses (see Chapters 8 and 9). Still others provide no technical support at all to the buyer. *Before* you buy software, you should find out what level and types of help the vendor will provide after you buy the system.

---

[2]Suggested by Professor Albert L. Lederer, University of Kentucky.

If you know a lot about the software you want, you may choose to buy from mail-order companies. Ordinarily, mail-order prices are lower than prices from other sources. However, you may find that the software you buy is not what you wanted. You need to find out before you buy what options are available for returning software. When you buy from the company that produces the software, you are often allowed to use the software for 30 days on a trial basis. If you are not happy at the end of the 30 days, you can return the software for a full refund. If you buy from mail-order companies, you may have to pay a small charge to return the software.

As in buying hardware, it is important, especially for large purchases, to investigate every vendor you are seriously considering. How long have the vendors been in business? What has been the history of customer satisfaction with the software the companies produce? How financially sound are the vendors? Do they have training centers? How often do they run classes? What level of training do they offer? How comprehensive are their course offerings? What level of technical support do they offer? How do they deliver technical support?

MANAGEMENT CONCERNS

Many management concerns pertaining to software have already been described in previous sections of this chapter. For example, the cost of software has been discussed, including whether it would be better to acquire a software package and place it on each workstation, to buy a site license for the software so that it could be placed on any workstation (including mobile notebook), or buy a concurrent license that would restrict simultaneous use of the software to a specific number of workstations. The comparative costs of installing software on each workstation rather than allowing many users to contend for a limited number of available licenses can be significant when the number of workstations in an organization becomes large.

Another factor is the cost of upgrades to hardware that the software might require, such as larger display screens with higher resolution, more main memory, or more hard disk space. Computers with little hard drive space and little RAM do not work well with newer operating systems or sophisticated software. Costs in this category also include the cost of installing the hardware and training MIS personnel in the maintenance of the upgrades.

There is also the cost of upgrading the software to its latest version as opposed to remaining with the current version. Upgrades to newer versions of software may require not only upgrades to hardware but also that a new operating system be acquired. These costs must include the cost of installing the upgrades as well as training current MIS personnel in the maintenance of the new versions and users in the use of the new software. Some organizations that used Windows version 3.1 decided to skip Windows 95 and adopt Windows NT at a later date. They hoped that by skipping versions of the operating system they could substantially reduce acquisition, training, and installation costs. As you can see, an important management task is to plan for the transition from one version to its upgrade. This task may be magnified when MIS personnel are asked to move from one generation of development software tools to another. Clearly, moving from third-generation development tools to object-oriented tools requires a major shift in the way that MIS personnel approach the development process. The manager has to weigh the increased ease of use of the new programs and speed with which they can be developed by those experienced in the new tools to the temporary, but important, increase in development time required because developers are working with unfamiliar tools.

Deciding whether to custom build software or to buy a commercial package is also a management concern. Buying commercial software tends to be less expensive than developing custom software. In addition, commercial software, especially if it has been in the market for some time, is likely to have fewer bugs than custom-written software has. (Commercial software is often written by programmers who specialize in a certain type of software, whereas in-house development of the same software may be the staff's first attempt at writing programs of that type.) In general, when it satisfies an organization's needs, commercial software is usually less expensive and better written than custom software.

As you can see, user and MIS training is an important consideration in the acquisition of software. User training costs can be reduced when the software uses a graphical user interface and the software provides wizards or agents to help the user complete complex tasks. Purchasing software suites instead of stand-alone programs, can also help reduce user training costs. Software suites typically offer many of the same menus, prompts, and features for all programs in a suite. Thus, when a user learns one program, that user has learned a lot about the other programs in a suite. Furthermore, information produced by one program is likely to be readable by the others in the same suite, reducing the time and cost of data conversion.

The manager can also reduce user and MIS training costs by standardizing on specific operating systems, software programs, and software suites and upgrading to newer versions carefully. Standardizing on one word processor substantially reduces training and maintenance costs because every word processor requires special training programs for users and for MIS personnel. Clearly, one management task is to set standards for software and see that they are enforced.

MANAGEMENT SUMMARY

Computer programs are called software. Three major categories of software are systems programs, which control and supervise the activities of the computer system; application programs, which process your data; and development software, which are used to create systems and application programs. Systems software consists of operating systems programs, communications programs, and systems utility programs. Operating systems programs coordinate the hardware of the system and consist of supervisory programs, job management programs, and I/O management programs. Usually most supervisory programs are resident in main memory. Job management programs select, initiate, terminate, and schedule jobs to be processed. I/O management programs assign input and output devices to programs and manage the transfer of data between main memory and I/O resources. Utility programs handle repetitive activities and are usually transient programs.

Operating systems may be capable of serving a single user or multiple users. They may also be capable of running more than one program, seemingly at one time, through multiprogramming or time-sharing techniques. Operating systems may also be designed to run many programs concurrently by managing more than one CPU through multiprocessing. Some operating systems permit more than one CPU to perform the tasks needed for one program through parallel processing. Virtual memory is a method of expanding main memory by storing unneeded portions of programs in a direct access storage device.

There are two basic interfaces between the user and the systems software. Operating systems may require keyboarding commands or provide a graphical user interface. Operating systems may also provide dynamic data exchange between programs and desktop tools, such as calendars, calculators, and notepads. Application programs perform specific data, text, and image processing functions and are usually written for a specific operating system. Application programs may be developed in-house, by custom software firms or consultants, or by commercial software firms. Commercial software programs may stand alone or be part of a suite of integrated software programs.

Common application software suites include word processing, spreadsheet, database management, and presentation graphics programs. Application software is also available for specific types of organizations, such as medical clinics, construction companies, and law firms. Application software is also commonly available to serve functional business areas, such as accounting, finance, marketing, production, and human resources.

Development programs are used to create systems and application programs. Development programs include first-, second-, third-, and fourth-generation languages. Fourth-generation languages are a diverse group of programs, including query languages; report and application generators; decision support tools; CASE tools; object-oriented programming languages; and natural languages.

Software is becoming more user-friendly through improved interfaces, such as graphical user interfaces, wizards, and agents, and through easy-to-use installation programs. Software is also becoming more sophisticated, providing powerful features such as windowing, conversion, and data linking. Easier to use and more powerful software comes at the cost of increased hardware requirements (including faster and more powerful CPUs), increased memory (including main memory and secondary storage), and more powerful display screens.

Selecting a computer system should begin with a careful analysis of your application needs. The computer hardware should be chosen on the basis of whether or not it will run the application software that best serves these needs. Other factors to consider in selecting software are ease of use, compatibility with other software, compatibility with peripherals, portability, cost, memory requirements, group-work capabilities, and availability of site and concurrent licensing.

In this chapter you have learned a little about all kinds of computer software. In the next chapter, you will learn more about a type of software of great importance to managers: database management software. Database management software allows you to store, retrieve, and manipulate large amounts of data that managers use to make decisions.

KEY TERMS FOR MANAGERS

application software, 170
communications software, 173
compound documents, 194
computer-aided software engineering (CASE), 193
database management software, 184
development software, 170
fourth-generation languages (4GLs), 190
graphical user interface (GUI), 177
groupware, 196
menus, 180
multimedia systems, 187
multiprocessing, 173

multiprogramming, 172
multitasking operating systems, 174
natural languages, 192
object-oriented programming (OOP), 193
operating system, 171
parallel processing, 173
portable documents, 195
presentation graphics software, 185
programming languages, 187
prompts, 180
single-tasking operating systems, 174
software, 169

software suites, 181
spreadsheet software, 182
Standard Generalized Markup Language (SGML), 196
systems software, 170
task switching, 175
templates, 182
time-sharing, 172
user interface, 177
virtual storage, 173
visual programming, 193
windowing, 194
word processing software, 181

REVIEW QUESTIONS

1. What are the major components of systems software?

2. What is an operating system? What are the major components of an operating system?

3. List some examples of microcomputer operating system utilities. For each microcomputer operating system utility you list, briefly describe what the utility does.

4. What is a time-sharing operating system? How does a time-sharing operating system seem to run more than one program at the same time?

5. What is multitasking? How does multitasking compare with task switching?

6. What are foreground and background tasks?

7. What is a transient program? Is the kernel of a microcomputer operating system a resident or transient program?

8. Explain how virtual storage appears to expand the main memory of a computer system.

9. What is an operating system interface?

10. What is a command-line operating system interface? Name an operating system that uses a command-line operating interface.

11. What is add-on software? Who develops add-on software?

12. List five types of application programs. Briefly describe what each program type accomplishes.

13. List the four generations of programming languages. What two key characteristics separate each generation from the others?

14. What is the difference between industry-specific and function-specific software?

15. What is shareware? How does it differ from freeware?

16. Explain the difference between source code and object code.

17. What is meant by *booting a computer system?*

18. What is an on-line help feature?

19. List and describe the steps you might take in selecting microcomputer software and hardware.

20. List sources of information about software that the manager can use to help in selecting the right software.

21. Explain dynamic data exchange.

22. What is RAM resident software?

23. What are four types of fourth-generation languages?

24. What is a site-licensing agreement? Compare site licensing to concurrent licensing.

25. What is canned software?

26. What does GUI mean? What advantages does GUI provide to the manager?

27. What is portability? From the manager's viewpoint, what are the advantages of application program portability?

28. What is a menu? A prompt?

29. What is object linking? object embedding?

30. Which characteristics of software vendors are important in vendor selection?

QUESTIONS FOR DISCUSSION

1. How is a resident program different from a transient program?

2. How do systems programmers differ from application programmers? In what ways are they alike?

3. What is the difference between multi-programming and multiprocessing operating systems?

4. What is an application program? How does an application program differ from an operating system?

5. Compare command-line, windowing, and GUI operating system interfaces.

6. Explain the difference between stand-alone software and a software suite. What

advantages might each type of software offer a manager?

7. What is meant by *user-friendly software?* What are some features that make software user-friendly?

8. Explain why communications software is considered an extension to the operating system of a computer.

9. What are five general trends in software development today? What implications do these trends have for managers?

10. What is a software wizard? How do wizards help users?

PROBLEMS

1. **Crown Clinic, Ltd.**   Rob Seavers is an assistant consultant at B & L Associates, a computer consulting firm in Ontario, Canada. The firm is helping Crown Clinic, Ltd., a physical fitness chain, develop information systems. Rob has been asked by his firm to identify sources of commercial software that might contain information useful in the consulting project. What sources of information about software would you suggest?

2. **Riggens, Inc.**   Gwen Bradshaw is an office manager at Riggens, Inc., a marketing research firm. She is considering purchasing a desktop publishing software package to create final reports for clients. Her assistant, Jim Bernstein, has just read a review of 10 desktop publishing packages in *Tech Magazine,* a computer journal. He recommends that Bradshaw purchase the Publishing Company, one of the packages reviewed, because the magazine gave that package the highest rating among all 10 packages. What advice would you give Bradshaw?

3. **SuperNet Sports Shop.**   The SuperNet Sports Shop has decided that it needs to computerize its office functions, including the preparation, storage, editing, sorting, and printing of documents, budgets, and records. Irene Trevon, the owner, is thinking about purchasing a minicomputer and the following software: WordPrep (a word processor) from DocuPrep, Inc., Multisheet (a spreadsheet package) from HiTech, Inc., and ShowRite (a presentation graphics package) from Allorum, Inc. You are a new employee of SuperNet Sports Shop and the only one with anything more than casual information systems experience. Irene has asked you to review her pending purchases and make suggestions.

    a. What problems might occur if Irene acquires the programs she is considering?

    b. What criteria for operating system software and for application programs should Irene consider?

    c. What hardware features and components should be considered?

4. **TriTown Furniture Distributors, Inc.** Claude Ramsey is the owner of a small furniture distribution firm. He is considering purchasing a word processing software package for the firm's microcomputer systems to enable him to computerize document preparation, such as form letters, reports, and memos. He is trying to decide between purchasing Quicktype, a simple word processing program, and Secretariat, a complex word processing program. What questions would you ask of Claude to help him decide?

5. **Klines, Inc.**   Jill Brown manages a team of five people in the advertising department of Klines, Inc., who are developing an advertising program for a new product. What types of application software might Jill consider to help her and her team in their work? For each type of software you select, briefly describe how the software might be useful.

6. **Spreadsheet design problem.** Load the spreadsheet file "budget" into your spreadsheet program. Then take these steps:
   a. Identify the errors, omissions, and problems you find in the spreadsheet.
   b. Redesign the spreadsheet using the suggestions in Manager's Memo 6-3.

7. **Spreadsheet design problem.** Using spreadsheet software, develop a template for the budget report shown in Figure 6-7. Use the design suggestions in Manager's Memo 6-3. The Estimated Payments value for each budget line is computed by multiplying the Actual Payments by the percent in the Percent Change column and adding the result to the Actual Payments value. The spreadsheet should permit the user to enter a decimal number, such as 0.04, for each amount line of the budget and see the impact on the Estimated Payments, the Totals, and the Difference.
   a. Fill in the template you design with the data from Figure 6-7 to test the accuracy of your spreadsheet formulas.
   b. Create a bar graph of the actual payments for the year using the graphics portion of the spreadsheet program.

8. **Microcomputer utility programs.** Prepare a report on microcomputer utility programs. The report should include a brief description of 10 utility programs. Each description should identify the program's purpose, price, and features. You might start by obtaining issues of microcomputer magazines such as *Byte, PC Magazine, MacUser,* or *InfoWorld.* Examine the advertisements in microcomputer magazines that list and categorize the software offered for sale under "utilities" to develop a list of microcomputer utility programs. Then use Internet search engines or tools to find information about the utility programs. You might also use a computer database such as Computer Select and use "utility programs" as the initial key word search for the database.

9. **Groupware.** Complete a paper about one groupware software package by reading at least three articles or reviews about it. Your report should cover the package's features, shortcomings, and cost. To find information about the software package, you might examine issues of the following magazines: *Office Systems, Datamation, PC Magazine, Software Magazine, PC World, Byte,* and *Administrative Management.* You might also use Internet search engines or tools or a CD-ROM database such as Computer Select to find information about the program.

CASES

1. **Kriege Construction Company.** Kriege Construction Company (KCC) builds office and retail buildings in a two-province area in western Canada. KCC is considering automating its procedures for preparing bids for building jobs in response to customer requests for building proposals. The management of KCC has had little first-hand experience with computer systems. They use no computer systems currently, except for some IBM microcomputers that run word processing programs for the company secretaries. As a result, they contacted an information systems consulting firm that is partly owned by a friend of Mr. Kriege, the founder of KCC. The consulting firm, Reade & Owens, dispatched Tom Kaline, a systems analyst, to KCC. After spending some time talking with the management of KCC, examining the forms and procedures used in preparing bids, and learning the algorithms used in computing costs and charges, Kaline developed a list of specific application requirements that were needed for the bidding system. He suggested further that his consulting firm would develop a bid-proposal system using Insite, a database management system that his firm has used often for such purposes. Insite runs on Macintosh microcomputer systems. Kaline said both the

Macintosh and Insite are very easy to learn to use and should be just right for managers who have had little experience with computer systems. He felt that his firm could develop the information system in about two months and would like to get started right away on it.

a. If you were advising KCC, would you let Kaline get started?

b. What steps should Kaline have taken prior to recommending the Insite software to support his recommendation?

c. What problems might result if KCC gives the go-ahead to Kaline's recommendations?

2. **Bradford Lumber Products Corporation.** The management information systems (MIS) department of Bradford Lumber has been asked by the human resource management (HRM) department of the corporation to develop an information system to keep track of its employee evaluation program. Bradford Lumber employs more than 2,000 people, and the HRM department needs to ensure that each employee is evaluated at the right time, that the people who should be involved in the evaluation are included, that the pertinent information is distributed appropriately, and that the reports are stored for future use. Rita Verano, who heads the MIS department, has responded negatively to Jack Delaney, who heads the HRM department, about the HRM request. Rita tells Jack that she doesn't think that MIS has enough resources to do the job because her staff is bogged down developing two major applications for other departments. She feels that she won't be able to get to Jack's application for at least 18 months. Furthermore, she tells Jack that developing the system he wants will take many more months of programming and testing. The MIS department develops all company applications in-house using COBOL, a procedural language. Jack, of course, is very upset. Recent government rulings and legislation have required a number of reports regarding employee evaluation. Jack is concerned that the company will become vulnerable to legal action if a suitable system

is not developed shortly. However, Jack is not the only one at Bradford Lumber who is complaining. Many other departments are becoming increasingly annoyed at the time it takes the MIS department to address their information systems concerns. How can Rita speed up the development of applications at Bradford Lumber so that she can respond to everyone's needs sooner and complete programming projects faster, without adding full-time staff?

3. **Manfred Detweiler, Inc.**   You are a consultant for Manfred Detweiler, Inc., a small consulting firm. You are assigned to manage and complete projects with client firms in a geographic region. To manage and complete these projects, you often must prepare, or have prepared, project reports, project budgets, and both written and oral presentations to clients regarding the nature and progress of each project. Frequently you have to manage a number of projects at the same time. In addition, you are expected to generate business for the consulting firm by developing new clients, maintaining contact with your old clients, and identifying the problems these clients face. To help you with your work you are assisted by a full-time secretary. Write a report in which you explain to Mr. Detweiler why you need a new microcomputer system to improve the operational, tactical, and strategic activities in your office. Your report should include at least these elements:

a. Identify the applications that you believe should be considered for computerization.

b. For each application specified in the previous question, identify categories or types of software that would be appropriate to the applications in your office.

c. Following the steps for selecting software described in this chapter, identify by brand name one commercial software program that would be appropriate to each of the applications you specified for each computer workstation you are recommending. Use magazine ads to find the approximate cost for each software program. Make certain that each application program will run on the systems software you select.

   d. Using computer magazines or the Internet, select microcomputers and systems software for the consultant's workstation and the secretary's workstation. Specify the component parts of each microcomputer and also specify the peripherals for the computer systems you are recommending for the workstations. Include quoted or estimated prices for each component and peripheral for each workstation. Make certain that the software programs you recommended earlier will run on the computer systems and the system software you select here.

   e. Append to your report a list of your sources.

4. **Tel-West, Inc.** You are the owner of Tel-West, Inc., a small metals fabricating firm that has made the decision to automate its accounting and production activities. Tel-West had no one on its staff with computer expertise, so you have just hired Carla Wong, who was a system programmer for Canton Fabrics, Inc., in a nearby town. After being on the staff for a week, she comes into your office and is very upbeat. She has just learned that Maray Products Corporation, a wholesale distributor of hunting and fishing equipment, is upgrading its computer system and will be disposing of its old system, an Infotex 1000 mainframe computer. The system is equipped with multiple hard drives, proprietary systems software, several terminals, a tape drive for archiving purposes, and a high-speed printer. Carla feels that she probably can obtain this computer system very inexpensively, and the system should be more than adequate for whatever applications Tel-West may develop. She strongly recommends that Tel-West make a bid for the computer system so that she can start developing applications for the company.

   a. What concerns might you have with her recommendation?

   b. What stages should she have taken to obtain a computer system?

   c. (Optional) Prepare your report for this case using the word processing software available in your college or workplace.

SELECTED INTERNET REFERENCE SITES

Corel Corporation (http://www.corel.com)

Lotus Corporation (http://www.lotus.com)

Microsoft Corporation
   (http://www.microsoft.com/products/default.asp)

PC Today (http://www.pc-today.com)

PC World—multimedia edition
   (http://www.pcworld.com/workstyles/multimedia/index.html)

Portland State University's School of Business Information Systems
   (http://www.sba.pdx.edu/ug/is/isr/index.htm)

ZDNet (http://www.zdnet.com)

SELECTED REFERENCES AND READINGS

Applied Computer Research. *Computer Literature Index.* A monthly index of computer publications, including those covering mainframe, minicomputer, and microcomputer software.

Datapro Corporation. *Datapro Reports.* A series of reports pertaining to computer systems topics, including mainframe, minicomputer, and microcomputer software.

Holzberg, C. S. "Suite Success." *PC Today,* September 1996, p. 42.

Marshall, M. "Planning for Year 2000 Conversions." *Communications Week,* September 16, 1996, p. 15.

Salemi, J. "Kindler, Gentler Databases." *PC Magazine,* May 28, 1996, p. 117.

Ulanoff, L. "Business Graphics: Draw Your Own Conclusions." *PC Magazine,* February 6, 1996, p. 173.

Ulanoff, L. "The Ultimate Utility Guide." *PC Magazine,* May 14, 1996, p. 100.

7

FILE AND DATABASE MANAGEMENT SYSTEMS

CHAPTER OUTLINE

Manager's View

File Concepts

File Structures

Accessing Records

File Structures and Processing Methods

Database Concepts

Database Management Systems

Components of a Database Management System

The Database Administrator

Views of the Data

Database Models

Advantages of Database Management Systems

Problems of Database Management Systems

Specialized Databases

Universal Database Systems

Management Summary

Key Terms for Managers

Review Questions

Questions for Discussion

Problems

Cases

Selected Internet Reference Sites

Selected References and Readings

- The sales manager of your company wants to know the average number of calls each of her salespeople must complete to make a sale. She wants to use the information to help her decide how to define territories for her salespeople.

- A salesperson wants to know which of his customers he has not visited in the last month and what products those customers have already purchased. He wants to use the data to create his schedule for the week and wants to make sure that he knows what demonstration products he should take to each customer's site.

- The marketing manager wants to know which customers have already purchased a given product because she wants to implement a direct mail campaign to promote the sale of a supplement to that product.

- A human resource manager needs to know if any employees at the Witchita branch of the company have the skills and experience needed to fill a technical position at the Kansas City branch. He also needs to know if any of the employees who are qualified might be interested in moving.

- A human resource manager needs to estimate how many people are likely to retire in the next five years. She then needs to know what skills and experience are required for the positions to be vacated so that appropriate training and development programs can be developed in time to provide for a smooth transition.

- A store credit manager needs to identify the profiles of customers who are chronically late in making payments to their accounts. He wants to use the data to improve the credit application process and lower bad debts for the company.

- The top management of an organization is considering adding a new plant in a Midwestern state. The managers need to know what locations in that state will provide the best access to national highways, air and rail transportation, and well-trained and experienced workers. Once potential sites have been identified, they will then need specific information on labor and transportation costs, schools, housing, living costs, and other factors to narrow their choice further.

Managers, after all, are paid to make decisions. A major purpose of information systems technology is to improve managerial decision making by providing the right information at the right time. Managers need to know where to find useful information, how to access it, and how to use it in their decision making.

Much of the information that managers use is stored in a series of computer files or in computerized databases. This information may be stored on a company computer system or on the computer system of another organization. As a manager, you may use computerized data to complete day-to-day operational tasks, such as using payroll files to prepare the weekly payroll and produce payroll checks. You may use the files to decide if you are allocating your resources appropriately, such as monitoring a sales transaction file for salesperson performance. You may also use the files to assist in long-range planning, such as using the financial accounting files of the organization to identify divisions with high and low profitability. Regardless of the level of management activity for which you are using the information, knowledge of basic file and database concepts improves your ability to locate, access, and use the information available to you for the decisions you must make.

You have learned that data can be stored on many media, such as magnetic tapes; hard disks, and floppy diskettes; flash memory cards, optical storage media; computer output microfilm; and of course, paper media such as forms, letters, and reports. Storing data on magnetic instead of paper media has many advantages. For example, data stored on magnetic media can be stored compactly and easily, and the computer system can edit and check the data more efficiently than people can in a manual filing system. Also, the data produced as output from one system can be used as input to another system.

However, the main reason computerized files are so important to the manager is that data in magnetic files can be found and manipulated quickly and easily. Can you imagine searching through 2,000 file folders in an employee file to find those employees who have worked for the firm for more than 10 years? That type of search can be completed in seconds if the data are stored magnetically and searched by a computer program. This is why computer files and databases have changed the decision-making environment for managers. They simply make much more data available at the right time to assist managers in making their decisions.

FILE CONCEPTS

Data stored in paper-based, manual filing systems are organized into characters, data elements, records, and files (see Figure 7–1). Data stored in a computer-based, electronic filing system are usually stored in their most elementary form: binary digits, or bits. These bits are then organized into characters (or bytes), the bytes into data elements, the data elements into records, and the records into files (see Figure 7–2).

A **data element,** or **field,** is a logical collection of characters. For example, the data element for an employee's last or family name is a collection of characters that make up that name.

A **record** is a collection of logically grouped data elements. For instance, an employee record might contain these data elements: employee number, last or family name, first or given name, middle initial, street address, city, state or province, ZIP or postal code, date hired, department, job title, and hourly rate of pay (see Figure 7–3). A record is usually a collection of data elements describing an *entity.* For example, last or family name is an attribute of the entity employee.

Figure 7–1

Building blocks of a paper-based, manual filing system

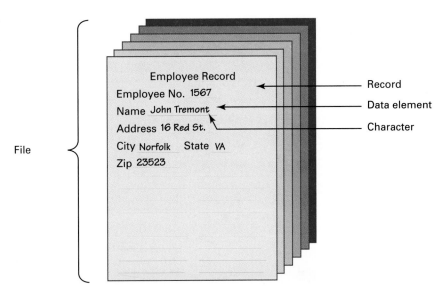

A **file** is a collection of records of one type. For instance, a set of employee records for a firm is usually called the *employee file*.

In computer files, each type of record and its associated data elements have a definite structure. That is, there is a set of data elements for each record type, and a sequence for those data elements. For example, in the employee record shown in Figure 7–3, the data element, ID, is the first data element.

Figure 7–2

Building blocks of a computer-based filing system

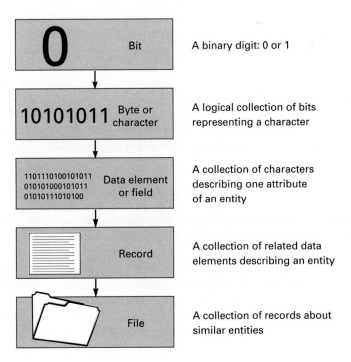

Figure 7–3

A screen showing part of an employee record

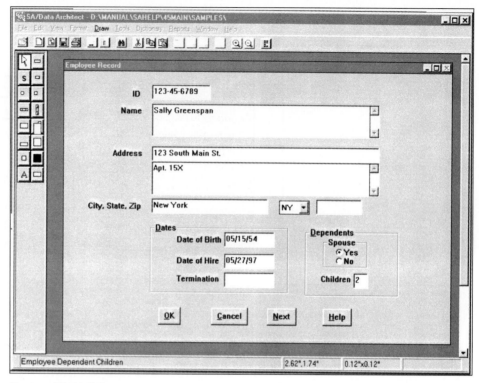

Courtesy of Popkin Software.

Each data element also has a set of characteristics. Two commonly used characteristics of a data element are the maximum number of characters and whether the data to be entered are alphabetic or numeric. Notice in Figure 7–3 that the data element, state, may not exceed two characters in length. This data element is also restricted to alphabetic characters, since no other type of character is required.

In a computer file, each record usually must have a **primary key.** A primary key is a field that is a unique identifier for the record that allows it to be stored and retrieved. For the ID in Figure 7–3, the data element employee number (123-45-6789) was chosen as the primary key because each employee has a unique ID. That way, when you ask for the record with a primary key of 123-45-6789, you will get only one record. (The employee's last or family name (Greenspan) was not chosen as the primary key because other employees might be named *Greenspan*.)

FILE STRUCTURES

The way you choose to store records on magnetic media is called the file structure. Employee records may be stored on magnetic media using several file structures.

Sequential File Structure

One way to store the employee records is *sequentially* by the primary key—in our example, the ID. With **sequential access** the computer system retrieves an employee record with the employee number 1567 by scanning all the records sequentially between the employee with the first record, 0001, and record 1567. If you were a manager in the personnel department and needed to examine individual employee records throughout the day as various employees visited you for advice, this method

Figure 7–4

An index of a file of records organized sequentially

```
                        INDEX
        PRIMARY KEY              DISK ADDRESS
            3548                    845528
            3549                    853658
            3550                    861788
            3551                    869918
            3553                    886178
            3554                    894308
            3557                    918699
            3558                    926829
            3559                    934959
            3560                    943089
            3561                    951219
            3565                    983739
```

would not prove to be a very efficient way to store employee records. With more than 1,500 records, you and the employee might fall asleep before the system retrieved the employee's record.

However, sequential access can be fast and inexpensive for storing files that are used only for batch processing operations (see Chapter 5). For example, if a payroll file is used only to produce paychecks in batch processing mode, sequential access may be satisfactory. Unfortunately, few of an organization's files are used *only* in batch processing operations. After all, employees also visit the payroll office with questions about their paychecks.

Direct File Structure

Another way to store the records is to store them *randomly*—that is, not in sequential order by primary key. To store records in this way requires using a storage medium that allows **direct access** to records, such as optical disk, magnetic disk, or floppy diskette. It also means that each record must be given a specific disk address so it can be found directly. One way to specify a disk address for records in a direct access file is to apply a *hashing algorithm* to the primary key. The algorithm might be simply using the last two digits in employee social security numbers for a firm of 80 employees. Or the algorithm might be more complex, such as dividing the primary key by another number. In any event, the result of the algorithm is used as the disk address for the record. By using a hashing algorithm and storing the data on a direct access medium, the computer system is able to retrieve the record with employee number 1567 directly, without having to scan records 0001 through 1566 first and without having you and the employee nod off.

One disadvantage of using hashing for file storage is that several record numbers may generate the same address. When this happens, two or more records may compete for the same storage space on disk. Several methods of handling this problem exist, but all of them require special processing, which may slow down the storage and retrieval of records.

Indexed Sequential File Structure

A third way to store records is sequentially on a direct access medium, such as a hard disk with a specific disk address for each record (or in some systems, every block of records). An **index** is maintained as records are added to the file and is used to keep track of the disk address of each record or block of records (see Figure 7-4). This method is called the **indexed sequential access method (ISAM)** and permits both sequential and direct access of records in a file.

The neat thing about storing records in an indexed format is that you can access these records in more than one way. You can access the records sequentially by starting at the beginning of the file and moving through it one record at a time to find the needed records. For example, suppose that a program was sequentially updating a batch of records, starting with the record with the lowest primary key. Suppose further that the record with the lowest primary key to be updated was 3559 in the index shown in Figure 7-4. In that case, the system would start at the record with the primary key of 3548 and read each record in order until it reached the correct one. However, the system can also access any record directly if you ask for it. In this case, the system looks up the record you have asked for in the index, finds the disk address of the block of records where the record is located, and goes directly to that block of records to capture the record for you. In our example, the system would look up record 3559 in the index, find that it is located in a block of records starting at disk address 934959, and search only that block of records to find that record.

On the downside, indexed files require maintenance of the indexes. That is, when records are added, the indexes must be revised, requiring at least some time and computer system resources. Thus, while indexed files are slower performers when direct access is needed, they provide an effective compromise because they also allow sequential processing.

ACCESSING RECORDS

The methods you use to store records in a computer file—sequential, direct, and indexed sequential—affect the way you can access those records. Ordinarily, you are interested in accessing records to complete these types of operations:

- Adding new records to a file.
- Deleting records from a file.
- Modifying records in a file.
- Viewing records from a file on a screen.
- Creating reports from records in a file.

Suppose that you are a personnel manager and you want to be able to view and modify an employee's record while you confer with the employee. Clearly, a sequential file structure would not be an effective choice because it would require you to arrange your interviews in sequential order by employee number. You would still have to wait for the computer system to scan the file sequentially until it locates the record you want, but at least you wouldn't have to start at the beginning of the file for each employee.

Compared to a sequential storage method, either a direct or an indexed sequential storage method would provide faster record access. If you used a direct storage method, the file program might apply a hashing algorithm to the primary key of the record whose disk address you want to find. The computer system would then go directly to that disk address and display the record on the screen. If you used an indexed sequential storage method, the computer system would consult an index to find the disk address of the record you want and then go directly to that record without scanning other records.

Inverted Files

The records in Figure 7–4 are indexed by the primary key, which might be student number, stock number, customer number, or the like. However, records can be indexed on any field. For example, you might wish to build an index of your records based on the ZIP or postal code field so that you can prepare mass mailings quickly and easily. These other indexes would be called *secondary indexes,* and the fields that are indexed would be called *secondary keys.* Files that have secondary indexes are called **inverted files.**

An important advantage of indexes is that they are usually much, much smaller than the actual data files themselves. It may be possible to be read the indexes into main memory in their entirety. This means that searching for record addresses can be done at main memory speeds instead of at secondary storage speeds.

Linked Lists

Sometimes access to records is not based on indexes. Instead, a pointer is embedded in each record that points to the next record with the same value in a field. In this system an employee record containing the value *night* in the shift field would also contain a pointer to the next record with the same value in the shift field. When you ask for a list of employees on the night shift, the program finds one record with that value and uses the pointer in that record to find the next record, and so on, until it builds a list of all records with *night* in the shift field. Thus, a list is built by linking each record with the value *night* in the shift field to the other records. This method for retrieving records is called **linked lists.**

FILE STRUCTURES AND PROCESSING METHODS

File structures affect not only the way that records can be accessed but also the efficiency with which records can be processed.

File Structures in On-Line, Real-Time Processing

The first four operations on the preceding list can be completed directly with either the indexed sequential structure or the direct structure. That is, you can go directly to the record you want and view it, delete it, or modify it immediately. As you learned in Chapter 6, this type of processing is called on-line, real-time processing because any processing occurs immediately. This type of processing is usually *interactive* as well. For example, if you make an error while modifying the employee record, the computer system will display an *error message* on your terminal. You could then correct your error immediately. Such processing is called interactive because you are interacting with the computer system while you are processing the record.

File Structures in Batch Processing

If you do not need to process employee records individually, then a sequential access file structure might be appropriate. Suppose that you can accumulate a batch of requests for additions, deletions, and modifications to employee records. These requests can then be sorted by employee number and processed in a batch.

Thus records stored on a sequential file are *batch processed.* Any other processing using this file is simply too inefficient. For the manager, this means that use of sequential file storage precludes the on-line, real-time processing of records. If you were a personnel manager and needed to view individual employee records directly, as opposed to sequentially, the use of sequential files for personnel records would not be appropriate for your decision needs.

DATABASE CONCEPTS

Whereas a file is a collection of related records, a **database** is a collection of related files (see Figure 7-5). To understand why database software was developed requires an understanding of the limitations of file systems. The business world turned to data processing in a big way in the 1960s. Many firms computerized their operations on an application-by-application basis. For example, they may have computerized their payroll activities first. Once that was completed, they may have computerized order processing and so on through their applications.

Converting a firm's manual applications one by one took time; the process was usually spread out over several years. Furthermore, the programs for each application were usually written specifically for that application. As a result, each program may have been written by different programmers, perhaps even in a different programming language. Thus the records in each file were designed specifically for each application and might not have been appropriate for the other application software the firm had developed (see Figure 7-6). For example, the payroll application program discussed earlier in this chapter was designed to read from and write to a record with the exact fields, arranged in the exact order, with the exact field lengths that the record contained. Other programs would be unable to read that record unless those programs were redesigned to that record's specifications.

Figure 7–5

Building blocks of a computer-based database

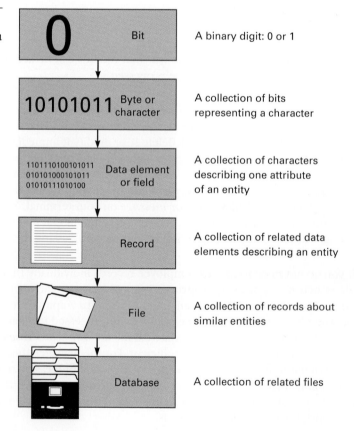

0	Bit	A binary digit: 0 or 1
10101011	Byte or character	A collection of bits representing a character
1101110100101011 010101000101011 01010111010100	Data element or field	A collection of characters describing one attribute of an entity
	Record	A collection of related data elements describing an entity
	File	A collection of records about similar entities
	Database	A collection of related files

**Data
Independence**

Thus many programs developed in-house were *dependent* on the data files created for them. Or in the language of information systems people, the programs lacked **data independence.** The lack of data independence meant that any time the record format of a file was changed (e.g., a field was dropped, added, or modified), every program that accessed that file had to be changed. You can imagine the work that was created when the nine-digit ZIP code replaced the five-digit ZIP code. All the application programs that accessed files with ZIP codes had to be changed so that they would be able to read and process the changed records! The same problem is now occurring because of the advent of the millenium (see Manager's Memo 6–7 in the previous chapter).

**Data
Redundancy**

Let's look at another problem associated with single record type file systems. Consider how many college or university offices maintain files on you as a student. You may have a file in the enrollment office, a file in the placement office, a file in the bursar's office, and a file in the office of your major field of study. Every file includes a record containing your first name, last name, middle initial, student ID number, home address, and college address. In other words, the files have considerable **data redundancy.**

**Data
Consistency**

As is often the case during your college days, you may decide to change your address. You would notify the placement office about your address change to ensure that they send job notices to the right location. The placement office would then bring up your record on a screen and update your college address. However, your address is still incorrect in all the other files at the college (see Figure 7–7). You can see that data redundancy not only leads to wasted disk space; it can also lead to data inconsistency. When many files contain records with the same or similar data fields, updating one record in one file will lead to inconsistency in those data in the other files. Inaccuracies in your data files, such as inconsistencies, mean that your files lack **data consistency.**

Furthermore, each office might run separate programs to process their files. The enrollment office might run a COBOL program to access its record on you to produce a transcript. The placement office might run an assembler-language program to

Figure 7–6

Dependence of application programs on files specifically designed for these programs

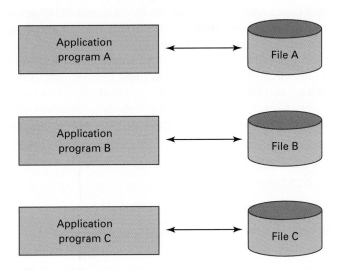

Figure 7–7

Multiple files lead
to data redundancy
and inconsistency

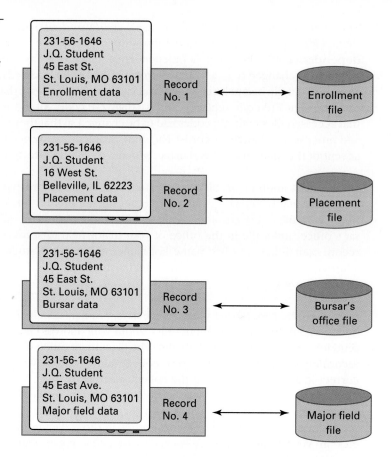

access its record on you to produce a list of job openings appropriate to your stated needs and qualifications. The bursar's office might run an RPG (report program generator) program to access its record on you to produce a tuition invoice. Because of the differences in the records and the programs that use them, there may be no easy way for a college administrator to produce a report showing how many students who owe tuition have found employment through the placement office. It was at best difficult and usually impossible for managers to obtain information useful for analysis and planning from the files of the entire organization. What they needed was a system that would eliminate data redundancy and provide data consistency—or make sure that data are accurate wherever they are stored. They also needed a system to provide data independence so a user could access data regardless of the record in which it was stored. To meet these needs, database management systems were developed.

DATABASE MANAGEMENT SYSTEMS

A **database management system (DBMS)** is a collection of software programs that

- Stores data in a uniform and consistent way.
- Organizes the data into records in a uniform and consistent way.
- Allows access to the data in a uniform and consistent way.

Figure 7–8

Relationship of application programs, a database management system, and a database

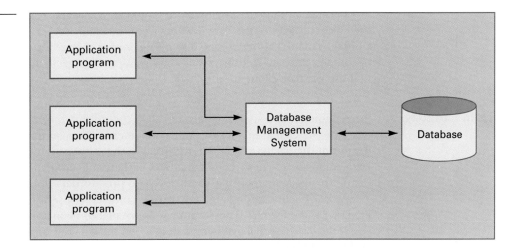

In a database management system, application programs do not obtain the data they need directly from the storage media. They must first request the data from the DBMS. The DBMS then retrieves the data from the storage media and provides them to the application programs. Thus a database management system operates *between* application programs and the data (see Figure 7–8).

COMPONENTS OF A DATABASE MANAGEMENT SYSTEM

Most organizations purchase database management system software from commercial vendors. The components of a particular DBMS will vary somewhat from one vendor to another. Some of these components are typically used by specialists in information systems. For example, information systems specialists typically use the data dictionary/directory, data languages, teleprocessing monitor, application development systems, security software, and archiving and recovery system components of database management systems. Programmers, managers, and various nonspecialists may use other components, such as report writers and query languages.

Data Dictionary/ Directory

A *data dictionary/directory* contains the names and descriptions of every data element in the database. It also contains a description of how data elements relate to one another. Through the use of its data dictionary, a DBMS stores data in a uniform and consistent manner, thus reducing redundancy. For example, the data dictionary ensures that the data element representing the number of an inventory item (named STOCKNUM) will be of uniform length and have other uniform characteristics regardless of the application program that uses it. The data dictionary also enforces consistency among users and application developers. It prevents users or application developers from adding data elements that have the same name but different characteristics to the database. For example, a developer would be prevented from creating a second inventory record and calling the data element for stock number INVNUM. Application developers use the data dictionary to create the records they need for the programs they are developing. The data dictionary checks records that are being developed against the records that already exist in the database and prevents inconsistencies in data element names and characteristics from occurring.

Because of the data dictionary, an application program does not have to specify the characteristics of the data it wants from the database. It merely requests the data from the DBMS. This technique may permit you to change the characteristics of a data element in the data dictionary without having to change all the application programs that use the data element.

Data Languages

Programmers use a special language called the *data description language* (DDL) to describe the characteristics of the data elements. To ensure uniformity in accessing data from the database, a DBMS will require that application programs use standardized commands. These commands are part of the *data manipulation language* (DML) that programmers use to retrieve and process data from the database.

A data manipulation language usually consists of a series of commands, such as FIND, GET, and INSERT. These commands are placed in an application program to instruct the database management system to get the data the application program needs at the right time.

Teleprocessing Monitors

A *teleprocessing monitor* is a communications software package that manages communications between the database and remote terminals. Teleprocessing monitors often handle order entry systems that have terminals located at remote sales locations. Teleprocessing monitors may be developed by database management systems software firms and offered as companion packages to their database products.

Application Development Tools

An *application development tool* is a program designed to help programmers develop application programs that use the database. Application development programs included in database management systems products often include computer-aided software engineering, or CASE, tools. CASE tools were briefly introduced in Chapter 6 and will be covered in more detail in Chapter 14.

Security Software

A *security software* package provides a variety of tools to shield the database from unauthorized access and from unwanted viruses. The security of data will be discussed in greater detail in Chapter 17.

Archiving, Backup, and Recovery Systems

Archiving programs provide the database manager with tools to make copies of the database, which can be used in case original database records are damaged or destroyed. *Restart/recovery systems* are tools used to restart the database and to recover lost data in the event of a failure. Backup systems automate making copies of data and work with restart/recovery systems to recover from database failures.

Report Writers

A **report writer** allows programmers, managers, and other users to design output reports without writing an application program in a programming language such as COBOL.

Query Languages

A **query language** is a set of commands used primarily for accessing data from a database. Query languages allow managers and other users to ask ad hoc questions of the database interactively without the aid of programmers. Three tools used to query a database are structured query language (SQL), natural language queries, and query by example (QBE).

51

SQL queries. One form of query language is **Structured Query Language (SQL).** SQL is a set of about 30 English-like commands that has become a standard in the database industry. Most vendors of DBMS software now provide SQL for their database software. Because SQL is used in most database management systems, managers who understand SQL syntax are able to use the same set of commands regardless of the database management system software that they must use. Knowing SQL provides the manager with access to data in many database management systems.

The basic form of an SQL command is SELECT . . . FROM . . . WHERE. After SELECT you list the fields you want. After FROM you list the name of the file or group of records that contains those fields. After WHERE you list any conditions for the search of the records. For example, you might wish to SELECT customer names and addresses FROM a customer record WHERE the state in the customer address is Michigan. So you would enter:

SELECT	NAME, ADDRESS, CITY, STATE, ZIP
FROM	CUSTOMER
WHERE	STATE = 'MI';

The result would be a list of the names and addresses of all customers located in Michigan.

Natural language queries. Some query languages use a *natural-language* set of commands. These query languages are structured so that the commands used are as close to standard English as possible. For example, the following statement might be used:

LIST THE NAMES AND ADDRESSES OF ALL CUSTOMERS WHO LIVE IN MICHIGAN

QBE queries. **Query by example (QBE)** is a query method that does not require writing statements directly. Instead, the user displays pictures of the records in the database and then drags and drops data elements from these records to a report form (see Figure 7–9a). The query is then run and the results displayed (see Figure 7–9b).

The upside and downside of query languages. Query languages allow users to retrieve data from databases without having detailed information about the structure of the records and without being concerned about the processes the DBMS uses to retrieve the data. Furthermore, managers do not have to learn COBOL, C, or other standard programming languages to access the database. The downside is that seemingly simple queries generated by naive users can take hours to execute. Knowing query shortcuts and strategies and the types of data in the database can improve the efficiency of retrieving data. In addition, managers who lack sufficient information about the nature of the data they are searching might create queries that do not return accurate data. Therefore, training managers and other users to use query languages efficiently for database retrieval is important.

Multiple-Platform Databases

Some vendors of DBMS software provide products that work on many different computer hardware and operating system platforms. For example, a DBMS software product might be offered in versions for mainframes, minicomputers, workstations, and microcomputers. The product may also be offered for several operating systems on each level of computer hardware. Having multiple versions of the DBMS software can be helpful. The versions often simplify downloading data from one system to another,

Figure 7–9

Query by example (a) Selecting the records (Employees, Orders, and Order Subtotals) and dragging the fields wanted to the report form (Employee Last Name and Order Subtotal) (b) Displaying the results of the query

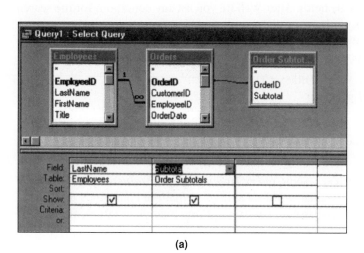

(a)   (b)

such as downloading mainframe database data to a microcomputer or minicomputer database for local processing. For example, the makers of the Oracle DBMS provide both microcomputer and minicomputer versions of their mainframe product that makes downloading and uploading data between these platforms more convenient. Some microcomputer and minicomputer versions even contain a communications program for transferring files between the mainframe and the microcomputer. By having versions for several platforms and operating systems, developers can create applications on one platform and use them on others with little modification.

Web Server Software

Recently many DBMS vendors have integrated World Wide Web (WWW) server software into their products (see Chapters 8 and 9). The software turns the computer system housing the database into a Web server and enables users with Web connectivity to access the data from wherever they are located. It also converts the data stored to a format that is readable by standard Web *browsers*. Browser software runs on computer systems that connect to the Web and lets users view the data in the local database as well as data on the World Wide Web itself. Thus personnel at remote and local locations who have appropriate authority can access the organization's data, as well as data on external computer systems, using only a standard Web browser. The use of Web software is discussed in more detail in the section "Intranet and Hypertext Databases" later in this chapter.

THE DATABASE ADMINISTRATOR

The development of DBMSs has created a need for organizational changes within firms. The focal point of these changes is the position of the **database administrator (DBA).** The DBA is charged with managing the organization's data resources, a job that often includes database planning, design, operation, training, user support, security, and maintenance. The role of the DBA requires a person who can relate to top management, systems analysts, application programmers, users, and systems programmers. Such a person needs both effective management skills and a fair amount of technical ability. Selection of the DBA and the organization of this important function are critical to the success of a DBMS.

The deployment of a database management system in a firm generates a number of changes in the way records and files are administered. The most prominent change is that now many users *share* data that were previously "owned" by one or more users. Thus payroll records no longer belong to the payroll department; they are part of the company's database. Giving up data ownership can be very painful for some units within an organization. The DBA must persuade "owners" to give up their data to a common database, and this task may not be easy.

Another change occurs when data are added to a database. Pooling data in a common database requires consensus concerning the structure of the data elements. The users of the database must agree on the nature of each data element and its characteristics, such as length and type of data. Though this matter sounds trivial, previous ownership of the data element may cause considerable problems for the DBA when seeking agreement on their definitions. However, uniform definitions of the data elements must be achieved before the elements are recorded in the data dictionary. In a very real sense, the data dictionary serves as a common discipline for all database users by requiring agreement on the data elements to be stored in the database. Thus the DBA should be involved to some extent in all applications under development because the DBA is the final authority on the structure of the database.

Another change pertains to data access. Maintaining data consistency and security is an important role of the DBA. The DBA must not only approve access to data stored in the database but also approve the access procedures. Because the data are shared, it is important to permit only those who need the data to have access to them. The ability to add, delete, or modify existing data must be tightly controlled. Consider the college file problem discussed earlier. If the placement file, enrollment file, bursar's office file, and major field file were reorganized under a DBMS, only one master record for each student would be necessary. This master record would contain the student's number, name, address, and other relatively permanent data. It also would include separate records for enrollment, placement, bursar, and major field data, but these records would not contain the data in the master record. They would contain only the student's number and the data pertinent to the department or unit. Thus the only connection between the various data elements pertaining to enrollment, placement, bursar, or major field and the student master record is the student number (see Figure 7–10).

Though such a scheme reduces redundancy and thereby reduces the threat to data consistency, consider what would happen if the student decided to drop the major field and the clerk in that department eliminated the student master record. The college would have enrollment data, placement data, even bills payable to the

Figure 7–10

Reduction of redundancy in a database

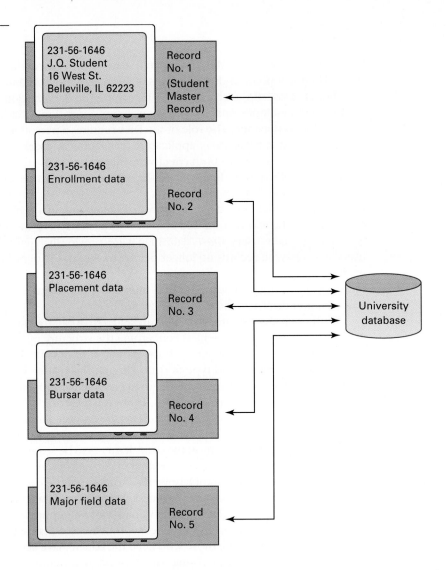

bursar's office with no student name and address to match. You can see why the DBA must tightly control the ability of users to add, delete, or modify information in the records. Also, because so much of the organization's data is in one resource, the organization is more vulnerable than before. The DBA is responsible for protecting the organization's data. Achieving this protection is complicated by the fact that many people within the organization view access to data as essential for success. Others view data access as a symbol of status. Restricting access to data then becomes a political problem for the DBA.

Another facet of database security is enforcing a policy for regular *backup* of the database. Backing up the database may take several forms. One of the most common is *archiving,* or making a complete backup copy of the database at regular intervals. Providing backup security for a database is essential to avoid total loss of data in the event of an equipment failure. Additional information about security is presented in Chapter 17.

VIEWS OF THE DATA

Any database contains two types of data: the actual data, such as employee names, hourly wage rates, and hours worked, and information about the data. That is, it contains (1) the definitions of each data element and (2) how each data element relates to other data elements. The data kept about data are called *metadata.*

The data in a database have two views. The *logical view* is the way users perceive records are structured and the relationships among records in the database. The *physical view* is the way the records are actually organized and stored on the storage media.

The Schema

A *schema* is a description of the logical view of a database. A common tool used to design schema is an *entity-relationship diagram*. A simple entity-relationship diagram showing the relationship between an equipment repair vendor and the equipment to be repaired demonstrates the complexity of database design (see Figure 7–11). Consider that these record types may be only two records in a database of hundreds or thousands of record types. Consider also that these two record types would undoubtedly have more data elements that those shown in the ellipses and that each record type would also be related to many other record types in the database. For example, the equipment record might be related to the vendor record (the company that sold the equipment to you), the manufacturer record (the company that built the equipment), a building record (the building in which the equipment is located), a room record (the room in which the equipment is located), and a department record (the department that purchased and uses the equipment).

Subschema

A less comprehensive logical view of the database is the *subschema*. The subschema is the view used by an application programmer, an application program, or a user. A subschema encompasses only a subset of the data elements in the entire database, those data elements needed by one user.

Figure 7–11

A simple entity-relationship diagram

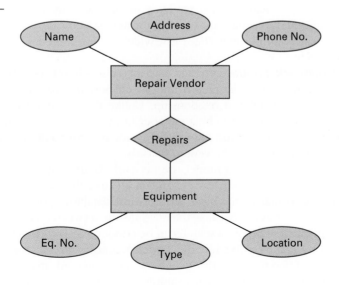

Subschema provide one means of making the database system secure. Users of one application program, for example, may be restricted to their own views of the database. The DBMS may not allow users of an application program to access data not within their view.

DATABASE MODELS

As you have seen, organizing a large database logically into records and identifying the relationships among the records are complex tasks. Most organizations will have many record types as part of a database, and each record type will have numerous data elements. Even a small business is likely to have many record types, each with several distinct data elements. Also, these records may have many relationships with one another. For example, an invoice can be related to the customer who purchased the merchandise, the salesperson who sold the customer the merchandise, the products included on the invoice, and the warehouse from which the merchandise was picked.

Four approaches have been implemented in commercial database products to organize records and their relationships. These organizational approaches are known as **database models.** The four database models are the

- Hierarchical database model.
- Network database model.
- Relational database model.
- Object-oriented database model.

Hierarchical and Network Database Models

In a **hierarchical database** records are organized into a hierarchy of relationships, like an inverted tree pattern. For example, an equipment database, diagrammed in Figure 7–12, may have building records, room records, equipment records, repair vendor records, and repair invoice records. Each record is related to others in a parent-child relationship. Each parent record may have one or more child records, but ordinarily a child record would not have more than one parent record.

The hierarchical database model is still in use in many existing information systems, but it is not being used as much for new systems development. IBM's Information Management Systems (IMS) is a widely adopted hierarchical database management system.

A **network database** model views all records in sets (see Figure 7–13). Each *set* is composed of an *owner* record and one or more *member* records, similar to the hierarchy's parent-children relationship. Unlike the hierarchical model, the network model permits a record to be a member of more than one set at one time. The network model would permit the repair invoice records to be the children of both the equipment records and the vendor records.

Like the hierarchical model, the network database model is still in use in older database systems. It is not, however, the model usually chosen in today's environment. The reason is that hierarchical and network database models are less flexible than other database models because the relationship between records must be determined and implemented before a search can be conducted. Thus the relationships between records are relatively fixed by the model. Managers' ad hoc queries that require relationships different than those already implemented may be difficult or time-consuming to accomplish. For example, a manager may wish to identify equipment

Figure 7–12
Hierarchical database model

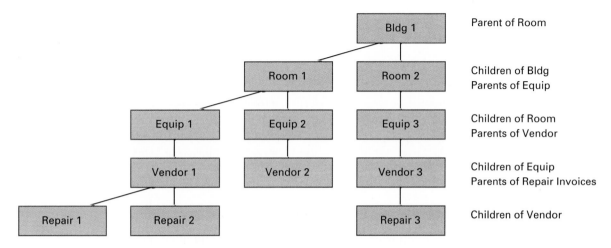

manufacturers whose equipment has a high frequency of repair. If the equipment record contains the name of the manufacturer, such a query could be performed fairly directly. However, data describing the manufacturer may be contained in a record that is part of another hierarchy or set. As a result, there may not be any established relationship between manufacturer records and repair records. Providing reports based on this relationship in a large database is not a minor task, and the data processing staff is not likely to undertake the job for a one-time management query. Managerial use of query languages to solve the problem may require multiple searches and also prove to be very time-consuming. Thus a hierarchical or network DMBS may not effectively support analysis and planning activities that frequently involve ad hoc management queries of the database. On the plus side, hierarchical and network DBMSs usually process structured, operational data rapidly. In fact, the relationships of records may be organized to maximize the speed with which large batch operations such as weekly payroll or sales invoices are processed.

Relational Database Model

The dominant database model in use today for developing information systems is the relational database model. Both the hierarchical and network data models require explicit relationships, or links, between records in the database. Both models also require that data be processed one record at a time. The relational database model departs from both these requirements.

Figure 7–13
Network database model

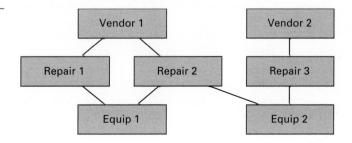

Figure 7–14
Repair vendor table
in a relational
database system

Repair Vendors Records		
Column 1	**Column 2**	**Column 3**
Repair Vendor Number	**Repair Vendor Name**	**Repair Vendor Address**
43623	Telo, Inc.	15 Tory Street
43890	A-Repair company	25 Vine Street
43118	Beeline, Ltd.	498 Olde Street
43079	Aspen, Inc.	12 Dome Avenue
43920	Calso, Inc.	5 Estes Street

A **relational database** is organized into a series of two-dimensional tables. Many managers often work with tabular financial data and often understand the relational database model easily. For example, our repair vendor records might be structured as shown in Figure 7-14.

The repair vendor table consists of the repair vendor master records, which contain the repair vendor number, name, and address. Each row in the table is analogous to a record, and each column represents one type of data element. A similar table for equipment could look like the table in Figure 7-15. The table contains the records for each piece of equipment in the firm. Each record also contains the number of the repair vendor who has a contract to repair that piece of equipment.

A manager could create a report showing the names of each repair vendor and the pieces of equipment that each vendor repairs by combining the needed data elements from both tables into a third table. The manager might join the two tables (REPAIR_VENDOR and EQUIPMENT) with a query statement such as this:

```
SELECT REPAIR_VENDOR.NAME, EQUIPMENT.NAME
FROM REPAIR_VENDOR, EQUIPMENT
WHERE REPAIR_VENDOR.NO=EQUIPMENT.REPAIR_VENDOR_NO
```

Figure 7–15
Equipment table in
a relational
database system

Equipment Records			
Column 1	**Column 2**	**Column 3**	**Column 4**
Equipment Number	**Equipment Name**	**Date Purchased**	**Repair Vendor Number**
10893	Typewriter	12/02/94	43623
49178	Microcomputer	01/31/87	43920
10719	Telephone	03/12/96	43079
18572	Copier	11/06/95	43890
60875	Calculator	08/01/94	43118

The manager might also use QBE instead. In that case pictures of both tables would be displayed and the data elements would simply be dragged to the report form, similar to Figure 7–9.

The manager might also produce a report by selecting from both tables only the rows for specific equipment types or for equipment purchased in specific years. The important things to notice are that you do not need to specify the relationships, or links, in advance and that you manipulate whole tables.

Relational databases allow the manager flexibility in conducting database queries and creating reports. Queries can be made and new tables created using all or part of the data from one or more tables. The links between data elements in a relational database do not need to be made explicit at the time the database is created—new links can be structured at any time. Thus the relational database model is more flexible than the hierarchical or network database model and provides the manager with rich opportunities for ad hoc reports and queries. However, because they do not specify the relationships among data elements in advance, relational databases do not process large batch applications as fast as hierarchical or network databases do.

Object-Oriented Databases

Generations of new file and database models evolved as the old models became less suitable to current applications (see Figure 7–16). When applications were built one by one over time, simple files were satisfactory. When a need arose for integrated databases, hierarchical, network, and finally relational models were developed. However, as flexible as the relational model is, it is not particularly well suited for many business and engineering applications today. The relational model still is based on data elements that describe rigidly defined records containing rigidly defined data elements.

Figure 7–16

The evolution of database structures

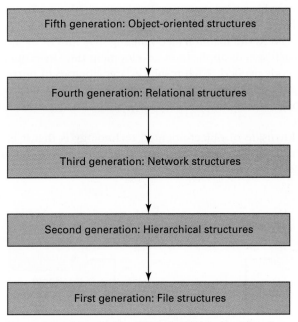

Source: Adapted from W. Kim, "A New Database for New Times," *Datamation* 36, no. 2 (January 15, 1990), pp. 35–42.

A great deal of the information managers use is stored in organization records and represents the results of the organization's transactions, such as sales invoices, payments to vendors, and payments to workers. However, an increasing amount of the information managers use is in the form of images, drawings, voice, sound, videos, and other nontext data. These data are produced by multimedia systems; computer-aided software engineering (CASE); computer-aided design (CAD); and other engineering, design, and manufacturing systems. These information systems produce information that may be scattered among letters, reports, memoranda, magazine articles, engineering drawings, charts, graphs, training films, or other "objects."

The data in these objects differ fundamentally from the data in a typical transaction-oriented database system. In the latter, specific information is entered in a very restricted manner, and the manager typically wishes to summarize, total, or list selected data from the records. In the former, the data may not be transactions, but instead include many complex data types that vary substantially in type, length, content, and form. At present, object-oriented database technology appears best suited to manage these data types.

Each object in an **object-oriented database (OODB)** is bound together with its own data and a set of instructions that describes the behavior and attributes of the object. Objects use *messages* to interact with one another. Every object is described by a set of *attributes*. For example, the object *building* in a database of architectural drawings may have the attributes type, size, and color, just as in any other database. Every object must also have a set of *methods,* or routines and procedures. For example, methods stored with an architectural drawing of a maintenance building might include instructions to display, rotate, shrink, or explode the drawing on a screen (see Figure 7–17).

Objects that have the same set of attributes and methods are grouped into a *class.* For example, building, floor, and room might be three classes of objects in the database of architectural drawings. Furthermore, the attributes and behaviors of one object can be *inherited* by other objects in the same class. Thus, another building in the same class as the maintenance building may inherit its attributes and behaviors. This approach speeds application development time by reducing the amount of programming code needed. What results is large libraries of *reusable objects,* which can be employed over and over again. New applications can be assembled by putting off-the-shelf objects from these libraries together, just as a car can be built from component parts.

One downside of object-oriented technology is that it is substantially different from other database technology. Because of that difference, it usually presents a considerable learning curve to practitioners.

Figure 7–17

Building, floor, and room objects in an object-oriented architectural database

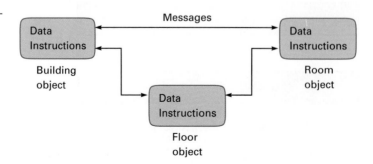

ADVANTAGES OF DATABASE MANAGEMENT SYSTEMS

Companies find a number of advantages in using a DBMS instead of having a series of separate files accessed by programs written specifically for those files.

Data Sharing

The data from the entire company are at the disposal of users who need them. Managers may analyze a much more extensive store of information than is available in the typical single record type environment (see Figure 7-18).

Reduced Data Redundancy

A database minimizes duplication of data from file to file. Thus a student's name and address might appear in only one record in a university database rather than in the files of many departments.

Improved Data Consistency

Because data redundancy is minimized, data inconsistency is substantially reduced. Data inconsistency naturally leads to conflicting reports. For example, a report derived from the student enrollment file may contain information that conflicts with reports generated from the university placement file. Where data redundancy must exist, as in the use of social security numbers to connect student records or in the use of vendor numbers to connect repair vendors and equipment records, the database system should maintain data consistency. If for some reason a vendor's number changes, the database system should change that number everywhere it exists in the database.

Figure 7–18

Reports produced from one record type and two record types in a database

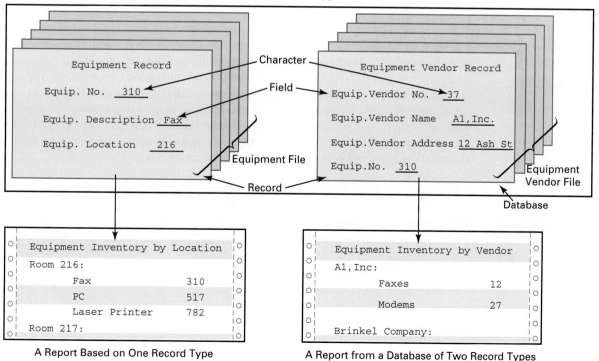

A Report Based on One Record Type

A Report from a Database of Two Record Types

Data Independence

A database system keeps descriptions of data separate from the applications that use the data. Thus changes in the data definitions can occur without necessarily requiring changes in every application program that uses those data. The result could be a substantial reduction in program maintenance costs—the costs to upgrade application programs in response to changes in the file structure.

Some databases also store data in ways that do not depend on the storage media used. Thus if new disk drives are purchased, the data may not need to be reorganized to remain accessible to the application programs using them.

Increased Application Programmer and User Productivity

Most DBMSs offer application program development tools that help application programmers write program code. These tools can be very powerful, and they usually improve an application programmer's productivity substantially. Some application development tools may increase the number of lines of code an application programmer can produce by as much as 5 to 10 times within a given period of time. Object-oriented databases provide developers with libraries of reusable code to speed development of applications. Nontechnical users also increase their productivity when query languages and report generators allow them to produce reports from the database without any help from MIS professionals, thus avoiding the long time period that a management information systems department may require to develop new applications. The result is greater use of the corporate database for ad hoc queries and managerial decision making.

Users also increase their productivity when they use microcomputer software designed to work with the mainframe database. This PC software allows them to acquire and manipulate data with ease without requiring the assistance of programmers. When users can obtain many of their reports and data without intervention by systems analysts or application programmers, demand on the services of these professionals for routine application requests decreases. Systems analysts and application programmers are thus freed to focus their attention on applications that require their talents, which increases their productivity to the organization.

Improved Data Administration and Control

Placing responsibility for the database in the hands of one person or department provides a number of advantages. It permits better enforcement of standards for defining data elements and data relationships. In this way the discipline of the data dictionary becomes easier to enforce and control. Access to data, the privacy of data, and updates and deletions of data are also easier to control. In addition, a person or department devoted to the supervision of data is more likely to archive the database and take other security measures than a department inexperienced with information systems management and preoccupied with its own problems.

Increased Emphasis on Data as a Resource

Establishing database administration and deploying a database management system emphasize throughout an organization the importance of information to the management function. The DBA acts as an advocate for the concept of information as a corporate resource. The result is likely to be greater corporate attention to information systems as an aid to managerial decision making and long-range planning using the database as the basic information resource.

PROBLEMS OF DATABASE MANAGEMENT SYSTEMS

DBMSs provide many opportunities and advantages, but these advantages may come at a price. DBMSs also pose problems.

Concurrency Problems

When more than one user utilizes a DBMSs, problems can occur if the system is not designed for multiple users. One of these problems is concurrent access to records, or **concurrency control.** Suppose that two of your salespeople are using terminals at two different company sites. Salesperson A is selling blue widgets to customer A, who wants to buy 200 of them. The salesperson retrieves the inventory record for blue widgets on the screen to see if there is enough stock on hand to make the sale. The blue widget inventory record shows a balance of 300 widgets.

At the same time, salesperson B is selling blue widgets to customer B at another location. Customer B wants to buy 150 of them. (Blue widgets are a popular item.) This salesperson also retrieves the blue widget record. In other words, both salespeople have retrieved and are viewing the blue widget record that shows 300 items on hand. Now salesperson B, being a fast talker, closes the sale first. The right keys are pushed on the terminal, and the blue widget file showing a balance of 150 is copied back to the database. Unfortunately, no change is made in the screen being viewed by salesperson A. Salesperson A, you will remember, is looking at the original blue widget record, which still shows a balance of 300 items. So salesperson A closes and records the sale of 200 widgets from the terminal, and that record shows a balance of 100 widgets. What happens next is that the record viewed by salesperson A, showing an old balance of 300, less a sale of 200, is now copied to disk. The sale by salesperson A overwrites the sale of salesperson B, and the blue widget record shows a balance of 100. But there is actually a shortage of 50 items in inventory. The problem of concurrent access can be solved in a number of ways. Some simple database systems merely lock a file when one user is using it. If salesperson A was using the inventory file, salesperson B would not be able to either view or write to that file. *File locking* is likely to be a poor choice to avoid the problem of concurrency, however. In our example, it would mean that only one of your salespeople could sell a product at any time.

Another way to avoid concurrency problems is to lock only the record being used. Thus salesperson B may view and write to any inventory item *except* the blue widget record because salesperson A is already using that record. *Record locking* still presents problems, though. Popular inventory items would frequently be locked and unavailable for use by other salespeople. Still another way to avoid concurrency is to lock a data element, or field, when it is being used. *Field locking* would permit more than one person to use a popular record but would allow only one person to make a change in a particular data element.

A more sophisticated means of handling concurrency problems is to use a DBMS that uses *versioning*. Versioning permits every user to view a record and make updates in that record. However, before any record update is actually saved, the system checks to see if the record (the prior version of the record) has changed. Before salesperson A would be able to close the sale, the system would recheck the blue widget record to see if any updates (newer versions of the record) have been made in the record. The system would notify salesperson A that there has been a change and update the screen being viewed to reflect that change. Salesperson A would then have to tell customer A that there are not enough blue widgets on hand. No doubt that would lead to a discussion of how nifty yellow widgets are.

A DBMS designed for a mainframe or minicomputer is usually designed to handle multiple users simultaneously; that is, it is a multiuser system, and the DBMS will usually provide for some form of concurrency control. Many microcomputer DBMSs, on the other hand, are designed for one user. Therefore, the single-user versions of microcomputer DBMSs will not have concurrency control. If you connect several microcomputers together in order to share data files on a hard disk, you should upgrade your DBMS software to a multiuser version with concurrency control.

Resource Problems

A DBMS usually requires extra computing resources. After all, the new DBMS's programs must be run. Much more data must be stored on-line to answer queries, which we hope will increase. As a result, you may need more terminals to put managers and other users on-line to the database. You may also need additional hard disk systems to put more data on-line and make it available to managers and more communication devices to connect the extra terminals to the database. You may even need to increase the size or number of CPUs to run the extra software required by the DBMS.

Security Problems

A database must have sufficient controls to ensure that only authorized personnel can access data and that only these personnel can add, delete, and update data in the database. The manager must realize that access security means more than merely providing login identification, account codes, and passwords. Security considerations should include means of controlling physical access to terminals, tapes, and other devices. Security considerations should also include the noncomputerized procedures associated with the database, such as forms to control the updating or deletion of records or files and procedures for storing source documents.

In addition, access to employee, vendor, and customer data should conform to various federal and state regulations, such as the 1971 Fair Credit Reporting Act, the 1974 Privacy Act, and the 1978 Right to Financial Privacy Act. Certainly the DBMS should contain an archiving feature to copy all important files and programs, and there should be procedures for regular update and storage of these archival copies. Also the DBMS should provide software to assist in recovering data lost when the system fails and in restarting the DBMS after the failure.

Additional information pertaining to database backup, archiving, and other security matters are presented in Chapter 17.

Specialized Databases

In addition to the traditional databases, such as the financial accounting and human resource databases, many organizations have developed or utilize specialized databases. The last few years has seen a growth in specialized databases as decision makers seek to use ever more data from both inside and outside their organizations to reduce the risk of their actions and improve the competitiveness of their organizations.

Intranet and Hypermedia Databases

Hypertext documents were defined in Chapter 6 as documents that are organized in document units such as cards, pages, or books and usually contain links to other cards, pages, or books. **Hypermedia databases** are systems in which hypertext documents are the records.

Hypermedia databases may consist of documents that are internal and external to an organization. For example, the documents may be located on one or more of the numerous computer systems connected to the World Wide Web (see Chapters 8 and 9). The Web is part of that complex of worldwide and interconnected computer systems called the **Internet.** Hypermedia databases may also consist of hypertext documents that are internal to an organization and available on a company's own network. In the latter case, the system is usually referred to as an **intranet.**

What makes hypermedia so appealing to most organizations is that a hypermedia document can contain text, images, sound clips, video clips, and other types of data and the document can be read by a single piece of software—a browser—whether the document is on a computer in your building or on a computer located in another country. Furthermore, the information stored in hypermedia documents may be accessed in a nonsequential fashion merely by clicking a mouse button on the links found in documents. In fact, the links in any hypermedia document may link to data, images, sound, and text from both internal and external sources.

The reason that any browser can read nearly any hypermedia document is that the documents are written in **hypertext markup language (HTML),** which is a subset of the standardized general markup language (SGML) described in Chapter 6. HTML replaces document-formatting code that is usually proprietary to each vendor with a standard set of formatting tags. For example, a word processing package will place a unique, proprietary formatting code before and after words that are to be underlined. HTML documents replace that unique code with a standard tag readable by nearly every browser. To create a word that will be displayed in underlined form by a browser, you merely add the following tags before and after the word:

<U>Word</U>

Most browsers will display that word this way:

<u>Word</u>

In fact, hypermedia documents have become so popular and useful that many word processors have added the ability to read and process HTML tags in addition to their own proprietary formatting codes.

Documents formatted in HTML can be read by any browser on any platform. It doesn't matter whether the user has a MacIntosh, IBM PC, or a UNIX workstation. All the user needs is a browser that runs on his or her machine to access and display the document. You can see why hypermedia documents have become so popular.

Recently, many DBMS vendors have added intranet software to their products. The software enables the computer on which the database runs to translate traditional records into HTML. It also allows any user with browser software and authority to access the database to read the records.

Organizations have found that they can make many existing documents, including compound documents, available to everyone in the organization swiftly merely by converting the documents to HTML and letting users access the documents over an intranet. One common set of documents are employee training materials, equipment and procedure manuals, and new-employee orientation documents. By keeping these documents in a database that can convert them to HTML, the documents can be made available throughout the organization and are quickly and easily updated. The cost savings to companies in terms of printing and distribution expenses can be very large. Furthermore, using an intranet is usually the fastest and least expensive way to ensure that everyone in an organization can obtain the information.

The Internet and intranets are described in more detail in Chapters 8 and 9.

On-Line Databases

A great deal of information is available to managers through thousands of commercial, government, and nonprofit organization computerized databases. These databases may be accessed directly through the sponsoring organizations or accessed through on-line information services, such as Microsoft Network (MSN), CompuServe, America Online, and Prodigy (see Manager's Memo 7–1). **On-line information services** are companies that provide a variety of information services to organizations or individuals who subscribe to their services. These services include access to many databases and also might include the use of a network over which your computer users may

Manager's Memo 7-1	EXAMPLES OF ON-LINE DATABASES

 ABI/Inform (data on over 1,000 business periodicals).

American Statistics Index (an index of federal agency statistical reports).

Business Wire (news from government agencies, universities, organizations, and companies).

CENDATA (data from the U.S. Census Bureau and Department of Commerce).

Computer Database (abstracts and other data on computer periodicals).

D&B Donnelly Demographics (demographic data from the census).

Dun's Financial Records Plus (financial data on nearly 700,000 companies).

Encyclopedia of Associations (data on 80,000 nonprofit organizations).

Federal News Service (information from federal news conferences, speeches).

GPO Publications File (data on publications for sale from the U.S. Printing Office).

Health Periodicals Database (an index of articles from health periodicals).

LEXIS (law libraries in all areas of the law).

Medline (a large index of articles relating to medicine).

Reader's Guide to Periodical Literature (index to English language periodicals from United States and Canada).

Reuters (news releases).

SEC Online (annual and financial reports and other stock-related reports from nearly 6,000 companies).

Social Sciences Index (index to periodicals for the social sciences, including economics).

Standard & Poor's Corporate Descriptions (data on over 9,000 companies).

Standard & Poor's Register—Biographical (data on 70,000 business executives).

The Wall Street Journal (issues since 1984).

Trade & Industry Index (abstracts and indexes of over 12,000 publications).

U.S. Copyrights (data on all current copyrights of the U.S. Copyright Office).

U.S. Patents (data on all U.S. patents issued since 1971).

Westlaw (data on statutory law, codes, regulations, decisions).

communicate with one another, such as a long-distance communications network that each of your branch managers might use to communicate data to headquarters (see Manager's Memo 7-2).

On-line databases are also available on the World Wide Web (see Chapters 8 and 9). However they are accessed, **on-line databases** enable managers to analyze and manipulate large quantities of information external to their organizations. Access includes searching the databases for information on key words or phrases, generating reports from information downloaded from the databases to the managers' computer systems, manipulating data downloaded from the databases to the managers' spreadsheets or database programs, and printing summaries of information selected from the databases.

On-line databases are essentially electronic libraries. They can offer managers a large variety of different types of information literally at their fingertips. These information sources help managers stay current on topics of importance to their organizations and give them a competitive edge over others who do not have such information immediately available. More information on the World Wide Web and its resources can be found in Chapters 8 and 9.

Some on-line information services allow you to tailor the service so it provides you with automatic updates whenever anything new is published on topics of interest to you. Using the search software provided with the service, you can develop

| Manager's Memo 7–2 | POPULAR ON-LINE INFORMATION SERVICES |

Major On-Line Services

America Online	CompuServe
Delphi Internet	Dow Jones
GEnie	Prodigy
Microsoft Network (MSN)	IBM Global Network (Advertising)

What They Typically Provide

Access to on-line databases.

Access to on-line libraries.

Electronic mail, including sending and receiving mail from and to the Internet.

Fax services, including sending and receiving faxes.

Teletype services, including sending and receiving Telex and TWX messages.

Access to forums on nearly every conceivable topic, including vendor support forums for popular hardware and software.

Software libraries, including the ability to download program updates to your software, program fixes, utilities, and shareware.

Investment and financial information and services.

News, weather, sports information.

Electronic shopping.

Travel information and services.

Reference information and services, including encyclopedias, thesauri, and biographies.

On-line games and programs.

Classified ads and career information, including job listings.

Health information, including drug databases and dietary information.

profiles for special topics. The on-line information service searches the appropriate databases whenever they are updated and sends you the results of the search. For example, you might set up a profile for artificial intelligence with several on-line information services to which you subscribe. Whenever anything new on artificial intelligence appears in sources that these information services monitor, it will automatically be identified and the reference, abstract, or even the full text will be transmitted to your computer system.

You may not wish to learn how to use, search, and manipulate these database services yourself. Though most on-line services are menu-driven, you may still have to learn quite a bit if you subscribe to more than one service because each has a slightly different set of software commands, key-word structures, and other procedures that you must know to use the service. Instead, you may wish to delegate the job of searching to a subordinate. In fact, many large organizations have search specialists to keep organization managers abreast of their areas of interest and their competitors. Smaller organizations may hire the services of an on-line information service search consultant. However, really creative searches of databases are best done by someone who is very knowledgeable and experienced in the specific field in which information is required. The synergistic effects of poking through references and documents inevitably lead to new key-word choices or whole new topics of interest for managers who take the time to do this work themselves.

Data Warehousing

Data warehousing is a term for any system that stores, retrieves, manages, or otherwise manipulates massive amounts of data. The data warehouse may contain data taken from the organization's databases as well as data obtained from external sources. The warehouse of data is often separate from the organization's production databases so that users can use this resource without reducing the response time for an organization's routine data processing operations.

A major difference between data in traditional databases and data in a data warehouse is that the organization of data in a data warehouse is subject oriented as opposed to transaction oriented. The purpose of a data warehouse is to make large amounts of data available to organizational personnel to support them in their decisions. The key to a successful warehouse is that it brings together information from many different and diverse company and external database systems into an integrated resource available to company personnel. For example, data from on-line databases may be integrated with company data into the data warehouse. Managers can then use tools to mine the data in this warehouse; that is, to retrieve data, analyze data, and find patterns in the data.

The major components of a data warehouse are

1. The data itself.
2. The hardware and network infrastructure that provides storage of and access to the data.
3. The software that extracts data from its original source, converts it into a uniform format, and places it into the warehouse.
4. Graphical query tools to permit data mining of the warehouse contents.
5. A user guide to the contents of the data warehouse.
6. Warehouse management software for information systems personnel to maintain and upgrade the warehouse.

To be most effective, the construction of the warehouse should be enterprisewide in design. As new information systems are developed or as important new external sources of data are identified, they should be integrated into the data warehouse. One result of a data warehouse is to integrate the islands of data that develop in an organization over time because information systems are developed that are not compatible with each other.

It is also important to ensure that the infrastructure provides for fast response time to users. The experience of organizations to date suggests that the use of data warehouses grows rapidly after their initial launch dates and that the infrastructure should be built with that in mind. In addition to fast response time to queries, the tools provided to managers should be easy to use, and the managers should receive training in the use of the tools.

One of the major uses of data warehouses by most organizations is marketing analysis—specifically, identifying customer buying preferences and trends and designing marketing programs that focus on customer profiles (see Chapter 10). For example, a women's lingerie chain with more than 1,300 stores hopes to save $3,000,000 in product markdown expenses by being able to identify how best to vary the promotions offered on merchandise. A global pharmaceutical company with thousands of employees is able to provide sales representatives with data about what affects physician drug-prescription decisions. This information provides the reps with a competitive advantage when developing sales messages and approaches tuned directly to each customer.

Data Marts

Creating a data warehouse that is enterprisewide can be a rather overwhelming task, especially in large organizations. For that reason, many organizations have tried to start small with *data marts*. What's the difference between a data warehouse and a data mart? The answer seems to be the scope of the data included. Data marts might be formed from data needed by one department in an organization. Some industry experts suggest that organizations might begin construction of their data warehouses by first building data marts for the needs of specific organization units and then combining these data marts later.[1] The bottom line is that data marts usually can be built faster and easier than data warehouses because they focus on a subset of an organization's data needs.

On-Line Analytical Processing

On-line analytical processing (OLAP) is a group of technologies that provide multidimensional views of a database; in fact, it is often referred to as *multidimensional analysis.* The technologies permit ad hoc questions to be asked of an OLAP database for tactical and strategic planning decision support. However, while typical databases contain transactions that are retrieved on a record by record or table by table basis, OLAP databases are data warehouses that may include filtered and aggregated data from many sources, including data from external sources.

Queries made against a typical relational database may take a long time to process because relational databases are not fast at retrieving a large number of records and summarizing, aggregating, or otherwise processing them concurrently. To avoid burdening these systems with queries that bring the databases to their knees, an OLAP database is created from subsets of the organization's database and placed on a separate host dedicated to managerial queries. Typically, these subsets are preprocessed data that filter out data that is not thought to be useful for management decision making and that provide more aggregate views of the database. OLAP database technology reflects the fact that in the 70s data to support business decisions was not easily available. In the 90s, however, managers are overwhelmed with data. Thus, there is a need to filter data from that available internally and externally to an organization.

Relational databases store data in two-dimensional tables, much like a spreadsheet. An OLAP database, on the other hand, stores and accesses data using several views, or *dimensions*. Data stored in this way is called a *hypercube*. Because the data have been preprocessed and aggregated in advance, OLAP hypercubes can be rapidly reorganized so that multiple views can be made. For example, while "a conventional spreadsheet can analyze sales by region, a multidimensional analysis tool can represent the same sales data by salesperson, geographic region, customer account, industry segment, and product line"[2]

However, because the hypercube data are often aggregates from other databases, the information in the OLAP hypercube may limit the ability of the user to "drill down" into the data. For example, a hypercube containing data from a student information system might only contain data on student's GPAs. The hypercube may not contain grades for every course the student completed during a metriculation. Thus, filtering and aggregation usually speed up user analysis, but may limit the ability of the user to obtain details. In fact, the user may have to query the underlying databases from which the hypercube was developed.

It should be clear that the usefulness of an OLAP database will depend on the ability of information systems specialists to understand and anticipate the user's need for information. If the data are not in the OLAP database, then the tool loses usefulness. It is often helpful to employ IS specialists with solid business knowledge. At the same

---

[1]K. Watterson, "Plug and Play Data Marts," *Client/Server Computing,* March 1997, p. 48.
[2]P. King, "The More Views, the Merrier," *Client/Server Computing,* May 1994, p. 49.

time, the user also must have a fairly comprehensive understanding of the nature of the data in the OLAP database. Knowledge of the content and structure of the data are major advantages to the user.

Leading database management systems vendors are beginning to integrate OLAP technologies into their relational database software, providing multidimensional analysis of relational data. As this integration occurs, the need for separate OLAP tools and databases may disappear.

Image Databases

Multimedia, CAD/CAM, presentation graphics, drawing programs, and a host of other software that produces images of one kind or another have created an avalanche of images that employees throughout an organization can use—provided the images can be found and translated into the format that the employee needs. The job of image management software is to store images in an **image database** so that they can be quickly found, easily accessed, and if needed, easily converted to the format needed.

Some database systems allow you to store images as well as data in a record. For example, some DBMSs let you store pictures taken by a VCR camera, scanned by a scanner, or copied from a computer screen in a record. Thus employee records managed by that software could contain pictures of employees as well as traditional text and numeric employee data. Consider how helpful photos of employees might be to members of the personnel department of a large company. After all, it's nice to be able to greet people by their names. Storing data and images pertaining to auto insurance claims is another useful application. Also, photos of stock items can help inventory clerks. You might expect fewer errors in taking inventory if you could be sure that the inventory clerks knew what they were looking at on the warehouse shelves.

Document Databases

The data in letters, memos, reports, and other documents in an organization—the organization's **document database**—may easily rival in quantity and sometimes in importance the financial data of that organization. However, an organization's stored documents are usually scattered across the filing cabinets, hard drives, and other storage media found in the departments and divisions of that organization. Finding what you want can be the equivalent of looking for the needle in the haystack. **Document management software** allows you to search, select, view, and otherwise manipulate these documents no matter where they are located. Search and select functions are usually completed through the use of key words.

Document management systems also organize compound documents, or those containing not only text, but also images, full-motion video, and sounds. Full-featured document management systems typically provide the means to perform all the following services: scanning, indexing, storing, converting, distributing, searching, viewing, and printing. Indexing may include providing key words to documents, images, sounds, and video. The conversion processes usually include scanning documents so that they are usable by a word processor. The conversion process may also include converting one form of graphics image format to another. For example, the systems may convert the image of a document received in fax format to the graphics format that can be imported by your desktop publisher. Because graphics files take up large amounts of disk space, document management systems also may provide compression utilities to reduce your storage space requirements.

When documents are created, users complete document profiles that include the names of the authors, the subject matter of the documents, and other data about the documents. The software maintains an index of key information about each document. The system searches documents using the index or by conducting brute searches for text strings. For example, a manager may retrieve numerous documents about one customer located in many files, including account information, reports, and correspondence. Some document management software, such as PageKeeper from Caere Corporation, searches each document and automatically creates indexes of words, screening out words that are considered "noise" as far as indexing is concerned. You can edit the list of noise words that you want PageKeeper to ignore in documents to improve the indexing capabilities of the system. The software search programs even produce a count of the important or key words in each document, displaying the count in a bar chart. You also can instruct the software to use one document as a model to find other documents with similar key words and frequencies of use.

Document management software can accept documents from a variety of sources, such as a scanner or a fax, and documents stored in a variety of text and graphics formats. It also may be able to accept documents directly from an e-mail system and let you annotate text and images. A key to user access for a document management system is the use of portable documents or SGML, described earlier in this chapter. SGML, especially, allows any user to share, view, and edit documents regardless of the hardware platform or software used to create the document.

UNIVERSAL DATABASE SYSTEMS

Recently, relational database management system vendors have been enhancing their products to incorporate many data types. These enhanced products are called universal database management systems. A **universal database management system** is a database system that handles all types of data—traditional transaction data as well as images, sound, video, hypermedia documents, and standard text. The universal database system is also typically marketed to fit multiple computer platforms. The resulting product can provide managers with a very versatile tool. For example, a real-estate agent trying to sell a lot in a new housing development to a prospect might click on the location of the home site and be able to show the customer a brief video clip of the development, a simulated walk-through of the home to be built, floor plans of the home, a detailed map of the area in which the development is located, a document describing the features of the home or development, and documents describing the financial status of the developer. That same system can also handle the sales transaction if the customer decides to buy the property.

Another application of the technology might be in banking. For example, a bank teller, asked to cash a large check, could view not only the customer's account but also the customer's photo and signature file.[3]

MANAGEMENT SUMMARY

To make decisions and plan for the future, managers need information. Much of the information they need is in the records their organizations keep. In the past these records have been kept in paper and computer files. More recently, organizations have used database management systems to increase the accuracy, timeliness, and quality of information available to their executives.

---

[3]M. Halper, "Universal Databases Are Still on the Bleeding Edge," *Datamation,* April 15, 1996 (on-line edition).

A database is a collection of related files. A file is a collection of one type of record. A record is a logical collection of related data elements. Data elements are attributes that describe an entity for which the business needs to keep records. Data may be stored by computers using file systems or database management systems. File systems are usually organized so that they can be accessed sequentially, directly, or through an indexed sequential access method. Database management systems are usually organized into a hierarchy, a network, relations or tables, or objects. File systems allow users to create records, manipulate data, search files, and create reports easily and rapidly without the aid of information systems personnel. However, file systems do not usually permit you to search data contained in files other than the file for which the software was specifically developed. Another problem is that the primary users of the file system may not allow others in the company to use the data. In addition, files usually contain data found in other files, which leads to data consistency problems among the files of the organization.

Database management systems provide a means of storing organization data, formerly stored in numerous individual files, in one system. This system reduces data redundancy and the threat to data consistency, and permits managers to search larger and more diverse amounts of data. Database management systems, however, may cause political problems within organizations, may require additional computing resources, and must be carefully managed to ensure data consistency and security. Like file systems, database management systems usually provide executives with a relatively easy-to-use query language to search for data, a report writer for reports, and support for downloading information from the database to their microcomputers.

Managers may also wish to access data located outside their organizations, especially managers making planning decisions. On-line information services provide subscribers with many services, including access to various on-line databases. On-line databases include diverse data, such as financial, market, census, newspaper, magazine, legal, and medical data, and data for a particular industry.

A great deal of an organization's data is contained in the images and documents it has stored throughout the organization. Organizing, managing, and making these images available to personnel in the entire organization provides enormous amounts of additional data to these personnel.

Recently, organizations are using Internet technology to store documents, images, records, sounds, and even video clips in hypertext form so that they can be viewed by browser software. When access to the documents is limited to the organization and its personnel, these networks are called intranets.

Universal database management systems promise to handle all types of data for organizations, including traditional transaction data and information in the form of sound, images, video, hypermedia, and standard text.

Files and database systems store information that many people want to access, whether they are in the next room, floor, building, state, or even the next country. You will learn how computer systems allow people to communicate with remote files, databases, and other users in the next chapter.

Key Terms for Managers

archiving programs, 222

concurrency control, 235

data consistency, 219

data element, 212

data independence, 219

data redundancy, 219

data warehousing, 239

database, 218

database administrator (DBA), 225

database management system (DBMS), 220

database models, 228

direct access, 215

document database, 242

document management software, 242

field, 212

file, 213

hierarchical database, 228

hypermedia databases, 236

hypertext markup language (HTML), 237

image database, 242

index, 215

indexed sequential access method (ISAM), 215

Internet, 236

intranet, 236

inverted files, 217

linked lists, 217

network database, 228

object-oriented databases (OODB), 232

on-line analytical processing (OLAP), 241

on-line databases, 238

on-line information services, 237

primary key, 214

query by example (QBE), 223

query language, 222

record, 212

relational database, 230

report writer, 222

sequential access, 214

Structured Query Language (SQL), 223

universal database management system, 243

REVIEW QUESTIONS

1. What are the building blocks of a computer-based electronic file system? database system?

2. Explain the three types of file structures and describe one application appropriate for each type.

3. What is an inverted file? What is one advantage of using an inverted file?

4. What is a linked list?

5. List and describe the three traditional database structures or models.

6. List five typical reasons that you might wish to access records in a file.

7. What is the role of the database administrator?

8. List and briefly describe the components that might be included in a database management software package.

9. List and briefly describe the disadvantages to an organization that employs a database management system.

10. What is the difference between interactive processing and batch processing?

11. What is meant by concurrency protection? Describe three levels of concurrency protection that might be provided in a database.

12. What is the difference between data and metadata?

13. Explain what is meant by data independence in a database management system.

14. What is the difference between a primary key and a secondary key?

15. Why are employee number and stock number often chosen for primary keys to employee and stock records rather than employee name or stock description?

16. Why is it important to archive files and databases?

17. How might choosing a multi-platform database management system help the manager?

18. What are the advantages of using Web server software that is integrated with database management system software?

19. Describe the possible services offered to a subscriber by an on-line service, such as America Online or CompuServe.

20. Describe the types of information commonly available to subscribers of on-line databases.

21. Explain how an on-line database might help a manager improve the quality of management planning. Provide one example of a decision in which the data from an on-line database might provide support for management planning.

22. What are the basic components of a data warehouse? Explain how a data warehouse can benefit a manager.

23. What is an image database? Can images be stored in records of a database management system? How might an image database provide an advantage to an organization?

24. How does a document database differ from a traditional database?

25. List the generations in the evolution of database structures.

26. What is a report writer? How might report writers shorten the time it takes for a manager to receive a report?

27. What is a query language? What do query languages provide for managers? What are the downsides to query languages for the manager?

28. What is the difference between SQL and QBE?

29. What two items does each object in an object-oriented database contain?

30. Which of the three database models permits you to link data elements together to create a report even though these linkages have not been specified previously?

31. What is an intranet? What types of data can an intranet make available?

32. What is a browser? Why is browser software important to a company?

33. Describe a hypermedia database. How does a hypermedia database differ from traditional databases?

34. What is on-line analytical processing?

QUESTIONS FOR DISCUSSION

1. Which of the three database models is best suited for ad hoc queries and reports and which is best suited for large, batch operations? Explain your choices.

2. What are the differences between a file system and a database management system?

3. What problems have been associated with file systems in the past?

4. Select three components of a database management system that you consider important to the decision-making capabilities of a manager. Explain why you think these components are more important than others.

5. What are the advantages to an organization of using a database management system rather than separate file systems?

6. What is meant by the ownership of data? How does the ownership of data change when an organization changes from a file system to a database management system?

7. What are the dangers of having many separate file systems that contain common data?

8. What may be the consequences to managers who do not archive their records regularly?

9. How might an on-line database help a manager to improve the quality of decision making? Provide one example of a decision in which the data from an on-line database might provide decision support.

10. Why might a loan manager at a bank want loan accounts for customers stored in an indexed sequential or direct access fashion rather than only sequentially?

11. What is SQL? What is the advantage to the manager of learning SQL as opposed to other query languages?

12. What is an object-oriented database? How does it differ from the traditional database models?

PROBLEMS

1. **Aztec Promotions, Inc.** You run a video store and wish to develop screen reports that would help your salesclerks help customers choose videotapes for viewing. You have noticed that people tend to ask for tapes based on several features. Some ask for the latest tapes received by the store. Others ask for tapes based on the actors that star in them. Still others ask for tapes by type, for example, westerns, horror, science fiction, drama, and comedy. Many ask for tapes based on combinations of these features. For example, a customer may ask if the store has a western starring John Wayne or a recent comedy starring Dan Aykroyd.

   a. Outline four reports as they might look on a computer screen to allow your salesclerks to respond to each of the typical requests your customers make. The screen report should contain the report title, the column headings, and possible data.

   b. Create a record that could be used to provide the reports you outline in part a. The record should contain all the data elements that are needed to complete the reports you outlined. Name each data element and indicate a recommended field length and data type (alphabetic, numeric, date). Finally, identify or create a primary field that will be used to distinguish one record from another.

c. (Optional) If you have a PC database management system available, create the record you developed in part *b*, populate 20 records with fictitious values, and print out the reports you developed in part *a*.

2. **Velor Sporting Goods, Inc.** You are the sales manager for Velor Sporting Goods, Inc., a sporting goods wholesaler. You wish to use a database management software package to maintain vendor and customer records. The records do not contain financial data, but rather the names, addresses, past buying preferences, past product portfolios, and other important data about vendors and clients. Your current manual files include these records:

a. 350 vendor records, each of which may contain a maximum of 225 characters of information.

b. 735 customer records, each of which may contain a maximum of 430 characters of information.

Further, suppose you estimate that the data about the data in your database (the metadata) will take 20 percent of the space occupied by the records themselves and that you are not using any compression storage methods.

c. What is the minimum storage capacity, stated in kilobytes, that the database management software package you buy must be able to handle to meet the maximum of your current record needs?

d. If you estimate that your files will increase by 5 percent each year, what will be the estimated maximum capacity in kilobytes of your database system in five years?

3. **Talbot Company (A).** The Talbot Company uses a file of manually prepared stock record cards to manage its inventory. Each record contains the following data elements: the name of the stock, a description of the stock, the stock number, the unit of

purchase (e.g., dozen, gross, crate), the minimum amount required that should be on hand, the maximum amount to have on hand, the warehouse section number, and the aisle location number. The firm now wishes to computerize these records to improve the management of its inventory.

a. Which data element(s) should be used as the primary key for the record? Why?

b. Which data elements might be used as secondary keys for the record? Why?

c. Which of the three file structures discussed in this chapter would you recommend for these records? Why?

d. Do you recommend that in-house programmers develop the inventory system or that a commercial software package be selected? Why?

4. **Talbot Company (B).** After the inventory system was developed and implemented, the Talbot Company considered computerizing two of its other files: the stock vendor file and the stock quotation file. The records in the vendor file contain the following data elements: vendor number, vendor name, vendor address, and vendor product using Talbot stock name and number. The stock quotation file contains these data elements: stock number; stock name; stock description; vendor name; vendor number; vendor address; and the date, quantity, and price of each quotation obtained from the vendor.

a. If the inventory, vendor, and stock quotation files are developed into separate computerized files instead of using database management software, what problems are likely to occur?

b. What do you recommend that the firm do before developing two more computerized files?

5. **Talbot Company (C).** Using a microcomputer database management system, develop a simple database containing the stock record and stock vendor record described in problems 3 and 4. Then create 10 actual records for each record type using fictitious data. Once the 20 records are completed, prepare the following:

a. A report listing stock numerically by stock number.

b.   A report listing each vendor alphabetically by name.

c.   A report listing each vendor with the number and name of each stock item purchased from the vendor.

6. **Software evaluation project (A).**   Prepare a report about a database management system software package for a microcomputer. The report should contain (a) the cost of the package, (b) the features of the package, and (c) some evaluation of the ease with which a manager might learn to use the query features of the package. Refer to the "General Features of Software" in Chapter 6 for additional help in preparing your report. Use Internet search tools to locate articles, reviews, and vendor descriptions of the product. If possible, download a demonstration package for the database management software and use it to learn about its features.

7. **Software evaluation project (B).**   Prepare a report on one microcomputer image management software package. The report should contain (a) the costs of the package, (b) the features of the package, and (c) some evaluation of the ease with which the retrieval features of the package can be learned. Refer to the "General Features of Software" in Chapter 6 for additional help in preparing your report. Use Internet search engines to find articles and reviews of the package. If possible, download a demonstration package for the image management software and use it to learn about its features.

8. **On-line database project.**   Identify and describe five business-related on-line databases. Prepare a report describing the contents of the databases, along with details of the companies that provide them, the cost, and the method of access. You may wish to use Internet search engines to locate the company home pages and obtain the information needed for this project.

CASES

1. **Urban Advantages, Inc.**   After a successful career as an advertising executive in a large corporation, Jill Roncine left that world to start her own consulting firm. The firm, Urban Advantages, Inc., advises communities and states on attracting and holding new businesses. At the start, Roncine ran her firm from her home. She purchased a microcomputer, a presentation graphics package, a desktop publishing package, and Busio, a financial database software package. Her husband Fred, who helped her as a part-time bookkeeper, used Busio to record the firm's transactions into a financial database and prepare its financial statements.

Over the next two years, the firm grew rapidly. Roncine hired five professionals in marketing, management, public planning, and other specialties to help her serve her clients. She also hired a full-time bookkeeper and two full-time secretaries. The firm's workload has grown so much, however, that she is now considering adding two more office workers: a part-time bookkeeper/secretary and a general office clerk. Because of the increased staff, she is considering buying more personal computers and connecting them to allow both bookkeepers, the general office clerk, and her husband to enter transactions into the financial database using the Busio software at the same time. She plans to place the new personal computers in the open office area that separates her office and those of the professional staff from the client waiting and meeting room area.

Because she knows little about personal computers and financial software, she has asked Lammert and Associates, a computer consulting firm, for advice. If you were the consultant, what problems would you suggest she is likely to encounter with her plan?

2. **Roget College Affirmative Action Office.**   Ms. Martha Radcliff is the director of Roget College's Affirmative Action Office. Radcliff's office is responsible for identifying the organization's affirmative action goals, assisting the organization in carrying out the

goals, and reporting on the goals to various organization units and state and federal agencies. The reporting requirements have increased considerably in the last few years. Numerous federal and state agencies and college units require information about minority status, affirmative action goals, compliance with state and federal regulations, and similar matters for the college's clerical, professional, and teaching personnel. Each agency seems to want similar information in different formats at different times during the year. Providing these agencies with the information required has become a clerical headache.

Currently, the college maintains information about employees in payroll files and some personnel files on its mainframe. The management information systems department developed these files at the request of payroll and the personnel departments using a mainframe database management system. Radcliff and her employees use the mainframe system for a variety of applications. However, although the current mainframe database management files contain some of the data Radcliff needs for the affirmative action reports, they do not contain all the necessary data. Radcliff and her employees have been using the mainframe system to obtain what data they could, but these data were insufficient to prepare the reports needed. So Radcliff approached the management information systems department about the problem last year and was told that they were completely overwhelmed by the development of a student information system, which was already behind schedule. The administration was breathing down their necks over the student information system, and they simply would not be able to devote any resources to Radcliff's project—although they would like to very much. The MIS department suggested to Martha that she hire a consultant to develop the information system she needed.

As a result, Radcliff contacted an information systems consultant, Robert Ahmed. Ahmed suggested that he could develop a system for her quickly and inexpensively, although it would involve re-creating some of the files that already exist on the mainframe. He proposed purchasing a microcomputer with hard disk drive and Microsoft Access, a microcomputer database management software package. He felt that he could develop a database of personnel files that would provide her with all the reports that she needed with this package. He estimated that the costs would include $2,900 for the microcomputer, $1,000 for a laser printer, $500 for all the software, and $3,000 for development of the applications she required. He estimated that it would take him about one month to complete the programming for the project.

Radcliff has the $8,000 in her budget to fund Ahmed's plan. Since neither Radcliff nor any member of her staff has had any experience with microcomputers, she has asked you to evaluate Ahmed's plan. Prepare a report identifying the concerns you have with Ahmed's plan and how those concerns might be reduced or eliminated.

3. **Pelegrin Industries.** Pelegrin Industries has been in business for more than 70 years. The company manufactures sports equipment, and its specialty is hunting and fishing equipment. The firm has its headquarters and manufacturing plants in Dayton, Ohio. It ships directly to sporting goods wholesalers and a number of large retailers located throughout North America. Pelegrin has grown rapidly during the last few years as a result of close attention to quality products and customer satisfaction. As the company has grown, it has become increasingly difficult for the production department to assess the market success of its increasingly larger product line. As a result, production has not always matched demand, resulting in crisis production runs or large overruns of unpopular products. A major contributor to this situation is that sales data are buried in paper invoices that are not analyzed easily. To support its information needs, the company has a large number of paper file systems for its financial, personnel, marketing, and production records. Recently, the slowness of processing

paper files has become painful to the company. Some customers have canceled orders because they were taking too long to fill. In addition, the managers have been finding it difficult to make decisions or develop long-range plans simply because the paper files do not permit the timely construction of reports useful for decisions.

At a recent executive meeting, the problems with the paper recording system were discussed. Alice Noel, the production officer, felt that developing a computerized file system for the company's various paper records was long overdue. She stated that computerizing the files would speed up order processing and shipping and allow for many timely reports. She felt that a great deal of commercial file system software was available from which the company could choose and that it would be relatively easy to identify the best file system software for each application that the firm had. She also stated that the company was not so unique that it had to develop its own programs in-house. She felt that it should hire some consultants, buy the different programs, and get the computerized files implemented as soon as possible.

Clyde Morehouse, the personnel officer, felt that it was silly to go to the expense of purchasing commercial software and hiring "a bunch of consultants." He felt that the firm should hire its own programmers on a full-time basis to develop the software in-house. That way, the company would also have the programmers available to develop additional programs in the future. Furthermore, in-house programmers could develop software specifically designed for the firm. He felt it was high time that Pelegrin had its own management information systems department.

John Akers, the financial officer, suggested that there was really nothing seriously wrong with Pelegrin information systems that a few more people wouldn't cure. He recommended that additional order-entry and shipping clerks be hired to move the products out the door faster. He argued that computerizing the files would take a lot of money and a lot of time, and during the developmental stages of the project, the company would still require additional help to meet its immediate needs for speedier order processing.

You are the new assistant to the chief executive for the firm, and you have just completed a number of seminars on the use of computers to support managerial decision making. Your boss, Claire Williams, has asked you to prepare a report on the filing systems at Pelegrin for the next meeting. She would like to know what you think about each of the other officer's views and what you would recommend that they do to solve their paper problems.

Prepare a memo to Claire Williams (a) analyzing each of the other officers' ideas and (b) detailing the approach you would recommend to solve the problem. Make certain that you justify each of your recommendations.

4. **Babcock Valve Corporation.** Janice Kalimeyer is the personnel manager of the Babcock Valve Corporation. She has spent a number of years developing a series of files to help her manage the personnel function within Babcock. Among the files developed are an employee skills inventory file, a personnel history file, and an employee placement file. Last year, however, the corporation hired Betty Fuller as the database administrator. Janice wants the management information systems department to develop a new file to help her manage her recruiting activities and to maintain data for reports to various federal agencies. When Janice requested the help from the department, however, Jason Culver, the MIS director, told her that she would have to clear her plans for the file with Betty Fuller. Janice was at first surprised, then outraged. She said to the director, "What right has Fuller to tell me what my files should look like? I've been working on these information systems for years. Who is she to tell me what to do with my files?" Culver said that it was the new policy for the database administrator to clear all file structures and that he had no choice. When she returned to her office, Janice had cooled down only slightly but made an appointment with Betty Fuller for the afternoon to talk about the new file she

wanted. When Kalimeyer arrived at Fuller's office, the personnel manager described the history of the development of her files and the need she had for the new file. She next told Fuller that she felt that she could handle the new file herself, with the help of the MIS department. She asked Fuller why the new database administrator had to have anything to do with the personnel files, and why she couldn't just proceed as usual.

a. What reasons justify Betty Fuller's involvement in Janice Kalimeyer's new files?

b. If you were Betty Fuller, how would you approach Janice Kalimeyer?

SELECTED INTERNET REFERENCE SITES

DB2 Database, IBM Corporation (http://www.software. ibm.com/data/info/uni-server/db2unidb.html).

Halper, M. "Universal Databases Are Still on the Bleeding Edge." *Datamation,* April 15, 1996 (on-line version: http://www.datamation.com/PlugIn/issues/1996/april15/04bsoft1frame.html).

Informix Software, Inc. (http://www.informix.com).

Oracle Corporation (http://www.oracle.com).

Oracle Magazine Interactive (http://www.oramag.com/).

Radding, A. "Support Decision Makers with a Data Warehouse." *Datamation,* March 15, 1996 (on-line version: http://www.datamation.com/PlugIn/workbench/ dw-house/stories/03bsw100.htm).

Sybase, Inc. (http://www.sybase.com).

Sybase Archive, Administrative Computing Resources, North Carolina State University (http://www.acs. ncsu.edu/Sybase/Archive.html).

Sybase Information Server, Pacific Northwest National Laboratory (http://sybase.pnl.gov:2080/Sybase/).

SELECTED REFERENCES AND READINGS

Cole, B. "Document Management on a Budget." *Network World,* September 16, 1996, p. 59.

Dorshkind, B. "Microsoft Scales up Data Warehouse." *LAN Times,* November 25, 1996, p. 14.

Eckerson, W. W. "Drilling for Data." *Computerworld,* December 2, 1996, p. 95.

Hayes, G. M. "4 OLAP Tools." *Computerworld,* December 2, 1996, p. 101.

Hoffer, J. A. and F. R. McFadden. *Modern Database Management.* 4th ed. Redwood City, CA: Benjamin/Cummings, 1994.

Huttig, J. W. "The ABCs and SQLs of Client/Servers." *PC Today,* April 1995, p. 18.

King, P. "The More Views, the Merrier." *Client/Server Computing,* May 1994, p. 49.

Mattison, R. *Data Warehousing: Strategies, Technologies, and Techniques.* New York: McGraw-Hill, 1996.

Moser, K. "Natural Language Tool to Support Windows." *PC Week* 9, no. 3 (January 20, 1992), pp. 45 and 48.

Oakes, B. "Database Platforms: Examining the Options." *Netware Connection,* November/December 1994, p. 52.

Remington, M. "Mining the Database." *PC Today,* July 1995, p. 64.

Salemi, J. "Kinder, Gentler Databases." *PC Magazine,* May 28, 1996, p. 117.

Schussel, G. "Database Replication: Watch the Data Fly." *Client/Server Today,* October 1994, p. 80.

Smith, L. "Developers Eye Object Databases." *Development Tools,* a special supplement to *PC Week,* February 15, 1993, p. S8.

Steeves, R. "Smoothing the Flow of the Paper Stream." *PC Today,* April 1995, p. 11.

Tweney, D. "Online Services." *PC World,* August 1996, p. 153.

Varhol, P. D. "Three Routes to OLAP." *Datamation,* August 15, 1995, p. 57.

Watterson, K. "Plug and Play Data Marts." *Client/Server Computing,* March 1997, p. 48.

COMMUNICATIONS SYSTEMS BASICS

CHAPTER OUTLINE

Manager's View

Communications Systems Elements

Communications Modes and Codes

Communications Media

Sources and Products

Common Network Components

Network Topologies

Network Types

Remote Access

Reasons Managers Implement Networks

Network Concerns for the Manager

Voice Systems

Communications Standards and the Manager

Management Summary

Key Terms for Managers

Review Questions

Questions for Discussion

Problems

Cases

Selected Internet Reference Sites

Selected References and Readings

IN RECENT YEARS, the world of communications has undergone enormous changes. In fact, the term *paradigm shift* has become hackneyed in the information systems field. However, it is definitely an appropriate descriptor of the communications industry. The primary focus of computer technology in the past was to provide processing power for increasingly hungry but traditional applications, such as word processing, spreadsheet, and database applications. While computing power for application processing is still important, today's computer buyers are paying at least as much if not more attention to the computer's ability to connect to networks. In fact, some computer systems (for example, network PCs and Web TVs) have been developed *primarily* to connect to networks. These computers rely on other computer systems connected to a network to do most of the processing. This change in emphasis is affecting how computer systems impact individuals, organizations, and society by placing more information, even more computing power, at everyone's fingertips.

The laws governing communications also have been changing rapidly, opening up opportunities for competition between industry giants who had enjoyed monopolies in their areas or were at least restricted from entering other communications areas. The most recent change is the Telecommunications Act of 1996. The basic purpose of this act is to permit any business to compete in any communications market. The law blurs traditional demarcations in industry "turf." For example, cable TV companies used to be confined to offering TV entertainment. These same companies are now considering offering voice communications over their cable system and have already begun to enter the arena of data communications by providing Internet access to their subscribers. At the same time, more and more video and voice conversations are being transmitted over the Internet, and telephone companies have been given the right to provide cable service to their customers. Entertainment firms have begun to purchase or make alliances with telephone, cable, and satellite broadcasting companies. Major TV networks have created alliances with major software firms, and local telephone companies have entered the long-distance telephone market. Some PBS stations have begun to embed data in their TV broadcasts, allowing PCs with a special card installed to receive the data. Even power companies are considering entering the communications business because of the important rights of way to our homes and businesses that they already possess.

The tumult in the communications industry has created a situation in which the transmission of voice, data, text, sound, and images pervades computer information systems regardless of the size of a manager's computer resources. Consider the diversity of organizational tasks that now depend on some form of communications system.

- A company wishes to speed up its order-entry system by developing a network of order-entry terminals at its branch sales offices in several major cities. Each sales office is to have terminals that permit salespeople to be on-line directly with the computer at the home office. Salespeople will be able to enter an order at a remote terminal, immediately determine the customer's credit status and the availability of the stock the customer wants, and provide both a hard copy invoice to the customer at the remote site and a hard copy shipping order to the shipping department at the warehouse within seconds.

- A company wishes to equip its on-the-road salespeople with laptop microcomputers to implement an order-entry system such as the one previously described. However, the salespeople will complete orders via the laptops from their hotel rooms, from their cars, or from the customer's premises, using whatever phone is available at any of these locations.

- A company wishes to have data about production on an assembly line input directly from the assembly line. It wants to place terminals on the factory floor at key locations so that workers can enter data about the raw materials they use, the products they are working on, and the products they have finished making. Management hopes to use the system to better control inventory and materials costs.

- A department in a large corporation wishes to develop an in-house publication capacity so several secretaries can use inexpensive desktop publishing software to create documents on networked microcomputers. Also on the network is a special laser printer that they will use to produce hard copy containing text, charts, and drawings.

- A number of executives want to access the organization database using the microcomputers they have in their offices and homes. Sometimes they want to view information in the database. At other times they want to transfer information from the database to programs they are running on their microcomputers. They hope that the increased quantity and quality of data available to them will improve their decision making.

- Some employees want to work at home on projects and send electronic reports to their offices for hard copy printout and distribution. This plan will allow parents with sick children, workers with long commutes to the office, and others who may have to stay home for a time to continue working. Working at home but staying in touch with the office using communications systems is called *telecommuting*.

- Some managers want to use the information from on-line databases for planning. Sometimes they only want to view the information. At other times they want to download the information to the programs they are running on their microcomputers. They hope to use the on-line databases to bring increased knowledge of the competition, the market, and the customer to their decision making.

- The field representatives of one company are concerned because they spend too much time dialing and redialing the home office to leave routine phone messages. At the same time, home office personnel are frustrated because they have difficulty getting messages to the field reps. The company wants to install a voice mail system so voice messages can be delivered where and when they are needed.

- An express package delivery firm wants to get immediate data on the location of every delivery truck in its fleet. Managers place microwave transmitters/receivers on each vehicle and give each driver a handheld computer with a wand that can scan the bar codes on packages. They use the system to track every shipment. Later, they provide major customers with on-line access to their tracking data so customers can track their own shipments.

These few examples (more are presented in Chapter 9) demonstrate that communications systems are likely to have an impact on every possible information system the manager uses. The ability to create, send, and receive voice, data, text, sound, video, and images electronically has become as important today as the ability to create, send, and receive paper documents was in the recent past. Information is the lifeblood of the effective manager. Accurate, timely, and appropriate information is necessary for managers to make effective decisions. Communications equipment and software play an important part in delivering the information managers need when they need it. Managers must understand the basics of communications so they can use communications resources for their operations and their planning needs.

The goal of this chapter is to provide you with a basic understanding of communications systems. Additional information pertaining to electronic communications is presented in Chapter 9, which covers distributed systems, client/server systems, interorganizational information systems, the Internet, intranets, facsimile, electronic mail, voice mail, electronic conferencing systems, and computer-supported telephony.

COMMUNICATIONS SYSTEMS ELEMENTS

Communications systems are often defined as systems for creating, delivering, and receiving electronic messages. To accomplish these tasks, every communications system comprises at least three elements, as shown in Figure 8–1: (1) a device to send the message, (2) a **channel,** or communications medium, over which the message is sent, and (3) a device to receive the message.

Communications systems are also referred to as **telecommunications systems,** or networks. Very simply, a **communications network** is a group of devices connected to one or more communications channels. The devices could send signals, receive signals, or do both—such as telephones, terminals, printers, mainframe computers, or microcomputers. The devices also could encode, decode, relay, or otherwise manipulate signals so that they may be transmitted and received.

Figure 8–1

Basic elements in a communications system

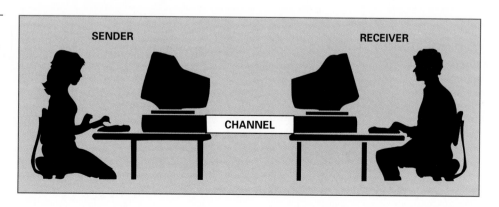

COMMUNICATIONS MODES AND CODES

You may select from a number of transmission modes and data codes for transmitting signals from a sending device to a receiving device. In fact, many networks use a variety of transmission modes and data codes for signaling.

Analog and Digital Transmission

The majority of computers communicate with digital signals. Digital signals are discrete "on" and "off" pulses of electricity that most computer systems use to create the bits that make up bytes, or characters (see Chapter 5). For example, a computer may create an on bit by placing a short positive signal of 5 volts on a channel. Conversely, it may create an off bit by placing a short negative signal of 5 volts on the channel (see Figure 8–2a). Sending data with digital signals is called **digital transmission.**

Sound, including the human voice, travels over analog signals. Analog signals are continuous sine waves. In a communications system, an analog signal may send a continuous 5-volt signal on a channel, but the signal will vary continuously from +5 volts to −5 volts (see Figure 8–2b). Compare, for example, the effect of using the loudness dial on your radio versus the on/off button. If you continuously move the loudness dial from maximum to minimum loudness, you would be simulating the action of an analog signal. If you turn the radio on and off, however, you would receive discrete bursts of radio sound waves and be simulating the action of a digital signal.

Many voice telephone lines still use **analog transmission** because the telephone system was originally designed to carry the human voice. Radio signals also are analog transmissions. Many data channels use digital signaling because computers use digital signals. However, today's technology allows both voice and data to be transmitted by either analog or digital signaling, although many new telephone lines are digital.

Digital transmission offers advantages over analog transmission because it is usually easier to reduce and clean up noise and errors in digital transmission, especially when messages must be sent over long distances. Another advantage is that digital transmission is compatible with digital computer systems. Thus it is not necessary to convert data messages to and from analog to digital form when computer systems use digital transmission channels.

Data Codes

You know that computers use codes to represent data, which can be alphabetic, numeric, or special characters. Two frequently used data codes for communications systems are ASCII and EBCDIC (see Chapter 5). In fact, many communications networks have devices that use both codes.

Figure 8–2

(a) Digital signal and (b) analog signal

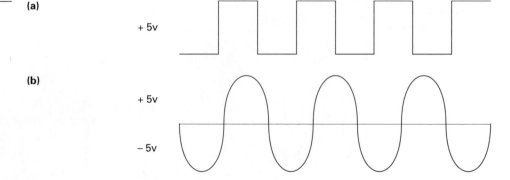

(a)

+ 5v

(b)

+ 5v

− 5v

Asynchronous Transmission

Still another choice is whether your messages will be sent as a series of single characters or as a block of characters. In *asynchronous transmission* each character is sent down a channel separately; that is, each transmission unit is only one character in length. The character is headed with a start bit and ends with one or more stop bits. The start and stop bits tell the receiving device that a character is coming and that the character has been sent.

The character usually contains a *parity bit,* which the receiving device uses to verify that the transmission was received correctly. In a system using even parity, the number of 1 bits in all characters sent must equal an even amount. So the sending device will place a 1 bit in the parity slot whenever it sends a character whose 1 bits don't add up to an even number. The receiving device checks each character it receives by summing the 1 bits. If the character arrives with an even number of 1 bits, the device assumes that it has received a correct character. If the number of 1 bits is odd, the device assumes that a transmission error has occurred. Some systems verify transmissions using an odd-parity procedure.

Many terminals send messages asynchronously in ASCII code (see Figure 8–3a); that is, they send messages by transmitting a series of separate, single characters composed of these elements:

1. A start bit.
2. Seven bits that represent an ASCII-coded character.
3. A parity bit.
4. A stop bit.

In this method to send one character, the terminal actually must send a total of 10 bits. Thus the overhead to send a character is 30 percent of the total bits sent or 3 bits out of 10. For the manager, this overhead means that 30 percent of the transmission costs paid to the common carrier are for nonmessage bits. That's a pretty hefty percentage of your costs for sending nothing but start, stop, and parity bits. If the terminal uses EBCDIC code—an 8-bit code—11 bits are sent for each character: 8 character bits plus 1 start bit plus 1 stop bit plus 1 parity bit.

Synchronous Transmission

To reduce the overhead costs of data transmission, some networks send messages using synchronous transmission. *Synchronous transmission* blocks many characters together for transmission (see Figure 8–3b). Several bits precede the message block so the receiving device knows what is coming and can prepare for the message. Several bits also follow the block so the receiving device can verify what it received. However,

---

Figure 8–3

(a) A character in asynchronous format and (b) a synchronous message

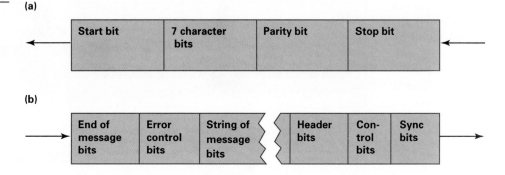

the beginning and ending bits are a small percentage of the total number of message bits sent. Synchronous transmission reduces the overhead costs of communications. It should be noted, however, that the cost of synchronous equipment is usually higher than the cost of asynchronous equipment. The manager must be sure that the higher investment in the synchronous equipment will be justified by the reduced overhead costs of using synchronous transmission.

Simplex, Half-Duplex, and Full-Duplex Transmission

Some networks have communications channels that send messages only one way, which is called *simplex transmission* (see Figure 8–4a). Commercial radio networks are simplex networks. You can listen to your favorite station, but you cannot communicate back to the station on the same radio frequency. Simplex channels are often used to connect fire and smoke alarm devices in offices and factories to nearby fire stations. Simplex transmission is also used for airport monitors.

Many networks use transmission channels that permit messages to be sent both ways, but only one way at a time—like a CB radio. This process is known as *half-duplex transmission* (see Figure 8–4b). Other networks use transmission channels that permit simultaneous transmission of messages in both directions, or *full-duplex transmission* (see Figure 8–4c). The public voice telephone network uses many full-duplex channels. Many companies have networks that include all three types of channels.

Circuit Switching

Many voice telephone networks link a sender and receiver over a channel that is dedicated to their communications for the length of their session. It does not matter if the sender and receiver remain silent for long periods of time; the channel is still theirs until they hang up. That type of channel mode is called *circuit switching*. A circuit-switching network may use a different route to make the connection between sender and receiver each time they call each other. However, once the connection is made, the parties may use the channel as long as they wish. Both dial-up lines and leased lines offer circuit switching.

Message Switching

Message-switching networks differ from circuit-switching networks in that the connection from sender and receiver is not kept open unless there are messages to send. The networks also differ in that in circuit switching, if a route from the sender to the

Figure 8–4

(a) Simplex, or one-way transmission, (b) half-duplex, or transmission in two directions but not at the same time, and (c) full-duplex transmission, or transmission in both directions at the same time

receiver is not available, the sender gets a busy signal. In message switching each message from the sender may be sent immediately to the receiver if a route to the receiver is available. If a route is not available, the message will be *stored and forwarded* later when a route does become available or when the receiver demands its stored messages.

Packet-switching networks offer a type of message switching. Packet-switching networks transmit messages in one or more fixed-size packets, or message blocks. Packet-switching networks consist of a series of channels that are connected to *nodes,* or computer-controlled switching centers. A voice, data, text, or image transmission is first broken into packets, and then each packet is sent to its destination via the fastest or shortest route. The packets may travel different routes to the destination. At the destination the packets are put in sequential order and delivered to the receiver (see Figure 8–5). Compared to circuit switching, packet switching provides better use of the network. If the packets are small and if the network has enough alternative routes, the packet-switching system can balance the traffic loads on the channels by routing packets appropriately.

Figure 8–5

Delivery of packets on a packet-switching network

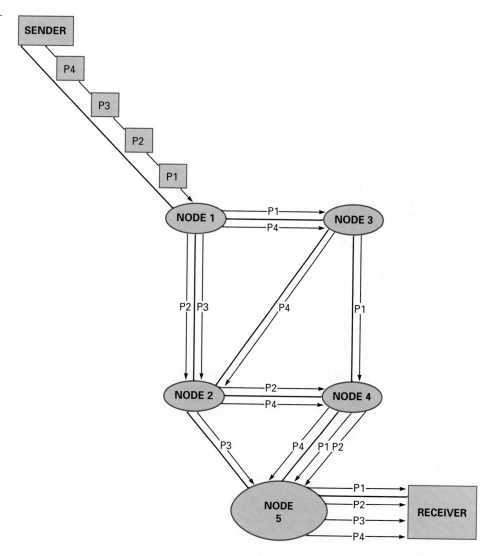

COMMUNICATIONS MEDIA

Communications media represent the types of channels over which messages are transmitted. You may choose from many types of communications media, including, for example, twisted-pair wire, fiber optic cable, coaxial cable, microwaves, and radio waves. Many communications systems, including telephone systems, use several different media. When you call a friend, for example, your voice may travel over twisted-pair wiring, fiber optic cabling, and microwaves to reach its destination.

Speed and Capacity

One of the most important characteristics of communications channels is capacity, which may be expressed in bits per second, or by the speed of the line. A channel that can transmit 56 kilobits per second (56 Kbps) has a larger capacity than one that can transmit only 28 Kbps.

Many networks today are suffering from insufficient capacity for the work that users wish them to perform. Much of this problem is due to two major factors: increased numbers of users who are now connected to networks and the nature of the data sent over the channels. The latter problem has arisen as more and more people transmit images, sounds, and video over a network designed for short, bursty voice conversations.

Twisted Pair

Twisted-pair wiring or cabling is the same type of cabling system used for home and office telephone systems (see Figure 8–6a). It is inexpensive and easy to install. Recent technological improvements have increased the capacity of twisted-pair wires so that they can now handle data communications with speeds up to 100 Mbps over limited distances. Many telephone companies have recently introduced Asymmetric Digital Subscriber Line (ADSL) service that, using telephone wiring, is capable of speeds of 640 Kbps for uploading and more than 6 Mbps for downloading.

Coaxial Cable

Coaxial cable is a well-established and long-used cabling system for computer systems. This cabling comes in a variety of sizes to suit different purposes. Coaxial cable is commonly used to connect computers in a local area, such as an office, floor, building, or campus (see Figure 8–6b) and, of course, to deliver cable TV.

Fiber Optics

Many common carriers are replacing older, copper wire cables in their networks with *fiber optic cables,* which use light as the communications medium. To create the on-and-off bit code needed by computers, the light is rapidly turned on and off on the channel. Fiber optic channels are lightweight, can handle many times the telephone conversations or volumes of data handled by copper wire cabling, and can be installed in environments hostile to copper wire, such as wet areas or areas subject to a great deal of electromagnetic interference. They are also less susceptible than copper wire to spying; that is, conversations or data are more secure in a fiber optic network (see Figure 8–7).

Wireless

Wireless communications media use microwaves, radio waves, and even infrared waves to transmit text, data, images, and sound. They are often referred to as *wireless channels*.

For heavy users, *microwave transmission* channels provide what amounts to bulk-rate service. You can lease long-distance microwave transmission facilities from common carriers or acquire short-haul microwave networks and run them yourself,

Figure 8–6

(a) Twisted-pair wiring and telephone plug and (b) coaxial cable

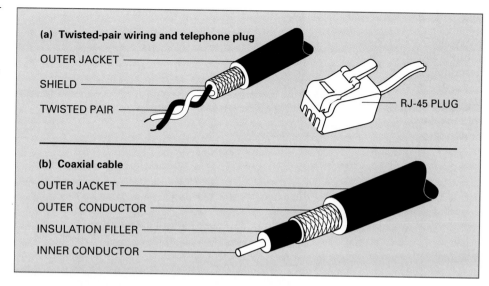

(a) Twisted-pair wiring and telephone plug

OUTER JACKET

SHIELD

TWISTED PAIR

RJ-45 PLUG

(b) Coaxial cable

OUTER JACKET

OUTER CONDUCTOR

INSULATION FILLER

INNER CONDUCTOR

for example, to transmit large amounts of voice and data between buildings on a large campus. Microwave transmission may involve "dishes" located on top of buildings or on towers, or it may involve transmitting data and voice to and from satellites placed in stationary earth orbits (see Figure 8–8).

Recent improvements in technology have shrunk the satellite receiving dish from 3 feet in diameter to a mere 18 inches, making the dish more acceptable in residential subdivisions, less expensive to buy, and easier to install.

Radio channels are increasingly used for short-distance voice and data telephone communications (see the section "Wireless Networks" later in this chapter). Infrared light signals are also used for data transmission, especially for transmissions in a local area such as a room or floor of a building. In fact, radio and infrared signals are used for remote TV control devices, for wireless computer keyboards, and for remote computer mice. Wireless devices allow the user to get rid of the usual desktop tangle of mouse and keyboard wires.

Figure 8–7

Fiber optic cabling

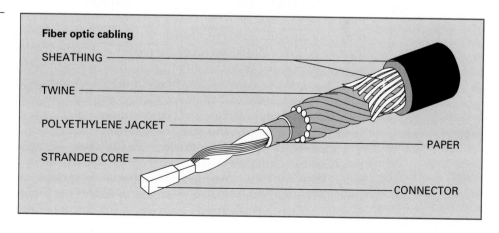

Fiber optic cabling

SHEATHING

TWINE

POLYETHYLENE JACKET

STRANDED CORE

PAPER

CONNECTOR

Figure 8–8

(a) A campus-to-campus satellite-based microwave network and (b) a satellite-based microwave network

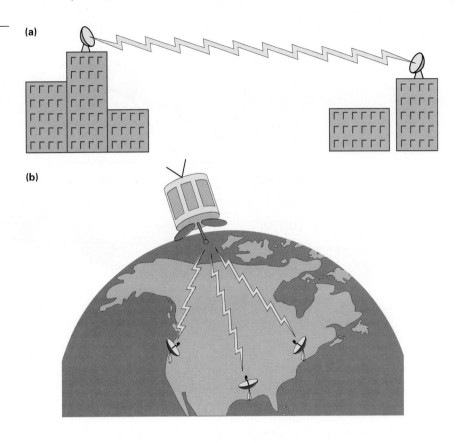

Sources and Products

If your channels will be confined to your own building or campus, you might purchase and install the channels yourself, which will usually save you a considerable amount in leasing fees over the long haul. If your network is larger than your own building or campus, you will have to obtain your communications channels from other sources. For example, you can lease both analog and digital channels from a **common carrier,** which may be the local telephone company or a long-distance carrier such as AT&T, Sprint, or MCI. You may also purchase channels from **value-added networks (VANs),** such as Telenet or Tymnet. Value-added networks may supply their own channels or lease channels from other common carriers and then re-lease them to others. Value-added networks usually add value to those channels by providing special features for their customers, such as packet-switching services, electronic mail, data code conversion, matching the speed of transmissions to the receiving equipment, or the use of their own computers by their customers. Many on-line database and information service companies connect their computer systems to packet-switching, value-added networks.

Other types of common carriers are the cable TV network and the satellite broadcasting companies. These companies in the past have offered live video and radio. However, cable companies have begun to provide Internet access to subscribers, and satellite firms are expected to follow suit. Analysts expect cable and satellite carriers to increase their presence in both voice and data transmissions in the near future, providing competition to the traditional phone company carriers. One advantage of cable systems is that they are always "open," that is, you do not have to dial in to gain access to the system. Also, you do not need to tie up one of your telephone lines when you are connected. The most important advantage of cable systems, however, will be speed (see "Modems" later in this chapter).

Common carriers offer many types of products (see Manager's Memo 8-1). Two of the most common are dial-up lines and leased lines. Another group of products growing in popularity is wireless network service.

| Manager's Memo 8-1 | SOME FAST CARRIER PRODUCTS |

◣ The increased use of networks has put pressure on managers to provide faster ways to connect to networks and to allow users to download files, images, and other data swiftly. Moving data through the common carrier networks is often the bottleneck. For example, a typical speed of a network connecting computers in an office is 10 Mbps. Connecting a network in an office in one city to a network in a branch office in another city using ordinary modems over analog lines will reduce that speed to 56 Kbps—a substantial reduction. Managers who must connect networks to other networks are constantly seeking better and faster "pipes" or channels.

Identifying and acquiring the right products to relieve capacity pressures is not an easy task because managers *always* seem to face a bewildering choice among many existing communications products and standards. Apprehension over their choice is increased because several more promising standards are always "on the horizon." Choosing an existing technology will get the job done quickly but will likely mean the acquisition of a system that may become outmoded very soon. Waiting for emerging technologies will mean sacrificing fast connectivity immediately and investing in unproven systems later.

Common carriers currently offer several products that you can use to connect to networks or to connect one network with another.

T line service. T line service provides users with high-speed digital service capable of carrying voice, data, images, and sound at 1.544 Mbps. The circuits can be combined to provide even higher speed levels. T2 services provide speeds up to 6.3 Mbps by combining 4 T1 lines, T3 provides speeds up to 44.4 Mbps by combining 28 T1 circuits, and T4 provides 274 Mbps by combining 178 T1 circuits.

ISDN. Integrated Services Digital Network (ISDN) allows users to transmit voice, data, sound, and images at rates up to 128 Kbps. Because of differences in analog and digital transmission and the differing characteristics of voice, data, image, video, and other transmissions, many specialized networks and communications devices have evolved over the years. Specialized analog networks are now available for voice and data, specialized digital networks for voice and data, and specialized digital networks for facsimile transmissions (see Chapter 9). Specialized networks for cable television, videotext, teleconferencing (see this chapter), and local area networking are also available. And this is not a complete list of all the specialized networks available. The specialized networks have evolved because the technology to transmit data, text, voice, image, facsimile, and video over a single network did not exist. AT&T and the other major communications organizations in the world have developed ISDN to replace current analog technology with digital technology. With ISDN, voice, data, facsimile, image, and video communications are all encoded digitally and can be transmitted through a single set of standardized interfaces.

Proponents of ISDN hope that the network will cover the world and allow users to transmit simultaneously the various information types through a single network. Because the effort is international and because of its complexity, it will take many years to implement fully. The final goal, however, is to provide a totally digital communications system that will link public and private networks on a worldwide basis so that users can access any system remotely from anywhere on earth. The intention is to have ISDN network computers handle conversion for incompatible computer systems so that users will be able to share data worldwide without regard to computer system or data differences. However, ISDN has been slow to catch on, primarily because telephone carriers have failed to make the capability available in many areas. Recently, however, ISDN services have become more available, and more organizations are using ISDN to connect remote LANs. At the same time, asynchronous

Manager's Memo 8–1	CONTINUED

transmission mode facilities may simply make ISDN obsolete or at best a bit player in the communications marketplace.

SMDS.   Switched multimegabit data service (SMDS) is a standard for data transmission that has been around for over a decade but has been offered on only a limited basis by commercial carriers. SMDS offers speeds of 1.544 Mbps and 45 Mbps, and in the future it may offer speeds of 155 Mbps and 600 Mbps.

Frame relay.   Frame relay is a form of packet switching that uses small packets that can vary in length. It gets its high speed by performing error detection and correction procedures only at the sending and destination nodes rather than at each node on the network. Many common carriers currently offer frame relay on a flat-rate basis or a usage basis at speeds of 64 Kbps to 1.544 Mbps.

ATM.   ATM, or asynchronous transfer mode, uses fixed-length packets and offers speeds from 45 Mbps to 600 Mbps. Future speeds are anticipated in the gigabit range. Because of its high speeds, ATM can handle multimedia traffic.

ADSL.   Asymmetric Digital Subscriber Line (ADSL) service is a recent offering of telephone companies that is likely to challenge cable companies by providing telephone, video, fax, and other data over ordinary telephone lines to both businesses and individuals. Furthermore, unlike current cable channels, ADSL allows bidirectional signaling, thus permitting interactive TV and Internet use. Speeds for downloading reach more than 6 Mbps, while speeds for uploading are limited to 640 Kbps.

SONET.   Synchronous Optical Network (SONET) offers fiber-based products that reach very high speeds. OC-1 channels reach speeds of about 52 Mbps, OC-2 channels reach about 156 Mbps, and OC-12 reach speeds of about 622 Mbps.

Dial-Up Telephone Lines

Dial-up telephone lines are telephone lines that you rent from the local telephone company and pay for largely on a usage basis. Dial-up lines are often called *switched* lines because the route used to connect your phone or your workstation to the party called may be different each time you call; that is, your call may be routed through different telephone switching centers each time.

Dial-up lines represent the telephone service you typically have in your home. Although you pay for installation of the lines and a small flat monthly fee to keep them in service, your telephone bill largely depends on how much you use them. That is, the cost of the lines is usage sensitive. For example, suppose that you need to make a long-distance connection between a remote terminal and a host computer. Suppose further that the terminal needs to be connected to the host only occasionally during the day. Rather than lease a line that is dedicated to communications between the terminal and the host for the entire day, you would probably simply dial up the host on the ordinary public switched telephone network when communications need to occur. You would then pay for the line only for the time you actually used it. Dial-up lines thus use the public telephone switched network—a very large network indeed. Dial-up lines often use analog signaling and are not usually employed when a user needs frequent or high-speed data communications. Typical data communications speeds on dial-up analog lines are measure in **bits per second (bps)** and include 9.6 kilobits per second (Kbps), 14.4 Kbps, 19.2 Kbps, and 56 Kbps.

Leased Telephone Lines

When you need high-speed data communications or frequent data communications between a sender and receiver, you usually lease the use of a telephone line. You then receive from the carrier use of a dedicated circuit. **Leased telephone lines** typically provide more error-free communications and much higher transmission speeds than dial-up lines. Leased-line speeds range from 9.6 Kbps to multiples of 45 Mbps.

Wireless Networks

A **wireless network** is just that: a network that uses a medium other than wire or fiber cable. As you have already learned, that medium may be radio waves or infrared light waves. A number of communications firms provide radio-based voice, paging, and data networks. One type of wireless network is a **cellular telephone system** that provides mobile telephone service (see Figure 8–9). Employees who must spend a great deal of time in their cars and away from their offices often use cellular telephone service. For example, salespeople can use mobile telephones in their cars to maintain contact with their clients. Salespeople can also use cellular modems to communicate with the computer systems in their home offices (see "Modems" in the next section).

However, wireless networks are not limited to voice communications (see Manager's Memo 8–2). A number of communications companies permit mobile computer systems to connect to other computers and to other networks. The connection can be made using circuit-switched data service (dial-up lines) or *cellular digital packet data* (CDPD) networks. The latter is a packet-switched cellular network. Other companies offer packet radio networks. In a packet radio network, a laptop connected to a wireless radio modem transmits packetized data to a radio base station. The data then travels over a private network to its destination. The RAM Mobile Data network

Figure 8–9

Cellular phone system

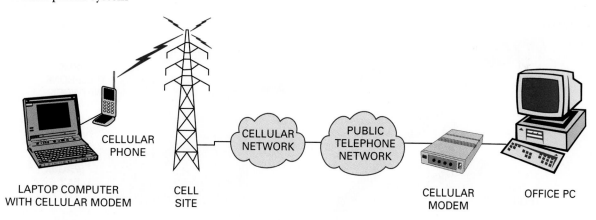

CELLULAR PHONE

LAPTOP COMPUTER WITH CELLULAR MODEM

CELL SITE

CELLULAR NETWORK

PUBLIC TELEPHONE NETWORK

CELLULAR MODEM

OFFICE PC

| Manager's Memo 8–2 | **MANAGING VENDING MACHINES REMOTELY** |

Ameritech wireless data networks and Skyview, Inc., are enabling vending machine companies to manage their equipment remotely. Managers, using a remote wireless connection to each vending machine, can determine the current status of the products and cash in each machine and also whether the machine needs any maintenance. Furthermore, they can use a software package to load and route trucks, plan itineraries for vending machine personnel, and produce financial reports pertaining to vending machine operations.

is an example of a packet radio network. Packet radio networks are slower than the newer CDPD networks for transmitting data.

Another wireless system is the **personal communications service (PCS) network.** PCS networks and cellular networks are both radio-based systems. The phones used in both systems are two-way radios. The systems differ primarily in the radio spectrum they use for communications. Also, while some cellular systems provide digital handsets, all PCS units use digital technology. The digital technologies, however, used by major PCS carriers are not necessarily compatible, for example, a handset from one carrier may not be able to work on another carrier. Furthermore, the cellular networks, being older, cover more of the country. It will take some time before some PCS carriers are able to provide the same breadth of coverage.

Personal communications networks use high-frequency radio waves to create very short-range networks, often with a broadcast radius of about 8 miles, to allow voice and data communications for persons close to each other. These systems use small, easily carried, and relatively inexpensive communication devices called **personal communicators.** Some personal communications networks, such as Planet 1 from Comsat Corporation and Iridium from Motorola Corporation, are global (see Figure 8–10) and will eventually provide fax, paging, e-mail, and cellular phone features from anywhere in the world. That is, the lid of one commercially available PCN device is an antenna, which the device uses to connect to a satellite. The user

Figure 8–10

(a) A global personal communications network; (b) Comsat's PCN device; and (c) the handset of the PCN device

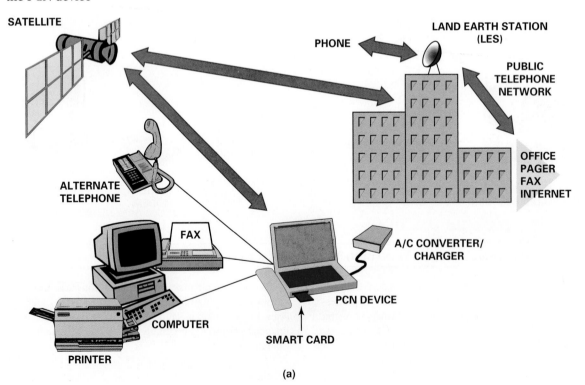

(a)

(b)

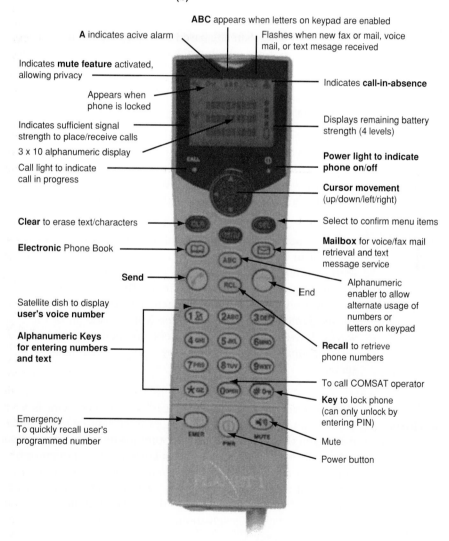

ABC appears when letters on keypad are enabled

A indicates acive alarm

Flashes when new fax or mail, voice mail, or text mesage received

Indicates **mute feature** activated, allowing privacy

Indicates **call-in-absence**

Appears when phone is locked

Indicates sufficient signal strength to place/receive calls

Displays remaining battery strength (4 levels)

3 x 10 alphanumeric display

Power light to indicate phone on/off

Call light to indicate call in progress

Cursor movement (up/down/left/right)

Clear to erase text/characters

Select to confirm menu items

Electronic Phone Book

Mailbox for voice/fax mail retrieval and text message service

Send

Alphanumeric enabler to allow alternate usage of numbers or letters on keypad

Satellite dish to display **user's voice number**

End

Alphanumeric Keys for entering numbers and text

Recall to retrieve phone numbers

To call COMSAT operator

Emergency To quickly recall user's programmed number

Key to lock phone (can only unlock by entering PIN)

Mute

Power button

Courtesy of Comsat Corporation.

(c)

points the antenna at the equator (using the built-in compass), and an on-screen icon indicates that the antennae is locked on the satellite. Communications can then begin.

Personal communicators, notebook computers, personal digital assistants, pen-based computing devices, cellular phones, and cellular modems make remote and portable computing convenient. Motorola even offers wristwatch pagers that can receive short messages from anywhere in the United States. Seiko's MessageWatch beeps you when you receive voice mail and lets you receive weather reports, stock reports, sports scores, even information on the winning lottery tickets from a device that is much like the one Dick Tracy used for years.

Wireless communications systems are expected to grow swiftly in the next 10 years because more people are working away from the office, new networking technologies are making connections from anywhere to anywhere at anytime possible, and convenient, handheld computing devices are proliferating. Currently, cellular networks allow you to call or transmit data from anywhere your system can reach a cellular tower. That location could be your home, your car, a taxi, or airport limo, or your friendly skies. Satellite-based PCS systems, when finished, promise to bring communications systems within reach of a person anywhere on Earth.

COMMON NETWORK COMPONENTS

A typical network might be constructed of a variety of communications hardware devices, software, and communications channels. For example, Figure 8–11 provides a schematic drawing of a mainframe-based order entry system showing the typical hardware that would be needed to serve the home office and two of the branch offices. The following paragraphs explain the equipment found in this system.

Hosts and Servers

A **host** or **server** may be a PC, a minicomputer, or even a large mainframe computer. The host or server computer system typically provides other users on the network with computing services, such as application processing, printing services, and access to database management systems. These computers are called *hosts* or *servers* because they serve terminals attached to them much like party hosts serve their guests. Sometimes a host or server will provide all of these services. In large networks, however, usually computers are dedicated to special tasks, such as file servers, e-mail servers, print servers, fax servers, database servers, and application servers.

Terminals or Workstations

Many types of terminals can be placed on a network. One is a simple *dumb terminal*. This terminal is called "dumb" because it has limited intelligence and memory; that is, it relies on the host or server computer for its memory and its brains. A dumb terminal usually provides the user with a keyboard and a monitor or screen. Another type of terminal is the *intelligent terminal*. Such a terminal usually has a keyboard and a screen, but it also has the memory and computing power to process data by itself. One type of intelligent terminal is the microcomputer. PCs on networks may also be called "workstations," even though they are not high-end computer systems, as described in Chapter 5.

Figure 8–11

A communications system for an order-entry system

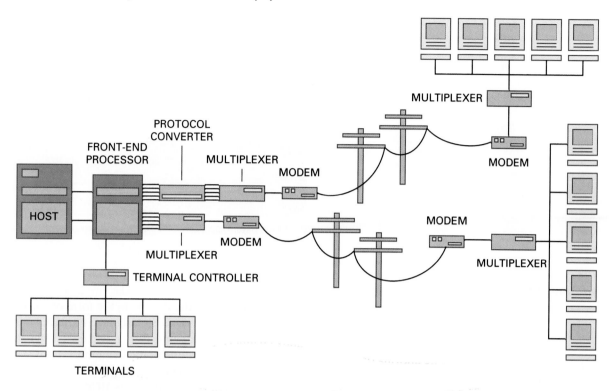

Another common device found on a network is a printer. This device is often a high-speed laser or line printer that provides rapid output of invoices, checks, and other documents.

Protocol Converters

Networks are often eclectic in design because they have grown over a period of years. During those years the organization may have gone through several mergers and acquisitions and experienced many changes in technology. The result is that networks are often a mixture of many different types of devices, channels, transmission modes, and transmission codes. To permit diverse system devices to talk to one another, *protocol converters* are used to translate the signals from one system to another. For example, a protocol converter permits dumb terminals transmitting ASCII code in asynchronous mode to talk to IBM hosts using EBCDIC code and synchronous transmission mode.

A *communications protocol* is a convention, or a set of rules or procedures, for completing a communications systems task. For example, the use of ASCII code is a convention; so is the use of even parity for checking errors or of asynchronous transmission for sending characters. Protocol converters are aptly named because they change the protocols used in a message from one convention, rule, or procedure to another.

Figure 8–12

(a) An external modem and (b) an internal modem

Courtesy of US Robotics.

(a)

Courtesy of Hayes Corporation.

(b)

Modems

Many telephone channels that carry voice communications today are analog channels. To send data over these channels requires that the data be in the form of analog signals. However, computers produce digital signals, not analog signals. To place host-generated digital signals on a voice, or analog, channel means that the digital signals must first be converted into analog form. At the other end of the communications system, the analog signals must be converted back to digital form so that they are acceptable to the terminals. To provide for the conversion, **modems** MOdulate and DE-Modulate the analog signals to represent digital signals. Modems that are on boards to be placed inside a computer system are called *internal modems*. Modems that are housed in boxes and connected to the back of a computer system are called *external modems* (see Figure 8–12).

Cable modems are modems designed to be used on the cable TV network and promise to deliver access to networks, such as the Internet, at very high speeds when compared to telephone modems. Current cable-modem speeds range from 500 Kbps to 10 Mbps. However, 300-Mbps cable modems are under development. To grasp the significance of these speeds, to download a 10 Mbps file using a telephone modem with a speed of 28.8 Kbps would take 46 minutes; at 56 Kbps, 24 minutes; at 128 Kbps using an ISDN line, 10 minutes; and at 10 Mbps using a cable modem, 8 seconds. Or a cable modem could transmit a 900-page book in about 2 seconds. In the same time, an ISDN system would transmit 10 pages, and a 28.8 modem would still be transmitting page 3.[1]

Terminal Connection Equipment

Among the connection devices that allow multiple terminals or workstations to access a network or a server are terminal controllers, multiplexers, hubs, and concentrators. These devices may simply allow servers to broadcast to each terminal attached to the connection device, or they may allow the terminals to reach the

---

[1] Krantz, M. "Wired for Speed," *Time*, September 23, 1996, p. 54.

Figure 8–13

A multiplexer combines the signals from many terminals on one line

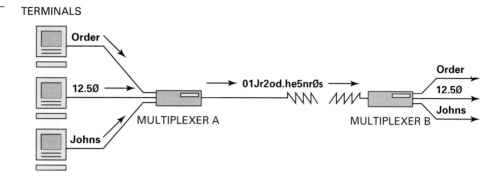

TERMINALS

Order

12.5Ø

Johns

MULTIPLEXER A

01Jr2od.he5nrØs

MULTIPLEXER B

Order

12.5Ø

Johns

server. However, some connection devices provide other features. For example, when terminals and printers are located at a remote site, telephone lines may be used to connect the terminals to the hosts. If a separate telephone line were used for each device, the communications system could get very expensive. Not only would the manager have to pay for the installation and rental of one line for each terminal, but each line would not be busy most of the time.

Consider how fast a typical typist is able to enter order-entry data on a terminal; with coffee breaks, keystroke corrections, and normal office interruptions, a rate of 20 to 30 words per minute is likely to be a reasonable rate of data entry. If it takes 10 bits to send each character over a telephone line, then one order-entry clerk would average about 200 to 300 bits *per minute.* The speed of the telephone line attached to the terminal, however, is measured in bits *per second.* As you can see, one line per terminal is not apt to be cost-effective. Most communications systems take advantage of the difference between the speed of the operator and the speed of the line by placing signals from several slow terminals on one fast line. One device that implements this procedure is called a multiplexer. A *multiplexer* accepts data from many terminals and places them over one or more communications channels networked to the host (see Figure 8–13) so the company can connect many remote terminals to a host while paying only for a few telephone lines. Because a modem is needed for each incoming or outgoing telephone line, a multiplexer saves more than the cost of phone lines; it saves the cost of additional modems, too.

Like modems, multiplexers are usually used in pairs so that the signals from lines that are combined at one end of the system can be *demultiplexed,* or sorted back out at the other end of the system.

One of the most time-consuming tasks for a host or server to perform is input and output tasks (I/O). These tasks involve accepting data input from terminals and providing data output to printers or other terminals. Because these tasks are time-consuming and because a data communications system requires that they be done constantly, communications systems designers often place a special intelligent terminal controller in front of a mainframe host and program it to do as many of these I/O tasks as possible. These intelligent terminal controllers are minicomputers placed between the remote terminals and a host; they are called *front-end processors.* Their job is to take away, or *off-load,* as many of the communications tasks from a host as possible, thereby allowing a host to concentrate on processing data.

Network Connection Equipment

Other devices allow one network to connect to one or more other networks. Examples of network connection equipment include switches, routers, bridges, and repeaters. When distance weakens a communications signal, repeaters are used to boost the signal. Thus *repeaters* may be used to connect two distant networks. However, when two networks are connected by repeaters, the signals from *each* network are shipped to the other. Two networks with moderate traffic, then, can become two networks with heavy traffic and slow response time. To avoid that problem, bridges are used. *Bridges* will repeat signals to avoid the loss of the signal. However, a bridge passes signals from one network to another only when the addresses to which the messages are sent are not local. Thus a message from one workstation in network 1 (see Figure 8–14) to another workstation in network 1 will not be repeated to network 2. A message from a workstation on network 1 to a workstation on network 2 will be allowed to pass through the bridge.

Bridges, however, are not effective devices for connecting multiple networks. Since bridges pass on messages that are not destined for their own network, connecting many networks with bridges would flood the networks with traffic from other bridges. To avoid this problem, routers are used. *Routers* do not indiscriminately forward the messages they receive. They first confirm that the destination address of a message exists. They then determine the available paths to the destination address. Finally, they route messages from sender to receiver by plotting the fastest way, the shortest way, or some other method.

Bridges and routers typically provide shared network service to workstations on a network. That is, on many networks today, the workstations must share access to the medium over which signals are sent. Because workstations must share access, any one workstation cannot use the full capacity of the network medium. To reduce that impediment to speed, switching hubs can replace bridges and routers. A *switching hub* connects each workstation attached to it directly; that is, point to point. One workstation communicating with another workstation on the same switch can transmit at roughly the full speed of the medium.

Figure 8–14

Bridges can be used to connect two networks

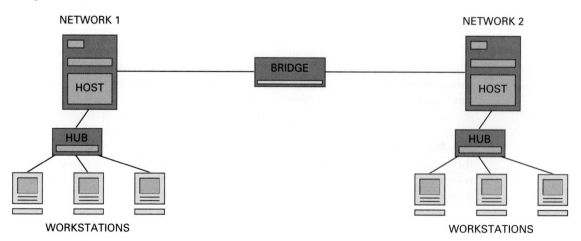

NETWORK TOPOLOGIES

All networks are arranged in topologies, or configurations. A *topology* is simply a method or methods by which devices on the network are laid out and connected.

Point-to-Point or Star and Hierarchical Topologies

One basic topology is a *point-to-point network* in which two devices or points on the network are connected. Point-to-point networks often connect devices such as terminals, or clusters of terminals connected to a terminal controller, to a host (see Figure 8–15). A point-to-point topology is also called a **star topology.**

One basic advantage of a star topology is that multiple devices on the network do not have to contend for access to the media. Each device has its own channel to the central point or host on a network. A disadvantage is that you have to pay the cost of installing or leasing each channel. Another disadvantage is that if the central point in a star network fails, the entire network fails.

A variation of the star topology is the hierarchical topology (see Figure 8–16). In a *hierarchical network* devices are connected to their host, and these hosts are then connected to other hosts. The hierarchical network can provide a number of advantages in certain situations. For example, suppose that your firm owns stores throughout the country. Having a line from each store computer to the host computer at headquarters would be expensive. However, if some store computers act as regional hosts to their surrounding stores, less lengthy channels would be needed to connect to the headquarters computer. Also, the stores may transmit all their data to the regional hosts, but the regional hosts may transmit only summary data to the headquarters computer. Thus the amount of network traffic may also be reduced.

Multidrop or Bus and Ring Topologies

Another basic topology is a multidrop network, which is similar to a party line. In a *multidrop network* a number of devices are connected to a single host channel. Multidrop networks may be arranged in the form of a bus or ring. In a **bus topology** more than one device shares a single channel, but the ends are not con-

Figure 8–15

A point-to-point or star topology

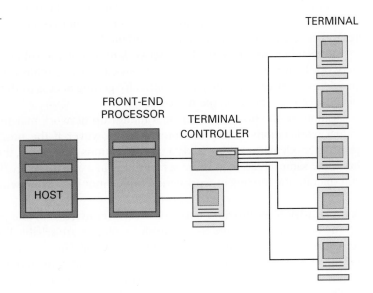

Figure 8–16

A hierarchical topology

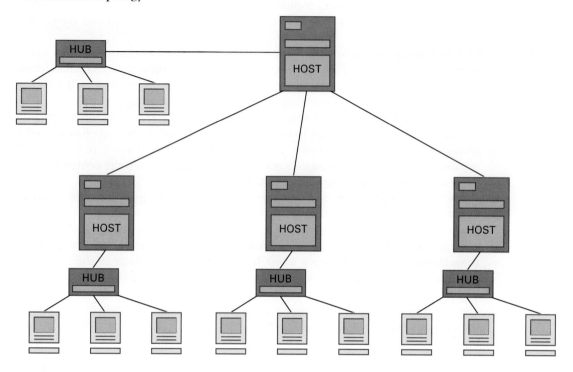

nected (see Figure 8-17). In a **ring topology** more than one device also share a single channel, but the ends of the channel are connected (see Figure 8-18).

Multidrop networks can offer savings to firms because many devices share one channel, reducing line costs. A disadvantage, however, is if that channel fails, none of the devices can transmit data to or receive data from the host. Another disadvantage is that the devices must contend for access to the network cable as well as network resources, such as printers, hard disks, and modems.

Remember, the capacity of any network to handle the volume of messages on the network is important to its success. A low-capacity multidrop network may create problems for users; they may have difficulty getting access to the network resources because of high traffic on the network.

Failure of the host or server on a multidrop network may not bring down individual workstations if they are intelligent. However, if the host or server controls printers, modems, or access to data or applications processing, the network user will be in the same situation as if the server failed in a star topology. That is, the user can still operate the intelligent workstation but cannot get any network services.

Mesh

A **mesh topology** provides networks that offer more than one path between nodes on the network (see Figure 8-19). Mesh topologies are reliable because they offer alternative paths to workstations if line failures occur. They also improve response time for high-traffic paths. Most networks are eclectic and contain both point-to-point and multidrop channel topologies. The network shown in Figure 8-19, for example, includes a point-to-point channel and a multidrop channel.

Figure 8–17

A bus topology

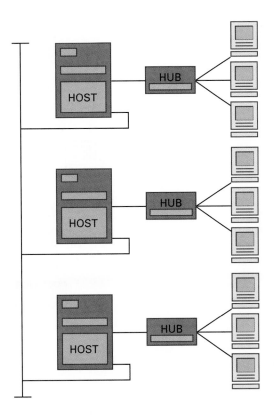

Figure 8–18

A ring topology

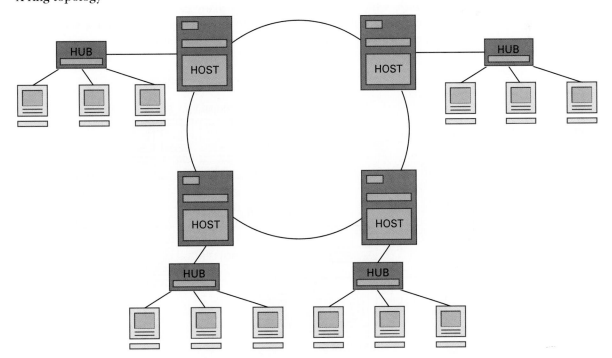

Figure 8–19

A mesh topology

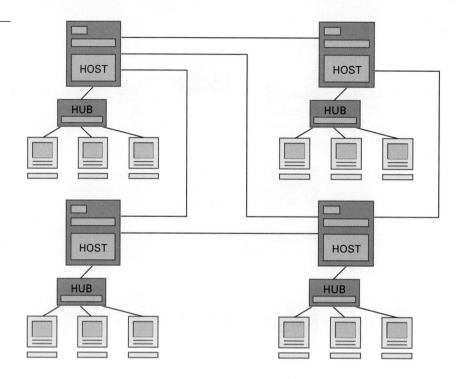

In practice, network topologies may be mixed—that is, a bus topology may be connected to a star topology, a wireless network may be connected to a bus network, or a ring topology may also include a bus topology. For example, to provide for rows of workstations in a classroom, you may run cables from the file server to a multiport *hub,* which is a box that permits many cables to be attached to it. You may run individual cables from the hub to several workstations for a star pattern. However, you may use a bus cable to daisy chain several workstations in a row (see Figure 8–20).

Figure 8–20

Point-to-point and multidrop topologies

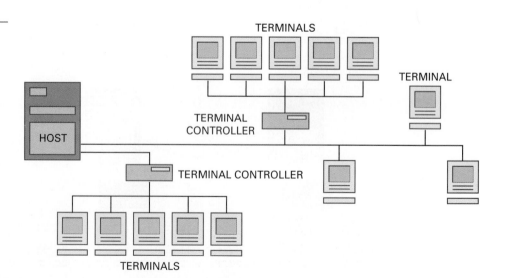

Figure 8–21

A wireless topology

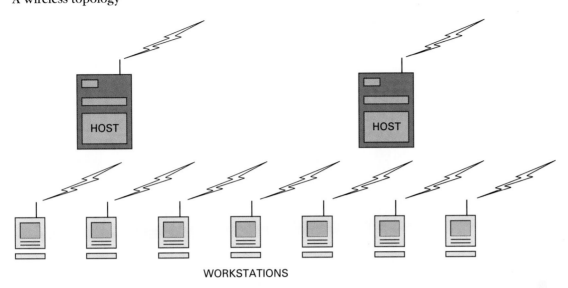

WORKSTATIONS

Wireless Topology

When wireless network systems are used (see Figure 8-21), the initial cost of the hardware is typically higher than for other media. However, the costs of installing a wireless system, especially in older buildings, may save far more than the initial hardware cost differential. Wireless networks can be especially useful when network workstations are moved about frequently. For example, wireless networks allow retail store managers to place workstations, including checkout workstations, on the showroom floor. When displays, counters, and other store furniture are changed for a new line or a new season, the workstations are easy to move. Kmart, for example, uses thousands of wireless systems in its stores.

NETWORK TYPES

There are many types of networks including those that serve computer users in a local area, in an enterprise, in a wide area, and in an international area. There are also voice networks and networks that carry all kinds of messages, including data, voice, images, and video.

Local Area Networks

A **local area network (LAN)** (see Figure 8-22) is an interconnected group of microcomputers or other terminals within a small geographic location such as a single room, office suite, floor, building, or campus. Typically, the devices attached to local area networks are intelligent, rather than dumb. In fact, a major reason for the development of LANs was the proliferation of personal computers. Given the continuing drop in microcomputer costs, however, more and more microcomputers will probably serve as terminals on all types of networks.

Because LANs have proliferated in organizations, it has become necessary to connect LANs to each other and to other networks. To connect LANs on a campus, organizations frequently use fiber optic cabling within buildings or between buildings as a **backbone network.** Each LAN is connected to the backbone, and the

Figure 8–22

A bus topology
LAN

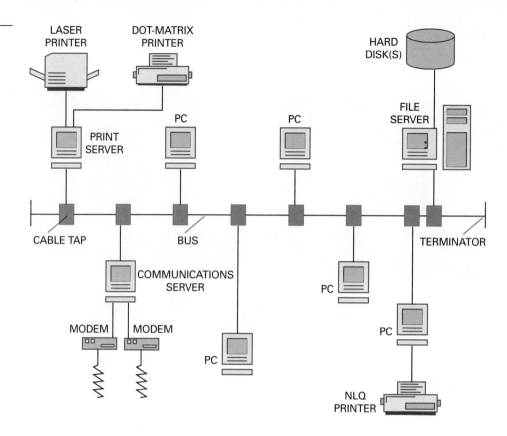

Figure 8–22

A bus topology
LAN

backbone is then connected to one or more of the organization's other networks (see Figure 8–23). Fiber optic cabling is a good choice for backbone networks because it has high capacity and can usually handle the traffic of many LANs. Typically, fiber backbone networks conform to the industry Fiber Distributed Data Interface (FDDI) standard.

Wide Area Networks

A **wide area network (WAN)** is simply a network spread out over a wide area. For example, the telephone networks in the United States, Canada, and Mexico are wide area networks. The order-entry system shown in Figure 8–11 is a wide area network and uses a telephone network to provide channels for the system. A host computer attached to this network might be in the home office, which might be in the United States. The terminals might be placed in each of the company's offices, which might be located in a number of major cities throughout the United States, Canada, and Mexico. When an organization connects local area networks from many different locations, it is creating a wide area network.

Enterprise Networks

As LANs proliferate, WANs expand, and other networks grow in an organization, attempts to make these various networks work together occur. That is, organizations attempt to build *internetworks*. Internetworking for an entire organization is called **enterprise networking.**

For small firms, enterprise networking is a relatively easy task because small firms are likely to have fewer networks and fewer, different types of networks than larger firms. For large firms that have grown over time, developing an enterprise network

Figure 8–23

A backbone network connecting LANs

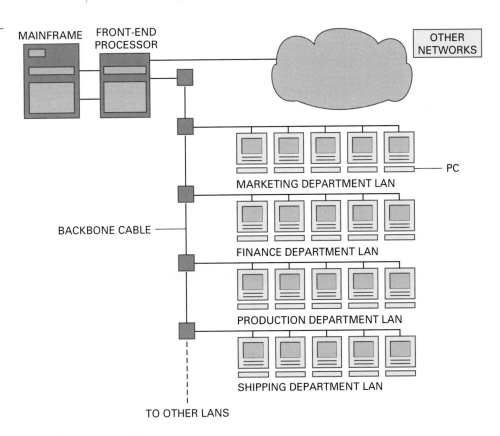

can be daunting because many different networks, many of which use their own protocols, may be in place.

Enterprise networking includes developing the means by which different networks can exchange data. It also includes setting standards for communications for the entire organization so that future internetworking tasks are easier to handle. Developing a backbone network system for all an organization's networks and agreeing on a comprehensive set of communications standards for connecting to the backbone cabling system are major steps to enterprise networking. (See "Communications Standards and the Manager" later in this chapter.)

International Networks

International networks may generate various problems for managers. These problems may range from simply trying to connect to a bewildering array of equipment specifications, managing power differences, and handling time differences to the more complicated task of handling multiple non-English character sets (Kanji in Japan and China, Hongul in Korea, and Farsi in Arabic countries). Problems in codes arise because 7-bit ASCII codes can accommodate only 128 distinct characters, whereas the number of Kanji characters, for example, exceeds 30,000.

Problems with international networks may also be politically based. Most countries have governmental agencies that regulate telephones and other communication networks. These agencies usually have regulations that favor, subsidize, or protect certain national interests. For example, some governments may restrict equipment attached to the network to equipment made in their countries. Governments may also levy duties on software passed over the network. Other governments may be more concerned about the nature of the information about a country that becomes more accessible over international networks. In fact, some countries are considering regulating the information that may be placed on international networks because their governments consider these networks a threat to national security.

REMOTE ACCESS

Many people who use portable microcomputers away from their offices need to connect them to their office LANs, their desktop microcomputers, their office host computer systems, and to other networks. Managers who are working at home in the evening or at the airport and need to obtain information on other computer systems; salespeople who need to communicate with the host computer system to complete sales orders; and technicians, drivers, and repair persons who are working away from the office and must report their activities to the home office or who need data from the home office computer systems to complete their assignments are all in this situation.

Transferring Data Files between Microcomputers

One of the simplest forms of communications is PC-to-PC communications. When the two microcomputers are distant, communication usually requires that each PC be equipped with a modem and the appropriate communications software (see Figure 8–24). Most microcomputer software is capable of transferring ASCII code in asynchronous format, which is the common mode of communications by microcomputers.

When transferring data between microcomputers that are close together, you usually don't use a modem. Instead you attach a special cable, known as a *null modem,* to the serial ports of each computer system and use special software to transfer files. This situation often occurs when you wish to transfer data from your laptop to your office microcomputer after returning from a trip or the field. Null modems and software are usually bundled with laptop computer systems.

You should remember that transferring data from one microcomputer to another is one thing; having both microcomputers understand the communications is another. A person who transfers a document prepared with one word processing software package to a microcomputer equipped with another word processing package may encounter problems. That is, one word processing package may not be able to read the document prepared with the other unless the document is converted to a different format. The conversion may not include special features of the original software, such as tab and column settings, and special print features, such as bold-faced letters. A secretary may have to go through the converted document and reformat it.

Figure 8–24

PC-to-PC communications using modems

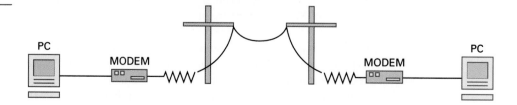

For long documents with many special tabs, columns, and other format features, reformatting is a tedious and potentially expensive task.

Connecting Your Remote PC to Your Office Desktop

Another type of PC-to-PC communications involves communicating remotely from your home or laptop computer to your office microcomputer. A number of remote communications software packages (for example, Carbon Copy Plus) allow you to connect to your office PC, and all of its on-line data files and programs, from your other microcomputer system. The effect is as if you were sitting at your microcomputer at the office, even though you may be at home or on the road. Remote access is an invaluable service to sales representatives, executives, field auditors, and others who travel a great deal.

Connecting to the Internet and On-Line Databases

Many mobile managers need to access information utilities, the Internet, commercial, on-line databases (see Chapter 7), or electronic bulletin boards (see Manager's Memo 8-3). To connect to a bulletin board system from a remote PC usually requires a modem, modem software, and membership in a user group.

Connecting to a Remote Local Area Network

Some people need to connect their microcomputer, which might be at home, in a hotel, or in a car, to their organization LAN. This connection can be made easily with a modem and software for the PC. At the LAN end of the network, you will usually find a *dial-in server*, which is another computer equipped with a network interface card, one or more modems, and software to manage the dial-in communications system (see Figure 8-25).

| **Manager's Memo 8–3** | **ELECTRONIC BULLETIN BOARD SYSTEMS** |

Electronic *bulletin board systems* (BBS) exist for almost any imaginable area of interest. BBSs allow users to read and write messages to the bulletin board. A message might ask a question of other users or share information about special areas of interest. BBSs may also allow users to upload and download files or documents.

An example of a bulletin board system is the Health Information Network, offered by US Telecom, which provides 24-hour access to information on drugs, physical fitness, exercise, and other health-related topics to physicians and dentists. It includes specialized databases and bulletin board systems from such agencies as the Center for Disease Control and the Food and Drug Administration.

Conversely, many firms provide bulletin boards for their customers. These systems allow customers to ask questions of salespeople or technicians and receive prompt answers without having to be connected on a real-time basis. A customer who might need information about a product can drop a note to the firm at any time of day and then read the answer anytime that is convenient.

A manager also may want access to *users' groups* that provide bulletin board services for members about different software packages and computer systems. Members can send questions or problems to the group's bulletin board and receive answers or solutions through the same bulletin board. User groups provide tips and problem-solving assistance from experienced users of the hardware or software.

Figure 8–25

Connecting a remote PC to a LAN

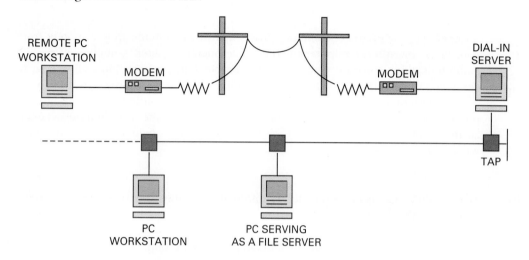

Connecting to a Minicomputer or Mainframe

Many managers need to connect a mobile PC to the company minicomputer or mainframe, for example, to use data from the company database in a spreadsheet. Making the connection is relatively easy in terms of the technology. However, the database administrator is not likely to welcome many naive users rummaging around the company database on weekends. Procedures for protecting the integrity of the database must be developed to ensure that zealous executives who play what-if games using data from the mainframe database do not create a disaster.

Figure 8–26

Connecting a remote PC to a mainframe computer system

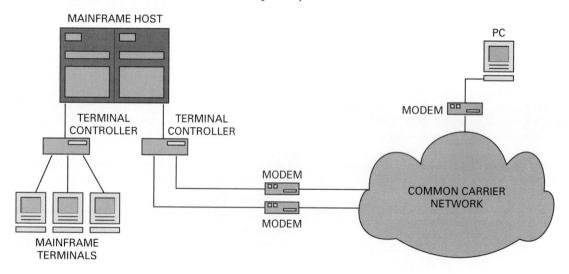

Connecting a remote PC to a minicomputer or mainframe computer usually involves making the microcomputer *emulate,* or look like, an ordinary terminal on the mainframe network. For example, if a mainframe computer network uses IBM 3270 terminals, then one way to connect the microcomputer to the network is to install 3270 emulation hardware and/or software in the PC. This may mean buying an **emulation board** and an **emulation software** package for the micro (see Figure 8-25). If the PC and the mainframe are both on an enterprise network, running emulation software on the PC may be all that is needed (see Figure 8-26).

REASONS MANAGERS IMPLEMENT NETWORKS

Networks are often very expensive additions to a computer system. Such expenses would not be incurred if an organization did not have important reasons for them. Many of the reasons for networks are implied by the examples described earlier in "Manager's View." A brief discussion of these reasons follows.

Sharing Peripherals

Laser printers, line printers, and plotters are often expensive, especially when they are large and fast. Providing fast or specialized printing devices for each microcomputer is usually prohibited by cost. Connecting workstations to a network that includes specialized or expensive printers spreads the cost of the printing devices over many workstations and enables users to access these devices regardless of where or how they are connected.

Some other peripherals that users can share are optical disks readers, especially optical disk towers that provide access to many optical disks; fax machines; modems; and large, fast, hard drives.

Sharing Data Files

When several order-entry clerks need to enter data that affect sales, inventory, and accounts receivable records, these records have to be available to each worker. When workers must have concurrent access to the same records, as they usually must in accounting and database applications, a network is necessary.

Sharing Applications

Many programs have been designed specifically for networks. Some examples include groupware, electronic mail software, and multiuser database software. Network versions of common software may also provide more features than the single-user version of the same software. For example, a network version of a word processing package may allow multiple users to share and edit a single document on which they are all working simultaneously. A network version of accounting software allows many salespeople to enter orders, access the same inventory files, and access the same customer files simultaneously. The ability to send messages to electronic mailboxes stored on a network server may prove to be an important productivity tool for managers.

Electronic mail provides a mailbox for each person on the network and allows users to send messages to individuals or groups of people or even to broadcast messages to everyone on the network. Users can view the contents of their own mailboxes from a terminal attached to the network locally or from a terminal attached at a remote location (see Chapter 9).

Networks of groups of employees engaged in common work or a common project make a lot of sense—especially when the group is supported by groupware software (see Chapter 6) that allows them to share scheduling, document creation and review, electronic mail, and commonly used programs and files. Groupware, or software designed to support groups at work on common projects, requires a network.

Reducing the Costs of Acquiring, Installing, and Maintaining Software

Acquiring and installing a software package, such as a statistical software package, on every workstation in an organization can cost a great deal of money. The expenses are the cost of the software and then the cost of installing the software. In the current software environment, most software will probably be upgraded within a year or two, which means that the organization has to acquire and install the upgrade. In large firms with thousands of PCs, this daunting task can overwhelm technical staffs. Acquiring one copy of the software and placing it on a host or server accessible by all workstations can substantially reduce these costs for two reasons. First, in most organizations all users do not need to use the software at the same time. Therefore, instead of purchasing one copy for each user, the firm can reduce its costs by purchasing a concurrent license only large enough to handle the number of users who need to use the software at the same time. Second, the software needs to be installed on only one machine (the host or server), instead of thousands.

Connecting to Other Networks

Connecting to other networks through your organization network can save money because the hardware and software needed to make the connection can be spread over all the workstations on your network. You don't have to buy hardware and software for each workstation to make the connection. One of the most important networks today is the Internet (see Chapter 9). An Internet connection allows managers to create and view e-mail, connect to the computer systems of other firms, including competitors, and gather information from computer systems around the country and the world.

Capturing Data at Its Source

A network permits the use of remote terminals in sales offices, factory production lines, cars, and even on customer premises. Remote terminals allow employees to enter data into a computer system immediately, eliminating the need to rekey data captured originally by hand or by typewriter. For the manager, source data capture reduces the errors and costs associated with copying data from one form to another several times. Input controls, available to remote users, guard against incorrect entries made by your staff and reduce errors made at the time of original entry.

Increasing Productivity

A salesperson who uses a portable computer at a customer location may find that the merchandise the customer wants to purchase is not in stock. Knowing that, the salesperson may choose alternative products that are in stock to satisfy the customer's needs. Furthermore, instant distribution of the sales invoice completed by the salesperson to the warehouse, shipping, and accounting departments means the customer order is filled faster and the customer is billed faster. Thus both merchandise turnover and cash flow increase. Also, since the salesperson completes the sales order directly, sales order-entry clerks, supervisors, and other supporting resources are not needed.

Managers with portable terminals at home or in their cars can use this equipment for planning and decision making whenever they get ideas, not just when they are in the office. Managers with such resources are *always* at the office.

Permitting Expansion

Organizations that expand often do so by purchasing or constructing facilities at other locations. Also, many organizations are so large that they span several buildings. Communications networks allow these remote and dispersed sites to be connected.

Increasing Timely Communications	Networks permit organizations with dispersed personnel to distribute information quickly to the right people, thereby aiding decision making. Using the interoffice mail system and the postal system may delay critical information as much as three to five days. Using the voice telephone system for rapid communications to a large number of people individually would be very labor intensive. Also, the price per character of information sent over a manual mail system or a voice telephone system may far exceed the cost per character of an electronic data communications system. The ability to communicate new prices, stockouts, or changes in organizational policy to dispersed salespeople, managers, other employees, and customers instantly is very important to many organizations.
Increasing Management Control	Instant feedback of data from the assembly line allows supervisors to avoid major problems or to attend to potential problems before they become major crises. Timely knowledge of salespeople's accomplishments may affect raw materials purchases and production schedules. Communications networks provide managers with early information to permit them to react swiftly to potential problems.

NETWORK CONCERNS FOR THE MANAGER

The most important network concerns for managers include network reliability, network response time, network costs, compatibility, and network access and security.

| **Network Reliability** | A network of remote terminals used for order entry that is constantly down loses sales for the organization. How well the network can be relied on to be up and running during work hours is very important. One study estimates that the typical LAN in an organization fails about 27 times each year and that this downtime costs the organizations about $3,500,000 in worker time and about $600,000 in lost revenue.

Network reliability is also affected by the rate of errors encountered on the channels during transmissions. High error rates slow down throughput on the network because they usually require that messages be retransmitted, thereby increasing the load on the network and increasing the associated costs of transmitting messages. The quality of the channels and devices used on the network contributes greatly to network reliability. The experience, training, and tools given to the organization's network management personnel also contribute significantly to network reliability. |
|---|---|
| **Network Response Time** | The time it takes for an order-entry clerk to send a request for information to the host and receive a reply is called **response time.** Obviously, the response time of the network is important to the productivity of the manager's staff. When you use a terminal to find out if stock a customer wants is on hand, you must get a response before the customer leaves or falls asleep.

Among the many factors that affect response time on networks are the distance the signal must travel, the amount of traffic on the network, and the capacity of the network channels. High error rates, of course, slow down response time and increase line traffic because messages must be retransmitted. When large files—as opposed to a single record, such as a sales order—must be transferred, the capacity of the channel and the capacity of the equipment attached to the channel become very important. Sending a 4MB file over a network with a capacity of 4,800 bits per second will take more than two hours. Sending that same file over a network capable of handling |

56 Kbps will take only about 12 minutes. High-speed channels and equipment cost more money than low-speed channels and equipment, but slow networks require more transmission time, thus increasing common carrier costs. Slow networks also reduce worker productivity and may even lose sales—customers are likely to leave rather than fall asleep.

Network Costs

Networks cost money (see Manager's Memo 8–4). Network costs include the costs of installing and renting the channels, installing and acquiring the equipment, hiring network maintenance and management personnel, training employees to use the network, and repairing and maintaining the equipment and channels. Using multiplexers, transmitting noncritical data during low-cost evening hours, using multidrop channels, reducing transmission errors, and even slowing response time by a fraction may result in large savings. Configuring networks or comparing various network design alternatives is a complex undertaking. Network design software is available, but basically network design is still an art. Therefore, the quality of the network management staff available to the manager is critically important to the efficiency of the system.

Compatibility

A major problem with most networks is the incompatibility of the equipment and software used on the system. This incompatibility results from the fact that networks grow over time, with the associated problems of changing technology. The lack of central control over equipment and software purchases or the acquisition of new firms with established networks or computer systems are also causes of incompatibility. Solving incompatibility problems usually means buying equipment that converts the signals from one system to another or developing software to make the conversion. Either solution can require a lot of money and time. Furthermore, the conversion software or equipment adds to system processing time and, of course, reduces response time.

Manager's Memo 8–4	THE COSTS OF LOCAL AREA NETWORKS

The costs of acquiring and installing LAN equipment and software are pretty steep. However, it is in the maintenance and management of LAN resources that the bill really soars to great heights. According to Gartner Group, the cost of supporting a LAN PC averages about $13,200 annually. This includes the costs for hardware and software, and other costs pertaining to technical support, training, services, and administration.

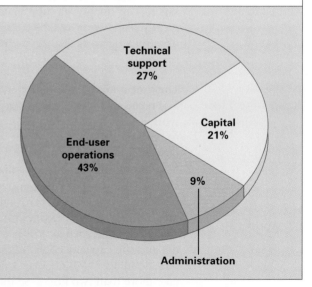

Source: David Simpson, *Datamation*, January 1997 (on-line version).

Network Access and Security

Many organizations store confidential data, such as long-term company plans, product development and marketing information, employee information, and customer information. Organizations that manufacture products for a nation's defense must secure much of the data they use from unauthorized access. Unfortunately, networks may increase the accessibility of host data to people who are not authorized to access those data. Managers must pay careful attention to the security of the network.

Network security may include these actions:

1. Providing log-on codes to authorized personnel to prevent unauthorized access from a remote computer terminal.

2. Issuing passwords for access to certain files to restrict employees to those data that they are authorized to view.

3. Providing physical access protection to remote terminals, such as locking offices or locking the terminal keyboards.

4. Encrypting, or coding, the information so that if it is stolen it may not be understood.

Probably the most unsettling security issues involve using microcomputers to access the host through "dial up" or switched lines. Frequently, executives and salespeople are allowed to access the host database using their portable or home microcomputers through the use of a simple modem and a telephone line. Security is often maintained through the use of log-on codes and passwords. In addition, the host system may, when called, dial back the calling microcomputer to make certain that the caller is authorized. These measures and others have discouraged inexperienced callers from penetrating the system. However, anyone who reads the papers knows that computer hackers routinely break log-on codes, passwords, and other security measures used even in our most tightly controlled defense networks. When microcomputers have access to host databases through dial-up lines, little real security is available to keep out the persistent computer expert.

VOICE SYSTEMS

The telephone system was designed as a voice system and engineered for short conversations between people. Voice transactions still constitute a substantial amount of the traffic over common carrier networks. Voice conversations are also critical to many organizations. The telephone system represents the "front door" of many firms, including mail-order firms. Two tools for helping firms manage voice communications are PBX systems and Centrex systems.

PBXs

A **private branch exchange (PBX),** is a computer system that provides for the switching of telephone signals for voice and data on your company's premises rather than at the telephone company's office (see Manager's Memo 8-5). A PBX actually takes the place of comparable equipment located in the nearest local telephone office (called the *central office*).

Centrex

For managers who do not want to incur the initial costs associated with acquiring their own PBX and who also do not want the headaches of operating and managing a telephone switch, there is Centrex. **Centrex** provides PBX-like functions and services to the user on a lease basis. Basically, it gives the user dedicated central office (CO)

| Manager's Memo 8–5 | USING A PERSONAL COMPUTER AS A PBX |

TouchVoice Corporation makes a PBX adapter card that fits into any IBM compatible personal computer and turns it into a PBX. The card, called a PCBX, can support from 4 outside lines and 12 extensions up to 64 outside lines and 225 extensions.

The system provides existing commercial telephone sets with many of the special features found on larger PBXs, including software for automatic call distribution.

Source: The TouchVoice Corporation Web site
(http://www.deltanet.com/touchvoice/index.html).

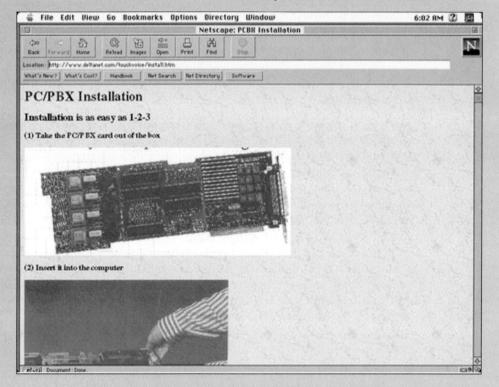

telephone lines and a varying set of features, such as intercom, call forwarding, least-cost routing, toll restrictions, and call hold. These features vary with the telephone company and the state in which the service is offered. The local telephone company's central office switch, rather than a switch on the customer's premises, does the switching.

The trade-offs seem to be that Centrex offers a lower initial cost, lower costs of telephone system management, and the ability to vary the telephone features leased from the telephone company. The PBX offers better usage and management reporting and usually lower costs over the long term (see Figure 8–27).

Reasons for Implementing a PBX

You might wonder why a manager would acquire a PBX facility for voice telephone service when such service is available from the local telephone company. One reason is to reduce costs. Purchasing a PBX may be more cost-effective for a company than leasing telephone service from a telephone company.

Figure 8–27

Centrex versus PBX

Centrex Services	PBX
Regulated environment	Unregulated
Functions in telephone company central office (CO)	Functions on user premises
Leased only	Lease or buy
Reliable because of redundancy	Reliable when user pays for redundancy
Full maintenance always available	Maintenance not always on site (may require user personnel for service)
Growth practically unlimited	Finite growth limitations
No capital outlay necessary (installation may be amortized)	May require purchase or significant up-front cash outlay
Multiple buildings may be connected to same Centrex through CO	Separate PBXs usually required
Upgrade features can be continuous	Significant upgrade may require new PBX
Simultaneous voice/data available	Simultaneous voice/data available
Relatively limited station message detail recording (SMDR) information	Full SMDR information available
All wiring twisted-pair	Wiring may be twisted-pair or coaxial cable
May have high monthly cost per line	Line cost amortized over time in service
No space or power required	User space and power required
Telephone company personnel provides maintenance	User may need dedicated maintenance personnel
Rate stability plans available	Rate stability not available

Source: Adapted from K. Sherman, *Data Communications: A User's Guide,* 3rd ed. (Englewood Cliffs, NJ: Prentice Hall), 1990, p. 309

Another reason is that PBXs may be used for more than merely voice communications. PBXs have become very powerful—they are sophisticated, programmable computers, even though they are specifically designed for telephone traffic. PBXs are powerful enough to switch not only voice messages for an organization but also data messages. A third reason is to obtain features that are not available from the local telephone company. In fact, the features of PBXs have broadened their use. Consider the following possibilities:

Using telephone keypads as data terminals. You may connect an organization's PBX and mainframe computer to allow the telephone keypad to be used as a terminal. Salespeople, customers, managers, and others who have been given authority to do so may address the host computer through the telephone set in their office, home, car, or even airport.

Offering a voice mail system. A *voice mail system* (see Chapter 9) digitizes, stores, routes, and forwards voice messages under the control of the PBX's computer. Telephone users may listen to voice messages that have been digitized and stored in their voice mailboxes. Users may access their voice mailboxes from any telephone handset—anywhere. A salesperson or field agent can always be in touch with the home office, other salespeople, or even customers. Users may also leave voice messages in other mailboxes or even broadcast messages to many users of the voice mail system. Consider how easily a manager with voice mail can announce meetings. A sales manager can use voice mail to broadcast messages to all or selected groups of salespeople about product price changes or changes in product availability.

Telephone companies now offer some voice mail functions to users at a monthly fee without the need to purchase special equipment.

PBX Hardware and Software

A PBX has at least one central processor and main memory like any other computer system. Of course, its switching capabilities are extensive and require specialized hardware. The PBX system also includes telephone handsets, central operator consoles, cabling, and distribution boxes for the cabling. The PBX provides software to install, monitor, and control incoming and outgoing telephone lines, telephone handsets, and other devices attached to it.

Older PBXs were large systems, occupying a significant amount of floor space. However, like computers in general, PBXs have become smaller in size and price, and models are available for even the smallest of offices. Some specialized hardware and software that may be added to a PBX system include the following.

Call conferencing.   Call conferencing allows many people to talk together without being in the same room. PBXs offer various ways to serve this form of electronic conferencing. You may define the parties to the conference beforehand and have the PBX call and connect everyone automatically, the conference originator may call each person and add him or her to the conference, or each participant may be given a number to call at a given time to connect to the conference. One vendor allows up to 100 people to be connected in a conference call at one time.

Call directors.   A *call director* may be provided to put customers on hold when all incoming lines are busy. A call director would then connect the oldest incoming call to the next available operator. Usually it provides music or information to the caller who is waiting on hold. Sales managers make effective use of call directors to avoid losing customers at busy hours during the day or during busy seasons. You have probably been placed on hold many times when you called airlines or stores during rush hours or holiday seasons.

Network access hardware and software.   The manager may wish to access the organization host from a local microcomputer or to access another computer system that uses different codes and is located at a remote location. The PBX can be used to provide protocol conversion and routing to other networks for those computer systems attached to the PBX. These systems include the hardware—usually an interface board—and the software to provide communications to another computer, another computer network, or a value-added network (such as Tymnet or Sprintnet).

Voice mail software.   PBX vendors and other vendors offer voice mail systems, like the one described earlier that run on a PBX.

Station message detail recording software.   *Station message detail recording* (SMDR) software provides an organization with detailed reports of telephone usage and costs for each department. The software also allows an organization to manipulate the telephone usage data. Thus the organization can locate high-cost telephone users or identify the amount of time spent talking to clients on the phone. In firms that bill clients by the hour, the latter capability is very important. Knowledge that every call is being monitored and that a report will show who made what phone calls, when, and for how long usually reduces employee abuse of the phone system for personal phone calls substantially. Some organizations have found that SMDR reduces their long-distance phone bills by as much as one-third. In addition to the costs of personal phone calls, the organization usually saves more money because reduced traffic allows the company to eliminate extra outgoing lines.

Data entry software. A number of vendors provide software that allows telephone keypads to become data entry terminals. The software uses the PBX to provide switching to a host database. You have already read how such a system might allow salespeople to use any convenient telephone to enter an order or allow students to use their home telephones to register for classes. Some banks have used this type of software to allow customers to access their checking accounts, pay bills, and move money from their checking to their savings accounts.

Computer telephony integration. In the past computer systems and voice systems used separate networks. The integration of these networks, or computer telephony integration (CTI), has widened the horizon for new applications that provide new functionality and lower costs for organizations. For example, with the advent of PC-board PBXs, a single computer system, containing the organization's customer database, can serve as both a PBX and a server. When a customer calls, the originating phone number can be looked up in the customer database, the call transferred to the customer's sales representative, and the customer's record displayed on the sales representative's screen. Now when the rep answers the phone, he or she can be fully prepared to greet the customer. This feature is called *intelligent call processing*.

CTI technology will also allow organizations to supply employees with inexpensive phones and let the CTI software running on a local PC to which a phone is attached provide features normally associated with expensive phone sets: hold, transfer, flash, conference calls, and speed dialing. Furthermore, the software usually provides an easy to understand interface for these features. The user points and clicks with a mouse instead of memorizing the typically cryptic phone keypad combinations used on older systems.

CTI technology will also allow even small companies to create *interactive voice response* systems (see Chapter 9). These systems are automatic telephone attendant systems that answer the phone and lead the caller through a series of menus to reach the party they are calling. Because of the integration of the database with the phone system, CTI technology will allow the caller to reach the database, assuming the caller has the proper authority. This permits technicians to interact with technical manuals, service employees and customers to interact with the service and repair schedules, customers to find out their account balances, and salespeople to find out order information.

Even home users can find a use for CTI technology. Single multimedia workstations equipped with sound cards, speakers, and microphones can run software that will make the workstation into a standard, full-duplex speakerphone and answering machine.

Voice Systems Concerns for the Manager

The use of the PBX as a switching device for both data and voice messages holds real promise for increasing productivity. Voice mail and the use of telephone sets as data entry devices for short messages that are sent in bursts seem especially promising. However, the manager should recognize that the typical PBX today is still designed for the type of traffic associated with voice communications. Where data communications are sporadic, short in length, and "bursty" in nature, combining voice messages with data messages through a PBX should be considered. But using the current generation of PBXs to process voice communications along with large, batch operation data processing jobs will seriously degrade communications services. Neither the channels nor the switching capacity of the typical PBX system is designed for such activity. The manager must also be concerned with the resources necessary to operate and maintain the PBX system. Large PBX systems do not run by themselves. They require the attention of skilled technicians, and they require training workers to use sophisticated features. The firm must allocate more resources to a PBX system than merely the price of acquisition and installation of the system.

Additional information about applications of telephone systems to the office and the convergence of telephone systems and computer systems appears in Chapter 9.

COMMUNICATIONS STANDARDS AND THE MANAGER

The field of communications is extremely complex and includes many diverse technologies. It also includes many organizations that set standards, and thus many sets of often incompatible standards. In fact, the usual quip of communications professionals is that what makes communications standards so nice is that there are so many of them from which to choose. Such a diverse environment makes it difficult for the manager to make decisions regarding communications systems, including hardware, software, and media. However, two major sets of communications standards, which are called *communications architectures,* might help managers bring some degree of order to the current chaos: Systems Network Architecture (SNA) from IBM and Open Systems Interconnect (OSI) from the International Organization for Standardization (ISO) (see Manager's Memo 8-6).

Each of these architectures is really an organized set of specifications for handling communications tasks, allowing software developers and manufacturers who use these specifications to create products that "fit" together. Communications networks built on the foundation of a comprehensive architecture, or set of standards, present fewer problems because they are built within a coherent framework of specifications. Hardware and software, built according to the architecture's specifications, usually will work together.

Because of the widespread use of computer systems built on the Wintel (Microsoft Windows operating system and the Intel family of chips) standard and the widespread acceptance of the OSI standards, systems built on either of these two architectures provide many options for acquiring communications components that work together and a sound basis for handling future expansion and technological change. That is, the future hardware and software products, built according to the specifications of an architecture, are apt to be compatible with an existing network built on the same architecture.

| Manager's Memo 8–6 | THE LAYERED STANDARDS OF OPEN SYSTEMS INTERCONNECT ARCHITECTURE |

The OSI network standards group all communication tasks into seven layers. Each layer describes specifications about how these tasks will be accomplished (the protocols). On an OSI-based network, messages pass from one computer system to another through all seven layers.

Because of the widespread use of IBM computer systems and the widespread acceptance of the OSI standards, systems built on either of these architectures provide many options for acquiring communications components that work together and a sound basis for handling future expansion and technological change. That is, future hardware and software products, built according to the specifications of an architecture, are apt to be compatible with an existing network built on the same architecture.

Layer	Protocols
Application	Provides network services to users and user applications, including file transfer.
Presentation	Formats data between different systems.
Session	Establishes and terminates links between computers.
Transport	Controls data transfer for the complete path, from sending point to receiving point.
Network	Controls the routing of data through the channels of a network.
Data link	Controls grouping data into blocks and transferring blocks from one network point to another.
Physical	Handles voltages, electrical pulses, connectors, and switches.

MANAGEMENT SUMMARY

The transfer of voice, data, text, and images through communications networks has become very important to the success of organizations. The solutions to numerous business problems can involve a variety of communications systems. Every communications system consists of at least a sender, a channel over which the message is sent, and a receiver. However, communications systems, or networks, are likely to be a good deal more complex than that. One reason for complexity is the number of differing sources of communications channels, the variety of communications channels available, the diversity of communications equipment, and the variety of communications modes and data codes used.

Many types of communications networks are found in organizations: local area networks, enterprise networks, wide area networks, international networks, voice networks, and specialized networks that handle different types of messages, including voice, data, images, and video. Networks are often implemented to allow PCs to share peripherals, data files, and programs as well as to capture data at its source, increase productivity, permit organizations to expand, increase management control over enterprise activities, and provide timely communications.

Networks may be laid out in a point-to-point, hierarchical, multidrop, or mesh topology, and network hardware can include hosts or servers, terminals or workstations, devices that permit many terminals to connect to the network, and devices that connect one network to another.

The manager must be concerned about the reliability of networks, the response time of networks, the high cost of networks, the compatibility of network hardware and software, and the security of networks.

PBX networks are designed primarily for voice communications, but increasingly they include some capability to process data and text communications as well. PBXs are often acquired to reduce voice communications costs, to process a limited amount of data and text communications over the voice system, and to secure features that may not be available from the local telephone company. Besides the ability to handle both voice and data communications, PBXs may also provide gateways to other computer networks, allocate calls more efficiently among receivers, provide voice mail systems, furnish call accounting systems, provide better management of line use, provide conferencing capabili-

ties, and provide access to company databases using the telephone keypad.

Developing communications systems based on widely accepted technologies (such as Ethernet protocols) and comprehensive communications standards architectures (such as OSI) helps an organization to construct communications systems that can work and grow together.

Key Terms for Managers

analog transmission, 256
backbone network, 277
bits per second (bps), 264
bus topology, 273
cellular telephone system, 265
Centrex, 287
channel, 255
common carrier, 262
communications media, 260
communications network, 255
dial-up telephone lines, 264

digital transmission, 256
emulation board, 283
emulation software, 283
enterprise networking, 278
host, 268
leased telephone lines, 264
local area network (LAN), 277
mesh topology, 274
modems, 270
personal communications service (PCS) network, 266

personal communicators, 266
private branch exchange (PBX), 287
response time, 285
ring topology, 274
server, 268
star topology, 273
telecommunications systems, 255
value-added networks (VANs), 262
wide area network (WAN), 278
wireless network, 265

Review Questions

1. Identify and describe at least five business applications for which data communications systems are appropriate.
2. List and describe the basic components of any communications system.
3. Explain the difference between asynchronous communications and synchronous communications.
4. Explain the difference between simplex, half-duplex, and full-duplex transmission. Provide an example of each type of transmission.
5. What is a communications network?
6. Identify and describe at least five types of communications media.
7. What is a communications protocol?
8. What is wireless communications? What are some common types of wireless communications?

9. What is a personal communications systems? A personal communicator?
10. Can a cell phone system be used to transmit and receive data as well as voice? If so, what equipment is involved?
11. What are some common network components?
12. What are some common types of servers on a network?
13. Identify some examples of terminal connection equipment.
14. What are some examples of network connection equipment?
15. Compare the functions of a repeater to a bridge. What does a bridge do that a repeater does not?
16. Compare the functions of a bridge to a router. What does a router do that a bridge does not?

17. Explain the purpose of a front-end processor.
18. Explain why a manager might want the organization to use multiplexers.
19. Why would an organization need one or more protocol converters?
20. Explain why a modem is usually needed when communications must take place over voice lines.
21. What are the differences between intelligent and dumb terminals?
22. What is a microcomputer terminal emulation board? What is it used for?
23. Describe the basic types of network topologies.
24. What does the term *response time* mean on a network?
25. What is a central office?
26. What is data entry software for PBXs? How might a manager apply data entry software?
27. What is SMDR software? What benefits does SMDR offer the manager?
28. What are some common carrier products that managers can use to connect two networks that are distant from each other?
29. Explain the difference between circuit switching and packet switching. What advantage does packet switching offer?
30. What are six concerns a manager should have about a communications network?
31. What is a local area network? Compare a local area network to a wide area network.
32. What is an enterprise network? Why are enterprise networks important to managers?
33. What is a file server? What is its purpose?
34. What are print servers and communications servers?
35. Explain the term *backbone network*.
36. What are internal and external modems? How do they differ?
37. What is a PBX?
38. What is a call director? How can a call director help an organization?

QUESTIONS FOR DISCUSSION

1. Why might an organization send messages using a synchronous transmission mode?
2. Why might an organization use a dial-up telephone line, rather than a leased line, for data communications?
3. What factors might make organizations utilize a wide area network?
4. Why might a manager want to connect microcomputers into a local area network?
5. Why might a manager decide not to develop a LAN?
6. Why might managers want to connect their microcomputers to the company mainframe?
7. What is a PBX? Why might a manager consider buying a PBX?
8. Why might a manager consider acquiring a Centrex system instead of a PBX system?
9. What problems can occur in an international network?
10. Why are communications standards important to the manager?

PROBLEMS

1. **Bear-Reece, Inc.** Bear-Reece, Inc., is considering placing six remote terminals at a site in another city to be used to enter sales orders on-line. The company wants to connect the terminals to the host at the home office. Company management is considering installing six lines at the home office and at the remote site so that each

terminal can be directly connected to the host. The company will also need 12 modems for the installation—6 at the host end and 6 at the terminal end.

  a. Develop and draw an alternative configuration of communications equipment and channels for the company's remote site to save the company lines and modems.

  b. What concerns should Bear-Reece, Inc., have regarding the communications system it is considering?

2. **Centix, Inc.**   Bill Franke is a sales manager with Centix, Inc. His desktop computer system is connected to the office LAN. Bill travels quite a bit and wants to connect his notebook computer system to the office LAN while he is away.

  a. Describe two methods that he can use to connect his notebook computer to the office LAN.

  b. Describe, in general, the hardware and software Bill would need to buy for each method.

  c. List actual brand names and prices of one set of hardware and software for each method you described. To gather these data, use a CD-ROM database, such as *Computer Select* or use one or more search engines to examine the Internet for products. You may also use *Computer Literature Index,* published by Applied Computer Research, Inc., Phoenix, Arizona, to find PC magazines that have recently featured articles on remote computing.

3. **Anastasi Imports, Inc.**   Anastasi Imports, Inc., wants to develop a communications system to link its branch office with its home office. At the home office, it has a mainframe computer that uses EBCDIC as a data code.

  a. Assume that the company wants to use six dumb ASCII terminals at the branch office site. Draw a configuration of a network that might connect the dumb terminals at Anastasi's branch office to its home office mainframe computer system

using multiplexers to save telephone lines. Make sure that you draw and label each piece of equipment you feel should be placed on the network, including the host mainframe computer and the terminals at the branch office. Use Figure 8–11 as a guide.

  b. Assume that the company wants to use six microcomputers as terminals at the branch office site. Draw a configuration of a network that might connect the microcomputers on the LAN at Anastasi's branch office to its home office mainframe computer system. Make sure that you draw and label each piece of equipment you feel should be placed on the network, including the host mainframe computer, the servers on the LAN, and the microcomputers at the branch office. Use Figure 8–25 as a guide.

4. **PCS Evaluation Problem.**   Identify and compare two personal communicator devices. List and compare their features, limitations, and prices. Present your findings in a report. To gather data for your report, use a CD-ROM database, such as *Computer Select,* or use one or more search engines to examine the Internet for products. You may also use *Computer Literature Index,* published by Applied Computer Research, Inc., Phoenix, Arizona, to find PC magazines that have recently featured articles on personal communicator devices.

5. **Cellular Phone Evaluation Problem.** Compare the features and costs of using cellular phones and PCS phones in your area for voice and data. Present your findings in a report. To gather data for your report, contact cellular and PCS carriers in your area. Also, use one or more search engines to examine the Internet for general information pertaining to these two systems.

CASES

1. **Advanced Financial Services, Inc.**
   Advanced Financial Services, Inc. (AFS) is a partnership that provides accounting and financial planning services to small and medium-sized businesses and organizations in Oakland, California. Its home office in Oakland employs 94 people and is supported by a mini-computer system. AFS is considering opening a second office in San Francisco, which is just across the bay from Oakland. Advanced Financial plans to start with an office that will be home to approximately 50 people, including one partner, managers, financial planners, field agents, and office support personnel. The field agents visit firms, collect accounting data, and prepare accounting and tax reports. The financial planners advise firms on financial and tax matters and usually conduct their business in the office.

   Identify and describe several communications systems that AFS might consider using at its San Francisco office.

2. **Northern Paper Company.** Oki Sumio, the plant manager of Northern Paper Company, is upset with the cost and performance of her telephone service. Customers, salespeople, and vendors have complained that they cannot reach the company between 10 AM and 2 PM. The phone lines are almost always busy during those hours. People who only want to leave a message for someone at Northern are especially annoyed when they have to call and recall many times. Ms. Sumio is also upset with the cost of her plant's long-distance charges. She suspects that many employees are using Northern's long-distance lines to telephone friends, relatives, and stores for personal reasons. Ms. Sumio is considering purchasing a PBX for the company to improve the telephone service and reduce the cost.
   a. What special equipment and software for PBXs might Ms. Sumio consider for the new system?
   b. How will each piece of equipment and each type of software you list in part *a*

   solve a specific telephone system problem Ms. Sumio has identified?
   c. What concerns should she have regarding the acquisition of a PBX for the Northern plant?

3. **Cloris, Inc.** Cloris, Inc., employs 120 field representatives who visit customers by car. They often stay overnight in hotels and motels as they sweep their sales territories. Currently, field reps mail in sales orders at the end of each day. It takes about three days for the orders to reach the home office and another day for the orders to be processed. Cloris field reps can usually promise the customer that their orders will be shipped within five days. Rush orders are handled over the telephone. Problems arise when an item is out of stock or discontinued. Delays with such orders can exceed several weeks because the salesperson does not learn of the problem for several days. The customer then has to be contacted and sold alternative stock. It is also difficult to locate salespeople on the road or to keep up with their itineraries. Cloris has no way to contact all its salespeople quickly when stockouts occur, when stock is discontinued, or when special pricing policies have been implemented. The company wants to implement a communications system that would permit its field representatives to maintain close contact with the home office. The field reps need to contact the home office daily to pick up and deliver messages, and the home office also needs a way to contact the field reps when customers call or to advise them on the stock and price conditions.
   a. Identify and describe several communications systems that Cloris might explore to solve its problems. Your description should include how each system solves each problem.
   b. Identify and describe concerns that the Cloris management should be aware of for each communications system you included in your answer to part *a*.

SELECTED INTERNET REFERENCE SITES

ActiveX Web site (http://www.activex.com/).

AT&T Wireless Services Web site (http://www.airdata.com/assist/cds/index.htm).

Baynetworks home page (http://www.baynetworks.com/Products/).

BC Tel Wireless Data Services Web site (http://www.bctm.cdpd.net:80/switch/toc.htm).

Client/Server Computing magazine (on-line version) (http://www.sentrytech.com).

Data Communications magazine (on-line version) (http://www.data.com/).

Ericsson Web site (http://www.ericsson.com).

Hotwired Magazine (on-line version) (http://www.hotwired.com).

Institute of Electrical and Electronics Engineers, Inc. (http://www.ieee.org).

International Telecom Center home page (http://www.telematrix.com).

Internet Society's home page (http://www.isoc.org).

Java Web site (http://www.sun.com/java/).

LAN Magazine (on-line version) (http://www.lanmag.com).

LAN Times magazine (on-line version) (http://www.lantimes.com).

LookSmart Mobile Computing Web site (http://mulwala.looksmart.com:8080/r?l3,f,f&show=framesmall).

LookSmart Networking Standards Web site (http://mulwala.looksmart.com:8080/r?l3,f,f&show=framesmall).

LookSmart Networks and Communications Web site (http://mulwala.looksmart.com:8080/r?l3,f,f&show=framesmall).

Lycos search engine page (http://www.lycos.com).

NEC home page (http://www.nec.com).

Net Search search engine page (http://home.mcom.com/home/internet-directory.html).

Network Computing Magazine Online (http://techweb.cmp.com/nwc).

Spry, Inc., home page (http://www.spry.com).

Telecommunications Research Guide (http://www.quik.com/~certconsut/travel.html).

World Pages Web directories page (http://www.worldpages.com).

Yahoo! search engine page (http://www.yahoo.com).

ZD Anchordesk (http://www.zdnet.com/anchordesk/).

ZD Net Tech Locator (http://www.zdnet.com/locator/).

SELECTED REFERENCES AND READINGS

Boardman, B. "Global Network Management." *Network Computing,* August 15, 1996, p. 63.

Boardman, B. "Good Things Come in Small Packages: Combo PC Cards." *Network Computing,* April 1, 1996, p. 108.

Boardman, B. with M. Fratto. "Industrial Strength Remote Access." *Network Computing,* June 1, 1996, p. 56.

Case, T. L. and L. D. Smith. *Managing Local Area Networks.* New York: McGraw-Hill, 1995.

Conover, J. "CTI on Call: At Work with Voicemail/Soundcards." *Network Computing,* April 15, 1996, p. 76.

Freed, L. "Fast Connections." *PC Magazine,* June 11, 1996, p. 143.

Friedman, R. "Anywhere, Anytime: The Wireless Office of Today." *The Office,* August 1993, p. 8.

Goldman, J. E. *Local Area Networks: A Client/Server Approach.* New York: John Wiley & Sons, 1997.

Gunn, A. "Wireless Communications: Connecting over the Airwaves." *PC Magazine,* August 1993, p. 359.

Harbison, R. "Let Your Computer Do the Talking." *NetWare Solutions,* October 1996, p. 28.

Keen, P. G. W. and J. M. Cummins. *Networks in Action: Business Choices and Telecommunications Design.* Belmont, CA: Wadsworth Publishing Company, 1994.

Krantz, M. "Wired for Speed." *TIME,* September 23, 1996.

Mayer, J. H. "Bringing Remote Access Closer to Home." *Client/Server Computing,* April 1996, p. 45.

Molta, D. "How Far Is It to 802.11 Wireless LANs?" *Network Computing,* June 1, 1996, p. 126.

Pawlak, A. S. "Remote Node and Remote Control: Like Peanut Butter and Chocolate." *Network Computing,* May 15, 1996, p. 98.

Rogers, A. "Chicago Realtors Tap Remote Access." *Communications Week,* September 16, 1996, p. 35.

Rysavy, P. and A. Wittmann. "Wireless Data Made to Order." *Network Computing,* March 15, 1996.

Stamper, D. A. *Business Data Communications.* 4th ed. Redwood City, CA: The Benjamin/Cummings Publishing Co., 1994.

Trimm, J. "Priming the Pump: A Primer on ISDN and Frame Relay." *NetWare Solutions,* August 1996, p. 33.

Trulove, J. E. "Wired for Speed on Cat 5 Cable." *NetWare Solutions,* June 1996, p. 36.

Willis, D. "The State of the WAN." *Network Computing,* April 15, 1996, p. 50.

Willis, D. and J. Newman. "ISDN: PRIme for the Enterprise." *Network Computing,* May 15, 1996, p. 45.

Zgodzinski, D. "Enter ADSL." *Internet World,* October 1996, p. 72.

9

DISTRIBUTED SYSTEMS, THE INTERNET, AND OFFICE COMMUNICATIONS

CHAPTER OUTLINE

Manager's View

Distributed Processing

Distributed Databases

Client/Server Computing

Interorganizational Information Systems

Internet Communications

Internet Commerce

Intranet Communications

Office Communications

Management Summary

Key Terms for Managers

Review Questions

Questions for Discussion

Problems

Cases

Selected Internet Reference Sites

Selected References and Readings

As desktop computing equipment became more powerful and wide-spread, managers moved away from depending on a large, centralized host, for example, the large mainframe located at the home office. Instead, they began to move computing down to the department levels of organizations, and to the departments went not only computer systems but also the data used by those systems. Widespread acquisition of smaller computer platforms scattered enormous amounts of computing power and data across enterprises to laptops, desktops, workstations, and minicomputers. This situation has led organizations to connect and coordinate those computing resources so that they are accessible to employees throughout the organization and can be used collaboratively to solve organization problems.

As computing power and data spread to more and more departments, more and more offices were affected. Thus the distribution of computing power and data not only affected the way traditional computing was completed but also how office work was completed.

The need to network an organization's computers has become a key component to the success of many organizations. However, the need to connect your own organization's computers is just part of the picture. Organizations are finding that it is critical for them to connect to their customers and vendors as well as to the larger worldwide computer and organizational community.

Consider these now-common scenarios:

- An organization's mainframe is nearing its capacity to handle the organization's work. One computer vendor offers to sell the company a larger mainframe so that the organization can continue to grow. Another vendor offers to help the company use micro and minicomputers to expand the capacity of its information system. The second vendor's system will allow the organization to grow in smaller, less costly increments and cause less operational disruption, since the existing mainframe can continue to operate.

- A computer printer manufacturer and its major suppliers connect their computers so that the suppliers can detect when inventory items are low and resupply the company automatically. The connected computer systems complete the inventory resupply process without the need for paper forms and with a minimum of human intervention.

- An accounting firm spread out over 15 offices in 10 cities replaces its centralized database at its home office with databases kept at each office. Each office keeps detailed information about its work and its clients locally, sending only summary data to the home office. The new system saves the organization a great deal of money in common carrier costs.

- A sales representative wants to gather information about his clients. An executive in the same company wants to gather information about her competitors. Both use notebook computers to connect to the Internet to gather the data from computer systems across the nation, including computer systems run by the clients and competitors.

- A human resource manager wants to provide information to employees about company benefit packages. The package benefits and other information useful to employees change frequently, and it is costly for the manager to update this information. The revision process usually takes many weeks because brochures and manuals containing the updated information must be printed and distributed. The manager is considering using a company network called an intranet to distribute the information instead of printing hard copy brochures and manuals. The intranet would save the company the costs of printing and distributing the information and would reduce the entire update procedure to a matter of minutes.

- An organization wants its production engineers to attend a three-hour seminar and have an opportunity to question an industry expert. However, the engineers are scattered across the country, and the costs associated with travel and time away from work for the engineers would make the seminar too expensive. The organization is considering using the videoconferencing facilities of a hotel chain or movie theater chain to reduce these costs. The engineers could gather at local hotels or theaters and take part in a *teleconference* conducted from a facility near the home office. The conference system would allow engineers throughout the country to see, hear, and communicate with the expert and with each other without having to travel far.

- A national discount store wants to improve the way it receives goods and places the goods on store shelves. It appoints a task force of five inventory managers from different regions to study ways to improve the system. The managers "meet" regularly and share their ideas, reports, and other documents using the electronic mail, voice mail, fax, and audioconferencing. The project leader manages the team using group scheduling software, group to-do list software, and group calendar software.

- A small company wants to expand its customer base but lacks the financial clout for a national marketing campaign. The company decides to construct a company presence on the Internet that allows customers and potential customers around the globe to learn about the company, view pictures and information about its products, and place orders.

This chapter describes how organizations are using networking to leverage the computing power located in all their locations. It also describes how organizations are using networks to reach customers and suppliers and to help their own employees work collaboratively and more efficiently.

DISTRIBUTED PROCESSING

Distributed processing can be defined as a system in which both computer power and data occur at more than one site, and application programs are run at more than one site. Using that definition, distributed processing is associated with all types of networks, including WANs, PBXs, LANs, and even the Internet. For example, when users of mainframes, minicomputers, microcomputers, or smart terminals located over a large geographical region are connected to a WAN but process data locally, the network provides distributed processing (see Figure 9–1). When users of microcomputers located in different buildings on a campus are attached to a minicomputer system but still use their microcomputers to run application programs, the network is a distributed processing system. When microcomputer users on different floors of a building are connected to a LAN and run application software such as word processors, spreadsheets, or databases, the LAN is a distributed processing network (see Figure 9–2). A network doesn't have to be large or widely scattered geographically to be distributed.

Reasons for Implementing Distributed Processing

Distributed processing systems once were considered uneconomical because of the economies of scale associated with large, centralized computer systems. In recent years, however, distributed processing systems are becoming commonplace for a number of solid reasons.

Improved response time.   When data and processing power are located close to users, response time improves. Many of the delays associated with centralized systems are reduced, including the delays that occur when users contend for the use of an overloaded central host or when slow communications channels are used. Distributed processing may also reduce the variability of response time caused by high demand for services at certain times; for example, when the system is fast at 8 AM but slows down considerably at 11 AM as more employees log on.

Reduced costs.   It costs money to transmit data across distances, and transmission costs (leased lines, dial-up services, and so on) have been declining at a much slower rate than the cost of computer power. When branch offices can key in, edit, and

Figure 9–1

A geographically distributed processing system

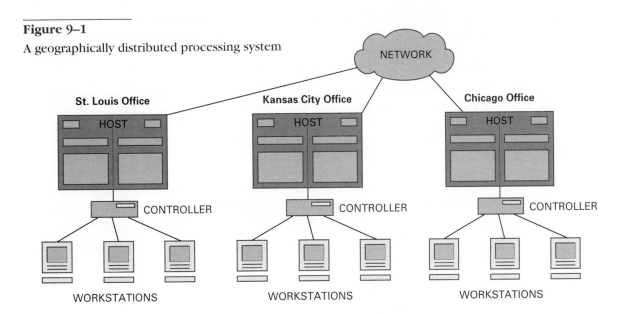

Figure 9–2

A locally distributed processing system

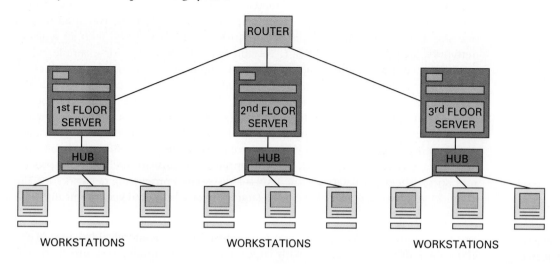

process much of the data locally, those transmission costs are substantially reduced. Keeping data needed only by one department or user with that department or user eliminates transmission costs.

Improved accuracy and currency. Giving control of data entry and data storage to local users frequently results in higher degrees of data accuracy and currency. A branch department clerk entering branch data is likely to know more about the data and therefore to spot errors more frequently. For example, the branch clerk is more likely than a clerk at a remote site to know how to spell a branch customer's name, who should be included in the branch payroll, or whether the stock number of a branch product is correct.

Reduced mainframe costs. Many local processors reduce the burden on a centralized host by distributing the work to local sites. Therefore, a larger computer system may not have to be added to the system to meet increased computing demands. A computer system that is nearing maximum load can provide a great incentive for distributed processing. Reducing the burden on the central host also improves the response time for those users who must use it.

Smoother growth. When a large computer system is acquired, the operational dislocation that results can be enormous. The system has to be installed, programs converted or developed and debugged, data converted or reentered, and new commands and procedures learned by everyone in the organization. The installation of a new system that uses a new operating system can be especially disruptive. On the other hand, if a new, small system is added at a remote site, only the remote site may be affected. In this way, growth and change in computing resources can be incremental and easier to manage, rather than all-pervasive and disruptive of the entire organization. The addition of distributed power may eliminate the need for a new central system.

Increased reliability. In a centralized system, if the host fails, the entire system fails. In a distributed system, failure of one processor disrupts only the operations dependent on that processor. Furthermore, because other processors are available on the network and because users may be able to switch processing to those sites, the disruption may not last long.

Resource sharing.   In a distributed system many users can share the computing resources located anywhere on the network, including expensive printers, large or fast data storage devices, other processors, or other peripherals. For example, a branch office in California might use the processor of a branch office in Florida because at 4 PM the California processor is very busy and the Florida processor (where it is 7 PM) is relatively idle.

Increased user satisfaction.   Because a centralized application-program development staff usually faces a large backlog of application development tasks, users may be dissatisfied with the staff's responsiveness. Users may welcome more control over computing power so that they can reduce the time they must wait for their tasks to be addressed.

Distributed Processing Concerns for Managers

Although distributed processing has become a welcome necessity for many organizations, it is not without problems. Some of the problems with a distributed processing system are discussed next.

Lack of professional MIS staff.   Small branch sites on the distributed network may be run by personnel with little or no training or experience with computing systems. The local employees may lack the knowledge or skills to manage their computing resources with the same care that professional MIS personnel normally associated with a centralized computing facility can provide.

Standardization.   When computing power is distributed, managers must maintain some form of organizationwide control over the acquisition of computer resources. Without control, local units might acquire incompatible equipment and software, and the system will be unable to provide integrated computing resources to everyone on the network. For example, compatibility problems occur when a network uses multiple operating systems and application software for the same level of computing power. Compatibility problems also occur when different communication protocols exist because of differing standards used in equipment acquisition. Solving conversion problems is almost never easy or inexpensive.

Given that some or all of the branches may not have computing professionals on site, local purchasers may be naive about costs and the appropriateness of the computing resources they are acquiring.

Documentation.   Application-program development at remote sites increases the risk that these programs may not be fully documented. Therefore, these "homegrown" programs could be difficult to update or maintain, especially if the original program developer is no longer an employee of the firm. Centralized application development departments are likely to enforce minimum program documentation standards; the single application developer at a remote site may not.

Data loss.   Archiving or backing up computer files is a tedious but necessary activity. In centralized computing departments, archiving is an established routine, and someone in the department is responsible for carrying out the routine systematically and regularly. Without some form of central control or enforcement of archiving procedures, inexperienced users of minicomputers and microcomputers at remote sites may treat the archiving of data too casually, and data loss is likely to result. Also, restarting a computer system and recovering data lost from a system failure is not an easy task. Professional MIS personnel, trained in restart and recovery procedures and equipped with the appropriate software tools, can handle system failure much easier and with much greater success than inexperienced and untrained personnel.

Security.   Most organizations keep data that are sensitive in one way or another. For example, all organizations keep confidential data on employees, customers, and vendors. Many organizations store data about new products, new production techniques, product and customer research, or marketing plans that they do not wish their competitors to obtain. Some organizations store data about national security matters or military equipment specifications. Centralized computing departments normally establish procedures for security, including the use of physical and electronic security procedures and devices, to keep confidential data confidential. Without some form of organizationwide control, security procedures for confidential data at small, remote computing sites may easily become lax, or they may not exist at all. Because distributing power usually means that local sites may view or download information from other sites, very confidential data could be written to a 3½-inch diskette and carried out the door of a branch office. In these locations the data may have been transferred to diskettes that are casually stored in an unlocked diskette caddy in an open office area.

Data consistency.   Distributed data processing usually means that both data and computing power are distributed. Without careful planning, monitoring, and controls, this situation invites increased risks of data redundancy and therefore data inconsistency, resulting in inconsistencies in the reports prepared by various units on the system.

System maintenance.   Large, centralized data centers have trained professionals who are experienced in program and system maintenance. They also usually have contracts with equipment and software vendors for maintenance of computer hardware and software. When computing power is distributed to small, remote sites, such on-site talent is less likely to be available. It may be very difficult to provide system maintenance swiftly or at all at every distributed site.

An Effective Distributed Processing System

Distributed processing systems must be managed very carefully to be effective. Usually some form of organizationwide monitoring, supervision, training, and control is necessary to ensure that the system does not get out of hand.

An effective system should also be easy to use. Users should not have to be concerned with where the data are or where the processing is occurring when they make a request of the system. To produce a report, for example, a manager should not have to know where the system will find the necessary data or which processors and communications systems it needs to use. This feature of a distributed system is usually referred to as *location transparency.*

An effective system should also guard against loss of data consistency. The software and procedures should provide automatic systemwide updates. A user who updates a record in a file should not have to be concerned with whether or not the system updates the data wherever those data exist in the system. This feature of a distributed system is usually called *update transparency.*

A major concern of computer system professionals is in the explosion of computing power resulting from the availability of inexpensive computing systems such as minicomputers and microcomputers. Many departments or individuals within organizations, dissatisfied with the responsiveness of the centralized computing department, are going it alone with their own equipment. Though this response provides short-term solutions, it often creates major long-term problems for the organization. As a manager, you need to understand not only the advantages of local computing power but also the need for professional organizationwide help in managing that computing power.

The nature of the organization is another consideration in planning for distributed processing. Organizing information systems in a distributed processing fashion is often likely to be effective in organizations that are decentralized in other ways. For example, a large firm may acquire a number of other firms as subsidiaries that produce different, though related, products. The large firm may choose not to meddle in the way that the subsidiaries function, delegating to each a great deal of decision-making authority. These subsidiaries may even use many different types of computer systems to support their functions. In such a environment, distributed processing is likely to make a great deal of sense because it fits the way the total organization is structured and operates.

DISTRIBUTED DATABASES

In a centralized system, the computer system and the database of an organization are both found at one location under the management of one group. Databases in this setting are called **centralized databases.** Organizations that need to decentralize their computer processing may also need to decentralize their databases. When computing databases are scattered rather than centralized, they are called **distributed database systems.**

Replicated Databases

When processing is distributed, the data to be processed usually must be located at the processing site. This means that the database, or parts of the database, must be distributed. There are basically two ways to distribute a database. The first is to provide duplicates of all data at all sites (see Figure 9-3). This approach is called a **replicated database.** If every location must have frequent access to the same data, replication of

Figure 9–3

A replicated database

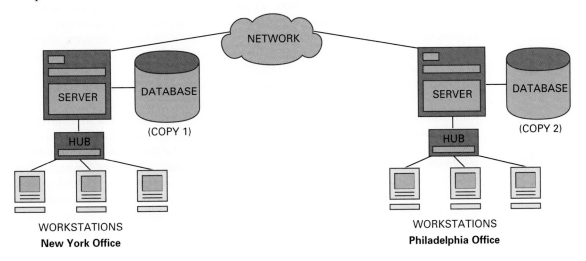

WORKSTATIONS
New York Office

WORKSTATIONS
Philadelphia Office

the database may be recommended. However, replication of a database is very expensive in terms of computer system resources, and it can be difficult and costly to maintain consistency for each data element. On the other hand, replication does provide some measure of security by providing duplicates of the database in case of failure at one location.

Partitioned Databases

Another means of distributing the database is to partition it. The database may be divided into segments that are appropriate for certain locations and distributed only to those locations (see Figure 9-4). This approach is called a **partitioned database.** The database may be partitioned along functional lines; for example, financial, marketing, and administrative data may be kept at corporate headquarters, and relevant production and personnel data may be kept at each manufacturing plant and office site.

Partitioning may also be achieved along geographical lines. That is, all locally relevant information—financial, marketing, administrative, production, and personnel—may be kept at each location of an organization. If an organization has four divisions, each quite different in purpose and each located at a different site, partitioning on a geographical basis may make a lot of sense. If a distributor maintains seven warehouses for storing merchandise at seven locations, partitioning the inventory database on a geographical basis also may make sense.

Many organizations with many locations partition the database hierarchically. Detailed data, such as payroll and sales data, are kept close to their source—the local site. Regional and national locations receive increasingly less detailed summaries of the detailed data as these data are transmitted up through the organization's hierarchy. For example, the detailed information on customer orders, salesperson commissions, and product inventory status may be kept at each store location for a national department store chain. Only summary data on total sales, total commissions, and total inventory may be kept at the home office.

Advantages and Disadvantages of Distributed Databases

Distributed database systems usually reduce costs for an organization because they reduce the costs of transferring data between remote sites and the organization's headquarters.

Distributed database systems may also provide organizations with faster response times for filling orders, answering customer requests, or providing managers with information. However, distributed database systems also magnify the problems of databases. They compound the problems of control over the database, increase problems of security for the database, increase data redundancy and the resulting danger to data consistency, and increase the need for more computer resources. Unless the distribution of a database is done very carefully, many of the advantages of having a database in the first place can be lost.

The increased power and use of microcomputers by managers and professionals have created additional problems for database administrators. When managers download data from a centralized database to their microcomputers, a truly centralized database no longer exists. Parts of the database are segmented and distributed to these microcomputers. Because of the backlog of requests to be filled at many management information systems departments, other departments may become so frustrated that they decide to acquire their own minicomputers or microcomputers to provide their own information services. Consequently, additional files and databases are established throughout an organization, creating much of the same redundancy, inconsistency, and incompatibility that characterized corporate data in the 1960s and 1970s.

Figure 9–4

A partitioned database

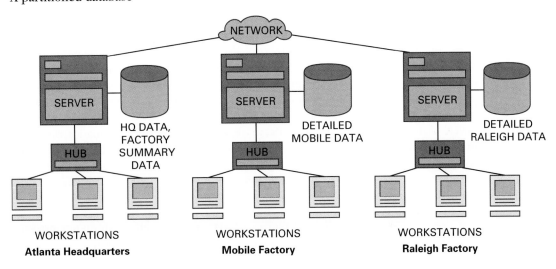

CLIENT/SERVER COMPUTING   *57*

Many organizations are now adopting a form of distributed processing called **client/server computing.** The basic notion of a client/server computing system is that application processing is divided between a *client,* which is typically a personal computer, and a *server,* which may be a file server on a local area network, a minicomputer, or a mainframe. The client processes run on the personal computer and make requests of the server processes, which, as noted, may run on several computer platforms. Typically components of client/server computing are a relational database, a powerful server or servers, personal computer workstations, a network, and client software for the workstations.

SQL Servers

A common application of client/server computing is the use of special relational database software called Structured Query Language, or a SQL server. A *SQL server* is a software package that usually runs on a dedicated networked computer that is also called a SQL server. The SQL server computer usually devotes all its energies to managing the database software and does not handle other network tasks. SQL server software performs database applications faster and more reliably than typical LAN-based database management software. A major reason for this efficiency is that SQL servers process client workstation requests for data differently than other types of LAN database management systems do. For example, when you request a record for a LAN database that is on a file server, the typical LAN database management system sends a large block of records from the server over the network to your workstation. Your workstation then must sort through the block of records to find the one you wanted. Furthermore, you won't use much of the traffic placed on the network—only one of the records in the block. In other words, typical LAN database management systems treat file servers as not much more than remote hard disk drives for the workstation. This system is equivalent to asking a bat boy to get you your favorite bat and then having him drag the whole bat rack to the on-deck circle so that you can pick the one you want.

In contrast, a client workstation might ask SQL server software to send all records that match certain selection parameters; for example, all employees who earn an hourly rate of more than $15. The SQL server software processes the request *at the SQL server* and sends only those records that meet the selection parameters. The client workstation then displays the records for the user. The SQL server not only stores but also processes the records. This feature reduces traffic on the network and also might improve processing performance because the workstation may be a less expensive, slower microcomputer than the file server where the processing occurs.

Because SQL servers perform the bulk of the processing, the machines they are placed on are usually fast and powerful microcomputers. To ensure fast performance on LANs that make heavy use of a database, many SQL servers are loaded on multiprocessor microcomputers. A LAN-based client/server system might contain client workstations, a SQL server computer, a printer server, a communications server, and a file server for network control and management and the remaining applications (see Figure 9–5).

In a SQL server environment, records may be sorted on the server running the SQL server database software and sent to a workstation, or client, running a different version of the same database software or another application program for additional processing. For example, a dedicated SQL file server (also called the *back-end processor*) running SQL Server from Oracle may sort and send records requested by a workstation (also called the *front-end processor*). The workstation then reads the records and further processes them by placing them into a Lotus 1-2-3 spreadsheet template.

In client/server computing, the back-end processor provides access to the database and a variety of database services, such as remote connectivity and data security. The front-end processor often provides data entry and data validation and also formats and displays the data. Both the back-end and the front-end processors may perform operations on the data, such as sorting and calculating.

Client/server computing, however, is not limited to local area networks. The basic plan of client/server models is to permit workstations to access data wherever they are found and to have many processors perform whatever processing needs to be done according to their availability and capability. Thus client/server computing may include WANs as well as LANs, and mainframes and minicomputers as well as microcomputers. These systems can use mainframes to perform large, repetitive processing

Figure 9–5

A LAN-based client/server system

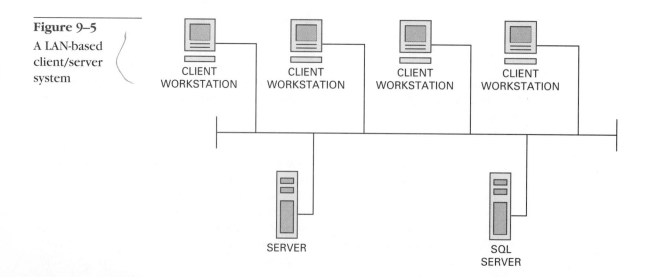

operations, such as sorting, while leaving the formatting and display of the results to microcomputers, which typically use more user-friendly and easier-to-understand GUI software. For example, you might search a database for specific records using a relational database management system on an IBM mainframe, but the final results of the search might be displayed on a client microcomputer system running a GUI-based, microcomputer spreadsheet package.

Downsizing

The bottom line is that client/server computing can make the data in any of the databases that exist on an organization's networks available to any end user who has a microcomputer workstation and the authority to use the data. Furthermore, client/server computing promises to allow whatever computing resources on the networks can best perform a service do so, using each network computing resource to its best advantage.

Because of the power and efficiency of SQL servers, client/server computing systems running on local area networks have been replacing mainframe-based information systems in many organizations. Organizations faced with high maintenance costs on existing mainframe computer hardware and software or the need to upgrade those systems are increasingly **downsizing** to LAN-based, client/server computing systems from older, preexisting or "legacy," mainframe-based information systems to reduce costs. Downsizing can provide substantial reductions in systems costs, including equipment costs, software purchase costs, annual hardware and software maintenance costs, and application development costs. The greatest cost reduction is likely to occur when an organization proposes to downsize applications to equipment already in place, such as microcomputers, LANs, and the supporting operating systems and applications software. By using its current equipment, the organization manages to partially protect existing system investment.

Many organizations now view client/server systems as vehicles for replacing or expanding costly mainframe systems with the less expensive power of personal computers. Most practitioners do not suggest replacing mainframe systems that are operating efficiently and effectively. They do suggest that mainframe systems be migrated down to mini and micro systems when the mainframe becomes inadequate to its tasks or obsolete, or when new application systems need to be developed.

INTERORGANIZATIONAL INFORMATION SYSTEMS

Information systems in the past have been largely confined to organization boundaries. For example, an accounting information system was typically confined to accepting data from employees of the organization, processing the data, and then providing reports about the data to employees. Although accounting reports might be shared beyond the company (for example, with the IRS and the SEC), the initiation and distribution of reports were in the hands of organization staff. Information system boundaries today, however, are increasingly distributed over more than one organization. These types of distributed systems are called **interorganizational information systems** and are another application of client/server technology. In this case, the servers may be in one organization and the clients in another.

Interorganizational information systems can be defined as information systems that permit an employee of one organization to allocate resources and initiate business processes in another organization directly. The two broad types of interorganizational information systems are electronic data interchange and electronic market systems.

Electronic Data Interchange

Electronic data interchange (EDI) systems are primarily bilateral information systems that allow two organizations to exchange information electronically. Typically, an EDI is an information system that links an organization to its customers or suppliers. For example, a buyer and a seller might create links between the databases of each organization to exchange purchase and sales information electronically, thereby eliminating many paper forms and procedures, such as purchase orders and sales receipts. In such a system, the supplier's computer system monitors the buyer's computerized database to determine when inventory levels of a product need replenishing. When this level occurs, the seller's computer system initiates a purchase order process within the buyer's computer system. EDI handles purchase orders, payments, and inventory and account updates automatically between the two computer systems.

In fact, an important application of communications technology by organizations has been the reduction of costs pertaining to the management of inventory and purchasing. Many large firms have required their smaller suppliers to use EDI to monitor the large company's inventory levels and deliver inventory only when it is needed. EDI used in this way passes the burden of large inventories with their accompanying maintenance, interest, insurance, and tax costs to the supplier. The buyer's inventories become lean. In addition, EDI substantially reduces all the procedures and paper forms that were printed, examined, mailed, stored, and otherwise managed. As paper purchase orders and sales orders and other forms become relics of the past, business processes become faster, more efficient, and less costly. The cost savings are shared by the sellers, too.

EDI systems may be classified into supplier-focused systems and customer-focused systems. For example, Wal-Mart has created a supplier-focused EDI system that requires suppliers to query Wal-Mart inventory databases and deliver the appropriate inventory in amounts and within delivery times set by prior agreements. Suppliers are fined for not meeting their agreements and can, if failures occur more than a certain number of times, lose the right to sell to Wal-Mart. There are obvious advantages to the suppliers in these systems, although, at the very least, suppliers gain increased sales and a more efficient sales order system.

You have seen how EDI can be used to reduce inventories and costs to an organization through supplier-focused EDI systems. In addition, companies can use EDI to increase sales through customer-focused systems. Levi Strauss, for example, hoped to use EDI as a means of turning around declining sales patterns. The company developed Levilink, an EDI system that processes orders and deliveries. The system allows customers to order products in small amounts, as they are needed, instead of in large orders. The orders are then delivered by UPS within two days. The system allowed Design, Inc., a Levi Strauss customer with a chain of 60 stores, to eliminate its entire warehouse system. Thus a firm can use EDI to gain a competitive advantage.

In other cases, where most of an organization's competitors already possess EDI systems, developing an EDI system with a customer or a supplier may be a competitive necessity. For example, R. J. Reynolds Tobacco Co. (RJR) sent letters to 1,500 vendors in December 1992, informing them that unless they had EDI capabilities within about a month they would get no new business from RJR. The company took this drastic step because each purchase order costs the company about $75 to process, whereas processing EDI purchase orders costs the company only $.93. At the time, the 1,500 companies produced 11,000 orders a year, which at a savings of about $74 each, meant an annual savings of almost $815,000 to RJR.[1]

---

[1]"EDI or Else," *Datamation*, February 15, 1993, p. 15.

Electronic Market Systems

Electronic market systems are multilateral information systems that allow two or more organizations to share data about products, services, and prices. An example of an electronic market system is the electronic version of the Official Airlines Guide, which allows sellers (the airlines) to share flight information and prices with buyers.

Electronic market systems usually reduce the power of sellers by providing market data to buyers in a convenient form. However, sellers do get the opportunity to present information about promotions, prices, products, and services. If the electronic market system is popular, such as an airline reservation system, it is imperative for an organization to participate; failure to do so reduces the availability of its products or services to potential buyers and could so disable the company that it becomes unable to compete effectively. For the buyer, however, electronic market systems hold many advantages. The systems inherently put price and feature pressures on sellers and generate better, less expensive products and services for buyers. The systems also reduce the costs of purchasing because they reduce the costs of searching for products and comparing features, prices, delivery methods, and terms.

INTERNET COMMUNICATIONS

Many people describe the **Internet** as a network of networks or a relatively ungoverned aggregation of millions of computers and computer networks located throughout the world. In fact, the Internet provides yet another example of client/server computing. The Internet allows you to connect your PC (the client) to computers (the servers) located at sites around the world to use their services.

The Internet began in the 1960s as a means to connect research institutions and laboratories with military and government agencies. Originally called ARPANET, for the Advanced Research Projects Agency that managed it in the beginning, the network has joined with other public and private networks over the years to create a vast, worldwide connection of computer systems. The Internet now connects millions of subscribers, including government agencies, military agencies, educational institutions, small businesses, corporations, and individuals to thousands of interconnected networks. Hundreds of thousands of new subscribers join the Internet each year, with the number doubling every 12 to 15 months. Membership is expected to reach the hundreds of million by the millennium.

Access to the Internet can be gained easily if your organization already is a member. All you need to do is gain an ID and password from your organization. Technically, access can be achieved in many ways including using a modem or using a local area network with Internet access. Private companies and individuals can also gain access to the Internet by subscribing to organizations that provide access and special software, such as America Online.

The organization providing access is known, fittingly, as an **Internet service provider (ISP).** An ISP has one or more banks of modems to allow you to connect to them from remote locations. ISPs, in turn, connect to network service providers, or NSPs, that run area, national, or worldwide high-speed networks (see Figure 9-6).

Internet Features

So what can you find on the Internet? Just about anything is the answer. For example, the Internet has magazines, databases, bulletin boards, music, weather, sports information, forums or discussion groups, news in print, news in video, news in sound, shopping malls, and electronic mail. You can view college course materials on the Internet, take courses on the Internet, even earn degrees on the Internet. You can visit museums

Figure 9–6

Connecting to the Internet by modem

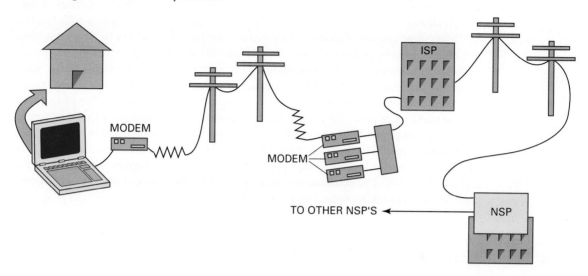

and view exhibits; you can visit libraries and check out books. You can also find information about job openings and careers on the Internet (see Manager's Memo 9-1). The Internet allows you to upload and download shareware, to transfer files between Internet users, to take part in discussions of topics from Zen to world trade, to receive and send e-mail messages, to shop, to bank, and of course, to browse documents.

Browsing Documents

One of the most appealing and useful features of the Internet is the **World Wide Web,** or more simply, the Web. The Web is a subset of the computer systems on the Internet consisting of those computer systems (the servers) that store documents that can be viewed by other computer systems (the clients). The server computers run Web server software, and the client computer systems run Web browser software. Browser software, or more simply, a **browser,** lets users view documents, called **Web pages,** on the servers, which are often called **Web sites** (see Figure 9-7).

Web sites have Web addresses, which in typical computerese, are called *universal resource locators* (URLs). You will probably find *Web address* a more straightforward term. In Figure 9-7 the Web site address is *http://www.irwin.com.* The *http* stands for hypertext transfer protocol, which is the set of rules and procedures for sending and receiving hypertext documents. The *www* stands for the World Wide Web. *Irwin* is the name given to the computer that contains the Web documents, and *com* stands for the type of Web site—in this case, commercial.

Recently, the vendors of office suites (a package of integrated software including word processing, spreadsheet, database, presentation, and other software) have made all of their programs web enabled—capable of viewing Web documents and of translating the documents they produce into Web documents. Using these suites, the manager can view a Web document from a word processor or convert a spreadsheet document into a Web page for viewing by browsers.

Managers can find a great deal of useful information on the Web. Various Web sites provide stock prices, stock price histories, and news and information about the companies themselves. Some Web sites even allow the manager to buy and sell stock. There are many web sites that provide information about competitors. Managers can gather the SEC financial statement reports that a competitor filed, as well as company

Manager's Memo 9–1	FINDING A JOB ON THE WEB

The Web is full of information about jobs, including job openings, typical salaries, and career information. The Web addresses below contain a great deal of job and career information that you may find useful. Beware, however. Web sites come and go. Some of the sites listed may have gone out of existence before you read this book. They may also have changed their web address.

Some Web sites let you post your resume so that employers can read it and contact you if they are interested, some Web sites post job openings for your review, and some post both resumes and openings. Some sites post job openings for one organization and others contain job openings from many organizations. Some sites limit themselves to resumes and openings and others provide general information about careers, career paths, and typical earnings. Some sites provide information about a narrow range of occupations; others restrict themselves to openings in a specific city, state, or region.

The list below is just a sample to give you an idea of the richness and diversity of the Web sites that contain job information. The list includes the name of each site, its Web address, and a brief description of its contents.

- *NationJob Online Jobs Database*
  (http://www.nationjob.com)

  This Web site provides thousands of job listings and profiles of the companies that have the openings. Employers use the site to post openings; job seekers use it to find them. You can select a set of criteria for your job search, including type of work, location, salary range, and educational requirements.

- *Entertainment Recruiting Network*
  (http://www.showbizjobs.com)

  Provides job listings, resumes, and career advice for the entertainment industry, including film, TV, radio, gaming, theme park, and recording industries. The jobs listed are not just performing jobs. The site lists jobs in the entertainment industry comprehensively: jobs for accountants, sales personnel, human resource management, information systems specialists, legal personnel, etc.

- *Yahoo! (Metro-New York)*
  (http://www.ny.yahoo.com)

  One site from Yahoo!'s many sites pertaining to jobs and careers. Contains resumes and classified ads for job openings for people and organizations in the metropolitan New York City area. You can search for jobs by job function, industry, or even organization name.

- *Marketing Classifieds*
  (http://www.marketingjobs.com)

  This site accepts resumes and job opening information in the field of marketing. It contains a resume database, a job-listing database, and company profiles. The site uses a search engine that lets users search these databases using key words. It also contains links to other, related Web sites containing information about resume preparation, professional marketing associations, and other marketing sites.

- *JOB Source* (http://www.jobsource.com)

  This site provides not only searchable job listings and company profiles but also opportunities for job internships and part-time jobs. The site specializes in listing resumes of college graduates and provides information about the preparation of resumes, career trends, salary trends, and graduate studies. Many links to other job and career sites are provided, as well.

- *Saludos Web* (http://www.saludos.com/)

  A site containing career information, resume postings, and job listings especially relevant to the Hispanic community. Jobs in more than a dozen fields are listed by field and by state. Career information, resume help, and company information is available. Like many other sites, this site contains links to other Web sites pertaining to jobs and careers.

Many other job and career sites can be found by using a search engine. Simply enter careers, jobs, employment, or other key words that might narrow the results you get so that the site listings are more pertinent to your job and career interests.

announcements, news about company sales, products, legal actions the company is defending against as well as pursuing, and changes in the organizational structure. Managers can also gather information from the competitor's own Web site and from on-line news magazines that carry stories about the competitor. In fact, the problem of Web browsing is the tremendous amount of information contained in the millions

Figure 9–7

A Web page at a
Web site viewed by
a browser

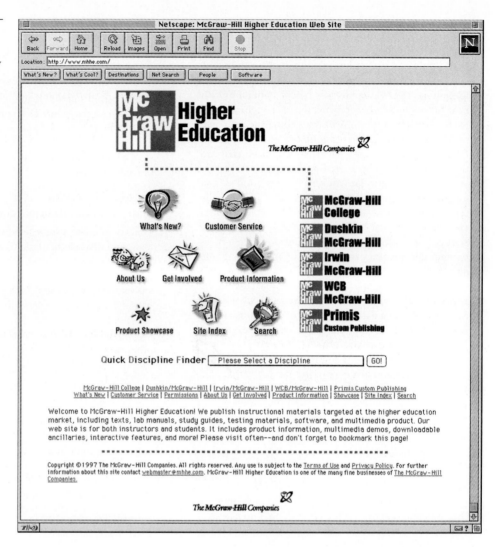

of Web sites. What you need is a means of sifting through all these Web sites and finding the information you need. Here is where the search engine enters—stage right.

Searching for Information

To help you find what you want on the Web, some Web sites provide search tools, or as information systems professionals call them, search engines. A **search engine** (see Figure 9-8) allows you to enter one or more key words describing the topic of your search. The search engine then scans computers throughout the world to find information containing those key words. For example, if you want information about a competitor, such as General Motors, you would enter General Motors in the text box and click on "search." The search engine would then search for information about General Motors and display a list of Web sites that contain information about the company. To view the information found at any site, you would simply click on the link to it. In Figure 9-8b, each underlined phrase is a link. (The first one is General Motors Links.)

Documents on the Web are usually hypertext documents, which means they may contain links to other documents. A link may be highlighted or underlined text or an image or icon. Clicking on the link transports you to the other Web page. The linked documents may be on the same computer or on computers in other continents. The

Figure 9–8

(a) The key words entered into the text box and (b) the results of a search

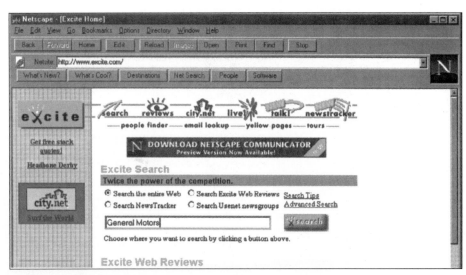

Courtesy of Excite Inc.

(a)

Courtesy of Excite Inc.

(b)

Figure 9–9

A PointCast page
showing news
about a company

documents are also likely to be hypermedia documents in that they contain not only text, but also sound, voice, images, and video clips. Furthermore, the document may contain animated text or images and even 3-D images.

A new specification for the Internet, which was under discussion at the time this text was written, would allow a person using a browser to make a telephone call, fax a message, or view a television show directly from the browser. The telephone, fax device, and television channel would be just another linkable Web address on the browser. For example, you might click on the highlighted name of a customer, and that name would actually be a link to your telephone which would dial the number of the customer.

Push versus Pull Internet

Ordinarily, when users want information, they search for it by scouring Internet servers and "pulling" Web pages from the servers down to their workstations. This approach requires time, especially the time to seek out the Web pages on topics of interest to the user. Recently, however, companies providing Internet services have begun to "push" Web pages to users based on the users' stated interests. For example, PointCast, Inc., allows users to pick topics of interest to them, such as news, sports, weather, and business information, and then sends Web pages containing information about those topics to users daily (see Figure 9–9). A user may wish to be kept up-to-date about the weather in St. Louis, the news about the St. Louis Cardinals, and the news about selected companies, including their stock prices and price histories. Each day, the user receives information about these topics from PointCast's browser. The free service is paid for by the advertisements that appear on the browser as the user views the information. Some companies are providing more in-depth searches to users, including searching not only Internet servers but also on-line databases. These companies then push the information to the user via the Internet for a fee.

Figure 9–10
Internet
connection choices

Connection type	Speed
Standard telephone (analog) modem	28.8 Kbps to 56 Kbps
Integrated Services Digital Network (ISDN) modem	56 Kbps to 128 Kbps
Direct Broadcast Satellite line	400 Kbps for downloading; 28.8 Kbps for uploading
Asymmetric Digital Subscriber Line (ADSL)	6 Mbps for downloading; 640 Kbps for uploading
Cable TV modem	500 Kbps to 10 Mbps

Note: ISDN, ADSL, and cable TV lines and modems are described in Manager's Memo 8–1 in Chapter 8. Telephone modems are also described in Chapter 8.

Internet Connection Problems

The tremendous increase in Internet use has led to two major problems. First, it has led to difficulty connecting to Internet service providers. For example, America On-line (AOL) in January of 1997 decided to offer its subscribers a flat monthly rate for unlimited access time, much like Internet service providers offer their subscribers. The response from AOL's members was overwhelming. The number of hours AOL members spent on-line in September 1996 was 1,500,000. That figure jumped to 4,200,000 hours in January 1997. AOL was so overwhelmed that many subscribers were unable to gain access at all, and a number of them, along with states attorneys general, filed suit against the service. The AOL case illustrates both the tremendous demand that exists for low-cost unlimited access to Internet and on-line services and also the inadequacy of the current communications systems available to provide those services. In the AOL case, subscriber demand greatly exceeded the banks of modems and the number of lines available from AOL. Some ISPs believe that a ratio of about 10-15 lines per subscriber is sufficient to provide reasonably swift access. In January 1997 AOL had about 300,000 lines for about 8,000,000 subscribers, or roughly 26 lines for each subscriber.[2]

Second, the more sophisticated features of the Internet have led to huge increases in the size of the Web pages sent over the channels to Internet users. It takes a lot more capacity to send a Web page full of images, animations, and photographs than it does one filled only with text. A major problem has been the capacity of the channels that connect you to an ISP, the ISP to an NSP, and NSPs to each other. Of those channels, the one with the lowest speed, and thus with the greatest capacity problems, is usually the channel from you to your ISP. Connecting to an ISP with a modem that runs at 28.8 Kbps or 56 Kbps can become a bottleneck when you wish to download graphics-intensive Web pages or listen to an on-line TV program. Common carriers, including cable companies, are beginning to provide alternative technologies that would allow you to connect to your ISP at much higher speeds (see Figure 9–10).

To solve the capacity crunch problem, some companies are turning to privately run networks. These Internet networks are offered by ISPs that guarantee capacity to their subscribers. Some industry analysts suggest that the Internet will be divided into a two-tier service in the future. One tier will be inexpensive, designed for the masses,

[2]V. B. Hick, "AOL's Problems Highlight Online Growing Pains," *St. Louis Post-Dispatch,* February 2, 1997, Section E, p. 1E.

and will use the current Internet system. The other will be privately run Internets that offer much higher capacity and greater reliability and performance. These private Internets will connect large organizations willing to pay the higher service fees.

Sending E-Mail

A number of Internet e-mail software packages are available, and some browser software also has e-mail features. Unlike a company e-mail package, which might be deliberately limited to communications within and between company employees, Internet e-mail allows you to correspond with the millions of Internet users around the globe.

Managers can use Internet e-mail for both internal organization messages and external messaging. E-mail can be extremely useful, allowing members of project teams to keep up-to-date, allowing field personnel to maintain vital links to their home offices, and allowing sales representatives to reach customers. E-mail can also improve customer service by allowing customers to reach customer support and sales personnel within the firm quickly and easily. E-mail can even be used by marketing departments to gather information from current or prospective customers.

E-mail is discussed in more detail in the section on office communications.

Electronic Discussion Groups

One feature of the Internet is the user group feature, usually called **usenet newsgroups.** A newsgroup is an electronic discussion group that permits people with a mutual interest in a topic to conduct a "virtual" conversation. The Internet offers thousands of newsgroups covering every imaginable topic. Newsgroup conversations are virtual because the participants do not talk to each other in real time; rather, they "post" messages to the newsgroup and read the responses to their messages—usually at a later time. Newsgroup members may use e-mail or browser software to post and read these messages.

A newsgroup is often monitored or managed by a person called a *moderator.* The moderator may, from time to time, synthesize commonly asked questions and their answers into a **frequently-asked-question (FAQ) file.** Customers can use this file to see if the problem or question they have has already been answered. That way, they can get immediate help without waiting for other newsgroup members to respond to their inquiry.

Managers can use newsgroups in a variety of ways. Newsgroups can be formed around a company's product lines or by customer service representatives. A product newsgroup allows customers to post questions that other customers and product support personnel can answer. A newsgroup is like a worldwide bulletin board where interested people ask questions, post information, and read the postings of others. The problems and questions that customers post can provide valuable information to product engineers and advertising personnel.

A local form of newsgroup, one that can be used only by people who are allowed to subscribe to the group, can be an effective project management tool. By allowing team members to post and read information, these newsgroups allow broad and swift communication. These types of newsgroups are called *listservs.* Many college instructors provide listservs for each of their classes so that students and instructors can discuss course topics, changes of assignment, and study tips.

Transferring Files

Another popular feature of the Internet is the ability to share files with other users. This feature is called **file transfer protocol (FTP).** FTP is a procedure by which you can upload (send) or download (receive) a file to or from another computer system. This feature can be very helpful to collaborative work in an organization, allowing team members to share their documents, spreadsheets, and slide presentations. FTP can also be helpful for customer service. Many software vendors allow customers to download updated versions of their software. When the original version of the software has bugs, the vendor can make available the updated software, containing fixes to the bugs, to customers quickly and easily.

Running Programs on Remote Computers

If you have the authority to do so, you can run programs on the computer systems on the Internet to which you connect. For example, Pine is a popular e-mail program that Internet users can run on distant computer systems. To connect to the host computer system to run a program, the user runs **Telnet,** which is a client communications program that interacts with the server Telnet program running on the host. Using Telnet, the client acts like a terminal attached to the host. The program, the data, and all the processing is completed on the host. The results are simply displayed on the client computer system.

Network PCs and the Internet

One expected use of the network computer is to connect to a host on the Internet and use the host's superior computing power and storage capacity to perform most of the work. In that way, the network computer system does not need as much power as the usual desktop PC. Having a network PC telnet to a host to run programs and process data can make a lot of sense in some business environments. The system allows managers to purchase much less expensive client machines and place most of the power and storage capacity on the server.

This strategy is the exact opposite of today's large office suites. The typical computer system you buy today comes already loaded with a suite of software programs, such as Microsoft Office. These programs occupy a large amount of storage space on the desktop's hard drive, and take a lot of power to run swiftly. An opposite strategy is to load the minimum amount of software on a network computer and download whatever programs are needed on the fly. That is, a network computer might have a small word processing program installed on it. If the user needed to perform more sophisticated tasks, the necessary additional programming code would be downloaded from the host to which the network computer is attached—automatically, without the user having to take any action (see Manager's Memo 9-2).

Internet Telephony and Desktop Conferencing

A use of the Internet that is expected to grow is conducting real-time telephone conversations and providing desktop conferencing with video on the Internet. (See the section on videoconferencing later in this chapter.) At present, real-time telephone conversations are a bit scratchy sounding, and delays in the conversations can occur because all parts of the conversation are not necessarily routed together. Another problem is that both parties must use the same software.

The business applications for Internet telephony would be very great because it would permit voice and data to travel over the same line. A customer who is shopping on the Internet could click on a telephone icon and talk to a salesperson, or a customer could talk to a customer support person while viewing a FAQ file. A surgeon might even talk to a radiologist who is at another location while viewing an X-ray of a patient.

As you can see, the Internet can be used effectively to support collaborative effort among employees and to improve customer service. The Internet can also be used to gather information on a wide range of topics of interest to managers and employees, including intelligence pertaining to competitors. In addition, the Internet can provide a major means of advertising and selling products and services. In other words, the Internet can be used for commerce.

Manager's Memo 9–2	THE JAVA REVOLUTION

Java from Sun Microsystems, Inc. is a client/server application development system that promises to change the way we think about the Internet, intranets, or extranets. Java allows application developers to create software that can be run not only on any machine but also over the Web. Whole office suites have been developed in Java code; for example, Corel Office for Java. However, the basic thrust of Java is to allow the development of "applets," or small applications that can be downloaded from a server to a client from an Internet or intranet server when it is needed. Java applets let system designers place "thin" clients on users' desks, since the usual RAM, hard drive capacity, and CPU power are not needed to store and run full-blown, integrated office suites on the desktop. Instead, the parts of a program that are needed are downloaded as needed to the client workstation. In other words, application software is stored on the server and supplied to the client in small doses on demand.

Java applets are designed to run on any machine that runs a browser that supports Java. Ideally, very thin clients, such as network computers, running Java would be able to run any applet software that is on any server to which the client can connect. In fact, Java clients can include "smart" telephones with built-in displays, personal digital assistants, TV set-top devices, kiosk devices, and point-of-sale computer systems.

Some analysts envision Java as a potential Microsoft killer because Java can reduce an organization's dependence on full-blown operating systems (such as Microsoft Windows) and office suites (such as Microsoft Office). However, Microsoft has developed ActiveX, which it is positioning as a Java competitor. Also, creating a set of Java applets that offer the maturity, complexity, and comprehensiveness of existing office suites may take several years.

Java information systems are platform independent; therefore, they allow organizations to leverage their existing computer systems, including those that are not powerful enough to run the newer office suites well. In fact, Java allows an organization to shift its emphasis from being desktop centric to network centric.

Java was introduced in 1995 and has already seen incredible acceptance in the corporate world. One survey reported that more than 60 percent of Fortune 1000 companies already have developed Java applications and that more than 40 percent expect Java to play a strategic role in application development in their organizations within the year.

Source: Christopher Barr, "Will Java End Microsofts' Hegemony?" *CNET (Online)*, February 3, 1997.

INTERNET COMMERCE

The Internet represents a major lure to the business world. Through one connection—a Web site containing advertising about a company and its products—even a small organization can reach millions of potential customers throughout the world. That prospect has many companies working feverishly on ways to achieve it. However, advertising is not the only commercial venture on the Internet. Electronic commerce, or **e-commerce,** over the Internet is being explored on a wide front by many organizations. The appeal of the Internet is especially high to companies that sell their products to customers via similar media, such as catalog firms that use mail order and firms that use TV shopping program formats. Unfortunately, sales to the public via the Internet have been disappointing so far. However, some types of e-commerce are doing well. For example, at this writing some 60 percent of the electronic magazines on the Web were reporting profits. So were many of the Web companies that provide services such as search tools and market reports. These firms were making money from a variety of sources, including advertising revenue, that is, they were charging other companies to advertise on their Web pages.

Many reasons have been suggested for the low rate of success experienced in some forms of e-commerce. First, many Internet users are suspicious of purchasing over the net. When organizations can promise secure transactions over the net, analysts expect net sales to grow rapidly. Second, Internet reliability must be improved; the capacity of the system must be increased and the ability of one computer to contact ano·.her quickly and reliably must be assured. Companies are reluctant to place their mission-critical, revenue-earning information systems on an overloaded, poorly performing, insecure system. Third, some customers prefer to purchase certain types of items in stores. This cultural bias may not last long, however, as more and more people use the Internet and become accustomed to it. Also, if web TV takes off (see Chapter 5), sales over the Internet will probably increase as families become familiar with the system.

Despite slow progress in sales over the Internet, for many organizations the Internet offers low-cost advertising, improved public relations, increased productivity, and lower costs of doing business.

Another commercial application that may hold promise is on-line banking. Fifteen banks and IBM are building an extranet (see "Extranet Communications" later in this chapter) that will allow their customers to pay bills, check their accounts, and transfer funds between accounts all on-line. A number of other banks are introducing similar services.

It is expected that e-commerce will alter the way we do business in many other ways. For example, on-line discount brokerage firms are an area of e-commerce that is expected to grow. In fact, an ad in the *Wall Street Journal* by E*Trades, a Web-based discount brokerage firm, declared that stockbrokers were obsolete. While that statement is obviously advertising hype, the company at that time was charging $14.95 for a stock trade that would have cost nearly $400 from a full-service broker.[3]

The number of airline, hotel, and travel reservations are also increasingly being made over the Web, as are real-estate transactions (at least the act of searching for a home). Increasingly, home owners are advertising their homes directly over the Web. Although it is unlikely that many real-estate firms, travel firms, and brokerage firms will go out of business, it is very likely that they will lose business if they do not adapt to e-commerce over the Web. At the very least, Web-based e-commerce will put price pressure on current institutions.

INTRANET COMMUNICATIONS

Providing Internet access to employees can benefit companies in many ways already described. However, by connecting the company network to the global Internet, the company also opens itself up to increased security problems (see Chapter 17). Connecting a computer to the Internet puts that computer at risk. Hackers may be able to penetrate the company computer network for fun or ill. Employees may unwittingly download virus programs along with Web pages and files. In addition, companies can expect to incur new costs when they connect their computer systems to the Internet. Perhaps for these reasons, some companies have chosen to use Internet technology within their organizations without connecting to the Internet. Such a system is called an **intranet.** Intranets are designed to provide many of the same features and benefits of the Internet (e-mail, file transfer, document browsing, electronic discussion groups) while avoiding some of the costs and risks.

Intranet technology allows data developed and stored in older or legacy information systems to become widely accessible using a simple browser. Intranets allow users in a company who formerly had to use one kind of terminal to reach data on

---

[3]E. B. Baatz, "Will the Web Eat Your Job," *WebMaster,* May/June 1996, p. 43.

one system and another type of terminal to reach data on another system to use one browser to reach all the data. The reason is that many software vendors provide tools to convert existing database information on mainframes, minicomputers, and other data storage sources to hypertext format "on the fly." And the applications in all new versions of the major software suites (such as Microsoft Office) are also browsers.

Dynamically converting data on the fly means that the resulting Web pages reflect the latest revisions in the records converted. Also, data entry forms can be placed on Web pages so that, for example, salespeople can enter sales orders using a browser.

The savings to firms that use intranet technology can be substantial. Information systems developers report that applications that provide access to existing databases can be developed in days rather than weeks or month, end users can use inexpensive or free software to access the data, and end users need little or no training in the use of the software.[4]

The first applications of intranet technology in many organizations have been the many documents that organizations make available to employees: technical manuals, handbooks, employee manuals, orientation manuals, personnel and telephone directories, employee newsletters, job opening announcements, product descriptions, organization charts, and location maps. Training materials have also been included as common applications for a company intranet.

Forms are also frequently made available through an organization intranet. This technology allows employees to complete different types of paperwork—benefit plan choices, travel expense forms, vacation request forms, and office supply request forms—quickly and easily.

When an organization has thousands of employees, the intranet provides a quick and easy route to reach them. Manuals and other company materials are usually in constant flux. The ability to make immediate changes to these materials without having to rekey or reprint them is an important advantage and provides real cost savings. On-line forms make form printing and distribution unnecessary.

This rosy scenario is basically reserved for document publishing, that is, making relatively static documents, records, and reports available to users, as opposed to providing the ability to sort or otherwise manipulate a large group of records to obtain a quantitative answer to a problem. In addition, intranets take time, effort, and money to create and maintain. Hundreds of thousands of document pages must be converted to hypertext format, unless they are converted dynamically, or "on the fly." These pages may require that their content be updated in a timely manner. Furthermore, the links between documents will require constant maintenance because pages are dropped, changed, or added all the time. Thus a change in one document can have an impact on many other documents.

Extranet Communications

While an intranet is confined to your own organization and the Internet is open to the world, an **extranet** lies somewhere between these extremes. A typical extranet is an intranet that allows the organization to connect to a wider group, such as an organization's customers and suppliers. The idea of an extranet is to let a select group of external entities, such as an organization's business partners, access selected areas of an organization's Web site that are not open to the general public. Probably the most

---

[4]M. Grygo, "Intranet Reality Check," *Client/Server Computing,* May 1996, p. 23.

commonly known extranet is Federal Express Corporation's Web-based package tracking system. Turner Broadcasting Sales, Inc., has made information available to its business partners (mostly ad agencies) that helps those agencies find the best use of TBS for the ad agencies' clients. This, in turn, encourages the ad agencies to use TBS for their client advertising.

Organizations today are beginning to integrate the Internet with intranets and extranets. For example, a nonprofit organization may develop Internet Web pages describing its charitable activities to current and potential donors, along with the means by which donors can contribute (contribution forms that can be e-mailed or organization telephone and fax numbers). The nonprofit organization may also have an intranet for employees that provides information on current and potential donors, the status of current fund drives, and internal memos and documents. Its extranet may be designed for current donors and contain a newsletter, list of current donors, information about discounts available at stores, air and car rentals, and hotel and motel chains that donor status provides, and information about upcoming events to which donors are invited.[5]

In another example, about 1,000 field technicians at Southern New England Telephone Company use laptop PCs and cellular phones to access and update work orders, receive new assignments, report their status to the home office, and send and check on their e-mail from remote locations. They dial into the company intranet using the Internet.

OFFICE COMMUNICATIONS

Information technologies, including communications systems, have had a major impact on office work, our perception of what an office is, and how office work is done (see Manager's Memo 9–3). Of course, many people still work in traditional offices; that is, offices that are places or rooms in a building. With the advent of modern telecommunications and laptop computers, however, it has become increasingly obvious that the "office" is wherever you perform your work. Your office may be your home, an airport terminal, a seat on a plane, a parked automobile, or wherever it is that you conduct the activities for which you are responsible. A sales representative who connects to his or her company computer network to preview contact files in a hotel room on the evening prior to sales visits is doing office work. Executives who use notebook computers and cell phones to create and send letters and reports to customers and colleagues from an airport en route to a conference are doing office work. Managers who use home computers to monitor their subordinates' progress by viewing their reports are doing office work.

These people are viewing the office as a function, not a place. Communications systems have allowed them to be more concerned about the tools and information required to perform their work than where their office is located. In fact, because of inexpensive computers and readily available electronic communications systems, telecommuting has become a reality (see Manager's Memo 9–4). **Telecommuting** is the process by which office workers and executives work part-time or full-time out of their homes and communicate with their offices through their computers using some sort of communications network.

---

[5]From SharNews, a newsletter by SharWest, Inc. (http://www.sharwest.com/nettools.html).

| Manager's Memo 9–3 | THE EFFECTS OF TECHNOLOGY ON OFFICE ORGANIZATION |

 Because of increasing technological innovation, the traditional office and the role of the traditional secretary have undergone substantial changes. Some foresee a time when the traditional office may disappear entirely in the wake of technological and social changes affecting the activities of both the boss and the secretary. In fact, computer-based technology is increasingly eroding the traditional organization and distribution of office functions because computer systems are changing the way managers and other office personnel work. Managers query databases instead of having secretaries search files. Managers use spreadsheets instead of having secretaries prepare budgets. Many managers key in their own memos on their office computer terminals or away-from-office laptops rather than dictate those memos to secretaries. Many are more comfortable developing reports at a word processor than writing them out for secretaries to key in later. Managers order their own plane tickets using on-line travel services and schedule their own meetings using on-line calendaring software. They often find it more convenient to work at home using a remote terminal or a personal computer with a modem than to stay late at the office. In many offices, in short, the traditional work of administrative support staffs is increasingly being performed by executives. Whether this change is a more or less productive use of managers' time is a legitimate question. However one answers that question, it is clear that one effect of office automation has been to redistribute office tasks and one effect of communications technology has been to redefine the physical office.

| Manager's Memo 9–4 | TELECOMMUTING |

 Employees and employers may choose telecommuting for several reasons:

- A mother and father in a two-income household want to spend more time with their children and want to switch days going to their offices.

- People want to reduce the number of times they must spend long hours commuting to and from work.

- Organizations want to hold on to capable employees who live long distances from work or who move away from the organization's home office.

- Executives and professionals want to work while they are away from the office, such as on trips to customers or conventions.

- Some professionals, such as writers and programmers, do not always need to be at the office to do their work.

- The Clean Air Act of 1990 requires organizations with more than 100 employees to reduce the number of employees who drive to work alone.

Telecommuting provides one way to comply with the act. Organizations can count telecommuting workers as employees who get to work in zero vehicles.

Some telecommuting data:

- There were 7,000,000 telecommuters in 1994, and experts estimate that number will grow to 25,000,000 in 2000.

- Videoconferencing, desktop conferencing, and other technologies will boost the prevalence of telecommuting.

- The Telecommuting Advisory Council (which can be reached at 619-688-3258) serves as a clearinghouse for information about telecommuting.

- The software that telecommuters most frequently use at home is word processing software.

Source for some of the above: C. Levin, "Don't Pollute, Telecommute," *PC Magazine*, February 22, 1994, p. 32.

Many information systems that are based on communications systems have changed the nature of office work. These include e-mail, voice mail, fax machines, teleconferencing, groupware, and workflow automation. In the remainder of this chapter, each of these technologies will be described.

Figure 9–11

A screen from an e-mail software package

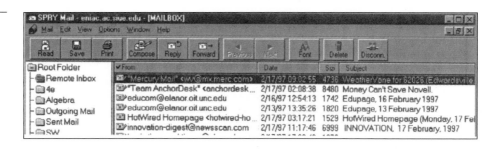

Electronic Mail Systems

Electronic mail systems may include any system of transmitting messages electronically rather than in hard-copy form. For example, electronic mail may include transmissions of text by facsimile, teletype, or any other device that transmits text electronically on a network. Among the fastest growing segments of electronic mail are computer-based systems that provide for the transmission of short messages between stations on a computer network, especially e-mail systems over the Internet. Some organizations are predicting that by 2001, about half the U.S. population (135,000,000 people) will have e-mail accounts.

Computer-based electronic mail systems generally allow a user to transmit messages to any or all of the other users on the network without having to produce hard copy. You may transmit, view, save, share, edit, or erase memos, letters, and even short reports without ever engaging a printer. These systems let you transmit messages immediately, rather than using the postal service or your organization's interoffice mail service to deliver the "dead tree" versions of those messages several days later.

When electronic mail systems share existing data transmission networks or local area networks that are operating at less than full capacity, electronic mail provides an extremely inexpensive form of mail service. Adding an electronic mail service to a local area network is likely to cost only the purchase price of the software because the existing network is already in place. Adding electronic mail to a wide area network is likely to increase transmission costs only marginally if the network is composed primarily of leased lines.

An electronic mail system is often a client/server system that requires an e-mail server, some clients, and a computer-based network. The software to manage and control the mail system is loaded on the server. Each user or mail client, which is usually a PC, runs the client software that allows the PC to connect to the server, read and download mail, and create and send messages (see Figure 9–11). Each user is allocated so much disk space on the server for a mailbox and is given an identifying number or name so that the user and other people may address the user's mailbox.

If you have a notebook computer or personal digital assistant with a modem, you can access your mailbox while you are mobile. For example, a salesperson in the field would be able to send and receive mail at any time of the day and at almost any location. To assist in e-mail access from remote sites, you may use *remote e-mail software*. This software creates a mailbox on your remote computing device and enables you to dial the home office e-mail system.

Remote e-mail software may provide security by encrypting IDs, passwords, and messages. It also may filter mail messages. The *filtering feature* automatically selects e-mail messages according to criteria you have chosen in advance, such as the name of the sender, the file size, and message type, or if the message is marked urgent. "The filters can also be set to select messages with key words you have chosen. E-mail filtering is not unique to remote e-mail systems but it can be especially useful to field employees, or "road warriors," because it saves them telephone line charges. Only the type of mail you want will be downloaded from the home office to your remote computing device.

In addition, some remote e-mail software allows you to synchronize automatically the contents of your home office mailbox with your remote computer's mailbox.

A number of telecommunications and information utility firms provide *public electronic mail systems.* For example, MCI offers MCI Mail, AT&T offers AT&T Mail, and America Online offers an electronic mail system to subscribers. In addition, the Internet provides a network for public e-mail and many Internet service providers provide the server part of the system.

Commercial electronic mail systems and the Internet allow individuals who do not have or cannot afford their own networks to communicate with others. For example, a sales manager may provide MCI Mail accounts to all of her sales staff, along with notebook computers equipped with modems. The sales group can then exchange messages and files over the MCI e-mail network. The commercial systems also allow users connected to private e-mail networks to communicate with others outside their private networks, including Internet subscribers. Electronic mail systems allow you to address messages to a single user, to a group of users (multicast), or to all users (broadcast). A sales manager may, for example, broadcast a price change to all salespeople or a note to only one person. To speed their work, users typically construct mailing lists so that they can mail messages to groups of people quickly and easily.

Many electronic mail systems also allow users to construct bulletin boards on topics of interest to users. For example, an organization might develop an e-mail bulletin board when a desktop publishing software package is introduced. Users of the software could then share ideas, helpful hints, and solutions to problems.

Many electronic mail systems also allow users to attach files to mail messages so that users can transfer document and data files accompanied by a written note. Also, some systems allow you to attach voice messages to electronic mail messages. Managers can use this feature to soften or personalize memos to staff. Some e-mail software will even translate text messages to voice so that you can access the system and "read" your messages via telephone.

One of the major advantages of electronic mail is that it is one way to avoid **telephone tag.** Telephone tag occurs when one person calls another to give a short message and the other person is out or the line is busy. The first person then leaves a message to return the call. When the other person returns the call, the original caller may be out or the line could be busy. The two players may end up playing telephone tag for some time before a simple message can be conveyed. Telephone tag is very frustrating, eats up a great deal of time, and is costly to the organization. Many messages, such as price changes, do not really require two-way communications. Simply depositing a note about the price change in the salesperson's mailbox eliminates telephone tag.

A fast growing trend in e-mail is an application of "push" Internet technology discussed earlier in this chapter. Ordinarily, information e-mail for a user is placed on the user's server. The user then "pulls" or downloads his or her mail from the server to his or her workstation. In contrast, e-mail push technology provides customized information to users via their e-mail accounts. Subscribers to this type of service choose topics of interest to them. Then each day a user's e-mail inbox is automatically filled with relevant messages. If someone is using an Internet browser for e-mail functions, the messages may be in hypertext form instead of merely being in standard text format. Thus, e-mail messages can be very rich in context, allowing the receiver to browse related web pages from links embedded in e-mail.

Voice Processing Systems

Voice processing systems include voice mail systems, voice messaging systems, and interactive voice response systems. **Voice mail systems (VMS)** usually employ software that runs on PBX equipment rather than on the organization's mainframe computer. However, some voice mail systems are PC-based (see Figure 9–12). PC-based systems typically come installed on multimedia computer systems and include a full-duplex speakerphone, answering machine, and the ability to set up many levels of voice mailboxes for different callers.

Voice mail systems are very similar to electronic mail systems except that the stored message is a digitized version of the voice message rather than a text message. In a reverse of e-mail systems, some voice mail systems will translate voice messages to text. Like e-mail systems, voice mail systems are another means of eliminating the annoying and sometimes costly problem of telephone tag.

Voice mail systems are usually client/server systems and require a computer to act as a server and provide disk storage space for the software and mailboxes, just like electronic mail systems do. The sending and receiving terminal or client for voice mail, however, may be a telephone. The digitized voice message can be played back; sent to one address, a group of addresses, or all addresses; and saved or erased, just like text in the electronic mail system. Users may access their own mailboxes by dialing from any telephone and using the telephone keypad to listen to a list of the messages in the mailbox, "scroll" through the mailbox messages, go directly to a priority message, listen to one or more messages, save a message, or send a message to another person or group of persons. These capabilities permit field representatives or executives who are at a conference to keep up with their messages, to deliver messages, and in general, to maintain contact with the home office (see Figure 9-13). People may not like some of the messages they receive from their bosses, but at least they do receive them in a timely manner.

Voice mail systems can also be interconnected with the mainframe computer, and telephone keypads then can be used to enter data directly into the computer system, permitting salespeople to enter orders directly over the telephone or letting customers order products directly. Some universities allow students to enroll using their home phones with a voice mail system. The students call the system's special enrollment

Figure 9–12

PC-based voice mail system

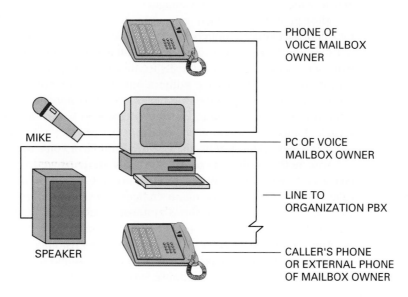

MIKE

SPEAKER

PHONE OF
VOICE MAILBOX
OWNER

PC OF VOICE
MAILBOX OWNER

LINE TO
ORGANIZATION PBX

CALLER'S PHONE
OR EXTERNAL PHONE
OF MAILBOX OWNER

Figure 9–13

Transactions in a
voice mail system

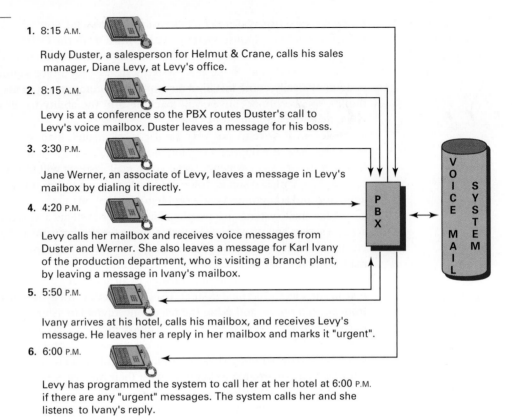

1. 8:15 A.M.

Rudy Duster, a salesperson for Helmut & Crane, calls his sales
manager, Diane Levy, at Levy's office.

2. 8:15 A.M.

Levy is at a conference so the PBX routes Duster's call to
Levy's voice mailbox. Duster leaves a message for his boss.

3. 3:30 P.M.

Jane Werner, an associate of Levy, leaves a message in Levy's
mailbox by dialing it directly.

4. 4:20 P.M.

Levy calls her mailbox and receives voice messages from
Duster and Werner. She also leaves a message for Karl Ivany
of the production department, who is visiting a branch plant,
by leaving a message in Ivany's mailbox.

5. 5:50 P.M.

Ivany arrives at his hotel, calls his mailbox, and receives Levy's
message. He leaves her a reply in her mailbox and marks it "urgent".

6. 6:00 P.M.

Levy has programmed the system to call her at her hotel at 6:00 P.M.
if there are any "urgent" messages. The system calls her and she
listens to Ivany's reply.

number, enter their social security numbers, and then enter the section numbers for
the classes they wish to attend. The voice system prompts them through the enrollment process and confirms whether the sections are open. If a section is not open, alternative sections are given. Enrolling by voice mail sure beats waiting in long enrollment lines at the beginning of each semester and, especially for commuter institutions,
may provide a competitive advantage.

Most people have called an organization and heard, "Good morning. Thank you
for calling Detweiler Products, Inc. If you are calling from a touch phone, please press
one now . . . " **Voice messaging system** allows an organization to set up voice menus
that route a customer automatically to the correct department, person, or mailbox or
provide the correct message without any human intervention. They save organizations money by reducing the number of operators needed for routine inbound calls.
They also provide after-hours service to customer's who need to leave a message or
receive standard information about company's product or business hours. As you can
see, voice messaging systems include the features of voice mail systems.

Interactive voice response systems are enhanced voice messaging systems
(see also "Computer Telephony Integration" in Chapter 8). Interactive systems allow
callers to respond to voice menu choices and obtain information, products, or services automatically. Such systems automate routine sales calls, such as requests for
free demonstration diskettes, free literature, or information about seminars, products,
or other company services. They also provide customer service by allowing customers to obtain information about their accounts and order status. Some organizations use interactive voice response systems for routine order processing, allowing

the customer to order products or services directly, without any intervention by order clerks or salespersons. Other organizations' interactive systems are structured to fax information about products and services directly to customers if they make the appropriate menu selections. The latter systems are usually referred to as *fax-on-demand systems.*

Electronic Conferencing Systems

Electronic conferencing, or **teleconferencing systems** permit many participants to engage in two-way communications without having to travel to a common site. These systems eliminate the costly travel expenses and wasted travel time.

Electronic conferencing does not eliminate the need for one-to-one meetings. Such meetings are especially useful when the participants have not met each other or when personal camaraderie or esprit de corps are objectives. Ordinarily, meetings with customers or vendors for price negotiations are better handled face to face. However, teleconferencing is useful when the participants all know each other and when the meeting should last only a short time. For example, when branch managers who are located all over the nation must meet, teleconferencing may prove very cost-effective if their meeting is likely to take only an hour or so.

Electronic conferencing has evolved into four types:

1. Audioconferencing
2. Videoconferencing
3. Desktop conferencing
4. Computer conferencing

Audioconferencing uses the telephone system to provide multiple parties with a chance to meet electronically. The system typically uses a speakerphone at one or more locations and patches together groups of people who are meeting at different sites, such as branch offices. To supplement an audioconference, illustrations, charts, or other graphics may be shared by means of facsimile devices (see next section) at each location. Another device for supplementing audioconferencing is the electronic blackboard, or **whiteboard.** This system captures the writing on a board in digital form and uses the telephone system to transmit the data to television screens at the remote locations. The system is particularly useful for training sessions.

Videoconferencing combines both voice and television images to provide two-way conferencing between groups (see Figure 9-14). Videoconferencing is especially useful when groups of participants are able to gather at local sites, such as branch offices. Videoconferencing facilities can then be limited to a small number of locations, minimizing travel for the participants. Because videoconferencing systems and facilities are expensive, some companies prefer to rent videoconferencing services from hotel and movie theater chains. Common carriers also make videoconferencing services available to their subscribers. In this way, organizations that do not need to use such facilities often do not need to acquire and maintain videoconferencing systems themselves.

Recent hardware and software innovations have allowed videoconferencing to move to the desktop computer system. **Desktop conferencing,** as these systems are called, typically allow users on a network to use their workstations to conduct meetings without physically getting together (see Manager's Memo 9-5). The simplest systems allow users simultaneously to view and edit reports, charts, images, and other documents from their workstations. For example, one system provides real-time, interactive conferencing and tools for annotating documents, including drawing tools so

Figure 9–14

A teleconferencing system with presenter in New York and participant groups in Chicago and St. Louis

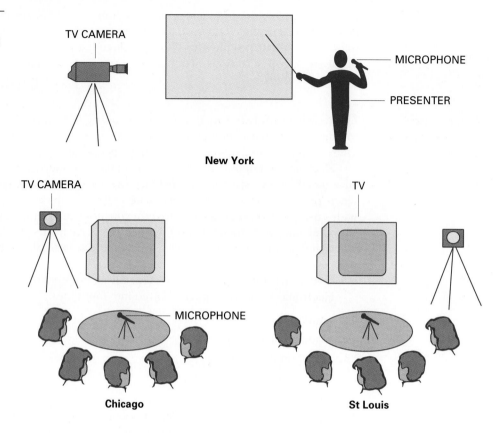

users can circle or underline parts of a screen image. The system also allows conferees to send written messages to each other using a notepad. Other products permit users to connect to the conference remotely via a dial-up connection, which means that people do not have to be connected to a local area network to participate in a conference.

More sophisticated forms of desktop conferencing add the capabilities of full-motion video and sound to the conference (see Figure 9–15). These systems are sometimes called multimedia conferencing. For example, IBM Corporation's Person-

Manager's Memo 9–5	DESKTOP CONFERENCING OVER THE INTERNET

Some PC manufacturers are selling their multimedia computer systems loaded with the MMX, or multimedia chip, an inexpensive video camera, and VDOPhone software from VDONet. The software allows the user to make a videoconferencing connection through an ordinary telephone connection or an Internet connection. If you use the latter connection, you can find other videoconference participants by connecting to a server that VDONet operates. If you

know the Internet address of the participant, you can simply type in that address.

The system costs between $99 and $149, depending on the features you buy. Reflecting the low cost, the number of frames per second is between 7 and 12. Also, the frames are small—about the size of a playing card. Thus, the size and resolution of the images may not be sufficient to use for some types of conferences, such as customer conferences.

Figure 9–15

A desktop
conferencing
system

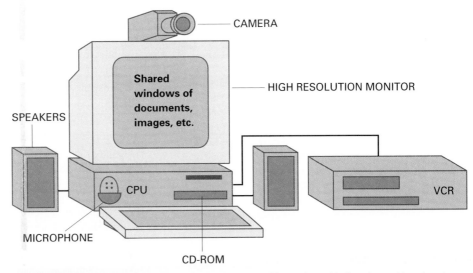

CAMERA

Shared
windows of
documents,
images, etc.

HIGH RESOLUTION MONITOR

SPEAKERS

VCR

CPU

MICROPHONE

CD-ROM

Notes: Each PC is connected to a local area network, and each PC contains a videoboard, sound board, and desktop conferencing software

to-Person/2 software lets conferees use these features:

- A whiteboard for conferees to share reports, images, and other documents.
- A message feature that allows users to broadcast short messages on top of the current display.
- A pointer to highlight parts of a screen display.
- File transfer capability to allow users to share document, data, image, and other files during the conference.
- Real-time video capability that lets users display images of conferees or other full-motion video material.

U S West, a regional Bell operating company, offers a desktop videoconferencing system called PictureTel. The PictureTel system provides live videoconferencing and includes a video camera, audio system, and the expansion boards for a PC. The user must also have a 56 KB network connection. The system allows users to share screens, files, and live TV images; talk to each other; and mark up or annotate shared documents or images.

Desktop conferencing systems are relatively inexpensive replacements for full-motion teleconferencing systems. They allow people to collaborate as well as to be relatively passive participants, as at an ordinary conference. As networked multimedia PCs become commonplace, desktop conferencing is likely to become very popular. In anticipation of that growth in interest, Internet browser producers are modifying their products to provide groupware (see "Groupware Systems" in this chapter), that includes desktop conferencing features (see Manager's Memo 9–6).

Computer conferencing is similar to electronic mail except that instead of the communications flowing from one participant to one participant, or from one participant to many participants, the sessions allow many participants to communicate with many participants. The "conversations" are all keyed-in messages displayed on computer screens. Basically, participants attend a joint conference through their keyboards and display screens, sending messages to all participants. Computer

| Manager's Memo 9-6 | BROWSERS EXPAND THEIR FUNCTIONS |

The newest versions of Netscape Navigator and Microsoft's Internet Explorer, two popular Internet browsers, offer a number of features designed to help local work groups collaborate on projects using a company intranet and to help separated group members collaborate from a distance using the Internet. In fact, Netscape has renamed its browser Netscape Communicator and Internet Explorer now includes Hot Meeting, a phone conferencing program.

These new products allow organizations to conduct virtual meetings, provide job training, expand and enrich telecommuting, and enhance customer service. The products include such features as:

- Expanded e-mail messaging.
- The ability to create user groups and conduct work-group discussions, similar to Internet news group programs.
- Real-time single or multiparty voice group conferencing.
- Real-time text chat capabilities.

- The ability to share data through file transfers.
- The ability to share data through a group or shared clipboard.
- Application sharing, which allows users to share the data on their PC screens with other users who can edit or take control of the program.
- The ability to share sketches, drawings, and other data through a shared whiteboard.
- Group scheduling software.

The first version of Netscape Communicator was not as feature rich as Microsoft's Internet Explorer. For example, it supported only a single, point-to-point telephone conference as opposed to Microsoft's NetMeeting, which provides multipoint conferencing. Netscape Communicator also does not offer video; Microsoft's NetMeeting does. Clearly however, both Netscape and Microsoft have set their sights on capturing the organization intranet market, and we should expect that each company will continue to enhance its product to provide more groupware features.

conferencing also differs from audio- and videoconferencing in that the latter two approaches are in real time. Computer conferencing is a store-and-forward technology, as is electronic mail. This system allows people to participate in conference proceedings at times convenient for them, rather than according to a specific schedule of events. User groups on the Internet are examples of computer conferencing.

Fax Systems

Facsimile, or **fax,** machines are one type of digitizing equipment that has been available for many years. The facsimile device is an **optical scanner** that reduces text or graphic images recorded on paper to electrical impulses that can be transmitted to compatible facsimile devices over your telephone or other network. Basically, a fax system is an electronic document delivery system that combines scanner technology with modem technology.

Facsimile devices may be analog or digital devices. Analog devices scan and transmit an entire document, including its unused or white-space portions. Digital fax devices compress the material to be transmitted and are much faster than analog devices. High-speed fax machines can transmit a page in about 20 seconds (see Figure 9-16). The newest generation of fax machines uses laser technology for speed and high-resolution reproduction. To increase office productivity, fax machines may be equipped with automatic dialers and automatic sheet feeders so that they can send and receive transmissions unattended.

Fax machines can easily save organizations money. Typically, organizations use fax equipment to replace same-day or overnight mail services. The telephone line costs of sending a few pages by fax is generally substantially less than sending those same pages by same-day mail. If the fax equipment transmits the pages after 11 PM in unattended mode, the savings over next-day mail can be greater.

Figure 9–16

A digital facsimile machine

Courtesy of CANON USA, Inc.

Facsimile devices can be merged with teleconferencing systems to permit sharing of hard-copy materials. Photographs of chalkboards, copies of transparencies, and copies of other documents can be sent quickly to all participating locations, even in color. Combining fax technology with local area networks not only allows any network user to fax documents to others but also allows incoming fax documents to be routed directly to the fax mailbox of the intended recipient, thus avoiding delivery delays.

PC fax/modem boards.   Fax technology today is commonly added to modem technology to create **fax/modem boards** that are placed in an expansion slot of a PC or external fax/modem devices that connect to a PC's serial port. PCMCIA fax/modem devices are available for laptop or notebook computer systems (see "PC Cards," Chapter 5). These boards or devices, with their associated software, allow your PC to send documents stored on disk to other fax devices; to receive and store fax images on disk; and to edit, display, and print the images.

Fax technology is also being combined with other office technologies into multifunction machines. For example, fax technology is being combined with laser-driven copying technology to produce machines that provide facsimile transmission, document copying, and document printing—thus merging facsimile, printing, and copying functions in one device.

People without fax/modems or stand-alone fax machines can create and send faxes by using an on-line or common carrier fax service. For example, CompuServe, America Online, and MCI subscribers can send messages and transfer existing files to fax machines from their modems. The on-line service converts the message or file to a fax format and delivers it.

Fax systems deliver documents as images—a series of black dots on a white page—rather than as numbers and letters. Images of pages of text cannot be manipulated by word processors unless the images are converted back into number and letter form. That conversion is the job of optical character recognition systems.

Optical character recognition.   Optical recognition systems include **optical character recognition (OCR)** technology and **optical mark recognition** technology. OCR technology has been used in offices since the 1950s. The technology may take the form of OCR software running on a PC that also has a fax device and scanner attached. The technology also may take the form of a dedicated OCR machine that contains a scanner and OCR software. Dedicated OCR machines usually have sheet feeders so that large amounts of hard copy can be scanned and converted quickly.

Companies can use OCR technology to avoid costly rekeying of hard-copy text. OCR software along with an optical scanner can convert hard-copy text to digital information and store it on disk as numbers and letters. Once on disk, word and data processors can edit and otherwise process the information. If the information is an image of text stored in a computer file, like a fax transmission received through a PC fax/modem board, OCR software running on that same PC can convert the image file to a text file so that it can be read and manipulated with word processing software.

The accuracy, speed, and versatility with which OCR software can read text have continually increased during the last decade. OCR software is now able to read images of text in both upper- and lowercase, in different font styles, with paragraph indentation and in columnar form, with varying pitch and line spacing, and even in handwriting. Desktop-size optical scanners are now available (see Figure 9–17), as are handheld models that scan 4 inches or so of a document at one time.

The Virtual Office

Networking technologies enable managers to supervise employees spread out over many locations—even worldwide—creating **virtual offices** composed of these employees. This flexibility permits managers to choose staff for projects on the basis of

Figure 9–17

Desktop optical scanner

Courtesy of Hewlett-Packard Company

competence and experience rather than convenience. It also allows managers to tap a world pool of talent when needed. For example, virtual offices permit project members in several locations across the globe to work on a project together and to keep in close touch using such technologies as electronic mail, fax, electronic bulletin boards, electronic white boards, audioconferencing, computer conferencing, voice mail, videophones, desktop conferencing, videoconferencing, and Web sites (see Manager's Memo 9–6).

Audioconferencing may be used for small meetings of 10 to 15 participants who are reviewing a project or discussing a budget. Electronic bulletin boards or faxes may be used for sharing a particularly difficult problem with all project members. Personal messages or progress reports may be handled by e-mail or voice mail. Fax and Web sites may be used to share more static data such as organization charts, project descriptions, and job descriptions. Desktop conferencing and videoconferencing may be used to share real-time presentations.

Groupware Systems

Special software, called groupware, is designed to help project teams and other groups complete their tasks more easily, whether the group members work in the same office suite or in a virtual office. **Groupware** can be defined very simply as software that provides support for groups of workers and is designed to work over a network.

Many managers and other office workers work in a group environment for all or part of the day. For example, a group of managers and support personnel may be formed to complete a specific project. Some team project members may be members of more than one team or group. For example, a marketing manager may lead a task force to review the advertising program of an organization. That same manager may also serve as a member of a computer information systems steering committee. Work groups may be relatively fixed departmental or committee structures or temporary groups formed to complete projects or ad hoc tasks.

Groupware software products provide many or all of these functions:

- Electronic mail services, including attaching files and voice annotations to messages.
- Voice mail services.
- Web services to allow groups to share documents.
- Teleconferencing services, including audio-, video-, computer, and desktop conferencing.
- Fax services, including group faxing and OCR conversion of faxed documents.
- Word processing services, including multiuser document viewing, editing, and annotation.
- Group calendaring and scheduling services, including room scheduling and meeting agendas.
- Shared to-do lists for tracking the status of assignments.
- Shared phone lists.
- Group project management services for optimizing human and other project resources and for monitoring group progress.
- Transparent file, document, and data retrieval services.
- Personal utilities (appointment books, calculators, auto-dialers, notepads, outliners, file managers, personal to-do lists, and expense reporting).

Group project management services may include multiuser project management programs, which help group managers track work assignments by spotting assignments that are overdue, reminding group members when task due dates pass, and even urging members to complete required paperwork.

Groupware and the definition of what groupware represents is still evolving. No package seems to offer all or even most of the features useful to group projects or work tasks. Many vendors of traditional software have begun to add group work features to their products. For example, network versions of word processors now have group annotation features. The annotation features allow multiple users to view and edit a document but provide a clear trail of the editing and revision process. Edited text is identified by strikeovers, underlines, or some other formatting feature, and the date, time, and name of the reviser is noted right on the document.

Some spreadsheets permit *versioning* so that several people may create different scenarios for an event using the same spreadsheet template. For example, a team might examine the different outcomes of an event as predicted by each team member using different assumptions. One spreadsheet package lets one member of a team send a range of cells to a colleague for completion using a "delegate" function. Once completed, the colleague returns the range using a "return to sender" function.

Many software vendors have expanded their office suites, teleconferencing software, and e-mail software to include features that support work groups over networks. Even vendors of browser software are following suit, expanding the features of their products to support group work.

Major groupware developers are expanding the software they offer. Groupware products are becoming more comprehensive in terms of the group tasks they support and more integrated in terms of the work flow between these tasks. In fact, a new form of groupware that addresses the need to integrate work-group tasks, workflow software, is expanding rapidly (see the following "Workflow Automation").

Workflow Automation

One type of groupware software lets developers create programs to perform routine tasks at preset time periods. This software is called **workflow software** because it allows developers to create a program that automates a series of actions in a flow of work. In short, the software allows the developer to automate a series of tasks that would ordinarily have been completed by the manager and office clerks. For example, a developer may create a program that automatically collects data from several files located on different networks and then automatically compiles the data and distributes a report each month.

Workflow software has the potential for changing how businesses, especially work groups, are organized because the software directly alters the processes and the flow of work in an organization. If the software is used intelligently, it provides an opportunity for firms to reengineer their business processes. Workflow software may be built around e-mail systems, word processing software, database software, and even fax systems.

E-mail workflow software allows you to create forms and then automate routing the forms to those who must use them. The e-mail portion of the software provides a rapid transportation medium for the forms. E-mail–based workflow software also provides two types of development tools: a *forms creation tool* that lets users create the forms used in the business processes and a *scripting language* that allows users to create a "script," or the play-by-play procedures through which the forms will be processed. The user first develops a form, like a purchase order, and then builds a script of who does what with the purchase order and when they do it. The software then follows the script to process each form.

Typical applications for e-mail–based systems are order processing, expense account reporting, and document review and approval. Let's look at a typical example of how, in a manual system, a manager might file an expense report (see the first column, Figure 9–18). The manager completes a travel expense form in pencil to report expenses incurred at a recent training seminar. The manager then places the form in the in-basket of a secretary, where the form sits until the secretary gets to it. At that

Figure 9–18

Completing an expense report manually and with workflow software

Steps in manual system	Steps in e-mail–based workflow system
1. Manager fills out travel expense form in pencil.	1. Manager completes and signs expense form on computer.
2. Manager places form in secretary's in-basket.	2. Workflow automation software verifies arithmetic and completeness, checks amounts against company guidelines, checks total against manager's budget, and places form in superior's e-mail box.
3. Secretary types expense form.	3. Superior signs form.
4. Secretary verifies arithmetic.	4. Workflow automation system places signed form in accounting clerk's e-mail box.
5. Secretary checks amounts spent against company guidelines.	5. Accounting clerk initiates check.
6. Secretary places form on desk of manager for signature.	
7. Manager signs form and returns to secretary's in-basket.	
8. Secretary places signed form in outbox.	
9. Interoffice mail picks up, sorts, and delivers form to accounting.	
10. Form is placed in clerk's in-basket.	
11. Clerk verifies arithmetic.	
12. Clerk checks amounts against company guidelines.	
13. Clerk checks total amount against manager's budget.	
14. Clerk places form in outbox.	
15. Interoffice mail picks up, sorts, and delivers to superior.	
16. Superior's secretary opens and place on desk for review.	
17. Superior reviews and signs form.	
18. Superior's secretary places in outbox.	
19. Interoffice mail picks up, sorts, and delivers to accounting.	
20. Clerk completes check.	

time the secretary types a copy of the expense report, verifies the accuracy of the arithmetic, and makes certain that the amounts spent are within company guidelines. The secretary then takes the form to the manager's desk to be signed; the manager signs it and returns it to the secretary, who places it in the out-basket to await mail pickup. Eventually, it will be picked up and sent via interoffice mail to the mailbox of the accounting office, where it is opened and placed in the in-basket of a clerk, who once again reviews the expense form for completeness and accuracy and once again checks the amount spent against company guidelines. The accounting clerk also compares the total amount requested against the balance in the manager's travel budget to ensure that the manager has enough money in the travel line of the budget to pay for the seminar. The form is then placed in an out-basket again, awaits pickup, and is forwarded to the manager's superior for review and a signature of approval, once again by interoffice mail. At the superior's office, it is placed in the in-basket of a secretary until it is opened and placed on the desk of the superior who reviews it. Once signed by the superior, it is picked up by the secretary and placed in another out-basket awaiting mail pickup. After pickup, it is routed back to the accounting department, once again through interoffice mail, where yet another clerk with yet another in-basket and out-basket completes a check to the manager.

Using workflow software, (see second column, Figure 9–18) the life of the same expense form might take quite a different path. The manager completes the travel expense form on an expense report form displayed on a computer screen. The manager signs the form using a light pen. The workflow automation software immediately verifies the completeness of the form, compares the amounts listed to a file of company guidelines for approved expense limits, and using information obtained from another information system, verifies that the manager's travel budget is sufficient to cover the expenses reported. Seconds later, the workflow software places the verified document in the superior's e-mail box for review and signature. Once the superior signs off on the form using a light pen, the workflow software immediately places the form in the e-mail box of an accounting clerk so that the clerk may initiate a check. The new process eliminated several redundant steps and automatically completed several routine verification steps. In addition, the workflow software eliminated many in-baskets and out-baskets, and reduced the interoffice mail delays from days to seconds. Overall, the process has taken just a few minutes rather than many days. The major reason for the improved productivity is that the workflow automation software squeezed out the delays between steps.

As you can see from the example, some workflow products allow developers to use scripting tools to extract needed data from existing information systems, such as a budget system, inventory system, or accounts receivable system. Some workflow software also provides libraries of forms and scripts for common business processes that users can modify to fit their needs. Still other workflow software adds management and reporting tools that tell managers the status of work in the flow and that provide statistics on the number of documents processed, the average time for processing documents, the average time each step in the process takes, and so on. Information of this type allows developers to identify bottlenecks in the system, improve productivity, and streamline workflows even further.

The Paperless Office

This chapter has described numerous technologies that are being applied to office work. At the present time, many of these technologies are not being integrated in any significant way. That is, they often are not deployed in an office in such a way that the output of one technology provides input to another. Merging these technologies into an integrated information system to support office work is sometimes referred to as the **paperless office,** or the *office of the future.* Groupware, document management systems, and workflow software applications represent rudimentary forms of the paperless office because they integrate multiple technologies into systems to get office work done. Electronic data interchange is another rudimentary form of the paperless office.

For decades, people in the office industry have been predicting a time when office automation would make possible a paperless office—that is, an office in which hard copy is rarely produced or processed. The paperless office, or office of the future, will be one in which documents are received in electronic form; processed in electronic form; and stored, replicated, and distributed in electronic form within and between organizations. Keys to the paperless office are a common architecture for application software and telecommunications to ensure that the systems adhere to a common set of standards. Providing for the complete electronic processing of information means that a variety of LANs, WANs, and other electronic networks will link various office personnel inside and outside of every organization. Complete electronic processing of information will require that networks become ubiquitous and that the application and communications protocols for creating, editing, storing, and transmitting electronic documents become standardized.

The paperless office will use networks to link intelligent copy machines, optical scanners, facsimiles, word processors, computers, printers, optical and hard disk storage facilities, and many other office technologies to each other and to the outside world via wide area networks. In such a system, the need to produce hard copy will be almost nonexistent because documents can be displayed, edited, and stored on magnetic media and transmitted anywhere within the system.

The technology to provide a nearly paperless office is available today. LANs, WANs, PBX networks, intranets, the Internet, and other networks are increasingly being used to link various kinds of office equipment to provide an electronic path for every document or message, including voice messages. However, given the penchant of most organizations for hard copy, the cost of the technology to make the paperless office, the resistance that some people have to technology, and the plodding speed of the standardization of communications protocols, it seems unlikely that the paperless office will be implemented in the near future. Still, office functions are yielding to integration in increasing numbers of firms of all sizes each year, especially through the Internet, groupware, document management systems, and workflow automation. A reasonable view is that although the office of the future is still clearly that, the rate and extent of technological development in office equipment and the concurrent change in office work seem to make the "paperleast" office a hope for the near future and the paperless office of the future inevitable.

One necessary precursor of this development is the establishment of WANs, LANs, or both as a common feature of almost every office. As networks become commonplace, the most important link for electronic information transfer within offices will be in place.

In addition, comprehensive information system architectures, including IBM's Systems Application Architecture (SAA), which provides, among other things, a common user interface for applications regardless of the computer platform through which a user encounters the applications, and HTML, which allows users to share many types of documents, are important developments supporting the paperless office.

To this chorus has been added the voice of Microsoft Corp., with its plan for Microsoft at Work (MAW), which promises to add a new operating system for office machines, new communications software to link the machines, and common file formats so that the machines can easily exchange and use data. The office machinery that MAW plans to integrate includes faxes, printers, personal digital assistants, scanners, copiers, and PCs.

MANAGEMENT SUMMARY

Many organizations process data at more than one site. These organizations must wrestle with the problem of distributing their data to make distributed processing possible. At the same time they must maintain management control over their databases. Databases may be replicated at each processing site, or they may be partitioned with the parts distributed selectively to appropriate sites.

Distributed database systems offer the opportunity for lower costs and faster response time but carry the burden of increasing security, redundancy, consistency, and compatibility problems for an organization.

A growing form of distributed information systems is a client/server system in which clients (often PCs) make requests of servers (may be PCs, minicomputers, or mainframes). In a client/server system, clients and servers may share the responsibility of information systems tasks, such as the storage and processing of data.

Interorganizational systems are distributed information systems that extend beyond the boundaries of a single organization. Electronic data interchange systems are interorganizational information systems that allow the direct sharing of information between two organization's computer systems, typically between a buyer and a seller. Electronic marketing systems are muiltilateral information systems that permit many organizations to share information about products, services, and pricing. These systems permit sellers to inform potential buyers of their offerings and allow buyers to comparison shop efficiently.

One form of client/server computing has been exploding in terms of use: the Internet and its variants, intranets and extranets. The Internet is a network of networks that places vast amounts of information and services in the hands of those connected to it, including libraries of documents, files, images, sounds, videos, and live presentations. The major application that permits users to access these data is a browser. Browsers allow users to view documents, transfer files, send and receive e-mail, and participate in group work. Search engines help users find data located on the Internet on the basis of key words or topical searches by directories.

An intranet is a network that is confined to a single organization and offers Internet-like services with less expense and with less risk to organizational security than the Internet. Intranets have become popular means of providing information to employees. Extranets are also limited forms of the Internet. These networks typically connect an organization and its customers and business partners, such as vendors or suppliers.

The explosive growth of the Internet, intranets, and extranets is expected to continue because these systems offer users valuable services and opportunities. One area of expected growth is the use of the Internet for electronic commerce, including shopping, advertising, banking, and investing.

Many communications technologies have been applied to the office. These technologies include electronic mail, voice mail, voice messaging systems, facsimile, audioconferencing, videoconferencing, computer conferencing, desktop conferencing, groupware, and workflow software. These technologies have led already to the virtual office and may someday lead to the paperless office.

KEY TERMS FOR MANAGERS

audioconferencing, 331

browser, 314

centralized databases, 307

client/server computing, 309

computer conferencing, 333

desktop conferencing, 331

distributed database systems, 307

distributed processing, 303

downsizing, 311

e-commerce, 322

electronic conferencing, 331

electronic data interchange (EDI), 312

electronic mail systems, 327

electronic market systems, 313

extranet, 324

facsimile (fax), 334

fax/modem board, 335

file transfer protocol (FTP), 320

frequently-asked-question (FAQ) file, 320

groupware, 337

interactive voice response systems, 330

Internet, 313

Internet service provider (ISP), 313

interorganizational information systems, 311

intranet, 323

optical character recognition (OCR), 335

optical mark recognition, 335

optical scanner, 334

paperless office, 341

partitioned database, 308

replicated database, 307

search engine, 316

telecommuting, 325

teleconferencing systems, 331

Telnet, 321

telephone tag, 328

usenet newsgroups, 320

videoconferencing, 331

virtual offices, 336

voice mail systems (VMS), 329

voice messaging systems, 330

voice processing systems, 329

Web page, 314

Web site, 314

whiteboard, 331

workflow software, 338

World Wide Web, 314

REVIEW QUESTIONS

1. Explain the term *distributed processing*. How does distributed processing differ from a distributed database?

2. What are the two basic ways to distribute a database? Explain how these methods differ.

3. What is client/server computing? What are the typical components of a client/server computing system?

4. What is a SQL server? How do SQL servers differ from ordinary networked database management system software?

5. How can client/server systems improve response time and reduce transmission costs to organizations?

6. Explain what the term *downsizing* means in a client/server environment. What might be the advantages of downsizing to an organization with a mainframe system?

7. What are interorganizational information systems? What are two types of interorganizational information systems?

8. What are the differences between a supplier-focused EDI system and a customer-focused EDI system?

9. What is EDI? Compare an electronic market system to an EDI system.

10. What is the Internet?

11. What is an ISP? How does an ISP differ from a NSP?

12. What is the World Wide Web? How can a manager use the Web to track the competition?

13. What is a search engine and how can search engines help you find information on the Internet?

14. What is a browser?

15. What is a Web site?

16. What are some popular features offered on the Internet?

17. What is a FAQ file?

18. What is the difference between a newsgroup and a listserv?

19. How might an organization use FTP to improve customer service?

20. Explain what a voice mail system is. How can a manager use a voice mail system?

21. What is an interactive voice response system? How can such a system benefit an organization?

22. What is electronic mail and what features does it provide?

23. What does a fax device do? Why are digital fax devices faster than analog fax devices?

24. What are four means of providing teleconferencing? Describe an application that might be appropriate for each teleconferencing method.

25. What is an electronic mail system? What are the components of an electronic mail system?

26. Explain how users might communicate through an electronic mail system.

27. What is a voice mail system? What are the components of a voice mail system?

28. Explain how users communicate through a voice mail system.

29. Describe an application for which a voice mail system might be appropriate.

30. Explain the difference between optical character recognition devices and optical scanning devices.

31. What is groupware? What features might a groupware package offer?

32. Explain telecommuting. What benefits does telecommuting offer the employee? the employer? the environment?

33. What is e-mail filtering? How does e-mail filtering save common carrier costs?

34. Explain the term *telephone tag*. How can elimination of telephone tag save time?

35. What is a voice message system? How do interactive voice response systems differ from voice messaging?

36. What is workflow software? What steps in a manual system does workflow software usually eliminate?

37. What is an electronic whiteboard? How might an organization make use of this device?

38. What is a virtual office? Describe how the virtual office might improve project team work.

QUESTIONS FOR DISCUSSION

1. Why might an organization want to have a distributed database system? What problems might a distributed database system generate for the organization?

2. What are some client/server information systems described in this chapter? Explain how client/server information systems can help managers.

3. Why might a manager want to create a Web site for his or her organization?

4. How might a manager save time and money using an intranet?

5. What is the difference between pushing and pulling information on the Internet? How might pushing Internet data to a manager's desk be of use?

6. How might a network PC be used with the Internet to reduce costs?

7. What are some reasons that a manager might hesitate to use the Internet for electronic commerce?

8. What advantages might a large buyer gain from developing electronic data interchange systems with its major suppliers?

9. Describe some communications technologies and the impact they have had on office work.

10. Explain the term *paperless office*.

11. What are the essential characteristics of the paperless office?

PROBLEMS

1. **Daniel Distributors, Inc.**   Daniel Distributors, a wholesaler, has a home office in Los Angeles and 95 field representatives and seven warehouses scattered in three western states. The bulk of the administrative and clerical staff is located in the home office. The field reps work out of offices in the warehouses. How do you recommend that the organization distribute

   a. Payroll and personnel data?
   b. Inventory data?
   c. Sales data?

2. **Landcrest Realtors, Inc.**   Landcrest Realtors, Inc., a national real-estate chain, has offices across the United States and headquarters in St. Louis, Missouri. The home office provides corporate-level services. Each of the chain locations has a manager, several

real-estate agents, and the necessary supporting staff. How do you recommend that the organization distribute

    a. Commercial property listing data?

    b. Home or family property listing data?

    c. Sales data?

    d. Payroll data?

3. **Job and career information Web sites.** Use an Internet browser to connect to a search engine, such as Yahoo!, InfoSeek, or Lycos. Using the search engine, identify Web sites that provide information about jobs and careers in your area of interest. Prepare a report that provides an annotated list of at least 10 Web sites containing job or career information in your major field. You should provide a name for each site, its Web address (or URL), and two or three sentences describing its contents.

4. **Office communications technology.** Identify one or more office technologies that might be considered for each situation:

    a. Transmitting text, pictures, or charts in hard-copy form to branch offices in hard-copy form.

    b. Sending memos and files from one office employee to one or more other office employees.

    c. Communicating by phone to another employee or group of employees who are not at their desks.

    d. Meeting with a group of persons who are located at multiple distant locations.

    e. Meeting with a group of persons who are located at multiple distant locations, but who may not be able to be present at the same time.

5. **Groupware.** Complete a paper about one groupware software package by reading at least three articles or reviews of it. Your report should cover the package's features, shortcomings, and cost. To find reviews, you might examine issues of the following magazines: *Office Systems, Datamation, PC Magazine, Software Magazine, PC World, Byte,* and *Administrative Management.* You might also use a search engine to scour the Internet for documents that review groupware products.

6. **Office communications.** Complete a paper about one of the following office communications technologies: electronic mail, voice mail, facsimile, or teleconferencing. The paper should identify the current hardware and software available for the technology and their capabilities. Also identify office applications for the technology and describe new trends or forecasted changes in the technology. You may wish to examine Applied Computer Research's *Computer Literature Index* for leads, Datapro Corporation's *Datapro Reports* on office automation for technology reviews, and some of the following magazines for product reviews: *Modern Office Technology, Office Systems, Datamation, Telecommunications, PC Magazine, Byte, Today's Office, The Office,* and *Administrative Management.* You may also use a search engine to identify documents on the Internet containing product reviews.

7. **Workflow software.** Compare two workflow software packages by reading articles that review the packages. Prepare a report evaluating the two packages on the basis of

    a. Cost

    b. Features

    c. Ease of use

CASES

1. **Jay Stuart, Inc.** Jay Stuart, Inc., was a small retail furniture firm located in the city of Barrett. Jay Stuart Sr., the founder, started the store in 1968. At that time the furniture warehouse was simply the back end of the original store.

In 1984 the firm decided to automate some of its operations. Jay Stuart Jr., who had recently taken over management of the store, contracted with Data Advisors, Inc., a computer consulting firm, to develop a database application that maintained data on, among other things, sales orders, purchase orders, and inventory levels. The automation decision paid off for the Stuarts. The store grew in sales consistently throughout the rest of the 1980s and early 1990s. The automation reduced the firm's costs and allowed it to offer quality merchandise at a lower price than many stores in the city and surrounding towns.

As its sales volume grew, the firm decided to add a small MIS department to handle its automation needs, rather than to depend on the computer consulting firm. In 1991 Jay Jr. hired Vicky Penn as head of the department. She promptly hired a small staff to handle the maintenance of existing programs and to operate what now was being called the Data Center. By 1995, however, Jay Jr. and his management staff recognized that they had saturated the firm's local market. If revenues were to increase, they would have to add other product lines, other services, or other locations. After a lengthy analysis of marketing data, some of which were obtained from on-line databases, Jay Jr. decided to expand geographically by adding three stores, each located in a city to the north of the original store and just over the line to another state. He also decided to add one centrally located warehouse to serve as an inventory hub for the three stores. Suddenly, the firm had decided to grow from one store and one warehouse to four stores and two warehouses. It had also shifted from a store serving a local area to a regional store serving customers in a two-state geographical area. As these decisions were made, Vicky Penn began to consider the implications of them for the Data Center. She began to realize that she would have to make decisions about how she would handle the data processing and data storage needs of the new store and warehouse locations.

To help her formulate a sound decision, she has asked Arif Buhkta, a member of her staff, to prepare a report on her options. Assume the role of Arif Buhkta and prepare a report of Vicky Penn's options for organizing the firm's database. Your report should include a list and brief description of her options and a brief analysis of the advantages of each.

2. **Pine Products Company.** Pine Products Company is a small but growing furniture manufacturer. Its principal product is pine bunk beds, but it has recently expanded its line to include a small number of other pine furniture items, such as dressers, lamps, tables, and chairs. The company is located in Jacksonville, Florida.

The company began operations five years ago with one factory in a converted building and has since spread out into three other buildings within the city and four others in neighboring cities. The home office is located on 10th Street, above the first factory. This office serves as the sales office for the factories in Jacksonville. Each of the other factory buildings also houses sales offices and administrative offices.

Business has been very good. In the last few years, sales to stores within a three-state area surrounding Atlanta, Georgia, and a three-state area surrounding Lexington, Kentucky, have provided enormous growth for the company. To meet the demand in these two areas, the company has had to operate the four Jacksonville factories on two shifts. Pratt Williams, the founder and president of Pine Products Company, is considering starting factories in two more cities—Atlanta and Lexington—in order to locate production closer to the company's customers in these two areas and to reduce the burden on the Jacksonville operations. He also hopes to reduce shipping costs, and thereby lower the total delivered prices, for its products for dealers in the Lexington and Atlanta territories. Based on previous sales, Williams estimates that production at each of the new sites will start at nearly 25 percent of the old sites but grow rapidly to 50 percent within three years.

The company has been using a minicomputer located in the home office to handle its data processing needs. Each of the other factories has several terminals that are connected to the home office through telephone lines. The system provides accounting software for sales orders, invoices, purchase invoices, inventory, payroll, and similar accounting functions.

Pratt Williams wants to establish two remote data entry and printing stations at each of the new factories. He recommends specifically that three data entry terminals and one printing terminal be placed at the two new sites and that the minicomputer at the Jacksonville office be upgraded to handle the communications and the extra processing from the new sites.

John Williams, Pratt's son, is in charge of the financial information systems for the firm. John has told Pratt that the company's minicomputer is nearly at the limit of its ability to expand, and in fact, that response time on the present system has already begun to slow down. John Williams believes that the current computer system is totally inadequate for the firm and feels that the company should scrap it and purchase a much larger computer system so that it will be in a position to meet planned growth.

a. Do you believe that Pratt's recommendations are better than John's? Why or why not? Be specific; provide reasons for choosing one plan or the other.

b. What other options are open to Pine Products? Specifically, how might these options be better than either Pratt's or John's plans?

3. **Feinstein Publishing Company.**
    Feinstein Publishing Company produces business textbooks for the collegiate market. The company has a particularly good reputation in the field of quantitative business texts. It markets textbooks throughout the United States, maintaining a large sales force whose members typically live in the city, state, or region they serve.

Salespeople visit the faculty at various colleges and universities to discuss the firm's texts and to take orders for examination copies of texts from faculty members. The firm also sets up booths at various business conferences during the year. The booths are filled with the firm's textbooks and are staffed by salespeople who live in the area of the conference. Salespeople at these conferences also spend most of their time taking orders from faculty for examination copies. Many faculty members also request examination copies by completing prestamped and preaddressed forms detached from textbook advertising brochures. If everything goes well, requests for examination copies will eventually turn into book orders issued from college bookstores.

Because the sales force is far-flung, the firm holds a sales conference at the home office only once a year. At that time, new products are introduced and explained to the salespeople, and salespeople get a chance to discuss successful sales tactics they have used during the previous year. However, the firm also introduces new products at several other points in the year, and salespeople receive written sales documents that explain the new products. The firm has never been happy with this tactic, but it does not wish to spend the money to bring every salesperson back to the home office for several sales conferences each year.

The marketing director is anxious to improve sales next year and to improve the productivity of her functional area. What Internet and office technologies can she use to improve productivity in the tasks that have just been described?

SELECTED INTERNET REFERENCE SITES

Alta Vista search engine (http://www.altavista.digital.com).

Bruno, L. "Groupware vs. Webware," *Data Communications* (on-line version), March 1996 (http://www.data.com).

Client/Server Computing Magazine (on-line version) (http://www.sentrytech.com).

CNET (http://www.cnet.com).

Cooltalk (http://www.netscape.com).

CyberCoin (http://www.cybercash.com).

Excite search engine (http://www.excite.com).

InfoSeek search engine (http://www.infoseek.com).

Internet Phone (http://www.vocaltec.com).

InterTrust Commerce Architecture
(http://www.intertrust.com).

NetMeeting (http://www.msn.com).

Netscape Communicator (http://www.netscape.com).

Rupley, S. "Videoconferencing Comes Home," *Trends On-line,* October 18, 1966.

Sharkews (http://www.sharwest.com/nettorb.com).

WebMaster Magazine (on-line version)
(http://www.web-master.com).

Yahoo! search engine (http://www.yahoo.com).

SELECTED REFERENCES AND READINGS

Anderson, H. "Net Talk." *PC Today,* October 1996, p. 81.

Baatz, E. B. "Will the Web Eat Your Job." *WebMaster,* May/June 1996, p. 41.

Banta, G. "Internet Pipe Schemes." *Internet World,* October 1996, p.62.

Brousell, D. R. "Client/Server Is Getting Stronger." *Client/Server Computing,* January 1997, p.25.

Covell, A., and T. Tannenbaum. "Video Servers: Live from Your Network!" *Network Computing,* October 15, 1996, p. 60.

Drummond, R. "Safe and Secure Electronic Commerce." *Network Computing,* December 1, 1996, p. 116.

"EDI or Else," *Datamation,* February 15, 1993, p. 15.

Frey, A. "Internet Servers: How the Latest Ones Are Stacking Up." *Network Computing,* October 15, 1996, p. 125.

Frey, A. "Making the Right Web Connection," *Network Computing,* July 15, 1996, p. 176.

Gaskin, J. E. "The Surprising Costs of Internet Connections." *NetWare Solutions,* August 1996, p. 28.

Grygo, E. M. "Intranet Reality Check." *Client/Server Computing,* May 1996, p. 22.

Halper, M. "The New Politics of Client/Server." *Client/Server Computing,* November 1996, p. 26.

Hick, V. B. "AOL's Problems Highlight Online Growing Pains," *St. Louis Post-Dispatch,* February 2, 1997, Section E, p. 1E.

Kantor, A., and M. Newbarth. "Off the Charts." *Internet World,* December 1996, p. 44.

King, K. "Real-World ATM." *NetWare Connection,* February 1997, p. 40.

King, K. "Understanding the Big ATM Picture." *NetWare Connection,* February 1997, p. 30.

Liebmann, L. "Talk, Talk, Talk: Internet Telephony Promises to Make Speech Truly Free, or Does it?" *NetWare Solutions,* January 1997, p. 28.

Maddox, K. "Accessing Corporate Data." *Communications Week,* September 16, 1996, p. 69.

Martin, M. H. "When Info Worlds Collide." *Fortune,* October 28, 1996, p. 130.

Messmer, E. "Intranets & the 'Net." *Network World,* September 16, 1996, p. 73.

Riggs, B. "Getting Off the Beaten Internet Path." *LAN Times,* February 3, 1997, p. 16.

Salamone, S. "Telecom." *LAN Times,* December 18, 1996, p. 1.

Schreiber, R. "Glue Enterprise Apps Together." *Datamation,* August 15, 1995, p. 41.

Snyder, J. "Groupware: Colonizing New Ground for Networks." *Network Computing,* March 15, 1996.

Stuart, A. "Business in the Wake of the Web." *WebMaster,* December 1996, p. 46.

Thé, L. "Workflow Tackles the Productivity Paradox." *Datamation,* August 15, 1995, p. 65.

Trimm, J. "Priming the Pump: A Primer on ISDN and Frame Relay." *NetWare Solutions*, August 1996, p. 33.

Trumbo, J. and J. Snyder. "Big, Bad E-Mail." *Network Computing,* October 15, 1996, p. 98.

Wiggins, R. "How the Internet Works." *Internet World,* October 1996, p. 54.

Willis, D. with J. Milne. "Domestic ISPs: Adapt or Perish." *Network Computing,* June 1, 1996, p. 100.

Zgodzinski, D. "Enter ADSL." *Internet World,* October 1996, p. 72.

Ziems, C., et al. "Intraware Solutions: Notes Wins the First Bout." *InfoWorld,* December 9, 1996, p. 88.

Upgrading Computer Information Systems for the U.S. Army Reserve Personnel Center

Background

The U.S. Army Reserve Components Personnel Administration Center (RCPAC) is located in St. Louis, Missouri. Its primary mission is to maintain personnel records for members of the U.S. Army Reserve. In total, there are more than 200,000 active reservists and more than 1,000,000 inactive reservists. The center is responsible for maintaining each reservist's entire career file. This file is used for individual promotion decisions, to record the receipt of awards for meritorious service and for heroism, and, most important to many reservists, to record the accumulation of creditable retirement years toward that important 20-year retirement goal. Additionally, the center maintains records on reservists in other than active and inactive status, such as reservists who are in the retired reserve. With this large volume of records to maintain, the center must rely extensively on computer technology.

The Software Reengineering Company (SRC), Inc. (see Integrated Case 1) recently negotiated a contract with RCPAC to upgrade the computer facilities for the main headquarters building, which is not far from SRC's St. Louis office. Malivai Washington manages the St. Louis regional office of SRC; he reports to the corporate president, Joseph Pyszynski at SRC's corporate headquarters in Arlington, Virginia. SRC organizes its regional offices along divisional lines. Each office has three divisions: defense contract software division, corporate contract software division, and contract training support division. The defense contract software division is responsible for developing information systems on an outsourcing basis for various agencies of the Department of Defense (DOD). The corporate contract software division performs similar services for private industry client firms. The contract training/support division provides training and support on an outsourcing basis for both DOD and private industry clients.

Mr. Washington has assigned the RCPAC contract to Priscilla Lundy, the division chief for the contract training/support division of the SRC St. Louis regional office. Ms. Lundy supervises a division composed of four training/support project teams. Each project team has a team leader, two to three programmer/analysts, and a number of additional computer specialists, with college degrees in the areas of management information systems (MIS) and computer science (CS), including scientific programmers, fourth-generation-language experts, systems programmers/administrators, database administrators, data communications engineers, and client/server systems administrators. These computer professionals know how to work with many operating systems including UNIX, Microsoft Windows, and Microsoft NT. Some of them have training on Novell network software. Others have skills in administering various types of database management systems including Oracle, Informix, Sybase, and Microsoft's SQL Server. The division also has numerous computer personnel who are assigned to projects in client firms on an outsourcing basis as technical experts in their respective specialties.

Current Situation

Mr. Washington normally meets with his division chiefs each Monday morning to review the status of ongoing contracts as well as any new projects. On this particular morning, Mr. Washington had completed his business with the division chiefs of the defense contract software and corporate contract software divisions. He asked Ms. Lundy to remain after the meeting to discuss the RCPAC contract.

"I had an interesting discussion with General Weimer at the golf course this weekend," said Malivai as he sipped his coffee. "He's the head honcho over at RCPAC. You may not know this, but Mike (the general) and I were cadets together in the Reserve Officer Training Corps (ROTC) over 20 years ago. In fact, I'm a retired reservist myself."

"Mike was telling me how excited he is about the prospect of upgrading his office computing facilities. The workers are having so much trouble with their old existing mainframe systems, and it's almost impossible for the office workers to share information on a timely basis. They're looking for solutions to their office information systems needs that can be delivered quickly. Further, they want standard systems that are supported by leading manufacturers of computer hardware and software. Of course, you'll have to examine the military standards for computer technology acquisition. Regardless of what the General wants, we have to stay within government regulatory standards."

Priscilla nodded her head at Malivai, but she had a sly smile, an I-know-something-you-don't-know type of smile. "I'm ahead of you on this project, Mr. Washington," Priscilla said grinning. "I've negotiated with the DOD agency in Washington that oversees computer technology acquisition standards for the military. I suggested and the agency agreed that there's a need to rewrite the standards in the area of office computer technology in light of the tremendous advances that have been made in the last few years."

"The existing standards outline details for acquiring mainframe and minicomputer technology with little mention of integrated microcomputer technology. There are few standards for client/server computer networks. The DOD agency believes that the existing standards are obsolete, and so we have received what amounts to carte blanche authority to acquire whatever General Weimer needs. Of course, we'll have to cost justify everything that is acquired under the contract, but it is a cost-plus type of contract. In addition, the agency will probably ask us to provide input when it rewrites DOD office technology standards later this year."

A cost-plus contract guarantees SRC a certain percentage of profit above the costs of the contract. This type of open-ended contract is used only in situations where the contract requirements have a high element of uncertainty.

"Well, that's excellent Priscilla," beamed Malivai. "I guess I don't have to tell you that our approach to the upgrade for RCPAC must be well organized so that we don't throw money down the drain buying equipment that they don't really need or that may cause compatibility problems later. Everyone seems to have increasing problems sharing information on the different microcomputer platforms that are used in offices these days. I'd like you to get to work on the project and brief me on the initial draft of the office technology specifications you're suggesting for Weimer in, let's say, two weeks. After that we'll brief the general together. We only have three months to complete the project."

THE CURRENT OFFICE ENVIRONMENT AT **RCPAC**

Priscilla assigned the multimillion dollar project to her senior project team leader, Tom Berry. Tom decided that the best approach to identifying RCPAC's requirements was to select two floors from the total of 12 floors at the RCPAC headquarters building to serve as a prototype for the project. He selected the floor that housed General Weimer's office, as he wanted the general's direct input on the project. Tom also wanted to showcase what current technology could accomplish. He also selected the floor below where the senior staff officers for RCPAC worked. Figure C2–1 gives an organizational chart for the major functional areas at RCPAC. Figure C2–2 shows a layout of these two office floors.

Current office support is provided via an IBM AS/400 minicomputer. This computer is about six years old and is actually located in the basement of the building. Computer terminals are located on various administrative desks, although none of the senior officers in RCPAC has a terminal available at their desks. This configuration makes it difficult for them to access key information. The AS/400 has dedicated printers at multiple locations on each floor of the building.

Figure C2–1

RCPAC organization chart

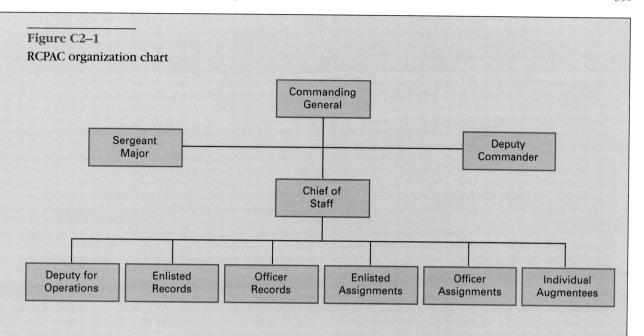

Figure C2–2

Office layouts for the two prototype office floors

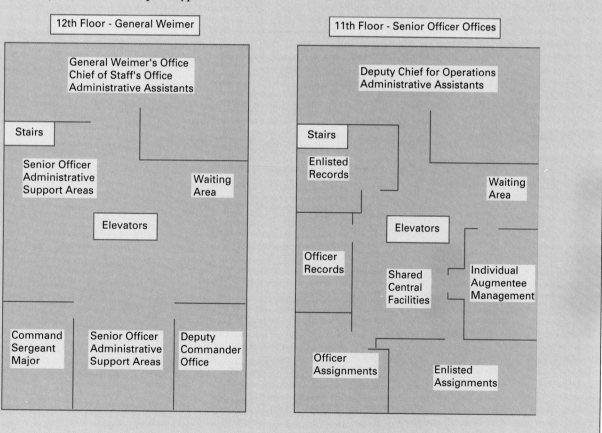

Terminals connected to a mainframe computer that is also located in the MIS data processing center in the basement of the building serve both the enlisted records section and officers records section. This computer can process millions of records and produces hundreds of standard reports for various offices in the building each month. The line printers attached to the mainframe computer are located in the basement, and the reports are delivered according to an established schedule on a daily basis.

Administrative managers and clerical workers on the two floors selected for the prototype study use a mixture of stand-alone microcomputers, primarily older 80486 computers running Microsoft Windows, that were purchased from various vendors. Most of the microcomputers have individual dot-matrix printers, although numerous administrative workers have their own laser printers.

THE DESIRED OFFICE ENVIRONMENT

In completing her analysis of RCPAC's office technology requirements, Priscilla determined that each functional area within the center needs to be supported as a work group. Within functional groups, computer-based support should be provided for a number of work-group activities, including the ability to

- Share files, reports, and other documents.
- Access common databases.
- Share calendars.
- Allow group members to access files, documents, and reports concurrently.
- Coordinate group meetings.
- Provide electronic mail, bulletin board, and voice mail services.
- Provide project management software.
- Share special hardware resources such as high-speed laser printers, scanners, and a fax server.

Some work groups, such as the enlisted assignments functional area, have specialized needs. Tom noted the need to improve the coordination of assignment activities across various military occupational specialties. Most enlisted personnel have multiple specialties; for example, a sergeant might be qualified as a missile repair technician and also be qualified as a motor vehicle repair supervisor. Since different assignment officers handle the different specialties, they needed to access a common database of recent assignments to ensure that they didn't assign the same enlisted reservist to two different units.

Most administrative workers expressed an interest in learning how to use software programs that would provide a 'what-you-see-is-what-you-get' approach to word processing and other office software. They were tired of using older computer packages that required them to print samples of their documents to determine if the format of the output would be satisfactory.

Other workers wanted integrated software packages. One captain in the operations area said, "I need to pull up aggregated data about recent operations such as those we've supported with individual reservists and troop units overseas in the Middle East. Then I may need to prepare graphs of the data that make the various trends clear during my briefings to senior officers. Finally, I need to be able to transfer the graphs into word processing documents that my administrative assistant can use to produce reports to meet ad hoc reporting requirements. I'm tired of having to use scissors and tape to cut and paste my presentations and reports together. I know civilian firms have software that speeds up this process dramatically. We need that type of software." Tom noted this requirement for dynamic data exchange between packages.

Several senior officers in the officer assignments functional area noted the need for improved on-line access to officer records. "We're continually getting telephone calls from officer reservists requesting a review of their personnel records prior to a new assignment or consideration for promotion in the U.S. Army Reserve. Our existing system is based on entering the Social Security number. We need a system that can pull up an individual record or groups of records based on alternative search fields. For example, I want to access officer records of reservists who are eligible for consideration for promotion on the next lieu-

Figure C2–3

Draft list of office technology requirements

Work group	Group size	Current computers and other equipment	Computers and other equipment needed
Command group	15	8 stand-alone older personal computers.	15 new personal computers. Laser printer access. Color printer access.
Operations	22	5 stand-alone personal computers with terminal-emulation hardware/software to link to the AS/400. Various printers.	22 new personal computers. Laser printer access. Scanner access.
Enlisted records	28	14 older stand-alone personal computers. Various printers. 6 mainframe terminals. 4 AS/400 terminals.	14 or more new personal computers. High-speed laser printer access. Scanner access.
Officer records	11	11 older stand-alone personal computers. 3 laser printers. 8 dot-matrix printers. 2 mainframe terminals. 2 AS/400 terminals.	5 or more new personal computers. High-speed laser printer access. Scanner access.
Enlisted assignments	18	12 current technology stand-alone personal computers. Various printers. 4 mainframe terminals. 2 AS/400 terminals.	6 new personal computers. High-speed laser printer access. Scanner access. Fax/modem access.
Officer assignments	9	4 older stand-alone personal computers. 5 current technology personal computers. 2 laser printers. 7 dot-matrix printers. 3 mainframe terminals. 3 AS/400 terminals.	9 new personal computers. Laser printer access. Scanner access. Fax/modem access.
Individual augmentee management	8	2 older stand-alone personal computers. 6 dot-matrix printers. 3 mainframe terminals. 1 AS/400 terminal.	8 new personal computers. Laser printer access. Scanner access. Fax/modem access.

tenant colonel promotion board. We also need the system to display the most current official photograph for an officer." Tom noted the need for improved database technology with OLE data fields. He also thought the group might need computer image scanning technology. Preliminary requirements are outlined in Figure C2-3. The group size column refers to the number of administrative and clerical workers and senior officers who need office technology support.

Case Questions and Exercises

1. Consider General Weimer's floor as a work group. The general wants to acquire the necessary equipment to implement a local area network. You've decided to recommend a network with multiple Windows NT–based servers. List some of the hardware and software (application package, operating system, and network operating system) components needed for the network.

2. The general wants each functional area to continue to use the existing reports and information from the AS/400 system. You've decided to recommend linking all existing and new microcomputers into a set of functional area networks (one network for each functional area), with each functional area network having a link to the existing AS/400. Assume that the functional area networks are similar, and that there will eventually be several functional area networks. Describe some of the computer hardware and software that could provide the linkages to the AS/400 for the functional area networks.

3. Select a software package to support work-group activities such as calendar sharing, file sharing, electronic mail, bulletin boarding, and other group activities as mentioned in the case. Identify specific software packages that are advertised on the Internet and the current price of these packages if that information is available from the Internet. Assume that enough copies would be acquired to support each functional area and that each functional area would have a work-group LAN that is also connected to the network on General Weimer's floor.

4. Use the Internet to search for and identify two alternative full-page scanners that RCPAC could acquire and the associated price of the hardware and software needed to operate the scanners. Identify two brands of high-speed laser printers that will produce letter quality grayscale printing and graphics. Printing output for nongraphical documents must be at least 20 pages per minute. After recommending a printer for purchase, and assuming each functional area would have at least one high-speed printer, how would you plan on using the expensive printer as a shared resource?

APPLICATIONS OF INFORMATION SYSTEMS TO FUNCTIONAL BUSINESS AREAS

SO FAR, YOU HAVE LEARNED about information systems, the role of systems within organizations, the strategic uses of information systems, and the basic computer resources available to the manager. What you learned generally emphasized the organization as a whole, rather than the major areas of decision making commonly found in organizations. Part 3 focuses on these areas. You will apply what you have learned about information systems and computer system resources to problems in managerial decision making, accounting and finance, marketing, production, and human resources. You will also learn about information tools such as artificial intelligence and expert systems that are used to solve managerial problems.

At the end of Part 3, you will understand the nature of the decisions to be made in these areas and the nature of the information systems that are designed to support these decisions.

CHAPTER 10

APPLICATIONS OF OPERATIONAL INFORMATION SYSTEMS TO BUSINESS

CHAPTER 11

APPLICATIONS OF TACTICAL AND STRATEGIC INFORMATION SYSTEMS TO BUSINESS

CHAPTER 12

DECISION SUPPORT SYSTEMS AND EXPERT SYSTEMS

10

APPLICATIONS OF OPERATIONAL INFORMATION SYSTEMS TO BUSINESS

CHAPTER OUTLINE

Manager's View

Operational Accounting and Financial Information Systems

Operational Marketing Information Systems

Operational Production Information Systems

Operational Human Resource Information Systems

Management Summary

Key Terms for Managers

Review Questions

Questions for Discussion

Problems

Cases

Selected Internet Reference Sites

Selected References and Readings

Consider these activities of typical organizations:

1. Paychecks are calculated, printed, stuffed in envelopes, and distributed each week.

2. Sales invoices are verified, calculated, printed, stuffed in envelopes, and mailed each month.

3. Purchase orders are verified, calculated, printed, stuffed in envelopes, and mailed each day.

4. Checks to vendors are calculated, printed, stuffed in envelopes, and mailed each day.

5. Potential customers are identified and called each day.

6. Employees, floor space, and pieces of equipment are scheduled for specific times and tasks each day.

7. Parts manufactured are scanned, viewed, measured, or otherwise inspected for faults continuously.

These are just a few of many information tasks that must be completed accurately, swiftly, and repeatedly on a regular basis in many organizations. In large organizations, thousands of these tasks are completed daily.

The information systems that perform or support the completion of these tasks are often referred to as operational information systems, or **transaction processing systems.** In fact financial transactions typically come to mind when you think of operational information systems because many operational information systems focus on the routine, repetitive financial transactions that are an important part of the basic activities of most business enterprises. However, operational information systems include more than the financial transactions of an organization. Operational information systems record, process, and report all routine and repetitive activities or organizations. These activities occur not only in accounting and finance but also in human resources, production, and marketing (see Figure 10–1).

The Nature of Operational Information Systems

Operational information systems primarily produce routine, repetitive, descriptive, expected, and objective data that describe past activities. The information they produce is usually detailed, highly structured, accurate, derived from internal sources, and produced regularly. To some, these systems may appear to represent pure drudgery for employees who must complete them. However, the application of information systems technology to operational information systems has reduced this drudgery to a great extent and provided managers with a number of major advantages.

Management Advantages

Automating operational information systems usually increases the efficiency of these systems; they typically run faster and require less personnel and other business resources than manual systems. Organizations that automate operational information systems usually receive several benefits for their efforts.

Figure 10–1

Examples of operational information systems in four business functions

Accounting/finance	Marketing	Production	Human Resources
Fixed assets	Prospect leads	Purchasing	Position control
Sales order processing	Contact information	Receiving	Employee profiles
Accounts receivable	Micromarketing and data warehousing	Quality control	Employee skills inventory
Accounts payable	Telemarketing	Shipping	Performance management
Inventory control	Direct mail	Automated materials handling	Government reporting
Purchase order processing	Point-of-sale	Computer-aided design/manufacturing	Selection and placement
Payroll	Delivery tracking and routing	Image management	Training
Billing/Invoicing	Electronic shopping	Material selection	
	Electronic advertising	Shop-floor scheduling	
		Mass customization	
		Shop-floor control	

1. *Reduced Cost* Information technology reduces the cost of operational information systems, often substantially. Consider the time and manpower a large firm would need to read each time card manually; compute the amount of time worked each day and for the whole week; and calculate regular pay, overtime pay, gross pay, deductions, and net pay for each employee. The worker hours needed to produce weekly paychecks and their associated records have been substantially reduced in most firms through information technology. In fact, information technology applied to operational systems may help an organization become a low-cost leader and improve its competition position.

2. *Increased Speed* Information technology also vastly increases the speed with which operational tasks are completed, thereby increasing the service levels that an organization can offer to its customers and clients. For example, information technology can speed up processing and filling sales orders, allowing organizations to ship orders the same day they are received. Selling inventory that you don't have because your inventory data is not kept current leads to backorders and dissatisfied customers. Sending invoices to customers as soon as goods are shipped leads to faster cash flow.

3. *Increased Accuracy* Copying data from one record to another, such as copying data from a sales order to a sales invoice, often generates errors. Manually calculating order totals and discounts can lead to errors in customer invoices and, subsequently, to disgruntled customers. Capturing employee work times electronically as they report for work and leave work reduces errors when these data are subsequently used to calculate total hours, total pay, deductions, and net pay.

4. *Increased Customer Service* The application of information technology has also improved an organization's ability to respond to each customer's or client's unique product or service needs. Computer systems can help an

organization record, process, and keep track of the many details needed to provide customers with what they want, when they want it, and in the manner that they want. Information technology also helps organizations track customer shipments, allowing them to answer customer queries faster and to keep on top of customer deliveries.

5. *Increased Data for Decision Making* Operational information systems are also important for decision making. The data from operational information systems not only represent the basic activities of most organizations but also serve as the raw material for tactical and strategic information systems. Reports that compare, extrapolate, and otherwise massage operational-level data, to help managers make tactical and strategic decisions. Tactical and strategic information systems are difficult to build for an organization that does not already have a well-developed set of operational-level information systems.

This chapter examines the application of information technology to some of the operational information systems common to four organizational functions: accounting/finance, marketing, production, and human resource management.

OPERATIONAL ACCOUNTING AND FINANCIAL INFORMATION SYSTEMS

63, 64

Typically, the first applications that organizations computerize are operational-level financial accounting systems. **Operational financial accounting information systems** are typically task oriented. They focus on processing financial transactions to produce the routine, repetitive information outputs that every organization finds necessary. These outputs include paychecks, checks to vendors, customer invoices, purchase orders, stock reports, and other regular forms and reports.

Financial Accounting Systems

The heart of an organization's operational financial information system is its financial accounting system. A computerized **financial accounting system** is composed of a series of software modules or subsystems that may be used separately or in an integrated fashion. The system modules typically include

- General ledger
- Fixed assets
- Sales order processing
- Accounts receivable
- Accounts payable
- Inventory control
- Purchase order processing
- Payroll

When these computerized financial accounting systems are integrated, each system receives data as input from some systems and provides information as output to other systems. The financial accounting systems and how they might be integrated are shown in Figure 10–2.

Importance to Decision Making

The fact that operational financial accounting systems are predominantly routine and repetitive in nature does not mean that they do not contribute to decisions that are important to the organization. For example, the accounts receivable system may

Figure 10–2

An integrated financial accounting system and its major components

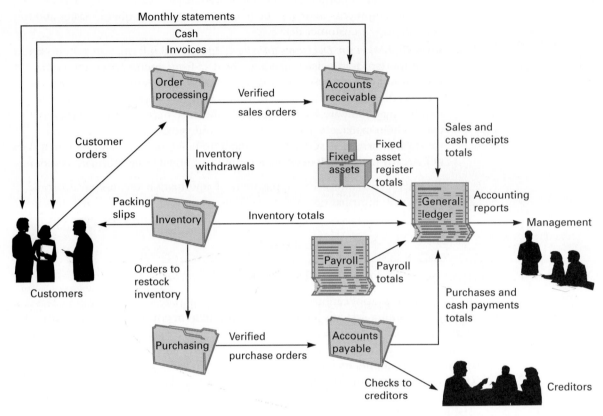

routinely process credit information about customers, which may include comparing the balance of customer accounts to customer credit limits. Though this comparison might seem trivial, it is essential to a common decision faced by the sales force: Should the customer be allowed to make this purchase on credit? Organizations that can provide *on line* credit information to salespeople reduce the risk of incurring bad debts, which lowers their cost of operations.

Let's briefly examine each of the financial accounting systems.

General Ledger System

The **general ledger system** provides managers with periodic accounting reports and statements such as the income statement and balance sheet. The general ledger system also permits general ledger accounts to be created, defines the organization's fiscal period, and produces a chart of accounts maintained by the accounting system. Other financial accounting systems periodically provide input to the general ledger system. For example, after processing the weekly payroll, the payroll system provides the general ledger system with data to update the various payroll accounts.

Fixed Assets System

The **fixed assets system** maintains records of equipment, property, and other long-term assets that an organization owns. The records include the original cost of the assets, their depreciation rates, the accumulated depreciation to date, and the *book value* of the assets, or the original cost less accumulated depreciation. The general ledger system uses this information to maintain current balances in the various long-term asset accounts of the organization. The system also may maintain and process data pertaining to the gain or loss on the sale of fixed assets and may prepare various special income tax forms for fixed assets that the federal government requires.

<table>
<tr><td>

Sales Order Processing System

</td><td>

The **sales order processing system,** or order-entry system, routinely records sales orders and also provides data to other systems that fill those orders, maintain inventory levels, and bill the customer. This system provides sales tax data to the general ledger system for posting to taxing agency accounts, stock data to the inventory system for updating inventory balances, and sales data to the accounts receivable system for posting to customer accounts.

A computerized sales order system usually tracks the sales made by each salesperson and provides input to the payroll subsystem so that salespersons' commissions can be calculated. The system should also provide information to the shipping department to ensure that the correct stock is sent to the customer; provide for backorders when not enough stock is on the shelves; accurately figure prices, totals, discounts, and taxes on the order; and allow a quick and accurate response to customer inquiries about the status of an order.

When the sales order system is on-line, the salesperson can immediately verify customer credit and inventory levels. This system gives the salesperson a competitive advantage over salespeople without an on-line order-entry system. Consider, for example, a field sales representative who carries to the client's premises a laptop PC equipped with a modem allowing a connection to the organization's mainframe. Using the PC, the salesperson can verify immediately whether the customer can be granted the credit needed for the sale and also determine if enough stock is on hand to fill the order. The sale can be closed while picking and packing slips (see Manager's Memo 10–1) are delivered electronically to the warehouse. Because the system is on-line, the customer should get the goods much faster than if a manual order-entry system were used.

</td></tr>
<tr><td>

Accounts Receivable System

</td><td>

The **accounts receivable system** allows you to enter, update, and delete customer information such as sales made on account, credit terms, cash payments received, credit memorandums, and account balances.

Inputs to the accounts receivable system include sales invoices, credit memorandums, and cash received from customers. Typical outputs of this system are monthly customer statements of account and a schedule of accounts receivable listing each account and its balance (see Figure 10–3).

Many accounts receivable systems produce *aged accounts receivable reports.* These reports classify account balances into several categories, such as more than 30 days, 60 days, and 90 days overdue (see Figure 10–4). That output may seem rather lackluster, but an aging report identifies customers with overdue balances, allowing managers to use the computer system to prepare collection letters, start collection procedures, and disallow additional credit to poor credit risks. Without aging data, an organization may continue to grant credit to customers who are already overdue on their payments.

The accounts receivable system may also provide data to the direct mail advertising system of the organization. For example, customer names and addresses may be *imported,* or copied, from the accounts receivable file stored on the organization's mainframe to a word processing file stored on the marketing departments local area network to produce sales promotion letters. This process can be especially effective

</td></tr>
</table>

| Manager's Memo 10-1 | HOW AN ON-LINE ORDER-ENTRY SYSTEM WORKS |

◢ To illustrate how an on-line order-entry system works, let's examine how a manufacturing firm might use one to process orders. At this firm, salespeople with notebook computers equipped with modems are responsible for entering customer orders at the customer site. To create an order, salespeople bring up an order-entry screen like the one shown.

The salespeople enter the customer's name, and the computer system at the home office supplies the customer's number, address, city, state, ZIP code, and

plays these data on the screen. When the salespeople enter the quantity ordered, the inventory system is queried to determine if enough stock is on hand to fill the order.

The salespeople continue this sequence of entries and responses until the last item ordered has been entered. Then the order-entry system immediately subtotals the order and verifies that the customer's credit is good. It then produces immediately, at the appropriately located printer, a picking slip for ware-

```
                    ENTER CUSTOMER ORDER

        ACCOUNT NUMBER _
        NAME
        ADDRESS
        CITY
        STATE/ZIP
        CREDIT TERMS
        STOCK NUMBER
        STOCK NAME
        STOCK DESCRIPTION
        QUANTITY ORDERED
```

credit terms in the correct places on the screen. The order-entry system obtains these data from the accounts receivable system.

The salespeople then enter the stock number of each item the customer orders. The order-entry system obtains the stock name, stock description, and price for each item from the inventory system and dis-

house personnel to use to fill the order from inventory shelves, a mailing label for the carton, and a packing slip to be included in the carton with the completed order. The accounts receivable system then uses the completed sales order to bill the customer and create and print the sales invoice.

Figure 10–3

Typical inputs and outputs for an accounts receivable system

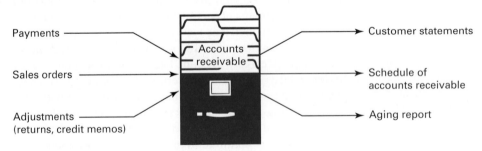

if the customers can be linked with the products or services they have bought. Organizations can often increase sales by targeting sales appeals for product upgrades or services to customers who have purchased the basic product.

For example, suppose that Enbloch, Inc., a large national retail department store chain, wishes to contact all recent charge account purchasers of humidifiers to offer a special savings on annual maintenance contracts. Using a query language like the

Figure 10–4
An aged accounts
receivable report

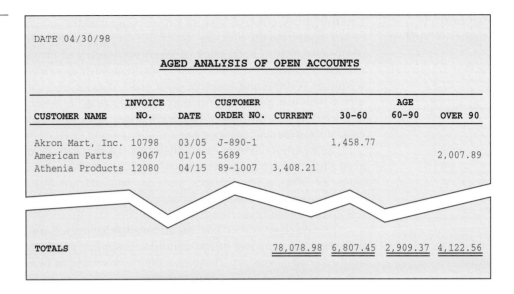

DATE 04/30/98

AGED ANALYSIS OF OPEN ACCOUNTS

CUSTOMER NAME	INVOICE NO.	DATE	CUSTOMER ORDER NO.	CURRENT	30-60	AGE 60-90	OVER 90
Akron Mart, Inc.	10798	03/05	J-890-1		1,458.77		
American Parts	9067	01/05	5689				2,007.89
Athenia Products	12080	04/15	89-1007	3,408.21			
TOTALS				78,078.98	6,807.45	2,909.37	4,122.56

one discussed in Chapter 7, the manager electronically completes a search of the sales order file for the customer numbers on all recent orders that contain humidifiers. Using those numbers, the manager directs the system to search for matches in the Customer Number field of the accounts receivable file. The names and addresses of all customers whose numbers match are copied to a new file that is sent to the marketing department's local area network file server. There, using a word processing system, the names and addresses are merged with a sales promotion letter.

Accounts Payable System

The **accounts payable system** processes much the same routine, repetitive information as the accounts receivable system, except that in this case the information is about the organization's creditors rather than about its customers (see Figure 10-5). For example, the system maintains creditor account information, prepares checks to creditors, and produces the accounts payable schedule. The accounts payable system provides data directly to the general ledger system and receives data from the purchase order system.

The accounts payable system may also find the due dates for purchases on account and the last date on which cash discounts may be taken on those purchases. This system provides important operational-level information that can be used to schedule cash payments to creditors. The effect of such a system is to allow the organization to keep its money working as long as possible while ensuring that the firm takes all cash discounts.

Figure 10–5
The accounts
payable subsystem

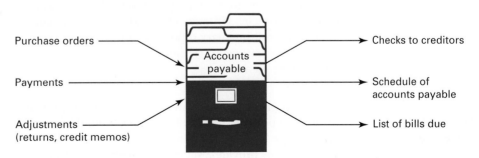

Purchase orders — Accounts payable — Checks to creditors

Payments — Schedule of accounts payable

Adjustments (returns, credit memos) — List of bills due

Inventory Control System

The **inventory control system** provides input to the general ledger system and receives input from the purchase order and the sales order systems. The basic purpose of the system is to keep track of inventory levels and inventory costs. The system maintains information about each stock item, such as stock numbers and stock descriptions, receipts and issues of stock, stock damage, and stock balances. The inventory system may also notify the purchasing department when stock items need to be reordered. It may maintain information about stock item costs, selling price data on each stock item, and the location and distribution of stock within the organization.

The inventory system maintains stock balance data by obtaining stock receipts from the purchase order system and stock issues from the order-entry system. Updates for other stock changes, such as damaged goods, lost stock, shrinkage, or spoilage, are usually entered directly into the system by inventory clerks after a physical inventory has been completed.

Specialized inventory systems are needed for manufacturers to provide information regarding the cost of raw-materials inventory, goods-in-process inventory, and finished-goods inventory. These systems are described in more detail later in the section on production information systems.

Accountants regard inventory as an asset. Other managers, however, may regard inventories as a burden. Stock has to be stored, heated or cooled, counted, and otherwise husbanded. These tasks all represent expenses to an organization. Inventory represents a substantial amount of funds for many organizations, and managers may wish to deploy these funds elsewhere in the firm. Furthermore, many state and local agencies tax inventories. Maintaining as lean an inventory as possible while suffering from minimal stockouts is an important goal, and computerized inventory systems assist managers in achieving this goal. Lowered inventory costs for an organization may mean that the organization can lower its prices and achieve a competitive advantage over firms without computerized inventory systems.

Purchase Order Processing System

The **purchase order processing system** processes purchase orders and tracks which purchase orders have been filled, which stock items ordered are on backorder, which stock items have been damaged or do not meet the specifications of the original order, and which orders are still on order and when those orders are expected to arrive.

The purchase order system provides information to the accounts payable and inventory systems. The system produces a variety of reports, including a list of all stock on backorder and an open-order report that lists all purchase orders not yet received and their expected arrival dates.

Payroll System

The **payroll system** processes wage and salary information such as payments to employees; deductions from employee paychecks; and payments to federal, state, and other taxing agencies for taxes owed. The payroll system produces such reports as the weekly payroll summary report, overtime reports, forms for taxing agencies such as wage and tax statements (Forms W-2), payroll checks, and checks for payroll taxes owed to taxing agencies.

Financial Accounting Software

Commercially packaged accounting system software contains the operating-level programs used to produce the invoices, checks, monthly financial statements, and other regular, routine output necessary to run an organization. Many computerized accounting systems provide a variety of features (see Manager's Memo 10–2), including financial analysis tools for the tactical decision maker and strategic planner, such as

| Manager's Memo 10–2 | SELECTED FEATURES OF COMPUTERIZED ACCOUNTING SOFTWARE |

Computerized accounting software typically includes a general ledger module and subordinate modules such as payroll, inventory, purchase order, sales order, accounts receivable, accounts payable, job cost, and fixed assets. When buying accounting software, examine the features and specifications of each module to ensure that what is offered matches your organization's needs. Some possible features and specifications of accounting software include these:

FEATURES

1. Handles multiple companies.
2. Processes multicompany consolidated reports.
3. Maintains budgets.
4. Allows entries outside the current period.
5. Allows data export to spreadsheet files.
6. Allows unbalanced entries.
7. Provides billing-cycle functions.

8. Reconciles checking accounts.
9. Provides financial reports at any time for any period.
10. Allows multiuser access.
11. Provides on-line help.

SPECIFICATIONS

1. The maximum number of accounts it handles.
2. The highest account balance it accepts.
3. The maximum number of account number digits it accepts.
4. The maximum number of departments it allows.
5. How it processes purchase discounts.
6. How it processes aging of accounts receivable.
7. What tax form reports it produces.
8. What access security it provides.
9. What auditing features it provides.

various financial statement ratios. The manager automatically can produce data simply by selecting a report from a menu displayed by the software.

Vertical accounting software responds to the unique concerns and problems of firms in specific industries. For example, organizations in the health industry often must collect their payments not only from the patient but also from third parties, such as insurance companies or government agencies. The ability of software to handle accounts receivable from third parties and to provide third-party billing is important to these organizations. This ability is usually a standard feature in accounting software designed for organizations in the health industry.

OPERATIONAL MARKETING INFORMATION SYSTEMS

The marketing function occurs in all organizations, including profit and not-for-profit, manufacturing, agricultural, financial, educational, and service organizations. The basic goal of the marketing function in any organization is to satisfy the needs and wants of its customers. To achieve that goal, marketing personnel engage in activities such as planning and developing new products; advertising, promoting, selling, storing, and distributing goods and services; providing financing and credit to customers; and conducting market research.

Operational marketing information systems include systems such as sales systems, advertising systems, sales promotion systems, warehousing systems, and pricing systems. The systems collect data that describe marketing operations, process those data, and make marketing information available to marketing managers to help them make decisions. To be effective, marketing information systems must be coordinated with other organizational information systems, such as purchasing systems, production systems, inventory systems, accounts receivable systems, credit systems, and order-entry systems.

Computer information systems have been widely applied to operational-level marketing tasks. Information technology has increased the productivity of salespeople; helped firms manage customers better, locate prospective customers, customize marketing efforts to specific groups and individuals, and reduce costs; and vastly widened the reach of many organizations in terms of the geographic territory they serve. Computer technology applied to operational-level marketing systems also captures data useful for tactical and strategic decisions. These examples are listed in Figure 10–1.

Sales Force Automation Systems

Sales force automation systems are designed to increase the productivity of salespeople. Bread-and-butter sales activities usually include identifying potential or prospective customers, contacting customers, calling on customers, making sales pitches, closing the sale, and following up on sales. Sales force automation systems may address only the administrative tasks of salespeople, such as customer contact management, customer call reports, and travel expense reports. The systems may also support the sales process itself by managing the sales cycle, providing electronic catalogs, or providing electronic sales presentations. Typically, automating a sales force involves equipping salespeople with notebook computers and software to support their activities.

Prospect information systems.   Locating potential customers is often a time-consuming and frustrating part of the salesperson's work. The sources of information used to obtain sales leads are diverse and may include other customers, other vendors who sell supporting or ancillary products, newspaper notices, telephone directories, and customer inquiries. Searching directories and other customer lists may take a lot of time and yield few actual customers.

Files of sales leads are called prospects files. When these files are stored on magnetic media, they are easier for the salesperson to search or summarize. **Electronic directory** databases are one source of sales leads. Many of these directories are inexpensive and available on CD-ROMs for use on PCs. For example, American Business Information offers a CD-ROM directory of 88,000,000 U.S. households, Pro CD's Select Phone Deluxe lists 95,000,000 individual and business phone numbers and addresses, and MarketPlace Information Corporation provides a directory of more than 10,000,000 firms. Outputs of **prospect information systems** may include lists of prospects by location, by product category, by income or gross revenue, or by other classifications important to the sales force.

On-line databases also provide prospect information systems. On-line databases may be searched by database query software or plotted by mapping software (see Figure 10–6), which displays prospects on a map.

Contact management systems.   Customer **contact management systems** (see Figure 10–7) provide information to the sales force pertaining to customers, their product or service preferences, sales history data, and a historical record of sales calls and/or visits. One output of these systems may be a *call report* showing the number of sales calls made by a salesperson categorized by size of organization, previous sales, or some other characteristic, and the number or amount of sales made per customer, per visit, and/or per category.

If the information is kept on magnetic media, it is a relatively simple matter for the salesperson to identify all those customers who prefer certain types of products or who may be ready to purchase accessories for previous purchases. Sorting the dates

Figure 10–6

Mapping software

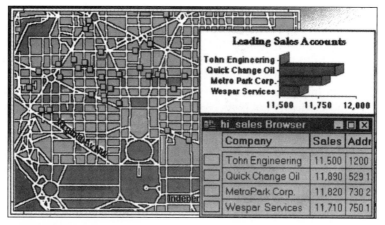

Courtesy MapInfo Corporation

of previous visits allows the salesperson to identify customers who may be running out of a product and need to place another order. When stock has been placed on sale, contact file records permit the salesperson to notify customers who are interested in or who regularly purchase these items about the price reductions.

Other sales force automation systems.   Sales force automation systems may also provide support for many other routine, repetitive salesperson activities, for example, travel expense reports, appointment calendars, telephone and address rolodexes, sales letter creation and distribution, e-mail, and fax. Internet access may also be provided so that salespeople can keep current on business news at any hour, especially news

Figure 10–7

A screen from Act! showing the report of contacts with a customer

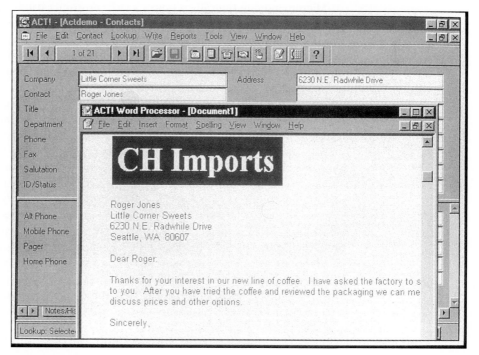

Courtesy Symantec Corporation

about the industry, competitors, and customers. The notebook computers may be equipped with CD-ROM drives that allow salespeople to display company catalog data and use presentation graphics software for sales presentations.

Sales force automation systems may not succeed if implemented poorly. In fact, industry analysts report a failure rate of between 25 and 60 percent by those companies implementing such systems.[1] Automating people's work requires change, and those who do not perceive an advantage to the change may resist. It is important that the sales force perceive that the system will benefit them by improving their productivity. One way that some firms have attempted to achieve acceptance of sales force automation is to select key salespeople to test the system. Their success then feeds through the firm grapevine to others, creating interest and demand for similar systems. Careful and thorough training in the use of the system hardware and software is also critical to success.

Micromarketing and Data Warehouse Systems

Pitching sales or advertising campaigns to very narrowly defined customer targets is called **micromarketing.** Computer systems have made micromarketing possible. They can be used to identify and target specific customers or prospects from large databases. For example, advertisements can be inserted into magazines targeted to each person who has purchased a product before and might be willing to buy an upgrade. You might receive your favorite news magazine one week and find it contains an insert with your name on it, asking you how you are enjoying a product you had bought previously, and wondering if you might be interested in an accessory to that product. You might also receive a catalog from a mail-order firm that contains only data about products you have purchased before or products related to your purchases. Micromarketing avoids the waste of resources that occurs when marketing efforts cannot be so narrowly focused. It also can dramatically raise the probability of a successful marketing effort.

Micromarketing typically requires a large customer database, called a **data warehouse.** The information in the data warehouse can be sorted and massaged, or *mined,* to discover customer preferences and trends, sorted by geographic region, income level, sex, age, and occupation. The purpose of **data mining** a customer database is to identify new marketing opportunities and to allow marketing departments to focus sales, advertising, and promotional campaigns on tightly drawn market niches. Firms may use their own customer records as their data warehouse. Many firms, however, augment their own customer database with customer data purchased from other companies (see Figure 10–8). Some companies with large data warehouses, such as polling and survey companies, credit rating firms, and credit card companies, sell their data warehouses. For example, one major credit card company, which has data on millions of credit card customers, sells its customer transaction information to thousands of its business partners.

Large department stores have begun data mining their huge customer databases to identify their most profitable shoppers. The stores then provide these customers with a great deal of personal attention and special offers. One retail firm provides "client books" containing the preferences and sizes of its most frequent customers. Sales clerk are then able to call these customers and provide them with information about or complete orders for merchandise these customers regularly order. A major department store executive estimated that one-fifth of its credit customers were responsible for 75 percent of its sales.[2]

---

[1]Scott Inks, University of Memphis, June 16, 1996.
[2]*Wall Street Journal,* March 3, 1995, p. B1.

Figure 10–8

Compusearch
Micromarketing
Data & Systems

Some firms provide software to mine customer data. That software may include statistical analyses software, mapping software, charting and graphics software, and reporting software. Other firms provide the customer data. Some provide both. For example, a Canadian firm, Compusearch Micromarketing Data & Systems, provides customers with software that performs each of those tasks as well as many different types of databases. Here is a list of some of them:

Demographic databases

Census data
Estimates and projections of census data
Consumer spending potential data
Household facilities and equipment data

Cartographic databases

Geographic files
Street and highway files
Place names and location files

Segmentation systems

Geodemographic data files
Lifestyles
Wealth styles

Location databases

Businesses
Shopping centers
Restaurants
Financial institutions
Grocery stores
Drugstores
Physicians
Dentists
Hospitals
Nursing homes

Marketing databases

Daytime population
Business activity
Home values
Tax filer data
Vehicle registrations
Traffic volumes
Health data
Prospects unlimited
Lifestyle selector
International Surveys Limited (ISL)
Homescan
Market facts

Media links

Television
Magazines
Newspapers
Cable
Radio

Mexican data
Market Mexico

Telemarketing Systems

You have probably received many calls hawking products or services or soliciting donations. Use of the telephone to sell products and services, or *telemarketing,* has become a common and important means by which organizations improve the productivity of their sales force. The telephone allows salespeople to initiate contacts, offer products and services, or follow up on sales without travel costs or travel time and also lets salespeople reach many more customers in a given time period than they could have through conventional means.

Telemarketing systems usually include support for the automatic dialing of parties and/or delivering voice messages to the answering party under the control of a computer system. Some systems allow you to make notes about the calls, to generate follow-up letters, and to view a customer file while a call to that customer is in progress.

Telemarketers also use electronic directories and on-line databases to gather names, addresses, telephone numbers, and other data on potential customers. Using these databases, telemarketers can quickly create lists of people and organizations that meet their marketing criteria. Telemarketing systems usually provide computer support for identifying customers and automatically calling them from disk-based telephone directories or from customer files maintained on a database. This software may then provide a digitized message about a product to people who answer the phone, or permit the salesperson to make the sales pitch.

Telemarketing has moved down from mainframe systems to microcomputer systems. One manufacturer even provides a LAN-based system that permits more than 200 telemarketers to use the system at the same time. It also includes management features for analysis of data pertaining to calls, contacts, sales approaches, and sales transactions.

Telemarketing technology has allowed many firms to increase their sales substantially—and gain market share—while decreasing costs per sale.

Direct Mail Advertising Systems

Many organizations generate sales by mailing sales brochures and catalogs directly to customers using **direct mail advertising systems.** To distribute sales documents rapidly to large numbers of potential customers, most marketing departments maintain customer mailing lists that are used for mass mailings. The lists may be drawn from customer files; accounts receivable records; prospect files; commercial databases of households, businesses, and organizations; or they can be purchased from other firms. Sources of lists include telephone directories; membership rosters from trade publications; private membership rosters of clubs, unions, and associations; government records, including registrations for each state for all licensed trades such as doctors, cosmetologists, contractors, and teachers; vehicle registrations and driver's license lists in states where these files are released, and house-to-house canvasing, mail surveys, and warranty card data.

In addition to data files describing addresses, mass mailing systems usually require automated mailing equipment, such as envelope stuffers, collating equipment, and postage equipment.

Point-of-Sale Systems

Point-of-sale (POS) systems are another facet of the order-entry system. POS systems capture data about orders at the point of sale and are frequently found in fast-food chain stores, department stores, and grocery chain stores. The information obtained from point-of-sale systems becomes input to the financial accounting systems, which then supplies data to marketing information systems (see Figure 10–9).

POS systems provide immediate updates to sales and inventory systems and allow firms to monitor sales trends minute by minute. They also allow firms to capture customer data and preferences and add the information to their data warehouses.

Some organizations provide their customers with terminals that have direct access to the organization's sales order system. The idea is to make ordering easy and convenient for the customer. Once customers have learned how to order using the system, they tend to be reluctant to learn the system of a competitor. As a result, some firms have achieved an important competitive advantage through their sales order system.

Delivery Tracking and Routing Systems

Customers like to receive their merchandise on time. In a manual system, customers called in to a customer representative to check on the delivery of their merchandise. The customer rep would then have to call the delivery vehicle driver who uses a cell phone to tell the rep where he or she is and how soon the merchandise might be delivered. That process took time, frequently frustrated the customer, and cost the firm money to support. Today, some delivery systems place small satellite dishes on their delivery vehicles and use the satellite-based global positing system (GPS) to monitor the movement and location of every vehicle in their fleet. Some firms even provide customers with **tracking system** software to monitor the status of their packages. FedEx even lets customers use a Web site on the Internet to track their packages (see Figure 10–10).

Figure 10–9

Point-of-sale (POS) system

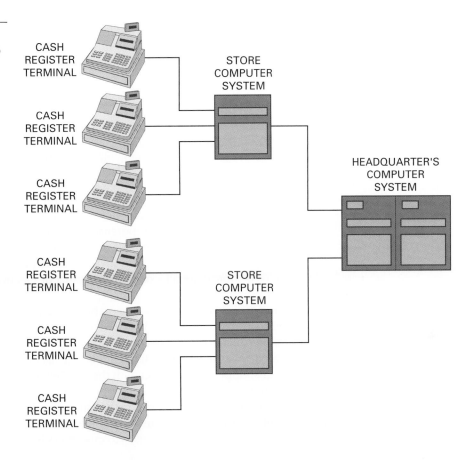

Figure 10–10

Federal Express Web site that lets customers track merchandise shipments

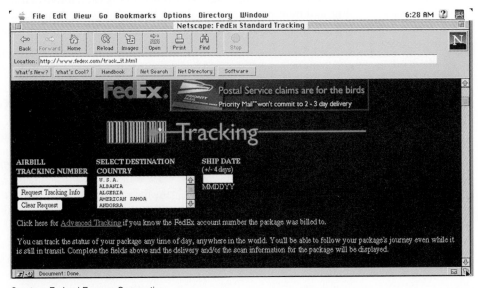

Courtesy Federal Express Corporation

Firms also like to route their delivery vehicles in the most efficient manner. Being able to lay out deliveries on an electronic map and then to have mapping software identify the best routes for the delivery vehicles saves firms a great deal of time and money (see Manager's Memo 10–3).

Electronic Shopping and Advertising

Firms have been able to advertise and customers to shop via TV, radio, and the telephone for many years. The computer age, however, has made other avenues for shopping and advertising available, the most dramatic of which is clearly the Internet.

Virtual shopping.   When people view, select, and purchase products and services from a store in another location using electronic means, they are virtually shopping at that store. **Virtual shopping,** or electronic shopping, allows organizations to present information about goods and services to potential customers who are connected to their electronic "store." Selecting and buying goods using an electronic kiosk (described in the next section), from an organization's Internet site, and from a "virtual mall" of Internet Web "stores" are all examples of virtual or electronic shopping (see Figure 10–11).

A future feature of virtual shopping is likely to be interspace technology. *Interspace technology* is a virtual environment that is shared by many users and in which they can interact. In interspace technology, *avatars* represent users who move around within a computer-generated environment, which might be a virtual city. Through your avatar, you can meet other shoppers and interact with the "city" environment. You can also interact with the avatars of other shoppers. Shoppers have the ability to see and talk to each other as they stroll along store fronts on the same virtual streets. You can select a store, enter through the front door, and interact with other customers as they shop.

The advantage of virtual stores and malls to customers is that they eliminate parking problems, crowds, and the need to travel to a real store or mall (see Manager's Memo 10–4). Also, customers can find products quickly by searching for them electronically, and they are always on the electronics shelves. Video clips and still images display goods to users, and purchases are made with credit cards.

Interspace technology is currently being used for virtual shopping, distance learning, and multiplayer games. Tower Records has used interspace technology to create virtual music stores, where avatars can shop, interact with sales clerks, and preview

---

Manager's Memo 10–3	**TRACKING BUS ARRIVALS: AN *INNOVATIONS* NEWS SUMMARY**

▶ In Minnesota, winter temperatures of minus-30 Fahrenheit can freeze flesh in minutes—and discourage commuters from cooling their heels (and everything else) waiting at the bus stop. So Minneapolis's Metropolitan Council Transit Operations has started a pilot bus tracking system that combines military satellite, radio and PC technologies to pass on up-to-the-minute information on where any bus in the system is at any given time. Commuters can then time their arrival to coincide with the bus's, and stay out of the cold as long as possible. The information is displayed at public kiosks and on outdoor signs near bus stops. Commuters at Park and Rides can stay in their cars, watch the signs, and make a last minute dash as the bus rounds the corner. The new system is aimed at clearing up traffic jams by boosting the city's current 5% ridership.

Source: J. Gehl and S. Douglas, *Innovations,* an on-line electronic magazine, *January 9, 1995.* Abstracted from Investor's Business Daily source 1/4/94 A6.

Figure 10–11

A virtual mall

CDs and videos. Levi Strauss is using the system for a virtual reality game that's part of its ad campaign.[3]

By offering virtual shopping opportunities, organizations vastly stretch their marketing areas. Literally, a world full of customers, providing they have the systems for access, can stop at a virtual store. However, customers must have a PC equipped with a video camera to enter interspace, some users have difficulty navigating the virtual environments, and others prefer the social activity associated with "real" shopping.

Manager's Memo 10–4

ELECTRONIC SHOPPERS SHOPPING ELECTRONICALLY: AN *INNOVATIONS* NEWS SUMMARY

"Instead of flying to the Mall of America and having a nice time, you also may use digital servants to seek out best buys from network-savvy vendors while you soak in the tub. General Magic CEO Marc Porat says the future will allow an ordinary consumer to put out a request-for-proposal into the market and have vendors bid on it. He asks: What if consumers could use their electronic agents to find discount coupons for corn flakes, pet food, toothpaste, laundry detergent, toilet paper, and all their other necessities without having to spend their lives cutting through newspapers—which is a major roadblock to the efficient use of coupons? The economic effects would be great. Porat acknowledges, though, that may take 30 years or so before we really know how to do electronic markets.

Source: J. Gehl and S. Douglas, *Innovations*, an on-line electronic magazine, January 9, 1995. Abstracted from *Wired* Jan. '95, p. 108.

---

[3]*New York Times,* March 4, 1996, p. C3.

Figure 10–12
Advertising on the
Internet

Courtesy Yahoo! Corporation

Electronic kiosks.   **Electronic kiosks** are another form of electronic commerce. Kiosks are computer terminals placed in walls or other structures on streets and public places and can be used for a variety of marketing purposes, such as multimedia presentations and electronic catalogs. They can also be used for computer-based training. Kiosks replace salespeople and provide 24-hour access to products and product information to customers. Museums have used touch-screen kiosks for years to give their patrons information about exhibits.

Some organizations use kiosks to provide information. Many other organizations allow customers to select and purchase products and services interactively. For example, Sears stores use kiosks that provide on-line catalogs from which customers can select Sears products using a touch screen and pay for the products using a credit card. Baseball fans in Minneapolis can buy tickets to Twins's home games at kiosks. What is more, the kiosks show buyers the view from the seats they have selected before they finalize their purchase. The U.S. Postal Service uses kiosks to sell stamps, let people submit address changes, and produce address labels for packages.

Some stores are planning to use in-store kiosks to display slower-moving models or merchandise, saving the floor space for their best-selling items. For example, Sears plans to use in-store electronic kiosks for some of its high-priced products. Sears expects to be able to present three times the array of products to customers without using any additional floor space. The kiosks will let customers view a wide range of color and style options, allowing Sears to provide more customized service.[4]

Internet advertising.   Organizations without Web sites today are likely to feel somewhat disadvantaged. Nearly every type of organization maintains a Web site to provide information about itself and its work, products, or services. Universities, hospitals, research labs, manufacturers, religious organizations, retailers, professional service providers, and governmental units have Web sites. In addition, some firms advertise on Web sites that are popular with potential customers. For example, many providers of search tools, such as Yahoo!, sell advertising space to organizations (see Figure 10–12). Advertising rates for space are usually based on the number of "hits" a

---

[4]*Investor's Business Daily,* January 25, 1996, p. A8.

Web site can claim, that is, number of times people connect to a site. **Internet advertising** has become a popular means for organizations to reach new customers.

OPERATIONAL PRODUCTION INFORMATION SYSTEMS

Production systems are designed to produce the goods and services to meet marketing system projections. Production information systems support decision making for the operation, allocation, and planning of production resources.

Operational production systems are diverse; they include continuous flow production, mass production, job order production, and project production. In addition, operational production systems include the production of services as well as hard goods. The purpose of the production system is to acquire the raw materials and purchased parts; test the materials for quality; acquire the appropriate human resources, work space, and equipment; schedule the materials, human resources, space, and equipment; fabricate the products or services; test the product or service outputs; and monitor and control the use and costs of the resources involved.

Numerous operational information systems support the production function. Some are part of the financial accounting system of an organization. For example, the purchasing, accounts payable, inventory, order entry, accounts receivable, and payroll subsystems of the accounting system provide information to support production activities. This section briefly describes some of the major operational information systems used in production. The systems described are listed in Figure 10-1.

Purchasing Systems

To produce goods and services, you must have the right quantity of raw materials and production supplies on hand. Furthermore, you will want to procure these materials and supplies at the lowest cost and have them delivered at the right time. To assist in this function, the **purchasing system** has to maintain data on all phases of the acquisition of raw materials and purchased parts used in production. For example, the purchasing system must maintain vendor files with price quotation information on all production materials and supplies so that intelligent choices can be made among suppliers. The system also maintains records of goods that are already on order. Such records, often called an *open order file* (see Figure 10-13), are used to monitor the ordering and delivery of production materials and supplies to keep you from exceeding budget allocations and correct inventory levels.

Figure 10–13

An open order report showing the stock of raw materials and purchased parts on order

```
OPEN ORDER REPORT
11/15/98


REQUISITION        REQ.          DATE          RECEIPT        REMARKS
   DATE            NO.           WANTED         DATE

  11 05 98        30789         11 21 98

  11 08 98        30790         11 25 98

  11 08 98        30791         11 23 98      11 22 98

  11 09 98        30792         11 27 98
```

Figure 10–14
A sample receiving report

```
ZUMAR-READE
Receiving Report


   DATE RECEIVED:   09/04/98

   VENDOR NO:   803

   VENDOR NAME:   Vineta Fabrication, Inc.

   OUR PURCHASE ORDER NO:   38097

   VENDOR INVOICE NO:   9077


   ITEM       DESCRIPTION    QUANTITY   QUANTITY       REMARKS
   NO.                       ORDERED    RECEIVED


   T-345    4" Brace           1000       1000
   T-500    8" Brace            200        100     100 backordered
   T-750    Angle brace         500        499     1 damaged
```

Receiving Systems

When shipments of purchased goods and supplies are received, they must usually be opened, inspected, and verified against purchase orders, and the information about their status passed to the accounts payable, inventory, and production departments (see Figure 10–14). Delivery dates should also be noted for several reasons, including collecting data on the delivery-time reliability of suppliers. This type of information is supplied by **receiving systems.**

Quality Control Systems

Quality control systems provide information about the status of production goods as they move from the raw materials state, through goods in process, to finished goods. Quality control systems ensure that raw materials or parts purchased for use in the production processes meet the standards set for those materials. The systems also monitor quality during the production cycle.

Quality control data may be collected using **shop-floor data collection systems,** which can include a rich assortment of input devices—counters, assembly-line data entry terminals, process control sensors, and so on. Workers may use assembly-line data entry terminals to enter data regarding the status of goods in process and the amount of worker time devoted to each phase of the production process. Process control sensors frequently monitor the gauge of metal as it is fabricated into such final products as sheets, bars, or wire.

Shop-floor data collection devices can be connected to a **factory local area network (LAN)** (see Figure 10–15). The LAN may in turn be connected to a minicomputer or mainframe computer system. A factory LAN is a communications network that often connects very different devices found on a factory floor, such as robots used to handle, load, or weld parts; programmable controllers used to sequence processes; vision systems used to inspect or sort parts; bar code readers used to count or sort parts; and microcomputers with keyboards or voice recognition systems to allow factory floor personnel to enter data such as the time spent on a job order, piece counts, and the number and types of waste and scrap material.

When inspection, testing, or monitoring identifies items that fail to meet the standards that have been set, a *variance* occurs. If the variance occurs in raw materials or purchased parts, it may be reported on the receiving report. If it occurs during the production processes, the quality control system may shut down the production sys-

Figure 10–15

A factory LAN

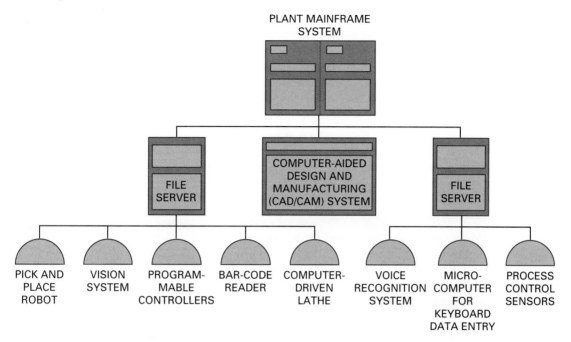

tem or report the variance in some way to employees or supervisory personnel. If the variance occurs in finished goods, the goods must not be placed in inventory and the nature of the variance must be reported to the production manager. For example, the standards for sheets of copper rolling off a mill may demand that the sheet thickness never vary more than 0.01 mm positively or negatively. If, at any time during the production process, failures occur in equipment, raw materials, or human procedures that result in the sheets exceeding this *tolerance,* the quality control mechanisms in place may activate a warning light or bell, print a report, or shut down the production equipment entirely.

The product development and design system can use quality control information to determine realistic specifications for a product under development. The purchasing system can also use this information to set effective specifications for raw materials, purchased parts, and production supplies. In addition, quality control systems allow managers to identify vendors who consistently ship poor-quality materials or whose material quality is highly unreliable. These systems can also help managers identify production machinery that is unreliable or faulty and workers whose training, procedures, or attention is not sufficient for their work. At the same time, quality control systems should include an information stream from the customer service department to ensure that customer complaints and concerns about quality are directed back to the production system.

Two management approaches that require organizations to improve quality are just-in-time systems and **total quality control (TQC).** Just-in-time systems are discussed in the next chapter.

In a traditional manufacturing environment, quality control tasks and production tasks are separated. In an organization using TQC and committed to the fabrication of quality products, quality control information pervades the production processes—everyone in the production chain is responsible for quality. Furthermore, emphasis is placed on the prevention of defects rather than on measurement and inspection.

Quality control systems embedded in the production processes are typically continuous and automatic and may not require direct management decisions. Systems designed for raw materials and finished goods usually consist of routine and repetitive sampling and tasting procedures. These procedures are used to sample the raw materials and parts received and the finished goods produced to determine if their specifications fall within the standards that have been previously set.

Shipping Systems

At the other end of the production process, finished goods are placed in inventory and/or shipped to customers. Many records and documents are used to assist and monitor in the inventorying and shipping processes—for example, shipping reports and packing slips. The information from the shipping system affects the inventory and accounts receivable systems.

Cost Accounting Systems

Many operational-level financial accounting systems collect and report information about the resources that are used in the production processes so that managers can obtain accurate costs of production on products and services. Cost accounting systems monitor the three major resources used in production: human resources, materials, and equipment and facilities.

Workers, supervisors, and managers are one of the most important resources available to managers. Payroll systems collect and report information about the costs of these resources and how much of their time has been allocated to different products and services. Human resource time and costs are often collected manually through employee time card or job ticket systems, or electronically through employee badge systems. Accurate information about the allocation and costs of direct and indirect labor are required to control existing production processes and to plan and schedule future production activities.

Materials management systems provide information on current inventory levels of production materials, use of these materials in the production processes and their locations, and specifications of how these materials are employed in products. The latter system is usually called a **bill-of-materials (BOM) system** (see Figure 10–16). A bill-of-materials system produces a list of the raw materials, subassemblies, and component parts needed to complete each product. It provides, in essence, a list of ingredients for the end product.

In addition to getting information about the use of materials and human resources, production managers must get information about the use of equipment and facilities in the production processes. The information systems need to provide operational-level information about what equipment and facilities have been used for what length of time on what products and services and at what costs. Materials usage, human resource usage, and equipment and facility usage information systems provide input to job costing systems. Reports from each of these information systems allow managers to monitor production costs and the allocation of production resources.

Inventory Control Systems

The management and control of raw materials, goods-in-process, and finished goods inventories is an important part of the production system. Careful management and control of these inventories will usually provide considerable savings to the organization. Inventory control systems use information from operational information sys-

Figure 10–16

A bill of materials needed to produce a product (1046), subassemblies (C120, D250, R250), and subassembly parts (1201–1205 and 2501–2503)

Vasquez Industries, Inc.
Bill of Materials
Stock No. 1046

Part Number	Description	Quantity	Unit
C120	Shaft assembly	1	Each
1201	1/2-2 bolts	4	Each
1202	1/2" nuts	4	Each
1203	1/2" washers	4	Each
1204	1" shaft	1	Each
1205	Base plate	1	Each
D250	Motor assembly	1	Each
R250	Casing assembly	1	Each
2501	Sides	4	Each
2502	Top/bottom	2	Each
2503	1/4-1 screws	16	Each

tems, such as the shipping and receiving systems, purchasing systems, and order-entry systems.

Maintaining inventories at their proper levels eliminates production shutdowns from lack of raw materials and lost sales from lack of finished goods. However, maintaining inventories also represents a number of costs to the organization, including the costs of procuring and carrying the inventory, and stockout costs, or those costs that result when the right amount of the right item is not on hand at the right time.

In a conventional production system, two basic information tools are used to manage inventories: a *reorder-point system* and a system for determining the least expensive quantity to order, or **economic order quantity (EOQ)** system. A reorder-point system is used to make certain that production materials are ordered in sufficient lead time to arrive at the plant when they are needed in the production process. The system uses predefined levels of inventory to initiate the purchasing process. The predefined levels of inventory are the levels necessary to cover the organization while waiting for new orders of the stock to be delivered. Some organizations do not wish to cut their timing this close, however. They maintain an additional amount of stock, called *safety stock,* on hand in case shipments are delayed, some stock items are defective, or some other foul-up occurs.

The EOQ system helps managers reduce total inventory costs by identifying the most economic quantity in which to order each item of inventory. Ordering in small quantities reduces taxes, insurance, and other carrying costs but increases ordering, shipping, receiving, and other procurement costs. Ordering in large quantities reduces procurement costs but increases carrying costs. The best or *economic order*

Figure 10–17

Inventory costs graphed to show the balancing of stocking costs and carrying costs, or the economic order quantity (EOQ)

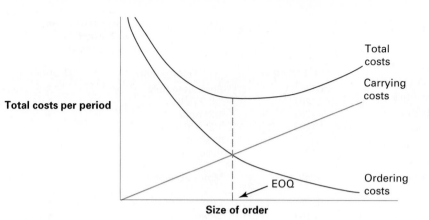

quantity (EOQ) strikes a balance between carrying costs and procurement costs (see Figure 10-17).

Computing EOQ manually for each item in inventory would be a very large and tedious task. Also, for many inventory items, the manager may wish to ask what-if? questions about the values in the EOQ formulas. Without computers, these tasks would be laborious and perhaps too time-consuming to keep the order process fine-tuned to current data.

Automated Material Handling Systems

Keeping count of and ordering inventory are important tasks for an organization. However, monitoring inventory from the time it is received to the time it is shipped is also important. **Automated material handling (AMH) systems** track, control, and otherwise support the movement of raw materials, work-in-process, and finished goods from the receiving docks to the shipping docks. AMH software combines with various materials handling equipment, including conveyors, pick-and-place robots, and automated guided vehicles, to get this job done.

Computer-Aided Design and Manufacturing Systems

A great deal of software has been developed to aid product engineers design new products and improve old products. One type of software that helps product engineers is **computer-aided design/computer-aided manufacturing (CAD/CAM) software.** CAD software normally falls into two categories. One category helps mechanical engineers and architects construct and modify complex drawings, blueprints, diagrams, or illustrations quickly and easily (see Figure 10-18). For example, AutoCAD, a software package from Autodesk, assists engineers and architects to complete drafting tasks on a computer.

Another category of CAD software includes programs that help electrical engineers produce schematics quickly and easily, alter the schematics, and then produce a final draft of the electrical circuits. Of course, both types of CAD software require that your computer system be equipped with terminals and printers capable of graphic output.

CAD software may provide the engineer with simulation capabilities. That is, he or she may be able to simulate the use of the product under many different conditions or various amounts of stress. For example, an engineer might design a handle for a vacuum cleaner and then test the handle's resistance to failure by simulating selected stress conditions. By simulating design faults early in the process, a company

Figure 10–18

An AutoCAD drawing

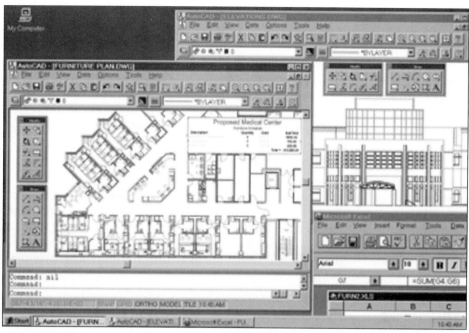

Courtesy Autodesk Inc.

can save a great deal of development money, avoid bringing a product to market that will later fail, and ensure that the product will be reliable. Simulation also allows an organization to bring products to market faster (see Manager's Memo 10-5). The result is a better product that costs less to develop, reaches the market faster, and reduces returns and repairs, all of which may provide an organization with a competitive advantage.

CAM software converts CAD drawings into finished products with little human intervention. For example, a bolt may be designed using CAD software. A compatible CAM software package reads the design and instructs lathe machinery to turn out bolts with the parameters specified in the CAD drawing. CAD/CAM software has been

---

Manager's Memo 10–5

THE VIRTUAL CAR SHOWROOM: AN *INNOVATIONS* NEWS SUMMARY

Carmakers are looking to virtual reality and holographic display technology to cut short the time it takes to move products from concept to production, and to make more informed decisions about which vehicles to build. A Ford Motor Co. designer is working on a prototype CAD/CAM workstation that will display car models in 3-D, using a holographic projector instead of a conventional video display. 'We want to be able to project a full-size hologram,' enabling Ford management to judge the models 'as if they were real,' he says. Meanwhile, GM is getting into the act, teaming up with subsidiary EDS to build a technology showcase in Detroit which includes 'the cave,' where you can don special glasses, sit down, and the image of a new car surrounds you, making it seem that you're actually sitting in it. Using a special handgrip, you can manipulate the instrument panel and gauges. The cave is being used to provide GM with customer feedback on future product designs.

Source: J. Gehl and S. Douglas, *Innovations*, an on-line electronic magazine, March 13, 1995. *Investor's Business Daily* 3/10/95 A5.

enhanced by software providing computer-aided engineering (CAE), computer-aided testing (CAT), computer-aided process planning (CAPP), and computer-aided inspection (CAI).

Image Management Systems

Engineering and architectural drawings are difficult to store and retrieve in hard-copy form. Parts of one design may be useful in another if you can find the design that contained the useful element. **Image management systems** are designed to manage the storage and retrieval of engineering and architectural drawings using optical disk storage media. The software also maintains controls over changes made to drawings and distributes the drawings to users with PCs on a LAN.

Material Selection Systems

Many programs are available that aid the engineer in choosing materials for the product under design. These programs are called **material selection programs (MSP).** Selecting the best materials to account for stress, heat humidity, and other conditions can be laborious. Sawyer and Pecht (1986) note that in the metals category alone, an engineer might choose from more than 100,000 materials with more than 80 properties.

Shop-Floor Scheduling Systems

A common operational task for factory supervisors is to schedule production jobs. This task includes scheduling the time, building and rooms, tools and equipment, inventory, and personnel to complete factory orders. Scheduling must take into account the constraints of setup time, or the time it takes to get ready for the production run, take down time, or the time it takes to return the area to its original state, tool requirements, equipment requirements, and operator requirements. Because it involves many subtasks and relies on many parts of the organization, **shop-floor scheduling** can be very complex. Computer systems can help the supervisor reduce complexity by completing some subtasks automatically.

Outputs of a shop-floor scheduling system might include a GANTT chart showing the major phases of the job and tables showing the resource requirements. Other outputs may serve as inputs to other information systems. Shop-floor scheduling software is most effective when the inputs and outputs of the system are integrated with inventory management systems, the factory LAN, production planning systems, job costing systems, and payroll systems.

One of the most important advantages of using computer systems to assist in scheduling job runs is the ability it gives the supervisor to optimize the use of sources, as opposed to using the first acceptable schedule that works. When problems occur, such as a strike of key operators, late shipments of raw materials, or equipment failures, the supervisor can use the software to alter the schedule quickly.

Mass Customization and Agile Manufacturing Systems

Computer systems are often criticized for "dehumanizing" our society. In fact, evidence abounds that computer systems have contributed a great deal to the opposite outcome. Without computer systems, fitting an insurance policy to the specific needs of one person is usually difficult or impossible. Before they had computer systems, many insurance organizations, out of necessity, used a "one size fits all" approach. That approach has been true for many large corporations, and it certainly has been a criticism of large government agencies for many years. Using computers to tailor employee compensation and benefits to each employee has provided some employers with a competitive edge in hiring skilled workers in high-demand fields (see Chapter 11). Tailoring advertising and sales pitches to the quirks of each customer has allowed many marketing departments to reach new highs in sales. Media organizations are examining how they can provide a portfolio of entertainment shows, news, movies, sports, and other events to masses of individuals—allowing each person to view whatever he or she wants at any time. Production departments are using computer systems to vary products—right on the production line—to fit the demands of individual customers. This ability to use mass production techniques to tailor products to each customer is called **mass customization** or **agile manufacturing.** Computer systems applied in this way are no longer making the organization just more efficient. They are also making these organizations more effective and even transforming some firms.

Usually, to ensure efficiencies in production, mass production of standard products is necessary. That approach requires customers or customer requirements to fit the standard products. By being able to alter each product—to make a production run of one unit, for example—organizations can reach many new customers who don't fit the standard mold. The ability of a firm's production facilities to respond to runs of one or to change the volume to be produced quickly to meet the swiftly changing demands of consumers requires firms to change the way they do business.

> The impact of mass customization permeates the extended enterprise. It requires the committed involvement of employees, suppliers, manufacturers, distributors and end users in identifying and fulfilling the latest needs of highly diverse buyers. "When you supply a custom product to someone who wants to ramp to very high volume in a certain period of time, you have to revamp all your systems—systems for putting capacity in place, for product development, for order processing, for forecasting demand" Roe [Cliff Roe, VLSI's vice president of strategic programs] said. "You reduce cycle times throughout the design-and-manufacturing process to avoid delay and waste. All systems must be in sync."[5]

Mass customization often also requires that the firm become tightly synchronized with its suppliers and buyers. The firm may have to outsource production to others when demand grows too swiftly for its capacity. Surely it will have to integrate its inventory needs closely with its suppliers. It may also have to synchronize its production capacity with its major buyers, which usually requires that electronic data interchanges be developed between it and all the other players.

> Agile enterprises are totally integrated organizations. Information should flow seamlessly among manufacturing, engineering, marketing, finance, inventory, sales, and research departments. There should be transparent flow of information between agile manufacturers and their suppliers, who play an active role in product design and development under agile manufacturing.[6]

OPERATIONAL HUMAN RESOURCE INFORMATION SYSTEMS

Human resource departments are responsible for many facets to human resource management, including recruiting, assessment, selection, placement, training, performance appraisal, compensation and benefit management, promotion, termination, occupational health and safety, employee services, compliance with legal constraints, helping managers with human resource problems, and providing top management with information for strategic planning.

---

[5] VLSI Technologies, Inc., Web page (http://www.vlsi.com/), 9/27/96.

[6] Candadai, Arun, Loventopoulos, Marios, Mirza, Azhar, *Computer Aided Decision Support System for Agile Manufacturing (CADSAM),* http://www.glue.umd.edu/~azzaro/cadsam.623/CADSAM.html#A2.1, last updated, 1994.

To manage this diverse, expensive, and important human resource within a complex environment, human resource departments have increasingly made use of computer-based **human resource information systems (HRIS).**

Operational human resource information systems provide managers with data to support the routine, repetitive human resource decisions that occur regularly in the management of an organization's human resources. There are many operational-level human resource information systems, including systems that help managers keep track of the organization's positions and employees, conduct performance evaluation, provide alternative or flexible scheduling, recruit new employees, place employees, train employees, relocate employees, terminate employees, provide employee benefits, and provide reports to governmental agencies. To be effective, human resource information systems must be integrated with other information systems within an organization, such as the payroll system.

Several examples of operational-level human resource information systems are discussed here. The systems discussed are also listed in Figure 10–1.

Position Control Systems

A *job* is usually defined as a group of identical positions. A *position,* on the other hand, consists of tasks performed by one worker.[7] For example, one job in an organization may be given the job title of Data Entry Clerk III. However, 20 Data Entry Clerk III positions may be available within the organization. The purpose of a **position control system** is to identity each position in the organization, the job title in which the position is classified, and the employee currently assigned to the position. Reference to the position control system allows a human resource manager to identify the details about unfilled positions. For instance, routine, repetitive outputs of the position control system include *position inventories,* or lists of positions by job category, by department, by task content, or by job requirements. Another output of the system includes lists of unfilled positions, which might be organized in a similar manner.

Categorized lists of unfilled positions can be very useful to the human resource staff. These lists allow staff members to plan recruiting activities. By listing unfilled positions in terms of their job requirements, for example, recruiting personnel may advertise the openings in appropriate media, such as magazines, newspapers, and journals, and plan visits to labor sources, such as educational organizations, that prepare workers to meet those job requirements.

Position control systems also allow the human resource manager to identify human resource problems. The list of unfilled positions, for instance, may identify vacant positions with the same job title scattered throughout the firm. On investigation, the human resource manager may find that positions with this job title experience a high rate of turnover. On further investigation, the manager may learn that the positions are not compensated sufficiently to retain employees, that these positions do not have a clear promotion path within the firm, or that these positions involve the performance of duties that employees view as overly tense, boring, frustrating, or difficult. The investigation may lead to tactical decisions regarding the composition of the duties in these positions; the nature of the training for employees in these positions; the compensation plans used for these positions; or the skills, knowledge, and abilities of the employees recruited for these positions.

---

[7] G. T. Milkovich and J. W. Boudreau, *Human Resource Management,* (Burr Ridge, IL: Irwin, 1994), p. 137.

Employee Information Systems

The human resource department must maintain information on every employee for a variety of reporting purposes. One part of the **employee information system** is a set of employee profile records, or employee inventory. An **employee profile** usually contains personal and organization-related information, such as name, address, sex, minority status, marital status, citizenship, years of service or seniority data, education and training, previous experience, employment history within the organization, salary rate, salary or wage grade, and retirement and health plan choices. The employee inventory may also contain data about employee preferences for geographical locations and shifts.

Another part of an employee information system is an employee **skills inventory.** The skills inventory contains information about every employee's work experience, work preferences, test scores, interests, and special skills or proficiencies. The skills inventory provides the human resource manager with valuable data for completing operational tasks. For example, the skills inventory can be used to

1. Identify potential internal applicants for open positions in the organization.
2. Identify employees for transfer, promotion, or training and development programs.
3. Identify employees who are "underemployed," in that their skills far exceed their present assignments.

Performance Management Systems

Many organizations review the work of employees on a regular basis to make decisions regarding merit pay, pay increases, transfer, or promotion. Typically, a new employee is evaluated at the end of the first six months of employment, and other employees are evaluated annually. These reviews are often called **performance appraisals.** The data for performance appraisals are frequently collected by asking each employee's immediate superior to complete an employee appraisal form. The forms may also be given to peers, the employees themselves, and even customers or clients. An example of an appraisal form is found in Figure 10-19.

Employee appraisals may also be based on performance measures. That is, worker effectiveness may be measured in terms of productivity on the job. Numerous productivity measures have been used in the past. Some are straightforward measures of productivity, such as counting the number of units of work performed within the hour, day, shift, or other time period. For example, purchase order clerks may be measured by the number of purchase orders they process in a day, or office clerks may be measured by the number of document lines they enter during a day. Other measures of productivity are less direct; they include the number of customer complaints received or the number of products returned (see Manager's Memo 10-6). For example, a trend in sales force management is to use customer evaluations to calculate employee compensation. The basic purpose of these systems is to encourage salespeople to focus on customer satisfaction.[8]

Performance appraisal information is frequently used as evidence in employee grievance matters. Careful documentation of employee performance and of how the performance was measured and reported is critical to acceptance of appraisal information in grievance hearings.

---

[8]*Selling,* January/February, 1995, p. 47. See also C. Lee, "Performance Appraisal," Training, May, 1996, p. 44.

Figure 10–19

The first page of an employee appraisal review form used for clerical employees

---

Time View, Inc.
Clerical Staff Performance Review

Review No. _____26_____ Date of Review _01_ / _15_ / _98_ SNN _335-16-1482_____

Employee Name _Dretsky, Alicia L._____

(Last, First, Middle Initial)

Department _Data Processing_____ Division _Western_____

Reviewer Name _Pallato, Paul R._____

(Last, First, Middle Initial)

Directions: Circle the letters that best characterize the employee.

If choices are inadequate, use the comments section.

I.   Productivity
   A.   Is Capable of handling a large volume of work.
   B.   Is capable of handling a normal volume of work.
   C.   Is not capable of handling a normal work load.
   Comments: _Always completes more work than co-workers_____

   _____

II. Quality of Work
   A.   Work produced is of high quality.
   B.   Work produced is of adequate quality.
   C.   Work produced is of poor quality.
   Comments: _____

   _____

III. Knowledge Required for Job
   A.   Demonstrates a high level of work-related knowledge.
   B.   Demonstrates knowledge adequate to do satisfactory work.
   C.   Demonstrates inadequate knowledge to do satisfactory work.
   Comments: _____

   _____

IV. Degree of Supervision Required
   A.   Works well without supervision.
   B.   Works adequately without supervision.
   C.   Works ineffectively without supervision.
   Comments: _Needs help in new situations or when learning new tasks_

   _____

Performance appraisal information can lead to a number of decisions beyond merely supporting the operational decision to retain, promote, transfer, or terminate a single employee. For example, the performance appraisal information may be sifted through to identify supervisors who have submitted a high number of appraisals on which employees are rated poorly. High numbers of poor appraisals may indicate that these supervisors need to be evaluated in terms of their ability to work with employees. The performance appraisal information may also be sorted to identify job titles with a high percentage of poor appraisals. Job titles that receive a high percentage of poor appraisals may mean that the requirements of the job have not

| Manager's Memo 10-6 | NEURAL NETWORK USED TO EVALUATE POLICE |

 The Chicago Police Department is using software to predict the behavior of its police force:

The system uses a predictive model called a neural network. The program forecasts whether each of the 12,500 officers on the force is likely to behave in a manner similar to their nearly 200 colleagues who were dismissed or resigned under investigation during the past five years for actions ranging from insubordination to criminal misconduct....

To make its predictions, the system uses data such as traffic accidents and citizen complaints.

Officers who the system indicates are likely to be dismissed or resign under investigation are sent to counseling.

As you might expect, Chicago's Fraternal Order of Police is upset. The order's president has suggested that, "... if this thing is so good, we should give it to all the detectives so they can solve all the murders and robberies."

Source: G. Stix, "Bad Apple Picker: Can a Neural Network Help Find Problem Cops?" *Scientific American* 271, no. 6 (December 1994), p. 44.

been described sufficiently or accurately to permit the selection of applicants with appropriate skills.

Performance appraisal information can also be used to identify labor sources that do not provide acceptable workers. Future recruiting campaigns can then avoid these sources. If the performance appraisal information indicates a lack of reliable sources of acceptable employees, the organization may need to develop training programs for certain types of workers.

Government Reporting Systems

Data secured from the payroll, position control, employee profiles, performance management, and other human resource information systems can be used to produce reports required by myriad governmental laws and regulations, including affirmative action and equal employment opportunity laws and regulations. Many federal, state, and local laws, regulations, and executive orders regulate the recruitment, selection, placement, promotion, and termination of employees. Many of these laws and regulations are designed to ensure that minorities, women, older workers, veterans, and the handicapped are given a fair shake at getting and retaining jobs and receiving promotions (see Manager's Memo 10-7).

Furthermore, the growth in the number and complexity of federal, state, and local regulations pertaining to employees does not seem to be abating. The Immigration and Nationality Act was extensively revised in the late 1980s and now requires employers to maintain information that will attest to the citizenship of their workers. More recently, the Family Leave and Medical Act was passed guaranteeing unpaid leave to care for family.

The various regulations not only prescribe how some human resource functions must be carried out but also require that a variety of records be kept and reports submitted on certain dates to specific governmental agencies demonstrating compliance with the regulations. For example, the Occupational Safety and Health Administration (OSHA) requires that information be kept about the health and safety of each employee, including information pertaining to each serious accident or illness connected with the workplace.

Though much information is necessary to complete government reports, the same information can be used in other ways to improve the organization. For example, information kept for OSHA reporting purposes can also be used to calculate the

Manager's Memo 10–7	SOME FEDERAL LAWS AND REGULATIONS PERTAINING TO EMPLOYMENT

 LAWS AND REGULATIONS

Age Discrimination in Employment Act—protects persons age 40 and over from arbitrary discrimination in employment practices, such as mandatory retirement based on age.

Americans with Disabilities Act—prohibits discrimination against disabled persons who can perform the essential tasks of a job.

Davis-Bacon Act—requires certain employers with federal contracts to pay employees the prevailing wage rates of the area.

Equal Pay Act—requires employers to provide equal pay for substantially equal work that requires equal skill, effort, responsibility, and working conditions.

ERISA (Employee Retirement Income Security Act)—regulates pension and benefit plans, including employee transfer of pension funds when switching jobs, and established the Pension Benefit Guarantee Corporation.

Executive Orders 11246 and 11375—prohibit discrimination based on race, color, religion, sex, or national origin by firms with government contracts of $100,000 or more and 100 or more employees.

Fair Labor Standards Act—regulates minimum wages, child labor practices, and overtime compensation.

Family Leave and Medical Act—requires employers with 50 or more employees to offer unpaid leaves of absence for up to 12 weeks to employees to care for newborn children or for ill family members or for the employee's own illness.

Immigration Reform and Control Act—prohibits employers from hiring or employing illegal aliens and from discriminating against employees, legally in the United States who are "foreign looking" or "foreign sounding." Also requires employers to maintain records documenting worker eligibility.

Occupational Safety and Health Act (OSHA)—regulates safety and health standards and working conditions in employment, including providing work environments that are free of known health and safety hazards.

Pregnancy Discrimination Act of 1978 (Amendment to Civil Rights Act)—prohibits discrimination in employment because of pregnancy, childbirth, or related medical conditions and requires medical insurance to cover pregnancy like other long-term medical conditions.

Title VII of the Civil Rights Act of 1964—prohibits employment discrimination because or race, color, religion, sex, or national origin and established the Equal Employment Opportunity Commission.

Vietnam-Era Veterans Readjustment Act—prohibits the federal government and federal contractors from discriminating against disabled veterans and requires them to hire and promote veterans of the Vietnam War era.

Vocational Rehabilitation Act of 1973—prohibits federal contractors from discriminating against physically or mentally disabled persons and requires them to make changes in the work environment to make their sites more open to the disabled.

Walsh-Healey Public Contracts Act—requires employers with federal contracts to pay employees overtime for work beyond eight hours in a day.

AGENCIES

Department of Immigration and Naturalization
EEOC (Equal Employment Opportunity Commission)
Employment Standards Administration
OFCC (Office of Federal Contract Compliance)
OSHA (Occupational Safety and Health Administration)

costs of work accidents and work-related illnesses. This information can be an important tool for persuading employees and line managers to emphasize safety procedures and to identify physical and other work factors that contribute to accident and illness.

Managers can also use this information to calculate averages for accidents and illnesses for the organization as a whole and for each unit, shift, project, location, and job title. A manager may then identify departments, shifts, projects, locations, job titles, or supervisors that are associated with a higher-than-average accident or illness rate. A manager can also identify employees who have higher-than-average accident experiences. These employees might require training or retraining in safety practices, or the supervisors of such employees might need retraining in safety procedures.

The manager may also wish to sort the records by type of accident or illness. This information may lead to further investigations to identify why there are more accidents or illnesses of certain types than others. The result may be changes in safety procedures or changes in the work environment.

Applicant Selection and Placement Systems

After jobs and the employee requirements for those jobs have been identified and after a suitable pool of job candidates has been recruited, candidates must be screened, evaluated, selected, and placed in the positions that are open. The primary purpose of the application selection and placement system is to assist the human resource staff in these tasks. Applicant selection and placement systems also help human resource staff members ensure compliance with federal, state, and local employment laws because the procedures followed in screening, evaluating, selecting, and placing employees must be fully documented and carried out in a structured manner. Thus data pertaining to interviews, examinations, and placement decisions should be collected and kept according to the requirements of the various laws and regulations of the acts previously described.

If any testing is performed on applicants to improve the selection or placement process, data on the applicants and their test scores should be maintained for later analysis. Follow-up analysis comparing the success of those selected to the scores they obtained on the tests should be completed. In this way test scores can be more useful to selection and placement of staff members, or if the tests are not found to be useful predictors of success, the tests can be dropped.

Human resource departments increasingly are using Internet technology for a growing number of human resource management tasks, including finding applicants for jobs. Some departments are building company intranets and using Web browsers to provide access to company human resource information. Others are providing on-line employee manuals, listing of job openings, self-directed training modules, and interactive benefit allocation documents (see Figure 10–20).[9]

Training Systems

Organizations are increasingly looking to information technology to reduce the cost of training new employees or updating experienced employees A great deal of software is available today providing on-line training for employees, including management training software, sales training software, microcomputer training software, and word processing training software. The human resource department can use this software to design **computer-based training** programs for both group and independent study programs. Computer-based training aids often simplify the trainer's job and allow the trainers to individualize instruction more easily than they can in traditional, group-based training classes. Computer-based training also allows employees to work at home or to review previous lessons without special help from human resource staff.

Many analysts predict that virtual reality software, which has been applied to the training of pilots, army tankers, and space vehicle operation, will be applied to more mundane training tasks, such as closing a sale, selecting a stock, and running a meeting.

---

[9] M. Frost, "HR Cyberspace," *HR Magazine* (on-line), September 1996.

Figure 10–20

An Internet site from the Human Resource Department of the University of California at San Diego

UCbencom

University of California • Employee Benefits Plan Administration   home   e-mail

 general info   health & welfare   retirement & savings   life events   online forms   annuitant news   benefit news

Top 10

1. Unit Values and Interest Factors

2. 403(b) and DC Plans Performance Information

3. Forecast Your Fortune

4. UC Retirement Income Estimator

5. Tax-Deferred 403(b) and Defined Contribution Plans

6. UC Retirement Plan

7. Online Forms

8. Benefit News

9. UCRP Summary Plan Description

10. The UCRP Buyback

What's New

1-800-888-8267: A Phone Number to Remember!
Now there's only one number to call for all your benefits information: 1-800-888-8267. *bencom.fone* has merged with our other automated telephone system, *At Your Service*. Call 1-800-888-8267 from any touch-tone phone and follow the simple instructions to receive information about your retirement accounts, health plans, and insurance enrollment.

New Tax-Deferred 403(b) Plan Loan Program Provisions
Read about the policy and procedural changes to the Tax-Deferred 403(b) Plan Loan Program-effective with loan applications received on or after September 1, 1997.

UC Retirement Income Estimator
Developed at Lawrence Livermore National Laboratory for employee use, this retirement modeling program works properly with Netscape 3.0, Microsoft Internet Explorer 3.0, or more recent versions of these browsers.

Forecast Your Fortune
This interactive modeling program lets you see how your 403(b) Plan savings can grow.

UCRS Distribution Kit
Use this kit to elect inactive membership or to request a distribution. You must read the Special Tax Notice to download the distribution forms.

Statement of Maximum Annual Contribution
Statement of Maximum Annual Contribution was mailed on April 16, 1997.

Please send questions, comments, and suggestions about this website to barbara.facey@ucop.edu

Home
E-mail

General Info
Health & Welfare
Retirement & Savings
Online Forms
Annuitant News
Benefit News

University of California
Employee Benefits Plan Administration
http://www.ucop.edu/bencom/
July 25, 1997

MANAGEMENT SUMMARY

Operational information systems are diverse and are used in all phases of an organization, including each functional business area. The systems record, process, and report the routine, repetitive transactions and other activities of the entire organization, including accounting and finance, marketing, production, and human resource management. These data help supervisory staff and operational-level managers perform their tasks and provide a foundation for many tactical and strategic information systems. Computerizing these information systems usually reduces the drudgery associated with their development and maintenance, reduces operational costs, increases the speed and accuracy with which they are performed, and improves customer service.

Operational financial information systems include systems such as fixed asset systems, accounts receivable systems, accounts payable systems, order-entry systems, purchase order processing systems, inventory systems, and payroll systems. Many operational financial information systems provide data to marketing, production, and human resources information systems.

Operational marketing information systems include systems that support the sale of the organization's goods and services. Examples of operational marketing information systems include sales force automation systems, micromarketing and data warehouse systems, telemarketing systems, direct mail advertising systems, point-of-sale systems, delivery tracking and routing systems, and electronic shopping and advertising systems. Operational-level financial information systems that provide important support include order-entry information systems, inventory systems, and customer credit systems.

Many operational information systems have been developed to support the production function; they include receiving systems, quality control systems, shipping systems, materials handling systems, image management systems, material selection systems, shop-floor scheduling systems, and mass customization systems. Many production information systems use operational data from the organization's financial accounting database, including purchasing, accounts payable, inventory, order entry, accounts receivable, cost accounting, and payroll subsystems.

Operational information systems that support the human resource function include position control systems, employee information systems, performance management systems, government reporting systems, applicant selection and placement systems, and training systems. Human resource information systems, like information systems in the other functional business areas, also use data from other functional areas, such as the financial accounting database, including the payroll information system.

Operational information systems are necessary precursors to the development of tactical and strategic information systems. Operational information systems provide much of the data used by tactical information systems and some of the data for strategic information systems. And the tactical and strategic information systems provide the support for managerial decision making in accounting/finance, marketing, production, and human resource management that you will learn about in the next chapter.

KEY TERMS FOR MANAGERS

accounts payable system, 363
accounts receivable system, 361
agile manufacturing, 383
automated material handling (AMH) systems, 380
bill-of-materials (BOM) system, 378

computer-aided design/computer-aided manufacturing (CAD/CAM) software, 380
computer-based training, 389
contact management systems, 366
data mining, 368

data warehouse, 368
direct mail advertising systems, 370
economic order quantity (EOQ), 379
electronic directory, 366
electronic kiosks, 374

employee information system, 385

employee profile, 385

factory local area network (LAN), 376

financial accounting system, 359

fixed assets system, 360

general ledger system, 360

human resource information systems (HRIS), 384

image management systems, 382

Internet advertising, 375

inventory control system, 364

mass customization, 383

material selection programs (MSP), 382

micromarketing, 368

operational financial accounting information systems, 359

operational marketing information systems, 365

payroll system, 364

performance appraisals, 385

point-of-sale (POS) systems, 370

position control system, 384

prospect information systems, 366

purchase order processing system, 364

purchasing system, 375

quality control systems, 376

receiving systems, 376

sales force automation systems, 366

sales order processing system, 361

shop-floor data collection systems, 376

shop-floor scheduling, 382

skills inventory, 385

telemarketing systems, 369

total quality control (TQC), 377

tracking system, 370

transaction processing systems, 357

vertical accounting software, 365

virtual shopping, 372

REVIEW QUESTIONS

1. What program modules are common to an accounting system software package? Describe the major functions of each module.

2. What are transaction processing information systems? Provide one example.

3. What are two ways in which the accounts receivable system of a computerized accounting system might be useful to the manager?

4. In what ways might a computerized inventory system provide a competitive advantage to an organization?

5. What is an aged accounts receivable report? What level of decision making does this report typically support? How would you classify the report—ad hoc, exception, detailed, or summary?

6. What is sales force automation? What types of support can sales force automation systems provide to salespeople?

7. What is a data warehouse? Define data mining.

8. What is a prospect information system? What computerized sources of information are available to identify prospects?

9. What types of outputs might a computerized prospect information system generate?

10. What is contact management software? Describe some features of contact management software.

11. What is micromarketing? What advantages does it provide to marketing?

12. Provide examples of electronic commerce. Describe how each form of electronic commerce might benefit the organization offering it.

13. Describe a telemarketing system.

14. What is a direct mail advertising system. From what sources might an organization obtain names and addresses for a direct mail advertising campaign?

15. Explain Internet advertising. Describe one form of Internet advertising.

16. What financial accounting systems provide data to operational production information systems?

17. What is a shop-floor data collection system?

18. What is an automated materials handling information system? With what kinds of equipment might this information system work?

19. Explain the function of quality control information systems.

20. What is TQC?

21. What two conventional information tools are used to manage inventories?
22. What is a bill-of-materials information system?
23. Explain mass customization, or agile manufacturing systems.
24. What is an HRIS? What are the typical components of an HRIS?
25. What types of information does an employee information system typically contain?

26. What is a skills inventory? Identify one report commonly produced by a skills inventory system.
27. What is a position inventory?
28. What information is contained in a position control system? What is one report typically produced by a position control system?

QUESTIONS FOR DISCUSSION

1. What is the nature of operational information systems? What kinds of data do these systems collect and process?
2. In what ways can operational information systems benefit organizations?
3. How might an accounts payable system provide information that could reduce the costs of payables to the manager?
4. Describe how computer systems might be helpful to a salesperson who maintains a manual prospect file.
5. How might a manager use the information supplied by a quality control information system?

6. How might a materials selection system benefit the product design process?
7. How might managers use the information found in a skills inventory?
8. Why is it important that payroll system and human resource system files be compatible and coordinated?
9. What types of operational decisions might be supported by performance appraisals?
10. In what ways can managers use information about employee health and safety that were originally collected to meet OSHA regulations?

PROBLEMS

1. **Spreadsheet problem: Aged accounts receivable report.** Create a spreadsheet that a credit manager of a small company might use to age accounts receivable. Assume that the manager will import the data from a host computer system. Assume also that the credit terms for customers is 30 days from the date on the invoice. You are to design a template to process and present the data. The spreadsheet should list customers, the date of their invoices, the amount paid so far, the amount due, and then place the amount due in one of four columns: 30 days overdue, 60 days overdue, 90 days overdue, more than 90 days overdue. Provide the credit manager with the totals of each column and the percentage of accounts receivable in each overdue category.

2. **Database problem: Customer call report.** Design a customer call record on which salespeople can record calls they make to their customers. To plan the record design, first identify three reports you, as a salesperson, would like to be able to generate from a file of the records. Then plan the fields in the record that will collect the data you need for those reports. If you have access to database software, implement your record using the software, populate the file with fictitious data for 20 records, and then produce the three reports you planned.

3. **Internet problem: Sales automation software.** Use an Internet search tool to identify two contact management software programs. Note the features of each program, including its cost. Create a memo to your boss, Andrea Baron, sales manager, comparing the two programs, recommending one to purchase, and justifying the software in terms of sales force productivity. Include the Web site addresses you used as references.

4. **Rollo Furniture Company.** Jane Williams is the purchasing manager for the Rollo Furniture Company, which makes inexpensive beds, dressers, and tables for distribution to furniture outlets in five southern states. Over the years the company has come to depend on the varnish sold by the Wesley Finishing Products Company because this product provides a superior finish for its furniture at a reasonable price.

   a. What information does the purchasing manager need in order to know when and how much varnish to buy?

   b. What tools might the purchasing manager use to decide how to maintain the varnish inventory at the lowest cost?

   c. What additional information might the company wish to maintain to ensure that the quality of varnish it buys is what it should be buying?

5. **Database problem: Employee record.** Using database management software, create an employee record that contains data fields such as employee number, social security number, last name, first name, middle initial, street address, city, state, zip code, home phone, office phone, birth date, hire date, job title, department, gender, and marital status. Then complete the record for 20 fictitious employees who work in the following departments: receiving, shipping, and accounting. Try to spread the employees as evenly as you can among the departments. Create the other data needed for the records as you go along. Finally, print out the following lists:

   a. The names of all employees who work in the shipping department.

   b. The names and phone numbers of employees who work in the accounting department.

   c. The names, job titles, and hire dates of all married employees who work in the receiving department.

   Submit the three lists along with a printout of all records in the database you created to your instructor.

6. **Internet Problem: Factory input devices.** Prepare a short paper that identifies and briefly describes common devices used to input data into production systems, such as sensors and factory terminals. The paper should include brief descriptions of the hardware and software the devices use and what type of information each device supports. Use Internet search tools to complete the assignment. Include the Web site addresses you used as references.

7. **Internet Problem: Mass customization systems.** Use Internet search tools to locate information about mass customization or agile manufacturing systems. Prepare a brief paper on the topic, with cover sheet. Include the Web site addresses you used as references.

8. **Internet Problem: Use of intranets for human resources.** Use Internet search tools to develop a report on the use of company intranets by human resource departments. Describe the trends you find in the use of this technology and provide examples from specific companies. Include the Web site addresses you used as references.

CASES

1. **Trexel Assembly, Inc.** Trexel Assembly (TA) is a firm that assembles inexpensive computer systems for small companies and retail chain stores. TA uses off-the-shelf parts to produce the computer systems it sells. The company's president and founder, Dell Anders, is proud that the company's business has been growing fast but is very worried

because it has encountered a number of problems that threaten future growth. Frank Walton in purchasing recently submitted a report detailing the numerous instances in which parts on order were reordered because the shipment of the original parts took more time than expected. The order system was developed by a consulting firm early in Trexel's life. Frank recommends hiring more purchase order clerks to stay on top of goods on order. Jane Feldman, an accounting manager, has reported that the total accounts receivable owed to the firm has been growing alarmingly of late, and she believes that the cause is a number of buyers who are not paying their invoices on time. She recommends that TA purchase an accounts receivable software package to provide her with better data on the status of accounts receivable. Tricia Velon, payroll supervisor, has reported many complaints from salespeople about errors in their gross pay. She feels that the problem lies with Richards Compensation Agency, the accounting firm that handles TA's payroll each week. The problem seems to be that the agency does not post sales made in one week quickly enough for the commissions on the sales to be reflected in the salespeople's paychecks even though Tricia provides Richards with a list of salespeople and their gross sales by fax each Friday. This situation has led to angry words between the salespeople and Tricia. She feels the problem is likely to lower the morale of the sales force. She suggests that the firm move their payroll business to another service company.

a. What is the underlying problem that the company faces?

b. Should Dell take Frank's advice and hire more purchase order clerks?

c. Should Dell heed Jane's advice and buy accounts receivable software?

d. Should Dell listen to Tricia and move the firm's payroll business elsewhere?

2. **Ralston Electric Company.** Melinda Kaikati, a sales manager for Ralston Electric Company, is considering providing computer support for her sales personnel. Her salespeople sell electric motors to manufacturing firms in seven Midwestern states and spend most of their time on the road. Most of them live in the area they serve.

While on the road, salespeople telephone in orders to order clerks located at the main office who use terminals connected to the firm's mainframe. This system allows the salespeople to confirm immediately that enough stock is on hand to meet each order and that the customer's credit is satisfactory.

Ms. Kaikati wants to know if there is computer support that she can provide to her salespeople to help them manage their sales activities so as to improve their productivity and performance. Ms. Kaikati has asked you for help.

Provide Ms. Kaikati with a list of potential operational-level information systems applications that might help her salespeople manage their everyday sales activities more efficiently and productively. For each application, describe how the application will improve the productivity and performance of the sales force.

3. **Triton Clothing Company.** Triton Clothing Company is headquartered in a city on the West Coast. The firm produces highly stylish models of men's and women's denim and khaki western pants for distribution to clothing wholesalers and retailers throughout the western states. Triton maintains clothing manufacturing plants in three of these western states. Terry Burroughs has just assumed the post of production manager at Triton's Vesta plant. Formerly he had been assistant production manager at Triton's plant at Sterling. Burroughs was moved to the post to see if the Vesta plant productivity and profitability can be revived after several years of decline. Top management is not quite certain what the production problems at Vesta are. However, the plant has not met its production goals for the last two years, and management is hoping that a new broom will sweep clean.

When Burroughs first arrived at the Vesta plant, he decided to ask some of his plant managerial and supervisory personnel what they believe are the strengths and weaknesses of Vesta's production operations.

In this way, he hoped to gain insight into the nature of Vesta's production operations and to isolate problems that he could prioritize and then attack. Excerpts of some of these meetings follow.

Darlow Pruitt, the purchasing manager, complained that the purchasing department has been asked to use expediters too often to rush the delivery of raw materials. He feels that his department is not given sufficient warning about the status of raw materials to allow it to obtain the goods on time through regular channels. Pruitt complains that he does not have enough expediters to ensure that purchase orders for raw materials that have been delayed by suppliers are filled on time to meet production schedules.

Pruitt also feels that production delays have been caused by too many stockouts for raw materials in the past. He thinks that these stockouts have occurred because there has been too much pressure to reduce inventories as a means of decreasing manufacturing cost. The result of the stockouts, as far as he is concerned, is that expediters must deal with raw materials acquisition in a crisis mode.

Levan Grant, supervisor of quality control, says that she does not have enough inspectors to ensure that the quality standards for raw materials and finished goods have been met. She notes that the variable quality of raw materials has caused too many delays in the production processes and that this variability has also produced a high level of rejections of finished goods.

Bergon Trout, warehouse manager, complains that he lacks enough stock clerks to manage the inventory of raw materials, parts, and finished goods the company maintains. He reports a number of instances in which raw materials that have been reduced to the reorder point were not identified and purchase orders for these materials were not cut. Trout is especially annoyed that even standard raw materials

from long-term suppliers are allowed to drop below the reorder point.

Tenlow Fenton, a shop-floor supervisor, charges that there are too many breakdowns in equipment—breakdowns that then delay production schedules. Fenton believes that the workers are reasonably satisfied with their work and are experienced at their jobs. He argues that equipment, not labor, is causing the delays.

Ruby Kent, the finance manager, thinks that too much money is being tied up in inventory and that these high inventories generate higher inventory taxes that must be paid to the local community.

a. Given the data obtained in these interviews, what production problems seem to be occurring at the plant?

b. How do you think these problems ought to be prioritized?

c. What information systems should be considered to solve the problems?

d. What software do you recommend that Burroughs consider to assist in solving these problems?

4. **Ambrose Technologies, Inc.** I-Chen Yi is the new manager of the product design department of Ambrose Technologies, Inc. She supervises a large staff of design engineers and drafting personnel. During her first month as manager, Yi has noted that the operations in the department are entirely manual. Requests for new products are designed according to the specifications received, and a preliminary draft of the product is manually prepared. This draft is critically reviewed by numerous company personnel, and a second, revised draft is drawn. If the second draft is satisfactory, a physical model is put together for testing. This testing usually generates several more drafts of the product and several revised physical models that are tested.

Yi is a strong proponent of rigorous testing and thus fully supports the iterative model building and product drafts that such testing requires. She feels that thoroughly tested products are likely to be well-received by customers and to save on warranty costs for the firm. However, Jason Schmidt, the marketing manager is concerned with the long lead time that the new-product development cycle takes. In several instances recently, the company has taken a very long time to develop new products. As a result, these products entered the market long after those of the competition, allowing the competition to develop a well-established customer base. Schmidt has complained strongly to Yi about the lengthy new-product development procedures. He feels that the process must be speeded up or the company will continue to lose market share to its competitors.

Yi has asked Clara Wilson from the management information systems department to examine the product development cycle and to recommend changes that can bring products to market faster. As part of her recommendations, Wilson plans to present to Yi some recommendations for computer software that can be used in the development cycle. Wilson has asked you to prepare the software recommendations for the report.

a. Identify the parts of Yi's development cycle that might prove to be suitable applications for computer software.

b. Identify types of software that could be used for each of the applications you listed in (a).

c. Describe how each software type identified in (b) can be used to improve the applications listed in (a).

5. **Minitek, Inc.**   You work in the training unit of the Human Resource Department of Minitek, Inc., a distributor of computer storage devices located in Glen Carbon, Illinois. Your job involves using an information system that tracks employees and the seminar programs in which they have enrolled. It is now fall 1997, and you are using a database that describes employees, seminar programs, instructors, seminar registrations, and seminar schedules. To complete this case, you will query the database. You can use any database software that is able to read dbf, or dBase files, such as Microsoft Access. If you are using dBase, you may choose to query the database using the command interface, the query-by-example interface, or the SQL interface.

To get started, you will need these items:

1. A copy of a database program that will read and process the dBase (dbf) files listed below.

2. The following database files stored on your Student Data Disk:

   a. An EMPLOYEE file, which describes the employees.

   b. A SEMINAR file, which describes the seminars that are classified into Professional Development, Management Training, Technical Training, Sales Training, and Specialized Training categories.

   c. An INSTRUCT (instructor) file describing the instructors.

   d. A REGISTER file describing the employees registered in various seminar programs for the fall semester of 1997.

   e. A SCHEDULE file describing the seminars schedules for the spring and summer semesters of 1998 to be held in certain rooms and their capacity.

Directions:

1. Load dBase or your database software on your computer system.

2. Place your data disk in your computer's disk drive. If you are using dBase, get to the dot prompt(.) and key in these commands:

   .SET DIRECTORY TO N (where N is the letter of the disk drive in which you inserted your data disk)

.SET CATALOG TO MINITEK

Change to the dBase Control Center screen by entering ASSIST at the "." prompt.

3. Scan the contents of records in the database so that you understand the nature of the data in the database. If you are using dBase, you can move the cursor to each file in the Date panel or column of the Control Center, press enter, and select Display Data. Move about each file by using the Home, End, Page Up, and Page Down keys.

4. Print the answers to each of the following queries:

Query 1: You are considering offering some seminars off-site in Belleville, Illinois. Produce two lists: one list of the last names and telephone numbers of all students who live in Belleville, Illinois, and another list of the last names and telephone numbers of all instructors who live in Belleville, Illinois.

Query 2: You wish to improve revenues for the training unit by encouraging enrollment in seminars with high fees. Produce a list of all seminars with fees greater than $350 that will be offered in spring 1998. The list should contain the seminar ID, the seminar description, and the seminar fee.

Query 3: Produce a list of all employees registered for PRO108 for fall 1997. The list should include last name, phone number, and department of each employee in the seminar.

Query 4: Employees who register in seminars have their fees paid by the departments in which they work. Produce a list of all employees enrolled in a fall 1997 seminar who have not yet paid their fees. The list should contain the employee's last name, the department, the seminar ID, and the fee owed.

Query 5: Produce a schedule of seminars for summer 1998 showing the Seminar ID, seminar description, building, room number, and instructor's last name.

Hand in each of your lists to your instructor. Add your name and the query number to each list.

To help you understand the records you will work with, the names and characteristics of the fields in each type of record follow.

1. **EMPLOYEE file (EMPLOYEE.DBF)**

Field Name	Type	Width
EID	Character	9
ELNAME	Character	10
EMI	Character	1
EFINAME	Character	10
EDOB	Character	6
ESEX	Character	1
ESTR	Character	15
ECITY	Character	15
ESTATE	Character	2
EZIP	Character	5
EPHONE	Character	10
EDEPT	Character	3
EEOC	Character	3

2. **SEMINAR file (SEMINAR.DBF)**

Field Name	Type	Width	Dec
SID	Character	6	
SDESC	Character	22	
SPROG	Character	18	
SFEE	Numeric	7	2

3. **INSTRUCT file (INSTRUCT.DBF)**

Field Name	Type	Width	Dec
IID	Character	9	
ILNAME	Character	10	
IMI	Character	1	
IFNAME	Character	10	
IJOBTITLE	Character	23	
ISTR	Character	15	
ICITY	Character	15	
ISTATE	Character	2	
IZIP	Character	5	
IPHONE	Character	10	

4. REGISTER file (REGISTER.DBF)

Field Name	Type	Width Dec
RSEM	Character	4
RSID	Character	6
RSID	Character	9
RTPAID	Character	1

5. SCHEDULE file (SCHEDULE.DBF)

Field Name	Type	Width Dec
SCSEM	Character	4
SCSID	Character	6
SCIID	Character	9
SCBLDG	Character	2
SCROOM	Character	4
SCCAP	Numeric	4

Data Entry Codes:

File: Employee; Field: EDEPT:

ACC	Accounting
MIS	Management Information Systems
PUR	Purchasing
SAL	Sales
SHI	Shipping

File: Employee; Field: EEOC:

CAU	Caucasian
BLA	Black
HIS	Hispanic
ASI	Asian
IND	Indian

SELECTED INTERNET REFERENCE SITES

Interesting Web Sites about Financial Accounting

CTSNET Business and Finance Center (http://CRASH.CTS.COM/biz/).

Dow Jones Industrial Average (http://www.secapl.com/secapl/quoteserver/djia.html).

FinanceNet (http://www.financenet.gov).

FINWeb (http://riskweb.bus.utexas.edu:80/finweb.html).

NETworth Information Page (http://networth. galt.com/www/home/networth.htm).

Security APL Quote Server (http://www. secapl.com/cgi-bin/qs).

SEC's EDGAR Database (http://www.sec. gov/edgarhp.htm).

Wall Street News (http://www.netmedia. com:80/ forecasts).

Wall Street Research Net (http://www.wsrn.com).

Interesting Web Sites about Marketing

Advertising Age (http://adage.com).

Electronic Malls on the Web (http://www.ro.com/ShopInternet/malls.html).

Federal Trade Commission Guidelines on Advertising (http://www.ftc.gov).

International Markets (http://www.odci.gov/cia/publications/95fact/index).

[The] Internet Marketing Archive (http://galaxy,einet.net:80/hypermail/inet-marketing).

Links to Marketing Sites (http://nsns.com/MouseTracks).

MarketPlace Resource Center (http://www.mktplace.com/home1022).

Interesting Web Sites about Production

Agile Manufacturing Home Page (http://www.sandia.gov/agil/home_page.html).

Computer Aided Decision Support System for Agile Manufacturing (CADSAM) (http://www.glue.umd.edu/~azzaro/cadsam.623/CADSAM.html#AI).

Project Management Institute (http://www.pmi.org).

Quality Management Library (http://vector.casti.com/qc/QY95/QY95.html).

VLSI Technology, Inc. (http://www.vlsi.com/).

Interesting Web Sites about Human Resource Management

American Compensation Association
(http://www.ahrm.org/aca/aca.htm).

Americans with Disabilities Act Document Center
(http://janweb.icdi.wvu.edu/kinder/).

Benefits Link (http://www.benefitslink.com/).

Brian Croft's Guide to Technology and HR
(http://www.inforamp.net/~bcroft/index.html).

Bureau of Labor Statistics (http://stats.bls.gov/).

Bureau of Labor Statistics: Occupational Outlook
Handbook (http://stats.bls.gov/ocohome.htm).

Bureau of Labour Information (Canada)
(http://www.hrdcdrhc.gc.ca/hrdc/bli/eng/
bli.html).

Department of Labor (http://www.dol.gov/).

Employee Relations Web Picks
(http://www.webcom.com/~garnet/labor/).

HR News Online (http://www.shrm.org/hrnews/).

Labor Law News (http://www.ljextra.com/
practice/laboremployment/labcol.html).

Links to Important HRIS Web Sites
(http://www.shrm.org/hrlinks/hris.htm).

Links to Important HRM Web Sites
(http://www.shrm.org/hrlinks/).

Occupational Safety and Health Administration
(http://www.osha.gov/).

Social Security Administration (http://www.ssa.gov/).

Society for Human Resource Management
(http://www.shrm.org.).

Training Net (http://www.trainingnet.com/).

Ultimate Employee Handbook
(http://www.courttv.com/seminars/handbook/).

SELECTED REFERENCES AND READINGS

Bylinksy, G. "The Digital Factory." *Fortune,* November 14, 1994, p. 93. How the use of software and factory networks is changing the face of production in the United States.

Conroy, C. "People, by the Numbers." *CompuServe Magazine* 13, no. 10 (October 1994), p. 32. Describes numerous sources of on-line demographic databases.

Davis, S. M. "Mass Customization." *Harvard Business Review,* April 1994, p. 180.

Gable, M. ""Spotlight on Marketing Lists: When Does Direct Marketing Interfere with Consumers' Privacy?" *PC Today* 8, no. 1 (January 1994), p. 20. Discusses the ethical issues surrounding the use of electronic directories. A sidebar describes how American Business Information was formed.

Huttig, J. W. "'X' Marks the Spot: Geographic Information Systems Turn Databases into Marketing Treasure Maps." *PC Today* 8, no. 1 (January 1994), p. 16. Reviews mapping software and its application to the marketing function.

Levin, C. "Virtual Prototyping: New Tools to Build New Products." *PC Magazine* 14, no. 16 (September 26, 1995), p. 32. Briefly describes several applications of simulation to product design.

Noe, R. A.; J. R. Hollenbeck; and B. Gerhart. *Human Resource Management: Gaining a Competitive Advantage.* Burr Ridge, IL: Irwin Publishing Company, 1994. A human resource management textbook, a major theme of which is how human resources can contribute to an organization's competitiveness. Chapter 19 is devoted to human resource information systems. In addition, each chapter has a section devoted to "Competing through Technology & Structure."

Ottolenghi, H. H. "Hot New Personal-Finance Services." *Your Money,* August/September 1995, p. 24. Describes some on-line sources for investing.

Perera, P. A. "Sales Automation: Re-engineering Gone Awry." *ComputerWorld,* October 21, 1996, p. 37.

Pine, B. J. Illinois *Mass Customization: The New Frontier in Business Competition.* Boston, Harvard Business School Press, 1993.

Samyer, Thomas and Michael Recht. "A Material Selection Program," *BYTE,* July 1986, p. 235.

Strangelove, M. "The Walls Come Down: Net Age Advertising Empowers Consumers." *Internet World* 6, no. 5 (May 1995), p. 39. Analyzes effective and ineffective Internet advertising.

Washburn, B. "The Problem with Advertising." *Internet World* 6, no. 5 (May 1995), p. 32. Presents the problems and opportunities for Internet advertising.

11

APPLICATIONS OF TACTICAL AND STRATEGIC INFORMATION SYSTEMS TO BUSINESS

CHAPTER OUTLINE

Manager's View

The Nature of Tactical and Strategic Information Systems

Tactical Accounting and Financial Information Systems

Strategic Accounting and Financial Information Systems

Tactical Marketing Information Systems

Strategic Marketing Information Systems

Tactical Production Information Systems

Strategic Production Information Systems

Tactical Human Resource Information Systems

Strategic Human Resource Information Systems

HRIS Software

Management Summary

Key Terms for Managers

Review Questions

Questions for Discussion

Problems

Cases

Selected Internet Reference Sites

Selected References and Readings

AS YOU MOVE UP THE ORGANIZATIONAL LADDER from supervisory positions to middle- and upper-management positions, you will make decisions that have an increasingly greater impact on the organization. The decisions you may face along the way are diverse and could include decisions similar to these:

1. Should you purchase a new piece of equipment or lease the equipment for a three-year period?

2. Is the idle cash of your firm being invested wisely?

3. Should you invest money in new computer equipment or in additional merchandise for resale?

4. What criteria will you use to create territories for your salespeople and how large of a territory should each salesperson cover?

5. What products should be emphasized through advertising or promotion to reach the firm's sales goals?

6. What are the best potential sites for a new retail store location?

7. How many and what types of workers will be needed to staff a new plant in another state?

This chapter examines the types of tactical and strategic decisions that you may make as you move up the ranks of middle and upper management. Specifically, the chapter examines the application of information technology to some of the tactical and strategic information systems frequently used by middle and upper management in four organizational functions: accounting/finance, marketing, production, and human resource management (see Figure 11-1).

THE NATURE OF TACTICAL AND STRATEGIC INFORMATION SYSTEMS

Tactical information systems support management decision making by providing managers with regular summary reports, regular exception reports, ad hoc reports, and other information that helps them (1) control their areas of responsibility and (2) allocate their resources to pursue organization goals. While the focus of operational information systems (see Chapter 10) is on the completion of tasks, the focus of tactical information systems is on resource allocation; that is, how do you allocate the resources available to you to reach organizational goals.

In contrast, strategic-level information systems are goal oriented. That is, these systems are designed to support organizational goal and direction setting.

Figure 11–1

Examples of tactical and strategic information systems in four business functions

Accounting/Finance	Marketing	Production	Human Resources
TACTICAL:			
Budgeting	Sales management	Materials requirements planning	Job analysis and design
Cash management	Advertising and promotion	Just in time	Recruiting
Capital budgeting	Pricing	Capacity planning	Compensation and benefits
Investment management	Distribution channel	Production scheduling	Succession planning
	Competitive tracking	Product design and development	
		Manufacturing resource planning	
		Computer integrated manufacturing	
STRATEGIC:			
Financial condition analysis	Sales forecasting	Site planning and selection	Workforce planning
Long-term forecasting	Market research	Technology planning and assessment	Labor negotiations
	Product planning and development	Process positioning	
		Plant design	

It is difficult at times to categorize some information systems as clearly tactical or clearly strategic. For example, some marketing information systems, such as marketing research systems and competitor tracking information systems, clearly could support both tactical and strategic planning decision making. Sometimes the decision to categorize a decision as tactical or strategic comes down to the length of time the decision is likely to impact an organization. That is, decisions that will impact an organization for a year or less are often viewed as tactical, while decisions that will impact an organization for more than a year are often viewed as strategic.

The computerization of financial accounting systems was a major event for most large organizations in the 1950s and 1960s. Many large organizations developed data processing departments during those decades to install computer systems and develop computerized versions of their financial accounting systems to handle the great volume of transactions that needed to be processed. The advent of microprocessors and the stunning drop in the cost of computer systems enabled most small organizations to computerize their financial accounting systems in the 1980s.

The computerization of financial accounting systems changed the way managers viewed accounting information. A large database of information became available in computerized form, and it could be viewed or manipulated much more easily than data in traditional hard copy form. So managers began to view this information as a resource for tactical planning. Suddenly managers could obtain important summaries and comparisons of financial accounting data easily and swiftly. In the past this information would have taken a great deal of time to extract from a manual financial accounting system. The result was that managers began to view the financial accounting system as more than merely a transaction-processing system, a producer of checks, invoices, and statements. It became a repository of important data that assists management in tactical decision making and long-range strategic planning.

The computerization of financial accounting systems helped spawn the development of other corporate databases to support tactical decisions and strategic planning in other functional business areas.

TACTICAL ACCOUNTING AND FINANCIAL INFORMATION SYSTEMS

It is possible to design many computer-supported, tactical-level information systems for the financial decisions that managers must make. Budgeting systems, cash management systems, capital budgeting systems, and investment management systems are common examples. Each system will be briefly described to give you an idea of the nature and use of these tactical-level information systems in the financial arena.

Budgeting Systems

The **budgeting system** permits managers to track actual revenues and expenses and compare these amounts to expected revenues and expenses. It also allows managers to compare current budget amounts to those of prior fiscal periods, other divisions, other departments—even to industrywide data. Comparisons of budget data against such standards allow managers to assess how they use their resources to achieve their goals. For example, a manager may view the budget to find the amount of money actually spent in the purchasing department on supervisory versus clerical staff. The manager may then compare those amounts to the amounts spent by other purchasing departments in the organization or in the industry.

The general ledger system of computerized financial accounting systems often permits budget amounts to be entered by account number. Periodically (weekly, monthly, quarterly, or annually) these budgeted amounts (**allocations**) and the actual amounts spent or received (**actuals**) for each account are compared and reports are prepared. The difference between the allocation for an account and the actual amount spent, called a **variance,** is also identified and reported.

For example, the general ledger system of a financial accounting system may provide these reports:

1. Current budget allocations, expenditures, and variances by budget line item.
2. Current budget allocations compared to the previous year's allocations.
3. Current revenues and expenditures compared to the previous year's revenues and expenditures.
4. Current revenues and expenditures compared to the average of the other units or divisions of the organization.
5. Projected expenditures and variances for each budget line item for the entire year based on the expenditures incurred to date.

Reports such as these may be prepared for a department, a division, a subsidiary, or the entire organization. Sometimes, however, the manager may wish to download the data from the financial accounting system to a spreadsheet so that additional processing can be completed. An example of a budget variance report prepared using a spreadsheet is shown in Figure 11–2.

Figure 11–2

A budget variance report

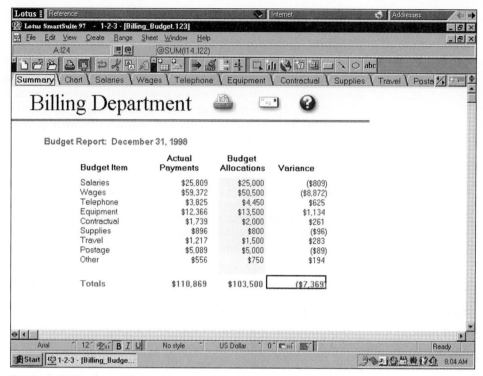

Courtesy Lotus Development Corporation.

Regularly produced tactical-level reports, such as budget variance reports, often generate managerial questions and concerns. These in turn may lead managers to query the financial accounting database for answers or solutions. Suppose, for example, that you are an accounting manager and supervise several departments, including the billing department. Suppose further that the regular budget report shows that the wages line of the billing department report is much higher than in prior years. To find out why, you might query the financial accounting database for answers. If the database stores the number of statements produced each month, the number of employees in the billing department, and the costs associated with the billing department, you might obtain various measures of the productivity of that department, such as the average number of statements produced per billing department employee and the average cost per statement. If you found poor productivity results, you might then examine the productivity of each billing supervisor compared to the average for the organization or the productivity of each billing clerk compared to the average for the department. This information might lead you to decisions about changing supervisory personnel, providing training for specific billing clerks, acquiring new equipment to produce customer statements, or other possible remedies. Notice that the system does not make the decisions for you; it provides information to help you identify and remedy problems. It is a decision-support system, not a decision system.

When the standards against which budgetary data are compared are well known, the manager can generate regular comparative reports using the organization's data processing system. For ad hoc reports, the organization's financial accounting database might be accessed by the manager using a query language or report writer. Many managers also find it helpful to use spreadsheet software to analyze their departments' budgetary data (see Chapter 6).

Figure 11–3

A spreadsheet cash flow report

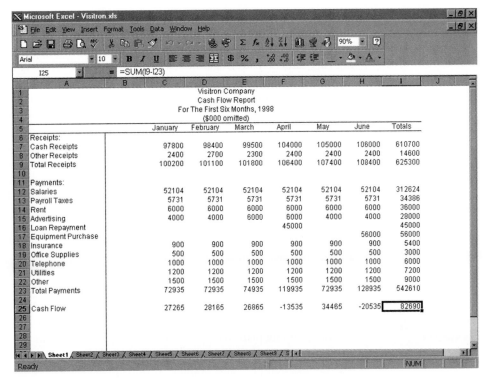

Courtesy Microsoft Corporation.

Cash Management Systems

Important functions of financial management include ensuring that the organization has sufficient cash to meet its needs, putting excess funds from any period to use through investments, and providing borrowing power to meet the organization's cash needs in periods of insufficient cash flow.

An organization needs cash for two major reasons: for working capital (cash needed for day-to-day operations) and for the acquisition of long-term assets. To determine if adequate cash is available for its working capital needs and its long-term asset acquisition plans, the organization must prepare a report of its expected cash flow for the time periods being considered. Typically this report shows the cash flow for each month of the coming year.

A **cash flow report** (see Figure 11–3) shows the estimated amount of cash that will be received and spent each month. The report shows which months will have excess funds that might be put to use and which months will have insufficient funds, which may require the organization to borrow cash to meet its working capital or fixed asset acquisition needs.

A cash flow report supplies information that helps the manager make decisions about investing, purchasing, and borrowing money. If this information is placed on an electronic spreadsheet, the manager may simulate a number of possible business conditions, such as (1) increasing or decreasing revenue, (2) increasing or decreasing customer credit, (3) deferring the acquisition of an asset, or (4) repairing existing fixed assets instead of replacing them. By simulating many possible business conditions, the manager is able to make more informed decisions about the use of or need for cash for the short term. In short, the manager can study various reallocations of the resources of a department, division, or other units.

Cash management systems are more difficult to sustain for smaller organizations that may not be able to afford the resources necessary to track cash balances on a day-to-day basis and invest the excess to maximize organization income. Recognizing that difficulty, Merrill Lynch, a brokerage house, created a product in the 1970s that offered business customers an account combining the attributes of a money market account, a brokerage account, a margin credit account, and a checking account. The product, called the cash management account (CMA) provided business customers with automatic deposits of cash and dividends from other accounts into a money market account. This option gave organizations high interest rates on idle cash resulting from sales of stock, receipts of dividends, or deposits made for the purchase of stock. Organizations could also use a debit card and checks to withdraw money from the money market account. The result was that a small organization could use the service to maximize its income from idle cash sometimes available in its normal cash flow.

The CMA gave Merrill Lynch an enormous competitive advantage and resulted in a large increase in new accounts until other brokerage houses, banks, and financial institutions developed similar products.

Capital Budgeting Systems

A **capital budget** contains information about the planned acquisition or disposal of major plant assets during the current year. The manager may compare the various capital spending plans using three commonly used evaluation tools: net present value, internal rate of return, and payback period. Before the plant asset is acquired, the manager should compare and evaluate various plans for its acquisition using some financial software tool, such as an electronic spreadsheet.

For example, suppose a manager is considering acquiring a large electronic printer and estimates that her firm will keep the machine for five years. The printer may be purchased or leased. Each method requires the manager to spend different amounts of money over different periods of time. The manager can improve the decision to buy or lease by evaluating the present value of the funds each method requires.

 Net present value (NPV) is the current value of cash that will be received at some future time. For example, $10,000 spent now is worth more than $10,000 spent one year from now. If you did not spend the money now, you could invest it and earn interest or other income. For example, if the current discount or interest rate is 10 percent, then the present value of $10,000 one year from now would be only $9,090.91. That is, the latter amount, if invested now, would produce $10,000 at the end of one year. Thus the present value of $10,000 to be spent one year from now is only $9,090.91. Using net present value, the manager must first identify all yearly cash inflows and outflows that would result from the lease or purchase of the printer. Cash inflows might include earnings of the asset, expenses saved through the use of the asset, and tax deductions resulting from the lease or purchase of the asset. Tax deductions could include operating expenses, maintenance, and annual lease costs if the equipment is leased, or operating expenses, maintenance, and annual depreciation if the equipment is purchased.

The manager also must determine the current discount or interest rate for money. Then she will be able to compare the discounted value of the net cash flows to the organization from leasing and purchasing the printer. These discounted values represent the net present values of leasing versus buying the equipment.

Many financial analysis software packages and spreadsheet software packages provide for the computation of net present value. A spreadsheet that the manager might use to evaluate the net present value of the cash flows for the lease or purchase of the electronic printer is shown in Figure 11–4.

Figure 11–4

A printout of a spreadsheet showing net present values for leasing and purchasing an electronic printer

```
                    ASSET ACQUISITION EVALUATION
                         LEASE VS. PURCHASE

    Purchase Price    $17,500
    Sales Tax Rate       0.05
    Resale/Trade-In   $6,000
    Interest Rate        0.1
    Mo. Maintenance     $270
    Mo. Lease Pay.      $450
    Lease Deposit          0
    Mar. Tax Rate       0.45
    Deprec. Rate         0.2


                           Purchase Option

    Year                     0        1        2        3        4        5
    Total Cost         $18,375
    Main. Net of Tax            $1,458   $1,458   $1,458   $1,458   $1,458
    Total Outgoing     $18,375  $1,458   $1,458   $1,458   $1,458   $1,458

    Tax. Sav. Deprec.          $1,571   $1,571   $1,571   $1,571   $1,571
    Sale/Trade Amt.                                                $6,000
    Total Incoming             $1,571   $1,571   $1,571   $1,571   $7,571

    Net Cash Flow      $18,375   -$113    -$113    -$113    -$113    -$113
    NPV                $14,221


                            Lease Option

    Year                     0        1        2        3        4        5
    Deposit                  0
    Mo. Pay Net Tax            $2,430   $2,430   $2,430   $2,430   $2,430
    Main. Net of Tax          $1,458   $1,458   $1,458   $1,458   $1,458
    Net Cash Flow            0 $3,888   $3,888   $3,888   $3,888   $3,888
    NPV                $14,739
```

The **internal rate of return (IRR)** method uses the same types of data as the net present value method. The manager needs to identify the cash inflows and outflows that result from acquiring an asset by the various methods and to identify the present discount or interest rate that the organization can earn on its money. The purpose of the internal rate of return calculation is to find the discount rate that generates a present value of the earnings or savings equal to the present values of initial investment. The IRR can be compared to the rate of return the organization has decided it must make on its investments. Basically, you use IRR to determine whether the organization will make a better return by acquiring the asset than by investing its money in some other venture.

The manager may also wish to estimate the payback period of the investment of her firm's funds in the electronic printer. The **payback period** is how many years or months the increase in revenues or the savings from reduced operating expenses obtained from the asset will take to match the investment in the asset. Suppose that the purchase of the new printer is projected to provide $3,500 annual savings over the old equipment. If the new equipment costs $17,500 to purchase, deliver, and install, then the payback period is estimated to be $17,500/$3,500, or five years. The way the manager calculated the payback period here does not consider the time value of annual savings.

Using payback period, net present value, internal rate of return, and other asset acquisition analysis tools, the financial manager can make informed decisions on the utility of acquiring assets and how these acquisitions may best be funded. Software tools, such as spreadsheets and financial analysis software, assist the manager in accomplishing these tasks quickly. The manager also can see the results when various factors are varied. For example, varying the discount rate, the length of time the asset is held, the amount of down payment, or other variables can help determine the optimum factors for use in negotiating with vendors.

Investment Management Systems

Investment management—overseeing the organization's investments in stocks, bonds, and other securities—is an important part of cash management. Managing investments is also an important part of managing the organization's pension plan. Whatever their source of investment funds, most organizations invest money in securities of one kind or another. Careful management of these investments is necessary to ensure the achievement of organization goals.

Computer information systems provide unique ways to manage stock and bond portfolios. These ways typically involve the use of on-line databases that furnish immediate updates for stock and bond prices, information about the history of each invest-

---

Manager's Memo 11–1	**SOME ON-LINE AND INTERNET FINANCIAL SERVICES**

◢ A wealth of financial information and services is available to financial and other managers on the Internet today. Below is a list of just a few on-line sources of financial data. Some of the items listed have fees. In those cases the Web address provides information about the service and how to become a subscriber.

Product and Web address (http://omitted)	Description
FinWeb (www.finweb.com)	Contains links to finance journals and magazines, databases, working papers, financial and economic Web servers, and other financial data. Also has search engines, references, and newspaper links.
Department of Finance, Ohio State University, Financial Data Finder (www.cob.ohio-state.edu/~fin/osudata.htm)	A vast array of financial data and information including dozens of downloadable data sets pertaining to many topics in finance.
Barra (www.barra.com)	Articles, news, and U.S. and Canadian market data sets.
Canada Net Stocks and Bonds (www.cyberion.com/canadanet/stocksbonds/)	Articles, stock quotes, and a searchable mutual fund database on Canadian organizations.
Finance Net (www.financenet.gov)	Information about state and local, federal, and international public finance, including organizations, networks, and resources.
Dow Jones News/Retrieval (bis.dowjones.com/online-lib/index.html)	Provides financial news, company financial information, earnings per share estimates, mutual fund and stock quotes, and other financial data.
S & P Online (www.stockinfo.standardpoor.com)	Standard and Poor's on-line database providing a wide variety of company data including earnings estimates. Also provides stock pick recommendations.
Value Line Corporate Reports (www.publishingresources.com:80/valueline/vlprof.htm)	Financial and statistical information about 5,000 stocks and 6,000 mutual funds on CD-ROM disks and through CompuServe.

ment, and various portfolio investment analysis tools to help the manager stay on top of the organization's investments. The system may be a simple one in which the manager has a computer system with a modem and a subscription to an investment service.

For example, companies that provide on-line services, such as Dow Jones and CompuServe, typically provide a host of data about investments, including current and past security prices and company information such as financial statistics, earnings estimates, and brokerage reports, Securities and Exchange Commission filings, and even financial statements and other analyses. Investment databases are also available through other means (see Manager's Memo 11-1).

For example, Value Line is an investment service company that provides investment data on regularly updated CD-ROM disks. The system also allows you to download current stock prices to your microcomputer using a modem. The data can be analyzed using your own software or with Value/Screen software provided by Value Line. This software provides data on many different variables for about 1,700 stocks (see Figure 11-5). Value/Screen permits the manager to view the data on individual companies or to compare data on companies or groups of companies against the entire database of 1,700 firms. It also permits the manager to analyze and maintain data on the organization's current stock portfolio. When you input the current price of each stock, the software calculates the gain or loss the portfolio would generate if sold now, provides the income and yield of the portfolio, and offers a variety of other measures for each stock owned and the entire portfolio. The data and analyses the software provides allow investment managers to make more-informed decisions regarding the sale or acquisition of investments.

Figure 11–5

A screen from Value/Screen software

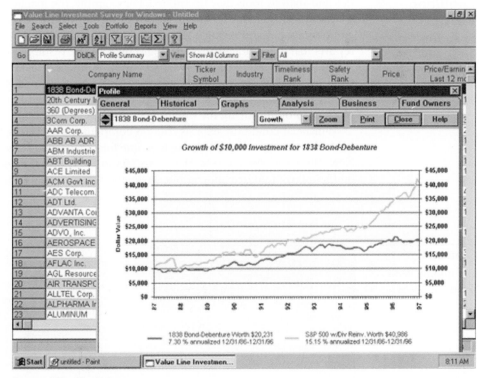

Courtesy Value Line Software.

STRATEGIC ACCOUNTING AND FINANCIAL INFORMATION SYSTEMS

Strategic accounting and financial information systems typically include several types of information flows:

1. Internally generated financial condition analysis data, describing the status of the organization.
2. Externally generated economic, demographic, and social data describing the present and future environments for the organization.
3. Forecasts of the future of that organization in those environments.

Two major outcomes of financial strategic planning are the setting of financial goals and directions of the organization. The former may include setting goals for investments and return on investments. The latter may involve deciding on new investment opportunities or on the mix of capital sources used to fund the organization.

A major source of computerized information about the current and future status of the organization is the organization's own financial accounting database. A major source of computerized information on the present and future environments in which the organization must operate are on-line databases that contain economic, social, demographic, technological, and political information. Projecting likely scenarios for the organization using these two categories of data is the art of forecasting. A major purpose of strategic decision making is to use long-range forecasts to reduce the risk involved in major organizational decisions.

Financial Condition Analysis Systems

Computerized accounting systems provide the user with many reports to which ratios and analysis tools may be applied. For example, the manager may use a variety of analysis tools, including those shown in Figure 11–6, on the data reported on the income statement and balance sheet. Many computerized accounting systems supply reports that automatically calculate and present the results of these tools and ratios. Along with the data and reports, these tools and ratios make up the organization's **financial condition analysis system.** This system provides management with a variety of measures of the soundness of the organization and makes it possible to explore ways of improving the organization's financial condition.

Financial condition analysis data on competitors, suppliers, buyers, and other organizations is also available through on-line financial databases such as the Dow Jones News/Retrieval Service (see Manager's Memo 11–1) and through information found on the Internet. Information about on-line databases was also presented in Chapter 7

Figure 11–6

Commonly used financial ratios

RATIO NAME	RATIO FORMULA
Current ratio	Current assets ÷ current liabilities
Working capital	Current assets − current liabilities
Inventory turnover	Cost of goods sold ÷ average inventory
Debt-to-equity ratio	Stockholder equity ÷ total liabilities
Rate earned on stockholder's equity	Net income ÷ average stockholder's equity
Earnings per share	Net income ÷ number of shares

in the section entitled "On-Line Databases," and information on the Internet was also presented in Chapter 9.

Long-Range Forecasting Systems

Strategic planners demand forecasts on a variety of factors that will affect organization performance in the future. Some forecasts may involve the use of internally generated data. For example, past sales data may be used to project future sales. Other forecasts may use only external data or both internal and external data. For example, forecasting economic indicators helps planners understand the likely economic environment in which the organization must operate in the future. Forecasting the financial health of the organization through long-range budget estimates—including a variety of possible wage negotiation settlements, actions by competitors, interest rate fluctuations, fuel cost changes, and different inflation rates—provides planners with opportunities to consider actions that will help the organization survive bad times or take advantage of a future environment.

Information used in forecasting the future environment includes descriptions of the past activities of an organization, data on the present economy and forecasts of the future economy, information on the present demographic structure of the region or country and forecasts of the future demographic structure, and descriptions of the current social structure and social mores and predictions of the future structure of society and societal mores.

For example, suppose that Juan Aponte is superintendent of a small school district and wishes to predict the economic and demographic conditions in the school district five years from now. He forecasts the school-age population for the next five years using hard data obtained from present census figures adjusted for the life expectancies of the population and the dropout rate of the district. These figures allow him to project the number of classes, teachers, and school facilities the district will need. The data also allow Aponte to project state aid to the district, a major source of its revenue.

Aponte forecasts that part of the district's budget in five years will come from an expanded tax base. This prediction is made using economic projections for the district, including new home construction, new family formations, business additions and failures, and the estimated rate of price increases on real property.

Aponte also uses the current ages of the staff and the district's past retirement experience to project staffing needs five years from now, indicating how many new staff members must be acquired because of retirements and growth or how many present staff members must be let go. Aponte projects the salary increases for the previous five years in the district to the next five years, adjusting those figures for the estimated effects of the projected supply and demand of teachers.

Aponte hopes that these projections will permit him and his staff to identify potential resource problems for the district in time to solve them without needing crisis management. Notice that some of the information he needs can be generated using internal data from the district's computerized database. However, other information critical to strategic planning is external to the organization. Some of this information may be available from an on-line database.

After Aponte acquires the information, he builds a spreadsheet to allow him to forecast the financial condition of the school district. He develops the spreadsheet so he can make changes in assessed values, property tax rates, student enrollment, state aid, interest rates, supplies and expenses, union-negotiated salaries, and the student/teacher ratio (see Figure 11-7). This spreadsheet allows Aponte to simulate how a variety of demographic and economic conditions will impact the financial condition of the school district next year or five years from now.

Many financial analysis tasks involve forecasting future events and require that you use statistical tools. Sometimes these tools are available in general purpose software, such as spreadsheets. In other cases, you may need to use software specifically designed to complete statistical tasks. Selecting statistical or **forecasting software** to aid you in tactical-level decisions and long-range planning requires that you carefully analyze your applications so that the software you buy has these features:

1. It contains the statistical procedures or forecasting methods you wish to use. If the software does not do what you want it to do, no discount given for the software will allow you to paper over the problem.

Figure 11–7

A printout of a spreadsheet used to forecast the financial condition of a school district

```
                    GASPE SCHOOL DISTRICT
                    BUDGET WORKSHEET, 1998

INCOME:
Assessed Value: Residential Property   $24,625,000.00
Assessed Value: Business Property       $5,495,000.00
Property Tax Rate per $1,000                   $65.00
Residence Property Taxes                $1,600,625.00
Business Property Taxes                   $357,175.00
     Total Income from Taxes                            $1,957,800.00
Student Enrollment                                823
State Aid per Pupil                            $37.00
Enrollment State Aid                       $30,451.00
Other State Aid                             $6,000.00
     Total State Aid                                       $36,451.00
Funds Invested                             $90,000.00
Investment Interest Rate                        7.00%
Interest Income                             $6,300.00
Other Income                                $4,500.00
     Total Interest and Other Income                       $10,800.00
     Total Income for District                          $2,005,051.00

EXPENSES:
Student/Teacher Ratio                              24
Number of Teachers Needed                          35
Number of Special Professionals                     2
Number of Administrators                            3
Number of Clerical Staff                            3
Number of Other Staff                               2
Average Teacher Salary                     $29,807.00
Average Professional Salary                $32,867.00
Average Administrator Salary               $43,082.00
Average Clerical Salary                    $19,253.00
Average Staff Wages                        $20,982.00
     Total Salaries and Wages                           $1,337,948.00
Instructional Supplies                    $210,000.00
Curriculum Supplies                       $440,000.00
Office Expenses                            $26,000.00
Equipment Expenses                         $56,000.00
Other Expenses                              $5,000.00
     Total Non-Salary Expenses                            $737,000.00
     Total Expenses                                     $2,074,948.00

SURPLUS/DEFICIT                                           ($69,897.00)
```

2. It presents the procedures and methods at a level appropriate to your sophistication with statistics and forecasting techniques. Software designed for statistically unsophisticated users helps users select statistical procedures and enter data.

TACTICAL MARKETING INFORMATION SYSTEMS

As you learned in Chapter 10, the marketing function is the satisfaction of the needs and wants of customers—current and potential. Marketing managers engage in many planning activities in the pursuit of the marketing function (see Figure 11-8). These planning activities result in a combination of products, services, advertising, promotion, price, and product delivery methods ultimately offered to the organization's customers, which is referred to as the **marketing mix.**

Tactical marketing information systems differ from operational marketing information systems because in addition to producing information on a regular basis, they also generate ad hoc reports, create unexpected as well as expected output, produce comparative as well as descriptive information, provide summary information as

Figure 11–8

A planning model for marketing management

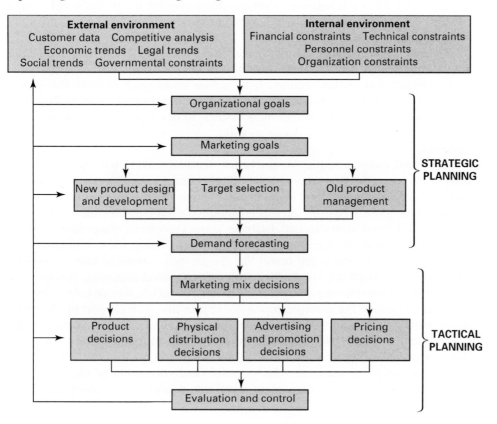

opposed to detailed data, include both internal and external data sources, and process subjective as well as objective data.

A great deal of the data that tactical marketing information systems utilize are collected by operational financial information systems. Tactical marketing information systems often combine operational-level financial data with other data to support tactical decision making by marketing managers. Tactical decisions are often made by managers when they prepare and implement marketing plans through which they hope to reach top management's sales and profit goals. For example, tactical decisions regarding market focus for the coming year may be partly based on the sales history of market segments derived from the sales order-entry system. This information may then be compared to information about the competition's success with those same market segments gleaned from sources outside the organization.

Examples of tactical marketing information systems that will be discussed in this chapter include systems that support deploying and managing the sales force, managing advertising and promotion campaigns, distributing and delivering products sold, and pricing products.

Sales Management Systems

A major objective of marketing managers is to reach the sales goals set by top management. To accomplish this objective, marketing managers must make many tactical decisions, such as how sales territories should be shaped, how the sales force should be allocated within those territories, and what emphasis should be placed on the products offered and customers served. Marketing managers must decide how to reward salespeople to encourage increased sales efforts, which market segments should be emphasized to best reach sales goals, and which products and services will best appeal to each segment. They also must monitor the progress of the sales effort to determine if their decisions were correct or if they need to change their tactical plans.

To make these decisions effectively, marketing managers should have at their disposal a great deal of data about the sales histories of each customer, salesperson, territory, product, and market segment. The various information systems that supply these data to marketing managers are called **sales management systems.** Managers can use the data from sales management systems to develop reports analyzing sales activities that help them make decisions about salespeople, territories, products, and customers.

The trend today is to provide marketing decision makers with access to *data warehouses,* described in earlier chapters. These data warehouses contain customer information; salesperson information; and information about territories, products, and market segments derived from internal organization databases; they may also contain information derived from external databases about customers, competitors, and the economic environment (see Manager's Memo 11–2). Mining these warehouses for data on past sales efforts might reveal that the greatest volume of sales is obtained when certain products are emphasized with certain market segments. This information may be obtained from a query that correlates product or service categories with customer categories. For example, you would expect that such a report produced for an automobile dealership would show that older, wealthier customers would be the most frequent buyers of the dealership's most expensive four-door sedans. You might also expect that younger, professional customers might be the most frequent buyers of the dealership's recreational vehicles. Additional correlation of the data, using finer classifications of customers, might reveal that younger customers from certain

Manager's Memo 11–2	ON-LINE AND INTERNET MARKETING DATABASES

■ The following databases are only a few of the many on-line or Internet databases of use to marketing decision makers. The databases listed show the diversity of resources available.

Database name	Description
CENDATA (http://waffle.nal.usda.gov/agdb/cendata.html)	U.S. census bureau database.
SuperSite (Sales and Marketing) (http://supersite.net/)	Provides demographic data and data for retail store sales potential.
Findex Directory of Market Research (http://www.csa.com/details/findexlo.html)	A Dialog database providing summaries of market studies.
Donnelley Consumer Database (http://www.rrdonnelley.com)	A demographic database.
IMarket, Inc. (http://www.imarketinc.com/)	Marketing database and marketing tools.
NeighborhoodID (http://www.neighborhoodid.com)	Data organized by street address, zip code, city, and country. Includes population data by sex, ethnic background, age, labor force, household type, education and school spending, crime rate, income, home values, and occupancy.
Hispanic Market Site (http://rodcom.com/)	Information about Hispanic markets, media, population, and more.
Nielsen Station Index (http://www.nielsenmedia.com)	Ratings on local TV stations.

professions do not act like the younger group as a whole. Younger members of some professions may be the most frequent purchasers of traditional family sedans, whereas younger members of other professions are the primary purchasers of recreational vehicles. By mining data warehouses, marketing managers may adjust advertising media, promotion schemes, sales calls, and sales approaches to emphasize selected products to very narrowly defined market segments in order to maximize gross sales (see Manager's Memo 11-3).

In addition to planning future campaigns, marketing managers need information to control current campaigns. The manager monitoring sales progress may wish to receive daily, weekly, or monthly reports on the sales achievement of each salesperson with averages calculated for the entire sales force. The manager can use this information to evaluate salesperson effectiveness, the success of the sales reward system, or the appropriateness of the shape of the territories assigned. Key information might be downloaded into a sales performance spreadsheet template for analysis (see Figure 11-9).

In addition, a report showing the percentage of each salesperson's sales by market segment and by product along with averages for the total sales force would display the current effectiveness of each salesperson in selling the organization's products to each customer group.

Sales management systems enable marketing managers to assess the productivity of the sales force; the fertileness of sales territories; and the success of products by salesperson, territory, and customer type. Sales management systems keep track of salesperson call activities, sales orders, and customer activity. The systems allow the

---

Manager's Memo 11–3 | ## THE NEXT STEP IN DATA MINING

◤ While companies rush to data mining as a way to predict more accurately what their customers will want and when, the latest wrinkle on this strategy involves a collaborative process between retailers and manufacturers based on a software product called CFAR—collaborative forecasting and replenishment. The process allows a manufacturer and retailer to calculate anticipated demand for a product, based on past sales trends, promotion plans, and variables such as holidays and weather. The numbers are exchanged over the Internet using the CFAR software. If the numbers differ by more than 10%, the seller and supplier continue their electronic dialogue, exchanging more data until they reach a unified forecast model. "So far, supply-chain partners have cooperated only over the

short term, via orders," says Michael Hammer, co-author of *Reengineering the Corporation.* "What they need to do is get their overall forecasting and planning systems integrated for a long-term view." Currently, it's estimated that $715 billion of consumer goods are gathering dust on warehouse shelves, tying up capital and running up interest charges, according to Bench-marking Partners Inc. Benchmarking says that if retailers and manufacturers could coordinate their forecasts, they could reduce that overage by about a quarter, saving $179 billion.

Source: *Innovation Digest,* October 21, 1996; a summary of an article in *Business Week,* October 21, 1996, p. 140.

---

manager to identify weak territories or weak products in a territory; to compare salesperson performance by product and customer type; to compare salesperson performance against salesperson goals; to analyze salesperson calls within territories or by customer type; to identify trends in customer purchases; to identify potential shortages or excess stock in inventory; and to perform other planning, controlling, and organizing tasks with ease and speed.

The marketing manager can also compare sales, product, customer, and territory information from one department against external benchmarks of success, such as the organization as a whole or industry averages. The manager, for example, may wish to compare staff deployment to the deployment of marketing staffs in other marketing departments within the organization or to major competitors. The manager might

---

Figure 11–9

A spreadsheet used to analyze sales-force performance

Name	Number of Orders	Number of Calls	Orders per Call	$ Total of Orders	Average Order per Call	Calls per Day	Monthly Quota	Percent of Quota
For July, 1998								
08/02/98	MONTHLY SALESFORCE PERFORMANCE ANALYSIS							
Andrews	28	58	0.48	41104	$709	2.5	40,000	103%
Bali	24	47	0.51	96256	$2,048	2.0	38,000	253%
Chiang	31	38	0.82	50964	$1,341	1.7	50,000	102%
D'Arcy	17	42	0.04	52708	$1,255	1.8	50,000	105%
Evans	22	59	0.37	03008	$522	2.6	45,000	68%
Ferino	10	64	0.16	18750	$293	2.8	30,000	63%
Garcia	29	44	0.66	55013	$1,205	1.9	45,000	122%
Hull	32	41	0.78	65088	$1,588	1.8	55,000	118%
Averages	24	49	0.6	51335	$1,126	2.1	44125	117%
Ave/Mo Last Yr.	23	52	0.44	47397	$911	2.4	41238	101%
No. of Working Days in Current Mo.	23							

also view the amount of money spent in the department on salespeople versus support staff and then compare those amounts to the amounts spent by other marketing departments in the organization or to the industry as a whole. If sales data are added to expense data, the manager can compare the productivity of the department to the productivity of the organization and the productivity of the industry. Comparisons that indicate poor productivity might lead the manager to compare the productivity of each salesperson to the average for the department. This comparison, in turn, might lead to decisions changing the configuration of sales territories, training for specific salespeople, product emphasis for certain territories, market segment emphasis for certain sales personnel, or a variety of other remedies.

At the same time, information on the productivity of the present sales force permits managers to estimate annual sales budgets given a set of sales goals from top management. Knowing the sales figures that top management wishes to reach, the manager may use previous productivity information to estimate the number of salespeople or salesperson days needed to achieve success.

These examples should not imply that the manager's job can be performed merely by projecting historical information on current problems. If all marketing decisions could be made merely by referring to the past performance of salespeople with customers and products within territories, managers would not be needed at all. The manager must bring to the table not only historical information, trends, and probabilities but also considerable knowledge of the current environment. In the end, the manager must make decisions based on less than all of the information desired. Marketing information systems do not make the decisions for marketing managers; they provide information to support those managers in the decision-making process.

The marketing manager may use general purpose software such as statistical software and spreadsheet software as information systems tools. The manager may use a query language to access information in data warehouses or commercially designed sales management and mapping software (see Manager's Memo 11-4). The marketing manager may also have information systems specialists design reports specifically for his or her decision making.

To support sales management decisions, marketing managers may develop or acquire sales management software. **Sales management software** may be a module of the sales-force automation software described in Chapter 10. The software may access data from the financial information system or from the database created by salespeople using sales-force automation software. Sales management systems may bring together the islands of data contained in, for example, contact files, prospect files, and order-entry files to enhance decision support. The wide variety of data available through such systems are helpful to many marketing personnel, including marketing researchers and those who develop strategic marketing plans.

Sales managers will also find that the use of geographic information systems (see Figure 10-6) can be of great help in allocating sales territories.

Advertising and Promotion Systems

Marketing managers also need to develop advertising and promotional tactics to implement strategic sales goals set by top management. Managers must decide which advertising media and promotional devices to use to reach the selected market segments, when to use these media and devices, and what overall mix of promotional activities to deploy to achieve sales goals. **Advertising and promotion systems** assist managers in these tasks.

Manager's Memo 11–4	GEOGRAPHIC INFORMATION SYSTEMS

Mapping software, also called *geographic information systems* software, is software that allows managers to arrange or place data from a database onto a map of a country, region, state, city, county, or even city street. Some of the software comes with its own prepackaged data. More sophisticated packages offer customizable maps and are bundled with high-end databases. Basically, the software consists of maps and the programs that convert data into map coordinates so that the data can be displayed on the maps. The software differs from traditional database report writers or query languages in that instead of merely listing companies or individuals that meet a query, a manager can also visually present these entities on a map (see Figure 10–6).

Mapping software has been used in the past for land-use analysis and geology. Applications to marketing quickly followed mapping software's development for microcomputers. For example, as a marketing manager you might wish to explore a market around a city. You would draw a circle around the city with a light pen and query the database about all firms in that circle that employ more than five workers and have gross sales in excess of $500,000 or about all firms in the circle that use plywood as raw material.

The Democratic National Committee used mapping software to find areas of the country with concentrations of voters who had voted Democratic in previous congressional elections but who had voted Republican for president. It then targeted these voters with special advertising materials and used the maps to route then-candidate Clinton's bus tours for the 1992 presidential election. Marketing personnel today are using mapping software to carve out sales territories; plan direct-mail promotion campaigns; identify new store and warehouse locations; analyze the market potential of cities, towns, and neighborhoods; allocate advertising funds; generate mailing lists; and plan delivery routes. Mapping software, thus, can provide support for both tactical and strategic marketing decisions.

The order-entry system contains the raw data to identify which products or services are selling poorly or well. Managers can use reports based on the order-entry system data to decide which products and services need the help that advertising and promotion can supply. If marketing managers receive these reports at the right time, they can identify which products and services are falling behind projected sales goals for the year in time to attempt corrections. Managers may then devise tactical advertising and promotional plans to close the gap between actual and projected sales. The reports may also identify products and services selling better than expected that should be pushed. The reports may take the form of summary reports simply listing the sales of each product or service by time period. To be more useful, however, they should compare current sales with sales forecasts for the time period (see Figure 11–10).

Tactical reports based on data from the order-entry system also can provide advertising and promotion managers with information about the effectiveness of current advertising campaigns and promotional devices so they can make timely corrections in these marketing systems and in the production and distribution of stock if needed.

To decide what advertising and promotional tactics to use, marketing managers need information such as market segment history, the effectiveness of previous advertising and promotional efforts on each market segment, and the sales history of products by market segment. Historical data on the effectiveness of various advertising and promotional instruments and the sales of products by market segment are not foolproof methods for forecasting future success. Past profiles and trends may not necessarily be projected into the future. The areas of advertising and promotion contain too much managerial art for projection of past data to be perfectly successful. However, the past success of specific advertising and promotion campaigns for

Figure 11–10

A tactical marketing report comparing current sales to forecasted sales

Liang Manufacturing Company Sales for first quarter (1998)			
Stock no.	Current sales	Projected sales	Percent on target
T128	243,891	265,000	92.0%
T129	128,933	129,000	99.9
T218	50,311	54,500	92.3
T219	45,208	45,000	100.5
T251	157,244	152,600	103.0
T310	98,156	95,500	102.8
Totals	723,743	741,600	97.6

specific products and customers is very important information for the manager. For example, a marketing manager may construct a model of the types of advertising media that have been used in the past to advertise certain products. The model may display success in terms of dollars of sales generated per dollars spent on each type of media. Using these historical relationships, the manager might decide on the **media mix** (media types used and time or dollars devoted to each) appropriate for this year's sales effort. Another manager may have sufficient historical data to show which advertising instruments within each media type are the most effective for reaching particular market segments. For example, if the manager wishes to sell a product to newlyweds, he or she will know not only which types of media but also which companies have been most successful in the past in reaching this market segment.

The marketing manager may use many of the same tools for tactical decision support in advertising and promotion as were used in sales management: data warehouses, query tools, spreadsheet software, statistical software, on-line databases, the Internet (see Figure 11-11), and custom-written reports. Some software vendors provide products specifically designed to mine data warehouses for the analysis of advertising and promotion data.

Managers may also use information from marketing research firms that specialize in advertising and promotion data collection and analyses. For example, Information Resources, Inc. can provide a variety of analyses of data from household panels from which TV viewing and purchasing data are collected electronically. The data can be analyzed to determine trends in purchasing brand merchandise in relationship to advertising media and times, to learn whether ads are reaching intended markets, and to predict whether market segments might increase purchases as a result of additional advertising.

Pricing Systems

Pricing systems provide information to managers that helps them set prices for their products and services. These information systems are important because the price of a product or service affects the sales volume and profitability of the organization. The marketing manager usually selects a price that will recover production costs and provide a profit, but the price chosen in constrained by the prices of competitors for similar products or services and for alternative products or services. To make pricing decisions, the marketing manager should know the expected demand for the product or similar products, the desired profit margin for the organization, the costs of producing the product or providing the service, and the prices of competing as well as substitute products. *Substitute products* refer to products that might be

Figure 11–11

A portion of a Web page from *Ad Age*'s Web site showing magazine circulation

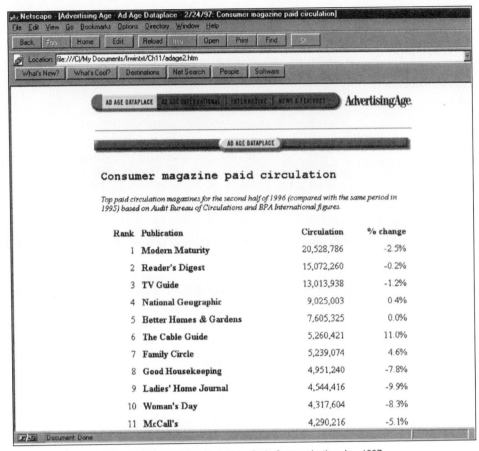

used instead of the original product, particularly when that product is viewed as too expensive by the customer. For example, a person might drive to a destination if the price of an airline ticket is viewed as too expensive.

Price may also depend on other organization objectives. An organization may choose to increase its market penetration by setting much lower prices than competitors for the same or similar products and services. Once the organization has developed a larger market share or a larger customer base, it may then raise prices slowly relative to its competitors, counting on customer satisfaction and customer inertia to retain the market share.

Pricing decisions also include what types of discounts to give at various levels of the channels of distribution and what promotional devices to use, such as financing options and rebates.

To help the marketing manager price products and services, some organizations develop a pricing model that allows the manager to input data on a variety of forces affecting prices, such as expected competitive prices, expected consumer price indexes, expected consumer disposable income, volume of products produced, costs of labor, costs of raw materials, and the value of expected advertising expenditures. The model then uses arithmetic algorithms that represent the organization's assumptions about the interrelationship of each of these factors. A pricing model enables the manager to vary the inputs to identify the best price for a product under a variety of possible conditions.

Distribution Channel Systems

Deciding how the organization's products and services will be delivered to the ultimate consumer is another important tactical decision. The organization needs to determine if it wishes to sell all or some of its products and services directly to its customers, use middlemen, or do both. If it considers direct sales, then the trade channel or channels within that delivery mode—for example, sales force, direct mail, telemarketing, and so on—must be chosen. If middlemen are chosen to distribute the product or service, the choice of trade channel will be affected by how well the channel distributes the products or services among the targeted market segments.

To support the marketing manager, the marketing information system should provide **distribution channel decision-support systems.** These systems should provide information on the costs of using the various distribution channels, the time lags caused by the various channels, the reliability of the various channels in delivering the products and services, and the market segment saturation provided by the channels. The systems should also track the demand and inventory at all levels of the distribution channels so that the manager may anticipate excess inventories or shortfalls.

The manager can derive a great deal of the information necessary for these decisions from data generated by the organization's operating systems, including sales order entry, telemarketing, sales force automation, inventory, and customer information systems. If these data are placed in a data warehouse, the manager can use query tools to extract the information needed. He or she may then use a variety of other software tools, including statistical software, spreadsheet software, and graphics software, to massage and display the data.

Because of the importance of channel decisions to some firms, commercial software may be acquired or custom software developed to track and monitor channel data.

Competitive Tracking Systems

To ensure that your organization's marketing mix will continue to satisfy customers, you must keep abreast of major competitors and their marketing activities. In the end, market share is likely to be greatest for the organization that provides the marketing mix most closely matching a given market segment's needs and wants. *Competitive intelligence,* or knowledge of competitor prices, products, sales, advertising, and promotions, must be gathered if the organization is to avoid falling behind the competition in the eyes of the customers. Gathering competitive intelligence is carried out through **competitive tracking systems.** It should be noted that data about competitors can be used *both* tactically and strategically by managers.

Information about competitors is readily available through most trade journals and newspapers. The *Wall Street Journal,* for instance, publishes a great deal of information on various industries, product and service types, and organizations that produce the products and services. These publications often provide information about a new product under development by a competitor. Knowledge that a competitor is developing a new product may result in new research into customer preferences. A change in the advertising agency used by a competitor may be a harbinger of new advertising themes. A growing oversupply of products in your competitor's inventory might mean that a price reduction, rebate, or other promotional campaign is likely to occur soon and signal that you should explore promotional campaigns that preempt your competition. Information about competitor activities is also obtained from informal sources, through such activities as visiting competitor sales outlets and talking to the firm's employees at conventions. Salespeople in most organizations are encouraged to provide feedback about competitor activities by filing field reports. They may obtain information by observing competing salespeople or by asking seemingly casual questions of customers.

Information about the competition may also be gathered more systematically by conducting keyword searches in on-line databases or Internet search engines. You can use a general database, such as the Dialog Information Services database, to gather business and industry news. IQuest is another comprehensive information service that provides access to more than 850 databases of articles and other data about companies, product news, technology, and industry trends within the U.S. and global markets. CompuServe offers access to IQuest as well as to Business Database Plus. The latter allows you to track information about companies, trends, industries, technologies, and products found in journals and other publications. Specialized marketing databases are also available. For example, Interactive Market Systems provides on-line access to more than 300 marketing and advertising databases, and C-Systems offers Ad-Line, which provides data on ads placed by more than 20,000 companies in 185 publications. Searching the Ad-Line database can reveal information about such topics as where your competitors are placing their ads, what kind of ads they are running, what the ads cost, and what products are advertised in what magazines.

One of the easiest ways to collect competitor data is to use the push technology of the Internet. Push services will gather information about specific topics for you from journals, magazines, newspapers, news broadcasts, and other sources on the Internet. Once or more each day, the Internet links to those documents will be downloaded to your PC. You can then view, save, or otherwise process the documents. Some of these services are free (see Figure 11–12). However, free services generally

Figure 11–12

NewsPage screen showing partial result of push document search for General Motors

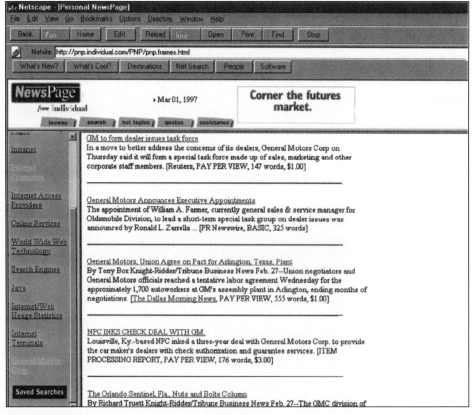

Courtesy of Individual, Inc.

limit their searches to a substantially reduced set of journals, newspapers, and other electronic publications.

STRATEGIC MARKETING INFORMATION SYSTEMS

To develop an overall marketing plan, an organization may engage in a variety of tactical and strategic planning activities (see Figure 11-8). The strategic activities may include segmenting the market into target groups of potential customers based on common characteristics, needs, or wants; selecting those market segments the organization wishes to reach; planning products and services to meet those customers' needs; and forecasting sales for the market segments and products. The tactical activities have already been described and include planning the marketing mix—the best combination of product, price, advertising, promotion, financing, and distribution channels to reach the chosen target groups. The strategic activities revolving around sales forecasting and product planning decision making will now be discussed.

Sales Forecasting Systems

Strategic **sales forecasting systems** usually include several varieties of forecasts: forecasts of sales for the industry as a whole, forecasts of sales for the entire organization, forecasts of sales for each product or service, forecasts of sales for a new product or service, and forecasts for market segments. The results of these sales forecasts are often further categorized by sales territory and sales division. Regardless of type, sales forecasts are usually based on more than historical data; they are not merely projections of past trends. Sales forecasts are also based on assumptions about the activities of the competition, governmental action, shifting customer demand, economic trends, demographic trends, and a variety of other pertinent factors, including even the weather.

Developing the sales forecast for an organization for the coming year is an extremely important undertaking. From that one forecast, tactical decisions regarding the directions of many other organizational functions will flow. For example, based on that sales forecast, management will decide to keep or cast aside products and services in the organization's current marketing mix. Research and development personnel may plan and develop new products and services. Marketing managers will allocate sales personnel, divide territories, plan advertising, and devise promotional campaigns. Production managers will allocate the use of plant facilities; plan the purchase of raw materials; and decide on the size, composition, and allocation of the work force. Financial managers will acquire or reserve the necessary capital to support the expected levels of production and marketing planned by other departments within the organization, project profits for the year, and plan for the use of the organization's cash flows.

Clearly, a lot rides on an organization's sales forecasts. Errors in forecasting sales will have an impact on nearly all facets of the organization. If actual sales are well below expectations, considerable loss may result from excess inventory, excess personnel, and other unnecessary operational expenses associated with gearing up for levels of production and sales that never materialize.

Given that sales forecasts are predictions of the future, any forecast must have a margin for error, even when the forecast is made using very sophisticated statistical procedures. Attempting to predict the future is always difficult, and attempting to predict future sales of new products is clearly the most difficult of all sales-forecasting activities. Since new products have no prior track record, no data are available from which to project trends. Estimates of sales must be made from the fate of similar products introduced in past years and from customer surveys; market testing of the product; and economic, demographic, and other data external to the organization.

Errors in sales forecasting are compounded by the fact that these forecasts usually attempt to describe sales activity for a two- to five-year period. The further out the forecast is extended, the greater likelihood of error. For that reason, sales forecasts are regularly revised based on data from the financial operating system and from data external to the organization.

Managers use a variety of information systems to support forecasting. They use the data internal to the organization including the financial accounting database and the customer database. They also gather information from the organization's marketing research and from on-line databases and the Internet pertaining to the competition and to the external environment. Data from these sources may be mined using query languages and processed with statistical, mapping, graphics, forecasting, spreadsheet, and other software tools (see Figure 11–13).

Marketing Research Systems

In large organizations, research departments conduct and manage marketing research. In smaller companies, marketing research may be completed by outside consultants or by personnel who must wear several hats. Regardless of how the function is completed, the results of **marketing research** provide important input to *both* tactical and strategic decision making.

Inputs to marketing research are heavily derived from sources external to the organization, including customers, potential customers, census and demographic data, industry or trade data, economic data, social trend data, environmental data, and scientific and technological data. Data may be obtained through such means as direct mail customer surveys, Internet surveys, personal and telephone interviews of consumers, library or Internet searches of governmental and industry reports, searches of external databases, and reports filed by sales personnel.

Figure 11–13

A sales forecast completed using spreadsheet software

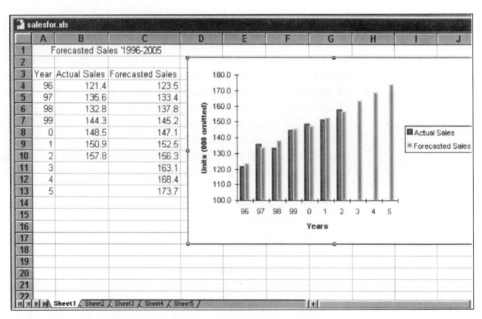

Courtesy Microsoft Corporation.

Marketing research personnel make heavy use of statistical methodology in analyzing the data collected and in reporting the information to the organization. Obtaining totals, counts, and averages in terms of consumer responses to questions, correlating social and economic characteristics of customers with their buying practices, completing time series analyses of past industrywide sales to determine the projected sales of a product, and testing hypotheses about consumer responses to differing product packaging represent only some of the statistical procedures marketing managers use to analyze information for other marketing managers.

These activities are typical of a marketing research department.

1. Conducting trend analyses of industry sales of products and services identical or similar to those offered by the organization to identify products or services that are on the ascent or descent.

2. Analyzing population and target group characteristics, especially for trends or changes in data that could affect the organization.

3. Analyzing and identifying consumer preferences, including testing products and services.

4. Determining and analyzing customer satisfaction with the organization's existing products and services.

5. Estimating market share for all of each product and service offered.

Many companies, especially small companies, often hire marketing research firms to help them assess such topics as customer reactions to a new product or customer desires for product alternations. However, new software for PCs has made conducting market research much easier for any organization. *Desktop survey software* lets you create survey questions and then helps you sum, tabulate, and otherwise treat statistically the answers collected to those questions.

The subjects of the surveys or the researchers can enter the answers to the questions. Some companies even distribute their surveys on floppy disks, having subjects return the disks by mail. Or the answers can be copied from completed surveys or directly input as subjects answer questions during telephone interviews. Computer-aided telephone interview (CATI) software can select subjects for interviews automatically from an electronic directory using preselected demographic criteria and quotas. Usually CATI software automatically dials subjects, too.

Some companies use handheld PCs in survey research—subjects complete forms displayed on the handheld PCs using light pens, and the results are stored or transmitted to a larger computer system. Many other companies use the Internet to gather survey data. They provide survey forms that current or potential customers can complete on a Web site. The data are then stored in a database for later analysis. In fact, the Internet has many organizations that provide free software or services if only the user will "register" by completing a form. The form, of course, contains a variety of questions about the user's age, buying preferences, and so on.

Although software can help you write, collect, and compile data from surveys, the process still requires you to know quite a bit about constructing effective and valid survey questions, how to create an appropriate sample, and how to interpret the survey results.

Product Planning and Development Systems

The major objective of **product planning and development systems** is to make information about consumer preferences obtained from the marketing research system and from customer inquiries available for the development of new products. The primary output of planning and development activities is a set of product specifications. In a manufacturing organization, these specifications would be given to the engineering department, which would try to design a product to meet them. Similar activities occur in service organizations. For example, a survey of bank customers may indicate that customers would like a checking account that also acts like a savings account—an account in which they could place all their money, maximize the amount of cash earning interest, avoid multiple statements, and avoid the need to shift funds between savings and checking accounts. Bank personnel charged with product development may then identify specifications for such a product that meet current banking laws and regulations. These specifications may require the new account to carry the same rate of interest as a passbook savings account, earn interest on the average balance on deposit during a month, not limit the number of deposits or withdrawals during a month, maintain a minimum balance of $500, and pay interest monthly. The specifications can be tested and refined through additional consumer surveys and focus groups or through testing the product in a subset of the market, such as one branch of the bank.

When new product specifications are developed, the legal concerns for that new product must also be addressed. The product development system must provide appropriate organizational personnel with sufficient information to ensure that they accurately and completely address patent and copyright concerns, consumer product safety concerns, and a host of other legal issues pertaining to the new product.

TACTICAL PRODUCTION INFORMATION SYSTEMS

Production systems encompass all the activities necessary to ensure the manufacture of products or services. To perform its functions, the production system must locate production sites, plan the layout of those sites, and produce a production plan. The production system has to acquire the raw materials, parts, and subassemblies needed to produce the products or services described in the plan and to identify how many workers of each type are required. The system must then allocate or acquire workers with the appropriate skills, make certain that sufficient work space and production equipment are available, and schedule an integrated use of these resources to produce the correct quantity of goods at the correct time to meet the marketing system's forecasted needs. While production is under way, the system also must monitor the use and cost of those resources.

Production systems provide the data necessary to plan, organize, operate, monitor, control, and otherwise manage production systems (see Figure 11-14). Production systems may differ from other information systems in the variety of input and output devices used and the nature of data typically included in the system. For example, production systems may include robotics as well as heat sensors, pressure sensors, and other process control devices that measure the temperature and thickness of steel wire as it is produced in a mill.

Typically, tactical production information systems collect and report information relevant to the management and control of resources, and strategic planning production information systems support managers who are developing long-range production plans and setting long-term goals.

Production costs are a major cost component of any organization. It should not be surprising, therefore, to find that many systems are available to help managers (1) monitor and control production processes and (2) allocate resources to achieve production goals set through the strategic planning process. This section includes a

Figure 11–14
Production processes and information systems

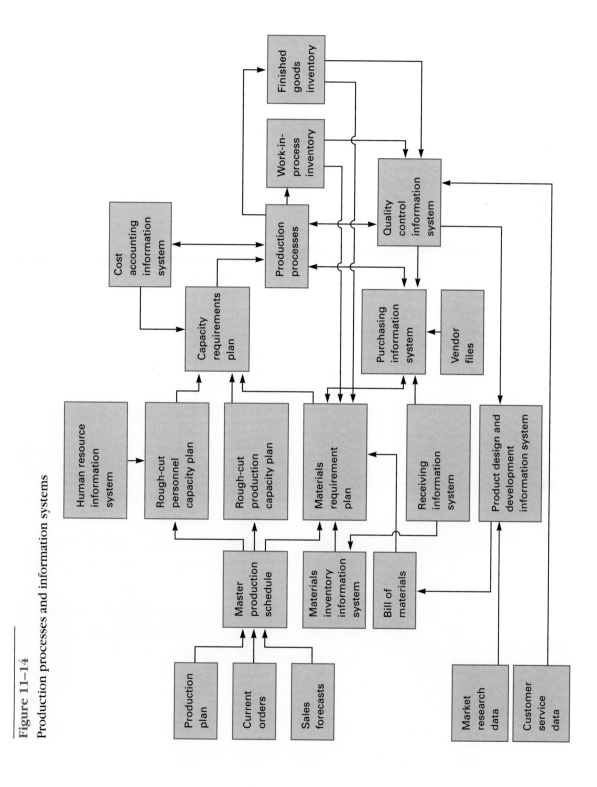

discussion of several tactical information systems: materials requirements planning systems, just-in-time systems, capacity planning systems, production scheduling systems, and product design and development systems.

Materials Requirements Planning Systems

Inventory management can be taken a step further so that the system automatically produces purchases orders for stock that needs to be reordered. **Materials requirements planning (MRP)** software is basically a set of programs that use data from the master production schedule, inventory files, and bill-of-materials systems—or lists of raw materials and components needed to create each product—to help manage production and inventory.

MRP systems perform a great deal of calculation and record keeping. When quantities of raw materials and parts are large, the calculations and record keeping become too time-consuming to complete manually, except at high costs. The computer, however, has made such calculations and purchase-order preparation possible for all sizes of organizations, and in recent years, software to implement materials requirements planning has become abundant.

The basic purpose of MRP software is to ensure that the proper amount of the right materials are available for the production processes at the right time (see Figure 11-15). The primary objective is to meet the customer's delivery requirements. Ancillary objectives of the system are to ensure that an unnecessary buildup of materials does not occur and that overtime or other extra costs are not incurred to provide the materials on time. One output of the software is a series of purchase orders along with information on when these purchase orders should be released to ensure that the right materials are ordered at the right times in the most economical quantities.

Figure 11–15

A screen from the MAX MRP software system alerting the manager to shortages of parts needed for production

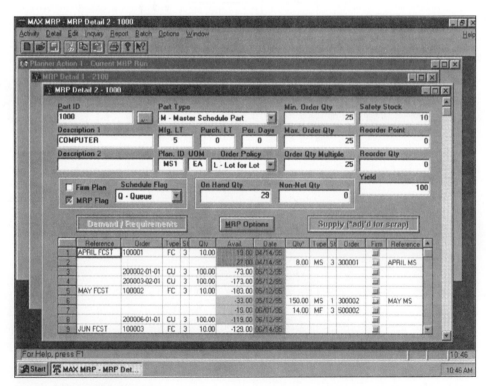

Courtesy of Micro MRP Incorporated.

Just-in-Time Systems

The **just-in-time (JIT) system** is not a tactical information system, but a tactical approach to production. The just-in-time approach was created by the Toyota Motor Company of Japan and has generated many advantages to organizations, especially those that do repetitive production. The purpose of the approach is to eliminate waste in the use of equipment, parts, space, workers' time, and materials, including the resources devoted to inventories. The basic philosophy of JIT is that operations should occur just when they are required to maintain the production schedule. To assure a smooth flow of operations in that environment, sources of problems must be eradicated. That means that quality must be emphasized because quality problems interfere with the even flow of work. For inventory management, JIT translates into having just as much inventory on hand as is absolutely needed, which is achieved by developing efficient and effective production controls. One of these controls is to develop close working relationships with suppliers and require them to deliver just enough acceptable materials to meet the day's or week's production schedule. To assist in this process, manufacturers and their suppliers may use electronic data interchange (EDI). EDI lets suppliers monitor the manufacturer's inventory levels by allowing them to access the manufacturer's inventory files electronically. Suppliers then ship the raw materials or parts to the manufacturer only as needed (see Chapter 9).

Capacity Planning Systems

In addition to ensuring that enough raw materials will be on hand for planned production, the production manager must also see to it that enough production capacity will be available to meet production goals. The purpose of capacity planning is to make certain that sufficient personnel, space, machines, and other production facilities are available at the right time to meet the organization's planned production. Managers also utilize capacity planning to minimize excess production capacity.

Capacity planning decisions are tactical production decisions and include allocating personnel and production facilities. Selecting sites for constructing plant facilities, acquiring plant facilities, and planning those facilities to meet long-term production goals are usually categorized as strategic planning production decisions.

One capacity planning technique is called **rough-cut capacity planning.** Rough-cut capacity planning provides an overall estimate of capacity needs using the information provided by the master production schedule as inputs. Rough-cut capacity planning is used to convert the production goals included in the master production schedule into capacity needs by using historical measures of production or shop-floor standards for producing end products. Rough-cut capacity planning produces estimates of the capacity needed, such as the hours of labor and the hours of machine time necessary to meet the production goals. These estimates of labor and machine hours are then allocated to specific work groups and factory locations to determine the feasibility of meeting the production goals with current facilities (see Manager's Memo 11–5).

The basic purpose of rough-cut capacity planning is to identify whether there is enough, too little, or too much capacity based on the information from the master production schedule. If the rough-cut capacity plan detects too little capacity to meet the needs of the master production schedule, then existing resources must be expanded or resources external to the organization must be used. For example, if you do not have enough equipment or workers to meet the planned production needs of the master production schedule, then you may rent or buy more floor space, rent or buy more equipment, or employ workers from temporary employment agencies. Alternatively,

| Manager's Memo 11–5 | ROUGH-CUT CAPACITY PLANNING: AN EXAMPLE |

Production goals for a data entry department require that 30,000 sales orders be processed daily at three locations. You know from historical production records kept by the department that you can expect a data entry clerk to type sales orders at a rate of one character per second for an effective day of six hours, given breaks, lunch, interruptions, and delays. You also know that the average sales order requires 300 keystrokes to complete. Thus you can estimate the number of data entry clerks and terminals to produce the 30,000 sales orders.

1. 30,000 orders $\times$ 300 characters per order = 9,000,000 characters per day (CPD) to be produced.
2. 1 character per second $\times$ 60 seconds $\times$ 60 minutes $\times$ 6 hours per day = 21,600 characters produced per data entry clerk (CPDEC) per day.
3. 9,000,000 CPD/21,600 CPDEC = 416,667, or 417 clerks and terminals needed.

If the demand forecast estimates that 20 percent of the orders will be received at location A and 40 percent each will be received at locations B and C, then the data entry clerks and terminals will need to be allocated as follows:

1. 417 clerks and terminals $\times$ .20 = 83.4, or 84 clerks and terminals at location A.
2. 417 clerks and terminals $\times$ .40 = 166.8, or 167 clerks and terminals each at locations B and C.

Furthermore, your production records may indicate that, on average, 5 percent of the terminals are defective and 2 percent of the clerks are ill or absent on any one day. Thus you should plan on providing the following:

1. 84 $\times$ .05 = 4.2, or 5 extra terminals at location A.
2. 167 $\times$ .05 = 8.35, or 9 extra terminals each at locations B and C.
3. 84 $\times$ .02 = 1.68, or 2 extra data entry clerks at location A.
4. 167 $\times$ .02 = 3.34, or 4 extra data entry clerks each at locations B and C.

The procedures used to estimate production capacity just described assume that direct labor hours, the percentage of sales orders each location receives, and when they are received during the day occur rather evenly and remain relatively constant. When these assumptions are not true, more complicated methods of rough-cut capacity planning must be used. For instance, the example assumes that the entry of sales orders can be evenly spread throughout the day because of batch processing of orders. However, if the sales order system were an on-line system, it is likely that there would be busy hours of telephone sales order traffic; that is, customers would telephone most of the orders to the locations during specific hours, such as between 10 and 11 AM and 2 and 3 PM. It might also be true that there are different types of orders, some of which require more time to enter than others do. When the goods to be produced are more complex, more complex rough-cut capacity planning tools must be used.

if you find that you will have excess equipment, workers, and facilities, you may choose to reallocate these resources to other production tasks or rent, sell, retire, lay off, or terminate those resources.

You may also choose to meet capacity needs by subcontracting all or some of the production tasks to other organizations. Organizations frequently use external production resources, or *outsourcing,* to meet peak demands. Outsourcing is also used by organizations that wish to reduce costs by subcontracting with firms in third world countries.

Rough-cut capacity planning allows you to identify your needs in time to adjust capacity to the master production schedule. Alternatively, it allows planners to estimate how realistic the master production schedule is. Where production resources are constrained, such as when few workers with the special skills needed are available, marketing forecasts of demand simply may not be fulfilled; demand may exceed the ability of the production system to supply it.

Figure 11–16

An example of a Gantt chart

Activity name	May '98			June '98				July '98	
	9	16	23	30	6	13	20	27	4	11
Design phase										
Brainstorming	△——▽									
Marketing		△——▽								
Engineering		△——▽								
Design			△——▽							
Testing phase										
Prototype										
Renderings					○══○					
Build						○══○				
Final review						◆				
Production phase										
Retooling							■			
Materials delivery								■		
Production phase									████	
Begin shipping										◇

From FastTrack Schedule for Windows software, courtesy AEC Software, Inc.

A more refined tool for capacity planning is capacity requirements planning. **Capacity requirements planning** provides detailed estimates of production capacity availability. This form of capacity planning requires human resources and bill-of-materials information. Capacity requirements planning also necessitates detailed information on the status of raw materials, goods-in-process inventories, finished goods inventories, orders in the plant, lot sizes, lead times for orders, and routing plans for products as they work their way through the production line. The result is a set of detailed, time-phased plans for each product and each production work area. Since cost accounting reports often provide detailed direct-labor hours for each end product produced, these cost accounting records are often the source of the standards used in capacity estimation.

Personnel capacity planning is that part of rough-cut capacity planning that estimates the numbers and types of workers, supervisors, and managers needed to meet the master production plan. To plan for the allocation of personnel resources, managers need information from the human resource information system maintained by the personnel department. This system provides information about the members, skills, and experiences of current employees, applicants, and workers available from other personnel sources, such as temporary employment agencies. Managers also need information on employment constraints imposed by unions and regulatory agencies.

Production Scheduling Systems

The purpose of the **production schedule** is to allocate the use of specific production facilities for the production of finished goods to meet the master production schedule. To manage the scheduling process, a number of scheduling tools have been developed. Two of these tools are Gantt and PERT (Program Evaluation and Reporting Technique) charts (see Figures 11-16 and 11-17).

These tools allow managers to control projects and project completion times and also to determine the impact problems will have on project completion dates. For example, top management may ask a manager to complete a project sooner than originally planned. The manager may then consider ways to shorten the duration of the project by completing two tasks at once. However, to complete two tasks concurrently may raise production costs substantially, because two production teams and two production facilities may be needed. To solve the problem, the manager may create what-if scenarios with the project conditions using the PERT chart tool. However,

Figure 11–17

An example of a PERT chart prepared using Microsoft Project software

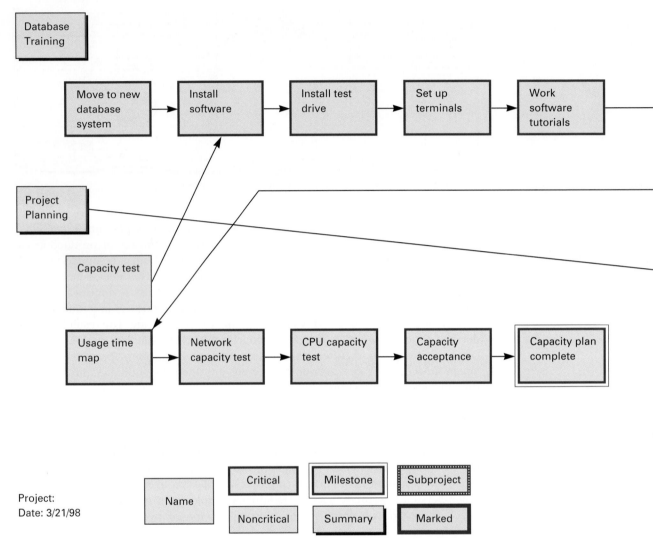

Project:
Date: 3/21/98

Courtesy Microsoft Corporation

completing multiple PERT charts manually requires extensive calculations and may prove frustrating to the manager. Computer-generated PERT charts let the manager simulate many scenarios with speed and ease (see Figure 11–17). The use of project management software for this purpose is discussed later in this chapter.

Product Design and Development Systems

Many tactical decisions must be made to design and develop a product, especially a new product. The design engineering team usually depends on product specification information derived from customer surveys, target population analysis, or other marketing research systems.

The primary objective of the design engineering team is to develop a product that meets perceived needs of customer. However, the team's tactical task is to

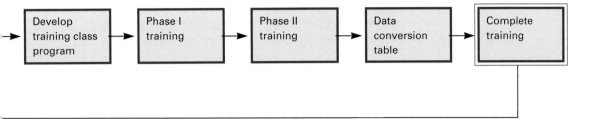

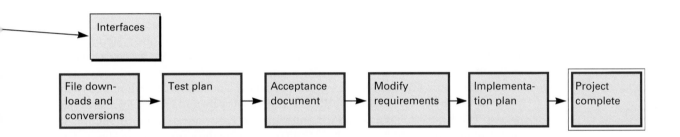

achieve that objective with the least demand on company resources. Designing products to contain or reduce costs often results in ingenious uses of raw materials, labor, and machinery. Through careful design, an engineering team can often design a product that can be produced at lower costs than competitors can produce it. Careful design may also lead to a simpler product, which leads in turn to fewer maintenance problems, better customer acceptance, fewer product returns, and increased product repeat sales. Through the use of **product design and development systems,** the engineering team may provide the company with important competitive advantages.

Manufacturing Resource Planning Systems

More recently, software that provides for **manufacturing resource planning (MRP-II)** has become available. MRP-II software extends the production information system to finance, marketing, human resource management, and other organizational functions. A fully developed MRP-II system includes modules that provide material requirements planning, shop-floor control, inventory management, and capacity planning. The system also accesses cost accounting data through integration with the financial accounting system. MRP-II systems usually accept data from a wide range of shop-floor data collection equipment, including voice recognition equipment, factory robots, production-line sensors, process control systems, bar code readers, and CAD workstations.

MRP-II systems use market projections to generate inventory requirements. During production, design data and output data, including process control, work-in-process, and finished goods inventory data, are fed back to the system.

Many vendors offer MRP-II software for organizations of all types, including mass-production manufacturers, job-order producers, and distributors. Vendors also offer the software for computer platforms of all types and sizes. The software usually consists of many modules, including modules for bill of materials, inventory management, purchasing, capacity planning, production scheduling, shop-floor control, and financial planning. Some MRP-II software is designed so that its modules will work with specific financial accounting software packages. For example, one vendor has developed a series of MRP-II modules that integrate with another vendor's financial accounting modules, thus eliminating the need for the user to make duplicate entries. Other MRP-II software is sold as part of a financial accounting software package.

Computer-Integrated Manufacturing Systems

Many production professionals envision a day when factory and product planning, control, design, and operation will be totally integrated and almost totally computerized. Some software and hardware firms that provide MSP, MRP, MRP-II, CAD, CAM, CAE, CAT, CAPP, CAI, robotics, and related information systems are joining forces through mergers, acquisitions, and joint projects to integrate current production hardware and software products into systems that provide **computer-integrated manufacturing (CIM).** A growing number of manufacturers are utilizing CIM—or at least a great many components of CIM—to run their factories. Implementing CIM can lead to considerable cost savings, improvement in quality, and more flexible responses to customers.

CIM implementations typically include process control sensors and systems, shop-floor terminals, bar code readers, factory local area networks, CAD workstations, robots, machine tools, automated factory equipment, minicomputers and mainframe computers, the software modules listed previously, and the organization's existing databases. The heart of CIM is usually the MRP-II software and factory local area networks. The key is to integrate all the software and hardware used in production, to merge numerous production databases, and to eliminate the paperwork, delays, and errors that occur when systems are operated wholly or in part manually. CIM eliminates the islands of automation created in an organization when each department operates its own system using different hardware, communications protocols, and software.

Although some organizations have developed computer-integrated manufacturing systems, for many, CIM remains an ideal. Organizations with machine-based production that turn out standard products and use repetitive production processes are likely candidates for CIM.[1] Other organizations may find it best to limit their automation to phases of the production process. The tasks involved in both implementing and integrating so many technologies have proven difficult for many organizations or have appeared so daunting to others that they have opted not to consider the concept.

STRATEGIC PRODUCTION INFORMATION SYSTEMS

Strategic production information systems provide support for top-management-level production decisions such as:

- Selecting a plant site.
- Constructing a plant addition.

---

[1] J. C. Polakoff, "The Factory Foreman: Alive and Well in the Age of Automation," *The Journal of Manufacturing,* Winter 1990, p. 59.

- Building a new plant.
- Designing and laying out a production facility.
- Choosing the technologies that will be used in the production processes.
- Choosing responsibility for production processes—deciding basic policies on vertical integration and outsourcing.

Decisions of this magnitude require the commitment of a large amount of capital and other resources over a long period of time and thus are strategic in nature. Clearly, such decisions must not be made lightly.

Site Planning and Selection Systems

Site planning systems usually rely on a variety of internal and external sources. Some of the external information needed is relatively objective and quantitative, such as the availability and cost of trained or experienced labor and the degree to which it is unionized, the availability and cost of transportation for raw materials and finished goods, the availability of suitable sites, the cost of land, the proximity of raw materials suppliers and finished goods customers, the availability and costs of power, and the rate of property and income taxation.

Other information used in locating a plant may be subjective and qualitative in nature, including community attitudes toward the organization and the quality of community services, such as education and training opportunities.

Internal information sources may include human resource information systems, financial accounting information systems, and production information systems. External information sources may include on-line or Internet databases maintained by government agencies, industry groups, private research groups, and consulting organizations. External sources may also include CD-ROM databases and traditional libraries.

The final decision concerning plant location may be made using some form of weighted-average technique, in which factors such as those listed above are ranked and the total scores for several potential sites calculated. Mapping software, similar to that used in marketing, may be used to support site decisions.

Technology Planning and Assessment Systems

Having access to information on new production technologies allows top management to make better and more informed decisions about which production technologies to use for a product or service. **Technology assessment systems,** which identify new technologies and assess them for their strategic advantage, can help top management in many areas, not merely production. Like site planning, technology information systems may include CD-ROM databases, traditional library resources, Internet sites, and on-line databases maintained by government agencies, industry groups, private research groups, and consulting organizations. They may also include technology assessment groups within the production or engineering arms of the organization.

Process Positioning Systems

An important part of any organization's strategic production plan is the span of production processes it decides to perform for any given product or product line. Decisions of this nature are called **process positioning,** or *vertical integration*. An organization might purchase raw materials, fabricate parts, assemble parts into subassemblies, and then assemble and test the complete product. It may, on the other hand, decide to purchase already constructed subassemblies and parts from others and limit its internal span of production processes to assembling and testing the completed product. Outsourcing subassemblies, for example, to production facilities in third world countries, may allow the organization to gain a competitive advantage by being a low-cost leader for its products.

Deciding on the degree to which the organization vertically integrates—that is, which parts of the material or goods chain it chooses to own, lease, or rely on other organizations to supply—requires a great deal of internal and external information from a variety of information systems. Useful internal information may include the production skills and experience of the organization's existing personnel, the financial condition of the firm, and the quality of current inventories.

External information useful to the process positioning decision may include information about the skills and experience levels of personnel at the new site, the competitive structure of the organizations within the material or goods chain in the industry, the risks and reward associated with each link in the production chain, an assessment of future technological developments and their effects on production processes, an assessment of future competitor plans, and the stability of organizations proposed as suppliers.

The sources of external information for process positioning are similar to those used for site planning and selection and technology assessment.

Plant Design Systems

Designing and laying out a manufacturing plant requires large amounts of diverse information about the proposed plant, including engineering data on the proposed site, proposed production technologies, the number and duties of plant personnel, the expected schedule for the use of the facility, the area transportation system, choices of water and power systems and their costs, the cost and availability of construction materials, the plans for shop-floor information systems, and the need for physical security. Much of this information is available to the **plant design system** from the site planning, technology assessment, and process positioning decision processes.

TACTICAL HUMAN RESOURCE INFORMATION SYSTEMS

An organization's human resources usually represent its largest operating expenditure, often between 40 and 60 percent of total operating expenses. However, in service organizations, salaries and wages may account for as much as 85 percent of total operating expenses. Cost alone would make human resources a very important element of any firm. However, the skills, knowledge, and attitudes of any organization's employees shape that organization in fundamental ways and represent its human capital. Because people are the most basic and the most important component of any organization, the wise management of an organization's human resources, or **human resource management (HRM),** is critical to the organization's success.

To assist managers in managing human resources, a number of information systems, called **human resource information systems (HRIS),** have been developed (see Figure 11–1). Human resource information systems contain personal information about the employees of an organization, and securing this information against unwanted or unwarranted access, use, or distribution is terribly important to the individuals involved. Unwarranted access, use, or distribution is also likely to be illegal under current legislation and can subject the organization to serious legal liability. Security issues surrounding databases, such as the human resource information database and the computer systems that house these databases, are discussed in greater detail in Chapter 17.

Human resource information systems include a number of tactical and strategic information systems. Tactical HRIS include job analysis and design, recruitment, training and development, and employee compensation. Strategic HRIS include information systems that support workforce planning and labor negotiation.

Job Analysis and Design Systems

Job analysis and design includes describing the jobs needed in an organization and the qualities of the workers needed to fill those jobs. These tasks involve the development of *job descriptions* for every type of position in an organization. Each job description specifies the purposes, tasks, duties, and responsibilities of each job and the conditions and performance standards under which those duties and responsibilities must be carried out. (A job description for an office position is shown in Figure 11-18.) Job analysis and design also includes the development of *job specifications* for each type of job. A job specification describes the skills, knowledge, experience, and other personal characteristics required to perform the jobs that are listed in job descriptions. In short, job descriptions describe the jobs, and job specifications describe the workers needed to fill those jobs. (An example of a job specification is shown in Figure 11-19.)

The information inputs to the **job analysis and design system** include data from interviews with supervisors and workers and affirmative action guidelines. Inputs also include information from sources external to the firm, such as labor unions, competitors, and governmental agencies. The outputs of the job analysis information system are job descriptions and job specifications. These outputs provide managers with the basis for many tactical human resource decisions. For example, job descriptions and specifications allow managers to set a job's relative worth in relation to similar work performed elsewhere within the organization, perhaps by classifying the job into one of the organization's pay grades. This process permits a manager to provide, as nearly as possible, equal pay for equal work within an organization. When equal pay for equal work does not exist within an organization, low morale may occur, resulting in poor performance and low productivity.

Figure 11–18

A job description for an office position

```
                          JOB DESCRIPTION

JOB TITLE:  Office Clerk I          REVISION DATE:  3/22/98
JOB NO.:  109
PAY GRADE:  6
REPORTS TO:  Office Supervisor
SUPERVISES:  No one
GENERAL DESCRIPTION:
     Performs general office tasks under close supervision.
DUTIES AND RESPONSIBILITIES:
     Files, keyboards, answers the telephone, uses calculator, enters
data into a terminal, and performs other general office tasks. Checks
work, completes forms, requisitions, and memos, and supplies
information on request.
     Must be able to handle confidential information about employees,
customers, and creditors.
JOB CHARACTERISTICS:
     Proficiency in use of keyboards.
```

Figure 11–19

A job specification for the office position described in Figure 11-18

JOB SPECIFICATION

JOB TITLE: Office Clerk I   **REVISION DATE:** 3/22/98

JOB NO.: 109

PAY GRADE: 6

JOB REQUIREMENTS:

EDUCATION: Minimum, high school education, preferably with emphasis in business subjects

PHYSICAL AND HEALTH: Good health, emotionally stable

APPEARANCE: Neat, well groomed

SPECIAL SKILLS AND ABILITIES: Passing score on keyboarding test, clear and pleasant voice.

WORK EXPERIENCE: None

The information from job analysis and design information systems also can be used to increase the flexibility with which human resources are deployed in the organization. For example, if you were a human resource manager, you might find that a comparison of office jobs with titles such as Records Clerk I, Data Entry Clerk I, and Clerk Typist I reveals identical or nearly identical duties, responsibilities, and requirements. You may decide, therefore, to collapse these three job titles into a single title such as General Office Clerk I. This action simplifies the job structure of the firm and permits managers to move people more easily among positions in this general job title; it also simplifies recruiting, testing, and placement activities. Job analysis and design information can also be linked to the position control system (see Chapter 10). This linking allows position openings, for example, to be listed by job content or by the skills, knowledge, and experience needed for the open positions.

Job analysis and design information helps determine the qualities and types of employees to be recruited, which applicants should be selected, and where new employees should be placed. This information also provides a basis for determining how employees will be paid, evaluated, promoted, or terminated. In fact, the job analysis and design information system provides a legal basis for many human resource management practices. Thus the information system supports many tactical decisions about the allocation of human resources within an organization. Nearly every manager can use information from the job analysis and design information system. For example, managers can refer to current job descriptions and specifications when they want to add new positions within their departments. They also need to be aware of positions to which they can recommend outstanding workers for promotion.

Recruiting Systems

A **recruiting system** should provide the organization with a bank of qualified applicants from which it may fill vacant positions identified through the position control system and described by the job analysis and design information system. The recruiting function should also ensure that the organization is in compliance with various federal, state, and local statutes and contract regulations for affirmative action and equal employment opportunity.

To direct the recruiting function, the organization needs to develop a recruiting plan. The plan specifies the positions to be filled and the skills required of the employees for these positions. To develop the plan and to monitor its success, many different types of information are needed, including a list of unfilled positions; the duties and requirements of these positions; lists of planned employee retirements, transfers, or terminations; the skills and preferences of current employees; and summaries of employee appraisals. Other inputs to the recruiting plan include data about turnover rates and about the success of past placements. For example, if the goal of a recruiting campaign is to improve the quality of the organization's human resources, information about the past success of employee placements is essential. It is also important to identify departments that have had high employee turnover and to determine if this turnover represents poor-quality placements or is a result of other factors. Recruiters need to know whether their past selections have been well received by the supervisors for whom these employees work. Identifying employee factors that have led to past success and failure is essential to improving the recruiting function.

Organizations of a certain size are required to develop affirmative action plans to ensure compliance with various laws. The affirmative action plan requires an analysis of the number of minorities employed in specific job categories and reports the organization's recruiting and hiring goals for meeting deficiencies. The information for this plan is obtained from data in the position control system, the employee information system, and the recruiting system. The recruiting plan should reflect the organization's affirmative action goals. A recruiting system also provides the manager with information that helps to control recruiting activities. Thus, in addition to information about applicants, the system may include information from these sources:

- Schools and colleges, including placement officers.
- Federal, state, and local employment offices.
- Private placement services.
- Journal, magazine, and newspaper advertisements.
- Standard job advertisements and recruiting brochures.
- Prospect files.

Information about the success of recent placements and recruiting drives is essential to evaluate the effectiveness of past recruiting campaign tactics, the media used for advertising positions, and the recruiting sources used. For example, you may wish to know what recruiting sources provided you with the most job applicants who were hired, were of a minority status, or are currently rated highly by their supervisors.

Compensation and Benefits Systems

The wage and salary systems, or compensation plans, an organization can offer vary widely and include hourly wage plans, piece-rate plans, incentive pay plans, merit pay plans, monthly salary plans, commissions, and profit sharing. Special plans for part-time employees and those in job-sharing programs are also possible. Benefit plans include a wide range of fringe benefits, such as stock options, health insurance, life insurance, dental insurance, medical services, day care services, tuition for approved courses, and retirement plans.

Although government reporting requirements are an important reason that organizations have implemented computerized human resource information systems, they are not the only reason. The costs of employee benefits have soared in recent years, now averaging more than one-third of wages, and the need to control these costs has become a second major reason for the use of computerized human resource information systems (Stamps, 1990). In addition, many benefit plans are mandated by governmental units. For example, the federal government mandates coverage for social security, Medicare, disability, unemployment, and other benefit plans for certain workers. These plans may require payments by employees, employers, or both. The social security plan requires that employees and employers split the cost of social security and Medicare. Thus, the total cost of an employee to an employer is the sum of the amounts paid for work and the amounts paid for the various benefits the employee receives, including those benefits that are mandated by governments. The total cost of each worker is an important factor in human resource decision making and should be provided by the HRIS.

To help human resource managers control their compensation and benefit plans, organizations must keep and maintain information describing the various pay plans and fringe benefits as well as the choices of each employee. The **compensation and benefits system** may support a variety of tactical human resource decisions, especially when compensation and benefits information is related to information from internal and external sources. For example, you may wish to relate the pay received by employees with the same job duties or job titles to identify employees who are paid more or less than they should be for the skills they have and the duties they must complete. Some organizations have implemented cafeteria style, or flexible, benefits systems that allow employees to choose or change their benefits. In some of these systems, employees may also query the benefits system to ask their own what-if questions. For example, they can see the effect a change in their benefits package would have on their take-home pay. For instance, employees can add or remove dependents, change their marital status, redirect payroll deductions to other benefit programs, or find out what happens if they retire at 55 instead of 65. Some human resource professionals feel that cafeteria-style benefits programs provide their organizations with a competitive edge in acquiring and retaining high-demand employees. Flexible or cafeteria-style benefits administration usually requires computer system support. These self-service employee systems may be provided through standard on-line terminals, touch-screen kiosks, and even interactive voice response systems. These systems relieve human resource personnel from answering many routine and repetitive questions employees have about their benefits.

You may also wish to evaluate the effect of various pay plans on retention, promotion, and termination of employees. For example, compensation and benefit plans may be increased to attract or to retain highly marketable or highly skilled employees. In recent years, special retirement benefits have been used by many companies to induce older workers to retire early, thereby lowering payroll costs. Compensation and benefit plans can play an important part in improving an organization's productivity. Tying employee productivity to pay or encouraging increased productivity with incentive pay plans can often improve an organization's productivity substantially. Thus, these information systems provide important support to managers for tactical decisions.

Human resource managers may also wish to keep abreast of the changing benefits and legal environment by tapping into on-line databases pertaining to human resource management and issues (see Manager's Memo 11–6).

Succession Planning Systems

An important role of human resource departments is to make certain that replacements for key organizational personnel are available when the positions key personnel occupy become vacant because of death, injury, retirement, or other reasons. Planning for the succession of these key people means identifying replacement employees

Manager's Memo 11–6	HUMAN RESOURCE INFORMATION NETWORK

The Society for Human Resource Management offers the Human Resource Information Network (HRIN) a rich collection of databases containing information ranging from personnel policies and practices to labor-related news and statistics. HRIN provides immediate access to the latest information from over 100 databases and 65 news services on eight categories of HRMS data:

- Administration, systems, and planning.
- Affirmative action.
- Benefits and compensation.
- Employment and recruiting.
- Labor and legal matters.
- Labor–management relations.
- Safety and health.
- Training and development.

Of special interest, the administration category contains directories and reviews of more than 10,000 business, professional, and system software packages for all computer platforms, reviews of computer hardware and books, and a directory of 400 micro-based HRIS software packages.

Users can retrieve information, automatically track human resource issues, manipulate data, and analyze data on the system. In addition, HRIN provides users with on-line HRMS software to use in their work, electronic mail, bulletin boards, a calendar of professional human resource events, and even flight and hotel reservation services. HRIN can be accessed through any microcomputer or terminal with a modem 24 hours a day.

and providing them with the appropriate training and experience to fill openings. **Succession planning systems** help human resource personnel with these activities and are increasingly included as part of human resource information systems.

STRATEGIC HUMAN RESOURCE INFORMATION SYSTEMS

Human resource planning ensures that the organization has the right kinds and the right numbers of people at the right places at the right time to achieve its objectives (see Figure 11–20). Several types of human resource planning are strategic in nature, including workforce planning and labor negotiations.

Workforce Planning Systems

Organizations involved in long-term strategic planning, such as those planning to expand into new market areas, construct factories or offices in new locations, or add new products, will need information about the quantity and quality of the available workforce to achieve their goals. Information systems that support **workforce planning** serve this purpose. This type of planning involves identifying the human resources needed to meet the organizational objectives specified in the strategic plan and that means forecasting the supply and demand of the required workforce. These forecasts are estimates of the characteristics, quantity, and pricing of the labor force needed to achieve the long-term plans of the organization. Forecasting human resource needs requires information to answer a number of planning questions, including the following:

1. What should the labor force of the organization look like to meet the strategic plan? What skills, experiences, knowledge, and other qualities should the organization's human resources possess? In other words, what job descriptions and specifications does the strategic plan require?

Figure 11–20

A model showing human resource information systems (HRIS) support for a workforce plan

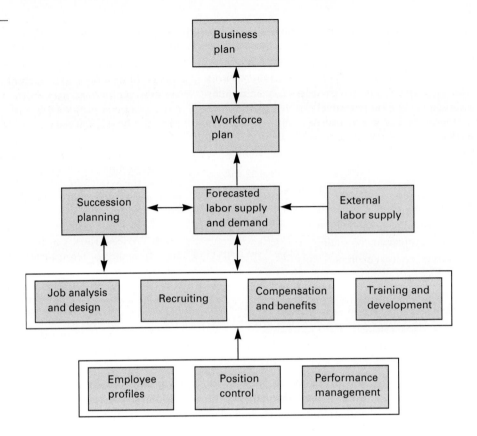

2. What quantities of human resources with the qualities already identified are needed to carry out the strategic plan? In other words, how many positions for each job title does the strategic plan need?

3. What are the current human resources of the organization and how well do they satisfy the organization's strategic needs for human resources?

4. What other human resources are available to achieve the strategic plan?

Identifying the types and quantities of workers needed for the strategic plan is forecasting the demand for human resources. Identifying the human resources available internally and externally is forecasting the supply of those human resources. Forecasting demand and supply can be done on a macroeconomic level or a microeconomic level. Macroeconomic forecasts of supply and demand for workers in various job categories can be obtained for states and regions from a variety of national and state agencies. Microeconomic forecasts involve using data more specific to the organization.

The data for microeconomic human resource forecasts may be obtained from internal and external sources. For example, suppose that a company plans to expand its business by constructing a new factory in an adjacent state. The company's planners examine the economic data relevant to the probable success of this plan and also examine a variety of sites for the new factory. To complete their planning, the planners will need demand data on the types of jobs and the number of positions required to manage and operate the new factory. They will also need supply data about the availability and cost of the workforce with the essential skills and experiences required to fill those positions. To prepare the forecast, the company planners will have to estimate the demand for each type of job the new factory will require. Demand data may be developed by asking current managers to forecast their workforce needs. Data also may be obtained from industry associations that provide guidelines for estimating worker needs. For instance, industry associations may provide guidelines, based on surveys of its members, for the number of salespeople per square mile of territory or per million dollars of sales, or the number of supervisors per 10 lathe operators, and so on.

Data may also be obtained by using industry or organization performance standards. For example, if the company's production plan for the new factory is 1,000 widgets per day, planners can use performance data taken from current workers to estimate the numbers of each type of worker needed to produce that number of widgets each day (see the section on capacity planning). To estimate supply, the company's planners may start by examining the current workforce to identify employees with the necessary skills and a preference for the geographical region where the new factory will be located. Planners can obtain this information from the company's skills inventory and its human resource file. They can then prepare a forecast to show how many of these employees will still be working for the company at the time of the move.

The company can also identify current employees who have a preference for the location but who do not have the skills needed. With additional training, these employees may be able to transfer to the new site. The company must also estimate the pool of workers with the essential skills available near the new location as well as the pool of workers near the present site who must be hired to fill the positions of those who do transfer. This estimate will usually require information about the numbers of each type of worker employed by competitors or other organizations from which the company may recruit.

Information Systems Supporting Labor Negotiations

Negotiating with craft, maintenance, office, and factory unions requires information gathered from many of the human resource information systems already discussed. In addition, negotiators need information from the financial accounting system and from external sources, including competitor wage agreements and appropriate economic data for the industry, employee group, and geographical region. Much of the external information required by a negotiating team can be obtained from the on-line databases discussed in Chapter 7. The human resource team completing the negotiating needs to be able to obtain numerous ad hoc reports that analyze the organization's and union's positions within the framework of both the industry and the current economic situation. The negotiating team must receive these ad hoc reports on a very timely basis because additional questions and tactics will occur to the team while they are negotiating.

Other Strategic Uses of Human Resource Information Systems

In addition to workforce planning and labor negotiations, human resource information systems data also support other strategic decisions. For example, organizations that are planning to restructure, downsize, sell off divisions, or merge with other organizations need to know what impact these decisions will have on their workforce profiles, the overall cost of their personnel, and the specific costs of benefit plans, such as retirement and health plans. Companies can also use workforce forecasts strategically to negotiate for concessions from local governments when making decisions about organization locations.

HRIS Software

Computerizing human resource information allows human resource managers to sift through it on an ad hoc basis to pursue answers to what-if questions. This capability supports managers' tactical decision-making and policy-making activities. For example, human resource managers can use information systems to minimize the costs of employee compensation and benefits and to increase the fairness of an organization's compensation and benefit plans. Forecasting and analyzing trends in accidents, pay rates, and position openings; identifying problems in pay grades, job titles, or supervisory skills; and assessing the impact of various pay increases, benefit plans, or retirement plans for employees are just a few of the many information-seeking activities that a computerized HRIS facilitates.

Software to support the HRM function comes in two flavors: limited function software or comprehensive and integrated software. Numerous commercial software packages are sold for use on mainframes, minicomputers, and microcomputers designed to handle one or a small number of human resource functions (see Figure 11–21).

Take care if you follow the single-function software route, though. The success of the first venture and the ease with which you complete it will likely lead you to add other single-function software packages to automate other human resource activities. If these additional software packages are not compatible with one another, you may be left with a series of data files and software packages that cannot be used in an integrated fashion. Thus you will not be able to produce reports or ask what-if questions that require more than one data file for completion.

Many products organize the various human resource information systems into integrated software referred to as human resource information system, or HRIS, software. In general, the computerization of HRIS has resulted in an integrated database of human resource files. This integrated database allows application programs or users to produce reports from any or all of the records.

Figure 11–21

Some types of limited-function human resource information systems software

Applicant tracking	Immigration reform
Attendance tracking	Job analysis
Benefits administration	Job description
Career development	Labor relations
Compensation administration	Payroll administration
Comprehensive Omnibus Budget Reconciliation Act (COBRA) administration	Pension and profit-sharing administration
	Performance evaluation
Computer-based training	Relocation management
Employee manual and handbook preparation	Stress management
Employee relations	Substance abuse management
Equal Employment Opportunity/Affirmative Action	Succession planning
Flexible benefits administration	Temporary services management
Health and safety management	Training administration and management
Human resources forecasting	Turnover analysis
	Workforce planning

MANAGEMENT SUMMARY

Tactical information systems support managers in the allocation of resources to meet top management's goals. Strategic planning information systems, in contrast, support the setting of organization goals. There are many applications of information systems to tactical and strategic planning in businesses and organizations. This chapter briefly describes applications to tactical and strategic planning decisions in finance, marketing, production, and human resources.

Financial information systems include tactical systems, such as budgeting, cash management, capital budgeting, and investment management, and strategic systems, such as financial condition analysis and long-term forecasting. A wealth of internal and external sources of information exists for these information systems, and many general-purpose and specialized software tools are also available.

Tactical marketing information systems support marketing managers in the management and control of the sales force, sales campaigns, advertising and promotion campaigns, pricing, and the distribution and delivery of goods and services, as well as in tracking competitors. Strategic marketing information systems include sales forecasting, market research, and product planning and development.

Many tools are available to assist marketing managers in tactical and strategic decision making, including data warehouses, geographic information systems, on-line and Internet databases, and CD-ROM databases.

Tactical and strategic production information systems support decision making for the allocation and planning of manufacturing and production resources. Many information systems have been developed to assist in controlling inventories; estimating, assigning, and monitoring production capacity; designing products and services; scheduling production facilities; allocating human resources; controlling production projects; assessing production technologies; planning for the development of new plants; deciding on the level of vertical integration; and designing plant facilities. These information systems use data from the organization's financial accounting and human resource databases. In addition, many external sources of information, such as on-line government, scientific, and industry databases and Internet sites, provide support for strategic planning.

The continued use and refinement of computer support for manufacturing and production operations and decisions is leading organizations to an integrated approach to the management of manufacturing and production systems.

Human resource departments are responsible for many facets of human resource management, including tactical decision making in the areas of recruiting, training, compensation, benefit management, and job analysis and design. HR managers also provide top management with information for strategic planning, including providing workforce plans and support for labor negotiations.

KEY TERMS FOR MANAGERS

actuals, 405

advertising and promotion systems, 419

allocations, 405

budgeting system, 405

capacity requirements planning, 433

capital budget, 408

cash flow report, 407

cash management systems, 408

compensation and benefits system, 442

competitive tracking systems, 423

computer-integrated manufacturing (CIM), 436

distribution channel decision-support system, 423

financial condition analysis system, 412

forecasting software, 414

human resource information systems (HRIS), 438

human resource management (HRM), 438

internal rate of return (IRR), 409

investment management, 410

job analysis and design system, 439

just-in-time (JIT) system, 431

manufacturing resource planning (MRP-II), 435

marketing mix, 415

marketing research, 426

materials requirements planning (MRP), 430

media mix, 421

net present value (NPV), 408

payback period, 409

plant design system, 438

pricing systems, 421

process positioning, 437

product design and development systems, 435

product planning and development systems, 427

production schedule, 433

production systems, 428

recruiting system, 440

rough-cut capacity planning, 431

sales forecasting systems, 425

sales management software, 419

sales management systems, 416

site planning systems, 437

succession planning systems, 443

technology assessment systems, 437

variance, 405

workforce planning, 443

REVIEW QUESTIONS

1. What types of information flows are typically associated with strategic planning systems? What are the sources of those information flows?

2. What information would a manager need to compute net present value? What types of tactical decisions can net present value information assist the manager in making?

3. Identify the information a manager would need to compute payback period. What kind of tactical decisions can payback period calculations help to support?

4. How can on-line databases be used to support financial decisions at the tactical level?

5. How can on-line databases be used to support financial decisions at the strategic planning level?

6. Describe how spreadsheet software can be used to support financial decisions at the tactical and strategic planning levels.

7. What precautions should you take when acquiring forecasting or statistical software?

8. What are two major outcomes of financial strategic planning?

9. What is the marketing mix?

10. What kinds of information, internal to an organization, might be found in a data warehouse that would be useful to marketing personnel?

11. What is sales management software? What information does sales management software usually provide to managers?

12. Describe ways in which a marketing manager might use a spreadsheet software package for tactical decision making.

13. Describe ways in which a marketing manager might use query languages and report writers for tactical decision making.

14. What major types of decisions do advertising and promotion systems support?

15. What is media mix? What types of decisions relate to the media mix of an organization?

16. What information might a marketing manager use to make a decision about the price of a product or service?

17. What is a distribution channel system? What types of information should this system provide to managers?

18. How might the Internet be used to obtain information about competitors and competitive products?

19. What is competitive intelligence? What tasks do competitive information professionals complete? What information systems support gathering competitive intelligence?

20. Describe five activities frequently performed by marketing research departments. How might computer information systems support each of these activities?

21. Identify ways in which marketing research departments can support marketing managers' tactical decision making and strategic planning.

22. What internal and external sources of information might managers use to prepare a sales forecast for a new product? What computer-based information systems and software provide support for this activity?

23. Why are sales forecasts important? What other organizational personnel or systems use sales forecast reports?

24. Describe desktop survey software. What are some of its typical features?

25. What is a materials requirements planning system? How can an MRP system help an organization?

26. What are the basic inputs and outputs of an MRP system?

27. What is a bill-of materials information system? How does this system relate to MRP systems?

28. What information tools does MRP software often use to identify when and in what quantities raw materials should be purchased?

29. What is JIT?

30. What is the purpose of capacity planning?

31. What basic categories of information do managers need for capacity planning decisions?

32. At what decision level are capacity planning decisions?

33. What types of production decisions may be classified as strategic planning in nature?

34. What is MRP-II software and how does it differ from MRP software?

35. What is CIM?

36. What types of software and hardware systems might be included in a CIM system?

37. What are the objectives of a recruiting system? How do various human resource information systems support these objectives?

38. How might a compensation and benefits information system be used tactically?

39. Differentiate between comprehensive human resource software and limited-function human resource software.

40. How can a job analysis and design system contribute to an organization?

41. What is a succession planning system?

42. What are the outputs of a workforce planning forecast? What may be the types and sources of inputs to a workforce forecast?

QUESTIONS FOR DISCUSSION

1. How do operational, tactical, and strategic planning information systems differ in their orientation?

2. How has the computerization of accounting information changed the views of managers toward that information?

3. Explain what information a cash flow report contains. How might a financial manager use a cash flow report? What tactical decisions might the cash flow report support?

4. Describe one summary report and one exception report that might be useful for these types of managers:
   a. Accounting manager
   b. Budget officer
   c. Investment manager

5. How might on-line databases assist a manager responsible for managing a portfolio of stock and bond investments for an organization?

6. What categories of information might be useful for strategic planners concerned about the environment in which the organization may find itself 5 to 10 years from now?

7. Explain how a spreadsheet may prove useful to a manager for financial decision making. That is, what characteristics of a spreadsheet make it helpful for tactical decision making and strategic planning decision support? Provide examples of the use of spreadsheets in financial decision making.

8. Compare operational and tactical marketing information systems in terms of the type of data they process and the types of output they produce.

9. Describe how computer systems might be used to support the sales management function of the organization.

10. Compare the characteristics of a competitive tracking system to a contact information system. In what ways are these information systems different?

11. Are projections of past sales an effective measure of future sales? Why or why not? If not, what other types of information might prove helpful?

12. Describe how a marketing manager might use the Internet to monitor competitors.

13. What are the objectives of an MRP system?

14. Compare the approach of JIT and MRP-II systems to inventory, quality, and workers.

15. How might project management software aid a production manager? What advantages does the software provide that are hard to obtain in a manual planning system?

16. What is process positioning?

17. How can product design information systems contribute to an organization's competitive edge?

18. Name some production decisions that are strategic planning decisions.

19. What are the advantages of CIM? Why does there seem to be a lack of interest among production executives in CIM?

20. What are the advantages of implementing comprehensive human resource software as opposed to limited-function human resource software?

PROBLEMS

1. **Spreadsheet problem: Accounts receivable department budget estimate.** Using any spreadsheet program that can read or import an Excel spreadsheet file, load the file labeled budtemp.xls on the applications diskette provided by your instructor. The file is a template for estimating the budget expenses for an accounts receivable department. The template contains the column and row headings for estimating the budget. You must enter the goal for the rate of increase or decrease in the total budget amount for next year as a decimal in cell C20. You must also enter the rate of increase or decrease that each budget line amount is estimated to change in cells D8–D16 (for example, enter .03 in cell D8, the Salaries line in the Possible Changes as Percent column).

    a. Enter percentages in columns C and D to reflect these estimates for next year:
       1. The goal is to keep the overall budget to no more than a 5 percent increase over last year.
       2. Salaries will increase by 3 percent.
       3. Wages will increase by 5 percent.
       4. Postage will increase by 12 percent.
       5. All other budget items will increase by 3.5 percent.

    b. After entering the values in (a) above, answer these questions:
       1. What is the total of the estimated budget expenditures for next year?
       2. What is the difference in dollars between the goal for next year and the total estimated payments for next year?

    c. What would be the answers to (b) if both wages and salaries increased by 6 percent?

    d. Using the spreadsheet amounts developed in (c) above, develop a budget estimate that meets the 5 percent overall increase goal stated in (a) and also maintains the 6 percent increases in wages and salaries stated in (c). The increase or decrease in all other budget items can be varied to achieve the results needed.

2. **Spreadsheet design problem: Budget analysis.** Acquire the current-year budget of an organization such as a town, a school, a university, a department, the business of a relative or friend, or even an extracurricular activity, such as the university newspaper.

    a. Describe the information you would like to have to analyze the budget you acquired.

    b. Identify at least one source for each type of information you described in (a).

    c. Explain what type of analysis each type of information allows you to make and why such an analysis might prove fruitful.

    d. Develop a spreadsheet template for the budget. Use the design suggestions in Manager's Memo 6–3. Then test your template by inputting the data from the actual budget and comparing the results.

3. **Tactical decision-making tools.** Using the Internet, periodical literature, CD-ROM or on-line databases, or other sources, identify

three software packages that provide the manager with financial, marketing, production, or human resource management tools. For example, you might identify software packages that provide support in cash management or sales management.

a. If they are available, send for or download a demonstration diskette for each package. Use the demonstration diskettes to view the features of the packages.

b. Prepare a report describing each package, including the package's features, cost, ease of use, and hardware requirements.

4. **Barrington Distributors, Inc.** You are the sales manager for Barrington Distributors, which distributes more than 100 different outdoor furniture products to discount stores, department stores, and other retail outlets in a 24-state area. You supervise 42 salespeople who must cover territories as narrow as a large metropolitan area and as wide as an entire state. Barrington is implementing a computer system, and the systems analysis group is in the process of questioning managers to determine their reporting needs. You have been asked to identify five reports that would help you make the tactical decisions regarding the allocation and control of your sales force. Then develop an outline of each report; show the main headings; the column headings; and the types of totals, counts, averages, or other statistical results you want to see in each report. Finally, indicate the internal or external source for the data you want in each column.

5. **Forecasting problem: Forecasting sales.** You are the sales manager for Media Sources, Inc. The following table shows the gross annual sales for your firm for the last 10 years:

Year	Gross Sales	Year	Gross Sales
1	$145,340	6	$157,180
2	$140,389	7	$159,210
3	$142,580	8	$156,950
4	$151,190	9	$162,560
5	$151,440	10	$174,810

a. Forecast the sales for years 11, 12, and 13 using the forecast function of your spreadsheet software. Use the data for years 1 through 10 in your forecast.

b. After reviewing the sales for the last 10 years, you decide that the last 5 years are probably more representative of sales than the last 10 years because in the first 5 years the company was just getting off the ground. Forecast the sales for years 11, 12, and 13, using sales data from years 6 through 10.

6. **Spreadsheet design problem: Salesperson performance.** Design a spreadsheet like the one shown in Figure 11-9 to analyze salesperson performance. Provide cells to input the number of orders, the number of calls, the total dollar amount of orders, the monthly quotas for each salesperson, the number of working days in the month (Mondays through Fridays), and the monthly averages for each column for last year. Then provide cells to calculate the number of orders per call, the average order per call, the number of calls per day, the percent of sales made to quota, and averages for each column for the entire firm for the month. Test the accuracy of your spreadsheet design by entering the values found in Figure 11-9 and comparing the results you get in your calculated cells. Then evaluate your spreadsheet design by reviewing Manager's Memo 6-3. Adjust your spreadsheet, if necessary.

7. **Spreadsheet design problem: S & I Manufacturing Company.** S & I Manufacturing Company assembles braces and brackets from component parts purchased from suppliers. The company's sales forecast predicts sales of 100,000 braces and 300,000 brackets for the coming year. You are the production manager for the firm, and your production records from previous years indicate that an experienced assembly-line worker can assemble 10 braces or 20 brackets per day. Your records also show that workers who can assemble braces can also assemble brackets. There are no skills to learn, nor are there any union restrictions on moving personnel from the assembly of one

product to another. You need to know how many assembly-line workers the company will need to meet the sales forecast under these circumstances:

a. Each worker is given two weeks off for vacation.

b. Each worker is given eight days off for holidays in the year.

c. An average of 2 percent of the workers are ill or absent from work each day.

d. The company estimates that 1 percent of the braces and brackets produced each day are defective.

Using any spreadsheet software, develop a template for calculating the number of assembly-line workers needed. Design the spreadsheet so that the manager can easily change the number of weeks of employee vacation, the number of holidays, the percent of workers ill or absent, and the percent of defective products. If you don't have spreadsheet software available, construct rows and columns on a sheet of paper. Then, using a pencil, sketch the template, showing the row and column labels you would use, and write in the formulas you would need for the template.

8. **Project management problem: Richard's Painting Company.** Richard's Painting Company's (RPC) major market consists of large business firms and large public sector organizations. Tanya Martin, a project manager for RPC, has been trying to schedule a work crew to complete the painting of a large, two-story, rectangular, wood-sided commercial building. The building's external walls are to be repainted. However, before the final coat of paint is applied, all loose paint and dirt must be removed from the walls. Next a primer coat of paint must be applied. Then the primer coat must be left to dry for one full day before the final coat of paint is applied.

Tanya has visited the site and learned that the building's north and south walls are twice the length of its east and west walls. She has measured the areas to be painted and estimates that a crew of two workers will need two days to remove loose paint from and clean the east wall and that two workers will

need another two days to do the west wall. Two workers will need four full days to do the north wall and another four days for the south wall. She estimates that four workers will have to spend two full days to paint a primer coat on each of the east and west walls, and four days each for the north and south walls. Then these workers will spend an equal time applying the final coat of paint.

Tanya would like to start the project on May 5 and has been authorized to use four workers for the project. She is authorized to schedule her work crew for eight-hour days, Monday through Friday. She is not authorized to schedule overtime or weekend work without prior permission of her supervisor. The union contract for her workers does not include any holidays during the first three weeks of May.

Develop a Gantt chart for the project. Maintain the needed sequence of phases for the project: (1) the preparation phase (remove loose paint and clean walls), (2) the primer phase (apply a primer), (3) the drying phase (allow the primer to dry), and (4) the final coat phase (apply a final coat). However, schedule the tasks to be performed in such way that the project is completed in as short a time as possible given the assigned workers. You may complete the Gantt chart manually or use a project management software package.

9. **Averill & Barnes, Inc.** Averill & Barnes, Inc., manufactures lead and colored pencils at one plant in Kansas City, Kansas. Sales have been growing consistently over the last few years to the point that the plant is working three shifts each day. To meet estimated demand three years from now, the company will have to expand its production capacity. Sales growth has been especially strong in the northeastern United States, and the company is considering locating a second plant in the area of their growth market. Saratoga and Rochester, New York, are two locations that appear promising after a preliminary survey of data from the standpoint of proximity to wood supplies and customer density. Top management also wants to assess the manpower situation in

and around those two cities. You are to provide the managers with this information:

a. Topics that should be searched in on-line databases or the Internet to provide

information useful to workforce planners.

b. Two on-line databases and two Internet Web sites to start their search.

CASES

1. **Munson Beverage Corporation.** Munson Beverage Corporation owns 30 warehouses and the distribution equipment necessary to supply a variety of soda products to retailers throughout the Midwest. The headquarters of the corporation are in Muncie, where its largest warehouse is located. You have just been appointed vice president of finance for the Munson Beverage Corporation. The information system that the corporation currently uses provides you with accounting information gleaned from the typical accounting system database. This system includes modules for accounts receivable, accounts payable, order entry, purchase order, inventory, payroll, fixed assets, and the preparation of statements and reports. At regular intervals the following periodic statements are sent to your office for your examination:

   - Aged accounts receivable reports.
   - Balance sheets.
   - Current merchandise inventory lists.
   - Employee earnings records.
   - Fixed assets and equipment inventories.
   - Income statements.
   - Payroll sheets.
   - Schedules of accounts payable.
   - Schedules of accounts receivable.
   - Sources and uses of funds.
   - Stockout lists.

   a. Do you believe that the current reports you receive are appropriate to your tasks? Be specific: Describe which reports are appropriate or inappropriate and why.

   b. Outline on separate sheets of paper three new reports that might be helpful to you in tactical-level decision making. On each sheet show the title of the report, the column headings (if any), the nature of the data to be included, and the processing needed on the report (percentages, totals, formula results, and so forth). For each type of data to be included, indicate a possible source.

   c. Outline on separate sheets of paper three new reports that might be helpful to you in strategic planning. On each sheet show the title of the report, the column headings (if any), the nature of the data to be included, and the processing needed on the report (percentages, totals, formula results, and so forth). For each type of data to be included, indicate a possible source.

   d. Specify any additional types of software you would consider acquiring to assist you in your tactical decisions and strategic planning. Then describe how you would use each type of software you identified to help you in your work.

2. **Dell competitor analysis.** You are an assistant to the vice president of marketing for a large computer company that produces microcomputer hardware, including desktop and notebook PCs. Your boss has asked you to prepare an analysis of Dell Computer Corporation, a major competitor and producer of PCs. Your boss wants your report to analyze the nature of the competitive threats posed by Dell, based on the data collected. It should also recommend specific actions that your company might take to counter or reduce these threats. The report should be limited to five pages, not including cover or reference pages. The report may be enhanced with illustrations from a presentation graphics package, including charts on sales trends, margins, market share, revenues, or similar data. To gather data for the report, use the Internet,

CD-ROM, or on-line databases available to you, such as ABI/Inform, Computer Select, Lexis/Nexis, and Dialog. The competitor analysis report should contain the following types of information about Dell:

- Market share.
- Financial statistics.
- Sales history.
- Product lines.
- Territories served.
- Advertising themes.
- Plans for expansion in products or territories.
- New products.
- Products under development.
- Product margins.
- Market strategy.
- General market outlook for the industry.
- Marketing mix.
- Competitor strengths.
- Competitor weaknesses.
- Best-and worst-selling product lines.
- Trends in U.S. and world markets affecting products.

3. **Merrill's.** Ralph Johnson and Teresa Merrill are partners in Merrill's, a fashion clothing retailing firm. Teresa Merrill has been primarily concerned with the marketing aspects of the firm, and Ralph Johnson has concentrated on the accounting and finance functions. The firm has three stores in the Dallas/Fort Worth area, two stores in Houston, and two stores in El Paso, Texas. Merrill's has been very successful, growing from one store three years ago to its current total of seven stores. Its success has been largely due to Teresa's ability to guess what fashions customers will like and to stock these items in the stores as well as her persistence in identifying stock that is moving too slowly or very fast and adjusting inventories accordingly. Until recently, Teresa did all the buying, and it was relatively easy for her to stay on top of inventory turnover when there were only one or two stores. As the firm grew, however, Teresa has had to hire

professional buyers and increasingly delegate these duties to them.

The partners are now considering establishing their own data processing department and computerizing the accounting system, including the order-entry and inventory subsystems. Ralph recently attended a two-day seminar on the use of computers for decision support. He has become interested in using the computer system to help him manage the financial activities of the firm and to help Teresa manage the marketing functions in some way, especially in helping her forecast product sales. When Ralph discussed this idea with Teresa, Teresa became agitated. She felt that there was no way that a computer system could help her or her buyers forecast the sales of individual products. After all, they were in the fashion business, and predicting customer acceptance using a computer would be impossible. Teresa believes that the fashion business is simply too erratic for computer support.

However, Ralph still believes that the use of the computer system in marketing is a real possibility. He simply does not have the background, though, to show Teresa how the computer could help her. As a result, Ralph has asked you to serve as a consultant to the firm to identify how a computer system could be used to assist Teresa in marketing, especially in the area of forecasting product sales and controlling inventory levels.

Prepare a report for Ralph in which you take these steps:

a. Identify and describe at least three ways in which a computer system might help Teresa in her tactical decision making.

b. Develop the layouts for two reports that will help her with her tactical planning. The report layouts should include report, row, and column headings and show totals, averages, or other ways in which column data are to be treated. Make certain that your report addresses Teresa's forecasting and inventory control activities.

4. **Southern States Manufacturing Company.** Gilbert Hawthorne is the

human resource director for the Southern States Manufacturing Company of Atlanta, Georgia. Southern States is a very traditional, well-established company, having been incorporated in 1888. Hawthorne will be celebrating his 25th year with the company this year, and he has been the human resource director for Southern States for the last 20 years. During that time, the company has grown to 600 employees, and Gilbert now manages the work of several assistant human resource directors. Hawthorne's assistants are charged with the following areas of responsibility: personnel benefits, personnel health and safety, wage and salary administration, and affirmative action. Though Southern States has had a data processing department to handle the accounting and payroll functions of the company for a number of years, the use of computers has not spread to other departments or functions within the firm. Elizabeth Lucas, current president of Southern States and granddaughter of the firm's founding father, is concerned about making the firm more technologically current and thereby maintaining its competitive edge. As a result, she has asked Wylder Washington, an information systems consultant, to explore with the firm's managers how they could use computerized information systems to improve their operations.

Hawthorne missed his scheduled appointment with Washington. When Washington telephoned Hawthorne to ask why, Hawthorne explained that he was tied up because of pressing discussions with his assistant human resource director in charge of personnel benefits. Hawthorne added, however, that "I do not feel an appointment is really necessary. After all, human resource management is a people function and, as such, cannot be computerized. Furthermore, the company's human resource function has been operating very well for the last 20 years without the aid of computers." Hawthorne suggested that Washington pursue the computerization of other functions within the company, as he felt that those functions would be more likely to yield results. Despite Hawthorne's objections, Washington insisted on setting up

another meeting and extracted from Hawthorne the promise that he would attend.

a. Hawthorne's opinion about computers is not uncommon. What approach might you use to persuade him that the computerization of the human resource information system might be worth exploring?

b. What operational, tactical, and strategic planning human resource activities might be plausible applications for computerized information systems in the firm? For each application, spell out how the computerization of these activities might benefit Hawthorne's operation.

c. Which application identified in (*b*) should be given first priority for development? Explain why you chose this application as the first one to develop.

5. **Chase Media, Inc.** The human resource department staff at Chase Media, Inc., serves a labor force of 750 employees, including office workers, factory workers, sales workers, technicians, and professionals. Because the workforce is growing and because of the complexities of governmental reporting, the staff has been considering computerizing its human resource activities. Valerie Epstein, the training director, has been reading articles about full-blown human resource information systems in professional journals and is interested in acquiring a comprehensive commercial HRIS package. Epstein suggests that the department ask the MIS department for help identifying, evaluating, and selecting a commercial package to be used on its mainframe. She feels MIS expertise is needed in this project because none of the human resource staff has much computer training or experience.

Tyrone Wilson, the benefits administrator for the department, feels that such a move would be too much, too soon. He suggests that it would be easier and faster if the department computerized only one HRIS activity first to see how effective computerization would be and what problems staff would have moving to computer-based systems. Wilson suggests that the department evaluate and acquire commercial benefits management software to see how things go before plowing ahead with a comprehensive package of software. If the benefits software works satisfactorily, the department can proceed to acquire and implement software packages for the other human resource functions one at a time.

Elicia Watson, the recruiting director for the department, complains that the MIS department may defer the computerization it needs now to manage an increasingly large labor force with some degree of efficiency. Watson points out that the human resource department does not have the highest priority in the firm's pecking order and that its requests for MIS services are likely to be placed behind those of the marketing and production departments. She suggests that the department acquire a microcomputer human resource system so that it can implement the software immediately and not

have to worry about the priorities of the MIS department. Watson also believes that use of the microcomputer system will give the human resource department greater control over the system's use and its security. She points out that the microcomputer system is much less expensive than purchasing a mainframe human resource system and should be easy for staff members to implement without help from the MIS department.

Marcia Dobbins, director of human resource services for Chase, decides that they all need some expert advice and decides to call in a consultant. You are the consultant:

a. How would you assess each of the suggestions by Epstein, Wilson, and Watson? What are the strengths and weaknesses of each suggestion?

b. What plan of action would you recommend and why?

SELECTED INTERNET REFERENCE SITES

Accounting Resources on the Internet (http://www.rutgers.edu/Accounting/raw/internet/internet.htm).

Ad Age home page (http://www.adage.com).

Advanced Personnel Systems HR Software Directory (http://www.hrcensus.com/html).

American Accounting Association (http://www.rutgers.edu/Accounting/raw/aaa/aaa.htm).

American Institute of Certified Public Accountants (http://www.rutgers.edu/Accounting/raw/aicpa/home.htm).

American Marketing Association home page (http://www.ama.org).

American Production and Inventory Control Society's home page (http://www.industry.net/apics).

American Production and Inventory Control Society's links to general manufacturing Web sites (http://www.industry.net/c/orgunpro/apics/link3gen).

Dun & Bradstreet (http://www.dbisna.com).

IndustryNet home page (http://www.industry.net).

FinanceNet (http://www.financenet.gov).

FINWeb Home Page (http://riskweb.bus.utexas.edu:80/finweb.html).

HR Links—Society for Human Resource Management (http://www.shrm.org/hrlinks/).

International Association for Human Resource Information Management (IHRIM) (http://www.ihrim.org).

LookSmart's Advertising Agency page (http://mulwala.looksmart.com:8080/?comefrom=netscape&divert).

LookSmart's Marketing Research page (http://mulwala.looksmart.com:8080/?comefrom=netscape&divert).

Mechanical.Com(http://www.mechanical.com:80/index.html).

Mercury Mail stock quotes and news Web site (http://www.merc.com/cb/cgi/cb_merc.cgi?).

Microsoft's Business and Financial Sites (http://library.microsoft.com/finance.htm).

Microsoft Investor Web site (http://investor.msn.com/contents.asp).

NETworth Information Page (http://networth.galt.com/www/home/networth.htm).

PAWWS, the stock market simulator (http://pawws.secapl.com/G_phtml/top.html).

Rutgers University's Accounting Web Introduction (http://www.rutgers.edu/Accounting/raw.htm).

Society for Human Resource Management
(http://www.shrm.org/).

Society of Manufacturing Engineers—Manufacturing
Web sites link page
(http://www.sme.org:80/memb/associations.html).

Stetson University Marketing Department's Guide to
Professional Organizations
(http://www.stetson.edu/~market/mktgrps.html).

Wall Street Research Net (http://www.wsrn.com/).

Selected References and Readings

Attaran, "Barriers to Effective CIM Implementation." *Information Systems Management,* Fall 1996, p. 52.

Berkowitz, E.; R. Kerin; S. Hartley; and W. Rudelius. *Marketing.* 5th ed. Chicago: Irwin, 1997.

Bernardin, H. J., and J. E. A. Russell. *Human Resource Management: An Experiential Approach.* New York: McGraw-Hill, 1992.

Block, S. and G. Hirt. *Foundations of Financial Management.* 8th ed. Chicago: Irwin, 1997.

Bovee, C. L.; M. J. Houston; and J. V. Thill. *Marketing.* 2nd ed. New York: McGraw-Hill, 1995.

Brealey, R. A.; S. C. Myers; and A. J. Marcus. *Fundamentals of Corporate Finance.* New York: McGraw-Hill, 1995.

Chambers, N. "Beyond MRPII: A New Approach to Manufacturing Planning and Simulation." *Industrial Management & Data Systems,* April 1996, p. 3.

Cope, J. "Tracking Advertising Effectiveness." *PC Today,* July 1995, p. 41.

Diamond, J. "Production and Inventory Control: The Move to the PC." *IIE Solutions,* January 1997, p. 18.

Dilworth, J. B. *Production and Operations Management: Manufacturing and Services.* 5th ed. McGraw-Hill, 1993.

Doolittle, S. "Desktop Logistics: GIS Software Streamlines Marketing and Sales." *PC Today,* January 1996, p. 112.

Doolittle, S. "Desktop Marketing." *PC Today,* October 1995, p. 116.

Eckerson, W. W. "Drilling for Data." *Computerworld,* December 2, 1996, p. 95.

Egan, R. "Online Clipping Services Deliver." *PC Today,* March 1995, p. 20.

Flanagan, P. "Getting the Paper out of the Marketing & Sales Pipeline." *Management Review,* July 1995, p. 53.

Fox, M.; V. Nilakant; and R. T. Hamilton. "Managing Succession in Family-Owned Businesses." *International Small Business Journal,* October–December 1996, p. 15.

Goldenberg, B. "The Benefits of Sales & Marketing Automation." *Sales & Marketing Management,* April 1995, p. S6.

Gumaer, R. "Beyond ERP and MRP II: Optimized Planning and Synchronized Manufacturing." *IIE Solutions,* September 1996, p. 32.

HRMagazine, February 1996, p. 91.

Henson, Row, "HRIMS for Dummies: a Practical Guide to Technology Implementation." *HR Focus,* November 1996, p. 3.

Holzberg, C. "Mapping the Way to Success." *PC Today,* April 1996, p. 80.

Leinfuss, E. "Employees Empowered by Direct Access HRMS." *Software Magazine,* April 1993, p. 83.

Milkovich, G. T. and J. W. Boudreau. *Human Resource Management.* 8th ed. Chicago: Irwin, 1997.

Morris, J. S. and L. J. Morris "Problems in CIM Implementation: A Case Study of Nine CIM Firms." *Computers & Industrial Engineering,* September 1994, p. 147.

Remington, M. "Mining the Database." *PC Today,* July 1995, p. 64.

Slack, N. *The Manufacturing Advantage: Achieving Competitive Manufacturing Operations. Industrial Management and Data Systems,* January–February 1994, p. 30.

Slick, B. "Technology and the Human Factor." *PC Today,* March 1995, p. 10.

Stearman, S. W. "Financial Analysis Software." *PC Today,* April 1995, p. 26.

Stone, R. W. and D. J. Good. "Information Support for Sales Managers." *Industrial Marketing Management,* October 1994, p. 281.

Thomas, P. and D. Wainwright. "Gaining the Benefits of Integrated Manufacturing Technology—Just Who Benefits and How?" *International Journal of Production Economics,* June 1994, p. 371.

Townsend, A. M. and A. R. Hendrickson. "Recasting HRIS as an Information Resource." *HRMagazine,* February 1996, p. 91.

Turbide, D. A. "MRP II: Still Number One!" *IIE Solutions,* July 1995, p. 28.

Vine, D. "I $py: Gathering Business Intelligence." *Internet World,* March 1997, p. 48.

Weston, F. C., Jr. "Three Dimensions of CIM." *Production & Inventory Management Journal,* Winter 1994, p. 59.

Decision Support Systems and Expert Systems

Chapter Outline

Manager's View

Managers' Systems Needs

Characteristics of the Decision-Making Process

Important Features of Decision Support Systems

Components of a Decision Support System

The Tools of Decision Support

Cases in Managerial Decision Support Systems

The Development of Decision Support Systems

The Benefits of Decision Support Systems

The Risks of Decision Support Systems

Group Decision Support Systems

Artificial Intelligence and Expert Systems

Expert Systems and Decision Support Systems

The Characteristics of Expert Systems

How an Expert System Works

Expert Systems Applications in Business

The Advantages of Expert Systems

Management Summary

Key Terms for Managers

Review Questions

Questions for Discussion

Problems

Cases

Selected Internet Reference Sites

Selected References and Readings

THE EARLIEST INFORMATION SYSTEMS were operational information systems designed to automate payroll, accounts payable, and other accounting transactions. In the early 1970s operational information systems that processed orders, scheduled production, and managed transportation needs were developed. Many of these applications allowed businesses to reduce clerical effort, to control administrative costs, and to provide better service. Designed by systems development professionals, most of these systems ran on centralized mainframe computers with large databases.

In the 1980s and 1990s a new concept of information systems has evolved because managers increasingly need information to make decisions about how to organize and control resources effectively. These systems, known as decision support systems, are quite different from the information systems of the past. They are designed by managers themselves, sometimes with the help of data processing professionals serving as user-consultants.

This chapter explains the evolution and development of managerial decision support systems. Because decision support systems are designed to support managers' information needs, you should also be familiar with the process of decision making. Decision support systems must constantly evolve because the decisions that managers need to make change from day to day. This chapter also describes how expert systems support less structured decisions.

MANAGERS' SYSTEMS NEEDS

One reason for the emergence of decision support systems is that many existing information systems do not support the information needs of managers. In a study of managers' systems needs, Alloway and Quillard asked 529 managers in 13 firms to describe how effectively current information systems supported their decision-making needs. Of the information systems in the 13 organizations they studied, Alloway and Quillard learned that 63 percent were operational information systems designed to produce standard reports on a fixed schedule. An additional 16 percent were exception reporting systems designed to support tactical decision making. An *exception report* produces information about deviations from planned activity, such as identifying all customer accounts doing 25 percent more business this year than last year. Although exception reporting systems can highlight trends affecting the business, the exception conditions are usually fixed; that is the logic for reporting exceptions is explicitly coded in the computer programs that prepare the exception reports. If a manager wants a report of all customers doing 10 percent less business this year than last year, for example, reprogramming would be required.

Although operational and exception reporting systems were helpful to the managers Alloway and Quillard surveyed, the managers considered inquiry and analysis systems far more useful in supporting decision-making needs. According to these authors, an inquiry system provides a database that can be used to make ad hoc queries. Using a query language, a manager can ask, List the names of all customers in the

Figure 12–1

Appropriateness of
information
systems used by
managers

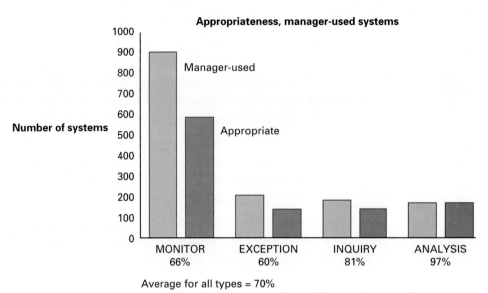

Appropriateness, manager-used systems

Source: Adapted from R. Alloway and J. Quillard, "User Managers' Systems Needs," *MIS Quarterly* 7, no. 2 (1983), p. 32.

Midwest region who have overdue account balances of more than $500. The next day, the same manager might ask, List the names and addresses of customers in the Southwest region who have done more than $10,000 worth of business with us in the past year. The types of queries managers want answered change as information needs change.

In their study Alloway and Quillard learned that only 12 percent of the information systems they surveyed were inquiry systems and that the managers considered most of these systems useful. Managers also wanted to use data in existing databases for analysis purposes, and information systems providing data analysis capabilities, using modeling, simulation, and statistical routines, were in great demand with them. Figure 12–1 shows that of the 1,403 information systems used by managers in the Alloway and Quillard study, 70 percent were considered appropriate. The inquiry and analysis systems in particular were considered valuable. For inquiry systems 81 percent were appropriate, and for analysis systems 97 percent were appropriate.

In short, the Alloway and Quillard study demonstrates an increase in demand for inquiry and analysis systems relative to the demand for operational and exception reporting systems. In another study of managers' information needs, Rockart and Treacy (1981) also concluded that senior managers want to be able to manipulate and analyze existing databases to obtain the information they need to support important decision-making tasks.

CHARACTERISTICS OF THE DECISION-MAKING PROCESS

Before learning about the purpose and features of decision support systems, you should become acquainted with the decision-making process, the types of problems addressed in decision making, the attributes of decision makers, and strategies for decision making. All these concepts have implications for the design of decision support systems.

| Phases of Decision Making | According to Simon (1960) and Mintzberg, Raisinghani, and Theoret (1976), decision making involves three phases. During the first phase, **intelligence,** the decision maker searches for conditions calling for a decision. The decision maker may be reacting to problems or may recognize opportunities. In either case a gap between the existing state and a desired state is a necessary condition for the existence of a decision problem. |

Design is the second phase of decision making. During design, the decision maker develops and analyzes alternative courses of action by either searching for ready-made alternatives or developing a custom-made solution. The third phase of decision making is **choice.** During this phase, the decision maker selects the best alternative.

For a decision situation to occur, the decision maker must be aware of a gap between the existing state and the desired state, must be motivated to solve the problem, and must have the resources to do so. The type of decision problem and the attributes of the decision maker both influence the decision-making strategy.

| Types of Decision Problems | Problems are structured, or semistructured, depending on how familiar the decision maker is with the existing state, the desired state, and the transformation necessary to get from one state to the other. Structured problems are well understood. Pricing customer orders, reordering office supplies, and specifying the wage rate for a new employee are examples of structured decisions. They are routine and can be addressed using standard operating procedures in the form of **algorithms** or **heuristics.** *Algorithms* are sets of standard operations that guarantee a solution to a problem in a finite number of steps. *Heuristics* are rules of thumb that offer procedures or outlines for seeking solutions. |

In organizations, managerial decision problems are semistructured because the decision environment is uncertain, complex, and unstable. A decision maker may be uncertain about the nature of the problem, about the alternative actions he should take, and about how external events may affect the outcome.

| Attributes of the Decision Maker | The attributes of decision makers also affect the types of decision strategies used. These attributes include perceptual ability, information capacity, risk-taking propensity, and aspiration level. |

Perceptual ability refers to the way a decision maker perceives a decision problem. If a decision maker has experience dealing with a similar problem, the problem-solving situation will not seem as complex and as uncertain as in a case where her background with a similar situation is limited.

Information capacity is important because all decision making requires an information base. In complex decision-making situations, decision makers who are receptive to new information are better prepared to handle the cognitive demands of information search when they are faced with difficult or uncertain tasks. In contrast, dogmatic decision makers tend to make rapid decisions based on little information. In either case decision makers resist changing a decision once it has been made.

The other two attributes that account for differences in decision-making behavior are risk-taking propensity and aspiration level. In risky situations, decision makers are more uncertain about outcomes and possible loss of resources. The aspiration level of decision makers also influences their effectiveness in identifying problems, evaluating alternatives, and making choices. In general, decision makers attempt to achieve an optimal standard, and prior experiences of success or failure and knowledge of results influence this standard.

Strategies for Decision Making

The type of decision problem and the attributes of the decision maker influence whether the decision maker will use a **maximizing, satisficing,** or **incrementalizing** strategy (MacGrimmon and Taylor, 1976).

Maximizing.   When the outcome of a decision is clear and the alternatives are well established, the decision maker will make the decision that *maximizes* the desired outcome. Let's say that you are faced with a choice between two alternatives. One of these alternatives offers a 1 percent chance of winning $20,000, and the other alternative offers a 50 percent chance of winning $500. If you multiply the probability of each alternative by its outcome, you will see that the second alternative has a higher expected value.

$$\text{Probability} \times \text{Outcome} = \text{Expected Value}$$
$$.01 \times \$20,000 = 200$$
$$.50 \times 500 = 250$$

A rational decision maker will select the second alternative to optimize the expected value. The maximizing approach assumes that the decision maker is rational and is aware of the probabilities of each alternative.

Satisficing.   Because many decisions are made in situations of uncertainty, decision makers are willing to settle for less than maximum utility. According to Simon, decision makers display rationality only within limits imposed by their experience, background, and awareness of alternatives in a given decision situation. A decision maker will set up a reasonable aspiration level and search for possible alternatives until he finds one that achieves this level. Simon calls this behavior *satisficing* because the decision maker will terminate the search as soon as he or she finds a satisfactory alternative.

Incrementalizing.   In the third decision-making strategy, the decision maker attempts to take small steps away from the existing state toward a desired state. This approach may neglect important outcomes because the alternatives considered are generally familiar to the decision maker.

Implications of Decision Making for Decision Support Systems

Decision support systems are designed to support semistructured decisions in situations in which information is incomplete and where satisficing is a goal. They are developed to support decisions that are so different each time that it would be hard to develop a standard set of procedures for programming them. Such decisions may be specific and may relate to a one-time-only situation.

A decision support system should enable the decision maker to apply the right decision rules to a problem rather than using standard rules that may not apply because of changing conditions. For example, to apply an inventory reorder model designed for slow-moving items to a problem situation involving fast-moving items would be ineffective. As you'll see in the next section, a decision support system provides the decision maker with the flexibility to explore alternatives by using appropriate data and models.

IMPORTANT FEATURES OF DECISION SUPPORT SYSTEMS

The design of a decision support system must take into account the characteristics of decision makers and of the decision-making process. An effective decision support system needs to incorporate a number of features.

Support of Semistructured Decisions

To begin with, a decision support system must support semistructured decisions. Semistructured problems involve a decision-making process that can't be defined before actually going through the process of making the decision. In Chapter 1, a framework for information systems describing operational, tactical, and strategic planning systems was discussed. Although traditional data processing applications support structured decision-making requirements at each of these levels, decision support systems need to support less-structured decision processes.

For example there is a difference between budget analysis and budget preparation, two tactical applications. Budget analysis is a much more structured procedure than budget preparation. Budget analysis requires knowledge of possible cost factors, alternative resource requirements, and future needs. Although budget analysis can be accomplished easily with current or cumulative budget data with a spreadsheet or database program, budget preparation is considerably more challenging. Those responsible for budget preparation tend to be managers with considerable experience in managing projects and with knowledge of the possible cost factors to be considered on a long-term basis.

Support for Database Access and Modeling

Decision support systems (DSS) attempt to combine the use of models or analytic techniques with traditional data access and retrieval functions. A manager can overcome some of the problems associated with traditional information systems by determining what databases can be used, by defining what data analysis techniques are required, and by identifying what outputs are meaningful.

In building a decision support system, you first need to define your information requirements. Ideally, a decision support system should provide a database that serves as a repository of data for easy access and change. Subsets or copies of databases that support transactions information systems are often used in decision support systems. For example, an order history database detailing customer orders over the past 18 months may provide an excellent source of data for a decision support system.

Support for All Phases of the Decision-Making Process

An effective decision support system should support the three phases of the decision-making process: intelligence, design, and choice. As you recall, during the intelligence phase a situation requiring a decision is visualized. During the design phase the problem is defined and alternative solutions are considered. During the choice phase a course of action is selected.

At each phase of the decision-making process, different operations occur. During the intelligence phase, data are collected as a basis for diagnosing a problem or a situation requiring a decision. When alternatives are weighted during the design phase, data may be manipulated or values may be assigned to each alternative. A simulation of the results of the alternatives or statistics describing them may be useful operations for choosing the best option.

An example, making a decision about a new automobile, illustrates some of the activities that take place during the decision-making process. If you were going to buy a new car, you might go through the following steps:

- **Intelligence**—Review automobile maintenance records showing chronic transmission problems. Seek information from dealers and friends about new automobiles.

- **Design**—Establish objectives and criteria for evaluating automobiles. Establish weights illustrating the relative importance of these criteria. Analyze alternative possibilities.
- **Choice**—Generate summary statistics on the evaluation of each automobile.

Chronic problems with an existing automobile might create a situation in which you need to make a decision about purchasing a new car. During the design phase, you may select safety, price, and performance as three important criteria for buying a car. Weights establishing the importance of each of these factors, such as safety (25 percent), price (25 percent), and performance (50 percent), also need to be set. You could get information from consumer reports, dealers, owners, and magazines to help you make comparisons among alternatives and then use summary statistics to provide overall scores for each alternative. These scores should provide evidence supporting a reasonable choice on your part.

A decision support system, as defined previously, provides data for inquiry and analysis. These data can be used in different ways during each phase of the decision-making process. In making a decision about bad debts, different kinds of data are used at each of the three phases of the decision-making process:

- **Intelligence**—a listing of customers with bad debts; a graph of bad debts over time.
- **Design**—a scatterplot of customers by two attributes associated with bad debts used to partition customers into risk groups.
- **Choice**—a report on simulated bad debt losses for each alternative risk group.

Different types of data and analytical techniques are useful at different phases of the decision-making process. A listing of customers with bad debts might create an awareness of the bad debt expense problem. In an analysis of the bad debt situation, the number of customers under 25 years old with bad debts might be contrasted with those over 25 to determine the risk of these two groups. Projecting these bad debt losses over time might provide insight into policies and procedures that could help control losses. For example, if customers under 25 make up a high-risk group and if projections indicate that this risk group will continue to grow, management may take steps to cut policy approvals and to raise premiums to this risk group. Management may also decide to reallocate sales efforts to more profitable buyer groups.

Support for Communications among Decision Makers

Decision support systems must support decision making at all levels of the organization. Because some decisions require communications among decision makers at all levels, decision support systems need to support group decision making. In some cases decisions are made sequentially, with each decision maker responsible for part of the decision before passing it on to the next decision maker. The process of approving a marketing program might be one example. Senior management may decide to expand an advertising budget by 20 percent for two new product lines. In turn, middle management may seek to develop an advertising program, approving media choices and commercial messages. Operational management may need to make further decisions about timing and frequency of commercials.

Other decisions require pooling knowledge and result from negotiation and interaction among decision makers. An example of this kind of decision might be the choice of a conference site for a professional meeting. Each member of the conference planning committee might have specific preferences based on geographical location and travel-related expenses for conference participants. Negotiations might bring out the advantages and disadvantages of several alternative sites. After these options are evaluated, the decision can be made in everyone's best interest. A decision support system should support interaction among decision makers.

Availability of Memory Aids

In making decisions managers constantly have to recall information or the results of operations conducted at previous times. Decision makers need *memory aids,* so a decision support system should provide them. Work spaces for displaying data representations or for preserving intermediate results from operations are useful. For example, monthly budget data stored in spreadsheets from prior months could be used for reference. Triggers reminding a decision maker to perform certain operations are also helpful. A trigger, for example, may remind the user to calculate and project the costs of various investment alternatives before trying to complete a cash flow analysis.

Availability of Control Aids for Decision Making

A final important feature of a decision support system is the availability of *control aids* for training and system use. Many managers feel some anxiety about using computer-based systems. Without effective training in the early phases of computer operation, managers may give up and return to paper-and-pencil methods. Help screens, menus, and prompts are valuable software features that make the training process easier and contribute to the development of language skills.

In summary, a decision support system should support all phases of the decision-making process, have short- and long-term memory aids, provide effective control aids, and support semistructured and unstructured types. It should also support data access and modeling and should facilitate communications among decision makers.

The design of decision support systems creates opportunities for managers to determine their information needs, to select appropriate tools, and to develop outputs they can use. In the next section you will learn about the tools for decision support systems.

COMPONENTS OF A DECISION SUPPORT SYSTEM

Data Components of a Decision Support System

The main database concern for a decision support system is that the right data are available and that these data can be manipulated in the desired fashion. This is sometimes difficult because data that is gathered from transactions processing systems must be reorganized and verified before becoming useful for decision support. This problem is addressed using the data warehouse concept.

Building a Data Warehouse

Most databases that support business information systems are not organized to meet the decision support needs of managers. Some of the problems with existing databases are that data are often stored in highly technical formats and the same data may be represented differently in different systems. Most important, managers cannot get the answers they need to day-to-day questions, such as What is the impact of a pricing special for a specific product line this month, as compared with the impact of a special promotional offer on that same product line for the same month last year?

Most existing operational-level databases are not organized to make them appropriate for general analysis-type and query applications. Originally, companies addressed this problem by creating frozen data extracts for query purposes. The problem with this approach was that these extracts were frozen for one point in time, and they could become outdated readily.

A data warehouse is a database that exists separately from operational-level systems. With access to a data warehouse, managers can make fact-based decisions addressing many business issues, such as which pricing strategies are most effective, which customers are most profitable, and which products have the highest margin.

The process of creating a data warehouse is straightforward. First the data are "scrubbed" to ensure that they are meaningful, consistent, and accurate. Then the data are loaded into relational tables so that they can be used to support both analysis and query applications. Often data must be pulled from multiple production systems and external sources. For example, in one data warehouse application, data had to be pulled from 3,000,000 customer records housed in seven legacy systems. This difficult process includes identifying the relevant data, blending them, and scrubbing them to ensure validity. Ultimately, the data need to conform to the logical data model that has been established.

Data Mining and Intelligent Agents

Once the data warehouse is created, managers need to use tools that enable them to access and to query the data they need. This process is called data mining, and the tools are referred to as intelligent agents. Intelligent agents are pieces of software that managers can use to search through relational databases for relevant data. They can be used to analyze trends, to identify exception conditions, and to track results. Data mining tools can also be used to identify patterns in the data, to infer rules from these patterns, and to refine these rules based on the examination of additional data.

The types of results which can come from data mining include:

- Associations—the process of linking together events. For example, you might want to link two courses that students often take together so that they are not scheduled at the same time.
- Sequences—the process of identifying patterns. For example, you might want to identify a sequence of courses that students take over multiple semesters.
- Classifications—the process of organizing data into patterns. For example, you might want to classify students into subgroups, based on criteria such as length of time spent in degree completion (less than or equal to four years; over four years, etc.).
- Clusters—the process of inferring rules about certain subgroups that distinguish them from other subgroups. For example, you might want to cluster students by area of interest, age, and job experience.

The major advantage of a data warehouse is that it can provide managers with the data they need as well as the tools that are useful in analyzing these data. The concept of the data warehouse frees information systems professionals from dealing with day-to-day custom programming of reports and queries and provides managers with the real keys to decision support. It takes the theory of decision support and puts it into practice. In addition, many data warehouse tools are equipped with graphical user interfaces to provide ease of use.

Model Component

The goal of model management is to help decision makers understand a phenomenon about which they are making a choice. For example, in developing an advertising campaign, it is useful to know whether a product appeals to young, unmarried professionals or to young, married blue-collar workers. Dozens of business questions require the analysis of alternative design options, and models are useful tools in establishing a framework for this type of analysis.

Each type of model has a slightly different application context. For example:

- Statistical models include regression analyis, analysis of variance, and exponential smoothing.
- Accounting models include such processes as depreciation, tax planning, and cost analysis.
- Personnel models include in-basket simulations and role-playing exercises.
- Marketing models include analysis of advertising strategy, consumer choice, and consumer switching behavior.

The challenge of creating a decision support system entails knowing what models to include and knowing how to make them meaningful for the decision maker.

Models also have different characteristics. Some are experiential, and some are objective. Experiential models include judgments and expert opinions. For example, a physician might use an experiential model to diagnose a heart condition. Objective models mean that data are analyzed independently of the decision-maker's experiences. For example, using the Bridge Information System, an analytical tool for investment portfolios, a securities analyst can obtain access to real-time quotes, historical data, and models for analyzing these data. If one investment advisor plots the return on an investment option, the results will be the same as those received by another investment advisor plotting the return on investment on that same investment option.

Complete enumeration, algorithmic, heuristic, and simulation are among the methodologies used to build models.

Complete enumeration is often supported by the use of neural networks. A neural network consists of many simple processing elements which cooperate in an interconnected network. Each processing element is responsible for generating an output, based upon the nature and weighting of the inputs it receives.

Neural networks can help solve problems which involve complex pattern matching, incomplete information, and large numbers of transactions. A neural network uses a set of cases to "train" itself. After the network is trained with training samples, another set of cases is used to test its performance. Rather than deducting rules, a "trained" neural network may land on decision criteria which may even come into conflict with traditional or conventional rules, but the results of the decision may be good. Neural networks can be successfully "trained" to make decisions using historical data such as credit approval and mortgage insurance underwriting. For example, a neural network system was constructed for a major bank in Chicago to identify suspicious credit card transactions as a basis for locating stolen cards. Before the use of the neural network, an expert system had been used to identify dubious transactions through an analysis of rapid increases in the number of transactions affecting certain cards. When the neural network was used, the analysis showed that numerous small-volume transactions were a more effective indicator of stolen cards because many credit card thieves were using small purchases as a means of determining whether or not stolen cards were still being accepted.

Algorithms, or algorithmic models, include a set of procedures that can be repeated in order to achieve a result. Algorithms support many types of business decisions, including decisions on how to place investments, on when to advertise products, and on how to assign staff to projects.

Another basis for establishing models is heuristics. Heuristics are rules of thumb that are applied to the analysis of large or ill-structured problems. Heuristic models are often used in the design of expert systems because these models enable users to apply rules to replicate a solution technique that an expert would use in solving such an ill-structured problem.

The fourth approach to modeling is simulation. In simulation, the goal is to imitate reality. You could simulate the workings of a factory, the operations of a business, or the governmental climate of a country. In so doing, you could develop preliminary analyses of changing strategies in each of these environments. For example, what would happen if the business had to face a major shortage of an important raw material for a long time? What would happen if the market for products and services were to dramatically change? What would happen if international competition were markedly different? Simulation can address all these questions.

THE TOOLS OF DECISION SUPPORT

The tools of decision support include database query, modeling, data analysis, and display software. A comprehensive tool kit for Decision Support Systems would include software supporting all these application areas. Examples of software tools falling into these four categories are given in Figure 12–2.

Tools supporting *database query and report generation* use mainframe-, minicomputer-, and microcomputer-based databases. Ingres, Oracle, and Informix are database systems on mainframes, minicomputers, and microcomputers. Managers frequently use microcomputer-based database tools such as Access and Paradox. Using a database query tool, the user could also generate a report with a title, page headings, column headings, subtotals, and totals. See Figure 12–3.

Figure 12–2

Software tools for decision support systems

DATABASED SOFTWARE	MODEL-BASED SOFTWARE	STATISTICAL SOFTWARE	DISPLAY-BASED SOFTWARE
Access	Excel	SAS-PC	PowerPoint
Paradox	QuattroPro	SPSS-PC	Freelance Graphics
Approach	Lotus 1-2-3		

Figure 12–3

A database query

LIST OF PRODUCTS BY CATEGORY
13-Apr-97

Category:	Product:	Product ID:	Quantity per Unit:	Units in Stock:
BEVERAGES				
	Chai	1	10 boxes × 20 bags	39
	Chang	2	24–12 oz bottles	17
	Chartreuse verte	39	750 cc per bottle	69
	Côte de Blaye	38	12–75 cl bottles	17
	Ipoh Coffee	43	16–500 g tins	17
	Lakkalikööri	76	500 ml	57
	Laughing Lumberjack Lager	67	24–12 oz bottles	52
	Outback Lager	70	24–355 ml bottles	15
	Rhönbräu Klosterbier	75	24–0.5 l bottles	125
	Sasquatch Ale	34	24–12 oz bottles	111
	Steeleye Stout	35	24–12 oz bottles	20
Total: 11				
CONDIMENTS				
	Aniseed Syrup	3	12–550 ml bottles	13
	Chef Anton's Cajun Seasoning	4	48–6 oz jars	53
	Genen Shouyu	15	24–250 ml bottles	39
	Grandma's Boysenberry Spread	6	12–8 oz jars	120
	Gula Malacca	44	20–2 kg bags	27
	Louisiana Fiery Hot Pepper Sauce	65	32–8 oz bottles	76
	Louisiana Hot Spiced Okra	66	24–8 oz jars	4
	Northwoods Cranberry Sauce	8	12–12 oz jars	6
	Original Frankfurter grüne Soβe	77	12 boxes	32
	Sirop d'érable	61	24–500 ml bottles	113
	Vegie-spread	63	15–625 g jars	24
Total: 11				
CONFECTIONS				
	Chocolade	48	10 pkgs.	15
	Gumbär Gummibärchen	26	10–250 g bags	15
	Maxilaku	49	24–50 g pkgs.	10
	NuNuCa Nuβ-Nougat-Creme	25	20–450 g glasses	76
	Pavlova	16	32–500 g boxes	29
	Schoggi Schokolade	27	100–100 g pieces	49
	Scottish Longbreads	68	10 boxes × 8 pieces	6
	Sir Rodney's Marmalade	20	30 gift boxes	40
	Sir Rodney's Scones	21	24 pkgs. × 4 pieces	3
	Tarte au sucre	62	48 pies	17
	Teatime Chocolate Biscuits	19	10 boxes × 12 pieces	25
	Valkoinen suklaa	50	12–100 g bars	65
	Zaanse koeken	47	10–4 oz boxes	36
Total: 13				

Model-based analysis tools such as spreadsheet software enable managers to design models that incorporate business rules and assumptions. Microcomputer-based spreadsheet programs such as Excel and QuattroPro are designed to support financial modeling and analysis.

A good example of a spreadsheet application is a cash flow analysis. Figure 12–4 shows a cash flow statement for a small business. The spreadsheet includes formulas that calculate expenses, profits, and cash flow. In developing this spreadsheet, the manager projected an inflation rate of 10 percent. Using this assumption, the free cash flow at the end of five years is $3,351. By building in different assumptions, such as changes in inflation, operating expenses, and revenues, the manager could use the formulas in the spreadsheet to recalculate values such as total expenses, pretax profit, and cash flow. A spreadsheet is a valuable analysis tool because it enables managers to analyze the impacts of different 'what-if?' situations.

Figure 12–4

Cash flow analysis using a spreadsheet

	Year 1	Year 2	Year 3	Year 4	Year 5
REVENUE	50,000	55,000	60,000	66,550	73,205
EXPENSES					
General & Admin.					
Salaries	19,500	21,450	23,595	23,955	28,550
Payroll Taxes	5,000	5,500	6,050	6,655	7,320
Office Expenses	6,500	7,150	7,865	8,652	9,517
Professional Fees	1,000	1,100	1,210	1,331	1,464
Travel	1,500	1,650	1,815	1,997	2,196
Ent. and Promo.	6,000	6,600	7,260	7,986	8,785
Total G & A	39,500	43,450	47,795	52,574	57,832
Total Financing	8,318	8,318	8,318	8,318	8,318
Interest	8,125	8,094	8,057	8,015	7,966
Principal	193	224	261	303	352
Principal Remaining	49,807	49,583	49,322	49,019	48,666
TOTAL EXPENSES	47,625	51,543	55,852	60,589	65,797
PRE-TAX PROFIT	2,375	3,457	4,648	5,961	7,408
Income Tax	1,188	1,728	2,324	2,980	3,704
AFTER-TAX PROFIT	1,188	1,728	2,324	2,980	3,704
Repayment of Debt	193	224	261	303	352
FREE CASH FLOW	995	1,504	2,063	2,677	3,351

Source: Adapted from A. Williams, *What IF* (New York: John Wiley & Sons, 1984).

Statistical analysis software such as SAS-PC and SPSS-PC supports market researchers, operations research analysts, and other professionals using statistical analysis functions.

The final category of decision support software is *display-based software*. Graphic displays of output generated from Excel spreadsheets, for example, are very effective in management presentations. Microcomputer-based tools such as Harvard Graphics and PowerPoint display graphics output in the form of pie charts, bar charts, and graphs.

You can get a better understanding of the nature and scope of decision support systems by learning about the experiences of managers who have developed them. The following case studies will give you insight into the reasons that managers develop decision support systems.

CASES IN MANAGERIAL DECISION SUPPORT SYSTEMS

The following cases describe decision support applications in a food marketing company, a commercial bank, an insurance company, and a financial services company. All these systems were developed by users serving as computer specialists within various functional areas, including production, finance, and marketing.

A Production Planning System

The first case involves a food marketing company that produces food products in regional plants and distributes them to branch warehouses around the country. Two production planning analysts with considerable computer skills designed a decision support system to determine target inventories in branch warehouses. To build this system, the user-developers used FOCUS, a database query language, to access a sales history database consisting of 3,500,000 records. Based on the analysis of sales trends of various food products in certain regions, managers developed a sales forecast depicting how much inventory of each product would be needed in each branch warehouse each month. The sales forecast indicated, for example, the number of boxes of spaghetti sauce needed to accommodate sales orders that would be filled by a branch warehouse in the Northeast region.

An example of the sales forecast is shown in Figure 12–5. This report shows the difference, or variance, between the target inventory level for each product and its actual inventory. In the case of regular spaghetti sauce, for example, the variance shows that actual inventory is 9,000 cases less than target inventory. The target inventory established in this report is used as an input into the production plan, and the production planner may want to increase production of regular spaghetti sauce because she knows that the potential demand for the product is greater during the summer months.

Inventory levels are determined for each branch warehouse not only to serve distribution requirements but also to minimize transportation costs. If demand for spaghetti sauce increased in the Southeast, for example, management would know to redistribute target inventory levels for this product to a branch warehouse in the Southeast region. Continuing to maintain high inventory levels in the Northeast warehouse would require shipping goods much too far to accommodate consumer demand.

After the sales forecast and target inventory levels for each branch warehouse were determined, these data became input into planned production requirements for

Figure 12–5

Forecast of target
inventory levels

```
SALES FORECAST
NORTHEAST REGION
June 1, 1998


PRODUCT     PRODUCT          SALES       TARGET      ACTUAL
CODE        DESC             FORECAST    INVENTORY   INVENTORY   VARIANCE
                            (IN CASES)


SS101       SPSAUCE-REG      60,000      22,000      13,000      (9,000)
SS102       SPSAUCE-GARLIC   35,000      18,000      27,000       9,000
SS103       SPSAUCE-MUSH     52,000      25,000      20,000      (5,000)
SS104       SPSAUCE-VEG      22,000      15,000      18,000       3,000
```

the various plants serving the warehouses. This system greatly minimized the cost of excess inventory being produced and shipped to branch warehouses. The production planning system also minimized distribution costs and produced overall better service to customers.

A Financial Control System

The second case is a financial decision support system developed at a commercial bank. A functional specialist within the corporate controller's office designed a cost measurement system to provide unit cost data for each bank service. These cost data were originally created and used to determine how to price the bank's products (for example, how much to charge for 2,000 wire transfers).

After several months of using the cost measurement system, its developer recognized that its value was potentially greater than originally anticipated. The availability of cost data for every bank product allowed the bank to allocate the unit costs of its products to expense centers such as lending areas. Because expense centers were aware of the costs of the products they sold, they were able to determine which products provided the highest profit margins. Figure 12-6 shows a profitability analysis of financial services based on unit cost data. For example, if offering traveler's checks was a much more profitable service than providing money orders, bank personnel could demonstrate greater profitability by focusing their sales efforts on marketing traveler's checks. What was originally designed as a monitoring system to store unit cost data became an effective tactical system for marketing the most profitable services.

An International Loan System

A third case depicts a decision support system designed to monitor existing international loan portfolios. Its developer, a computer specialist in the international loan operations department, set up a database of international loan accounts using a database query and reporting language. This database provided loan information, such as interest income and loan balances, by geographical area and by type of obligor. The system enabled users to extract the names of all obligors with loan balances over a certain amount or within a certain geographical region. A sample query, shown in Figure 12-7, requests the names of all loan accounts with balances over $250,000 in Central American countries.

Although the original purpose of the international loan system was to create timely access to loan account information, the system fulfilled a much more useful purpose. By analyzing current loan balances by type of obligor and by type of credit

Figure 12–6

Profitability analysis of financial services

```
MIDTOWN BRANCH
PROFITABILITY ANALYSIS
MARCH 16, 1998                                              GROSS
                                                           MARGIN
             NUMBER OF  TOTAL     UNIT    TOTAL            AS A %
SEVICE       TRANS      CHARGES   COST    COST    PROFIT   OF SALES
TYPE

MONEY ORDER   12,000   $ 2,160    .13    $1,560   $  600    28%
WIRE TRANS   120,000   $ 4,800    .20    $2,400   $2,400    50%
TRAV CHECKS   87,000   $ 7,830    .06    $5,250   $2,580    33%


TOTAL        219,500   $14,790           $9,210   $5,580    38%
```

Figure 12–7

A sample query of an international loan database

```
INTERNATIONAL LOANS
CENTRAL AMERICA
MARCH 1, 1998

ACCT  ACCOUNT      CREDIT   LOAN        LOAN        YTD        OVERDUE
NO    NAME         RATING   AMOUNT      BALANCE     INTEREST   AMOUNT

0311  RF CHEMICAL     B    $2,500,000  $1,450,000  $125,000   $ 25,000
0422  DIAZ CONSTR    AA    $1,780,000  $1,700,000  $ 10,500          0
0673  PANAM HOSPITAL  A    $3,325,000  $2,850,000  $ 68,650   $450,000
```

rating, the user could determine the riskiness of the current loan portfolio. This information could then be used to monitor future loan decisions. For example, if the current loan portfolio showed large outstanding loan balances for accounts in Latin American countries with credit ratings of B, then it might be risky to loan additional funds to accounts in this area.

The financial decision support systems designed to determine the unit costs of financial services and to monitor the riskiness of loan portfolios were effective tactical systems. Each system was designed to improve the profitability of banking services and international loan operations by providing information that would enable management to allocate resources effectively. These systems were decision support systems because they supported ad hoc query and reporting requirements. In each case outputs were generated when they were needed, not according to a fixed schedule. Each system was designed to be flexible and changeable so that different questions could be asked. The characteristics of these decision support systems in the production planning, financial control, and international loan functions are summarized in Figure 12–8.

These case studies illustrate a number of points about the development of decision support systems. First, in all of these examples, relevant databases were identified and constructed. User-friendly database and spreadsheet tools were used to extract and to manipulate these data as needed.

Second, users were responsible for designing these decision support systems. Data processing personnel would not have designed these projects because of their low priority or because of insufficient resources. However, each of these systems sup-

Figure 12–8

Decision support systems

	FOOD MARKETING COMPANY	COMMERCIAL BANK	INTERNATIONAL LOAN OPERATIONS
Primary users	Production analysts	Financial analysis	Loan analysts
Databases utilized	Sales history	Unit cost data	International loan accounts
Key tasks	Determining target inventory levels for products	Assessing unit costs of financial products and services	Assessing risk of international loan accounts
Software	FOCUS (4GL)	Lotus 1-2-3 (Spreadsheet)	Microcomputer-based database

ported important business decisions such as production planning, product marketing, and loan applicant screening.

Third, some of these decision support systems were in constant evolution. Most of these projects were initiated by constructing simple databases for query and reporting purposes, but several of them evolved into important analysis systems. For example, the original purpose of the international loan system was to provide easy access to loan account records. The system eventually evolved into an analytical system providing information about the potential riskiness of future loan decisions.

In this section you have learned about the nature and scope of various decision support systems. The next section explains how decision support systems are developed.

THE DEVELOPMENT OF DECISION SUPPORT SYSTEMS

The development of decision support systems requires an **adaptive design** process that involves the interaction of a user and builder with the information system. Decision support systems development starts when a user identifies a problem area and begins to think of information that would contribute to an understanding of it. A model decision support system is built with close cooperation between a builder and a user. This decision support systems is designed by a builder, tried out by a user, and continually modified based on the user's evaluation. This continuous or iterative process encourages short-lived ad hoc systems that can be junked when they are no longer needed and refined as the user's needs change.

The dynamic relationship among the user, designer, and system is depicted in Keen and Gambino's adaptive design framework, shown in Figure 12–9. This framework illustrates links among the user, designer, and system. The first link is the cognitive loop between the system and the user. The system-user link shows managerial learning as the decision support systems stimulates changes in the user's problem-solving process. The user-system link illustrates how the user envisions new approaches to problem solving as she uses the system.

The second link is the implementation loop between the user and the designer. The designer is a facilitator who attempts to understand the user's requirements and to customize the system accordingly, as illustrated in the designer-user link. The user,

Figure 12–9

Adaptive design framework

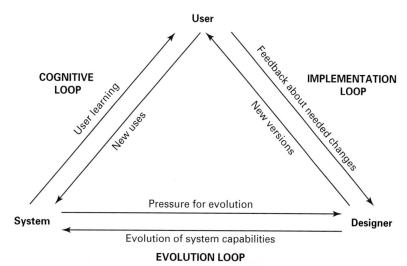

Source: Adapted from P. G. W. Keen and T. J. Gambino, "Building a Decision Support System: The Mythical Man Month Revisited," In *Building Effective Decision Support Systems,* eds. R. Sprague and E. Carlson (Englewood Cliffs, NJ: Prentice Hall, 1982), p. 153.

in turn, provides feedback to the designer on needed adaptations, as shown in the user-designer link.

The third loop is the evolution loop, which refers to the continuing evolution of system functions. As managerial learning occurs and personalized uses of the system evolve, pressure for evolution (system-designer link) develops. This pressure results in adding new capabilities to the system, as illustrated by the designer-system loop.

Keen and Gambino's adaptive design framework provides a conceptual view of the decision support systems development process and the roles involved. The framework illustrates the flexibility of the decision support systems approach. Users' concepts of the problems they are addressing change as they use their systems. As a result the actual decision support system is likely to differ from the original version. One of the key elements of this process is experimentation because trying new versions provides the learning required for the system to evolve.

The Decision Support Systems Development Life Cycle

As a user you will be involved in many phases of the decision support systems development process. These phases are summarized in Figure 12–10. The first step is *planning,* or diagnosing a problem requiring the development of a decision support system. A user may need information that is not available in weekly or monthly exception reports. Users often react to concrete, immediate information needs when they recognize a decision support systems requirement.

Once a need is defined, the user begins to identify relevant approaches to addressing it. This process is called *application research.* The user must pay some attention to whether information can be obtained from present information systems, perhaps exploring whether microcomputer-based software or mainframe-based database systems might be possible alternatives to satisfying the need. Vendors and consultants might also be considered.

Figure 12–10

The decision support systems development life cycle

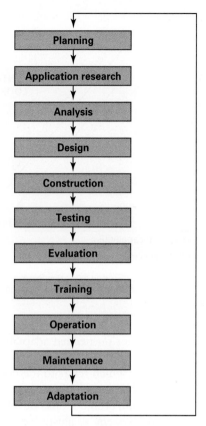

Source: Adapted from C. L. Meador and P. G. W. Keen, "Setting Priorities for DSS Development," *MIS Quarterly* 8, no. 2 (1984), p. 125.

During the *analysis* phase, the user considers the overall feasibility of pursuing the project—in technical resources, support requirements, and hardware and software needs. If enough benefits are envisioned to justify developing a prototype or preliminary model of the system, the project moves to the *design* phase, during which system components are specified.

During *system construction* the technical design is implemented and then *tested* to determine whether the system performs in accordance with its original design. Assuming the system is technically adequate, the designer can determine how well the system satisfies the users' needs during system *evaluation*. The capabilities of the system can be demonstrated to other members of the user community, and top-level managers can be oriented to the system and its features. Actual users of the system must then be *trained* in its structure and operations. Finally, the system goes into operation.

Because decision support systems are constantly modified, *maintenance* is ongoing. Changes are made during *adaptation* that can reinitiate the entire decision support systems design cycle and the activities already described.

As users are given the tools to develop their own systems, systems designers must respond by providing consulting, training, and ongoing support. Systems analysts must be retrained, and user-developers within functional areas must take on the responsibility of encouraging learning among their peers and maintaining critical departmental systems.

The Benefits of Decision Support Systems

Investments in decision support systems technology, development efforts, and support are growing substantially. Because new versions of decision support systems are constantly evolving, their costs are difficult to quantify. Measuring the benefits of decision support systems also is difficult because many of these benefits are qualitative. Some of these benefits follow.

The ability to examine more alternatives.   Spreadsheet tools make it possible to analyze alternative ways of allocating resources in a business and to visualize the impact of these options on cash flow. Scenarios that would have taken days to construct and analyze can be viewed in minutes.

The ability to achieve a better understanding of the business.   A decision support system can help managers analyze the long-range impact of a new marketing venture or a potential acquisition decision in a reasonable time, making it possible to foresee possible pitfalls and to avoid future problems.

The ability to respond quickly to unexpected situations.   Confronted with new tax legislation, many companies have to analyze the impact of new requirements on profitability. Without decision support systems tools, this type of analysis would be time-consuming and limited. With decision support systems, businesses can construct new models and quickly adapt them to changes in business policy and market share. The models can generate new results in days, not weeks.

The ability to carry out ad hoc types of reporting and analysis.   Many managers want to ask questions of existing databases and to pull out data relevant to current business operations. For example, a marketing manager can extract data on sales of a new product line to department store customers in the Northeast within minutes, rather than waiting for a monthly report that overaggregates these sales data and fails to highlight important market trends.

The ability to provide timely information for control of ongoing operations.   Information from a decision support system, for example, can provide a better picture of detailed expenses by company, by division, and by department. A report of energy expenses, broken down by division, enables managers to spot deviations from prior years more quickly and to take remedial action to conserve resources.

The ability to save time and costs.   If a manager takes five hours to make a budget forecast using a spreadsheet when this analysis would have taken 20 hours to complete using a calculator, the time-effectiveness of accomplishing this task improves substantially. The ability to perform what-if analyses improves the quality of a budget forecast.

The ability to make better decisions.   Decision support systems allow managers to consider issues and alternatives that they may not have explored before. Increased depth and sophistication of analysis are possible. Decision support systems help managers explore complex issues, such as marketing strategy and personnel productivity, using relevant data analysis. Access to these data gives managers an opportunity to make better-informed decisions and to substantiate the decisions they have made.

The Risks of Decision Support Systems

One of the major motivations behind the development of decision support systems is users' frustration with long systems development cycles, frozen requirements specifications, and unresponsive maintenance procedures. With the availability of fourth-generation languages and microcomputer-based software, managers can design information systems that would not have had high priority because of their departmental scope and limited number of users. One of the major benefits of decision support systems is that users can analyze their own requirements, rather than rely on a systems analyst to understand and to specify these requirements for them.

However, user development has risks. You should be aware of these risks and how to deal with them. The following issues occur when users try to develop their own information systems.

Lack of Quality Assurance

Quality assurance refers to procedures for data validation and testing, documentation, and backup and recovery that are an integral part of a good system. Without adequate validation of input data, output printed on reports may not be correct. Inadequate documentation may result in losing hours spent designing a system. In one organization, for example, a user spent six months developing a system for sales analysis that everyone began to depend on for weekly reports. When the developer suddenly left the firm, the application was lost because no documentation existed. Lack of backup and recovery—another problem—may result in loss of critical data and time-consuming manual rebuilding of these files.

Lack of Data Security

Lack of data security is another issue affecting user-developed decision support systems. Password security for microcomputer-based data management systems may be inadequate or nonexistent, leaving many users to resort to such procedures as key access to hardware or physically locking up diskettes.

Failure to Specify Correct Requirements

Users can visualize their immediate, short-term needs but find it more difficult to understand ongoing or long-term requirements. In one firm, for example, a user failed to keep a log of monthly transactions that was needed for year-end reporting. A systems analyst, serving as a technical expert in systems design, could have recommended keeping that log.

Requirements analysis generally involves validating the logic of a model or calculation used in data analysis. In the design of decision support systems, outputs are constantly modified and the logic used in data analysis often changes. These changes introduce the chance of error, especially if the logic being used is not continually reviewed and documented. If their logic is not validated, computer-based decision support systems may be no better than their paper-and-pencil counterparts of the past.

Failure to Understand Design Alternatives

One of the common problems in user development is a mismatch between software and design requirements. Users in one office, for example, designed a microcomputer database to store information about prospective students without anticipating the growth in file size. After six months, the prospect data file had expanded to close to 100,000 records, and simple operations such as sorting records by ZIP code were no longer feasible to run on a microcomputer. If a systems analyst had assessed the short- and long-term needs of the users in advance, the feasibility of various design options, including microcomputer, minicomputer, and mainframe approaches, could have been considered.

GROUP DECISION SUPPORT SYSTEMS

Up to now, you have learned about decision support systems that managers use individually to make decisions. However, many decisions occur in groups, and computer-based technology now supports group decision making, too. A **group decision support system (GDSS)** is an interactive computer-based system that facilitates the solution of semistructured problems by a set of decision makers working together in a group.

Just like a decision support system, a group decision support system includes a database, a model base, and software supporting group processes. Software might be used to summarize members' ideas, to report votes, to calculate the weights of decision alternatives, and to anonymously record ideas. In the group decision support situation, a group facilitator coordinates the use of the technology in the process of conducting the meeting.

Group decision support can take place in four scenarios: the decision room, the local decision network, teleconferencing, and remote decision making. See Figure 12–11.

The decision room is like a traditional meeting room, with the addition of computers. Each member has a computer terminal. Members can interact with each other, both verbally and by computer. A display screen in the front of the room is used to present ideas and to analyze alternatives. Take, for example, a set of executives meeting to make a merger/acquisition decision. Computer-generated information on projected sales, cost constraints, and market statistics may be available while members are discussing personnel and organizational considerations.

The second type of group decision-making scenario is the local decision network. In this situation, the group members are located at workstations in the privacy of their offices. A central processor stores the group decision support software, and the local area network provides intercommunication. At Chemical Bank, one executive used the local decision networking idea to gain insight about fears and anxieties related to the potential merger between Chemical and Manufacturer's Hanover Bank. He instituted the Rumor Mill, a shared electronic database where employees could express their views. He even took time to answer their questions via the network, thus quieting fears about job loss and circumventing the gossip mill.

The third situation is teleconferencing. Here, decision rooms are located in major cities so that groups can meet with each other. At the University of Minnesota Medical School, for example, scientists meet regularly with their colleagues via videoconferencing. At BASF, a group vice president for carpet products meets with his counterparts at 24 BASF sites via videoconferencing—he and his peers jointly view carpet samples, edit memos, and sign approvals on capital budgeting projects.

Figure 12–11

Models for group decision support

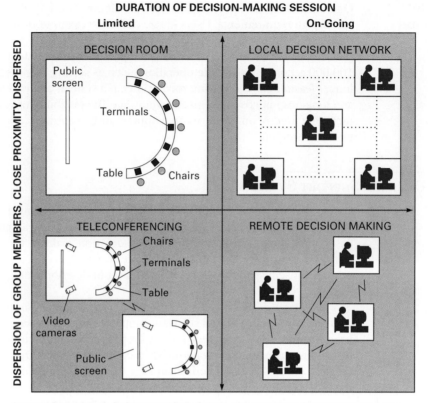

DURATION OF DECISION-MAKING SESSION

Source: Adapted from G. DeSanctis and R. B. Gallupe, "Group Decision Support Systems: A New Frontier," *Database,* Winter 1985, pp. 190–201.

In the fourth situation, remote decision-making groups in geographically remote locations are tied together via a long-distance telecommunications network. At Johnson and Higgins, the largest privately held insurance brokerage firm in the world, customized group decision support software is used for electronic problem solving. Electronic forums tie together brokers in remote locations. These electronic forums allow brokers to request help on sticky problems or to volunteer solutions to issues that are troubling other brokers. A request for help goes out to and comes back from 50 sources, and everyone benefits from the interaction.

Group Decision Support Software. Group decision support systems are designed to facilitate active participation by all members. The software does everything from facilitating the exchange of information among members to providing automated tools for discussion and problem solving. Some of the facilities for group decision support are shown in Figure 12–12.

Some of the advanced features that group decision-making software supports are planning, uncertainty reduction, resource allocation, and consensus building. Some systems provide automated tools for meeting management, such as automated parliamentary procedures or automated *Roberts' Rules of Order* (see Figure 12–13).

As you can see, group decision support systems can facilitate planning through the use of electronic brainstorming tools and planning tools such as PERT. Group decision support systems also encourage choice, using tools for weighing preferences, voting, and consensus building. Tools that are used for resolving conflicts include displaying members' opinions and automatic mediation.

Figure 12–12

Basic features of GDSS software

GROUP PROBLEM	GDSS FEATURE
• Sending and receiving information	• Electronic messaging
• Display of notes, graphs, and tables	• Common viewing screen
• Reluctance of some members to speak	• Anonymous input
• Failure to organize ideas	• Summary and display of votes
• Failure to quantify preferences	• Display of ranking schemes

Figure 12–13

Advanced features of GDSS software

GROUP PROBLEM	GDSS FEATURE
• Need for planning and scheduling	• Planning models (PERT, CPM)
• Decision aids for dealing with uncertainty	• Probability assessment models
• Decision analytic aids for resource allocation problems	• Budget allocation models
• Desire to enhance formalized decision procedures	• Automated parliamentary procedures

Without question, group decision support systems change the nature of meetings. Anonymous input methods encourage people to participate more openly and equally in group discussions. Anonymous communications also reduce the probability that any one member will dominate the discussion and facilitate "democratic" interaction. Members are more willing to suggest controversial views. Because diverse ideas are offered, achieving a consensus view in a group decision support environment can be difficult.

Use of group decision support technology can improve the quality of decisions by encouraging open input of ideas, evaluation of various solutions, and selection of an alternative based upon its merits rather than just a compromise. Participants may sense a more democratic environment in which power and influence are difficult to gain. Overall, the effectiveness of the group's decision making should improve.

ARTIFICIAL INTELLIGENCE AND EXPERT SYSTEMS

Artificial intelligence (AI) is concerned with the creation of computer programs that do things that require intelligence. In other words, artificial intelligence means programming a computer to perform activities that if done by a person would be thought to require intelligence. The field of artificial intelligence includes the areas of natural-language processing, robotics, machine vision, and expert systems.

Natural-language processing means programming computers to understand language. For example, a bank customer could ask a computer, What is my bank balance? and the computer would respond with the proper amount. The problem with natural-language processing systems is that English can be unclear. For example, if a traveler asked a natural-language system, What is the temperature in New York? the computer would have to know if the traveler meant the state of New York or New York City. Other English statements, such as We saw the ship with a telescope, can be interpreted in several ways and cause further natural-language processing problems.

Another application of artificial intelligence is robotics. Robots can be programmed to handle specialized tasks such as cutting, drilling, painting, and welding. They are particularly good at performing the same motions, again and again, day after day. They can also perform dangerous or difficult tasks that humans prefer not to do.

In Japanese factories, robots have been put on the assembly line to assemble copiers, automobiles, cameras, and electronic equipment. They are also being introduced into the factories of such American manufacturers as IBM and General Dynamics Corporation. General Dynamics, for example, uses robots to drill holes and to insert rivets in its F-16 aircraft. Other manufacturers view robotics as key to the improvement of manufacturing productivity in the 1990s.

Machine vision, another application of artificial intelligence, has been used to improve the capabilities of robots. For instance, robots with machine vision in an electronics assembly plant can take a snapshot of the circuit board being worked on and then insert components in the proper place. Robots also use machine vision systems to determine where to insert rivets in Ford trucks on the assembly line. The major limitation of machine vision at the present time is that it can handle only very specific tasks.

Expert systems development is the application of artificial intelligence that is having the greatest impact on the business community. In this chapter you learned how managers use decision support systems to analyze information for problem solving. An expert system differs from a decision support system in that the former uses rule-based or expert knowledge to solve problems. The expert system acts like an expert consultant, asking for information, applying this information to the rules it has learned, and drawing conclusions.

EXPERT SYSTEMS AND DECISION SUPPORT SYSTEMS

Managers build decision support systems to obtain the data they need to solve unstructured problems. Many of these applications use database query and modeling tools to generate reports and to perform straightforward data analysis tasks. Expert systems tools and techniques can be built into a decision support system in order to improve the quality of the decision-making process. One way to improve this process is by including heuristic modeling techniques that replicate the reasoning processes of an expert and allow the system to address poorly structured problems more effectively.

A decision support system gives control to the decision maker for acquiring and evaluating information and for making the final decision. In contrast, an expert system provides the intelligence to solve problems within a specific domain. That is, the system makes the decision, not the individual. In Figure 12-14 you can see some of the characteristics that distinguish an expert system from a decision support system.

Expert systems tools can be added to a decision support system to extend its capabilities for performing functions that a regular decision support system cannot perform. An expert system can build a knowledge base to help the decision maker understand problems and alternatives. Unlike traditional decision support tools, which are used to invoke a series of procedures in a predetermined manner, expert systems tools can apply rules depending on the situation and the variables to be considered. Many decision makers deal with incomplete data, and an expert system provides rules of thumb for situations in which some of the factors are uncertain. Figure 12-15 summarizes some of the features of decision support systems and expert systems that support decision-making processes.

Figure 12–14

Differences between decision support systems and expert systems

	DECISION SUPPORT SYSTEMS	EXPERT SYSTEMS
Objective	Assists the human	Provides "expert" consulting
Who makes decision	The human	The system
Query type	Human queries the machine	Machine queries the human
Problem area	Complex, wide	Narrow domain
Database	Includes factual knowledge	Includes procedures and data
Evolution	Adapts to the changing environment	Supports a fixed problem domain

Source: Adapted from E. Turban and P. Watkins, "Integrating Expert Systems and Decision Support Systems." In Ralph H. Sprague Jr and Hugh J. Watson, *Decision Support Systems: Putting Theory into Practice* (Englewood Cliffs, NJ: Prentice Hall, 1986).

Figure 12–15

A comparison between expert systems and decision support systems

PROCESSES	FEATURES	
Specify objectives	Modeling syntax	DSS
Retrieve data	Data entry	DSS
Generate alternatives	"What-if" analysis	DSS
Infer consequences of alternatives	Modeling syntax with IF/THEN/ELSE logic	ES
Assimilate numerical and graphical information	Statistical functions	ES
Evaluate sets of consequences	Financial evaluation functions; optimization	ES

Source: Adapted from L. Meador et. al., "Personal Computer and Distributed Decision Support." *Computerworld,* May 7, 1984.

Managers in sales, finance, and manufacturing are now using expert systems as expert consultants to help them make decisions about how to allocate resources, how to control costs, and how to develop more accurate production plans. Today, for example, staff accountants at Coopers and Lybrand use ExperTAX, an expert system for supporting the corporate tax accrual and planning process. ExperTAX functions like an intelligent questionnaire, guiding the accountant through the information gathering process and providing explanations for why questions are being asked. In this way the accountant not only gathers the data but also learns about its ramifications. In addition to gathering relevant information, ExperTAX uncovers some of the most important tax accrual and planning issues.

As you can see from this example, an expert system does not replace the manager. Rather, it can augment the manager's capabilities, accelerate training, and provide quick analysis of important issues. In the future, expert systems tools are likely to be used in many environments.

THE CHARACTERISTICS OF EXPERT SYSTEMS

An expert system is composed of a *knowledge base,* an *inference engine,* a *knowledge acquisition subsystem,* and an *explanation subsystem.* A schematic diagram of the components of an expert system appears in Figure 12-16.

Figure 12–16

The components of an expert system

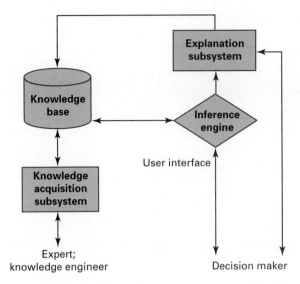

The Knowledge Base

The **knowledge base** contains the information and the rules of thumb that the expert system uses to make decisions. This information should represent high-level expertise gained from top experts in the field. In many expert systems, knowledge is represented using rules. An example of a rule is If Mobil Oil stock drops below $150, then buy 1,000 shares. Most decisions cannot be based on applying a single rule, however. In the case of buying the Mobil Oil stock, other related questions may have to be asked, such as Do I have enough money? or Can the money be obtained from selling another stock?

Depending on the nature of the decision, the expert system will use different rules. These rules are applied in a different order in different decisions. For example, a simple expert system may include 40 rules. Decision 1 may use rules 1, 3, 6, and 7 and decision 2 may use rules 6, 3, 12, and 22. Each time a rule is executed, a change in the database is triggered, new questions are asked, and new rules are applied.

An expert system is quite different from a data processing system, even though both may use if/then logic. In a data processing system, the data structures are defined and programmed code is used to express procedures. These procedures are executed in the same way and in the same order on all the data that are processed. In contrast, an expert system does not execute its rules in the same order. When an expert system receives input data, it selects the rules that apply to the problem. As it asks the user additional questions, it learns more about the situation and applies further rules.

For example, a manufacturer has developed an expert system to diagnose potential failures in an automobile's transmission system. The user may key in information about the problem, and the system may respond with a series of questions. If the user asks, Can it be repaired in two hours? the system may have to check to see what parts are available and how long it will take to make the repair to recommend a course of action.

The Inference Engine

The **inference engine** is the central processing unit of the expert system. The inference engine conducts the dialogue with the user, asking for information and applying it. It uses the knowledge base to draw conclusions for each situation. The structure of the inference engine depends on the nature of the problem and the way knowledge is represented in the expert system.

The inference engine represents both the knowledge base and the procedures to be used for a particular application. The inference engine contains an interpreter that decides how to apply rules to infer new knowledge. It also contains a scheduler that determines the order in which the rules are applied. An example of an inference engine is the Texas Instruments Personal Consultant.

The Knowledge Acquisition and Explanation Subsystems

Most expert systems continue to evolve over time. New rules can be added to the knowledge base by using the **knowledge acquisition subsystem.** The process of developing an expert system involves building a prototype using a simple problem and continually refining this prototype until the expert system is perfected. As the system matures, new rules may be added and others deleted. The knowledge acquisition subsystem makes this process possible.

The **explanation subsystem** explains the procedures that are being used to reach a decision. In this way the user can keep track of the methods being used to solve the problem and can understand how the decision is reached.

HOW AN EXPERT SYSTEM WORKS

Knowledge is represented in an expert system in the form of rules or in the form of frames. Rule-based systems consist of sets of rules (if/then) that describe how knowledge is used to reach a conclusion. Frame-based systems are frames, or networks of nodes, that are organized in a hierarchy to represent knowledge.

Rule-Based Systems

The knowledge base of a rule-based system consists of rules (for example, if/then) and a database that is continually updated as the problem is being solved. An example of how an engine-system fault-diagnosis system for an automobile would work will give you an idea of how an expert system operates. Although automobiles today do not have this type of expert system, you may find it to be a feature of future cars.

In our example, the expert system continually cycles through a series of rules to determine if a problem exists. If the temperature in the engine is too high, if gas is vaporizing too soon, if the engine is firing too soon, or if the engine is running roughly, the system is alerted. To determine such problems, the system uses data about temperature, air pressure, and voltage to the cylinder.

If the temperature in the engine is too high, for instance, the car self-corrects this problem by turning on a fan. If this action doesn't work, the data (for example, gas vaporizing, and so on) are reviewed again. The expert system knows that the first corrective action—turning on the fan—did not work, and so it continues through the rules until it flashes on a light to warn the driver about insufficient fluid levels.

The major characteristics of an expert system are summarized in Figure 12–17. An expert system is designed to achieve a *goal.* In the case of the fault-diagnosis system, the goal is to avoid engine problems. The *domain* is the mechanics of an automobile engine system. The *task* is the diagnosis and correction of engine-system faults. Information about temperature, air pressure, and voltage to the engine's cylinder provides *input* to the system, and procedures or messages that are used to correct the problem are its *output.*

Figure 12–17
Characteristics of
an expert system

CHARACTERISTIC	DEFINITION
Goal	Reason for building the system
Domain	General area of application
Task	Specific task the system is to accomplish
Input	Data needed to accomplish the task
Output	Results of the system
Paradigm	Conceptual problem-solving model used to structure the system
Tools	Software environment in which the system is implemented
Methodology	Method used to build the system

The **paradigm** refers to the problem-solving model that the system applies to diagnose and correct engine-system faults. The knowledge base includes the rules that consist of data and procedures relevant to the problem. The database is continually updated with new information about the problem. For example, when the fan did not correct the problem, the database was updated to indicate this condition.

The *tools* describe the software that builds an expert system. This software includes the knowledge-acquisition subsystem, the explanation subsystem, the knowledge base, and the inference engine. Finally, the *methodology* used to build an expert system, knowledge engineering, uses a prototyping approach in which rules are developed, applied, and reviewed. You'll learn more about the knowledge engineering process in a later section.

Frame-Based Systems

A frame-based system represents knowledge using a network of nodes. Each node represents a concept that may be described by attributes and values associated with the node. A *frame* is a collection of facts and rules about a thing or concept that the computer needs to know. A frame describing the unit Gary Gaetti would tell the computer that he is a person, that he is a baseball player, that he belongs to the St. Louis Cardinals, and that he plays in the National League.

A frame might look like a fact sheet. In building a frame, the *knowledge engineer* decides what kinds of information about a unit might be valuable to the program. These information categories can be typed in as a list, and each category can be filled with a value. For example, a frame for a unit EATING might contain the following values:

EATING:

WHAT HAPPENS WHEN DELAYED: HUNGER

PERFORMED BY: ANIMALS

THINGS CONSUMED: FOOD

MORE GENERAL PROCESS: CONSUMING

Units can also be interrelated. The unit SLEEPING may also be a bodily function. The computer needs to know that both sleeping and eating are part of the unit BODILY FUNCTIONS. This is the same thing as telling the computer that Bob and Paul are neighbors and that Bob's house is in Texas. If the computer knows that Bob's house is in Texas, it will probably know that Paul's house is there too.

How an Expert System Differs from a Conventional Information System

Expert systems differ from conventional information systems in four ways.

First, an expert system must demonstrate expertise—it must achieve levels of performance that a human expert can achieve.

Second, an expert system must be able to represent knowledge symbolically. A symbol may represent a product, a defendent, or an electric motor. The expert system must also be able to depict relationships among symbols, such as a product is defective.

Third, an expert system must be able to handle difficult problems, using complex rules. In other words, it must work in-depth to simulate the reasoning of an expert problem-solver and to produce useful solutions.

Fourth, the expert system must demonstrate self-knowledge—it must be able to examine its own reasoning and to estimate the accuracy of its own conclusions. The system uses its explanation facility to explain how it arrived at its answers. Even though an expert system will eventually make mistakes, its developers can work toward correcting these mistakes because the assumptions used in its knowledge-based programs are explicitly stated in code.

The Kinds of Problems an Expert System Can Solve

Expert systems can be designed to solve certain types of problems: problems that have a specific scope, lend themselves to a particular type of analysis, and draw upon available human expertise.

The scope of expert systems. Expert systems are generally developed to address a specific area of expertise. For example, it would be impossible to design an expert system to be an expert doctor, because the realm of knowledge is much too large. However, an expert system could be designed to diagnose infectious blood diseases, a specific area of expertise.

It is interesting to contrast expert knowledge with general knowledge. We see programs that are expert in diagnosing infectious diseases but know nothing of general medicine. Expert systems have been designed that diagnose faults in atomic power plants but are ignorant of freshman physics. A simple task like answering the telephone is almost impossible for the computer to do because of the vast range of possible responses and topics. But expert systems are routinely designed to attack problems that are difficult for humans. Most people consider diagnosing infectious diseases difficult because physicians need years of training in medical diagnosis. However, diagnosing diseases actually takes far less information than answering the telephone.

In general, an expert system should be designed to focus on a rather narrow domain of knowledge. Expert systems may be very smart in very narrow fields of expertise but will be practically ignorant in areas outside their domain of knowledge. One of the most difficult challenges in artificial intelligence is teaching machines to understand simple, everyday language—even though most children understand spoken language at the age of two.

Types of problems. Expert systems are good at problems that require diagnosis, prediction, and planning. One of the best uses of expert systems is **diagnosis.** Rule-based technology is well suited to describing many routine diagnostic decisions made by professionals such as doctors and engineers. Their decisions are based upon a large collection of rules of thumb that are well described by situation-action rules.

Some diagnostic systems are designed to detect system malfunctions from facts that are supplied. For example, expert systems have been developed to diagnose faults in electrical systems, gas turbine engines, electronic equipment, and automotive subsystems. An expert system called ACE detects faults in telephone networks and recommends appropriate repair and maintenance work. In the computer field a system called DART helps diagnose faults in computer hardware systems.

Expert systems have been used extensively in medical diagnosis. For example, MYCIN was developed to assist physicians in diagnosing infectious blood diseases using knowledge of patient history, symptoms, lab test results, and the characteristics of the infecting organisms. MYCIN diagnoses the cause of the infection and recommends appropriate therapy.

The if/then logic of MYCIN might go something like this:

If (1) the stain of the organism is grampos and (2) the morphology of the organism is coccos and (3) the growth conformation of the organism is chains, then there is suggestive evidence (0.7) that the identity of the organism is streptococcus.

Another expert system, BLUE BOX, helps diagnose and treat various forms of clinical depression. The system uses data about the patient's symptoms and information about medical, drug, and family histories to suggest a plan that includes hospitalization and drug treatments.

A second area in which expert systems excel is **design work.** Expert systems can configure computers, circuits, and organic molecules. One of the most successful expert systems is XCON, which Digital Equipment Corporation (DEC) uses to configure its computers. XCON uses information on the customer's order to determine which components to use. The system has enabled DEC to cut down on costly configuration errors and has given it a competitive edge in the computer business.

A third category of expert systems applications is **interpretation.** Expert systems are widely used to interpret situations from information provided. Many expert systems in medicine use measurements from patient monitoring (heart rate, blood pressure, and so on) to diagnose and treat illnesses. For instance, an expert system named PUFF interprets data from pulmonary function tests to diagnose lung diseases.

Another application, MUDMAN, helps geologists analyze mud. Mud at drilling sites has to be sampled and analyzed for viscosity, specific gravity, and silt content. If mud contamination is misdiagnosed, drilling operations can be doomed at a particular site. N. L. Baroid, a drilling services firm, used MUDMAN to diagnose a mud contamination problem that had gone undetected by human experts for more than 10 years. DIPMETER ADVISOR, another geological interpretation system, uses measures of rock conductivity in and around holes drilled in the earth to determine subsurface geological structure.

A fourth area in which expert systems excel is *prediction.* Prediction is the ability to infer the likely consequences of given situations. Prediction systems can estimate global oil demand, forecast possible areas of international political unrest, and simulate bad debt losses from faulty credit decisions. Farmers can benefit from an expert system that predicts insect damage to crops. PLANT, an expert system, predicts black cutworm damage to corn crops using a simulation model. There is a rule that PLANT uses to make its predictions:

If (1) the black cutworm versus leafstage table has been computed, (2) whether there are greater than four weeds per foot of row is known, (3) the corn variety is known, and (4) the soil moisture in the field is known, then compute the corn yield without insecticide treatment and assign it the variable Yield 1.

However, expert systems cannot solve all prediction-type problems. One of the best examples of expert system predictive limitations is in oil drilling. In the early 1980s, a team of experts wanted to design an expert system to determine the probable value of oil wells based upon measurements taken during drilling. The project sounded like an excellent opportunity for the development of an expert system for two reasons: Millions of dollars rested on these decisions, and an elite group of petroleum geologists was responsible for doing these analyses. After making significant investments in designing an expert system to predict the yield of oil wells, the developers recognized that their system had no more knowledge than a junior geologist. However, the project was not a total waste because it produced a number of intelligent support tools that the expert geologists could use.

Though many of these systems seem sophisticated, expert systems are currently being developed to address a number of business applications. The cost of expert systems development has decreased with the availability of minicomputer- and microcomputer-based expert systems software. As a result expert systems development is no longer just applicable to problems in engineering, medicine, and electronics, where the investment and returns are large. Simple, less costly expert systems are being developed to address business problems.

EXPERT SYSTEMS APPLICATIONS IN BUSINESS

American Express Company employs credit authorizers to analyze credit card transactions for clues to determine if charges outside of typical credit patterns are likely to be paid and if they have been incurred by the true cardholder. The knowledge of professional credit authorizers was used to develop an expert system for credit authorization. The purpose of this system was to minimize credit losses from incorrect authorizations. Since the rules of credit authorization could be defined, an expert system was feasible. American Express has been able to make more accurate credit authorizations with this system.

An expert system for personal financial planning named PlanPower is currently available. Using information about its clients' objectives, taxes, prior investments, insurance coverage, and real estate holdings, PlanPower develops financial plans for its clients. To develop these strategies, PlanPower uses its knowledge of interest rates, expected inflation rates, tax laws, and standard investment strategies. Clients can use PlanPower to make what-if? projections to compare the impacts of alternative financial decisions.

Expert systems also are being used in aircraft design, which requires the development of process plans detailing the steps in manufacturing. The design process involves thousands of parts. If design errors occur, considerable costs result from production delays, the reworking of tools, and the scrapping of parts.

Northrop Engineering has designed an expert system to convert descriptions of parts into process plans. These process plans are permanently stored for future referral, preventing future designers from reinventing the wheel. Before the development of this expert system, much of this aircraft design expertise was in the heads of design engineers. When designers left the company, their expertise went with them.

Expert systems are also being applied in the financial services business. For example, the insurance industry is using expert systems for claim estimation, credit analysis, and underwriting. In each of these applications, expertise is available and can be used to develop a knowledge base consisting of rules and data. Other expert systems applications include financial statement analysis, tax advising, conflict-of-interest consulting, and inventory management.

The Kinds of Opportunities Expert Systems Address

As you have learned from our description of expert systems in medicine, engineering, business, and other fields, expert systems technology presents an opportunity to capture the knowledge of experts and to share it as a resource throughout an organization.

The initial step in the development of an expert system is the selection of a project in which a recognized expert can be found. This expert should be 10 times better than an amateur problem solver in the particular area. The task involved should be primarily cognitive, such as medical diagnosis, financial planning, or insurance underwriting. Expert systems do not have common sense and cannot address problems requiring common sense.

The task also must be narrowly defined so that specialized knowledge can be used. It wouldn't be possible to build an expert system to be an expert lawyer, but one could be developed to provide legal advice in a specialized area like personal tax law. In addition, the task should be one that an expert could accomplish in a relatively short period of time—in a few minutes to a few hours. If a task is too time-consuming, it should probably be broken down into subtasks.

For other reasons, some problems aren't feasible for expert systems development. Simple problems with fewer than 10 rules aren't good candidates because they can be solved by most people. However, problems with thousands of rules may be too complex and time-consuming to develop. Problems that are too complex for experts or problems involving a great deal of disagreement among the experts are also not feasible for expert systems development.

Because of the massive investments in time and effort in developing an expert system, managers should realize that only certain projects are justifiable. High-payoff applications such as oil exploration and computer configuration are excellent opportunities for building expert systems. In situations where expert knowledge may be lost because of retirement or job transfer, or in cases where human expertise is very scarce, an expert system can be a good investment.

Even though an expert system may be possible and justifiable, it may not be appropriate unless the task at hand is appropriate. The task must require a heuristic solution, that is, one that uses rules of thumb to achieve a solution. Second, the task must be sufficiently narrow to make the problem manageable yet broad enough to be of practical interest. Third, the task must be a serious problem that may take years of study for a human expert to address well.

How Expert Systems Are Developed

The development of expert systems involves the process of knowledge engineering, which means the creation of a knowledge base. The **knowledge engineer** builds the pieces of the knowledge base by working with experts who use their experience to develop rules applying to a problem.

Expert systems development entails the acquisition of knowledge, and several factors related to knowledge acquisition apply to their development. First of all, knowledge is inexact. No one has perfect knowledge, including the expert. An expert auto mechanic, for example, may be able to identify the correct problem with an air-conditioning system only about 75 percent of the time. Making errors can be useful, though, because the expert can learn more about factors involved in diagnosing the problem. An expert system can be no more certain than the expert.

Second, knowledge is incomplete. Knowledge is acquired in pieces, a little at a time and through trial and error. For instance, expert platform divers learn their skill after hundreds of hours of practice. Gradual learning takes place throughout the college curriculum as well. In the freshman year, an economics major may take a survey course in microeconomics. It isn't until the student takes advanced courses that some of the reasons behind the basic concepts learned in the survey course are conveyed.

Expert systems development is also incremental. In the initial development phase, a preliminary set of rules is defined and applied to a simple problem. However, as experience with the system grows, new rules are incorporated into the knowledge base. An expert system ultimately acquires a great deal of knowledge.

The Stages of Building an Expert System

The process of building an expert system involves five stages. The first stage, *identification,* is the stage during which the problem is defined. The problem must be appropriate in type and scope. At this time an expert and the required computing resources must be acquired.

The next phase is *formalization.* The knowledge engineer must determine how knowledge will be formally represented. A number of questions must be addressed. Will a rule-based or frame-based approach be used? What key concepts and relationships must be addressed? At what level of detail will the knowledge be represented? During this phase, the knowledge engineer will also select appropriate system building tools.

During the third stage, *implementation,* the knowledge engineer will work with the expert to identify the rules of thumb that make up the formalized knowledge of the expert system. These rules are used to construct a workable computer program using the system building tools or language.

Testing of the system is its final phase. During this phase, the system builder supplies a number of test cases to evaluate whether the prototype system makes decisions that other experts would deem to be appropriate. The system builder must check the rules to see that they are consistent, correct, and complete. She must check to see if the explanations the system provides for reaching its conclusions are sensible and adequate.

The Roles of the Knowledge Engineer and the Expert

The process of expert systems development involves a knowledge engineer and an expert. At first, the expert is presented with a simple problem. Past experience allows him to identify the variables and rules that apply to it. After some of the rules are defined, the expert and knowledge engineer apply the rules to several simple problems.

As new problems are presented, the expert refines the knowledge base by adding more rules and data. After a number of sessions, up to 100 rules may be defined. The knowledge base is continually revised and refined to include the most relevant rules. A final version of the expert system may condense the original 100 rules to 30 or 40 rules. However, producing a final version doesn't mean that the expert system will remain static. As the system is used, its rules continue to be refined. This iterative process is similar to the prototyping approach in systems development.

One of the reasons that expert systems development employs an incremental approach is that the working memory of humans is a surprisingly short six seconds. Working memory consists of knowledge that the person can access immediately. The expert has immediate access to her working memory but needs to refer to long-term memory as well. The simple problems the knowledge engineer uses help the expert extract knowledge from this long-term memory. In general, experts are not very good at describing what they know. The knowledge engineer must be highly trained in order to help the expert identify the rules and test cases that are relevant to the problem.

The Prototyping Approach in Expert Systems Development

As you can see, the expert systems building effort involves exploratory prototyping. The knowledge engineer keeps building the rule base to see if the rules that have been accumulated provide enough information to reduce uncertainty. The expert must constantly review each version of the system to compare it with his own reasoning.

You might want to think of the prototyping approach in terms of a number of stages. The first working prototype of the system might be designed to solve a portion of the problem. Success at this initial phase may suggest that the project is feasible and may lead to the development of a research prototype. The research prototype is designed to address the whole problem, but it may not be of practical value because it has not been thoroughly tested. After continued testing and revision, a field prototype may emerge. The field prototype should display good performance and reliability on practical problems. Prior to commercial use, however, continued testing is needed to create a production version. XCON, Digital Equipment's expert configuration system, is an example of a commercial expert system. XCON, which has over 3,000 rules and is correct more than 95 percent of the time, took over six years to develop.

How Knowledge Is Acquired from Experts

The process of acquiring knowledge from an expert may take systematic interviews over a period of months. During these interviews, the knowledge engineer presents the expert with a series of realistic problems. Let us say that the knowledge engineer is building a system to assist attorneys in settling product liability cases. The knowledge engineer provides the expert with descriptions of actual cases, including statements by witnesses and medical reports. The knowledge engineer then questions the expert in detail about how she would evaluate these cases.

The goal of this effort is to determine how the expert organizes knowledge about each problem. A number of questions arise. What kind of data does the problem require? What kinds of solutions are adequate for the problem? What kind of knowledge is needed to solve the problem? How does the expert handle inconsistent or inaccurate information? What is an adequate explanation for a problem solution?

As the knowledge engineer asks the expert to solve a series of problems, she probes the expert's reasoning and keeps track of the information the expert uses to solve the problems. After an initial prototype of the system is built, the expert attempts to solve sample problems using these rules and makes adjustments in the prototype system's rules to achieve an acceptable level of performance.

Throughout the system building process, the knowledge engineer has to deal with certain obstacles to capturing the expert's knowledge. First, experts tend to state their conclusions in general terms, without providing each step in the reasoning process that was used in reaching these conclusions. An expert may ascribe a judgment to intuition when actually this judgment is the result of a very complex reasoning process based upon a large amount of data and experience.

The more adept an expert becomes, the less able he is to describe the individual steps it takes to solve a problem or to arrive at a conclusion. The role of the knowledge engineer is critical because the expert needs outside help in clarifying and explicating her expert knowledge. The knowledge engineer must decompile or break down the expert's knowledge into the hundreds of rules that are part of a complex reasoning process. Although the knowledge engineer may be able to gain some insight into this reasoning process by observing the expert's methods of solving problems, the best way to extract knowledge is to present the expert with representative problems and to discuss the strategies used to solve them.

One of the risks of developing an expert system is that it is difficult to estimate the time and effort it will take to complete. At some point the prototype version must be transported into a production version. But even the production version will have a certain amount of uncertainty and will have to be constantly reviewed and revised. The expert must review each version of the system and compare it with his own thinking. The expert should also validate the system by comparing its performance with the thinking of other experts.

The Advantages of Expert Systems

Expert systems have definite advantages. An expert system can capture the knowledge of an expert and serve as an expert consultant in the absence of a real expert. If the expert system draws on the knowledge of several experts, it may actually be superior to a single consultant. Once this expertise is acquired, it can be used forever.

Expert systems can provide advice that is more consistent than the advice of consultants, who may be affected by stress and time constraints. An expert system can be trained to process information more efficiently and to provide a recommendation more quickly than its human counterparts. An expert system can also be put to work in a hostile environment (e.g., a nuclear power plant or space station) where you could not afford to keep a human expert on hand.

Another advantage of an expert system is that its knowledge can be transferred or reproduced. An expert system can be used for consultation and training in numerous locations simply by duplicating the necessary hardware, software, and data disks. Once the expert system is constructed, it should be documented to prevent losing the valuable expertise of experienced technical experts who may retire. The knowledge of employees who might leave a firm can also be captured. In either case the expert system prevents system users from having to reinvent the wheel.

Finally, an expert system may be less expensive than an actual expert, particularly if the expertise is needed again and again. Human experts are highly valued and are able to obtain large salaries as consultants. Though an expert system may be costly to develop, its ongoing value should provide benefits that outweigh these initial development costs.

The Limits of Expert Systems

Although the benefits of expert systems are great, you still need to be acquainted with certain limits to the technology and its uses. First, expert systems cannot truly replace experts. Rather, systems can be used to augment experts' capabilities. In the former example of an expert system to identify the probable value of oil well sites, the expert system could not replace the knowledge of an elite group of petroleum engineers. Ultimately, the expert system was used as an expert consultant to the geologists in their work.

Expert systems are used as consultants in various lines of work. Financial planners use the expert advice of financial planning systems, and physicians use expert systems for medical diagnosis. For example, at Stanford Medical School, ONCOCIN, an expert system, assists physicians in prescribing chemical treatment for cancer patients.

Finally, expert systems are not truly intelligent. They cannot learn new concepts and rules. They cannot address problems that lack focus and careful definition. They cannot demonstrate common sense. Teaching an expert system the most basic common sense would take thousands of instructions. In a very real sense, expert systems don't know what they don't know. They will demonstrate unacceptably high levels of uncertainty in situations requiring knowledge outside their very narrow range of expertise.

The practical use of expert systems may be limited by the extent to which humans are willing to let computer systems become accountable for the decisions they make. How to ascribe legal and ethical responsibility to the workings of expert systems is a difficult issue. You have learned that expert systems can excel at medical diagnosis and even surpass human physicians in accuracy. But if a patient dies because of a bad diagnosis by an expert system "doctor," who is responsible? You may already know that computers "fly" many airplanes—in simulations, computers actually make fewer mistakes than their human pilot counterparts. Both the real pilots and the computer pilots make mistakes, however. Somehow, humans are willing to accept, if not tolerate, a plane crash that is due to pilot error. But if a plane crashes because of a bad computer decision, is that acceptable? The legal implications are enormous.

Because of issues such as these, expert systems are being confined to consulting and assisting roles in such activities as medical diagnosis, computer configuration, and oil exploration. If Digital's XCON makes a mistake, it is not a life or death matter. An occasional mistake can be remedied by an extra shipment of parts. In general, expert systems may be restricted to low-responsibility decision-making applications until legal and ethical responsibilities associated with their use can be resolved.

Expert System Tools

Expert systems can be developed using problem-oriented languages such as LISP or PROLOG. These are symbol-manipulation languages designed for artificial intelligence applications. As you can see from the English and LISP versions of a simple relationship, LISP is an effective language for implementing rule-based logic.

English: If the spill is in a building, call the fire department.

LISP: (IF (LOCATION SPILL BUILDING) THEN (CALL FIRE DEPARTMENT)

A second type of expert system tool is the expert system shell. An expert system shell includes a knowledge base that specifies the parameters and rules and an inference engine that processes these parameters and rules. A diagram of the components of an expert system shell is shown in Figure 12–18. Expert system shells also include an uncertainty module that conveys information about the certainty of the recommendations being made and an explanation module that keeps track of the rules and procedures that have been accomplished in solving a problem.

Rule-based systems can address a number of business problems, such as tax auditing, insurance underwriting, product pricing, and credit authorizing. For a project to be appropriate for expert systems development, the type of reasoning involved in performing the task must be heuristic or symbolic, as opposed to quantitative. Heuristic knowledge is judgmental, which means that the objective is to make a reasonably good decision.

Figure 12–18

The elements of an expert system shell

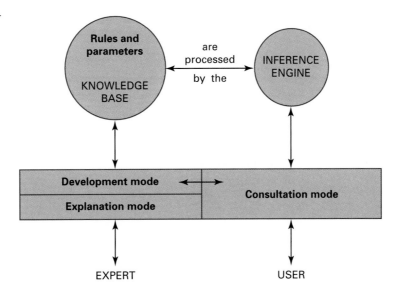

For an expert systems development project to be feasible, expertise must be available. Experts must be able to articulate the methods they use to reach conclusions and to make decisions. In addition to expertise, a project must be useful and have a practical business application. A practical system can help repair products, can provide sales assistance to customers, and can help train or retrain employees. If expertise is available and if the project is useful, then the system is a good candidate for expert systems development.

MANAGEMENT SUMMARY

Decision support tools enable managers to construct databases for ad hoc query and reporting of data and to develop models for analyzing these data. Decision support systems must be able to address semistructured and unstructured problems because the decision-making process is usually not known up front and because different managers make decisions in different ways.

One of the most important features of a decision support system is its ability to support the three phases of the decision-making process: intelligence, design, and choice. Intelligence is the awareness that a decision needs to be made. Data on declining sales, increasing bad debt expenses, or rapidly growing student numbers may all support this first phase. Design is the process of identifying and analyzing alternatives. Tools such as spreadsheet programs make it possible to evaluate alternative ways of allocating resources and support the

design phase. Finally, summary statistics or a graph depicting the preferred alternative may support the selection of an appropriate course of action.

The Decision Support Systems design process involves a user, who identifies an information need, and a designer, who develops an initial version of the proposed system and continues to modify it as the user's needs change. According to the adaptive design process, the system continues to evolve as the user gains experience and as the designer continues to incorporate new features into its design.

Expert systems have been developed to perform diagnostic and design tasks such as medical diagnosis, computer system configuration, and fault detection in telephone networks. Business-related applications of expert systems, such as financial planning, insurance underwriting, and inventory management, are becoming more common.

KEY TERMS FOR MANAGERS

adaptive design, 474
algorithms, 461
artificial intelligence (AI), 481
choice, 461
decision support systems (DSS), 463
design, 461
design work, 488
diagnosis, 487
expert systems, 482

explanation subsystem, 485
group decision support systems (GDSS), 479
heuristics, 461
incrementalizing, 462
inference engine, 484
intelligence, 461
interpretation, 488
knowledge acquisition subsystem, 485

knowledge base, 484
knowledge engineer, 490
machine vision, 482
maximizing, 462
natural-language processing, 481
paradigm, 486
satisficing, 462

REVIEW QUESTIONS

1. What activities occur during each of the three phases of the decision-making process?

2. Give an example of a semistructured decision and of an unstructured decision.

3. What is an algorithm?

4. What are several attributes of decision makers that influence decision-making strategy?

5. Compare the maximizing and the satisficing strategies for decision making.

6. Which of the following are decision support systems? Explain the reasons for your answers.
   a. A marketing system that provides a weekly sales report summarized by product line.
   b. A sales prospect database that managers can use to make queries, such as List the names of all prospects in the 63166 ZIP code.
   c. A personnel information system that provides a listing of all new hires, changes, and terminations at the beginning of each week.
   d. A financial system that projects the cash flow impacts of two investment decisions.

7. What is a limitation of the exception reporting systems that Alloway and Quillard describe?

8. What is an inquiry system?

9. What are three important features of a decision support system?

10. What information could you use to help you decide which college to attend? Identify the information that would be helpful in supporting each phase of the decision-making process.
    a. Intelligence
    b. Design
    c. Choice

11. Give an example of a memory aid that should be built into a decision support system.

12. Give an example of a control aid that can assist managers in learning how to use decision support software.

13. What is meant by adaptive design?

14. What is the role of the systems designer in building a decision support system?

15. Name four types of group decision support systems and describe the characteristics of each.

16. Define *artificial intelligence.*

17. Why are natural-language processing systems so difficult to develop?

18. What is the function of the inference engine in an expert system?

19. What are the two methods of representing knowledge in an expert system?

20. Explain this statement: Computers can be very stupid.

21. Can expert systems make mistakes?

22. Give an example of an expert system that does diagnosis.

23. What is an expert system shell and how is it used?

24. What are two characteristics of a "good" expert system project?

25. Why is the prototyping approach used in expert systems development?

QUESTIONS FOR DISCUSSION

1. Describe the three phases of decision making with respect to selecting a career.

2. What are three important features of an effective decision support system?

3. Can you think of an application in sales or marketing for the development of a decision support system?

4. Would an information system designed to keep track of maintenance calls on office equipment be an example of a decision support system?

5. Why does the development of a decision support system work best using an adaptive design approach?

6. What are some of the qualitative benefits of decision support systems?

7. What risks may occur because of lack of quality assurance in building a decision support system?

8. What are some of the organizational impacts of group decision support systems? How does the decision-making process change when automated tools are used to support groups?

9. Explain the statement: The more competent domain experts become, the less able they are to describe the knowledge they use to solve problems. What are the implications of this statement for the process of knowledge engineering?

10. Describe the phases of building an expert system.

11. Compare the intelligence of an expert system with the intelligence of a two-year-old child.

12. Give two ways in which expert systems programs differ from conventional data processing programs.

13. Name two key skills the effective knowledge engineer should have.

14. Name several characteristics of an expert.

15. Could expert systems tools be used to develop a decision support system?

16. Why is knowledge sometimes difficult to extract from experts?

17. What advantages can expert systems provide business?

18. What are some of the limitations of expert systems?

PROBLEMS

1. **Amalgamated Stores, Inc.** John McDonald is the director of data processing for Amalgamated Stores, Inc., a chain of 35 discount stores with locations in the West and Southwest. Recently he has received a number of complaints from store managers that monthly sales reports do not provide meaningful information. The store managers want to be able to analyze sales trends for various product lines on a timely basis. They receive weekly sales summary reports, but they want a more responsive output. John has been exploring some options. Should he hire a consultant? Should he buy microcomputers? Should he hire more programmers to redesign the existing sales summary reporting systems to be more responsive to the needs of managers? Should he acquire tools that would enable managers to extract the information they need themselves? Which option would you choose? Explain the reasons for your choice. In your answer, you may want to examine the advantages and disadvantages of some of the options given.

2. **Purcell Industries.** Bob Lobdell, a financial analyst at Purcell Industries, would like to develop a profitability report showing the profit margins on sales for various product lines on a weekly basis. Current MIS systems show sales by product line this month versus last month, but existing reports do not calculate the profit margin on sales for various products. Bob believes that the profit margins on certain product lines are greater than the profit margins on others. The system he proposes would give sales managers information on product profitability and would enable them to promote the most

profitable products. Bob wants to build a decision support system to examine product profitability. What steps should he take to develop such a system? What kind of assistance will he need?

3. **United National Insurance Company.** In the marketing department of a major insurance company, Joan Phillips, a user-developer, set up a system with information about prospective insurance customers. The system made it possible to query the database to extract information about customers with certain characteristics. It also made it possible to generate mailing labels for various mailings to these customers. Phillips also developed management reports summarizing the number of inquiries about various types of insurance programs. Salespeople, clerical employees, and managers used the system extensively. After the system had been in operation for about six months and many users had grown dependent on it, Joan Phillips left to take a position in another firm. Soon after, someone tried to select customers in a certain ZIP code from the database but was unable to do so. Though this capability had been built into the system, no one had been trained to select records with specific characteristics. As time went on, the users of the system could not figure out how to perform many of its functions. Eventually, a consultant was brought in to study the system and to develop several new reports that were needed. How could the situation in this case have been avoided?

4. **A job selection decision.** Demonstrate your understanding of the decision-making process by outlining the approach you would take in making a decision about a prospective job as a management trainee. Use your own preferences to establish criteria for making the decision. You have three offers from which to choose. Each is described below.

The first offer is for the position of management trainee with a large manufacturing firm in a major metropolitan area. The firm has an excellent training program that lasts about six months. The position offers a competitive starting salary and good raises with annual reviews. After two to three years at the corporate office, most junior managers have opportunities to transfer to first-line division-level management positions. The job requires a minimum of travel during the first two to three years and travel mainly between division offices and the home office after that.

The second offer is for a position as a junior management consultant with a well-established consulting firm in a major metropolitan area. The firm offers a high starting salary and profit sharing. The position requires between 50 percent and 70 percent travel to clients' offices throughout the Midwest. Advancement is based on performance and entrepreneurial skill, and successful consultants have an opportunity to earn six-figure incomes within five to seven years of being employed with the firm. The firm employs between 35 and 40 professionals; it does not have a formal training program.

The third offer is for a position as a management trainee with a mid-sized organization in the high-technology telecommunications business. The firm is located in a small city of approximately 350,000 people. It offers a good starting salary and a chance for participating in an exciting high-technology sales environment. Training includes on-the-job tutorials and one to two weeks of workshops during the year. Moderate travel is involved to regional clients. The firm is in a very competitive industry, and the job potential depends on its ability to provide state-of-the-art products, effective marketing, and excellent service.

5. **Clark Consulting.** A client has just asked John Robertson, a partner in Clark Consulting, Inc., about the feasibility of developing several expert systems. Clark Consulting is a firm specializing in the development of managerial information systems, and the area of expert systems development represents a relatively new

business opportunity. Assume that the client has asked about the feasibility of each of the following projects. Do you feel that each of these projects is a good candidate for expert systems development? Why or why not?

a. An expert system to qualify sales leads.
b. An expert system to select potential store sites.
c. An expert system to diagnose problems with plant production equipment.
d. An expert system to develop an effective sales incentive program.
e. An expert system to supply legal advice about corporate taxes.

CASES

1. **Universal Widgets, Inc. (A).**   Following are extracts from four different reports that are currently produced at Universal Widgets, Inc.

Report 11
Sales report

SALES BY REGION							
Product	Price	NE	SE	Central	West	Total units	Dollar totals
Widgets	$ 80	120	60	130	90	400	$ 32,000

Report 44
Production report

		QUANTITY			
Product code	description	Plan	Actual	Unit MFG cost	Unit PNT cost
303-B-AL	Black alloy widget	100	120	20	4
303-B-FE	Black iron widget	100	100	20	4
303-N-AL	Natural alloy widget	200	240	20	0
303-R-FE	Red iron widget	120	140	20	8

Report 77
Materials purchasing report

Material Name	Quantity	Unit Cost	Budget	Variance
Iron billets	240	20	6,000	1,500
Aluminum rods	400	30	10,000	2,000
Paint	500	4	2,000	0

Report 98
Profitability report

			COST			
Product	Sales ($)	MFG($)	PNT($)	MAT($)	Profit(s)	PCT of Sales
Widgets	32,000	12,000	2,000	15,600	2,400	7.5

Notes to the reports

1. Alloy widgets are made out of aluminum rod, one rod per widget.
2. Iron widgets are made out of iron, one billet per widget.
3. If a widget is to be painted any color at all, it must first be painted black; every coat of paint uses $4 in paint.

Further notes:

1. Actual widget sales by type were
   Black iron 0
   Black alloy 100
   Red iron 60
   Natural alloy 240

2. During the last sales period, 550 widgets were sold. Profit as a percent of sales was 9.6 percent.

Instructions: Obviously, Universal Widgets is having problems. As a manager who receives the four reports shown, George Phillips does not have a good idea of how well widgets are doing, what the most profitable lines are, and what the least profitable lines are. Construct a mock-up of a report (or reports) that will help George understand widget profitability and make decisions about sales and production. Use your own judgment about what the report should contain. You may use data that is on one or more of the current reports. In creating the mock-up of your report, try to use as much real data in constructing the new report(s) as possible. Explain why you believe the report(s) you propose will be helpful to the manager.

2. **Universal Widgets, Inc. (B).**   Use the mock-up of the report you designed in Case 1 to develop a spreadsheet. Using the spreadsheet, develop another version of the profitability report using different sales figures. The new sales figures are

   Black iron 100
   Black alloy 50
   Red iron 120
   Natural alloy 100

What recommendations would you make about the sales and marketing strategy for various lines and for inventory management?

3. **Using Microsoft Access for Windows for database projects**
   Introduction
   Use the NorthWind database to find the solutions to the queries you must complete. First, browse the database by looking at the types of records (tables) in the database, the fields (columns) in each record, and the relationships among the records and fields. Examine also the types of data found in the fields. To help you find your way around the database, a layout of the 8 tables in the database is included, along with their fields, below. You should study this layout and then use it to plan your queries.

To get started on your queries

- Select the NorthWind database, click on the Tables tab, and then select the first of the eight tables in the database (Customers, Orders, etc.) by double-clicking on it.

- Click on the angle icon in the upper-left corner of the screen to display the types of fields in the table and the nature of those fields. This view of the tables is called the *design view*. Compare what you see with the layout diagram of the database.

- Click on the spreadsheet icon next to the angle icon to browse the actual data in each table. This view is called the *datasheet view* of the table. You can move back and forth between the design view of the table and the datasheet view of the table by clicking on these icons. When you are through with a table, close it by double-clicking on the bar button in the upper-left corner of the table.

  Browse the rest of the tables, in both design and datasheet views, and compare what you see with the layout diagram of the database.

Practice exercises

- Print a list containing only the last and first names of every employee. Do this by "adding" the employee table to your query and closing the Add Table screen. Then drag the employee last name and first name fields from the Employees table in the top part of the screen to the first line of the first and second columns of the blank table in the bottom of the screen. Now click the datasheet view icon to see the data.

- Print a list of the last and first names of every employee who is a sales representative. Do this by clicking the design view icon to get back to your original query design screen. All you have to do is drag the title field from the Employees table on the top to the third column in the table at the bottom. Then, on the Criteria line of the third column, type "Sales Representative." Now click on the datasheet view icon to get the results of your query.

- Print a list of the names of customers located in London.

- Print a list of the names of customers located in London or Paris.

- Print a list of the English names for stock items that have been discontinued.

- Print a list of *only* those customers with fax numbers. Print their names and fax numbers.

Queries requiring more than one table

- Print a list of the English names for stock items that have been discontinued and the names of their suppliers.

- Print a list of the English names for stock items that are discontinued from the supplier, Tokyo Traders.

- Print a list of the English names for each product carried, the quantity on hand, and supplier's name.

- Print a list of the English names of *only* those products whose units in stock are less than or equal to their reorder levels.

Practice: Using /combining tables and tables created from existing queries

- List the order numbers and subtotals for sales representative Fuller.

- Print a list of the dates and gross order amounts for all orders from customer Quick-Stop. Arrange your data by the largest order first.

- List the salesperson, order date, order subtotal, and city to which the order was shipped. First arrange the data by order subtotal with the highest order amount listed first. Then arrange the data by order date with the most recent order listed first.

Assignment queries

- Print a list of the English names for each product and the quantity on hand of each item.

- Print a list of the English names for the products and quantities on order from Exotic Liquids.

- List the last names, phone numbers, and photos of every employee.

- List the last names, city, and phone numbers of every employee serving London or Tacoma.

- List the company names of only those customers who paid freight charges. Show the company names and the amount of freight charges. Arrange your

list first by company name in ascending order. Then arrange your list by the largest freight charge.
- List the order numbers and order subtotals for sales representative King.
- List the order numbers, order date, and order subtotals for sales representative Buchanan. First order your list by the most recent order date; then by the largest order amount.
- Count the number of customers in the database.
- Find the average order for each customer. Order your list by the highest average.
- Find the average order for each sales representative. Order your list by the highest average.

4. **Computer-based sales management.**   In his article, "Computerized Sales Management," G. David Hughes describes spreadsheet applications that can enable the sales manager to determine the potential of

various accounts and to test different assumptions about account management. In this exercise, you will learn about several spreadsheets and assess the impact of changing assumptions.

Spreadsheet 1: Sales forecast
One of the first questions sales managers must address is, What is the potential of an account? In Spreadsheet 1 you should enter the figures shown in brackets, which are the account requirements for the previous period, estimated growth rates per period, sales for the previous period, estimated share points for the next period, and an estimate of the number of calls necessary to achieve these share points.

a. Use the spreadsheet program to estimate the total requirements for the forecast period, the share points for the previous period, company sales, and sales per call. Your output should match the output shown as Spreadsheet 1.

Spreadsheet 1:
Sales forecast

FOR I PERIOD(S) ACCOUNTS					
	CENTRAL MFG. CO.	WESTERN TOOL INC.	NORTHERN ENG. LTD.	OTHER ACCTS.	TOTALS
TOTAL REQUIREMENTS LAST PER	[500]	[1230]	[713]	[6245]	8708
ESTIMATED GROWTH/PERIOD	[1.2]	[1.95]	[.95]	[1.00]	1.01
FORECSTD TOTAL REQRMTS./PER.	600	1312	677	6245	8835
OUR SALES LAST PERIOD	[200]	[125]	[214]	[1249]	1788
OUR SHARE POINTS LAST PER.	40.00	10.00	30.01	20.00	20.24
FORECASTS					
SHARE POINTS	[47.50]	[20.00]	[30.00]	[20.00]	22.63
SALES ($000)	285	262	203	1250	2000
CALLS/PERIOD	[11]	[10]	[20]	[839]	880
SALES/CALL ($000)	25.91	26.25	10.16	1.49	2.27

Note: Planner enters figures in brackets; computer produces in other figures.

As you can see from the resulting model, the projections made into the future show that the Central Manufacturing account will generate more sales per call than the other accounts because of its higher growth rate.

Spreadsheet 2: Account contribution and product mix
The sales manager also wants to know which accounts buy the highest-margin products because those accounts may be

most profitable. Spreadsheet 2 shows the profit margins on different products, including axles, bars, clutches, and drums. Account profitability also depends upon the product mix an account buys. As you can see, 50 percent of Central Manufacturing's purchases are axles, the lowest-margin product. In contrast, Northern Engineering buys mostly clutches and drums, which have profit margins of .3 and .4, respectively. As a result, Northern Engineering is the most profitable account, based on its product contribution.

a. Develop Spreadsheet 2, Account Contribution and Product Mix, to generate the output shown below. You will need to enter the data in brackets, including the product margins and the product mix ratios. The other data can be generated by using formulas within the spreadsheet.

Spreadsheet 2:

Account contribution and product mix

		FOR I PERIOD(S)
		CENTRAL MFG. CO.		WESTERN TOOL INC.		NORTHERN ENG. LTD.		OTHER ACCTS.		TOTALS	
SALES FORECAST ($000)		285		262		203		1249		2000	
PRODUCT	PRODUCT MARGIN	PRODUCT MIX	CONTRIB ($000)	PRODUCT MIX	CONTRIB ($000)	PRODUCT MIX	CONTRIB ($000)	PRODUCT MIX	CONTRIB ($000)	PRODUCT MIX	CONTRIB ($000)
AXLES	[.1]	[.5]	14.25	[.3]	7.87	[.1]	2.03	[.3]	37.47	0.31	61.63
BARS	[.2]	[.3]	17.10	[.3]	15.75	[.1]	4.06	[.3]	74.94	0.28	111.85
CLUTCHES	[.3]	[.1]	8.55	[.3]	23.62	[.5]	30.48	[.2]	74.94	0.23	137.60
DRUMS	[.4]	[.1]	11.40	[.1]	10.50	[.3]	24.38	[.2]	99.92	0.18	146.20
TOTAL CONTRIBUT		1.00	51.30	1.00	57.75	1.00	60.96	1.00	287.27	1.00	457.28
CONTB.% OF SALES			18.00		22.00		30.00		23.00		22.87
CALLS/PERIOD			11		10		20		839		880
CONTB/CALL ($000)			4.66		5.77		3.05		0.34		0.52

b. Modify the product mixes for Central in the spreadsheet:

Axles .1

Bars .1

Clutches .4

Drums .4

How does this modification change Central's total contribution? Which firm now makes the greatest contribution to sales? Using this spreadsheet, the sales manager can allocate resources to maximize account profitability. For example, he can develop strategies to encourage certain accounts to buy higher-margin products. Because Central Manufacturing has a high growth rate, it should be encouraged to buy higher-margin products.

Spreadsheet 3: Account costs and contribution

The sales manager needs to know which accounts are more costly in terms of freight, inventory, technical services, advertising, and interest on accounts receivable. The net contribution of an account depends upon these costs. Even if an account purchases a high percentage of higher-margin products, high account costs may lower its overall net contribution and diminish its profitability. Spreadsheet 3 shows how account costs can factor into the net contribution of various accounts. As you can see from the spreadsheet, the net contribution of Western Tool is greater than the net contribution of Northern Engineering ($33,590 vs $29,420) because Western Tool has lower account costs.

Spreadsheet 3:

Account cost and contribution

<table>
<tr><td colspan="11" align="center">For I Period(s)</td></tr>
<tr>
<td></td>
<td colspan="2" align="center">CENTRAL
MFG. CO.</td>
<td colspan="2" align="center">WESTERN
TOOL INC.</td>
<td colspan="2" align="center">NORTHERN
ENG. LTD.</td>
<td colspan="2" align="center">OTHER
ACCTS.</td>
<td colspan="2" align="center">TOTALS</td>
</tr>
<tr>
<td></td>
<td>ISALES</td><td>($000)</td>
<td>ISALES</td><td>($000)</td>
<td>ISALES</td><td>($000)</td>
<td>ISALES</td><td>($000)</td>
<td>ISALES</td><td>$(000)</td>
</tr>
<tr>
<td>SALES FCST. ($000)</td>
<td>100.00</td><td>285</td>
<td>100.00</td><td>262</td>
<td>100.00</td><td>203</td>
<td>100.00</td><td>1249</td>
<td>100.00</td><td>2000</td>
</tr>
<tr>
<td>ACCT·PROD CONTRIB.</td>
<td>18.00</td><td>51.30</td>
<td>22.00</td><td>57.75</td>
<td>30.00</td><td>60.96</td>
<td>23.00</td><td>287.27</td>
<td>22.87</td><td>457</td>
</tr>
<tr><td colspan="11">ACCOUNT COSTS</td></tr>
<tr>
<td>FREIGHT (DIRECT)</td>
<td>[1.00]</td><td>2.85</td>
<td>[3.00]</td><td>7.87</td>
<td>[6.00]</td><td>12.19</td>
<td>[3.00]</td><td>37.47</td>
<td>3.02</td><td>60</td>
</tr>
<tr>
<td>INVENT. (IMPUTED)</td>
<td>[3.00]</td><td>8.55</td>
<td>[4.00]</td><td>10.50</td>
<td>[2.00]</td><td>4.06</td>
<td>[1.30]</td><td>16.24</td>
<td>1.97</td><td>39</td>
</tr>
<tr>
<td>ACT REC (IMPUTED)</td>
<td>[3.00]</td><td>8.55</td>
<td>[2.00]</td><td>5.25</td>
<td>[4.00]</td><td>8.13</td>
<td>[3.00]</td><td>37.47</td>
<td>2.97</td><td>59</td>
</tr>
<tr>
<td>TEC SVC (DIRECT)</td>
<td>[1.00]</td><td>2.85</td>
<td>[0.00]</td><td>0.00</td>
<td>[1.00]</td><td>2.03</td>
<td>[1.00]</td><td>12.49</td>
<td>0.87</td><td>17</td>
</tr>
<tr>
<td>ADV/PRO (DIRECT)</td>
<td>[0.00]</td><td>0.00</td>
<td>[0.00]</td><td>0.00</td>
<td>[2.00]</td><td>4.06</td>
<td>[1.00]</td><td>12.49</td>
<td>0.83</td><td>17</td>
</tr>
<tr>
<td>TOTAL ACCOUNT COST</td>
<td>8.00</td><td>22.80</td>
<td>9.00</td><td>23.62</td>
<td>15.00</td><td>30.48</td>
<td>9.30</td><td>116.16</td>
<td>9.65</td><td>193</td>
</tr>
<tr><td colspan="11">PERSONAL SELLING</td></tr>
<tr>
<td>COST/CALL ($000)</td>
<td></td><td>[.053]</td>
<td></td><td>[.053]</td>
<td></td><td>[.053]</td>
<td></td><td>[.053]</td>
<td></td><td></td>
</tr>
<tr>
<td>CALLS/ACCOUNT</td>
<td></td><td>11</td>
<td></td><td>10</td>
<td></td><td>20</td>
<td></td><td>839</td>
<td></td><td>890</td>
</tr>
<tr>
<td>SALES COST/ACCT.</td>
<td>0.20</td><td>.583</td>
<td>0.20</td><td>.53</td>
<td>0.52</td><td>1.06</td>
<td>3.56</td><td>44.47</td>
<td>2.33</td><td>.47</td>
</tr>
<tr>
<td>TOTAL MKTG. COSTS</td>
<td>8.20</td><td>23.38</td>
<td>9.20</td><td>24.15</td>
<td>15.52</td><td>31.54</td>
<td>12.86</td><td>160.62</td>
<td>11.99</td><td>240</td>
</tr>
<tr>
<td>NET CONTRIBUTION</td>
<td>9.90</td><td>27.92</td>
<td>12.90</td><td>33.59</td>
<td>14.48</td><td>29.42</td>
<td>10.14</td><td>126.65</td>
<td>10.98</td><td>218</td>
</tr>
<tr>
<td>% OF TOTAL CONTRB.</td>
<td>12.83</td><td></td>
<td>15.44</td><td></td>
<td>13.52</td><td></td>
<td>58.21</td><td></td>
<td>100.00</td><td></td>
</tr>
<tr>
<td>% OF TOTAL CALLS</td>
<td>1.25</td><td></td>
<td>1.14</td><td></td>
<td>2.27</td><td></td>
<td>95.34</td><td></td>
<td>100.00</td><td></td>
</tr>
<tr>
<td>NET CONTRB./CALL $000</td>
<td></td><td>2.54</td>
<td></td><td>3.36</td>
<td></td><td>1.47</td>
<td></td><td>0.15</td>
<td></td><td>0.25</td>
</tr>
</table>

In the lower right portion of the spreadsheet, you will see that 95.34 percent of the sales calls are generating only 58.21 percent of the net contribution. Most of the profits are coming from the three large accounts. Perhaps the sales manager should reallocate these calls to the accounts with greatest potential. Other methods, such as telemarketing and direct mail, might be used to distribute information to many of the other, smaller accounts.

a. Develop Spreadsheet 3. You can enter the data shown in the brackets and develop formulas for the other cells. As you can see, the average cost per sales call is $53. Your output should match the output shown here.

b. Change spreadsheet 3 to reflect different account costs for Western Tool, as follows: Freight 13.00 Tech Svc 5.00

How does this modification change Western Tool's net contribution? Which firm now makes the greatest net contribution? As you can see from these spreadsheets, the sales manager can use a number of models to determine the potential profitability of each account. These models can be continually adjusted to reflect market conditions and account characteristics. Spreadsheets are invaluable tools for supporting decisions on how to allocate resources most effectively.

SELECTED INTERNET REFERENCE SITES

-Decision Support Systems

  -Decision Support Systems

    http://dsc.gsu.edu/dss.html

  -Decision Support Systems & Services

    http://www.decisioninfo.com/

  -Decision Support Systems: A Knowledge-Based Approach

    http://www.uky.edu/BusinessEconomics/dssadba/

  -Decision Support Systems

    http://sunsite.nus.sg/ORSS/dss.html

  -ISWorld Decision Support Systems Teaching Resources

    http://power.cba.uni.edu/isworld/dssteaching.html

  -1994 Annual Research Summary - Information & Decision Support Systems

    http://pasture.ecn.purdue.edu/~afenhtml/research/research94/RP7.html

  -Decision Support Systems: An Overview

    http://wwwedu.cs.utwente.nl/~uilenree/dss.html

  -Decision Support Systems by Vicki L. Sauter

    http://www.umsl.edu/~sauter/book.html

  -DSS - New and Interesting Web Sites

    http://www.umsl.edu/~squter/DSS/dss-links.html

-Executive Information Systems

  -Executive Information Systems Home Page

    http://www.tm.tue.nl/tm/vakgr/it/ozt 1/index.htm

  -Executive Information Systems

    http://www.origin.nl/origin.ext/facts/company/homepages/eiscc/eiseis.htm

  -Computer Information Center - Executive Information Systems, Report Writers, Data Warehousing

    http://www.compinfo.co.uk./tpeis. html

-Expert Systems

  -Building Expert Systems

    http://pasture.ecn.purdue.edu/~agenhtml/agen-565/es.htm

  -The International Journal of Applied Expert Systems

    http://info.abdn.ac.uk/~acc025/ijaes.htm

  -Expert Systems Assist in Fraud Detection

    http://wwwcob2.acad.emich.edu/~s129475/estask.html

  -Expert Systems Online Resources

    http://www.cbu.edu/~pong/624es.htm

  -Expert Systems Capability (Diagnosis and Design)

    http://krusty.eecs.umich.edu/cogarch0/common/capa/expert.html

  -Expert Systems in Agriculture

    http://potato.claes.sci.eg/claes/wes.htm

  -Expert Systems in Medicine

    http://amplatz.uokhsc.edu/acc95-expert-systems.html

  -The Problem with Expert Systems

    http://www.ils.nwu.edu/~e_for_e/nodes/NODE-22-pg.htm

  -Expert Systems Review for Business and Accounting - Table of Contents

    http://www.bus.orst.edu/faculty/brownc/isafm/tocesr.htm

  -Expert Systems with Applications (Special Issues)

    http://www.elsevier.nl:80/inca/publications/store/3/0/3/7/7/

  -Legal Expert Systems Limited Home Page

    http://www.demon.co.uk/lesl/

  -The Impact of Expert Systems

    http://www.morebusiness.com/other/v2n8.html

SELECTED REFERENCES AND READINGS

Alloway, R. and J. Quillard. "User Managers' Systems Needs." *MIS Quarterly* 7, no. 2 (1983), pp. 27–41.

Carlson, E. D. "An Approach for Designing Decision Support Systems." In *Building Effective Decision Support Systems,* eds. R. Sprague and E. Carlson. Englewood Cliffs, NJ: Prentice Hall, 1982.

Davis, D. B. "Artificial Intelligence Goes to Work." *High Technology* 7, no. 4 (April 1987), pp. 16–27.

Davis, G. "Caution: User-Developed Systems Can Be Dangerous to Your Organization." MISRC Working Paper 82-04. Minneapolis: Management Information Systems Research Center, University of Minnesota, February 1984.

Dennis, A.; J. George; L. Jessup; J. Nunamaker; and D. Vogel. "Information Technology to Support Electronic Meetings." *MIS Quarterly,* December 1988, pp. 591–624.

DeSanctis, G. and R. B. Gallupe. "A Foundation for the Study of Group Decision Support Systems." *Management Science* 33, no. 5 (May 1987), pp. 589-609.

DeSanctis, G. and R. B. Gallupe. "Group Decision Support Systems: A New Frontier." *Database,* Winter 1985, pp. 190-201.

Gorry, G. A. and M. S. S. Morton. "A Framework for Management Information Systems." *Sloan Management Review* 13, no. 1 (1971), pp. 55-70.

Keen, Peter G. W. "Value Analysis: Justifying Decision Support Systems." *MIS Quarterly* 5, no. 1 (1981), pp. 1-15.

Keen, P. G. W. and T. J. Gambino. "Building a Decision Support System: The Mythical Man Month Revisited." In *Building Effective Decision Support Systems,* ed. R. Sprague and E. Carlson. Englewood Cliffs, NJ: Prentice Hall, 1982.

Keim, R. and S. Jacobs. "Expert Systems: The DSS of the Future?" *Journal of Systems Management* 37, no. 12 (December 1986), pp. 6-14.

MacGrimmon, K. R. and R. N. Taylor. "Decision Making and Problem Solving." In *Handbook of Industrial and Organizational Psychology,* ed. M. D. Dunnette. Chicago: Rand McNally, 1976, pp. 1397-1453.

Meador, C. L. and P. G. W. Keen. "Setting Priorities for DSS Development." *MIS Quarterly* 8, no. 2 (1984), pp. 117-129.

Meador, L. et al., "Personal Computer and Distributed Decision Support." *Computerworld,* May 7, 1984.

Mills, C. "The Information Center." *DRS Journal* 1, no. 1 (1983), pp. 1-104.

Mintzberg, H.; D. Raisinghani; and A. Theoret. "The Structure of 'Unstructured' Decision Processes." *Administrative Science Quarterly* 21 (June 1976), pp. 246-75.

Newquist, H. P. "American Express and AI: Don't Leave Home without Them." *AI Expert* 2, no. 4 (April 1987), pp. 63-5.

Nolan, R. L. "Managing the Advanced Stages of Computer Technology: Key Research Issues." In *The Information Systems Research Challenge: Proceedings,* ed. F. W. McFarlan. Boston: Harvard Business School Press, 1984, pp. 195-210.

Nunamaker, J. F.; A. Dennis; J. Valacich; D. Vogel; and J. George. "Electronic Meeting Systems to Support Group Work." *Communications of the ACM* 34, no. 7 (July 1991), pp. 40-61.

Rockart, J. "The CEO Goes On-Line." *Harvard Business Review,* January-February 1982, pp. 82-88.

Rockart, J.; and M. Treacy. "Executive Information Support Systems." Sloan Working Paper 1167-80. Cambridge: Center for Information Systems Research, Massachusetts Institute of Technology, April 1981.

Turban, E. and P. Watkins. "Integrating Expert Systems and Decision-Support Systems." In *Decision Support Systems: Putting Theory into Practice,* R. H. Sprague Jr. and H. J. Watson. Englewood Cliffs, NJ: Prentice Hall, 1986.

Waterman, D. A. *A Guide to Expert Systems.* Reading, MA: Addison-Wesley, 1986.

Analyzing the Computer Personnel Allocation Problem at Software Reengineering Company (SRC), Inc.

Background

The Software Reengineering Company (SRC), Inc., develops computer software and installs computer information systems for client firms and organizations on a contract basis. For many years SRC focused on contract software development for various agencies of the U.S. government, primarily the Department of Defense (DOD). DOD contract development is still SRC's "bread and butter" business. Today, however, the firm also has divisions that supply contract software solutions to client firms in the private sector of the economy.

The original owner of SRC, Mr. Stanley Pyszynski, organized the firm's first office in St. Louis, Missouri. SRC has grown since that time to its current stature as a nationwide provider of computer software solutions. (See Integrated Case 1 for more background information.)

SRC provides a full-line of contract computer information system solutions. SRC's main selling strength is its ability to help client firms and organizations integrate existing information systems that do not currently enable data sharing. When SRC finishes a job, various managers and computer systems users throughout the client firm are better able to share data. SRC especially focuses on installing computer systems that support operational- and tactical-level decision making through the use of database management system technology.

Even though typical data processing systems for organizations such as order entry, human resource management, inventory management, purchasing, and the like can be described in fairly generic terms, actual computer information systems that exist within different client firms and organizations are quite unique. The management processes that computer systems support can vary considerably from one firm to another. For this rea-

son, information systems specialists who actually design, program, and implement the solutions provided by SRC are faced with very complex development tasks.

When SRC contracts with a client firm to build or reengineer an existing computer information system, SRC and the client firm must agree on a set of computer system specifications. These specifications detail the various components of the information system that SRC will deliver. In order to meet contract specifications and manage the development process, SRC regional office divisions are organized into project teams. Since a division can have a dozen or more different projects underway at one time, each project team is usually responsible for many projects at the same time.

The complex nature of the computer systems development environment makes project management at SRC a very important issue. The project team leader must coordinate the development of the various components of a computer information system. In a typical project, certain development tasks must be completed before other tasks can be started. For example, a computer programmer cannot write a program to access data in a database until the database design/implementation task is completed. Sometimes tasks can overlap during their development. For example, two different systems analysts could be developing computer screen layouts and report layouts for different parts of an information system at the same time.

The primary resources to be managed in this environment are the specialized computer personnel who actually build the various components of the client's project. The project team leader must ensure that personnel resources are allocated to appropriate tasks on a timely basis or else projects will fall behind schedule.

See Figure C1-2 for the typical allocation of computer specialists and other personnel to a regional office contract division of SRC. This figure shows a situation in which two project team leaders report to the division chief. A pool of computer specialists are available for assignment to various projects. Each project team leader may be responsible for from three to eight projects at a time. The division chief allocates computer specialists to the various projects, and the project team leaders supervise their work according to the projects that they are managing.

Recently SRC has experienced problems competing with other firms in the contract software development industry. In particular, firms located in Seattle, Washington, have been bidding contract software prices lower than SRC is bidding them. Further, these competitors are bidding to complete projects faster than SRC has been able to complete them. SRC is also failing to complete projects by the estimated completion date. Contract sales negotiators at SRC are responsible for estimating project completion dates and cost figures. To prevent the loss of contracts, the negotiators have begun to promise shorter delivery times than those offered by competitors whenever a potential client firm complains about the estimated completion date. In order to meet these promised project completion dates, division chiefs have pushed project team leaders to give these projects "special" attention.

A project's estimated completion date is a reflection of the amount of actual work that is required to complete the design, programming, testing, and installation of a computer information system. Often a project installation includes new hardware and network components. When contract sales negotiators at SRC bid on projects, they estimate the time requirements based on a number of factors. They factor in the initial system requirements that are specified by the client firm. Unfortunately, system requirements may vary somewhat as the design process unfolds. New, unforeseen requirements may arise. Sometimes SRC can adjust the contract price as a result of new requirements, and other times it cannot, especially with fixed-price government requirements. Of course, SRC's goal is to satisfy the customer, so

sometimes SRC absorbs the extra work as a cost of doing business.

A key factor affecting SRC's ability to complete projects on time is the availability of appropriately trained computer system specialists to work on the project. The project team leader's role is of paramount importance to projecting success and to meeting the estimated completion date. If the project team leader fails to allocate personnel resources properly among competing projects that he or she is managing, some projects will fall behind schedule. At this point the project team leader is faced with a difficult decision: to reallocate computer personnel from other projects in order to focus on the project that is late or to incur the penalties associated with delivering a project late to a client. Penalties may be intangible, such as lost goodwill, or they may be very tangible, such as a monetary penalty. The pressure that division chiefs put on project team leaders often causes them to reallocate computer personnel from the project task the computer specialist is currently working on to tasks that are part of the "late" or "special" projects. Although this approach may speed up completion of a project, it can lead to havoc with the scheduling of personnel and tasks for other projects.

CURRENT SITUATION

Marvin Albert is the St. Louis regional office chief of the defense contract software division. On this particular Tuesday afternoon, Marvin is reviewing the month's software development productivity figures. Yesterday Marvin met with Malivai Washington, executive vice president in charge of the St. Louis regional office, to discuss the productivity figures. Malivai Washington directed Marvin to investigate the firm's recent apparent drop in software developer productivity. Washington was also concerned with the division's seeming inability to meet contract software expected completion dates. Marvin recalled the meeting vividly.

"Marvin, I don't know what is going on with the software development specialists working in your defense contract software division, but this latest report shows unacceptable results," complained Malivai at the meeting. The St. Louis office cannot continue to accept this level performance. We're losing market share in the defense contract software area and have been for at least six months. Do you have any idea what the problem is?"

"Well, sir," said Marvin. "I think the problem is a direct result of the high level of rush orders we're receiving. Our contract sales negotiators are simply promising more than we can deliver. They're bidding contracts promising we can produce software and install computer information systems faster than we can. I think they need a shake up—maybe firing the senior contract sales negotiator will fix the problem."

"Well, before I take some action like that, I'd have to have some proof that their contract bids are definitely out of line," replied Malivai. "You may not be aware of this, but the other two divisions here in St. Louis are able to complete their projects within the estimated completion dates specified in our bids. Further, they're not experiencing the overtime your division is experiencing. And you know that the same contract sales negotiators who negotiate your contracts are negotiating the contracts of the other two divisions."

"Further," added Malivai, "our competitors are also beating us to the punch in the defense contracting area. So I'm not certain that your reasoning is accurate. What proof can you give me that the contract bids are out of line?"

Marvin was definitely in a pickle as he tried to formulate his answer to Malivai's question. "Well, the level of rush orders we're receiving for contract software development is simply overwhelming," answered Marvin. "It seems like every time one of my programmers or software specialists begins working on a development task on one project, he or she gets pulled off of that task to work on some other task for a project that is behind schedule. Of course, when the programmer returns to the original task, sometimes days later, he or she has difficulty starting again. It takes some time to get reoriented and to remember the complex logic that was required in writing the computer program or specifications for the task. I think this description is causing us to incur a lot of unproductive work time because we lose the

hours the computer specialists spend trying to get going again for the project tasks that are not being rushed."

"Marvin, I don't want you to tell me what you *think* the problem is. I want you to tell me that you *know* what the problem is, and you don't have to lecture me about the problems associated with computer programming," growled Malivai. "I've been in the industry for more than 20 years, and you know that I've written a lot of computer code and delivered a lot of software myself over the years. I think I understand computer programming and software development as well as anyone. You know we have to give personnel allocation priority to projects that are behind schedule; otherwise, we won't be able to beat the competition, and we'll incur large penalties."

"Besides, I don't think that moving computer specialists from one task to another is the problem," Malivai continued. They're professionals, and they like a challenge. That's why they're often here late at night working on projects—they just love solving computer problems no matter how long it takes. I was the same way when I was younger. I think the problem is that you need to reorganize your division into a larger number of project teams and balance the skill levels of the workers on the various teams by providing more training to your computer specialists. In fact, I've been thinking about mandating an increase in the number of project teams for all of the divisions in St. Louis. If it works here, the same approach could be applied to the other regions, and the likely end result is that I'd be moved to corporate headquarters in Arlington to supervise the new approach. The bottom line is you either get me the evidence I need to back up your perspective on the problem or make the reorganization and personnel changes necessary to get these productivity figures back in line."

Marvin was still stewing about the meeting. He knew that most of his computer professionals had years of experience on the job and were quite adept at solving complex computer systems development problems. Fortunately, he had a plan to prove that reallocating personnel from one task to another in a haphazard fashion was the problem.

THE PLAN

Marvin knew that if reallocating computer professional resources from one task to another without allowing them to complete tasks they had already started was the root problem, then projects where this type of personnel allocation was not used should tend to be completed fairly close to the estimated completion date called for in the contract bid. Projects where workers were pulled to work on other projects would tend to fall behind schedule and incur overtime costs. Also Marvin knew that he could compare average actual task times required to complete tasks against average estimated task times. In order to prove this point, Marvin needed to select an appropriate set of comparable projects; otherwise, Malivai might argue that Marvin was comparing apples to oranges.

Marvin worked with his two project team leaders to select an appropriate set of projects. He didn't explain to them the nature of his quest because he didn't want them to be biased in the selection of projects. The data for the projects that were selected is shown in Figures C3-1 and C3-2. Marvin obtained data for projects that were completed over the last six months.

Figure C3-1 gives data for 70 selected tasks. These tasks are divided into four categories and coded as follows: A = analysis task; D = design task; P = programming task; and T = test/implementation task. Data for each task shows the actual hours required to complete the task versus the original estimated hours required to complete the task. The last column indicates whether the computer specialist(s) assigned to complete each task was interrupted in order to work on other tasks. If Marvin is correct, tasks that were interrupted prior to completion should, on average, take longer to complete than their original estimate.

Figure C3-2 gives data for 36 projects. Of these, 18 are projects that were completed by Marvin's division. The remaining 18 projects were completed by project teams assigned to the corporate contract software division. From talking to Ms. Juliet Hartman, division chief of the corporate contract software division at the St. Louis regional office, Marvin knew that Juliet's division tended to avoid moving personnel resources from one task to another until they completed their work. Marvin had selected projects from his division where he knew significant personnel reallocation took place.

Each project in Figure C3-2 is identified by a project number. The second column identifies the projects from the two divisions. The estimated total number of hours to complete each project is given in the next column. This figure is equivalent to the total work in a project. The actual total number of hours required to complete each project is given in column 4. Projects that required overtime would tend to have an actual number of hours that exceeded the estimated number of hours. The last two columns indicate whether or not each project was completed by the estimated completion date. If the plus-or-minus column indicates a plus, then the project exceeded the estimated completion date by the number of days indicated in the last column. If a minus appears, then the project was completed that many days early.

Marvin decided to analyze the data by using two microcomputer software packages with which he was familiar—a spreadsheet package and a database management system package. He eventually planned to build a decision-support system that would help him identify potential projects that were going to fall behind schedule, but this was a task best left to the future. For now he planned to use these tools to analyze his division's productivity figures. Marvin believed this would enable him to determine if the problem was related to giving priority for personnel resources to one project over another one.

Case Questions and Exercises

For this exercise you will use a microcomputer database management system (DBMS) and/or a microcomputer spreadsheet package. Your instructor will direct you as to the particular DBMS and/or spreadsheet selected. You will have to create your data files and enter the data into the records. You need to be careful not to make mistakes entering the data.

Figure C3–1

Task data

Task #	Task type	Estimated hours for task completion	Actual hours for task completion	Task was interrupted (yes or no)
1	P	10.2	14.4	Yes
2	A	18.8	17.7	No
3	T	21.4	20.1	Yes
4	P	22.4	20.8	No
5	D	8.4	8.2	No
6	D	12.4	12.5	No
7	T	22.8	20	No
8	P	8.4	9	No
9	A	19.2	19.4	Yes
10	D	48.4	40.4	No
11	D	22.8	28.2	Yes
12	T	8.5	9.1	Yes
13	D	12	12	No
14	A	17.2	16.8	No
15	P	7.2	14.4	Yes
16	P	4	4.8	Yes
17	A	12.3	8.1	Yes
18	D	15.2	18.2	Yes
19	P	4.2	3.8	No
20	T	28.5	27	No
21	A	18.4	21.2	No
22	D	22.3	28.8	Yes
23	P	18.4	21.7	Yes
24	A	23.4	27.2	Yes
25	P	17	14.4	No
26	P	17.1	15.8	No
27	T	22.8	28.8	Yes
28	A	27.4	26.5	No
29	P	48.4	61.2	Yes
30	T	28.4	28.5	No
31	D	33.4	37.5	No
32	P	41.3	40.1	No
33	A	33.4	33.7	Yes
34	T	45.5	40.3	No
35	P	37.3	47.1	Yes
36	D	12.4	21.4	Yes
37	A	36	34.3	No
38	D	12.8	10.1	No
39	A	41.2	44.3	Yes
40	P	12	11.9	No
41	D	4.4	5.2	Yes
42	T	45.3	38.9	Yes
43	P	12.1	13.9	Yes
44	A	18.2	15.8	No
45	T	30.3	31.2	No
46	D	4.3	4.5	No
47	P	8.4	15.5	Yes
48	A	19.2	19.8	Yes
49	P	9.9	11.8	No
50	D	19.9	25.6	Yes
51	P	15.5	19.9	Yes
52	T	51.5	52.3	Yes
53	D	18.4	21.6	Yes
54	A	28.8	30.5	No
55	P	14.1	15.3	Yes
56	D	15.4	14.2	No
57	T	8.9	9.2	No
58	A	37.3	41.2	Yes
59	P	22.8	29.2	No
60	D	8.8	4.5	No
61	D	9.2	10.4	No
62	T	4.3	4.5	No
63	A	38.5	35.5	No
64	P	28.8	37.8	No
65	T	17.2	18.2	Yes
66	P	12.4	15.5	Yes
67	D	18.2	25.6	Yes
68	D	19.2	19	Yes
69	A	40.2	33.8	Yes
70	P	8.8	6.2	No
	TOTAL	1463.5	1546.3	

Task type codes: P = programming; A = analysis; D = design; T = testing/implementation

Figure C3–2

Project data

Project #	Project code	Estimated total hours to complete project	Actual total hours to complete project	+ or –	Days of deviation from the estimated completion date
1	D	1255	1450	+	15
2	D	850	910	+	16
3	D	725	710	+	13
4	D	1250	1290	–	4
5	D	1300	1375	+	9
6	D	1475	1500	–	6
7	D	450	400	–	5
8	D	790	780	–	3
9	D	950	970	+	12
10	D	1200	1245	+	13
11	D	1250	1275	+	9
12	D	1800	1785	–	3
13	D	1650	1620	+	1
14	D	1475	1575	+	5
15	D	1800	1810	+	12
16	D	1700	1710	+	10
17	C	1245	1240	–	4
18	C	900	875	+	6
19	C	700	710	–	5
20	C	1275	1300	–	8
21	C	1260	1265	+	3
22	C	1485	1500	+	11
23	C	440	400	–	4
24	C	800	855	+	2
25	C	930	875	–	6
26	C	1210	1250	+	3
27	C	1240	1205	–	8
28	C	1830	1855	–	2
29	C	1610	1570	–	1
30	C	1500	1500	–	1
31	C	1775	1755	+	5
32	C	1750	1790	+	7
33	C	1190	1095	–	3
34	C	950	960	–	6
35	C	650	675	–	1
36	C	1275	1310	+	7

Project codes: D = defense division; C = corporate division
Deviation from the estimated completion date code: + indicates the
project took longer than originally estimated; – indicates the
project was completed earlier than was originally estimated.

Microcomputer DBMS Exercises

1. Create a database in which to store the data given in Figures C3–1 and C3–2. You will need two different DBMS tables. You must determine an appropriate data structure.

2. Use the DBMS query generator feature to create queries that give the following average productivity figures.

   a. Compute a separate set of averages and standard deviations for each task type given in Figure C3–1 as follows: (1) the average (and standard deviation) estimated hours for task completion and (2) the average (and standard

   deviation) of actual hours for task completion.

   b. Compute the same averages as in (a) above except you should compute separate averages by task type for tasks where the task was interrupted versus tasks where no interruption took place.

3. Assume you are Marvin. Write a one-page memorandum to Malivai explaining your results and answering the question: Does interrupting tasks tend to increase the time required to complete tasks beyond the original estimate? Attach documentation to support your explanation.

Microcomputer Spreadsheet Exercises

4. Create a spreadsheet with the data from Figures C3–1 and C3–2. If you created the database required in question 1, you may elect to either import the data from the microcomputer DBMS file you created or restructure the layout for the data in your spreadsheet to facilitate your analysis. You must decide upon the appropriate layout for the data.

5. Compute the averages outlined in question 2.

6. Complete the memorandum requirement outlined in question 3. In addition to evidence provided in the spreadsheet computations, develop appropriate graphs that support your explanation. For example, if your analysis supports Marvin, you might develop bar graphs that show estimated versus actual completion times for tasks by type.

PLANNING AND DEVELOPMENT OF INFORMATION SYSTEMS

IN THIS PART OF THE TEXT, you will learn about information systems planning, analysis, and design. Managers need to think about how information technology can be used to support business plans. By learning about planning methods, you will develop a better understanding of how information systems can be used to provide feedback on overall business performance.

In addition, managers must become directly involved in analyzing current business systems, in recommending necessary changes in business processes, in evaluating alternative hardware and software options, and in judging the financial and technical feasibility of a project. You will learn about these issues in the chapters on systems analysis, systems design, and alternative application development approaches.

CHAPTER 13
INFORMATION
SYSTEMS PLANNING

CHAPTER 14
SYSTEMS ANALYSIS
AND DESIGN

CHAPTER 15
ALTERNATIVE
APPLICATION
DEVELOPMENT
APPROACHES

INFORMATION SYSTEMS PLANNING

CHAPTER OUTLINE

Manager's View

Information Systems Planning Strategies

Problems with Determining Information Requirements

Managing by Wire in a Complex Business Environment

Critical Success Factors

Business Systems Planning

Ends/Means (E/M) Analysis

Technology Planning in an Age of Uncertainty

Organizing the Information Systems Plan

Management Summary

Key Terms for Managers

Review Questions

Questions for Discussion

Problems

Selected References and Readings

As a manager, you will make decisions on the types of information systems that should be developed to support important business plans. The emergence of new technologies, such as office automation, expert systems, personal computers, and robotics, has created new opportunities for improving productivity. To take advantage of these opportunities, you must understand and be able to use appropriate information systems planning methods. Information systems planning methods help managers plan and organize information resources, including data processing systems and new information technology.

INFORMATION SYSTEMS PLANNING STRATEGIES

The major focus of this chapter will be to familiarize you with methods the manager can use to specify information requirements. Today's manager needs information to make decisions on pricing, product development, marketing strategy, and resource allocation. Most managers suffer from too much information—they get too many computer-generated printouts and too much e-mail. Yet much of the information they need to make decisions is not available on a timely basis.

Managers need to take a proactive role in defining their requirements for computer-based information systems. But first, they need to determine what information they need. Most managers do not know what information they need, and as a result, they put the systems analyst in the position of producing too much information.

In this chapter you will learn about the major problems involved in determining management information needs. Then you will learn about three methodologies a manager can use to determine these needs more effectively (see Figure 13–1): critical success factors (CSF), business systems planning (BSP), and ends/means (E/M) analysis. Each of these approaches is fundamental to establishing information systems plans that serve the needs of managers.

PROBLEMS WITH DETERMINING INFORMATION REQUIREMENTS

Two important problems with information requirements definitions are the failure to understand information needs from a cross-functional perspective and the limited use of joint application design in interviewing and data collection. In Chapter 4 you learned how business process reengineering is being used as a strategy to define data requirements that must be shared across functional lines. For example, when a con-

Figure 13–1
Information
planning methods

METHOD	PURPOSE	DEVELOPER
Business Systems Planning (BSP)	To specify problems and decisions.	IBM
Critical Success Factors (CSF)	To define critical success factors.	Rockart
Ends/Means(E/M) Analysis	To specify effectiveness criteria for outputs and efficiency criteria for processes.	Wetherbe

solidated accounts payable, warehousing, and purchasing database was designed at Ford Motor Company, much of the paperwork for reconciling incoming shipments with invoices and purchase orders was eliminated. Instead, when a shipment was received into the warehouse, an individual checked the database to determine if the shipment matched a purchase order. If it did, an accounts payable check was generated to pay for the goods received.

As another example, let us say that a computer manufacturer has hundreds of orders pending. The manager must determine how to allocate existing inventory in the most effective way. The question the warehouse manager needs to ask is, Which customer orders should we fill first? Should inventory be allocated to the customers who do the most business with the company, who need prompt delivery, who provide the greatest profit margin, or who are most likely to pay their bills on time? In order to make the decision on inventory allocation, the warehouse manager will need the following information:

How important is each customer to the business?

Which customer accounts are most profitable?

Which customers need prompt delivery on their orders?

What is the credit status of the customers requiring shipment?

The information that the warehouse manager needs to make allocation decisions comes from sources outside the warehouse. For example, information on customer importance and profitability would come from the sales and marketing department. Information on credit history would come from accounting, and information on delivery requirements would come from customer service representatives.

In developing information requirements for the warehouse, other functional areas must be taken into account. Perhaps a cross-functional database with information accessible to sales, accounting, customer service, and warehouse personnel will have to be designed. Because information is needed for intelligent decision making within many departments, the old concept of information "ownership" (e.g., sales information being owned by sales) is outmoded and counterproductive. Without shared information, the organization ends up in a situation where the right hand does not know what the left hand is doing.

The concept of shared information also applies to the importance of joint application design as a process for determining the information requirements of managers. Obtaining a cross-functional perspective in defining information needs requires input from managers in a number of departments. It is difficult to achieve an overall organizational perspective if each manager is interviewed individually.

Take, for example, the case of a direct-mail catalog company. Prior to joint application design the credit department viewed its mission as minimizing credit losses and as a result accumulated more and more information about customers—including credit references, credit bureau checks, and internal credit history files. The cost of maintaining credit records was excessive.

After an exercise in joint application design, the company decided it was better off not doing any credit checks. Why? Because it could send catalogs to first-time buyers on a trial basis. Those who made orders and paid for these orders could be maintained as catalog customers; those who didn't pay could be dropped from any future mailings immediately.

Using this logic, the company could use its own credit experience to generate mailings. It quickly learned that its losses from nonpaying customers were actually much less than the former cost of doing all the credit checks themselves. Furthermore, it turned out that people who were often depicted as higher credit risks were generally the best catalog buyers, and people who were better credit risks rarely purchased goods from the company's catalogs. If the company had continued to use creditworthiness as a criterion for making mailings, it would have continued to send out catalogs to people with excellent credit ratings—who seldom bought anything. In effect, the company was better off marketing to people who were higher credit risks and then establishing their ability to pay through experience with these accounts.

The lesson learned from this case is that if the credit department had been the sole group interviewed, the old system would have remained in place; the company would have continued to maintain expensive credit files and to send catalogs to individuals who were least likely to make purchases. It was the joint work of sales management and the credit department that provided the insight into making a change in the business process and in the information requirements.

MANAGING BY WIRE IN A COMPLEX BUSINESS ENVIRONMENT

In today's business environment, flexibility, responsiveness, and sensitivity to changing customer needs are critical for competitive survival. Stephen Haeckel and Richard Nolan compare today's management challenges to "flying by wire," using computer systems to augment a pilot's ability to assimilate and react to rapidly changing environmental information.[1] When a pilot makes a decision to veer sharply to the left, for example, the pilot's command translates into thousands of detailed orders that orchestrate the plane's behavior in real time.

"Managing by wire" is the same thing. Like a plane at high speeds, a company must be able to respond to a turbulent business environment. The manage-by-wire environment means being able to modify business plans based upon changes in market conditions. It means using information as feedback by sensing environmental conditions, interpreting them, and selecting a plan of action that can be sent out to subsidiary units such as manufacturing and sales.

The Air Force assesses a pilot's ability to learn with the concept of the OODA loop, a model for the mental processes of a fighter pilot. OODA stands for *observation,* the ability to sense environmental signals; *orientation,* the ability to interpret these signals; *decision,* the ability to select from a repertoire of available responses; and *action,* the ability to execute the response selected. A pilot's ability depends upon this learning loop, which constantly processes information and uses it to take action.

An enterprise must create learning loops that enable it to sense changes in the external environment, to interpret them, to decide how to respond to them, and to take action. Feedback from the external environment must provide measures of how well the business is performing. If market needs change, then the information system must provide feedback to trigger changes in the internal mix of activities and in the outputs the system generates.

Let's see how the concept of learning loops can be applied to a business situation. *At Mrs. Fields Cookies,* local managers enter projected sales information into a microcomputer each morning. The software analyzes the data and responds with

---

[1]Stephen Haeckel and Richard Nolan, "Managing by Wire," *Harvard Business Review,* September–October 1993, pp. 122–33.

Figure 13–2
Information
requirements
definition methods

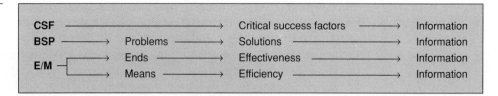

information on how many batches of cookies to make, how to adjust cookie distribution (e.g., chocolate chip versus oatmeal raisin) as the pattern of customer buying unfolds, and how to schedule workers. This decision support system provides a learning loop that can adapt and change in the course of the day's business activity.

Sometimes the learning loop can generate feedback to suppliers. *Wal-Mart,* for example, transmits information about sales of jeans to Wrangler, its supplier, each day. This information translates into a distribution plan that sends specific quantities of sizes and colors of jeans to designated stores from certain warehouses. This learning loop lowers logistics and inventory costs and allows Wal-Mart stores to stock the sizes and styles their customers need.

The concept of a learning loop is basic to identifying the information requirements of managers. In order to react on a timely basis, managers need feedback from the external environment that provides data on changing sales and market trends. The ability to define these feedback requirements is an essential element in all three strategies for information requirements definition that you will learn about in this chapter. Figure 13-2 provides a framework that briefly summarizes the techniques used to gather information requirements in each method: CSF, BSP, and E/M analysis.

CRITICAL SUCCESS FACTORS

The **critical success factors (CSF) method,** developed by John Rockart of the Massachusetts Institute of Technology, addresses the information needs of senior management. In particular, it is meant to deal with the frustration of senior managers who receive dozens of computer-generated reports each month, but find little information of value in these reports.

Traditional approaches to helping managers define their information needs are ineffective, Rockart argues.[2] One such method, which he calls the "by-product technique," uses the by-products of transactions processing systems to support managers' needs. However, reports such as sales summaries and monthly budget summaries may not zero in on current business problems.

A more effective way of spotting problems is to develop key indicators of the health of the business and to focus on significant deviations from planned performance. A report comparing the unit margins on various product lines, this March versus last March, is an example of an exception report that may help managers focus on problems and opportunities. One limitation of this type of report is that it may fail to address issues brought on by changes in the business environment and competitive strategy.

---

[2]John Rockart, "Chief Executives Define Their Own Data Needs," *Harvard Business Review,* March–April 1979, pp. 81-93.

As a result of their frustration with current management reporting systems, many managers fail to use computer-generated information to make decisions. They argue that the business environment is so dynamic that no information system could be designed to provide them with the information they need.

Defining Critical Success Factors

The CSF method attempts to overcome the limitations of the by-product technique and other reporting methods by focusing on the information needs of individual managers. The first step in the CSF method is for the manager to identify his or her goals. The next question the manager must answer is, What are the critical success factors underlying these goals? A critical success factor defines "what has to go right" to achieve a business goal. An example of goals and critical success factors for three profit-making organizations appears in Figure 13–3. Even though the business goals of these three organizations are the same, the strategies that must be implemented effectively to achieve these goals vary.

The nature of an industry may determine some of the critical success factors. For example, succeeding in the paperwork-intensive insurance business requires cost-effective back-office operations and clerical productivity. In the automobile business, manufacturing cost control is an important critical success factor.

In addition, the competitive strategy of a particular business may determine other critical success factors. For example, two department stores may have similar objectives but different strategies. One, an established department store like Saks Fifth Avenue, may view effective customer service, styling of merchandise, and quality control as key to its competitive success. A discount department store like Kmart would have different critical success factors such as pricing, high turnover of seasonal merchandise, and advertising effectiveness.

Figure 13–3

Critical success factors

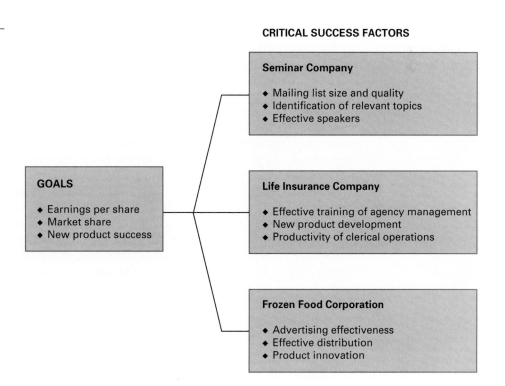

Figure 13–4
Critical success factors and measures for a discount department store

CRITICAL SUCCESS FACTORS	MEASURES
Pricing	Margin percentage for various product lines
High turnover of seasonal merchandise	Inventory turnover by product line
	Inventory analysis, by item, this year versus last year (for example, March 1998 versus March 1997)
Advertising effectiveness	Change in market share, by product line

Defining Measures

The critical success factors help managers define their information needs. Information that is valuable to the manager should support achievement of these critical success factors by providing measures of how well they are being achieved. As an example, a discount department store's critical success factors and the methods of measuring them are given in Figure 13–4. Pricing is important in the discount business because margins are low. A report on the margin percentage for various product lines enables sales management to make pricing decisions that ensure an adequate margin on sales. Inventory turnover, another important indicator, could be analyzed by product line so that stockouts could be minimized and year-to-year sales trends evaluated.

Each of these measures can be used to define an information systems requirement. After these needs are established, existing information systems can be analyzed to determine if reports providing the needed information currently exist or if they can be generated from existing databases.

If the necessary reports cannot be generated from existing information systems, the manager can identify "new" information requirements. If the organization provides access to databases for database query and reporting applications, some of these information needs may be satisfied by user-developed systems. Other projects, however, may require full-scale systems development projects.

Advantages and Limitations

An advantage of the CSF method is that it enables managers to determine their own critical success factors and to develop good measures for these factors. As a manager, you can develop an information system that is meaningful to you. The costly accumulation of unnecessary data is limited. Reports that list data on sales, customers, and inventories, often generated because the data are available and easy to print out, are minimized. The focus of information systems developed to support CSFs is effective control and monitoring of existing operations. If inventory levels are too high or if sales figures of a particular product line are below expected levels, you can use reports that highlight these conditions to take remedial action.

Finally, the CSF method accommodates changes in competitive strategy, business environment, and organizational structure. In a dynamic business environment, the information needs of managers change. Managers cannot wait six months to a year for an information system to be built that helps them determine how well a particular competitive initiative is doing. By the time the system is built, a completely different strategy may be in effect. The CSF method enables managers to define information needs that can be supported by flexible inquiry and reporting systems. These systems, which use existing databases to generate a variety of on-demand reports, are commonly known as decision support systems.

The main limitation of the CSF method is that it focuses on manager-specific information needs, rather than on organizationwide information requirements. Its original objective was to help senior executives define the information they needed for effective planning and control. The CSF method doesn't try to recommend a data architecture planning strategy to accompany the analysis of managerial information needs, and it doesn't address the MIS management responsibilities associated with implementing these systems projects.

BUSINESS SYSTEMS PLANNING

The **business systems planning method** assists a business in developing an information systems plan that supports both short- and long-term information needs.[3] This method provides a formal, objective way for management to establish information systems priorities that support business needs. In the process of participating in a BSP study, top management should improve its relationships with information systems professionals and make a commitment to the development of high-return information systems projects.

One of the underlying objectives of BSP is to develop a data architecture that supports information systems development activities. Most organizations build their information systems one piece at a time. As each system is built, a new database is constructed to store data elements needed to generate reports. After dozens of systems are built, the organization has to grapple with the problem of maintaining dozens of databases. Many of these databases store the same data elements, contributing to problems of data redundancy and data inconsistency.

For example, customer-related data elements may be used in 33 different reports and stored in 18 different databases. When a customer's address changes, the relevant data elements have to be changed 18 times. The BSP approach attempts to overcome this problem by analyzing data requirements for major business processes and proposing a data architecture that supports multiple applications. In the next section, you'll learn how this is accomplished.

BSP Study Activities

The major activities that are involved in a BSP study are these:

Make a commitment.

Prepare for the study.

Hold a kickoff meeting.

Define business processes.

Define data classes.

Determine executive perspective.

Assess business problems.

Define an information architecture.

Determine priorities.

---

[3]"IBM Business Systems Planning." In J. Daniel Couger, Mel Colter, and Robert Knapp, *Advanced Systems Development/Feasibility Techniques.* New York: John Wiley & Sons, Inc., 1982.

Review information systems management.

Develop recommendations and action plans.

Report results.

The Study Team   At the outset of the BSP study, a study team is organized to participate in gathering data. The study team consists of managers from different functional areas to do the required interviewing. The first step is to identify the major business processes of the organization. (A *business process* is an activity needed to manage the resources of the business.)

Methods of Analysis   These business processes become the basis for understanding information systems needs and for identifying key data requirements. The BSP methodology uses a number of matrices to establish relationships among the organization, its processes, and data requirements. The process/organization matrix shown in Figure 13–5 relates the activities of the organization to people responsible for these activities.

One of the major objectives of BSP is to identify the data classes that support business processes. These relationships are graphically depicted in the data class/process matrix shown in Figure 13–6. This matrix enables management to determine which data classes support multiple business processes. Identification of shared data creates a basis for developing a data architecture to support multiple applications. Borders enclose clusters of shared data that support multiple business processes in Figure 13–6. The *C* in certain cells of the matrix indicates that a process creates certain data. For example, you can see that the business planning process creates planning data by looking at the upper-left cell. The *U* in some cells indicates that

Figure 13–5

The process/ organization matrix

PROCESS / ORGANIZATION	Plan administration	Plan review	Receipt	Edit	Entry	Processing	Tracking	Territory management	Selling	Administration
	Business plan		Order servicing					Sales		
General manager	+	+					+	+	+	+
Sales manager		+	+				+	+	+	+
Marketing manager		+		+	+		+	+	+	+
Controller	+	+		+						
Purchasing manager		+								
Service manager		+								
Manufacturing operations manager		+		+	+	+	+			

Figure 13–6

Data-class/process matrix

PROCESS / DATA CLASS	Planning	Financial	Product	Parts master	Bill-of-material	Vendor	Raw material inventory	Fin. goods inventory	Facilities	Work in process	Machine load	Open requirements	Routings	Customer	Sales territory	Order	Cost	Employee
Business planning	C	U															U	
Organization analysis	U																	
Review and control	U	U																
Financial planning	C	U								U								U
Capital acquisition		C																
Research			U												U			
Forecasting	U	U												U	U			
Design and development			C	C	U									U				
Product specification maintenance			U	C	C	U												
Purchasing						C											U	
Receiving						U	U											
Inventory control							C	C		U								
Work flow layout			U						C				U					
Scheduling			U			U				U	C	U						
Capacity planning						U				U	C	U	U					
Material requirements			U		U	U						C						
Operations										U	U	U	C					
Territory management			U											C		U		
Selling			U											U	C	U		
Sales administration															U	U		
Order servicing			U											U		C		
Shipping			U					U								U		
General accounting		U				U								U				U
Cost planning						U										U	C	
Budget accounting	U	U								U							U	U
Personnel planning		U																C
Recruiting/development																		U
Compensation		U																U

a process uses certain data. You can see that the business planning process uses financial data.

A BSP study also accomplishes other types of analyses. One of the objectives is to determine how effectively current information systems support major business processes. Another part of the analysis studies the data classes supporting various information systems. If common data support a variety of current information systems, opportunities for designing integrated databases can be defined.

Assessment of Business Problems

Once business/system relationships are established, the BSP study team undertakes in-depth interviews with managers throughout the organization to determine problems and priorities. Managers are asked to identify their problems, possible solutions, value statements, processes impacted, and processes causing the problems. For example:

What major problem have you encountered that has made your job difficult?

What is needed to solve this problem?

What would be the value to your function or to the overall business if the problem were solved?

How satisfied are you with the current level of information systems support?

What additional information do you need to help you do your job?

What would its value be?

Once interviews are conducted, information is analyzed and consolidated into a summary report. An example of the results of an executive interview appears in Figure 13-7. The interviews conducted during a BSP study are critical in obtaining an executive perspective on information systems needs. The interview process may take months to complete, but the participation of key managers is vital.

Determining Priorities

Defining the information architecture involves analyzing the relationship of data classes to business processes. In Figure 13-6 we noted the clusters of data classes supporting multiple processes. This analysis helps identify a number of systems development projects. These projects need to be prioritized according to their benefit, impact, success, and demand. *Benefit* is measured in terms of the expected financial returns that will occur if the project is implemented. *Cost-benefit analysis,* using return on investment or net present value, can help to determine the potential benefits of a project.

The *impact* of a project means the number of people affected, its qualitative effect, and its effect on accomplishing overall objectives. *Success* refers to the probability of the project's being implemented successfully, given the risk and the resources available. Finally, *demand* measures the need for and the value of the proposed system.

Figure 13–7
BSP interview

MAJOR PROBLEM	Lack of ability to identify qualified people
PROBLEM SOLUTION	Better information on personnel resources
VALUE STATEMENT	Retain good people; improve morale
INFORMATION NEEDS	Skills inventory system
AFFECTED PROCESS	Human resources

Figure 13–8
Subsystem ranking

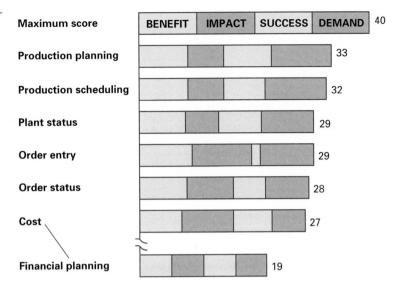

Each of the proposed information systems projects is rated using these four factors, and an overall ranking of projects is developed. Figure 13–8 shows such a ranking. Projects with the highest ratings become candidates for implementation and become part of the short-term information systems architecture plan.

Information Systems Management

An important step in planning is to review the capability of the existing information systems organization to develop the proposed information systems. Since the BSP study identifies opportunities for the development of an integrated database environment in which shared data support multiple applications, the information systems group will need to establish plans to move toward this kind of environment. New technology, new personnel, and new procedures may have to be introduced to make this transition.

The Action Plan

The final step of a BSP study is to develop an action plan in which the first subsystem project is scheduled for development, appropriate MIS personnel are assigned, and the project justification is completed. Once this project is underway, longer range plans for designing the information architecture of the firm can be developed.

Implications of the BSP Method

The major thrust of BSP is data architecture planning. The method includes identifying business processes, listing information requirements supporting each process, and establishing data element needs. From this analysis it is possible to define data elements that support multiple business processes and to develop an information architecture using a shared database approach. The BSP method ultimately defines a way of achieving an integrated database architecture by implementing one system at a time. The BSP approach also paves the way for management of data as a resource.

Although the BSP methodology is one of the most comprehensive planning techniques, it can be time-consuming and expensive to implement. It is designed to address data architecture planning rather than issues such as information systems organization and project management and control. Some criticisms of BSP include the fact

Figure 13–9

Ends/means analysis

ENDS	EFFECTIVE	INFORMATION
Fill customer orders	• Customer orders delivered when expected, and as soon as or sooner than the competition's	• Summary and exception reports on customer deliveries; comparative statistics on delivery service vs. competition's
Provide customer service	• Promptly provide credit to qualified customers • Quick response to and reduction of customer complaints	• Customer credit status and payment history • Report of number and type of complaints by customers and average time to resolve complaint

Source: Adapted from J. Wetherbe, "Executive Information Requirements: Getting It Right," *MIS Quarterly,* March 1991, pp. 51–65.

that it does not identify opportunities for the effective use of new information technology and the integration of the technology with traditional data processing systems. Managers who want to use BSP need specialized training in the technique.

ENDS/MEANS (E/M) ANALYSIS

The third technique, **ends/means (E/M) analysis,** was developed by Wetherbe and Davis at the University of Minnesota.[4] The purpose of E/M analysis is to determine effectiveness criteria for outputs and to specify efficiency criteria for processes used to generate outputs.

The first question in E/M analysis is, What is the end or good or service provided by the business process? As you can see from Figure 13–9, the "end" might be to fill customer orders.

The next question is, What makes these goods or services effective to the recipients or customers? The effectiveness criteria is that these orders be delivered when expected, and, if possible, as soon as or sooner than the competition.

The final question is, What information is needed to evaluate that effectiveness? In this case information about customer deliveries and comparative statistics on delivery service versus the competition's will provide the feedback management needs to determine how effectively they have achieved their result.

In the other part of E/M analysis, the manager needs to specify efficiency criteria for processes used to generate outputs. This analysis asks three questions. First is, What are the key means or processes used to generate or provide good or services? A key process might be to process orders, as you can see from Figure 13–10. Second, What constitutes efficiency in providing these goods or services? Efficiency for processing orders might mean lowering transactions costs for orders and minimizing shipping costs. Third, What information is needed to evaluate that efficiency? Information needed to assess efficiency might include cost per transaction, cost per credit transaction, and shipment costs.

As you can see, E/M analysis seeks to determine information requirements using a simple, straightforward approach.

---

[4]James Wetherbe, "Executive Information Requirements: Getting It Right," *MIS Quarterly,* March 1991, pp. 51–65.

Figure 13–10
Ends/means
analysis

MEANS	EFFICIENCY	INFORMATION
Process orders	Low transaction cost	Cost per transaction with historical trends
Process credit request	Low transaction cost	Cost per transaction with historical trends
Make shipment	Minimize shipment costs	Shipping cost categorized by order, customer, and region

Source: Adapted from J. Wetherbe, "Executive Information Requirements: Getting It Right," *MIS Quarterly,* March 1991, pp. 51–65.

Figure 13–11
Critical success
factors for order
processing

CRITICAL SUCCESS FACTORS	INFORMATION
Adequate inventory to fill customer orders	Percentage of orders filled on time, by customer and by product
Prompt shipment of orders	Delivery time—overall and categorized by customer
High percentage of customer payments	Delinquency report on nonpaying customers
Vendors promptly filling reorders	Exception report of vendor reorders not filled on time

Source: Adapted from J. Wetherbe, "Executive Information Requirements: Getting It Right," *MIS Quarterly,* March 1991, pp. 51–65.

Figure 13–12
Business systems
planning interview
for order
processing

PROBLEMS	SOLUTION	INFORMATION
Out of stock too often	Better inventory	Out-of-stock and below-minimum reports
Ordering department allocates limited inventory to the least important customers and/or customers with credit problems	Let warehouse know relative importance and credit status of different customers	Customer-importance rating and credit rating

Source: Adapted from J. Wetherbe, "Executive Information Requirements: Getting It Right," *MIS Quarterly,* March 1991, pp. 51–65.

Comparison of the Three Methods

You can compare the three methods, CSF, BSP, and E/M analysis, most effectively by considering how each method is used to gather information requirements for the order processing example. In the CSF method, information is used as feedback indicating the extent to which the critical success factors have been achieved (see Figure 13-11).

The BSP method starts with a problem statement. The solution to the problem states the business objectives that must be achieved. The information requirements specify the feedback needed to determine how well these business objectives are being accomplished (see Figure 13-12).

Figure 13–13
Ends/means
analysis for order
processing

ENDS	EFFECTIVE	INFORMATION
Fill customer orders	• Customer orders delivered when expected, and as soon as or sooner than competition.	• Summary and exception reports on customer deliveries; comparative statistics on delivery service vs. competition's.
Provide customer service	• Promptly provide credit to qualified customers • Quick response and reduction of customer complaints.	• Customer credit status and payment history. • Report of number and type of complaints by customers and average time to resolve complaint.

Source: Adapted from J. Wetherbe, "Executive Information Requirements: Getting It Right," *MIS Quarterly,* March 1991, pp. 51–65.

As you can see, the E/M interview also specifies objectives (ends), factors that are important for success (effectiveness criteria), and measures used to determine whether or not these factors have been achieved successfully (information). Figure 13–13 reviews the E/M analysis for the order processing example.

The E/M method seems to be most similar to the CSF method. The goals in the CSF approach are similar to the ends in E/M analysis. The critical success factors are similar to the effectiveness criteria ("what has to go right") in E/M analysis, and the information requirements in both approaches provide feedback on the extent to which the critical success factors or effectiveness criteria are being achieved. In either case, the information requirements are designed to provide feedback on the responsiveness of the business to the environment.

Although the BSP approach starts with a problem statement, it also specifies business outcomes to be achieved (solutions) and identifies information requirements that are designed to provide feedback on the extent to which these solutions are being achieved. All three approaches use information requirements as a barometer to determine whether or not business outcomes are being successfully accomplished.

Each of the information systems planning methodologies you have learned about so far in this chapter has different objectives, methods, and outcomes. The selection of a planning methodology may determine the outcome of the information systems plan. If the CSF methodology is used, the outcome will be a strategy for designing executive information systems for better planning and control. If the BSP methodology is used, a data architecture plan will result.

Information Systems Planning at the Organizational Level

In this chapter you have already learned how managers can use planning methods such as BSP and CSF to define their information needs. These methods can also be applied at an organizationwide level. To understand how information systems plans are developed at the organizationwide level, it is important to first understand the connection between information technology plans and business plans.

How Information Technology Supports Business Strategy

The information planning grid developed by McFarlan and McKenney at Harvard Business School (see Figure 13–14) will help you understand the connection between information technology and business strategy.

Figure 13–14

Information planning grid

STRATEGIC IMPACT OF APPLICATION DEVELOPMENT PORTFOLIO

		Low	High
STRATEGIC IMPACT OF EXISTING SYSTEMS	Low	Support	Turnaround
	High	Factory	Strategic

Source: Adapted from Fig. 2–4: "Categories of Strategic Relevance and Impact," J. Cash, F. W. McFarlan, J. L. McKenney, and L. M. Applegate, *Corporate Information Systems Management* (Burr Ridge, IL: Richard D. Irwin, 1992), p. 39.

The Information Planning Grid

Strategic quadrant. In the **strategic quadrant** of the information planning grid, you will find companies that are critically dependent on the smooth functioning of information technology for their competitive success. Both existing applications and applications that are under development are closely linked with business plans. Information technology is closely linked with corporate planning.

An example of a firm in the strategic quadrant is a financial services company that uses information processing to manage its loan portfolios, including loan application screening, payment processing, and account management. Without information technology, the firm would literally drown in a sea of paperwork. Financial services that are on the drawing boards cannot be developed and offered to potential customers without a significant information technology infrastructure and management capability.

Turnaround quadrant. Companies in the **turnaround quadrant** need a substantial information technology planning effort because the impact of applications under development is critical to their ability to achieve strategic business plans. Although information systems plans have not been closely linked with business plans in the past, future uses of information technology are "strategic."

Let's take the example of a four-year comprehensive university. In the past information systems have been used to handle accounting functions and the management of student information, including registration, grade reporting, transcript generation, and student tuition and fees. These financial and student information systems are critical to the day-to-day operations of the university, but they are not necessarily connected with the institution's ability to recruit students, address the needs of new markets, and build new academic programs. Technology has not been critical to the university's ability to implement its strategic plans.

However, the situation is changing. The university is now designing distance-learning classrooms so that it can deliver its courses and programs to remote locations via interactive videoconferencing systems over telecommunications networks. Information technology is being used to recruit new students and to address the needs of new markets. Via the distance-learning network, for example, the university will be able to develop academic programs with other four-year institutions in the state; these programs would not have been possible before. A graduate program in nursing will be electronically transmitted to distance-learning classrooms in remote sites so that nursing students in other locations will be able to get the training they need without driving hundreds of miles. Without question, distance learning is closely linked with the institution's ability to achieve its strategic goals. The change from using technology to support administrative information systems to using technology to achieve strategic objectives places the university in the turnaround quadrant.

Factory quadrant.   The third quadrant of the information systems grid is the **factory quadrant.** Factory firms are in the situation in which existing applications of information systems have a strategic impact, but future applications are not critical to their ability to achieve strategic business plans. In other words, strategic systems have already been built.

An example of a firm in the factory quadrant is a regional commercial bank that has already developed major backbone systems for demand deposit accounting, savings accounting, mortgage accounting, and trust accounting. Now that these information systems are in place, the bank has no current plans for developing other applications that will leverage the use of technology. Although management has considered organizing an at-home banking network, most of the bank's feasibility studies do not cost justify this approach based upon the potential return on investment.

Support quadrant.   For firms in the **support quadrant,** the uses of information technology are not connected with competitive success either in the past or in the future. A firm in this quadrant is a soft-drink distributor. Although the distributor uses information systems to support back-office administrative functions such as inventory control, accounts receivable, and accounts payable, it does not see information technology as strategic. Investments in marketing, advertising, and promotion are more closely linked with its ability to achieve sales goals, as compared with investments in additional uses of information technology.

Management Strategies

Information systems planning strategies are different in each of the four environments. In organizations in the strategic quadrant, it would make sense for the information technology manager to have a higher status and to actively participate in the corporate strategic planning process. For example, if establishing a distance-learning network is critical to achieving institutional goals at a university, the manager of information technology (IT) should be involved in the strategic planning process. Without input from the IT manager, the university may envision technological capabilities that cannot be successfully implemented without training, specialized personnel, and significant financial resources. The network may involve other costs as well, such as training faculty to teach on a distance-learning network and adding administrative staff who can schedule distance-learning classes with other colleges and universities on the network.

Figure 13–15 shows the variation in management strategies for companies in the support and strategic quadrants.

As you can see from this table, the management strategies needed in a strategic environment are much different from those needed in a support environment. Project management, leadership, and effective allocation of resources to high-potential projects are necessary. Firms in the strategic quadrant need to maintain state-of-the-art technology know-how because their competitors do.

Let's take the example of two defense contractors. Both organizations adopted computer-aided design and manufacturing (CAD/CAM) systems during the mid-1970s to provide automated support for manufacturing defense aircraft such as the F-16 fighter. In the 1980s investments in integrated database management systems made it possible to exchange data with subcontractors so that major defense projects could

Figure 13–15
Managerial
strategies for
support and
strategic
companies

FACTOR	SUPPORT COMPANY	STRATEGIC COMPANY
Planning	• Less urgent. • Mistakes in resource allocation not fatal.	• Critical—must link to corporate strategy.
IT management	• Can be low.	• Should be very high.
Technical innovation	• Conservative posture one to two years behind state-of-art is appropriate.	• Critical to stay current and fund R and D. • Competitor can gain advantage.
User involvement	• Lower priority. • Less-heated debate.	• Very high priority. • Active debate.
Expense control	• System modernization expenses are postponable in time of crisis.	• Effectiveness is key. • Must keep applications up-to-date; save money in other places.
Uneven performance	• Time is available to resolve it.	• Serious and immediate attention needed.
Project risk	• Avoid high-risk projects because of constrained benefits.	• Some high-risk, high-potential-benefit projects are appropriate if possibility exists to gain a strategic advantage.

Source: Adapted from Table 13–1: Managerial Strategies for "Support" and "Strategic" Companies, J. Cash Jr., F. W. McFarlan, J. L McKenney, and L. Applegate, *Corporate Information Systems Management,* 3rd ed. (Burr Ridge, IL: Richard D. Irwin, 1992), p. 634.

be completed in a timely manner. In the 1990s future investments in computer-aided software engineering tools are forecast as a means of improving application development productivity and guaranteeing an information architecture for the future. Both firms are organized to keep abreast of the latest technologies in networking, software development, and database design so that they are technologically capable of winning future contracts.

Another major difference between organizations in the support and strategic quadrants is the willingness to take risks. Clearly, companies in the support quadrant justify information systems design projects in terms of cost-savings and administrative efficiency. In contrast, firms in the strategic quadrant may pursue projects that cannot be cost justified up front but that might provide a long-term competitive advantage if they are pursued.

A case in point is the competition between Frontier and United Airlines. Even though these two organizations were both in the airline business, one was in the support quadrant and the other in the strategic quadrant. Frontier Airlines used the cost-benefit approach to justify investments in information systems development and focused on developing information systems aimed at cutting costs through operational efficiency. While the company was investing in accounting systems, its competitors were developing sophisticated airline reservations systems that eventually put Frontier out of business.

The situation at United Airlines was quite different. United invested in a computer-based airline reservations system called APOLLO. As United gradually added more and more travel agents to the APOLLO system, it gained a significant strategic advantage because these travel agents had an incentive to book United flights. Without a reservation system of its own, Frontier became a user of the APOLLO system. With information about Frontier's flights on APOLLO, United could cut fares in strategic markets and "accidentally" drop Frontier flights from its system. Inevitably, Frontier lost significant market share to United in the Denver market.

The story of Frontier Airlines illustrates a mismatch between competitive strategy and information technology. In the 1970s major airlines such as American and United were building reservation systems in order to achieve a strategic advantage. Frontier was making investments that were consistent with a support posture, even though its competitors were in a strategic mode. Using information technology for support while its competitors were using technology as a strategic weapon was Frontier's mistake.

TECHNOLOGY PLANNING IN AN AGE OF UNCERTAINTY

Schein's Theory of Technology Assimilation[5]

Organizations must learn to manage many diverse technologies, for example, videoconferencing, fiber optics, distributed databases, local area networks, mainframe-based administrative information systems, and multimedia. Some technologies are older and well understood, whereas others are new and unfamiliar. In Schein's view technology assimilation occurs in four phases, and each phase creates different management challenges.

Phase 1: Technology identification and investment. When an organization invests in a new technology, it must focus on staff development, training, and management of pilot projects. The planning challenge here might mean mobilizing a special team to deal with the new technology implementation and evaluation. Let us say, for example, that a university wishes to introduce videoconferencing capability. The first step may be to organize a team of professionals, consisting of a telecommunications analyst, a TV-radio specialist, a multimedia development consultant, and a project manager, to undertake a pilot project.

Phase 2: Technological learning. The focus of planning during this phase is to facilitate learning by encouraging users to examine the technology and its applications. Because phase 2 is an experimentation phase, the major goal is to gain experience. During this phase the university may encourage faculty to use the videoconferencing center to practice teaching classes to students in remote locations. A consultant may help faculty members learn how to use the technology.

Phase 3: Rationalization/management control. Planning at this phase is short-term because the objective is to define uses of the new technology and to implement it in a cost-effective way. Technical support staff for the videoconferencing center

[5]Edgar Schein, "Management Development as a Process of Influence," *Industrial Management Review* 2, 1961, pp. 59–77.

may be appointed on a permanent basis, and faculty users may be assigned classes. The major focus is day-to-day implementation of the project.

Phase 4: Maturity/widespread technology transfer.   In the final phase of new technology assimilation, a technology such as videoconferencing can be transferred throughout the organization. Once faculty members learn how to use the system and standards for technology integration are achieved, it is time to develop longer term objectives for using the technology. The dean of the business school may foresee using videoconferencing as a way of transmitting courses in the MBA program to conference rooms at local corporations. The nursing school may want to transmit courses to two-year colleges in remote locations of the state to enhance educational opportunities for students interested in nursing careers. An entire range of opportunities is possible once the technology is considered workable.

Planning in a Dynamic Environment

In most organizations planning for the use of information technologies is difficult for two reasons. First, the competitive environment is so dynamic that competitive strategy and technology strategy are constantly changing. Second, the manager of information technology is responsible for managing multiple application portfolios: data processing, microcomputers, office automation systems, and factory automation. Each of these systems is evolving at a different rate and may be at a different stage of automation. The challenge is to use different management strategies to manage multiple application portfolios.

Let's take the university as a case in point. Mainframe-based administrative systems, such as the student information system and the human resource information system, were developed in the 1980s, putting data processing at a phase 4 level of evolution in 1994. The evolution of microcomputers and local area networks was in its phase 2 learning phase in the mid-to-late 1980s and is evolving into a management control phase by the mid-1990s as software, local area networking, and operating systems are being standardized. An electronic mail system, introduced in the early 1990s, is still in its experimentation phase. However, new technologies such as computer-based videoconferencing are just being introduced in the mid-1990s and are clearly at the first phase of evolution. Figure 13–16 depicts these phases.

As already noted, each stage of evolution requires different management planning and control strategies. Because the videoconferencing project is a pilot project, it may require a team approach. In contrast, the administrative information systems that have already been built may need to be accessible to the offices of faculty advisors via a campus network. In the latter case connectivity standards provide a context within which technology transfer can occur. In other words, faculty members who want access to the network will need to obtain standard network interface cards and communications software.

Figure 13–16
Technology assimilation at a university

PHASE 1: Investment	Videoconferencing facilities for distance education
PHASE 2: Learning	Electronic mail
PHASE 3: Management control	Microcomputer local area networks
PHASE 4: Technology transfer	Administrative information systems

ORGANIZING THE INFORMATION SYSTEMS PLAN

Rapid changes in technology are creating enormous opportunities, but these opportunities cannot be pursued without effective planning. Without planning, the wrong systems will be developed. Without planning, a proliferation of incompatible hardware, software, operating systems, and database management systems will evolve. Technology is expensive, and mistakes can be costly. For these reasons, an information systems strategic plan must be developed.

The strategic planning process for information systems enables senior management to determine what information technology opportunities will support competitive strategy, what applications will bring about the highest returns, and what patterns of organization are most effective. Once these initiatives are defined, MIS managers must develop tactical plans that organize application development, technology, and organizational resources to achieve these objectives.

Application Development

As you learned in this chapter, one of the major purposes of information systems planning is to define application development projects that support the strategic goals of the organization. MIS management must work with users to set priorities for accomplishing these projects and must also look for methods of improving software development productivity so that critical systems are completed on time. Alternative systems development approaches, such as software packages and prototyping with fourth-generation languages, need to be evaluated. Computer-aided software engineering tools (CASE), which provide automation support for the systems designer, may also improve productivity.

Moving toward a data-driven application development environment in which shared data support multiple applications is another challenge. MIS management has to determine what applications are appropriate to the data-driven approach, what technologies will support this approach, and how the systems development process needs to be modified. Many new technologies, including database management systems, fourth-generation languages, and code generators, need to be evaluated.

Once new systems development approaches have been identified during the planning phase, MIS management must also allocate its resources to make sure that new methods are used successfully. Traditional life-cycle methodologies must be re-examined and modified to support data-driven development approaches. Systems analysts and programmers must be retrained to learn how to use new tools such as fourth-generation languages and CASE tools. Both users and systems professionals must be trained to use the prototyping approach to systems development. Some of the issues involving application development that need to be addressed in the information systems planning process are summarized in Figure 13–17.

New Technology

The strategic planning process for information management helps senior management identify new technology opportunities that support business plans. These new technologies include office automation, teleconferencing, factory automation, client server, and others. One of the biggest problems MIS managers face today is supporting incompatible hardware and software in decentralized user environments. A technology plan must address strategies for linking mainframe-based operational data systems and decentralized decision support systems. The plan must address the architecture that will make it possible to design interfaces between data processing and office au-

Figure 13–17

Application development issues in the MIS planning process

STRATEGIC ISSUES	TACTICAL ISSUES
• What applications will bring about the highest return? • What applications will support the strategic goals of the organization? • Should we move toward a data-driven application development environment? • Can CASE tools be used to improve productivity? • Should software packages be used? • Should fourth-generation languages be used?	• Are the phases of the systems development life cycle being successfully accomplished? • Are projects being completed within time and cost constraints? • Do user-managers have an opportunity to review project activities and outcomes at checkpoints in the systems development process?

Figure 13–18

New technology issues in the MIS planning process

STRATEGIC ISSUES	TACTICAL ISSUES
• What opportunities does new technology provide? • Do we invest in personal computers? factory automation? office automation? • How do we integrate mainframe-based data systems with personal computers?	• What equipment selection strategy should be designed? • What vendor strategy is needed? • What controls over equipment acquisition must be introduced?

tomation systems, between administrative data processing and manufacturing systems, and between telecommunications networks and local personal computers.

At the tactical level, MIS management must establish an equipment selection strategy and a vendor policy that ensures compatibility between centralized and decentralized systems and enables local computers to share centralized data and network devices. Some of the technology issues that must be addressed in an information systems plan are summarized in Figure 13-18.

Organization and Management of Information Processing

One of the major strategy decisions that senior management must make is how to organize information processing to make it responsive to the needs of the organization. In the 1980s, most organizations experienced a shift in processing, database, and application development from centralized groups to distributed organizational levels. This process was driven by the introduction of less-expensive, more powerful technologies and the growth of workstations, software packages, and user-friendly languages.

The centralization of information systems architecture, network management, and database management functions and the decentralization of systems development and operations responsibilities have created some challenges that the MIS planning process must address. The MIS plan must establish central standards and guidelines for managing the organization's database, communications, and computer utilities. It also must identify the skills that information systems professionals need to fill consulting and support roles in the end-user environment.

Tactical plans must address training and professional development strategies. The information systems professional needs communications skills, business understanding, and project management skills. Personnel already in the MIS field must prepare for roles as consultants and business systems analysts. With the increasing decentral-

Figure 13–19
Organization and management issues in the MIS planning process

STRATEGIC ISSUES	TACTICAL ISSUES
• How will information processing be organized? • What will be the respective roles of user-managers and information systems professionals? • What skills will user-managers need? • What skills will information processing professionals need?	• What project management guidelines must be followed by user-managers in accomplishing local projects? • What training and professional development strategies are needed to prepare information processing professionals for their roles?

Figure 13–20
Distribution of information systems activities (greater than 60 percent consensus by CIOs)

CENTRALIZED INFORMATION SYSTEMS ACTIVITIES	DISTRIBUTED INFORMATION SYSTEMS ACTIVITIES
• Strategic planning for information systems • Technology planning • Management of voice and data communications • Establishing standards for mainframes and minicomputer systems • Providing end-user support	• Selection and approval of application software • Operation of office systems • Selection and operation of personal computers • Planning what applications to develop • Establishing budgets and project plans

Source: Adapted from R. Benjamin, C. Dickinson, Jr., and J. Rockart, "Changing Role of the Corporate Information Systems Officer," *MIS Quarterly* 9, no. 3 (1985), p. 181.

ization of systems development, MIS professionals also need to provide guidelines for the management and control of local projects. Some of the organizational issues that must be addressed in the information systems plan are described in Figure 13–19.

In summary, an information systems planning methodology must establish technology and application development opportunities that support business plans. The MIS plan also must outline tactical plans for developing applications, selecting new technology, and designing organizational structures to meet overall objectives. These tactical plans also must establish the criteria for performance that can be used as a basis for evaluating whether information systems are responsive to the needs of the business.

The Changing Role of the Chief Information Officer

In a study of computing environments in 25 large organizations, Benjamin, Dickinson, and Rockart (1985) found that the development and operation of application systems and the management of hardware and software had become distributed to subsidiary information systems groups and to user-managers. Figure 13–20 shows information systems activities that 60 percent of the chief information officers (CIOs) surveyed agreed were either centralized or distributed. As you can see, key systems development activities such as application software selection have been decentralized to local information systems groups or to line managers.

In spite of this decentralization pattern, some key activities remain in the hands of centralized information systems professionals. These activities include responsibilities for designing and managing voice and data communications networks, for creating and maintaining the information utilities, and for providing user consulting and training. MIS professionals are also responsible for technology planning and strategic planning. They will continue to play a major role in determining how information technology can be used to support business strategy.

MANAGEMENT SUMMARY

In this chapter you have learned about information systems planning methods with different objectives, techniques, and outcomes. The CSF approach is a planning method directed at helping senior managers define their information needs. In this approach, executives are asked to define their critical success factors (i.e., what has to go right) and to develop measures of how well these factors are being achieved. If reports satisfying these needs are not currently available, then new information systems are developed.

IBM's BSP methodology helps MIS management develop a data architecture that supports information systems needs. In the BSP method, a study team identifies the key data classes supporting business processes and recommends a data architecture that supports high-priority applications. In (E/M) analysis, information systems planners define the ends, effectiveness criteria, and information requirements needed to achieve business objectives.

At a time when the competitive environment is very dynamic and competitive strategy is changing, an organization needs to rely on planning strategies that are flexible and adaptable. Managers of information technology need to be able to plan by wire. That is, they need to rely upon the information systems plans to identify the feedback mechanisms they need to survive in a rapidly changing business environment.

KEY TERMS FOR MANAGERS

business systems planning (BSP) method, 523

critical success factors (CSF) method, 520

ends/means (E/M) analysis, 528

factory quadrant, 532

strategic quadrant, 531

support quadrant, 532

turnaround quadrant, 531

REVIEW QUESTIONS

1. Explain the objectives of the business systems planning methodology.

2. What factors are used to rank potential BSP projects?

3. Define *critical success factors*.

4. How are critical success factors used to determine information systems opportunities?

5. What questions are asked during an interview using ends/means analysis?

6. How can an automobile manufacturer differentiate its products by using information technology?

7. What are characteristics of organizations in the support quadrant of McFarlan's information planning grid?

8. Identify some differences between the management strategies used in firms in the strategic quadrant as compared with firms in the support quadrant of the information planning grid.

9. What are the characteristics of phase 2, technological learning, in Schein's model of technology assimilation?

10. What types of decisions does MIS management need to address in developing a tactical-level plan for application development?

11. What types of tactical-level decisions are made with regard to new technology?

12. What types of information systems responsibilities have been distributed to line managers and local information systems groups?

13. What skills does the distribution of computing activities demand of information systems professionals?

QUESTIONS FOR DISCUSSION

1. What are two critical success factors for an automobile dealership?

2. Why would the critical success factors for an automobile dealership differ from those for a grocery store chain?

3. Could the critical success factors for two different computer hardware manufacturers (for example, IBM and Digital) be different? Explain your answer.

4. Which information systems planning methodology do you feel is more effective: The CSF approach, the BSP approach, or E/M analysis? Explain why.

5. Why is it important for senior managers to be involved in information systems planning?

6. What are the characteristics of a firm in the turnaround quadrant of the information planning grid?

7. What kind of role should the MIS manager play in an organization in the strategic quadrant of the information planning grid?

8. What types of planning issues are relevant to the technology transfer phase of Schein's technology assimilation model?

PROBLEMS

1. **Sterling Industries.** Sterling Industries is a $200 million company in the textile manufacturing industry. The director of data processing, Malcolm Rogers, has been with the firm for 20 years. Most of the information systems that have been developed use traditional files. Because many of these systems have been developed piecemeal, many of the data elements about customers, products, vendors, and orders are stored in many different databases. Managers at Sterling Industries are demanding that new applications be developed in the areas of sales and distribution. Conversion of an old batch order entry and inventory control system to an on-line system is a major need. However, managers in virtually every area have their own critical needs and are becoming impatient with the five- to six-year backlog of information systems development projects that currently exists. Explain how you would use the business systems planning method to remedy some of the problems that Sterling Industries is experiencing. In your answer, describe the steps and the outcomes of such a study. What would be the roles and responsibilities of data processing management and user management in conducting the study?

2. **Software Associates, Inc.** Software Associates, Inc., is a vendor that develops custom-designed software for large and small businesses in the St. Louis metropolitan area. The firm has grown very rapidly and now employs more than 100 systems analysts and programmers. Almost all the code for application development projects is written in BASIC programming language. Software Associates both develops and maintains its custom software products. The president of Software Associates, Edward Rosen, has very little information available for determining how well the firm is doing, whether new marketing efforts are paying off, and whether projects are being completed on time and within budget. Because the firm has grown so rapidly, internal information systems are crude and almost no management reporting systems exist. Ed has decided to use the critical success factors method to determine his information needs for planning new activities for the firm as well as for monitoring existing operations. With the help of a consultant, Ed

has been able to determine the following critical success factors:

Ease of use of software products.

Company morale.

Project completion within budget and time constraints.

Quality of sales literature.

Risk recognition in major contracts for software development.

In the software design business, software products must be easy to use to ensure that information systems will be accepted and used. Company morale is important because Software Associates relies heavily on the technical know-how of its experienced programmers and analysts. One of the major CSFs of the firm is the ability to complete software projects within budgetary and time constraints. In addition, Ed wants the sales literature to provide a high-quality image of the firm. Ed does not want to take on projects with such a high risk that they might not be completed successfully. A significant project cost overrun or a project failure would hurt the company's reputation in a highly competitive marketplace. Given this situation, recommend measures that Ed can use to determine how well the firm is doing in achieving each of the critical success factors.

3. **The information planning grid.** Indicate which cell of the information planning grid each of the following firms would fit into and explain reasons for your answers.

Firm A: This uniform manufacturer has developed operational systems supporting order entry, inventory control, and purchasing. Most of the work in the information systems department is making changes and enhancements to existing systems.

Firm B: This financial services company implemented an on-line telecommunications network linking branch offices and the home office in the late 1970s. Systems projects are underway to analyze buyer and product profitability, to develop a profile of potentially delinquent accounts, and to develop a management control system for cash management.

Firm C: This food marketing company has designed information systems to support accounting applications such as payroll and general ledger. The firm is now designing more effective control systems for sales forecasting, computer-assisted manufacturing, and branch inventory control.

SELECTED REFERENCES AND READINGS

Benjamin, R. C. D., Jr. and J. Rockart. "Changing Role of the Corporate Information Systems Officer." *MIS Quarterly* 9, no. 3 (1985), pp. 177–88.

Cash, J; F. W. McFarlan; J. L. McKenney; and L. M. Applegate. *Corporate Information Systems Management: Text and Cases.* 3rd ed. Burr Ridge, IL: Irwin, 1992.

Haeckel, S. and R. Nolan. "Managing by Wire." *Harvard Business Review,* September–October 1993, pp. 122–33. "IBM Business Systems Planning."

Colter, M. A. and R. W. Knapp. *In Advanced Systems Development/Feasibility Techniques,* ed. J. D. Couger, New York: John Wiley & Sons, 1982.

Porter, M. *Competitive Strategy: Techniques for Analyzing Industries and Competitors.* New York: The Free Press, 1980.

Rockart, J. "Chief Executives Define Their Own Data Needs." *Harvard Business Review,* March–April 1979, pp. 81–93.

Schein, E. "Management Development as a Process of Influence." *Industrial Management Review,* 2nd issue 1961, pp. 59–77.

Wetherbe, J. "Executive Information Requirements: Getting It Right." *MIS Quarterly,* March 1991, pp. 51–65.

SYSTEMS ANALYSIS AND DESIGN

CHAPTER OUTLINE

Manager's View

The Systems Development Process

Systems Analysis

Structured Systems Analysis and Design

Evaluating Alternative Design Options

Analysis of Alternative Design Options

The Organizationwide Data Dictionary

Management Summary

Key Terms for Managers

Review Questions

Questions for Discussion

Problems

Cases

Selected References and Readings

AS A MANAGER, you will be a user of information systems. If you are a sales manager, you probably get printouts detailing sales activity in different regions. If you are a retail store manager, you may receive inventory reports describing the inventory turnover of various items in stock on a weekly basis. If you are a college administrator, you may get a report listing the number of students enrolled in various classes on a semester-to-semester basis. If you are a county welfare department administrator, you may receive a report listing welfare recipients who have been added to the welfare rolls in the past month.

Many users of information systems believe that the systems they are using do not meet their needs. One user argues, "The system that was built is technically accurate, but the reports I get don't give me the information I need." Still others argue that systems analysts themselves are out of touch with business requirements. One user comments that "the systems analyst had good technical training but really didn't understand the marketing business." Another says, "The system that was designed cost over $100,000 and took more than six months to build, but the reports I get don't help me identify business opportunities."

These problems, though they have plagued systems analysts for a long time, have partly been solved by the use of structured systems analysis and design techniques, by increasing user involvement in information systems development, and by better techniques for project management and control. In this chapter you'll learn about the process of systems development, beginning with problem definition and systems analysis. You'll also become acquainted with structured analysis and design techniques that allow the systems analyst to communicate more effectively with users and to understand their requirements better. Most important, you'll see that systems must be built to make it possible for management to achieve important business objectives. Without an understanding of these objectives, no information systems design project can succeed in serving the users' needs.

THE SYSTEMS DEVELOPMENT PROCESS

Systems analysis and design is a process that is similar to problem solving. Long before the introduction of computers, systems analysts were responsible for analyzing work methods and procedures to simplify work and to improve work flow. You've probably been involved in many systems analysis and design studies without even realizing it. The process of systems analysis involves a number of steps that can be applied to any study. These are the steps in a systems study:

1. Define the problem.
2. Develop an understanding of the system.

3. Identify and evaluate the alternatives that can be used to achieve the organization's objectives.

4. Select and implement one of the alternatives.

5. Evaluate the impact the changes have made.

All these steps were applied to a systems study in Chapter 2. In this chapter you'll learn how they are applied to an information systems design project.

The Systems Development Life Cycle

The steps followed in designing an information system are known as the **systems development methodology.** A systems development methodology establishes a set of procedures that conform with a life cycle. Without a methodology specifying what events and activities should occur in what order, systems development projects are likely to be out of range in cost and time. When projects are completed, the results may not meet the needs of the business. Adequate documentation may be lacking, making modifications difficult to design and implement. Lack of standardization from project to project may make it necessary to reinvent the wheel again and again.

One reason for introducing a systems development methodology is to make sure that users have an opportunity to review and to sign off on system requirements at each phase in the life cycle. These checkpoints make it possible to detect and correct errors at the end of each phase of the project. If errors in analysis are not detected, they may become inputs into errors in systems design and in detailed design. These errors may not even be detected until the system is up and running and a manager points out a missing data element on a report or an erroneous calculation on a financial statement. Each phase in the systems development life cycle is a checkpoint. Users have an opportunity to review progress and can modify time and cost estimates after each phase of the life cycle. They can choose to cancel the entire project at one of these checkpoints if they believe progress has been unsatisfactory. However, the "sunk cost" syndrome—the emotional resistance to canceling anything on which money has already been spent—is a major deterrent to project cancellation.

The steps and key activities to be accomplished at each phase of the systems development life cycle are shown in Figure 14-1. Most organizations use methodologies similar to this one, though some slight variations from one methodology to another may occur. **Problem definition,** the process of determining the nature and scope of the problem, is the first step. If the problem is incorrectly or incompletely defined, the entire study could address the wrong issues. The major methods used in problem definition are interviewing and using questionnaires.

Most organizations conduct a **feasibility study** to determine whether a solution to the problem is feasible to prevent wasting many months of effort and many thousands of dollars in cost if the project is too large, too uncontrollable, or simply impossible to carry out. The feasibility study is a miniature systems analysis and design effort that entails an exploration of alternative design options and an analysis of the costs and benefits of each alternative. If several alternatives seem to be realistic in terms of their potential costs and benefits, the project proceeds to the next phase, **systems analysis.** However, if no feasible alternatives exist, the project can be terminated. During systems analysis the current system is studied in detail. Interviews and questionnaires are used to collect information on existing procedures, information requirements, and methods of work organization and control. Interview findings are used to detect inefficiencies in work methods, inequities in work distribution, and inaccuracies in reports and other documents. These findings are used to develop a logical model of the present system by using a logical data-flow diagram. The logical

Figure 14–1

The systems
development life
cycle

STEP	SYSTEMS DEVELOPMENT ACTIVITIES
Problem definition	Examination and evaluation of the problems of the current system.
Feasibility study	• Development of objectives and a logical model of the proposed system. • Preliminary analysis of alternative design options, including the technical and economic feasibility of each alternative. • Development of recommendations for the systems project, including a projected schedule and proposed costs.
Systems analysis	• Detailed study of the current system, including its procedures, information flows, and methods of work organization and control. • Development of a logical model of the current system.
Systems design	• Development of objectives for the proposed system. • Development of a logical model of the proposed system, including process logic definition, logical data dictionary, and logical database design. • Evaluation of alternative design options. • Development of a cost-benefit analysis to evaluate the economic implications of each alternative.
Detailed design	• Development of specifications for the physical system; including report design, file design, input design, and forms design. • Design of program specifications. • Development of an implementation and test schedule.
Implementation	• Coding and documentation of programs. • Evaluation and selection of hardware. • Development of security, audit and control, and test procedures. • Development of training programs.
Maintenance	Ongoing support, changes, and enhancements for the system.

data-flow diagram, a tool that graphically depicts the system, its procedures, and information flows, will be discussed in the next section, which covers structured tools for systems analysis and design.

The analysis of the problems of the current system is used at the beginning of **systems design** to develop objectives for the proposed system. These objectives must state the business objectives of the information systems design project. If the system doesn't enable management to accomplish important business goals, such as improving profitability, cutting costs, or improving customer service, then it might not be worth the time and cost to design and implement. Assuming that the system will bring benefits that are measurable in business terms, the next step in systems design is to evaluate alternative design options. This step may mean evaluating batch versus on-line systems design options, mainframe-based versus minicomputer-based alternatives, or in-house development versus the purchase of a software package. The nature and type of design alternatives to be considered depend on the characteristics of the project. The evaluation of alternative design options is a major issue and deserves user management attention.

Systems design also involves the development of a logical model of the proposed system. The proposed **logical data-flow diagram** becomes a model of the new system. By using structured tools and techniques, the logic of major system processes can be defined, a **logical data dictionary** can be developed, and a logical database design of systemwide data requirements can be specified. **Detailed system design** is the process of developing specifications for the proposed physical system. This process includes the design of report layouts, screens and input documents, forms, and physical file structures. It also includes detailed data dictionary specifications documenting data names and data definitions for all data elements used in the system. During detailed design, any one of many procedures for program design is used to outline program specifications. Structure charts, Warnier-Orr diagrams, structured flowcharts, and pseudocode are all methods of documenting the design of structured programs. Systems flowcharts depicting the data processing procedures to be implemented are also developed as a part of detailed system design. By the end of detailed design, the blueprints for the proposed system—its programs, reports, screens, and procedures—have been finalized.

Implementation is the process of coding, testing, and documenting programs that are a part of the system. This process may take as much as 60 to 70 percent of the overall systems development effort. It involves development of quality assurance procedures, including data security, backup and recovery, and system controls. It also involves testing programs using both artificial and live data and training users and operating personnel. The development of an information system includes all the activities that begin with problem definition and end with system implementation. **Maintenance** includes whatever changes and enhancements are necessary after the system is up and running. Systems development activities encompass about 20 percent of the overall lifetime cost of an information system, and maintenance takes up about 80 percent of this overall cost. This breakdown of effort and the percentage breakdown of cost for various phases within the development life cycle are shown in Figure 14–2. These data show that a great deal more time is spent on maintenance than is spent on initial development. This situation is analogous to a construction engineer building a building and having its owners request ongoing modifications that cost many times more than the original building.

However, information systems require modifications for many reasons. Some of these reasons are within the control of information systems designers; some are not. Many information systems design projects do not spend enough time in analysis. Errors not caught in analysis and design become a permanent part of the system, and the system goes into operation before users see the results of these design errors and request changes. Some of the changes in information systems design are impossible to prevent. Competitive forces may require a company to introduce new products, to reorganize its sales force, or to change reporting relationships. These changes may

Figure 14–2
Lifetime cost of an information system

	SYSTEM ACTIVITIES (%)	LIFETIME DEVELOPMENT COST (%)
Development		
Analysis/design	35 ⎤	
Coding	15 ⎬	20
Testing	50 ⎦	
Maintenance		80
Changes and enhancements		

affect business procedures, data requirements, and reporting requirements. New managers may enter the business requesting different types of reports for planning and control purposes. Government regulations may require reporting new types of information. All these changes may render existing information systems obsolete or make major modifications necessary. These factors mean that the systems designed today must be flexible and changeable. They must also provide adequate documentation because systems designers who inherit projects must be able to understand these programs and procedures in order to adjust them.

As a user of information systems, you'll have a major role to play in the systems analysis and design process. In fact, lack of user involvement in systems development almost guarantees that an information system will fail because it will not serve the requirements of the business. The major responsibilities of users occur during the phases of problem definition, systems analysis, and systems design.

SYSTEMS ANALYSIS

The major objective of systems analysis is to understand the current system and to determine the importance, complexity, and scope of problems that exist. The scope and boundaries of the system, including its people and procedures, must be defined. Much of this phase involves collecting data about what is being done, why it is being done, how it is being done, who is doing it, and what major problems have developed. The systems analyst cannot presume to understand a system's procedures and interactions until existing methods have been thoroughly examined. He needs to avoid the tendency to mistake symptoms of the problems for the real problems. In manual systems common problems are job duplication, job overlap, and job inconsistencies. Job duplication is a frequent problem. Two or three people may be checking credit on incoming orders without knowing that this process is being duplicated. Secretaries within different offices may be editing and retyping manuscript copy several times as it makes its way over to the publications office. Poor workload distribution is another common problem. One office worker may be overloaded with work while another one sits idle day after day. Without knowledge of their tasks and reporting relationships, however, it is difficult for an analyst to suggest alternative patterns of work distribution.

Paperwork bottlenecks, lack of systematic procedures, and inaccuracies are also problems systems analysts frequently run into in manual systems. A purchase order may sit on a supervisor's desk for 10 days before it is signed and passed on to the next office. Time-consuming loan application screening procedures may delay credit approval for weeks. In addition, lack of systematic procedures may mean that different people within the same organization are using different methods to apply discounts, to approve credit, and to select authorized vendors for purchasing. Lack of standardized procedures may mean that workers reinvent the wheel, establish their own criteria for making decisions, or simply make mistakes. All these problems lead to errors that cost the organization time and money. They cause a firm to lose customers and business opportunities. It is important for the systems analyst to collect information about current procedures, controls, and information needs. Interviews, questionnaires, work samples, work distribution analyses, and systems and procedures analyses are all methods of collecting information about the current system. A short case will provide a basis for examining these methods of data collection.

Case Study: A Law School Admissions Office

You are Roger Peterson, a systems analyst. You have been called in by Dr. George Blake, director of admissions for the School of Law. The admissions office is organized into three functions: admissions, financial aid, and student activities.

During an initial interview, George has expressed some of the following concerns. The office is inundated with paperwork, and the current administrative staff, consisting of four secretaries, cannot handle the hundreds of letters—including admissions decision letters, recruiting letters, public relations letters, interview request letters, and financial aid letters—that go out each month. George thinks that much of this correspondence is standardized, but currently it is handled on a piecemeal basis, one letter at a time. Updating files is another problem. Applicants to the law school change their addresses from two to four times from the point of initial contact to actual entry into the school. According to George, files are not kept up-to-date. Although he would like to be able to select applicants with certain characteristics from the files so that he can send them information related to their specific interests, he doesn't believe that the current administrative staff can handle this added responsibility.

Finally, he thinks that the work of the office is poorly organized and managed. Some of the secretaries are overwhelmed with work, whereas others are idle much of the time. He is concerned about the poor morale on the part of some of the less experienced secretaries who are overworked. As the systems analyst, your first task is to collect information relevant to the problems in the office.

The Systems Interview

Although the interview is one of the most important sources of information about the current system and how it operates, it is not always used effectively. People being interviewed may feel threatened by the systems analyst or fearful that the changes management is proposing may affect their jobs. As a result, management must let everyone know that the purpose of the systems study is to improve the current situation. The systems analyst should be introduced to all participants, and they should be aware of the purpose and scope of the study. Guidelines for successfully conducting an interview are summarized here:

1. Prepare for the interview by learning about the individuals to be interviewed and the overall function of the organization.
2. Introduce yourself and outline the purpose and scope of the study.
3. Begin with general questions about the overall function of the office, its organization, and work methods and procedures.
4. Bring up specific questions about procedures that might lead to information about areas of improvement.
5. Follow up on topics and issues raised by the interviewee.
6. Limit the amount of notetaking to avoid distracting the person being interviewed.
7. At the end of the interview, summarize the information gathered during the session and suggest a way of following up.

Even though some of these steps may seem obvious, many systems analysts don't follow them. One of the most common mistakes is to neglect learning about the office and its function. In the law school admissions case, the systems analyst should learn a little about the school, its students, its reputation, and its graduates. If the analyst were interviewing an advertising executive in a major food marketing company, it would help to learn about the products the firm sells and the market share it currently enjoys. Otherwise, the interviewee will think that the systems analyst is ill-prepared or, at worst, uninterested in the organization and its needs.

Figure 14–3

Questions in a
systems interview

Volume	• How many repetitive letters are sent out each week? • How many address changes are made to the admissions master file each week?
Processes	• Once a prospective student applies to the law school, what steps are taken to process this application? • What are the procedures used in making a financial aid decision?
Data	• What data do you keep about each applicant? • What data are needed to make a financial aid decision?
Control	• Are there any precautions in place to safeguard against improper access to applicant financial data? • What procedures are in effect to make sure that transcript data sent in by applicants are accurate?
Organizational factors	• Who is currently responsible for supervising office systems and procedures? • What are the current reporting relationships of the secretarial and clerical employees in this office?

Another common mistake systems analysts make is glossing over key issues and failing to ask for a detailed description of work methods and procedures. Asking yes/no type questions does nothing to reveal hidden issues. For example, if Roger Peterson asked a secretary, "You seem to have an overwhelming volume of letters, don't you?" the likely answer would be yes. A similar result would occur if he asked a question such as, "You seem to have difficulty maintaining up-to-date information in the files of applicants, don't you?" Questions worded this way would not only bring about yes/no answers but also might be viewed as critical of current practices and be addressed with hesitation or resistance. The analyst can develop a more comprehensive view of the current system by asking fact-finding types of questions. These types of questions are far less threatening and encourage people being interviewed to examine existing practices on their own. Fact-finding questions can relate to volume, processes, data, control, and organizational factors. Examples of questions in each of these categories relating to the law school office case are summarized in Figure 14-3. The systems analyst can learn a great deal by just pursuing questions about how, why, where, when, and by whom activities are being done. Most users are fully aware of the shortcomings of their current situation and are more comfortable diagnosing these issues if they are challenged to do so.

Still, some users may rush through an interview, provide irrelevant information, withhold important information, and be generally uncooperative. In this kind of situation, the systems analyst should try to diagnose the reason for the uneasiness and allay any anxieties interviewees may have. Instead of asking direct questions, the interviewer could ask workers to describe the current situation in detail, seek other sources of information, and crosscheck answers with other people in the office. The systems analyst can't expect full cooperation in all cases.

Using Questionnaires in Systems Analysis

Another way to collect data in a systems study is to use questionnaires. When detailed information about the nature and volume of work in an office is needed, questionnaires can provide uniform responses to standard questions. Using questionnaires, for example, can save the interviewer the time it would take to gather data about work volumes from more than 100 office workers. However, the systems analyst needs to make sure that all respondents answering the questionnaire understand the objectives and scope of the study, or their responses may not be valid. The design of an effective questionnaire takes careful preparation, pretesting, and evaluation. If the systems analyst does not have training in questionnaire development, she should work with an experienced researcher to develop questions and appropriate data analysis procedures. Some general guidelines for questionnaire design follow.

1. Identify the group to be surveyed.
2. Write introductory material clearly so that respondents know the purpose of the study and the use that will be made of the data.
3. Determine what facts need to be collected.
4. State questions with sufficient clarity so that respondents will understand them. Structure the response format to minimize the amount of time the respondents must spend writing.
5. Limit the length of the questionnaire so that respondents will be encouraged to take the time to respond.
6. Implement a pilot test of the questionnaire to determine if all questions are clearly understood and if all responses are of the expected type.
7. Design and implement a data collection plan.
8. Determine the method of data analysis that will be used.
9. Distribute the questionnaire, follow up to obtain desired responses, and analyze the results.

As an example, a questionnaire could be designed to collect data on the nature and volume of keyboarding and filing work in the law school admissions office. The resulting data could be used to calculate the percentage of repetitive keyboarding requirements. Using a questionnaire would also make it possible to collect standardized data over a period of time and in this way ensure that actual requirements were reported. Figure 14-4 lists questions that might appear on an office survey.

Similar questions could be asked to determine the volume and nature of filing requirements, procedures followed in making admissions and financial aid decisions, and information requirements for students and applicants. The specific data gathered from a questionnaire could be used to determine overall typing and filing requirements, to develop patterns of work distribution, to suggest new procedures, and to identify opportunities for automating certain applications, such as database requirements and standardized letters and documents. For many types of studies, the systems analyst needs to do more than conduct a straightforward data collection effort. Structured tools and techniques, discussed in the next section, can be used to analyze existing work procedures, information requirements, and methods of work organization.

Figure 14–4

Office systems questionnaire

1. What areas need to be improved?
2. What information do you need that is currently not available or difficult to access?
3. What unnecessary information do you have?
4. What bottlenecks occur in day-to-day work procedures?
5. How can these bottlenecks be avoided? How would you change current processes to avoid these bottlenecks?
6. If the time you now spend on redundant or overlapping processes were freed up, how would you use this time?

STRUCTURED SYSTEMS ANALYSIS AND DESIGN

The major objective of structured systems analysis and design is to determine the exact system requirements so that the "right" system is designed. The structured approach employs a series of graphic tools and techniques that the user can fully understand. This method enables analysts to catch errors in analysis before they become inputs into the design and subsequent phases of the systems development process.

If an error is caught during the analysis phase of a project, the cost of correcting it is many times lower than the cost of correcting the same error once the system has been designed and is in operation. For example, if a necessary data element is not identified during the analysis phase, it may be left out of system files during the design phase. Once the system is in operation, a user may notice that certain information is missing from a report. The designer may look into the situation and find out that a data element is missing from a master file. Redesigning the file and the report would take much more time than adding the data element to a data dictionary during the analysis phase of the project. Figure 14-5 summarizes the effect of undetected errors on the cost of systems development. The process of structured systems analysis helps analysts catch errors early. Instead of giving users pages of system specifications that they cannot understand, the structured systems analysis process uses tools that depict a logical model of the current system and of the proposed system that the user can clearly understand.

The structured approach to systems development is compared to the traditional approach in Figure 14-6. The traditional approach calls for studying the current system, including its data files, reports, procedures, and decisions, and developing an automated version of the system. Although this approach is efficient, there is a tendency to automate the inefficiencies of the current system. Reports could be produced for no reason in the current situation. Information about applicants could be incomplete, out of date, or simply inaccurate. If the current system is automated, many of these problems could be left undetected. In contrast, in the structured approach to systems analysis and design, the analyst collects information about current procedures,

Figure 14–5

Relative costs of correcting systems analysis errors

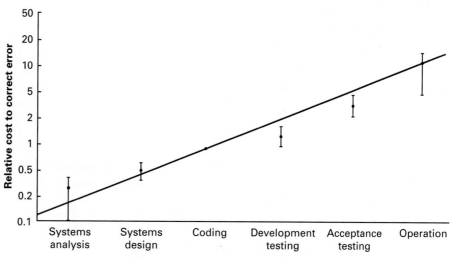

Source: Adapted from McDonnell Douglas Professional Services Company.

Figure 14-6
Structured approach to systems analysis and design

TRADITIONAL APPROACH	STRUCTURED APPROACH
• Study the current physical system.	• Study the current physical system.
• Devise a new physical system.	• Build the current logical model.
	• Analyze the objectives of the new system.
	• Derive a new logical model.
	• Draft alternative designs.
	• Finalize the new physical system.

information flows, decision-making processes, and reports and builds a logical model of the current situation, using a tool called the logical data-flow diagram.

The data-flow diagram is used because it depicts *logical* business processes, information requirements, and information flows—not the *physical* view of these elements of the system. The user doesn't need to know if personnel records are stored in a tape file, a disk file, or paper files. These are physical types of storage media. The choice of whether to store personnel records in a disk or tape file is a technical design decision that the systems designer should make. The user doesn't need to make technical design decisions. However, the user should have an opportunity to see a logical view of the data. In a logical data-flow diagram, personnel records are depicted as a personnel data store, not in their physical representation. The logical data-flow diagram provides a graphic model of the current system and can be used to analyze areas of improvement and to develop objectives for the new system. These objectives should be visualized in terms of the business results that need to be achieved in the design of a new system. Major modifications in current procedures, information needs, and decision-making processes, all of which are designed to accomplish desired objectives, are built into the model of the new logical system that is graphically depicted in the proposed logical system data-flow diagram.

The logical data-flow diagram of the proposed system becomes the basis for developing and evaluating alternative design options for the proposed system. Systems design alternatives could include mainframe-based batch and on-line systems, distributed systems, dedicated minicomputer- and microcomputer-based systems, and a range of software to support these configurations, including software developed in-house, package programs, and software developed using fourth-generation languages. Once the best design alternative has been selected, the detailed design and implementation of the proposed system can begin. This process involves designing output and input specifications, file requirements, and control procedures. These technical tasks are largely the responsibility of information systems professionals. Each step in the structured analysis and design process is covered in greater detail in the following sections of this chapter.

Developing a Logical Data-Flow Diagram of the Current System

The systems analyst uses information collected from interviews and other data collection efforts to develop a logical data-flow diagram of the present system. A logical data-flow diagram illustrates system processes, information flows, and data requirements using easy-to-understand graphic symbols (see Figure 14-7).

The "external entity" (square) depicts a source or a destination of data. It often specifies the boundary of the system. Processes (rounded rectangle) identify the major activities of a system, such as verify customer credit or send invoice to customer. They are usually best described using action verbs such as *create, produce, compute, determine,* or *verify.* Data stores are the logical repositories of data that are

Figure 14–7

Data-flow diagram symbols

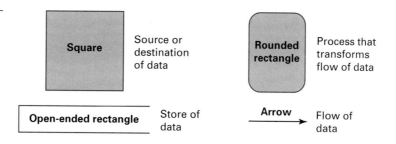

used throughout the system. Data about customers, vendors, shipments, and suppliers may all be housed in data stores. Data-flows represent data or information that is being transmitted from process to process, from an external entity to a process, or from a process into a data store. The best way to understand how a data-flow diagram works is to view one. Figure 14–8 illustrates a simple data-flow diagram showing order processing, purchasing, receiving, accounts payable, and accounts receivable activities.

The data-flow diagram graphically depicts what happens when a customer sends in an order for a part. The part order goes into a verify-orders-as-valid process, which involves checking customer credit status against a customer data store and checking for the availability of the part being ordered in a part data store. If the order is validated, it is temporarily stored in a pending orders data store. One reason for creating this pending orders data store is to accumulate enough orders to receive a quantity discount from a supplier. Batching all the orders to a particular supplier also minimizes the paperwork involved in preparing purchase orders for the supplier. After the pending orders have been held for a given interval, they are used to prepare purchase orders to suppliers. This process uses two data stores: a suppliers data store, which is used to obtain the supplier's address, and a purchase orders data store, which is used to file a copy of the purchase order being sent to the supplier.

The supplier ships the parts to the company along with shipment advice indicating the contents of the shipment. In the verify-shipment-correct process, the company checks the purchase order data store to make sure that the shipment contains everything that was ordered. If the company has received the correct shipment, it can verify the accuracy of the invoice that has been sent by the supplier, update the accounts payable data store, and prepare a vendor payment to the supplier. When a shipment is received, parts are assigned to specific orders and individual customer orders are assembled. A shipping note and an invoice are sent to the customer, and the invoice amount is used to update an accounts receivable data store for that customer. When the customer receives the invoice, payment is made and applied to the accounts receivable balance.

This system is fairly easy to understand with the graphic techniques of a logical data-flow diagram. The users should be able to detect any missing procedures or data requirements. The overall logical data-flow diagram has a number of subsystems, including order processing, purchasing, accounts receivable, and accounts payable. The data-flow diagram helps users and analysts visualize the relationships among these subsystems. The outputs of some of the subsystems, for example, become inputs into other subsystems. Pending orders, which are outputs of the order processing subsystem, become inputs into both the purchasing and order filling subsystems. The purchasing subsystem produces outputs that become inputs into the accounts payable subsystem. Understanding these relationships is important because data requirements need to be visualized on a systemwide basis. The data-flow diagram in Figure 14–8 shows a system without any particular flaws.

Figure 14–8

A system data-flow diagram

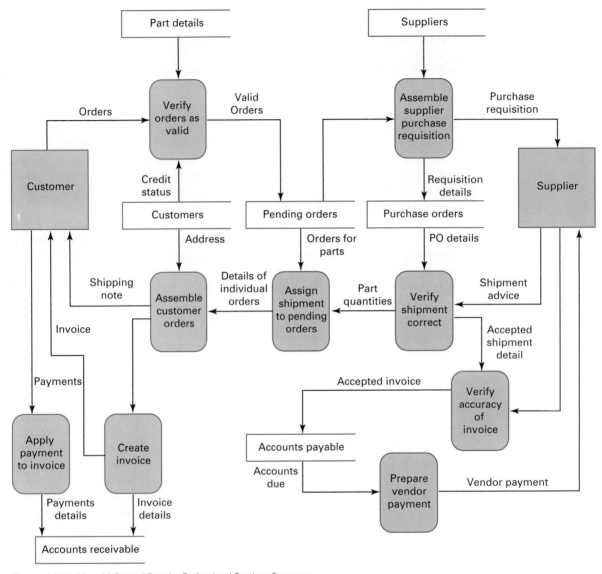

Source: Adapted from McDonnell Douglas Professional Services Company.

Case Study: The Reliable Finance Company

Background. The Reliable Finance Company (RFC) started in a small mid-Western town in the 1890s, lending money to farmers and small businessmen. Reliable Finance assumed risks that the commercial banks were unwilling to take and charged slightly higher interest rates. At the current time, Reliable Finance has 178 branches, spread from Denver to Cleveland and from Detroit to Houston. The company is committed to making loans to individuals to assist them in making purchases such as automobiles, appliances, and home improvements.

The company is managed by Ed Clarkson, grandson of its founder, along with a new management team. Management has decided on a growth plan that would expand the number of RFC branches to 400 within three years and to 1,000 within the next eight-year period. The locations will be selected in growing suburbs—especially in Texas, Florida, California, and Arizona.

These expansion plans will clearly require an enhanced information system to support transactions processing for loans, payments, and settlements. The president has asked the MIS department to develop recommendations for the redesign of the existing consumer loan system.

Analysis of the current system.   The current systems to be analyzed are the loan application screening system, the payment processing system, the delinquency analysis and reminder system, and the settlement accounting system. As indicated earlier, the company currently has 178 branches. The local branches handle some of the activities for loan processing, payment processing, and reminder processing, and the home office, which is located at Centerville, Indiana, also handles some of these activities. (See Figure 14-9 for a logical data-flow diagram.) The following narrative describes the processes that make up the loan application screening, payment processing, delinquency analysis, and settlement accounting subsystems.

Loan application screening.   Each RFC branch has a manager, several customer service advisors, and clerical staff. Applicants for loans complete a loan application form, with the assistance of a customer service advisor. The branch checks local income and bank references, and the branch manager gives the application a preliminary screening prior to sending the materials to the home office in Centerville. At the home office, a clerk in the screening department checks on whether the applicant has defaulted on any prior loans with Reliable Finance and also checks on outstanding and delinquent loans to make certain that all current loans held by the applicant are in good order. Finally, the screening clerk obtains a credit report from TRW to determine the applicant's creditworthiness based upon his or her other loan activities. The loan officer in the home office uses the data from the branches and the home office credit searches to determine whether to accept or reject the loan application.

If the loan application is accepted, the loan department generates a check for the amount of the loan and sends a confirmation of the loan's acceptance to the branch. The loan department also sends loan paperwork to the accounting department, which sets up a new loan account in the outstanding loans file. The accounting department prints a voucher booklet and sends it to the branch. The branch notifies the customer to come in and collect the check and voucher booklet.

The branch keeps copies of the vouchers in a local outstanding loans file for each customer. These voucher copies are organized in order by due date. This system enables the branch manager to see what payments are due each day. The information systems department produces monthly management reports summarizing new loans by branch.

When a new loan is confirmed, the branch also sets up an index card file for each customer, with details such as name, address, loan ID, and principal amount. This information is not shown on the voucher copies, and it is often useful in identifying accounts to which payments should be applied.

Payment processing activities.   Once the loan is set up, customers can pay in three different ways. First, customers can bring their payments into the branch in the form of cash, check, or money order. Second, they can mail their payments to the branch. The branch verifies the loan ID by checking the customer card file and then updates the local outstanding loans file by pulling the voucher copy corresponding to

Figure 14–9

Current system data-flow diagrams for Reliable Finance Company

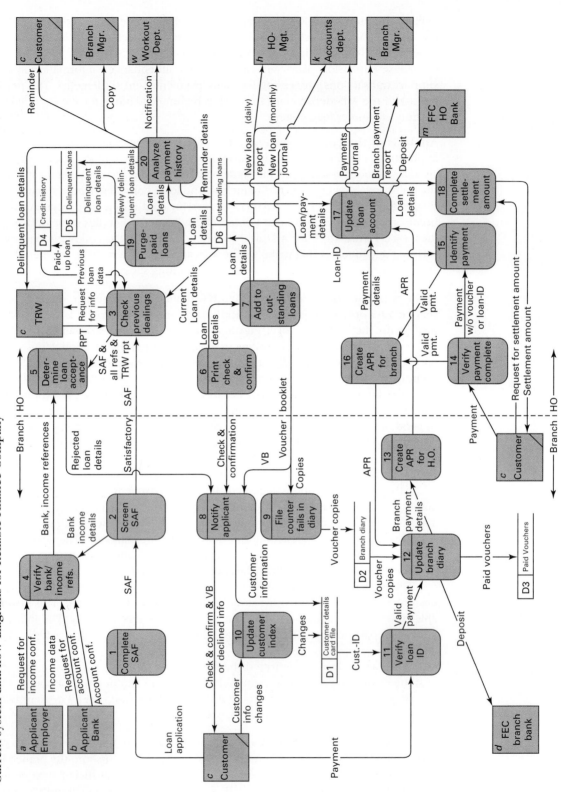

the payment, stamping it "paid," and then filing it in the paid vouchers file in sequence by loan ID and due date. The actual payments are then batched and deposited in the branch bank each afternoon. An advice of payment received form (APR) is filled out for each payment and mailed to the home office.

Customers may also make payments directly to the home office. The home office payment processing department verifies that each payment is complete by checking the enclosed voucher. If the voucher is missing, the payment processing clerk uses a printout of the central outstanding loans file to look up the loan ID corresponding to the account. Then the branch is notified by mail of the payment by means of an APR.

The details of the payment are used to update the outstanding loans file in the home office. Each evening, a batch payment processing run updates all the accounts centrally, based on payments received during that working day. In addition, the branch uses the APRs from the home office as well as its own internal records of payments that have been sent directly to the branch to update its own local outstanding loans file.

Payments made directly to the home office are batched and sent directly to the Home Office bank. The payments processing system produces a payment report for the accounting department and a branch-by-branch payment report for each branch manager.

Delinquency analysis system.   The delinquency analysis system is run once a week. It checks the outstanding loans file in the home office and determines whether any payments are overdue. It generates an aged trial balance report that indicates which payments are 15-, 30-, 45-, and 60-days overdue. When a payment is 15-days overdue, a polite first reminder is sent. When a payment is over 30-days overdue, a second (less polite) reminder is sent. Four reminders, with increasing degrees of insistence, are sent. All of these reminders are computer generated. When the loan becomes 60-days overdue, it is moved to the collections department, and collections agents begin to follow up.

Settlement accounting system.   From time to time, customers want to repay a loan early. The customer requests a settlement figure, which is the amount required to settle the outstanding balance on the loan. If the request is urgent, the branch manager will phone the request to the home office. The information systems department now prepares a settlement run, which is processed nightly, with the urgent request for the settlement balance. The settlement balance is sent back to the branch manager the next morning.

Current problems.   In order to accommodate the expansion plans, the current system will need to be streamlined, modified, and enhanced. These are some of the problems with the current system:

- The various steps in the loan approval process typically take 10 to 13 working days. In many of the cities where RFC has branches, commercial banks approve or disapprove loan applications in two or three days. Consequently, some of the best loan candidates (e.g., people who are the best credit risks) obtain approval for their loans at least a week before RFC gets around to approving them. RFC is losing some of its best loan prospects to the commercial banks.

- About 80 percent of the payments are made to a branch, and the rest are mailed to the home office. Of the payments that are mailed, the payment voucher from the voucher booklet is missing in about half the cases. The missing voucher does not matter so much at a branch, because each branch maintains a local customer card file with the name and loan ID. However, the home office, has trouble tracing payments. At the current time, incoming payments without an accompanying voucher are identified by checking against a printout of the outstanding loans file. However, APRs for voucherless payments are sometimes sent to the wrong branch, and the entire process causes more clerical work and error correction.

- The bottlenecks in processing payments trigger additional problems. People who do not pay until 10 days after their due date, create considerable clerical overhead. Because of various delays, their late payment does not actually get posted to the outstanding loans file until after the delinquency analysis run has sent them their first reminder. When these customers call the branch to protest, the branch has to call the home office to trace the payment. Forty-four people are currently tied up in the customer service section at the home office, and much of their time is spent dealing with late and missing payment matters.

- Instances of excessive clerical overhead exist throughout the system. In 129 of the 178 branches, a full-time clerical person was engaged in maintaining the local branch loans file, in pulling voucher copies, in recording payments, and in preparing APRs. In the other 49 branches, these activities take between two and five hours per day.

- Since the outstanding loans file is always several days out-of-date, it is often difficult to isolate loans that are genuinely delinquent until it is too late. About 2.5 percent of all loans are never repaid. Last year $4,795,000 was written off as uncollectible. Although processing delays account for not flagging late payers sooner, management feels that RFC could do a much better job of weeding out potential delinquents during the initial approval process. RFC wants to build a picture of the potential delinquent, including age, occupation, income, family size, location, mobility, and a host of other criteria yet to be specified. A "delinquency profile" will aid in identifying high-potential-for-delinquency accounts. Operations research personnel can develop, maintain, and modify this profile on an ongoing basis.

- Because of error and adjustment activities, RFC rarely balances its books for month end before the 12th of the following month. This delay greatly complicates planning for cash flow and frequently requires RFC to borrow more money than it really needs (and at higher interest rates).

A summary of the major problems of the current system illustrates the following:

- The loan application screening process is too time-consuming.

- Excessive clerical overhead is invested in maintaining the local and central outstanding loans files, in preparing APRs, in handling late and missing payment matters, and in tracing loan IDs for checks without vouchers.

- Some customers receive delinquency notices after they make their monthly payment because of the delays and bottlenecks in the payment processing subsystem.

- An excessive number of loans are written off as uncollectible.

- Cash-flow projections are difficult to determine because account balances are not known until the 12th of the following month.

New system requirements.   As you have already learned, Reliable Finance has ambitious expansion plans. In addition, the key priorities of management include:

- Eliminating APRs. The current APR paper chase creates many bottlenecks, excessive paperwork, and delays in posting payments to the outstanding loans file.

- Developing a delinquency profile and using it to screen new loan applications. This tool should eventually decrease the percentage of uncollectible accounts.

- Receiving up-to-date cash-flow information based on outgoing loan amounts and incoming payments. Right now, this cash-flow information is delayed. The cash-flow reporting system should show how much profit each branch makes each week. This report should incorporate interest earned, fees earned, delinquent loans written off, salaries, overhead, and branch expenses.

Analysis of the current system. As you can see from the logical data-flow diagram, the current system (Figure 14–9) has a number of bottlenecks. In the loan application screening process, you can see local credit checking in the branch, followed by the checking of credit history, delinquent loans, and external credit references in the home office. The extra time required to conduct two sets of credit checks—in the branch and in the home office—puts RFC at a competitive disadvantage because the banks can approve loans much more rapidly.

As you can see from the diagram, payment processing in the current system is very inefficient. When a customer pays the branch, clerks verify the loan ID, update the local branch loans file, and create an APR for the home office. When a customer pays the home office, clerks there verify the completeness of the payment, update the central outstanding loans file, and create an APR for the branch. The local loans file duplicates the information in the central outstanding loans file. In addition, the branch and home office perform other redundant recordkeeping and updating procedures.

Two more smaller subsystems are shown on the data-flow diagram. A daily delinquency analysis run is conducted against the outstanding loans file in the home office. A number of reminder letters are generated, and eventually the case is referred to the collections department in the home office. This routine raises the question of effectiveness: Are customers more likely to pay their overdue accounts when the notice comes from the home office or when it comes from the branch?

Finally, the settlement accounting system is not working. When a customer wants to make a settlement payment on a loan, the branch manager needs to contact the home office and wait at least 24 hours while a settlement data processing program is executed. The system is ineffective. If a client wants to make a payment, RFC should be able to compute the settlement balance immediately. The 24-hour delay in the current system is unacceptable and gives the client time to find other uses for their funds.

Developing Business and System Objectives

At the end of the analysis phase of the systems study, the user should be able to identify objectives that address the needs of the business. These business objectives should state the business outcomes that need to be achieved. The business outcomes should be measurable so that the user understands the extent of the changes that will be necessary to make them occur. In most cases a profit-making concern is trying to increase revenues and minimize costs. An example of a measurable business objective is: Increase sales by 25 percent within the next five years.

System objectives describe the major capabilities of the information system to be designed. Computer-based information systems can process information faster and more accurately than manual systems can. For example, a person responsible for manually checking the credit for hundreds of customer orders per day is likely to make an error, but a computer-based system will be almost totally accurate. Information

Figure 14–10
Business and
system objectives
for Reliable Finance
Company

BUSINESS OBJECTIVES	SYSTEM OBJECTIVES
• Complete loan authorizations in less than three days.	• Create decentralized responsibility for loan application screening and decision making in the branch; design distributed databases (credit history, delinquent loans) that are accessible in the branch to support decision making.
• Reduce the delinquency rate from 2.5 to 2 percent within one year.	• Develop a more accurate delinquency profile that identifies "high-potential-for-delinquency" accounts; provide for more data on the loan application form.
• Reduce clerical expense associated with maintaining duplicate files, processing APRs, and handling late-payment matters.	• Force all payments to be made through the branch; provide posting of all payments before any payment reminders are generated.
• Reduce by 50 percent the cost of short-term borrowing within one year.	• Provide a cash-flow reporting system that identifies current cash position.
• Offer a carefree bill-paying program at no net cost.	• Process 30,000 bills per night for an average cost of less than 50 cents per bill.

maintained by a computer-based information system is also more likely to be up-to-date. Finally, a computer-based system can introduce new functions for management reporting and analysis purposes. Although it's very difficult to perform many of these analytical functions manually, computer-based procedures can easily summarize and aggregate sales data, accounts receivable data, and inventory data for analytical purposes.

In developing business and system objectives, each problem in the current system needs to be addressed. Business objectives deal with the business outcomes of the proposed system, and system objectives deal with the changes in processes, information flows, and databases that are needed to realize the business objectives.

A listing of the business and system objectives for RFC appears in Figure 14–10.

Preparing the Proposed System Data-Flow Diagram

The proposed system data-flow diagram in Figure 14–11 shows the changes in processes, data flows, and data stores that are needed to implement these business and system objectives.

A new database, the customer profile, has been added to find new loan applications that fit the "high-potential-for-delinquency" criteria. This customer profile is developed by the Operations Research Group, as shown by an external entity. Another subsystem within that entity has detailed processes and data stores.

The payment processing subsystem has been streamlined and simplified because all payments must now be made to the branch. When a customer sends a payment into the branch, a clerk edits and batches the payments. Valid payments are transmitted once a day to the home office, where they are posted to the outstanding loans file prior to the next business day. This system prevents reminders from being sent to individuals who have paid their account balances on time. The payment processing system is vastly improved. Instead of seven processes and three data stores, the procedures can be accomplished with two processes and one data store in the new subsystem. You can see the subsystem boundary by looking at the proposed data-flow diagram.

Figure 14–11

Proposed system data-flow diagrams for Reliable Finance Company

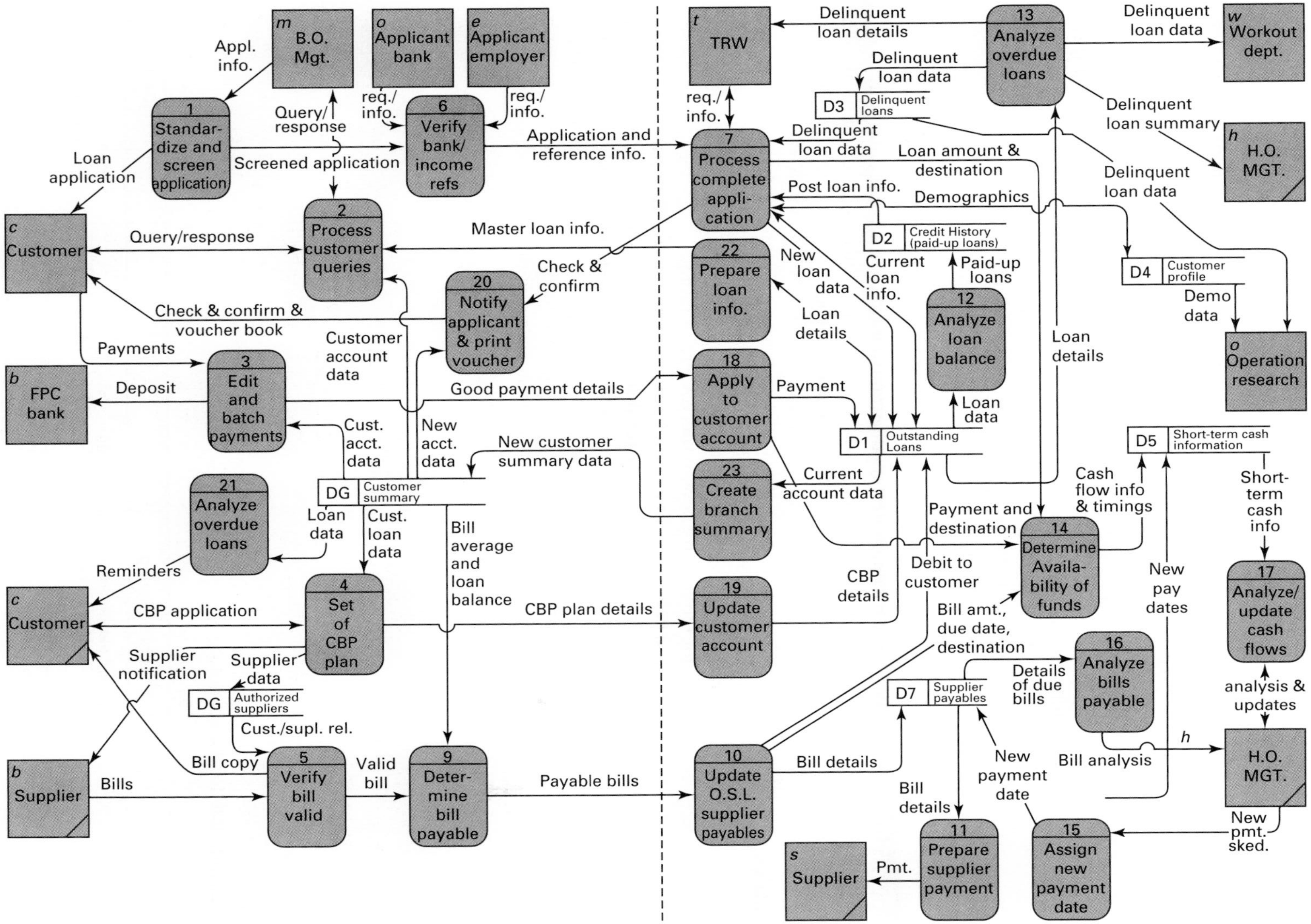

The proposed system has two new subsystems: the cash management reporting subsystem and the carefree bill payer (CBP) subsystem. The cash management reporting subsystem provides management with an analysis of cash flows. It uses income (e.g., incoming payments) and outgoing funds (e.g., new loans and payments to suppliers) to determine RFC's current cash position.

The carefree bill payer program requires a new subsystem. This plan enables an RFC client to set up an additional loan to cover all monthly payments to vendors, such as rent, automobile financing, credit cards, electrical utilities, the gas company, and so forth. The client establishes a loan that covers the average amount of these monthly bills. In turn, RFC collects the suppliers' bills, determines if they are payable, and generates checks to each supplier each month. RFC takes advantage of the "float" because it receives loan payments from each client at the beginning of each month, and can hold many supplier payments until a later date.

Specifying Process Logic Using Decision Trees and Tables

One new procedure RFC might want to introduce is a discount policy for loan applicants with exceptionally good credit histories. This policy might be as follows:

The interest rate discount to clients with a "AAA" credit rating is 2 percentage points (e.g., 8 percent to 6 percent). Customers with a "AA" credit rating get a 1 percent discount on loans of $10,000 or more, a .75 percent discount on loans of $7,500 or more, and a .50 percent discount for loans of $5,000 or more. Loans of $10,000 or more would receive an additional .50 percent interest rate discount over the regular discount for customers with the "AA" credit rating.

Although this policy may appear straightforward, in its narrative version it could be misinterpreted. A **decision table** or **decision tree** is a useful tool for specifying the logic of a process such as this one. The decision tree and decision table for RFC's discount policy are shown in Figure 14-12. A decision table or tree enables the user to make sure that the systems analyst has interpreted a business policy or procedure correctly. In turn, the systems analyst can use a decision table or tree to explain the logic of a procedure to a programmer.

Figure 14–12

Decision table for a discount policy

C1: Credit Rating	AAA			AA		
C2: Loan Amount	≥10,000	≥ 7,500 <10,000	≥5,000 <7,500	≥10,000	≥ 7,500 <10,000	≥5,000 <7,500
A1: 2% discount	X	X	X			
A2: 1% discount				X		
A3: .75% discount					X	
A4: .50% discount						X

Describing Data Flows and Data Stores in the Logical Data Dictionary

The data flows and data stores in the logical data-flow diagram consist of data elements that the user must identify. The characteristics of these data elements also must be defined—the systemwide data elements and their characteristics are described in a data dictionary.

Data flows are data in motion. In the RFC case, one of the data flows is the loan application form. This data flow consists of many data elements, each of which needs a unique data name and a standard data definition. Some of the data elements are customer name, customer street address, customer bank, customer employer, and customer income range. Once the data elements of the system have been defined, the user must be involved in determining the contents of data stores. Data stores are data at rest. The data stores house the data that become the basis for designing files throughout the system. The most commonly used approach to defining data store contents is to take inventory of the data elements that are used in outgoing data flows. These are typically the data elements that are printed in some kind of output report. The user must be directly involved in determining these output requirements, particularly the nature of management reports for such functions as sales and inventory analysis. The data stores then become whatever is necessary to support the agreed-upon outputs.

Structured tools for systems analysis and design allow users to identify their systems requirements. The user must provide and the systems analyst must understand the logic of decisions, the definition of data elements, and the description of reports. These tools enhance communication between the analyst and user and provide logical specifications that become inputs into the detailed design phase of the project.

EVALUATING ALTERNATIVE DESIGN OPTIONS

One of the most important elements in systems design is the evaluation of alternative design options. The input of managers who will be using the system is critical at this point. The range of systems design options that should be evaluated includes batch versus on-line systems, mainframe-based versus microcomputer-based systems, and systems developed in-house versus packaged systems. In each systems design project, the alternative design options are slightly different.

Alternative Processing Modes

One range of alternatives to be considered in developing a systems design proposal is the mode of processing that the system will support. Processing modes include batch, on-line, distributed, and decentralized options.

Batch processing. **Batch processing** normally uses a central computer system to process all transactions against a central database and to produce reports at fixed intervals. Payroll is a good example of a batch processing application because all time cards are used to update a payroll master file, calculate pay amounts, and produce checks and other payroll reports at fixed times.

On-line processing. In **on-line processing,** transactions can be keyed in at terminals at remote sites and transferred to the computer system via telecommunications channels. Users at remote sites can also receive outputs that have been processed by the central computer system and display them at their terminals. An on-line order-entry system, for example, allows a local sales clerk to check a customer's credit against an accounts receivable master file at a central office. In on-line processing, transactions can be edited against a central database or at the local workstation. If transactions are edited by a program running on the central system, error transactions are printed in an error report and sent back to the local office that originated them. However, many local data entry terminals have built-in data validation capabilities so that transactions are edited on-site and only accurate data are transmitted to a central system, where it is used to update a central database.

On-line processing has two types of update procedures: **on-line with batch overnight update** and **on-line immediate update.** The following examples explain these procedures. In batch overnight update, transactions are entered locally at remote terminals, transmitted to the central system, and used to update the central database overnight. A loan company may accept loan payments at branch offices. Payment transactions could be entered and validated at the local branches, transmitted to the central home office, and used to update the central loan file overnight. In this mode of processing, a record of payments made on any given working day is not available until the next day. However, batch overnight update is an efficient method for most business data processing applications.

Although batched update is normally associated with overnight update, there is no reason that updates cannot be batched more or less frequently than overnight. Updates can be deferred and batched twice a day, once during lunch hour and once overnight. There is no reason why updates cannot be done once a week if the users of the application find that satisfactory. In contrast, an on-line system with immediate update enables transactions to update the central database on a real-time basis, or as they occur. Inquiries to the database reflect business that has taken place that same day. Examples of information systems requiring on-line immediate update capabilities are airline and hotel reservations systems.

Distributed data processing.   In a distributed data processing situation, local transactions can be used to update local files, and summary results can be transmitted to a central system. The point-of-sale processing systems used by stores such as Sears and JC Penney are good examples of this approach. In these systems sales transactions update local inventory databases, and summary sales and inventory results are sent to the central office for management reporting and analysis.

Decentralized processing.   A dedicated minicomputer or microcomputer with its own database can serve as a decentralized system. When communications with other systems are not necessary and the application is relatively self-contained, decentralized processing is appropriate. A local word processing system in an office and a dedicated production planning system in a plant are good examples of decentralized processing.

Improved manual operations.   Another alternative that needs to be considered in systems design is improving manual operations. Introducing an automated system into a situation in which work is disorganized, procedures are unclear, and job responsibilities are not equitably allocated may actually worsen the situation. Work procedures must be simplified, methods of work organization and control improved, and work responsibilities distributed equitably before a computer-based information system is introduced. Each alternative must be evaluated on the basis of user needs, the characteristics of the application, the trade-off between local and central control, and cost-effectiveness. The availability of microcomputer-based workstations has improved the technical and economic feasibility of distributed and decentralized processing approaches.

Computer Design Alternatives

The three major computer design alternatives that should be considered are acquiring an in-house computer system, using a time-sharing service, or contracting for service with a service bureau.

An in-house computer system. A number of in-house computer options exist, including mainframe-based, minicomputers, and microcomputer alternatives. The improving capabilities of minicomputers and microcomputers make them excellent candidates for distributed, decentralized, and departmental computing options. Frequently, these minis and micros can be linked to mainframe-based databases via telecommunications networks. Earlier chapters have discussed these computer configurations in greater detail. The choice of computer system depends on processing requirements, including processing mode, the nature and scope of applications, the number of applications, file sizes, number of users, and other capacity needs. As discussed in earlier chapters, large mainframe-based systems support multiple users and multiple applications and provide economies of scale in processing and support. In contrast, distributed or dedicated minicomputer and microcomputer options provide opportunities for user control over hardware, software development, operations, and maintenance.

Time-sharing services. Sometimes it is not feasible to purchase an in-house computer system. A few users may want access to statistical analysis software, but their requirements do not justify purchasing the hardware and software to support this system in-house. In a **time-sharing** situation, the user pays only for the computer resources—including processing time and access to computer programs—that he or she uses. Normally, the user has a terminal and a local printer tied to the time-sharing computer. He uses programs, sends data, and receives output on an on-demand basis. The advantage of this approach is that many users can share computer resources and have access to programs and computer capacity that would not otherwise be available to them. The disadvantages of this approach are (1) the user does not have control over the system and (2) the associated cost. Powerful desktop workstations and more cost-effective solutions have largely replaced time-sharing services. The only significant use of time-sharing today is to access highly specialized, expensive resources such as supercomputers.

Service bureaus. Many organizations have no experience with selecting and managing a computer system. **Service bureaus** provide services ranging from full-scale support for applications from accounts receivable and payroll to data entry and distribution of output. The job of application development, processing, maintenance, and support is in the hands of technical professionals working for the service bureau. Some service bureaus rent or sell their customers computers so that some data processing can occur locally.

The biggest advantage of a service bureau is that it allows the use of computer services without incurring the time and expense of organizing and managing an in-house computer operation. A service bureau can be contracted, for example, to maintain a database of 450,000 names and addresses and to generate mailing labels from this database quarterly. Since the computer capacity to handle this application is needed only four times a year, the fund-raising organization would benefit from using the service bureau approach. However, service bureau customers are not totally in control of the processing and maintenance of their applications and may have to tolerate poor service levels and lack of responsiveness to their needs. Some of the advantages and disadvantages of the various computer design alternatives are summarized in Figure 14-13.

Software Development Alternatives

A final range of alternatives deals with software development. Many software packages on mainframes, minicomputers, and microcomputers provide excellent alternatives to in-house software development. In addition, software vendors or software

Figure 14–13
Computer design
alternatives

	Advantages	Disadvantages
IN-HOUSE COMPUTER SYSTEM	• Control over hardware. • Control over systems development.	• Cost of systems development. • Cost of hardware operations and maintenance.
	• Control over priorities. • Optimum configuration possible; limited to what is needed.	• Cost of staffing and training computer personnel.
	Advantages	**Disadvantages**
TIME SHARING SYSTEM	• Variable cost; pay only for what is used.	• Lack of control over system service levels.
	• Access to computer programs and capacity not otherwise available.	• Lack of control over charges for system use.
	Advantages	**Disadvantages**
SERVICE BUREAU OPTION	• Use of computer systems without having to bring systems development and operations functions in-house. • Availability of specific services.	• Lack of control over priorities. • Data in the hands of an external organization. • Lack of control over data processing expense.

houses offer systems design and programming services that make it unnecessary for an organization to hire in-house programmers.

In-house software development.   In large organizations with MIS systems development professionals, software for information systems development projects that are sophisticated, unique to the organization, and maintainable by MIS professionals is usually developed in-house. Unique user requirements can be satisfied more readily with in-house development. However, the time and cost of developing software from scratch argue against using this approach in many projects.

Software houses.   **Software houses** offer specialized systems design and programming services as well as help with implementation, including conversion and training. In cases where the in-house development staff does not have the time or expertise to support a project, contracting for software development services can be a cost-effective approach. In most cases software houses also support maintenance and enhancements to the current system. Although contract personnel may have specialized expertise in the application area, they may not be familiar with the business requirements of the user.

Software packages.   The use of software packages can save considerable time and effort in systems development. Software packages must be evaluated in detail to make sure that they support the users' requirements. If modifications are substantial, then in-house development may pay off more effectively in the long run. Figure 14–14 summarizes some of the advantages and disadvantages of various software development approaches.

The selection of an appropriate systems design alternative requires user involvement. A systems design proposal will include an analysis of each alternative, its tech-

Figure 14–14

Software
development
alternatives

	Advantages	Disadvantages
IN-HOUSE SOFTWARE DEVELOPMENT	• Can manage and control the program development process. • Internal professionals can serve unique user requirements. • Internal systems designers can provide more effective training, evaluation, and follow-up.	• Time and cost greater than other options. • In-house staff may lack specialized expertise needed for the project.
	Advantages	**Disadvantages**
SOFTWARE HOUSES	• Can contract and pay for specific services that are needed. • Can obtain experts to do design work.	• External project management, including time, cost, and performance considerations. • Implementation may be difficult for "outsiders."
	Advantages	**Disadvantages**
SOFTWARE PACKAGES	• Save the time and cost of in-house development. • Availability of detailed documentation and training materials.	• Package may not fit users' needs. • May incur time and cost necessary to modify the package to meet users' needs.

nical feasibility, its economic feasibility, and its impact on the organization. The development time and cost for each alternative suggest trade-offs that also need to be evaluated. For example, a package software solution may not meet 100 percent of the users' requirements, but it could be implemented within six months, compared with a system developed in-house, which might take two years to design, program, and implement. Businesses need information systems to obtain a competitive edge or to provide needed services to customers. These considerations enter into the selection of an appropriate design alternative.

ANALYSIS OF ALTERNATIVE DESIGN OPTIONS

Any systems study includes an analysis of alternative design options selected from a "menu of alternatives." In the RFC case, numerous processing options can support the company's business requirements.

A review of some of these processing options follows.

• *On-line data entry with batch overnight update.* In this situation data entry clerks in the branches would enter payment transactions locally. Each afternoon, these transactions would be transmitted to the home office, where they would be used to update the central outstanding loans database. Any error transactions would be printed out on an error report and would be returned to the branch. When branch personnel received a copy of the error report, they would rekey the transactions. Local branch personnel would be able to check the balance in the customer loan accounts by querying the outstanding loans file from their terminals. Reminders about overdue accounts would be generated at the home office after each night's update and then forwarded to

Manager's Memo 14–1	TAKE A LOOK AT OUTSOURCING

Outsourcing of information systems is a trend that is receiving a great deal of attention. Firms that outsource often hire external vendors to perform almost any kind of data processing service, including data center operations, telecommunications, software maintenance, hardware support, or even application development. One of the main reasons for outsourcing is cost reduction. External contractors can often offer services at a lower cost than a company would spend to manage its data center internally. A firm considering an outsourcing arrangement should be aware of both the benefits and pitfalls.

One of the major benefits of outsourcing is the ability to redirect MIS staff members away from traditional, maintenance-type projects to application development projects that have strategic value. At Talman Federal Savings and Loan, for example, management decided to outsource data center operations so that the internal information systems staff could develop sophisticated branch-banking products and services to give Talman a competitive advantage in the savings and loan market. One of these services was a bank-at-home service that let customers transfer money between their accounts and conduct other banking business at home. Another service enabled customers to do their banking via a touch-tone phone. As you can see from this example, a firm can outsource nonstrategic activities such as data center management and refocus its attention on projects that have an important business impact. This approach is consistent with an overall business strategy of downsizing operations to essential core business activities.

Outsourcing has its pitfalls, too. Once management has decided to outsource its data center operations, it may be difficult to organize them again. Without careful initial planning, the services provided through an outsourcing arrangement may not be any better than the services provided by an internally managed operation. At Farm Credit Banks of St. Louis, management initiated an outsourcing program in the mid-1980s. The outsourcing contract supported network management, data center operations, computer processing, application development, PC support, systems maintenance, staffing, and database management. However, the services provided by the outsourcing arrangement were ineffective. The major problem was the lack of business systems analysts who understood the bank's business. To correct the situation, Farm Credit Banks purchased a midsized computer and hired staff developers who had good knowledge of bank operations. These internal developers focused on key information systems projects. External contractors handled data center management and operations on an outsourcing basis.

Another pitfall to avoid is locking yourself into an inflexible contract. Contracts need to be evolutionary so that companies can pursue new technology and development methods. Contracts must also weigh the partnership as a mutually beneficial and cooperative arrangement. If a fixed-cost contract is negotiated, the vendor may not be motivated to provide anything other than minimum service. However, if revenues are tied to the success of a project, both the firm and the outsourcing vendor win. In one case, Andersen Consulting, an outsourcing vendor, placed an accounts receivable system in a client company. The new system didn't make any money for Andersen until its clients' revenues grew from better ability to track receivables. When its clients' revenues grew, Andersen's revenues grew as well. For an outsourcing arrangement to work, the contract should be a two-way street. Without question, outsourcing will pave the way for many companies to refocus their MIS missions toward projects that are critical to achieving business results.

the branch managers for distribution to local accounts. This system would cost between $300,000 and $400,000 to design and implement. It would be written in COBOL and maintained by the information systems department.

- *Distributed processing with a PC-based terminal.* In this case each branch would have a microcomputer that could also serve as a data entry terminal for inputting and editing payment transactions. At the end of each business day, the branch computer would transmit the file of payment transactions to the home office. Once these transactions had been used to update the central file, the home office could write a new customer summary file listing the up-to-date balances of each customer account for each branch. The advantage of having a

Figure 14–15

An analysis of alternative design options

	Advantages	Disadvantages
ON-LINE SYSTEM WITH OVERNIGHT UPDATE	• Least expensive. • Uses simple technology. • No local DP expertise needed.	• Requires rekeying of error transactions, causing further delays. • Local branches do not have access to data for analytical purposes. • Local branches do not generate reminder letters.
	Advantages	**Disadvantages**
DISTRIBUTED PROCESSING WITH A PC-BASED TERMINAL	• Provides access to data for generating reminders and for analytical purposes. • Avoids rekeying of error transactions and avoids unnecesary delays.	• More expensive than on-line system. • Local branches do not control access to a database of their accounts.
	Advantages	**Disadvantages**
DISTRIBUTED PROCESSING WITH A LOCAL PC DATABASE	• Local branches maintain a decentralized database of their loan accounts. • Local branches can generate their own reminder letters and reports. • Branch controls access to data.	• Most expensive. • Requires a dedicated systems person in the branch to handle systems administration and reporting.

microcomputer-based workstation is that the branch could also download a file of overdue accounts and use a mail-merge program to merge these records with reminder letters. This system would cost about $5,000 per branch. The total cost of this option is about $950,000.

- *Distributed processing with a local PC database.* In this alternative each branch would have a microcomputer that would store a decentralized outstanding loans file for that branch. Customers would send their payments to the branch, and these payments would be entered into a microcomputer-based file and used to update the local database. At the end of each business day, the local branch would transmit a summary report of total payments to the home office, but the details of the individual transactions would not be sent. In addition, local branch personnel will be able to query the local outstanding loans database for customer records and generate payment reminder notices. Because of the costs of software development and operations, this alternative would cost about $1,215,500.

You can use the brief descriptions in Figure 14–15 to analyze the advantages and disadvantages of each alternative. As you can see from this preliminary analysis, each alternative is feasible and has merit. The determination of the best design alternative also depends on its financial feasibility, which will be determined using a cost-benefit analysis.

Manager's Memo 14–2 | COMPUTER-AIDED SOFTWARE ENGINEERING

Computer-aided software engineering tools are software programs that automate part of the application development process. First introduced in the mid-1980s, these tools range from graphical tools that can be used to depict software designs to systems that can be used to produce code from detailed design specifications. These tools provide the software engi-neer with support similar to the computer-aided design and manufacturing (CAD/CAM) workstations that engineers use.

One type of CASE tool enables the systems designer to produce schematic designs of the proposed system producing data-flow diagrams, data dictionary specifications, logical data models, and the design of

Figure 14–16

Data-flow diagram using a CASE tool

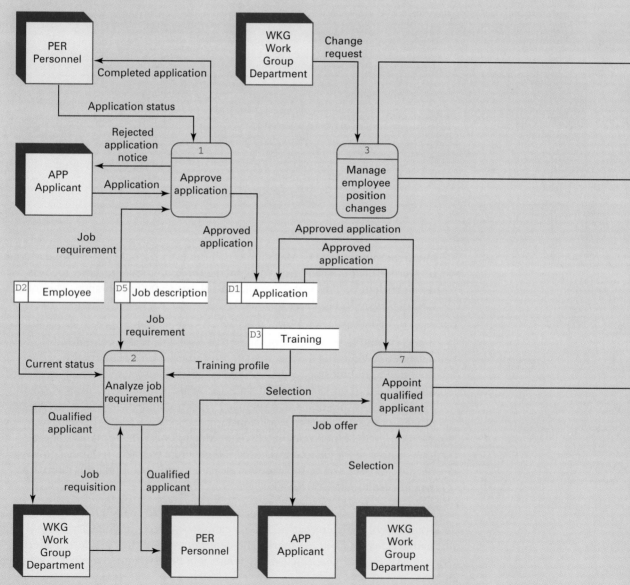

input and output formats. The systemwide data dictionary that many CASE tools support enables the analyst to create standardized data names and data definitions for data elements used throughout the system. If a data definition changes in the data dictionary, the change will be made wherever this data element is used. A logical data-flow diagram prepared using a CASE tool is shown in Figure 14–16. One of the main advantages of using a CASE tool is the ability to catch design errors. For example, the tool can check whether data elements included in output data flows are present in the source data store. If a data element has not been created and stored, the system will indicate the error so that it can be corrected.

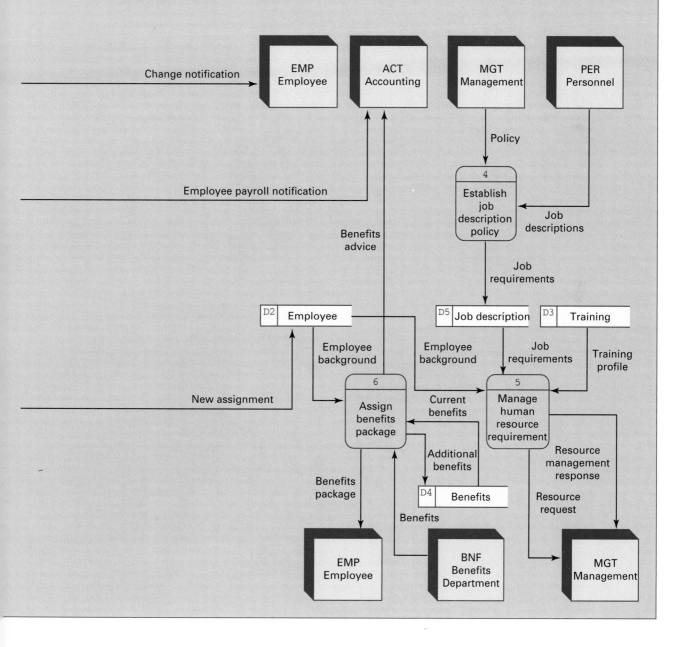

Some integrated software tools providing similar capabilities for software design include Visible Analyst Workbench from Visible Systems, Inc., the Applications Development Workbench from Knowledgeware, and Composer from Texas Instruments. CASE tools that support software design have a number of advantages. Their use forces the systems analyst to design and document algorithms, data flows, data element definitions, and database descriptions. Once these diagrams have been constructed, CASE tools make it possible to make additions, deletions, and changes without completely redrawing them. Most CASE systems provide a standardized set of tools addressing each phase of the systems life cycle. The analyst uses these tools to create design documentation that people responsible for maintaining the system can understand.

CASE tools enable analysts to generate and analyze alternative design possibilities. Changes in data-flow diagrams, data dictionary specifications, and input/output forms can be made and incorporated into the system design. The result may be a better quality design that requires less maintenance. Using CASE tools to graphically depict system processes and data requirements allows the analyst to involve the user directly and to make modifications based on the user's suggestions. CASE tools support the prototyping approach by allowing the analyst to document the characteristics of various versions of the system and to make revisions until the system meets the user's needs.

One of the current issues regarding CASE tools is that many different tools exist. Although the majority of the tools focus on schematic design at the front end, some tools generate code from software designs. Examples of code generators are Gamma from Knowledgeware and VAX Cobol Generator from Digital Equipment Corporation. The ideal CASE tool would provide an integrated set of tools supporting software design and coding. It would include front-end software to pictorially represent data-flow diagrams, structure charts, and other design constructs consistent with the methodology being used. The product should also support the prototyping of screens, sample databases, and reports. The central component of a CASE tool is a data dictionary that stores the data names and data definitions of data elements used throughout the system. The tool should also include a code generator that transforms software designs into code. The key elements of a CASE environment are shown in Figure 14-17.

Most CASE tools support specific software design methodologies, such as the Information Engineering Methodology. An organization should select a CASE tool that is consistent with its current systems devel-

Figure 14-17

Elements of a CASE environment

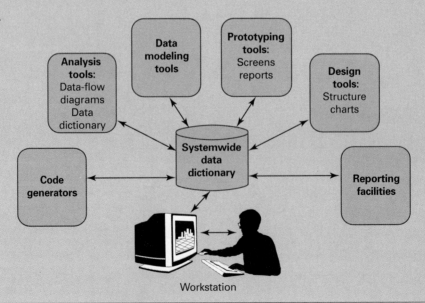

Workstation

Manager's Memo 14–2	**CONTINUED**

Figure 14–18
Benefits of CASE

- Provides checks on design errors.
- Provides a systemwide data dictionary.
- Prevents redrawing of diagrams.
- Provides opportunities to make design changes.
- Ensures conformance with design and documentation standards.
- Increases user involvement in systems design.
- Creates a repository of systems design documentation.
- Improves system reliability and maintainability.
- Aids project management and control.

opment methodology. CASE tools mechanize some of the systems analyst's more repetitive chores, such as drawing and redrawing data-flow diagrams. As a result, analysts have more time for important tasks such as analysis of alternative design options and checking of accuracy. CASE tools also enable the designer to spend more time addressing organizational issues in systems design, which should ultimately result in improved designs and more effective use of information systems. Some of the benefits of CASE are summarized in Figure 14–18.

THE ORGANIZATIONWIDE DATA DICTIONARY

During the systems analysis process, systems analysts collect information about the data elements that make up records and reports. Over the past 20 to 25 years, many information systems have been developed, and the data used in these systems has been defined and redefined many times. For example, the data element CUSTOMER-NAME may be called CUST-NAME, C-NAME, CUS-NAM, NAME-OF-CUST, and IN-C-NAME in various programs and records. To compound the situation, the characteristics of the data may also be defined differently in different systems. In one system, CUSTOMER-NAME may be defined as a 26-digit alphabetic field, and in another, NAME-OF-CUST may be defined as a 32-digit alphanumeric field. The result is a Tower of Babel situation in which the same element is called different names and described in different ways in different information systems. Some of the problems of the Tower of Babel situation are illustrated in the following examples. Lawrence Peters describes the experience of a flight instructor who had taught hundreds of private pilots. On one occasion, when he was training a new pilot to land a B-17 that had been converted for use in fighting forest fires, the instructor noticed that the pilot was coming in too low. He waited for the trainee to detect and correct the problem, but when he didn't, the flight instructor shouted "takeoff power." In the military, the instructor had learned that *takeoff power* meant to apply full power to the engines. However, the student interpreted *takeoff power* to mean to cut the engines further back. The plane crashed, but the instructor and student pilot survived. The lack of a common definition for the phrase *takeoff power* was certainly felt in this incident.

Other problems occur when a data element has multiple names. Gordon Davis, a professor of management information systems at the University of Minnesota, tells of a situation in which a business analyst was asked to assess the feasibility of offering a tuition-reimbursement program to the employees of a firm. To determine the number of employees who might use such a program to pay for their children's college education, the analyst queried the employee master file for the number and ages of children. Based on his analysis of children who would be eligible for benefits from the proposed program, he concluded that the program was feasible. However, the analyst made a serious mistake. In doing his study, he used one data name to extract employee information. But three different data names for the data element EMPLOYEE existed in various files. As a result, the program affected three times as many employees and potentially three times as many children as the number he projected. When the program was implemented, requests for tuition reimbursement tripled the original projection. The president quickly realized that the company could not afford to support the program and withdrew these benefits. Employees were bitter about the outcome because their children's education was a sensitive personal issue. Plant workers went out on strike, demanding that the tuition benefit program be reinstated. In the midst of the turmoil, the president himself resigned.

Scenarios like this one depict the potential dangers of nonstandardized data element names and definitions. Most organizations today are moving toward a centralized database approach and, along with this approach, are implementing organizationwide data dictionaries. These dictionaries enforce standard data names and data definitions for the data elements used in the enterprise. For example, CUST-NAME may be established as a standard data name, and 26 alphabetic digits may be set as the standard data definition for the data element *customer name*. Any other data names used to describe customer name in other programs and records are called *aliases,* or other data names by which customer name is known. The organizationwide data dictionary concept has many benefits. For one thing, programmers and analysts can use the dictionary to look up the standard data names and definitions for data elements used in information systems under development. This method minimizes the Tower of Babel problem. The dictionary also saves time and effort in maintenance. For example, if the data element EMPLOYEE-ZIP, representing ZIP code, has to be changed from a five-digit numeric field (63121) to a nine-digit numeric field (63121–1106), the programmer must be able to search for each occurrence of the ZIP code field in all existing programs and records. If this field is called different names in different programs, the search can be very time-consuming. However, with a data dictionary, the programmer can identify the standard data name (EMPLOYEE-ZIP) as well as aliases (EMP-ZIP, EMP-ZIP-CODE, and so on) for that data element and then make the necessary changes. As you can see, knowing the data element name to look for can greatly reduce the maintenance process.

The organizationwide data dictionary approach also allows managers throughout the organization to learn the data names and definitions of data they need to generate reports and to make queries from existing databases. It is a critical strategy in moving toward using data as a corporate resource.

Manager's Memo 14-3	**INFORMATION ENGINEERING**

You have already learned that a structured systems development methodology establishes a set of policies and procedures for accomplishing a systems design project. A methodology attempts to add structure and control to a project so that activities are completed on time and within budgetary constraints. First and foremost, a methodology enables systems designers to create an information system that meets the needs and priorities of the users. The structured methodologies were introduced in the late 1960s, after years of experience with information systems projects that were out of control in terms of budgets and schedules and that failed to meet users' objectives. The increased complexity of systems and the increased need for maintainability spurred the introduction of structured programming in the 1970s. Structured programming forced the issue of structured design and the concepts of modularity and stepwise refinement. Programmer teams and structured walk-throughs were introduced as organizational strategies for achieving better quality designs.

During the 1970s and 1980s, two major schools of structured design emerged. The first school, led by such teachers as Yourdon, Constantine, and Gane and Sarson, introduced a process-oriented structured design approach, using the data-flow diagram as a principal tool. You learned about a number of tools and techniques using the data-flow approach in this chapter. The second school of thought, represented by the Warnier-Orr methodology, used a design approach based upon the structure of the data. Most systems designers use a variety of tools and techniques to represent both the data flows and data structures within an information system. Depending upon the nature and scope of the design problem, they may mix and match methodologies. Good designers know how to use a variety of methods and how to match the methods they choose to the type of design problem.

In the 1980s a methodology known as information engineering incorporated both process-oriented and data-driven tools into a single approach. Information engineering includes four phases: information strategy planning, business area analysis, systems design, and construction. These phases are depicted in Figure 14-19.

Information strategy planning. The purpose of information strategy planning is to investigate how a firm can use information technology to gain competitive advantage. Therefore, planners must establish goals and critical success factors that senior management can understand. At the planning stage, the analyst develops an enterprise model depicting what critical business functions exist and how current information systems support these functions. Then the users identify information systems needs that address important business opportunities. During the information strategy planning phase, planners use information planning matrixes, organization charts, and entity relationship diagrams (see Figure 14-20).

Figure 14-19

The phases of information engineering

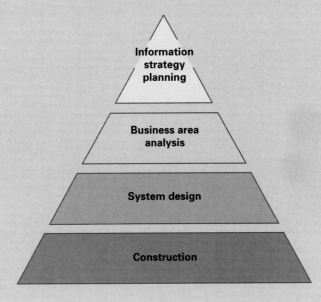

Manager's Memo 14–3 | **CONTINUED**

Figure 14–20
An entity relationship diagram

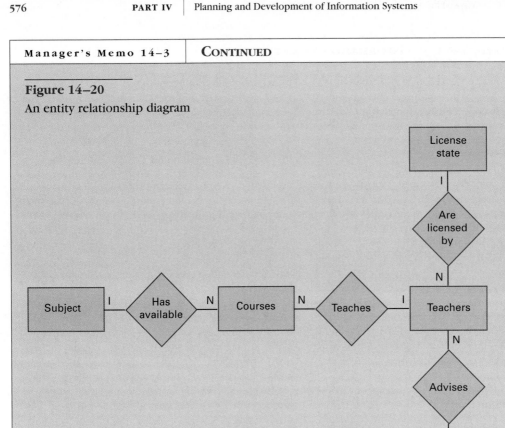

Business area analysis. During the business area analysis phase, the analyst determines the processes and data needed to support the enterprise. As the analyst and user study each business area, they may rethink existing systems and procedures and identify areas for systems design. The results are recorded in a detailed process model and a detailed data model. At this phase, an entity/process matrix may be used to illustrate which data entities support various business processes. The analyst may decompose the functions described in the planning phase into a detailed process model and may depict the interrelationships among processes using a process dependency diagram. The fully simplified data model illustrating the relationship between data structures is also developed during this phase (see Figure 14-21).

Systems design. After business area analysis, the information systems design process can begin. In the information engineering methodology, systems design uses a prototyping approach in which users work jointly with designers to develop report designs, screen designs, and other specifications. Throughout the process, the users are responsible for establishing system specifications. The analyst works with the user to revise and refine prototypes until the user's needs are met.

During the design phase, design automation tools are used to the greatest extent possible. The data models and process models are stored in a central design repository, or encyclopedia, and are used to generate prototypes. Design automation tools are used to prototype screens and reports and to store design documen-

Manager's Memo 14–3	CONCLUDED

Figure 14–21
A simplified data model

CUSTOMER

CUST NO	CUST NAME	CUST ADDR

ORDER

ORDER NO	CUST NO	ORDER DATE	REQ DEL DATE	SHIP METH

ORDER ITEM

ORDER NO	ITEM NO	QTY

ITEM

ITEM NO	ITEM NAME	PRICE

tation in the encyclopedia. Information engineering advocates using code generators and fourth-generation languages to implement the design wherever possible.

Construction. During the last phase of information engineering, construction, the actual code is generated to implement the system. Report and screen layouts, action diagrams of code, and prototypes are used to implement the design. In some cases users can access databases and generate reports to meet their needs using high-level languages. If end-users are going to design their own systems, they should be encouraged to use the common data models and standardized data definitions stored in the common repository or encyclopedia. Otherwise, redundant definitions for common data elements will eventually create a Tower of Babel and data management will be almost impossible.

In summary, the information engineering approach combines a variety of tools and techniques to accomplish strategic planning, business analysis, sys-

tems design, and construction. One of its main advantages is the linkage between business plans and information systems plans using the critical success factors method. Another advantage is the focus on establishing design blueprints through the development of data models and process models maintained in a central encyclopedia. Systems designs are implemented using code generators and fourth-generation languages to the extent possible. As a result, systems are easier to build and to modify, and users have an opportunity to be directly involved in systems design from beginning to end. The information engineering approach is supported by a variety of computer-aided software engineering (CASE) tools, including Knowledgeware's *Information Engineering Workbench (IEW)* and Texas Instruments' *Information Engineering Facility (IEF)*. Information engineering will continue to be an important information systems development approach throughout the 1990s.

MANAGEMENT SUMMARY

The systems development process involves a series of steps that must be accomplished if the systems analyst is to be able to develop an information system that meets the users' needs, satisfies business objectives, and can be designed and implemented within time and budgetary constraints. The systems development life cycle provides a methodology for accomplishing these activities. The life cycle begins with problem definition, during which the systems analyst works with the user to identify the nature and scope of current problems. The next step is a feasibility study, intended to deter-

mine whether realistic systems design alternatives exist. If the systems project is feasible, the analyst investigates the current system, its procedures, information flows, decisions, and methods of work organization and control during the systems analysis phase. At the end of the systems analysis phase, the problems of the current situation are identified and the objectives for the new system are proposed. The systems design phase involves the process of determining how the proposed system will be designed and implemented. During this phase, a number of alternative design options, such as batch, on-line, and packaged software alternatives, are studied and evaluated, and the best option is selected. This option creates the framework for detailed design, during which application specifications are established. Reports, screens, files, and procedures all need to be designed. During implementation, programs are coded and tested, training is implemented, and new procedures are introduced to put the new computer-based system into operation.

One of the problems in systems development is that many systems are technically accurate but do not meet the users' needs. Structured methods for systems analysis and design provide logical tools enabling users to participate in systems development activities. According to the structured approach, information about the current system is used to construct a logical data-flow diagram. Problems with current procedures are studied and used to develop a set of business and system objectives for the proposed system. The business objectives state what business outcomes must be achieved, and the system objectives define what capabilities the information system must have. Modifications are made to the existing logical data-flow diagram, and a proposed logical data-flow diagram is developed. The

proposed logical data-flow diagram becomes the blueprint for establishing further system requirements. Decision tables and trees specify the logic of business processes. A logical data dictionary identifies the names and definitions of data elements that compose the data flows and data stores of the proposed system. Finally, the contents of the data stores are analyzed and simplified to construct the beginnings of systemwide data files.

The final step in systems design is to evaluate systems design alternatives. A number of alternatives exist for selecting processing modes, computer configurations, and software development methods. Each of these alternatives must be evaluated in light of proposed system requirements. At every phase in the systems analysis and design process, user involvement is critically important. The systems development life cycle methodology builds in a number of checkpoints that enable users to review activities that have been accomplished. Structured methods enable users to contribute to the design process. Finally, users are ultimately responsible for identifying and evaluating the feasibility of alternative design options for the proposed system.

KEY TERMS FOR MANAGERS

batch processing, 563
decision tables, 562
decision trees, 562
detailed system design, 546
feasibility study, 544
implementation, 546
logical data dictionary, 546

logical data-flow diagram, 545
maintenance, 546
on-line transaction processing, 563
on-line immediate update, 564
on-line with batch overnight update, 564
problem definition, 544

service bureau, 565
software houses, 566
systems analysis, 544
systems design, 545
systems development methodology, 544
time-sharing services, 565

REVIEW QUESTIONS

1. What are the steps in a systems study?
2. What are the phases of the systems development life cycle?
3. What activities occur during the problem definition phase of the systems development life cycle?
4. What activities occur during the systems design phase of the systems development life cycle?
5. Identify five guidelines for conducting a successful systems interview.
6. What is the purpose of a feasibility study?

7. Why is system maintenance a large percentage of the life span of an information system?
8. What are the major reasons for using structured methods in systems analysis and design?
9. What are the advantages of developing a logical data-flow diagram for the proposed system?
10. What are four processing modes in information systems design?
11. What are the characteristics of an on-line system with batch overnight update?

12. What kind of business data processing application would be supported by on-line with immediate update?

13. What are the major advantages and disadvantages of using a service bureau?

14. What are the main advantages and disadvantages of in-house software development?

15. What are the advantages of using packaged software?

QUESTIONS FOR DISCUSSION

1. What are some of the benefits of using structured tools and techniques in systems analysis and design?

2. What are some of the reasons organizations choose outsourcing as a method of supporting data processing activities?

3. What are some of the methods used in business area analysis as a part of information engineering methodology?

4. Why should organizations have a systems development methodology in place before they introduce computer-aided software engineering (CASE) tools?

5. What are some of the benefits of CASE tools?

PROBLEMS

1. **Southern Oil Company.** Southern Oil Company uses the following credit card procedure: The customer presents a credit card to the service station attendant who completes the invoice and gives one copy to the customer. The station manager batches the accumulated invoices, together with an adding machine tape, and sends them to the company's regional office once a week. The company verifies the amounts, credits the station's account with the amount of the batch, and holds the invoices until the end of the month. At the end of the month, the company batches the invoices by customer number, microfilms them, adds the invoices to the customer account tape file, prints the monthly statement, and mails it to the customer with the invoices. On receipt of the payment, the company verifies the amount of the check against the payment stub, batches the daily stubs by customer number, and subtracts the payment from the customer account on the tape file. Develop a logical data-flow diagram for this case.

2. **Processing Modes.** Select the processing mode that would support each of the following applications and give reasons for your answers. You may choose from these alternatives:

   a. Batch.
   b. On-line with batch overnight update.
   c. On-line with immediate update.
   d. Distributed processing.
   e. Decentralized processing.

   The applications are as follows:

   a. An airline reservations system.
   b. A demand deposit accounting system (that is, a system that processes deposits and withdrawals from checking accounts).
   c. A point-of-sale inventory system that updates local inventory files based on sales transactions and transmits summary sales and inventory data to a central office computer system.
   d. A payment processing system for a loan company. Loan payments are made directly to branch offices, where they are entered and validated, and then these loan payments are transmitted to the home office computer, where the central loan files are updated.
   e. A word processing system that a university development office uses to generate fund-raising letters.

3. **Package Software versus Custom Software Development.** Emily Martin, an owner of an art supply store, wants to acquire an accounts receivable system. Her

main requirements for accounts receivable are to set up and maintain a customer master file, to update account balances, to generate monthly statements, to apply cash receipts to customer balances, and to generate overdue account notices. Because she doesn't have a computer background, she is considering two alternatives. The first is the purchase of an accounts receivable software package that could run on a microcomputer. The package would provide many extra features, such as sales analysis, customer analysis, and various overdue account notices and reminders. The other option Emily is considering is custom software development. Because the system she needs is fairly simple, she feels that software could be developed using Access database program on a microcomputer. Although the cost might be greater, the software could be modified. Examine the advantages and disadvantages of the software package option versus the custom software development option. Which would you choose? Give reasons for your answer.

4. **Alro Uniform, Inc.**   Donald Hudson, the manager of systems and programming for Alro Uniform, Inc., a major manufacturer of uniforms for health care professionals, was preparing for a meeting with user-managers in the production department. The purpose of the meeting was to enable the users to review systems design specifications for a proposed production planning and scheduling system. Donald's main concern was that the users had not been involved in the systems design process because they did not have sufficient time and resources to participate in the project. Donald was looking over pages of detailed design specifications that outlined reports, screens, forms, files, and program design requirements. He knew that the users would have a difficult time understanding these technical documents. Donald was afraid that if he went ahead with the meeting the users would simply sign off on the specifications because they would not understand them. As a result, he would not be able to obtain any input into the design. The users wouldn't be aware of any mistakes until after the system was implemented and major costs had been incurred. Donald wants to develop some documents that the users could understand and approve before moving ahead on the project. Should he involve the users? What approach might he use to describe the proposed system to the user-managers so that they can understand the new system and make their suggestions?

CASES

1. **Movies Unlimited, Inc.**   Movies Unlimited, Inc., is a large St. Louis–based company in the videocassette rental business. It has an inventory of over 15,000 movies in 20 branches. The management of Movies Unlimited, Inc., wants you to conduct a systems investigation. During your interviews, you learned about the following checkout, check-in, and inventory procedures.

A customer joins Movies Unlimited, Inc., by paying a $25 membership fee. At the time of joining, the following information is recorded in a customer card file: driver's license number, major credit card, home address, and phone number. There is no method in place at present to update this information. After joining Movies Unlimited, Inc., the customer receives a membership card that he or she uses to check out movies.

The boxes of available movies are arranged in alphabetical order on shelves. The actual videocassettes are kept in boxes in a storage area behind the reception desk. To check out a movie, the customer takes a box to the counter and the clerk looks for the movie on the back shelves. Sometimes a movie is not filed in correct order, and the clerk needs to hunt for it. The customer pays a one- or two-day rental fee at the time of checkout. The clerk is supposed to ask if the customer has changed his or her address and phone but rarely takes the time to do so.

When movies are returned, the clerks try to determine whether they have been brought back on time or if a late charge is due. Sometimes a customer leaves a movie in the stack of returned films without informing the clerk whether it is overdue.

By the time the clerk who is responsible for reshelving returned movies discovers overdue movies, the customer has left the store. Sometimes a clerk tries to reach a customer by phone, but very little can be done to force payment on overdue returns. Sometimes renters return movies late but are not assessed for late charges because they drop off their movies in an off-hours collection box and there is no way to verify the time and date of a movie's return.

Another problem occurs with returns during particularly busy times. Returned movies may stack up because clerks do not have enough time to reshelve them. Sometimes customers want to check out movies they find in the stack of returned films. A customer probably will not be able to locate a movie if it has not been reshelved.

One of the major problems is inventory control. Most of the new releases are out of stock, particularly on weekends when many customers want to rent them. Management wants to make more copies of these videocassettes. However, Movies Unlimited does not have any way to keep track of sales trends in order to reallocate inventory effectively. Also, many of the slow-moving titles remain in stock when they should be discontinued.

Finally, the movie rental business is very competitive. Management wants to develop ways to promote the business and increase the number of renters without incurring unnecessary costs.

Develop a systems analysis study for Movies Unlimited that includes the following elements:

a. Five questions for a systems interview.

b. A statement of major findings based on the case.

c. Business and system objectives for the proposed system.

d. Alternative design options for implementing the proposed system. (Identify two alternatives and describe the advantages and disadvantages of each.)

2. **Thinktank University.** After obtaining permission from their advisers, students must prepare a five-part form requesting withdrawal from a course and a refund of money. The adviser has to sign the request form. The student gives the first three copies to him or her and delivers the remaining two copies to the bursar in the business office. The bursar decides whether a refund is due and prepares a refund check. Copy 5 of the form is returned to the student with the refund check. Copy 4 is marked with the action taken and then filed. If no refund is due, the bursar stamps "no refund" on copy 5 and returns it to the student. The adviser sends copy 1 to the registrar, files copy 2, and sends copy 3 to the instructor who teaches the course. The registrar cancels the course from the student's schedule and subtracts the hours dropped from the total hours carried on the student's record. The instructor records a grade of 'W' for the student on the class roster. At the end of the semester, the instructor updates the class roster with grades for the remaining active students and sends it to the registrar. The registrar uses this final grade report from the instructors to update student records. Develop a logical data-flow diagram for this case.

SELECTED REFERENCES AND READINGS

Davis, W. S. *Systems Analysis and Design.* Reading, MA: Addison-Wesley, 1983.

Couger, J. D.; M. A. Colter; and R. W. Knapp. *Advanced Systems Development/Feasibility Techniques.* New York: John Wiley & Sons, 1982.

Gane, C., and T. Sarson. *Structured Systems Analysis: Tools and Techniques.* Englewood Cliffs, NJ: Prentice Hall, 1979.

Peters, L. *Advanced Structured Analysis and Design.* Englewood Cliffs, NJ: Prentice Hall, 1987.

Whitten, J. L.; L. D. Bentley; and V. Barlow. *Systems Analysis and Design Methods.* 2nd ed. Burr Ridge, IL: Richard D. Irwin, 1989.

ALTERNATIVE APPLICATION DEVELOPMENT APPROACHES

CHAPTER OUTLINE

Manager's View

Strategies to Overcome the Systems Development Bottleneck

Project Management and Control

A Portfolio Approach to Project Management

Cost-Benefit Analysis

Detailed Design: Transforming Logical Specifications into Physical Specifications

Implementation

User Involvement in System Selection

Management Summary

Key Terms for Managers

Review Questions

Questions for Discussion

Problems

Cases

Selected Internet Reference Sites

Selected References and Readings

IN THE LAST CHAPTER you learned about the systems analysis and design process. Users participate in the phases of problem definition, analysis of the existing system, development of objectives for the proposed system, and evaluation of alternative design options. After a design option is selected, detailed design begins. During this phase the user helps the systems analyst design reports, screens, and files. Users and MIS professionals also evaluate hardware and software and establish an implementation schedule.

Many companies are now experiencing software development backlogs of between two and three years. More than 70 percent of the time spent in information systems development occurs during the detailed design and implementation phases. Coding and testing of programs are among the most time-consuming phases of a project. Under pressure from management to complete information systems projects on a more timely basis, MIS management has begun to explore alternative application development approaches, including software packages, user development, prototyping in systems design, and automated tools for software engineering. You'll learn about these alternative development methods in this chapter.

STRATEGIES TO OVERCOME THE SYSTEMS DEVELOPMENT BOTTLENECK

In this chapter and in Chapter 14, we use a life cycle methodology to show how systems development projects are accomplished: problem definition, systems analysis, systems design, and implementation. Though a life cycle methodology ensures that information systems requirements are carefully studied and that alternative design options are evaluated before detailed design gets underway, these activities are time-consuming. Programming and testing, which may encompass as much as 70 percent of a project, are labor-intensive activities.

A systems development backlog of projects exists in many organizations today. Users, frustrated with the high cost and time commitment involved in traditional development, are anxious to seek alternative development strategies. Many of the information systems design projects in the backlog, they feel, are critical to achieving a competitive advantage by providing better service to customers, by offering new products and services, and by developing better internal information about products, customers, and suppliers.

Requirements documents, the blueprints of the proposed system design, are frozen once a systems proposal has been approved, making changes or modifications difficult and costly. Although these requirements documents are necessary to move to the detailed design phase, users want the opportunity to propose changes.

Three alternative development strategies can substantially decrease the systems development bottleneck. These are the purchase of *software packages,* the use of *prototyping* in systems design, and the creation of *user-developed systems.* Each of these approaches has advantages and disadvantages that you should understand. For certain types of projects, each of these approaches can provide an effective alternative to traditional development.

Software Packages

The purchase of software packages has already been discussed as an alternative design option. Without question, **software packages** provide economies of scale in development and maintenance. In-house development of a payroll system, for example, would cost more than the purchase of a payroll package. The software package business is a billion-dollar business, and hundreds of payroll programs exist for microcomputer-, minicomputer-, and mainframe-based systems. The main task of the user is to evaluate alternative packages to determine which one best fits his requirements. For a major package, this process of evaluation may take months.

If modifications are needed, most software houses can provide programming support. Sometimes, source code is made available so that in-house development personnel can make modifications. However, if many of the programs need to be modified, in-house development may be more cost-effective than purchasing a software package. Another possible disadvantage of a software package is that it may also require the purchase of new hardware or the upgrade of existing hardware. The major advantages and disadvantages of software packages appear in Figure 15–1.

Prototyping

Prototyping is the process of developing a model of the proposed system design and working with the user to modify it until the user's requirements are met. The availability of fourth-generation languages that can be used to develop on-line screen designs and report mock-ups has made prototyping a practical reality in information systems development. Using prototyping, a systems designer can determine a user's requirements much more efficiently and cost-effectively than with traditional methods. The step-by-step refinement of designs provides opportunities for active user participation and avoids the problem of frozen requirements.

Prototyping may be used in several ways. It can be used to design and implement an information system using a fourth-generation language. This approach works well when system requirements are constantly changing because users can use fourth-generation-language tools to make ad hoc queries and to generate reports from existing databases. In some cases, however, fourth-generation languages may be inappropriate because of high transaction volumes in a production version of the information system. In these cases, a fourth-generation language may be used to develop a version of the system requirements and a third-generation language (e.g., a procedural language like COBOL) to actually implement the system.

The main problem with prototyping is that unending iterations and revisions of the system may be proposed because changes are so easy to make. Fourth-generation languages consume a high level of CPU resources and are generally not efficient for developing high-volume transactions-based systems. A summary of the major advantages and disadvantages of prototyping appears in Figure 15–2.

Figure 15–1
Advantages and disadvantages of software packages

ADVANTAGES	DISADVANTAGES
• Economies of scale in development • Economies of scale in maintenance	• Major modifications may be necessary • May require hardware upgrades or additions

User Development of Information Systems

User-managers today have the opportunity to use microcomputer-based spreadsheet and database software and mainframe-based ad hoc query and reporting languages to develop their own information systems. Many of these systems fall under the general category of decision support systems because they support the decisions managers need to make. Using a mainframe-based order history database and a fourth-generation language like FOCUS, for example, a manager can analyze sales trends by product line, by customer, and by territory. Additional types of analyses can include sales forecasting and production planning. Such **user-developed systems** usually address specific individual or departmental-level information needs and would not be developed by information systems professionals. However, user-managers believe that these systems are critical to their needs.

User development has been an issue for several years now. Many experts argue that user-developed systems do not decrease the systems development backlog because they consist of one-time-only projects that never become part of the backlog. These projects are not evaluated to see whether a business need exists for them or whether they are cost justified. In addition, many of these projects, particularly those developed using microcomputer-based software, are poorly designed and lack quality assurance. Many of these systems lack data validation, testing, documentation, and controls in their design. In addition, the logic of internal algorithms used in making spreadsheet calculations or in generating data into reports is poorly documented.

Another problem with user-developed systems is that procedures for backup and recovery, data security, and system maintenance are seldom laid out. If a user-developer leaves a company, the users of the system he or she developed may not have adequate documentation to use it or to manage it successfully. The advantages and disadvantages of user development appear in Figure 15–3.

Figure 15–2
Advantages and disadvantages of prototyping

ADVANTAGES	DISADVANTAGES
• Rapid development of a working system • Step-by-step refinement of designs • Costs 25 percent of traditional approach • Allows experimentation	• Unending iterations may occur • Fourth-generation-language products require excessive machine resources • Not realistic for high-volume transactions systems

Figure 15–3
Advantages and disadvantages of user development

ADVANTAGES	DISADVANTAGES
• Increases user satisfaction • Provides users with needed decision support systems • Allows ad hoc query and reporting • Addresses specialized problems	• Doesn't attack the backlog problem • Questionable cost-effectiveness • Inferior development methods • Poor transferability of systems • Poor quality assurance

Figure 15–4
Development
strategy proposed
by Gremillion and
Pyburn

PROPERTIES OF A PROJECT			
Commonality	**Impact**	**Structure**	**Method**
Common	Broad	High	Package
Uncommon	Broad	High	Traditional
Uncommon	Broad	Low	Prototype
Common	Limited	High	Package
Uncommon	Limited	High	User-developed
Uncommon	Limited	Low	User-developed

Factors to Consider in Selecting a Development Approach.

Each of these development strategies—software packages, prototyping, and user development—has advantages and disadvantages. Each can work to reduce the backlog of systems development projects. The decision to choose one of these methods depends on the nature and scope of the projects to be accomplished.

Gremillion and Pyburn cite three factors to consider in evaluating projects that are candidates for development using one of these approaches: commonality, impact, and structure.[1] *Commonality* means the extent to which other organizations could use the system's solution to the problem. A word processing package would have high commonality because many organizations could benefit from using it.

The second factor to consider in selecting a development approach is *impact*. The more widespread the impact and the more important an information system is, the greater the demand for involving information systems professionals. If a company is planning to develop a national network tying its customers to its order entry system, for example, the major impact of this project on customer service and sales would dictate professional MIS involvement.

The third factor to consider is *structure*. Gremillion and Pyburn define structure as a measure of how well the problem and its solution are understood. An accounts receivable system is a highly structured system because its operations are clearly defined and well understood. However, a decision support system used to make a corporate acquisition decision would be unstructured and complex.

Gremillion and Pyburn suggest that a development approach can be selected on the basis of the commonality, impact, and structure of an information systems design project. Figure 15-4 summarizes their recommendations.

If a project is common to many organizations, is high in structure, and has a broad impact on the organization, a package is a good solution. An example of this type of project is a prospect information system for sales and marketing analysts. Many organizations need a prospect system, and its use would have a substantial impact. Because it is a highly structured system, a package could probably be found to do the job. If a system is common, high in structure, and has limited impact, a package is also a good choice. An example of this type of project is a plant production scheduling system for a single plant.

If a project is not common to many organizations, has a broad impact, and is low in structure, Gremillion and Pyburn argue that prototyping is an effective approach.

---

[1]Lee L. Gremillion and Phillip Pyburn, "Breaking the Systems Development Bottleneck," *Harvard Business Review*, March–April 1983, pp. 130-37.

Prototyping can give the users an opportunity to define their requirements. A decision support system for cash management is a good example of a project whose impact is broad and structure is low.

If a project is not common to many organizations or to many other users throughout the organization, has a limited impact, and has either high or low structure, user development is appropriate. The limited scope and impact of such projects make them ideal for user development. This category encompasses many of the individual decision support systems in organizations today.

However, if a project is not common, has a broad impact, and has high structure, a traditional approach will be the best alternative. Prototyping is not necessary because the requirements are well-defined. In addition, MIS involvement is warranted because of the uniqueness and impact of the project on the overall organization. An example of this type of project is an international order billing system for a chemical company.

In summary, one way to attack the systems development bottleneck is by using alternative development methods such as software packages, prototyping, and user development. However, these methods are not the solution for all types of projects. The characteristics of various systems development projects must be studied to determine whether any one of these approaches is realistic.

PROJECT MANAGEMENT AND CONTROL

One of the major responsibilities of a project manager in information systems design is project management and control. The project manager assumes responsibility for the completion of systems design and implementation activities within time and budgetary constraints. In major projects, involving dozens of systems designers and programmers, million-dollar budgets, and years of duration, project management is a challenging task. But even in smaller-scale projects, the project manager has to schedule activities, establish completion dates, supervise project team members, monitor progress, and make sure that activities are being completed successfully. When problems occur, he must reallocate resources and reschedule personnel. In addition, the project manager must see that users have an opportunity to review design work and to provide feedback.

The project manager's first duties are to define the tasks to be accomplished, the order in which they should be done, and their interdependence. For example, file design must be accomplished before programming can begin. Many project activities will occur simultaneously, whereas some must be completed before others begin. The systems development life cycle methodology will identify major activities, but it will not necessarily show the interdependencies among various tasks.

Once activities and completion dates have been established, the project manager should prepare a project management plan showing activities, completion dates, and concurrent tasks. Techniques such as Gantt charts and a project network using the Critical Path Method (CPM) are useful in establishing these goals. Figure 15–5 shows a Gantt chart for a systems development project. The chart shows estimated start and end dates for major tasks. If progress is not on schedule, the project manager can take necessary action to accomplish necessary activities. One advantage of the Gantt chart is that both nonsystems personnel and project participants can understand it. The Gantt chart also depicts which systems development tasks overlap. Individual Gantt charts can be developed for project team members, too.

Figure 15–5

A Gantt chart

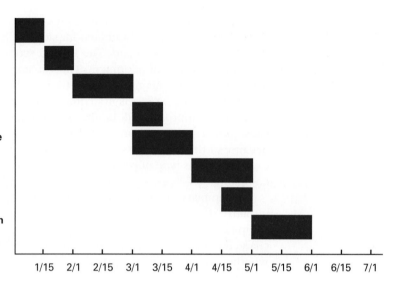

A. **Problem definition**

B. **Feasibility study**

C. **Analysis of current system**

D. **Evaluation of design options**

E. **Evaluation of hardware and software**

F. **Development of detailed design specifications**

G. **Coding and testing of programs**

H. **Development of implementation plan**

I. **Implementation**

1/15 2/1 2/15 3/1 3/15 4/1 4/15 5/1 5/15 6/1 6/15 7/1

One of the limitations of the Gantt chart is that it does not illustrate how activities depend on each other. The project network shows not only start and completion times for project tasks but also the interdependencies among the tasks. In addition, the project network identifies slack times, or the amount of time a project can slip from its original schedule without affecting the overall project's completion time. Also, if a major task is not completed on schedule, the project network can detect its impact on the overall project. A project network is shown in Figure 15–6. In this project network, you can see the description of each event, beginning with project initiation. You can also see the description of each project task, including developing a problem definition, conducting a feasibility study, and evaluating alternative design options. Some tasks must be completed before subsequent ones begin; others can occur simultaneously. For example, the feasibility study must be completed before a detailed analysis of the current system can begin. But coding and testing and the development of an implementation plan can occur simultaneously. Using the project network, you can determine the earliest completion time for each event, the latest completion time for each event, and the expected duration of each task. For example, task A is the problem definition phase of the project. Its duration is 10 hours. The earliest completion time for event 2, the problem statement, is 10 hours. The latest completion time for this event is also 10 hours because no other prerequisite tasks are involved in reaching the completion of the problem statement.

As the diagram in Figure 15–6 shows, the slack time for each event is the latest completion time minus the earliest completion time. For example, the latest completion time for the design proposal (event 5) is 120 hours, and its earliest completion time is 95 hours. The slack time is 25 hours for completion of the design proposal because two other tasks must be completed before event 7, the design specification report, can be concluded. These tasks are E, evaluate hardware/software, and F, develop detailed design specifications. Tasks E and F can be accomplished in 10 hours and 40

Figure 15–6

A project network

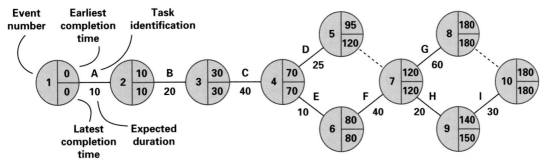

SLACK TIME FOR EVENT = LATEST COMPLETION TIME – EARLIEST COMPLETION TIME

Event	Description	Task	Description
1	Project initiated	A	Problem definition
2	Problem statement	B	Conduct feasibility study
3	Feasibility study report	C	Detailed analysis of the current system
4	Systems analysis report	D	Evaluation of alternative design options
5	Design proposal	E	Evaluate hardware and software
6	Hardware and software evaluation	F	Develop detailed design specifications
7	Design specification report	G	Code and test programs
8	Completed programs	H	Design implementation plan
9	Implementation plan	I	Implement the system
10	Post-implementation review		

hours, respectively. In total, since tasks E and F must be completed prior to event 7, the design specification report, the tasks leading up to event 7 entail 120 hours.

The project network approach is a useful approach because it takes into account prerequisite activities and their relationship to accomplishing project events. The network can be used to assess the impact of delayed tasks on the completion of project events. This information is important in managing a project in which tasks are dependent upon each other and when project outcomes must be constantly updated as a result of delays, manpower changes, and scheduling difficulties.

The project manager and users need to use these checkpoints to review progress regardless of the project management method being used. During system reviews, people working on various components of the project can communicate with each other and discuss unforeseen problems. User-managers must have an opportunity to review interim design documents, to approve changes in schedule, and to suggest changes. Users also must be informed of the impact of desired changes on time and cost estimates. You can gain more insight into what project management strategies should be used in projects with varying degrees of risk by learning about the portfolio approach to project management.

A Portfolio Approach to Project Management

One of the issues in information systems development is how to assess risk. With high-risk projects, hundreds of thousands of dollars can be spent without ever achieving anticipated benefits. McFarlan describes a situation in which a large consumer-products company budgeted $250,000 for a new personnel information system to be ready in nine months. After two years and $2,500,000, the company projected that another $3,600,000 would be needed to complete the project. In another case a sizable financial institution went $1,500,000 over budget and lagged 12 months behind schedule on the development of a new financial systems package. When it was installed, the average transactions response times were much longer than expected.

The history of information systems development tells of hundreds of projects that have failed or have suffered severe cost and time overruns. Many of these problems occur, McFarlan suggests, because user managers and MIS professionals take on projects without assessing risk. McFarlan's portfolio approach helps managers identify risk factors and strategies for minimizing risk. Risk may not be all bad. Risky projects, if successful, are often the ones that provide the greatest benefits. Risk must be recognized and managed for these projects to be successful.

Risk Factors

Three major risk factors are (1) project size, (2) experience with the technology, and (3) project structure. The greater the time and expense involved in a project, the greater the risk. If a project team is not familiar with the hardware, operating system, database management system, or telecommunications network, risk increases. Projects whose managers who have ill-defined ideas of the outputs and who change their minds throughout design incur greater risk. These are low-structure projects.

Strategies for Minimizing Project Risk

Management strategies to minimize project risk include external integration tools, internal integration tools, formal planning tools, and formal control tools (see Figure 15–7). External integration tools enable the project team to communicate effectively with users. Internal integration tools manage the internal interactions among project team members. Formal planning tools estimate the time, cost, and resources needed to complete a project, and formal control tools help managers evaluate

Figure 15–7
Project management tools

EXTERNAL INTEGRATION TOOLS	• Selection of user as project manager. • Participation of users on steering committee. • Users responsible for approving changes in design.
INTERNAL INTEGRATION TOOLS	• Selection of experienced DP professional as project manager • Regular reviews of project status. • Selection of team members with previous work relationships
FORMAL PLANNING TOOLS	• Use of network project management tools, such as PERT and critical path. • Selection of project phases and activities. • Formal project approval processes.
FORMAL CONTROL TOOLS	• Comparisons of project status with plans. • Development of strategies for change control. • Regular presentations on outcomes.

progress on completing project activities. Depending on the type of project, managers must use one or more of these strategies.

Using Appropriate Strategies to Manage Projects

McFarlan identifies four major types of projects, as shown in Figure 15–8. *High-structure-low-technology* projects have relatively low risk because the outputs are well understood and the technical problems are familiar. An example of this type of project is purchasing an accounts receivable system to run on a minicomputer. Accounts receivable is a highly structured application, and the technology is familiar. Internal integration strategies should be used to manage the project team, and life cycle planning tools should be introduced to ensure that tasks and resources are defined.

High-structure-high-technology projects involve new technology and require technical expertise and effective internal integration. The project manager must be able to manage technicians, maintain teamwork, and make sure that all design decisions are well understood. An example of this type of project is converting from one mainframe-based operating system to another. Even though the outputs are clearly defined, users need to be aware that project outcomes may be postponed if technology-related problems occur.

Low-structure-low-technology projects require user involvement and direction to reach consensus on project design specifications. If these projects are not managed by users, continual change requests will result in time and cost overruns. A good example of this type of project is a personnel information systems project that resulted in millions of dollars of cost overruns because users kept changing their minds about the types of reports they wanted to generate from the database. These projects must enlist a user as a project leader and a user steering committee to evaluate the design at each phase.

Low-structure-high-technology projects have the greatest risk. Project managers undertaking these projects must have technical experience and the ability to communicate effectively with users. Internal integration is necessary because teams need to keep abreast of technical issues. Users must also commit to design specifications to keep these projects on track.

Figure 15–9 summarizes strategies that information systems professionals and users can use to successfully manage projects with various levels of risk.

Figure 15–8

Project types

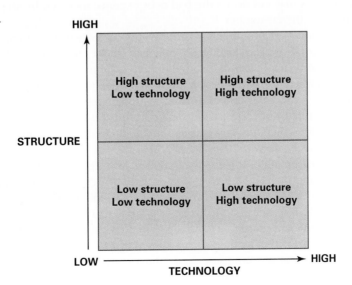

Figure 15–9
Tools contributing
to project success

PROJECT TYPE	STRATEGIES
High-structure–low-technology	• Formal control • Formal planning • Moderate internal integration
High-structure–high-technology	• High internal integration • Moderate formal planning • Moderate formal control
Low-structure–low-technology	• High external integration • High formal control • Moderate formal planning
Low-structure–high-technology	• High external integration • High internal integration

COST-BENEFIT ANALYSIS

The purpose of **cost-benefit analysis** is to determine the economic feasibility of various systems design alternatives. Information systems are investments just like any other business investment, such as building a new warehouse or developing a new marketing program. The benefits of information systems projects must be compared with the benefits of other capital budgeting projects. Cost-benefit analysis is the best way of measuring the financial impact of an information systems design project proposal.

The Benefits of Information Systems

The benefits of an information system have to be measured in terms of their business impact. **Tangible benefits** can be measured in terms of hard dollar savings or profits. Increased revenues and decreased costs are examples of tangible benefits. An on-line order entry system that enables a company to service more orders on a timely basis may generate increased revenues. On-line access to credit information about customers may cut down the bad debt expense incurred by shipping orders to noncreditworthy customers.

Another tangible benefit is the ability to reduce processing errors. A rental car company whose clerks manually calculate charges may incur a much higher error rate than a company that uses a computerized system. Another benefit of information systems is faster turnaround. A nationwide order processing system can enable order-entry clerks to enter order information, update inventory levels, and generate invoices to be printed out at a distribution center nearest the customer location. Orders are filled more efficiently and invoices are generated more rapidly, making it possible to improve cash flow.

Other tangible benefits are reduced inventory cost, reduced administrative expenses, and the reduced cost of paperwork processing. For example, let's consider a university admissions office that processes 6,000 applications a year. In the current manual system, the time it takes secretaries to retype and recompile the same data about applicants amounts to about 30 minutes per application, or about 180,000 minutes a year. If the average secretary makes $12 an hour, the cost of the problem is $36,000 a year. If a computerized database system were developed to house applica-

Figure 15–10
The benefits of
information
systems

TANGIBLE BENEFITS	INTANGIBLE BENEFITS
• Fewer processing errors	• Improved customer goodwill
• Increased throughput	• Improved employee morale
• Decreased response time	• Improved job satisfaction
• Elimination of job steps	• Better customer service
• Reduced expenses	• Better decision making
• Increased sales	
• Faster turnaround	
• Better credit	
• Reduced credit losses	

tion data, much of this rekeying would be avoided and at least $36,000 in savings would occur.

Information systems also have many **intangible benefits.** Intangible benefits cannot be measured in terms of hard dollar savings, but they are important. An on-line order inquiry system, for example, may enable customers to inquire about delivery dates on orders and can increase customer goodwill. Employee morale may also be improved by the ability to provide information to customers. Without access to this type of information, a customer service clerk may have to handle dozens of complaints per day.

Other intangible benefits of information systems are improved employee job satisfaction and better decision making. If a sales manager uses sales history data to identify the most profitable products and the most profitable buyers, then the marketing strategy she develops can maximize business opportunities. If a production planner can analyze regional sales trends for various products and recommend target inventory levels in branch warehouses, proper inventory levels are more likely to be available. Figure 15-10 summarizes the benefits of information systems.

The Costs of Information Systems

The costs of information systems include development costs, equipment costs, and operations and maintenance costs. Some of these costs are nonrecurring and others are recurring. Development costs are the one-time costs of systems analysis, design, and implementation. Development also includes the costs of training, conversion, testing, and documentation.

Equipment and other start-up costs include the cost of new equipment, packaged software, equipment installation, and materials and supplies. A computer acquisition may also require new facilities, air-conditioning, and space. Equipment costs are generally considered nonrecurring costs, although additional costs can be incurred as the original system is upgraded, new software is acquired, or new peripheral devices are purchased.

Operations and maintenance costs are recurring costs and start being incurred once the system is installed. Operating costs include the costs of computer usage; overhead costs such as power, insurance, and space; and the cost of supplies. Ongoing personnel costs, such as the salaries of supervisors, clerical staff, and maintenance programmers, are included in operating costs. Personnel training costs are additional ongoing costs. Maintenance costs for hardware typically run about 10 to 12 percent of the costs of the equipment configuration. Many software companies

Figure 15–11

The costs of information systems

DEVELOPMENT COSTS	EQUIPMENT COSTS	OPERATING COSTS
• Systems analysis (interviewing, etc.) • Systems design (file design, etc.) • Coding, testing, and debugging • Training and conversion • Inspections and walkthroughs • Documentation (systems design and user documentation)	• New equipment • Packaged software • Equipment installation, testing, and debugging • File conversion • Materials and supplies • Facilities, light, heat, and space	• Equipment (I/O operations, maintenance) • Personnel costs (supervisory, clerical) • Overhead (power, insurance, space) • Computer program maintenance • Standby facilities • Training • Materials

offer maintenance contracts that entitle users to enhancements and modifications of software packages and their documentation. Figure 15–11 summarizes the costs of information systems.

Performing a cost-benefit analysis requires the systems analyst and user to estimate the development costs, equipment costs, operating costs, and maintenance costs of the proposed system. The development and equipment costs occur during the systems design and implementation phases of the project, and the operating costs occur over time. Normally, the benefits of the proposed system will be realized over its life span. Although the costs will outweigh the benefits during the original system investment, the benefits should eventually overtake the costs.

An example will help you understand how cost-benefit analysis works. Let us say that the one-time development and equipment costs for a new microcomputer system for each branch office at Reliable Finance Company is $10,000. The proposed system will save each branch approximately $5,000 per year by reducing bad debt. Enabling each branch to generate its own reminder letters is a major factor in eliminating many currently uncollectable accounts. If these were the only costs and benefits, we could assume that the $10,000 cost would be made up in two years, because the benefits of the new system would be $5,000 per year.

However, this kind of analysis would not take into consideration the time value of money. In other words, How much you would be willing to invest to get $5,000 after one year? The answer would probably not be $5,000. You would expect to invest less than $5,000 because money has a time value and can earn interest. If the interest rate is 12 percent, an investment of $4,468.28 will return $5,000 after one year.

The present value of a $5,000 benefit five years from now—assuming the same 12 percent interest—is calculated from the following formula:

$$P = \frac{F}{(1-i)^n}$$

where F is the future value of the investment, P is the present value of the investment, i is the interest rate, and n is the number of compounding periods.

In this case, if we invest $2,837.14 at 12 percent interest for five years, we'll have $5,000 after the five years.

Figure 15–12

Cost-benefit analysis for an RFC branch

	Year 0	Year 1	Year 2	Year 3	Year 4	Year 5
Development costs	$ 5,800	$ 0	$ 0	$ 0	$ 0	$ 0
Maintenance	0	0	0	0	0	0
Operations	0	100	100	100	100	100
Equipment	6,500	0	0	0	0	0
Total costs	12,300	100	100	100	100	100
Total savings	0	4,500	4,500	4,500	4,500	4,500
Net balance	−12,300	4,400	4,400	4,400	4,400	4,400
DCF factor*	1.000	.893	.797	.712	.636	.567
Discounted balance	−12,300	3,929	3,507	3,133	2,798	2,495
Cumulative discounted	−12,300	−8,371	−4,864	−1,731	+1,067	+3,562

* The discounted-cash-flow factor assumes an interest rate of 12 percent.

Now you can apply this principle to the cost-benefit analysis for each branch's computer system. Let us say that the original investment cost of the branch microcomputer is $12,300. This amount includes $6,500 in hardware and software; $4,800 in systems development; and an additional $1,000 for installation setup, data entry, and testing.

The major tangible benefit of the proposed system is avoidance of some bad debt that will result from generating personalized reminder letters to customers with overdue accounts. During the first year, management believes that losses from bad debt could drop by $4,500 per branch.

Figure 15–12 illustrates the cost-benefit analysis for an RFC branch. The analysis assumes that an interest rate of 12 percent will prevail during the period of the investment. According to this analysis, the break-even point can be derived by looking at the cumulative discounted balance at the bottom line of the worksheet. The branch will break even by year 4 of this investment. In year 4, the benefits will have accrued to +$1,067. If intangible benefits occur, the break-even point may occur even sooner.

DETAILED DESIGN: TRANSFORMING LOGICAL SPECIFICATIONS INTO PHYSICAL SPECIFICATIONS

Structured Design

Structured design is the process of taking a set of logical specifications for the proposed information system and transforming them into a set of physical specifications. One of the chief objectives of design is changeability. A changeable design allows the system to be changed to meet the users' needs. Changes in management structure, changes in lines of business, and changes in pricing and salary plans may bring about changes in information systems. If the designer can produce a changeable, flexible system, he can dramatically reduce its overall lifetime cost.

A changeable system is built from a set of small modules that are independent of each other in function. If a module is independent in function, it can be taken out of the system, changed, and put back without disrupting the other modules in the system. A *module* is a set of instructions that perform a specific function within a program and can be invoked by name.

A *structure chart* is a set of modules organized into a hierarchy. As you can see from the structure chart depicted in Figure 15–13, the series of modules is organized into a hierarchy with a commander module at the top. The commander module is the "boss," which ultimately controls each module in the chart.

Within a system, the commander delegates functions to supervisory modules and to worker modules. Some of the modules are responsible for input functions, some for transforming input into output, and others for output functions. An input supervisor module may delegate work to Read and Edit modules. An output supervisor may delegate detailed output functions to Format and Print modules.

One of the major characteristics of a good design is cohesion. *Cohesion* refers to the degree to which a module carries out a single, well-defined function within a program. A module designed to read a record or format an error message carries out a specific function. A program that consists of cohesive modules is more changeable and more maintainable. For example, if users want to change a discount policy, the designer could go to the Compute Discount module and change its logic without affecting the workings of any other modules. Changing a cohesive module that carries out an independent function has little or no effect on other modules within the program.

In contrast, if a module takes on too many functions or combines many different processes, it will lack cohesion. Large, complex modules are difficult to modify and almost impossible to reuse. If a module takes on too many functions, the chance of triggering errors is much greater. The degree to which modules are interconnected is called *coupling*. If modules are interconnected with each other, a system will be difficult to maintain. Extensive coupling leads to the "ripple effect," in which a bug in one module generates bugs in other modules. As you can probably imagine, maintaining a program with extensive coupling among modules is troublesome.

One of the major objectives of good structured design is reusability. In a highly cohesive system, individual modules are reusable within the same program and within other programs because they execute a single, self-contained function. A module such as Edit Customer Number or Format Print Line can be reused whenever these functions are needed. Today, a programmer can use "canned" modules with code designed to execute a variety of common functions, such as editing, updating, and reporting. The major job is to design a program structure within which these modules can be used and reused.

Figure 15–13

A structure chart

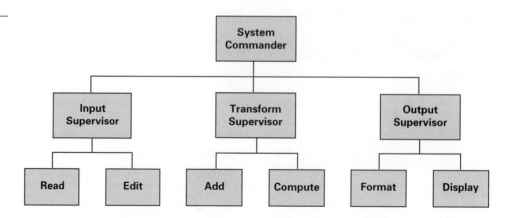

In summary, the systems designer is a systems architect. The designer must be able to organize processes into a hierarchy of modules, using the structure chart as a modeling tool. A good structure chart is a blueprint for transforming input data into output data. Within the structure chart, the designer must include processes that take care of data validation, editing, and other functions that assure the correctness and completeness of the system. Specific module-level logic can also be documented using tools such as structured flowcharts and decision tables.

Physical Design Specifications

After the structure charts for various programs within a system are documented, the systems designer can work on the physical design specifications for the system, including the design of reports, screens, and forms. Although the systems analyst is primarily responsible for accomplishing these tasks, user input is still important. If the user is not satisfied with the layout of reports or has trouble using the data-input screens, that user is less likely to use the system.

The logical database design developed during the logical design phase of the project should be used to construct physical files during the detailed design phase. The detailed **data dictionary** for the proposed system is also created during this phase. The detailed data dictionary contains the data names and data definitions for all data elements to be maintained in data files, to be generated as output, and to be created as input. The detailed data dictionary is also known as the project dictionary because it includes data elements used in a specific systems design project. Some of the data elements in the data dictionary for the RFC loan application system are shown in Figure 15–14.

Report design is one of the most important aspects of detailed design. Reports must provide managers with the information they need to monitor day-to-day activities, such as the reporting of payments by branch. A daily payments report is an

Figure 15–14

Data dictionary record for RFC loan application

LOAN-DETAIL
- Customer-loan-number
- Amount-loan-principal
- Loan-term-in-months
- Loan-security-type
- Date-loan-approved
- Date-loan-check-issued
- Loan-interest-percent

CUSTOMER-DETAIL
- Customer-name
- Customer-address
- Customer-date-of-birth
- Customer-social-security-num

CREDIT-DETAIL
- Customer-annual-salary
- Customer-employer-name
- Num-years-with-employer
- Customer-other-income
- Source-of-other-income
- Name-credit-source

COLLATERAL-DETAIL
- Collateral-description
- Collateral-current-value-amount
- Collateral-purchased-price

PAYMENT-DETAIL
- Date-payment-due
- Monthly-payment-amount
- Monthly-interest-amount
- Voucher-payment-number
- Date-payment-received
- Amount-payment-received

REMINDER-DETAIL
- Reminder-code
- Date-reminder-issued

DATE-FINAL-PAYMENT
DATE-LOAN-DELINQUENT

operational-level report. Managers also need information enabling them to control resources more effectively. A delinquency analysis report, depicting overdue accounts by age group and marital status, may help branch managers develop policies for screening high-risk applicants. This type of report is an example of a *tactical* report.

In designing these reports, the systems analyst would use a printer spacing chart. A good report has a heading, page number, date, column headings centered over data elements, and subtotal and total lines. The report should be easy to read. A mock-up of a report may be more useful to a manager than the printer spacing chart.

Output design, including report design and screen design for terminal output display, is critical to a good system. To the end user, the output represents the true system. Ideally, the output should be designed by the end user and the systems analyst.

The systems analyst also needs to design screens for data input and for terminal display output. One of the tasks that branch clerks perform every day is entering data from the standard application form. You can see a screen for the application form in Figure 15–15.

Program Specifications

If the system is to be programmed, then program specifications need to be designed to produce the various outputs from the files and input data. These program specifications can use any one of a number of techniques, including structure charts, pseudocode, or Hierarchical Input-Processing-Output (HIPO) charts. The program specifications would be given to the programmer along with the data dictionary.

Documentation

Documentation is one of the most critical aspects of an information system. It tells the story of a system, its design and construction, and its objectives. Without documentation, it is difficult to make changes or modifications to the system because no one knows how files, reports, and procedures were designed.

The first type of documentation is **systems design documentation.** Systems design documentation includes the specifications for the new system, such as the design of reports, screens, files, programs, and procedures. It should include program design specifications such as structure charts, pseudocode, Warnier diagrams, flowcharts, or decision tables. Systems design documentation specifies the logic used at the module level. In addition, it documents test methods, test data, and test results. Systems design documentation explains manual procedures, such as data validation and source document data entry, and is essential to anyone who will ultimately become responsible for enhancing and modifying the system.

User documentation provides users with the training they need to understand and use the new system. Users need to be familiar with data entry and validation procedures, the interpretation of computer output, methods of dealing with errors, and procedures to follow during testing and conversion activities.

Finally, **operations documentation** includes a systems flowchart identifying programs and the order in which they are executed. The input files, processing requirements, output files, and output reports for the system are identified. The tool used to depict these processing requirements is the systems flowchart. Systems flowcharting symbols depict the physical storage devices and data processing procedures that are implemented as a part of a data processing system.

Figure 15-15 Application form

STANDARD APPLICATION FORM

RELIABLE
Finance Company

"As long as you pay, we'll be friends"

APPLICATION COMPLETED BY: _____ DATE _____

PURPOSE OF LOAN _____

AMOUNT REQUESTED $ _____

☐ UNSECURED ☐ SECURED BY: _____

Complete This Block If Applying For Secured Credit
☐ Married ☐ Unmarried ☐ Separated
Collateral Is Owned Or To Be Owned By:

APPLICANT:

	FIRST	M.I.	LAST
FULL NAME			

HOME ADDRESS			APT NO.

CITY	STATE	ZIP

SOCIAL SECURITY NUMBER		DATE OF BIRTH

HOME PHONE AND DEPENDENTS	Area Code No. ( )	NO. OF DEPENDENTS (Include Yourself)

YEARS AT PRESENT ADDRESS	YEARS	☐ OWN ☐ RENT	RENT OR MTG. PMT $

FORMER ADDRESS	IF LESS THAN 2 YRS AT PRESENT ADDRESS	YEARS THERE

EMPLOYER	FIRM NAME		YEARS THERE
	EMPLOYERS ADDRESS		PHONE

OCCUPATION & SALARY	POSITION	MO. SALARY $

Do Not List Alimony, Child Support, Or Separate Maintenance Income If You Do Not Wish To Have It Considered As A Basis For Repaying The Loan.

OPTIONAL QUESTION	ALIMONY AND CHILD SUPPORT	☐ Wkly ☐ Mo ☐ Qtrly	AMOUNT $

OTHER SOURCES OF INCOME	SOURCE	AMOUNT $

COMPLETE THIS SECTION ONLY IF:
☐ (a) You Are Relying On The Income Of Your Spouse Or Other Person As A Basis For Repayment.
☐ (b) You Are Relying On Alimony, Child Support Or Separate Maintenance Payments From Your Spouse Or Former Spouse As A Basis For Repayment.
☐ (c) Your Spouse Or Other Person Will Be Contracturally Obligated To Repay The Loan.

NAME BELOW IS:
☐ Spouse ☐ Former Spouse ☐ Other

	FIRST	M.I.	LAST
FULL NAME			

HOME ADDRESS			APT NO.

CITY	STATE	ZIP

SOCIAL SECURITY NUMBER		DATE OF BIRTH

EMPLOYER		YEARS THERE

OCCUPATION & SALARY	POSITION	MO. SALARY $

BANK & CREDIT REFERENCES. IF THE ABOVE SECTION HAS BEEN COMPLETED, PLEASE MARK REFERENCES RELATED TO APPLICANT WITH "A", SPOUSE OR FORMER SPOUSE "S", JOINT "J", OTHER "O".

A/S/J/O	FIRM NAME	MO. PAYMENT	BALANCE

BANK NAME		☐ Checking ☐ Savings ☐ Loan

I Certify That The Information Contained In This Application Is Correct. FFC Is Authorized To Obtain Any Information It Deems Necessary For Approval.

SIGNATURES	DATE
	DATE

FOR FFC USE ONLY:

TF _____
Approved By: _____ Date: _____

_____

Release Limit $ _____

599

Documentation is a time-consuming task, and many systems analysts and programmers leave it to the last minute or fail to do it properly. Because of its importance, many MIS organizations hire documentation specialists who are responsible for compiling, maintaining, and updating systems design, user, and operations documentation.

At the end of the detailed systems design phase of the project, the blueprints for the proposed system are in place. The users of the proposed system should have an opportunity to review all design documents, including report mock-ups, input screens, and forms, so that their feedback can be used to make improvements before implementation.

An implementation plan is developed during the detailed design phase of the project. If the software is to be written in a procedural or nonprocedural language, the time, cost, and machine resources needed to implement the proposed system have to be determined. If a software package is purchased, provisions for making modifications and enhancements in reports, files, and screens must be determined. During this time, plans for testing and conversion may also be established. Implementation is the most time-consuming aspect of the project and requires careful planning and control of resources.

IMPLEMENTATION

The implementation phase of the project includes programming, testing, training, conversion, and documentation. In this section, you'll learn about implementation procedures that are of interest to the user-manager.

Programming and Testing

Programming and testing software developed in-house are the most time-consuming aspects of a systems development project. Because changes are inevitable, one of the major objectives of program design is to develop modular, changeable systems. Structured programming techniques, introduced in the early 1970s, helped to eliminate the problems caused by transfers of control and data among the various procedures in programs. Transfers had caused a ripple effect: When a programmer attempted to correct a bug in one part of a program, this bug would create a second bug in another part of the program, the second bug would create a third bug, and so on. In structured programming, three control structures governing program logic are implemented through different kinds of procedures. These control structures are *sequence, selection,* and *iteration.* In COBOL, for example, the selection control structure is implemented using the IF THEN ELSE statement, and the iteration procedure is implemented using the PERFORM UNTIL statement. The PERFORM UNTIL statement, which makes it possible to execute one module at a time, minimizes the interference of modules with each other.

A program module should execute a self-contained function within a program. Functions can be reading records, performing edit checks, writing records, and doing calculations. If each module performs a unique function, it is less likely to interfere with the inner workings of other modules. The more functionally independent a module is, the more likely the module can be reused in different parts of the program or in many different programs. The art of designing a program becomes a matter of constructing a hierarchy of self-contained modules that are organized to carry out the major functions of a program.

In the 1970s many programmers were independent workers who resisted using the new structured programming methods. As a result, two organizational strategies were introduced into organizations. One of these was the programmer team, consisting of programming specialists and a programming project manager.

The other organizational strategy (which was introduced in the late 1970s) was the **structured walkthrough.** The structured walkthrough provides an opportunity for programmers to have peers review their work. Its objective is to catch errors and to improve work at all phases of systems design and implementation. Participants in walkthroughs provide feedback, not criticism. Structured walkthroughs are used extensively today.

The purpose of program testing is to catch errors in programs. Often, when programmers provide test data for their own programs, they are not testing all the possible conditions that could affect their programs. For example, let us say that a programmer wanted to test a program that would read customer invoice numbers. Because an invoice number is a numeric field, one edit check would be for nonnumeric data. But that would not be enough. Test input data should also include unusual situations such as the existence of symbols, decimal digits, quantities that may be out of range, and blank fields. To get around the problem of inadequate testing, teams are sometimes organized to test programs so that programmers who may be hesitant to develop comprehensive sets of test data can get ideas from other programmers. Users can also provide test data consisting of erroneous transactions.

After programs are tested using artificial data, they should be tested using "live" data. Once individual program modules and programs are tested, subsystem- and system-level tests can begin. Many of the problems are likely to occur because of the interfaces of high-level and lower-level modules and because of the integration of programs into the overall system. Highly modularized system designs make it easier to catch and to fix integration type errors.

Training

Everyone who will be affected by the new system should have an opportunity to participate in training. Training may make the difference between system acceptance and failure. If people do not understand the new procedures they will be responsible for conducting or if they are unsure about how the new system will affect their jobs, they will be more likely to sabotage its performance than to make it work.

Managerial, supervisory, and clerical personnel all need some kind of training. Managers may need an orientation on how the system works, how to use and interpret its reports, and how it will affect their business activities. Supervisory personnel need to understand the system, its functions, and its impact on the jobs of the people they supervise in various functional areas, such as order entry and accounts receivable. They should be thoroughly familiar with methods of data input, file maintenance, handling output, and troubleshooting.

Clerical workers may be directly responsible for validating data input, maintaining files, and generating output documents. They need thorough training in these procedures. Procedures manuals must be developed to give workers continuing guidance on how to conduct many day-to-day operations, such as file backup and system security.

Training programs should have specific objectives; relevant, job-related materials, and effective measures of successful performance. Companies can use training technologies such as computer-based training to train system operators and clerical workers in multiple sites.

Conversion

Conversion from the old to the new system can be accomplished by one of four methods. In the **parallel systems method,** the old and new systems are operated simultaneously until the new system works well. Ideally, the end users and the systems analyst would have already come to an agreement about the performance measures used to evaluate whether the new system is operating successfully. Conversion to the new system occurs when the new system performs as well as the old system. If the new system does not work, the parallel approach guarantees that ongoing operations won't be disrupted. However, the evaluation of the new system is not based on its running independently.

In a slightly different approach, the **phased method,** the new system is phased in as the old system is phased out. Phased conversion may call for the use of temporary file conversion modules at the interface between old and new modules. The cost of this approach may be as great as that of the parallel method. In addition, this approach may be confusing to both the user and customers. When a system has multiple modules, such as inventory control, accounts receivable, and accounts payable, one module at a time can be introduced at periodic intervals, such as every six months. This approach may avoid the shock of introducing the entire system at once.

When the **cut-over method** is used, a complete, one-time conversion from the old to the new system occurs. Although this approach may be risky, it can be accomplished quickly. A fairly simple microcomputer-based system can normally be introduced by this method.

Finally, the **pilot systems method** entails introducing a new system to a small part of the organization. In this way the pilot system can be evaluated and modified before being introduced to other users. New technologies like electronic mail are often introduced using the pilot approach because their impact and benefits are not really known. Experiences during a pilot project can help systems designers anticipate the impact of new technology on work methods and procedures.

Human Factors in Systems Implementation

One of the main reasons that information systems fail is that users resist change. Common reasons for resistance to change include uncertainty about new expectations for performance, unfamiliarity with new tasks, and anxiety about potential displacement. When computer-based word processing systems were introduced into many offices in the late 1970s, for example, many secretaries felt that their jobs would be eliminated. Many resisted learning new skills and reorganizing work activities to integrate the new technology into office work.

However, in most cases, word processing did not replace secretaries. Rather than making their jobs less skilled, it mechanized much of the routine, repetitive work that they were responsible for and created opportunities for handling new administrative tasks. Some secretaries were able to provide more effective administrative support for professionals. Others learned technical skills and managed to organize departmental databases and text files to support a variety of applications.

When new technology is introduced into an organization, many people perceive threats to their jobs, their status, and their relationships with others. Feelings of insecurity may cause them to sabotage the success of a system at worst or simply to resume traditional work methods. If new methods of work organization and control are not accepted, then few productivity gains are likely to occur with the introduction of an information system. For example, if a word processing system is introduced into an office, few productivity gains will occur unless clerical and secretarial jobs are redesigned and new procedures for preparing and filing documents are developed. If the system is superimposed on the traditional office, where work is unspecialized and unstandardized, productivity gains will be limited.

One reason for resistance to change is that existing work methods are comfortable. Employees have a **work psychological contract,** which means that they accept the organization's expectations for their performance. When these expectations change, they feel insecure. If the reward system does not change to provide incentives for them to acquire the new skills needed to use new information systems effectively, they may feel frustrated. A good example of this problem occurred in the 1970s when secretaries were expected to become word processing operators. Job classifications for word processing operators were lower than those for secretaries, creating very little incentive to learn the new technical skills needed in the workplace. Word processing operators who were recruited at the clerical level often lacked the educational background and technical know-how to perform well in these jobs. After years of high turnover in the word processing field, many organizations changed the reward system to recruit capable candidates. To reduce resistance to change brought on by an information system, the systems analyst needs to serve as a change agent. The manager of the department or area into which an information system is being introduced must also fill the role of a change agent. A change agent has to understand the feelings of inadequacy and loss of control that can occur. If new technologies are to succeed, people have to accept them and want to make them work. The systems analyst and the manager should understand strategies for planning, designing, and implementing change.

Planning for change.   Planning for change occurs from the moment that the necessity for change is recognized. This planning should not be put off until the information system is being implemented because by then employees will realize that introducing a computer-based system is a foregone conclusion. They need to become involved in diagnosing problems in work methods, organization, and effectiveness during the problem definition and systems analysis phases of the project. If they recognize a disparity between current and potential methods, they will want to become involved in the design and implementation of a new information system. However, it may be necessary to move slowly and to limit introducing technological advances. Recommended changes should be based on thorough research, including information gathered from questionnaires and interviews. Users should have an opportunity to study this information, to assess alternatives, and to recommend changes.

Designing for change.   During systems design, alternative design options are studied and the blueprints for the new information system are developed. Users should have an opportunity to participate in design, including the evaluation of software packages, the development of reports and screens, and the set-up of new work methods and procedures. In situations where jobs are to be redesigned, workers should help redefine jobs in ways that preserve job satisfaction, skill, and status. Finally, new work procedures and job expectations must be thoroughly documented. If employees do not know what to do or how to do it, the new system will never succeed.

Implementing change.   Implementation must begin with complete communication about the goals and benefits of the new system. Everyone who will be affected by the change should understand the implementation schedule. Thorough training in technical and operating procedures is absolutely necessary for any system to work effectively. After the system is in operation, expectations for users' performance should be reasonable. It may even be necessary to designate a period during which performance will not have a negative impact on employee reviews. Finally, if problems occur, systems designers should react quickly so that unfavorable attitudes do not develop.

The role of the systems analyst as a change agent requires an understanding of the effects of technology on work attitudes and behavior. Even though the systems analyst may be able to put together a technical design, she also has to be able to deal with people-related issues. People who are affected by potential changes should be involved in making design and implementation decisions. The systems analyst may be able to solicit the help of employees who are in favor of innovation and in this way lay the groundwork for leadership after the system is in operation.

USER INVOLVEMENT IN SYSTEM SELECTION

One of the major responsibilities of users in information systems development is the evaluation of alternative design options. This process may include the development of a **request for proposal (RFP),** followed by the evaluation of software and hardware design options.

Developing an RFP

Many users don't have time to shop around for hardware and software to fit their needs. Developing an RFP can save time and provide valuable information. In an RFP the user outlines major system requirements, including mandatory features, data requirements, and support needs, and asks vendors to respond to these needs with a proposal. The user also indicates necessary reports, forms, and special interface requirements to existing systems.

Normally, after an RFP is issued, vendors have a deadline within which to respond with a proposal. Vendors provide documentation on technical and systems development support and give the names of contact persons who can provide demonstrations and further information.

Evaluating a Database Program

Let us assume that each branch office microcomputer system at RFC needs to be equipped with a database package. In the process of system evaluation, a manager would probably want to evaluate at least three alternative microcomputer-based database packages. A relational database package would enable the manager to create files storing information about customers, loan payments, and loan payment history. A database package would also provide query and reporting features.

Figure 15–16

Weighted factors in a consideration of data management software

PARAMETERS	WEIGHTED FACTORS
1. COST (30%)	
• Price (50%)	$.50 \times .30 = .150$
• Implementation (50%)	$.50 \times .30 = .150$
2. SUPPORT (20%)	
• Maintenance (30%)	$.30 \times .20 = .060$
• Training (30%)	$.30 \times .20 = .060$
• Installation (40%)	$.40 \times .20 = .080$
3. SOFTWARE FEATURES (30%)	
• Report writer (25%)	$.25 \times .30 = .075$
• User-friendliness (30%)	$.30 \times .30 = .090$
• Query capability (20%)	$.20 \times .30 = .060$
• Documentation (25%)	$.25 \times .30 = .075$
4. CAPACITY (20%)	
• Record volume (50%)	$.50 \times .20 = .100$
• Number of active files (50%)	$.50 \times .20 = .100$

In evaluating alternative programs, the manager would want to use an objective method of evaluation. The weighted-factor method is a useful approach. The first step in this approach is to develop a series of selection parameters, or criteria, to use in determining the value of alternative products. The major parameters in evaluating a database package might include cost, support, software features, and capacity. Figure 15–16 provides a list of the parameters, subfactors, and relative weights for each parameter that could be considered in evaluating alternative database packages.

However, just weighting the parameters to be considered in a software decision doesn't determine the outcome. The software packages must be evaluated according to these criteria. In order to assign performance scores to each software product, the user must establish the basis for making performance judgments. Figure 15–17 shows a relative performance chart that can be used to make this kind of assessment.

The next step in the software evaluation process is scoring the alternative software products. Given two database management systems (DBMSs), A and B, the scoring might appear as shown in Figure 15–18. Based on these scores, the final

Figure 15–17

Relative performance chart for software products

PERFORMANCE SCORE BY PERCENTAGE			
Parameters	**0**	**50**	**100**
1. COST			
• Price	• Greater than $1,000	• Greater than $500	• Less than $500
• Implementation (training and setup)	• Greater than $1,000	• Greater than $500	• Less than $500
2. SUPPORT			
• Maintenance	• None	• Telephone help 9:00 A.M–5:00 P.M.	• 24-hour hotline
• Training	• None	• Workshops available at user's expense	• On-site training; tutorial included
• Installation	• None	• Documentation only	• On-site installation help
3. SOFTWARE FEATURES			
• Report writer	• Command-driven; limited options	• Command-driven; broader options	• Menu-driven; wide capability of user-defined reports
• User-friendliness	• Low; command-driven	• Moderate; command-driven with help features	• High; menus and prompts; help features
• Query capability	• Command-driven; limited options	• Command-driven; broader options	• Menu-driven; wide variety of options
• Documentation	• Limited	• Moderate	• Extensive
4. CAPACITY			
• Record volume	• Less than 10,000 records	• 10,000 to 100,000 records	• More than 100,000 records
• Number of active files	• One at a time	• Less than five at a time	• More than five at a time

weighted-factor evaluation would result in a total score of 79.88 for DBMS A and 72.25 for DBMS B, as shown in Figure 15–19.

The weighted-score method is one method of evaluating both hardware and software options. The process of establishing weighted parameters and the process of candidate scoring force the user to establish objective criteria for decision making. The candidate software scoring process may require the user to conduct research by consulting software reviews in various trade publications. Microcomputer publications such as *Infoworld, PC Week,* and *Byte* feature buyers' guides comparing popular microcomputer-based software packages. Independent reviews of mainframe and minicomputer-based hardware and software are compiled by research firms such as Datapro in Delran, New Jersey.

The weighted-score method can be somewhat subjective. Initially, the selection of parameters and the percentages allocated to these parameters can be subjective. Further, the scores assigned to the two or more alternatives (e.g., software packages, hardware) also can be subjective. If the systems analyst is careful to guard against a subjective evaluation of parameters and scores, the weighted-score method can be a very useful approach to analyzing alternative design options.

Hardware Evaluation

Hardware evaluation and selection take place after software selection because the hardware has to be compatible with software that has been selected. Software packages generally run in specific operating system environments. For example, Microsoft Access runs in the Windows operating system environment.

Some of the factors to consider in making a hardware choice are memory size, the capacity of hard disk storage, and the type of **peripheral devices** that can be supported. Where growth is anticipated, the user may need to analyze the maximum memory size and maximum capacity of hard disk storage. The cost of installation, training, and maintenance is also an important factor in decision making. Vendor reputation and financial stability should be taken into consideration because local service and support may be needed.

Figure 15–18

Software scoring of two database management systems

PARAMETERS	DBMS A	DBMS B
1. COST		
• Price	90	80
• Implementation	65	70
2. SUPPORT		
• Maintenance	85	70
• Training	70	55
• Installation	95	80
3. SOFTWARE FEATURES		
• Report writer	85	90
• User-friendliness	90	45
• Query capability	75	80
• Documentation	90	70
4. CAPACITY		
• Record volume	80	80
• Active files	60	70

Figure 15–19
Weighted-score
rating summary

PARAMETERS	WEIGHTED FACTORS	DBMS A	DBMS B
1. COST			
• Price	.150	13.50	12.00
• Implementation	.150	9.75	10.50
Subtotal	.300	23.25	22.50
2. SUPPORT			
• Maintenance	.060	5.10	4.20
• Training	.060	4.20	3.30
• Installation	.080	7.60	6.40
Subtotal	.200	16.90	13.90
3. SOFTWARE FEATURES			
• Report writer	.075	6.38	6.75
• User-friendliness	.090	8.10	4.05
• Query capability	.060	4.50	4.80
• Documentation	.075	6.75	5.25
Subtotal	.300	25.73	20.85
4. CAPACITY			
• Record volume	.100	8.00	8.00
• Active files	.100	6.00	7.00
Subtotal	.200	14.00	15.00
Grand Total	100.000	79.88	72.25

Figure 15–20
Hardware and
software
recommendations

HARDWARE	AMOUNT*
• P166 microcomputer system with 32 MB RAM and 1.2 GB hard drive	$2,700.00
• 1.44MB 3 ½ disk drive	
• Serial port, parallel port	
• Enhanced keyboard	
• VGA monitor and graphics card	Included
• Laser printer	600.00
• Tape backup system	1,499.00
Hardware Total	**$5,498.00**
SOFTWARE	
• Windows 95	Included
• Microsoft Office Pro	$200.00
Software Total	**$995.00**
Grand Total	**$6,493.00**

*Prices may not reflect current market prices.

Once decision-making criteria are established, the user can analyze alternative hardware using the weighted-factor method of evaluation. The hardware would be selected and a specific hardware configuration developed. A hardware configuration for a microcomputer-based system with a database management program might look like the one shown in Figure 15–20.

The final decision relevant to a hardware choice is whether to purchase training, installation support, and ongoing maintenance from the vendor. In the case of RFC, the corporation may want to rely on a national vendor that can provide on-site technical expertise, training, and installation support for all the branches. RFC will also need to evaluate the trade-offs between the cost of a maintenance contract for all its machines and the cost of maintenance on an as-needed basis. The cost of a maintenance contract for the hardware may run about 10 percent of the total hardware cost.

MANAGEMENT SUMMARY

In this chapter you have learned about the activities that take place during the detailed design and implementation phases of a project. Users are responsible for an analysis of alternative design options and for an assessment of project risk. Once an alternative design option is selected, a cost-benefit analysis is used to determine the economic feasibility of the proposed system. Benefits of an information system include increased revenues, decreased administrative costs, and better customer service. Costs include development, equipment, and ongoing operations and maintenance. The present value method of cost-benefit analysis considers the time value of money in determining the costs and benefits of a project over a three- to five-year time frame.

The blueprints for the physical design of the new system are established during detailed design. Reports, screens, files, and forms are designed.

Implementation includes programming, testing, training, documentation, and conversion. Methods such as programmer teams and structured walkthroughs help programmers catch design errors in programming and testing. The three types of documentation include systems design documentation, user documentation, and operations documentation. Conversion can be accomplished by the parallel systems method, the phased method, the cut-over method, or the pilot systems method.

Human factors must be taken into account in designing and implementing an information system. New technologies affect work methods, procedures, and interpersonal relationships. Managers need to anticipate and manage anxiety, uncertainty, and resistance by involving users in planning, designing, and implementing information systems.

KEY TERMS FOR MANAGERS

cost-benefit analysis, 592
cut-over method, 602
data dictionary, 597
intangible benefits, 593
operations documentation, 598
parallel systems method, 602
peripheral devices, 606

phased method, 602
pilot systems method, 602
prototyping, 584
request for proposal (RFP), 604
requirements documents, 583
software package, 584
structured walkthrough, 601

systems design documentation, 598
tangible benefits, 592
user-developed system, 585
user documentation, 598
work psychological contract, 603

REVIEW QUESTIONS

1. What are the advantages of using the weighted-factor method to evaluate alternative hardware and software options?

2. Give some examples of intangible benefits of information systems.

3. Give some examples of development costs in an information systems design project.

4. Define the time value of money. Why should it be considered in conducting a cost-benefit analysis?

5. Describe two guidelines in designing reports.

6. Identify one guideline for designing input screens.

7. What is the *ripple effect?*

8. What are the reasons for conducting a structured walkthrough during various phases of an information systems design project?

9. Explain the advantages and disadvantages of the parallel systems method of conversion.

10. In what situations would the pilot system method of conversion work effectively?

11. What are the components of systems design documentation? Why is it important?

12. What are the components of user documentation? Why is it important?

13. Compare the Gantt chart and project network diagram as tools used in project management.

14. Name several risk factors that are associated with systems development projects.

15. Give some examples of internal integration tools that can be used to successfully manage projects.

16. What are some strategies that can be used to minimize the risk of low-structure-low-technology projects?

17. What are the advantages of the prototyping approach in systems design?

18. What are some of the disadvantages of user development of information systems?

19. Name three factors that must be considered in determining whether an information system can be created using a software package, prototyping, or user development.

20. What are the characteristics of an information systems project where prototyping could be used effectively?

Questions for Discussion

1. Why should a manager develop a request for proposal for a new information system?

2. What kinds of benefits of an information systems project are most difficult to measure? Should these benefits be included in the justification for a new information system?

3. How can the structure chart be used to create a changeable, flexible system design?

4. Why is systems design documentation so important?

5. What kinds of human factors can cause resistance to systems implementation?

6. What kinds of control mechanisms can be used to minimize the risk of a high-technology-high-structure project?

7. Why are external integration strategies useful in a low-structure project?

8. What are some of the characteristics of an information systems project in which software packages can be used effectively?

Problems

1. **Detailed design for RFC, Inc.** RFC is interested in setting up a delinquency analysis reporting system to identify the characteristics of high-risk loan applications. Imagine that you are a branch manager. You want to have a delinquency analysis report that indicates which characteristics of loan applicants are most highly correlated with risk. Design a mock-up of a delinquency analysis report that identifies these risk factors and divides loan applicants into low- and high-risk groups based upon these factors. Once you design your report, design a data dictionary describing the data names and data definitions of data elements in your report.

2. **The MacMillan Manufacturing Company.** The MacMillan Manufacturing Company has a systems development backlog of 52 months. Managers are very anxious to accomplish some information systems development projects and are beginning to seek the help of consultants. The information systems department, headed by Richard Price, does not want to lose critical projects that should be developed by MIS professionals. Richard also wants to investigate the possibility of

using alternative development approaches to accomplish some of the projects. A list of some of MacMillans projects follows. Use Gremillion and Pyburn's framework to determine the best development approach for each project. Traditional development, software packages, user development, and prototyping are possible development alternatives.

a. A manager in the production planning department wants an information system to help branch managers determine target ending inventory levels for their respective branch distribution centers. The production planners need access to a sales history database for the past 18 months consisting of 3,500,000 records. Using these data, they would determine sales trends for various product lines. The sales analysis information would be used to determine the target ending inventory levels.

b. The accounting department needs an information system to maintain records on funded government contracts. The budgets for each contract have to be updated weekly to reflect charges for manpower and equipment, transportation, services, and overhead expense. Monthly reports have to be prepared for the government agencies funding the contracts.

c. The members of the corporate strategic planning department need an information system to enable them to analyze alternative capital budgeting decisions, including investments in real estate, new acquisitions, and new facilities.

d. Senior management proposes developing an international order entry and billing system, making it possible to enter orders and to invoice customers from all 12 district offices.

e. The personnel office wants a computerized job applicant information system. This system would make it possible to identify prospective candidates for job openings (for example, Give me a list of all the job applicants with MBAs in finance). In addition, the personnel director wants a database of current job openings so that the criteria for selecting candidates for particular positions could be matched with the applicant data file. In this way, lists of candidates with the qualifications for each job opening could be generated automatically and used to set up interview schedules.

3. **Using McFarlan's portfolio approach.** Use McFarlan's portfolio approach to identify the risk category of each of the following projects. Give reasons for selecting the risk category you choose. Then recommend strategies to help minimize the risks and maximize the chances of success for each project.

Project 1: A major corporation is designing a human resources information system that will enable managers throughout the firm to query personnel files with such questions as, Give me the names of all employees who have been with the firm for at least 15 years and who have degrees in chemical engineering. The system will support more than 3,000 users. In addition, the system will enable employees to make queries about employee benefit programs and job openings throughout the firm. The system will be designed using a mainframe-based database management system and a fourth-generation language, NOMAD II. The fourth-generation language will replace current COBOL programs used to extract personnel reports. Using the fourth-generation language, managers will be able to make queries and to generate reports directly from the database.

Project 2: The chairperson of the department of nursing wants to set up a database system storing information about all current nursing students, including their grades, internship sites, and areas of specialization. The system will be designed using a centrally located personal computer housing the student information database. A local area network will be used to link the central PC to PCs in faculty offices so faculty members can query the database. The local area network will use the Windows NT 4.0 network operating system, which will enable the PCs on the network to share data and access to a laser printer. The nursing faculty plans to query the database and to ask questions such as, Give me the names of students who are serving internships at St. Mary's Hospital. The database maintains between 75 and 100 records per semester. It will be updated to reflect changes in addresses, internship locations, and interests.

Project 3: A major insurance company is developing a prospect information system for its sales agents. The sales agents will receive portable PCs with Microsoft Access for a database management program. Using a custom-designed program, they will be able to store customer prospect information and to make queries. For example, they will be able to ask questions such as, Give me all the prospects who have not been called on in the past 60 days. They will also be able to generate reports listing customer prospect records in order by ZIP code, age, occupational category, interest category, and socioeconomic group. The database will maintain records on more than 20,000 prospects and will be continually updated. The sales agents will also be able to generate reports indicating prospects with the highest sales potential based upon industry growth, product mix, and account service costs. Each sales agent will receive training on the query and reporting language and standardized reports to be generated from the database.

Cases

1. **Sunset Valley Country Club.** Sunset Valley Country Club is considering a proposal to design and implement a point-of-sale system for its shops and restaurants. The proposed system would include electronic cash registers in the club's two shops, the golf shop and the tennis shop, and in its two restaurants, the Thunderbird Room and the Arrowhead Room. Sales transactions would be entered at each of the shops and restaurants, and summary sales data would be transmitted to a central minicomputer system and used to update a central member accounts receivable file. At the end of each month, members would receive their monthly statements. In addition, the system would update inventories for each of the shops and restaurants, making it possible to reorder items on a timely basis. Sales analysis reports, depicting monthly trends, would also be available. The total cost of the proposed system, including four electronic cash registers, a central minicomputer, point-of-sale inventory and accounts receivable software packages, a text-quality printer, and a 1 gigabyte hard disk storage device, would be $23,000. The systems development costs, including analysis, evaluation of software packages, testing, and user documentation, will run about $4,500. The main benefit of the proposed system is inventory management. With an inventory control program, the golf shop expects to increase its profits by $4,800 per year, and the tennis shop estimates an increase in profits of $2,500 per year. The two restaurants estimate that their profits can be increased by $6,000 each because of more effective sales analysis, more accurate entry of sales transactions, and reduction in excess inventory. Another benefit of the proposed system is more timely monthly billing and receipt of payments on member accounts. At the current time, some bills are not mailed until 12 days after month-end closings, and checks are not received until a week later. With the proposed system, bills can be mailed out within 24 hours of the month's end, and payments can be recorded much more quickly. Interest charges will be applied to overdue accounts, bringing in an additional $2,800 of revenue per year.

The other savings will come from decreased clerical time, aggregating various bills for each member, and preparing monthly statements. Additional clerical time is spent applying payments to account balances. It is expected that a part-time clerical worker responsible for these tasks could be eliminated for a savings of $8,000 per year. With the new system, the hardware and software maintenance contracts will run about $2,300 per year. The operating costs, including supplies, part-time clerical help, and ongoing training, will be about $2,000 per year. A part-time data processing supervisor will be paid $13,000 per year. Other benefits of the proposed system include improved member relations because of faster point-of-sale service and more accurate billing procedures. Employees working in the golf and tennis shops and restaurants should be able to input sales transactions more efficiently. Managers of the shops and restaurants will be better informed for planning sales and controlling inventory. Based on these facts, can the proposed point-of-sale inventory and accounts receivable system at Sunset Valley Country Club be cost-justified? Conduct a cost-benefit analysis of the proposed system using the present-value method. Assume an interest rate of 12 percent. Conduct the analysis using a five-year period of time.

2. **A university admissions information system.** A new information system is being developed within the admissions and financial aid offices of a major university. The system will analyze application data, apply criteria for admissions and financial aid decisions, and generate various reports on applicant characteristics. In addition, the system will generate various letters and documents about admissions and financial aid details to applicants and their parents. The system will enable the university to recruit applicants more effectively, process their financial aid applications more quickly, and ensure their successful matriculation. Up to now, all of these procedures have been handled manually. A senior admissions supervisor, Francine Minor, has meticulously handled each application individually. Francine believes that her personal familiarity with each application enables her to answer questions more effectively as candidates call. She believes that good judgment is as

important as the standard admissions criteria in making admissions decisions. The new computer system, she believes, will treat each applicant as a "punched card" and fail to make good admissions decisions based on judgment and experience, especially in borderline cases.

Another senior administrative supervisor, Malcolm Blake, handles the financial aid decisions. Malcolm feels threatened by the proposed system because it will take away some of the autonomy he has had over financial aid decisions. He, too, feels that a computer system will ignore judgmental factors. Both Francine and Malcolm plan to circumvent the new system in any way they can. They do not plan to support efforts to train the clerical personnel in both the admissions and financial aid offices who will be responsible for keying in data and generating various reports. Dean Robert Walters suspects that the new system may fail because of user resistance and hires you as a consultant. What factors do you think are creating the resistance to the proposed system? What strategies could you use to deal with them effectively? If you had been the systems analyst at the very outset of the project, what steps would you have taken to minimize potential resistance to the proposed information system?

3. **A student intern tracking system.** Phillips Agricultural Supplies Company hires interns from many universities every summer to work in the accounting, marketing, information systems, and personnel departments. Louise Miller, director of personnel, asked one of her assistants to design a database management system to keep track of these interns. The system would generate reports on interns, their responsibilities, their qualifications, and their evaluations. Louise hoped the system would provide summary reports by functional area and by university program. Her assistant, David Conklin, had taken a course in Microsoft Access and was able to develop the student intern tracking system by the end of the summer. Then David left the firm to attend graduate school in another state. A few

months later, Louise asked one of the secretaries in the personnel office to use the system to obtain a report of all that past summer's interns. The secretary found the program and data disks, but she was not able to get any of the reports to work. To everyone's amazement, David had not prepared any documentation. No one could find copies of sample outputs or any evidence of the logic used in their design and implementation. Finally, in frustration, Louise hired a programmer to reprogram the reports. What steps could have been taken to prevent this problem from occurring? In your answer, list some useful types of documentation that would help the user understand the purpose of the system, the logic of the programs, and the data requirements.

SELECTED INTERNET REFERENCE SITES

Hardware/software references
    http://www.ronin.com:80/SBA/
    http://www.iol.ie/~kmagee/compco.html
    http://www.mindspring.com/~gis/vendor.html

Software evaluations
    http://benchin.com/cgi~win/$br.exe/cat/1

Software site
    http://www.edsonent.com/

Download software
    http://www.linknet.net/dload.htm

Microsoft Library
    http://library.microsoft.com/

Software Web search
    http://www.softsearch.com

Software Publisher's Association
    http://www.spa.org/

Hardware research
    http://www.u~net.com/~sysdoc/hardware.htm

SELECTED REFERENCES AND READINGS

Davis, W. S. *Systems Analysis and Design.* Reading, MA: Addison-Wesley, 1983.

Gremillion, L. L. and P. Pyburn. "Breaking the Systems Development Bottleneck." *Harvard Business Review,* March–April 1983, pp. 130–37.

Isshiki, K. R. *Small Business Computers: A Guide to Evaluation and Selection.* Englewood Cliffs, NJ: Prentice Hall, 1982.

McFarlan, F. W. "A Portfolio Approach to Information Systems Development." *Harvard Business Review,* September–October 1981, pp. 142–50.

Whitten, J. L.; L. D. Bentley; and V. Barlow. *Systems Analysis and Design Methods.* 2nd ed. Burr Ridge, IL: Irwin, 1989.

SYSTEMS DEVELOPMENT BY SOFTWARE REENGINEERING COMPANY (SRC), INC.

BACKGROUND

This particular morning Juliet Hartman, division chief of the corporate contract software division for the St. Louis regional office of the Software Reengineering Company (SRC), Inc., was sitting in her office contemplating a new contract her division had just received. The contract was with the St. Louis Steel Company. The small steel firm maintains a fairly profitable product line by focusing on niches within the industry. In particular, the firm specializes in the production of cold-rolled steel products that are made to order.

Managers at the St. Louis Steel Company recently determined that their competitive position was deteriorating. The primary problem was an aging computerized order processing system. The existing system simply failed to support management's information requirements. To continue to be competitive, management decided that the system needed to be reengineered as soon as possible. Unfortunately, the managers also determined that their in-house management information systems (MIS) department was overloaded with work, so they elected to *outsource* the reengineering project to SRC.

Ms. Hartman suspected that St. Louis Steel had never before handed over a project to a contract software development firm like SRC. She speculated that if SRC did a good job, then her company would probably obtain several additional contracts from St. Louis Steel.

Order processing at St. Louis Steel is similar to order processing in most make-to-order manufacturing firms. Customers place orders through the product sales department or by direct contact with salespeople. Steel products are manufactured according to customer specifications. When an order is finished, it is shipped to the customer by truck; in addition an invoice is prepared and mailed. St. Louis Steel does not maintain a fleet of trucks to handle shipping; rather, the firm contracts with a well-known freight company to transport finished orders to the customer's site. Many of St. Louis Steel's better customers are in the automobile and recreational vehicle production industry.

Although one might suspect that order processing is fairly standardized across firms, different factors affect the way customer orders are handled in different industries. For example, St. Louis Steel, as a manufacturing firm, processes orders differently than a service industry firm or retail outlet firm processes orders. Further, St. Louis Steel has three production facilities around St. Louis. The sales office at the main corporate headquarters site receives all orders. After processing each sales order, the production manager at the main production facility decides which mill will actually produce the order.

The main corporate headquarters office maintains responsibility for all invoicing operations. Even within the steel industry, St. Louis Steel processes orders in a unique way because of the size of its product line and because of internal factors that prevent its managers from accessing information that affects their decision-making activities.

Order processing is a complex system composed of numerous subsystems. In a manufacturing environment, order processing encompasses all activities from the time that an order is received through final product delivery and customer billing. This system cuts across functional areas. At St. Louis Steel, order processing involves activities in several departments including: marketing and sales, engineering and quality assurance, shipping, operations and manufacturing, and finance.

The St. Louis Steel Company is experiencing tremendous problems in managing order processing because it cannot integrate data from several stand-alone existing information systems. SRC's goal is to reengineer these systems in order to develop a single integrated order processing system that is based on an enterprise database using database management systems technology.

CURRENT SITUATION

"This meeting of the contract software division will come to order," announced Juliet Hartman, division chief. "Let the record show that all members are present." Those present included the division's two project team leaders, Yei Mei (Emily) Yen and Jonathan Branson, their primary assistants, Roberto Gonzales and Karen Gronchak, respectively, and Malivai Washington, executive vice president in charge of the St. Louis regional office of SRC. Malivai was present because he considered this contract to be very important to the regional office's success.

"Our agenda today is restricted to a single item, the problem of reengineering the order processing system for the St. Louis Steel Company," began Juliet. "I assume everyone has read Mr. Branson's report on the initial contract specifications.

"I also want to take this opportunity to congratulate Jonathan on his fine work in helping land this contract. He was instrumental in working with the contract software negotiators in drawing up the initial specifications and requirements for the new integrated system. You should also know that Jonathan was able to identify this potential client because of his membership in the local information systems professional society where he met the director of the MIS department at St. Louis Steel."

Jonathan Branson beamed his pride in receiving recognition and praise from his boss. "I suspected the client was experiencing trouble with order processing when I overheard a discussion during the social hour at the latest society meeting," said Jonathan with an air of braggadocio. "Although he is not present, I want to give credit to Bobby Socks, the contract negotiator representative who helped us land this contract. Initially we

thought St. Louis Steel might have problems related to its old mainframe hardware technology, but after doing a preliminary investigation, we determined that the firm's order processing system needed a complete overhaul. This contract includes new hardware and software. The current system has 52 computer programs, many of which were written more than 20 years ago. The programs access data stored in about 75 different files that are not well integrated. Managers at St. Louis Steel are unable to do any type of ad hoc decision-support analysis."

The meeting continued with a discussion of the contract's requirements. Each member of the committee discussed how SRC might proceed with the contract. After about an hour, the committee decided to assign the next step in the development process to Karen Gronchak. Karen's task is to conduct a detailed analysis of the order processing system at St. Louis Steel.

"Karen, I realize that this question may be premature, but what do you see as our alternatives for improving St. Louis Steel's order processing system?" asked Juliet. She was extremely concerned about the timetable established for the project and thought that the project might result in cost overruns.

"One usual option is to maintain the status quo," answered Karen. "Clearly that option has been eliminated or else we wouldn't have the contract. There are two viable alternatives. Regardless of which way we go, the current system appears to need reengineering to include the design and installation of a new relational database. I tend to favor the Oracle DBMS technology (the Oracle Database Management System is a product produced and sold by Oracle Corporation), since many of our computer specialists have training on Oracle's information systems development tools (computer-aided software engineering, or CASE, tools).

"This database," continued Karen, "will store all information about order processing, invoicing, and other related data. The system will be integrated in that managers will be able to do ad hoc queries in order to analyze sales order data, determine the current status of an order, or obtain other data needed to support decision making. The relational DBMS technology will enable the development of a combined new order processing and manufacturing process flow control system. The manufacturing process flow control system is outside of the specifications/scope for this project, but it is a natural extension that we should try to sell to St. Louis Steel once we have the current contract well under way. It could easily result in a follow-on contract.

"The first alternative is for our project team to analyze, design, program, test, and install a new system. The second alternative is to purchase a customized system from another firm and write the computer programs needed to adapt the package to St. Louis Steel's requirements. Before making a decision, I recommend developing a logical model of the current system in order to understand its weaknesses. This model should capture the way St. Louis Steel does order processing. We need both a process model and a data model. This may also help us refine their system requirements if we decide to examine customized packages from software vendors."

STEEL MANUFACTURING

Steel manufacturing follows a common process. The typical steel mill must be able to smelt raw iron ore into steel. Steel is manufactured by using a recipe. Different ingredients produce different types and qualities of steel. The actual smelting (boiling all ingredients together) process uses a very large iron pot—such as the pot you might see on an old cook stove, but enormously larger. In fact, the pot used to make steel is lined on the inside with special fire brick to keep the pot itself from melting. This fire brick is replaced quite regularly.

In order to achieve the temperature needed to smelt iron ore, a special fuel is required. This fuel is named *coke* and is itself created at the steel mill in large outdoor ovens called coke ovens. The raw material used to create coke is baked in a coke oven, and then the coke is transferred to the steel smelting area for use as fuel.

As the raw material (ore) is boiled to remove impurities, additional ingredients are added to the recipe to achieve the desired product. The liquid steel is poured off into molds that create very large ingots (sometimes a foot or more in thickness and dozens of feet in length) of steel. These ingots cool and then are moved to a cold-rolled steel machine that uses thousands of tons of hydraulic pressure to compress the steel ingots into thin sheets of steel plating. Some of these rolls are used to manufacture doors and fenders for automobiles, which gives you some idea of how much pressure is used to compress the steel ingots. Much of this production process is computer controlled.

DETAILS OF THE SYSTEM

In developing a logical model of St. Louis Steel's existing order processing system, Karen conducted interviews with managers at all levels within the client firm. She also gathered and examined copies of documents, such as sales order forms, work order forms, and shipping documents, so that she could identify the type of information managers used in controlling the subsystems that make up order processing.

Karen developed the high-level context diagram for the system shown in Figure C4–1. This context diagram can be further decomposed into

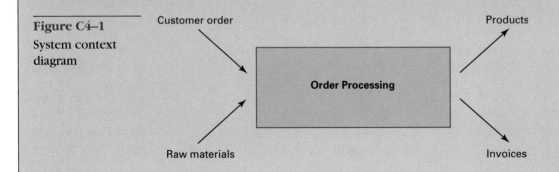

Figure C4–1
System context diagram

Customer order → Order Processing → Products

Raw materials → Order Processing → Invoices

four subsystems: (1) order-entry subsystem, (2) engineering subsystem, (3) manufacturing subsystem, and (4) shipping and billing (invoicing) subsystem.

Order-Entry Subsystem

Orders are received in two ways. The most common approach is for salespeople to make sales calls on established or new customers. Salespeople transmit order information either via telephone or fax machine to the order-entry group in the marketing and sales department. An order-entry clerk uses an on-line computer program to record the orders. The order information is batched into a transaction file. A separate computer program eventually merges information in the order transaction file with the existing order master file, and the result is an updated order master file.

If the customer has established credit, an order-entry clerk will telephone a credit manager to obtain credit approval for the amount of the order. Customers typically pay for the order within 30 days of receipt of finished orders. The clerk waits on the telephone for credit approval and then enters the approval (or disapproval) into the order record. Next a computer program automatically prints a *sales order report* form. The clerk forwards a copy of this report for filing in the credit approval section's actions-completed file. All activities associated with order approval for an established customer take one day, on average.

When the customer is new, the order-entry clerk accesses a different computer program and completes a data entry screen labeled *new customer screen*. To use this program, the clerk must print an incomplete copy of the sales order report and then exit the order-entry program. This step is quite tedious. The clerk would prefer to switch between two windows on the computer screen—one for order entry and the other for entering new customer data. A *new customer report* is printed showing new customer information.

The clerk forwards this new customer report and a printed copy of the incomplete sales order report to a credit manager, who establishes a line of credit for the new customer. Since steel cus-

tomers tend to place very large orders, establishing credit with vendors is very important. At the same time it is a very sensitive topic because the vendor must conduct a detailed investigation of the customer's credit history.

Once credit is established, approval/disapproval of the order is indicated on the sales order report, which is returned to the order entry section. An order-entry clerk enters approval/disapproval information into the computer using still another computer program and then prints the completed sales order report for distribution as appropriate. A preferable alternative would enable the credit approval manager to access the sales order record directly and indicate approval/disapproval of the order. This approach would speed up processing.

The new customer report is filed in the customer-credit file, and a photocopy of the sales order report is filed in the actions-completed file, both files belong to the credit department. All activities associated with order approval for new customers take two-and-one-half days, on average. The reports must be filed because the current information system does not allow for ad hoc retrieval of order information; however, a weekly order summary report is produced for management use.

The second way orders are received is for customers to call the order-entry section directly. An order-entry clerk transfers the call to the marketing section of the marketing and sales department. When the call is received, the salesperson on duty processes the order and becomes the key contact for the customer for this particular order. This salesperson takes down order information and ensures that all details are complete. In all cases the salesperson is responsible for negotiating a promised delivery date for the order. The salesperson delivers the information usually by telephone, to the order entry section for processing as indicated above.

After approval of an order, a copy of the sales order report is filed in the pending-orders file in the order-entry section. The salesperson also forwards two copies of the sales order report to engineering and one copy to the manufacturing process control office. He or she forwards another copy to the payroll section of the finance department to receive the correct commission.

Engineering Subsystem

An engineer in the engineering and quality assurance department uses information on the sales order report to establish an *engineering design order*. This preprinted form is typed manually. It is necessary in case St. Louis Steel does not have an established engineering *recipe* for the product. New steel orders may require the engineering department to design a new recipe.

A copy of the engineering design order is attached to the sales order report and is used to record the manufacturing specifications for the product being ordered. The engineering design order references the recipe. Engineers also refer to the firm's standard product book for guidance in developing the product's manufacturing specifications.

The engineer assigned responsibility for the engineering design order also contacts the customer in order to verify that the manufacturing specifications are satisfactory. Sometimes the customer will transmit additional information and other requirement specifications for the steel product to the engineer.

The engineering design order and other documentation are duplicated on a copy machine and attached to the two copies of the sales order report. One copy of the sales order report and accompanying documentation is filed in the engineering-design file. Another copy of the sales order report and accompanying engineering documentation is forwarded to the manufacturing process control office. The activities that comprise this subsystem take two days, on average.

Manufacturing Subsystem

Don Strock, the manufacturing process control manager for the main production facility of St. Louis Steel, is responsible for coordinating all activities required to manufacture steel orders. Strock procures raw materials, establishses a detailed daily work schedule, and supervises all work shifts for the main production facility. He also supervises the order shipping section. His staff includes the production managers at all three St. Louis facilities.

When a copy of a sales order report is received, a production manager analyzes the order requirements. The production manager follows the company's manufacturing policy guidelines to determine which facility should handle an order.

When the order is to be completed at one of the other steel mills, the production manager of that particular steel mill notifies the engineering department at the main production facility, and copies of all paperwork for the order (sales order report and any engineering specifications) are transferred via facsimile to the appropriate steel mill. The assigned manufacturing site is noted on one copy of the sales order report, which is filed with any accompanying documentation in a subsidiary-production file. This file tells Don which manufacturing site to contact to determine the status of any order. The plant managers at the other manufacturing sites are responsible for contacting the customer if any questions arise regarding the order.

If the order is manufactured in the steel mill at the main production facility, a shop control office clerk files the copy of the sales order report in a pending-production file. This is a type of suspense or action-pending file. If someone questions the status of a sales order and if the sales order report is in this file, Don knows that the sales order is being produced at the main facility.

When a copy of a sales order report and accompany documentation are received from Engineering, a raw material acquisitions clerk reviews the *list of raw materials* required to manufacture the product. (Engineering attaches this list to the form.)

If the necessary raw materials are not in stock, the clerk uses an on-line computer information system to enter data required to produce a *purchase requisition form*. A printer in the raw materials acquisition section prints multipart copies of the purchase requisition form. The clerk forwards one copy of the purchase requisition form to the purchasing section of the operations and manufacturing department. Purchasing managers use the information on the form to acquire the raw materials from a supplier.

Figure C4–2
Work order form

> **Manufacturing Control Process Work Order**
>
> Work order #: ————————   Manufacturing site: ————————
>
> Sales order #: ————————   Order date: ————————
>
>   Promise date: ————————
>
> Product recipe#: ————————   Completion date: ————————
>
> Quantity to produce (short tons): ————————————————
>
> Remarks:

All of St. Louis Steel's raw material vendors are required to use electronic data interchange (EDI) to speed up the raw materials acquisition process. St. Louis Steel managers want the existing EDI process to be integrated into the new system. Karen determined that the purchasing process is not really central to sales order processing and product manufacturing because 98 percent of the time the raw materials needed are already on hand as bulk stock. She plans to try to get managers at St. Louis Steel to alter the contract specifications to eliminate the EDI portion of the contract.

Next a shop floor control clerk types a two-part *work order form* (see Figure C4–2). One copy (white) is printed on cardboard stock. The harsh work environment in a steel mill makes it difficult to work with flimsy paper, so cardboard stock is used. A better approach would be to place computer terminals and screens around the manufacturing facility so that managers could check the status of work orders.

The work order helps control work flow during the steel production process. Since steel is manufactured in batches, one batch after another (kind of like baking Christmas cookies), it is necessary to determine the appropriate sequencing of production batches. A production manager can use the work order forms to specify sequencing for the day's production of steel. Sometimes a batch will not turn out as desired, even though the actual production process and addition of recipe raw materi-

als to the steel baking process is computer controlled. In these situations the production manager may determine that a batch of steel that is not appropriate to meet the needs of one customer may, in fact, meet the needs of some other order.

A green copy of the work order is attached to a copy of the sales order report in case it is necessary to coordinate some aspect of the production process with the customer. This enables cross-referencing the work order to the sales order. The sales order report, green copy of the work order, and engineering specifications are filed in a production-in-process file.

The white copy of the work order and a copy of the engineering specifications are forwarded to the worker who actually operates the large cooking pot where the steel is cooked. As each order is completed, the work order form, engineering specifications, and work-in-process are forwarded to the appropriate cold-roll steel line. The St. Louis Steel Company has several types of cold-roll steel lines.

When the cold-rolling process is finished, the work order and engineering documentation is forwarded to the shipping office where a shipping clerk notifies the production control office that the work order is finished.

Actual manufacturing time varies considerably. If the work order is expedited, manufacturing may be completed in as little as one to three weeks. Routine work orders require about five to seven weeks for the steel manufacturing process.

Shipping and Invoicing Subsystem

When a clerk in the shop control office learns that a work order is finished, he or she pulls a copy of the sales order report and all accompanying documentation from the production-in-process file. The clerk notes that the work is complete on the copy of the sales order report and forwards the report to an accounts receivable clerk in the finance department. Another copy of the sales order report and accompanying documentation is filed in a finished-order file.

The accounts receivable clerk uses an on-line computer system to prepare and print a multipart *invoice form*. The clerk files one copy of the invoice in the accounts-receivable file and mails one copy to the customer.

The computer system that prepares the invoice forms also prints shipping forms on a second printer in the accounts receivable area. This form is forwarded to the shipping clerk who coordinates shipping activities with the various trucking firms that St. Louis Steel uses. The work order white copy and accompanying documentation is returned to the shop control office for filing with the other related documents in the finished-order file.

When a sales order is manufactured at one of the other two steel mills, the shipping clerk at that site faxes a copy of the work order to the shop-floor control clerk at the North Alton facility. Three clerks coordinate paperwork that is used to manage and track sales orders that are assigned to other manufacturing facilities. One of these clerks will pull the file copy of the sales order report from the subsidiary-production file and send it to the accounts receivable clerk to notify the clerk to produce an invoice for the sales order. The invoice is filed and forwarded to the customer as noted above. Other documentation is filed in the finished-order file as indicated above. All billing services are provided through the mail production facility.

Case Questions and Exercises

1. Given the context diagram in Figure C4–1:
   a. Draw a first-level data-flow diagram depicting the processing that takes place in terms of the major subsystems and major data flows between the subsystems.
   b. Draw a detailed data-flow diagram depicting the processing for each major subsystem and the internal data flows, data stores, sources/destinations of data, and processes that transform the flow of data.

2. Working individually or as a member of a student team (as assigned by your instructor), brainstorm the different ways that computer technology can be used to track work orders.
   a. Don Strock has reported problems in tracking the status of a work order once it is released for production. He cannot determine what percentage of work orders scheduled for a given day are complete without touring the production facility. He also cannot easily determine if a work order will be completed by the promised delivery date given on the sales order.
   b. How would a computer system that can track work orders as they progress throughout the manufacturing facility affect Don's ability to determine the status of a work order at any time during the day and to prioritize work orders? Would Don be able to incorporate the need to expedite certain orders? What would be the effect on his ability to manage work orders that were close to their promised delivery date?

3. Review the textbook material on batch versus on-line information systems. Given your data-flow diagrams from question 1, discuss which parts of the subsystems might be based on (1) batch processing, (2) on-line with batch overnight update processing, (3) on-line with immediate update processing, or (4) distributed processing. Explain your answers.

4. Assume the order processing and manufacturing shop-floor control system is to be reengineered. Design the following sample screen layouts:
   a. A screen for a worker in the manufacturing facility to use to enter

information about a particular job activity for a work order, such as completion of the steel baking process.

b. A screen that gives the status of an individual work order so that an order-entry clerk can report that information to a customer.

c. What fields did you identify on the screens for (4a) and (4b) that must be stored in data files?

5. Karen identified two methods for acquiring a new combined order processing and manufacturing shop-floor control system: (1) build the system in-house by the current MIS staff or (2) purchase a customized, vendor-supplied package system. Discuss the general relative advantages and disadvantages of these two approaches.

V

THE MANAGEMENT OF INFORMATION SYSTEMS

IN AN EFFORT TO REDUCE COSTS and improve service, managers are constantly debating strategies for organizing information system resources. You will find all forms of organization approaches—centralized, decentralized, distributed, and recentralized—for information systems in use today. In Chapter 16 you will learn about these approaches and how information systems professionals and line managers can share information systems tasks and responsibilities.

Securing those systems from the many threats that exist in our world is one of the most important managerial responsibilities pertaining to information systems. Chapter 17 explores these threats and explains how managers can make information systems more secure. In the process, the ethical issues infusing and surrounding information systems are analyzed and the manager's responsibilities for the ethical use of information systems are considered.

CHAPTER 16

ORGANIZATION OF INFORMATION SYSTEMS AND END-USER COMPUTING

CHAPTER 17

SECURITY AND ETHICAL ISSUES OF INFORMATION SYSTEMS

ORGANIZATION OF INFORMATION SYSTEMS AND END-USER COMPUTING

CHAPTER OUTLINE

Manager's View

The Organization of Data Processing

Departmental Computing

Management Summary

Key Terms for Managers

Review Questions

Questions for Discussion

Problems

Cases

Selected Internet Reference Sites

Selected References and Readings

ORGANIZATIONS TODAY are facing a tough set of problems related to managing the computing function. Indeed, how to organize data processing is one of the major strategic issues of the 1990s and beyond. In many organizations the tremendous demand for computer-based information systems has created application development backlogs ranging from two to five years. Core business systems need to be replaced, and the shortage of *application programmers* and *systems analysts* continues to be a major constraint.

Accompanying the pressure for application development is the rapid pace of technological change. The related technologies of telecommunications, office automation, and computer-aided manufacturing pose difficult management problems. These technologies and their organizational effects need to be managed if organizations are to avoid technological obsolescence.

As a manager, you will be confronting the issue of how to organize information resources within a firm. Which information resources should be centralized and which should be decentralized? Which information systems should be managed centrally and which should be managed locally? Today many managers are becoming responsible for acquiring hardware and software and for developing information systems at the departmental level. Decentralization of these responsibilities has created some new challenges, such as system selection and maintenance.

In this chapter you will learn about how computing is organized and managed in centralized, decentralized, and distributed environments. You will also learn about the roles and responsibilities of MIS professionals and users for systems development and operations in these different environments. Finally you will learn how information systems professionals are assuming new functions as consultants and facilitators to support users.

THE ORGANIZATION OF DATA PROCESSING

The Evolution of Computing

Different ways of organizing data processing have evolved over the past 25 years. In the 1960s data processing was a back-office function, staffed primarily by specialists working directly for departments that were automating various accounting functions, such as accounts receivable and accounts payable. To most users of these systems, data processing was a mystery. "Computer people" spoke their own language and had the technical skills to keep data processing operations running smoothly. These early systems automated many routine paperwork-intensive operations and were considered very successful.

Success with accounting systems projects led to demands for the development of more data processing systems. Users left the development of these systems up to technical specialists, who didn't always understand the business functions they were attempting to automate. Many users began to question the high cost and disappointing results of these data processing projects. These concerns forced senior management to become directly involved in planning and controlling data processing projects. As a result MIS departments were formed, and MIS professionals were trained to use project management methods to make sure that systems would be developed within budget and on schedule. Functional managers themselves became responsible for selecting the most critical projects and for approving expenses for these projects.

In the 1970s computing technology became much less expensive. Minicomputers with software packages to handle applications such as accounts receivable and inventory control were aggressively marketed directly to users by vendors who argued that user departments could manage their own computers. Users, motivated by the opportunity to control their own hardware and data, acquired many of these minicomputer systems. The result was an era of decentralized computing.

However, problems such as incompatible hardware, lack of local systems analysts, and lack of capable technical professionals led many of these users to rethink the job of running their own computer systems. By the late 1970s most organizations had centralized their data center operations. A centralized group of computer professionals managed hardware, computer operations, and technical support for database and communications systems. In many firms systems development functions were decentralized, with systems analysts working within functional areas of the business. This approach gave users more control over application development projects.

In the 1990s most organizations have to manage multiple technologies. Computing technology is in the hands of virtually every manager in the form of microcomputers, computer-based telephone systems, CAD/CAM systems, and expert systems. The availability of new technology has created new roles for end users, as well as for information systems professionals. Many MIS professionals have become involved in training end users to use new technologies such as fourth-generation languages and microcomputer-based software.

To understand the evolution of data processing and its future development, you need to learn about the characteristics, advantages, and disadvantages of the major approaches for organizing information systems activities. You also need to recognize the factors to consider in selecting an appropriate organization strategy. These questions are discussed in the next section.

Centralized Data Processing

In the **centralized data processing** environment, a large mainframe computer system supports multiple users and multiple application programs. Users have access to computer resources via hundreds of remote computer devices, including on-line terminals used to input data and printers used to obtain reports.

Applications with a centralized store of data that are helpful to many different users are well suited to a centralized system. For example, numerous departments could use a personnel information system with data about the characteristics and job histories of employees. Corporate personnel data may be utilized to generate payroll checks and reports. Users may want to query personnel records to locate employees with certain characteristics. A personnel administrator, for example, may want to locate all employees who have secretarial skills and can speak Spanish.

A staff of highly trained technical specialists, including people responsible for computer operations, systems analysis and design, programming, and telecommunications, supports a centralized data processing facility. These responsibilities are described later in this chapter.

Computer resources are organized centrally for a number of good reasons. One reason for centralization is that it allows economies of scale. A large computer system can provide large-scale processing capacity for many users. Complex applications such as large linear programming models and statistical analysis programs require the largest available computer capacity. A large computer system supporting many applications can reduce operating and maintenance costs that would result if small processors and operations personnel were dispersed throughout the organization.

Other factors supporting centralization are multiple access to common data and the assurance of data integrity and security. In the airline industry, for example, hundreds of reservations agents need multiple access to centralized databases on seats, fares, and schedules. Organizationwide databases, such as personnel data and financial data, require security and integrity safeguards that can be effectively managed by specialists like database administrators. Problems such as loss of data, access to data by unauthorized personnel, and duplicate data may be minimized in this way.

Decentralized data can create problems of redundancy and inconsistency. An example that you might encounter after graduation concerns alumni information systems, which maintain records on all graduates of a university. Most universities use central alumni records to generate fund-raising letters and to mail various publications. If the particular school of the university that you have attended (such as the business school or the engineering school) decides to set up its own alumni information system, you may receive two fund-raising requests—one from the university and one from the individual school. Maintaining correct information in both these files can also be a problem. When you change your address after you graduate, you could inform either the university or your particular school, thus creating lack of consistency between the centralized and decentralized databases.

If alumni data were stored only on a central university system, your school could still have access to data on you and your classmates. A procedure could be introduced to enable school personnel to edit and to update their own records and to print out mailing labels and letters locally using the names and addresses of alumni stored in central files. This system would maintain the integrity of the centralized alumni database, and allow users to have access to the data they need.

The centralized approach requires a large, specialized MIS staff. Central MIS organizations attract new recruits by offering a chance to work on a variety of challenging projects, to share knowledge with other data processing professionals, and to enjoy richer career paths. Data processing personnel can also find better prospects for training and more diverse career opportunities within a central MIS group. Turnover problems have less impact in a central organization.

A major motivation toward centralization is control of data processing expense. The ability to control the costs of systems development and operations is a strong reason for central MIS units. A central operation is often more cost-effective than multiple smaller operations.

However, centralized data processing has some disadvantages, too. Many central groups have a backlog of application development projects ranging from three to five years. As a result users find it difficult to get small, locally important projects accomplished within a reasonable time frame or at all. Users, frustrated by central data center charges, lack of responsiveness of central personnel to their needs, and lack of control over their data, may turn to decentralized data processing as an answer to their problems. Although centralized computing has been an effective approach historically, it is rare today. Figure 16–1 lists the advantages and disadvantages of centralized data processing.

Figure 16–1
Advantages and
disadvantages of
centralized data
processing

CENTRALIZED DATA PROCESSING	
Advantages	**Disadvantages**
• Economies of scale. • Access to large-scale capacity. • More professional operation and management. • Multiple access to common data. • Security, controls, and protection of data. • Better recruitment and training of specialized personnel. • Richer career paths. • Control of data processing expense.	• Lack of user control over systems development and operations. • Limited responsiveness to small development projects. • Frustration with corporate charges for DP services.

**Decentralized
Data Processing**

In a **decentralized data processing** environment, minicomputers or microcomputers support local applications. Local systems and operations personnel are responsible for developing and maintaining programs and for managing computer operations. If software packages are used to support application requirements, a programming staff may not be necessary. A local computer and local staff often support a single application such as plant production scheduling.

The main motivation for decentralized data processing is local control of hardware, software, and data. If a user department wants to develop a management reporting system for sales analysis, for example, management does not have to wait for centralized personnel to get around to its project. Furthermore, local systems analysts may have a better understanding of departmental needs and management preferences for the system.

Decentralization of hardware also allows users to escape corporate data processing charges for both systems development and operations. Many users believe that they can actually cut their data processing costs by purchasing a single-purpose minicomputer or microcomputer programmed to support a single application. Reasonable hardware costs often justify local operations. Efficiency of hardware operations on a large mainframe is no longer a convincing issue. Decentralized computing also reduces the telecommunications costs associated with on-line access to centralized data files. In addition, users of decentralized systems are shielded by fluctuations in response time on corporatewide computer networks.

Another factor supporting the decentralized data processing approach is better access to local data. If divisions of an organization do not share applications and data, maintaining a centralized data center may create more frustration than benefit. Users who need local control and local access to data may avoid the red tape associated with centralization by entering and editing their own data. Finally, if each division is relatively autonomous, the various operating units may have no reason for sharing access to data.

One reason for centralization is the development of highly trained technical professionals. In contrast, information systems professionals in a decentralized organization may have excellent opportunities to cross-train themselves in business areas. Better understanding of business functions may improve their ability to define systems requirements and to work with users. MIS professionals in rural divisions, moreover, are isolated from the pressures of urban-based search firms. Thus user-managers in division settings may be able to reduce the turnover of information systems professionals that commonly affects centralized urban MIS groups.

Effective user-managers understand their information systems needs and are capable of managing local hardware and data. In companies with relatively autonomous operating divisions, the decentralized approach is consistent with the organizational structure. For example, even though airline reservation data must be maintained on a centralized system, much data can be effectively managed at the local level. A network of distributed minicomputers can keep local operations moving and reduce a main corporate computer system's chances of failure.

However, decentralization of computing creates many new responsibilities for user-managers who decide to manage their own hardware, software, and data. First of all, they need to manage their own computer operations. User-managers might have to hire clerks to handle routine procedures, such as backing up data files, and programmers to develop and to enhance software. These staff members may not be fully utilized. Furthermore, local staff members may not have the training to design systems with proper data security, documentation, controls, and backup and recovery procedures.

When users acquire their own data processing systems, they put their local needs above the needs of the organization as a whole. Local departments may select computer equipment, including hardware, software, and operating systems, that is not compatible. If this situation is allowed to continue, some users may not be able to share data and computer network resources, such as hard disk storage devices and high-speed printers.

Figure 16–2 summarizes some of the main advantages and disadvantages of decentralized data processing.

Distributed Data Processing

As you have seen, one of the driving forces behind decentralized data processing is that users want more control over their data processing activities. However, decentralization may lead to inefficient operations and to duplication of data processing expense. One way to solve the problem of organizing data processing is to distribute some data processing activities to users but to maintain centralized control over other activities. This approach is known as **distributed data processing.** Earlier in the text, you learned that distributed data processing refers to a system in which application programs are run and data are processed at more than one site. This approach means that both computer power and data can be distributed to local user sites. Distributed data processing can also mean distributing responsibility for other computing activities to the user. Responsibilities for systems development, such as systems

Figure 16–2

Advantages and disadvantages of decentralized data processing

DECENTRALIZED DATA PROCESSING	
Advantages	**Disadvantages**
• Local autonomy and user control. • Responsiveness to user needs. • Reduction in telecommunication costs. • Immediate access to decentralized databases. • Local systems analysts more attuned to local needs. • Opportunity for career paths within user's functional area. • Consistent with decentralized corporate structure.	• Loss of central MIS management control. • Incompatible data, hardware, and software. • Failure to follow standard systems development practices. • Duplication of staff and effort.

design and training, as well as responsibilities for data processing operations can be distributed to the user. The following case studies of a financial services firm, a retail store chain, and a hospital illustrate some forms of distributed data processing.

A financial services system.   One method of distributed data processing is to give the responsibility for data entry and data validation to user departments. A financial services company successfully used this distributed processing approach to process loan payments. Local personnel in more than 250 branch offices around the country entered payment transactions at local microcomputers. These microcomputers had storage and processing capabilities. All transactions were edited locally and transmitted once a day to the home office computer, where they were used to perform a batch overnight update of the centralized outstanding loans database.

This division of effort enabled local personnel to offload work from the centralized computer system through local data entry and validation. Users in branch offices could query customer loan account files and get immediate responses. However, because new payments were not posted to the outstanding loans file until each evening, data accessed by personnel making queries were one day out of date.

To make this system work, centralized MIS personnel set standards for a nationwide telecommunications network linking all the terminals to the central computer system and provided local personnel with local data entry programs, validation programs, and data transmission procedures. Local personnel had control over and access to the data they needed to service customer accounts and were able to manage local computer operations.

A retail point-of-sale system.   In the case of the financial services organization, responsibility for data entry and editing was decentralized. In other forms of distributed data processing, responsibility for computer operations can be decentralized as well. A good example of such decentralization is a retail department store chain with point-of-sale processors in each store. At Sears stores, for example, clerks enter sales transactions at local point-of-sale terminals. These transactions are used to update a local minicomputer-based inventory database and to generate local reports on inventory turnover so that buyers can purchase needed merchandise on a timely basis. Summary totals of sales and inventories are transmitted to a host computer system at corporate headquarters.

As you can see from this example, all processing of local sales and inventory data is decentralized. It would make no sense to transmit sales transactions to a central computer system because the costs of telecommunications from each store to a central system would be prohibitive. Furthermore, local store management personnel would not have timely access to information on sales trends and inventory levels. In the Sears example, central management personnel also have access to the information they need. A communications network links local store point-of-sale systems to a central host computer, making it possible for company management to receive summary reports periodically.

An accounts receivable system.   The retail store chain example shows how responsibility for computer operations can be decentralized to user organizations. In many other cases responsibility for systems development activities is decentralized, whereas computer operations are managed centrally. The visiting nurse division of a major hospital acquired a software package to handle its own accounts receivable. The package enabled the division to invoice clients and to generate reports on overdue accounts. Because the central MIS department did not have the time to develop programs for this application, the visiting nurse staff found a package that fit its needs.

Figure 16–3

Distributed data processing in three organizations

	CENTRALIZED	DECENTRALIZED
Financial Services Company Loan Payment Processing System	• Telecommunications planning, design, and implementation. • Systems development, including requirements analysis and programming. • Central computer operations. • Technical support. • Data security and integrity.	• Data entry. • Data validation. • Local computer operations. • Hiring of local data-entry personnel.
Retail Store Chain Point-of-Sale System	• Systems development, including requirements analysis, programming, and testing. • Telecommunications and network design. • Technical support.	• Computer operations. • Local sales order entry. • Local inventory update. • Training of store personnel.
Visiting Nurse Division Accounts Receivable System	• Computer operations. • Technical support.	• Requirements analysis. • Software package evaluation and selection.

However, the manager of the visiting nurse division did not want to acquire a minicomputer system to support the accounts receivable application. The manager chose to run the application on the centralized data processing system and to pay the MIS department for the time needed to run the program. Consequently, the central MIS staff was responsible for managing computer operations, but the division was able to identify its information systems needs and to acquire the package best suited to its needs.

Figure 16-3 summarizes the division of data processing responsibility in these three organizations. In the first two cases, MIS professionals were responsible for systems development. The loan payment processing application was a corporatewide system developed totally by MIS professionals. The complexity of the application, which included on-line edit and batch update procedures as well as various management reports, warranted MIS development. Experienced technical personnel also designed password security procedures for data entry and coding procedures to protect data being transmitted over telecommunications lines. Knowledgeable MIS professionals handled database design and administration, including precautions for backup and recovery of both the payment transaction file and the outstanding loans master file.

Systems development activities were also handled centrally in the case of the retail point-of-sale system. A central MIS development team identified the requirements, selected the point-of-sale configuration, and developed the software to support this application. The point-of-sale system that was developed centrally was designed for use in hundreds of retail stores. If each store had designed its own point-of-sale system, users all over the country would have needlessly reinvented the wheel. In addition, each of the decentralized local store systems had to be networked to a central corporate computer system for management reporting purposes. This process required technical expertise. Telecommunications specialists within the MIS department provided telecommunications planning, network design, and implementation. In both this case and in the financial services case, it would have been impossible to find local technical personnel to handle the technical requirements of designing these systems. Centralized MIS personnel also handled the ongoing maintenance and technical support of these applications.

Only in the third case were some responsibilities for systems development distributed to the users. In this case central systems development personnel did not have the time to design and write programs for the system. Visiting nurse personnel were familiar enough with their needs to identify criteria for selecting an appropriate software package. In fact, a package for outpatient nursing services had already been developed by a software vendor and could be utilized effectively by the visiting nurses, saving a great deal of time and expense in potential development.

There are advantages and disadvantages to users being responsible for certain systems development activities. As illustrated by the visiting nurse case study, users are familiar with their needs and are interested in controlling information processing expenditures. As a result, they are more likely to invest in training their own personnel to use a system effectively.

However, when users assume responsibility for systems development, they incur some risks. User-managers may develop a system, only to discover that they have reinvented the wheel. User-managers may find it more difficult to recruit and retain competent information systems professionals both for application development and for ongoing technical support and maintenance. Data security, backup and recovery, and control procedures may be difficult to develop and maintain in user areas. The next section explains how to determine the best mix of responsibility between users and MIS professionals.

Allocation of Responsibilities in Distributed Data Processing

Much of the motivation for decentralization of data processing stems from users' desire to control certain data processing activities. Increasing exposure to computing technology encourages user-managers to set up data processing activities within their own departments. However, distributing responsibility for data processing does not mean that users have to acquire minicomputers and microcomputers. They can take on additional responsibility by sharing systems development and operations functions with MIS professionals.

Figure 16–4 depicts the kinds of responsibilities users and MIS professionals can assume. These responsibilities deal with hardware operations, telecommunications, database administration, systems analysis, systems documentation, and user training.

For a particular application, users need to select the level of responsibility they want to have for various data processing activities. A decentralization pattern describing user responsibilities for various information systems development and operations activities appears in Figure 16–5. In this example users are largely responsible for user training, systems analysis, and systems responsibility for such functions as database administration and application programming. MIS professionals and users share documentation. However, MIS professionals handle all technical responsibilities such as hardware operations, telecommunications, and systems programming.

The decentralization pattern described in this example builds on the strengths both of users and of MIS specialists. Users are more likely to understand functional requirements and can play an effective role in systems analysis. They have a greater stake in successful training and in the development of adequate documentation and are likely to want to play a major role in these activities. However, they rarely have the technical know-how or interest to play an effective role in hardware operations, telecommunications planning and network design, and systems programming. The strengths of users lie in the systems development area; the strengths of MIS professionals lie in the technical and operations management functions.

However, the distribution of responsibility for systems development and operations management functions may vary depending on the nature of the application.

Figure 16–4

Range of
responsibilities
involved in
information
systems activities

DATA PROCESSING RESPONSIBILITIES			
LOW RESPONSIBILITY	**INCREASING USER RESPONSIBILITY**		**HIGH RESPONSIBILITY**
Hardware Operations — Prepare source documents	Manage data entry	Operate a satellite processor with database	Manage an independent facility
Telecommunications — Specify communications needs	Design network configurations	Implement network	Maintain network
Database Administration — Control source documents	Carry out logical data-base design	Carry out physical database design	Manage all databases
Application Development — Use turnkey system	Communicate needs to programmers	Participate on programming team	Select and develop system-building tools
Systems Analysis — Conduct preautomation interviews	Define user data and functional specifications	Evaluate system relative to functional specifications	Carry out program-level system design
System Documentation — Write functional specifications	Write user's manual	Write program design specifications	Write detailed description of data structures
User Training — Conduct preautomation interviews	Prepare user training materials	Conduct user training	Maintain adequate user competence

Source: Adapted from J. R. Buchanan and R. G. Linowes, "Making Distributed Data Processing Work," *Harvard Business Review,* September–October 1980, p. 146.

Certain self-contained applications can be run on dedicated minicomputers and managed exclusively by users themselves. For each application, users should select the level of responsibility they want for a variety of data processing functions.

Using the scheme of responsibilities (Figure 16-4) to identify various data processing activities, the user can select appropriate levels of responsibility for each activity and depict these responsibilities using the decentralization pattern (Figure 16-5). These tools demonstrate how users can increase their involvement in information processing activities without necessarily acquiring their own hardware or managing computer operations and technical functions. Distributed data processing means distributing certain information processing responsibilities to the user. The best mix is achieved when users assume a greater role for systems development activities while MIS professionals maintain control over hardware, computer operations, and technical functions.

Effective Organization of Information Processing Activities

In many organizations today, information technologies, such as office automation, expert systems, microcomputers, and decision support systems are being introduced. These technologies are frequently acquired by user departments without any input from MIS management. These technologies may create many of the same problems experienced with traditional decentralized data processing systems: incompatibility, lack of data standards, lack of organizationwide planning, and lack of control over systems development.

Figure 16–5

Decentralization pattern for data processing activities

Hardware operation
The user prepares source documents and manages data entry through terminals to DP center.

Telecommunications
The user specifies the volume and scheduling requirements for communications through his or her configuration of terminals.

Systems programming
The user uses only the DP centers operating system, compilers, and utilities.

Application system maintenance
The user both documents and assists in diagnosing system errors.

Database administration
The user determines his or her data requirements and develops a logical database design.

Applications programming
The user assigns some internal personnel to participate in the programming team.

Systems analysis
The user is quite involved in most analysis work including some program-level system design.

System documentation
The user develops his or her own manuals and shares in writing program design specifications.

User training
The user alone is responsible for all internal training activities.

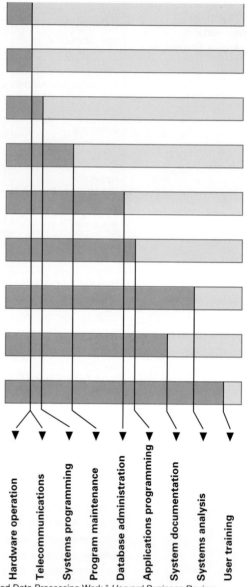

DECENTRALIZED

CENTRALIZED

Source: Adapted from J. R. Buchanan and R. G. Linowes, "Making Distributed Data Processing Work," *Harvard Business Review*, September–October 1980, p. 151.

MIS management must share responsibility with users for managing and controlling systems development activities involving these technologies. MIS responsibilities include developing hardware standards, providing support and training, and offering technical assistance. In the area of standards, MIS management should establish mandatory standards for hardware, telecommunications, programming languages, and documentation. The systems that users propose to develop must meet corporate communications standards. Systems development projects that users undertake must be reviewed to make sure that they don't conflict with corporate needs. Any projects implemented outside the firm should also follow appropriate professional standards for project control and documentation.

With regard to many end-user projects, information systems professionals can serve as consultants, facilitators, and technical specialists. Training programs can be developed to explain the possibilities and pitfalls of new technologies as well as to train users in specific skills.

Users also have important responsibilities when it comes to managing new information technology projects. Users should define the level of responsibility they want to take in these projects, such as providing guidelines for local network design, implementing filing procedures for word processing systems, or designing programs for user training. Users should work closely with information systems professionals to evaluate and select the best mix of support services, including the use of prepackaged software, the hiring of contract personnel, and the use of centralized MIS personnel. Finally, user-managers should perform periodic audits to ensure that systems are reliable, meet security requirements, and satisfy documentation requirements.

As a user-manager, you'll need to rely on information systems professionals for many systems and technical services. The next section covers the roles and responsibilities of these professionals.

Roles and Responsibilities of Information Systems Professionals

The data processing organization includes three major functions: systems development, operations, and technical support, as shown in Figure 16-6.

Systems development. The systems development group is responsible for analyzing the business system and designing a computer-based information system that will enable users to achieve their objectives. The **systems analyst** is responsible for the analysis of the current business system, its organization, procedures, work flow, information requirements, and problems. As a result of the systems study, the systems analyst develops objectives for a computer-based information system. She evaluates alternative design options, such as batch, on-line, and distributed systems; determines whether software will be purchased or programmed; and develops design specifications for the proposed system, including report layouts, data dictionary requirements, CRT display screen design, and necessary controls and procedures.

Figure 16–6

The functional organization of data processing

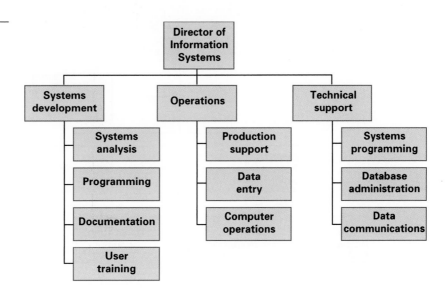

The **application programmer** is responsible for designing, coding, testing, and debugging programs to implement new applications. The application programmer can use both procedural languages, such as COBOL, and nonprocedural tools, such as fourth-generation languages. The **maintenance programmer** works with users to modify or make corrections in existing programs. In many data processing organizations, maintenance programming is about 70 percent of the programming work.

Other roles in systems development include the **documentation specialist** and the **user training specialist.** Systems analysts and programmers often neglect documentation of programs, reports, screens, and procedures. Documentation specialists record systems design specifications, including program specifications, report layouts, screen designs, file descriptions, systems flowcharts, operating procedures, user procedures, and control procedures. The person responsible for training the user on how to use a new system is called a user training specialist. A training specialist may instruct users on procedures for entering data, interpreting output, and backing up data files.

Finally, the **project manager** supervises programmers and analysts working on a systems development project. The project manager assigns responsibilities, monitors progress, and makes sure that activities are completed within cost and budget requirements. Sometimes the project manager is from the user department because user leadership in project planning and control decisions is critical for project success.

Systems development groups are organized by type of skill and by type of system. Figure 16-7 shows systems development organized into two skill areas: systems analysis and design, and programming. In this arrangement the project manager can come from the systems analysis side or from the programming side. This approach makes it possible to recruit specialists and to maintain their competence in each of these areas.

Systems development activities can also be organized by type of system, as shown in Figure 16-8. In this type of organization, systems analysts and programmers are organized into teams responsible for specific types of projects. One team may work on financial information systems and another on marketing information systems. The advantage of this approach is that systems development personnel become very knowledgeable in the functional requirements of the area for which they are responsible.

Figure 16–7

Systems development organized by skills

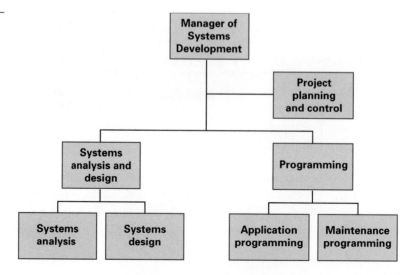

Figure 16–8

Systems development organized by type of system

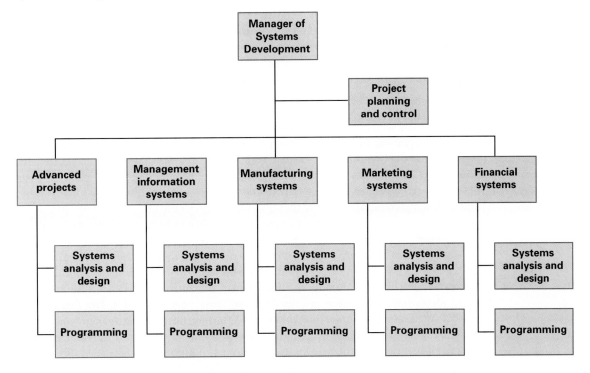

Operations. Responsibilities for operations relate to the day-to-day operations of the computer system. The **operations manager** is responsible for scheduling the running of programs and for making sure that output is distributed in a timely manner to users. The operations manager also supervises data entry personnel and equipment operators.

Data entry personnel are responsible for keying in data to be input into the computer system, using key-to-tape and key-to-disk devices as well as remote terminals. Today users handle most data entry themselves, and the number of data entry operators has diminished. **Equipment operators** work in the computer room performing such tasks as mounting tapes, reels, and disk packs, putting paper into output devices, and running the computer console. Using the console, operations personnel can determine the data needed by programs that are going to be run and can alert equipment operators to mount necessary tapes or disks. Finally, operations personnel are responsible for production support, including maintaining production schedules and distributing output to users according to schedule.

Technical support. Technical support personnel are responsible for systems programming, system evaluation, user services, database administration, and communications systems design and maintenance. **Systems programmers** are responsible for maintaining the operating system environment, including the selection, evaluation, and maintenance of operating systems and utilities. They try to optimize the performance of the computer by monitoring hardware and software and by identifying and streamlining inefficient programs. Personnel assigned the task of **system evaluation**

examine new technologies and hardware and software alternatives that will improve performance. These assessments help identify preferred vendors for hardware and software.

Two very important positions in the technical support group are the **database administrator (DBA)** and the **data communications specialist.** The database administrator is responsible for analyzing the organization's data requirements, developing a logical database design to support application needs, and maintaining the organizationwide data dictionary. The database administrator is also charged with establishing data security and integrity procedures and providing for database backup and recovery. Because of the increasing emphasis on organizationwide data management, the roles of database administrators and designers have grown in importance.

The increasing need for telecommunications planning and design has created positions for data communications specialists and analysts. Many organizations have centralized mainframes communicating to hundreds of remote terminals via large networks. Applications such as electronic mail, electronic document distribution, and videoconferencing have further increased the need for data communications. Other technologies, such as microwave and satellite communications, may need to be explored.

Data communications specialists are responsible for designing data communications networks, selecting appropriate channels for voice and data communications, and evaluating various communications hardware and software. They define standards for network operation and establish security procedures for data being transmitted over communications lines. The need to plan, design, and manage voice communications systems and to integrate voice and data communications has brought new responsibilities to the telecommunications function.

Career Paths and Management of Data Processing

The traditional career path in the data processing field has been from programmer to programmer/analyst and systems analyst. Experienced systems analysts have a chance to move into a project management position, which requires organizational and leadership skills. First-line management positions, such as manager of information systems development and manager of computer operations, also require organizational and managerial skills.

The MIS director is responsible for overall MIS planning, for selecting appropriate organizational structures, for working with user-managers to determine application development priorities, and for managing equipment and staffing needs. The MIS director is responsible for developing the MIS strategic plan, which identifies application development priorities, the operations needs that support these application requirements, and the implications of these needs for staffing and equipment. The main task of the MIS director is to explain computing to top management and thus to sell top management on its potential for the organization. In large firms the MIS director may be a chief information officer (CIO) at the vice-presidential level.

New technologies can affect the development of MIS strategy. When the microcomputer was introduced into organizations in the early 1980s, MIS management needed to assess what opportunities this new technology provided, how the technology could be interfaced with existing data processing systems, and how user-managers could be trained to use it effectively. The emergence of microcomputers meant that MIS professionals needed to assume roles as trainers and technical support specialists. Applications requiring interfaces between micros and mainframes presented new technical challenges.

The MIS director must be able to evaluate alternative organizational arrangements for information systems development and operations, including centralized, decentralized, and distributed approaches. Much of this chapter has been spent examining the advantages and disadvantages of these approaches. The MIS director needs to evaluate these arrangements in terms of their flexibility and responsiveness to user needs, their cost-effectiveness, and their ability to provide adequate service levels. The key issue in organizing data processing is control: central control versus local control. As described earlier, users can gain responsibilities for many data processing functions without necessarily running their own local MIS departments.

The MIS director is ultimately responsible for managing systems development and operations. As a general rule, the director must establish a method for identifying organizationwide application development priorities. One common procedure is to have users and information systems professionals work together on a corporate steering committee. The MIS director is also responsible for making sure that data processing operations meet production schedules, provide adequate response time, and provide effective controls over errors and possible data loss.

In addition, the MIS director must handle equipment and staffing needs. New technologies constantly require recruiting new staff and retraining existing staff in new methods and new skills. Microcomputers, fourth-generation languages, and expert systems development tools are just a few of the tools that have challenged the resources of the MIS function. The effective use of these technologies generated new roles for many MIS professionals. MIS professionals responsible for training and supporting users are known as end-user support consultants and analysts. Their roles will be discussed next.

The Organization and Management of End-User Computing

In many organizations end-user computing has been growing at the rate of 50 percent to 70 percent per year, compared with the growth rate of 10 percent to 20 percent for data processing. Throughout the text, the term *user* describes user-managers who are responsible for planning, developing, and using information systems. To be consistent, this chapter uses the term *user computing* instead of the term *end-user computing*. Users, frustrated with long systems development cycles, frozen requirements specifications, and unresponsive maintenance procedures, have taken advantage of such tools as report writers and microcomputer-based software to develop their own applications.

MIS organizations have responded to this situation by organizing user support or PC support centers responsible for facilitating and coordinating user computing. Consultants provide tools, training, and support services for users.

The role of the user support center.　The major role of the user support center is to provide users with training and consulting services. Consultants are responsible for defining the market for services, providing appropriate hardware and software facilities, offering support for application development, and conducting training programs. Other duties of user support analysts include hardware and software evaluation, technical support, data management, and help desk support. Help desk support means providing technical assistance via telephone from a central desk known as a "help desk."

Most user support centers offer mainframe-based query languages and report generators as well as tools for statistical analysis, graphics, financial modeling, and office automation. They also support microcomputer-based software packages for word processing, spreadsheet, and database applications. In most cases, only approved vendor packages are supported, providing an incentive for users to purchase and use standard software. Hardware and software standards are established primarily to prevent a proliferation of incompatible systems.

A study by Brancheau, Vogel, and Wetherbe surveyed the critical success factors related to effective user support. One of the major CSFs identified by users was that a

Figure 16–9

Critical success factors for the information center

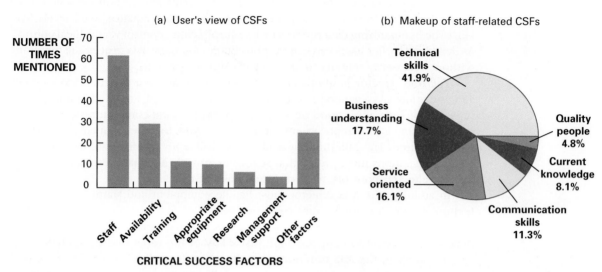

(a) User's view of CSFs

(b) Makeup of staff-related CSFs

Source: Adapted from J. C. Brancheau, D. R. Vogel, and J. C. Wetherbe, "An Investigation of the Information Center from the User's Perspective," *Database,* Fall 1985, p. 11.

technically competent staff member must be available at all times to answer questions and to provide support. Important skills for consultants were technical skills, business understanding, communications skills, and service orientation. These critical success factors are summarized in Figure 16–9.

Users and User-Developed Applications

The market for user support services consists largely of user-managers who have begun to develop their own applications using microcomputer-based software and fourth-generation languages. These users vary in sophistication from novice learners who know a few commands to sophisticated users who build their own systems. John Rockart and Lauren Flannery identified six types of users, including nonprogramming users, command-level users, user programmers, functional support personnel, user computing support personnel, and data processing programmers. The characteristics of each of these user groups are described in Figure 16–10.

The largest percentage of the 140 users studied by Rockart and Flannery were functional support specialists, sophisticated programmers supporting users within functional areas. Even though these specialists spend a good deal of their time developing information systems, they are not DP professionals; they are market researchers, financial analysts, production planners, and so forth.

Most of the applications developed by users in Rockart and Flannery's study and in other studies were designed for inquiry and analysis. This indicates that users were anxious to address the invisible backlog of inquiry and analysis systems demonstrated by Alloway and Quillard's findings. Rockart and Flannery's findings are summarized in Figure 16–11. The complex analysis applications, making up 50 percent of the overall applications studied, included financial analysis, operations research, engineering calculations, and simulations. The majority of the user-developed applications studied were departmental or personal in scope, indicating that users were building applications that would be considered low priority on an organizationwide basis.

Figure 16–10

Types of users

Nonprogramming users	Use software provided by others.
Command-level users	Perform simple inquiries and simple calculations.
User programmers	Use both command and procedural languages for their own personal information needs.
Functional support personnel	Write sophisticated programs and support users within their functional areas.
User computing support personnel	Located in a central support organization such as an information center.
DP programmers	DP professionals who program in user languages.

Source: Adapted from J. Rockart and L. Flannery, "The Management of End-User Computing," *Communications of the ACM* 26, no. 10 (1983), p. 778.

Figure 16–11

Types of user-developed applications

PURPOSE	NUMBER	PERCENTAGE
1. Operational systems	24	9
2. Report generation	39	14
3. Inquiry/simple analysis	58	21
4. Complex analysis	135	50
5. Miscellaneous	15	6
TOTAL	271	100

Source: Adapted from J. Rockart and L. Flannery, "The Management of End-User Computing," *Communications of the ACM* 26, no. 10 (1983), p. 779.

Management and Control Issues

The emergence of user-developed applications creates risks as well as opportunities. The most pressing concern is lack of **quality assurance,** including data validation and testing, documentation, controls, and backup and security procedures. Other specific concerns with systems developed by users are the failure to specify correct requirements, mismatches between hardware and software, and the failure to consider systems design alternatives.

A number of studies indicate that many user-developed applications are developed without proper review and discipline. In a study of 33 user-developed applications, Sumner found that documentation consisted primarily of copies of programs, screens, and reports. Fewer than 20 percent of the users studied had developed controls, backup and recovery, and data security procedures for their applications. Davis and Alavi also point out that lack of documentation, data validation and testing, controls, audit trails, backup and recovery, and data security measures are all concerns with user-developed applications.

In response to these concerns, user support consultants are developing policies and procedures to guide user development. Corporate guidelines for hardware and software acquisition are being established to prevent a proliferation of incompatible systems and to provide links between microcomputers and mainframe-based resources. Many organizations are introducing policies for quality assurance to motivate users to follow procedures for data validation, documentation, and backup and recovery.

Policies are also being formulated for data management. Whereas users cannot update "live" data in production databases, they can request sequential extract files. Using these extract files, which are actually copies of production databases, users can make queries and generate reports. To gain access to up-to-date data, users can request new extracts on a periodic basis.

In many organizations PC and user support centers have been successful in introducing policies governing hardware and software acquisition. In many cases incentives are used to obtain acceptance of these policies. Users adhering to hardware and software guidelines are offered technical support, training, and access to centralized service facilities such as color laser printers.

DEPARTMENTAL COMPUTING

Although many user applications are designed for management reporting and data analysis, departmental-level production projects are growing. Departmental systems projects are occurring for reasons similar to those that led to decentralized data processing in the 1970s. Users are frustrated with application development backlogs and anxious to gain control over their own data, and they feel that MIS departments have not been responsive to departmental-level projects. These projects support multiple users and serve important decision-making needs. These systems require good security, thorough documentation, effective backup and recovery procedures, and validation of data and processing logic.

Assessing the costs and benefits of centralized versus decentralized computing will be one of the major challenges of the era of user computing. User-managers must consider the alternative costs and benefits of developing internal systems development specialists and of relying upon MIS professionals to do systems development work for them. In the future functional support specialists will oversee the development and maintenance of many departmental systems.

The roles and responsibilities of MIS professionals will also change. MIS professionals will need to specify hardware and software options that are compatible with the corporate data processing network. The network will create the opportunity to develop applications linking microcomputers in decentralized business sites with corporate repositories of data. For example, customers of a commercial bank in St. Louis are already able to use their microcomputers to issue letters of credit that are in turn transmitted to overseas customers via the bank's international communications network.

User computing will require a distribution of responsibility between MIS professionals and users in much the same way that data processing applications have required a division of responsibility in the past. The same issues that were raised in the 1970s during the era of distributed data processing are reemerging in the 1990s with the era of user and departmental computing. As users begin to assume greater responsibility for requirements analysis and systems development, MIS professionals will provide technical support services, telecommunications planning, central database management, training, and user support.

The Future of the Information Systems Organization

In the 1980s there was a transition to decentralized forms of organization. The evolution of strategic business units, organized around product lines or markets, was a common strategy. In contrast, the bywords of the 1990s are recentralization, networking, and teamwork. The evolving organizational structure recognizes the contribution of multidisciplinary teams consisting of specialists in various disciplines.

In the organizations of the 1990s, management hierarchies have flattened and horizontal networking has come of age. Entrepreneurial teams work on multidisciplinary projects with a business purpose. Projects are geared to supporting customer service, introducing innovative new products, or competing effectively on a multinational basis.

Where does the MIS organization fit in? In the 1980s many companies decentralized their MIS organizations within the strategic business units. In the 1990s MIS functions are becoming recentralized for a variety of reasons. Centralized computing operations, network operations, and software licensing are more cost-effective than multiple decentralized facilities. Centralization also improves the bargaining position with vendors and enables DP management to obtain special terms and extra support that might not otherwise be possible. In addition, centralized operations provide better career paths for DP personnel. Finally, the increasing emphasis on corporatewide information systems that provide value-added services to customers is causing a recentralization of many important systems development projects.

However, the forces behind decentralization are still very real. In the early days of data processing, centralized DP shops were bureaucratic and unresponsive to the needs of user organizations. What resulted were decentralized MIS groups responsible for setting their own priorities and for developing their own computer applications. The recentralization that is occurring in the 1990s is not a return to the entrenched, unresponsive MIS bureaucracies of the 1970s. What is emerging is a hybrid organizational model based upon power sharing between information systems professionals and user-managers. In the new model the central MIS function supports the consolidated data center and communications network—the technological spinal cord of the enterprise. MIS professionals establish and disseminate standards for application development, database design, and networking. They also provide central staff recruitment and training.

Within the decentralized MIS entities, systems analysts and user-managers select project priorities and develop information systems in conformance with application development standards. In one Fortune 500 company, a new crop of college graduates is brought into the central MIS organization and trained in the standard systems development methodology and tools. When they move out into the various business units on a series of apprenticeships, these MIS professionals transfer the standards they have learned.

The recentralization of MIS activities has made it possible to "grow" integrated business systems that transcend departmental boundaries in purpose and scope. Three projects are examples of the new integrated systems.

One firm created a new customer service unit to provide customers with a central contact point for tracking shipments, handling service activities, and resolving questions about billing. Because these customer support representatives needed access to integrated databases, MIS had to reintegrate a number of once-separate computer systems.

An insurance company is streamlining the application screening process. In the original system an application crossed 20 separate desks and many different computer systems—taking as long as 25 days to process. Streamlining these processes requires computer systems and databases that span departmental boundaries.

A highly decentralized company in which each business unit addresses different products and different markets is designing a new integrated purchasing database to pool purchasing information from heretofore isolated purchasing systems. To accomplish this type of project, a strong central MIS organization with a strategic overview of the business must be able to overcome the more parochial objectives of individual business units.

The recentralization of MIS organizations is closely connected with building integrated systems that support important business goals. As you have learned throughout this chapter, the ongoing implementation of strategic business information systems requires MIS to be responsible for managing the infrastructure and user management to be responsible for identifying systems priorities that have a business impact. The new hybrid type of organization combines these responsibilities so as to reengineer important business functions.

MANAGEMENT SUMMARY

In this chapter you have learned that the issue of how to organize information systems activities is a major business and MIS strategy question. The evolution of data processing has seen centralized, decentralized, and distributed approaches to organizing both systems development and operations functions. Each approach has advantages and disadvantages. Most projects require a division of responsibility between MIS professionals and users. Users need to determine the level of responsibility they want to take for certain data processing activities, particularly systems development, database design, training, and user documentation. MIS professionals are more likely to assume responsibility for such functions as operating hardware, designing the telecommunications network, and providing technical support.

The emergence of user computing has created new roles for MIS professionals. Users are developing their own applications using fourth-generation languages and microcomputer-based database and spreadsheet software. User support professionals are responsible for "helping users help themselves"

by offering training, consulting help, hardware and software evaluation, and purchasing help. In many organizations, they provide guidelines for application design, including quality assurance, documentation, backup and recovery, and security procedures.

MIS professionals establish standards for hardware and software that can be supported by the corporate data processing network so users don't purchase incompatible equipment, database management systems, and operating systems software. MIS professionals are ultimately becoming responsible for managing and maintaining the integrity of centralized organizationwide data respositories—large "file cabinets" of information housed in central mainframe-based computer systems. Users are building local databases supporting departmental functions and also utilizing data housed in central repositories. In almost every application, users and MIS professionals are finding themselves cooperating with each other to achieve common organizational goals.

KEY TERMS FOR MANAGERS

application programmer, 636

centralized data processing, 626

database administrator (DBA), 638

data communications specialist, 638

data entry personnel, 637

decentralized data processing, 628

distributed data processing, 629

documentation specialist, 636

equipment operator, 637

maintenance programmer, 636

operations manager, 637

project manager, 636

quality assurance, 641

system evaluation, 637

systems analyst, 635

systems programmer, 637

user training specialist, 636

REVIEW QUESTIONS

1. What are some of the advantages of centralized data processing?

2. What are some of the disadvantages of centralized data processing?

3. List some of the advantages of decentralized data processing.

4. Give some of the disadvantages of decentralized data processing.

5. What are the characteristics of distributed data processing?

6. What is the difference between the job of application programmer and that of maintenance programmer?

7. Describe the responsibilities of the systems programmer.

8. Briefly discuss the responsibilities of the documentation specialist.

9. What is the career path most likely to be for a programmer?

10. What major responsibilities does the MIS director have for managing systems development activities?

11. Describe some data processing responsibilities that can be distributed to users in each of the following areas:
    a. Hardware operations.
    b. Telecommunications.
    c. Systems documentation.
    d. User training.
    e. Database administration.

12. Why have MIS departments organized PC support centers?

13. What are the major responsibilities of user support consultants?

14. What future challenges does the user support center face?

15. Discuss some of the potential risks of users developing their own applications.

16. What policies have MIS professionals introduced to guide user computing?

17. What are the characteristics of the command-level end user? Of the functional support specialist?

QUESTIONS FOR DISCUSSION

1. What are some of the motivations for users to set up their own departmental data processing systems?

2. What kinds of data processing responsibilities might a local sales organization assume in planning and organizing a prospect database information system?

3. What kind of central technical expertise might a local insurance agent seek from home office information systems professionals in setting up a sales call reporting system? This information system would monitor each client's current insurance portfolio and keep track of all inquiries and sales calls having to do with new insurance programs.

4. Should a user attempt to design an information system that houses financial records on government contracts that may be subject to audit? Why or why not?

5. What types of skills should an effective PC support analyst have?

6. Should an organization encourage end-user computing? Why or why not?

7. Why is the chief information officer (CIO) a vice-presidential-level position many large corporations?

PROBLEMS

1. **Western National Bank.** A major bank, Western National, centralized all its information processing activities in the 1970s to take advantage of economies of scale in supporting computer resources. It made economic sense to have one large computer system rather than many small processors. Some of Western National's managers have recently attempted to reverse the trend toward complete centralization. In one case a

trust department manager found a trust accounting software package on a minicomputer that could maintain a local database on trust accounts and provide management reports on a timely basis. On-line access to trust account records would be available to all managers in the department. The entire system—including hardware, software, a database management system, and operating system—could be purchased and maintained, he argued, for less cost than the trust department currently was being charged for the trust accounting system running on the central mainframe computer. Furthermore, managers in the trust department would have greater control over their information processing activities with a dedicated minicomputer. The MIS director of Western National argued that the software and hardware acquisition being proposed by the trust department manager was not com-patible with the corporate data processing system and would create many unanticipated operational and personnel problems.

a. Evaluate the advantages and disadvantages of the trust department's proposal to acquire its own hardware and software for trust accounting.

b. What pitfalls may the trust department experience if the manager decides to decentralize its data processing activities?

c. How could the trust department gain more responsibility for its data processing activities without necessarily acquiring its own hardware?

2. **Amalgamated Can Company.** The director of information systems at Amalgamated Can Company is considering how to divide responsibilities for the development and operations of several information systems between user and MIS professionals. The characteristics of each of these projects are briefly described below. Develop a decentralization pattern for each project by identifying which responsibilities in each case could be distributed to users in these functions. Which information processing activities should be in the hands of MIS professionals?

a. *Employee information systems.* This system maintains data on all employees, including personnel, job history, and payroll information. The system produces personnel reports required by the government; annual reports on salaries, promotions, and terminations; and payroll-related information, including paychecks and W-2 forms. Users would like to be able to make queries about employees for job placement purposes. They also would like to have access to employee names and addresses in order to generate mailing labels for various internal activities. Which responsibilities for developing, using, and maintaining this system should MIS professionals handle and which could users of the system handle?

b. *A word processing system.* Secretaries throughout the company want to use word processing systems to automate their repetitive and heavily revised documents and letters. Ideally, the system that is selected would be compatible with laser printers for high-speed document printout, particularly for repetitive letters and newsletters. Local printers would also be needed at each secretarial workstation for day-to-day letters and reports. Each secretary could purchase a word processing software package independently, learn how to use it, and purchase upgrades and maintenance according to the department's needs. MIS could also take on a role by planning for and designing a corporatewide word processing system. Describe the appropriate role and responsibilities of users and MIS professionals in this system.

c. *A sales order entry system.* A new system is being developed to enable salespeople to enter sales data more effectively. According to the marketing director who is proposing the system, salespeople would use OCR-scannable order-entry forms to record information about customer orders. This system would eliminate the bottleneck created by data entry operators having to transcribe order information from sales order entry forms handwritten by salespeople. The proposed system would make it possible to receive sales order input information more rapidly. As a result orders could be processed faster, invoices generated more quickly, and inventory levels updated more efficiently. Salespeople themselves would be able to receive reports from the system describing sales trends within their respective territories. Describe the best mix of responsibility between the salespeople and the MIS development staff in the design, operation, and maintenance of this system?

d. *A sales forecasting system.* Users in the production planning department want to design a sales forecasting system to enable them to depict sales trends based on order history data and to use this information to plan target inventory levels in the branch warehouses around the country. The information on target inventory levels would be used to determine plant production requirements in regional plants. The production planners believe they could develop a forecasting model and an inventory plan using a spreadsheet program on a microcomputer. They would need to have access to order history data stored in a mainframe-based database. These data could be analyzed using a mainframe-based database query language or else downloaded to a microcomputer. Once the target inventory plan was developed, it could be distributed to branch warehouses using the corporate telecommunications network. What responsibilities should the production planners and MIS department take in the development and implementation of this sales forecasting system?

CASES

1. **Hudson Industries.** Users in the marketing and finance departments acquired microcomputers for various kinds of sales and financial analyses at Hudson Industries about a year ago. The microcomputer-based software handles many routine calculations and produces management reports on marketing and financial trends. The initial success of some of the users in these departments has caused other managers throughout the organization to want to acquire microcomputers as well. Bill Clarke, the director of data processing at Hudson Industries, is concerned about the imminent proliferation of microcomputers within the corporation because he is aware of some of the problems that have resulted. First of all, in the corporate finance department, a user named Carol Carlson spent more than six months developing a budget analysis system using a microcomputer-based spreadsheet program. Many of the department's managers began to use the reports from this system. When Carol left the firm for a job with a competitor, the system was "lost" because no documentation existed and no one knew how to reconstruct the system. In the marketing department, users created a database of 20,000 customer records using a microcomputer-based database package. Simple operations such as sorting the database in ZIP code order took hours because the processing capacity of the new microcomputer was not sufficient to handle this kind of data volume. Transferring the data to a larger mainframe-based system could be accomplished by transferring the PC database file into an ASCII sequential file for transmission over an asynchronous communication line. But then the users would need to learn how to use a mainframe-based query language. Another problem occurred when a secretary using a word processing program on one of the

microcomputers in the finance department forgot to back up a data file containing a 50-page financial report. The disk on which the file was stored was accidentally destroyed. The report had to be completely reconstructed from a rough draft, and an important meeting was delayed. Bill is concerned about some of the problems of users developing their own applications. Inadequate documentation, failure to create backup copies of data files, and lack of sufficient security procedures are just a few of the problems he visualizes. More serious problems could occur if major financial and marketing decisions were made using erroneous data on reports generated from user-developed systems.

a. What steps should Bill take as director of data processing to manage and control user computing more effectively?

b. Should he control the acquisition of microcomputers, including both hardware and software?

c. What kinds of policies and guidelines should be introduced with respect to user computing?

2. **C. F. Industries.**   At C. F. Industries, the backlog of systems development projects is two and a half years and the pent-up demand for small projects is probably two to three years beyond that. The MIS department has selected a fourth-generation language tool to enable users to obtain access to mainframe-based data and to generate some of their own reports. However, few users are benefiting from the fourth-generation language program. Most users do not know how to obtain copies of the databases they need or how to use the tools. You have been asked to organize a user support center to address the needs of users. Develop a plan that includes this information:

a. The objectives of the user support center.

b. The responsibilities of the consultants.

c. The tools to be supported.

d. The policies for managing user computing.

SELECTED INTERNET REFERENCE SITES

MIS careers

MIS employment opportunities

http://www.umsl.edu/usr/local/Web/business/mis/mis_employ.html

Advanced computer careers

http://www.nash.mindspring.com/~accjobs/index.html

Careers OnLine—computers/information technology positions vacant

http://www.careersonline.com.au/vacancies/infosci.html

MIS consultants—career placements

http://www.careersonline.com.au/vacancies/infosci.html

MIS career opportunities

http://www.cob.ohio-state.edu/~acctmis/deg/mis/oppsmis.html

Computer placement services home page

http://careers4u.com/

Career development

http://www.espan.com/salary/edp/edpdev.html

BSA CareerMart

http://www.careermart.com/

Help desk

Information technology help desk

http://www.sju.edu/COMPUTING_NETWORK_SERVICES/HELP_DESK/

ActionWare help desk

http://www.actionware.com/HelpDesk.html

CSU computing resource center help desk

http://www.csupomona.edu/crc/mainmenu/userserv/helpdesk.html

MindSpring help desk

http://help.mindspring.com/

The Training Registry—Help Desk Institute

http://www.tregistry.com/ttr/hdi.htm

The Help Desk home page

http://helpdsk.com/

IBM Internet Connection help desk

http://www.ibm.net/helpdesk.html

PLAnet Help Desk—useful sites

http://www.planet.eon.net/HelpDesk/useful.html

SELECTED REFERENCES AND READINGS

Alavi, M. "Some Thoughts on Quality Issues of End-User Developed Systems." *Proceedings of the Twenty-First Annual ACM Computer Personnel Research Conference.* Minneapolis: University of Minnesota, May 2, 1985, pp. 200–207.

Brancheau, J. C.; D. R. Vogel; and J. C. Wetherbe. "An Investigation of the Information Center from the User's Perspective." *Database,* Fall 1985, pp. 4–17.

Buchanan, J. and R. Linowes. "Making Distributed Data Processing Work." *Harvard Business Review,* September–October 1980, pp. 143–61.

Carlyle, R. "The Tomorrow Organization." *Datamation* 36, no. 3 (February 1, 1990), pp. 22–29.

Davis, G. *Caution: User-Developed Systems Can Be Dangerous to Your Organization.* Working Paper 82–04. Minneapolis: Management Information Systems Research Center, University of Minnesota, February 1984.

Rockart, J. and L. Flannery. "The Management of End-User Computing." *Communications of the ACM* 26, no. 10 (1983).

Sumner, M. "The Impact of User-Developed Applications on Managers' Information Needs." *Proceedings of the Annual Meeting of the American Institute of Decision Sciences,* Las Vegas, Nov. 12, 1985, pp. 328–30.

Sumner, M. "Organization and Management of the Information Center." *Journal of Systems Management* 36, no. 11 (1985), pp. 10–15.

Sumner, M. and R. Klepper. "Information Systems Strategy and End-User Application Development." *Database,* Summer 1987, pp. 19–30.

von Simson, E. M. "The Centrally Decentralized IS Organization." *Harvard Business Review* 68, no. 4 (July–August), 1990, pp. 158–62.

SECURITY AND ETHICAL ISSUES OF INFORMATION SYSTEMS

CHAPTER OUTLINE

Manager's View

Viewing Information Systems Security

Risks

Common Controls

Common Threats

Protecting Information Systems

Ethical Issues and Information Systems

Management Summary

Key Terms for Managers

Review Questions

Questions for Discussion

Problems

Cases

Selected Internet Reference Sites

Selected References and Readings

Issues and concerns pertaining to security and ethics typically permeate any manager's job, especially when information systems are involved. For example, consider these situations:

1. A marketing manager is searching the company database to determine what types of customers are buying a product the firm introduced two months ago. She is in the process of matching customer location, size, and industry to volume of purchases when her screen clears and displays a strange message. Then she sees that letters on the screen are vanishing. As she reads the disappearing message, she slowly realizes that the database has been invaded by a virus program. What she doesn't realize, however, is that the virus is in the process of destroying the very files she is accessing.

2. A field technician, using a notebook computer, has recorded on his hard disk the fourth customer on-site visit for the day. The data about the visit, which was made to repair a piece of electronic equipment, along with data about all the on-site visits for the week, have been meticulously entered and stored on the notebook's hard disk. The data include time and materials data necessary for billing purposes. The data are also used for technician scheduling, product improvements, and marketing campaigns by the various departments of the technician's firm. The technician usually transfers the data to the local area network serving his office when he reports in at the end of the week. When he arrives this time, however, for some reason the hard disk has failed, and he is unable to transfer the critical data. Asked by his manager if he has made a backup to a 3 1/2-inch diskette, the man flushes and admits that he has not made a backup diskette since last week.

3. An angry employee, just fired from her job because she was caught with her hands in the till, decides to get even with her employer. While she is supposed to be packing up her desk and leaving at the end of the day, she turns on her computer terminal and erases hundreds of important customer data files from the company's minicomputer system. She also removes the backup tape from the minicomputer and throws it in a trash container. It is not until the next day that other workers find that important customer files and the backup tape are missing.

4. Several employees of an organization are allowed back into what remains of their building after a blinding rainstorm and a series of tornadoes converged on their town. The storm hit during the peak of their busy season, tore the roof off the building, and broke every window. Descending apprehensively to the basement, they find the computer room filled with 2 feet of water. One

employee cries out in exasperation, "How will we ever get the system working again?" Another says, "Even if we are lucky enough to get it working in a few days, how will we process our work until then?"

5. A student in a finance class has not yet completed his homework assignment as closing time for the computer laboratory draws near. He must complete the assignment by tomorrow or lose valuable credit toward an already shaky grade in the course. He decides to copy the finance program that he is using to diskettes so that he can take them to his dorm room and work through the night on the assignment. He knows he shouldn't copy licensed software but decides that it is really OK because he promises himself that he will use the software only for this one assignment.

6. A manager of a data entry department is concerned about protecting her workers from carpal tunnel syndrome, an injury to the wrists that may occur from long-term use of keyboards or mice. To reduce the occurrence of this injury, she could spend the money to install wrist rests and adjustable tables and chairs for the operators. However, she is also under intense pressure to reduce the costs of the center and must constantly prepare reports about department costs and worker productivity.

Information systems have become ubiquitous in the organizational world. Through the data they process and store, they control enormous amounts of organizational assets. Because of their development costs and the costs of the hardware and software needed to run them, information systems are valuable assets in and of themselves. However, information systems also contain data about organizational assets with staggering value, critical organizational operations, employees with valuable talents, important customers and vendors, and other information that is vital to the health and welfare of an organization. These same information systems often contain data that are sensitive, personal, and private about people and must be protected from inquiring, unauthorized eyes.

It is no wonder then, that providing security for information systems has become a major concern of managers. Given the value of information systems to organizations and given the people, data, and assets that these information systems control, husbanding these systems to ensure their safety and proper use becomes critical. It is not a task that can be taken lightly. In fact, almost half of the companies responding to a survey reported that they had lost valuable information in the last two years and four-fifths now report having a full-time information security officer.[1]

---

[1] "Security—The good news . . . ," *Information Week,* November 27, 1995, p. 32.

Viewing Information Systems Security

How should a manager view information systems security? When you become a manager, how can you be sure that you have not overlooked a potential security problem? How can you avoid reliving one of the disaster scenarios previously described? One answer to these questions is to approach information systems security with many of the same attitudes and tools that electronic data processing (EDP) auditors bring to the task. *EDP auditors* are charged with the review and analysis of information systems to prevent, discover, and remedy security problems. The approaches and methods used in EDP auditing are an effective resource for managers seeking to remove their information systems from harm's way. In fact, the basic objectives of information systems security are the same as the basic objectives of EDP auditing. These objectives include the following:

1. To control the loss of assets.
2. To ensure the integrity and reliability of data.
3. To improve the efficiency/effectiveness of information systems applications.

To accomplish these objectives, the manager must make certain that the risks to information systems are identified and that appropriate security controls are used to eliminate or reduce the risks.

Risks

The various dangers to information systems and the people, hardware, software, data, and other assets with which they are associated necessitate security controls. These dangers include natural disasters, thieves, industrial spies, disgruntled employees, computer viruses, accidents, and even poorly trained or naive employees.

Risks, Threats, and Vulnerabilities

EDP auditors differentiate among risks, threats, and vulnerabilities. By **risk** they mean potential loss to the firm. Potential risk refers to potential monetary losses, whether those losses are direct or indirect. The monetary losses may result from total loss, partial damage, or even the temporary loss of an information systems asset. For example, monetary loss may result when a computer printer is stolen, when a computer system is damaged as it is moved, when an information systems person is injured in a fire, when a data file is partially destroyed by a virus, or when a line connecting a customer to a sales order-entry employee fails.

When EDP auditors use the term **threat,** they refer to people, actions, events, or other situations that could trigger losses. A thief is a threat; so is a sprinkler system placed over a mainframe computer system. Thus threats are potential causes of loss.

When EDP auditors use the term **vulnerabilities,** they mean flaws, problems, or other conditions that make a system open to threats. A firm's potential risk of losing all of its microcomputers occurs when the threat of a thief stealing the microcomputers becomes possible, for example, when inadequate locks and alarm systems are used in the building in which the PCs are housed.

Assessing Risks

The manager must use common business sense in applying controls to reduce the risks to information systems, and the controls used must be appropriate to the risks faced. It would not do to spend $1,000,000 to control the risk of losing an information system valued at only $50,000. Acceptable risks exist for any information system. Total

Figure 17-1

Costs of system downtime

Downed application	Financial impact of system failure per hour
Brokerage operations	$5,600,000–7,300,000
Credit card/sales authorization	$2,200,000–3,100,000 (seasonal)
Pay-per-view movies	$67,000–233,000
Home shopping (TV)	$87,000–140,000
Catalog sales	$60,000–120,000
Airline reservations	$67,000–112,000
Tele-ticket sales	$56,000–82,000
Package shipping	$24,500–32,000
ATM fees	$12,000–17,000

Source: Contingency Planning Research, Inc.

freedom from risk is not possible and certainly not affordable. By assessing potential losses, the manager can identify what risks are acceptable and what risks are not.

EDP auditors estimate potential loss in several ways. These methods usually include the amount of loss that could occur and the probability that the loss actually will occur. For example, suppose that the manager was considering the controls that ought to be used to reduce the risk posed by the theft of 100 microcomputers in locked offices on the 10th floor of an office building. Suppose further that the microcomputers had a book value of $200,000, which included any adapter boards and special peripherals. However, the manager knew that the replacement value of the equipment was $300,000, including not only the boards and peripherals but also the costs of installing the machines and their software and data files. The manager then considered the current location of the building, the fact that the office is on the 10th floor of the building, the current level of security such as locked offices and the use of keys to access the elevator, and the low incidence of crime in the neighborhood. Given these data, the manager estimated that the chance that such a theft would occur was 1 in 20. Using these data and inferences, the manager computed the potential loss due to theft as $15,000 ($300,000 × 0.05). The prudent manager would consider the potential for loss now at $15,000, rather than at $300,000. That assessment would materially affect the manager's level of concern.

Assessing risk means asking two basic questions. First, if a loss occurred, how would the organization respond? Second, what would the cost of the response be? Suppose, for example, that the microcomputers had been old, unused, and had no scrap value. Suppose further that if they were stolen, the organization would not replace them. Then the risk to the firm of their loss is zero, and the controls used to reduce or eliminate the threat of theft should be commensurate with the risk.

The manager should similarly assess the potential loss to the organization from the lack of availability or existence of a data file, key information systems people, in-house developed software, and other information systems assets. Furthermore, the manager must view potential loss in broader terms than the direct loss of assets. Potential loss also includes such risks as lost sales from a downed order-entry system (see Figure 17-1), wages spent to reconstruct data lost when storage devices fail, lost sales from an inaccurate inventory system that causes too many stockouts, and fines paid for violations of government regulations because an information system failed to deliver the right information to the right agency at the right time.

COMMON CONTROLS

If you examine EDP auditing forms and procedures used by major auditing firms, you are likely to be overwhelmed by the comprehensive lists of potential threats and controls that the auditors should consider. In this chapter, however, you will learn about threats that are commonly posed and controls that are commonly used in an organization's information system environment. Then you will read about the security decisions that were made by personnel at a branch office of a consulting firm. By stepping into the shoes of the decision makers in this branch office, you will see how security decisions can be made.

Controls are countermeasures to threats. Controls are the tools that are used to counter risks from people, actions, events, or situations that can threaten an information system. Controls range from simple deadbolt locks on office doors that reduce the threat of the theft of information systems equipment to devices that read the palm prints of personnel to prevent the threat of unauthorized access to sensitive data stored on a hard disk. Controls are used to identify, prevent, and reduce risk and to recover from actual losses. These controls can be classified in many ways. One useful classification is by type. Explanations of common types of controls follow.

Physical Controls

Physical controls are controls that use physical protection measures. Physical controls might include door locks, keyboard locks, fire doors, and sump pumps. Physical controls include controls over the access and use of computer facilities and equipment and controls for the prevention of theft. Physical controls also include controls that reduce, contain, or eliminate the damage from natural disasters, power outages, humidity, dust, high temperatures, and other environmental threats.

Electronic Controls

Electronic controls are controls that use electronic measures to identify or prevent threats. Electronic controls might include motion sensors, heat sensors, and humidity sensors. They may also include intruder detection and biological access controls, such as log-on IDs; passwords; badges; and hand, voice, and retina print access controls. Physical and electronic controls are often used together to counter a threat.

Software Controls

Software controls are program code controls used in information systems applications to identify, prevent, or recover from errors, unauthorized access, and other threats. For example, programming code may be placed in a payroll application to prevent a data entry clerk from entering an hourly pay rate that is too high. Software controls may also include programs that disable computer terminals during certain hours and that monitor who logs on, how long they connect, what files they access, and what type of access they make of those files (e.g., read from or write to).

Management Controls

Management controls often result from setting, implementing, and enforcing policies and procedures. For example, employees may be required to back up or archive their data at regular intervals and to take backup copies of data files to secure, off-site locations for storage. Also, management may enforce policies that require employees to take their vacation time or ensure separation of duties to reduce the threat of embezzlement. Required employee training may be used to reduce data entry errors, or background checks may be required for employees who have certain levels of access to information systems.

Some physical, electronic, software, and management controls can be implemented by the manager without any outside assistance. For example, the manager may have employees in every department regularly make backup copies of files and store them in a safe place. Other controls may require specialists in information systems, auditing, or security. For example, the manager may hire a security firm to provide guards or install a security alarm system in the office area where information systems are housed. The prevalence of information systems in most organizations usually means that the manager must consider using many controls to identify, reduce, prevent, or recover from potential losses.

Common Threats

A number of threats are common to computer systems and deserve the careful attention of managers. These threats include natural disasters, unauthorized access, theft, vandalism, invasion of privacy, computer crime, software piracy, and computer viruses.

Natural Disasters

In the ordinary course of business, organizations take precautions against the loss of assets from a variety of natural disasters such as fire, floods, water damage, earthquakes, tornadoes, hurricanes, mud slides, and wind and storm damage. Computer systems also are subject to these disasters and should be protected from them. Security planning should consider disaster prevention, disaster containment, and disaster recovery. For example, disaster prevention planning might include the use of backup power supplies or special building materials, locations, drainage systems, or structural modifications to avoid damage during floods, storms, fires, and earthquakes. Disaster containment planning might consider sprinkler systems, halon gas fire suppression systems, or watertight ceilings to contain water damage from fire hoses if fires do occur. Disaster recovery planning should consider how operations can be renewed quickly. Planning for recovery might include developing contingency plans for the use of the computer facilities of vendors or noncompetitors with similar computer systems in the event of disaster. A number of firms specialize in providing computer facilities to organizations in the event of disasters. These firms are called *hot-site recovery firms* because they provide a computer facility for others that can be used almost immediately.

Employee Errors

Ordinary carelessness or poor employee training represents one of the most common threats. An employee may destroy the contents of a hard disk by accidentally reformatting the hard drive of the computer system instead of formatting the floppy disk in drive A that was the intended formatting target. An employee may enter an incorrect amount in a data entry screen and that amount may then be added, subtracted, multiplied, or otherwise used in many other programs, compounding the error with frightening speed. Consider what would happen if an employee entered the wrong price for a popular product in a file used by the sales order system.

Middle-level managers have often created spreadsheets that contain major logic errors, resulting in seriously incorrect decisions. For example, an undetected spreadsheet error in the use of the SUM spreadsheet function at one construction company caused an erroneous bid on a contract, resulting in an underbid of $254,000. The company won the bid but lost its shirt. In another example, a consultant from an accounting firm discovered more than 100 errors in several of his clients' multibillion-dollar spreadsheets. In still another example, a spreadsheet designed to perform market forecasting produced a forecast that was incorrect by $36,000,000 because formulas rounded all amounts to whole numbers. Thus an inflation rate of 1.04 was eliminated from the calculations.

Figure 17–2

The computer crime law in Illinois

Illinois has passed legislation designed to prevent certain types of computer crime. The law identifies three categories of computer crime and defines them as misdemeanors or felonies.

Computer Tampering

The crime of computer tampering occurs when a person gains access to a computer system, a program, or a data file without the permission of the owner. The law defines unauthorized access by itself as a misdemeanor. When the tamperer obtains data or services from unauthorized access, the first offense is classified as a misdemeanor. Subsequent offenses are treated as felonies.

If the unauthorized access results in altering, destroying, removing, or damaging a computer, a program, or data, the offense is treated as a felony. Placing or attempting to place a computer virus on a computer system or computer network is included in these offenses as felonies.

Aggravated Computer Tampering

Aggravated computer tampering results when tampering is done with the intention of disrupting or interfering with vital services or operations of state and local governments or public utilities or when the tampering is likely to cause death or bodily harm to people. Aggravated computer tampering is classified as a felony.

Computer Fraud

When a person gains access to or uses a computer, computer program, or data to deceive or defraud others, that person is guilty of computer fraud. Computer fraud may be perpetrated to gain control of money, services, or property. Property is widely defined to include electronic impulses, electronic data, confidential or copyrighted material, billing information, and software. Computer fraud is treated as a felony.

The federal government has also created legislation pertaining to computer crime. PL 102-561 makes unauthorized copying of copyrighted software a criminal offense. The penalties are substantial and include fines in the hundreds of thousands of dollars.

Source: Office of Information Technology, Southern Illinois University at Edwardsville, and G. Lawton, "No Copying Allowed: The Software Publishers' Association," *PC Today,* March 1993, p. 71.

Computer Crime, Fraud, and Abuse

New technology breeds new crimes. Telephone fraud was impossible until the telephone was invented. With the spread of computer systems and the Internet have come electronic versions of old crimes: forgery, theft, and fraud.[2] Computer crime is hard to measure, basically because it has not been very clearly defined. A number of states have attempted to legislate against it (see Figure 17-2), and computer crime, fraud, and abuse have been the subject of numerous pieces of federal legislation (see Figure 17-3). Typical estimates of annual computer crime range from less than $1,000,000,000 to more than $15,000,000,000. Some important contributors to those numbers include a Florida stockbroker fraud case of about $50,000,000, the Volkswagen currency fraud that hit $261,000,000, and the Citibank fraud that amounted to $10,000,000.[3] In a recent survey, about 75 percent of U.S. corporate, government, financial, and academic organizations surveyed reported financial losses from computer crimes in 1996.[4] It is estimated that as much as 90 percent of computer crime is unreported because organizations do not wish to make known their vulnerability to their customers, suppliers, and stockholders.[5] After Citibank reported the crime, it lost 20 top customers to other banks that claimed to have better security.

---

[2]K. Ferrell, "Net Crime: Don't Be a Victim," *CNET.COM,* February 6, 1996 (online magazine).

[3]M. J. Major, "Taking the Byte Out of Crime: Computer Crime Statistics Vary as Much as the Types of Offenses Committed," *MIDRANGE Systems,* March 23, 1993, pp. 25.

[4]A. Gordon, "Study: Computer Crimes Grow, Losses Top $100 million," *USA Today,* March 7, 1997 (online version).

[5]M. J. Zuckerman, "Cybercrime against Business Frequent, Costly," USA Today, January 13, 1997 (online version).

Figure 17–3

Some legislation affecting computer security

- **Communications Decency Act** makes it a felony to transmit knowingly "indecent" or offensive sexual material over networks accessible to children. This act was struck down by the Supreme Court in 1997, but other attempts to enact similar legislation are expected.

- **U.S. Copyright Law** makes it illegal for anyone to make unauthorized copies of copyrighted software or to sell pirated copies.

- **Software Copyright Protection Act** of 1992 is aimed at software piracy on a large scale, not the home user who uses one pirated software package. The law makes selling or distributing more than 50 copies of pirated software a felony, rather than a civil matter between the violator and the software vendor.

- **Federal Computer Fraud and Abuse Act** of 1986 makes it illegal to tamper with computers that are owned by the federal government, government contractors, or interstate organizations. Currently the bill covers access to computer systems with the intent to defraud, damage, alter, or destroy data that results in losses over $1,000. Both the FBI and Secret Service may investigate crimes under this act, depending on the nature of the crime.

- **Fair Credit Reporting Act** of 1970 allows individuals to examine the contents of their own credit records and provides procedures for them to follow to correct errors. The act also restricts credit firms from sharing data on individuals or organizations with anyone else but their clients.

- **Privacy Act** of 1974 restricts federal agencies from collecting, sharing, using, or disclosing personal data that can be identified with a specific person.

- **Right to Financial Privacy Act** of 1978 specifies under what conditions banks can disclose financial information for individuals.

- **Electronic Communications Privacy Act** of 1986 makes it illegal for anyone except the sender or receiver to tap phone and data lines, including reading e-mail messages transmitted over public e-mail systems, such as MCI mail. It also grants exemptions to law enforcement agencies and employers. That means the law does not cover private e-mail systems, such as the electronic mail system of a company.

- **The Crime Control Act** of 1994 provides stiffer penalties for computer crimes, including intrusion, credit-card fraud, and the theft of computer services.

- **The Telephone Consumer Fraud Protection Act** of 1994 sets limitations on telemarketing and sets fines for violators. For example, the act prohibits calls before 8 AM or after 9 PM, prohibits calls to anyone on a "no sales call" list, and prohibits schemes that target prior victims of telemarketing fraud. The act also requires telemarketers to state up front that they are making a sales call and what products or services are offered, to maintain a database of people who have asked not to be called again, and to maintain a call log.

A major concern for those managing computer systems is the threat of intrusion by employees, competitors, and others. According to one survey, almost 60 percent of those organizations surveyed reported computer break-ins by hackers and competitors. The concern is that people might gain access to computer facilities, systems, software, and data to commit a variety of computer crimes, such as stealing data; damaging or vandalizing hardware, software, or data; using computer software illegally; or committing fraud.

Industrial espionage. The theft of organizational data by competitors is sometimes called **industrial espionage** or *economic espionage.* Foreign countries often conduct this type of espionage against U.S. companies. For example, Louis Freeh, FBI director, reported in 1996 that 23 countries were so engaged, including France, China, Canada, India, and Japan.[6] Some countries are known to be training agents specifically to be able to invade computer systems for industrial information.

Industrial spies may use a variety of computer systems as tools. For example, using an easily obtainable inexpensive scanner, spies can scan cellular conversations or data transfers. It is also easy for spies to tap into phone lines and snatch important

---

[6]R. Behar, "Who's Reading Your E-Mail?" *Fortune,* February 3, 1997, p. 64.

faxed documents. In some cases, hackers and spies gain their ideas and software tools from hacker Web sites on the Internet.

Any time a computer system provides dial-in access, that system is at risk of loss through unauthorized access and theft of data. Bruce Schneier, author of *E-mail Security*, says that "The only secure computer is one that is turned off, locked in a safe, and buried 20 feet down in a secret location—and I'm not completely confident of that one either."[7] When corporate employees use portable or notebook computers, spies can gain important information on the hard disks merely by stealing the computers. When employees are connected to networks, including the Internet, risks rise. Experts usually recommend that dial-in access be limited, that executives avoid toting portables or notebooks with valuable data unless absolutely necessary, and that all data stored on mobile computer systems and sent over communications systems be encrypted.

Hacking. **Hacking** sometimes called cracking because the person cracks the log-in codes and sequences of a system, is the unauthorized entry by a person into a computer system or network. **Hackers** (also called crackers), or people who illegally gain access to the computer systems, may simply enjoy the challenge of breaking into other computer systems and intend no harm. However, hackers also can insert viruses onto networks, steal data and software, damage data, or vandalize a system (see Manager's Memo 17–1).

In 1996 hackers invaded the U.S. Air Force Web site, as well as Web sites and systems at the Justice Department, NASA, and the CIA. The reason given for the Air Force Web site invasion, according to one of the hackers who did it, was to show how simple it is to break into government systems. In fact, one of the hackers was only 15 years old. The General Accounting Office reports that hackers attacked the Pentagon's networks 250,000 times last year. A hacker's magazine, *2600: The Hacker Quarterly,* recently provided step-by-step instructions that appeared to have been used to break into and disable New York's Public Access Networks Corporation, or PANIX. The attack issued 150 requests a second to the system and simply outran the system's ability to respond.

Toll fraud. Defrauding telephone companies out of long-distance toll charges has occurred for many years. Using slugs instead of real coins, letting the phone ring twice to mean you got home OK, and calling person-to-person for yourself with some cute message are all ways that people have swindled common carriers out of toll charges that were rightly theirs.[8]

Today's phone thieves, however, are big time, and they target organizations other than telephone companies. The national **toll fraud** bill to private or public organizations in the United States is estimated to be in the billions. That's a lot of slugs. Toll fraud thieves now use electronic means to gain free access to an organization's long-distance lines. Then they may sell the access codes or the use of the codes to others. For example, when the president of Alexon, a biomedical company located in California, examined the firm's monthly phone bill, he was astonished to find that the normal monthly bill of $1,000 had jumped to $42,000. But the toll thieves were not yet through with his company. The next monthly bill was for $118,000. When the firm was finally able to deploy some protective measures, it had been defrauded out of more than $230,000. Toll thieves even penetrated the Drug Enforcement Agency's

[7] R. Behar, "Who's Reading Your E-Mail?" *Fortune,* February 3, 1997, p. 58.
[8] T. Emma, "For Whom the Fraud Tolls," *Telecome Reseller,* April–May, 1993, p. 17.

Manager's Memo 17–1	CRIMES OF CRACKERS AND OTHERS

▶ Criminals have been inventive in applying their skills to computer systems resulting in losses sustained by all types of organizations and people. Here are just a few crimes they commit.

Data diddling. *Data diddling* involves the use of a computer system by employees to forge documents or change data in records for personal gain. Alan Krull describes a clerk who promised utility customers with overdue bills to make their bills disappear for sums that were substantially smaller than the amounts they owed. The clerk then changed the accounts of the customers so that they were identified as bankrupt. The clerk eventually changed 10,000 accounts in the system.[1]

A new twist on data diddling involves the use of high-resolution scanners and laser printers to counterfeit bank checks. Many people are amazed at the high quality of output available from computer systems today. These same scanning and printing tools can be used for forgery and fraud. For example, when financial officials at American Micro Systems, Inc., checked their monthly bank statement recently, they found four fake checks. A criminal had scanned one of their checks into a computer system, altered the scanned image, and reproduced it on a laser printer.

Trojan horses. *Trojan horses* are unauthorized changes to program code. The code is called a Trojan horse because it appears to be performing a proper task but may actually perform a variety of mischievous or criminal activities, such as printing checks to employees or vendors who don't really exist or who don't work for or sell products to the firm. For example, a Trojan horse program disguising itself as "install.exe," a program used by many software companies to help users install their software, was attached to an America Online e-mail message that was circulating through the company worldwide network. When users tried to install a software package, the program crashed their hard drives.

Salami slicing. Like a Trojan horse, *salami slicing* is also unauthorized program code. However, this code is added to a system in order to steal very small amounts of money from many customer or vendor accounts. The amounts stolen may be the remainders from rounding operations. When you have millions of transactions, partial pennies soon mount.

Trap doors. *Trap doors* are procedures or code that allows a person to avoid the usual security procedures for use of or access to a system or data. Originally used for computer maintenance personnel to gain legitimate entrance to information systems, the same type of code can be used for theft of data, vandalism, or malicious mischief by the less scrupulous. Michael Major describes an incident in which a software company that had a disagreement with Revlon used a trap door to disable the software the software company had developed. The problem caused a partial shutdown at one of Revlon's major distribution centers for three days.[2]

Electronic warfare. Criminals bent on shutting down your organization can employ various forms of *electronic warfare*. For example microwave "guns" called HERFs, for high-energy radio frequency guns, can shut down your computer system temporarily or permanently if they have sufficient energy. Other electronic warfare weapons are electronic magnetic pulse/transformer bombs, or EMPTYs. These devices, if they go off near a computer system, can erase the computer's memory.

Logic bombs. A *logic bomb* is code that a developer embeds in a program that he or she can set off if the customer fails to pay for the program.

Email bombs. *E-mail bombs* fill your in-box with hundreds or thousands of unwanted messages. In 1996 a student at a New Jersey college bombed university officials with more than 24,000 e-mail messages. Even President Clinton has received e-mail bombs. If one invades your in-box, call your Internet service provider, who will attempt to locate the source and take corrective action. Also, your ISP should be using e-mail filtering software to screen e-mail bombs from known senders.

[1] A. Krull, "Computer Rip-Offs and Foul-Ups: Is Management to Blame?" *edpacs (The EDP Audit, Control and Security Newsletter)*, May 1989, p. 10.

[2] M. J. Major, "Taking the Byte out of Crime: Computer Crime Statistics Vary as Much as the Types of Offenses Committed," *Midrange Systems*, March 23, 1993, p. 25.

phone system and stuck the taxpayers with a bill of about $2,000,000, some of which paid for calls to Colombia. You can only guess what transpired on those calls.

Toll hackers today are resourceful. They may use maintenance ports, modem pools, voice mail systems, automated attendants, or other facilities of the private branch exchanges (PBXs) that are the computerized telephone switches at customer sites. PBX manufacturers and common carriers are developing and implementing hardware and software devices that reduce toll fraud theft. In addition, hardware and software protection that reduces the risk of toll fraud substantially is available for any organization. However, preventive measures can never totally secure a communications system. Managers should be on the lookout for these signs of fraud:

- Numerous short calls.
- Simultaneous use of one telephone access code.
- Numerous calls after business hours.
- Large increases in direct inward system access dialing, or DISA.

DISA allows employees away from the office to dial into an organization and use the organization's telephone system features, including 800 lines and long-distance lines. To reduce toll fraud, managers might consider using access codes that require voice recognition or software that identifies the potential indicators of fraud mentioned in the preceding list.

Recently, phone thieves have been stealing the IDs of cell phones and then selling the IDs to others at low cost. The unlucky cell phoners then receive huge bills at the end of the month to places and people they never called. Some sophisticated authentication systems have been developed and put in place by the major phone companies to counter this scheme.

Computer viruses. Computer viruses have become a real threat to computer systems. Thousands of viruses exist, and hundreds more are being created each month. A study by the National Computer Security Association found that more than 60 percent of the computer users in their survey reported having experienced a virus on the system they were using. The Association estimates that viruses cost U.S. organizations about $5,000,000,000 in 1996.[9]

A **computer virus** is a hidden program that inserts itself into your computer system and forces the system to clone the virus. It can wreak havoc with your computer system. A virus can also travel from one computer to another over networks embedding itself in every system it touches. Sometimes a virus may disguise itself as a utility or other program. With names like alien, anthrax, and plague, viruses may simply play pranks by displaying messages on your screen. They also may cause serious damage by modifying your data, erasing files, or formatting disks. For example, the Michelangelo virus starts itself on March 6 of every year and wipes out the file allocation table on your hard drive. The file allocation table is essentially an index to the data on your drive. Without the index, your system cannot find your data.

Your computer system may become infected when you read your e-mail, download a program from a computer bulletin board, access a Web site, or copy a program or file from a floppy diskette to your system. You may download free public domain software from a Web or FTP site that ends up costing you a lot of money and time if the viruses it harbors ravage important data files. Because public domain software has been a source of viruses in the past, most publishers of public domain software take many precautions to be sure that the software they offer is free of viruses.

Some computer viruses can be pretty sophisticated. A virus might lie dormant until it can capture financial information and transmit the data to thieves. A virus might also provide a fake log-in screen in order to capture the IDs and passwords of

---

[9]S. Hanley, "Understanding Data Loss," *NetWare Solutions*, November 1996, p. 29.

Figure 17–4

Protecting your
computer system
from viruses

- Always get software, even commercial software, from sources you trust. A group of programmers in one country inserted virus code on diskettes containing illegally copied commercial programs that they sold to buyers in other countries.
- Assume that all floppy diskettes, even demonstration and commercial programs, are carrying viruses. Use a virus detection program to scan all floppy diskettes for viruses before you use them or load them. Some vendors of software place software returned by customers in shrink wrapped packages and resell or distribute them without checking the disks for viruses. If the seal has been broken on the software you receive, be especially wary.
- Avoid booting your system from a floppy drive. Do not borrow floppy diskettes from anyone. Floppy drives are a major source of computer viruses.
- Check new programs for viruses from a floppy diskette, not after they have been installed on your hard drive.
- Write-protect your systems and applications program diskettes so that they cannot be altered.
- Use only electronic bulletin board systems that check for viruses.
- Whenever your PC has been repaired or upgraded at the original vendor or a local PC store, scan your system for viruses.
- Buy antivirus software from vendors that update their software at least monthly because the many viruses created each month make antivirus software out of date quickly.
- Use more than one antivirus program. No single program can detect or protect against every virus.

users, especially of network supervisors who have near-total access to the systems. The virus then transmits the log-in data to the criminals. You can also use vaccination products, or **antivirus programs.** Antivirus programs may help in several ways: preventing a virus-laden file from being downloaded over a network, preventing the virus program from inserting itself in your system, detecting a virus program so you can take emergency action, and controlling the damage virus programs can do once they have been detected. For example, McAfee Associates produces a suite of antivirus programs and distributes them as shareware. One program usually runs when the system is booted and remains in the PC watching for viruses. Another program scans floppy disks for viruses, and a third program cleans the infected disks (see Figure 17–4).

Most security experts recommend that you use more than one antivirus program because few programs are able to detect all known viruses. You should also upgrade your antivirus software frequently to keep up with newly created viruses.

Hardware theft and vandalism.   Theft of hardware and damage from vandalism represent ever-present threats to organizations, especially when organizations employ easy-to-pilfer notebook computers and personal digital assistants. One estimate is that about 208,000 notebook computers were stolen in 1995, an increase of 39 percent over the previous year. The loss of the hardware is estimated to be $640,000,000, and that the real cost of the theft is many times the cost of the hardware because the systems, data, and programs must be replaced, which leads to substantial downtime for employees.[10] Theft of computer systems also presents problems because of the data that reside on the hard drives of the stolen systems. For example, these data may be critical competitively because they describe a product under development; sensitive

---

[10]Gambon, Jill, "Hold on to That Laptop!—Thieves Abound but Users Find Solutions," *Information Week,* May 13, 1996, p. 16.

Figure 17–5

Software piracy
and the copy cops

The SPA recommends that organizations take a number of steps to reduce or eliminate the illegal use of software. For example:

- Develop a software ethics code and software compliance program.
- Appoint a software manager to implement the ethics code and software policies and to monitor software license compliance.
- Store the original disks for software in a locked, secure place.
- Log all purchases and locations for software used in the organization.
- Audit your computer operations for violations of the software ethics code and license compliance program.
- Educate employees about license agreements, piracy, and the legal risks that violations cause the organization.

To counter software piracy, the SPA advertises regularly in computer journals and newspapers, provides speakers, and distributes leaflets and booklets. It also audits hundreds of schools, corporations, small businesses, organizations, and electronic bulletin boards each year. The SPA maintains an antipiracy hotline that individuals can use to report suspected illegal use of software.

To help organizations find out if they are violating the license agreements they have with software producers, the SPA created software called SPA Audit. The software permits organizations to inventory their software use and identify where they are in violation of their license agreements.

Source: Adapted from G. Lawton, "No Copying Allowed: The Software Publishers Association," *PC Today* 7, no. 3, March 1993, pp. 71–73; and P. Stephenson, "Negotiating a Cure for Viruses: What the Law Cannot Do," *LAN Times* 10, no. 8 September 6, 1993, p. 72.

because they include data about employees, customers, and vendors; or further damaging because they include IDs, passwords, and communication log-in codes.

Software piracy.   The Software Publishers Association (SPA) holds that "any reproduction of a copyright program is theft." That, of course, means that most people who copy programs from their organization for home use or who copy programs from friends are thieves. The SPA believes they are (see Figure 17–5). The SPA estimates that software thieves stole software valued at $13,200,000,000 in 1995 in the United States alone.

On an international scale, **software piracy** levies a much higher toll. In some countries, piracy is blatantly rampant. Peter Stephenson reports visiting a section of Hong Kong recently where copies of Windows, Lotus 1–2–3, and other software were being sold with mimeographed manuals for a few dollars.[11] An industry watchdog, the Business Software Alliance, estimates that 99 percent of the software used in Vietnam is illegal.[12]

Many people do not realize that when they acquire software they may not become the absolute owner of that software. Instead, they may be leasing the software, or they may be buying a license to use that software from the software producer. Software is usually licensed to an individual, to the computer on which it is loaded, or to a specified number of concurrent users. The license agreement usually specifies certain conditions under which the software can be used, on how many computers it can

---

[11]Peter Stephenson, "Negotiating a Cure for Viruses: What the Law Cannot Do," *LAN Times* 10, no. 8, (September 6, 1993), p. 72.

[12]Beth Davis, "Groups Gauge Value Of Pirated Software," *Information Week*, December 23, 1996, p. 26.

be loaded, how many copies may be made, or the maximum number of people permitted to use the software concurrently. Thus, if your division is bought by another company, the software on your computer systems may no longer be yours to use.

Managers must recognize that they jeopardize their organizations and themselves when they permit, either deliberately or by benign neglect, software piracy. Copying a program for use at home or for use on a machine for which it is not authorized is a crime. Discovery of the theft by groups such as the SPA may lead to major legal problems for the organization. It may also lead to the loss of the manager's job. Needless to say, software piracy is unethical.

Privacy violations.   *Privacy* has been defined as the capacity of individuals or organizations to control information about themselves. Privacy rights usually imply that the types and amounts of data that may be collected about individuals or organizations are limited; that individuals or organizations have the ability to access, examine, and correct the data stored about them; and that the disclosure, use, or dissemination of those data are restricted.

Violations to the privacy of records, especially records about people, may occur accidentally, through carelessness, or intentionally. Many organizations would like very much to secure the data about customers that other firms routinely keep. These data can be used for telemarketing and direct mail marketing. Data kept on customers, employees, and others is usually factual data, such as names, addresses, products purchased, and payments. However, some data may represent the opinions or remarks of others, for example, supervisory comments on employees or a creditor's remarks about a customer's credit capability. Ethical as well as legal questions have been raised about what kinds of information should be kept about people, what those data should be used for, and how the data should be distributed.

Privacy also extends to electronic mail messages. Organizations must ensure that employee e-mail is secure from the view of others. If certain e-mail is to be viewed by others, such as a supervisor, then the employees should be clearly warned in advance. A number of companies have been sued by former employees over the privacy of their e-mail messages. In general, courts have held that e-mail is the property of employers since it was created on employer time using employer resources.

Even the European Community (EC) has been forced to deal with the privacy issues involved in e-mail. EC members are developing policies that cover the transfer of personal information across the borders of the 12 member nations. Their rules cover not only e-mail but also EDI, or electronic data interchange, because it often contains personal information pertaining to financial accounts. The EC expects that American firms will implement rigid policies to protect e-mail messages. If that does not occur, U.S. firms may not be allowed to complete electronic business in the EC.

The rules currently under development are very stringent and treat as illegal nearly any transfer or commercial use of data about individuals without their prior consent. One proposed regulation would allow the EC to prohibit a company from transferring any electronic information into or out of the EC if that company does not have policies that meet the EC's standards. Because few companies in the United States have even considered policies surrounding the privacy of e-mail, such a provision would have drastic economic effects.

To ensure privacy, hardcopy output of sensitive reporting systems should be shredded and disks should be shredded or demagnetized before they are thrown in the trash. Hard disks should be demagnetized before computer systems are sent out for repair or sold as used equipment. For example, a man bought a used PC hard drive from a computer store in Edmonton, Alberta. After installing the drive, the man found all the personnel records of a provincial agency. The man could view salaries, supervisor evaluations, attendance, and other sensitive matters at his leisure. The government had traded in the equipment without erasing the disk's contents. There was quite an uproar when the story hit the papers. The government then ordered, as governments always seem to in these cases, a full investigation of the incident.

Automatic screen-blanking programs can also be used so that sensitive information is not exposed to anyone who happens to pass by a computer system that has been left running.

Program Bugs

A great deal of commercial software contains **bugs,** or defects, in programming code when the software is first offered for sale. After the software has been on the street for a few months, users usually discover the bugs and the software vendors provide "patches" to their code. These patches are often made available on the software vendors' electronic bulletin boards. Users can log in to the bulletin board and download the patches to their computer systems.

A recent example is the Microsoft Internet Explorer bug. Internet Explorer is Microsoft's Web browser software. After being on the market for some time, a serious flaw was discovered. The flaw would allow a person to create a hyperlink on a Web page that could ultimately activate a program on another person's hard drive as the person was viewing that Web page. That bug allowed unscrupulous people to do all kinds of things to your hard drive. Microsoft provided free patches to Internet Explorer users to fix the flaw.

Bugs vary in seriousness from those that crash your system when certain conditions are met to those that process data incorrectly, such as not calculating amounts correctly. To avoid getting buggy software and experiencing the various losses that the bugs can produce, many individuals and organizations make it a point to purchase software only after it has been on sale for quite a time and has evolved through more than the first version. Other organizations have extensive testing procedures that they use to test the software before they implement it generally in the organization. In any case most software licensing agreements stipulate that the vendor is not responsible for any errors, data loss, or other problems that the buyer encounters—so let the buyer beware.

Most commercial software is produced by software specialists with lots of experience in both the programming language and the business area for which the software is designed. It does not take much imagination to visualize the kinds of errors that might occur in the development of an in-house program designed by people who might have to wear many hats. Therefore, organizations need to develop quality control procedures to improve the reliability of the programs they develop.

A more recently noticed problem especially prevalent in in-house developed software, however, is the "bug" that has been built into many computer programs because the year field in these programs allowed only two digits (e.g., 96, 97, 98). The so-called year 2000 problem is a function of these older programs containing insufficient information to distinguish between the year 2000 and the year 1900 (see Manager's Memo 6–7). The bug has already produced problems for organizations that must calculate amounts for dates beyond the year 1999. A recent example was the premature release of prisoners whose prison time, according to computer calculations, were already up, even though their sentences should have kept them imprisoned for years to come.

PROTECTING INFORMATION SYSTEMS

As a manager you will need to identify potential risks and consider the use of controls for your information systems, including controls for your information systems facilities, your data, the communications systems you utilize, your applications, and even the applications development process itself.

Securing Information Systems Facilities

Facilities for information systems might include the buildings and rooms in which information systems are housed as well as the furniture, hardware, software, and documentation that make up the information systems. These facilities may place your organization at risk of potential loss from a number of common threats. When the probability of these threats becomes important to you, you must consider controlling the amount of loss your organization might suffer. Thus you will want to consider employing controls to prevent, reduce, or eliminate the threats or to reduce the loss that occurs if disaster actually strikes (see Figure 17–6).

Let's look at the security considerations that might be useful for a typical small business office facility. Sarah Weinstein is the manager of a branch office of the Teliram Corporation that has just opened in Orlando, Florida. The corporation provides consulting services in human resource management to organizations in northern Florida. The office consists of 10 employees: the manager, six consultants, a secretary, and two administrative assistants. Each employee has been given his or her own PC. The PCs are loaded with word processing and spreadsheet software. The consultants were given notebook computers so that they could take them on the road and prepare reports, budgets, and other documents easily. The office also has several dot-matrix printers and two laser printers. The hardware and software purchased so far have cost $35,000.

Sarah is concerned about the security of the PC investment the branch has made. As a result, she hires Nadeem Syed, an information systems security consultant, to review her computer facilities and recommend measures the company can take to reduce the risks. Nadeem spends some time at the branch office talking to employees and gathering data. Nadeem reviews the crime statistics for the part of the city in which the branch office is located, the current levels of fire and police protection, and the probabilities of other natural disasters. After the review, Nadeem believes that the major threats to the facilities are from fire, water damage, and theft; he suggests the following controls: (1) an alarm system for the doors and windows; (2) regular use of the keyboard locks that come with each desktop system during breaks, lunch, and closing hours; (3) password protection software that prevents use of any PC without keying in a password; (4) replacement-value insurance coverage for the hardware and software; (5) storage of the original software disks in a locked cabinet; (6) plastic covers for the systems to reduce dust in the machines and to prevent damage to the machines if the water sprinkler system is activated; (7) installation of deadbolt locks on all doors; and (8) installation of tie-down cables to lock the desktop computers to the desks. He recommends the cable system to reduce the number of machines that might be stolen while the police are enroute after a break-in.

For the notebook computers, Nadeem also recommends (1) training the consultants in the care and use of the systems, including not leaving them or data disks in a hot car during on-site visits, keeping them in their waterproof cases to prevent damage from rain, and storing disks properly, and (2) use of a cable locking system to secure the notebooks to the inside door armrests.

Figure 17–6

Information
systems facilities:
common threats
and controls

COMMON THREATS

- Earthquakes, hurricanes, tornadoes, and other storms.
- Fire and explosions.
- Power spikes, static electricity, power outages, and power overloads.
- Water damage from broken pipes or extinction of fires.
- Dust, smoke, heat, and humidity.
- Theft.
- Vandalism.
- Malicious damage by disgruntled employees.
- Industrial espionage.
- Unauthorized or illegal use of computer facilities.

COMMON CONTROLS

- Place systems on higher floors.
- Install water pumps and sump pumps.
- Arrange for backup facilities at another site.
- Buy insurance.
- Use special building-construction procedures.
- Store programs and data off-site.
- Install fire extinguishing systems and smoke detectors.
- Use noncombustible building materials.
- Provide security training for employees.
- Locate buildings close to a fire station or hydrants.
- Install surge protectors and antistatic mats.
- Install humidifiers.
- Install uninterruptible power supplies (batteries).
- Develop procedures for orderly shutdowns.
- Install dedicated power lines for major computer systems.
- Use waterproof covers for systems.
- Install air filters and air conditioning.
- Install window bars and deadbolt locks.
- Install alarm systems and closed-circuit TV cameras.
- Bolt equipment to desks.
- Hire security guards.
- Bond employees.
- Screen all job applicants.
- Develop procedures for identifying disgruntled employees.
- Use biological access controls.
- Use IDs, passwords, and PINs.
- Use a menu system to prevent use of the operating system so that files cannot be copied or deleted or the hard disk formatted.
- Lockout terminals in open areas and after hours.

Nadeem further recommends training for the entire staff in the use and abuse of software licenses. He believes that all employees should be instructed in the legal and ethical problems caused by software piracy.

In addition, Nadeem recommends that the firm develop a **disaster recovery plan,** which would consider how it would continue business if a disaster occurred and the computer facilities were destroyed or were inoperable for some time. With Nadeem's help, the firm examined some of its choices. Teliram could develop a **hot site** at which it could have identical computer facilities already loaded with its software so that the company could be up and running within a day or two. Or Teliram could make an agreement with a disaster recovery firm for hot site facilities. It could also develop a **cold site,** which would merely provide space and furniture at another location. The cold site would not be equipped with computers and software ready to go. Instead, the firm would rent the computer systems, install the software from the original diskettes, and load the firm's data files from the archive copies onto the systems. It would take longer to resume business at the cold site, but it would cost little more than rent in the meantime. Because the parent company had unused space on the third floor of a building on the other side of town, Sarah decided to go with a cold site disaster plan.

Securing Communications Systems

Communications systems provide many benefits for users, such as the ability to share data and printers. They also, however, present additional risks to the security of information systems (see Figure 17-7). The recent growth of the Internet, extranets, and intranets has placed many more systems at risk. Many firms have been scrambling to protect their networks against a swarm of hackers, competitors, and criminals both external and internal.

Encryption.   A major tool for protecting information systems, especially communications systems, is **encryption,** or the process of encoding data. Using encryption software, companies can scramble and encode e-mail messages, files, and other data so that they become unintelligible to anyone without proper authority to view the data. To reduce the risk of intrusion still further, all transmissions can be encrypted, including log-in IDs and passwords.

The United States has become a leader in encryption technology, and many firms would like to export encryption systems. However, they are prohibited from exporting the best of the lot because of U.S. government policy. The whole debate is about the "keys" that are used to encode and decode encrypted messages. The longer the key, the more difficult it is to break the encryption code. The White House doesn't want industry to export long-key systems. Analysts estimate that the export business could reach $60,000,000,000 in annual revenues and that foreign firms will reap those rewards if U.S. firms are hobbled indefinitely. Meanwhile, foreign competitors are allowed to sell long- or short-key systems not only abroad but also in the United States.

Export of encryption systems is not the only encryption issue in which the U.S. government, the private sector, and others are clashing (see Manager's Memo 17-2).

Electronic-commerce safety.   Many consumers believe that on-line purchasing by credit card is not as safe as purchasing something by credit card over the phone or through the mail. The accuracy of that perception is debatable. However, for electronic shopping and commerce to become widespread, electronic vendors must assure potential shoppers that their transactions are secure and tamperproof. Few people are willing to enter their credit card number to purchase a product on-line unless they are reasonably certain that no one can steal the number.

Another application of encryption is the encoding of order information, including the credit card numbers, sent by on-line shoppers. Encryption has become one method that electronic vendors use to provide the levels of safety that on-line shoppers and bankers demand.

Figure 17–7

Communications systems: common threats and controls

COMMON THREATS

- Incorrect or partial data received because of transmission errors or line failures.
- Loss of business from downed systems or downed lines.
- Loss of systems from overwhelming number of packets received.
- Intrusion by unauthorized persons.
- Intrusion by viruses and unwanted programs.
- Incorrect routing and receipt of data by unauthorized person.
- Signal interception.
- Poor network performance.
- Unnecessary communication lines.
- Slow communication lines.

COMMON CONTROLS

- Line conditioning and line shielding.
- Error detection and correction methods.
- Redundant lines and backup transmission lines.
- Archived files.
- Firewalls.
- Auditing software.
- Insurance to cover loss of business.
- Log of hardware and line failures on system.
- User IDs, passwords, and PINs.
- Modem dial-back.
- Use of nonradiating media.
- Access logs of users and terminals, including invalid access logs.
- Lockout of terminals after hours or after *x* number of failed log-in attempts.
- Encryption of transmitted passwords.
- Encrypted data transmission.
- Restricting access to other networks, file directories, and files.
- Locating terminals in secure areas.
- Training communications employees.
- Use of network management, diagnosis, and planning software.
- Enforcing information systems compatibility standards.

Firewalls.   When an organization connects to external networks, including the Internet, it provides many avenues for employees to find data vital to the organization's competitiveness. It also allows easy connectivity for partners and customers. However, connectivity also increases the risks that an organization's internal information systems will be accessed by intruders, invaded by viruses, or otherwise compromised. To reduce these risks from external sources, many firms use **firewalls.**

Firewall protection systems monitor all Internet or external communications activity at a site, closing all connection attempts from unauthorized users. Many also provide activity logs that can be used to identify intruders. Some also examine all programs and files that are downloaded to a company's network, looking for viruses and making sure that the users who are downloading the files and programs have the authority to do so. Firewalls can also look out for and block "denial of service" attacks. These are devices crackers use to flood a Web site with transmission packets and bring it to its knees, denying service to legitimate users.

Manager's Memo 17–2 | ## THE ENCRYPTION STANDARDS ISSUE

▶ The Department of Justice and the FBI have developed an encryption proposal that would require these steps from communications systems and service firms:

1. Ensuring that data and voice systems could be tapped by law enforcement agencies without having to decrypt the data.

2. Permitting the wiretaps to be implemented from remote locations, such as an FBI office.

3. Providing to law enforcement agencies selected real-time transmissions to and from people named in court orders obtained by the agencies.

Failure to cooperate could result in a $10,000 a day fine to a firm. As you might expect, neither communications firms nor civil rights groups are supporting the proposal.

The proposal results from the fact that recent digital transmission technology and fiber optic systems are not as amenable to tapping as previous communications systems. Law enforcement agencies fear losing the wire tap weapon in the fight against crime. It appears that the proposal will not give any greater rights to law enforcement agencies to conduct electronic surveillance of people than they already have under existing laws. It does give them greater rights in the collection of that information, however.

Liberals *and* conservatives in Congress have joined industry lobbyists to oppose the legislation. This legislative proposal is also likely to create real problems for international communications and trade. As you might expect, foreign governments do not like the idea of the U.S. government having the capacity to intercept and decode communications between their countries and U.S. embassies. Foreign firms don't like the idea of the U.S. government gaining access to their trade secrets or competitive plans.

At this writing, a compromise was put forth by the White House via an executive order that would permit the export of long-key encryption systems with some conditions that permit the government to obtain the keys to access the encrypted messages. Private industry would hold the keys, which government bodies could access only with a search warrant or similar legal support. However, a federal judge has already ruled that parts of the policy are unconstitutional, and Congress has proposed at least two laws to redefine U.S. policy.

We can expect a continuing debate on this policy as our nation continues to consider the complex ethical and legal issues that surround balancing citizens' rights to privacy and the public good in the age of technology.

Network auditing software. Ernst and Young Information Security Services reported the results of a survey showing that about 14 percent of security losses for most organizations occurred from external sources, 19 percent from hackers within the firms, and 43 percent from simple employee errors.[13] Given the large number of security problems occurring from internal sources, simply adding a firewall to your network is clearly not enough to safeguard your data.

Enter **network auditing software.** Network auditing software can identify and prevent many types of problems in local or wide area networks. The software is usually of two types: activity logs, which record all log-in attempts, failed or successful, and network scanning software, which looks for flaws or holes in network security.

Protecting communications systems assets means ensuring your system's confidentiality, integrity, and availability. Thus you should try to ensure that only authorized users can gain access to the data they are permitted to view or use, that programs and data cannot be tampered with, and that the communications system is reliable—that is, it remains up and running. To give you an idea of the planning issues involved, let's revisit Sarah Weinstein.

The management information systems group at Teliram has recently cabled the PCs in Sarah's branch office into a local area network so that files and printers could

---

[13]J. Bort, "When Firewalls Aren't Enough," *Client/Server Computing,* May 1996, p. 41.

Figure 17–8

How to manage your password

Managing the passwords of your employees is important. Intrusion Detection, Inc., recently surveyed more than 170 organizations for security vulnerabilities. It found that 85 percent of the users were not required to change their passwords frequently, 23 percent had easy-to-guess passwords, 21 percent had no passwords at all, and 14 percent of the IDs were inactive.[1] Some recommendations for managing passwords are:

1. Change your passwords often. Changing your password once a month is effective in many work situations.

2. Use a long password rather than a short one. If your system allows you to choose an eight-character password, create a password of eight digits. Short passwords are easier to uncover.

3. Don't use dictionary words, especially words that can be found in on-line dictionaries, thesauruses, and spell checkers. Intruders can use these programs to discover your password.

4. Don't use passwords made up of personally traceable characters, such as your initials, birthday, spouses's name, and street address. An intruder who knows you will quickly try these characters.

5. Create passwords composed of random characters with no meaning—for example, 2A0PQ7RT9. Such a password may be harder to remember, but it is also harder to discover. An intruder may simply use Crack, a public shareware program that helps "crack" your password.

6. Keep your password private. Don't share your password with your workmates or keep a note with the password on it in an obvious place, such as a desk drawer.

7. Do not recycle old passwords from previous years. Install a password system that logs all the passwords you have used and prevents you from using old passwords.

[1]M. Wagner and G. H. Anthes, "Underground Tools Aid Fledgling Hackers," *Computerworld*," November 13, 1995, p. 1.

be shared and an electronic mail system could be installed. In addition, the MIS group equipped the consultants' notebooks with modems and communications software so that they could connect to the office file server and use the electronic mail system from clients' sites. After discussing the new systems with Sarah, the MIS group recommended and later installed a number of security measures to reduce the risks posed by the new communications systems. For example, one concern was that the files of an employee stored on the file server of the local area network might be accessed by other employees who were not authorized to access those files. Thus an administrative assistant who was authorized to work on one client's files should not be able to access the files of other clients. Sarah believed that Teliram's clients had the right to expect that data on their organizations would be kept from the prying eyes of those who had no need to view the data. As a result, the MIS group set up IDs for each user and associated access rights to folders or directories on the file server with these IDs. MIS gave all employees exclusive access rights to their own subdirectories so that these employees could store information in their own directories privately. MIS also created subdirectories for the clients of the branch office and gave rights to these directories to the Teliram employees who were involved with those clients' contracts.

Furthermore, any user who wishes to use the services of the local area network must key in a valid password. The password is designed to keep nonemployees off the network, whether the nonemployee attempts to gain access in the branch office or from a remote computer system. The system requires employees to change their passwords every month. The MIS group also recommended that employees be warned to choose passwords that would not be obvious to intruders (see Figure 17–8). Finally, the MIS group used the local area network software to restrict log-in attempts to three so that an intruder would have to guess the correct ID and password within three tries or the terminal would be locked. Additional security provisions were considered for remote users. For example, one way to increase security for users accessing a computer system through a remote modem is to require the called modem to call the remote modem back. This **dial-back** procedure ensures that connections are made only to preauthorized locations. However, because the consultants frequently move from client to client, this call-back security procedure was not implemented. Instead, to ensure the safety of private, client information, the MIS group installed encryption-decryption software on the file server of the local area network and the notebook computers. In that way all transmissions are coded before they are sent. The receiving computer then decodes the messages. To further improve security for remote users, the remote users' IDs and passwords are also encrypted before they are sent to the file server.

The MIS group also used the local area network software to restrict access by users to the local area network by time. That is, they restricted each user to certain time periods in the day and evening. For example, the secretary and administrative assistants were given restricted access to the local area network from 8:00 A.M. to 5:00 P.M. Because the manager and consultants frequently work in the evenings and weekends, their access was not restricted to the normal workday. The MIS group also used the local area network software to create access logs or audit trails and trained the manager to print them out. They recommended that she examine the access logs regularly to detect unauthorized use, inappropriate use, or illegal attempts to gain access to the local area network.

Additionally, an antivirus program designed for a network was placed on the local area network. A virus scanning program was loaded onto each workstation, and the importance of virus protection was explained to each user. As policy, users were required to scan any floppy diskettes before they used them or stored their contents on the local area network file server. A software metering program was placed on the local area network to ensure that no more than the maximum number of authorized users used certain software at the same time. The software is designed to prevent violations of software licensing agreements. Finally, the MIS group recommended that Sarah develop an e-mail privacy policy that would prevent ordinary users and so-called superusers, or users whose password allows them total access to the network, from reading, copying, or otherwise interfering with the privacy of e-mail messages.

Teliram plans to provide Internet access for all employees so that they can send e-mail to and receive e-mail from vendors and customers and search the Web for information, such as information about competitors. Sarah wants to be as sure as possible that Internet access will not open Teliram's computer system to hackers, competitors, and criminals. The MIS group suggests acquiring a firewall system to connect the local area network to the Internet. The firewall system will prevent unauthorized users from entering the LAN from the outside and protect against Internet-born vandalism, industrial espionage, and other problems.

Securing Database Information Systems

Massive amounts of organizational data are stored today in electronic databases on computer systems. Consider the importance of the financial accounting database information stored on computer systems. Providing security for an organization's database information systems is usually critical to its survival. If an organization's accounts payable information is lost or destroyed, it is unlikely that the organization will be able to forget its debts to others. However, if accounts receivable information is lost or destroyed, a company is likely to lose a substantial amount of the revenue these accounts represent. An Ontario company recently charged a former employee with stealing the firm's entire customer database and using it to start a competing business. The theft, which was not then considered a crime in Ontario, was discovered when a mailing label was received by a spouse of another employee who recognized the label by its typographical errors.

Organizational databases also store important information about people: employees, customers, vendors, and creditors. It is both legally necessary and ethically proper to safeguard this information from prying eyes (see Figure 17-9).

Other information about the organization should also be kept secret. For example, financial information must be restricted to authorized personnel to prevent others from gaining information that might give them an unfair advantage in trading the organization's securities. Marketing and product information must be secured so that the tactical and strategic plans of the organization do not fall into the hands of competitors. When database data are restricted to authorized personnel, they are called **trusted systems.** Many client/server database vendors have begun to ship trusted versions of their database systems. These versions permit systems developers to keep unauthorized personnel from sensitive files, typically through log-in procedures, access rights, and audit trails, all of which have already been discussed.

Securing data from prying eyes is only one consideration, however, for the protection of databases. Many other security considerations are important, too (see Figure 17-10). Let's look in on Sarah Weinstein again and see how her firm is handling database security.

A number of important files are housed on the file server. Some of these files are sensitive and contain information about clients, employees, and vendors. Some of the files also contain information about the firm's strategic plans for marketing and growth. Sarah is concerned about the security of these files. She knows that IDs and passwords are required to gain access to the files on the server. She also knows that the files are protected against viruses through virus protection software and organization policies and that any data downloaded to consultant notebooks will be

---

Figure 17–9

Guidelines for database privacy

In 1973 the U.S. Department of Health, Education, and Welfare, through its Committee on Automated Personal Data Systems, published guidelines for handling information about people called the Code of Fair Information Practices. These guidelines are not law, but they do help the manager who is trying to store and use information about people in an ethical and legal manner. The guidelines suggest the following:

1. No secret files or databases about people should be created or allowed to exist in an organization.

2. Using information about people for other than its original purpose should not be permitted without the consent of the people themselves. Thus accounts receivable data about customers should not be sold to other organizations to use for direct mail advertising without the prior consent of the customers.

3. The people should have access to their records.

4. A procedure for amending or correcting records should be established, and this procedure should be communicated to the people whose records are being kept.

5. Every attempt should be made to ensure the accuracy of the data.

6. Every attempt should be made to prohibit unauthorized access or use of the data.

Source: Adapted from D. Van Kirk, "IS Managers Must Keep Customer Data Secure," *InfoWorld* 15, no. 11, March 15, 1993, p. 64.

Figure 17–10

Database
management
systems: common
threats and
controls

COMMON THREATS

- Loss or corruption of data by disgruntled employee.
- Loss or corruption of data by poorly trained employee.
- Loss or corruption of data by viruses.
- Theft of data by competitor or criminal.
- Malicious vandalism of data.
- Unauthorized access or loss of confidentiality of sensitive data.
- Embezzlement.
- Loss of data consistency from incomplete updates made to redundant or distributed data.

COMMON CONTROLS

- Physical facilities controls (see Figure 17–6).
- Antivirus software.
- Restart and recovery systems for disk failure.
- Backup copies of data and transaction logs.
- Off-site storage of archived media.
- Concurrency protection.
- Appointing a database administrator.
- Restricting record deletion and update authority.
- Maintaining deletion and update audit trails.
- Validating data input.
- Insurance to cover loss of business and re-creation of data.
- ID and password database, directory, file, and record access controls.
- Employee screening and bonding.
- Limiting physical access to database.
- Enforcing employee vacations.
- Encryption.
- Database access logs, including sensitive file access logs.
- Disk, file, and volume labels.

somewhat protected by the encryption system and the antitheft procedures of the organization. She still feels apprehensive, however, and decides to call in Nadeem Syed again for security advice.

Nadeem suggests that Sarah could take a number of precautions to increase the security of data on the local area network, the PC workstations, and the mobile notebooks. He recommends installing a tape drive and software on the file server so that the contents of the file server can be regularly archived to tape. He also recommends that one person be charged with this file server task and that Sarah should store the updated tape each day in a safe deposit box at the local bank, which is on the same block as the office. He also recommends that each workstation upload any workstation-specific files to the server daily for storage. He will write a simple "batch" program to perform that task automatically so that the tape drive system will provide archive copies of important data files stored on workstations as well as those ordinarily stored on the server. Furthermore, the program will eliminate the need to remind employees to back up their drives in order to prevent data loss (see Figure 17–11).

Nadeem is also concerned about disk failure on the file server and the impact on the business when important files are unavailable. He suggests installing a **disk duplexing system.** The disk duplexing system would require adding a second hard disk and hard disk controller to the server and installing software that will simultane-

Figure 17–11
Five major causes
of data loss

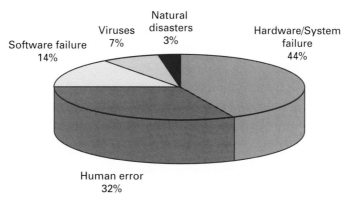

Source: Document Manager, Business and Technical Communications Ltd., March 1996 (on-line document: http://www.ltl.co.uk/disrec.html).

ously duplicate all writes to the original hard disk to the second hard disk. Thus the second hard disk will be a mirror image of the original hard disk. The software also switches from one disk drive to another in the event of a disk failure. The system would allow the business to continue to operate even if one of the hard disks or one of the disk controllers failed.

Nadeem also recommended purchasing an **uninterruptable power supply (UPS)** system for the file server. The UPS is a battery system that maintains power to a computer system in the event of a power failure, brownout, or serious reduction in power. If a power failure occurs, the file server can be shut down carefully to avoid any loss or corruption of data.

Securing Information Systems Applications

An important method of preventing security problems is to acquire secure applications or to build them from the ground up. Paying careful attention at the software acquisition stage or development stage can reduce or eliminate many security problems that might prove very difficult to find later on.

The make or buy decision. Before software is developed in-house, it is important to consider other design options. One important design option is the **make or buy decision.** For example, is thoroughly tested commercial software available to do the job? How does the cost of the commercial software compare with the expected cost of developing the same software in-house? Does the commercially available software fit the organization's needs? Often, software is cheaper to buy than to develop because the development costs of commercial software are spread over many companies. Commercial software also can be installed and implemented faster than software that is developed in-house from scratch. Because a commercial software company may specialize in particular types of software, its personnel are likely to be more experienced or expert in the software than are the information systems personnel at a company.

There are also potential problems with the buy decision. What does your firm do if the software vendor goes out of business? If you were dependent on the vendor for software maintenance and upgrades, how will you maintain and upgrade the software? Will the company allow you to purchase the source code (see Chapter 6) for the product so that you can have your MIS department or a consultant maintain and upgrade the software? What happens if your software vendor is purchased by a competitor? Will you feel secure allowing the competitor to maintain and upgrade your software? What happens if a dispute develops between your company and the vendor who developed and is maintaining your software?

Testing software.   If a company wants to consider buying commercial software, then the available software should be evaluated. Suggestions for evaluating commercial software are presented in Chapter 6. The commercial products that survive the evaluation process should then be tested thoroughly for appropriateness, stability, and security.

Appropriateness.   The software's appropriateness to the task to be performed should be evaluated. For example, some people spend inordinate amounts of time creating invoices, payroll registers, and other accounting forms using spreadsheet software. Spreadsheet software, however, was not really designed for transaction-processing financial information systems such as payroll and accounts receivable invoicing. Furthermore, each spreadsheet application is likely to be an island of data. That is, it is not likely that the various spreadsheet applications would be integrated so as to produce reports such as an income statement, sources and uses of funds, and a balance sheet. The appropriate software for this type of job is a comprehensive, integrated, financial accounting package that contains software modules pertinent to the task, such as accounts receivable and payroll, and also contains a general ledger module that produces financial statements.

Stability.   The software should be thoroughly tested to make certain at the very least that it is stable and doesn't crash the systems on which it runs. Some software and some hardware may not be compatible. You should test the software on *all* the computing platforms on which you plan to run it. For example, a university academic computing organization upgraded its Lotus spreadsheet program from one version to another. It tested the new version on one popular brand of microcomputers it had in some of its laboratories. The software ran fine on this computing platform. However, the new version froze up after students used the software for a certain length of time on another brand of popular microcomputers. The example illustrates that problems can arise even when highly reputable and popular software and hardware are used. Thorough testing is the only way to reduce or avoid these problems.

Security features.   The software's security features should be compared to the security features the application needs. For example, does the software provide automatic backup copies of documents, encryption and decryption, password protection, and the like?

When software is developed in-house, it is important to use or implant security measures into applications when they are developed. Thus an important part of information systems security should be implemented by systems analysts and programmers when they create, test, and debug programs. These developers might be assisted by an EDP auditor from the organization or from the outside who reviews the work of the developers at key stages of the development process. Some security measures might include the review of software code by several people and the use of structured design techniques for analyzing the business problem and designing the software. Another measure might include fully documenting programs so that future programmers can update the code without introducing errors into the software. Still another measure might include using external organizations, such as quality control firms, to complete quality control audits.

Access and update security.   Other important security measures surround access to and the right to update existing software. It is important to prevent unauthorized access and updates to current programs. Unrestricted access and update capability would allow programmers or others to change programs, permitting fraud or theft.

For example, an unscrupulous programmer might add code to a payroll program to send a paycheck to a fictitious person at a drop box. To ensure that access and update controls have been working, it is also important to store copies of the current software in a secure place and to check regularly the copies used to run applications for changes in size. You should also conduct regular comparisons of code and regular executions of the run copies of software using test data to ensure that no unwarranted changes are made in the software.

Input controls. At the home office of Teliram, the MIS department employs a number of development techniques to ensure the realibility and accuracy of the applications they create. Staff members also test commercial software to see if the programs contain similar techniques.

The techniques that the MIS department uses include **data validation,** or input controls. **GIGO** is an old information systems term that means **garbage in, garbage out.** The point of the term is that you must ensure accurate input if you wish to generate accurate output. **Input controls** are designed to prevent bad data from being entered into a program or a database. They are also used to prevent accurate data from being overlooked and not entered at all. Errors are identified at the source of data entry and eliminated if possible.

Careful programmers can use many input controls to reduce or prevent the chance of someone keying in inaccurate data, entering data for a record twice, or failing to enter data at all (see Figure 17–12).

Manual procedures and management policies can also be used to prevent or reduce input errors. For example, management might insist that personnel rotate jobs, take vacations, and segregate duties to prevent fraud or embezzlement.

Figure 17–12

Some input or data validation controls

- **Field type checks.** Data entered into a field are limited to certain types. For example, data entered into an hourly pay rate field must be numeric. Alphabetic letters or special symbols are not permitted.

- **Sign checks.** Data entered into a field are limited to positive or negative numbers. For example, negative pay rates are not permitted.

- **Field length checks.** Data entered into a field are limited to a certain number of digits or characters. For example, pay rates beyond five characters (99.99) may not be permitted.

- **Completeness checks.** Data must be entered into a field. The data entry clerk cannot continue entering data until data are entered in a certain field. For example, hourly pay rates or other data about an employee may not be entered into the employee record until the employee number field is completed.

- **Logic checks.** Data that are inconsistent with other data in a record are identified and prevented from being entered. For example, the entry of commissions earned into clerical employee records might be prevented, and the date entered into an employee termination date field must be later than the date entered into the employee's date of initial employment field.

- **File comparison checks.** Data entered must agree with data in certain files. For example, an employee number may not be entered in a payroll program unless that number already exists in an employee number file. This check prevents a person from paying fictitious employees.

- **Range or limit checks.** Data entered in a field must not be over a certain amount or must fall within a certain range of values. For example, hourly pay rate exceeding $80 an hour may not be accepted by the program. In fact, if employees are paid between $5 and $80 an hour, the data entered in a pay rate field must fall within that range or not be accepted.

- **File label checks.** All data files are labeled and programs that use these files include checks to see if the correct data diskette, data file, or data tape has been loaded.

Procedures can also be used to prevent input errors. For example, a sales order clerk might count the number of orders entered during a day and compare that sum with the number the sales order program says the clerk has entered. This procedure is called taking a **record count.** The clerk might also manually total the sales orders entered and verify that sum with the total sales orders the sales order program says have been entered. This procedure is called taking a **batch total.** Both record counts and batch totals are called **batch control** procedures. That is, totals or counts on an entire batch of source documents are compared with totals or counts generated by the application program.

Another batch control is the **hash total.** A *hash total* is a total that doesn't make any real sense but allows the data entry clerk to find out if the clerk has omitted a source document, entered one twice, or entered an important number incorrectly. For example, a payroll clerk might sum the employee numbers on the time cards being recorded. This sum will be compared to the sum generated by the payroll program, which also sums the employee numbers. If the amounts are different, the clerk may have entered an employee number incorrectly, left a time card out entirely, or keyed in one twice.

Process controls.   Processing errors may occur because of faulty logic in a program, incomplete transactions, or other events. For example, an auditor examining the water bills for a small town discovered that almost all the billed amounts were incorrect by a cent. When programmers examined the programming code, they discovered that the program had incorrectly rounded amounts that resulted when water usage amounts were multiplied by water rate amounts. The billing errors caused more than a little embarrassment to the city and the programmers. The auditor insisted on all payments being corrected. To correct errors of only a few cents per customer, the city had to spend several dollars per customer generating new bills, mailing them, and updating and correcting accounts.

The Teliram application developers include **process controls** to ensure the reliability and accuracy of the programs they develop. They also test commercial software for the presence of process controls. For example, when records entered cannot be processed because they contain errors or missing calculations, or for some other reason, **exception reports** list each transaction that failed to be processed. This report ensures that bad data or records are identified and allows the firm to correct them. To reduce the possibility that reports are generated before all records are processed, the developers insert **end-of-file checks** into their programs. Processing does not cease until all records are processed. To prevent certain processing from occurring on data out of order, they implant **sequence checks** in their programs.

Teliram developers also ensure that any transactions that are incompletely posted, perhaps because of a processing error or perhaps because of a power shortage, are identified. They also prevent processing errors by locking certain fields and records when they are being updated by one person to prevent others from updating the same records concurrently.

To test the programs they develop and the commercial programs they acquire, Teliram developers enter past data and compare the output from the new program with that of the old program or old manual procedure. Entering past payroll data, or a portion of those data, and then comparing new program output to old reports allows the developers to verify the accuracy of a payroll program.

In some cases, Teliram uses an outside software testing and quality control firm to verify the accuracy of the developers' work.

Output controls. Another security issue is protecting the hard copy output of computer applications. If the printouts of payroll files and other sensitive files are not protected, securing access to the data files or the machines that store the files may be futile. Typical **output controls** include the use of routing sheets to ensure that printouts only go to authorized persons. Shredding sensitive printouts when their useful life is over and storing sensitive printouts in locked cabinets or drawers are other safeguards that keep the data from falling into the wrong hands.

Outputs stored on disk or paper should be cleaned out regularly. Stored documents should be regularly scanned for destruction or transfer to other media. However, many businesses must retain records for long periods of time for operational needs, for legal protection, or to meet statutory requirements. To avoid destroying important documents before their legal or operational time periods are over, most firms establish a document or file **retention schedule.** The retention schedule for documents and files should conform to common practice, laws, and statutes.

ETHICAL ISSUES AND INFORMATION SYSTEMS

Information systems have become ubiquitous. People as well as organizations have come to depend on them not only for success and survival, but also for the conduct of everyday transactions and activities. Computer systems have invaded nearly every aspect of our daily lives. As information technology advances, it creates a continuing stream of new issues pertaining to those parts of our lives that it impacts. In the business arena, information technology has presented ethical issues in four areas. These areas, identified by Richard Mason, are privacy, property, accuracy, and access.[14] In addition, ethical issues surround the impact information technology has on us all.

Ethical and Contractual Behavior

Ethics may be defined as the study of the general nature of morals and of the specific moral choices to be made by an individual. Put somewhat differently, ethics can be viewed as the moral quality of a course of action.[15] However, what many people regard as ethical or unethical behavior pertaining to computer systems is often in reality legal or illegal behavior or behavior that is or isn't in violation of a contract. That is, when a person makes a copy of copyrighted software from his firm's computer system for use at home, that is unethical behavior. It is also illegal behavior and still further a violation of most software contracts. Thus a good part of behaving ethically is behaving legally and contractually, and much of the previous discussion in this chapter should be considered a discussion of ethical behavior. However, many ethical issues extend beyond the law and compel individuals to consider what is right, not just what is legal.

Privacy, Access, and Accuracy Issues

It is not illegal to view the electronic mail messages of employees produced and stored on a private, company-owned electronic mail system. However, the ethical considerations surrounding the invasion of the privacy of others would surely make most people pause and reflect about doing it. Organizations that do review the electronic mail of their employees may claim they have legitimate reasons for doing so. For

---

[14] R. Mason, "Four Ethical Issues of the Information Age," reprinted from *MIS Quarterly,* in R. Dejoie, G. Fowler, and D. Paradice, *Ethical Issues in Information Systems,* Boston: Boyd and Fraser, 1991.

[15] W. Morris, ed., *The American Heritage Dictionary of the English Language,* New York: The American Heritage Publishing Co., 1971.

example, organizations may have reason to believe that employees are selling trade secrets to competitors, or they may suspect that certain managers are engaging in biased behavior toward peers and subordinates. Organizations may take the position that electronic mail is produced on the organization's time and using the organization's resources and is thus organization property. They might further claim that if the notes, letters, and memos written using electronic means were prepared in the traditional paper-and-pencil manner, these documents would have been stored in the organization's files and would have been subject to review by appropriate organization personnel.

The caller ID feature of modern telephone systems is another example of the mixed blessing of technological advance. Caller ID permits better levels of customer service because it allows computer systems to identify callers and bring up their files on a customer representative's screen as the call is being answered. Caller ID can also severely reduce crank, harassing, and obscene calls. However, with caller ID anonymous calls to the police to provide leads to crimes are impossible. Likewise, people who have unlisted numbers may lose that privacy each time they make a telephone call.

The area of databases abounds with privacy issues. Consider these questions:

1. *What information on individuals and other organizations should any organization have the right to keep?* Although address and billing data seem like pretty safe bets for customers, what about salespeople's personal comments about customers? What about the personal opinions of purchasing agents about vendors when these data may influence credit ratings or bid acceptances? Many marketing organizations today are developing customer databases with an eye to identifying and serving customer needs better. However, the data gathered by such organizations may also intrude on customer privacy. Fingerhut, a large mail-order firm that targets households with annual incomes of less than $25,000, maintains a database of about 1,400 items of information on customers, including annual income; home ownership; appliance ownership; purchasing history of products by product types; the name, age, and sex of each occupant; and the credit history of households with the firm. It uses the data to identify customers likely to respond to certain promotions, purchase certain merchandise, or use certain credit terms. The company then targets individual customers for direct mailings and even individualizes the catalogs that are mailed to customers. (See Manager's Memo 17–3).

2. *What rights should these individuals and organizations have about the use to which these data are put?* A major bank may have narrowly avoided tremendous adverse publicity when a marketing department executive asked an IS executive for income and loan data in the bank's mortgage application file. The use of the information was not illegal, but others in the organization felt that it would have violated the privacy of many of the bank's customers and would have led to a loss of confidence in the bank. The company subsequently disallowed the use of these data by the marketing department. Lotus Corporation developed Lotus MarketPlace, a CD-ROM database of data on millions of people, to sell at a price acceptable to small and medium-sized organizations. However, Lotus received more than 30,000 telephone calls about the product from people complaining about the invasion of privacy. Lotus subsequently withdrew the product (although it is now offered by another firm).

Manager's Memo 17–3	COMPUTERS AND YOUR PRIVACY

▸ Many daily activities create computer records for government agencies, nonprofit agencies, and business firms. They often sell these records to other agencies and firms that use the records to create prospect lists, lists for direct mail advertising, or lists for telemarketing campaigns. A description of the kinds of data about you and the companies that keep the data follows.

Bank data. Chex-Systems keeps checking account data on individuals and firms, including the number and amount of checks written with insufficient funds. These data permit its customers—stores, vendors, and others that accept checks for payment—to verify the status of customer checks at the time of approval by entering the driver's license or checking account number. The Fair Credit Reporting Act requires that Chex-Systems allow a person to review his or her account. To do so, contact Chex-Systems at 12005 Ford Road, Suite 600, Dallas, TX 75234.

Auto data. Motor vehicle departments in many states provide data about you, your car, and your driving record to others for a small fee. Carfax, Inc., provides to anyone for a small fee, information about your car's history, including such details as whether it has been "totaled" before and any mileage inconsistencies that have been reported.

Property data. Local government agencies make information about any deeds that you hold available as part of the public record. Any claims on the property made by vendors seeking payment for past due bills are also public information.

Medical data. One organization, the Medical Information Bureau (MIB), stores medical information on millions of Americans that is used by medical insurance companies. Data from hospital stays and even your family doctor may find its way into MIB records. You can request the data MIB holds be sent to you or to your physician. Write Medical Information Bureau, PO Box 105, Essex Station, Boston, MA 02112, or in Canada: Medical Information Bureau, 330 University Avenue, Toronto, Ont. M5G 1R7.

Professional data. As a professional, you will often receive free trade publications. To get the free subscriptions, you usually must complete an annual questionnaire that asks for detailed information about your job and your company. In the computer field, this data includes how many and what types of computer systems your company has and how much the company spends each year on various computer products. In addition, the professional associations to which you belong ask you to complete membership forms. The professional organizations and trade magazine publishers usually sell these data to others.

Credit card data. If you have a standard credit card from American Express, Visa, or MasterCard, your credit card data is sold to many other companies. That's another reason you probably get more junk mail than you would like.

Credit data. A number of companies maintain detailed information about your credit history that they sell to other organizations. The information includes bankruptcies; unpaid bills; delinquent accounts; bank, boat, and car loan data; and information about your payment history to department stores, hotels, and many other product or service providers.

Other personal data. Birth and death certificate data are available as part of the public record. These data can often lead to telephone calls from salespeople. However, much more data may be available from firms from whom you have bought products or services. Product registration and warranty forms often ask for information about your age, salary, marital status, and where and why you bought the product. Most likely these data will wind up at National Demographics & Lifestyles, an organization that maintains and sells information about you to other database organizations. If you join some buying groups or get discount memberships at some stores, you provide even more data, including where you work, what products you are interested in, and your buying preferences.

Protecting yourself. Some tips on protecting yourself from these invasions of privacy or for reviewing your records held by others are available on the Web at several of the sites shown in the Selected Internet References at the end of this chapter. One place to start is by downloading the Consumer Protection Resource Kit. FTP to ftp.rahul.net and change to the /pub/jag/privacy directory. The files to download are cprkv1.doc and cprkv1.xls. Another good source is the Privacy Info Source (http://www.eff.org/pub/Privacy/HTML/monroe_priv.html).

Source for some of the data: C. Verdi, "Guarding Your Financial Data," *Your Money,* June–July 1994, pp. 22, 24, 61, 63.

Many companies sell the customer data they have collected over the years to other firms and organizations. Of course, newspaper and magazine publishers have sold their subscription databases for years. However, subscription databases contain far less data than the customer databases that are now kept by many organizations. The use of these databases leaves much room for ethical abuse, especially when there is no control over their use by the purchaser. It is one thing for an organization from whom you have purchased a product to know some of your preferences about the product and its use. It is another for such information to be exploited by other companies and intrude into your life via fax sales messages, mailed catalogs, telephone calls, and sales visits.

When individuals become members of bulletin board systems, visit certain on-line databases and Web sites, purchase goods and services on-line, and pay bills on-line, information about these individuals and their behavior often becomes available to other firms and organizations. More and more information about a person's marriages and divorces, the size and color of the sweater she just bought, the address and value of the person's home, the amount of the mortgage on that home, and the kind and age of the car he drives has become easily available through on-line databases. Gathering this information from the on-line databases is legal as long as you can afford the search time. The information comes from files on real estate transactions; auto transfers; motor vehicle records; court records on marriage, birth, death, and divorce; business credit files; and bankruptcy files, to name a few sources. However, the ethics of gathering, reading, using, and even selling such data may be questioned by those whose privacy has been invaded. Justifying these activities on the basis of gaining a competitive advantage or because many companies are doing them will hardly quell the typical customer's anguish over loss of privacy.

3. *When an organization is bought by another, what rights should the purchaser have to the data about individuals and organizations that the original firm maintains?* What are the responsibilities of the original firm to protect the privacy of its customers and vendors? There are some legal answers to the latter question, of course. Legislation to protect the privacy of information has been enacted. However, this legislation has not been sufficient to deter organizations from selling data about their customers or vendors to others. Managers are often caught in a crossfire here. On the one hand, managers may be under pressure to produce profits, and the data about individuals and organizations acquired from the purchased firm can be sold easily for a profit. On the other hand, managers are likely to recognize how they would feel if their data were being used in this manner. As a manager, you must recognize that you may be given access to extensive data about people. You are very likely to confront situations in which the best course for profit conflicts with the privacy of those people.

4. *What is the responsibility of the organizations that maintain data about others for ensuring the data's accuracy?* Keeping inaccurate records about customers may affect their credit ratings, their ability to secure loans, or their ability to obtain work. Inaccurate data about the financial well-being of vendors may prevent them from receiving contracts. Although people have some legal rights to review the accuracy of data kept by others on them, they often do not exercise these rights. Most people do not avail themselves of the right to check their credit ratings or their personnel data, for example.

Managers can take prudent steps to increase the accuracy of data about employees, customers, and vendors by using many of the security controls mentioned earlier, such as insisting on data validation controls, training employees, and testing programs. Managers can also emphasize the importance of accuracy to employees who create or update records about people and the consequences of errors in those records to the people involved.

Managers, as well as some other organization personnel, often have access to a vast amount of records pertaining to employees, customers, vendors, and other people. It is important that managers understand the ethical responsibilities that accompany that access, including the need to protect the accuracy of data describing people.

5. *What rights do people and organizations have to review the data kept about themselves?* Many records, such as school records and credit records, have by law become open to those whose data are being stored; other types of records have not. As a manager, you must consider how you will deal with peoples' right to know the contents of their files. Managers can use a variety of means, including neglect, to stonewall access to records. On the other hand, they can provide free and open access to those records to ensure that they are accurate.

6. *Who in an organization has the right to view the records of others that are stored by the organization?* What should constitute the right to know? What rules should be followed to establish the need to know? It may not be illegal for a manager to access the records of others within an organization, but that does not mean that it is always ethical to do so. For example, a manager in a human resource department may have access to the records of many employees. However, that access does not give the manager the right to invade the privacy of employees. Examining the record of an employee for promotion purposes is not the same as examining the record of a rival for a promotion with the aim of identifying weaknesses in that individual's past that can be exploited.

As technology advances, it becomes less expensive and easier for organizations to collect and maintain massive amounts of data on people and other organizations. Many firms are using these databases to identify the buying patterns of their customers and the customers of other organizations. Although this practice may allow organizations to serve their customers more efficiently and effectively, it also allows organizations to invade the privacy of those customers. Furthermore, use of these data has social consequences. For example, a firm may develop profiles of cigarette or liquor buyers and thus find ways to sell these customers more cigarettes or liquor. Although increased sales of these products may benefit the company, they also may lead to higher incidences of lung cancer and traffic deaths.

Property Issues   It may not be illegal for a person to use some shareware software without sending in a check to the developer of that software, but it is certainly unethical. Likewise, although it is not illegal in some countries to copy the software developed in another and sell it, it is clearly unethical. Respecting the property rights of the software developers in these cases is simply the right thing to do regardless of the lack of legal recourse available to developers.

Manager's Memo 17–4	TEN COMMANDMENTS OF COMPUTER ETHICS

▶ In an attempt to reduce piracy, privacy invasion, unauthorized access, and inaccuracy in records, the Computer Ethics Institute has formulated 10 guidelines for behavior.

1. Thou shalt not use a computer to harm other people.

2. Thou shalt not interfere with other people's computer work.

3. Thou shalt not snoop around in other people's computer files.

4. Thou shalt not use a computer to steal.

5. Thou shalt not use a computer to bear false witness.

6. Thou shalt not copy or use proprietary software for which you have not paid.

7. Thou shalt not use other people's computer resources without authorization or proper compensation.

8. Thou shalt not appropriate other people's intellectual output.

9. Thou shalt think about the social consequences of the program you are writing or the system you are designing.

10. Thou shalt always use a computer in ways that ensure consideration and respect for your fellow humans.

Furthermore, the implications of software piracy extend beyond simple crass behavior. The cost of stolen copies usually must be distributed over those who buy their copies legally. Thus, one result of software piracy is to raise the price of software to other organizations, including schools and charities. Widespread piracy also discourages developers from spending the enormous amounts of time necessary for software development by raising the risks of not receiving a fair return on the expenditure of that time.

Protecting the property rights of others, such as the rights of software developers, through ethical behavior as a student and an employee starts with using software at school and at work ethically. Ethical behavior means not copying or using software illegally or without compensating the developers (see Manager's Memo 17–4).

Information property issues are broader than software piracy, however. Most people understand that taking an object, such as a TV, from someone else without authorization is theft. However, some people's actions indicate that they fail to understand that making copies of copyrighted material, such as magazine articles or software, without permission from the authors is also theft. So is taking the ideas of someone else without authorization or citation, such as plagiarism. Whether these acts are defined as illegal in a society does not indicate whether or not these acts are unethical. Property rights cover intellectual property as well as tangible property.

Employees who leave their current employers may take with them ideas and trade secrets that have been developed at the expense of the employer. These secrets may be transferred to a new firm or to new enterprises begun by the employees. A recent legal case involved an executive of Borland International, Inc., who was hired by rival software vendor Symantec Corporation. Borland charged the executive with divulging confidential information and trade secrets to Symantec while he was still working for Borland and charged Symantec with hiring the employee in order to steal trade secrets and marketing plans. Symantec claimed the charge was an attempt to prevent other firms from hiring Borland personnel.

In many organizations a security guard or other employee routinely accompanies a fired employee from the termination interview back to the employee's office. The employee's access keys, badges, and cards are collected, and all his or her IDs and passwords are expunged from the computer system. The employee is then ushered out of the building. These practices, frankly, seem humiliating to employees. However, they not only prevent disgruntled employees from harming the system but also prevent the employee from taking key data. One disgruntled e-mail administrator for New Jersey's Clavin, Inc., "randomly deleted the network identification codes of his co-workers."[16]

Ethical behavior regarding intellectual property also extends to maintaining the integrity of that property. Consider the criticism that was leveled at the *St. Louis Post-Dispatch* when it ran a staff photographer's Pulitzer Prize-winning photograph on the front page. The paper was criticized because it had removed a soda can from the photograph using digital imaging technology. Understanding that creative work should be protected from theft and unauthorized modification is an important component of ethical behavior.

The Widespread Impact of Information Systems

Information systems have allowed organizations to increase the efficiency and effectiveness with which they produce goods and services. This has allowed some organizations to reduce their workforce and pass these savings on to customers in the form of lower prices. In the world of international competition, reducing costs is critical to survival. The impact of information systems in many organizations has been the elimination of jobs. However, organizations have responsibilities to employees as well as to owners and customers. Employees are also stakeholders in the organization. Thus managers must also consider ways to reduce the adverse impacts of information systems on employees. For example, employees whose jobs will be eliminated can be trained by their firms for different work in the organization or for different work in different organizations. Reductions in the workforce can be accomplished through the normal attrition that occurs from retirements, moves, and resignations, instead of by firing employees nearing retirement.

Information systems make it easy and inexpensive to transfer large amounts of data across a room, city, state, or country. They also make it possible to transfer information that is crucial to one nation's defense to others who may deliberately or inadvertently pass it on to that country's enemies. And they make it possible to transfer pornographic and violent images and text to any computer system with access, including computer systems used in the home by young children.

Dependable and swift information systems allow companies to develop software in third-world countries where programmers are paid a fraction of the wages paid in the original country. However, the cost to the original country of transferring and testing those programs may far overshadow the savings gained by using another country's cheap labor. Furthermore, the third-world country may lack labor laws that are adequate to protect the programmers from such work hazards as carpal tunnel syndrome or the affects of radiation emitted by cheap computer terminals.

Advances in information technology also enable many people to telecommute. The result has been a reduction in fossil fuel use by telecommuters and work opportunities for many people who would otherwise not be able to take jobs. Telecommuting also offers working spouses an opportunity to spend more time at home, reducing the dependence on child care centers or nursing homes. However, it also may offer irresponsible managers, through competitive pressure, opportunities to obtain more work from employees who no longer respond to the traditional plant closing whistle. For these workers, the inability to separate work from nonwork activities may reduce the quality of the time they actually spend with their families.

---

[16] B. D. Jaffe, "Disgruntled E-Mail Worker on Rampage," *Computerworld*, October 21, 1996, p. 37.

Information technology, including the inexpensive desktop computer system and the Internet, is already altering the way children learn. However, information technology costs money that many poor people do not have. It also costs money that many schools in poor areas cannot afford. If distributed widely, information technology can serve as a social leveler in the learning process. If not, it can serve to further distance the underclass from mainstream society. Computer literacy and information skills not only affect learning but also affect job success. Many jobs today assume certain levels of computer literacy on the part of job applicants. Students from underfunded schools who have not had the same opportunities as others to develop literacy and information skills face one more disadvantage in the marketplace.

Management Responsibility

When considering the ethical issues surrounding the impact of information systems, the bottom line is that organizations and their managers should develop and deploy information systems in a socially responsible way. They should consider the impact that information systems will have on employees, customers, vendors, other organizations, and the general public. That impact on people may be widespread and may affect their privacy, jobs, working conditions, health, property, home life, or future. Furthermore, organizations and managers should attempt to reduce or ameliorate the adverse impact of information systems by creating policies and procedures for acquiring, developing, using, and implementing information systems in a socially responsible manner.

Irresponsible behavior on the part of organizations frequently leads to legislation to correct the problem wrought by the behavior. Regulation of business is often a direct result of the abuse or neglect of social responsibility by business. Child labor laws, enacted much earlier in this century, are an obvious case in point.

MANAGEMENT SUMMARY

Computer information systems pose numerous security and ethical problems for managers. Managers must assess the risks, or potential losses to their organization, that their information systems represent and apply controls or countermeasures that are appropriate to those risks. Specifically, managers must identify the threats, or the events, people, actions, or other situations that could trigger a loss, that exist to the information systems and design controls that reduce the system's vulnerabilities, or the flaws, problems, and conditions that make a system open to threats. The controls used may be physical, electronic, software controlled, or a set of management policies and procedures. The threats posed to the information systems may be from natural disasters, employee errors, crime, fraud, abuse, and software bugs. Computer crime, fraud, and abuse are increasing and include industrial espionage, hacking, toll fraud, theft, viruses, vandalism, software piracy, and invasions of privacy.

Managers should consider security measures for a wide range of information system components, including information system facilities, the communications systems used to connect users, the database systems that store organization data, and the application development process.

Many ethical problems involved with computer information systems have been the subject of legislation and court action. The result is that much unethical behavior surrounding the use or abuse of information systems is also illegal behavior or behavior that does not conform to contractual agreements. Ethical issues still surround computer information systems, however, especially in the areas of software piracy, the privacy of individuals and organizations, the accuracy of information kept about individuals and organizations, and the right to access those data and why and when the data should be accessed.

Information systems also have adverse impacts on people through job reduction, changes in working conditions, and invasion of privacy. Managers must implement information systems in a socially responsible manner so as to reduce or ameliorate the adverse impact of their information systems.

The manager can expect that new technology will beget new ethical issues as well as new security concerns. Given the persistent change in technology, security and ethical concerns are likely to maintain a high profile for many years.

KEY TERMS FOR MANAGERS

antivirus programs, 662
batch control, 678
batch total, 678
bug, 665
cold site, 668
computer virus, 661
controls, 655
data validation, 677
dial-back, 672
disaster recovery plan, 667
disk duplexing system, 674
electronic controls, 655
encryption, 668
end-of-file checks, 678

exception reports, 678
firewalls, 669
garbage in, garbage out (GIGO), 677
hacker, 659
hacking, 659
hash total, 678
hot site, 668
industrial espionage, 658
input controls, 677
make or buy decision, 675
management controls, 655
network auditing software, 670
output controls, 679
physical controls, 655

process controls, 678
record count, 678
retention schedule, 679
risk, 653
sequence checks, 678
software controls, 655
software piracy, 663
threat, 653
toll fraud, 659
trusted systems, 673
uninterruptable power supply (UPS), 675
vulnerabilities, 653

REVIEW QUESTIONS

1. What is a *risk?* Provide two examples of potential losses to information systems.
2. What are the objectives of EDP auditors?
3. What is a *threat?*
4. What is a *vulnerability?* Provide an example of how an information system might become vulnerable.
5. Explain what a *control* is. How can controls be used?
6. List four types or categories of controls.
7. What are *electronic controls?* List four examples of electronic controls.
8. What are *management controls?* List three examples of management controls.
9. List four common types of threats to computer systems.
10. How might encryption be used to reduce threats for a communications system? For a database?
11. What is a firewall and how does it protect an organization?

12. What does the term *GIGO* mean? How can you reduce or eliminate the problems that GIGO represents?
13. List and describe five types of data validation controls.
14. What is an *exception report?*
15. What does an end-of-file check attempt to prevent?
16. Describe five types of computer crime, fraud, or abuse.
17. What is toll fraud?
18. What are batch controls? Describe three types of batch controls.
19. Explain what a *trusted system* is.
20. What does a hacker do? How does this practice threaten information systems?
21. What does the term *economic espionage* mean?
22. What is *salami slicing?*

QUESTIONS FOR DISCUSSION

1. How do threats differ from risks?
2. How do threats differ from vulnerabilities?
3. What is a hot site? a cold site? How may a hot site be used to provide security for an organization's information systems?
4. What are two important questions a manager must ask when assessing risks to information systems?
5. Explain why in some situations software piracy is illegal, in others a violation of a contractual agreement, and in all cases unethical.
6. What are some reasons a firm might buy commercial software rather than develop its own?
7. What does *appropriate to task* mean when referring to software testing?
8. What is a computer virus? How can viruses damage a computer information system? What can be done to prevent or recover from them?

PROBLEMS

1. **Avondale Shipping.**   Avondale Shipping Company is a small owner-operated firm that provides wrapping, shipping, and other services for individuals and businesses that wish to ship packages. The owner, Val Prior, hires part-time help for peak hours during the week and for the holiday seasons. She has two computers. One is an old PC that is no longer used and that has a book value of zero. The other is a new PC that cost $3,500, including the software, installation, and peripherals. Prior stores the old PC in a closet and does not plan to replace it. However, she estimates that the cost of replacing the new PC would be $4,400, including installing the hardware, software, and replacing the data. Prior currently has deadbolt locks on her store doors, uses an alarm system connected to the local police station, has bolted down the microcomputer to a desk in an interior, locked room, makes archive copies of her data, and takes the archive copies to her home each night. Two robberies have occurred in the last year in the strip shopping center in which Avondale is located. Prior estimates that the probability of loss of the computer systems from theft is only 1 in 20. She also estimates that if the computer were stolen, she could carry on business for a day or two without loss until the new system was acquired and installed.

    a. What is your estimate of the potential monetary loss of these PC systems from the threat of theft?
    b. What are some additional controls that Prior might consider to reduce the potential risk from the threat of theft?
    c. What threats other than theft might Prior consider?

2. **Gordon, Ford, & Little.**   Gordon, Ford, and Little (GFL) are partners in a small legal firm in the Midwest. They wish to develop a system that will track the time they spend with clients in the office and on the phone so that they can bill the clients on an hourly basis. Ford wants to buy a commercial time-billing software package from Detweiler Software, Inc. Gordon, the senior partner, does not want an off-the-shelf product. He thinks that the firm should hire a consultant to create a custom program. Little has become very adept at using spreadsheet software for budgeting and other decision support purposes. He believes that the partners could save a lot of money and time if he just used the spreadsheet software to develop a time-billing system. What are the advantages and disadvantages of the partners' proposals?

3. **Theona University.**   You are working on a computer assignment in the TU computer laboratory. It is 8:00 PM, and the lab closes at

8:30 PM. You must finish your project report so that you can hand it in to the instructor tomorrow. You have a computer system in your dorm room, but that computer system does not have the word processing program you are using in the lab. Your friend, who is using the computer at the next desk, suggests, "Just copy the program to your disk and load it on your dorm machine. Then you can finish the report tonight." You realize that that would be an easy solution, but you know the software you are using is copyrighted. It is also not a student edition that can be used by students in your course free of charge. Your friend sees that you are hesitating and says, "Oh, go on! That software company charges big bucks for a disk that costs them a few pennies. They will never miss it." You only have a half hour left.

    a. What should you do?

    b. What might the university do to reduce this problem?

4. **Virus protection software.** Prepare a report on virus protection software. Review at least one commercial software package that provides virus protection programs. As sources for your report, you might use the *Computer Literature Index,* published by Applied Computer Research, Inc., Phoenix, Arizona; the *Guide to Business Periodicals; Computer Select,* the CD-ROM database service; and Web search engines.

5. **Computer crime.** Prepare a report on computer crime. The report should contain information about dollar estimates of computer crimes and a discussion or explanation of several types of computer crimes that have recently been discovered. As sources for your report, you might use the *Computer Literature Index,* published by Applied Computer Research, Inc., Phoenix, Arizona; the *Guide to Business Periodicals; Computer Select,* the CD-ROM database service; or Web search engines.

6. **Internet security.** Your company is considering connecting its networks to the Internet in order to take advantage of Internet e-mail and to search for useful data, including information about competitors. What risks will the company's current networks face from Internet connectivity? What recommendations do you suggest to the company to reduce those risks?

CASES

1. **Babbitt, Inc.** Babbitt, Inc., is a wholesale sporting goods firm that serves clients in a two-state area. The sales department of the firm has a local area network that is used by all salespeople, including those who take orders over the phone from customers and those who visit customers in the field. Users of the LAN also have access to the firm's mainframe computer system. Until recently, field agents used the PCs on their desks to connect to the LAN only when they were at the home office. But the desktop PCs of the field agents have recently been exchanged for notebook computers, which the agents will use both at the home office and off-site. At the home office, the agents plug into the LAN directly. In the field, agents use a modem with software that connects to a dial-in server on the LAN. The agents will use the remote access to the LAN to query the mainframe financial accounting system on availability of stock and customer credit limits. They also will complete sales orders at customer sites by connecting through the LAN to the sales order system on the mainframe. The firm hopes that the system will result in increased sales because salespeople will have timely information about products and customer credit and because they can complete orders on the spot. The system also will allow field agents to send and receive e-mail to the firm through the local area network.

    However, the sales manager is concerned about the security of the new system. She has asked you, as a security consultant, to recommend some security procedures that might reduce the risks in the system. The manager is particularly concerned about these issues:

a. The threat of unauthorized access to the local area network and to the mainframe financial accounting database.

b. The threat of unauthorized access to the e-mail system.

c. The risks of theft of the notebook computers and the software and data stored on them.

Prepare a report describing the various options that the sales manager might consider to address her concerns.

2. **Werner Merchandise, Inc.** Werner Merchandise, Inc., is a catalog firm that provides a variety of stock for the home gardener, such as kneeling pads, wind chimes, garden statuary, and garden tools. The company sells directly to home gardeners by taking mail and phone orders. Werner Merchandise purchases the merchandise it resells from many domestic and foreign suppliers. The company's current purchase order system is completely manual (see the manual purchase order form below), and management is now considering automating the system.

If the purchase order system is computerized:

a. What input controls might be considered for the fields in the purchase order record?

b. What access controls might the firm consider for its purchase order records?

c. What additional controls might the firm consider for its purchase order records?

Does automation of the purchasing system pose any ethical issues to the company?

Werner Merchandise, Inc. 515 Sagamore Avenue Cincinnati, Ohio 45227-0515			No. **7923**
TO:		DATE: SHIP VIA: DATE WANTED: VENDOR NO: TERMS:	
QUANTITY	STOCK NO.	DESCRIPTION	UNIT PRICE
		Purchasing Agent —————————	

SELECTED INTERNET REFERENCE SITES

Antivirus.Com (http://www.antivirus.com/).

Business Software Alliance home page (http://www.bsa.org/index.html).

Business Software Alliance Virus FAQ page (http://www.bsa.org:80/piracy/virus/virusfaq.html).

Center for Democracy and Technology (http://www.cdt.org/).

Computer Operations, Audit, and Security Technology lab at Purdue University links to computer security, law, and privacy (http://www.cs.purdue.edu/homes/spaf/hotlists/csec.html)

DePaul University Institute for Business and Professional Ethics (http://condor.depaul.edu/ethics/resource.html).

Encryption Policy Resource Page (http://www.crypto.com/events/).

FBI's Computer Crime Squads (http://www.fbi.gov:80/programs/nccs/compcrim.htm).

Computer Emergency Response Team links (http://www.ncsa.com:80/ncsacert.html).

Computer Crime Research Resources (http://mailer.fsu.edu/~btf1553/ccrr/welcome.htm).

Data Logic's security references page (http://www. datlog.co.uk/security/external.html).

Electronic Freedom Foundation's links to information sources on privacy and other issues (http://www.eff.org/links.html).

Electronic Privacy Information Center (EPIC) (http://www.epic.org/).

Forum of Incident Response and Security Teams' (FIRST) page (http://www.alw.nih.gov/Security/first-papers.html).

Internet Firewalls Frequently Asked Questions (http://www.v-one.com/pubs/fw-faq/faq.htm).

Security and encryption links page (http://www.cs.auckland.ac.nz/~pgut001/links.html).

Software Publishers Association (http://www.spa.org/).

UCLA Online Institute for Cyberspace Law and Policy home page (http://www.gse.ucla.edu/iclp/hp.html).

UCLA Online Institute for Cyberspace Law and Policy links to other computer crime, privacy, and law web sites (http://www.gse.ucla.edu/iclp/resources.html).

SELECTED REFERENCES AND READINGS

Alexander, M. "The Real Security Threat: The Enemy Within." *Datamation,* July 15, 1995, p. 30.

Alexander, M. "Make It a Policy to Protect Yourself." *Datamation,* December 1, 1995, p. 59.

Behar, R. "Who's Reading Your E-Mail?" *Fortune,* February 3, 1997, p. 57.

Bort, J. "When Firewalls Aren't Enough." *Client/Server Computing,* May 1996, p. 41.

Bowers, D. M. "Equipment Protection: Lock It or Lose It!" *Modern Office Technology,* April 1993, p. 30.

Cheenne, D. "When Software Piracy Strikes Home: A True Story." *PC Today,* August–September 1993, pp. 41, 49.

Corrigan, P. "Planning for Disaster by Planning Ahead." *NetWare Solutions,* November 1996, p. 22.

Dejoie, R. G. Fowler; and D. Paradice. *Ethical Issues in Information Systems.* Boston: Boyd and Fraser, 1991.

Duffy, C. A. "Peace of Mind: LAN Administrators Juggle Long-Distance Data Security." *PC Week,* July 28, 1993, p. 98.

Dugan, S. "Cyber Sabotage." *InfoWorld,* February 10, 1997, p. 57.

Emma, T. "For Whom the Fraud Tolls." *Telecom Reseller,* April–May 1993, p. 17.

Godwin, M. "Sinking the CDA." *Internet World,* October 1996, p. 108.

Goree, K. *Ethics in American Life*. Cincinnati: ITP-South-Western Publishing Co., 1996.

Haight, T. "Thinking Through Secure Web Payments." *Network Computing,* February 15, 1996, p. 85.

Hanley, S. "Understanding Data Loss." *NetWare Solutions,* November 1996, p. 28.

Harwell, J. A. "Computer Piracy: Is Your Company Breaking the Law?" *NetWare Connection,* March–April 1993, p. 6.

Hudgins-Bonafield, C. "Will Spies Hold Your Keys?" *Network Computing,* March 15, 1996, p. 78.

Huttig, J. W., Jr. "Fear of Frying." *PC Today,* April 1993, p. 18.

James-Catalano, C. N. "Cyberlibrarian: Fight for Privacy." *Internet World,* January 1997, p. 32.

Krull, A. "Computer Rip-Offs and Foul-Ups: Is Management to Blame?" *edpacs (The EDP Audit, Control and Security Newsletter),* May 1989, p. 10.

LaPlante, A. "Turning Corporate Data into Profitability." *InfoWorld,* October 18, 1993, p. 63.

Lawton, G. "No Copying Allowed: The Software Publishers Association." *PC Today,* March 1993, p. 71.

Liebmann, L. "Are Intranets Safe?" *Communications Week,* August 5, 1996, p. 1.

Major, M. J. "Taking the Byte out of Crime: Computer Crime Statistics Vary as Much as the Types of Offenses Committed." *Midrange Systems*, March 23, 1993, p. 25.

McPartlin, J. P. "Loose Disks Sink Ships." *Information Week,* August 9, 1993, p. 60.

Morrissey, P. "Firewalls: Weapons for the New Cold War on Security." *Network Computing,* February 15, 1996, p. 54.

Morrissey, P. "Fortifying Your Firewall." *Network Computing,* February 15, 1997, p. 7.

Oz, E. *Ethics for the Information Age.* Dubuque, Iowa: Brown, 1993.

Paone, J. "Encryption Security Hits Wall," *LAN Times,* January 20, 1997, p. 1.

Quinn, B. "Dialing for Dollars." *Corporate Computing,* May 1993, p. 124.

Quittner, J. "Panix Attack." *Time*, September 30, 1996, p. 64.

Ricciuti, M. "Spy Proof Your Data!" *Datamation*, March 1, 1993, p. 101.

Rothfeder, J. "E-Mail Snooping." *Corporate Computing*, September 1992, p. 168.

Salamone, S. "Viruses Poised to Explode," *LAN Times*, November 11, 1996, p.1.

Schultheis, R. and M. Sumner. "The Relationship of Application Risks to Application Controls: A Study of Microcomputer-Based Spreadsheet Applications." *The Journal of End User Computing,* Spring 1994, p. 1.

Smith, H. J. *Managing Privacy: Information Technology and Corporate America.* Chapel Hill: University of North Carolina Press, 1994.

Sumner, M. and R. Schultheis. "Managing the Risks of User-Developed Database Applications." *The Journal of Manufacturing,* Winter 1990, p. 30.

Waltner, C. "Selling Security." *InfoWorld*, December 23–30, 1996, p. 49.

CLIENT COMPUTER SYSTEMS SUPPORT BY SOFTWARE REENGINEERING COMPANY (SRC), INC.

BACKGROUND

The Software Reengineering Company (SRC), Inc., develops computer software and installs computer information systems for client firms and organizations on a contract basis. Originally SRC was headquartered in St. Louis. As it grew to become a nationwide provider of computer software solutions, SRC opened offices in Chicago (Illinois), Tuscaloosa (Alabama), and San Jose (California). While a large regional office is still maintained in St. Louis, the corporate headquarters office is now located in Alexandria, Virginia.

Priscilla Lundy, the division chief for the contract training/support division of the SRC St. Louis regional office is examining a contract proposal she received that morning from a client. Like all regional offices, St. Louis is organized into three divisions: Defense Contract Software Division; Corporate Contract Software Division; and Contract Training/Support Division. The Contract Training/Support Division provides training and operational computer systems support for both Department of Defense (DOD) and private industry clients. The proposal in question was received from one of SRC's most important DOD customers, the Reserve Components Personnel Administration Center (RCPAC) located in west-central St. Louis. Recently SRC completely redesigned and upgraded the computer facilities at the RCPAC (see Integrated Case 2 for background information about upgrading the office information systems at RCPAC). This effort was spearheaded by Priscilla.

Apparently the upgrade in computer technology for the RCPAC offices stimulated even more demand for computer technology. The chief of RCPAC, General Weimer, reported in the cover letter to his latest support proposal that the center was now experiencing several significant problems associated with the increased use of computer technology, especially in the area of computer systems support and computer systems security.

Many of the workers at RCPAC are U. S. Army officers. Still others are full-time DOD civilian managers. Almost all of these officer-managers possess college degrees in fields related to their DOD/Army area of specialty. Their knowledge of their respective fields and the access to new computer technology has increased the demand for improved computer applications that support ad hoc decision making. Unfortunately, as General Weimer explained in his letter, the MIS Department within RCPAC is unable to meet this demand. RCPAC will need SRC's support on a new contract to solve the new problems.

OLDER RCPAC COMPUTER SYSTEMS

Prior to the completion of the recent office information systems upgrade, RCPAC tended to rely on older computer technology. The main headquarters building for RCPAC where all administrative activities take place is an older 12-story building, which still has a beautiful design both inside and out. An IBM AS/400 minicomputer provided most office support. This computer was about six years old and was located in the MIS data processing center in the basement of the building. Access to data on the AS/400 was by computer terminals. System users were required to enter an account name and password to access the system. All data for the AS/400 were stored on hard disk drives connected directly to the computer in the basement. Access to the MIS data processing center where the AS/400 was located was strictly controlled by control card readers that logged everyone who entered the facility. Data security was strictly enforced.

Terminals connected to a mainframe computer also served the enlisted records section and officers records section. Like the AS/400, the mainframe computer was located in the MIS data processing center in the basement of the building and access to the mainframe information systems was via entry of an account name and password on a dedicated computer terminal. Data security was also strictly enforced for this system as personnel data is considered to be private information requiring special access privileges.

CURRENT SYSTEMS

The recent office upgrade replaced older stand-alone microcomputers and some of the data processing that was formerly done on the AS/400 and mainframe systems with a mixture of new microcomputers that are connected to various local area networks (LAN). Each LAN is organized as a client/server network with powerful workstation server computers enabling the sharing of data both within and across networks. The AS/400 and mainframe systems still house much of the data that the RCPAC must maintain. Converting those systems to new client server systems will still take several years of work.

A word-group network of personal computers supports each functional area. Functional areas at RCPAC include the command group, operations section, officer records section, enlisted records section, officer assignments section, enlisted assignments section, and individual augmentee assignments section.

These work-group networks are linked to building a backbone network in order to enable the various system users to communicate more easily with one another. PC-based network software controls these networks, and the network end users have access to work-group software with a Windows-like graphical user interface. Since the functional area networks are fairly new, the MIS department has not yet had time to develop application systems that regularly download data from the centralized AS/400 and mainframe databases to departmental databases. The personal computers that replaced many of the computer terminals also support special purpose software, such as computer spreadsheets for model building and the development of end-user computing systems. This, as General Weimer pointed out in his letter, is part of the problem.

CURRENT SITUATION

Like many organizations, RCPAC is experiencing a literal explosion in the end-user development of information systems. This trend has General Weimer worried. He initially contacted Rebecca Byrnes, RCPAC's director of management information systems, to express his concern about potential security problems and about the growing number of complaints that he had received from his senior staff officers regarding what they perceived to be a lack of end-user systems support from the MIS department.

Rebecca was also concerned. One cause for her concern is that her department is understaffed in the personal computer systems support area. Fig. C5–1 shows an organizational chart for the MIS department at RCPAC. Although the MIS department has grown slightly since the completion of the earlier efforts to upgrade the center's computer systems technology, the MIS department still does not have sufficient personnel to support the number of requests that it is receiving for end-user technical support. The department receives between 100 and 150 requests for support each day. The average request requires anywhere from 5 to 60 minutes of attention on the part of current MIS staff members.

Rebecca has also noted an increase in PC-based systems problems that seem to stem from end-user systems development. For example, two months after the recent upgrade in office technology, Mary Ellen Goisdzinski, an enlisted assignments section supervisor, developed a very useful information system that could forecast the demand for various enlisted military occupational specialties for upcoming years. This information was forwarded through Reserve Component channels to the Recruiting Command for use in recruiting new enlistees. Mary Ellen developed this system herself by using a microcomputer DBMS and

Figure C5–1

MIS department organizational chart

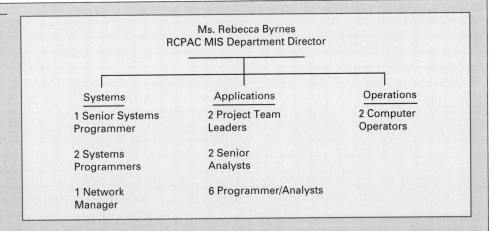

spreadsheet package that she interfaced with a common set of data files. Data for the system were downloaded regularly from the mainframe computer that was still being used to support large-scale batch-processing information systems.

For the first couple of weeks that Mary Ellen's forecasting system was in place, data for the system was obtained from a report produced by the mainframe computer. The data then had to be manually rekeyed into the system. After the first few weeks, Mary Ellen worked with one of the MIS systems programmers to develop a system to download enlisted occupational specialty data from the mainframe to her microcomputer data files once a week.

Last month, when Mary Ellen left RCPAC to move to California for a new job, the chief of the enlisted assignments section discovered that no one in the section knew how to operate the forecasting system. The system was not documented with the exception of the data-downloading component that the MIS staff developed. It now appears that the MIS department will have to devote personnel resources to redeveloping this system since the enlisted assignments chief considers it to be critical to RCPAC's ability to manage enlisted military occupational specialties. Unfortunately, not one of the other supervisors who still work in the enlisted assignments section knows anything about developing a forecasting system. The chief of enlisted assignments is now demanding that the MIS department give this system its immediate attention.

Rebecca also related a story to General Weimer about the newly formed MIS steering committee. The steering committee includes the chiefs of all of the functional areas within the center. At a recent meeting of the steering committee, LTC Denise Medeiros, chief of officer records, stated that her division was acquiring its *own* human resource management software package, even though the AS/400 continues to provide access to the current human resource management system. Denise claimed that the new software would run on the new personal computers in her department. The new human resource management software had a graphical user interface that she liked better than the text-based interface provided through the AS/400. She also felt that she could save money from her departmental budget in the long run by acquiring the new human resource management software because she wouldn't need to devote part of her departmental budget to paying the MIS department for support of the AS/400 human resource management software. Rebecca was worried that LTC Medeiros's new package wouldn't do everything that the current software would. Further, LTC Medeiros was talking about *her* department's officer records data as if no one else at RCPAC would need to access these data.

Similarly LTC John McEwen, assistant chief of staff for center administration, was complaining about problems he was experiencing with a new micro-based human resource management system software package that the personnel staff in the center administration department had acquired.

John signed and paid for a three-year software lease and site license before he discovered that the package would not operate on the new microcomputer hardware platforms. The software was an older, 16-bit version that tended to cause compatibility problems with the existing 32-bit network software that the department's work-group LAN ran on. John claimed that he wouldn't have encountered this problem if the MIS department helped him research the software purchase in the first place. Rebecca told General Weimer that having to support several human resource management systems was ridiculous and unproductive. Further, the situation was scary, especially since none of the packages had what Rebecca considered to be sufficient data security features.

Still other office personnel were complaining about the lack of support from the MIS department. These complaints covered a variety of topics. Some managers complained that MIS staff members had inadequate knowledge of the new personal computer hardware and software. Others managers complained about their inability to access RCPAC data that were still stored in centralized data files on the AS/400 and mainframe computer systems. Still others complained about insufficient technical support to aid end users in developing and debugging their own information systems. One user even complained that when he called the MIS department for help at 2:00 AM, no one was available! Rebecca knew that her existing personnel lacked training in new personal computer technologies, but she thought it was grossly unfair for end users to expect that MIS personnel never needed to sleep!

DEVELOPING THE INFORMATION CENTER

Priscilla worked with Rebecca to develop a plan to solve RCPAC's growing end-user support problems. Together, they determined that the firm needed to organize an information center. This initial analysis was used to develop the contract specifications that would enable SRC to provide the support that RCPAC's MIS department needed.

Priscilla's workload precluded her direct supervision of the project. Therefore, she assigned responsibility for developing and organizing the information center to Kyle Karensky, a recently hired senior systems analyst and project team leader at SRC. While Priscilla was getting her SRC project team ready for the contract, Rebecca was working at RCPAC to obtain initial approval from General Weimer to create six new staff positions for the MIS department's new information center. These personnel would be end-user, technical support specialists. At least two of them would have experience and training with client server network administration and support. Beyond that Rebecca was going to rely on Kyle to provide detailed plans for the type of skills that the new workers would be required to possess.

Priscilla gave Kyle only limited guidance. Specifically, she directed Kyle to do the following:

- Work with Rebecca as the client's main point of contact to identify the major roles and responsibilities of the information center.

- Use the critical success factors method to determine those factors that would be critical to the success of the information center.

- Determine whether the information center should be involved in setting standards for computer hardware and software acquisition within RCPAC.

- Determine the extent to which the information center should provide technical staff to support end-user technical requirements.

- Determine the characteristics that information center staff members should have in terms of technical competence, specific business knowledge, and general business knowledge.

- Identify the issues that are critical to the successful development of end-user systems and ways that the information center can work to help guide end-user systems development efforts.

Case Questions and Exercises

1. What should be the primary role and responsibilities of the new information center at RCPAC?

2. Answer Priscilla's question about the characteristics of information center staff members.

3. Discuss the issues in end-user systems development with respect to quality assurance. Include a discussion of data validation and testing, documentation, system controls, data backup, systems recovery, and security.

4. Discuss the *critical success factors* that are likely to determine whether the information center is adequate from the end-users' perspective.

5. One manager wants to decentralize information systems processing to the functional area level within RCPAC. Discuss whether a decentralized approach to information systems processing will or will not work. Justify your answer in terms of the RCPAC's mission to provide personnel support to the entire U.S. Army Reserve.

Glossary

accounts payable system An accounting system that manages information and tasks associated with paying an organization's creditors.

accounts receivable system An accounting system that manages information and tasks associated with collecting money from an organization's credit customers.

actuals The amount of money actually spent or received that is used as the basis of comparison in a budgeting system.

adaptive design A looping design method used in prototyping in which the prototype is developed, the user tests it, and then modifications are made.

add-on software products Programs that can be purchased to enhance the features of other software packages.

address Identifies the location of data in memory.

ad hoc report A one-time-only report that provides a manager with information to help solve a unique problem.

adhocracy A type of organizational structure that combines groups of specialists into small, market-based project teams.

advertising and promotion system A marketing information system that helps marketing managers decide what advertising media and promotion devices to employ to reach target markets.

affirmative action plan An organization's analysis of the number of minorities employed in specific job categories and its recruiting and hiring goals for meeting deficiencies.

affirmative action regulations Federal, state, and local laws and regulations pertaining to the recruitment, selection, placement, and promotion of minority employees.

aged accounts-receivable report A report that classifies customer account balances into categories, such as 30, 60, and 90 days overdue.

agile manufacturing *See* mass customization.

AI *See* artificial intelligence.

algorithm A set of standard operations that guarantees a solution to a problem in a finite number of steps.

allocations The amount of money budgeted to be spent or to be received, which is compared to actuals in an accounting system. *See also* actuals.

AMH software *See* automated material handling software.

analog channel A communications medium designed to carry continuous sine waves or voice communications.

analog transmission Sending information using analog signals, or continuous sine waves.

analytical capability The ability of information technology to bring complex analytical methods to bear in a business process.

antivirus programs Software that identifies the existence of viruses in a computer system and may also eliminate viruses the software recognizes.

applicant selection and placement systems Systems that assist human resource staff in screening, evaluating, selecting, and placing applicants in open positions.

application development system A set of programs designed to help programmers develop application programs.

application generators Fourth-generation languages that can automatically produce programs without requiring programming code to be written by people.

application programmers Trained personnel who use a programming language or a software package to create computer programs.

application programs Programs that perform specific data or text processing functions.

application software *See* application programs.

archive copy A second copy of data kept in case the first copy is destroyed or corrupted. *See also* backup copy.

archiving programs Programs that provide the database manager with tools to make copies of the database, which can be used in case original database records are damaged.

arithmetic/logic unit The part of the central processing unit that performs calculations and logical comparisons.

artificial intelligence (AI) A broad term for a category of software that simulates human reasoning and decision-making capabilities.

ASCII American Standard Code for Information Interchange. A common computer code that uses 7 bits to form each character.

assembler A language similar to machine language but that uses abbreviations, called *mnemonics,* to represent machine instructions.

assembly language same as Assembler.

asymmetric multiprocessing A method that permits the simultaneous processing of several application programs by allowing two or more CPUs to work together, sharing memory and peripheral devices. Each program is processed by separate CPUs dedicated to one program.

asynchronous transfer mode A type of communications that uses fixed-length packets and offers speeds of from 45 Mbps to 600 Mbps.

asynchronous transmission A type of communications mode in which each communication message consists of only one character.

ATM *See* asynchronous transfer mode.

audioconferencing Using a telephone system to provide multiple parties with a chance to meet electronically.

automated data processing The processing of data into information with the use of a computer.

automated material handling (AMH) software A production system that tracks, controls, and supports the movement of raw materials, work-in-process, and finished goods from the receiving docks to the shipping docks.

automating Converting something from manual entry or processing to entry or processing by electronic means. Usually applied to routine work (e.g., using computers to process payroll checks).

auxiliary memory Secondary storage, for example, storage on magnetic tape, hard disk, or optical disk.

backbone network A communications medium, usually high speed, such as fiber optic cabling, that allows an organization to connect local area networks.

back-end processor A dedicated processor that provides access to a database and database services, such as remote connectivity, data integrity, and data security. It also may perform operations on the data, such as sorting and calculating.

background task A task that the operating system performs while the user is working on another task.

backup copy *See* archive copy.

badge reader A scanner that reads magnetic data contained on a badge, such as an employee badge.

balancing feedback Information used to maintain stability in an organization or to correct progress toward a target.

bar-code reader A scanner that reads bar codes such as the universal product code.

BASIC Beginner's All-Purpose Symbolic Instruction Code. A commonly used high-level programming language.

batch controls A technique that compares totals or counts on a batch of source documents with totals or counts generated by the application program that processed the documents.

batch processing When transactions are accumulated into a group for processing at a later time.

batch processing with overnight update Transactions are accumulated throughout the day and then processed during the night to update the central database.

batch total The sum of the values from a field in a group of source documents.

BBS *See* bulletin board system.

benefit plans A wide range of fringe benefits, including stock options, insurance packages, tuition reimbursement, and retirement plans, that are offered to an organization's employees.

bill-of-materials (BOM) system A production system that produces listings of the raw materials, subassemblies, and component parts needed to complete each product.

binary digits (bits) The smallest unit of computer storage; used to store data and programs in primary and secondary storage media.

bits *Bi*nary dig*its.*

bits per second (BPS) A measurement of the speed of data communications transmissions.

BOM *See* bill-of-materials system.

boot To load part of the operating system, called the *kernel,* into main memory.

boundary The scope of activities to be supported by a system.

BPI Bits per inch; commonly used as a measure of the storage density of magnetic tape.

BPS *See* bits per second.

browser Software that lets users view documents created in HTML, or hypertext markup language.

BSP *See* business system planning.

budgeting system An accounting system that permits managers to track actual revenues and expenses and to compare these amounts to the revenues and expenses that were expected.

buffer A small amount of memory dedicated for special purposes. For example, a printer buffer holds data for printing. Buffers are often used to compensate for the differences in speed between devices.

bugs Defects in a program's code.

bulletin board system (BBS) A communications service that allows users to share information with other users about areas of special interest.

bus A set of wires or connectors between elements of a CPU or between a CPU and an add-in or expansion card.

business information systems Information systems that support the day-to-day operations within functional areas of a business.

business system planning (BSP) method A business information system planning technique developed by IBM that defines a technology plan.

bus topology A type of network configuration in which each component is attached to a single cable called a *bus*. The ends of the cable are not attached.

byte The set of bits that represents a character.

C A widely used, general-purpose programming language originally intended to develop system software.

cache A small part of a computer system's high-speed memory that is reserved for data that has been recently accessed.

CAD/CAM *See* computer-aided design/computer-aided manufacturing.

call director An optional feature of a PBX system that automatically places calls on hold when all incoming lines are busy and then connects the oldest incoming call to the next available operator.

call report A marketing report that provides information about the sales calls made by the sales staff.

canned programs Commercially developed application programs available for purchase; see commercial software.

capabilities-based competition An approach in which competitive success depends upon transforming key business processes into capabilities that provide superior value to the customer.

capacity requirements planning A planning tool that provides detailed estimates of production capacity availability.

capital budget An accounting report that contains information about the planned acquisition or disposal of major plant assets during the current year.

CASE *See* computer-aided software engineering.

cash flow report An accounting report that shows the estimated amount of cash that will be received and spent each month.

cash management system A system that monitors the flow of cash into and out of an organization.

CD-ROM Compact disk read-only memory; an optical-disk storage method that only lets you read data already stored on the disk.

cellular telephone system A communications medium that uses radio channels to transmit and receive short-distance voice and data communications to and from mobile telephones.

centralized databases The databases of an organization are located at one site under the management of one group of people.

centralized data processing Large mainframe computer systems that support multiple users and multiple application programs from one location.

central office A local telephone office.

central processing unit (CPU) The brain of a computer system. It contains the control unit, arithmetic unit, and logic unit.

centrex A telephone-system management service that provides clients with PBX-like features on a leased basis.

channel A communications medium over which a message is sent.

character printers Printers that print one character at a time. Include letter-quality printers using preformed characters and dot matrix printers, which form characters with rods.

children records Records in a hierarchical database that are owned by parent records.

choice The third phase in the decision-making process in which an alternative is chosen.

CIM *See* computer-integrated manufacturing.

circuit switching A type of channel mode in which the connection between the sender and receiver can vary each time a message is sent, but once the connection is established the channel is dedicated for the duration of the message.

client/server computing When application processing is divided between a client, which is typically a personal computer, and a server, which may be a PC, a minicomputer, or a mainframe. The client processes run on the personal computer and make requests of the server. The client and server may be in the same room or hemispheres apart.

clock speed The speed at which the CPU completes its internal processing tasks; measured in megahertz.

closed system A self-contained system that has little or no feedback from its external environment. Such systems tend to deteriorate rather than evolve.

COBOL COmmon Business Oriented Language. A third-generation language used extensively in the development of business application programs.

coding The process of writing programming instructions.

cold site A disaster recovery plan that provides space and furniture at another location for a computer facility when a disaster occurs that makes the original facility unavailable or unusable.

COM *See* computer output microfilm.

command-line operating environment An operating system in which the user must type commands to communicate instructions to the operating system.

commands Instructions that cause the computer to perform a task.

commercial software Software that has been developed by a software vendor that can be purchased and used by other organizations; canned programs.

common carrier A local telephone company or a long-distance carrier, such as AT&T, Sprint, or MCI.

communications architecture A set of communication standards. Two communications architectures are IBM's Systems Network Architecture (SNA) and the International Standards Organization's Open Systems Interconnect (OSI).

communications network A group of devices connected to one or more communications channels.

communications protocol A convention—a set of rules and procedures—for completing a communications systems task.

communications server A device that manages external communications for a communications network.

communications software Additional software required to allow a computer to communicate with remote devices or with other computers.

communications system A system for creating, delivering, and receiving electronic messages.

compatible Working with or being like another; for example, a microcomputer that works like an IBM-PC is called an *IBM-compatible computer system*. Software that runs on an IBM-PC is called *IBM-compatible software*.

compensation and benefits system A human resource system that describes and maintains an organization's various pay plans, fringe benefits, and employee choices.

compensation plan The wage and salary system offered by an organization.

competitive tracking system A marketing system that contains information about a competitor's products, prices, sales, advertising, and promotions.

compound documents Documents that contain several data types, such as text, graphics, photos, sound or voice annotations, and full-motion video clips. In a compound document, each type of data (text, graphics, voice, video) is linked to the program that created it.

computer-aided design/ computer-aided manufacturing (CAD/CAM) The use of computer systems with advanced graphics hardware and software to support engineering design and to convert CAD drawings into finished products with little human intervention.

computer-aided software engineering (CASE) A set of tools to help application developers complete the software development process more quickly and more accurately.

computer-based training The use of computer systems for instruction. Often these software packages are used to train employees in specific skills.

computer conferencing A computer system that allows participants in a group to communicate messages with all of the other participants in the group.

computer-integrated manufacturing (CIM) A concept that stresses the use of computer hardware and software to simplify, integrate, and automate all facets of production.

computerized accounting systems A series of software modules or systems that may be used separately or in an integrated fashion to automate accounting functions such as general ledger, fixed assets, sales order processing, accounts receivable, accounts payable, inventory control, purchase order processing, and payroll.

computer kiosk A form of electronic market system, usually small structures that contain a multimedia microcomputer system with a touch screen. Some allow customers to

get information about a company, its products, or its services. Others allow customers to select and purchase products and services interactively.

computer output microfilm (COM) Microfilm produced by devices that transfer computer data directly to microfilm; used for mass storage of data.

computer platform The type of computer system used for an organization's tasks. Size is one type of platform (e.g., mainframe, minicomputer, PC). The platform also could be the operating system (e.g., a Windows or UNIX system).

computer program A set of instructions that a computer system uses to process data.

computer terminal A common input/output device; often uses an attached keyboard for data entry and a screen to display commands, keystrokes, and system responses.

computer virus A hidden program that may cause damage to computer system files.

concurrency control That manner in which a database management system avoids problems from concurrent user access to data. *See also* field, record, and file locking and versioning.

contact information system A marketing system that provides the sales force with information about customers, their product and service preferences, and sales and visit history data.

contact management software A type of software used by salespeople to track information about clients, including their product and service preferences, visit information, and sales performance data.

continuous-flow production A production method that does not stop, producing output constantly.

control aids Features of a decision support system that allow the user to save intermediate results or that remind the user to perform certain activities.

controlling A managerial function that involves evaluating performance and controlling the organization's resources.

controls Tools used to counter risks from the people, actions, events, or situations that can threaten an information system. Controls may be used to identify risk, prevent risk, reduce risk, and recover from actual losses.

control unit The part of the CPU that interprets instructions and notifies other system components to carry out those instructions.

convergent computer system Computer systems that combine several technologies, such as technologies to view TV programs or control home appliances. An example would be a WebTV system.

co-processors Processors, other than the central processing unit, that help the CPU in its work; for example, an I/O channel used in a mainframe computer system and a numeric co-processor used in a microcomputer system.

cost-benefit analysis A study that determines the economic feasibility of various system design alternatives and the financial impact of an information system proposal.

CPU *See* central processing unit.

critical success factor (CSF) method A business information system planning technique that identifies key business goals and strategies that must be addressed with information technology.

CRT Cathode-ray tube; a type of computer screen. *See* display screen.

custom-written software Custom-designed software written by consultants or programmers outside to an organization.

cut-over method A method of conversion in which a complete, one-time conversion from the old to the new system occurs.

cylinder The collection of tracks accessible by a single movement of all the read/write heads of a disk drive.

cylinder storage method A method of storing data on the tracks of a cylinder to reduce the movement of the read/write heads of a disk drive.

DASD *See* direct access storage devices.

data Raw facts.

database A collection of related files.

database administrator (DBA) An MIS professional responsible for planning, designing, and maintaining an organization's data resources.

database management software A set of programs that creates and manages databases.

database management system (DBMS) A collection of software programs that allows users to organize and store data in a uniform way and to access data from more than one file.

database model The design by which a database management system organizes records.

data communications specialist A technical support person responsible for managing and maintaining an organization's data communication network.

data consistency When the same or similar data fields in files should contain the same data but contain different data.

data dictionary/directory A database management tool that contains the names and descriptions of all of the data elements within a database and how each data element relates to other elements.

data element A logical collection of characters that represents a basic unit of information, such as an employee's last name. Also called a *field*.

data entry personnel MIS professionals responsible for keying data into a computer system.

data independence The ability to define or describe data separately from an application program.

data manipulation language A specialized language used by programmers to retrieve and process data from a database.

data model An approach to organizing data in a database. Examples are hierarchical, network, relational, and object-oriented database models.

data processing department A unit responsible for operating and managing an organization's computer resources.

data redundancy When the same value in the same data element describing the same entity occurs in more than one file.

data validation Controls that are used to prevent incorrect data from being entered into a program or a database. Controls are also used to prevent accurate data from being overlooked and not entered at all.

data warehouse A system that stores, retrieves, manages, or otherwise manipulates massive amounts of data that may be from the organization's databases and external sources. The warehouse of data is often separated from the organization's production databases so that users can use this resource without reducing the response time for an organization's routine data processing operations.

DBA *See* database administrator.

DBMS *See* database management system.

DDE *See* dynamic data exchange.

decentralization An organizational pattern in which an information system or an office function is operated and managed by individual departments of an organization.

decentralized data processing A data processing environment in which microcomputers or minicomputers support local applications, systems, and operations personnel.

decision support systems (DSS)
Information systems that provide managers with ad hoc data on an on-demand basis.

decision table An analysis tool that uses a tabular structure to specify what action should be taken given a set of conditions.

decision tree An analysis tool that uses a treelike structure to specify what action should be taken given a set of conditions.

decryption Decoding data that has been encoded (*see* encryption).

dedicated server A computer system that performs one or a limited number of special tasks, such as communications, printing, or file management on a network.

delphi study A study that gives participants knowledge of group results so that they can reevaluate their own views and move toward the consensus view if they wish.

demonstration diskettes Limited-feature versions of software provided by vendors so that the user can try a software package before buying it.

design The second phase of the decision-making process during which the decision maker develops and analyzes alternative courses of action.

desktop Short for desktop computer system. A microcomputer system that fits on a desktop.

desktop conferencing A system that allows users on a network to use their workstations to conduct meetings without physically getting together.

desktop publishing software (DTP) Software that allows the user to design professional-looking documents with both text and graphics.

desktop survey software Software that lets you create survey questions and then helps you sum, tabulate, and otherwise treat statistically the answers collected to those questions.

desktop video technology Technology that permits you to capture video images from live TV or VCR tape as individual frames, store them on a hard disk or on optical disks, and manipulate the images or sequences of images.

detailed system design The process in the system development life cycle in which specifications for the proposed physical system are developed.

development software Easy-to-use software tools that allow programmers and nontechnical users to create programs for whatever jobs must be accomplished.

development tools Hardware and software used during the system development life cycle.

dial-back A security procedure that requires a called modem to call the remote modem back; it is used to ensure that connections made by remote users are restricted to preauthorized locations.

dial-up telephone lines Telephone lines rented from a common carrier and paid for on a usage basis.

digital cameras Devices that look like ordinary cameras but capture images digitally and store them on disk. The images can then be manipulated with graphics software. The technology allows you to insert the pictures you take into data files, documents, or presentations.

digital signals The discrete electronic pulses produced by a computer system that create the bits that make up a byte or character.

digital transmission Sending data as digital signals.

digital video disk A storage technology that uses what appears as ordinary CD-ROM disks but stores much more data than regular CD-ROM disks do (4.67GB vs. 0.6GB).

direct access A method of storing data in which each record is given a specific disk address so that it can be found directly without reading

every record sequentially from the beginning of a file.

direct access storage devices (DASD) Storage devices, such as floppy and hard disk drives, that allow data to be stored and retrieved directly as opposed to sequentially.

direct-mail advertising system A marketing system that utilizes mailing lists to distribute sales brochures and catalogs to a large number of potential customers.

disaster recovery plan A plan for restoring computer operations quickly when a disaster occurs. The plan might include a contingency plan for the use of alternative computer facilities. *See* hot site and cold site.

disintermediation capability The ability of information technology to connect two parties within a business process who would otherwise communicate through an intermediary.

disk drives Direct access storage devices used for auxiliary or secondary storage of data.

disk duplexing system The use of a second hard disk and hard disk controller in a server along with software that duplicates all writes to the original hard disk to the second hard disk simultaneously. Thus the second hard disk is a mirror image of the original hard disk. The system also switches from one disk drive to another in the event of a disk failure.

disk pack A collection of platters on which data can be stored. The disk packs may be removable.

display screen A visual output device that looks like a TV screen used for displaying computer commands, keystrokes, or the results of computer processing.

distributed database system Distributing a database to either a functional unit or a geographical location to support local processing requirements.

distributed processing A system in which computing power, data, and processing are located at more than one site.

divisionalized form A type of organizational structure that consists of a group of quasiautonomous entities coupled together by a central administrative structure.

DML *See* data manipulation language.

document database The data in letters, memos, reports, and other documents stored by an organization.

documentation specialist An MIS professional who records the documentation produced during the system development life cycle, including design specifications, flowcharts, file descriptions, operating procedures, user procedures, and control procedures.

document management software Computer software that lets users search for and retrieve documents from an organization's document database.

dot-matrix printer A character printer that uses rods to form characters on paper.

download The process of extracting data from a mainframe and sending it to an attached microcomputer.

downsize Changing your computer platform from a large computer system to a smaller one in order to save costs and provide less expensive units for increasing the size of the total system.

dual systems method *See* parallel systems method.

dumb terminals Terminals that do not have much intelligence or memory; dumb terminals rely on the intelligence and storage of the computer system to which they are attached.

duplication process A subset of reprographic processes that includes stencil, spirit, and offset duplication methods.

DVD technology *See* digital video disk technology.

dynamic data exchange (DDE) Automatically links data in one document with another so that manual updating is not necessary.

EBCDIC Extended Binary Coded Decimal Interchange Code. An 8-bit computer code commonly used on IBM computer systems.

e-commerce *See* electronic commerce.

economic order quantity (EOQ) An inventory management tool that identifies the least expensive amount to order for each item of inventory.

EDI *See* electronic data interchange.

EDP (electronic data processing) auditors Individuals responsible for auditing an electronic information system.

EEOC *See* Equal Employment Opportunity Commission.

effectiveness Doing the right things right.

efficiency Doing things right.

electronic blackboard A system that captures the writing on a chalkboard in digital form and uses the telephone system to transmit the data to television screens or other electronic blackboards at remote locations.

electronic commerce Any form of business conducted over the Internet including WWW advertising, shopping, and stock trading.

electronic conferencing Systems that permit many participants to engage in one- and two-way communications without actually having to travel to a common site. Also called *teleconferencing*.

electronic controls Controls that use electronic measures to prevent or identify threats, for example motion sensors, heat sensors, and humidity sensors, log-on IDs, and passwords.

electronic data interchange (EDI) Bilateral information systems that allow two organizations to exchange information electronically. Typically, EDI links an organization to its customers or suppliers.

electronic directory Lists of people and/or organizations in electronic form, such as an on-line database or a CD-ROM database. Often used by salespeople to locate new prospects and for direct-mail advertising campaigns.

electronic kiosk Kiosks are computer terminals placed in walls or other structures on streets and public places and can be used for a variety of marketing purposes, such as multimedia presentations, electronic catalogs, and electronic shopping.

electronic mail (E-mail) system Any system for transmitting messages electronically rather than in hard-copy form. Electronic mail may include transmissions of text by facsimile, teletype, intelligent copier, or any other device that transmits text electronically on a network. A popular form of electronic mail is a computer-based system that transmits of short messages between stations on a computer network.

electronic market systems Multilateral information systems that allow two or more organizations to share data about products, services, and prices; for example, the electronic version of the Official Airlines Guide that allows sellers (the airlines) to share flight information and prices with buyers and other sellers.

electronic meeting systems Interactive computer-based communications systems that are designed to help groups organize ideas, build consensus, and make effective decisions in meetings.

e-mail software Electronic mail software packages.

embedding Using information systems to support basic operations (e.g., using computer chips in microwave ovens and automobiles).

employee information system A human resource system that maintains information about employees.

employee profile A part of an employee information system. Usually contains personal and organization-related information.

emulation The process of making one computer system look like a terminal on another computer system.

emulation board A special expansion board that is added to one computer system to allow it to look like a terminal on another computer system.

emulation software The software required by an emulation board to make one computer system look like a terminal on another computer system.

encryption Encoding data so that it cannot be read or used without the decryption key.

end-of-file checks Code inserted in programs that reduces the possibility that reports are generated before all records are processed.

ends/means (E/M) analysis A method of determining management information requirements. Ends/means analysis uses effectiveness criteria to define outputs and specifies efficiency criteria for processes used to generate outputs.

enterprise networking Internetworking an entire organization so that different types of existing networks can exchange data.

entity A conceptual representation of an object, such as a person, place, or thing.

EOQ *See* economic order quantity.

Equal Employment Opportunity Commission The federal commission that monitors compliance with equal employment opportunity laws.

equal employment opportunity regulations Laws designed to ensure that minorities, women, older workers, veterans, and the handicapped are treated fairly when it comes to the hiring, retention, and promotion of employees.

equipment operator An MIS professional who works in the computer room performing tasks such as mounting tapes and disk packs, putting paper into printers, and running the computer console.

error message A brief message generated by the computer that notifies the user that a mistake has been made.

exception report A report that highlights results from an operation that exceed or do not meet the expected standard for the organization.

expert systems Systems that combine the knowledge of experts on a particular subject into a set of procedures that software can execute when faced with an appropriate problem. *See also* artificial intelligence.

explanation subsystem A component of an expert system that explains the procedures followed to reach a decision so that a user can understand how the decision was reached.

external modem A separate device that is attached to the serial port of a CPU to handle analog communications.

extranet A typical extranet is an intranet that allows the organization to connect to a wider group than the organization itself, such as an organization's customers and suppliers. The idea of an extranet is to let a select group of external entities, such as an organization's business partners, access selected areas of an organization's Web site not open to the general public.

facsimile (fax) A device that scans text or graphic images and converts the scanned data to electrical impulses that can be transmitted to compatible facsimile devices over a telephone or communications network.

factory firm The quadrant of the McFarlan-McKenney information planning grid in which a firm's current portfolio of information systems supports strategic goals but its future plans for information technology are not strategic.

factory local area network (LAN) A communications network that captures data about the production process by connecting different input devices found on a factory floor.

FAQ file *See* frequently asked questions file.

fax *See* facsimile.

fax/modem board A board that can be inserted into the bus of a microcomputer system that provides modem capabilities and many of the functions of a facsimile machine.

feasibility study The phase in the system development life cycle in which a brief analysis and design is conducted to determine if a feasible solution to the defined problem exists.

field A logical collection of characters that represent a basic unit of information such as a name. Also called *data element*.

field locking A data-handling method that permits more than one person to access a field at the same time but allows only one of them to make a change to the field.

fifth discipline The fifth discipline is systems thinking and is essential to achieving the vision of the organization.

file A collection of records all of the same type.

file locking A data-handling method that permits only one person at a time to update a file.

file server A computer system, attached to a network, that controls the network and manages access to one or more disk drives shared by the workstations on the network.

file structure The way in which records are organized and stored on magnetic media.

file transfer protocol Allows the user to connect to another computer and upload and download files from that computer.

financial accounting systems Systems that maintain and report information about the financial operations of an organization, including sales, payroll, purchasing, inventory, and cash transactions, budgeting, cash management, pensions, investments, plant assets, auditing, taxes, and credit.

financial condition analysis system An accounting system that provides management with a variety of measures on the financial soundness of the organization.

financial modeling software Specialized software that allows a financial manager to build financial models and manipulate those models to simulate various business scenarios.

firewall Protection systems that monitor all Internet or external communications activity at a site, closing all connection attempts from unauthorized users. May provide activity logs to identify intruders, examine programs and files as they are downloaded for viruses and to ensure that users downloading files and programs have the authority to do so.

firmware Computer programs stored in the form of electrical circuitry on ROM chips.

first-generation languages The lowest-level machine languages, written in binary representation.

fixed asset system An accounting system that maintains records of the equipment, property, and other long-term assets of an organization.

fixed disk *See* Hard drive.

flash memory Memory chips that, unlike RAM, do not require power to retain their data. Flash memory has been used as a substitute for hard drives and ROM in computer systems.

floppy diskettes A flexible, magnetic storage medium used on floppy drives.

floppy drives A direct access storage device that reads and stores data on floppy diskettes.

floptical drives Drives that store data magnetically, but use optical technology for precision.

fonts Sets of printable characters that vary in style, size, and spacing.

forecasting software Software that lets you predict future events using one or more statistical procedures.

foreground task The task that a user is actively performing on a computer.

formatted Describes a hard disk or floppy diskette that has been initialized and is ready to store information.

FORTRAN FORmula TRANslator. A third-generation language used extensively in the development of scientific application programs.

4GL *See* fourth-generation languages.

fourth-generation languages (4GL) Easy-to-use programming languages that allow relatively naive users to retrieve, manipulate, and analyze data.

freeware Software available free of charge, often through FTP sites, Web sites, and bulletin boards. Also called *public domain software.*

frequently asked question file A FAQ file contains the questions and answers that occurred most often on an electronic discussion group or newsgroup. People can review this file first before asking a question to see if their question has already been answered in the past.

front-end processor A dedicated processor that performs specialized tasks, such as handling communications to relieve the main processor of that work. In client/server networks, the term refers to a workstation on the network that provides data entry, validates data, formats and displays data, and performs operations on the data received from the back-end processor, such as sorting and calculating.

FTP *See* file transfer protocol.

full-duplex transmission A transmission mode that permits the simultaneous transmission of messages in both directions on a communications channel.

general ledger system An accounting system that manages an organization's general ledger accounts.

geographical capability The ability of information technology to transfer information quickly and easily across large distances making business processes independent of location.

gigabyte (GB) 1,000,000,000 characters or bytes.

GIGO (garbage in, garbage out) Refers to the importance of ensuring the accuracy of input into computer systems. If data with errors are permitted into a system, you can expect that the information generated by the system will have errors.

gopher Gopher is an information search and access method that lists different host computers and the subject areas of information they contain.

government reporting systems Systems that maintain records and produce reports required by governmental laws and regulations, including affirmative action and equal employment opportunity regulations.

graphical user interface (GUI) An operating environment that uses pictures, symbols, or menu selections to represent computer commands.

graphics software A software program that allows a user to manipulate, create, and/or display data in the form of a graph, chart, or image.

group decision support systems (GDSS) An interactive computer-based system that facilitates the solution of unstructured problems by a set of decision makers working together in a group.

groupware Software that electronically links people who work together so that they can share group-related information, such as documents, calendars, messages, and schedules.

GUI (pronounced "gooey") *See* graphical user interface.

hackers People (also called crackers) who illegally gain access to the computer systems or networks of others.

hacking Sometimes called *cracking* because the person cracks the log-in codes and sequences of a system to gain unauthorized entry into a computer system or network. *See* hacker.

half-duplex transmission A transmission mode that permits the transmission of messages in both directions on a communication channel but only one way at a time.

hard drive A magnetic disk storage device used for secondary storage of data.

hardware Computer equipment, such as disk drives, screens, keyboards, modems, and scanners.

hash total A total that doesn't make any real sense but allows the data entry operator to find out if the operator has omitted a source document, entered one twice, or entered an incorrect value.

hashing algorithm A special calculation performed on a record's primary key to determine its physical location on a disk when a random access file structure is used.

heuristics Rules of thumb that offer procedures or outlines for seeking solutions.

hierarchical database A database structure that organizes records into a hierarchy of relationships arranged logically in an inverted tree pattern. Each data element is related only to one element above it in the hierarchy.

host A computer system on a network that provides other computer systems or terminals with services. *See* also server.

hot keys Simple combinations of one or two keys that allow the user to suspend the operation of one program and move to another program.

hot site A disaster recovery plan that uses an identical computer facility located elsewhere that is already loaded with appropriate software so that an organization can be up and running within a day or two of a disaster.

HRIS software *See* human resource information system software.

HTML *See* hypertext markup language.

hub A device that connects many workstations to a network.

human resource information systems Provide managers with information to improve the quality of their human resource decisions and support the human resource management function.

human resource information system software Computer software that provides the information required to support one or more functions within the human resources department of an organization.

human resource management The function within an organization responsible for the acquisition and effective use of employees.

hypermedia database A database of documents organized in units such as cards, pages, or books and usually contain links to other cards, pages, or books. Hypermedia databases are systems in which hypertext documents are the records.

hypertext markup language A subset of SGML, the standardized general markup language. HTML replaces document formatting code that is usually proprietary to each vendor with a standard set of formatting tags.

image database A database of the images used by an organization including CAD drawings, scanned images, presentation graphics, presentation images, and digital camera images.

image management system A system designed to manage the storage and retrieval of images, for example, engineering and architectural drawings, using optical disk storage media. The system also maintains controls over changes made to drawings and distributes the drawings to users who are connected to a network.

imaging systems Two major types of systems are image digitizers and optical recognition systems. Image digitizers convert photographs, charts, and other illustrative materials to a series of dots and transfer those dots in magnetic form to disk or main memory. Images of text cannot be manipulated by word processors unless the images are converted back into characters. That conversion is the job of optical character recognition systems.

impact printer A printer that uses a print element that strikes the page.

implementation The phase in the system development life cycle in which program coding, testing, and documentation occur.

import To copy data from one computer file for use in another program.

incrementalizing A decision-making strategy in which the decision maker takes small steps away from the existing state toward a desired state.

index A table that shows the storage location of a record.

indexed sequential access method (ISAM) A method of storing records sequentially on disk that builds an index to show the storage locations so that the records can be retrieved directly.

industrial espionage The theft of organizational data by competitors.

industry-specific software Software programs tailored to the problems and needs of a particular industry, such as construction, accounting, and health care.

inference engine The "central processing unit" of an expert system that conducts a dialogue with a user, asking for information and applying the response.

informating Providing computing support for decision-making processes; for example, using spreadsheets and analytical tools.

information Data that have been processed and that have meaning.

information center An MIS unit that specializes in providing application development consulting, technical support, and training to users.

information management Managing information as an important organizational resource.

information system A system that converts data into information.

information utilities Companies that provide a variety of information services, such as on-line databases, to organizations or individuals that subscribe to their service.

informational capability The ability of information technology to bring vast amounts of information into a business process.

in-house programs Computer programs developed and written by application programmers who are employed in the management information system's department of an organization.

ink-jet printer A printer that forms characters by spraying ink on the paper.

input Data that are entered into a computer system.

input-bound When a computer system must stop because its input devices cannot keep up with the rest of the system.

input controls *See* data validation.

input device Devices that permit you to enter data into a computer system; for example, a keyboard, mouse, or scanner.

intangible benefit A benefit of an information system that cannot be measured in dollar savings, such as improved customer goodwill or employee morale.

Integrated Services Digital Network (ISDN) A communications service that encodes voice, data, facsimile, image, and video communications digitally so that they can be transmitted through a single set of standardized interfaces.

intelligence The first phase in the decision-making process in which the decision maker searches for conditions calling for a decision, such as a problem or opportunity.

intelligent terminal A smart terminal, often a microcomputer, that stores and processes data without host assistance.

interactive processing A type of real-time processing in which the user interacts with a computer system through on-line terminals.

interactive voice response systems Enhancements to voice messaging systems. Interactive systems allow callers to respond to voice menu choices and obtain information, products, or services automatically.

interface The link between either a user or a program and the computer. Also a connection between two or more systems or subsystems.

internal memory Random access memory (RAM) used to store data

and programs for processing; also called primary memory and main memory.

internal modem A device that handles digital/analog signal conversion and is placed on a board that fits inside a microcomputer.

internal rate of return (IRR) A financial calculation used by management to determine whether the organization will make a better return on its money by acquiring an asset or by investing in something else.

Internet The Internet is a network of computer networks. It provides the infrastructure for a variety of functions such as e-mail, Web access, file transfer, and discussion groups.

Internet advertising Using the Internet to advertise products or services. The advertising may be placed on the organization's Web page or the organization may pay to advertise on other Web pages, such as search engine web pages.

Internet service provider A company that provides access to the Internet.

internetworking Connecting networks together. That might mean connecting networks within and without an organization together.

interorganizational information systems (IOS) Information systems that permit an employee of one organization to allocate resources and initiate business processes in another organization directly; for example, electronic data interchange and electronic market systems. These systems provide electronic links between different organizations to streamline business processes.

intranet An Internet-like network that is confined to a single organization.

inventory control systems Systems that use information from operational inventory systems, such as the shipping and receiving systems, purchasing systems, and order entry systems, to assist managers in controlling inventory levels, costs, and availability.

inventory method *See* cut-over method.

inventory systems Subsystems of the financial accounting system that provide information about inventory levels, stockout conditions, stock receipts, stock issues, stock damage, and the location and distribution of stock within the organization.

inverted file A file that is indexed on one or more secondary keys.

investment The phase in information technological change in which a decision is made to invest in a new information technology such as office automation. Also called project initiation.

investment management An accounting system that assists management in overseeing an organization's investments in stocks, bonds, and other securities.

I/O bound When a computer system must wait because its input and/or output devices cannot keep up with its processing.

I/O channels Coprocessors that help the CPU handle input and output tasks.

I/O management programs Special operating system programs that assign input and output resources to programs and manage the transfer of data between main memory and devices such as disk drives, tape drives, and printers.

IOS *See* interorganizational information systems.

IOS facilitator Provides the information utility or the network that allows the exchange of information among IOS participants.

IRR *See* internal rate of return.

ISAM *See* indexed sequential access.

ISDN *See* Integrated Services Digital Network.

ISP *See* Internet service provider.

JIT *See* just-in-time system.

job A group of identical positions in an organization.

job analysis and design systems Systems that describe the jobs needed in an organization and the qualities of the workers needed to fill those jobs. Major outputs of the systems are job descriptions and job specifications.

job description Specifies the purpose, duties, and responsibilities of each job and the conditions and performance standards under which those duties and responsibilities must be carried out.

job management programs Programs that select, initiate, terminate, and schedule jobs that need to be processed in a way that maximizes the efficiency of a computer system.

job-order production A production method in which a product is produced in a batch when it is requested and according to the specifications of the particular request.

job specification Describes the skills, knowledge, experience, and other personal characteristics required of workers for the positions described in a job description.

jukebox storage Optical-disk storage devices that permit you to access many optical disks from a stack of disks; used for mass storage of data.

just-in-time (JIT) system An approach to production that performs operations only as required by the production schedule and sets inventory levels to meet only current production requirements.

KB *See* kilobytes.

kernel The required and most frequently used part of an operating system or application program that is always available in main memory. *See also* supervisory programs.

keyed in Entered into a computer system with a keyboard.

key-to-disk A terminal with a keyboard that allows an operator to enter data onto a magnetic disk.

key-to-tape A terminal with a keyboard that allows an operator to enter data onto a magnetic tape.

kilobyte (KB) 1,000 characters.

knowledge acquisition subsystem The component of an expert system that lets new rules be added to or deleted from the knowledge base.

knowledge base The component of an expert system that contains the information and the rules of thumb that the expert system uses to make decisions.

knowledge engineer An MIS professional who works with an expert to build the knowledge base of an expert system.

knowledge management capability The ability of information technology to capture and disseminate knowledge and expertise to improve a business process.

LAN *See* local area network.

language translator Translates application programs written in BASIC, COBOL, and other programming languages into machine language so the computer system can process them.

laptop computer A microcomputer system that is small enough to fit on your lap.

laser printer A printer that prints a whole page at once and is often used when drawings, photographs, and graphic images need to be reproduced with high quality or in color, when the number of pages to be printed is large, or when quality and speed are important.

LCD *See* liquid crystal display.

leading A managerial function that involves directing and motivating employees to achieve the organization's goals.

learning organization Organizations in which employees are continually learning how to learn together.

leased telephone line A dedicated communications circuit leased from a telephone company. Telephone lines are normally leased when high-speed transmissions or frequent data communications are needed.

line printers Printers that print whole lines of a document at a time.

linked list A file that uses pointers instead of indexes to relate records to each other.

liquid crystal display (LCD) A flat, lightweight screen display often used on laptop, notebook, and palmtop computer systems.

local area network (LAN) An interconnected group of intelligent microcomputers or terminals within a small geographic location.

location transparency A feature of a distributed system in which users submit a request to the computer system without being concerned with where the data are or where the processing will take place.

logical data dictionary A document that contains the names and descriptions of all the data elements to be developed in an information system. A logical data dictionary provides a list of data elements. This list is later refined in the development of a detailed data dictionary that records information about the physical characteristics of the data.

logical data-flow diagram An analysis tool that graphically depicts the system, its procedures, and the flow of information throughout the system.

low-cost leadership A competitive strategy that concentrates on reducing costs or improving productivity without incurring additional costs.

machine bureaucracy A type of organizational structure that has a clearly defined hierarchy of authority, centralized power for decision

making, and formal communications throughout the organization.

machine language Lowest-level programming language in which instructions are written in binary representation that the electronic circuits in the CPU can interpret and execute.

machine vision An application of artificial intelligence in robotics that allows the robot to "see" images electronically.

magnetic-ink character recognition (MICR) readers Scanning devices that read characters printed in magnetic ink.

magnetic storage media Media, such as tapes, diskettes, and hard disks, that store data in magnetic form.

magnetic tape A magnetic storage medium in the form of plastic tape.

magnetic tape drive A secondary storage device, used for sequential storage, that uses magnetic tape as its storage medium.

mainframe computer systems Large computer systems, often occupying a whole room, that are usually larger in size and power than minicomputer and microcomputer systems but smaller in size and power than supercomputers.

main memory *See* internal memory.

maintenance The process of changing and enhancing a system once it has been implemented.

maintenance fee A yearly fee that is paid to receive software updates and upgrades.

maintenance programmer An MIS professional who modifies or makes corrections to existing programs.

make-or-buy decision The choice faced by an organization to create an application or to purchase a commercial software package.

management control The phase in information technological change in which the organization recog-

nizes the importance of technology and introduces precise controls over systems development and implementation. Phase in which transfer of technology to other organizational units begins.

management controls In security planning, the setting, implementing, and enforcing of policies and procedures that will reduce the risk of loss to information systems; for example, requiring users to back up their computer files regularly.

manufacturing resource planning (MRP-II) software Software that extends a production information system to finance, marketing, and other functional areas; includes modules for material requirements planning, shop-floor control, inventory management, and capacity planning.

mapping software Software, also called *geographic information systems software,* that allows you to arrange or place data from a database onto a map of a country, region, state, city, county, or even city street. Some packages come with their own prepackaged data. More sophisticated packages offer customizable maps and are bundled with high-end databases.

marketing function A broad range of activities that identify current and potential customers; determine their needs and wants; plan and develop products and services to meet those wants; and price, advertise, promote, and deliver those products and services.

marketing information system An information system that collects and processes data to support the major activities of the marketing function within an organization.

marketing mix The combination of products, services, advertising, promotion, price, and product delivery methods offered to an organization's customers.

marketing research The process of gathering and analyzing data to identify product and service trends, target markets, and customer preferences and satisfaction and to estimate market share.

marketing research systems Information systems used by marketing personnel to collect and analyze data about such topics as an organization's market, customers, products, and sales regions.

market specialization A competitive strategy that concentrates on specializing in a particular market or finding a niche for a product.

mark-sense readers Scanners that read special optical marks.

mass customization The ability to use mass production techniques to tailor products for each customer.

mass production A production method that produces a good or service in a standardized fashion using assembly-line methods.

master production schedule The schedule of overall production requirements for an organization for a specific period of time.

material requirements planning (MRP) software A set of programs that use data from the master production schedule, inventory files, and bill-of-materials systems to help manage production and inventory.

material selection programs (MSP) Programs that aid the engineer in choosing materials for the product under design.

maximizing A decision-making strategy in which the decision maker makes the decision that maximizes the desired outcome.

MB *See* megabyte.

media mix The types of advertising media that are used to promote an organization's products or services.

megabyte (MB) 1,000,000 characters.

megahertz (MHz) A measure of the clock speed of a computer system.

member record In a network database structure, one of two types of records found in a set. A member record is owned by another record.

memory aid A feature of a decision support system that allows a decision maker to preserve intermediate results for future use or that reminds the decision maker to take certain actions at a particular time.

memory board A type of board that is added to a computer system and that contains random-access memory.

menu List of on-screen programming options from which the user can make a selection.

mesh topology A network configuration that provides more than one path between nodes on the network.

message switching A type of channel mode in which the connection between the sender and receiver is closed unless there are messages to send.

metadata Data about data.

methodology A set of methods, rules, and procedures to be applied.

MICR *See* magnetic-ink character recognition readers.

microcomputer systems Personal computing systems that are usually smaller in size and power than minicomputer and mainframe computer systems. Most personal computer systems are run by one or a few microprocessors.

micromarketing Pitching sales or advertising campaigns to very narrowly defined customer targets.

microprocessor A single chip containing the basic elements of a CPU: the control unit, the arithmetic unit, and the logic unit.

microwave transmission A mode of transmission that sends large amounts of voice and data messages in microwave form from sending dish to receiving dish.

millions of instructions per second (MIPS) The number of instructions that a computer system can process in a given time period; a measure of the power of a computer system.

minicomputer system A mid-sized computer system that is usually smaller in size and power than mainframe computer systems but larger in size and power than microcomputer systems.

MIPS *See* millions of instructions per second.

model-based analysis Decision support tools, such as a spreadsheet, that allow a decision maker to design a model that incorporates rules and assumptions about a particular business situation.

modem MOdulator/DEModulator. A communications device that converts signals from analog to digital and vice versa.

monitor *See* display screen.

motherboard The basic board of a computer system; often the board on which the CPU chip is placed or that contains the slots to which expansion boards are connected.

mouse A handheld input device connected to a computer terminal either with a wire or via radio, infrared, or other wireless transmission that lets you enter data or commands without a keyboard. The mouse may use a roller in its base, and the movement of the roller sends signals to the terminal that are converted into computer commands.

MRP *See* material requirements planning.

MRP-II *See* manufacturing resource planning.

MSP *See* material selection programs.

multidrop network A network configuration where a number of devices are connected to a single host channel.

multimedia systems A set of hardware and software tools for viewing or presenting information in many forms, such as data, text, images, live or taped video, and live or taped audio. Multimedia systems permit you to merge these information types into a presentation or file that can be accessed by users in any order they choose.

multiplexer A device on a communications network that accepts data from more than one slow-speed terminal and combines them for transmission across a higher-speed transmission channel.

multiprocessing When a computer system uses more than one central processing unit to process more than one program simultaneously.

multiprocessing operating system An operating system that can run on a multiprocessing computer system.

multiprogramming An operating system that partitions, or divides, main memory so that more than one program and its data can be available for processing.

multitasking operating system An operating system that allows a user to perform more than one task, or application, at a time.

multiuser operating system An operating system that allows more than one user to access a computer system at the same time.

natural language A query and programming language that has commands that are very similar to ordinary English.

natural-language processing Programming computers to understand language.

near-letter-quality printers Dot-matrix printers that simulate letter-quality output by making multiple print passes on each line or by using many rods to form the characters.

net present value (NPV) The current value of cash that will be spent or received at some future time.

network auditing software Software that identifies and prevents many types of problems in net-

works. The software is usually of two types: activity logs, which record all login attempts, failed or successful, and network scanning software, which looks for flaws or holes in network security.

network computer Also called a net PC. Low-cost computer systems that are designed to use the computing power, software, and intelligence of other computer systems to which they connect.

network database A type of database structure that supports many-to-many relationships and has multiple points of entry because any data element or record can be related to many other data elements.

network interface card (NIC) An adapter that connects workstations and servers to a network.

NIC *See* network interface card.

Node A record in a hierarchical database structure. In communications, a node is a computer-controlled switching center.

nonimpact printer Does not use keys or other devices to strike the paper. Two commonly used nonimpact printers are laser printers and ink-jet printers.

nonprocedural language A programming language that allows the user or programmer to identify what task is to be accomplished without concentrating on how to accomplish the task. *See also* fourth-generation languages.

notebook computer A computer system that is approximately the size and shape of a notebook.

NPV *See* net present value.

object An element that includes both data and the methods or processes that act on those data.

object code A compiled or assembled program of executable machine instructions.

object-oriented database (OODB) A database that stores and manages objects.

object-oriented programming (OOP) Using an object-oriented language to develop programs that create and use objects to perform information processing tasks.

Occupational Safety and Health Administration (OSHA) A federal agency that monitors compliance with laws that pertain to the health and safety of employees in the workplace.

OCR *See* optical character recognition.

office automation Automating and integrating office tasks through technology.

office of the future The merging of technologies into an integrated information system to support office work; the paperless office.

off-load The process of removing responsibility for processing certain tasks, such as communications, from a computer so that it can process more data.

OLTP *See* on-line transaction processing.

on-line communities Groups of people who communicate with one another through electronic means, such as chat groups, listservs, and newsgroups.

on-line database A database that specializes in a topic, such as medical information, legal information, and stock market information, and is available from a network.

on-line help feature On-screen definitions of commands and suggestions for how to use the commands.

on-line immediate update A processing mode in which transactions that are entered locally update the central database on a real-time basis or as they occur.

on-line information service Companies that provide a variety of information services to organizations or individuals who subscribe to their services. These services may include access to databases and the use of and access to a large network.

on-line transaction processing (OLTP) When a computer system immediately processes each transaction entered.

on-line transaction processing with batch update A computer system that immediately processes data at a local level. These local data later update a central database in batch mode.

on-line transaction processing with immediate update *See* on-line transaction processing.

OODB *See* object-oriented database.

OOP *See* object-oriented programming.

open system A system that operates in an external environment and that needs to receive feedback from that environment to change and to continue to exist.

operating system A set of programs that manages and controls computer resources, including the CPU, peripherals, main memory, and secondary storage.

operational financial information systems A classification of financial information systems that provide supervisory-level management with the routine, repetitive information required for day-to-day operations.

operational marketing information systems Systems that collect data that describe day-to-day marketing operations, process those data, and make the information available to marketing managers to help them make decisions.

operational system An information system that monitors and reports on the day-to-day activities of the firm.

operations documentation Systems documentation, such as system flowcharts, that documents how the system operates.

operations manager An MIS professional responsible for scheduling programs to run, seeing that output is distributed, and supervising data entry personnel and equipment operators.

optical character readers Scanning devices that convert characters from hard-copy documents into characters readable by a computer system.

optical character recognition (OCR) A method by which hand, typed, or printed characters are converted from hard copy into characters readable by a computer system.

optical disks A direct access storage medium that is written to or read by laser light beams instead of magnetic methods; used as the storage medium for CD-ROM drives.

optical mark recognition A technology that uses scanning devices to read marks placed in certain locations, such as marks made on a multiple-choice answer sheet.

optical scanner A device that optically scans characters, images, or marks and generates their digital representations.

order-entry system *See* sales order processing system.

organizing A managerial function that involves deciding how to use the resources available to achieve the goals of an organization.

OSHA *See* Occupational Safety and Health Administration.

output Information obtained from a computer system; examples include hard-copy documents and screen displays.

output bound When a computer system must stop because its output devices cannot keep up with the rest of the system.

output controls Procedures that secure the output of computer applications, including the hard copy output. Typical output controls include retention schedules, routing sheets, shredding old printouts, and locked filing cabinets.

output devices Devices that permit you to extract data from a com-

puter system; examples include a computer screen and printer.

outsourcing Contracting with external production resources for phases of the production process.

owner record In a network database structure, one of two types of records found in a set. An owner record owns one or more member records.

packet switching A type of channel mode in which messages are divided into packets, or blocks, that can then be transmitted across several different channels and reassembled at the destination.

page printers Printers that print whole pages of documents at one time, usually using a laser printing process.

palmtop Short for palmtop computer systems; computer systems that are small enough to fit in your palm. *See* personal digital assistant.

paperless office An office in which hard copy is rarely produced or processed.

paradigm A problem-solving model that an expert system uses to perform a process, such as diagnosis of a medical condition.

parallel processing A computer system that has more than one central processing unit and uses the CPUs to complete several tasks for a single program simultaneously.

parallel systems method A method of conversion in which both the old and the new systems are operated simultaneously until the new system works well.

parent record In a hierarchical database structure, one of two types of records. A parent record owns children records.

parity bit A bit added to each byte for checking purposes.

partitioned database A means of distributing a database by dividing it into segments that may then be distributed to the functional units or geographical locations to support local processing requirements.

Pascal A third-generation programming language.

payback period The time it takes for an asset to either generate increased revenues or to decrease operating expenses to match the amount of money invested in the asset.

pay grades A classification of jobs into categories based on pay.

payroll system Processes wage and salary information such as payments to employees, deductions from employee paychecks, and payments to federal, state, and other taxing agencies for taxes owed.

PBX *See* private branch exchange.

PC card A peripheral device, about the size of a credit card, that is often used with portable computer systems, such as notebook computers. Also called a *PCMCIA card.*

PCMCIA card *See* PC card.

PCS *See* personal communications services network.

PDA *See* personal digital assistant.

performance appraisal A formal review of an employee that is conducted on a regular basis.

performance management systems Systems that provide employee performance appraisal and employee productivity information to human resource managers.

peripherals Devices located next to or outside of the CPU; examples include keyboards, display screens, printers, disk drives, and mice.

personal communications services network (PCs) A cellular system that uses radio waves to create short-range networks for transmitting voice and data messages to inexpensive, handheld communication devices.

personal communicators Handheld radio-based phones used in personal communications services networks.

personal digital assistant (PDA) A type of palmtop computer system, including pen-based computers, electronic clipboards, pocket organizers, and other special function devices.

personnel capacity planning That part of rough-cut capacity planning that estimates the numbers and types of workers, supervisors, and managers needed to meet the master production plan.

phased method A method of conversion in which the new system is phased in as the old system is phased out.

physical controls Controls that use conventional, physical protection measures, such as door locks, keyboard locks, fire doors, and sump pumps.

physical view How records are actually stored on a storage medium as opposed to how people perceive they are stored.

pilot systems method A method of conversion in which a new system is introduced into a small part of the organization so that it can be evaluated and modified before being introduced to other users.

planning A managerial function that requires evaluating the organization's resources and environment to establish a set of organizational goals.

plant design system A system that provides information to support the design and layout of a manufacturing plant.

platform A level or family of computer hardware. For example, a minicomputer is a platform; so is an 80386 microcomputer system.

platters The individual, polished metal disks in a disk pack.

plotters Printers that use ink pens to draw maps, charts, and special graphs.

pointing device Any one of a number of tools for entering data or making selections from a computer screen, such as a mouse and trackball.

point-of-sale (POS) systems Computer systems used by salesclerks and others to record a sale at the counter or wherever the sale is completed; examples include cash registers used at fast-food stores, department stores, and supermarkets.

point-to-point network A network configuration with direct connections between the host and each device on the network.

portable documents Documents that can be read and printed by another user *exactly* like the original regardless of the software the other person is using.

position The tasks performed by one worker.

position control systems Systems designed to identify each position in the organization, the job title within which the position is classified, and the employee currently assigned to the position.

position inventory A list of positions by job category, by department, by task content, or by job requirements.

presentation graphics software Graphics software that allows the user to enhance standard graphs and charts with features such as sequencing, colors and shades, special print functions, and transition effects.

pricing system Systems that provide information to managers to help them set prices for their products and services, including information about expected demand, the desired profit margin, the costs of producing the product or service, and the prices of competing and substitute products.

primary key A unique identifier for a record.

primary storage The main memory of a computer system that stores the data and programs to be processed; *see* internal memory.

printing terminals Computer terminals that usually do not have screens but include a keyboard and a printer to permit the user to enter data into and gain information from a computer system.

print server A device that controls access to and manages printing resources on a network.

private branch exchange (PBX) A computer system that provides for the switching of telephone signals, both voice and data, on a company's premises.

problem definition The phase in the system development life cycle in which the nature and the scope of the problem are determined.

procedural languages Third-generation languages that require the programmer to provide detailed instructions about each step and the exact order in which the steps must occur in order to accomplish a task.

process controls Programming code that ensures that computer processes are completed accurately; for example, exception reports and end-of-file checks.

process positioning The span of production processes an organization decides to perform for any given product or product line. Also called *vertical integration.*

product design and development system A production information system that helps product designers and engineers create products appropriate for the targeted market at the least cost, including the maintenance costs resulting from returned products.

product differentiation A competitive strategy that concentrates on adding value or unique features to a product to improve its image, quality, or service.

product planning and development information system A marketing system that processes information about consumer preferences to create a set of specifications for developing a product or service.

product pricing systems A marketing system that helps to establish an optimum price for a product or service based upon production costs, competing product prices, and desired profit margins.

production information systems Computer systems that provide the data necessary to plan, organize, operate, monitor, control, and otherwise manage production systems for an organization.

production schedule A schedule that allocates the use of specific production facilities for the production of finished goods to meet the master production schedule.

production systems Systems that create the goods and services that the marketing system believes the organization will sell.

professional bureaucracy A type of organizational structure that consists of specialists who have control over their own work.

program bug *See* bugs.

program code Program instructions.

programmable read-only memory (PROM) A form of ROM that can be programmed with special equipment.

programming language Instructions that can be interpreted into commands that a computer can process. *See also* BASIC, COBOL, FORTRAN, Pascal, and fourth-generation language.

project initiation *See* investment.

project management software Programs that allow users to plan, schedule, track, and manage the resources associated with a project.

project manager An MIS professional who supervises programmers and analysts working on a systems development project.

PROM *See* programmable read-only memory.

prompts Helpful hints that appear on the screen and indicate what the user should do next.

prospect files Files of sales leads used by an organization's sales force.

prospect system A marketing system that captures and processes information about potential customers.

protocol converter A communications device that translates signals from one device or network to another, dissimilar device or network.

prototype A model of an information system created with advanced development tools.

prototyping An abbreviated system development life cycle that uses advanced development tools to create a prototype system in a very short period of time.

public domain software *See* freeware.

purchase order processing system An accounting system that processes purchase orders and tracks information on the delivery status of items ordered.

purchasing system Maintains data on all phases of the acquisition of goods and services by an organization.

QBE *See* query by example.

quality assurance Procedures, such as validation, testing, documentation, and backup and recovery, that help ensure that data is accurate, consistent, and reliable.

quality control system Provides information about the status of production goods as they move from the raw materials state, through goods in process, to finished goods.

query by example A query method that does not require the user to write query statements directly. Instead, the user displays pictures of the records in the database and then drags and drops data elements from these records to a report form.

query language A set of commands through which users can update, ask questions, and retrieve data from computer files.

RAID *See* redundant array of inexpensive disks.

RAM *See* random access memory.

RAM resident software Programs that are placed in RAM for immediate use.

random access memory (RAM) A type of memory in which data is stored in addressable locations so that the data can be accessed directly without having to move sequentially through all the data stored; random access memory is volatile.

read-only memory (ROM) Computer memory that can only be read, not written to or changed. Programs stored in ROM are not lost when power is shut off.

receiving systems Systems that identify anticipated delivery dates for goods on order and record when and in which condition they have been received.

record A collection of logically grouped data elements.

record count A procedure to help ensure that all source documents have been entered and that no source document has been entered more than once. The procedure involves counting the source documents entered into a computer system by hand and comparing that count with the count obtained from the computer system.

record locking A data-handling method that allows only one person at a time to update a record.

record set In a network database structure, the way in which the relationship between an owner record and a member record is determined.

recruiting system A system that collects and processes information about unfilled positions, the duties of those positions, and the skills and preferences of employees and candidates who may be interested in the unfilled positions.

redundant array of inexpensive disks The use of multiple, inexpensive hard drives so that more than one drive may be accessed at the same time. RAID systems work by spreading chunks, or blocks of data, across many hard disks.

reengineering The reanalysis and streamlining of business processes to achieve productivity improvements.

relational database A database structure in which all data elements in the database are viewed as simple tables that can be linked together through common data elements.

reorder-level system A system that uses predefined levels of inventory to make certain that production materials are ordered in time to arrive when needed by the production process.

replicated database A means of distributing a database by copying it and then sending the copy to either a functional unit or a geographical location to support local processing requirements.

report generator A tool that allows the user to generate reports from data quickly and easily.

report writer *See* report generator.

request for proposal (RFP) A document outlining major information system requirements that is distributed to vendors that are then asked to respond with a proposal.

request for quotation (RFQ) A request for bids or quotations from vendors for information system components.

requirements document The blueprint or definition of requirements used as a basis for designing a new information system.

resident Loaded and available in main memory.

resident programs Programs that have been loaded into main memory and are available for immediate use.

resolution The quality of the screen image in terms of the number of pixels (picture elements) per inch.

response time The total time it takes for a command to be sent to a host and to receive a reply.

restart/recovery systems Tools that restart a system or a database and recover any lost data in the event of a failure.

retention schedule A schedule for the destruction of documents that is used to avoid destroying important documents before their legal or operational time periods are over.

rewritable optical disks Optical disks that permit data to be written to them many times.

RFP *See* request for proposal.

RFQ *See* request for quotation.

ring topology A form of multidrop network configuration that uses cabling between all of the devices and is designed to pass messages through failed workstations.

risk A potential monetary loss to an organization.

robotics An application of artificial intelligence that builds machines with onboard computers that can be programmed to perform specialized tasks, such as cutting, drilling, painting, and welding.

ROM *See* read-only memory.

root record The top parent record in a hierarchical database structure.

rotational delay The time it takes for a location on a disk track to rotate underneath the read/write heads so that data can be written to or read from the location.

rough-cut capacity planning Provides an overall estimate of capacity needs based on information from the master production schedule.

safety stock The amount of extra stock maintained in case shipments are delayed, some stock items are defective, or some other foul-up occurs.

sales force automation system Systems that support the administrative tasks of salespeople, such as customer contact management, customer call reports, and travel expense reports. The systems may also support the sales process itself, including managing the sales cycle, providing electronic catalogs, or providing electronic sales presentations.

sales forecasting systems Systems that assist management in predicting future sales of an organization. The forecasts may include sales for the industry as a whole, for the entire organization, for each product or service, or for a new product or service.

sales management software Software that helps the sales manager manage the sales function. For example, the software may help to assess the productivity of the sales force; the fertileness of sales territories; and the success of products by salesperson, territory, and customer type.

sales management system A marketing system that can be used to develop reports analyzing sales activities such as sales volume by salesperson and by territory.

sales order processing system An accounting system that records sales orders, provides the documents that fill those orders, maintains inventory levels, and bills the customers. Also called *an order-entry system.*

SASD *See* sequential access storage devices.

satisficing A decision-making method in which the decision maker will terminate his or her search as soon as a satisfactory alternative is found.

scanners The general term for those devices that are able to convert text or images for use on computer systems; special scanners read and convert magnetic-ink charac-

ters, optical marks, bar codes, text, optical characters, and images.

schema Also called the logical view of a database. Includes all the data elements in the databases and how these elements logically relate to each other.

screen *See* display screen.

search engine A software tool used on the Web. A search engine allows you to enter one or more key words describing the topic of your search and then scans computers throughout the world to find documents containing those key words. The search engine displays the documents that it found in hypertext so that you can click on any document link and go to it to read the information.

search parameters A value or range of values in one or more fields that is used to select records.

secondary keys A field other than the primary key that is used to search and to sort a file.

secondary storage Auxiliary memory; examples include magnetic tape, magnetic disk, and optical disk.

second-generation languages Assembler languages. *See also* assembly language.

sector A subdivision of a track on a floppy or hard disk.

security software A type of systems software that provides a variety of tools to shield a system or database from unauthorized access.

seek time The time that it takes for the read/write heads to move to the track to which data is written or from which data is retrieved.

sequence check A processing control used to prevent certain processing from occurring on data out of order.

sequential access A method of storing records sequentially on a magnetic tape or disk.

sequential access storage devices (SASD) Devices that permit the storage and retrieval of data only in

sequential order; for example, tape drives.

sequential capability The ability of information technology to enable changes in the order of tasks performed in a business process allowing multiple tasks to be performed simultaneously.

server A computer system that provides other users on a network with computing services, such as application processing, printing services, and access to database management systems. *See also* host.

service bureau A computer service organization that provides information services that range from full-scale support for applications, such as accounts receivable or payroll, to data entry and output distribution.

shareware Relatively inexpensive software packages that are often produced by individuals and distributed through electronic bulletin boards or the Internet.

shop-floor data collection systems Input devices that capture data about the production process as it occurs.

shop-floor scheduling system A system for organizing and sequencing the resources needed to complete production jobs, including scheduling the time, building and rooms, tools and equipment, inventory, and personnel.

silicon chip A small electronic element made of silicon used for memory, processing, and other tasks; examples include the CPU chip and memory chips.

SIMM memory board A small board containing random access memory chips; the boards are placed in special slots to connect to the CPU of a computer system.

simple structure A type of organizational structure that has little or no technology in place, a small support staff and management hierarchy, and unspecialized, interchangeable operating jobs.

simplex transmission A communications transmission mode that sends a message only one way.

single-tasking operating system An operating system that allows only one program to run at a time.

single-user operating system An operating system that allows only one user at a time to access the computer.

site licensing agreement An agreement that allows an organization to pay a flat fee for a software package that can be used on many workstations.

site planning systems Systems that use a variety of internal and external sources to gather and analyze both quantitative and qualitative data useful to site planners. For example, the systems may collect information about the availability and cost of trained or experienced labor, the degree to which labor is unionized, the availability and cost of transportation for raw materials and finished goods, the availability of suitable sites, the cost of land, the proximity of raw materials suppliers and finished goods customers, the availability and costs of power, the rate of property and income taxation, community attitudes, and the quality of community services.

skills inventory A system that contains information about every employee's work experiences and preferences, special skills and proficiencies, test scores, and interests.

slide-show feature A graphics program feature that permits the timed and sequenced display of graphs or images on a display screen.

smart terminals *See* intelligent terminal.

SMDR *See* Station Message Detail Recording software.

software Detailed instructions or programs that make computer hardware apply itself to a task.

software controls Program code used in information systems to pre-

vent, identify, or recover from errors, unauthorized access, and other threats; for example, data validation and process controls.

software house A company that specializes in writing software packages that are used by other organizations to support information processing needs.

software piracy The unauthorized copying of a copyrighted program.

software suite Compatible and integrated programs that are sold as a set.

source code Program instructions that are written in a high-level language that must be converted into machine language.

spreadsheet software A software package that is frequently used to solve financial problems or create financial documents, such as budgets.

SQL *See* Structured Query Language.

SQL server A software package used on a network server to provide faster and more reliable performance of a networked database system. Also called a *back-end processor.*

stage assessment A process of determining the stage to which information systems have evolved within an organization so that the mix of application development opportunities and information management needs required for the next stage can be determined.

stagnation A slowdown in implementation or underutilization of information systems and resources.

stagnation A A form of stagnation that results from significant cost overruns, poor project management, and unanticipated technological problems and that indefinitely delays the evolution of new information technology.

stagnation B A form of stagnation that results from premature controls causing failure to learn how to use new technology.

stagnation C A form of stagnation that inhibits the transfer of technology into other organizational units.

stand-alone packages Software packages that function independently and are not part of a family of related packages.

standard generalized markup language (SGML) Provides standard rules and procedures for describing document formatting features. In other words, SGML codes documents by structure so that they can be exchanged for use with other software.

star topology A point-to-point network configuration that has a separate cable running between each component and the server or host.

Station Message Detail Recording (SMDR) software Software that provides an organization with detailed reports of telephone usage and costs for each department.

statistical software Software that enables a computer to perform statistical analysis, such as chi-square and regression analysis.

status access A database access method that allows the user menu-driven, read-only access to corporate data.

store and forward The ability to store a communications message and release it at a later time when either a channel becomes available or the receiver demands the stored messages.

strategic accounting and financial information systems Accounting and financial information systems that are used by top-level management to plan and set goals for an organization.

strategic firm A firm in which both the current and planned applications of information technology support strategic business goals and objectives.

strategic planning Long range analysis and prediction carried out by top management for the purpose of setting the organization's long range goals.

strategic planning system An information system that is future oriented, predictive, and supports an organization's strategic planning process.

Structured Query Language (SQL) A set of English-like commands that have become standard language for accessing data contained in a database management system.

structured walkthrough An exercise in which peers review the work of an analyst or programmer in an effort to identify errors and improve the work performed during the systems development life cycle.

subschema Consists of a subset of data elements in a database that are used by an application programmer, an application program, or a user.

subsystem A part of a system that performs specialized tasks related to the overall objectives of the total system.

succession planning systems Systems designed to assist human resource personnel in planning for the replacements of key organizational personnel, including identifying replacement employees and ensuring appropriate training and experience for these employees.

summary report A report that provides information to a manager on important totals, averages, key data, and abstracts on the activities of the organization.

supercomputers The largest, most powerful computer systems made; often used by military, scientific, and government agencies to process huge volumes of data quickly.

supervisory programs The portion of the operating system that must be resident in main memory. Supervisory programs are the heart of the operating system and are primarily responsible for managing computer resources.

support firm A firm in which current applications of information

technology and planned applications are not critical to the achievement of strategic business goals and objectives.

switched telephone line A method of transmission in which the route over which a telephone message travels between the sender and receiver is established every time a call is placed.

switching hub Hubs that connect each workstation attached to it directly; that is, point-to-point.

symmetric multiprocessing Using multiple CPUs; one CPU acts as the controller of the others and assigns any CPU any application task. The main CPU also provides control over I/O tasks.

synchronous transmission A transmission mode in which many characters are blocked together and sent as a single transmission. The block is preceded and followed by several bits of communications information that ensure that the block is transmitted correctly.

system A collection of people, machines, and methods organized to accomplish a set of specific tasks.

system entropy When systems run down because of lack of maintenance.

system feedback Information about the status of an information system or about the activities performed by an information system.

system prompt A character, symbol, or combination of the two that tells the user that the computer system is waiting to receive a command.

systems analysis The phase in the systems development life cycle in which the current system is studied in order to understand how the system works and to determine the scope of the problems that exist.

systems analyst An MIS professional responsible for the analysis of the current business system, its organization, procedures, work flow, information requirements, and problems.

systems design The phase in the systems development life cycle in which the specifications of a new system are developed.

systems design documentation All the specifications, including report design, screen design, file layouts, program logic, and operational procedures, that are used to develop the new system.

systems development The process of identifying an information need and developing an information system to satisfy that need.

systems development methodology A set of procedures that conform to the systems development life cycle and that identify what events and activities should occur, what order they should occur in, and what tools will be used.

systems evaluation The process of MIS professionals examining hardware and software alternatives to support specific information systems requirements.

systems programmers The programmers who write systems software and maintain the operating systems environment.

systems software A group of software packages that manage the hardware resources of a computer system.

systems utility programs Programs that handle repetitive tasks and that operating systems users find useful.

tactical accounting and financial information systems Accounting and financial information systems that provide information in a summary fashion to help middle-level managers allocate an organization's resources.

tactical system An information system that provides middle-level managers with information they need to monitor and control the allocation of resources. Designed to generate a variety of reports, including summary reports, exception reports, and ad hoc reports.

tangible benefits The savings or profits of an information system that can be measured in dollars.

tape drives Sequential access storage devices; a type of secondary storage device.

task switching The process of moving between a background task and a foreground task when more than one application is running on a computer.

technology assessment systems Systems that identify new technologies and assess them for their strategic advantage. They may include CD-ROM databases, traditional library resources, and on-line databases.

technology learning and adaptation The phase in information technological change in which users learn how to use technology for tasks beyond those initially planned.

telecommunications Electronically transmitting voice and/or data from one computer to another.

telecommunications system A group of devices connected to a communications channel that can send and receive messages to and from each other.

telecommuting Using a communications system to exchange information between the office and home so that a person may work at home.

teleconferencing systems Systems that permit many participants to engage in one- and two-way communications without actually having to travel to a single site.

telemarketing software Provides computer support for identifying customers and calling them from disk-based telephone directories or from customer files maintained on a database.

telemarketing systems A marketing system that uses the telephone, often coupled with computer support, to sell products or services.

telephone tag A situation that occurs when two people who wish to contact each other by telephone re-

peatedly miss each other's phone calls.

template A partially completed spreadsheet table or form that can be reused and completed as required.

terabyte (TB) A trillion characters or bytes.

terminal controller A device used in some communication networks to connect many terminals to a single line. Also called cluster control units.

testing The phase in the system development life cycle in which the system inputs, processes, and outputs are tested to make sure they work correctly.

third-generation languages High-level, procedural languages, used to develop application programs. *See also* BASIC, COBOL, FORTRAN and Pascal.

third-party software vendor A firm that develops software that can be used to supplement or replace a similar function performed by another software package.

threat People, actions, events, or other situations that could trigger losses.

time-sharing Providing computer services to many users simultaneously while providing rapid response to each. The user pays only for the services that are used.

time-slicing A CPU management method in which each user's application is allocated one or more fixed amounts of CPU time. When a user's time slice has expired, the operating system directs the CPU to work on another user's program instructions and the most recent user moves to the end of the line to await another slice.

toll fraud The act of defrauding telephone companies out of long-distance toll charges, including using slugs instead of real coins and obtaining illegal access to an organization's telephone lines and selling that access to others.

topologies Methods by which devices on the network are connected; how a network is configured.

total quality control (TQC) A commitment to the fabrication of quality products with an emphasis on preventing defects and placing responsibility for quality control at every point in the production process.

TQC *See* total quality control.

trackball A type of pointing device; often used with notebook computer systems.

tracking capability The ability of information technology to monitor business process task status, inputs, and outputs.

tracking system A system that monitors the location of packages or delivery vehicles.

tracks The concentric circles on a disk or diskette on which data are stored.

training software Computer-based training packages, including management training software, sales training software, microcomputer training software, and word processing training software.

transaction processing systems Operational-level information systems that process a large volume of routine and repetitive organization events.

transactional capability The ability of information technology to transform unstructured business processes into routinized transactions.

transfer time The time it takes for the read/write heads to read data from a location on a disk and place that data in main memory.

transformation Using information technology to change the way in which you do business.

transient programs The components of the operating system that are kept on a direct access storage device, such as a hard disk, so that they may be transferred to main memory quickly when needed.

trusted systems Systems in which database data are restricted to authorized personnel.

turnaround firm A firm in which past applications of information technology are not critical to achieving strategic business goals, but future plans do support the achievement of business strategy.

tutorial software Software packages that teach a user something, such as the commands and features of another software package.

uninterruptable power supply (UPS) A battery system that keeps a computer system powered up in the event of a power failure or brownout.

universal database management system A database system that handles all types of data—traditional transaction data as well as images, sound, video, hypermedia documents, and standard text.

universal product code (UPC) A bar-code standard adopted by the grocery industry.

update To add, change, or delete information to keep it current and accurate.

update policy A service offered by software vendors that usually provides users of registered software the opportunity to obtain the most recent version of their software free or at reduced prices.

update transparency A feature of a distributed system by which users can update data without being concerned with where the data is or where the processing will take place.

upload The process of sending data from a microcomputer to the host to which it is attached.

UPS *See* uninterruptable power supply.

usenet newsgroup A newsgroup is an electronic discussion group that allows people with a mutual in-

terest in a topic to conduct a "virtual" conversation with each other. Thousands of newsgroups cover every imaginable topic on the Internet. Newsgroup conversations are *virtual* because the participants do not talk to each other in real time; rather, they "post" messages to the newsgroup and read the responses to their messages—usually at a later time.

user computer analyst An information system professional who trains and provides consulting assistance to users who are developing decision support systems.

user-developed systems Information systems that are developed by users, sometimes with the assistance of MIS professionals.

user documentation Documentation that provides users with the training they need to understand and use the new system.

user-friendly When a software package has features that make it easy to use.

user group An affiliation of people who share common interests and problem-solving techniques for specific computer hardware or software.

user interface The features of a program through which the user interacts, or interfaces with it, is called the user interface.

user training specialist A person responsible for training the user to use a new system.

value activities The distinct activities a company must perform to do business. Value activities include primary activities and support activities.

value-added networks (VANs) Communication organizations such as Telenet or Tymnet that may lease channels from other common carriers, add services such as packet switching, electronic mail, and protocol conversion to the leased channels, and then re-lease the channels to others.

value analysis A method of justifying a decision support system that focuses on the benefits of the system rather than on the costs.

value chain A depiction of the value activities that are linked together to create, distribute, and maintain products and services. The primary activities of the value chain include inbound logistics, operations, outbound logistics, marketing, and service.

value system The larger system of activities within which the value chain of an industry works. The value system includes the value chains of suppliers, of the firm, of the channels through which the firm distributes its products and services, and of the ultimate buyer.

VANs *See* value-added networks.

variance In budgeting, the difference between the allocation for an account and the actual amount spent.

VDT *See* video display terminal.

versioning A method of controlling problems from concurrent access to data. Versioning permits every user to view and make updates in a record. However, before any record update is actually saved, the system checks to see if the record (the prior version of the record) has changed. If it has the system notifies the user and updates the screen display of the change.

vertical accounting software Commercial accounting software designed for the unique concerns and problems of firms in specific industries.

vertical integration The span of production processes an organization decides to perform for any given product or product line. Also called *process positioning*.

videoconferencing Combines both voice and television images to provide two-way conferencing between groups located at different sites.

video display terminal (VDT) A type of screen used on a computer terminal. Also called *monitor* or *screen*. *See also* CRT, display screen.

virtual office The use of electronic communications technologies to permit a group of people, widely scattered geographically, to work together on a project. Virtual offices usually employ such technologies as e-mail, the World Wide Web, facsimile, telephone, audio- and teleconferencing, whiteboards, and desktop conferencing to stay in touch.

virtual shopping When people view, select, and purchase products and services from a store in another location using electronic means.

virtual storage A way to overcome the size limitations of main memory by swapping data or programs between main memory and a hard disk.

visual programming Visual programming allows the programmer to use graphical tools to help construct information systems.

VMS *See* voice mail system.

voice mail system (VMS) A commercial software package that digitizes, stores, routes, and forwards voice messages for retrieval from any telephone handset.

voice messaging systems Voice menu systems that route a caller automatically to the correct department, person, or mailbox or receive the correct message without any operator intervention.

voice processing systems Voice mail systems, voice messaging systems, and interactive response systems.

voice recognition technology Sound board, microphone, and software used to convert the analog waves of sound into digital data so that they can be stored on disk, manipulated, and otherwise processed.

vulnerabilities The flaws, problems, and conditions that make an information system open to threats.

WAN *See* wide area network.

Web *See* the World Wide Web.

Web page A document on a server attached to the World Wide Web. Usually the document is in hypertext form.

Web site A computer system, attached to the World Wide Web, that allows people to access the hypertext documents it stores. The computer system is located by its universal resource locator (URL), or more simply, its Web address.

what you see is what you get (WYSIWYG) A term associated with word processing that allows the user to preview a document on the screen as it will appear when printed.

whiteboard An electronic blackboard that captures the writing on a board in digital form and uses the telephone system to transmit the data to television screens or other whiteboards at the remote locations.

wide area network (WAN) A communications network that is spread out over a wide geographical area.

widespread technology transfer The phase in information technological change in which new technology is transferred to other parts of the organization.

winchester drives Hard disks that are sealed in a container with the read/write heads to prevent dust, dirt, or other contaminants from damaging the data.

window One section of a computer's multiple-section display screen, each of which can display different data or programs.

windowing Splitting a computer's display into multiple sections with each section being able to run a different program or display different data.

wireless network A network that doesn't use physical cabling; for example, a wireless LAN may transmit

messages through radio waves or infrared waves.

word processing software A collection of application programs that permit the user to create, edit, and print documents.

word size A measure of the power of a computer system; the number of bits that a system can transfer between the CPU and main memory at one time.

workflow automation software Software that allows a user to create a program that automates a series of actions to complete a sequence of tasks.

workflow software *See* workflow automation software.

workforce planning Identifying the human resources needed to meet the organizational objectives specified in the strategic plan, including forecasting the supply and demand of the required work force.

work psychological contract When employees accept the organization's expectations for their performance.

workstation A high-end microcomputer that is used by technical and professional people who require fast, powerful computer systems with high-quality, high-resolution screens. The term can also be applied to any device connected to a network.

World Wide Web The World Wide Web is a subset of the computer systems on the Internet. The Web consists of those computer systems (the servers) that store documents that can be viewed by other computer systems (the clients).

WORM Write once, read many times; a method of storing data permanently on optical disks so that they may be read many times, but may not be altered.

WWW *See* the World Wide Web.

WYSIWYG *See* what you see is what you get.

Name Index

A

Alavi, M., 649
Alexander, M., 691
Alloway, R., 459, 460, 505, 640
Alsop, S., 166
Anderson, H., 348
Anthes, G. H., 671
Anthony, R., 28
Applegate, L. M., 531, 533, 541
Armstrong, A., 85
Attaran, 457

B

Baatz, E. B., 323n, 348
Banta, G., 348
Barlow, V., 581, 613
Barr, C., 322
Baum, D., 190
Behar, R., 658n, 659n, 691
Benjamin, R., 85, 107
Benjamin, R. C. D., Jr., 538, 541
Bentley, L. D., 581, 613
Berkowitz, E., 457
Bernardin, H. J., 457
Block, S., 457
Boardman, B., 298
Bort, J., 670n, 691
Boudreau, J. W., 384n, 457
Boulding, K., 55
Bovee, C. L., 457
Bowers, D. M., 691
Brancheau, J. C., 639, 640, 649
Brealey, R. A., 457
Bridges, W., 103
Brousell, D. R., 348
Brown, B., 166
Bruno, L., 347
Bruns, W. J. Jr., 13n
Buchanan, J. R., 633, 634, 649
Bylinksy, G., 400

C

Cahlin, M., 166
Candadai, A., 383n
Carlson, E., 475, 505, 506
Carlyle, R., 649
Case, T. L., 298

Cash, J., 85, 531, 533, 541
Cash, J. I., 97, 107
Chambers, N., 457
Champy, 91
Cheenne, D., 691
Clemons, E., 82, 85
Cole, B., 251
Colter, M. A., 523n, 541, 581
Conover, J., 298
Conroy, C., 400
Cope, J., 166, 457
Copy, J., 166
Cornette, W. R., 55
Corrigan, P., 691
Couger, J. D., 523n, 541, 581
Covell, A., 348
Cummins, J. M., 298

D

Davenport, T., 107
Davis, 528
Davis, B., 663n
Davis, D. B., 505
Davis, G., 505, 649
Davis, S. M., 400
Davis, W. S., 581, 613
Dejoie, R., 679n, 691
Dennis, A., 505, 506
DeSanctis, G., 480, 506
Diamond, J., 457
Dickinson, C., 107, 538
Dilworth, J. B., 457
Dock, V. T., 55
Doolittle, S., 166, 457
Dorshkind, B., 251
Douglas, S., 125, 372, 373, 381
Drucker, P., 97
Drummond, R., 348
Duffy, C. A., 691
Dugan, S., 691
Dunnette, M. D., 506

E

Eccles, R. G., 97, 107
Eckerson, W. W., 251, 457
Egan, R., 457

Emma, T., 659n, 691
Evans, P., 85

F

Ferrell, K., 657n
Flanagan, P., 457
Flannery, L., 640, 641, 649
Fowler, G., 679n, 691
Fox, M., 457
Fratto, M., 298
Freed, L., 298
Freeh, L., 658
Frey, A., 348
Friedman, R., 298
Frost, M., 389n

G

Gable, M., 400
Gallupe, R. B., 480, 506
Gambino, T. J., 474, 475, 506
Gambon, J., 662n
Gane, C., 581
Gaskin, J. E., 348
Gehl, J., 125, 372, 373, 381
George, J., 505, 506
Gerhart, B., 400
Germain, J. M., 166
Godwin, M., 691
Goldenberg, B., 457
Goldman, J. E., 298
Good, D. J., 457
Gordon, A., 657n
Goree, K., 691
Gorry, G. A., 506
Gremillion, L. L., 586, 610, 613
Grotta, D., 166
Grotta, S. W., 166
Grygo, E. M., 348
Grygo, M., 324n
Guest, R., 5
Gumaer, R., 457
Gunn, A., 298
Guterl, F., 125n

H

Haeckel, S., 46, 55, 519, 541
Hagel, J., III, 85

Haight, T., 691
Halper, M., 243n, 251, 348
Hamilton, R. T., 457
Hammer, 91
Hammer, M., 95, 107, 418
Hanley, S., 661n, 691
Harbison, R., 298
Hartley, S., 457
Harwell, J. A., 691
Hayes, G. M., 251
Henrickson, A. R., 457
Henson, R., 457
Hick, V. B., 319n, 348
Hirt, G., 457
Hoffer, J. A., 251
Hollenbeck, J. R., 400
Holzberg, C., 209, 457
Hopper, M., 79, 80, 82, 85
Houston, M. J., 457
Hudgins-Bonafield, C., 691
Hughes, G. D., 502
Huttig, J. W., 167, 251, 400, 691

I

Inks, S., 368n
Isshiki, K. R., 613
Ives, B., 69, 85

J

Jacobs, D. S., 167
Jacobs, S., 506
Jaffe, B. D., 685n
James-Catalano, C. N., 691
Jessup, L., 505

K

Kalakota, R., 73, 85
Kantor, A., 348
Keen, P. G. W., 298, 474, 475, 476, 506
Keim, R., 506
Kerin, R., 457
Kim, W., 231
King, K., 348
King, P., 241n, 251
Klepper, R., 649
Knapp, R. W., 523n, 541, 581

Konsynski, B., 85
Krantz, M., 270, 298
Krull, A., 660, 691

L
LaPlante, A., 692
Lawton, G., 657, 663, 692
Leavitt, 104
Lederer, A. L., 201n
Leinfuss, E., 457
Levin, C., 326, 400
Liebmann, L., 348, 692
Linowes, R. G., 633, 634, 649
Liu, C., 155n
Loventopoulos, M., 383n
Lucas, H. C., Jr., 107
Luchsinger, V. P., 55
Lyle, J., 139n

M
McFadden, F. R., 251
McFarlan, F. W., 13n, 22, 23, 530, 531, 533, 541, 590, 591, 610, 613
MacGrimmon, K. R., 462, 506
MacIntyre, T., 155
McKenney, J., 23, 530, 531, 533, 541
McPartlin, J. P., 692
Maddox, K., 348
Major, M. J., 657n, 660, 692
Malone, T., 85
Marcus, A. J., 457
Marshall, M., 209
Martin, M., 167
Martin, M. H., 348
Mason, R., 69, 85, 679
Mattison, R., 251
Mayer, J. H., 298
Meador, C. L., 476, 506
Meador, L., 483
Messmer, E., 348
Milkovich, G. T., 384n, 457
Millar, 57, 58, 59, 61, 63
Miller, H., 94
Mills, C., 506
Milne, J., 348
Mintzberg, H., 4, 5, 6, 26, 28, 55, 461, 506
Mirza, A., 383n
Molta, D., 298
Morris, J. S., 457
Morris, L. J., 457
Morris, W., 679n

Morrissey, P., 692
Morse, S., 129
Morton, M. S. S., 506
Moser, K., 251
Myers, S. C., 457

N
Nadel, B., 160
Neustadt, R., 6
Newbarth, M., 348
Newman, J., 299
Newquist, H. P., 506
Nilakant, V., 457
Noe, R. A., 400
Nohria, N., 97, 107
Nolan, R., 46, 55
Nolan, R. L., 18, 19–22, 26, 28, 97, 107, 506, 519, 541
Nunamaker, J. F., 505, 506

O
Oakes, B., 251
Ottolenghi, H. H., 400
Oz, E., 692
Ozer, J., 167

P
Paone, J., 692
Paradice, D., 679n, 691
Parsons, G., 61, 85
Pawlak, A. S., 298
Pecht, 382
Perera, P. A., 400
Peters, L., 581
Pine, B. J., 401
Polakoff, J. C., 436n
Porat, M., 373
Porter, 57, 58, 59, 61, 63
Porter, M., 63, 66, 67, 85, 541
Pyburn, P., 586, 610, 613

Q
Quillard, J., 459, 460, 505, 640
Quinlan, T., 160n
Quinn, B., 692
Quittner, J., 692

R
Radding, A., 251
Raisinghani, D., 461, 506
Recht, M., 401
Remington, M., 251, 457
Ricciuti, M., 692

Riggs, B., 348
Rockart, J., 107, 460, 506, 520, 538, 541, 640, 641, 649
Roe, Cliff, 383
Rogers, A., 298
Rothfeder, J., 692
Rudelius, W., 457
Rupley, S., 348
Russell, J. E. A., 457
Rysavy, P., 299

S
Salamone, S., 348, 692
Salemi, J., 209, 251
Samyer, T., 401
Sarson, T., 581
Sawyer, 382
Schein, E., 23, 534, 541
Schreiber, R., 348
Schulman, L., 85
Schultheis, R., 692
Schussel, G., 251
Senge, P., 49, 55
Sherman, K., 289
Simon, 461
Simpson, D., 286
Slack, N., 457
Slick, B., 457
Smith, H. J., 692
Smith, L., 251
Smith, L. D., 298
Snyder, J., 348
Sprague, R., 475
Sprague, R. H., 483, 505, 506
Stalk, G., 85
Stamper, D. A., 299
Stamps, 442
Stearman, S. W., 457
Steeves, R., 251
Stephenson, P., 663
Stix, G., 387
Stone, R. W., 457
Stoppard, T., 90
Strangelove, M., 401
Stuart, A., 348
Sumner, M., 649, 692

T
Tannenbaum, T., 348
Taylor, R. N., 462, 506
Thé, L., 348
Theoret, A., 461, 506
Thill, J. V., 457
Thomas, S. G., 167

Thomas, T., 457
Townsend, A. M., 457
Treacy, M., 460, 506
Trimm, J., 299, 348
Trulove, J. E., 299
Trumbo, J., 348
Turban, E., 483, 506
Turbide, D. A., 457
Tweney, D., 251

U
Ulanoff, L., 209

V
Valacich, J., 506
Van Kirk, D., 673
Varhol, P. D., 251
Verdi, C., 681
Vine, D., 457
Vogel, D. R., 505, 506, 639, 640, 649
Von Bertalanffy, 55
von Simson, E. M., 649

W
Wagner, M., 671
Wainwright, D., 457
Waltner, C., 692
Washburn, B., 401
Waterman, D. A., 506
Watkins, P., 483, 506
Watson, H. J., 483, 506
Watterson, K., 241n, 251
Weise, E., 155n
Weston, F. C., Jr., 457
Wetherbe, J. C., 528, 529, 530, 541, 639, 640, 649
Whinston, A., 73, 85
Whisler, 104
Whiting, R., 167
Whitten, J. L., 581, 613
Wiggins, R., 348
Williams, A., 470
Willis, D., 299, 348
Wittmann, A., 299

Y
Yates, J., 85

Z
Zgodzinski, D., 299, 348
Ziems, C., 348
Zuckerman, M. J., 657n

Subject Index

A

A. O. Smith, 69
ABC Industries, 26
Abuse, computer; *see* Computer crime, fraud, abuse
Access, and ethics, 679-683
Access database tool, 468
Access Market Square, 71, 85
Accessing records, 216
  inverted files for, 217
  linked lists for, 217
Accounting information systems; *see* Operational financial accounting information systems; Strategic accounting and financial information systems; Tactical accounting and financial information systems
Accounting models, 467
Accounts payable system, 363
Accounts receivable system
  distributed data processing and, 630-632
  operational systems and, 361-363
Accuracy
  in distributed processing, 304
  ethics, privacy, and, 682-683
  in operational information systems, 358
ACE expert system, 488
Acquisition, hardware; *see* Hardware, acquisition issues
Acrobat, 195
Action, OODA loop, 519
ActionWare, 648
ActiveX, 298, 322
Activities, 101
Actor language, 193
Actuals, 405
Ad hoc reports, 10
Adaptation, decision support systems, 476

Adaptive design, 474-475
Add-on software, 186
Address, memory, 129
Adhocracy, 22
Adobe, 195
ADSL; *see* Asymmetric Digital Subscriber Line service
Advanced Research Projects Agency, 313
Advertising
  in operational marketing systems, 370, 372-375
  in tactical marketing, 419-421
Advertising and promotion systems, 419-421
Aeroflot, 84
Aetna Life and Casualty, 84
Age Discrimination in Employment Act, 388
Aged accounts receivable reports, 361
Agents, intelligent, 198
Agile manufacturing, 382-383, 399
Airlines
  Internet reference sites for, 84
  reservation systems for; *see* APOLLO; SABRE
Alexon, 659
Algorithms, 461, 468
Allocations, 405
Allstate, 71
Allstate Motor Club, 84
Alta Vista search engine, 347
Alternative application development; *see also* Project management
  strategies for, 583-5
    prototyping, 583, 584
    selection factors, 586-587
    software packages, 583, 584
    user-developed systems, 583, 585
Alternative courses of action, 114

America Online, 71, 76, 237
  connection problems with, 319
  email service of, 328
  fax transmissions via, 335
  Internet access and, 313
  Trojan horses in, 660
American Accounting Association, 456
American Airlines, 81, 82
  competitive advantage and, 78, 79, 80
  competitive strategy and, 534
  information system risk at, 77
  interorganizational systems at, 70, 71, 72
  technological impact at, 65
  web site of, 84
American Business Information, 366
American Compensation Association, 400
American Express, 489, 681
American Hospital Supply, 57, 81
  competitive edge at, 78, 80
  information system risk at, 77
  interorganizational systems at, 71, 72
  technological impact at, 64
  value activities at, 61
American Institute of Certified Public Accountants, 456
American Marketing Association, 456
American Micro Systems, Inc., 660
American Production and Inventory Control Society, 456
American Standard Code for Information Interchange; *see* ASCII
Americans with Disabilities Act, 388, 400

AMH systems; *see* Automated material handling systems
Analog transmission, 256
Analysis, decision support systems, 476
Analysis system, 459
Andersen Consulting, 568
Antivirus programs, 662
APOLLO reservations system, 65, 72, 534
Apple Basket Antiques and Gifts, 85
Apple Computer
  in chip consortium, 126
  microcomputer sales of, 121
  web site of, 166
Applets, 199, 322
Applicant selection and placement systems, 389; *see also* Recruiting system
Application development, alternative; *see* Alternative application development
Application development tools, 222
Application generators, 192-193
Application programmers, 179, 625, 636
  productivity of, 234
Application research, 475
Application software, 40, 170
  add-ons, 186
  applets, 199
  categories of, by use, 180
  custom versus commercial, 179
  database management; *see* Database management systems
  desktop suites of, 180-181
  libraries of, 179
  for multimedia systems, 187
  multiprocessing and, 173
  other types of, 186, 188
  portability of, 179-180

Application software—*Cont.*
  presentation graphics, 185–186
  shareware and freeware, 179
  single-user versus multiuser, 180
  spreadsheet, 182–184
  word processing, 181–182
Applications
  sharing of, 283–284
  small (applets), 322
Architecture, and communications standards, 292
Archive copies, 135, 176
Archiving programs, 176
Arithmetic/logic unit, 125–127
Armed Forces Insurance, 84
ARPANET, 313
Artificial intelligence, 481–482; *see also* Expert systems
AS/400 minicomputer, 350, 354
ASAP system, 57, 77, 81
ASCII (American Standard Code for Information Interchange), 129, 256, 257
Aspiration level, 461
Assembly languages, 189
Asset management systems, 102
Associations, from data mining, 466
Asymmetric Digital Subscriber Line (ADSL) service, 260, 264
Asymmetric multiprocessing, 173
Asynchronous transfer mode (ATM), 264
Asynchronous transmission, 257
AT&T, 84, 262, 263, 328
AT&T Wireless Services, 298
ATM; *see* Asynchronous transfer mode
ATMs; *see* Automatic teller machines
Attributes, object, 232
Audioconferencing, 331
Auditing, EDP, 653–656
Auditing software, network, 670–672
Authoring software, 187

Auto data, privacy of, 681
AutoCAD, 380
Autodesk, 380
Automated design, 101
Automated material handling (AMH) systems, 380
Automatic teller machines (ATMs), 63, 66
Auxiliary storage, 129; *see also* Secondary storage

B
Back-end processor, 310
Backbone network, 278
Background tasks, 174–175
Backlog, systems development, 583–587
Backup copies, 135, 176
Backup systems, 222
Backward compatibility, 196
Badge readers, 148
Balancing feedback, 51
Banc One, 79
Bank data, privacy of, 681
Bar-code readers, 144
Barclay Square Shopping Mall, 71, 85
Barclaycard, 84
Barra, 410
BASF, 479
Batch control, 678
Batch processing, 133
  as a design option, 563
  file structures and, 217
Batch systems, in life cycle, 545
Batch total, 678
Baxter Healthcare System
  information system risk at, 77
  interorganizational systems at, 70, 71, 72
Baynetworks, 298
BC Tel Wireless Data Services, 298
Benchmarking Partners Inc., 418
Benefits
  in cost-benefit analysis, 592–593
  employee, 441–442
  project, 526
Better Business Bureau, 84
Bill-of-materials (BOM) system, 378
Binary digits, 129

Bits, 129, 138
Bits per second (bps), 264
BLUE BOX expert system, 488
Boards
  emulation, 283
  personal computer, 128
BOM system; *see* Bill-of-materials system
Book value, 360
Booting, kernel, 175
Borland International, Inc., 684
Bottleneck, systems development, 583–587
Boundary, 32
Bps; *see* Bits per second
Branch Mall, 71, 85
Bridges, 272
Browser software, 314
Browsers, Web, 224, 314–316
BSA CareerMart, 648
BSP (business systems planning); *see* Information requirements
Budget Rent-A-Car
  competitive edge at, 80
  information system risk at, 77
  interorganizational systems at, 70, 71
  technological impact at, 65
Budget variance, 405–406
Budgeting systems, 405–406
  capital, 408–410
Bugs, as security threat, 665
Builder-user interaction, 474–475
Building, object, 232
Bulletin boards, electronic, 281
Bundled software packages, 181
Burlington Coat Factory, 85
Burlington Industries, 100
Bus, 132
Bus topology, 273
Business area analysis, 576
Business process, 97, 524
Business process redesign, 97–98
  case studies in, 99–100
  information technology applications and, 101
  logistical processes, 102
  order fulfillment, 102
  product development, 101–102

  management challenges in, 103
  process types and, 100–101
  steps in, 98–99
Business Software Alliance, 691
Business systems planning (BSP); *see* Information requirements
By-product technique, 520, 521
Byte, 129
Byte, 167

C
C-Systems, 424
Cable media, 260
Cable modems, 270
Cable TV, 253, 262
Cache bit, 138
Cache memory, 138
Cache miss, 138
CAD/CAM (computer-aided design/computer-aided manufacturing), 380–382
Caere Corporation, 243
Call conferencing, 290
Call directors, 290
Call reports, 366
Canada Net Stocks and Bonds, 410
Canadian Airlines, 84
Canned programs, 179
Capabilities-based competition, 78–79
Capacity, channel, 260, 319
Capacity planning, 431–433
Capital budgeting, 408–410
Card readers, 148
Careers, Internet reference sites, 84
Careers OnLine, 648
Carfax, Inc., 681
Carpal tunnel syndrome, 160
CASE (computer-aided software engineering), 193, 222
  benefits of, 569, 573
  data-flow diagram using, 570–571
  elements of, 572
  information systems development and, 536, 615
Cash flow report, 407
Cash Management Account (CMA), 64, 80, 408

Cash management systems, 407–408

Cathay Pacific Airlines, 84

Cathode ray tube (CRT), 149

CBT; see Computer-based training

CD-ROM drives, 140

Cellular digital packet data (CDPD) networks, 265–266

Cellular telephone system, 265

Center for Democracy and Technology, 691

Central processing unit (CPU), 125–127, 128

  multiprocessing and, 173

  multiprogramming and, 172

  parallel processing and, 173

Centralization, systems development, 537, 538

Centralized data processing, 626–627

Centralized databases, 307

Centrex, 287–288

CFAR; see Collaborative forecasting and replenishment

Change, human factors of, 602–604

Change agent, 603

Changeability, in design, 595–596

Channel capacity, 260, 319

Channels, 255, 260, 261

Charles Schwab, 84

Chemical Bank, 479

Chex-Systems, 681

Chicago Mercantile Exchange, 84

Chicago Police Department, 387

Chief information officer, 538, 638

Chip, microprocessor, 126, 127

Choice phase, decision making, 461, 464

CIM; see Computer-integrated manufacturing

Circuit switching, 258

CIRRUS network, 70

CISC; see Complex instruction set computing

Citibank, 657

Civil Aeronautics Board, 65

Civil Rights Act of 1964, 388

Clark Products, Inc., 27–28

Classes, object, 232

Classifications, from data mining, 466

Clavin, Inc., 685

Client/server computing

  components of, 309

  downsizing in, 311

  SQL servers in, 309–311

Clip art, 185–186

Clock speed, 132

Closed systems, 35

Clothing, Internet reference sites, 85

Clusters, from data mining, 466

CMA; see Cash Management Account

CNET, 347

Coaxial cable, 260

COBOL language, 190

Coca-Cola, 26, 35

Code of Fair Information Practices, 673

Coding, 189

Cohesion, in design, 596

Coke, as fuel, 616

Cold site, for recovery, 668

Collaborative forecasting and replenishment (CFAR), 418

COM; see Computer output microfilm

Command-and-control structure, 90

Command-line user interfaces, 177

Commercial versus custom software, 179

Common carrier, 262

Commonality, in alternative application development, 586

Communication, protection of; see Protecting information systems

Communications Decency Act, 658

Communications network, 255; see also Networks

Communications protocol, 269

Communications software, 173–174, 188

Communications systems; see also Networks

  capacity of, 260

data codes for, 256, 257

elements of, 255

media for, 260–261

paradigm shift and, 253

remote access, 280–283

  to bulletin boards, 281

  to Internet, 281

  to mainframes, 282–283

  between microcomputers, 280–281

  to minicomputers, 282–283

remote access in

for LANs, 281

sources and products for, 262–268

speed of, 260

standards for, 292

transmission modes for

  analog, 256

  asynchronous, 257

  circuit switching, 258

  digital, 256

  full-duplex, 258

  half-duplex, 258

  message switching, 258–259

  packet switching, 259

  simplex, 258

  synchronous, 257–258

voice; see Voice systems

Compaq Computer, 125

Compatibility

  hardware, 155–156, 196–197

  in networks, 286

  software, 196–197

Compensation and benefits system, 441–442

Competitive tracking systems, 423–425

Complete enumeration, model building, 467

Complex instruction set computing (CISC), 126, 177

Compound documents, 194

CompUSA, 69

Compusearch Micromarketing Data & Systems, 369

CompuServe, 237, 335

  investment information on, 411

  marketing information on, 424

strategic uses of, 70, 71, 76

Computer-aided design/computer-aided manufacturing; see CAD/CAM

Computer-aided engineering, 382

Computer-aided inspection, 382

Computer-aided process planning, 382

Computer-aided software engineering; see CASE

Computer-aided telephone interview software, 427

Computer-aided testing, 382

Computer-based electronic mail systems, 327; see also E-mail

Computer-based training (CBT), 187, 389

Computer conferencing, 333–334

Computer crime, fraud, abuse, 657–658

  hacking, 659

  hardware theft and vandalism, 662–663

  industrial espionage, 658–659

  privacy violations, 664–665

  software piracy, 663–664, 684

  toll fraud, 659–661

  viruses, 661–662

Computer design options, 564–565

Computer-integrated manufacturing (CIM), 436

Computer output microfilm (COM), 153

Computer platforms; see Platforms

Computer power, 131–132

Computer program, 129; see also Software

Computer Shopper, 167

Computer systems; see Hardware, computer systems

Computer telephony integration (CTI), 291

Computer virus, 661–662

Comsat Corporation, 266

Concurrency control, 235

Concurrent engineering, 93

Concurrent-use licensing, 195

Consensus building, 480

Consistency, data, 219–220, 233

Constraints, problem solving, 114

Construction, information engineering, 577

Consultants
  expert systems as, 494
  for software selection, 200

Contact management systems, 366–367

Contagion stage, 19

Contractual behavior, ethics of, 679

Control aids, 465

Control issues, 655–656; *see also* Security
  in data processing organizations, 641–642
  in database management systems, 234, 235
  in networking, 285

Control stage, 19–20

Control tools, formal, 590

Control unit, 125–127

Controlling function, 4

Convergent computer systems, 123–124

Conversion, from old to new system, 602

Cookie Express, 85

Coopers and Lybrand, 483

Coprocessors, 128, 132

Copyright, 195, 658; *see also* Software piracy

Corel Corporation, 181, 209

Cost accounting systems, 378

Cost-benefit analysis, 526
  of design alternatives, 592–595
  benefits, 592–593
  costs, 593–595

Costs
  in cost-benefit analysis, 593–595
  of distributed processing, 303–304
  of networks, 286
  of operational information systems, 358
  of software, 199, 202–203, 284

Coupling, modules, 596

CPU; *see* Central processing unit

Credit data, privacy of, 681

Crime Control Act, 658

Critical success factors; *see* Information requirements

Croft, Brian, 400

CRT; *see* Cathode ray tube

CTI; *see* Computer telephony integration

CTSNET, 399

Currency, in distributed processing, 304

Custom versus commercial software, 179

Customer-focused EDI, 312

Customer service
  augmented, 69
  operational information systems and, 358–359
  personalized, 69

Cut-over method, conversion, 602

Cybercalifragilistic, 85

CyberCoin, 348

Cyberspace Malls International, 71, 85

Cylinder storage, 138

D

DART expert system, 488

DASD; *see* Direct access storage devices

DAT systems; *see* Digital audiotape systems

Data, 15
  consistency of, 306
  loss of, 305–306
  as a resource, 234
  scrubbed, 466
  views of, 227–228

Data administration stage, 20

Data class/process matrix, BSP method, 525

Data codes, 129, 256

Data communications specialist, 638

Data compression, 176

Data consistency, 219–220, 233

Data description language (DDL), 222

Data dictionary, 597; *see also* Logical data dictionary

Data dictionary/directory, 221–222; *see also* Logical data dictionary

Data diddling, 660

Data element, 212

Data entry personnel, 637

Data-flow diagram; *see* Logical data-flow diagram

Data independence, 219, 234

Data languages, 222

Data Logic, 691

Data manipulation language (DML), 222

Data marts, 240–241

Data mining, 368, 416, 466–467

Data processing, 110
  organization of
    career paths in, 638–639
    centralized, 626–627
    decentralized, 628–629
    distributed; *see* Distributed data processing
    end-user computing and, 639–640
    evolution of computing and, 625–626
    future of, 643–644
    information technologies in, 633–635
    management and control issues, 641–642
    management in, 638–640, 641–642
    responsibilities in; *see* Responsibilities, in data processing organization
    user-developed applications and, 640
    user support center in, 639–640
  stage evolution of, 19–21
    new information technology growth, 23–24
    updated framework, 21–22

Data processing era, 21–22

Data redundancy, 219, 233

Data security, 478; *see also* Information systems security

Data validation, 677

Data warehouses, 368, 416, 465–466

Data warehousing, 239–240

Database administrator, 225–226, 638

Database concepts, 218

data consistency, 219–220

data independence, 219

data redundancy, 219

Database management software, 184–185
  evaluation of, 604–606

Database management systems (DBMSs)
  advantages of, 233–234
  components of, 221–224
    application development tools, 222
    archiving systems, 222
    data dictionary/directory, 221–222
    data languages, 222
    multiple platform databases, 223–224
    query languages, 222–223
    report writers, 222
    security software, 222
    teleprocessing monitor, 222
    web server software, 224
  database administrator for, 225–226
  definition of, 220
  evaluation of, 604–606
  problems posed by, 234–235
  security of, 222, 226, 236
  universal, 243

Database query, 468

Databases, 60
  data marts, 240–241
  data warehousing, 239–240
  definition of, 218
  distributed; *see* Distributed databases
  document, 242–243
  electronic directory, 366
  hypermedia, 236–237
  image, 242
  intranet, 236–237
  models of, 228–232
    hierarchical, 228–229
    network, 228–229
    object-oriented, 231–232
    relational, 229–231
  multiple platform, 223–224
  OLAP, 241–242
  on-line; *see* On-line databases
  partitioned, 308
  protection of, 672–675
  replicated, 307–308

of software, 200
views of data in, 227–228
schema and, 227
subschema and, 227–228
Datapro, 606
Davis-Bacon Act, 388
DBMSs; see Database management systems
DDE; see Dynamic data exchange
DDL; see Data description language
DEC; see Digital Equipment Corporation
Decentralization, systems development, 537, 538
Decentralized data processing, 628–629
as a design option, 564
Decision analysis systems, 102
Decision-making process, 460–462
decision maker attributes in, 461
implications of, 462
OODA loop and, 519
operational information systems and, 359, 360
phases of, 461
problem types in, 461
strategies for, 462
Decision room, 479
Decision support systems (DSS)
benefits of, 477–478
cases in, 471–474
financial control, 472
international loans, 472–474
production planning, 471–472
components of, 465–468
data mining as, 466–467
data warehouse as, 465–466
intelligent agents as, 466–467
model building as, 467–468
development of, 474–477
life cycle of, 475–477
distribution channels and, 423
expert systems and, 482–483
features of, 462–465
communication, 464–465

control aids, 465
databases, 463
decision-making phases and, 463–464
memory aids, 465
unstructured decisions and, 463
group DSS, 479–481
Internet reference sites for, 505
need for, 459–460
risks of, 478–479
tools for, 468–471
Decision table, 562
Decision tree, 562
Decisional roles, 4, 5
Delivery tracking and routing systems, 370–372
Dell Computer Corporation, 453
Dellco Foods, Inc., 17
Demand, project, 526
Democratic National Committee, 420
Departmental computing, 642
Design; see also Systems design
computer-aided, 380–382
of jobs, 439–440
of plants, 438
project management and; see Project management
in tactical production, 434–435
Design, Inc., 312
Design phase, decision making, 461, 464
Design work, expert system, 488
Designer-user interaction, 474–475
Desired state, in problem solving, 113
Desktop computers, 121
Desktop conferencing, 321, 331–333
Desktop organizer software, 188
Desktop publishing software, 188
Desktop suites, 180–181
Desktop survey software, 427
Desktop video technology, 148
Detailed system design, 546
Development approaches, alternative; see Alternative application development

Development costs, 593
Development software, 170, 187
CASE tools for, 193
object-oriented programming for, 193
programming languages for, 187, 189–193
application generators, 192–193
assembly, 189
fourth-generation, 190–192
machine, 189
natural, 192
query, 192
report generators, 192
third-generation, 189–190
Diagnostic systems, 487–488
Dial-a-Gift, 85
Dial-back procedure, 672
Dial-up telephone lines, 264
Dialog Information Services, 424
Dictionary; see Data dictionary
Digital audiotape (DAT) systems, 142–143
Digital cameras, 148
Digital Equipment Corporation (DEC)
business process redesign at, 102
competitive advantage of, 82
EBCDIC and, 129
expert systems of, 488, 492, 494
PC speed of, 132
web site of, 166
Digital Review, 167
Digital transmission, 256
Digital video disk (DVD) technology, 140
Dillards, 100
DIPMETER ADVISOR expert system, 488
Direct access, 215
Direct access storage devices (DASD), 135
Direct file structure, 215
Direct mail advertising systems, 370
DISA (inward system access dialing), 661
Disaster recovery plan, 667
Disasters, natural, 656

Discussion groups, electronic, 320
Disk controller board, 128
Disk drives, 128, 135
Disk duplexing system, 674–675
Disk packs, 136
Disk storage; see Secondary storage, on disk
Display-based software, 471
Display screens, 149
Distributed data processing, 629–632; see also Distributed systems
accounts receivable system of, 630–632
as a design option, 564, 568–569
financial services system of, 630
point-of-sale system of, 630
Distributed database systems, 307
Distributed databases
advantages and disadvantages of, 308
partitioned, 308
replicated, 307–308
Distributed systems, 301–302; see also Distributed data processing; Internet; Interorganizational information systems
client/servers as; see Client/server computing
concerns about, 305–306
data consistency, 306
data loss, 305–306
documentation, 305
maintenance, 306
security, 306
staffing, 305
standardization, 305
definition of, 303
effectiveness of, 306–307
reasons for implementing, 303–305
accuracy and currency, 304
costs, 303–304
growth, 304
reliability, 304–305
resource sharing, 305
response time, 303
user satisfaction, 305

Distribution channel decision-support systems, 423

Division of labor, 90

DML; *see* Data manipulation language

Document databases, 242–243

Document management software, 242

Documentation
for detailed design, 598, 600
distributed processing and, 305

Documentation specialist, 636

Domain, expert system, 485

DOS, 175

Dot-matrix printers, 150–151

Dow Chemical, 102

Dow Jones News/Retrieval Service, 410, 411, 412

Downsized systems, 125

Downsizing, client/server computing, 311

DSS; *see* Decision support systems

Dumb terminals, 144, 268

Dun & Bradstreet, 456

Duplex, half- and full-, 258

DVD-ROM drives, 140

Dynamic data exchange (DDE), 178–179

E

E-commerce, 322–323

E/M analysis; *see* Ends/means analysis

E-mail, 283, 327–328

E-mail based workflow system, 338–340

E-mail bombs, 660

E-mail software, remote, 327–328

E*Trades, 323

Ease of installation, 198

Ease of use, 197

EBCDIC (Extended Binary Coded Decimal Interchange Code), 129, 256, 257

Economic espionage, 658–659

Economic order quantity (EOQ) system, 379–380

Economost system, 70, 81

EDGAR database, 399

EDI; *see* Electronic data interchange

EDP (electronic data processing) auditing, 653–656; *see also* Information systems security

EDS, 381

Effectiveness, 5, 7, 87

Efficiency, 5, 7, 87
E/M analysis and, 528

EISA bus; *see* Extended Industry Standard Architecture bus

Electronic advertising, 374–375

Electronic bulletin boards, 281

Electronic Car Showroom, 74

Electronic commerce, 73–76, 322–323
safety in, 668

Electronic conferencing; *see* Office communications

Electronic data interchange (EDI), 73, 312
just-in-time systems and, 431
order fulfillment and, 102
vendor use of, 619

Electronic data processing auditing; *see* EDP auditing

Electronic directory databases, 366

Electronic Freedom Foundation, 691

Electronic kiosks, 374

Electronic mail systems, 327–328; *see also* E-mail; Voice mail

Electronic market systems, 313

Electronic marketing applications, 102

Electronic Newsstand, 74

Electronic Privacy Information Center, 691

Electronic security controls, 655

Electronic shopping, 372–373

Electronic warfare, 660

Embedding, object, 194

Employee information system, 385

Employee profiles, 385

Employee relations; *see* Operational human resource information systems; Strategic human resource information systems; Tactical human resource information systems

Employee Retirement Income Security Act (ERISA), 388

Emulation board, 283

Emulation software, 283

Encryption, 668

End-of-file checks, 678

End-user computing, 639–640

Ends/means (E/M) analysis, 528–530

Energy Star systems, 159–160

Engineering design order, 618

Enterprise networking, 278–279

Entertainment Recruiting Network, 315

Entities, 100

Entity-relationship diagram, 227

Environment, 44, 159–160; *see also* Systems environments

EOQ system; *see* Economic order quantity system

EPROM; *see* Erasable programmable read-only memory

Equal Pay Act, 388

Equipment costs, 593

Equipment operators, 637

Erasable programmable read-only memory (EPROM), 131

Ergonomics, hardware, 160–161

Ericsson, 298

ERISA; *see* Employee Retirement Income Security Act

Ernst and Young Information Security Services, 670

Error messages, 217

Errors, as security threats, 656

Espionage, industrial, 658–659

Essex Industries, Inc., 26

Ethical issues, 651–652; *see also* Information systems security
contractual behavior and, 679
expert systems and, 494
information system impact and, 685–686
management responsibility for, 686
privacy and, 679–683
property issues and, 683–685

Ethics, definition of, 679

European Community, 664

Evolution loop, 475

Evolution of computing, 625–626

Excel, 194, 470

Exception reports, 10, 459, 678

Excite search engine, 348

Executive information systems, Internet reference sites for, 505

Expandability, hardware, 156

Expansion slots, 128

Expert systems, 188, 481–482
advantages of, 493
in business, 489–493
building of, 491
development for, 490–491
experts and, 491–493
knowledge engineer and, 491–493
opportunities for, 490
prototyping approach to, 492
characteristics of, 483–485
explanation, 485
inference engine, 484–485
knowledge acquisition, 485
knowledge base, 484
decision support systems and, 482–483
Internet reference sites for, 505
limits of, 493–494
shell for, 494
tools for, 494–495
workings of, 485–489
conventional systems and, 487
frame-based, 486
problem types for, 487–488
rule-based, 485–486

ExperTAX, 483

Experts, 490, 491–493

Explanation subsystem, 485

Extended Binary Coded Decimal Interchange Code; *see* EBCDIC

Extended Industry Standard Architecture (EISA) bus, 131

External integration tools, 590

External modems, 270

Extranets, 324–325

F

Facilities, protection of, 666–668

Factory local area network, 376

Factory quadrant, planning grid, 532

Fair Credit Reporting Act, 236, 658

Fair Labor Standards Act, 388

Family Leave and Medical Act, 387, 388

Famous Barr, 101

FAQ (frequently-asked-questions), 320

Farm Credit Banks, 568

Fax/modem boards, 335

Fax systems, 334–335
  on demand, 331
  printers and, 152–153

FDDI standard; see Fiber Distributed Data Interface standard

Feasibility study, 544

Federal Computer Fraud and Abuse Act, 658

Federal Express, 85, 325

Feedback, 35–36
  balancing, 51
  information systems for, 46–49
  in learning organization, 51–52

Fiber Distributed Data Interface (FDDI) standard, 278

Fiber optic cables, 260

Fidelity Investments, 84

Field, 212

Field locking, 235

Fifth discipline, 49

File, 213–214

File concepts, 212–214

File locking, 235

File structures
  accessing records and, 216–217
    inverted files for, 217
    linked lists for, 217
  direct, 215
  indexed sequential, 215–216
  processing methods and,
    batch, 217
    on-line real-time, 217
  sequential, 214–215

File transfer protocol (FTP), 74, 320–321

Filene's, 101

Files
  sharing of, 283
  transferred between microcomputers, 280–281

Filtering, e-mail software, 327

Finance, Internet reference sites, 84

FinanceNet, 399, 410, 456

Financial condition analysis system, 412–413

Financial information systems; see Operational financial accounting information systems; Strategic accounting and financial information systems; Tactical accounting and financial information systems

Financial services system, 630

Fingerhut, 680

FINWeb, 399, 410, 456

Firewalls, 669

Firmware, 131

First-line management, 7–8

Fixed assets system, 360–361

Fixed disks, 138

Flash memory, 139

Floppy diskettes, 135

Floppy drives, 128, 135

Floptical drives, 141–142

Florida Academy of Family Physicians, 166

FOCUS language, 471, 585

Ford Motor Company, 518
  accounts payable system at, 91–92
  business process redesign at, 102
  electronic commerce and, 74
  innovations at, 381
  reengineering at, 104, 106

Forecasting, 102
  long-range, strategic, 413–415
  sales, strategic, 425–426
  software for, 414

Foreground tasks, 174–175

Formalization stage, expert systems, 491

Formatting, 176

Forms creation tool, 338

Fourth-generation languages, 190–192

information systems planning and, 536
  prototyping and, 584

Frame-based systems, 486

Frame relay, 264

Fraud, computer; see Computer crime, fraud, abuse

Freeware, 179

Frequently-asked-questions; see FAQ

Front-end processors, 271, 310

Frontier Airlines, 65, 533, 534

FTP; see File transfer protocol

Full-duplex transmission, 258

Function-specific software, 180

G

Gantt charts, 433, 587–588

Garbage in, garbage out (GIGO), 677

Gateway, 67

GB; see Gigabyte

GDSS; see Group decision support systems

General Dynamics Corporation, 482

General Electric, 89

General ledger system, 360

General Life Insurance Company, 15–16

General Magic, 373

General Motors, 316, 381, 424

General purpose software, 180

Geographic information systems software, 420

Gifts, Internet reference sites, 85

Gigabyte (GB), 130

GIGO; see Garbage in, garbage out

Girard, 66

Global positioning system (GPS), 370

Goal, expert system, 485

Goodies from Goodman, 85

Gopher, 74

Government reporting systems, 387–389

GPS; see Global positioning system

Graphical user interface (GUI), 177
  ease of use and, 197
  trends in, 194

visual programming and, 193

Graphics software, 188

Graphiti T-Shirt Design, 85

Great-West Life and Annuity Insurance, 84

Green systems, 159–160

Group decision support systems (GDSS), 479–481

Groupware, 188, 196, 284, 337–338

GUI; see Graphical user interface

H

Hacking, 659

Haggar, 100

Half-duplex transmission, 258

Hard disks, 136–137

Hard drives, 128, 135

Hardware, 39–40, 119–120
  acquisition issues, 156–161
    environment and, 159–160
    ergonomics and, 160–161
    installation, maintenance, training, 159
    renting, leasing, buying, 157
    timing, 156–157
    vendor selection, 158–159
  central processing unit, 125–127
  computer platforms, 124–125, 194
  computer power and, 131–132
  computer systems, 120–124
    convergent, 123–124
    mainframe, 120
    microcomputer, 120–121
    minicomputer, 120
    network, 123
    smaller size, 121–123
    supercomputer, 120
    workstation, 121
  definition of, 120
  evaluation of, 606–608
  input and output devices; see Input devices; Output devices
  Internet reference sites for, 166
  memory, 129–131
  for multimedia systems, 187

Hardware—*Cont.*
  multiprocessing and, 132–133
  network; *see* Networks, components of
  PBX, 290–291
  processing types and, 133–134
  secondary storage; *see* Secondary storage
  standards for, 155–156
    compatibility and, 155–156
    expandability and, 156
    reliability and, 156
    theft and vandalism of, 662–663
Hardware demands, of software, 198–199
Hardware dependence, of software, 177
Harvard Graphics, 471
Hash total, 678
Hashing algorithm, 215
HDTV; *see* High definition television
Head switching, 138
Hecht's, 101
Help
  on-line, 197
  technical support hot-lines for, 201
Heuristics, 461, 468
Hewlett-Packard, 94, 95, 104, 106
Hierarchical database, 228–229
Hierarchical network, 273
Hierarchical storage, 143
High definition television (HDTV), 124
High-structure-high-technology projects, 591
High-structure-low-technology projects, 591
Hilton, 65, 77, 80
Holiday Inns, 62, 68
Honda, 79
Hosts, network, 268
Hot keys, 175
Hot-lines, technical support, 201
Hot site, for recovery, 656, 668
HRIS; *see* Human resource information systems
HRM; *see* Human resource management

HTML (hypertext markup language), 196, 237, 341
Hubs, network, 272, 276
Human factors, in implementation, 602–604
Human Resource Information Network, 443
Human resource information systems (HRIS), 384, 438, 446; *see also* Operational human resource information systems; Strategic human resource information systems; Tactical human resource information systems
Human resource management (HRM), 438
HyperCard, 193
Hypermedia databases, 236–237
Hypertalk, 193
Hypertext, 187
Hypertext markup language; *see* HTML

I
I/O (input/output)
  channels for, 132
  management programs for, 172
  network tasks of, 271
I/O bound systems, 154
IBM
  AS/400 minicomputer, 350, 354, 693–696
  BSP methodology of, 539
  in chip consortium, 126
  conferencing software of, 332
  interorganizational systems at, 70
  operating systems of, 175
  paperless office and, 341
  reengineering at, 92
  RISC technology of, 126
  robotics at, 482
  SNA from, 292
  web sites of, 166
  website of, 251
IBM clones, 121
IBM Credit, 79, 92
IBM Internet Connection, 648
Identification stage, expert systems, 491
Image databases, 242
Image management systems, 382

iMall, 71, 85
Immigration Reform and Control Act, 388
Impact printers, 149, 150–151
Implementation; *see also* Project management
  conversion in, 602
  of expert systems, 491
  human factors in, 602–604
  in life cycle, 546
  programming in, 600–601
  software testing in, 600–601
  training in, 601
Imported files, 361
Improved manual operations, 564
In-house computer system, 565
In-house software development, 566
Incrementalizing strategy, 462
Independence, data, 219, 234
Index
  file structure and, 215
  secondary, 217
Indexed sequential access method (ISAM), 215
Indexed sequential file structure, 215–216
Industrial espionage, 658–659
Industry-specific software, 180
IndustryNet, 456
Inference engine, 484–485
Information, 15, 39
Information capacity, 461
Information engineering, 575–577
Information planning grid, 531–532
Information requirements; *see also* Information systems planning; Information technology planning
  business systems planning method, 523–528
  action plan for, 527
  analysis method for, 524–526
  assessment interviews for, 526
  comparisons with other methods, 529, 530
  data class/process matrix for, 525
  implications of, 527–528
  priority determination for, 526–527

  process/organization matrix for, 524
  study activities for, 523–524
  study team for, 524
  comparisons of methods, 529–530
  critical success factors method, 520–523
    advantages of, 522
    comparisons with other methods, 529, 530
    defining factors for, 521
    defining measures for, 522
    limitations of, 523
  ends/means analysis for, 528–530
  managing by wire and, 519–520
  problems with determining, 517–519
Information Resources, Inc., 421
Information strategy planning, 575
Information systems, 15, 31; *see also* Information technology
  competition and, 77–78
  capabilities-based, 78–79
  expert systems and, 487
  failure to upgrade, 77
  for feedback
    change analysis, 46–48
    managing by wire, 46–49
  framework for, 9
    operational systems, 9–10
    strategic planning, 12, 14
    tactical systems, 10–12, 13
  impact of, and ethics, 685–686
  litigation and, 77
  planning; *see* Information systems planning
  risks of, 76–77
  as a system, 39–40
Information systems planning
  information requirements and; *see* Information requirements
  information technology and; *see* Information technology planning
  organization of the plan, 536–538

application
development, 536
centralization and,
537, 538
CIO's role in, 538
new technology and,
536–537
strategies for, 517
Information systems security,
651–652; *see also* Ethical
issues
common controls for,
655–656
common threats to
computer crime, fraud,
abuse; *see* Computer
crime, fraud, abuse
employee errors, 656
natural disasters, 656
program bugs, 665
objectives of, 653
protection for; *see*
Protecting information
systems
risks and, 653–654
Information technology; *see
also* Business process
redesign; Information
systems;
Interorganizational
systems
business activities
supported by, 57–61
for competitive advantage,
61–67, 77–78
capabilities-based, 78–79
customer service, 69
opportunities, 68–69
risk and, 76–77
strategy, 68
firm-level effect of
buyers, 63–64
new entrants, 64–65
rivals, 65–66
substitute products, 64
suppliers, 64
impact of, 87–88
on functional units, 89
on individuals, 88
on organizations,
89–90, 98
industry-level effect of
markets, 63
production economics,
62–63
products and
services, 62

organization of data
processing and,
633–635
organizational structure
and, 104
strategy-level effect of
low-cost leadership,
66–67
market specialization, 67
product
differentiation, 67
tactical decisions and, 13
Information technology era, 22
Information technology
planning; *see also*
Information systems
planning
in dynamic
environments, 535
information planning grid
and, 531–532
factory quadrant, 532
strategic quadrant, 531,
532, 533
support quadrant,
532, 533
urnaround quadrant,
531–532
management strategies and,
532–534
Schein's theory and,
534–535
Informational roles, 4, 5
Informix, 251, 349
InfoSeek search engine, 348
InfoWorld, 167
Inheritance, by objects, 232
Initiation stage, 19
Ink-jet printers, 151–152
Innovations Online, 85
Innovative Professional
Software, Inc., 185
Input, 143
Input bound systems, 153–154
Input controls, 677–678
Input devices, 143
input bound systems and,
153–154
pointing, 146
scanning, 144–146
terminals, 144
video technology, 148
voice recognition, 148
Input/output; *see* I/O
Input resources, 45
Inquiry system, 459, 460

Inspection, computer-
aided, 382
Institute of Electrical and
Electronics Engineers,
Inc., 298
Instruction set, 126
Insurance, Internet reference
sites, 84
Insurance Value-Added
Network (IVANS), 70,
71, 72
Intangible benefits, 593
Integrated Services Digital
Networks (ISDN), 263
Integration stage, 20
Intel
CISC chips of, 177
Merced chip of, 132
multiplatform capability
and, 194
Pentium chip of, 126
Intelligence phase, decision
making, 461, 464
Intelligent agents, 198,
466–467
Intelligent call processing, 291
Intelligent terminal, 268
Interactive processing, 217
Interactive Super Mall, 71, 85
Interactive voice response
systems, 291, 330
Interconnect architecture,
292–293
Interfaces, 31, 33, 170; *see also*
Graphical user interface
Interfunctional processes, 101
Internal integration tools, 590
Internal memory, 129
Internal modems, 270
Internal rate of return, 409
International Association for
Human Resource
Information
Management, 456
International networks,
278–279
International Organization for
Standardization, 292
International Telecom
Center, 298
Internet, 73–74; *see also*
Intranets; World Wide
Web
browsing on, 314–316
business uses of, 74–75
commerce on, 322–323
for competitive
tracking, 424

connection problems on,
319–320
desktop conferencing
on, 321
e-mail on, 320
features of, 313–314
file transfer on, 320–321
hypermedia databases on,
236–237
network PCs and, 321
push versus pull, 318, 328
remote access to, 281
remote programs run
on, 321
searching on, 316–318
telephony on, 321
usenet newsgroups
on, 320
Internet advertising, 374–375
Internet Explorer, 334, 665
Internet financial services,
84, 410
Internet Phone, 348
Internet reference sites
airlines, 84
careers, 84
clothing, 85
communications
systems, 298
databases and DBMSs, 251
decision support
systems, 505
ethics, 691
executive information
systems, 505
expert systems, 505
finance, 84
financial accounting, 399
gifts, 85
hardware sources, 166
help desks, 648
human resource
management, 400
insurance, 84
marketing, 399
MIS careers, 648
online malls and
catalogs, 85
production, 399
reference materials, 84
resource materials, 84–85
search engines, 347, 348
security, 691
software selection, 209
tactical and strategic
systems, 456–457

Internet service provider (ISP), 313, 319
Internet Shopping Network, 71, 85
Internet Society, 298
Internetworks, 278
Interorganizational communications systems, 102
Interorganizational information systems
    definition of, 311
    electronic data interchange, 312
    electronic market systems, 313
Interorganizational processes, 100–101
Interorganizational systems (IOSs), 59, 70; see also Internet
    electronic marketplace, 71–73
    information processing, 70–71
Interpersonal processes, 101
Interpersonal roles, 4–5
Interpretation, expert system, 488
InterTrust Commerce Architecture, 348
Interviews
    software for, 427
    systems, 548–549
Intranets, 236–237, 323–324
    extranets and, 324–325
Intrusion Detection, Inc., 671
Inventories
    of positions, 384
    of skills, 385
Inventory control systems
    in financial accounting systems, 364
    in production information systems, 378–380
Inventory levels, 471
Inventory Locator Service, 71
Inverted files, 217
Investment management, 410–411
Investment phase, 23
Invoice form, 620
Inward system access dialing (DISA), 661
IOSs; see Interorganizational systems

Iridium system, 266
ISAM; see Indexed sequential access method
ISDN; see Integrated Services Digital Networks
ISO facilitator, 70; see also Interorganizational systems
ISP; see Internet service provider
Iteration, structured programming, 600
ITT Hartford Insurance, 84
IVANS; see Insurance Value-Added Network

J
Java, 298, 322
JC Penney, 59, 564
Job analysis and design system, 439–440
Job descriptions, 439
Job management programs, 172
JOB Source, 315
Job specifications, 439
Jobs, compared to positions, 384
Johnson and Higgins, 480
Jukebox storage systems, 141, 142–143
Jungle Jim's Jungle Wear, 85
Just-in-time manufacturing, 13
Just-in-time system, 431

K
Kansas City Life Insurance, 84
Kaufmann's, 101
KB; see Kilobyte
Kenmore, 68
Kernel, 175
Keys
    primary, 214
    secondary, 217
Kilobyte (KB), 130
Kiosks, electronic, 374
KLM-Royal Dutch Airlines, 84
Kmart, 78, 521
Knowledge acquisition subsystem, 485
Knowledge base, 484, 485, 490
Knowledge engineer, 486, 490
    role of, 491–493
Knowledge engineering, 490

L
Labor negotiations, 445
Languages
    data, 222
    markup, 196, 237, 341
    programming; see Programming languages
    query, 192, 222–223
LANs; see Local area networks
Laptop computers, 121
Laser printers, 151
Laws
    copyright, 658
    employment, 387, 388
LCD; see Liquid crystal display
Leading function, 4
Learning loops, 47, 519–520
Learning organization, 49
    disciplines of, 49–50
    feedback in, 51–52
    learning disabilities of, 50
    transition to, 50–51
Leased hardware, 157
Leased telephone lines, 264–265
Legal responsibility, expert systems, 494
Legislation, employment, 387, 388
Levi Strauss, 312
Levilink, 312
Libraries, application software, 179
Library of Congress, 74
Licensing, software, 195, 202
Life cycle
    methodology of, 583
    in systems development, 544–547
Light pens, 148
Line printers, 150
Linked lists, 217
Linking, object, 194
Liquid crystal display (LCD), 149
LISP language, 494
Loan portfolios, 472–474
Local area networks (LANs), 277–278, 281
    distributed processing and, 303
    paperless office and, 341
    for shop-floor data, 376
    SQL servers as, 309, 310

Local bus architecture, 131
Local decision network, 479
Location transparency, 306
Locational systems, 102
Locking, concurrency control, 235
Logic bombs, 660
Logical data dictionary, 546, 563
    as organizationwide resource, 573–574
Logical data-flow diagram, 545
    for current system, 552–553
    for proposed system, 560–562
    using CASE tools, 570–571
Logical specifications, 595, 597–598
Logical view of data, 227
Logistical planning systems, 102
Long-range forecasting, 413–415
LookSmart, 298
Lord and Taylor, 101
Lotus Corporation, 209, 680
Lotus MarketPlace, 680
Low-cost leadership, 66–67
Low-structure-high-technology projects, 591
Low-structure-low-technology projects, 591
Lufthansa Airlines, 74, 84
Lycos search engine, 298

M
McAfee Associates, 662
McFarlan's portfolio approach, 590–591
Machine languages, 189
Machine vision, 482
Macintosh computers, 121
    chips in, 126
    Hypertalk for, 193
    operating system of, 175
    operating systems of, 177
McKesson, 70, 72, 78, 81
Macworld, 167
Magnetic-ink character recognition (MICR), 144, 146
Magnetic storage media, 135
Magnetic tape, 142

Main memory, 129

Mainframe computers, 120, 282-283

Maintenance
  costs of, 593-594
  of decision support systems, 476
  of distributed systems, 306
  of hardware, 159
  in life cycle, 546-547

Maintenance programmer, 636

Make or buy decision, 675

Mall of America, 373

Mall 2000, 71, 85

Management
  analysis of, 45
  in data processing organizations, 638-640, 641-642
  ethical responsibilities of, 686
  folklore and fact of, 6
  functions of, 3-4
  levels of, 7-8
  resource organization and, 38

Management control phase, 24

Management information systems (MIS)
  development sequence of, 15-18
  formerly termed data processing, 110

Management security controls, 655-656

Managerial activities, 101

Managerial performance, 5, 7

Managerial roles, 4-7

Managing by wire, 46-49

Manual operations, improvement of, 564

Manufacturer's Hanover Bank, 479

Manufacturing resource planning (MRP-II), 435-436

Mapping software, 419, 420

Mark-sense readers, 144

Market specialization, 66, 67

Marketing Classifieds, 315

Marketing information systems; see Operational marketing information systems; Strategic marketing information systems; Tactical

marketing information systems

Marketing mix, 415

Marketing models, 467

Marketing research systems, 426-427

MarketPlace Information Corporation, 366

MarketPlace Resource Center, 399

marketplaceMCI, 71, 85

Markup languages, 196, 237, 341

Marriott
  competitive edge at, 80
  information system risk at, 77
  interorganizational systems at, 70, 71
  technological impact at, 65

Mass customization, 382-383

Massachusetts Mutual Life Insurance Company, 65

MasterCard, 84, 106, 681

Matanuska Outfitters, 85

Material selection programs, 382

Materials requirements planning, 430

Math co-processor socket, 128

Maturity stage, 20-21

Maximizing strategy, 462

May Company, 101

Mazda, 91

MB; see Megabyte

MCI, 71, 85, 262, 328

MCT, 335

Med Facts, 72

Medequip, 79

Media, communications, 260-261

Media mix, 421

Medical data, privacy of, 681

Medical diagnosis, 488

Medical Information Bureau, 681

Megabyte (MB), 130

Megahertz (MHz), 132

MEMA/Transnet, 72

Member records, 228

Memory, 129-131; see also Secondary storage; Storage

Memory aids, 465

Memory boards, 130

Mental models, 49

Menus, 180

Merced chip, 132

Merrill Lynch, 64, 80, 408

Mesh topology, 274

Message switching, 258-259

Messages, object, 232

Metadata, 227

Methods, in object-oriented programming, 193, 232

Metropolitan Council Transit Operations, 372

Mexicana Airlines, 84

MHZ; see Megahertz

MICR; see Magnetic-ink character recognition

Microcomputer operating systems
  dynamic data exchange for, 178-179
  GUI for, 177
  hardware dependence of, 177
  interfaces for, 177
  kernel and, 175
  multitasking, 174-175
  single-tasking, 174
  task switching and, 175
  utilities for, 176
  vendors of, third-party, 176
  windowing for, 178

Microcomputers, 120-121, 128
  communications systems for, 280-281
  magazines for, 167
  software selection for, 199-202

Micromarketing, 368

Microprocessor, 127

Microsoft Access for Windows, 500-502

Microsoft at Work, 341-342

Microsoft Corporation; see also Windows; and names of other Microsoft products
  browsing and, 334
  bundling by, 181
  multiplatform capability and, 194
  paperless office and, 341
  spreadsheet products of, 185
  web site of, 209

Microsoft Network, 237

Microsoft NT, 349, 354

Microsoft Office, 181, 322

Microsoft Word, 181

Microwave transmission, 260-261

Middle-level managers, 7

Millions of instructions per second (MIPS), 132

MindSpring, 648

Minicomputers, 120, 282-283

Mining, data, 368, 416

MIPS; see Millions of instructions per second

MIS; see Management information systems

Missouri Pacific Railroad, 68, 71

Mobil Oil, 484

Model-based analysis tools, 470

Model building, decision support systems, 467-468

Modems, 270, 280, 335

Moderator, newsgroup, 320

Module, design, 596

Money Access Center, 66

Monitors, 149

Motherboard, 127, 128

Motley Fool, 76

Motor and Equipment Manufacturers Association, 72

Motorola
  in chip consortium, 126
  chips of, 126, 177, 194
  personal communicators from, 266

Mouse, 146

MRP-II; see Manufacturing resource planning

Mrs. Fields Cookies, 47, 82, 519-520

MS-DOS interface, 177

MUDMAN expert system, 488

Multidimensional analysis, 241

Multidrop topology, 273-274

Multimedia conferencing, 332

Multimedia systems, 187

Multiplatform capability, 194, 223-224

Multiplexer, 271

Multiport hub, 276

Multiprocessing, 132-133, 173

Multiprogramming, 172

Multitasking operating systems, 174-175

Multiuser application software, 180

Multiuser operating systems, 174–175

Mutual Benefit Life
business process redesign at, 99–100, 101
reengineering at, 95, 106

Mutual Fund Tracker Enterprises, 185

MYCIN expert system, 488

N

Namark Cap & Emblem, 85

Nation/Job Online Jobs Database, 315

National Business Association, 85

National Computer Security Association, 661

National Weather Service, 74

Nationwide Insurance, 84

Natural disasters, 656

Natural language, 192, 223

Natural-language processing, 481

NEC, 298

Neo Video Interactive Wear, 85

Net present value (NPV), 408

Net Search search engine, 298

Netgear E-mail Address Polo Shirts, 85

NetMeeting, 334, 348

Netscape Communicator, 334, 348

Netscape Navigator, 334

Network auditing software, 670–672

Network computer systems, 123, 195

Network database, 228

Network era, 22

Networks; see also Communications systems; Voice systems
backbone, 277
CDPD, 265–266
components of, 268–272
connection equipment, 270–272
hosts and servers, 268
modems, 270
printers, 269
protocol converters, 269
terminals, 268, 270–271

concerns about, 285–287
compatibility, 286
costs, 286
reliability, 285
response time, 285–286
security, 287
Internet as, 321; see also Internet
ISDN and, 263
packet-switching, 259
reasons to implement, 283–285
SONET, 264
standards for, 278
topologies of, 273–277
bus, 273
hierarchical, 273
mesh, 274
multidrop, 273–274
ring, 273–274
star, 273
wireless, 277
types of, 277–280
enterprise, 278–279
international, 278–279
LANs; see Local area networks
WANs; see Wide area networks
value-added, 262
wireless, 265–266, 268

NETworth, 399, 456

Neural networks, 387, 467–468

New customer report, 617

New Grolier Multimedia Encyclopedia, 187

Newsgroups, 320

Nodes, message switching, 259

Nonimpact printers, 149, 151–152

Nonprocedural languages, 190–191

Nonrecurring costs, 593

Northrop Engineering, 489

Notebook computers, 121

Novell, 349

NPV; see Net present value

Null modem, 280

O

Object code, 189

Object linking and embedding, 194

Object-oriented database (OODB), 231–232

Object-oriented programming (OOP), 193

Observation, OODA loop, 519

Occupational Safety and Health Act, 388

Occupational Safety and Health Administration (OSHA), 387, 400

OCR; *see* Optical character recognition

Off-loading, 271

Office communications, 325–326
e-mail systems, 327–328
electronic conferencing, 331–334
audioconferencing, 331
computer conferencing, 333–334
desktop conferencing, 331–333
videoconferencing, 331–333
fax systems, 331, 334–335
groupware, 337–338
OCR technology, 335–336
paperless office and, 340–342
scanning technology, 334, 335–336
virtual office and, 336–337
voice processing systems, 329–331
workflow automation, 338–340

Office of the future, 341

Official Airlines Guide, 313

Official Bubba Collection, 85

OLAP; *see* On-line analytical processing

Old Line Life Insurance, 84

OLTP; *see* On-line transaction processing

On-line analytical processing (OLAP), 241–242

On-line communities, 75

On-line databases, 237–239; *see also* Internet; World Wide Web
for competitive tracking, 424
for human resource management, 442, 443
for investment management, 410–411
for marketing, 416, 417
remote access to, 281

On-line help, 197

On-line immediate update, 564

On-line information services, 237–238

On-line order entry system, 361, 362

On-line processing, 217, 563–564

On-line systems, in life cycle, 545

On-line transaction processing (OLTP), 133

On-line with batch overnight update, 564, 567–568

ONCOCIN expert system, 494

1-800-FLOWERS, 85

Online malls and catalogs, 85

OODA loop, 519

OODB; *see* Object-oriented database

OOP; *see* Object-oriented programming

Open order file, 375

Open systems, 34

Open Systems Interconnect (OSI), 292

Operating systems; *see* Microcomputer operating systems; Systems software, operating systems

Operational activities, 101

Operational financial accounting information systems
accounts payable, 363
accounts receivable, 361–363
decision making and, 359–360
fixed assets, 360–361
general ledger, 360
Internet reference sites for, 399
inventory control, 364
payroll, 364
purchase order processing, 364
sales order processing, 361
software for, 364–365

Operational human resource information systems, 383–384
applicant selection and placement, 389
employee information systems, 385

government reporting systems and, 387–389

Internet reference sites for, 400

performance management, 385–387

position control, 384

training, 389

Operational information systems

advantages of, 357–359

nature of, 9–10, 40, 357

Operational marketing information systems, 365–366

data warehousing, 368

delivery tracking and routing, 370–372

direct mail advertising, 370

electronic shopping, 372–374

electronic kiosks, 374

virtual shopping, 372–373

Internet advertising and, 374–375

Internet reference sites for, 399–400

micromarketing, 368

point-of-sale, 370

sales force automation, 366–368

contact management systems, 366–367

prospect information systems, 366

telemarketing, 369–370

Operational production information systems

automated material handling, 380

CAD/CAM, 380–382

cost accounting, 378

image management, 382

Internet reference sites for, 400

inventory control, 378–380

mass customization, 382–383

material selection, 382

purchasing, 375

quality control, 376–378

receiving, 376

shipping, 378

shop-floor scheduling, 382

Operational systems, 9–10, 40

Operations activities, 8

Operations costs, 593

Operations documentation, 598

Operations manager, 637

Operations professionals, 637

Optical character recognition (OCR), 144, 146

for office communications, 335–336

Optical disks, 140

Optical mark recognition, 335

Optical scanners, 334

Optical storage, 140–142

Oracle, 251, 310, 349

Order-entry system, 361, 362

Order processing, 614–617

subsystems of, 617–620

Organization of data processing; see Data processing, organization of

Organizations

activities of, 8

disciplines of, 49

learning; see Learning organization

Organizing function, 4

Orientation, OODA loop, 519

OS/2, 175

OSHA; see Occupational Safety and Health Administration

OSI; see Open Systems Interconnect

Otis Elevator, 60, 89, 91

Output, 143

Output bound systems, 154

Output controls, 679

Output design, 598

Output devices, 143

COM, 153

display screens, 149

output bound systems and, 154

plotters, 153

printers, 149–153, 269

impact, 149, 150–151

nonimpact, 149, 151–152

voice synthesizers, 153

Outsourcing, 110, 432, 568, 614

Owner records, 228

P

Packet switching, 259

Page printers, 151

PageKeeper, 243

Palmtop computers, 121

Paperless office, 340–342

Paradigms, 253, 486

Paradox database tool, 468

Parallel processing, 133, 173

Parallel systems method, conversion, 602

Parity bit, 129, 257

Partitioned databases, 308

Password protection, 671, 672

Payback period, 409

Payroll system, 364

PBXs; see Voice systems, PBXs

PC cards, 138–139

PC fax/modem boards, 335

PC Magazine, 167

PC Today, 167

PC Week, 167

PC World, 167

PCMCIA (Personal Computer Memory Card International Association)

cards, 138–139

fax/model devices, 335

PCS; see Personal communications service

PDAs; see Personal digital assistants

Pen-based computers, 121–122

Pentium chips, 126, 132

People's Airlines, 83–84

People's Express, 51

Pepsi, 26

Perceptual ability, 461

Performance appraisals, 385–387

Performance management systems, 385–387

Performance objective, 113

Performance standard, 113

Peripheral Component Interconnect (PCI) bus, 131

Peripherals, 143, 606

sharing of, 283

software compatibility with, 196–197

Personal communications service (PCS), 266–268

Personal communicators, 266

Personal Computer Memory Card International Association; see PCMCIA

Personal computers, application software

types for, 188; see also Application software; Microcomputers

Personal data, privacy of, 681

Personal digital assistants (PDAs), 121

Personal information management software, 188

Personal mastery, 49

Personnel; see also Human resource information systems

allocation of, 507–510

in data processing organization, 635–638

Personnel capacity planning, 433

Personnel models, 467

PERT (program evaluation and reporting technique) chart, 433–434

Phased method, conversion, 602

Philadelphia National Bank, 66

Physical security controls, 655

Physical specifications, 595, 597–598

Physical view of data, 227

PictureTel, 333

Pilot systems method, conversion, 602

Piracy, software, 663–664

PLAnet, 648

Planet 1, 266–267

Planning, 3; see also Information systems planning

capacity, 431–433

in decision support systems, 475–476, 480

development and, in strategic marketing, 427–428

manufacturing resource, 435–436

materials requirements, 430

site, 437

strategic, 8, 12, 14

strategies for, 517

succession, 442–443

for technology, 437

workforce, 443–445

Planning tools, formal, 590

PlanPower expert system, 489

Plant design system, 438

PLANT expert system, 488

Platforms, 124–125, 194
  databases and, 223–224
Plotters, 153
Pocket organizers, 121, 123
Point-of-sale (POS) systems,
  144, 370, 630
Point-to-point network, 273
PointCast, Inc., 318
Pointing devices, 146
Pointing stick, 146
Portability, software, 179–180,
  195–196
Portable documents, 195
Portfolio approach, project
  management, 590–591
POS systems; see Point-of-sale
  systems
Position control system, 384
Position inventories, 384
Positions, compared to
  jobs, 384
Power supply, 128
PowerPoint, 181, 471
Prediction, expert system,
  488–489
Pregnancy Discrimination
  Act, 388
Present state, in problem
  solving, 113
Presentation graphics
  software,
  185–186
Pricing systems, 421–422
Primary key, 214
Primary storage, 129
Printers; see Output devices,
  printers
Printing terminals, 149
Privacy
  ethics and, 679–683
  financial, 236, 658
  violations of, 664–665
Privacy Act, 236, 658
Privacy Info Source, 681
Private branch exchanges; see
  Voice systems, PBXs
Pro CD, 366
Problem definition, 544
Problem-oriented
  languages, 494
Problem solving; see also
  Software Reengineering
  Company, Inc.
  by expert systems, 487–489
  systems approach to, 44–46
Procedural languages, 190
Process controls, 678

Process logic, 562
Process/organization
  matrix, 524
Process planning, computer-
  aided, 382
Process positioning, 437–438
Processing, types of, 133–134
Procter & Gamble, 59,
  93–94, 96
Prodigy, 70, 237
Product choice systems, 102
Product design and
  development systems,
  434–435
Product differentiation, 66, 67
Product planning and
  development systems,
  427–428
Product pricing, 421–422
Production information
  systems; see Operational
  production information
  systems; Strategic
  production information
  systems; Tactical
  production information
  systems
Production schedule, 433–434
Production systems, nature of,
  428–430
Productivity, 234, 284
Professional data, privacy
  of, 681
Professionals, roles of,
  635–638
Program bugs, as security
  threat, 665
Program code, 189
Program evaluation and
  reporting technique; see
  PERT chart
Program specifications, 598
Programmable read-only
  memory (PROM), 131
Programmers
  application, 179
  roles of, 636, 637
  systems, 170
Programming, structured,
  600–601
Programming languages, 187;
  see also Languages
  application generators,
  192–193
  assembly, 189
  fourth-generation, 190–192
  machine, 189
  natural, 192
  query, 192

report generators, 192
  scripting, 338
  third-generation, 189–190
  visual, 193
Programs; see Software
Progressive Insurance, 84
Project management, 587–589;
  see also Design;
  Implementation
  Gantt charts versus project
    networks for, 587–589
  portfolio approach to,
    590–591
    project types and, 591
    risk factors, 590
    risk minimization,
      590–591
Project Management
  Institute, 399
Project management
  software, 188
Project manager, 636
Project networks, 587–589
PROLOG language, 494
PROM; see Programmable
  read-only memory
Promotion systems, 419–421;
  see also Advertising
Prompts, software, 177, 180
Property data, privacy of, 681
Property issues, and ethics,
  683–685
Prospect information
  systems, 366
Protecting information
  systems
  for communication,
    668–672
    electronic-commerce
      safety, 668
    encryption, 668
    firewalls, 669
    network auditing
      software, 670–672
  for databases, 672–675
  for facilities, 666–668
  for systems applications
    access and update
      security of, 676–677
    appropriateness, 676
    input controls, 677–678
    make or buy decision
      on, 675
    output controls, 678
    process controls, 678
    security features, 676
    stability, 676

testing software
  for, 676
Protocol converters, 269
Prototyping, 583, 584
Psychological contract, 603
Public Access Networks
  Corporation, 659
Public domain software, 179
Public electronic mail
  systems, 328
PUFF expert system, 488
Pull technology, 318
Purchase order processing
  system, 364
Purchase requisition form, 618
Purchasing systems, 375
Push technology, 318, 424

Q
QBE; see Query by example
QIC systems, 142
Quality assurance, 478, 641
Quality control systems,
  376–378
Quantas Airways, 84
QuattroPro, 470
Query by example (QBE),
  223, 231
Query languages, 192,
  222–223
Questionnaires, system
  analysis, 549–550

R
R. J. Reynolds Tobacco Co.,
  312
Radio channels, 261
RAID (redundant array of
  inexpensive disks), 138
Random access memory
  (RAM), 129
Random record storage, 215
RCPAC; see U.S. Army Reserve
  Components Personnel
  Administration Center
Read-only memory (ROM),
  128, 131
Real-time transaction
  processing, 133
Receiving systems, 376
Recognition systems, 102
Record count, 678
Record locking, 235
Records, 212, 228; see also
  Accessing records
Recovery firms, 656
Recovery systems, 222

Recruiting system, 440–441; *see also* Applicant selection and placement systems

Recurring costs, 593

Reduced instruction set computing (RISC), 126, 177

Redundancy, data, 219, 233

Redundant array of inexpensive disks; *see* RAID

Redwood Country Unlimited, 85

Reengineering, 90; *see also* Business process redesign

changes and, 90–91

examples of, 91–94

of order processing, 614–615

organizational impacts of, 96

participants in, 96

process of, 94–95

Reference sites, Internet; *see* Internet reference sites

Relational database, 229–231

Reliability

in distributed processing, 304–305

of hardware, 156

of networks, 285

Remote access, 280–283

Remote decision making, 480

Remote e-mail software, 327–328; *see also* E-mail

Renting, hardware, 157

Reorder-point system, 379

Repeaters, 272

Replicated databases, 307–308

Report design, 597

Report generation, 192, 468

Report writers, 222

Request for proposal (RFP), 604

Requirements analysis, 478; *see also* Information requirements

Requirements documents, 583

Research prototype, 492

Resident programs, 171

Resolution, screen, 149

Resource allocation, 480

Resource issues

DBMSs and, 234, 236

distributed processing and, 305

Response time, 285–286

Responsibilities in data processing organization

allocation of, 632–633

professional roles in, 635–638

operations, 637

systems development, 635–636

technical support, 637–638

Restart/recovery systems, 222

Retail point-of-sale system; *see* Point-of-sale systems

Retention schedule, 679

Reusable objects, 232

Revlon, 660

Rewritable optical disk systems, 141

RFP; *see* Request for proposal

Right to Financial Privacy Act, 236, 658

Ring topology, 273–274

RISC; *see* Reduced instruction set computing

Risk-taking propensity, 461

Risks, 653

in decision support systems, 478–479

project management and, 590–591

security and, 653–654

Robotics, 482

ROM; *see* Read-only memory

Rosenbluth Travel, 67

Rotational delay, 138

Rough-cut capacity planning, 431, 432, 433

Routers, 272

Routing systems, 370–372

Rule-based systems, 485–486

Rules of thumb, 484

Ryder System, 71

S

S & P Online, 410

SABRE reservation system

competitive advantage and, 65, 79–80

interorganizational systems and, 72

strategic information and, 77

update on, 82

Safety stock, 379

Saks Fifth Avenue, 521

Salami slicing, 660

Salary systems, 441–442

Sales force automation systems, 366–368

Sales forecasting, 425–426, 471

Sales management systems, 416–419

Sales order processing system, 361

Sales order report, 617

Sales performance, 417–419

Saludos Web, 315

SAS-PC, 471

SASD; *see* Sequential access storage devices

Satellite broadcasting companies, 262

Satisficing strategy, 462

Scanner technology

as input devices, 144–146

for office communications, 334, 335–336

Schein's theory of technology assimilation, 534–535

Schema, 227

Scope International, Inc., 185

Screen capture, 188

Screen design, 598

Screen resolution, 149

Scripting language, 338

Scrubbed data, 466

Sea Lake County Welfare Department, 17–18

Search engines, 316, 347, 348

Sears

business opportunities at, 68

distributed data processing at, 564

information partnerships at, 81

interorganizational systems at, 70

point-of-sale system at, 630

technological impact at, 69

value activities at, 59

SEC; *see* Securities and Exchange Commission

Secondary indexes, 217

Secondary keys, 217

Secondary storage, 129, 134–135

on disk, 135–139

accessing data, 138

flash memory, 139

floppy diskettes, 135

hard disks, 136–137

PC cards, 138–139

RAID systems, 138

Winchester, 138

hierarchical, 143

optical, 140–142

CD-ROM drives, 140

DVD-ROM drives, 140

floptical drives, 141–142

rewritable systems, 141

WORM systems, 140

on tape, 142–143

Securities and Exchange Commission (SEC), 74, 84

EDGAR database of, 399

online information about, 411

Security; *see also* Data security; Information systems security

of DBMSs, 222, 226, 236

in distributed processing, 306

of networks, 287

Security APL, 399

Security software, 188, 222

Seek time, 138

Selection, structured programming, 600

Self-knowledge, 487

Semistructured decision, 463

Semistructured problems, 461

Sequence, structured programming, 600

Sequence checks, 678

Sequences, data mining, 466

Sequential access, 214

Sequential access storage devices (SASD), 135

Sequential file structure, 214–216

Servers, 268, 309

Service bureaus, 565

SGML (Standard Generalized Markup Language), 196

Shareware, 179

Sharing

information, 518

network, 283–284

Sharkews, 348

Shell, expert system, 494

Sheraton, 62

Sherwood Stores, Inc., 27

Shipping systems, 378

Shop-floor data collection systems, 376

Shop-floor scheduling, 382

Shopping, electronic, 372–373

Shopping In, 85

Silicon chip, 127

SIMM; *see* Single in-line memory module

Simplex transmission, 258

Simulations, 102, 468

Singapore TradeNet, 70–71

Single in-line memory module (SIMM), 128, 131

Single-tasking operating systems, 174

Single-user application software, 180

Single-user operating systems, 174

Site licensing agreement, 195

Site planning systems, 437

Skills inventory, 385

Slide-show software, 185–186

Slots, expansion, 128

Smart Software Inc., 185

Smart terminals, 144

SMDR; *see* Station message detail recording service

SMDS; *see* Switched multimegabit data service

SNA; *see* Systems Network Architecture

Social Security Administration, 400

Society for Human Resource Management, 400, 443, 457

Society of Manufacturing Engineers, 457

Software, 40, 169–170

application; *see* Application software

CAD/CAM, 380–382

communications, 173–174

computer-aided telephone interview, 427

cost of, 199, 202–203, 284

desktop survey, 427

development; *see* Development software

document management, 242

emulation, 283

evaluation of, 604–606

financial accounting, 364–365

forecasting, 414

geographic information systems, 420

human resource information systems, 446

Internet reference sites for, 209

manufacturing resource planning, 435–436

mapping, 419, 420

materials requirements planning, 430

for multimedia systems, 187

PBX, 290–291

sales management, 419

for security, 222

selection of, 199–202

statistical, 414

systems; *see* Systems software

testing of, 600–601

trends in, 194–199

applets, 199

compatibility, 196–197

cost, 199

ease of installation, 198

ease of use, 197

graphical user interface, 194

groupware, 196

hardware demands, 198–199

licensing, 195, 202

memory requirements, 199

network capabilities, 195

object linking and embedding, 194

portability, 195–196

sophistication, 197

windowing, 194

wizards and agents, 197–198

upgrading of, 202

vertical accounting, 365

web server, 224

Software Copyright Protection Act, 658

Software development options, 565–567

Software houses, 566

Software packages, 566–567

as alternative design option, 583, 584

Software piracy, 663–664, 684

Software Publishers Association, 663, 664, 691

Software Reengineering Company (SRC), Inc.

client support by

background, 693

current situation, 694–696

current systems, 694

information center development, 696

older RCPAC computer systems, 693–694

personnel allocation at

background, 507–508

current situation, 508–509

plan for, 510

problem solving at

background, 108–109

current situation, 109

processes and approaches to, 113–114

staff meeting, 112–113

three business areas, 110–111

systems development by

background, 614–615

current situation, 615–620

subsystems, 617–620

upgrades for RCPAC and, 349, 350

Software security controls, 655

Software suites, 180–181

Software vendors, 200

SONET; *see* Synchronous Optical Network

Source code, 189

Southern New England Telephone Company, 325

Southwest Airlines, 84

Specifications

logical to physical, 595, 597–598

program, 598

Speed

clock, 132

of communications channels, 260

Spreadsheets, 182–184

for decision support systems, 470

of sales performance, 417–419

Sprint, 262

Spry, Inc., 298

SPSS-PC, 471

SQL (structured query language), 223, 309–311

SQL Server, 310, 349

SRC; *see* Software Reengineering Company (SRC), Inc.

St. Louis Post-Dispatch, 685

Stand-along packages, 180

Standard Generalized Markup Language; *see* SGML

Standardization, and distributed processing, 305

Standards, 45

for communications systems, 292

for hardware, 155–156

Stanford Medical School, 494

Star topology, 273

State Farm, 71

State Mutual Life Insurance Company, 82–83

Station message detail recording (SMDR) service, 290–291

Statistical analysis software, 471

Statistical models, 467

Statistical software, 188, 414

S3PS, Inc., 185

Storage; *see also* Memory

primary, 129

secondary; *see* Secondary storage

virtual, 173

Strategic accounting and financial information systems

financial condition analysis in, 412–413

information flow types and, 412

long-range forecasting in, 413–415

Strategic human resource information systems

labor negotiations and, 445

workforce planning in, 443–445

Strategic information systems

Internet references sites for, 456–457

nature of, 403–405

Strategic marketing information systems
  marketing research in, 426–427
  product planning and development in, 427–428
  sales forecasting in, 425–426
Strategic planning, 8, 12, 14
Strategic production information systems, 436–437
  plant design in, 438
  process positioning in, 437–438
  site planning and selection in, 437
  technology planning and assessment in, 437
Strategic quadrant, planning grid, 531, 532, 533
Strategic systems, risks of, 76–77
Strowbridge and Clothier, 101
Structure, in alternative application development, 586
Structure chart, 596
Structured design, 595–597
Structured problems, 461
Structured programming, 600–601
Structured query language; see SQL
Structured systems analysis and design; see Systems analysis and design, structured
Structured walkthrough, 601
Subschema, 227–228
Substitute products, 421–422
Subsystems, 31, 32
  interfaces and, 33–34
  operational systems and, 40–41
Success, project, 526
Succession planning systems, 442–443
Suites, software, 180–181
Summary reports, 10
Sun Microsystems, Inc., 166, 322
Supercomputers, 120
Superflora, 85
Supervisory programs, 171
Supplier-focused EDI, 312
Support quadrant, planning grid, 532, 533

Survey software, 427
Swissair, 84
Switched multimegabit data service (SMDS), 264
Switching hub, 272
Sybase, 251, 349
Symantec Corporation, 684
Symmetric multiprocessing, 173
Synchronous Optical Network (SONET), 264
Synchronous transmission, 257–258
System
  defined, 31
  information system as, 39–40
  types of; see Hardware, computer systems
System construction, in decision support systems, 476
System evaluation personnel, 637–638
System-user link, 474
System utility programs, 174, 176
Systems analysis, 547–548
  in life cycle, 544
  questionnaires in, 549–550
  structured; see Systems analysis and design, structured
  systems interview in, 548–549
Systems analysis and design, structured
  business objectives and, 559
  case study of, 554–559
    current problems, 557–558
    current system, 555–557, 559
    new system requirements, 558–559
  compared to traditional approach, 551–552
  data dictionary and, 563, 573–574
  data-flow diagram
    of current system, 552–553
    of proposed system, 560–562
  process logic specifications, 562

    system objectives and, 559–560
Systems analysts, 625
Systems Application Architecture (SAA), 341
Systems applications, protection of; see Protecting information systems
Systems approach, 43, 114
  defining the problem, 44
  evaluating alternatives, 45–46
  follow up, 46
  gathering data, 44–45
  identifying alternatives, 45
  selection and implementation, 46
  steps of, 44
Systems concepts, 31–32
  boundaries, 32
  in business, 38–39
  enterprise structure, 43–44
  feedback, 42
  information system, 39–40
  interfaces, 33–34, 42
  internal controls, 42–43
  outputs and inputs, 32–33, 41–42
  subsystems; see Subsystems
  systems approach, 43
Systems design; see also Implementation
  alternative options for, 563–569
    analysis of, 567–569
    computers, 564–565
    processing modes, 563–564
    software development, 565–567
  alternative strategies for, 583–587
  cost-benefit analysis of; see Cost-benefit analysis
  prototyping, 583, 584
  selection factors in, 586–587
  software packages, 583, 584
  user-developed systems, 583, 585
  user involvement in; see User involvement in system selection
  changeability in, 595–596

  cohesive, 596
  cost-benefit analysis for, 592–595
  detailed, 546, 595–599
    documentation for, 598, 600
    physical specifications, 595, 597–598
    program specifications, 598
    structured approach, 595–597
  in information engineering, 576–577
  in life cycle, 545
  structured; see Systems analysis and design, structured
Systems design documentation, 598
Systems development, 543–544
  life cycle of, 544–547
  professionals in, 635–636
Systems development methodology, 544
Systems entropy, 36
Systems environments, 34
  entropy, 36–37
  feedback, 35–36
  open and closed systems, 34–35
  stress and change, 37
Systems interview, 548–549
Systems Network Architecture (SNA), 292
Systems programmers, 170, 637
Systems software
  as interface, 170
  operating systems, 171–179
    communications software for, 173–174
    for microcomputers; see Microcomputer operating systems
    multiprocessing and, 173
    multiprogramming and, 172
    parallel processing and, 173
    program types in, 171–172
    time-sharing and, 172–173
    virtual storage and, 173
  utility programs, 174
Systems thinking, 49

T

T line service, 263
Tactical accounting and financial information systems
budgeting in, 405–406
capital budgeting in, 408–410
cash management in, 407–408
investment management in, 410–411
Tactical activities, 8
Tactical human resource information systems, 438–439
job analysis and design in, 439–440
on-line databases for, 442, 443
recruiting in, 440–441
succession planning in, 442–443
Tactical information systems, 10–12, 42
Internet references sites for, 456–457
nature of, 403–405
Tactical marketing information systems, 415–416
advertising and promotion in, 419–421
competitive tracking in, 423–425
distribution channels in, 423
pricing in, 421–422
sales management in, 416–419
Tactical production information systems, 428–430
capacity planning in, 431–433
computer-integrated manufacturing in, 436
just-in-time systems in, 431
manufacturing resource planning in, 435–436
materials requirements planning in, 430
product design and development in, 434–435
production scheduling in, 433–434
Tactical systems, 10–12, 42

Talman Federal Savings and Loan, 568
Tampering, computer; see Computer crime, fraud, abuse
Tangible benefits, 592–593
Tape, as secondary storage, 142–143
Tape drives, 135
Tasks
analysis of, 510
expert system, 485
microcomputer operating systems and, 174–175
switching of, 175
Tax Cruncher Software, Inc., 185
TB; see Terabyte
Team learning, 49
Technical support
hot-lines for, 201
professionals in, 637–638
Technology assessment systems, 437
Technology assimilation, Schein's theory of, 534–535
Technology learning and adaptation phase, 23–24
Technology planning; see Information technology planning
Technology transfer phase, 24
Telcot, 72
Telecommunications Act, 253
Telecommunications systems, 255; see also Communications systems; Networks
Telecommuting, 254, 325
Teleconferencing, 331, 479; see also Office communications, electronic conferencing
Telemarketing systems, 369–370
Telephone Consumer Fraud Protection Act, 658
Telephone lines, 264–265; see also Communications systems; Networks
Telephone systems, 265, 289, 291, 321; see also Voice systems
Telephone tag, 328
Telephone toll fraud, 659–661
Teleprocessing monitor, 222
Television

cable, 253, 262
high definition, 124
web TV, 124, 323
Teliram Corporation, 666, 670, 672, 677, 678
Telnet, 321
Templates, spreadsheet, 182, 184
Terabyte (TB), 141
Terminals, 144, 149
in networks, 268, 270–271
telephone keypads as, 289, 291
Testing
computer-aided, 382
in decision support systems, 476
in expert systems, 491
as implementation step, 600–601
Theft, hardware, 662–663
Third-generation languages, 189–190
Third-party software vendor, 176
Threat, 653; see also Information systems security; Security
Throughput, 132
Time-sharing, 172–173, 565
Time slicing, 172
TitleWave Press, 185
Toll fraud, 659–661
Top-level management, 7
Topologies; see Networks, topologies of
Total quality control (TQC), 377–378
Touch screens, 148
TouchVoice Corporation, 288
Tower Records, 373
TQC; see Total quality control
Trackball, 146
Tracking systems, 102, 370–372
in tactical marketing, 423–424
Trade associations, 200
Training, 601
computer-based, 187
in decision support systems, 476
for hardware use, 159
in human resource information systems, 389
software for, 187, 188

Training Registry, 648
Transaction processing systems, 357; see also Operational information systems
Transfer time, 138
Transformation, 88, 95
Transient programs, 171
Transmission modes; see Communications systems, transmission modes for
Transparency, distributed systems, 306
Trap doors, 660
Triggers, 465
Trojan horses, 660
Trusted systems, 673
TRW, 555
Turnaround quadrant, planning grid, 531–532
Tutorial software, 187, 188
TWA, 65
Twisted-pair wiring, 260
2(x)ist Men's Underwear, 85

U

U S West, 333
Uncertainty reduction, 480
Uninterruptable power supply (UPS), 675
Union Pacific Railroad, 68, 71, 190
Union Pacific Technologies, 102
Unions, labor, 445
United Airlines
competitive strategy and, 533, 534
information system risk at, 77
interorganizational systems at, 72
technological impact at, 65
web site of, 84
United Parcel Service (UPS), 85, 312
U.S. Air Force, 47, 519, 659
U.S. Army Reserve Components Personnel Administration Center (RCPAC)
client support for, 693–696
upgrading for
background, 349
current office environment, 350–352

current situation,
349–350

desired office
environment,
352–353

U.S. Postal Service, 374

Universal database
management
systems, 243

Universal Product Code, 144

Universal resource locators;
see URLs

UNIX, 175, 177, 194, 349

Unstructured decisions, 463

Unstructured problems, 461

Update transparency, 306

Updates, on-line processing,
564, 567–568

Upgrades, software, 202

UPS; *see* Uninterruptable
power supply; United
Parcel Service

URLs (universal resource
locators), 314

Usenet newsgroups, 320

User-builder interaction,
474–475

User-developed
applications, 640

User-developed systems,
583, 585

User documentation, 598

User-friendly software, 197

User interfaces, GUI; *see*
Graphical user interface

User involvement in system
selection; *see also* Design
evaluation, hardware,
606–608
evaluation, software,
604–606
RFP development, 604

User satisfaction, in distributed
processing, 305

User support center, 639–640

User-system link, 474

User training specialist, 636

Utility programs, 174, 176, 188

V

Value activities, 57

Value-added features, 67

Value-added networks
(VANs), 262

Value chain, 57–61

Value Line, 410, 411

Value system, 58

Vandalism, 662–663

VANs; *see* Value-added
networks

Variance
in budgets, 405–406
quality control and, 376–377

VAX 9000, 129

VAX Professional, 167

VDONet, 332

VDT; *see* Video display
terminal

Vending machines, 265

Vendors
communications systems,
262–265
hardware, 158–159
software, 176, 200, 201

Versioning, 235, 338

Vertical accounting
software, 365

Vertical integration, 437–438

Video board, 128

Video display terminal
(VDT), 149

Video Electronics Standards
Association, 131

Video technology, 148

Videoconferencing, 331–333

Vietnamese-Era Veterans
Readjustment Act, 388

Views of data, 227–228

Village Software, 185

Virtual car showroom, 381

Virtual office, 336–337

Virtual shopping, 372–373

Virtual storage, 173

Virtual Vineyards, 75

Virus, computer, 661–662

Visa, 64, 106, 681

Visible Systems, Inc., 572

Vision, shared, 49

Visual programming
languages, 193

VL bus architecture, 131

VLSI, 383

VLSI Technology, Inc., 399, 400

Vocational Rehabilitation
Act, 388

Voice communications, 102

Voice mail, 289–290, 329

Voice messaging, 330

Voice recognition, 148

Voice synthesizers, 153

Voice systems
Centrex, 287–288

concerns about, 292
in office communications,
329–331
PBXs, 287
distributed processing
and, 303
hardware and software
for, 290–291
reasons to implement,
288–290

Volkswagen, 657

Vulnerabilities, 653

W

Wachovia, 79

Wage systems, 441–442

Wal-Mart
capabilities-based
competition and, 78–79
EDI and, 312
feedback mechanisms
at, 47
learning loop and, 520
reengineering at, 90–91,
93–94, 96
value chain and, 59–60

Walgreen's, 82

Walkthrough, 601

Walsh-Healey Public Contracts
Act, 388

WANs; *see* Wide area networks

Warehouses, data, 368, 416

Web; *see* World Wide Web

Web TV, 124, 323

Weighted-score method, 606

Wells Fargo, 84

Whirlpool, 91

Whiteboard, 331

Wide area networks
(WANs), 278
distributed processing
and, 303
paperless office and, 341
SQL servers and, 310

Winchester drives, 138

Windowing, 178, 194

Windows, 322, 349, 352

Windows 95, 175, 177

Windows 97, 175

Windows NT, 175, 177, 194

Wireless communications
media, 260–261

Wireless networks,
265–266, 268

Wireless topology, 277

Wizards, 197–198

Word processing software,
181–182

Word size, 131

Work methods and
procedures, 45

Work psychological
contract, 603

Workflow automation,
338–340

Workflow software, 338–340

Workforce planning, 443–445

Workstations, 121, 268,
270–271

World Wide Web (WWW),
71–72, 75–76; *see also*
Internet
addresses on, 314
advertisements on, 322
browsing of, 314–316
hypermedia databases on,
236–237
pages on, 314
push and pull of, 318
size of, 319
server software for, 224
sites listed, 84–85, 315; *see
also* Internet reference
sites

WORM (write once, read
many) systems, 140

Wrangler, 47, 520

WWW; *see* World Wide Web

X

XCON expert system, 488,
492, 494

Xerox Corporation
business process redesign
at, 100, 101
competitive advantage
at, 82
reengineering at, 93
value activities at, 60

Y

Yahoo! search engine, 298,
315, 348

Year 2000 problem, 190

Z

ZD Net, 298